W9-BAH-878

# enVision™ Geometry

## Student Edition

ISBN-13: 978-0-328-93158-3
ISBN-10: 0-328-93158-6

4 18

# Contents in Brief

enVision™ Geometry

# Reviewers & Consultants

## Mathematicians

**David Bressoud, Ph.D.**
Professor Emeritus of Mathematics
Macalester College
St. Paul, MN

**Karen Edwards, Ph.D.**
Mathematics Lecturer
Harvard University
Cambridge, MA

## Teacher Reviewers

**Jennifer Barkey**
K-12 Math Supervisor
Gateway School District
Monroeville, PA

**Miesha Beck**
Math Teacher/ Department Chair
Blackfoot School District
Blackfoot, ID

**Joseph Brandell, Ph.D.**
West Bloomfield High School
West Bloomfield Public Schools
West Bloomfield, MI

**Andrea Coles**
Mathematics Teacher
Mountain View Middle School
Blackfoot, ID

**Julie Johnson**
Mathematics/CS teacher (9–12)
Williamsville Central Schools
Williamsville, NY

**Tamar McPherson**
Plum Sr HS/Math Teacher
Plum School District
Pittsburgh, PA

**Melisa Rice**
Math Department Chairperson
Shawnee Public Schools
Shawnee, OK

**Ben Wilson**
Camille Casteel HS Teacher
Chandler Unified School District
Chandler, AZ

**Erin Zitka**
6-12 Math Coordinator
Forsyth County
Cumming, GA

**Jeff Ziegler**
Teacher
Pittsburgh City Schools
Pittsburgh, PA

# About the Authors

## Authors

### Dan Kennedy, Ph.D

- Classroom teacher and the Lupton Distinguished Professor of Mathematics at the Baylor School in Chattanooga, TN
- Co-author of textbooks *Precalculus: Graphical, Numerical, Algebraic* and *Calculus: Graphical, Numerical, Algebraic, AP Edition*
- Past chair of the College Board's AP Calculus Development Committee.
- Previous Tandy Technology Scholar and Presidential Award winner

### Eric Milou, Ed.D

- Professor of Mathematics, Rowan University, Glassboro, NJ
- Member of the author team for Pearson's **enVision**math**2.0** 6-8
- Member of National Council of Teachers of Mathematics (NCTM) feedback/advisory team for the Common Core State Standards
- Author of *Teaching Mathematics to Middle School Students*

### Christine D. Thomas, Ph.D

- Professor of Mathematics Education at Georgia State University, Atlanta, GA
- Past-President of the Association of Mathematics Teacher Educators (AMTE)
- Past NCTM Board of Directors Member
- Past member of the editorial panel of the NCTM journal *Mathematics Teacher*
- Past co-chair of the steering committee of the North American chapter of the International Group of the Psychology of Mathematics Education

### Rose Mary Zbiek, Ph.D

- Professor of Mathematics Education, Pennsylvania State University, College Park, PA
- Series editor for the NCTM *Essential Understanding* project

## Contributing Author

### Al Cuoco, Ph.D

- Lead author of CME Project, a National Science Foundation (NSF)-funded high school curriculum
- Team member to revise the Conference Board of the Mathematical Sciences (CBMS) recommendations for teacher preparation and professional development
- Co-author of several books published by the Mathematical Association of America and the American Mathematical Society
- Consultant to the writers of the Common Core State Standards for Mathematics and the PARCC Content Frameworks for high school mathematics

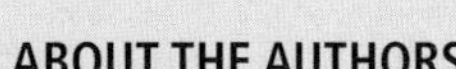

## enVision™ Geometry offers a carefully constructed lesson design to help you succeed in math.

**Step 1** At the start of each lesson, you and your classmates will work together to come up with a solution strategy for the problem or task posed. After a class discussion, you'll be asked to reflect back on the processes and strategies you used in solving the problem.

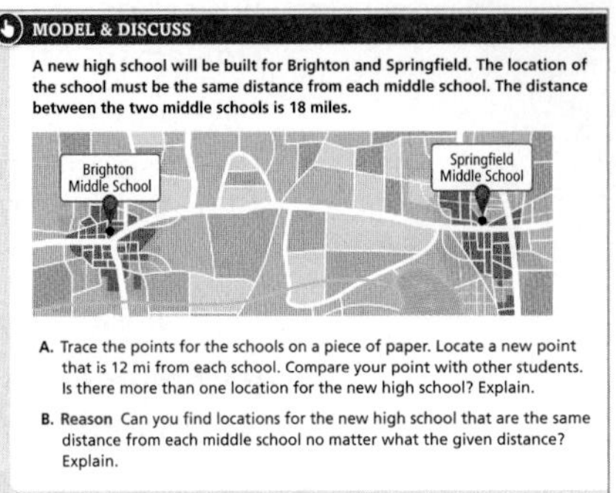

MODEL & DISCUSS
A new high school will be built for Brighton and Springfield. The location of the school must be the same distance from each middle school. The distance between the two middle schools is 18 miles.
Brighton Middle School
Springfield Middle School
A. Trace the points for the schools on a piece of paper. Locate a new point that is 12 mi from each school. Compare your point with other students. Is there more than one location for the new high school? Explain.
B. Reason Can you find locations for the new high school that are the same distance from each middle school no matter what the given distance? Explain.


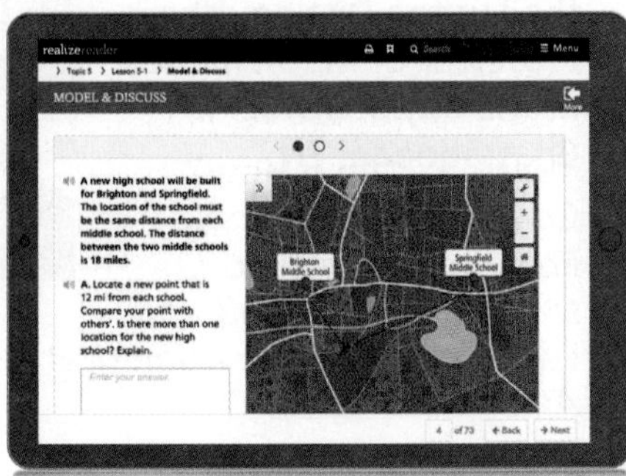


**Step 2** Next, your teacher will guide you through new concepts and skills for the lesson.

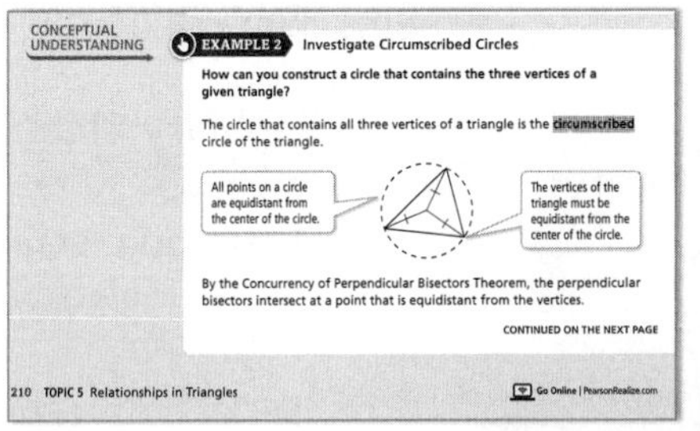

CONCEPTUAL UNDERSTANDING
EXAMPLE 2 Investigate Circumscribed Circles
How can you construct a circle that contains the three vertices of a given triangle?
The circle that contains all three vertices of a triangle is the circumscribed circle of the triangle.
All points on a circle are equidistant from the center of the circle.
The vertices of the triangle must be equidistant from the center of the circle.
By the Concurrency of Perpendicular Bisectors Theorem, the perpendicular bisectors intersect at a point that is equidistant from the vertices.
CONTINUED ON THE NEXT PAGE
210 TOPIC 5 Relationships in Triangles


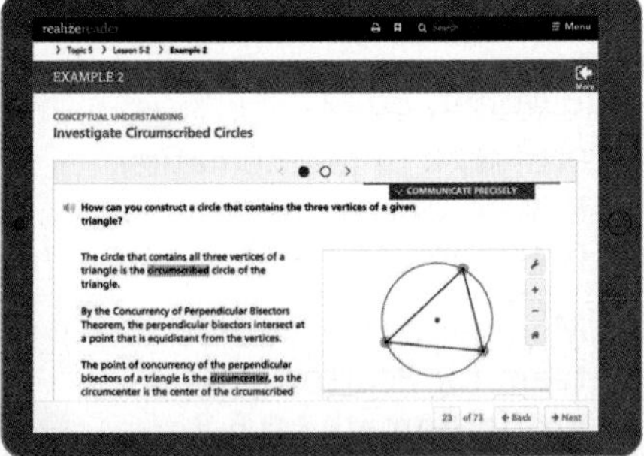


After each example, you work out a problem called the **Try It!** to solidify your understanding of these concepts.

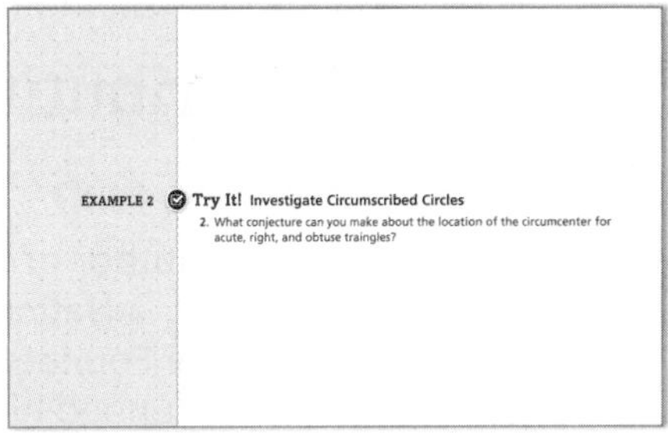

EXAMPLE 2 Try It! Investigate Circumscribed Circles
2. What conjecture can you make about the location of the circumcenter for acute, right, and obtuse traingles?

In addition, you will periodically answer **Habits of Mind** questions to refine your thinking and problem-solving skills.

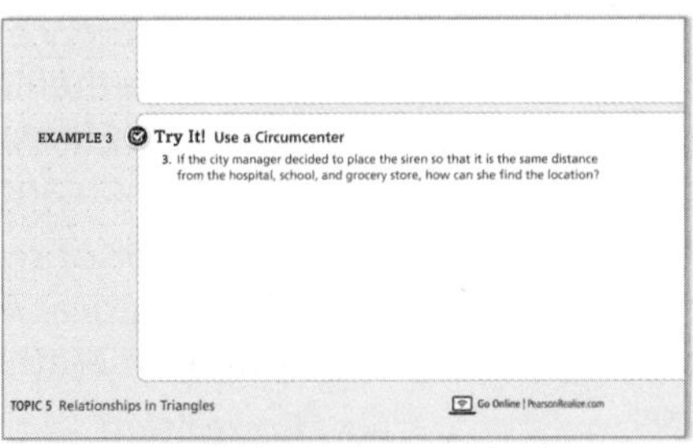

EXAMPLE 3 Try It! Use a Circumcenter
3. If the city manager decided to place the siren so that it is the same distance from the hospital, school, and grocery store, how can she find the location?
TOPIC 5 Relationships in Triangles

This part of the lesson concludes with a Lesson Check that helps you to know how well you are understanding the new content presented in the lesson. With the exercises in the **Do You Understand?** and **Do You Know How?**, you can gauge your understanding of the lesson concepts.

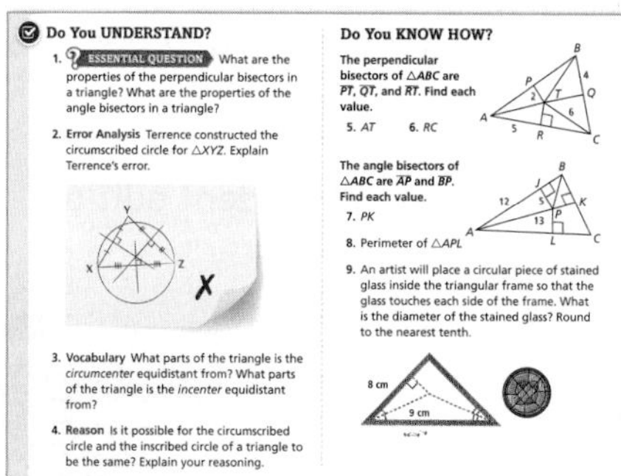

Do You UNDERSTAND?

1. ESSENTIAL QUESTION What are the properties of the perpendicular bisectors in a triangle? What are the properties of the angle bisectors in a triangle?
2. Error Analysis Terrence constructed the circumscribed circle for $\triangle XYZ$. Explain Terrence's error.
3. Vocabulary What parts of the triangle is the *circumcenter* equidistant from? What parts of the triangle is the *incenter* equidistant from?
4. Reason Is it possible for the circumscribed circle and the inscribed circle of a triangle to be the same? Explain your reasoning.

Do You KNOW HOW?

The perpendicular bisectors of $\triangle ABC$ are $\overline{PT}$, $\overline{QT}$, and $\overline{RT}$. Find each value.

5. $AT$
6. $RC$

The angle bisectors of $\triangle ABC$ are $\overline{AP}$ and $\overline{BP}$. Find each value.

7. $PK$
8. Perimeter of $\triangle APL$
9. An artist will place a circular piece of stained glass inside the triangular frame so that the glass touches each side of the frame. What is the diameter of the stained glass? Round to the nearest tenth.

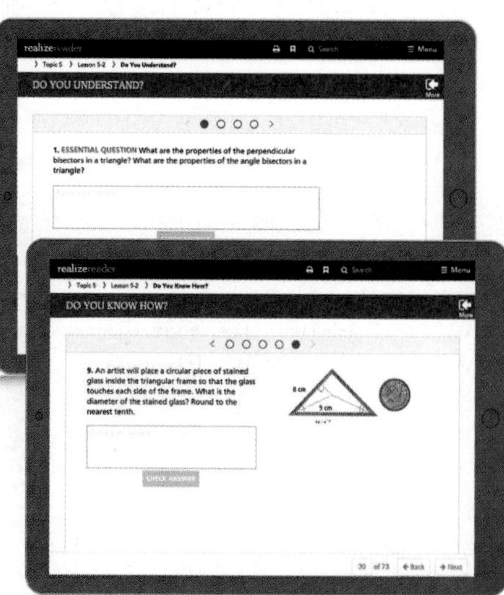


**Step 3** In Step 3, you will find a balanced exercise set with **Understand** exercises that focus on conceptual understanding, **Practice** exercises that target procedural fluency, and **Apply** exercises for which you apply concept and skills to real-world situations. The **Assessment Practice** exercises offer practice for high stakes assessments. Your teacher may have you complete the assignment in print or online at PearsonRealize.com

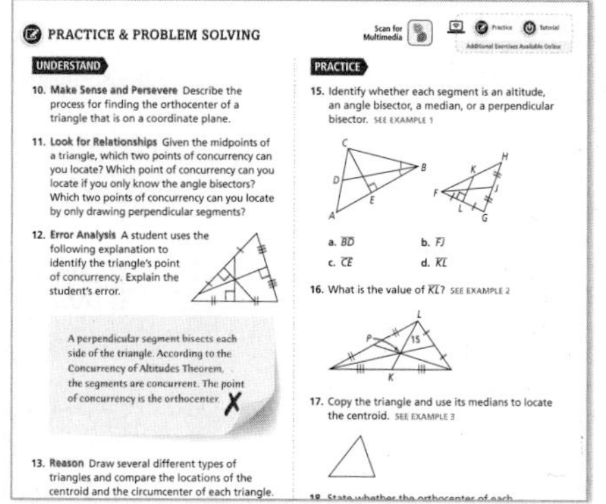

PRACTICE & PROBLEM SOLVING

UNDERSTAND

10. Make Sense and Persevere Describe the process for finding the orthocenter of a triangle that is on a coordinate plane.
11. Look for Relationships Given the midpoints of a triangle, which two points of concurrency can you locate? Which point of concurrency can you locate if you only know the angle bisectors? Which two points of concurrency can you locate by only drawing perpendicular segments?
12. Error Analysis A student uses the following explanation to identify the triangle's point of concurrency. Explain the student's error.

A perpendicular segment bisects each side of the triangle. According to the Concurrency of Altitudes Theorem, the segments are concurrent. The point of concurrency is the orthocenter.

13. Reason Draw several different types of triangles and compare the locations of the centroid and the circumcenter of each triangle.

PRACTICE

15. Identify whether each segment is an altitude, an angle bisector, a median, or a perpendicular bisector. SEE EXAMPLE 1

a. $\overline{BD}$ b. $\overline{FJ}$ c. $\overline{CE}$ d. $\overline{KL}$

16. What is the value of $KL$? SEE EXAMPLE 2
17. Copy the triangle and use its medians to locate the centroid. SEE EXAMPLE 3

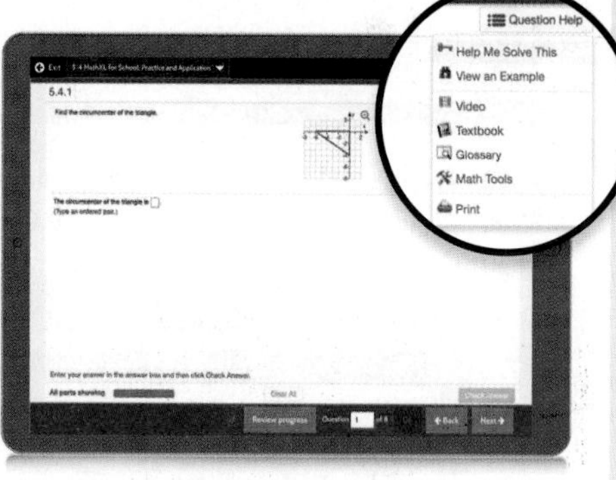


**Step 4** Your teacher may have you take the Lesson Quiz after each lesson. You can take the quiz online or in print. To do your best on the quiz, review the lesson problems in that lesson.

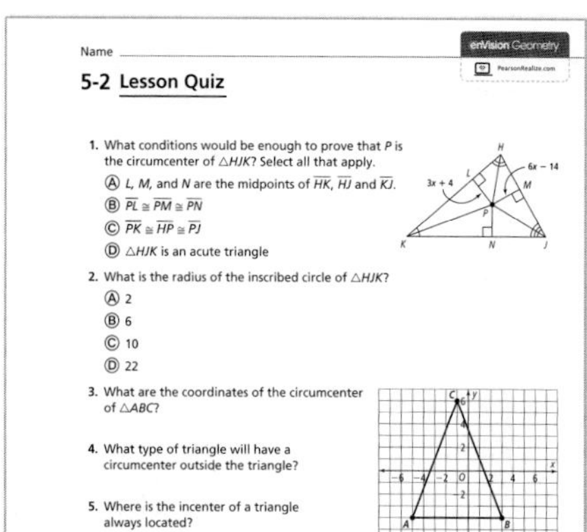

Name

5-2 Lesson Quiz

enVision Geometry

1. What conditions would be enough to prove that $P$ is the circumcenter of $\triangle HJK$? Select all that apply.
Ⓐ $L$, $M$, and $N$ are the midpoints of $\overline{HK}$, $\overline{HJ}$ and $\overline{KJ}$.
Ⓑ $\overline{PL} \cong \overline{PM} \cong \overline{PN}$
Ⓒ $\overline{PK} \cong \overline{HP} \cong \overline{PJ}$
Ⓓ $\triangle HJK$ is an acute triangle
2. What is the radius of the inscribed circle of $\triangle HJK$?
Ⓐ 2
Ⓑ 6
Ⓒ 10
Ⓓ 22
3. What are the coordinates of the circumcenter of $\triangle ABC$?
4. What type of triangle will have a circumcenter outside the triangle?
5. Where is the incenter of a triangle always located?

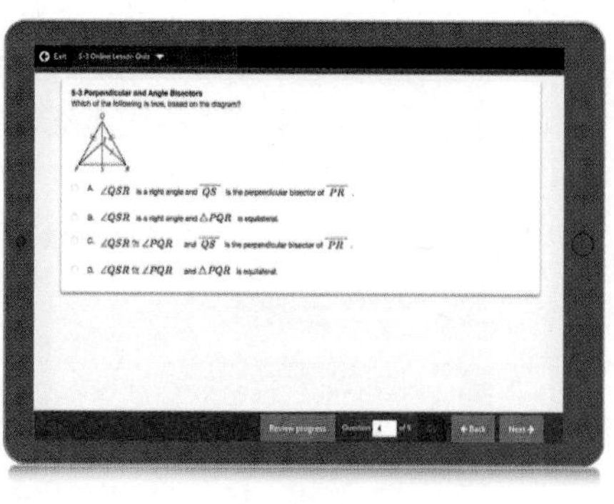

# Digital Resources

## Everything you need for math, anytime, anywhere.

PearsonRealize.com is your gateway to all of the digital resources for enVision™ Geometry. Log in to access your interactive student edition, called Realize Reader.

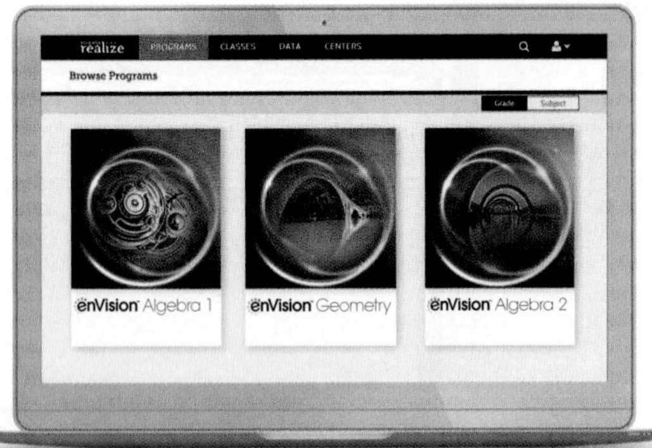


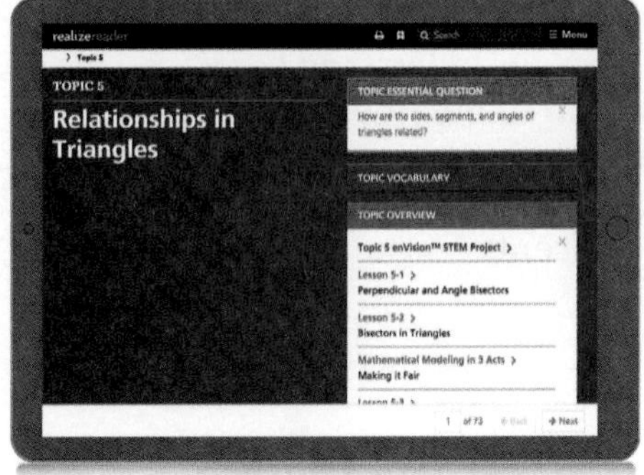


In PearsonRealize, you can:

**Activities** Complete Explore & Reason, Model & Discuss, Critique & Explain activities.

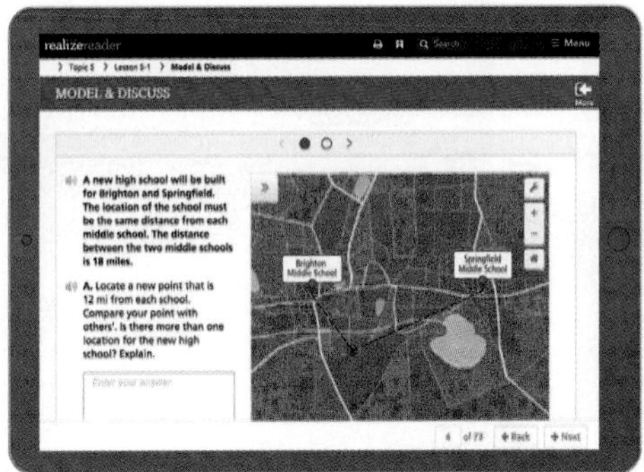


**Animation** View and interact with real-world applications.

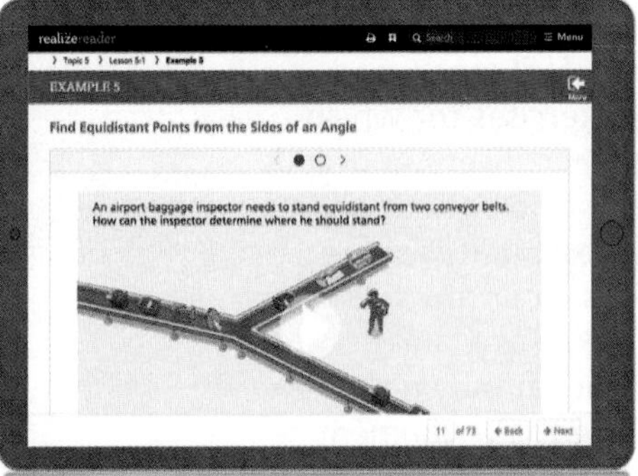


**Activities** Interact with Examples and Try Its.

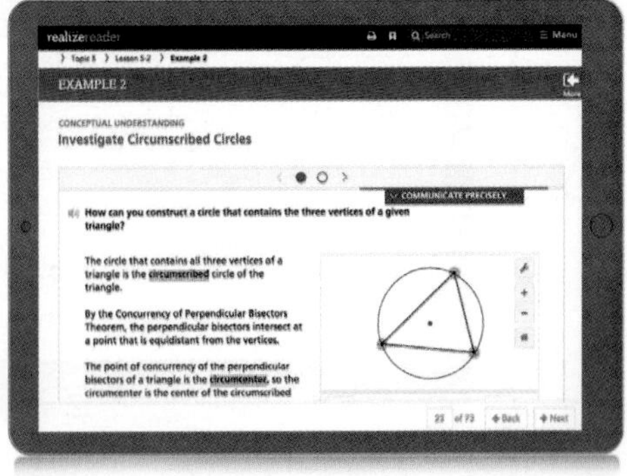


**Practice** Practice what you've learned.

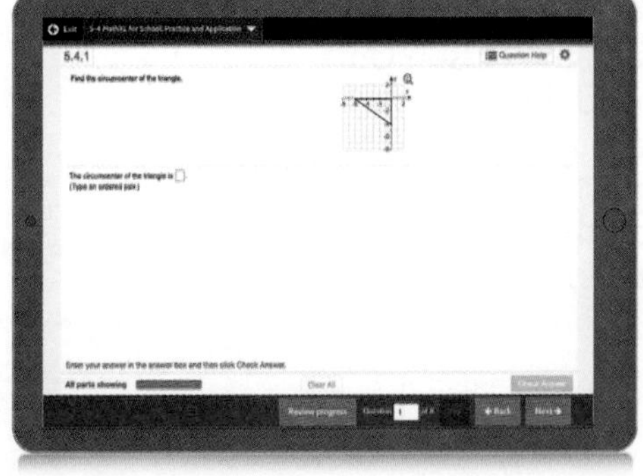

**Videos** Watch clips to support Mathematical Modeling in 3 Acts Lessons and enVision™ STEM Projects.

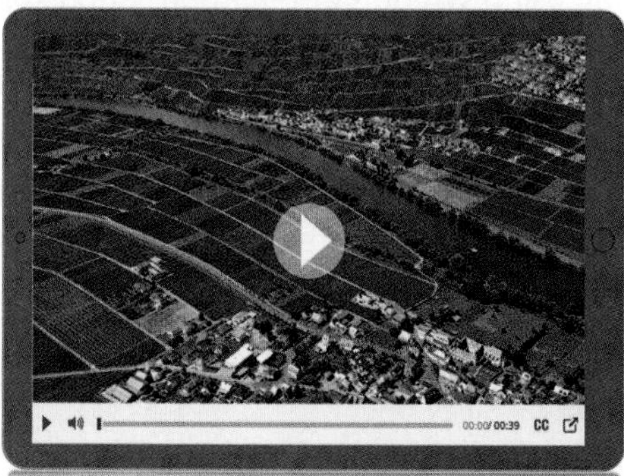

**Assessment** Show what you've learned.

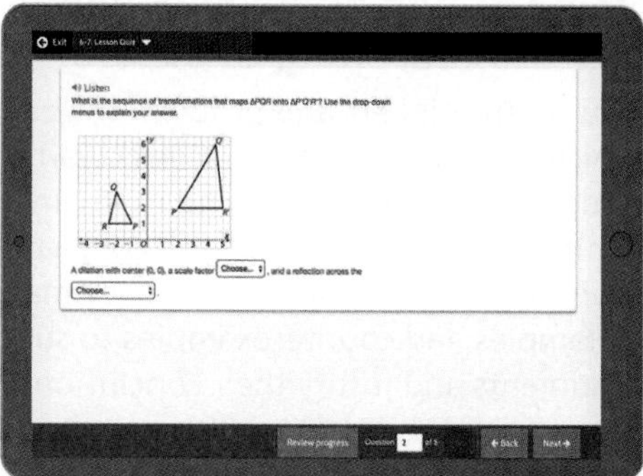

**Tutorials** Get help from Virtual Nerd, right when you need it.

**Concept Sumary** Review key lesson content through multiple representations.

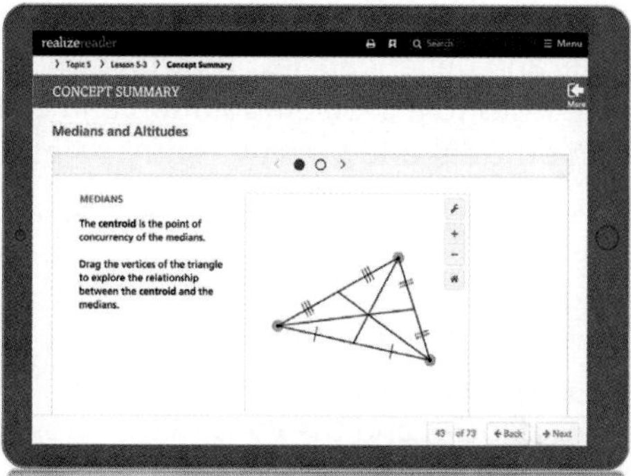


**Glossary** Read and listen to English and Spanish definitions.

**Math Tools** Explore math with digital tools and manipulatives.

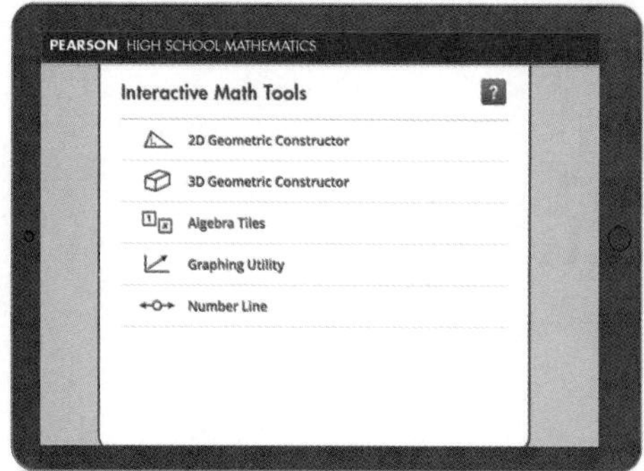

# Mathematical Practices and Processes

## Problem Solving

### Make sense of problems and persevere in solving them.

Proficient math thinkers are able to read through a problem situation and can put together a workable solution path to solve the problem posed. They analyze the information provided and identify constraints and dependencies. They identify multiple entries to a problem solution and will choose an efficient and effective entry point.

Consider these questions to help you make sense of problems.

- What am I asked to find?
- What are the quantities and variables? The dependencies and the constraints? How do they relate?
- What are some possible strategies to solve the problem?

### Attend to precision.

Proficient math thinkers communicate clearly and precisely the approach they are using. They identify the meaning of symbols that they use and always remember to specify units of measure and to label accurately graphical models. They use mathematical terms precisely and express their answers with the appropriate degree of accuracy.

Consider these questions to help you attend to precision.

- Have I stated the meaning of the variables and symbols I am using?
- Have I specified the units of measure I am using?
- Have I calculated accurately?

## Reasoning and Communicating

### Reason abstractly and quantitatively.

Proficient math thinkers make sense of quantities in problem situations. They represent a problem situation using symbols or equations and explain what the symbols or equation represent in relationship to a problem situation. As they model a situation symbolically or mathematically, they explain the meaning of the quantities.

Consider these questions to help you reason abstractly and quantitatively.

- How can I represent the problem using equations or formulas?
- What do the numbers, variables, and symbols in the equation or formula represent?

### Construct viable arguments and critique the reasoning of others.

Proficient math thinkers and problem solvers communicate their problem solutions clearly and convincingly. They construct sound mathematical arguments and develop and defend conjectures to explain mathematical situations. They make use of examples and counterexamples to support their arguments and justify their conclusions. When asked, they respond clearly and logically to the positions and conclusions of others, and compare two arguments, identifying any flaws in logic or reasoning that the arguments may contain. They ask questions to clarify or improve the position of a classmate.

Consider these questions to help you construct mathematical arguments.

- What assumptions can I make when constructing an argument?
- What conjectures can I make about the solution to the problem?
- What arguments can I present to defend my conjectures?

# Representing and Connecting

## Model with mathematics.

Proficient math thinkers use mathematics to represent a problem situation and make connections between a real-world problem situation and mathematics. They see the applicability of mathematics to solve every-day problems and explain how geometry can be used to solve a carpentry problem or algebra to solve a proportional relationship problem. They define and map relationships among quantities in a problem, using appropriate tools. They analyze the relationships and draw conclusions about the solutions.

Consider these questions to help you model with mathematics.

- What representations can I use to show the relationship among quantities or variables?
- What assumptions can I make about the problem situation to simplify the problem?

## Use appropriate tools strategically.

Proficient math thinkers strategize about which tools are more helpful to solve a problem situation. They consider all tools, from paper and pencil to protractors and rulers, to calculators and software applications. They articulate the appropriateness of different tools and recognize which would best serve the needs for a given problem. They are especially insightful about technological tools and use them in ways that deepen or extend their understanding of concepts. They also make use of mental tools, such as estimation, to determine the appropriateness of a solution.

Consider these questions to help you use appropriate tools.

- What tool can I use to help me solve the problem?
- How can technology help me solve the problem?

# Seeing Patterns and Generalizing

## Look for and make use of structure.

Proficient math thinkers see mathematical patterns in the problems they are solving and generalize mathematics principles from these patterns. They see complicated expressions or equations as single objects composed of many parts.

Consider these questions to help you see structure.

- Can I see a pattern in the problem or solution strategy?
- How can I use the pattern I see to help me solve the problem?

## Look for generalizations.

Proficient math thinkers notice when calculations are repeated and can uncover both general methods and shortcuts for solving similar problems.

Consider these questions to help you look for regularity in repeated reasoning.

- Do I notice any repeated calculations or steps?
- Are there general methods that I can use to solve the problem?
- What can I generalize from one problem to another?
- How reasonable are the results that I am getting?

# Key Concepts in Geometry

The focus of enVision Geometry is the study of Euclidian geometry. Studying plane figures both on and off the coordinate grid, students develop an understanding of the structures of geometry. They use postulates, corollaries, and theorems to write proofs for properties of two-dimensional figures, including triangles, quadrilaterals, and circles. Students use transformations to understand congruence in terms of rigid motions, and similarity in terms of similarity transformations. Students look at the relationships in right triangles to develop an understanding of trigonometry, and learn the Law of Sines and the Law of Cosines for all triangles. Students also build on prior knowledge from Algebra 1, expanding their knowledge of parabolas to include the focus and directrix. Once they have learned about two-dimensional figures, they use that foundation to learn the properties of three-dimensional figures such as prisms, cones, pyramids, and spheres.

## Foundations of Geometry

- The foundation of geometry is based on undefined notions of point, line, plane, distance along a line, and distance around a circular arc.
- Postulates and axioms are assumed to be true; whereas theorems and corollaries need to be proven.
- Theorems and corollaries about lines, angles, and figures can be proven using postulates, axioms, definitions, and other theorems.
- Two lines with the same slope are parallel while two lines whose slopes are opposite reciprocals are perpendicular.
- The coordinates of a polygon in a coordinate grid can be used to compute perimeters of polygons and areas of triangles and rectangles.
- Some geometric theorems can be proven algebraically by using coordinates of figures in a coordinate plane.
- Inductive reasoning is a tool to develop conjectures.
- Deductive reasoning is a way to formally construct a valid argument.
- Using laws of logic aids in the process of determining the validity of a statement.

## Angle and Triangle Relationships

- If the measure of one angle formed when a pair of parallel lines is cut by a transversal is known, then the measures of the other angles can be determined.
- The circumcenter of a triangle is the point that is equidistant from the vertices. This is where the perpendicular bisectors intersect.
- The incenter of a triangle is the point where the angle bisectors intersect. It is equidistant from the sides.
- Special angle pair measurements can be used to prove that two lines are parallel.
- Inscribed and circumscribed circles of a triangle are constructed to find the incenter and circumcenter of a triangle.

## Congruence and Similarity

- Transformations in the plane take points in the plane as inputs and give other points as outputs.
- Some transformations, such as translations, reflections, and rotations preserve distance and angle; others, such as dilations, do not.
- A series of transformations can carry a given figure onto another.
- The definition of congruence in terms of rigid motions can be used to determine whether two figures are congruent.
- Two triangles are congruent if and only if corresponding pairs of sides and corresponding pairs of angles are congruent.
- The criteria for triangle congruence – Angle-Side-Angle, Side-Angle-Side, and Side-Side-Side--follow from the definition of congruence in terms of rigid motions.
- Two triangles are similar if all corresponding pairs of angles are congruent and all corresponding pairs of sides are proportional.
- The properties of similarity transformations can be used to establish the Angle-Angle criterion for two triangles to be similar.
- Congruence and similarity criteria for triangles can be used to solve problems and to prove relationships in geometric figures.
- By similarity, side ratios in right triangles are properties of the angles in the triangle, leading to definitions of trigonometric ratios for acute angles.

## Trigonometric Relationships

- The sine of any acute angle is equal to the cosine of its complement.
- The cosine of any acute angle is equal to the sine of its complement.
- The relationship between the sine and cosine of complementary angles can be used to solve problems.
- The formula $A = \frac{1}{2}ab \sin(C)$ for the area of a triangle can be derived by drawing an auxiliary line from a vertex perpendicular to the opposite side.
- The Law of Sines states that $\frac{a}{\sin A} = \frac{b}{\sin B} = \frac{c}{\sin C}$. The Law of Sines can be used to solve real-world problems.
- The Law of Cosines states that $c^2 = a^2 + b^2 - 2ab \cos(C)$. The Law of Cosines can be used to solve real-world problems.

# Key Concepts in Geometry

## Circles and Parabolas

- All circles are similar.
- The length of the arc of a circle intercepted by an angle is proportional to the radius of the circle.
- The radian measure of an angle is the ratio of the arc length of a circle and the radius of the circle. It is a constant of proportionality between arc length and radius.
- The equation of a circle of given center and radius can be derived using the Pythagorean Theorem.
- The equation of a parabola can be derived given a focus and directrix.
- Tangent lines only intersect the circle at one point. They are perpendicular to the radius that intersects the circle at that point.
- When two segments are tangent to a circle and have a common endpoint outside of the circle, the segments are congruent.
- When a quadrilateral is inscribed in a circle, opposite angles are supplementary.
- When a tangent intersects the endpoint of a chord, the measure of the angle formed is half the measure of its intercepted arc.
- The measure of an angle inscribed in a circle is half the measure of the arc it intercepts.
- An angle inscribed on the diameter is a right angle.
- Two inscribed angles that intercept the same arc are congruent.
- If the chords in a circle are congruent, their central angles are congruent.
- If chords are the same distance from the center of a circle, they are congruent.
- If the diameter intersects the chord at 90°, then it bisects the chord.
- If arcs of a circle are congruent, their chords are also congruent.

## Geometric Figures and Measurements

- Volume formulas for cylinders, pyramids, cones, and spheres can help solve real-world and mathematical problems.
- The cross-sections of three-dimensional objects are two-dimensional figures.
- The properties and measures of geometric figures can be used to describe real-world objects.
- Concepts of density based on area and volume can be used to model real-world situations.
- Geometric methods can help solve design problems.

# Probability

- Probability events are subsets of a sample space. The outcomes can be categorized as unions, intersections, or complements of other events ("or," "and," "not").
- Two events *A* and *B* are independent if the probability of *A* and *B* occurring together is the product of their probabilities.
- The probability that event *A* occurs given event *B* is called a conditional probability. It is expressed $\frac{P(A \text{ and } B)}{P(B)}$.
- If *A* and *B* are independent events, the conditional probability of *A* given *B* is the same as the probability of *A*, and the conditional probability of *B* given *A* is the same as the probability of *B*.
- A two-way frequency table can show the frequency of events. It can represent a sample space. It can also be used to determine whether events are independent and to approximate conditional probabilities.
- When two events, *A* and *B* are mutually exclusive, the probability of *A* OR *B* occurring is the sum of the probability of each event, also known as the Addition Rule, that is $P(A \text{ or } B) = P(A) + P(B)$.
- When two events, *A* and *B* are not mutually exclusive, the probability of *A* OR *B* occurring is found using the Addition Rule, that is $P(A \text{ or } B) = P(A) + P(B) - P(A \text{ and } B)$.
- If *A* and *B* are dependent events, the probability of *A* AND *B* occurring is $P(A \text{ and } B) = P(A)P(B|A)$ or $P(B)P(A|B)$.
- Permutations and combinations are used to compute probabilities of compound events. A combination shows the probability of compound events when order does not matter while a permutation shows the probability of compound events when order does matter.
- An expected value is a predicted value of a random variable. It is a probability-weighted averages of all possible values.
- A random variable is a variable quantity whose possible values depend on random outcome events.
- The expected value of a random variable can be used to guide decisions about future events.

TOPIC 1

# Foundations of Geometry

TOPIC 2

# Parallel and Perpendicular Lines

TOPIC 3

# Transformations

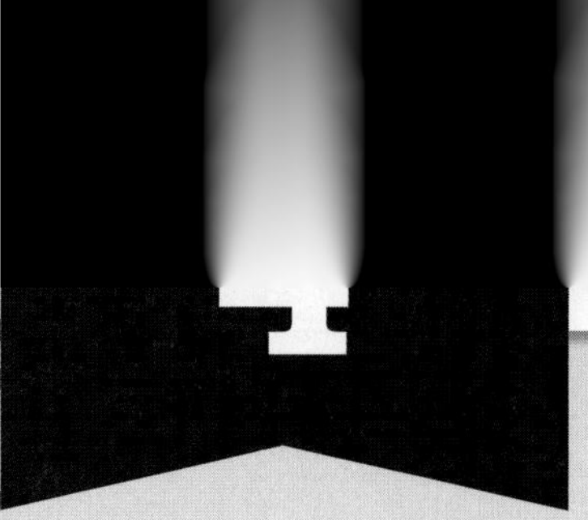

TOPIC 5

# Relationships in Triangles

TOPIC 6

# Quadrilaterals and Other Polygons

TOPIC 7

# Similarity

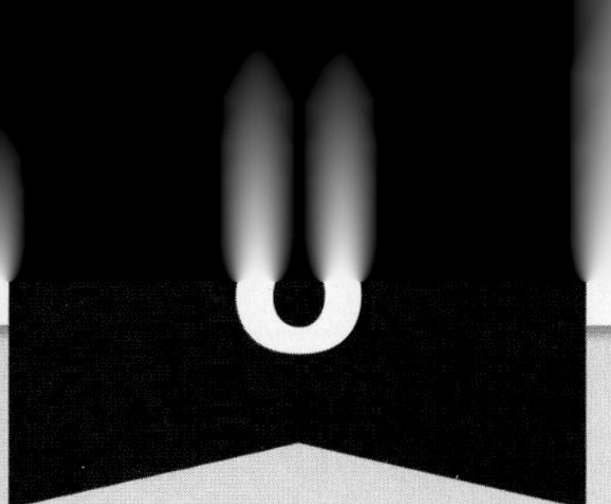

TOPIC 9

# Coordinate Geometry

TOPIC 11

# Two- and Three-Dimensional Models

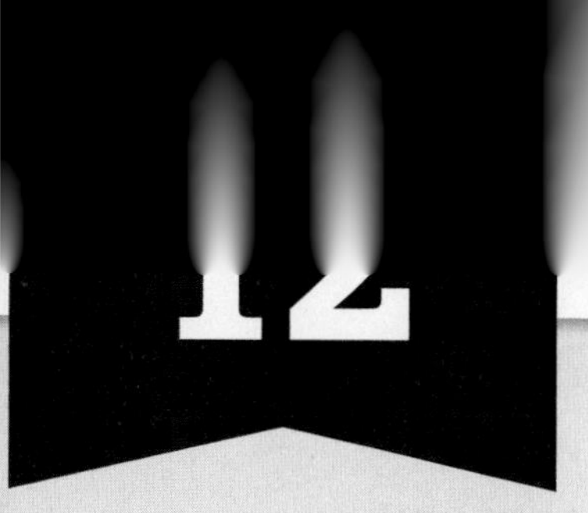

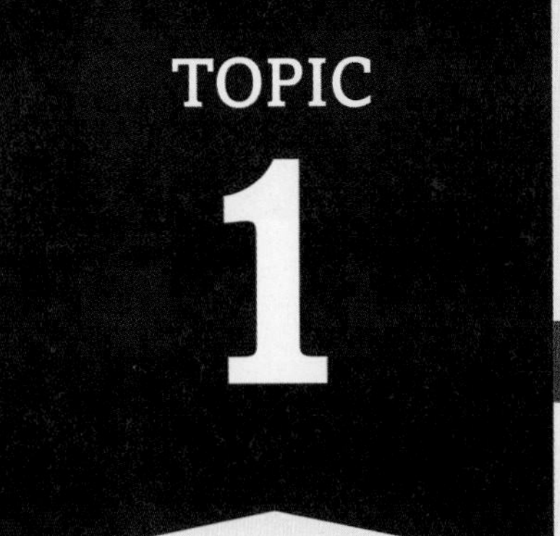


# Foundations of Geometry

## TOPIC ESSENTIAL QUESTION

What are some of the fundamentals of geometry?

## Topic Overview



## Topic Vocabulary

- angle bisector
- biconditional
- conditional
- conjecture
- construction
- contrapositive
- converse
- counterexample
- deductive reasoning
- inductive reasoning
- inverse
- Law of Detachment
- Law of Syllogism
- negation
- proof
- perpendicular bisector
- postulate
- theorem
- truth table
- truth value

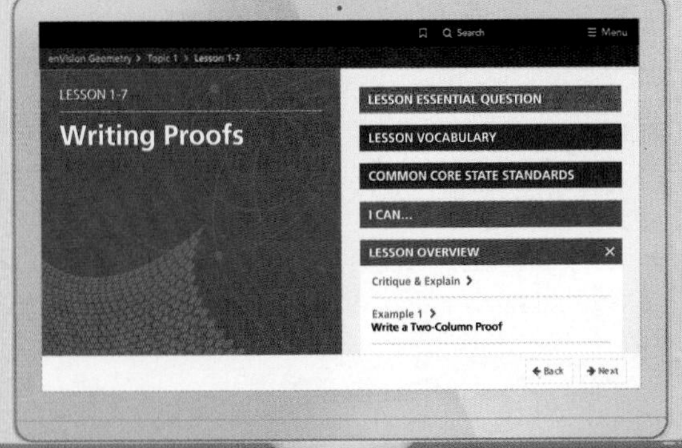

Go online | **PearsonRealize.com**

## Digital Experience

**INTERACTIVE STUDENT EDITION** Access online or offline.

**ACTIVITIES** Complete ***Explore & Reason, Model & Discuss***, and ***Critique & Explain*** activities. Interact with Examples and Try Its.

**ANIMATION** View and interact with real-world applications.

**PRACTICE** Practice what you've learned.

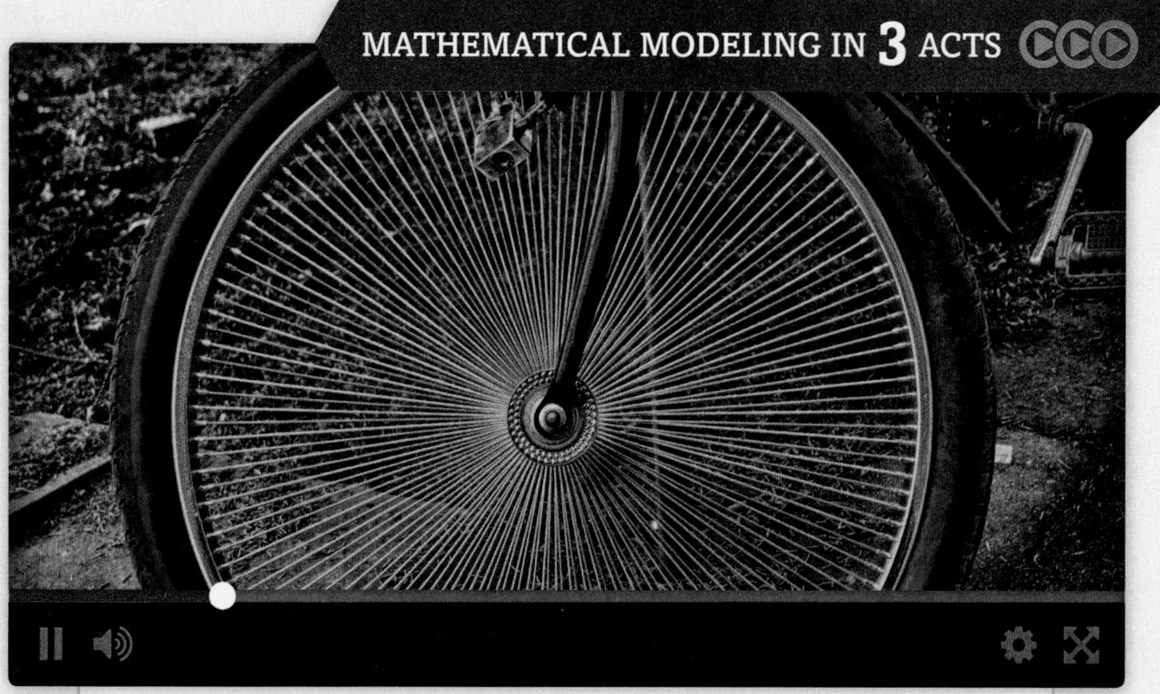


## The Mystery Spokes

Some photos are taken in such a way that it is difficult to determine exactly what the picture shows. Sometimes this is because the photo is a close up of an object, and you do not see the entire object. Other times, it might be because the photographer used special effects when taking the photo.

You can often use clues from the photo to determine what is in the photo and also what the rest of the object might look like. What clues would you look for? Think about this during the Mathematical Modeling in 3 Acts lesson.

TOPIC 1

**VIDEOS** Watch clips to support ***Mathematical Modeling in 3 Acts Lessons*** and **enVision™** ***STEM Projects.***

**CONCEPT SUMMARY** Review key lesson content through multiple representations.

**ASSESSMENT** Show what you've learned.

**GLOSSARY** Read and listen to English and Spanish definitions.

**TUTORIALS** Get help from ***Virtual Nerd***, right when you need it.

**MATH TOOLS** Explore math with digital tools and manipulatives.

## Did You Know?

The **golden ratio**, $(1 + \sqrt{5}) : 2$, has been explored in mathematics for over 2400 years. A golden rectangle has sides in the golden ratio.

$$(1 + \sqrt{5}) : 2$$

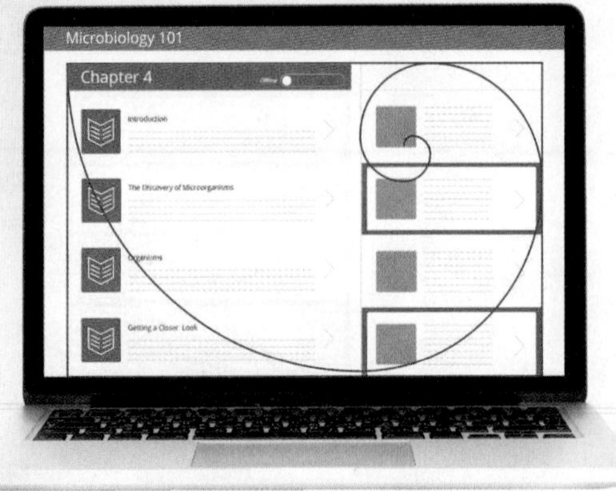


**Golden rectangles** are used in webpage design to allocate space for content areas.

The main door of the Taj Mahal, in Agra, India, is in the shape of a **golden rectangle**.

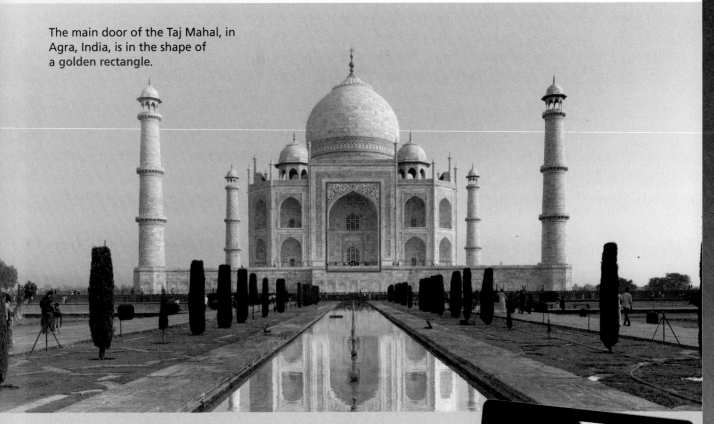

## Your Task: Design a Tablet

The tablet market is growing quickly. Each quarter, more than 38 million tablets are shipped around the world. By 2019, yearly shipping is expected to surpass 189 million. In this project, you'll design a new tablet using the golden ratio.

Activity Assess

# 1-1 Measuring Segments and Angles

PearsonRealize.com

**I CAN...** use properties of segments and angles to find their measures.

## VOCABULARY

- collinear points
- line
- plane
- point
- postulate

## EXPLORE & REASON

**A teacher labels two points on the number line.**

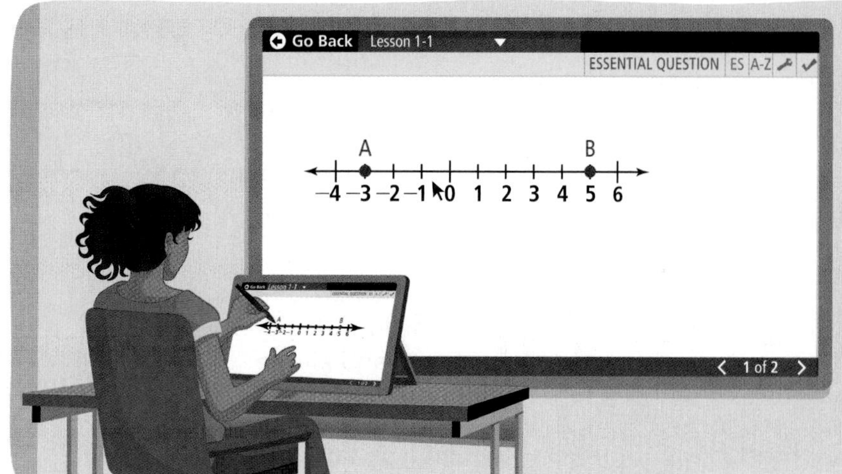


**A.** What are some methods for finding the distance between points *A* and *B*?

**B. Construct Arguments** Which method of finding the distance is the best? Explain.

## ESSENTIAL QUESTION

**How are the properties of segments and angles used to determine their measures?**

### CONCEPT Undefined Terms

Undefined terms are terms whose meanings are accepted without formal definition. The terms point, line, and plane are undefined terms that are the basic building blocks of geometry.

| Description | Diagram | Notation |
|---|---|---|
| A **point** is a location and has no size. | •P | *P* |
| A **line** is an infinite number of points on a straight path that extends in two opposite directions with no end and has no thickness. | A, B, ℓ | line $\ell$<br>$\overleftrightarrow{AB}$ |
| A **plane** is an infinite number of points and lines on a flat surface that extends without end and has no thickness. | X, Y, Z, M | plane *M*<br>plane *XYZ* |

## CONCEPT Defined Terms

In geometry, new terms are defined using previously defined or known terms.

| Description | Diagram | Notation |
|---|---|---|
| A segment is the part of a line that consists of two points, called *endpoints* and all points between them. | A B | $\overline{AB}$ |
| A ray is the part of a line that consists of one *endpoint* and all the points of the line on one side of the endpoint. | M N | $\overrightarrow{MN}$ |
| Opposite rays are rays with the same endpoint that lie on the same line. | S T U | $\overrightarrow{TS}$ and $\overrightarrow{TU}$ |
| An angle is formed by two rays with the same endpoint. Each ray is a side of the angle and the common endpoint is the vertex of the angle. | 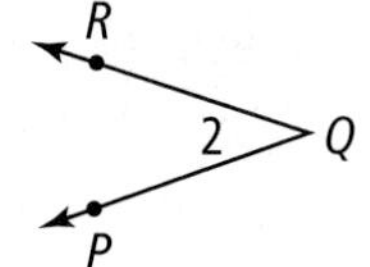  | $\angle Q$<br>$\angle PQR$<br>$\angle 2$ |

## EXAMPLE 1 Find Segment Lengths

**How can you find the length of $\overline{CD}$?**

The length of a segment is a positive real number. You can use the number line to find the length of $\overline{CD}$.

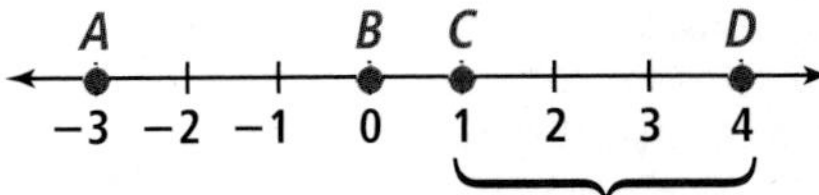


**COMMUNICATE PRECISELY**
Think about how notation and symbols are used. How might the notation for a segment and for the length of a segment help you remember their meaning?

To find the length of a segment, count the units of length between the endpoints. The length of $\overline{CD}$ is 3.

**Try It!** 1. Refer to the figure in Example 1. How can you find the length of $\overline{AC}$?

**POSTULATE 1-1** Ruler Postulate

Every point on a line can be paired with a unique real number. This number is called the *coordinate* of the point.

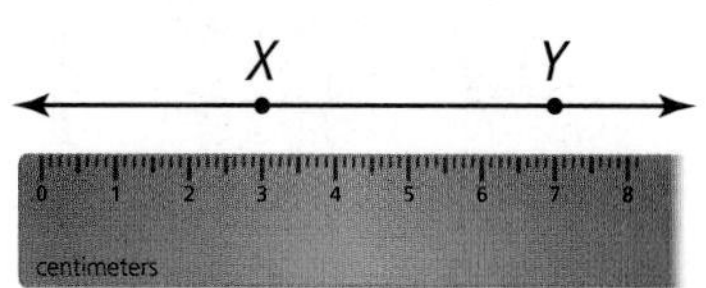


The coordinate of $X$ is 3.
The coordinate of $Y$ is 7.

**CONCEPT** Distance on a Line

The distance between any two points $X$ and $Y$ is the absolute value of the difference of their coordinates.

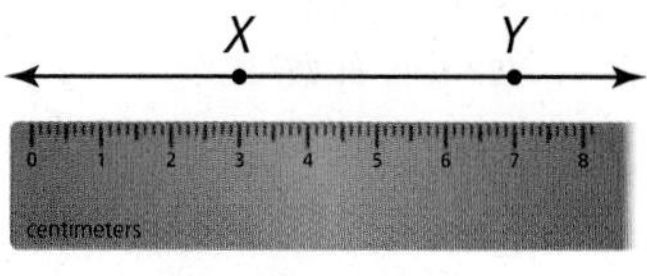


$XY = |7 - 3| = 4$

$XY = |3 - 7| = 4$

**EXAMPLE 2** Find the Length of a Segment

**What is $KL$?**

A **postulate** is a statement that is assumed to be true.

Use the Ruler Postulate to find the coordinates of $K$ and $L$.

**STUDY TIP**
Remember, when finding distance between two points, take the absolute value of the difference because distance is positive.

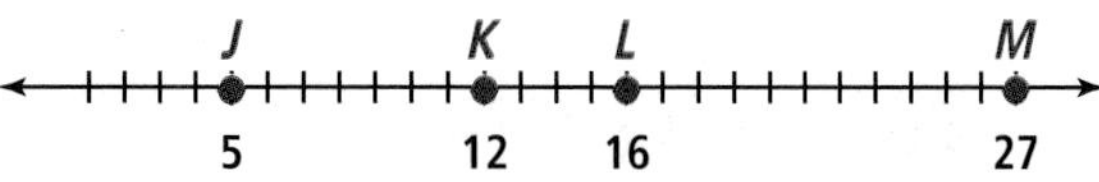


$KL = |16 - 12| = 4$ or $KL = |12 - 16| = 4$

**Try It!** **2.** Refer to the figure in Example 2.

**a.** What is $JK$?

**b.** What is $KM$?

**POSTULATE 1-2** Segment Addition Postulate

If points $A$, $B$, and $C$ are on the same line with $B$ between $A$ and $C$, then $AB + BC = AC$.

**If...**

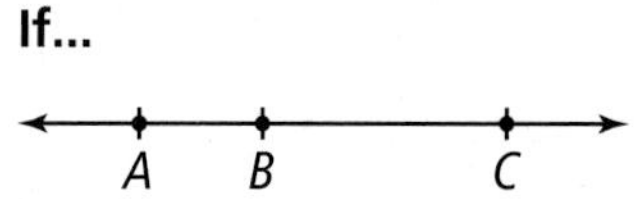


**Then...** $AB + BC = AC$

## EXAMPLE 3 Use the Segment Addition Postulate

**Points $F$, $G$, and $H$ are collinear.**
**If $GH = 16$, what is $FH$?**

Collinear points lie on the same line.

F G H

$3x - 1$ $2x + 2$

**Step 1** Use the expression for $GH$ to find $x$.

$$GH = 16$$
$$2x + 2 = 16$$
$$2x = 14$$
$$x = 7$$

**Step 2** Find $FH$.

$$FH = FG + GH$$
$$= 5x + 1$$
$$= 5(7) + 1$$
$$= 36$$

Apply the Segment Addition Postulate.

**COMMON ERROR**
Be sure to answer the question that is posed. You may state the value of the variable $x$ as the answer, but you use this answer to find $FH$.

 **Try It!** 3. Points $J$, $K$, and $L$ are collinear.

J K L

$3n$ $5n - 7$

a. If $JL = 25$, what is $n$?

b. What is $JK$? $KL$?

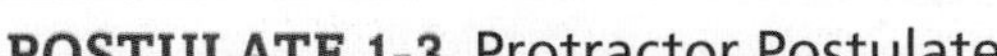

**POSTULATE 1-3** Protractor Postulate

Given $\overrightarrow{BA}$ and a point $C$ not on $\overrightarrow{BA}$, a unique real number from 0 to 180 can be assigned to $\overrightarrow{BC}$.

0 is assigned to $\overrightarrow{BA}$.

180 is assigned to $\overrightarrow{BD}$.

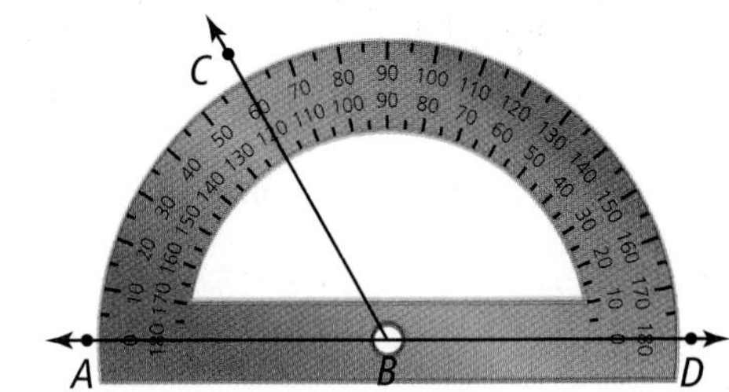


## EXAMPLE 4 Use the Protractor Postulate to Measure an Angle

**What is $m\angle BEC$?**

**STUDY TIP**
Remember, the measure of $\angle BEC$ is denoted as $m\angle BEC$.

Since $\overrightarrow{EA}$ lines up with 0 on the top scale, use the top scale for all of the other rays in the figure.

By the Protractor Postulate, real numbers are assigned to $\overrightarrow{EB}$ and $\overrightarrow{EC}$.

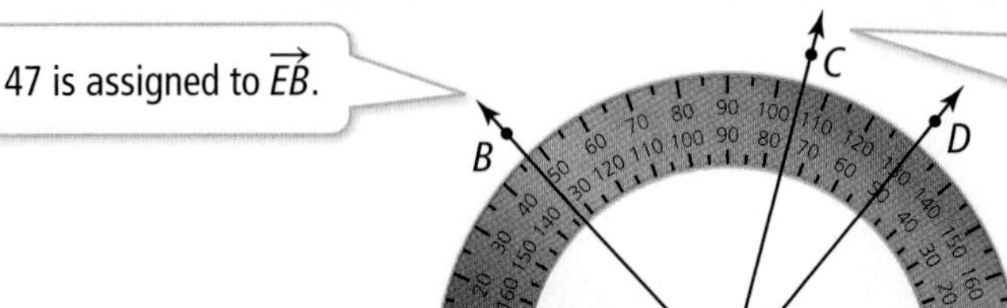


You can subtract $m\angle AEB$ from $m\angle AEC$ to find $m\angle BEC$.

$m\angle BEC = |105 - 47| = 58$

CONTINUED ON THE NEXT PAGE

EXAMPLE 4 CONTINUED

**Try It!** **4.** Refer to the figure in Example 4.

**a.** What is $m\angle AEC$?

**b.** What is $m\angle BED$?

**POSTULATE 1-4** Angle Addition Postulate

If point $D$ is in the interior of $\angle ABC$, then $m\angle ABD + m\angle DBC = m\angle ABC$.

**If...**

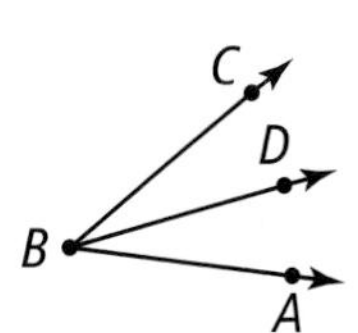


**Then...** $m\angle ABD + m\angle DBC = m\angle ABC$

APPLICATION

## EXAMPLE 5 Use the Angle Addition Postulate to Solve Problems

**A lighting designer is finalizing the lighting plan for an upcoming production. The spotlight can rotate 25° to the left or right from the shown starting position. The beam of light from the spotlight forms a 22° angle. Can the designer use the spotlight to light each of the objects on the stage?**

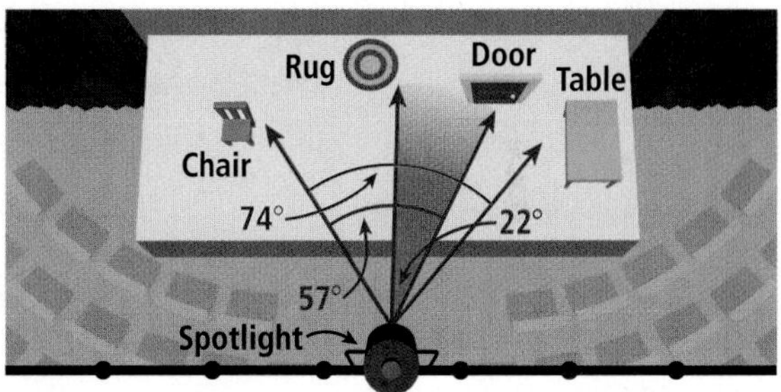


**Formulate** Draw and label a diagram to represent the beam angle, the angles given and the unknown angles.

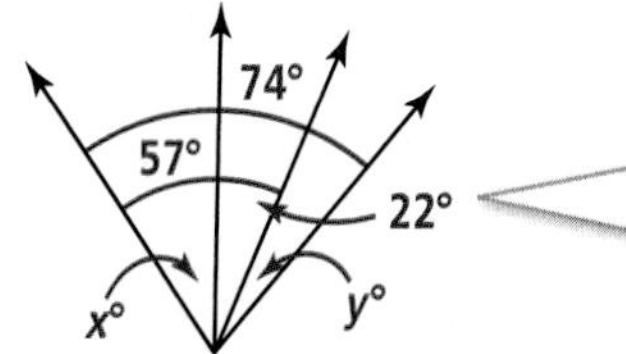


Use the Angle Addition Postulate to find the angles the light must rotate to the left and right to light the chair and table.

**Compute** Write and solve equations to find $x$ and $y$.

$x + 22 = 57$ $\qquad$ $y + 57 = 74$

$x = 35$ $\qquad$ $y = 17$

**Interpret** The spotlight can rotate 25° to the right or left, so the designer can use the spotlight to light the table but cannot light the chair.

**Try It!** **5.** Refer to Example 5. Can the lighting designer use a spotlight with a 33° beam angle that can rotate 25° to the left and right to light all of the objects on the stage?

## CONCEPT Congruent Segments and Congruent Angles

Segments that have the same length are congruent segments.

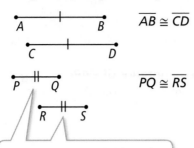

$\overline{AB} \cong \overline{CD}$

$\overline{PQ} \cong \overline{RS}$

The same number of *tick marks* shows congruent segments.

Angles that have the same measure are congruent angles.

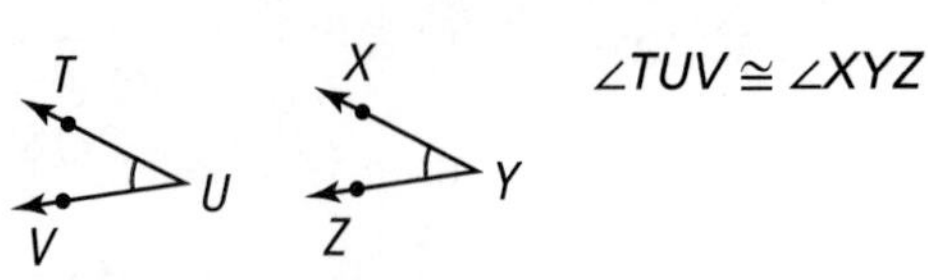


$\angle TUV \cong \angle XYZ$

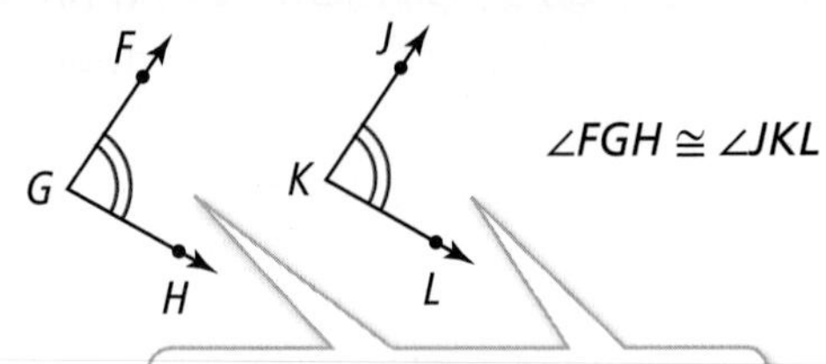


$\angle FGH \cong \angle JKL$

The same number of *arc marks* shows congruent angles.

## EXAMPLE 6 Use Congruent Angles and Congruent Segments

**STUDY TIP**
Be sure to read the congruency marks in the diagram carefully. Important information about a figure may be shown by using angle and segment congruence markings.

**A. If $m\angle XWZ = 127$, what is $m\angle YWV$?**

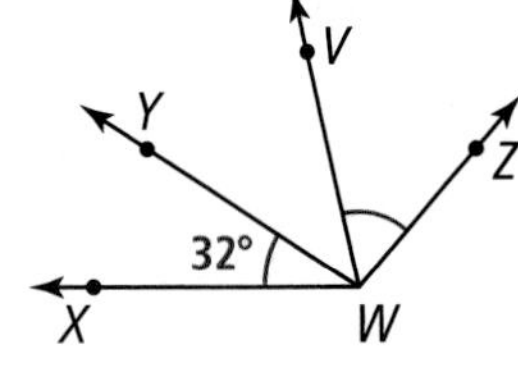


$$m\angle XWY + m\angle YWV + m\angle VWZ = m\angle XWZ$$

$$32 + m\angle YWZ + 32 = 127$$

$$m\angle YWV = 63$$

Apply the Angle Addition Postulate.

**B. What is *HF*?**

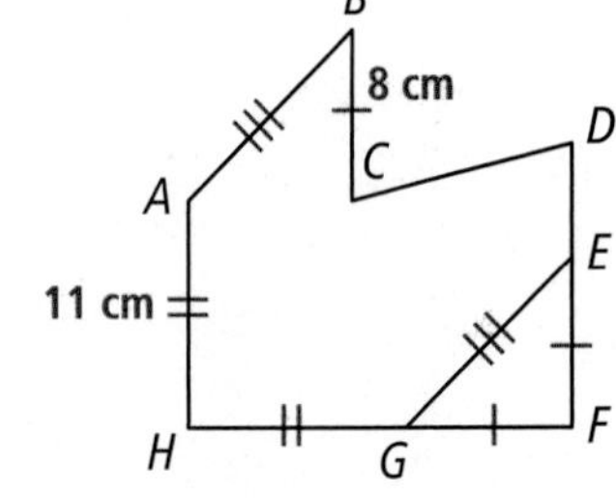


Apply the Segment Addition Postulate and substitute congruent segment lengths.

$HF = HG + GF$

$HF = AH + BC$

$HF = 11 + 8 = 19$ cm

**Try It!** **6. a.** If $m\angle NOP = 31$ and $m\angle NOQ = 114$, what is $m\angle ROQ$?

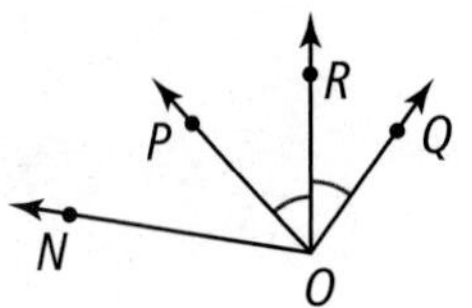


**b.** In the figure in Part B above, suppose $CD = 11.5$ cm, $DE = 5.3$ cm, and the perimeter of the figure is 73.8 cm. What is *GE*?

## CONCEPT SUMMARY Measuring Segments and Angles

| | Ruler Postulate | Protractor Postulate |
|---|---|---|
| WORDS | Every point on a line can be paired with a unique real number. This number is called the *coordinate* of the point. | Given $\overrightarrow{KL}$ and a point $J$ not on $\overrightarrow{KL}$, a unique real number from 0 to 180 can be paired with $\overrightarrow{KJ}$. |
| DIAGRAM | 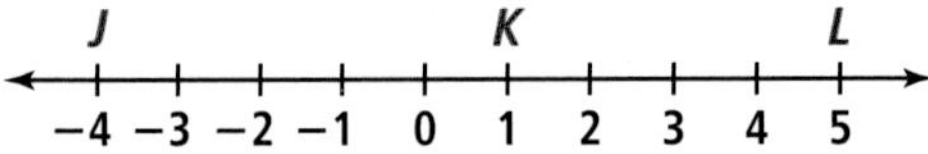  | 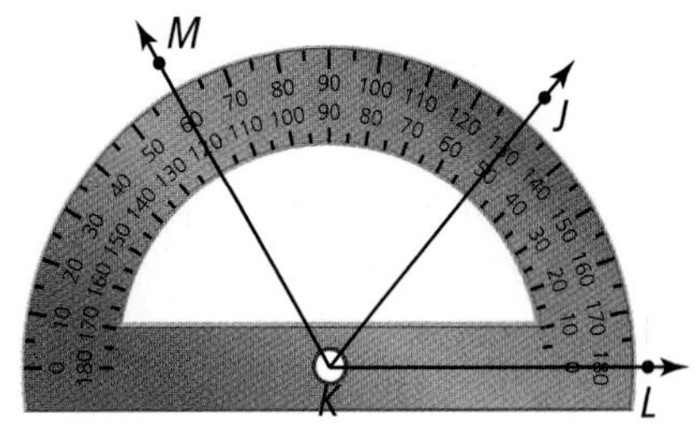  |
| SYMBOLS | $JK = 5$ $KL = 4$ $JL = 9$ <br> $JK + KL = JL$ | $m\angle JKL = 50$ $m\angle JKM = 70$ <br> $m\angle JKL + m\angle JKM = 120$ |

## Do You UNDERSTAND?

1. ESSENTIAL QUESTION How are the properties of segments and angles used to determine their measures?

2. **Error Analysis** Ella wrote $AB = |-1 + 5| = 4$. Explain Ella's error.

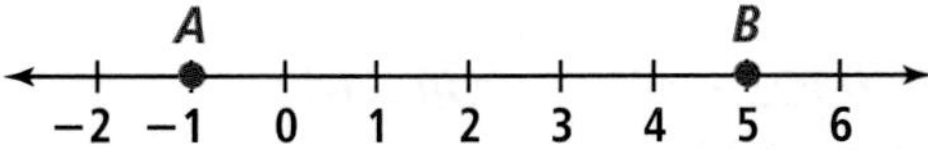


3. **Vocabulary** What does it mean for segments to be congruent? What does it mean for angles to be congruent?

4. **Make Sense and Persevere** Suppose $M$ is a point in the interior of $\angle JKL$. If $m\angle MKL = 42$ and $m\angle JKL = 84$, what is $m\angle JKM$?

## Do You KNOW HOW?

**Find the length of each segment.**

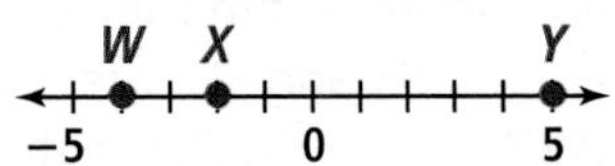


5. $\overline{WX}$

6. $\overline{WY}$

7. Points $A$, $B$, and $C$ are collinear and $B$ is between $A$ and $C$. Given $AB = 12$ and $AC = 19$, what is $BC$?

8. Given $m\angle JML = 80$ and $m\angle KML = 33$, what is $m\angle JMK$?

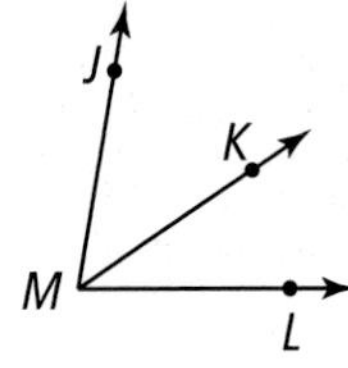

# PRACTICE & PROBLEM SOLVING

Scan for Multimedia | Practice | Tutorial | Additional Exercises Available Online

## UNDERSTAND

9. **Reason** The coordinate of point $M$ on a number line is 11. If $MN = 12$, what are the possible coordinates for $N$ on the number line?

10. **Construct Arguments** How can you use the Segment Addition Postulate to show that $AE = AB + BC + CD + DE$?

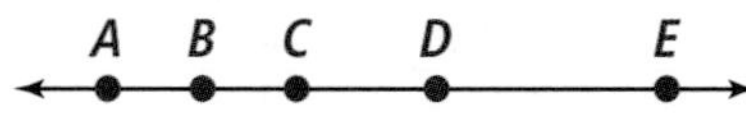


11. **Higher Order Thinking** If points $C$, $D$, and $E$ are on a line and $CD = 20$ and $CE = 32$, what are the possible values of $DE$?

12. **Error Analysis** Benito wrote the equations shown about the figure. Explain Benito's errors.

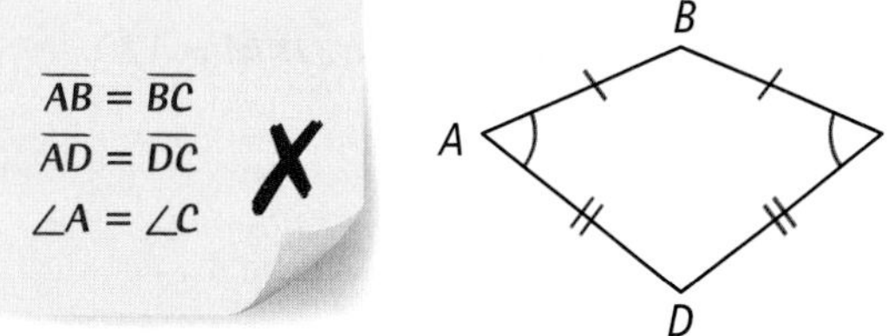


13. **Make Sense and Persevere** Point $Y$ is in the interior of $\angle XWZ$. Given that $\overrightarrow{WX}$ and $\overrightarrow{WZ}$ are opposite rays, and $m\angle XWY = 4(m\angle YWZ)$, what is $m\angle YWZ$?

14. **Mathematical Connections** The area of $ABED$ is 49 square units. Given $AG = 9$ units and $AC = 10$ units, what fraction of the area of $ACIG$ is represented by the shaded region? Give your answer in simplest form.

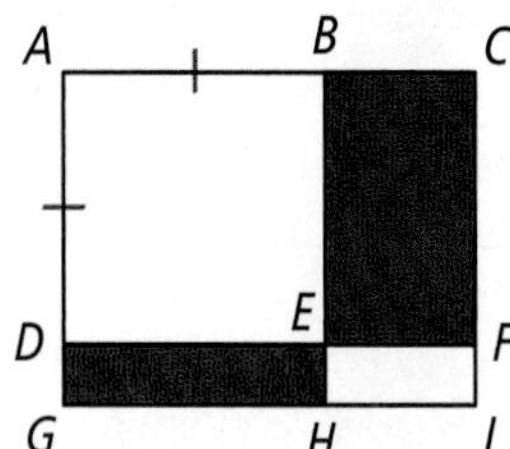


15. **Look for Relationships** In the diagram at the right, $m\angle LMN = 116$, $m\angle JKM = 122$, and $m\angle JNM = 103$. What is $m\angle NKM$?

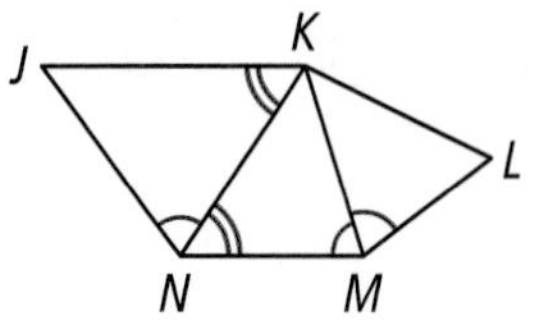


## PRACTICE

**Find the length of each segment.** SEE EXAMPLES 1 AND 2

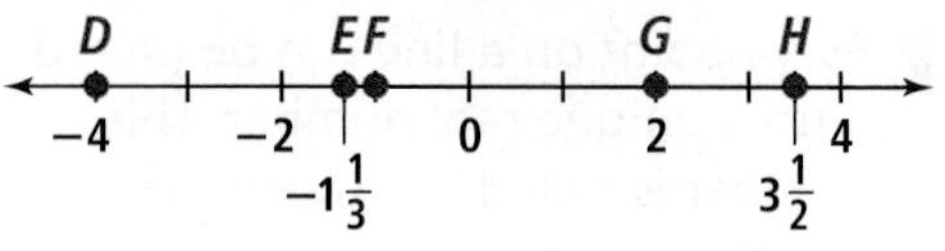


16. $\overline{DF}$
17. $\overline{DE}$
18. $\overline{FG}$
19. $\overline{FH}$
20. $\overline{GH}$
21. $\overline{EH}$

**Points $A$, $B$, $C$, $D$, and $E$ are collinear.** SEE EXAMPLE 3

A B C D E
$x + 7$ $2x$ $3x - 1$ $2x + 3$

22. If $AC = 16$, what is $x$?
23. What is $AB$?
24. What is $BD$?
25. What is $CE$?

**Use the figure shown for Exercises 26–28.**
SEE EXAMPLES 4 AND 5

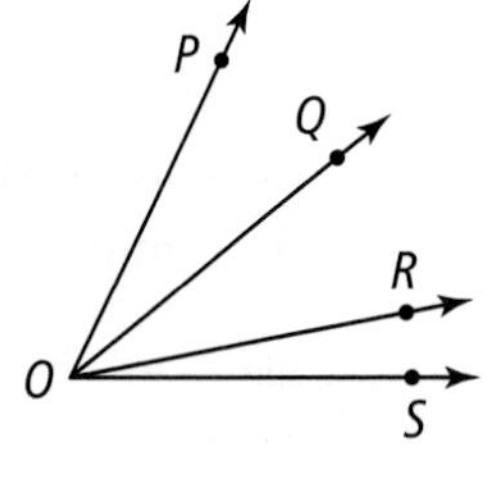


26. If $m\angle POQ = 24$ and $m\angle POR = 59$, what is $m\angle QOR$?

27. If $m\angle POQ = 19$, $m\angle QOR = 31$, and $m\angle ROS = 15$, what is $m\angle POS$?

28. If $m\angle QOS = 46$, $m\angle POR = 61$, and $m\angle POQ = 28$, what is $m\angle ROS$?

**Suppose $EG = 3$, $EB = 8$, $AF = 7$, $m\angle EBG = 19$, $m\angle EGF = 28$, and $m\angle CAE = 51$. Find each value.**
SEE EXAMPLE 6

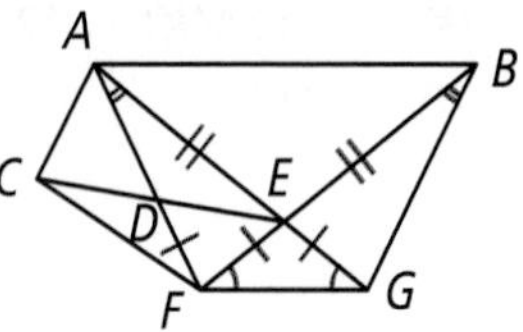


29. $EF$
30. $AG$
31. $AD$
32. $m\angle EFG$
33. $m\angle CAF$
34. $DF$

35. Points $P$, $Q$, $R$, and $S$ are collinear. Point $Q$ is between $P$ and $R$, $R$ is between $Q$ and $S$, and $\overline{PQ} \cong \overline{RS}$. If $PS = 18$ and $PR = 15$, what is the value of $QR$?

## PRACTICE & PROBLEM SOLVING

Practice Tutorial

Mixed Review Available Online

### APPLY

**36. Make Sense and Persevere** Dave is driving to Gilmore to visit his friend. If he wants to stop for lunch when he is about halfway there, in which town should he plan to stop? Explain.

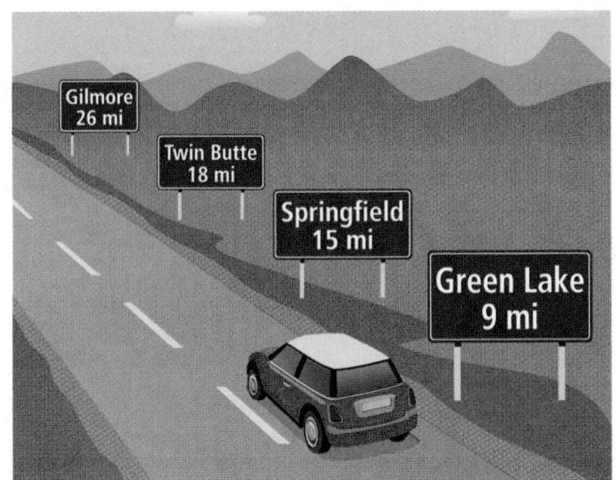


**37. Reason** A city planning commission must determine whether to approve the construction of a new building. The company wants to build in an area of the city that has a height limitation of 310 feet. The plans show that the first floor of the building is 20 ft high and each of the next 15 floors have a height of 11 ft, including the space between each floor needed for electrical, plumbing, and other systems. If the plan meets all other city code requirements, should the city commission approve the building plan? Explain.

**38. Reason** The city planning committee wants one tree planted every 20 ft along Dayton Avenue. If the perimeter of the plot of land is 234 ft, about how many trees will be planted? Explain.

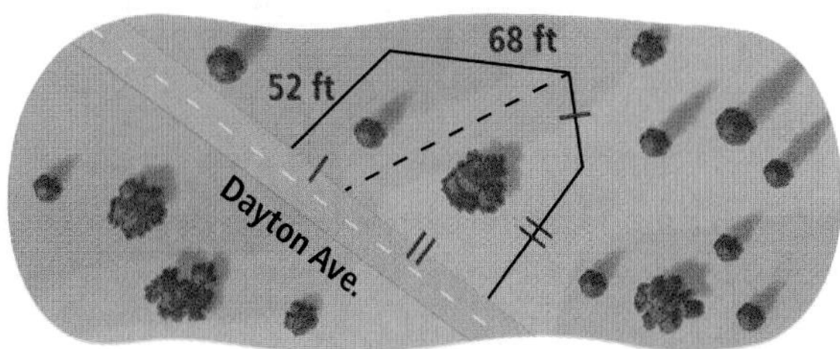


### ASSESSMENT PRACTICE

**39.** In the diagram, $FH = 2FG$, $GH = HI$, and $FI = IK$. Which of the following statements must be true? Select all that apply.

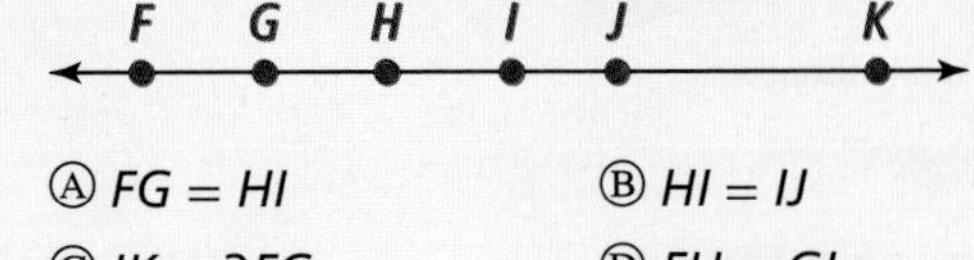


Ⓐ $FG = HI$  
Ⓑ $HI = IJ$  
Ⓒ $IK = 3FG$  
Ⓓ $FH = GI$  
Ⓔ $HJ = JK$  
Ⓕ $HK = 2GI$

**40. SAT/ACT** Point $C$ is in the interior of $\angle ABD$, and $\angle ABC \cong \angle CBD$. If $m\angle ABC = \left(\frac{5}{2}x + 18\right)$ and $m\angle CBD = (4x)$, what is $m\angle ABD$?

Ⓐ 12  Ⓑ 36  Ⓒ 48  Ⓓ 72  Ⓔ 96

**41. Performance Task** The American Institute of Architects is located in a historical building called "The Octagon" in Washington, DC. Octagonal houses became popular in the United States in the mid-1800s.

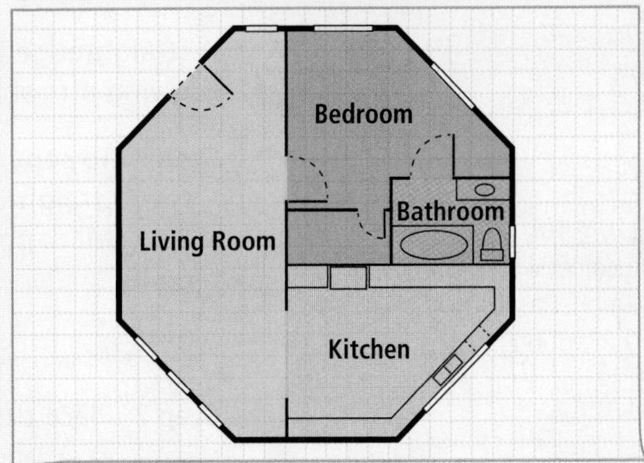


**Part A** Design your own plan for one floor of an octagonal-shaped house. Your plan should include at least four rooms, two walls of equal length, and two angles with equal measure. Draw your floor plan using the scale 1 cm = 1 m. Write the measures of the angles and lengths of the walls on your plan, and use appropriate marks to show congruent angles and segments. Label all the points in your diagram where the walls intersect.

**Part B** Write equations that show congruent angles and segments in your plan.

# 1-2 Basic Constructions

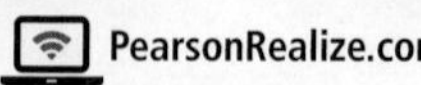

PearsonRealize.com

**I CAN…** use a straightedge and compass to construct basic figures.

**VOCABULARY**

- angle bisector
- construction
- perpendicular bisector

Activity Assess

## EXPLORE & REASON

**Using a compass, make a design using only circles like the one shown.**

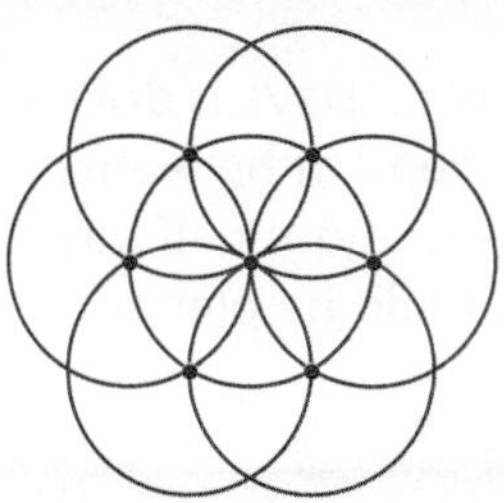

**A.** What instructions can you give to another student so they can make a copy of your design?

**B. Make Sense and Persevere** Use a ruler to draw straight line segments to connect points where the circles intersect. Are any of the segments that you drew the same length? If so, why do you think they are?

**ESSENTIAL QUESTION** **How are a straightedge and compass used to make basic constructions?**

CONCEPTUAL UNDERSTANDING

## EXAMPLE 1 Copy a Segment

**How can you copy a segment using only a straightedge and compass?**

A straightedge is a tool for drawing straight lines. A compass is a tool for drawing arcs and circles of different sizes and can be used to copy lengths.

**Step 1** To copy $\overline{AB}$, first use a straightedge to draw line $\ell$. Mark point $M$ on line $\ell$.

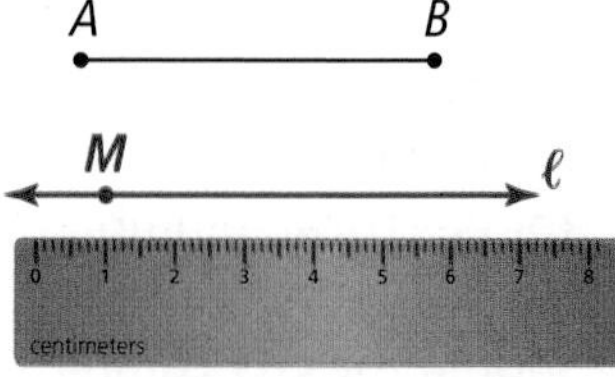


**STUDY TIP**
Remember, with constructions, only use a ruler as a straightedge, not as a measuring tool.

**Step 2** Place the compass point at $A$, and open the compass to length $AB$.

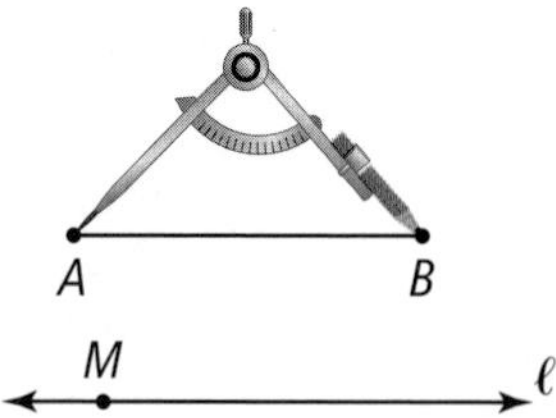


**Step 3** Using the same setting, place the compass point at $M$, and draw an arc through line $\ell$. Mark point $N$ at the intersection.

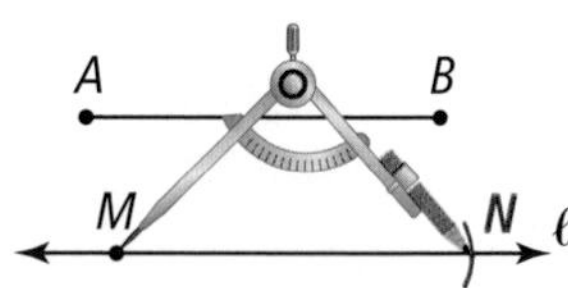


The constructed segment $MN$ is a copy of $\overline{AB}$. A copy of a line segment is a type of *construction*. A **construction** is a geometric figure made with only a straightedge and compass.

**Try It!** **1.** How can you construct a copy of $\overline{XY}$?

## EXAMPLE 2 Copy an Angle

**How can you construct a copy of $\angle A$?**

**Step 1** Mark a point $X$. Use a straightedge to draw a ray with endpoint $X$.

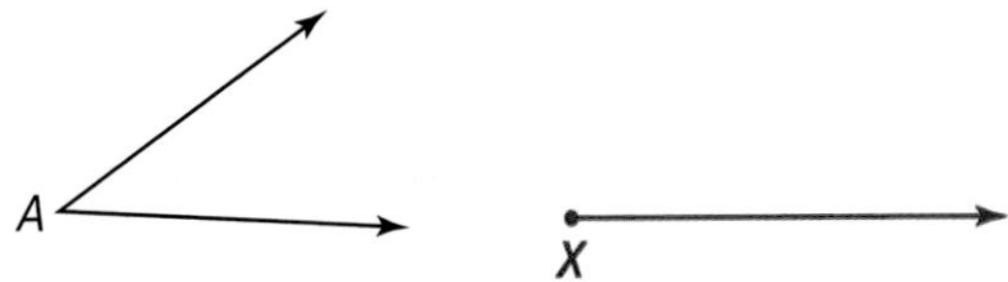


**Step 2** Place the compass point at $A$. Draw an arc that intersects both rays of $\angle A$. Label the points of intersection $B$ and $C$.

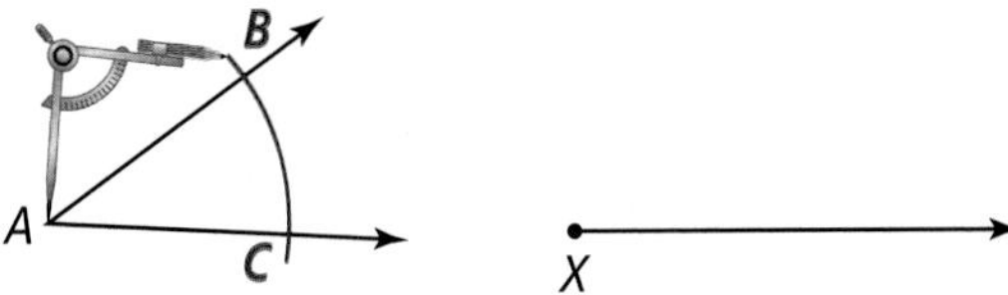


**Step 3** Without changing the setting, place the compass point at $X$ and draw an arc intersecting the ray. Mark the point $Y$ at the intersection.

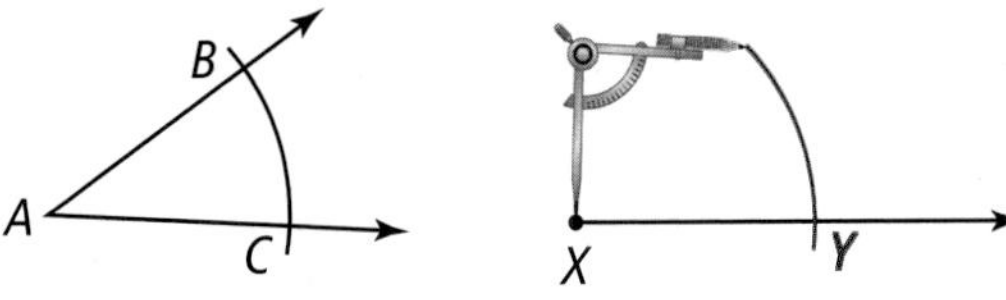


**Step 4** Place the compass point at $C$, and open the compass to the distance between $B$ and $C$.

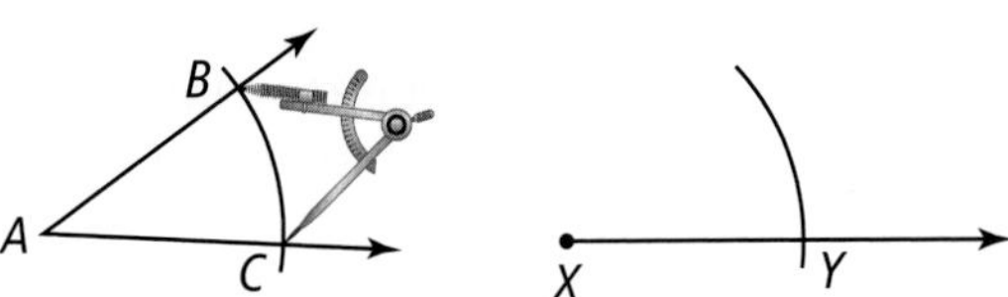


**Step 5** Without changing the setting, place the compass point at $Y$ and draw an arc. Label the point $Z$ where the two arcs intersect. Use a straightedge to draw $\overrightarrow{XZ}$.

**STUDY TIP**
You can use a protractor to confirm that the two angles are congruent.

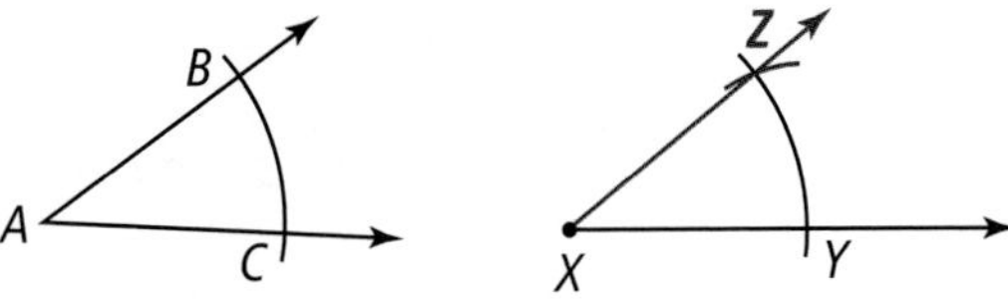


The constructed angle, $\angle YXZ$, is a copy of $\angle A$.

**Try It!** **2.** How can you construct a copy of $\angle B$?

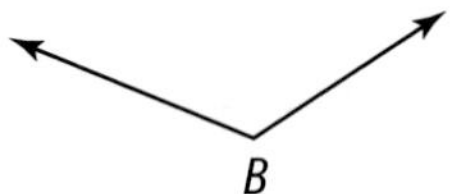

## EXAMPLE 3 Construct a Perpendicular Bisector

**How can you construct the perpendicular bisector of $\overline{AB}$?**

A **perpendicular bisector** of a segment is a line, segment, or ray that is perpendicular to the segment and divides the segment into two congruent segments.

You can use a straightedge and compass to construct the perpendicular bisector of a segment.

**Step 1** With a setting greater than $\frac{1}{2}AB$, place the compass point at $A$. Draw arcs above and below $\overline{AB}$.

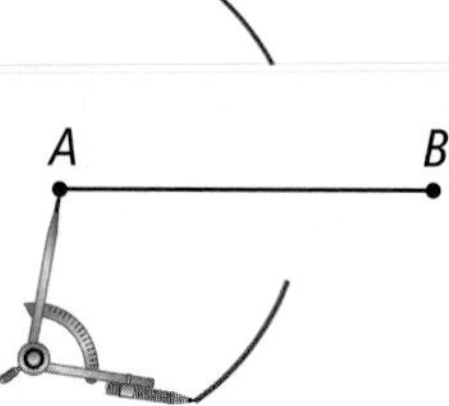


**Step 2** With the same setting, place the compass point at $B$. Draw arcs above and below $\overline{AB}$.

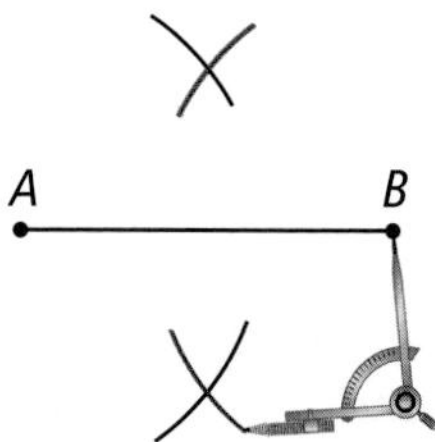


**Step 3** Label the points of intersection of the arcs $E$ and $F$. Use a straightedge to draw $\overleftrightarrow{EF}$.

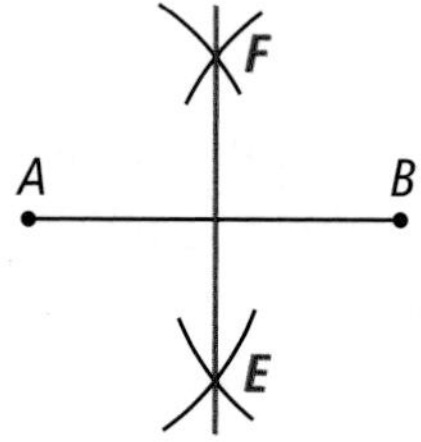


**USE APPROPRIATE TOOLS**
Consider the tools you can use to verify that a segment bisects another segment. What tool can you use?

The constructed line, $\overleftrightarrow{EF}$, is the perpendicular bisector of $\overline{AB}$.

**Try It!** 3. How can you construct the perpendicular bisector of $\overline{JK}$?

J K

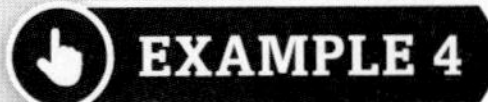


## EXAMPLE 4 Construct an Angle Bisector

**How can you construct the *angle bisector* of $\angle A$?**

An **angle bisector** is a ray that divides an angle into two congruent angles. You can use a straightedge and compass to construct an angle bisector.

**Step 1** Place the compass point at $A$. Draw an arc intersecting both rays of $\angle A$. Label the points of intersection $B$ and $C$.

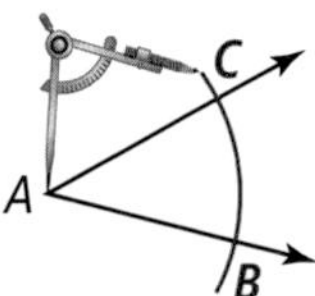


**COMMON ERROR**
Be sure to set the compass greater than $\frac{1}{2}$ the distance from $A$ to $C$.

**Step 2** Place the compass point at $B$. Draw an arc in the interior of $\angle A$. With the same setting, place the compass point at $C$ and draw an arc intersecting the arc drawn from $B$.

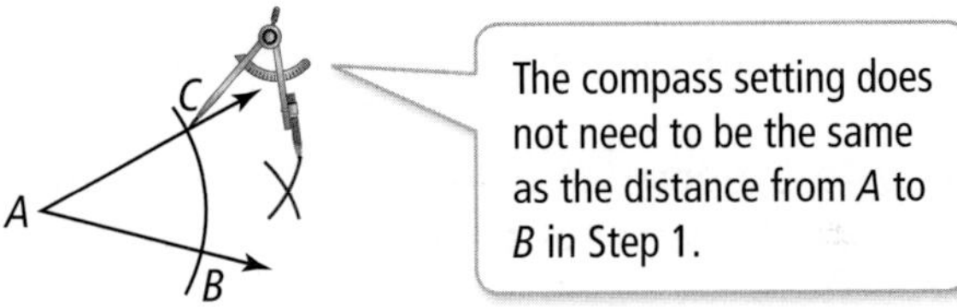

C
A
B
The compass setting does not need to be the same as the distance from A to B in Step 1.


**Step 3** Label the point of intersection of the two arcs $D$. Use a straightedge to draw $\overrightarrow{AD}$.

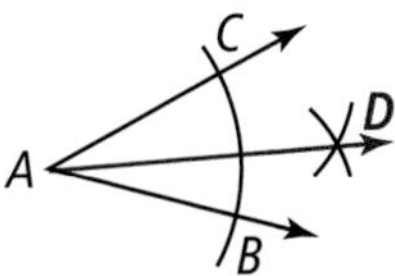


The constructed ray, $\overrightarrow{AD}$, is the bisector of $\angle A$.

**Try It!** **4.** How can you construct the angle bisector of $\angle G$?

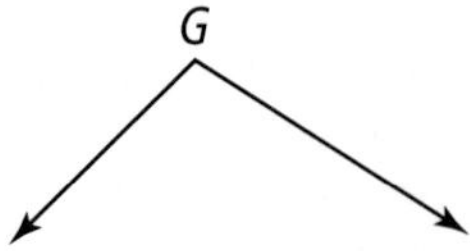

APPLICATION

## EXAMPLE 5 Use Constructions

**An artist wants to center-align a new sculpture with the bay window in the museum lobby. He also wants to center-align it with the entrance. Where should the sculpture be placed?**

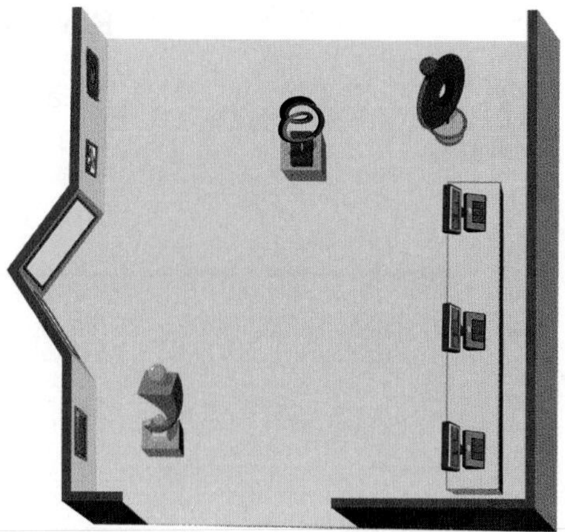

**Formulate** If the sculpture is center-aligned with the bay window, it lies on the angle bisector of the bay window. If it is center-aligned with the entrance, it lies on the perpendicular bisector of the entrance.

**Compute** Construct the angle bisector of the bay window and the perpendicular bisector of the entrance.

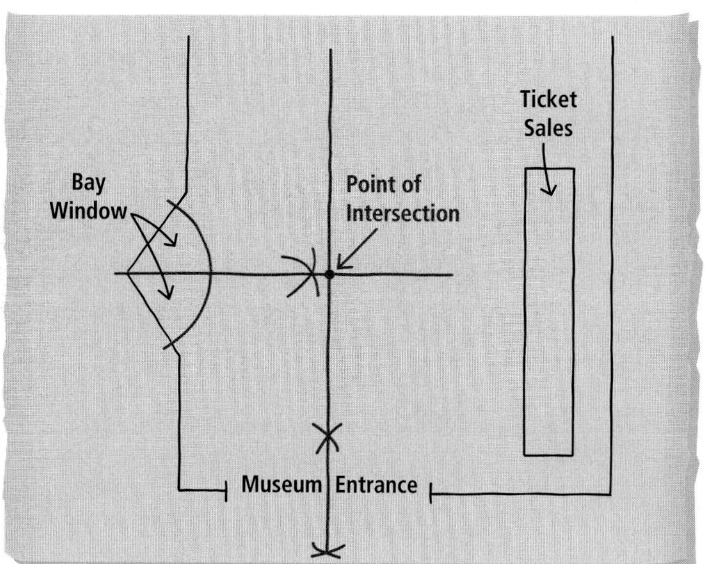


**Interpret** The center of the sculpture should be placed at the point of intersection of the angle bisector of the bay window and the perpendicular bisector of the museum entrance.

 **Try It!** 5. Where should the sculpture be placed if it is to be center-aligned with the museum entrance and the center of the ticket sales desk?

## CONCEPT SUMMARY Constructions

**WORDS** A **construction** is a geometric figure that can be made using only a straightedge and compass.

**Straightedge**
- is used to draw segments, lines and rays.

**Compass**
- is used to draw circles and arcs.
- is used to measure and copy length.

**DIAGRAMS** Construction of an Angle Bisector

**Step 1**

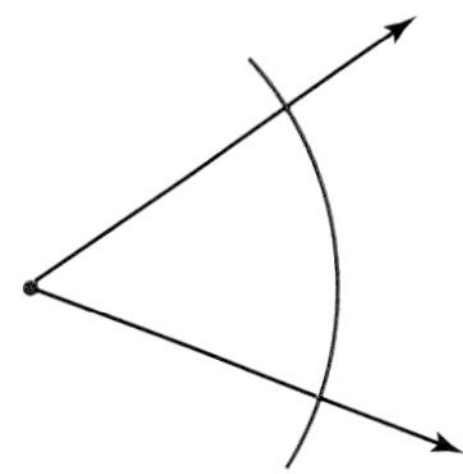

**Step 2**

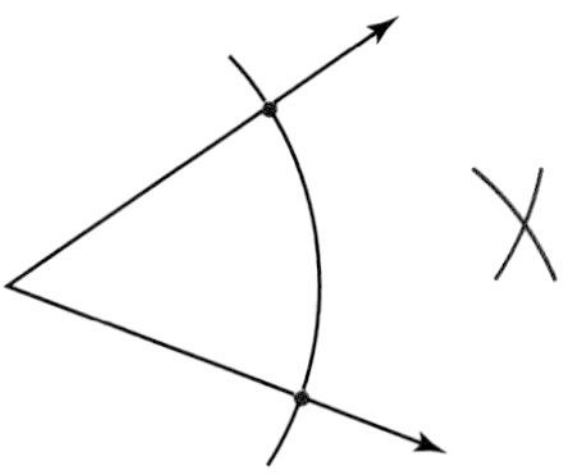

Use a compass to make arcs.

**Step 3**

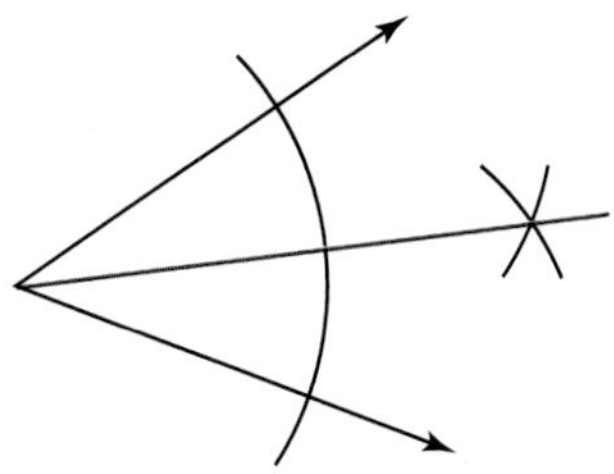

Use a straightedge to draw the bisector.

## Do You UNDERSTAND?

1. ESSENTIAL QUESTION How are a straightedge and compass used to make basic constructions?

2. **Error Analysis** Chris tries to copy $\angle T$ but is unable to make an exact copy. Explain Chris's error.

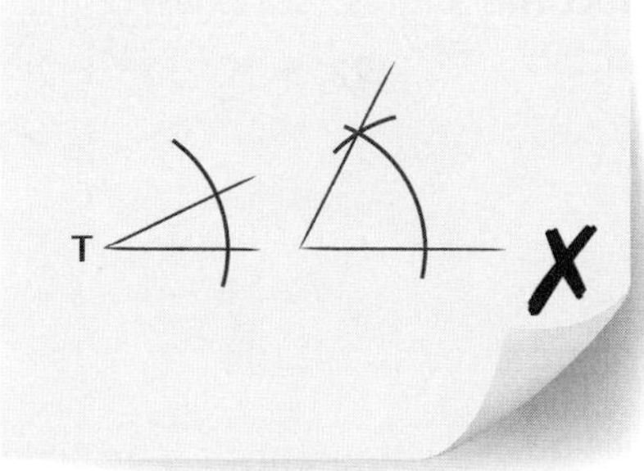


3. **Vocabulary** What is the difference between a line that is perpendicular to a segment and the perpendicular bisector of a segment?

4. **Look for Relationships** Darren is copying $\triangle ABC$. First, he constructs $\overline{DE}$ as a copy of $\overline{AB}$. Next, he constructs $\angle D$ as a copy of $\angle A$, using $\overline{DE}$ as one of the sides. Explain what he needs to do to complete the copy of the triangle.

A, B, C

## Do You KNOW HOW?

**Construct a copy of each segment, and then construct its perpendicular bisector.**

5. 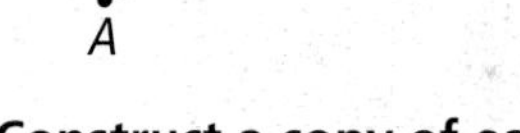


6. 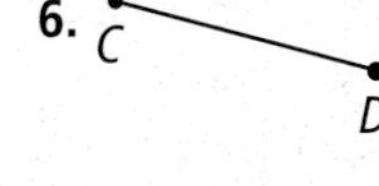


**Construct a copy of each angle, and then construct its bisector.**

7. 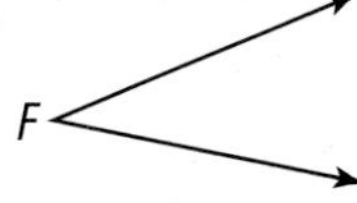


8. 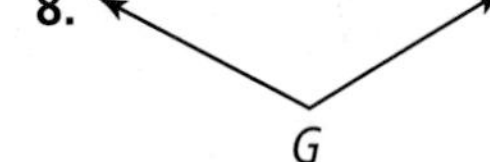


9. A new sidewalk is perpendicular to and bisecting the existing sidewalk. At the point where new sidewalk meets the fence around the farmer's market, a gate is needed. At about what point should the gate be placed?

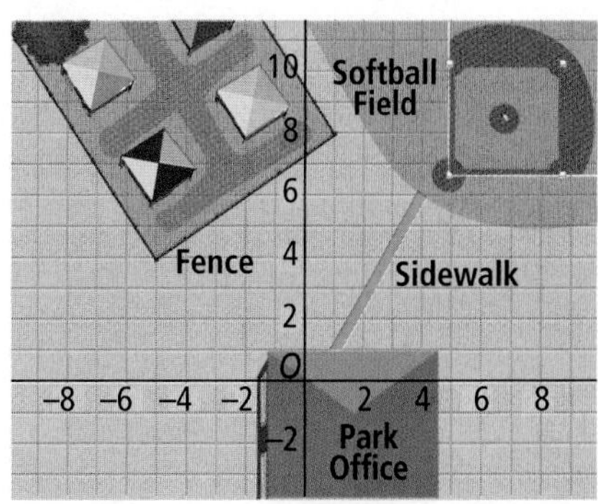

Scan for Multimedia

Additional Exercises Available Online

## UNDERSTAND

**10. Use Appropriate Tools** How could you use a compass to determine if two segments are the same length?

**11. Higher Order Thinking** You can divide a segment into $n$ congruent segments by bisecting segments repeatedly. What are some of the possible values of $n$? Give a rule for $n$.

**12. Make Sense and Persevere** In the figure shown, suppose $m\angle ABC = n$ and $m\angle ABD = 2(m\angle DBC)$. The angle bisector of $\angle DBC$ is $\overrightarrow{BE}$. What is $m\angle EBC$?

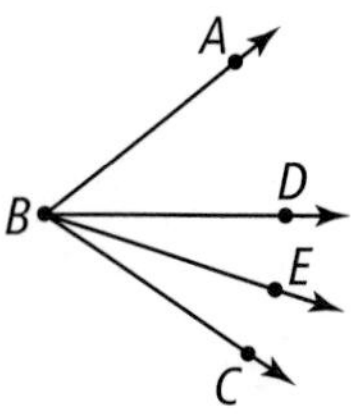


**13. Make Sense and Persevere** There are other methods for making constructions, such as paper folding. Follow the steps to use paper folding to construct the perpendicular bisector of a segment.

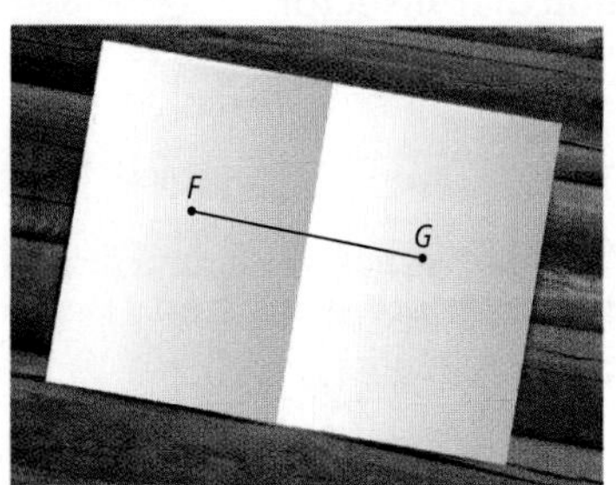


- On a sheet of paper, draw $\overline{FG}$.
- Fold the paper so that $F$ is on top of $G$.
- Crease the paper along the fold.
- Unfold the paper. The crease line represents the perpendicular bisector.

Why must $F$ and $G$ be aligned when you fold the paper?

**14. Error Analysis** Adam is asked to construct the bisector of $\angle R$. Explain the error in Adam's work.

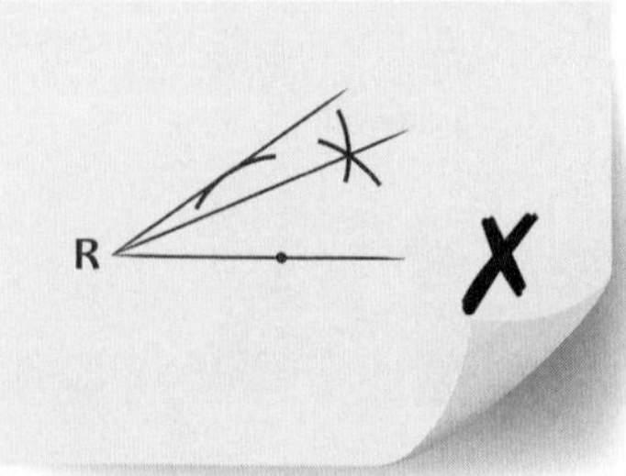


## PRACTICE

**Copy the segments.** SEE EXAMPLE 1

**15.** **16.**

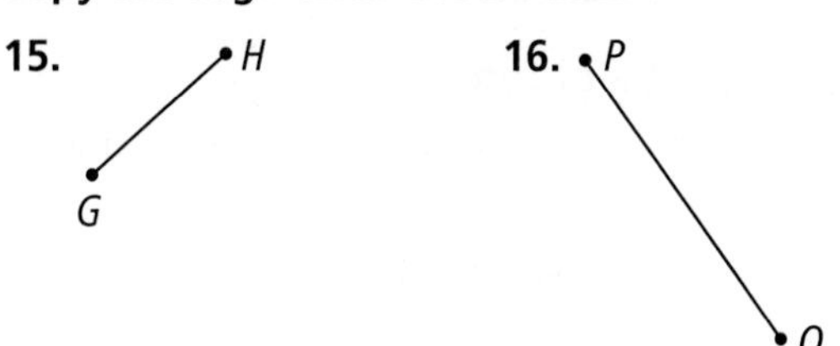


**Copy the angles.** SEE EXAMPLE 2

**17.** **18.**

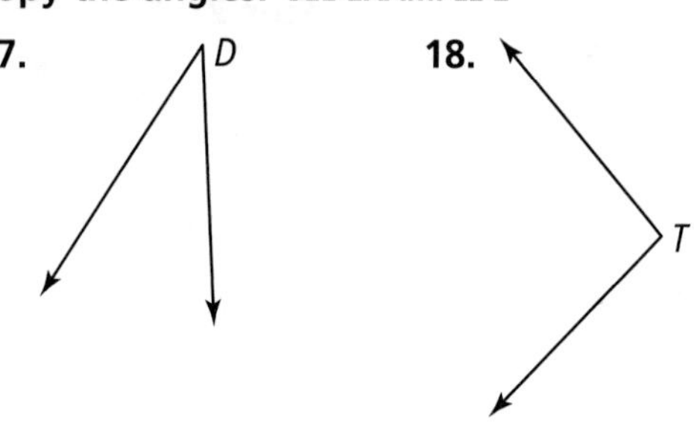


**Copy and bisect the segments.** SEE EXAMPLE 3

**19.** **20.**

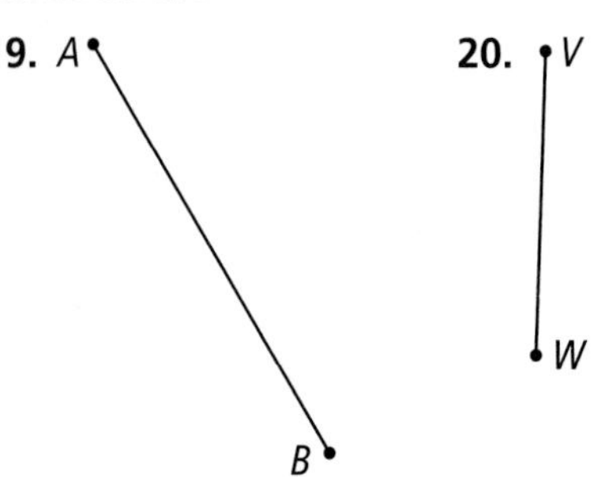


**Copy and bisect the angles.** SEE EXAMPLE 4

**21.** **22.**

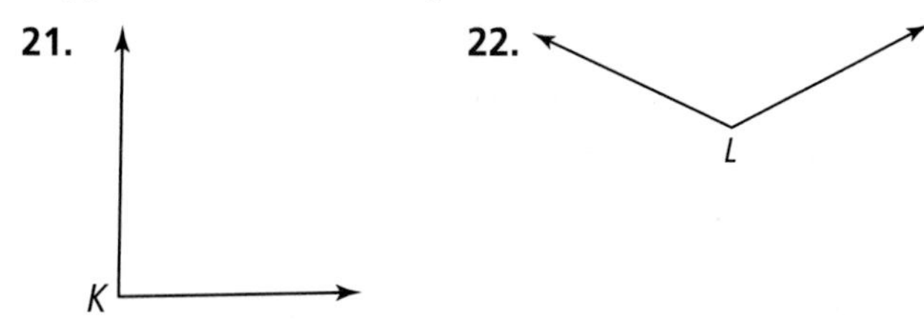


**23.** Where is the intersection of the perpendicular bisector of $\overline{GF}$ and the angle bisector of $\angle E$? SEE EXAMPLE 5

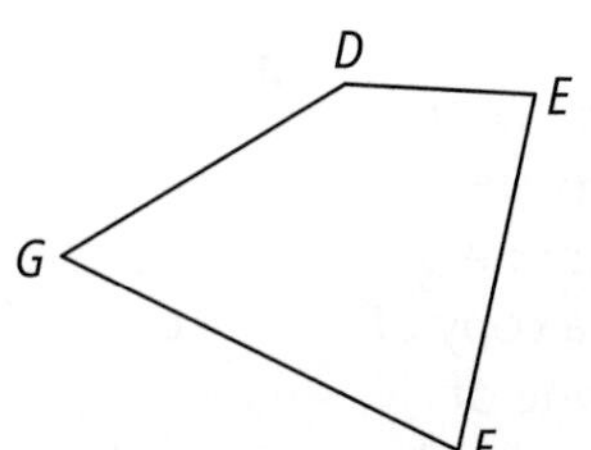

## PRACTICE & PROBLEM SOLVING

### APPLY

**24. Communicate Precisely** The quilt block is designed from a square using only perpendicular bisectors and angle bisectors. Write instructions for constructing the pattern in square $ABCD$. You may find it helpful to name some additional points.

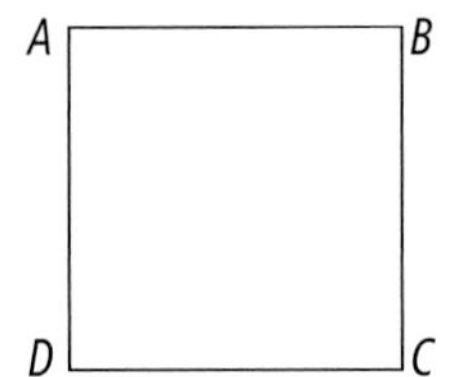


**25. Mathematical Connections** A school gym is divided for a fair by bisecting its width and its length. Each half of the length is then bisected, forming 8 sections in all. What are the dimensions and area of each section?

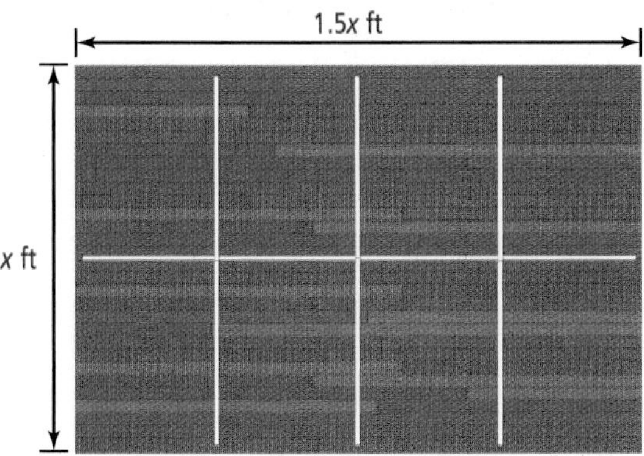


Perimeter = 300 ft

**26. Model With Mathematics** A sixth wind turbine will be placed near the intersections of the bisector of $\angle BCD$ and the perpendicular bisectors of $\overline{AE}$ and $\overline{ED}$. What is a possible location for the sixth turbine?

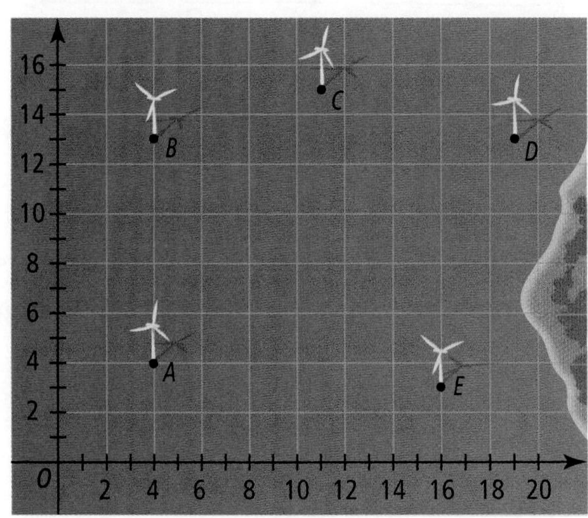


### ASSESSMENT PRACTICE

**27.** The angle bisector of $\angle NPM$ is $\overrightarrow{PQ}$. Write an equation to describe the relationship between $m\angle NPM$ and $m\angle QPM$

**28. SAT/ACT** A perpendicular bisector of $\overline{DC}$ is $\overleftrightarrow{AB}$, and a perpendicular bisector of $\overline{AB}$ is $\overline{DC}$. The intersection of $\overline{AB}$ and $\overline{DC}$ is at $E$. Which equation is true?

Ⓐ $AB = CD$

Ⓑ $CE = CD$

Ⓒ $DE = CE$

Ⓓ $AE = DE$

Ⓔ $EB = CD$

**29. Performance Task** Reducing or enlarging images can be useful when you need a smaller or larger version of a picture or graph for a report or poster.

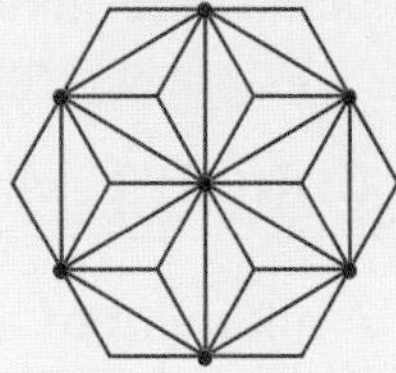

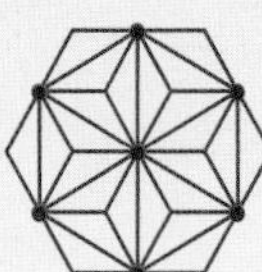

**Part A** Use a compass and straightedge to draw a polygon with at least 3 sides.

**Part B** Make a reduced version of your figure with sides that are half the length of the original figure. First, select one of the sides, bisect it, and then copy one of the halves. Next, copy one of the angles that is adjacent. Repeat until you have a reduced version of your figure.

**Part C** Think about how you can double the length of the line segment. Make an enlarged version of your figure with sides that are twice the length of the original figure. Describe how you made the enlarged figure.

Activity Assess

# 1-3 Midpoint and Distance

PearsonRealize.com

**I CAN…** use the midpoint and distance formulas to solve problems.

**VOCABULARY**

- midpoint

## MODEL & DISCUSS

**LaTanya is decorating her living room and draws a floorplan to help look at placement.**

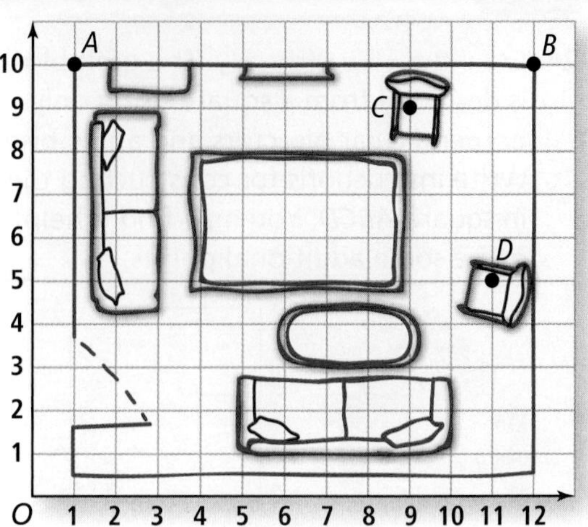


A. LaTanya wants to hang a picture at the center of the back wall. How do you find the point at the center between *A* and *B*?

B. **Communicate Precisely** LaTanya wants to place a lamp halfway between the chairs at points *C* and *D*. How can you find the point where the lamp should go?

## ESSENTIAL QUESTION

How are the midpoint and length of a segment on the coordinate plane determined?

### CONCEPT Midpoint Formula

A **midpoint** of a segment is the point that divides the segment into two congruent segments. The midpoint of $\overline{PQ}$ with $P(x_1, y_1)$ and $Q(x_2, y_2)$, is:

$$M = \left(\frac{x_1 + x_2}{2}, \frac{y_1 + y_2}{2}\right)$$

### EXAMPLE 1 Find a Midpoint

**What is the midpoint of $\overline{AB}$?**

Substitute the coordinates of the endpoints of $\overline{AB}$ into the Midpoint Formula.

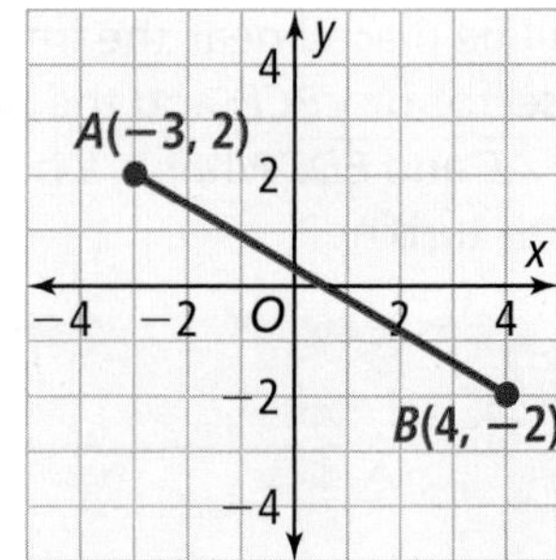


$$M = \left(\frac{-3 + 4}{2}, \frac{2 + (-2)}{2}\right)$$

$$= \left(\frac{1}{2}, 0\right)$$

The midpoint of $\overline{AB}$ is $\left(\frac{1}{2}, 0\right)$.

**COMMON ERROR**
Finding the midpoint is like finding the average of the *x*-coordinates and the *y*-coordinates, so be sure to add the coordinates before dividing by 2.

**Try It!** 1. Find the midpoint for each segment with the given endpoints.

a. $C(-2, 5)$ and $D(8, -12)$

b. $E(2.5, -7)$ and $F(-6.2, -3.8)$

**LOOK FOR RELATIONSHIPS**
Think about how number lines are related to the $x$- and $y$-axes. How can you relate partitioning on a number line to partitioning on a coordinate plane?

## EXAMPLE 2 Partition a Segment

**What are the coordinates of the point $\frac{3}{5}$ of the way from $A$ to $B$?**

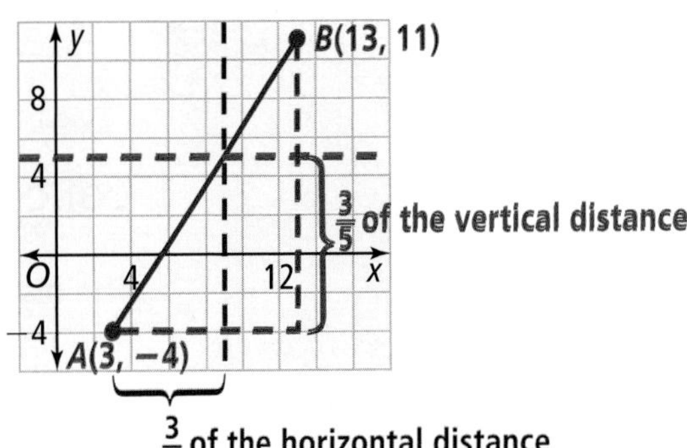


**Step 1** Find $\frac{3}{5}$ of the horizontal and vertical distances from $A$ to $B$.

Horizontal distance:
$\frac{3}{5}|13 - 3| = \frac{3}{5}(10) = 6$

Vertical distance:
$\frac{3}{5}|11 - (-4)| = \frac{3}{5}(15) = 9$

**Step 2** Add the horizontal distance to the $x$-coordinate and the vertical distance to the $y$-coordinate of point $A(3, -4)$.

$(3 + 6, -4 + 9) = (9, 5)$

The coordinates of the point $\frac{3}{5}$ of the way from $A$ to $B$ are (9, 5).

**Try It!** 2. Find the coordinates of each point described.

a. $\frac{7}{10}$ of the way from $A$ to $B$. b. $\frac{4}{5}$ of the way from $B$ to $A$.

CONCEPTUAL UNDERSTANDING

## EXAMPLE 3 Derive the Distance Formula

**How can you find the distance between $P(x_1, y_1)$ and $Q(x_2, y_2)$ on the coordinate plane?**

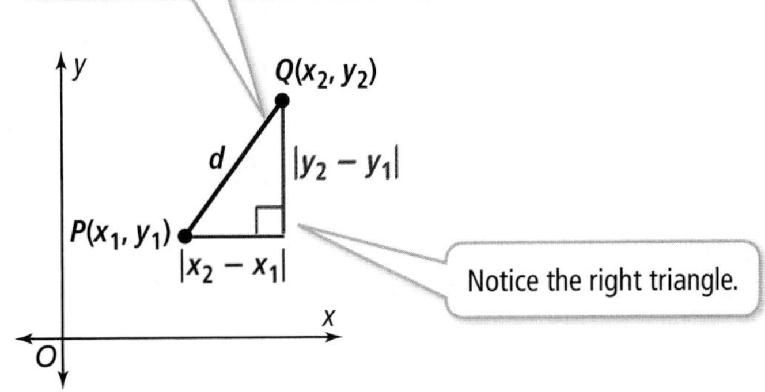


$$d^2 = |x_2 - x_1|^2 + |y_2 - y_1|^2$$
$$d = \sqrt{|x_2 - x_1|^2 + |y_2 - y_1|^2}$$

Apply the Pythagorean Theorem, $c^2 = a^2 + b^2$.

**STUDY TIP**
Recall that the square of any quantity is always nonnegative, so absolute value bars are not needed when an expression is squared.

The length of $\overline{PQ}$ is the distance between points $P$ and $Q$,
$d = \sqrt{(x_2 - x_1)^2 + (y_2 - y_1)^2}$.

CONTINUED ON THE NEXT PAGE

**Try It!** 3. Tavon claims that $d = \sqrt{(x_1 - x_2)^2 + (y_1 - y_2)^2}$ can also be used to find distance between two points. Is he correct? Explain.

## CONCEPT Distance Formula

The distance $d$ between two points $P(x_1, y_1)$ and $Q(x_2, y_2)$ is:

$$d(P, Q) = \sqrt{(x_2 - x_1)^2 + (y_2 - y_1)^2}$$

APPLICATION

## EXAMPLE 4 Find the Distance

**A pitcher throws a ball to a batter, who hits the ball to the shortstop. If the ball travels in a straight line between each, what is the total distance traveled by the ball? Round your answer to the nearest tenth of a foot.**

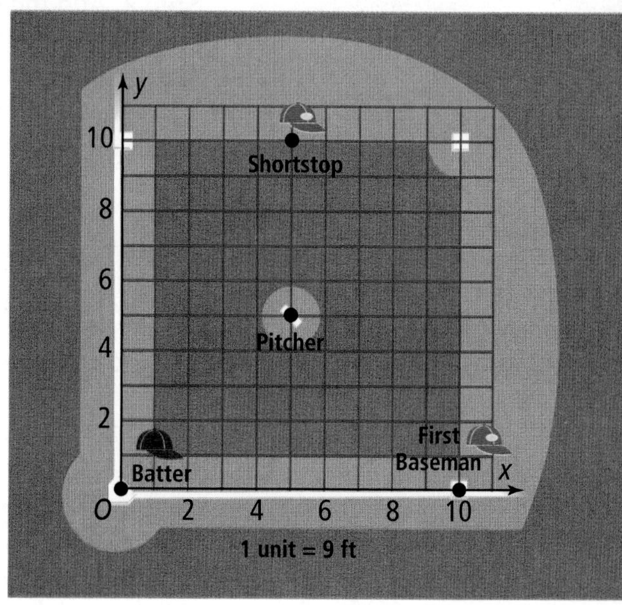


**Formulate** Represent the pitcher at point $P(5, 5)$, the batter at point $B(0, 0)$, and the shortstop at point $S(5, 10)$.

**Compute** Use the Distance Formula to find each distance.

$$\begin{aligned} d\text{ (pitcher to batter)} &= \sqrt{(0-5)^2 + (0-5)^2} \\ &= \sqrt{(-5)^2 + (-5)^2} \\ &= \sqrt{25 + 25} \\ &= \sqrt{50} \\ &\approx 7.1 \end{aligned}$$

Use the Distance Formula with $P(5, 5)$ and $B(0, 0)$.

$$\begin{aligned} d\text{ (batter to shortstop)} &= \sqrt{(5-0)^2 + (10-0)^2} \\ &= \sqrt{5^2 + 10^2} \\ &= \sqrt{25 + 100} \\ &= \sqrt{125} \\ &\approx 11.2 \end{aligned}$$

Use the Distance Formula with $B(0, 0)$ and $S(5, 10)$.

**Interpret** The total distance the ball traveled is about $7.1 + 11.2 = 18.3$ units, or about $(18.3)(9) = 164.7$ ft.

**Try It!** 4. How far does the shortstop need to throw the ball to reach the first baseman? Round your answer to the nearest tenth of a foot.

## CONCEPT SUMMARY Midpoint and Distance on the Coordinate Plane

**MIDPOINT**

$$M = \left(\frac{x_1 + x_2}{2}, \frac{y_1 + y_2}{2}\right)$$

**DISTANCE**

$$d = \sqrt{(x_2 - x_1)^2 + (y_2 - y_1)^2}$$

**EXAMPLE**

The endpoints of $\overline{PQ}$ are $P(-3, 4)$ and $Q(1, 7)$.

$$M = \left(\frac{-3+1}{2}, \frac{4+7}{2}\right)$$
$$= \left(-1, \frac{11}{2}\right)$$

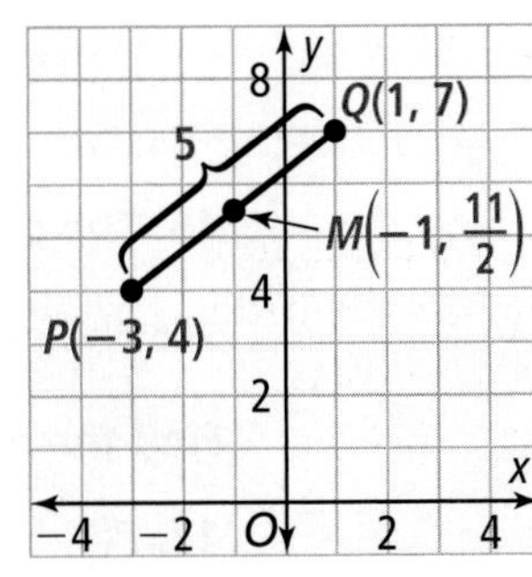


$$d = \sqrt{(-3 - 1)^2 + (4 - 7)^2}$$
$$= \sqrt{(-4)^2 + (-3)^2}$$
$$= \sqrt{25}$$
$$= 5$$

## Do You UNDERSTAND?

1. **ESSENTIAL QUESTION** How are the midpoint and length of a segment on the coordinate plane determined?

2. **Error Analysis** Corey calculated the midpoint of $\overline{AB}$ with $A(-3, 5)$ and $B(1, 7)$. What is Corey's error?

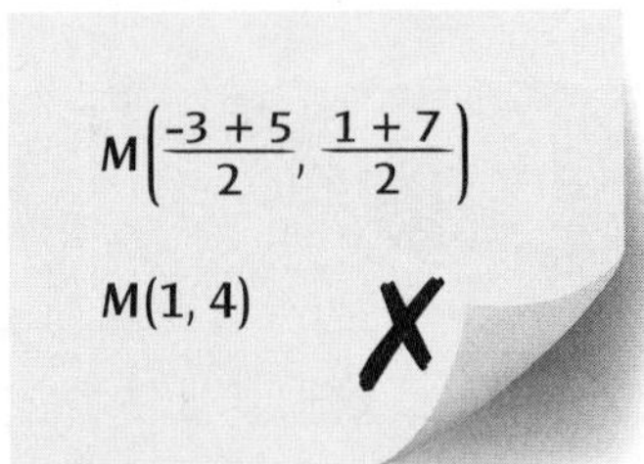


3. **Vocabulary** If $M$ is the midpoint of $\overline{PQ}$, what is the relationship between $PM$ and $MQ$? Between $PM$ and $PQ$?

4. **Reason** Is it possible for $\overline{PQ}$ to have two distinct midpoints, $M_1(a, b)$ and $M_2(c, d)$? Explain.

## Do You KNOW HOW?

**$\overline{PQ}$ has endpoints at $P(-5, 4)$ and $Q(7, -5)$.**

5. What is the midpoint of $\overline{PQ}$?

6. What are the coordinates of the point $\frac{2}{3}$ of the way from $P$ to $Q$?

7. What is the length of $\overline{PQ}$?

8. A chair lift at a ski resort travels along the cable as shown.

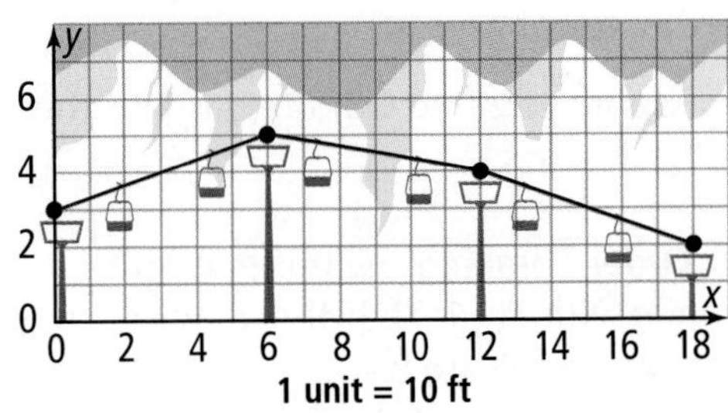


How long is the cable? Round your answer to the nearest whole foot.

## UNDERSTAND

**9. Use Structure** Point $K$ is $\frac{1}{n}$ of the way from $J(4, -5)$ to $L(0, -7)$.

a. What are the coordinates of $K$ if $n = 4$?

b. What is a formula for the coordinates of $K$ for any $n$?

**10. Error Analysis** Describe and correct the error a student made in finding the midpoint of $\overline{CD}$ with $C(-4, 5)$ and $D(-1, -4)$.

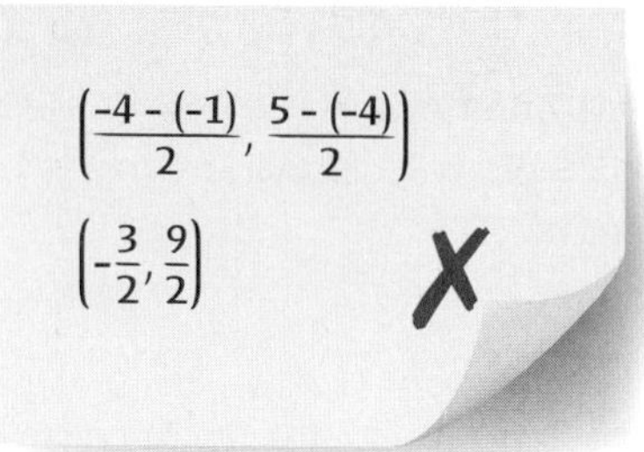


**11. Mathematical Connections** Point $M$ is the midpoint of $\overline{FG}$. Can you determine the value of $a$? Explain.

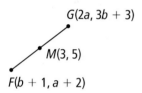

$G(2a, 3b + 3)$

$M(3, 5)$

$F(b + 1, a + 2)$

**12. Reason** Suppose $\overline{PQ}$ has one endpoint at $P(0, 0)$.

a. If $(2, 5)$ is the midpoint of $\overline{PQ}$, what are the coordinates of point $Q$?

b. How would you find $Q$ if $(2, 5)$ is $\frac{1}{4}$ of the way from $P$ to $Q$?

**13. Higher Order Thinking** $\overline{PQ}$ has a length of 17 units with $P(-4, 7)$. If the $x$- and $y$-coordinates of $Q$ are both greater than the $x$- and $y$-coordinates of $P$, what are possible integer value coordinates of $Q$? Explain.

**14. Make Sense and Persevere** Suppose $\overline{PQ}$ has $P(a, b)$ and midpoint $M(c, d)$. What is an expression for $PM$? Use the expression for $PM$ to find an expression for $PQ$.

## PRACTICE

**Find the coordinates of each given point on $\overline{AB}$.** SEE EXAMPLE 2

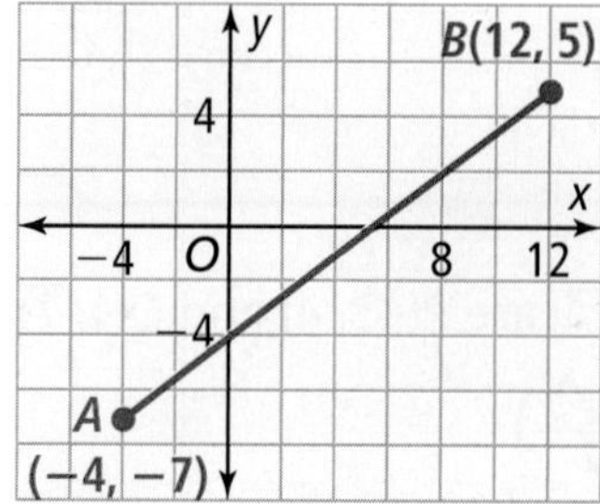


**15.** The point $\frac{3}{10}$ of the way from $A$ to $B$.

**16.** The point $\frac{1}{4}$ of the way from $B$ to $A$.

**Find the midpoint of $\overline{PQ}$.** SEE EXAMPLE 1

**17.** $P(3, 5)$, $Q(-2, 13)$

**18.** $P(-2, 2.5)$, $Q(1.4, 4)$

**19.** $P\left(4\frac{1}{3}, 3\frac{1}{6}\right)$, $Q\left(-2\frac{1}{5}, 3\frac{2}{3}\right)$

**Cameron, Arthur, and Jamie are playing soccer. Their locations are recorded by a motion tracking system. The distance between grids is 5 meters.** SEE EXAMPLES 3 AND 4

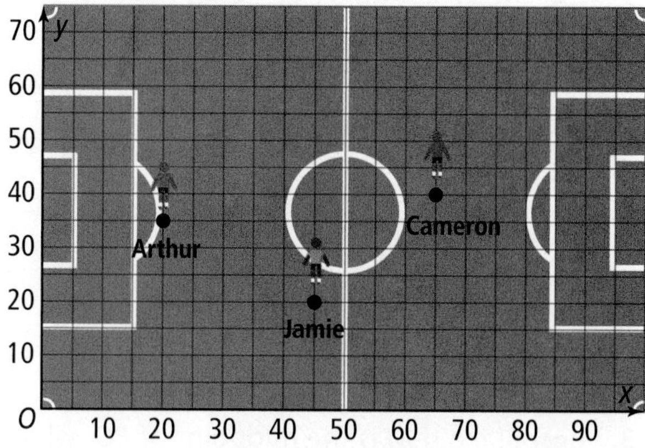


**20.** How far apart are Arthur and Jamie? Round to the nearest tenth of a meter.

**21.** Who is closer to Cameron? Explain.

**22.** The soccer ball is located at the point (35, 60). Who is closest to the soccer ball?

Mixed Review Available Online

## PRACTICE & PROBLEM SOLVING

### APPLY

**23. Model With Mathematics** A university is building a new student center that is two-thirds the distance from the arts center to the residential complex. What are the coordinates of the new center? Explain.

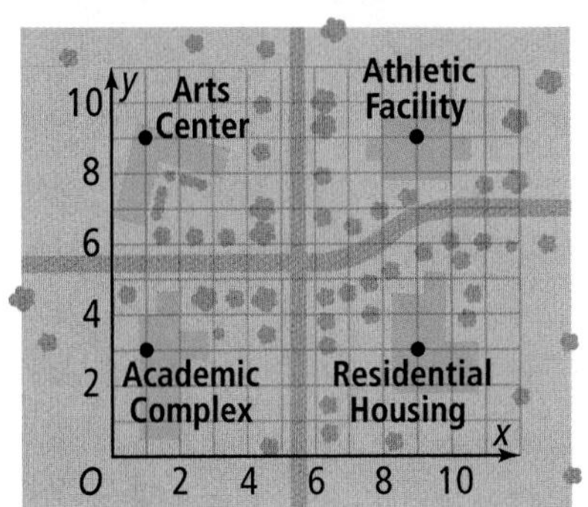


**24. Mathematical Connections** A lighthouse casts a revolving beam of light as far as the pier. What is the area that the light covers?

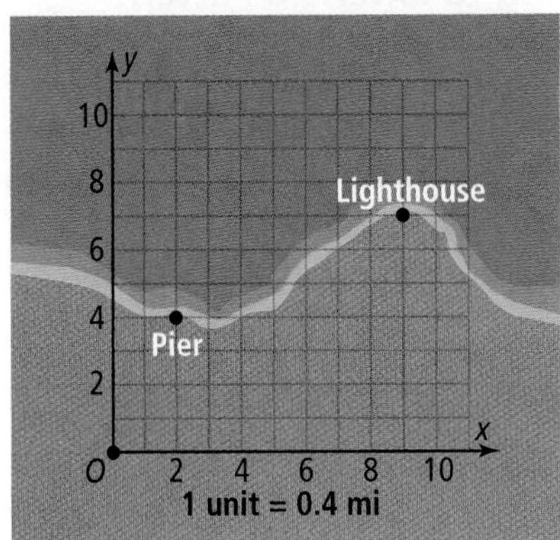


**25. Make Sense and Persevere** A ship captain is attempting to contact a deep sea diver.

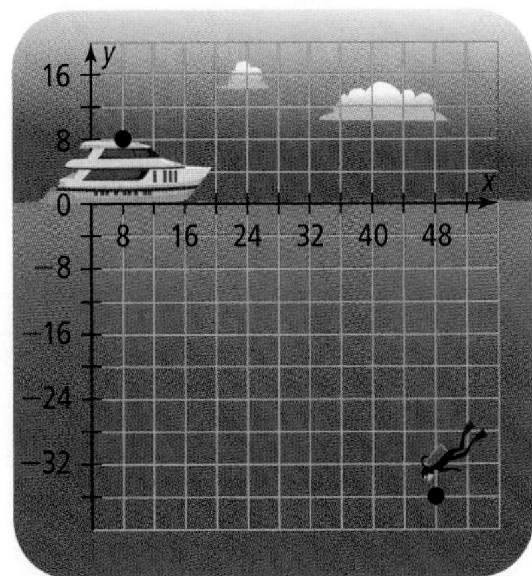

If the maximum range for communication is 60 meters, will he be able to communicate with the diver based on their current positions? Explain.

### ASSESSMENT PRACTICE

**26.** $\overline{AB}$ has an endpoint at $A(1, -2)$ and midpoint $C(3, 2)$. Graph $\overline{AB}$ and point $C$.

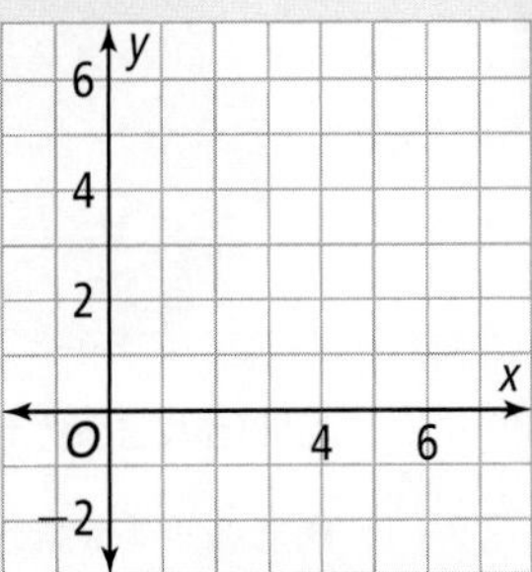

**27. SAT/ACT** $\overline{RS}$ has an endpoint at $R(6, -4)$ and length 17. Which of the following cannot be the coordinates of $S$?

Ⓐ (14, 11)
Ⓑ (6, 13)
Ⓒ (−9, −12)
Ⓓ (23, 13)
Ⓔ (23, −4)

**28. Performance Task** A parade route must start and end at the intersections shown on the map. The city requires that the total distance of the route cannot exceed 3 miles. A proposed route is shown.

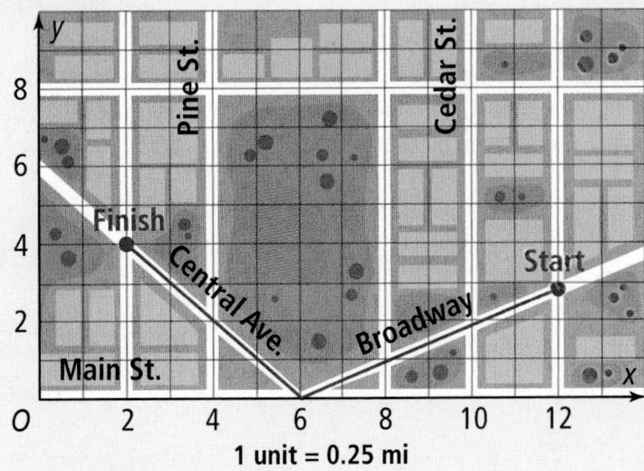


**Part A** Why does the proposed route not meet the requirement?

**Part B** Assuming that the roads used for the route are the same and the end point is the same, at what intersection could the parade start so the total distance is as close to 3 miles as possible?

**Part C** The city wants to station video cameras halfway down each road in the parade. Using your answer to Part B, what are the coordinates of the locations for the cameras?

# 1-4 Inductive Reasoning

PearsonRealize.com

Activity | Assess

## EXPLORE & REASON

**When points on a circle are connected, the line segments divide the circle into a number of regions, as shown.**

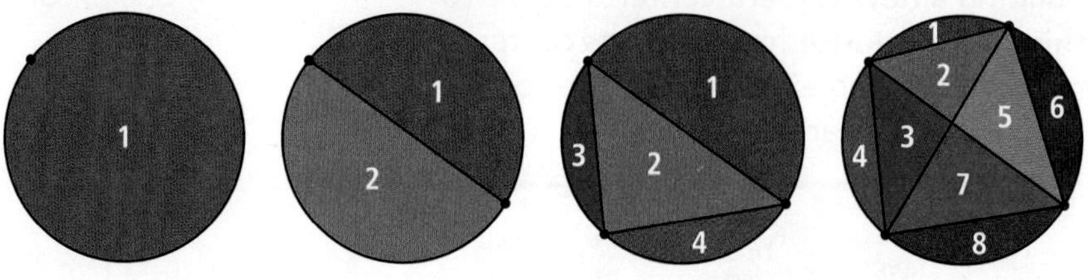


A. How does the number of regions change when another point is added?

B. **Look for Relationships** Using the pattern you observed, make a prediction about the number of regions formed by connecting 5 points on a circle. Make a drawing to test your prediction. Is your prediction correct?

**I CAN…** use inductive reasoning to make conjectures about mathematical relationships.

**VOCABULARY**
- conjecture
- counterexample
- inductive reasoning

## ESSENTIAL QUESTION

**How is inductive reasoning used to recognize mathematical relationships?**

## EXAMPLE 1 Use Inductive Reasoning to Extend a Pattern

**Inductive reasoning is a type of reasoning that reaches conclusions based on a pattern of specific examples or past events. How can you use inductive reasoning to determine what appears to be the next two terms in each sequence?**

**A. 88, 82, 76, 70, 64,…**

Look for a pattern. Observe that the terms decrease and the difference of the first two terms is 6.

Test whether the pattern continues with subsequent terms.

$82 - 6 = 76 \qquad 76 - 6 = 70 \qquad 70 - 6 = 64$

The rule works. Use the pattern to find the next two terms.

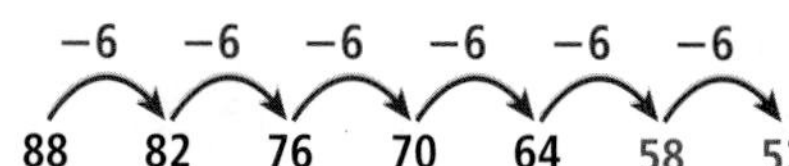


The next two terms in the sequence appear to be 58 and 52.

**B. 3, 5, 9, 15, 23,…**

Look for a pattern. Observe that the terms increase by successive multiples of 2.

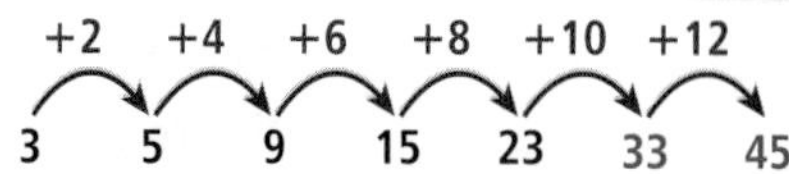


The next two terms in the sequence appear to be 33 and 45.

**STUDY TIP**
When looking for a pattern, remember to always test subsequent terms to be sure that you have found the correct rule.

**Try It!** 1. What appear to be the next two terms in each sequence?

**a.** 800, 400, 200, 100,…

**b.** 18, 24, 32, $\frac{128}{3}$,…

## EXAMPLE 2 Use Inductive Reasoning to Make a Conjecture

**A conjecture is an unproven statement or rule that is based on inductive reasoning. What conjecture can be made about the number of dots in the *n*th term of this geometric pattern?**

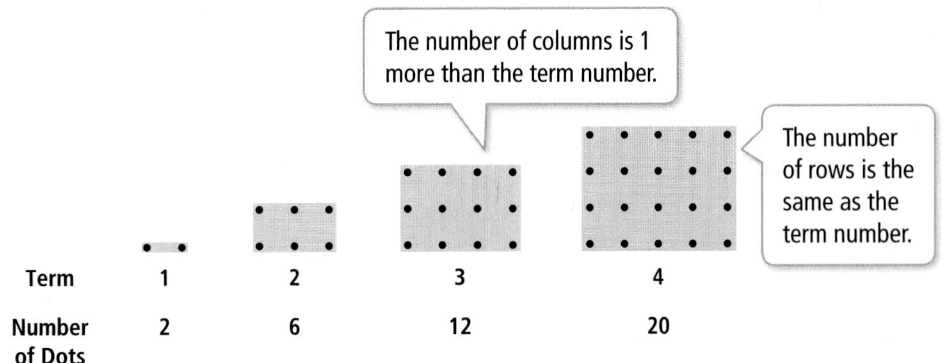
The number of columns is 1 more than the term number.
The number of rows is the same as the term number.
Term 1 2 3 4
Number of Dots 2 6 12 20

Write an algebraic expression to generalize the pattern for the *n*th term. Since the number or rows in the pattern is equivalent to the term number, use the n to represent the number of rows.

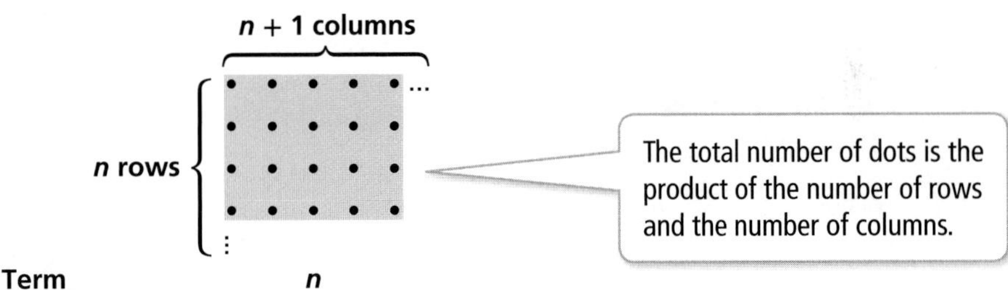
$n + 1$ columns
$n$ rows
The total number of dots is the product of the number of rows and the number of columns.
Term $n$

**MODEL WITH MATHEMATICS**
You can write an algebraic expression to represent a geometric pattern. What expressions can you write for the *n*th term?

Conjecture: The *n*th term of the sequence will contain $n(n + 1)$, or $n^2 + n$ dots.

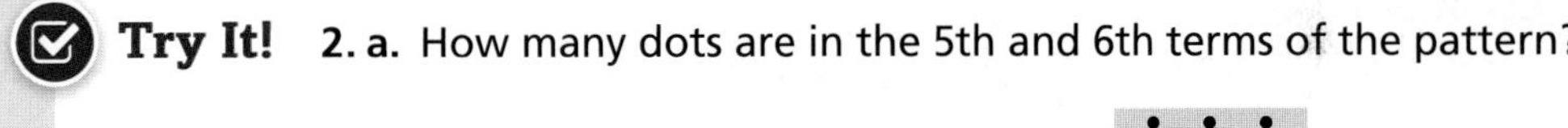

**Try It!** **2. a.** How many dots are in the 5th and 6th terms of the pattern?

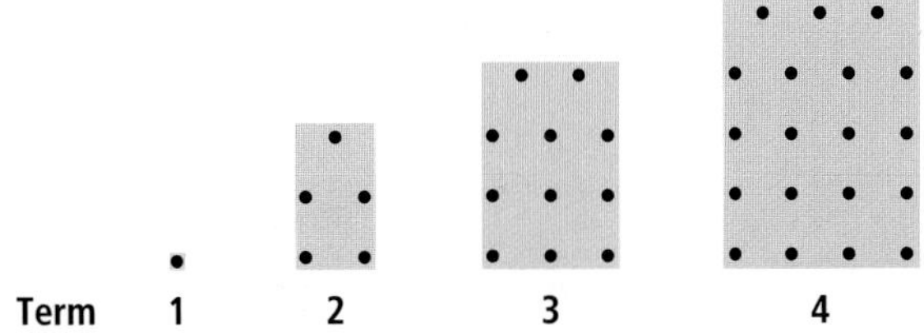
Term 1 2 3 4

**b.** What conjecture can you make about the number of dots in the *n*th term of the pattern?

APPLICATION

## EXAMPLE 3 Use a Conjecture to Make a Prediction

**Based on the data in the table, how many residents would you expect to vote in the 7th town council election?**

**Town Council Elections Voter Turnout**

| Year | Total Residents | Voters |
|---|---|---|
| 1 | 3,511 | 386 |
| 2 | 3,790 | 414 |
| 3 | 4,085 | 451 |
| 4 | 4,907 | 544 |
| 5 | 5,562 | 623 |
| 6 | 7,014 | 767 |
| 7 | 7,786 | ? |

Formulate

Look for a pattern by comparing the ratios $\frac{\text{number of voters}}{\text{number of residents}}$ for each year. Then use the pattern to make a conjecture about the number of residents who will vote in the 7th town election.

Compute

$\frac{386}{3{,}511} \approx 0.110$  $\frac{414}{3{,}790} \approx 0.109$

$\frac{451}{4{,}085} \approx 0.110$  $\frac{544}{4{,}907} \approx 0.111$

$\frac{623}{5{,}562} \approx 0.112$  $\frac{767}{7{,}014} \approx 0.109$

The number of voters each year is about 11% of the total residents.

Use the pattern to predict the number of voters in the 7th election.

$$7{,}786 \bullet 0.11 = 856.46$$

Interpret

About 856 people can be expected to vote in the 7th town council election.

**Try It!** 3. Based on the data, about how many members would you expect the chess club to have in its 5th year?

| Year | 1 | 2 | 3 | 4 |
|---|---|---|---|---|
| Club Members | 10 | 13 | 17 | 22 |

CONCEPTUAL UNDERSTANDING

## EXAMPLE 4 Find a Counterexample to Show a Conjecture is False

**Why does a *counterexample* show that a conjecture is false?**

A **counterexample** is an example that shows a statement or conjecture is false.

**Conjecture:** A polygon with diagonals has two fewer diagonals as sides.

To find a counterexample, you must find a polygon that has a number of diagonals that is not two fewer than the number of its sides.

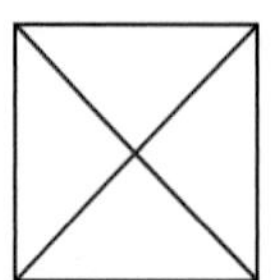

4 sides
2 diagonals

5 sides
5 diagonals

You only need to find one counterexample to show that a statement is false. A counterexample exists, so the conjecture is false.

**CONSTRUCT ARGUMENTS**
For a conjecture to be true, it must be true for every possible case, so if a counterexample is found, the conjecture is false.

**Try It!** 4. What is a counterexample that shows the statement, *the sum of two composite numbers must be a composite number*, is false?

## EXAMPLE 5 Test a Conjecture

**For each conjecture, test the conjecture with several more examples or find a counterexample to disprove the conjecture.**

**A. A polygon with four congruent sides is a square.**

A square has four congruent sides and four right angles.

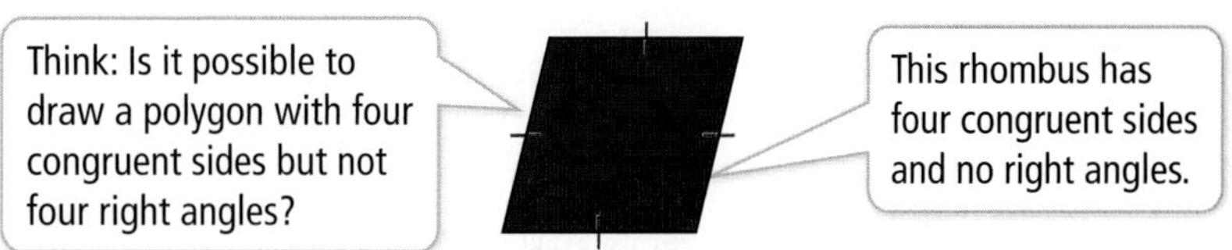

Think: Is it possible to draw a polygon with four congruent sides but not four right angles?
This rhombus has four congruent sides and no right angles.


A counterexample exists, so this conjecture is false.

**B. If a number is a multiple of 9, then the sum of its digits is a multiple of 9.**

To test the conjecture, list some multiples of 9 and find the sum of the digits of each multiple.

| Multiples of 9 | Sums of the Digits |
|---|---|
| $9 \bullet 12 = 108$ | $1 + 0 + 8 = 9$ |
| $9 \bullet 313 = 2{,}817$ | $2 + 8 + 1 + 7 = 18$ |
| $9 \bullet 1{,}105 = 9{,}945$ | $9 + 9 + 4 + 5 = 27$ |

The sums 9, 18, and 27 are multiples of 9.

The conjecture is true for the three cases tested.

**COMMON ERROR**
You may think that finding examples that support a conjecture shows that it is true. Remember that you must show that a conjecture is true for all cases, not just a few.

**Try It!** **5.** For each conjecture, test the conjecture with several more examples or find a counterexample to disprove it.

**a.** For every integer $n$, the value of $n^2$ is positive.

**b.** A number is divisible by 4 if the last two digits are divisible by 4.

Concept Summary

Assess

## CONCEPT SUMMARY Inductive Reasoning

### WORDS Inductive Reasoning

- leads to a conjecture by observing patterns.
- uses specific examples to make a generalization.
- does not show that a conjecture is true, so a conjecture could be disproven by a counterexample.

### DIAGRAM

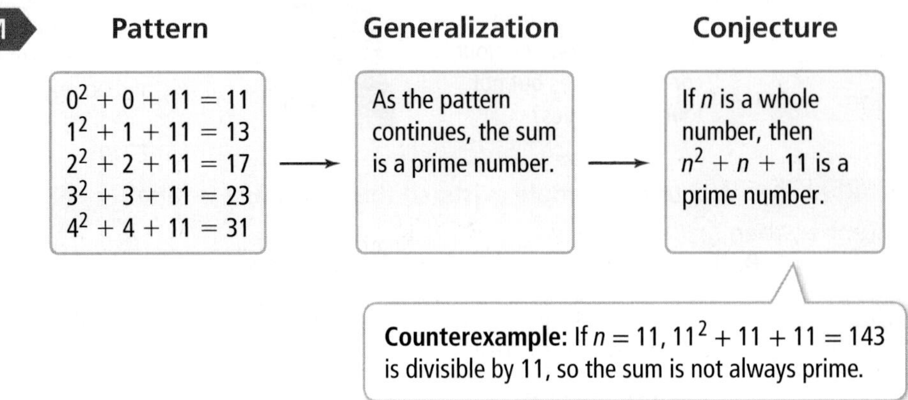

Pattern
Generalization
Conjecture
$0^2 + 0 + 11 = 11$
$1^2 + 1 + 11 = 13$
$2^2 + 2 + 11 = 17$
$3^2 + 3 + 11 = 23$
$4^2 + 4 + 11 = 31$
As the pattern continues, the sum is a prime number.
If $n$ is a whole number, then $n^2 + n + 11$ is a prime number.
**Counterexample:** If $n = 11$, $11^2 + 11 + 11 = 143$ is divisible by 11, so the sum is not always prime.

## Do You UNDERSTAND?

1. ESSENTIAL QUESTION How is inductive reasoning used to recognize mathematical relationships?

2. **Error Analysis** Esteban made the following drawing and then stated this conjecture: "The altitude of a triangle always lies inside of or along the side of the triangle." What error did Esteban make?

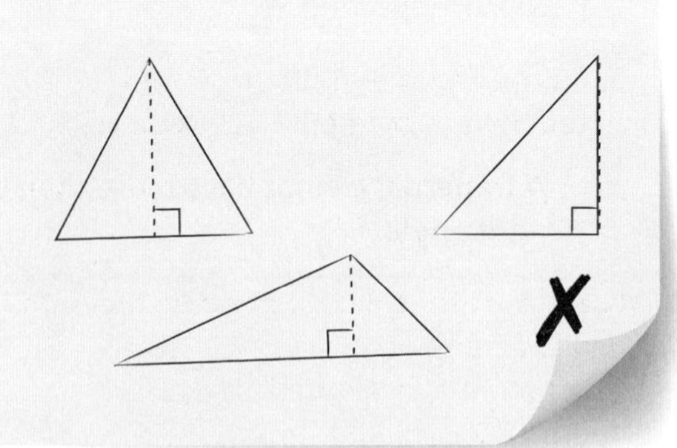

3. **Vocabulary** What type of statement results from inductive reasoning?

## Do You KNOW HOW?

4. What appear to be the next three numbers in the pattern?

   4, 11, 18, 25,...

5. What conjecture can you make about the number of regions created by $n$ unique diameters?

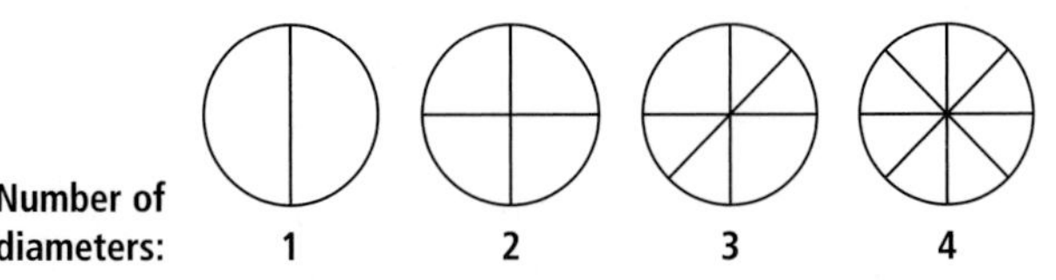


6. Can you find four examples that are true or a counterexample for the following statement?

   For every integer $n$, the value of $n^2 + 1$ is odd.

# PRACTICE & PROBLEM SOLVING

Scan for Multimedia

Practice Tutorial

Additional Exercises Available Online

## UNDERSTAND

7. **Mathematical Connections** Abby notices that for the first twenty perfect squares, each square is either a multiple of 5, one less than a multiple of 5, or one more than a multiple of 5.

| 1 | 4 | 9 | 16 | 25 |
|---|---|---|---|---|
| 36 | 49 | 64 | 81 | 100 |
| 121 | 144 | 169 | 196 | 225 |
| 256 | 289 | 324 | 361 | 400 |

She writes the following statement.

If $n$ is a natural number, then $n^2$ can be written as $5k - 1$, $5k$, or $5k + 1$, where $k$ is a whole number.

What type of statement did Abby make? Has she shown that her statement is true for all values of $n$? Explain.

8. **Error Analysis** Danielle tests the following conjecture.

If two angles share a common vertex, then they are adjacent.

Her work is shown below. What error does Danielle make?

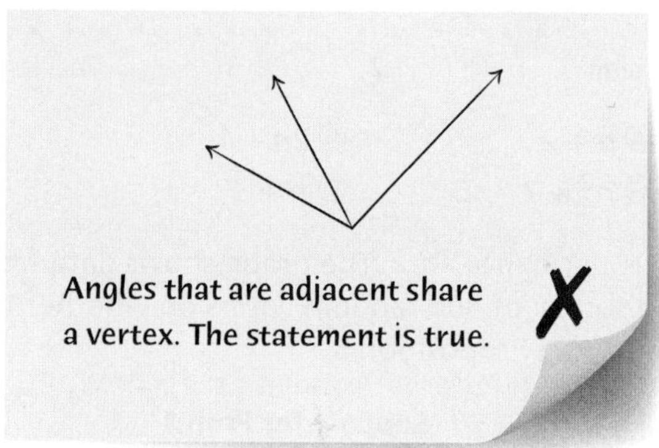

Angles that are adjacent share a vertex. The statement is true.
X


9. **Higher Order Thinking** Consider the following conjecture.

There are no prime numbers between 7,608 and 7,620.

How could you show that this statement is true or false? Would it still be a conjecture if you do not find a counterexample? Explain.

## PRACTICE

**For each sequence, what appear to be the next three numbers?** SEE EXAMPLE 1

10. 101, 89, 77, 65,...

11. 9, 6, 4, $\frac{8}{3}$,...

12. Observe the pattern made by the figures. Can you write a conjecture about the number of triangles formed by connecting one vertex of a polygon with $n$ sides to each of the other vertices? SEE EXAMPLE 2

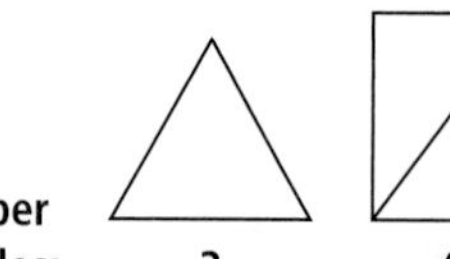

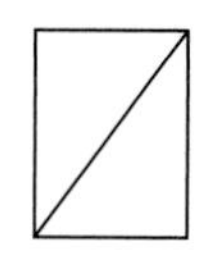

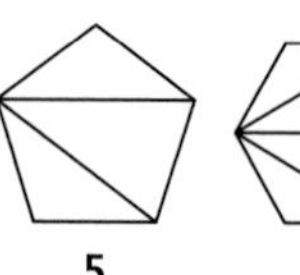


**The table shows the number of students in the senior class and the number of seniors who have their driver's license.** SEE EXAMPLE 3

| Year | 2014 | 2015 | 2016 | 2017 |
|---|---|---|---|---|
| Number of Seniors | 341 | 367 | 309 | 382 |
| Seniors With a License | 222 | 240 | 199 | 246 |

13. What pattern can you find between the number of seniors and the seniors who have a driver's license?

14. The class of 2018 has 413 seniors. How many seniors in the class of 2018 do you think will have a driver's license?

15. Can you find a counterexample for the following statement? SEE EXAMPLE 4

A trapezoid cannot have more than one right angle.

16. Support the following conjecture with 4 examples or disprove it with a counterexample. SEE EXAMPLE 5

The quotient of two rational numbers is a rational number.

# PRACTICE & PROBLEM SOLVING

## APPLY

17. **Model With Mathematics** Data from four identical trials on a new sleep herb are shown in the table.

| Group | Number of Subjects | Number Who Reported Better Sleep |
|---|---|---|
| A | 250 | 55 |
| B | 170 | 35 |
| C | 210 | 48 |
| D | 190 | 40 |

a. What conjecture can you make about the effectiveness of the herb?

b. The next trial will have 1,000 subjects. What is a reasonable prediction for the next trial?

18. **Make Sense and Persevere** Deshawn is given the following conjecture.

The first and third digits of a three-digit number are the same. If the second digit is equal to the sum of the first and third digits, then the number must be divisible by 11.

How can he determine whether the conjecture is true?

19. **Generalize** A graphic designer wants to know the number of regions that are formed when circles overlap in a particular way. Can she find a rule that describes how the number of regions increases when another circle is added to the design? How many regions would a design with 6 circles create?

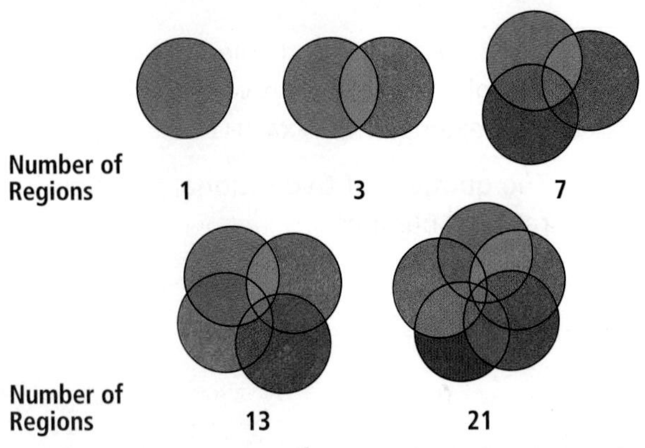


## ASSESSMENT PRACTICE

20. Consider the conjecture, "Any number divisible by 2 is also divisible by 4." Is each number a counterexample of the conjecture? Select *Yes* or *No*.

| | Yes | No |
|---|---|---|
| 12 | ❑ | ❑ |
| 19 | ❑ | ❑ |
| 22 | ❑ | ❑ |
| 28 | ❑ | ❑ |
| 30 | ❑ | ❑ |

21. **SAT/ACT** Which number is next in the following sequence?

1, 2, 2, 4, 8, 32,...

Ⓐ 64 Ⓑ 84 Ⓒ 106 Ⓓ 256

22. **SAT/ACT** How many dots are in the *n*th term of the following sequence?

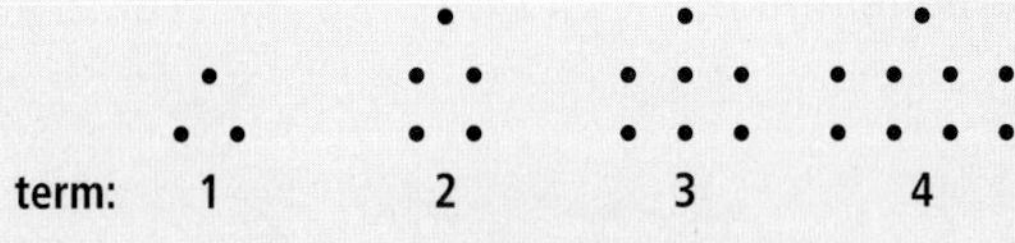


Ⓐ $n + 2$ Ⓑ $2n + 1$
Ⓒ $n^2 + 2$ Ⓓ $n + 3$

23. **Performance Task** The graph shows data from a survey of 300 random voters on whether they support Proposition 3.

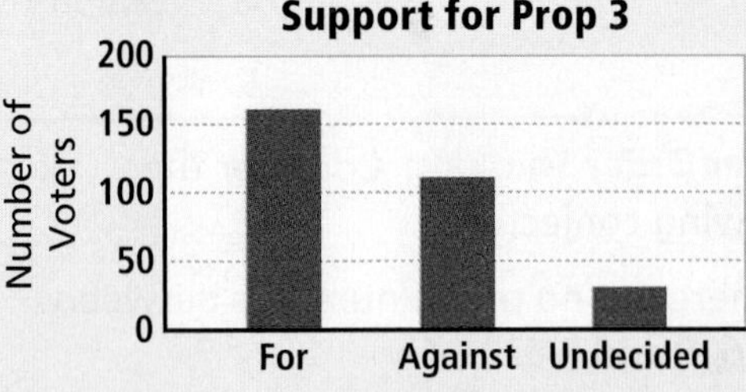


**Part A** Make a conjecture about the likelihood of Proposition 3 passing and explain your reasoning.

**Part B** If 7,500 people vote in the next election, how many people would you expect to vote for Proposition 3?

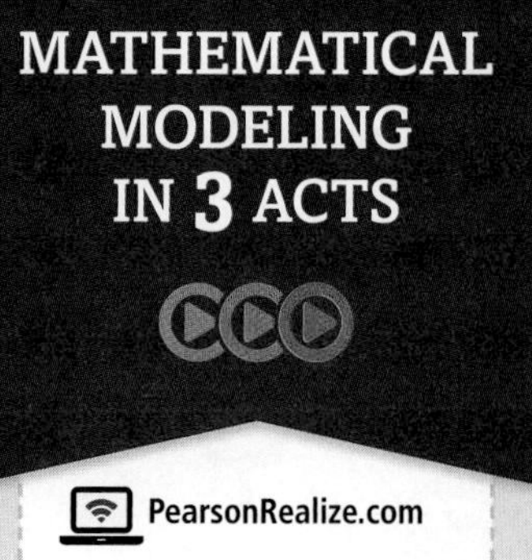


PearsonRealize.com

## The Mystery Spokes

Some photos are taken in such a way that it is difficult to determine exactly what the picture shows. Sometimes it's because the photo is a close up part of an object, and you do not see the entire object. Other times, it might be because the photographer used special effects when taking the photo.

You can often use clues from the photo to determine what is in the photo and also what the rest of the object might look like. What clues would you look for? Think about this during the Mathematical Modeling in 3 Acts lesson.

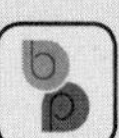

### ACT 1 Identify the Problem

1. What is the first question that comes to mind after watching the video?
2. Write down the main question you will answer about what you saw in the video.
3. Make an initial conjecture that answers this main question.
4. Explain how you arrived at your conjecture.
5. Write a number that you know is too small.
6. Write a number that you know is too large.

### ACT 2 Develop a Model

7. Use the math that you have learned in this Topic to refine your conjecture.

### ACT 3 Interpret the Results

8. Is your refined conjecture between the highs and lows you set up earlier?
9. Did your refined conjecture match the actual answer exactly? If not, what might explain the difference?

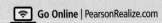

# 1-5 Conditional Statements

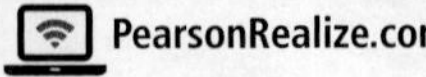
PearsonRealize.com

**I CAN…** write conditionals and biconditionals and find their truth values.

**VOCABULARY**

- biconditional
- conclusion
- conditional
- contrapositive
- converse
- hypothesis
- inverse
- negation
- truth table
- truth value

## EXPLORE & REASON

**If-then statements show a cause and effect. The table shows some if-then statements.**

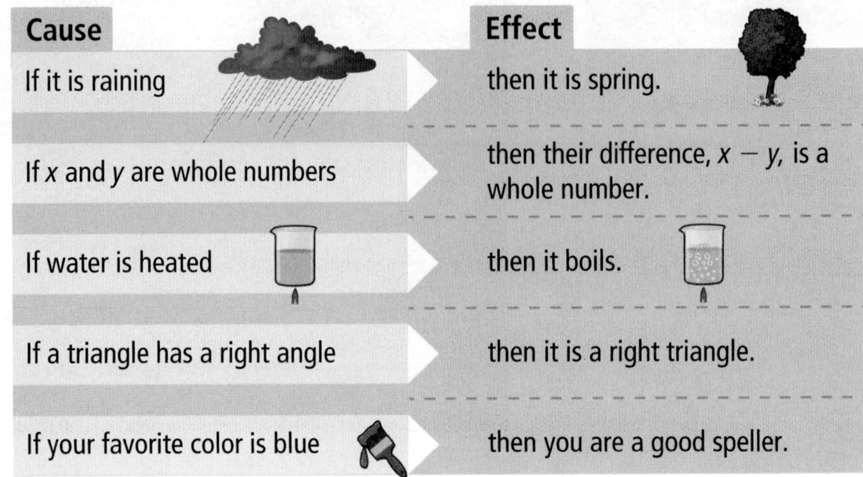

| Cause | Effect |
|---|---|
| If it is raining | then it is spring. |
| If $x$ and $y$ are whole numbers | then their difference, $x - y$, is a whole number. |
| If water is heated | then it boils. |
| If a triangle has a right angle | then it is a right triangle. |
| If your favorite color is blue | then you are a good speller. |

**A. Construct Arguments** Determine whether each effect is always true for the given cause, or is not necessarily true for the given cause. For the effects that are not necessarily true, how could you change them to make them always true?

**B.** Write some if-then statements of your own. Write two statements that are always true and two statements that are not necessarily true.

**? ESSENTIAL QUESTION** **How do if-then statements describe mathematical relationships?**

### CONCEPT Conditional Statement

A **conditional** is an *if-then* statement that relates a **hypothesis**, the part that follows *if*, to a **conclusion**, the part that follows *then*.

Conditionals can be represented as $p \rightarrow q$, read as "If $p$, then $q$," where $p$ represents the hypothesis and $q$ represents the conclusion.

## EXAMPLE 1 Write a Conditional Statement

**Write each statement as a conditional.**

**A. You can register to vote if you are at least 18 years old.**

Identify the hypothesis and conclusion.

The conclusion gives the outcome or result.

The hypothesis follows "if" and gives the condition.

**You can register to vote if you are at least 18 years old.**

**Conditional:** If you are at least 18 years old, then you may register to vote.

**COMMON ERROR**
Remember that in everyday language, the hypothesis does not necessarily come before the conclusion.

CONTINUED ON THE NEXT PAGE

EXAMPLE 1 CONTINUED

**B. A square must have four congruent sides.**

Identify the hypothesis and conclusion.

The hypothesis is that a polygon is a square.

The conclusion is that the polygon has four congruent sides.

**A square must have four congruent sides.**

**Conditional:** If a polygon is a square, then it has four congruent sides.

 **Try It!** **1.** Write each statement as a conditional.

**a.** A triangle with all angles congruent is equilateral.

**b.** Alberto can go to the movies if he washes the car.

CONCEPTUAL UNDERSTANDING

## EXAMPLE 2 Find a Truth Value of a Conditional

**The truth value of a statement is "true" (T) or "false" (F) according to whether the statement is true or false, respectively. A truth table lists all the possible combinations of truth values for two or more statements.**

**Truth Table for $p \to q$**

| Hypothesis $p$ | Conclusion $q$ | Conditional $p \to q$ |
|---|---|---|
| T | T | T |
| T | F | F |
| F | T | T |
| F | F | T |

A conditional with a false hypothesis has a value of true, regardless of the conclusion.

Only a conditional with a true hypothesis and a false conclusion has a value of false.

**How can you determine the truth value of each conditional?**

**A. If a number is even, then it is divisible by 2.**

An even number is always divisible by two, so when the hypothesis is true, the conclusion is always true.

The conditional is true.

**MAKE SENSE AND PERSEVERE**
To determine the truth value of a conditional, consider all of the options for the hypothesis and for the conclusion. For example, assume the hypothesis is true, then determine whether the conclusion must also always be true.

**B. If a quadrilateral has two pairs of congruent angles, then it is a parallelogram.**

Assume the hypothesis, a quadrilateral that has two pairs of congruent angles, is true. To decide whether the conclusion is true, determine whether the quadrilateral must be a parallelogram.

An isosceles trapezoid has two pairs of congruent angles, but is not a parallelogram. The conclusion is false.

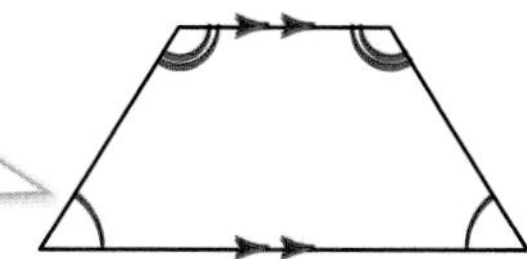

In this example, the hypothesis of the conditional is true and the conclusion is false, so this conditional is false.

CONTINUED ON THE NEXT PAGE

**Try It!** 2. What is the truth value of each conditional? Explain your reasoning.

**a.** If a quadrilateral has a right angle, then it is a rectangle.

**b.** If $X$ is the midpoint of $\overline{AB}$, then $X$ lies on $\overline{AB}$.

## CONCEPT Related Conditional Statements

| Definition | Symbols | Words |
|---|---|---|
| A conditional has a hypothesis and a conclusion. | $p \to q$ | If $p$, then $q$. |
| The **converse** reverses the hypothesis and the conclusion of a conditional. | $q \to p$ | If $q$, then $p$. |
| The **negation** of a statement has the opposite meaning of the original statement. | $\sim p$ | not $p$ |
| The **inverse** is obtained by negating both the hypothesis and the conclusion of a conditional. | $\sim p \to \sim q$ | If not $p$, then not $q$. |
| The **contrapositive** is obtained by negating and reversing both the hypothesis and the conclusion of a conditional. | $\sim q \to \sim p$ | If not $q$, then not $p$. |

## EXAMPLE 3 Write and Evaluate the Truth Value of a Converse

**Write and determine the truth value of the converse of the conditional.**

**If you play the trumpet, then you play a brass instrument.**

To write the converse, reverse the hypothesis and conclusion.

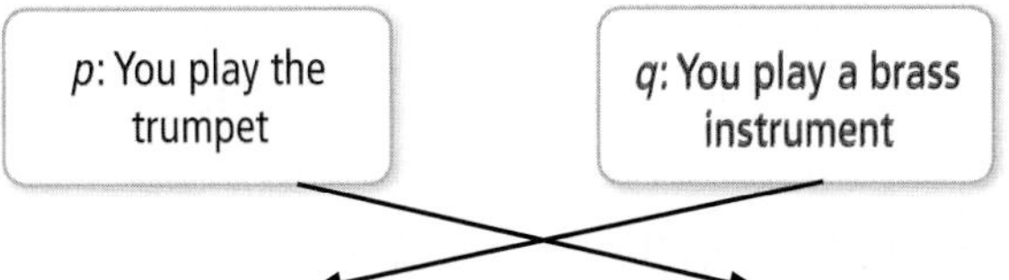

p: You play the trumpet
q: You play a brass instrument

If you play a brass instrument, then you play the trumpet.

If you play a brass instrument, then you may play a brass instrument that is not a trumpet. The converse is false.

**STUDY TIP**
To remember that the converse switches the order back and forth, remember that a *conversation* goes back and forth between two people.

**Try It!** 3. Write and determine the truth value of the converse of the conditional.

**a.** If a polygon is a quadrilateral, then it has four sides.

**b.** If two angles are complementary, then their angle measures add to 90.

## EXAMPLE 4 Write and Evaluate the Truth Value of an Inverse and a Contrapositive

**Write and determine the truth value of the inverse and contrapositive of the conditional.**

**If two whole numbers are both even, then their sum is even.**

**COMMUNICATE PRECISELY**
Consider how you can use clear and accurate reasoning to determine a truth value. What can you reason about a conditional if the conclusion is not true?

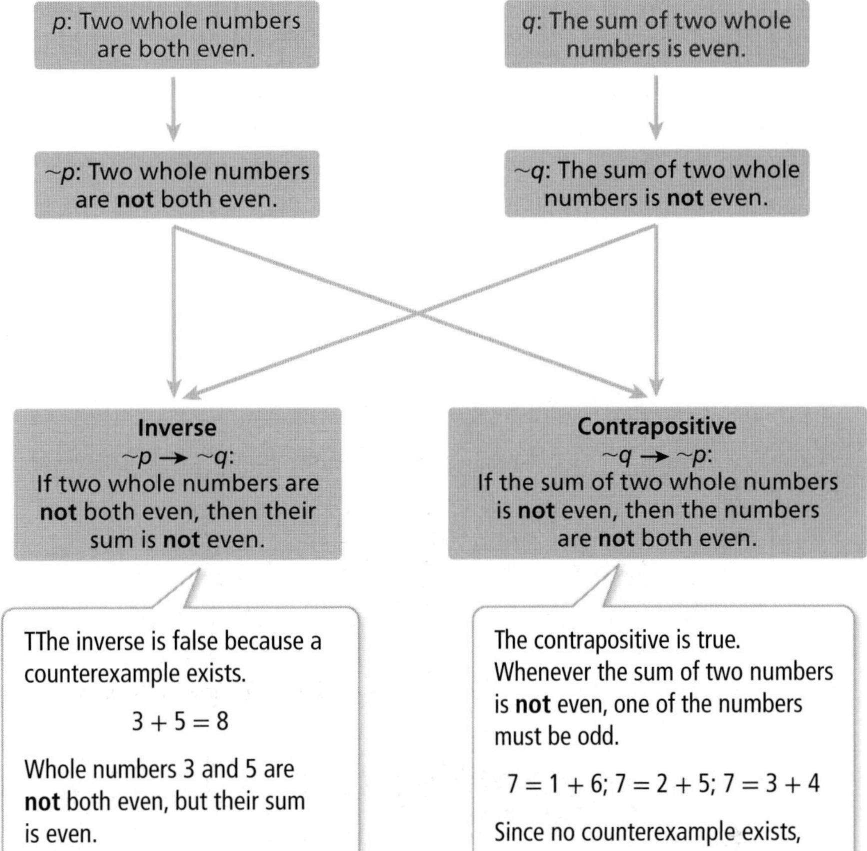

p: Two whole numbers are both even.
q: The sum of two whole numbers is even.
~p: Two whole numbers are **not** both even.
~q: The sum of two whole numbers is **not** even.
**Inverse**
~p → ~q:
If two whole numbers are **not** both even, then their sum is **not** even.
**Contrapositive**
~q → ~p:
If the sum of two whole numbers is **not** even, then the numbers are **not** both even.

TThe inverse is false because a counterexample exists.

$3 + 5 = 8$

Whole numbers 3 and 5 are **not** both even, but their sum is even.

The contrapositive is true. Whenever the sum of two numbers is **not** even, one of the numbers must be odd.

$7 = 1 + 6; 7 = 2 + 5; 7 = 3 + 4$

Since no counterexample exists, the contrapositive is true.

**Try It!** **4.** Write the converse, the inverse, and the contrapositive. What is the truth value of each?

If today is a weekend day, then tomorrow is Monday.

## CONCEPT Biconditional Statements

A **biconditional** is the combination of a conditional, $p \rightarrow q$, and its converse, $q \rightarrow p$. The resulting compound statement $p \leftrightarrow q$ is read as "$p$ if and only if $q$."

When $p$ and $q$ have the same truth value, the biconditional is true. When they have opposite truth values, it is false.

| $p$ | $q$ | $p \leftrightarrow q$ |
|---|---|---|
| T | T | T |
| T | F | F |
| F | T | F |
| F | F | T |

APPLICATION

## EXAMPLE 5 Write and Evaluate a Biconditional

**A marine biologist writes this conditional: "If a seahorse gives birth, then it is a male." Since it is true that, among seahorses, only the males can become pregnant and give birth, should the marine biologist state this as a biconditional in a paper she is writing?**

**Formulate** Identify the hypothesis $p$ and the conclusion $q$ of the conditional.

Combine the conditionals $p \rightarrow q$ and $q \rightarrow p$ in the form $p \leftrightarrow q$ to write the biconditional.

Then evaluate the truth value of the biconditional.

**Compute** **$p$: A seahorse gives birth.**

**$q$: A seahorse is male.**

**Biconditional** $p \leftrightarrow q$: A seahorse gives birth if and only if it is male.

**Determine the truth value of the biconditional.**

$p \rightarrow q$: If a seahorse gives birth, then it is male. **T**

$q \rightarrow p$: If a seahorse is male, then it gives birth. **F**

If each of the combined conditionals is true, then the biconditional is true.

**Interpret** The biconditional is not true; the biologist should not include the statement as a biconditional in her paper.

**Try It!** 5. Write a biconditional for the following conditional. What is its truth value?

If two lines intersect at right angles, then they are perpendicular.

## EXAMPLE 6 Identify the Conditionals in a Biconditional

**What are the two conditionals implied by the biconditional?**

**A triangle is equilateral if and only if it has three congruent sides.**

**STUDY TIP**
Remember that because the conditionals that form a true biconditional are also true, you can choose either part of the biconditional as the hypothesis and the other part as the conclusion.

Identify the two statements in the biconditional

**$p$:** A triangle is equilateral.

**$q$:** A triangle has three congruent sides.

Write the two conditionals.

$p \rightarrow q$: If a triangle is equilateral, then it has three congruent sides.

$q \rightarrow p$: If a triangle has three congruent sides, then it is equilateral.

**Try It!** 6. What are the two conditionals implied by the biconditional?

The product of two numbers is negative if and only if the numbers have opposite signs.

## CONCEPT SUMMARY Conditional Statements

| STATEMENT | Conditional | Converse | Inverse | Contrapositive | Biconditional |
|---|---|---|---|---|---|
| SYMBOLS | $p \rightarrow q$ | $q \rightarrow p$ | $\sim p \rightarrow \sim q$ | $\sim q \rightarrow \sim p$ | $p \leftrightarrow q$ |
| WORDS | If $p$, then $q$. | If $q$, then $p$. | If not $p$, then not $q$. | If not $q$, then not $p$. | $p$ if and only if $q$. |

## Do You UNDERSTAND?

1. ESSENTIAL QUESTION How do if-then statements describe mathematical relationships?

2. **Error Analysis** Allie was asked to write the inverse of the following conditional.

   If it is sunny, then I use sunscreen.

   What error did Allie make?

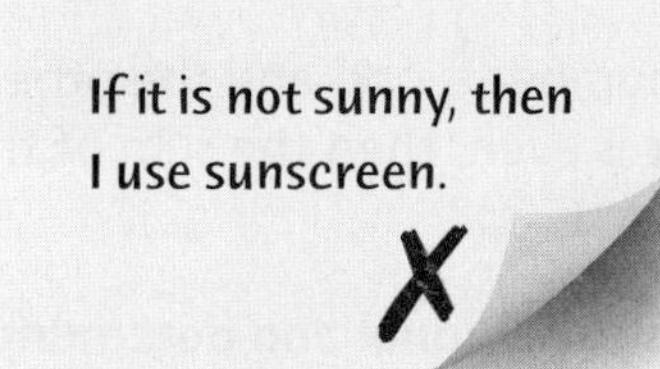

If it is not sunny, then
I use sunscreen.
X


3. **Vocabulary** Which term is used to describe the opposite of a statement?

4. **Generalize** How do you write the converse of a conditional? How do you write the contrapositive of a conditional?

5. **Communicate Precisely** Explain how the inverse and the contrapositive of a conditional are alike and how they are different.

## Do You KNOW HOW?

6. Write the following statement as a biconditional.

   A prime number has only 1 and itself as factors.

**For Exercises 7–9, use the following conditional.**

**If a rectangle has an area of 12 m$^2$, then it has sides of length 3 m and 4 m.**

7. What is the hypothesis? What is the conclusion?

8. Assume the hypothesis is false. What is the truth value of the conditional? Assume the hypothesis is true. What would be a counterexample?

9. What are the converse, the inverse, and the contrapositive? What are their truth values?

10. What two conditionals are implied by the following biconditional?

"The city can build new roads if and only if the sales tax is raised to 10%."

# PRACTICE & PROBLEM SOLVING

Scan for Multimedia 

Practice Tutorial

Additional Exercises Available Online

## UNDERSTAND

**11. Construct Arguments** Why is the following conditional logically true?

If 20 is a multiple of 3, then 101 is a perfect square.

**12** **Higher Order Thinking** Write a true biconditional and show that both implied conditionals are true.

**13. Error Analysis** Jacy was asked to write the following statement as a conditional.

Water freezes if it is below 0°C.

What error did she make? What is the correct conditional?

If water freezes, then it is below 0°C. ✗

**14. Higher Order Thinking** Write a true biconditional about angle bisectors.

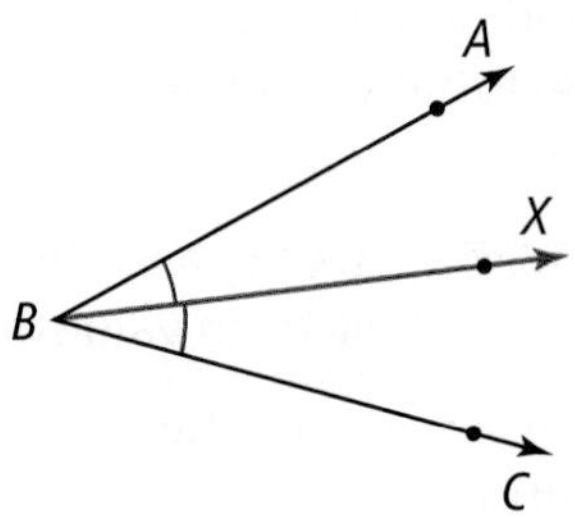


**15. Reason** Can an inverse and the contrapositive both have false truth values? Explain.

**16. Reason** If a biconditional is true, what are the truth values of the hypothesis and conclusion of the conditional? Explain.

**17. Look for Relationships** Emma found a counterexample to a given conditional. What are the truth values of the hypothesis and the conclusion? Explain.

**18. Mathematical Connections** Write the Pythagorean Theorem as a conditional. Then write a biconditional to include the Converse of the Pythagorean Theorem.

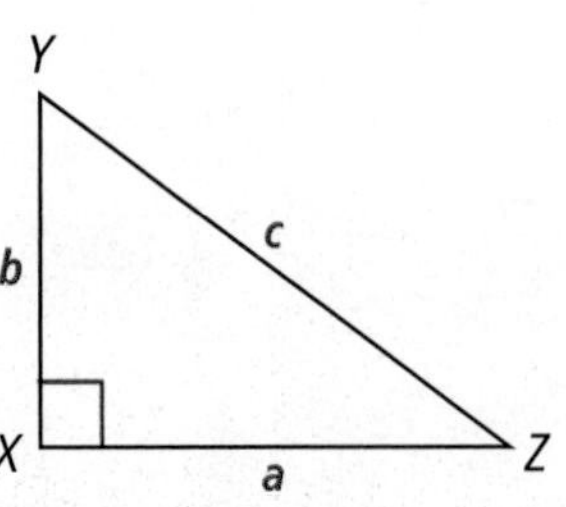


## PRACTICE

**Write each statement as a conditional.**
SEE EXAMPLE 1

**19.** My hair will be shorter if I cut it.

**20.** A number that is divisible by 6 is divisible by 3.

**21.** Movie tickets are half-price on Tuesdays.

**Find the truth value of each conditional. Explain your reasoning or show a counterexample.**
SEE EXAMPLE 2

**22.** If a pair of lines is parallel, then they do not intersect.

**23.** If the product of two numbers is positive, then the numbers are both positive.

**Write the negation of the hypothesis and the negation of the conclusion for each conditional.**
SEE EXAMPLES 3 and 4

**24.** If the sum of the interior angle measures of a polygon is 180, then the polygon is a triangle.

**25.** If one whole number is odd and the other whole number is even, then the sum of the two numbers is odd.

**Write each related conditional and determine each truth value for the following conditional.**
SEE EXAMPLES 3 and 4

**If an angle measures 100, then it is obtuse.**

**26.** converse

**27.** contrapositive

**28.** inverse

**29.** An employee at an animal shelter wrote the true conditional "If 47% of the dogs at the shelter are female, then 53% of the dogs are male." Can he rewrite this as a true biconditional? Explain. SEE EXAMPLE 5

**Write two conditionals from each biconditional.**
SEE EXAMPLE 6

**30.** A month has exactly 28 days if and only if it is February.

**31.** Two angles are complementary if and only if their measures add up to 90.

**32.** The area of a square is $s^2$ if and only if the perimeter of the square is $4s$.

# PRACTICE & PROBLEM SOLVING

Practice Tutorial

Mixed Review Available Online

## APPLY

33. **Model With Mathematics** In general, a person is 1% shorter in the evening than in the morning. Use your height to write a conditional that uses this fact.

34. **Communicate Precisely** In the year 1881, three different men were president of the United States—Rutherford B. Hayes, James Garfield, and Chester A. Arthur.

    a. Use this fact to write a conditional and a biconditional.

    b. There was one other year in which three different men were president of the United States. In 1841, Martin Van Buren, William Henry Harrison, and John Tyler were president. Using this information, determine the truth value of the conditional and the biconditional you wrote for part (a).

35. **Reason** The sign shows the hours for an art museum.

| MO ART | Modern Art Museum HOURS | |
|---|---|---|
| Monday | Closed | |
| Tuesday | 10:00 AM | 8:00 PM |
| Wednesday | 10:00 AM | 6:00 PM |
| Thursday | 10:00 AM | 8:00 PM |
| Friday | 9:00 AM | 6:00 PM |
| Saturday | 9:00 AM | 6:00 PM |
| Sunday | 12:00 AM | 5:00 PM |

    a. Write a conditional to describe the hours of the museum on Mondays.

    b. Write a conditional to describe the hours of the museum on Thursdays.

    c. Write the converse, inverse, and contrapositive of the conditional you wrote in part (b). Then give the truth value for each statement.

    d. Can each conditional you wrote for parts (a) and (b) be written as a true biconditional? Why or why not? If so, give each biconditional.

## ASSESSMENT PRACTICE

36. Consider the conditional $p \to q$, where $p$ is true and $q$ is false. Copy and complete the table to show the truth value of each statement.

| Statement | Truth Value |
|---|---|
| Conditional | F |
| Converse | |
| Inverse | |
| Contrapositive | |

37. **SAT/ACT** Which represents the contrapositive of $p \to q$?

    Ⓐ $p \leftrightarrow q$

    Ⓑ $q \to p$

    Ⓒ $\sim p \to \sim q$

    Ⓓ $\sim q \to \sim p$

    Ⓔ $\sim q \leftrightarrow \sim p$

38. **Performance Task** A group of students drew several different right triangles and found the measures of the two non-right angles. Their findings are shown in the table.

| Angle Measure | Angle Measure | Sum |
|---|---|---|
| 27 | 63 | 90 |
| 41 | 49 | 90 |
| 70 | 20 | 90 |
| 33 | 57 | 90 |

**Part A** Make a conjecture about the sum of two non-right angles in a right triangle. Write the conjecture in the form of a conditional.

**Part B** Construct several right triangles, and then measure the angles of each triangle. Do your measurements support your conjecture, or were you able to find a counterexample?

**Part C** Write the converse, the inverse, and the contrapositive of your conditional. Then, write a biconditional. Is the biconditional true? Explain.

# 1-6 Deductive Reasoning

PearsonRealize.com

**I CAN…** use deductive reasoning to draw conclusions.

## VOCABULARY

- deductive reasoning
- Law of Detachment
- Law of Syllogism

Activity Assess

## CRITIQUE & EXPLAIN

**A deck of 60 game cards are numbered from 1 to 15 on one of four different shapes (triangle, circle, square, and pentagon). A teacher selects five cards and displays four of the cards.**

**She tells her class that all of the cards she selected have the same shape and asks them to draw a conclusion about the fifth card.**

Chen

The fifth card is 11.

Carolina

The fifth card has a circle.

**A.** Describe how each student might have reached his or her conclusion. Is each student's conclusion valid? Explain.

**B. Make Sense and Persevere** What are other possibilities of the fifth card? What could the teacher say to narrow the possibilities?

## ESSENTIAL QUESTION

**How is deductive reasoning different from inductive reasoning?**

CONCEPTUAL UNDERSTANDING

## EXAMPLE 1 Determine Whether a Statement Is True

**Given that a conditional and its conclusion are true, can you use deductive reasoning to determine whether the hypothesis is true?**

**Deductive reasoning** is a process of reasoning using given and previously known facts to reach a logical conclusion.

**STUDY TIP**
Recall that in a conditional $p \rightarrow q$, $p$ is the hypothesis and $q$ is the conclusion.

You are given the facts that $p \rightarrow q$ is true and $q$ is true. Make a truth table for the conditional $p \rightarrow q$.

| $p$ | $q$ | $p \rightarrow q$ |
|---|---|---|
| T | T | T |
| T | F | F |
| F | T | T |
| F | F | T |

When $p \rightarrow q$ and $q$ are true, $p$ can be true or false.

You cannot determine whether the hypothesis is true.

**Try It!** **1.** Given that a conditional and its hypothesis are true, can you determine whether the conclusion is true?

  Activity  Assess

## CONCEPT Law of Detachment

The **Law of Detachment** is a law of logic that states if a conditional statement and its hypothesis are true, then its conclusion is also true.

**If...** $p \rightarrow q$ and $p$ are true.

**Then...** $q$ is true.

## EXAMPLE 2 Apply the Law of Detachment to Draw Real-World and Mathematical Conclusions

**Assume that each set of given information is true.**

**A. If Alicia scores 85 or greater on her test, she will earn an A as her final grade. Alicia scores 89 on her test. What can you logically conclude?**

To apply the Law of Detachment, determine the truth value of $p \rightarrow q$ and $p$.

$p \rightarrow q$: If Alicia scores 85 or greater on her test, then she will earn an A as her final grade.

This given conditional is true.

$p$: Alicia scores 85 or greater on her test.

The hypothesis is true because $89 > 85$.

The conditional and its hypothesis are true, so by the Law of Detachment, the conclusion $q$ is true.

You can conclude that Alicia will earn an A as her final grade.

**REASON**
If you cannot assume that given information is true, you can use deductive reasoning to determine whether the conditional and the hypothesis are true.

**B. If point $D$ is in the interior of $\angle ABC$, then $m\angle ABC = m\angle ABD + m\angle DBC$. What can you logically conclude about $m\angle ABC$?**

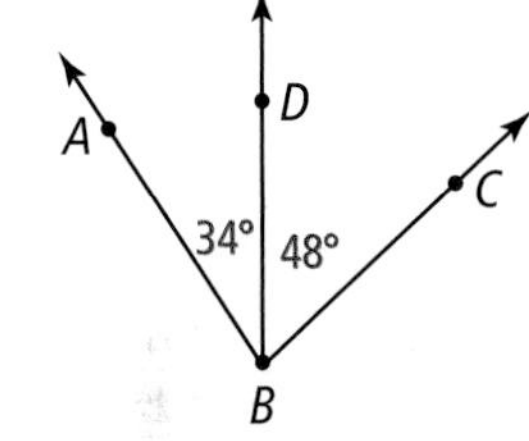


Determine the truth value of $p \rightarrow q$ and $p$.

$p \rightarrow q$: If point $D$ is in the interior of $\angle ABC$, then $m\angle ABC = m\angle ABD + m\angle DBC$.

The conditional is true by the Angle Addition Postulate.

$p$: Point $D$ is in the interior of $\angle ABC$.

This given hypothesis is true.

By the Law of Detachment, the conclusion $q$ is true.

You can conclude that $m\angle ABC = m\angle ABD + m\angle DBC$.

**Try It!** 2. Assume that each set of given information is true.

a. If two angles are congruent, then the measures of the two angles are equal to each other. Angle 1 is congruent to $\angle 2$. What can you logically conclude about the measures of $\angle 1$ and $\angle 2$?

b. If you finish the race in under 30 minutes, then you win a prize. You finished the race in 26 minutes. What can you logically conclude?

## CONCEPT Law of Syllogism

The **Law of Syllogism** is a law of logic that states that given two true conditionals with the conclusion of the first being the hypothesis of the second, there exists a third true conditional having the hypothesis of the first and the conclusion of the second.

**If...** $p \rightarrow q$ and $q \rightarrow r$ are true.

**Then...** $p \rightarrow r$ is true.

## EXAMPLE 3 Apply the Law of Syllogism to Draw Real-World and Mathematical Conclusions

**Assume that each set of conditionals is true. What can you conclude using the Law of Syllogism?**

**A. If Kenji plays the trumpet, then he plays a brass instrument. If he plays a brass instrument, he is a member of the marching band.**

To apply the Law of Syllogism, determine whether the conclusion of one statement is the hypothesis of the other statement.

$p \rightarrow q$: If Kenji plays the trumpet, then he plays a brass instrument.

$q \rightarrow r$: If he plays a brass instrument, then he is a member of the marching band.

The conclusion of one statement is the hypothesis of the other statement.

**Conclusion:** If Kenji plays the trumpet, then he is a member of the marching band.

**B. If points $A$, $B$, and $C$ are collinear and $B$ is between $A$ and $C$, then $\overrightarrow{BA}$ and $\overrightarrow{BC}$ are opposite rays. If $\overrightarrow{BA}$ and $\overrightarrow{BC}$ are opposite rays, then $AB + BC = AC$. What can you conclude?**

Apply the Law of Syllogism, determine whether the conclusion of one statement is the hypothesis of the other statement.

$p \rightarrow q$: If points $A$, $B$, and $C$ are colinear and $B$ is between $A$ and $C$, then $\overrightarrow{BA}$ and $\overrightarrow{BC}$ are opposite rays.

$q \rightarrow r$: If $\overrightarrow{BA}$ and $\overrightarrow{BC}$ are opposite rays, then $AB + BC = AC$.

The conclusion of one statement is the hypothesis of the other statement.

**Conclusion:** If points $A$, $B$, and $C$ are colinear and $B$ is between $A$ and $C$, then $AB + BC = AC$.

**COMMON ERROR**
You may confuse the hypotheses and conclusions of the given conditionals in writing the third conditional. Recall that the statement that is part of each conditional is not part of the conclusion.

**Try It!** 3. Assume that each set of conditionals is true. Use the Law of Syllogism to draw a conclusion.

**a.** If an integer is divisible by 6, it is divisible by 2. If an integer is divisible by 2, then it is an even number.

**b.** If it is a holiday, then you do not have to go to school. If it is Labor Day, then it is a holiday.

APPLICATION

## Apply the Laws of Detachment and Syllogism to Draw Conclusions

**What conclusions can you draw from the following true statements?**

**If you are climbing a mountain at an altitude of 28,500 feet or higher, then you are on the tallest mountain above sea level on Earth. If you are on the tallest mountain above sea level on Earth, then you are on Mount Everest. You are climbing a mountain at an altitude of 29,000 feet.**

Identify conditional statements and use the laws of logic to draw a conclusion.

**Use the Law of Detachment**

$p \rightarrow q$: If you are climbing a mountain at an altitude of 28,500 feet or higher, then you are on the tallest mountain above sea level on Earth.

This given conditional is true.

$p$: You are climbing a mountain at an altitude of 28,500 feet or higher.

$p$ is true because $29{,}000 > 28{,}500$.

By the Law of Detachment, the conclusion $q$ is true.

You are on the tallest mountain above sea level on Earth.

**Use the Law of Syllogism**

$p \rightarrow q$
If you are climbing a mountain at an altitude of 28,500 feet or higher, then you are on the tallest mountain above sea level on Earth.

$p \rightarrow q$ is true.

$q \rightarrow r$
If you are on the tallest mountain above sea level on Earth, then you are on Mount Everest.

$q \rightarrow r$ is true.

$p \rightarrow r$
If you are climbing a mountain at an altitude of 28,500 feet or higher, then you are on Mount Everest.

$p \rightarrow r$ is true by the Law of Syllogism.

**Use the Law of Syllogism and the Law of Detachment**

$p \rightarrow r$: If you are climbing a mountain at an altitude of 28,500 feet or higher, then you are on Mount Everest.

$p \rightarrow r$ is true by the Law of Syllogism.

$p$: You are climbing a mountain at an altitude of 28,500 feet or higher.

$p$ is true because $29{,}000 > 28{,}500$.

By the Law of Detachment, the conclusion $r$: is true

You are on Mount Everest.

 **Try It!** 4. Martin walks his dog before dinner every day. Martin is now eating his dinner. Using the Law of Detachment and the Law of Syllogism, what conclusions can you draw from these true statements?

## CONCEPT SUMMARY Deductive Reasoning

**WORDS**

**Law of Detachment**

If a conditional statement and its hypothesis are true, then its conclusion is also true.

**Law of Syllogism**

Given two true conditionals with the conclusion of the first being the hypothesis of the second, there exists a third true conditional having the hypothesis of the first and the conclusion of the second.

**SYMBOLS**

Law of Detachment:

**If...** $p \rightarrow q$ and $p$ are true.

**Then...** $q$ is true.

Law of Syllogism:

**If...** $p \rightarrow q$ and $q \rightarrow r$ are true.

**Then...** $p \rightarrow r$ is true.

## Do You UNDERSTAND?

1. **ESSENTIAL QUESTION** How is deductive reasoning different from inductive reasoning?

2. **Error Analysis** Dakota writes the following as an example of using the Law of Detachment. What is her error?

> If my favorite team wins more than 55 games, they win the championship. My team won the championship, so they won more than 55 games. ✗

3. **Vocabulary** What are the differences between the Law of Detachment and the Law of Syllogism?

4. **Use Structure** How can representing sentences and phrases with symbols help you determine whether to apply the Law of Detachment or the Law of Syllogism?

## Do You KNOW HOW?

**Assume that each set of given information is true.**

5. If you have a temperature above 100.4°F, then you have a fever. Casey has a temperature of 101.2°F. What can you conclude about Casey? What rule of inference did you use?

6. If points $A$, $B$, and $C$ are collinear with $B$ between $A$ and $C$, then $AB + BC = AC$. Use the information in the figure shown. What can you conclude about $AC$?



**Assume that each set of conditionals is true. Use the Law of Syllogism to write a true conditional.**

7. If you eat too much, you get a stomach ache. If you get a stomach ache, you want to rest.

8. If two numbers are odd, the sum of the numbers is even. If a number is even, then the number is divisible by 2.

# PRACTICE & PROBLEM SOLVING

Scan for Multimedia

Practice Tutorial

Additional Exercises Available Online

## UNDERSTAND

**9. Error Analysis** Samantha writes the following as an example of using the Law of Syllogism. Explain Samantha's error.

> If an animal is a dog, then it is a mammal.
> If an animal is a dog, then it has four legs.
>
> I can conclude that if an animal has four legs, then it is a mammal. ✗

**10. Look for Relationships** Make a truth table with statements $p$, $q$, $r$, $p \rightarrow q$, $q \rightarrow r$, and $p \rightarrow r$. How does the truth table support the validity of the Law of Syllogism and the Law of Detachment?

**11. Mathematical Connections** Consider the following conditional.

If all four sides of a quadrilateral are of equal length, then its diagonals intersect at right angles.

Which of the following figures can you use with the conditional to apply the Law of Detachment to draw the conclusion that its diagonals intersect at right angles?

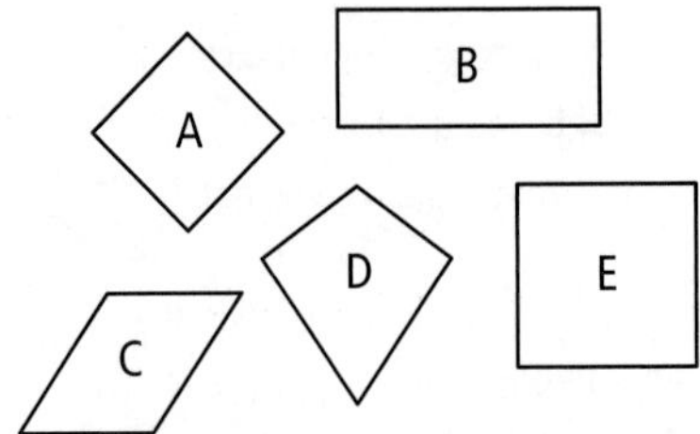


**12. Higher Order Thinking** Suppose you are given that a conditional is true but its conclusion is false. What can you conclude about the hypothesis? Explain your answer using the negation of the hypothesis and the conclusion with the Law of Detachment.

**13. Look for Relationships** To apply the Law of Detachment, a conditional statement and its hypothesis must both be true. Can you draw any conclusions if the conditional is true but the hypothesis is false? Explain.

## PRACTICE

**Determine the truth value of the following conditional.** SEE EXAMPLE 1

**14.** If two adjacent angles form a right angle, then the angles are complementary.

**Assume that each set of statements is true. Use the Law of Detachment to write a true statement. If the Law of Detachment cannot be used, explain why.** SEE EXAMPLE 2

**15.** If you can play the piano, then you can play a musical instrument. Kiyo can play a musical instrument.

**16.** If the endpoints of a segment are $P(x_1, y_1)$ and $Q(x_2, y_2)$, then the coordinates of the midpoint are $M = \left(\frac{x_1 + x_2}{2}, \frac{y_1 + y_2}{2}\right)$. The endpoints of $\overline{CD}$ are $C(2, -4)$ and $D(-3, 5)$.

**17.** If the graph of a linear function has a positive slope, then the function is not decreasing. The slope of the graph is 0.

**Assume that each set of conditionals is true. Use the Law of Syllogism to write a true conditional. If the Law of Syllogism cannot be used, explain why.** SEE EXAMPLE 3

**18.** If $\overrightarrow{BD}$ bisects $\angle ABC$, then $\angle ABD \cong \angle DBC$. If $\angle ABD \cong \angle DBC$, then $m\angle ABD = m\angle DBC$.

**19.** If a whole number is even, then it is divisible by 2. If the sum of the digits of a whole number is divisible by 3, then the whole number is divisible by 3.

**20.** If Zachary eats pasta for dinner, then he goes to bed early. If it is Tuesday night, then Zachary eats pasta for dinner.

**Use the Law of Detachment and the Law of Syllogism to draw conclusions from each set of true statements.** SEE EXAMPLE 4

**21.** If it is Thursday, then Charles has baseball practice. If Charles has baseball practice, then he eats grilled chicken for dinner. It is the day after Wednesday.

**22.** If the length of a segment is $PQ$, then the distance from $P$ to the midpoint of $\overline{PQ}$ is $\frac{1}{2}PQ$. If the endpoints of a segment are $P(x_1, y_1)$ and $Q(x_2, y_2)$, then the length of the segment is $PQ = \sqrt{(x_2 - x_1)^2 + (y_2 - y_1)^2}$. The endpoints of $\overline{PQ}$ are $P(3, -4)$ and $Q(-3, -12)$.

# PRACTICE & PROBLEM SOLVING

## APPLY

23. **Model With Mathematics** Represent each true statement with symbols. Use symbols to write related contrapositives of the conditionals. Then use the Law of Detachment and the Law of Syllogism to draw a conclusion.

    If Avery draws a numbered card from 4 to 10, then his game piece moves to home base. If his game piece moves to home base, he wins the game. Avery does not win.

24. **Mathematical Connections** The chart describes the number of tickets needed to win prizes at a family fun center.

| Numbers of Tickets | Prize Level | Sample Prizes |
|---|---|---|
| 0–100 | A | magnet, stickers |
| 101–200 | B | keychain, flashlight |
| 201–300 | C | earbuds, MP3 speaker |

   a. Write conditionals with sample prizes as the hypothesis and prize level as the conclusion. Write conditionals that relate the prize level to the number of tickets.

   b. Ines wins an MP3 speaker. Use the Law of Detachment and Law of Syllogism to write true statements about Ines based on the conditionals you wrote in part (a).

25. **Reason** The table shows the main dishes served each day at a cafeteria.

| | |
|---|---|
| Monday | hamburger, salad, pizza |
| Tuesday | hamburger, stir fry, pizza |
| Wednesday | fish and chips, stir fry, salad |
| Thursday | stir fry, salad, tacos |
| Friday | fish and chips, tacos, pizza |

Suppose you know that Joshua has a salad and Nora has stir fry. Is that enough information to determine what day it is? If not, what other piece of information can help you?

## ASSESSMENT PRACTICE

26. The following statements are true.

    - If you are over 54 inches tall, you can ride on the roller coasters.
    - If you can ride on the roller coasters, then you can go on the drop tower.
    - Cindy is 56 inches tall.

    Classify each of the following statements as *true* or *false*.

    - If Cindy can go on the drop tower, then she can ride the roller coasters.
    - Cindy can go on the drop tower.
    - Cindy can ride the roller coasters.
    - If Cindy rides on the roller coasters, then she goes on the drop tower.

27. **SAT/ACT** Which statement can you conclude from the given true statements?

    If you ride your bike to school, you exercise. If you exercise, you are happy.

    Ⓐ If you are happy, you exercise.
    Ⓑ You exercise.
    Ⓒ If you exercise, you ride your bike.
    Ⓓ If you bike to school, you are happy.

28. **Performance Task** In a game of exploration, rolling a cube numbered from 1 to 6 simulates asset acquisition. Some rules are listed.

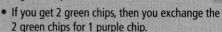

    - If you roll an even number, you get 1 red chip.
    - If you roll a factor of 6, you get 1 blue chip.
    - If you roll a number greater than 3, you get 1 green chip.
    - If you get 2 green chips, then you exchange the 2 green chips for 1 purple chip.
    - If you get 2 red chips, then you exchange the 2 red chips for 1 purple chip.

    Note that a roll can earn more than one chip.

    **Part A** Jacinta rolls a 2, 5, 1, and then 3. What chips does she have?

    **Part B** After four rolls, Kimberly has 1 purple chip, 1 green chip, 3 blue chips, and no red chips. What numbers could she have rolled?

# 1-7 Writing Proofs

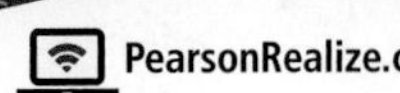
PearsonRealize.com

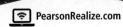

**I CAN…** use deductive reasoning to prove theorems.

**VOCABULARY**
- paragraph proof
- proof
- theorem
- two-column proof

Activity Assess

## CRITIQUE & EXPLAIN

**William solved an equation for $x$ and wrote justifications for each step of his solution.**

| | |
|---|---|
| $6(14 + x) = 108$ | Given |
| $84 + 6x = 108$ | Distributive Property |
| $6x = 108 - 84$ | Subtraction Property of Equality |
| $6x = 24$ | Simplify |
| $x = 4$ | Multiplication Property of Equality |

**A. Make Sense and Persevere** Are William's justifications valid at each step? If not, what might you change? Explain.

**B.** Can you justify another series of steps that result in the same solution for $x$?

## ESSENTIAL QUESTION

**How is deductive reasoning used to prove a theorem?**

### THEOREM 1-1 Vertical Angles Theorem

Vertical angles are congruent.

**If...**

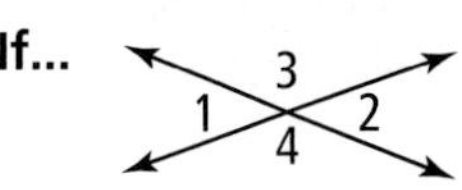


**Then...** $\angle 1 \cong \angle 2$ and $\angle 3 \cong \angle 4$

PROOF: SEE EXAMPLE 1.

CONCEPTUAL UNDERSTANDING

## EXAMPLE 1 Write a Two-Column Proof

**A theorem is a conjecture that is proven. Prove the Vertical Angles Theorem.**

**Given:** $\angle 1$ and $\angle 2$ are vertical angles

**Prove:** $\angle 1 \cong \angle 2$

A **proof** is a convincing argument that uses deductive reasoning. A **two-column proof**, in which the statements and reasons are aligned in columns, is one way to organize and present a proof.

| Statements | Reasons |
|---|---|
| **1)** $\angle 1$ and $\angle 2$ are vertical angles | **1)** Given |
| **2)** $m\angle 1 + m\angle 3 = 180$ and $m\angle 2 + m\angle 3 = 180$ | **2)** Supplementary Angles |
| **3)** $m\angle 1 + m\angle 3 = m\angle 2 + m\angle 3$ | **3)** Transitive Property of Equality |
| **4)** $m\angle 1 = m\angle 2$ | **4)** Subtraction Property of Equality |
| **5)** $\angle 1 \cong \angle 2$ | **5)** Definition of congruent angles |

**COMMON ERROR**
You may think that the proof is complete by stating that the measures of the angles are equal. You must explicitly state that the angles are congruent in order to complete the proof.

**Try It!** 1. Write a two-column proof.

**Given:** $\overrightarrow{BD}$ bisects $\angle CBE$.

**Prove:** $\angle ABD \cong \angle FBD$

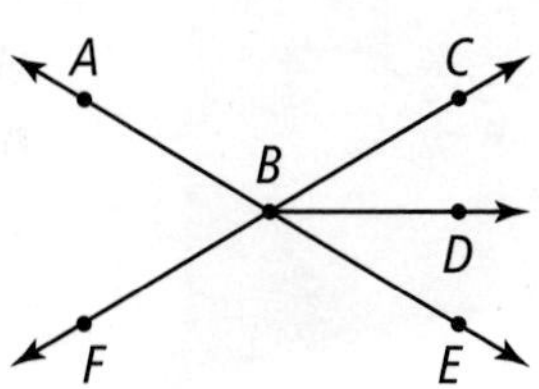


APPLICATION

## EXAMPLE 2 Apply the Vertical Angles Theorem

**The diagram shows how glass lenses change the direction of light rays passing through a telescope. What is the value of *x*, the angle formed by the crossed outermost light rays through the focal point?**

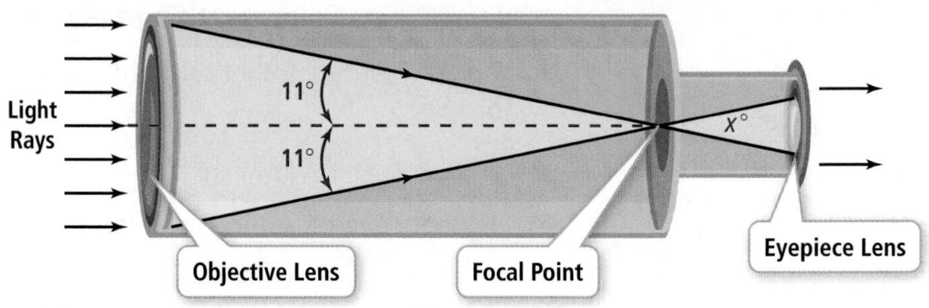


**Formulate** Draw and label a diagram to represent the telescope.

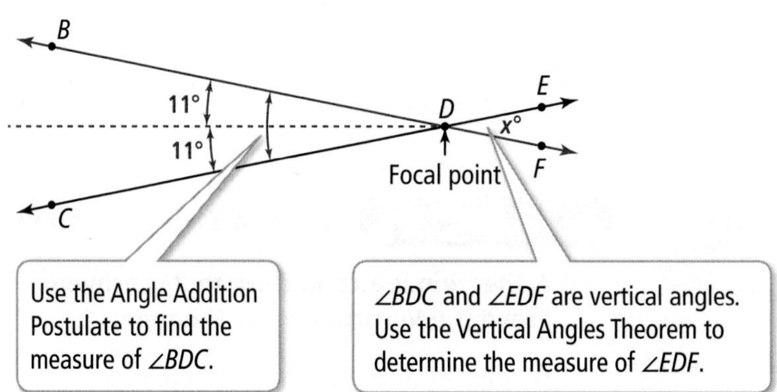


**Compute** $m\angle BDC = 11 + 11 = 22$ $\qquad m\angle EDF = m\angle BDC = 22$

**Interpret** The outermost light rays form a 22° angle as they leave the focal point, so the value of *x* is 22.

**Try It!** 2. Find the value of *x* and the measure of each labeled angle.

**a.** **b.**

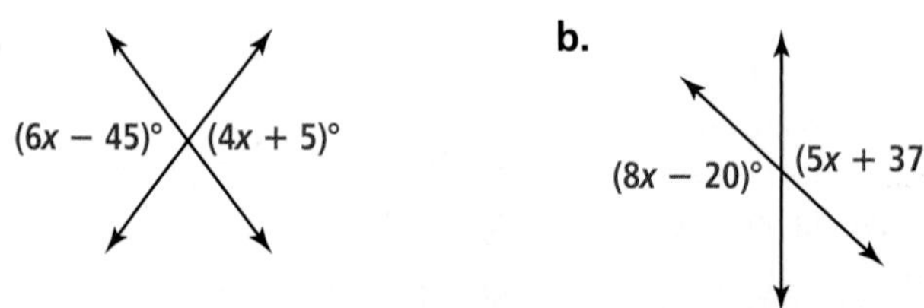

  Activity  Assess

## THEOREM 1-2 Congruent Supplements Theorem

If two angles are supplementary to congruent angles (or to the same angle), then they are congruent.

**If...** $m\angle 1 + m\angle 2 = 180$ and
$m\angle 3 + m\angle 2 = 180$

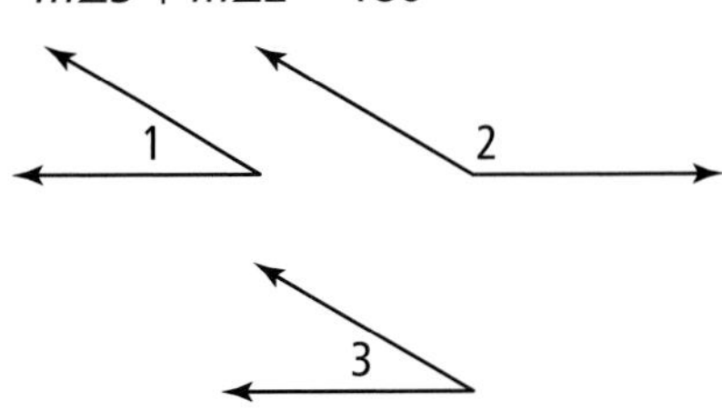

**Then...** $\angle 1 \cong \angle 3$

PROOF: SEE EXAMPLE 3.

## THEOREM 1-3 Congruent Complements Theorem

If two angles are complementary to congruent angles (or to the same angle), then they are congruent.

**If...** $m\angle 1 + m\angle 2 = 90$ and
$m\angle 3 + m\angle 2 = 90$

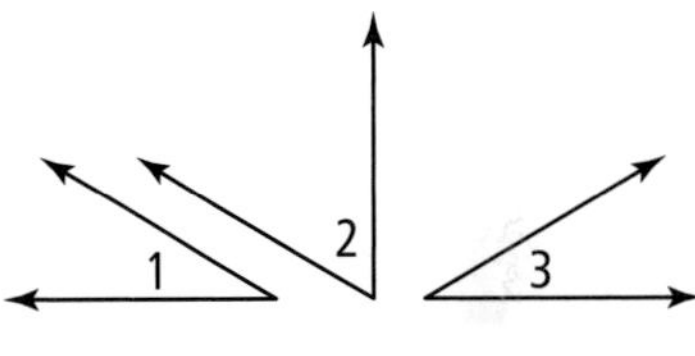

**Then...** $\angle 1 \cong \angle 3$

PROOF: SEE EXAMPLE 3 TRY IT.

PROOF

## EXAMPLE 3 Write a Paragraph Proof

**Write a paragraph proof of the Congruent Supplements Theorem.**

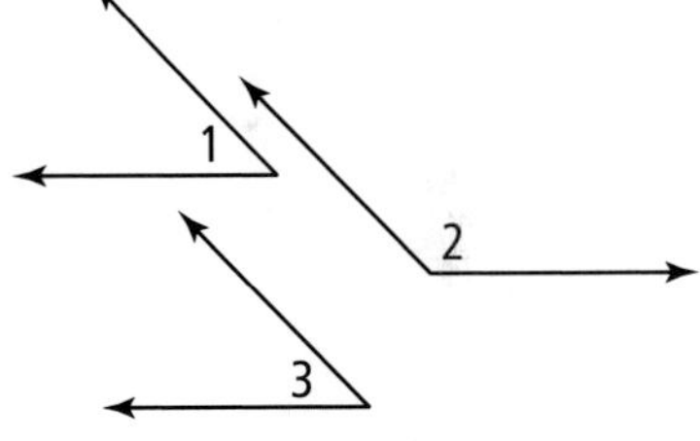

**Given:** $\angle 1$ and $\angle 2$ are supplementary.
$\angle 2$ and $\angle 3$ are supplementary.

**Prove:** $\angle 1 \cong \angle 3$

Another way to write a proof is a paragraph proof. In a **paragraph proof**, the statements and reasons are connected in sentences.

**Proof:** By the definition of supplementary angles, $m\angle 1 + m\angle 2 = 180$ and $m\angle 2 + m\angle 3 = 180$. Since both sums equal 180, $m\angle 1 + m\angle 2 = m\angle 2 + m\angle 3$. Subtract $m\angle 2$ from each side of this equation to get $m\angle 1 = m\angle 3$. By the definition of congruent angles, $\angle 1 \cong \angle 3$.

**STUDY TIP**
It may be helpful to confirm that a paragraph proof is complete by underlining each statement and then circling the corresponding reason.

**Try It!** 3. Write a paragraph proof of the Congruent Complements Theorem.

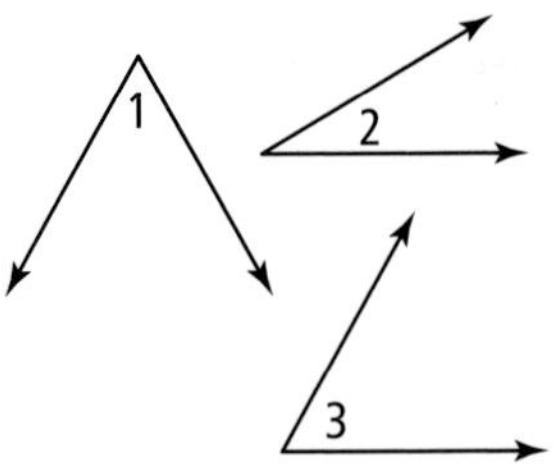

**Given:** $\angle 1$ and $\angle 2$ are complementary.
$\angle 2$ and $\angle 3$ are complementary.

**Prove:** $\angle 1 \cong \angle 3$

## THEOREM 1-4

All right angles are congruent.

If...

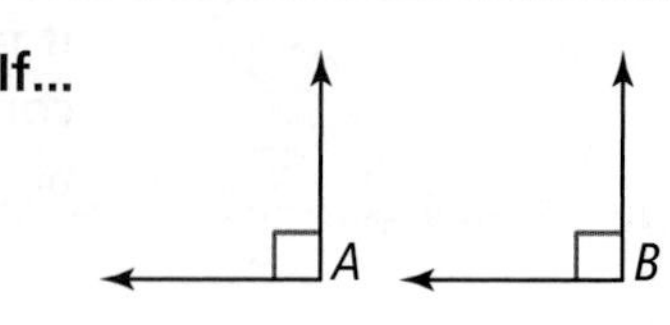


Then... $\angle A \cong \angle B$

PROOF: SEE EXERCISE 9.

## THEOREM 1-5

If two angles are congruent and supplementary, then each is a right angle.

If... $\angle 1 \cong \angle 2$ and $m\angle 1 + m\angle 2 = 180$

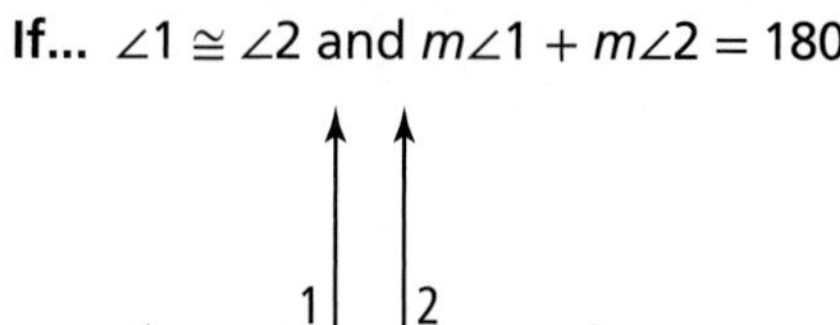


Then... $\angle 1$ and $\angle 2$ are right angles

PROOF: SEE EXERCISE 11.

## THEOREM 1-6 Linear Pairs Theorem

The sum of the measures of a linear pair is 180.

If... $\angle 1$ and $\angle 2$ form a linear pair.

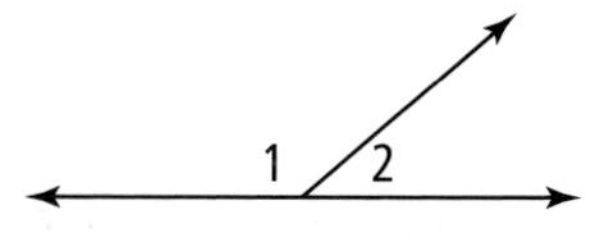


Then... $m\angle 1 + m\angle 2 = 180$

PROOF: SEE EXERCISE 12.

PROOF

## EXAMPLE 4 Write a Proof Using a Theorem

**Write a two-column proof.**

**Given:** $m\angle 1 = m\angle 2$, $m\angle 1 = 105$

**Prove:** $m\angle 3 = 75$

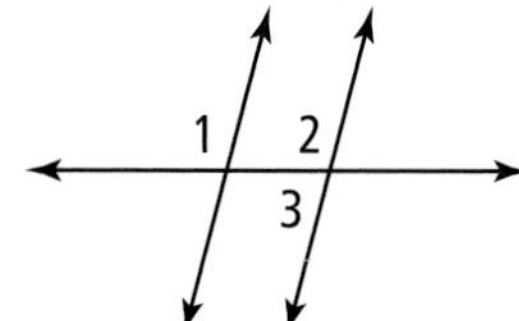


| Statements | Reasons |
|---|---|
| 1) $m\angle 1 = m\angle 2$ | 1) Given |
| 2) $m\angle 1 = 105$ | 2) Given |
| 3) $m\angle 2 = 105$ | 3) Transitive Property of Equality |
| 4) $\angle 2$ and $\angle 3$ are a linear pair | 4) Definition of a linear pair |
| 5) $m\angle 2 + m\angle 3 = 180$ | 5) Linear Pairs Theorem |
| 6) $105 + m\angle 3 = 180$ | 6) Substitution Property of Equality |
| 7) $m\angle 3 = 75$ | 7) Subtraction Property of Equality |

**CONSTRUCT ARGUMENTS**
Consider the logical flow for writing a proof. How can you be sure that each step in a proof follows logically from the preceding step or steps?

**Try It!** 4. Write a two-column proof.

**Given:** $m\angle 4 = 35$, $m\angle 1 = m\angle 2 + m\angle 4$

**Prove:** $m\angle 3 = 70$

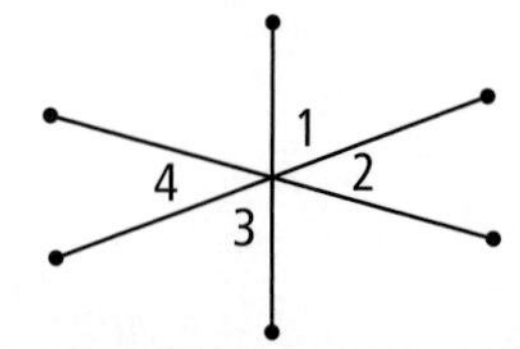

## CONCEPT SUMMARY Proofs

**Proofs** use given information and logical steps justified by **definitions, postulates, theorems,** and **properties** to reach a conclusion.

**Given:** ∠1 and ∠2 and are vertical angles

**Prove:** ∠1 ≅ ∠2

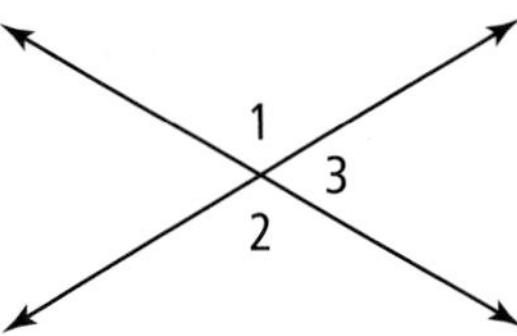


### PROOF Two-Column Proof

| Statements | Reasons |
|---|---|
| 1) ∠1 and ∠2 are vertical angles | 1) Given |
| 2) $m\angle 1 + m\angle 3 = 180$ and $m\angle 2 + m\angle 3 = 180$ | 2) Supplementary Angles |
| 3) $m\angle 1 + m\angle 3 = m\angle 2 + m\angle 3$ | 3) Subst. Prop. of Equality |
| 4) $m\angle 1 = m\angle 2$ | 4) Subtr. Prop. of Equality |
| 5) ∠1 ≅ ∠2 | 5) Def. ≅ angles |

### PROOF Paragraph Proof

By Supplementary Angles, $m\angle 1 + m\angle 3 = 180$ and $m\angle 2 + m\angle 3 = 180$. By the Substitution Property of Equality, $m\angle 1 + m\angle 3 = m\angle 2 + m\angle 3$. Subtracting $m\angle 3$ from each side of the equation gives $m\angle 1 = m\angle 2$. Then by the definition of congruent angles, ∠1 ≅ ∠2.

## Do You UNDERSTAND?

1. ESSENTIAL QUESTION How is deductive reasoning used to prove a theorem?

2. **Error Analysis** Jayden states that based on the Congruent Supplements Theorem, if $m\angle 1 + m\angle 2 = 90$ and if $m\angle 1 + m\angle 3 = 90$, then ∠2 ≅ ∠3. What is the error in Jayden's reasoning?

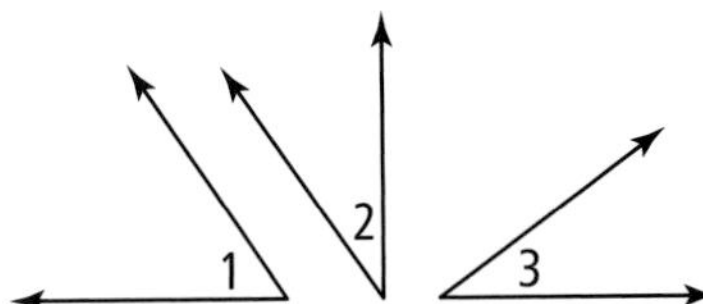


3. **Vocabulary** How is a theorem different from a postulate? How is a theorem different from a conjecture?

4. **Reason** If ∠2 and ∠3 are complementary, how could you use the Vertical Angles Theorem to find $m\angle 1$?

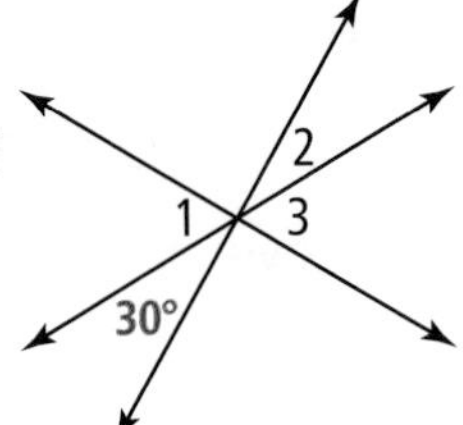


## Do You KNOW HOW?

**Use the figures to answer Exercises 5–7.**

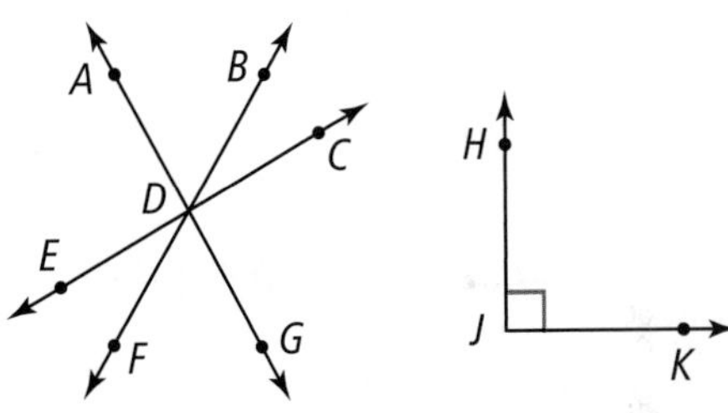


5. What statement could you write in a proof for $m\angle ADC$ using the Angle Addition Postulate as a reason?

6. Could you use the Vertical Angles Theorem as a reason in a proof to state $m\angle ADC = m\angle EDG$ or to state ∠ADC ≅ ∠EDG? Explain.

7. Given $m\angle ADC = 90$, what reason could you give in a proof to state ∠ADC ≅ ∠HJK?

8. The Leaning Tower of Pisa leans at an angle of about 4° from the vertical, as shown. What equation for the measure of $x$, the angle it makes from the horizontal, could you use in a proof?

# PRACTICE & PROBLEM SOLVING



## UNDERSTAND

9. **Construct Arguments** Fill in the missing reasons for the proof of Theorem 1-4.

**Given:** $\angle F$ and $\angle G$ are right angles.

**Prove:** $\angle F \cong \angle G$

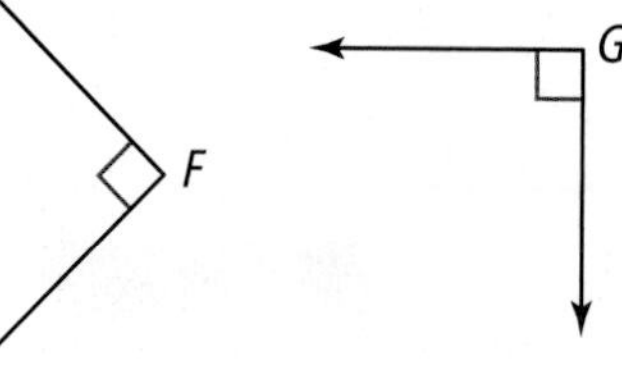


| Statements | Reasons |
|---|---|
| 1) $\angle F$ and $\angle G$ are right angles | 1) Given |
| 2) $m\angle F = 90$ and $m\angle G = 90$ | 2) |
| 3) $m\angle F = m\angle G$ | 3) |
| 4) $\angle F \cong \angle G$ | 4) |

10. **Error Analysis** A student uses the Vertical Angles Theorem and the definition of complementary angles to conclude $m\angle PTR = 50$ in the figure. What mistake did the student make?

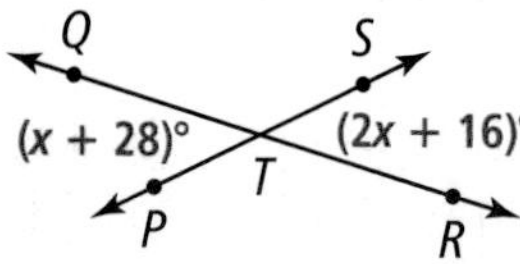


11. **Construct Arguments** Write a paragraph proof of Theorem 1-5. Given that $\angle N$ and $\angle M$ are congruent and supplementary, prove that $\angle N$ and $\angle M$ are right angles.

12. **Construct Arguments** Write a two-column proof of Theorem 1-6. Given that $\angle ABC$ and $\angle CBD$ are a linear pair, prove that $\angle ABC$ and $\angle CBD$ are supplementary.

13. **Higher Order Thinking** Explain how the Congruent Complements Theorem applies to the figure shown.

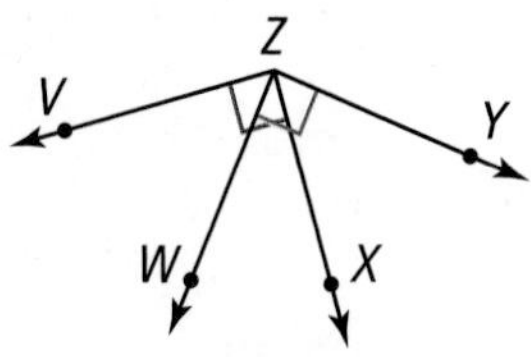


## PRACTICE

**Find the value of each variable and the measure of each labeled angle.** SEE EXAMPLES 1 AND 2

14.

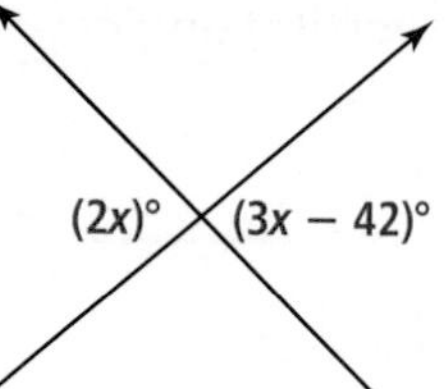


15.

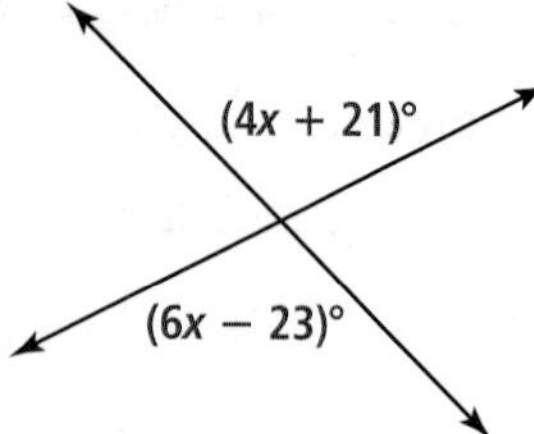


16.

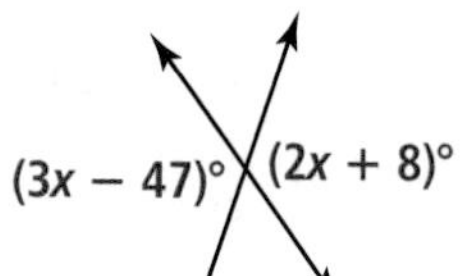


17.

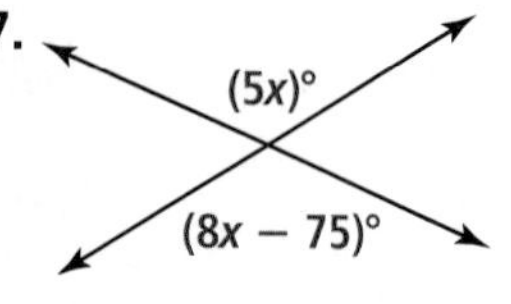


18. Write a paragraph proof. SEE EXAMPLE 3

**Given:** $m\angle ABC = 114$; $m\angle DHE = 25$; $m\angle EHF = 41$; $\angle ABC$ and $\angle GHF$ are supplementary.

**Prove:** $m\angle DHF \cong m\angle GHF$

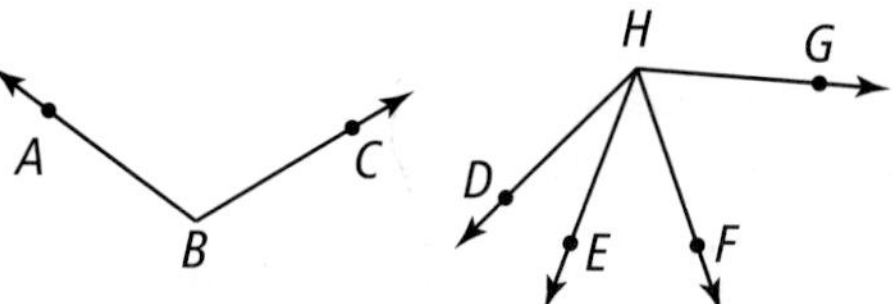


**Write a two-column proof for each statement.**
SEE EXAMPLE 4

19. **Given:** $\angle 1$ and $\angle 2$ are complementary.

$m\angle 1 = 23$

**Prove:** $m\angle 3 = 113$

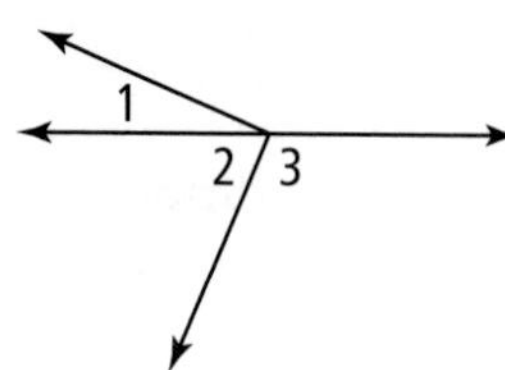


20. **Given:** $m\angle 2 = 30$

$m\angle 1 = 2m\angle 2$

**Prove:** $m\angle 3 + m\angle 4 = 90$

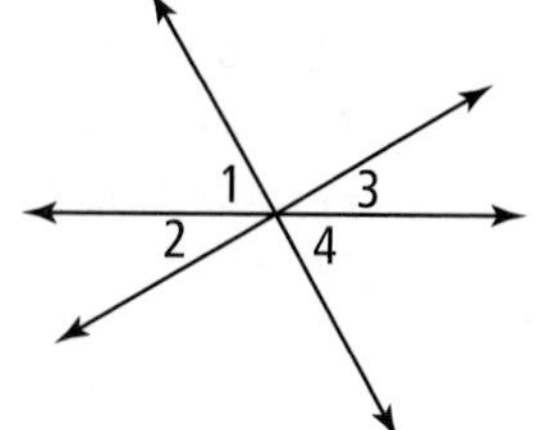

# PRACTICE & PROBLEM SOLVING

Mixed Review Available Online

## APPLY

**21. Mathematical Connections** The graph shows percentages of sales made by various divisions of a company in one year. What are the angles formed by the segments for each division? What are the missing percentages? Explain how you were able to determine each percentage.

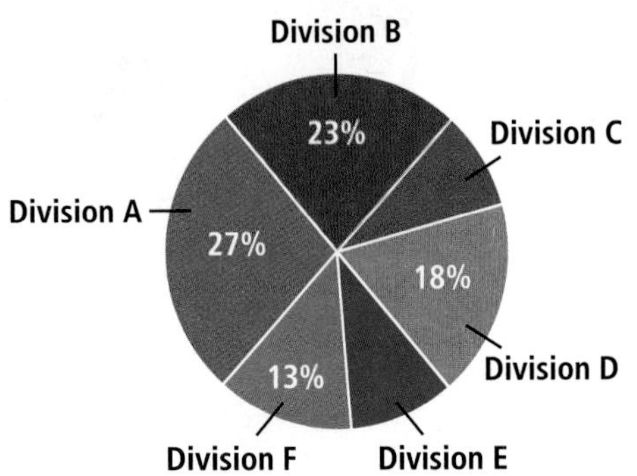


**22. Use Structure** A type of floor tiling is designed to give the illusion of a three-dimensional figure. Given that $m\angle 1 = 85$ and $m\angle 3 = 45$, what are the measures of the remaining angles?

**23. Reason** Consider the angles formed by the garden gate. Using theorems from this lesson, what can you conclude from each of the following statements? State which theorem you applied to reach your conclusion.

**a.** $m\angle 1 = 90$ and $m\angle 2 = 90$.

**b.** $\angle 3$ and $\angle 4$ are vertical angles.

## ASSESSMENT PRACTICE

**24.** Consider the figure shown.

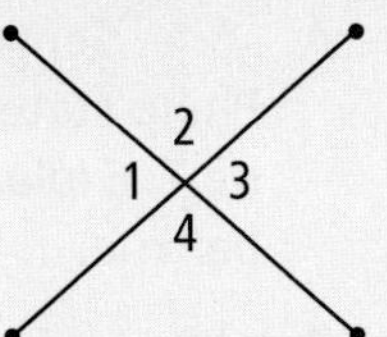


Classify each of the following statements as *always true, sometimes true,* or *never true.*

- $m\angle 1 + m\angle 4 = 180$
- $m\angle 1 + m\angle 2 + m\angle 3 = 180$
- $m\angle 2 + m\angle 4 = 180$
- $\angle 2 \cong \angle 3$
- $\angle 2 \cong \angle 4$
- $m\angle 3 = m\angle 4$

**25. SAT/ACT** Given $\angle ABC$ and $\angle DEF$ are supplementary and $\angle ABC$ and $\angle GHJ$ are supplementary, what can you conclude about the angles?

Ⓐ $m\angle DEF = m\angle GHJ$

Ⓑ $m\angle DEF + m\angle GHJ = 90$

Ⓒ $m\angle DEF + m\angle GHJ = 180$

Ⓓ $m\angle ABC = m\angle DEF$ and $m\angle ABC = m\angle GHJ$

**26. Performance Task** The figure shows lines that divide a designer window into different parts.

**Part A** Copy the figure onto a sheet of paper. Label each of the inner angles. Use a protractor to measure any two of the inner angles in the figure. Using your measurements, determine the measurements of the other angles.

**Part B** Choose two of the inner angles that you did not actually measure. How do you know the angle measures for these two angles? Write a two-column proof to show how you know their measures are correct.

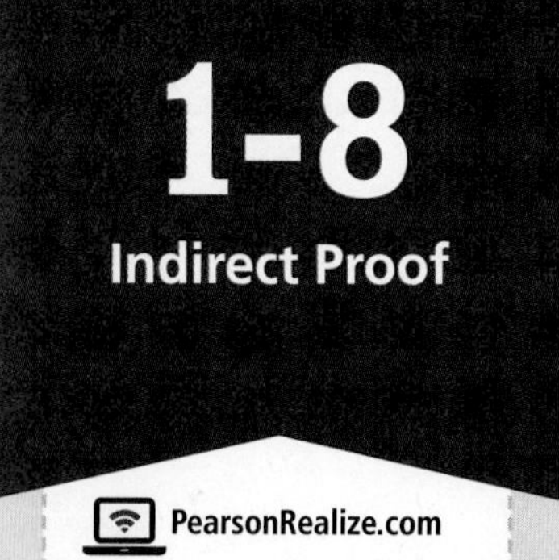

# 1-8 Indirect Proof

PearsonRealize.com

**I CAN…** use indirect reasoning to write a proof.

**VOCABULARY**

- indirect proof

Activity Assess

## CRITIQUE & EXPLAIN

**Philip presents the following number puzzle to his friends.**

**A. Make Sense and Persevere** Philip states that the number must be 7. Explain why this cannot be true.

**B.** Write your own number puzzle that has an answer of 5. Your friend says the answer is not 5. How do you use the statements of your puzzle to identify the contradiction?

The number is a prime number.
The square of the number is less than 100 and greater than 10.
The number is not a factor of 21.
What is the number?


## ESSENTIAL QUESTION

**What can you conclude when valid reasoning leads to a contradiction?**

APPLICATION

## EXAMPLE 1 Use Indirect Reasoning

**Beth is having dinner with Sarah and one of Sarah's friends—Libby, Kelly, or Mercedes. Beth orders a chicken and spinach pizza to share for dinner.**

Libby is a vegetarian.

Mercedes is at the library.

Kelly is allergic to mushrooms.

**Who is having dinner with Beth?**

Use indirect reasoning to determine who is having dinner with Beth.

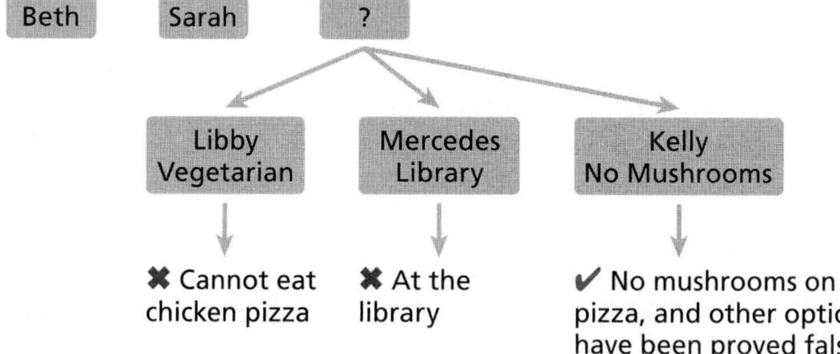


Beth must be having dinner with Sarah and Kelly.

**STUDY TIP**
Use a flow chart or table to keep track of details if you have difficulty following the logic in an indirect reasoning problem.

**Try It!** 1. Use indirect reasoning to draw a conclusion in the following situation.

A bagel shop gives customers a free bagel on their birthday. Thato went to the bagel shop today but did not get a free bagel.

## CONCEPT Writing an Indirect Proof by Contradiction

A proof that uses indirect reasoning is an **indirect proof**. Use an indirect proof when a direct proof is impossible. Two types of indirect proof are proof by contradiction and proof by contrapositive.

**Proof by Contradiction**

A statement is given as a conditional $p \rightarrow q$.

**Step 1** Assume $p$ and $\sim q$ are true.

**Step 2** Show that the assumption $\sim q$ leads to a contradiction.

**Step 3** Conclude that $q$ must be true.

PROOF

## EXAMPLE 2 Write an Indirect Proof by Contradiction

**Write an indirect proof of the following statement using proof by contradiction.**

**If Alani walks more than 8 kilometers over a two-day period, then she walks more than 4 kilometers on one or both days.**

Identify the hypothesis and conclusion.

$p$: Alani walks more than 8 kilometers over a two-day period.

$q$: She walks more than 4 kilometers on one or both days.

The statement has the form $p \rightarrow q$.

**Step 1** Assume $p$ and $\sim q$ are true.

$\sim q$: Alani does not walk more than 4 kilometers on either day.

**Step 2** Show that the assumption $\sim q$ leads to a contradiction.

If Alani does not walk more than 4 kilometers on either day, then the total distance she walks over the two-day period must be less than or equal to 8 kilometers. This contradicts the hypothesis, $p$.

**Step 3** Conclude that $q$ must be true.

Because the assumption leads to a contradiction, $q$ must be true.

Alani walks more than 4 kilometers on one or both days.

**LOOK FOR RELATIONSHIPS**
Consider what you can logically conclude from your assumption. What can you conclude from the negation?

**Try It!** 2. Write an indirect proof for each statement using proof by contradiction.

**a.** If today is a weekend day, then it is Saturday or Sunday.

**b.** If you draw an angle that is greater than 90°, it must be obtuse.

## CONCEPT Writing an Indirect Proof by Contrapositive

A conditional $p \rightarrow q$ and its contrapositive $\sim q \rightarrow \sim p$ are logically equivalent, so they have the same truth value.

If you prove the contrapositive, you have also proven the conditional.

**Proof by Contrapositive**

**Step 1** Assume $\sim q$ is true.

**Step 2** Show that the assumption leads to $\sim p$, which shows $\sim q \rightarrow \sim p$.

**Step 3** Conclude that $p \rightarrow q$ must be true.

CONCEPTUAL UNDERSTANDING

## EXAMPLE 3 Write an Indirect Proof by Contrapositive

**Write an indirect proof of the following statement using proof by contrapositive.**

**For two positive integers *n* and *m*, if *nm* > 16, then either *n* or *m* is greater than 4 or both are greater than 4.**

Write the negations of $p$ and $q$.

$p$: $nm > 16$

$\sim p$: $nm \leq 16$

This is the part of the contrapositive you prove.

$q$: $n > 4$ or $m > 4$ or both are greater than 4

$\sim q$: $n \leq 4$ and $m \leq 4$

This is the part of the contrapositive you assume.

COMMON ERROR
Be careful not to make assumptions that are not given in the statements.

**Step 1** Assume $\sim q$ is true.

Assume $n \leq 4$ and $m \leq 4$.

**Step 2** Show that the assumption leads to $\sim p$.

| | |
|---|---|
| $n \leq 4$ | $m \leq 4$ |
| $nm \leq 4m$ | $4m \leq 16$ |

By the Transitive Property, $nm \leq 16$.

Therefore, $\sim q \rightarrow \sim p$

Use properties of inequality to write equivalent expressions of $n \leq 4$ and $m \leq 4$ as $nm \leq 16$.

**Step 3** Conclude that $p \rightarrow q$ must be true.

Proving the contrapositive proves the conditional. Therefore, for two positive integers $n$ and $m$, if $nm > 16$, then either $n$ or $m$ is greater than 4 or both are greater than 4.

**Try It!** 3. Write an indirect proof of each statement using proof by contrapositive.

a. If today is Wednesday, then tomorrow is Thursday.

b. If a whole number is between 1 and 4, it is a factor of 6.

## CONCEPT SUMMARY Indirect Proof of $p \rightarrow q$

**BY CONTRADICTION**

**Steps**

1. Assume $p$ and $\sim q$ are true.
2. Show that the assumption $\sim q$ leads to a contradiction.
3. Conclude that $q$ must be true.

**BY CONTRAPOSITIVE**

**Steps**

1. Assume $\sim q$ is true.
2. Show that the assumption leads to $\sim p$, which shows $\sim q \rightarrow \sim p$.
3. Conclude that $p \rightarrow q$ must be true.

## Do You UNDERSTAND?

1. **ESSENTIAL QUESTION** What can you conclude when valid reasoning leads to a contradiction?

2. **Vocabulary** What are the two types of indirect proof? How are they similar and how are they different?

3. **Error Analysis** Consider the figure below.

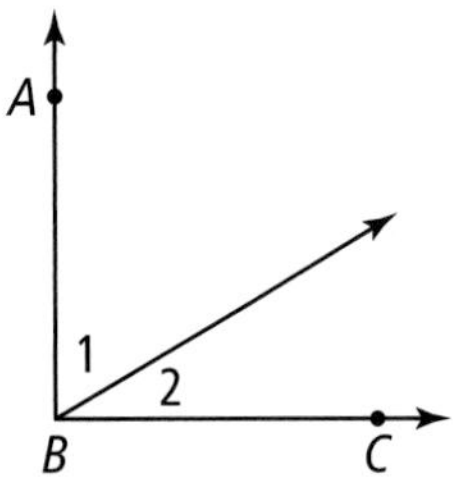


Consider the following conditional.

If $\angle ABC$ is a right angle and, $m\angle 1 < 60$, then $m\angle 2 > 30$.

A student will prove the contrapositive as a way of proving the conditional. The student plans to assume $m\angle 2 < 30$ and then prove $m\angle 1 > 60$. Explain the error in the student's plan.

4. **Make Sense and Persevere** How do truth tables explain why proving the contrapositive also prove the original conditional statement?

5. **Generalize** Explain how you can identify the statement you assume and the statement you try to prove when writing a proof by contrapositive.

## Do You KNOW HOW?

**Use indirect reasoning to draw a conclusion in each situation.**

6. Tamira only cuts the grass on a day that it does not rain. She cut the grass on Thursday.

7. Gabriela works at the library every Saturday morning. She did not work at the library this morning.

**Write the first step of an indirect proof for each of the following statements.**

8. $m\angle JKM = m\angle JKL - m\angle MKL$

9. $\overline{PQ}$ is perpendicular to $\overline{ST}$.

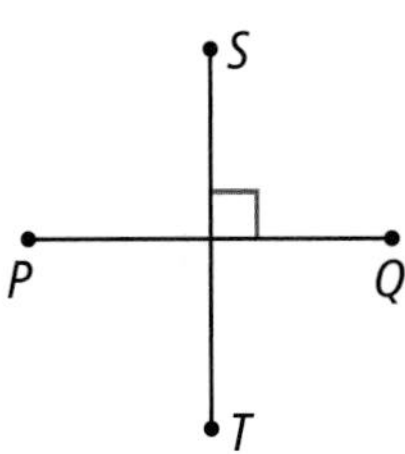


10. What can you conclude from the following situation using indirect reasoning? Explain.

- Nadeem spent more than \$10 but less than \$11 for a sandwich and drink.
- He spent \$8.49 on his sandwich.
- The cost for milk is \$1.49.
- The cost for orange juice is \$2.49.
- The cost for a tropical smoothie is \$2.89.
- The cost for apple juice is \$2.59.

## UNDERSTAND

11. **Construct Arguments** Write an indirect proof for this conditional statement about the given figure

    If $\overline{NJ}$ is the perpendicular bisector of $\overline{KM}$, then $LM = 6$.

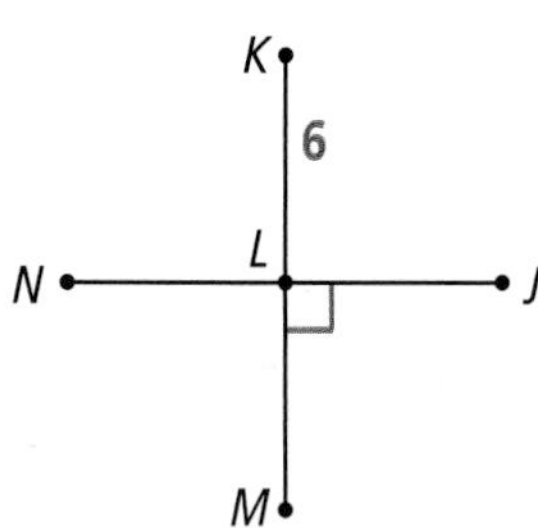


12. **Higher Order Thinking** Write an indirect proof about the given conditional using either contradiction or contrapositive. What is an advantage of the method you chose?

    Given that $x$ is a whole number, if $x$ and $3x$ are both less than 10, then $x \leq 3$.

13. **Mathematical Connections** Write a proof by contrapositive to prove the following conditional about the figures.

    If $\angle TUV \cong \angle WXY$, then $x \neq y$.

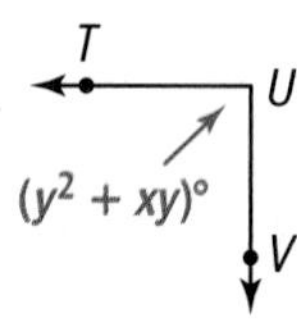


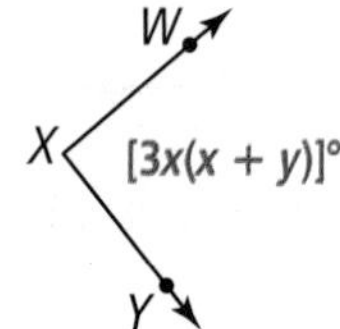


14. **Error Analysis** Consider the conditional, "If $x^2$ is even, then $x$ is even." Anna uses the contrapositive to prove the conditional. What is Anna's error?

> Assume $x$ is even. Then $x$ can be written in the form $2k$, where $k$ is an integer. Substitute this into $x^2$ to get $(2k)^2$, or $4k^2$. This expression can be written in the form $2m$, where $m$ is an integer, which proves $x^2$ is even. ✗

## PRACTICE

**Use indirect reasoning to draw a conclusion in each situation.** SEE EXAMPLE 1

15. Every student in Mr. Green's 2nd period class got an A on the math test. Paige got a B on the test.

16. Only students who studied at least 3 hours for the history test got an A on it. Derek studied 2 hours for the test.

**Write the first step of an indirect proof of each statement.** SEE EXAMPLE 2

17. $ST + TU + UV = 150$

18. Ray $DE$ is the angle bisector of $\angle ADC$.

**Identify the two statements that contradict each other in each set.** SEE EXAMPLE 2

19. **I.** $m\angle K + m\angle L = 150$
    **II.** $m\angle K - m\angle L = 20$
    **III.** $m\angle K = 180$

20. **I.** $\angle S$ is an acute angle.
    **II.** $m\angle S = 80$
    **III.** $m\angle S + m\angle T = 40$

21. **Write an indirect proof for the following conditional about the figure.** SEE EXAMPLE 2

    If $\angle EFG$ and $\angle HFJ$ are vertical angles, then $x \neq 3y$.

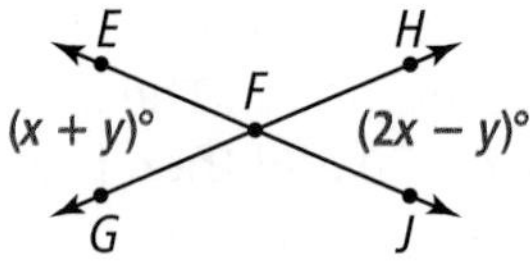


22. Write a proof of the contrapositive to prove the following conditional about the figures. SEE EXAMPLE 3

    If $AB + CD = EF$, then $EF = 14$.

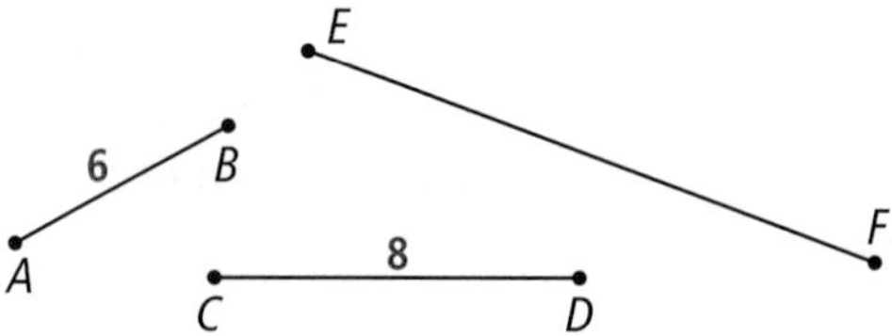

# PRACTICE & PROBLEM SOLVING

Practice Tutorial

Mixed Review Available Online

## APPLY

**23. Model With Mathematics** The lighthouse forms a right angle with the path of the boat.

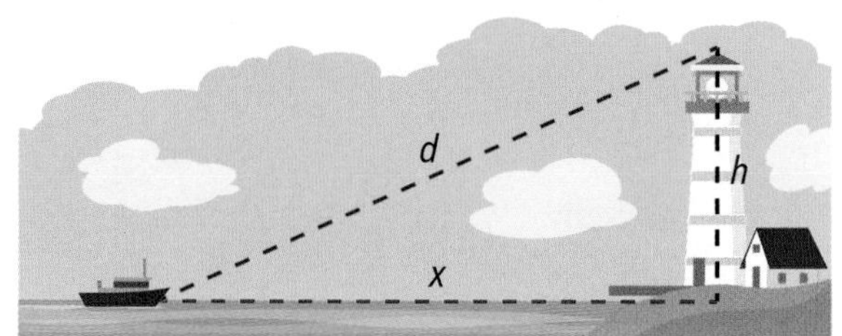


**a.** Write an equation relating *h, d,* and *x*.

**b.** Write an indirect proof of the statement by proving the contrapositive.

If *x* decreases, then *d* decreases.

**24. Reason** Friends eat the entire 6 slices of a pie. No slices are shared. Prove the following conditional by proving the contrapositive for the conditional.

If four friends share the pie, then at most two of the friends will have more than one slice of pie each.

**25. Reason** The library is at the midpoint between Nicky's home and the museum.

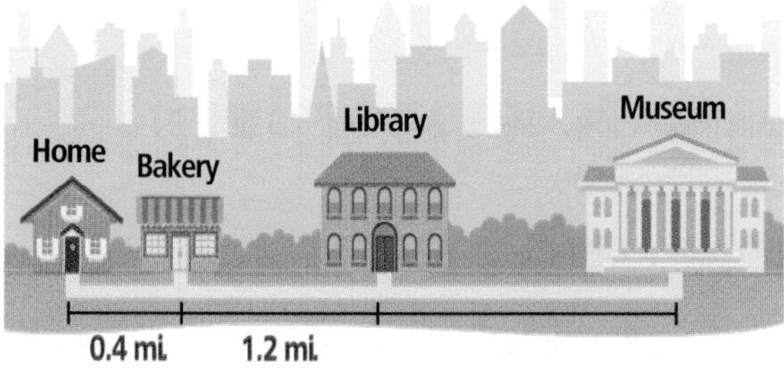


Nicky begins at her home and walks toward the museum. Write an indirect proof for this conditional: When she gets to the library, she will have less than 2 miles left to go.

## ASSESSMENT PRACTICE

**26.** Does this pair of statements contradict each other? Explain.

$\angle P$ and $\angle Q$ are both obtuse angles.

$\angle P$ and $\angle Q$ are supplementary.

**27. SAT/ACT** If you write a proof of the following conditional by proving the contrapositive, what should your assumption be?

If $\overrightarrow{JK}$ is the angle bisector of $\angle HJL$, then $m\angle HJK + m\angle KJL = 90$.

Ⓐ $\overrightarrow{JK}$ is the angle bisector of $\angle HJL$.

Ⓑ $\overrightarrow{JK}$ is not the angle bisector of $\angle HJL$.

Ⓒ $m\angle HJK + m\angle KJL = 90$

Ⓓ $m\angle HJK + m\angle KJL \neq 90$

**28. Performance Task** Customers who eat lunch at a diner have the following meal choices:

LUNCH MENU
cheese sandwich, carrot sticks, apple
ham sandwich, celery, fruit salad
chicken salad sandwich, orange, yogurt
cheese sandwich, celery, banana
ham sandwich, carrot sticks, yogurt


**Part A** Write an indirect proof of the following conditional.

If a customer chooses a meal with a banana, then the customer also has a cheese sandwich.

**Part B** Write another conditional statement related to which meal a customer has at the diner. Then write an indirect proof of your conditional statement.

TOPIC 1

# Topic Review

## TOPIC ESSENTIAL QUESTION

1. What are the fundamental building blocks of geometry?

## Vocabulary Review

**Choose the correct term to complete each sentence.**

2. A statement accepted without proof is a ________.
3. Arriving at a conclusion by observing patterns is ________.
4. A ________ is the combination of a conditional and its converse.
5. According to the ________, if a conditional statement and its hypothesis are true, then its conclusion is also true.
6. A conjecture that has been proven is a ________.
7. A statement of the form *if not q, then not p* is a ________ of the conditional *if p, then q*.
8. You use ________ when you logically come to a valid conclusion based on given statements.

- biconditional
- conjecture
- contrapositive
- converse
- deductive reasoning
- inductive reasoning
- Law of Detachment
- Law of Syllogism
- postulate
- theorem

## Concepts & Skills Review

### LESSON 1-1 Measuring Segments and Angles

#### Quick Review

If a **line segment** is divided into parts, the length of the whole segment is the sum of the lengths of its individual parts. **Congruent segments** have the same length.

Similarly, if an **angle** is divided into parts, the measure of the whole angle is the sum of the measures of the individual angles. **Congruent angles** have the same measure.

#### Example

**Given $SU = 60$, find $x$.**

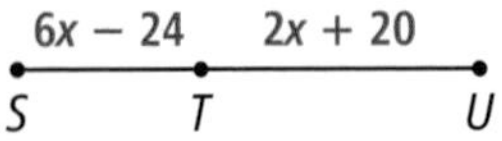


$$ST + TU = SU$$
$$(6x - 24) + (2x + 20) = 60$$
$$8x - 4 = 60$$
$$8x = 64$$
$$x = 8$$

#### Practice & Problem Solving

**Find each value.**

9. $LN = 45$. Find $x$.

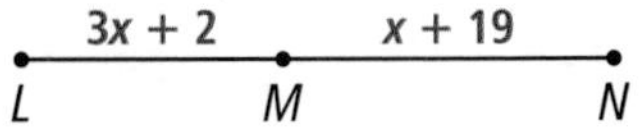


10. $RS = 27$. Find $QS$.

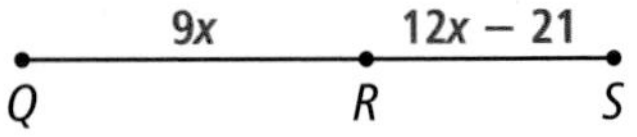


**Find the measure of each angle.**

11. $m\angle EBG = 60$; $m\angle FBG = 2m\angle EBF$; $m\angle EBF =$ ■

12. $m\angle ABE = 64$; $m\angle DBE =$ ■

13. $m\angle GBH = 28$; $m\angle GBC =$ ■

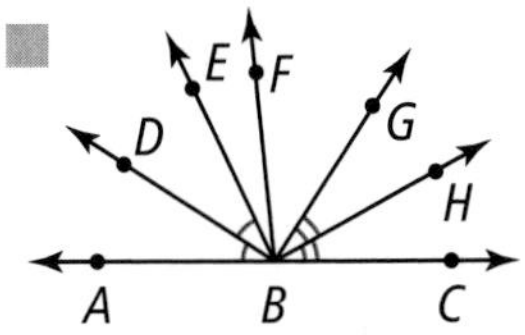


14. **Reason** Point $K$ is located at 7 on a number line, and $JK = KL$. If the coordinate of $L$ is 23, what is the coordinate of point $J$?

## LESSON 1-2 Basic Constructions

### Quick Review

You can use a compass and a straightedge to copy segments and angles, and to construct the **angle bisector** of a given angle and the **perpendicular bisector** of a given line segment.

Any geometric figure that can be constructed using a compass and straightedge is a **construction**.

### Example

**Construct the angle bisector of $\angle A$.**

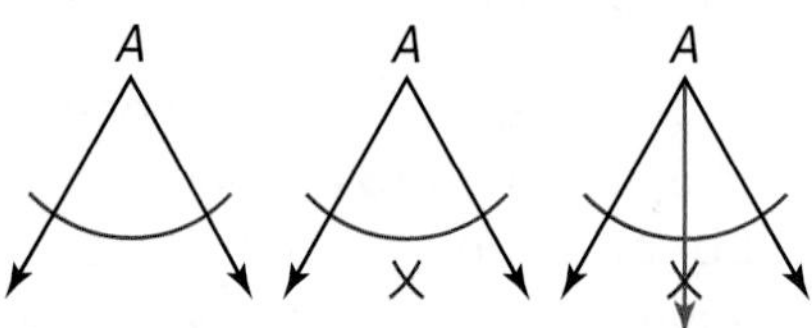


From the vertex, draw an arc that intersects both sides of the angle.

Next, using the same compass setting at each intersection, draw intersecting arcs within the angle.

Finally, draw the angle bisector from the vertex through the intersecting arcs.

### Practice & Problem Solving

**Copy each segment, and construct the perpendicular bisector.**

**15.** **16.**

**Copy each angle, and construct its bisector.**

**17.** **18.**

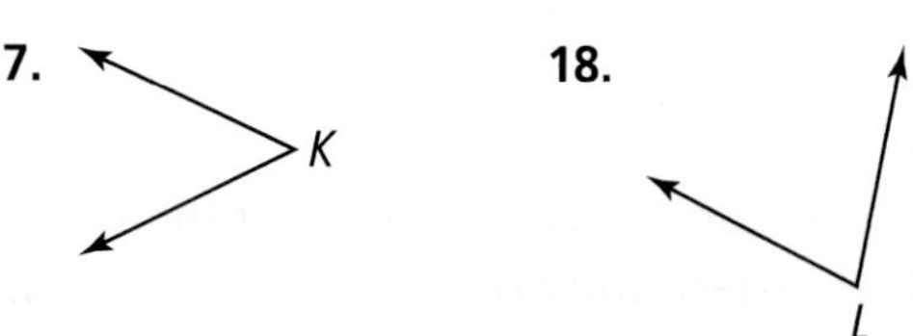


**19. Make Sense and Persevere** Why must the compass width be larger than half the segment width to draw a perpendicular bisector?

**20. Model With Mathematics** The sides of a roof meet at a 120° angle. A strip of wood extends down from the vertex so that it bisects the angle. Draw a diagram of the roof with the bisecting strip of wood.

## LESSON 1-3 Midpoint and Distance

### Quick Review

The midpoint formula gives the coordinates of the **midpoint** between two points.

$$M = \left(\frac{x_1 + x_2}{2}, \frac{y_1 + y_2}{2}\right)$$

The distance formula gives the distance between two points on a coordinate plane.

$$d = \sqrt{(x_2 - x_1)^2 + (y_2 - y_1)^2}$$

### Example

**What are the coordinates of point $K$ that is $\frac{2}{3}$ the distance from $J(8, 3)$ to $L(2, 6)$?**

Horizontal distance: $\frac{2}{3}(x_2 - x_1) = \frac{2}{3}(2 - 8) = -4$

Vertical distance: $\frac{2}{3}(y_2 - y_1) = \frac{2}{3}(6 - 3) = 2$

$K(x, y) = (x_1 + (-4), y_1 + 2) = (8 - 4, 3 + 2) = (4, 5)$

### Practice & Problem Solving

**Find the midpoint and length of each segment.**

**21.** $\overline{EF}$

**22.** $\overline{FG}$

**23.** $\overline{GH}$

**24.** $\overline{EH}$

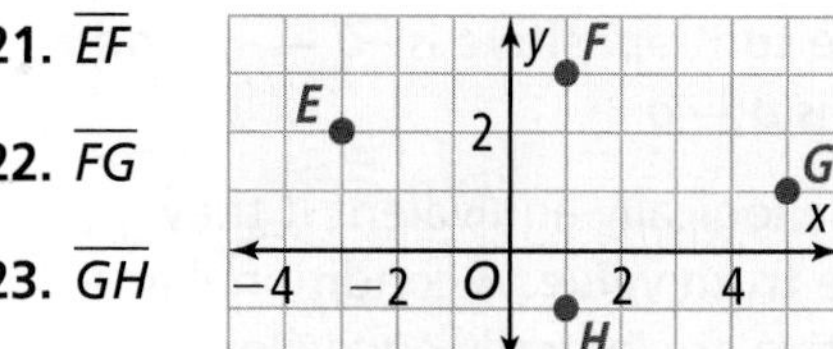


**25.** What are the coordinates of the point $\frac{2}{5}$ of the way from $H$ to $E$ on the grid?

**26. Make Sense of Problems** Sadie models her neighborhood on a coordinate plane so that her school is at (8, 12) and a store is at (14, 3). What are the coordinates of the point halfway between the school and the store?

## LESSON 1-4 Inductive Reasoning

### Quick Review

**Inductive reasoning** is the process of reaching a conclusion by observing patterns. A **conjecture** is a conclusion reached through inductive reasoning.

You can use several examples to support a conjecture, or you can disprove it by finding a **counterexample**.

### Example

**Make a conjecture about the shape of the *n*th term of the pattern shown.**

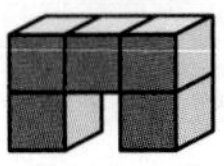
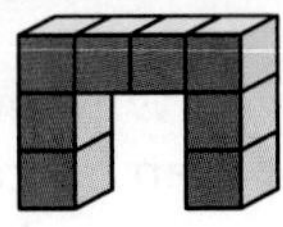

1st term: 2 blocks down each side, 3 blocks across

2nd term: 3 blocks down each side, 4 blocks across

3rd term: 4 blocks down each side, 5 blocks across

Conjecture: The *n*th term will have $n + 1$ blocks down each side and $n + 2$ blocks across.

### Practice & Problem Solving

**Use inductive reasoning to find the next two terms in each sequence.**

**27.** 1, 2, 6, 24, 120, ...

**28.** 3, 5, 8, 10, 13, ...

**29.** 2, 5, 9, 14, 20, ...

**30.** 17, 21, 25, 29, 33, ...

**Find a counterexample to disprove each statement, or support it with four examples.**

**31.** All triangles have three congruent angles.

**32.** If $p$ is an even number, then $p + 12$ is even.

**33. Construct Arguments** Explain why only one counterexample is sufficient to disprove a statement, but one example is not sufficient to prove a statement.

**34.** The table shows how much Jack saves in his bank account each week. At this rate, how much will he save on week 10?

| Week | Savings ($) |
|---|---|
| 1 | 1.75 |
| 2 | 3.50 |
| 3 | 5.25 |
| 4 | 7.00 |

## LESSON 1-5 Conditional Statements

### Quick Review

A **conditional** $p \rightarrow q$ relates a **hypothesis** $p$ to a **conclusion** $q$. The **converse** is $q \rightarrow p$, the **inverse** is $\sim p \rightarrow \sim q$, the **contrapositive** is $\sim q \rightarrow \sim p$ and a **biconditional** is $p \leftrightarrow q$.

Statements are logically equivalent if they have the same **truth value**. A conditional and its contrapositive are logically equivalent. A converse and an inverse are also logically equivalent.

### Example

**Find the truth value of the following conditional: All quadrilaterals have four congruent angles.**

A parallelogram that is not a rectangle is an example of a quadrilateral. It is a counterexample because its angles are not all congruent. The truth value for the conditional is false.

### Practice & Problem Solving

**For each statement, write a conditional and the converse, inverse, and contrapositive.**

**35.** A number that is a multiple of 4 is a multiple of 2.

**36.** Kona jogs 5 miles every Saturday morning.

**Find the truth value of each conditional. Explain your reasoning or show a counterexample.**

**37.** If a number is less than 4, then it is prime.

**38.** If $3x - 7 < 14$, then $x < 8$.

**39.** If it snows, then school will be cancelled.

**40. Communicate Precisely** A cafeteria only offers pudding on Tuesdays. Use this fact to write a biconditional about the pudding.

## LESSON 1-6 Deductive Reasoning

### Quick Review

**Deductive reasoning** uses logical steps based on given facts to reach a conclusion and can be applied through laws of logic, such as the following.

- **Law of Detachment:** If $p \rightarrow q$ and $p$ are true, then $q$ is true.
- **Law of Syllogism:** If $p \rightarrow q$ and $q \rightarrow r$ are true, then $p \rightarrow r$ is true.

### Example

**Given the following, use the Law of Syllogism to write a true conditional.**

- If $m\angle A < 90$, then $\angle A$ is acute.
- If $\angle A$ is acute, then it is not a right angle.

Conditional: If $m\angle A < 90$, then $\angle A$ is not a right angle.

### Practice & Problem Solving

**Assume the given information is true.**

**41.** If $AB = BC$, then $DE = 2(AB)$. $AB = 6$ and $BC = 6$. What can you conclude?

**42.** If it is a sunny day, the water park is filled with people. If the water park is filled with people, the lines for each ride are long. Use the Law of Syllogism to write a true conditional.

**43. Communicate Precisely** An advertisement says if you use their toothpaste for more than a week, you will have fresher breath. You use the toothpaste ten days. If the advertisement is true, what can you conclude?

## LESSON 1-7 & 1-8 Writing Proofs and Indirect Proof

### Quick Review

A **proof** uses deductive reasoning to explain why a conjecture is true. A conjecture that has been proven is a **theorem**.

For an indirect proof, assume the negation of what is to be proven, and then show that the assumption leads to a contradiction.

### Example

**Write a paragraph proof.**

**Given:** $m\angle BDC + m\angle ADE = 180$

**Prove:** $\angle ADB \cong \angle BDC$

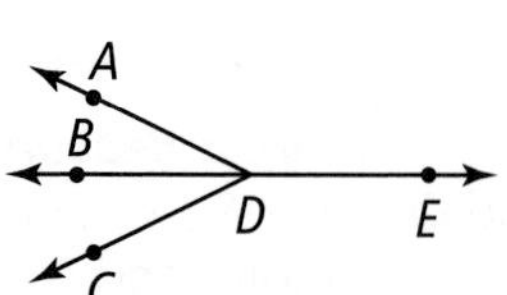


**Proof:** By definition of supplementary angles, $m\angle ADB + m\angle ADE = 180$. Since it is given that $m\angle BDC + m\angle ADE = 180$, by the Congruent Supplements Theorem, $\angle ADB \cong \angle BDC$.

### Practice & Problem Solving

**Find the value of each variable and the measure of each labeled angle.**

**44.**

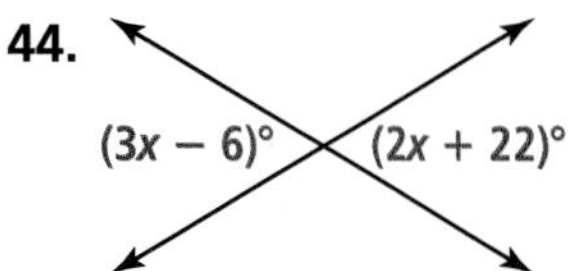


**45.**

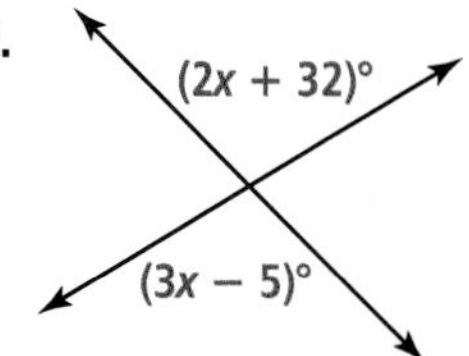


**46. Construct Arguments** Write a proof.

**Given:** $m\angle TUV = 90$

**Prove:** $x = 12$

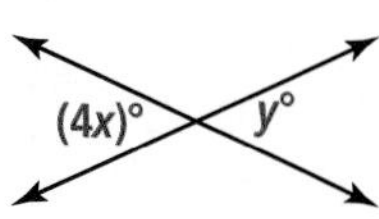


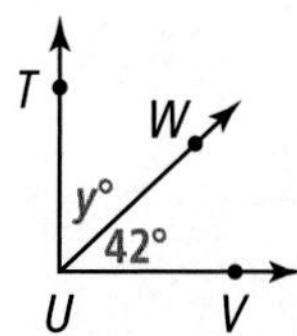


**47. Construct Arguments** Write an indirect proof by proving the contrapositive.

**Given:** $GJ = 48$

**Prove:** $x \neq 12$

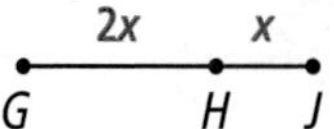


TOPIC 1 REVIEW

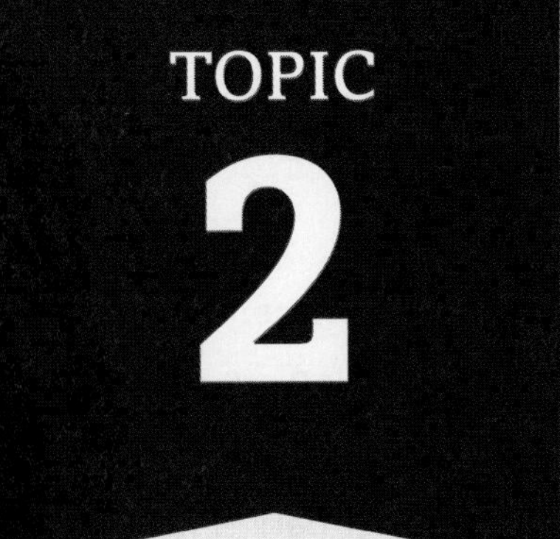


# Parallel and Perpendicular Lines

## TOPIC ESSENTIAL QUESTION

**What properties are specific to parallel lines and perpendicular lines?**

## Topic Overview

**enVision™ STEM Project:**
Build a Roof

**2-1** Parallel Lines

**2-2** Proving Lines Parallel

**2-3** Parallel Lines and Triangle Angle Sums

**2-4** Slopes of Parallel and Perpendicular Lines

**Mathematical Modeling in 3 Acts:**
Parallel Paving Company

## Topic Vocabulary

- flow proof

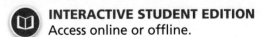

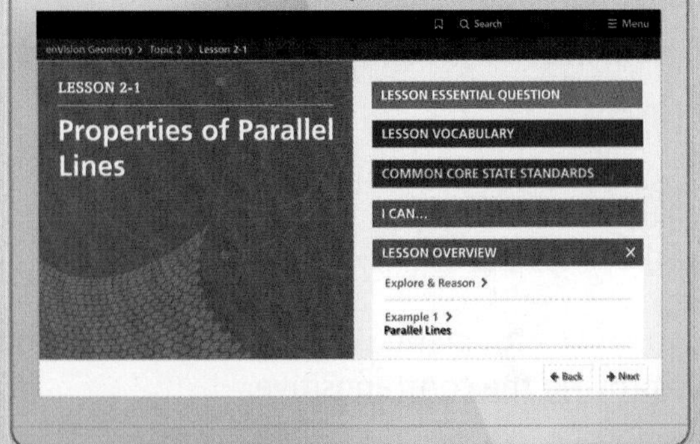

 Go online | **PearsonRealize.com**

## Digital Experience

 **INTERACTIVE STUDENT EDITION** Access online or offline.

 **ACTIVITIES** Complete ***Explore & Reason, Model & Discuss***, and ***Critique & Explain*** activities. Interact with Examples and Try Its.

 **ANIMATION** View and interact with real-world applications.

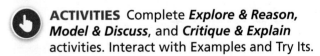

 **PRACTICE** Practice what you've learned.

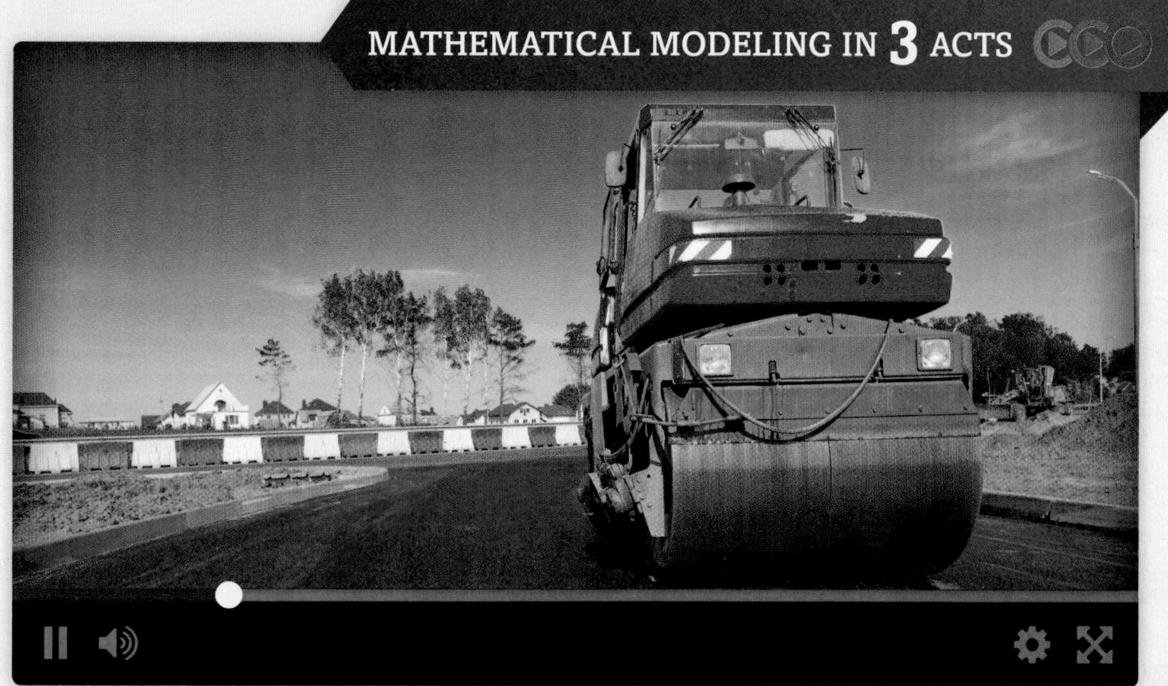


## Parallel Paving Company

Building roads consists of many different tasks. Once civil engineers have designed the road, they work with surveyors and construction crews to clear and level the land. Sometimes specialists have to blast away rock in order to clear the land. Once the land is leveled, the crews bring in asphalt pavers to smooth out the hot asphalt.

Sometimes construction crews will start work at both ends of the new road and meet in the middle. Think about this during the Mathematical Modeling in 3 Acts lesson.

TOPIC 2

**VIDEOS** Watch clips to support ***Mathematical Modeling in 3 Acts Lessons*** and **enVision™ *STEM Projects.***

**CONCEPT SUMMARY** Review key lesson content through multiple representations.

**ASSESSMENT** Show what you've learned.

A-Z **GLOSSARY** Read and listen to English and Spanish definitions.

**TUTORIALS** Get help from ***Virtual Nerd***, right when you need it.

**MATH TOOLS** Explore math with digital tools and manipulatives.

# Did You Know?

A roof is a critical component of shelter, one of humankind's most basic needs. Roofs vary depending on climate, local materials, and designs.

The front and back panels of a roof require a different, more complex, design than the rest of the roof and include vertical support beams called **gable studs**.

A **roof's pitch** determines the length of the rafters.

The **weight** of the roofing material affects the spacing of a roof's rafters and gable studs.

Bermuda has no fresh water other than falling rain, so roofs are designed to **funnel rain** down into underground holding tanks.

The weight of snow on a roof can be up to **21 lbs per square foot**.

A **green roof** is topped with earth and plants, which cools the building in the summer and insulates it in the winter.

## Your Task: Build a Roof

You and your classmates will plan the construction of a roof, including the location and cost of its ridge-board, rafters, and gable studs. How does the cost of the roof change based on on its pitch and the spacing between rafters?

# 2-1 Parallel Lines

PearsonRealize.com

**I CAN…** determine the measures of the angles formed when parallel lines are intersected by a transversal.

Activity
Assess

## EXPLORE & REASON

**The diagram shows two parallel lines cut by a transversal.**

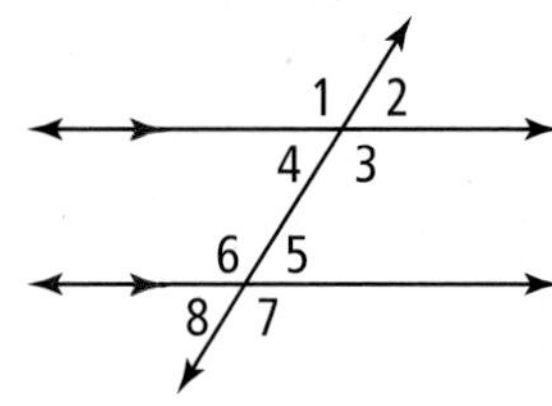
1
2
4
3
6
5
8
7

A. **Look for Relationships** What relationships among the measures of the angles do you see?

B. Suppose a different transversal intersects the parallel lines. Would you expect to find the same relationships with the measures of those angles? Explain.

**ESSENTIAL QUESTION** **What angle relationships are created when parallel lines are intersected by a transversal?**

## EXAMPLE 1 Identify Angle Pairs

**Identify the pairs of angles of each angle type made by the snowmobile tracks.**

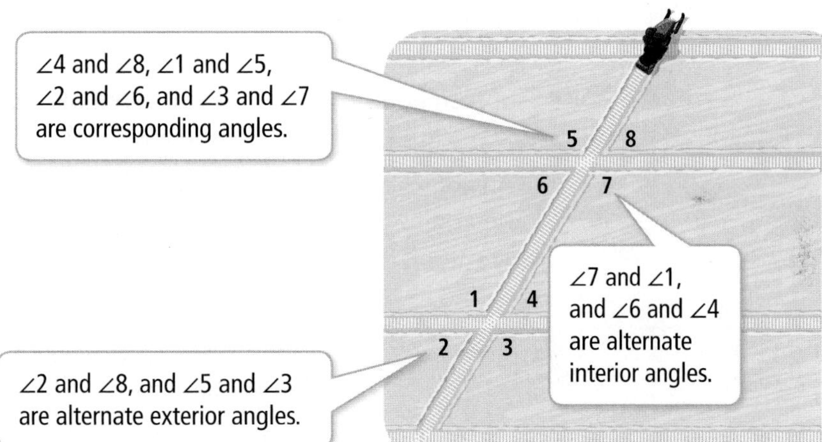
∠4 and ∠8, ∠1 and ∠5, ∠2 and ∠6, and ∠3 and ∠7 are corresponding angles.
∠7 and ∠1, and ∠6 and ∠4 are alternate interior angles.
∠2 and ∠8, and ∠5 and ∠3 are alternate exterior angles.
5
8
6
7
1
4
2
3

**STUDY TIP**
Transversals can intersect either parallel or nonparallel lines. The types of angle pairs remain the same.

**Try It!** 1. Which angle pairs include the named angle?

a. $\angle 4$

b. $\angle 7$

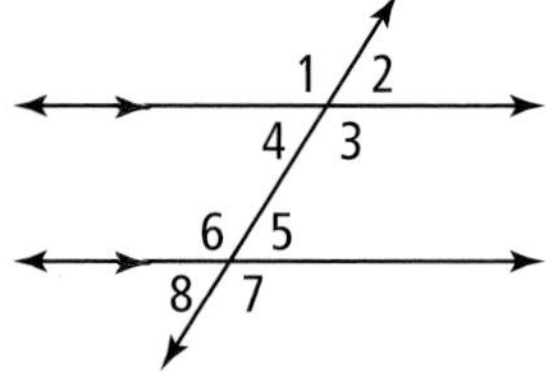
1
2
4
3
6
5
8
7

**POSTULATE 2-1** Same-Side Interior Angles Postulate

If a transversal intersects two parallel lines, then same-side interior angles are supplementary.

**If...**

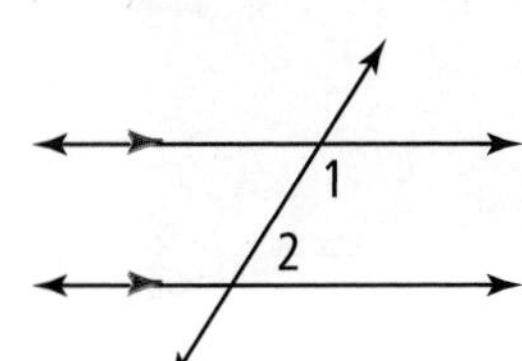


**Then...** $m\angle 1 + m\angle 2 = 180$

CONCEPTUAL UNDERSTANDING

**EXAMPLE 2** Explore Angle Relationships

**How can you express each of the numbered angles in terms of *x*?**

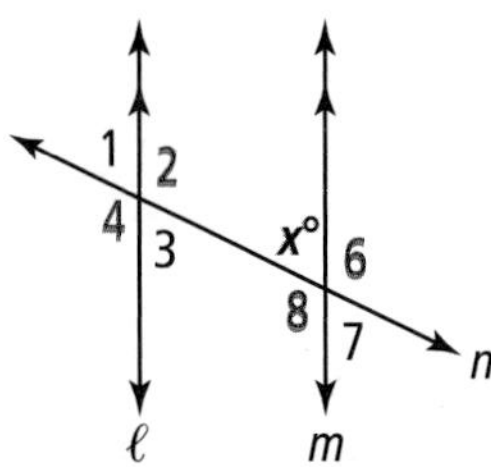


**LOOK FOR RELATIONSHIPS**
What patterns do you notice about the angles formed by two parallel lines cut by a transversal?

Angle 7 and the angle with measure $x$ are vertical angles. Both $\angle 6$ and $\angle 8$ each form a linear pair with the angle with measure $x$ and are therefore supplementary to it.

By Postulate 2-1 you know that $\angle 2$ and the angle with measure $x$ are supplementary. From that you can make conclusions about $\angle 1$, $\angle 3$, and $\angle 4$ like you did with $\angle 6$, $\angle 7$, and $\angle 8$.

The angles equal to $x°$ are $\angle 1$, $\angle 3$, and $\angle 7$.
The angles that are supplementary to the angle with measure $x$ have the measure $(180 - x)$. These are $\angle 2$, $\angle 4$, $\angle 6$, and $\angle 8$.

**Try It!** 2. If $\angle 4 = 118°$, what is the measure of each of the other angles?

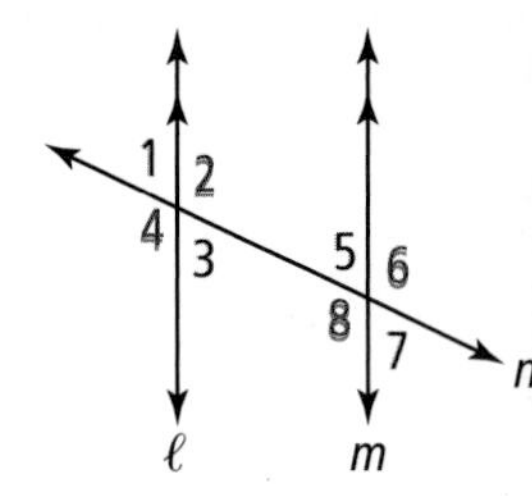


**THEOREM 2-1** Alternate Interior Angles Theorem

If a transversal intersects two parallel lines, then alternate interior angles are congruent.

PROOF: SEE EXAMPLE 3.

**If...**

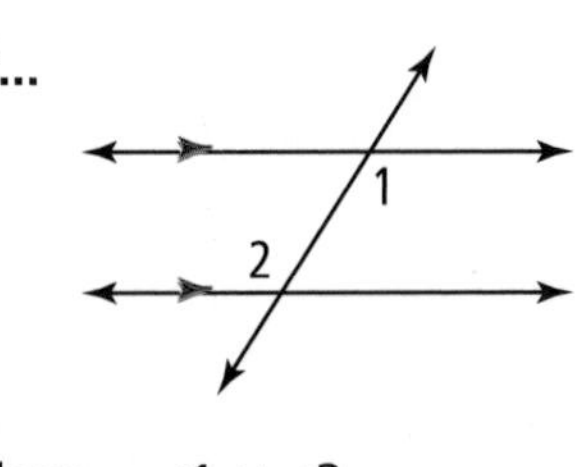


**Then...** $\angle 1 \cong \angle 2$

## THEOREM 2-2 Corresponding Angles Theorem

If a transversal intersects two parallel lines, then corresponding angles are congruent.

PROOF: SEE EXAMPLE 3 TRY IT.

If...

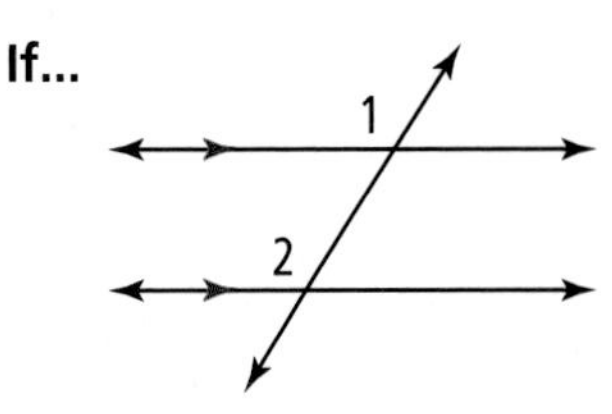


Then... $\angle 1 \cong \angle 2$

## THEOREM 2-3 Alternate Exterior Angles Theorem

If a transversal intersects two parallel lines, then alternate exterior angles are congruent.

PROOF: SEE EXERCISE 10.

If...

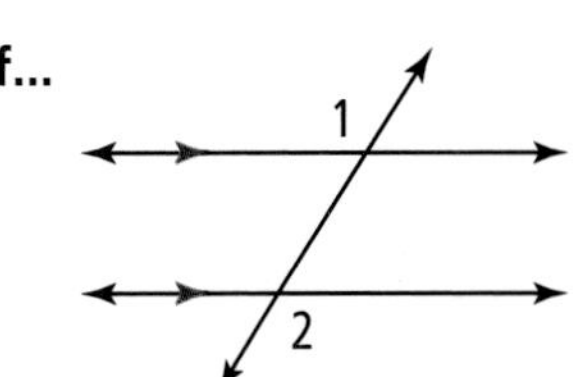


Then... $\angle 1 \cong \angle 2$

PROOF

## EXAMPLE 3 Prove the Alternate Interior Angles Theorem

**Prove the Alternate Interior Angles Theorem.**

**Given:** $m \parallel n$

**Prove:** $\angle 1 \cong \angle 2$

**Plan:** Use the Same-Side Interior Angles Postulate to show $\angle 1$ is supplementary to $\angle 3$. Then show that angles 1 and 2 are congruent because they are both supplementary to the same angle.

**Proof:**

| Statements | Reasons |
|---|---|
| **1)** $m \parallel n$ | **1)** Given |
| **2)** $\angle 1$ and $\angle 3$ are supplementary | **2)** Same-Side Interior $\angle$s Postulate |
| **3)** $m\angle 1 + m\angle 3 = 180$ | **3)** Def. of supplementary angles |
| **4)** $m\angle 2 + m\angle 3 = 180$ | **4)** Angle Addition Postulate |
| **5)** $m\angle 1 + m\angle 3 = m\angle 2 + m\angle 3$ | **5)** Transitive Property of Equality |
| **6)** $m\angle 1 = m\angle 2$ | **6)** Subtraction Property of Equality |
| **7)** $\angle 1 \cong \angle 2$ | **7)** Def. of congruence |

**COMMON ERROR**
Remember that for the proof to be complete, the last statement of the proof must match what you are trying to prove.

**Try It!** **3.** Prove the Corresponding Angles Theorem.

**Given:** $m \parallel n$

**Prove:** $\angle 1 \cong \angle 2$

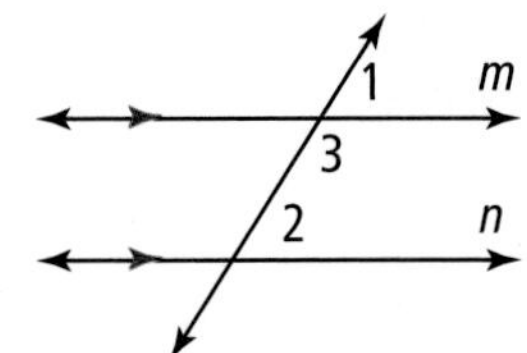

PROOF

## EXAMPLE 4 Use Parallel Lines to Prove an Angle Relationship

**Use the diagram to prove the angle relationship.**

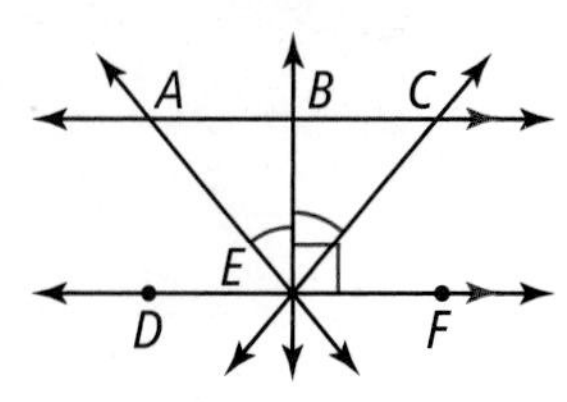


**Given:** $\overline{AC} \parallel \overline{DF}$, and $\overline{BE} \perp \overline{DF}$, $\angle AEB \cong \angle CEB$

**Prove:** $\angle BAE \cong \angle BCE$

**Proof:**

| Statements | Reasons |
|---|---|
| **1)** $\overline{AC} \parallel \overline{DF}$, $\overline{AC} \perp \overline{BE}$ | **1)** Given |
| **2)** $\angle BED$, $\angle BEF$ are rt. angles | **2)** Def. of perpendicular |
| **3)** $m\angle BED = m\angle BEF = 90$ | **3)** Def. of rt. angles |
| **4)** $m\angle AED + m\angle AEB = 90$, $m\angle CEF + m\angle CEB = 90$ | **4)** Angle Addition Postulate |
| **5)** $\angle AEB \cong \angle CEB$ | **5)** Given |
| **6)** $\angle AED \cong \angle CEF$ | **6)** Congruent Complements Thm. |
| **7)** $\angle BAE \cong \angle AED$, $\angle BCE \cong \angle CEF$ | **7)** Alt. Interior $\angle$s Thm. |
| **8)** $\angle BAE \cong \angle BCE$ | **8)** Transitive Prop. of Congruence |

**MAKE SENSE AND PERSEVERE** Look for relationships in the diagram not listed as given information. What angle relationships are shown in the diagram?

**Try It!** **4.** Given $\overline{AB} \parallel \overline{CD}$, prove that $m\angle 1 + m\angle 2 + m\angle 3 = 180$.

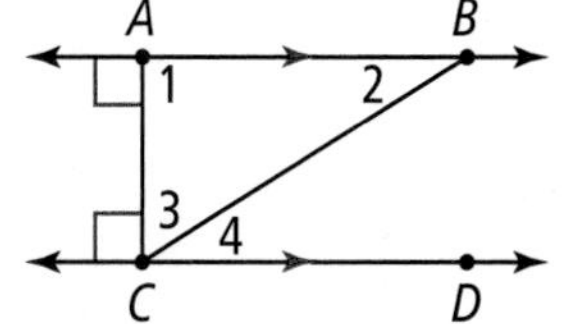

APPLICATION

## EXAMPLE 5 Find Angle Measures

**The white trim shown for the wall of a barn should be constructed so that $\overline{AC} \parallel \overline{EG}$, $\overline{JA} \parallel \overline{HB}$, and $\overline{JC} \parallel \overline{KG}$. What should $m\angle 1$ and $m\angle 3$ be?**

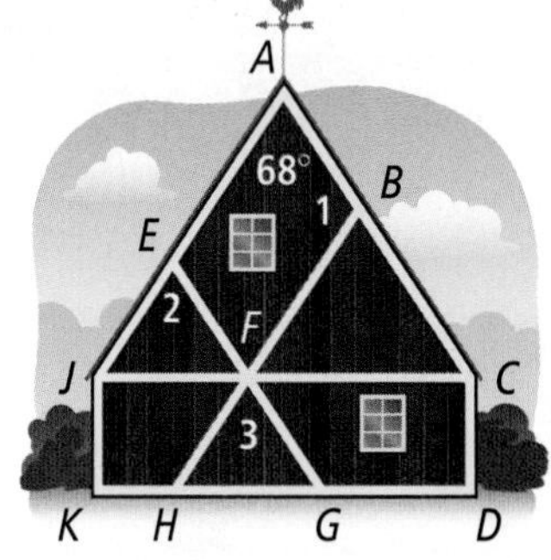


**Formulate** Look for relationships among the angles.

**Compute** By the Same-Side Interior Angles Postulate, $m\angle 1 + 68 = 180$.

$m\angle 1 = 180 - 68 = 112$

By the Corresponding Angles Theorem, $\angle EAB \cong \angle 2$ and $\angle 2 \cong \angle 3$, so $\angle 3 \cong \angle EAB$ by the Transitive Property of Congruence.

$m\angle 3 = 68$

**Interpret** So, $m\angle 1 = 112$ and $m\angle 3 = 68$.

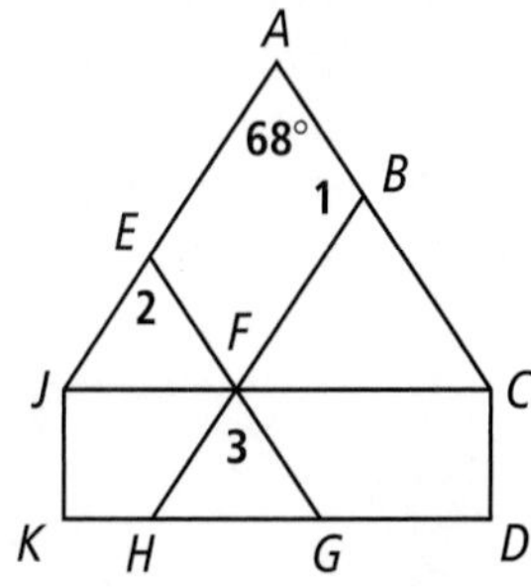

**Try It!** **5.** If $m\angle EJF = 56$, find $m\angle FHK$.

  Concept Summary 

## CONCEPT SUMMARY Parallel Lines and Angle Pairs

There are four special angle relationships formed when parallel lines are intersected by a transversal.

**POSTULATE 2-1** Same-Side Interior Angles Postulate

If...

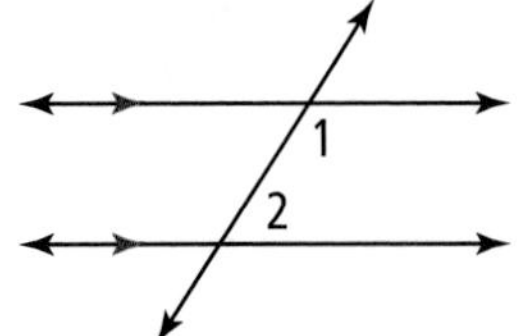


Then... $m\angle 1 + m\angle 2 = 180$

**THEOREM 2-1** Alternate Interior Angles Theorem

If...

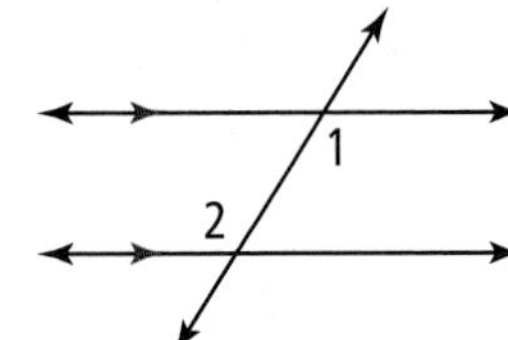


Then... $\angle 1 \cong \angle 2$

**THEOREM 2-2** Corresponding Angles Theorem

If...

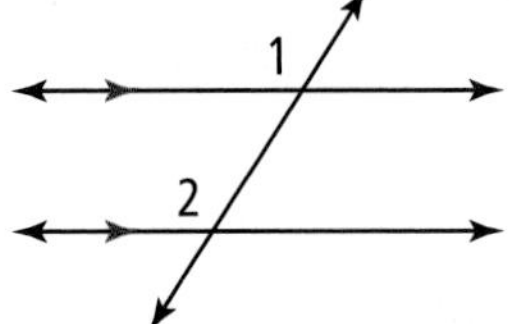


Then... $\angle 1 \cong \angle 2$

**THEOREM 2-3** Alternate Exterior Angles Theorem

If...

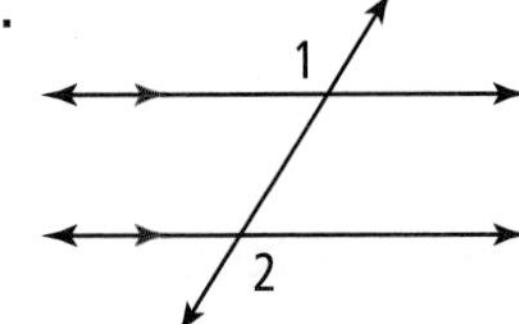


Then... $\angle 1 \cong \angle 2$

## Do You UNDERSTAND?

1. **ESSENTIAL QUESTION** What angle relationships are created when parallel lines are intersected by a transversal?

2. **Vocabulary** When a transversal intersects two parallel lines, which angle pairs are congruent?

3. **Error Analysis** What error did Leah make?

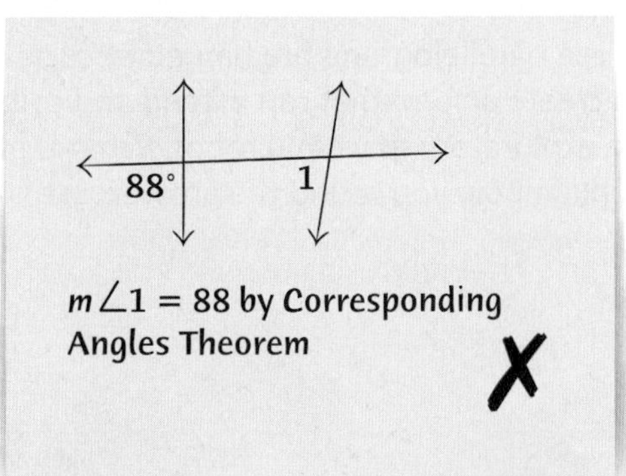


4. **Generalize** For any pair of angles formed by a transversal intersecting parallel lines, what are two possible relationships?

## Do You KNOW HOW?

**Use the diagram for Exercises 5–8.**

**Classify each pair of angles. Compare angle measures, and give the postulate or theorem that justifies it.**

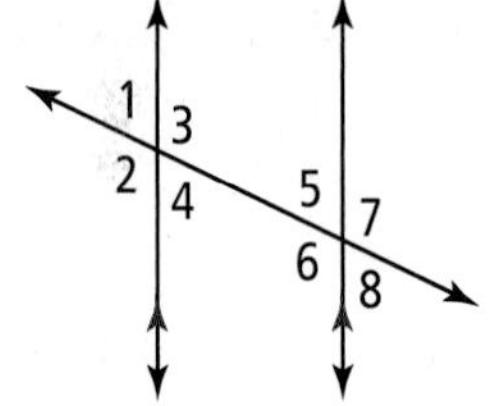


5. $\angle 2$ and $\angle 6$

6. $\angle 3$ and $\angle 5$

**If $m\angle 1 = 71$, find the measure of each angle.**

7. $\angle 5$

8. $\angle 7$

9. Elm St. and Spruce St. are parallel. What is $m\angle 1$?

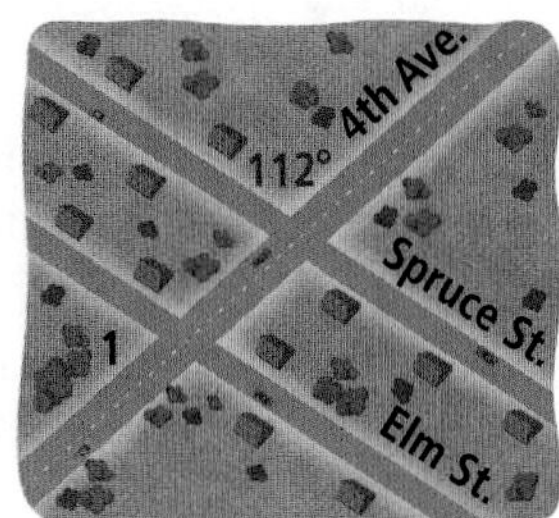

# PRACTICE & PROBLEM SOLVING

Scan for Multimedia

Practice Tutorial

Additional Exercises Available Online

## UNDERSTAND

10. **Construct Arguments** Write a two-column proof of the Alternate Exterior Angles Theorem.

**Given:** $m \parallel n$

**Prove:** $\angle 1 \cong \angle 2$

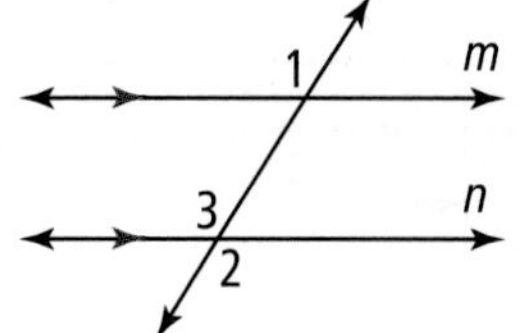


11. **Higher Order Thinking** Using what you know about angle pairs formed by parallel lines and a transversal, how are $\angle 1$, $\angle 2$, $\angle 3$, and $\angle 4$ related in the trapezoid? Explain.

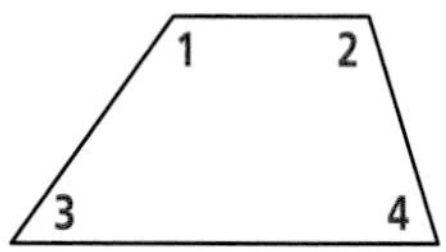


12. **Error Analysis** What error did Tyler make?

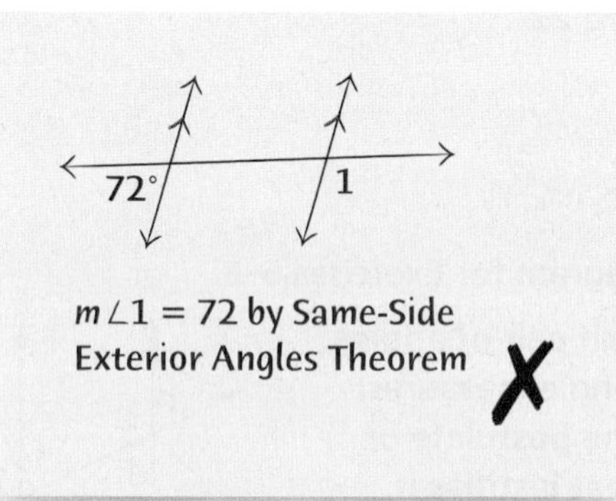


13. **Generalize** In the diagram shown, if $x + y = 180$, label the remaining angles as $x°$ or $y°$.

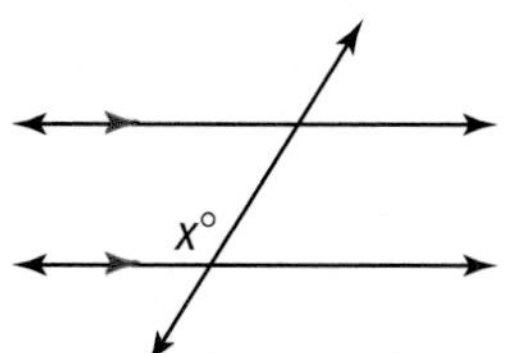


14. **Mathematical Connections** A transversal intersects two parallel lines. The measures of a pair of alternate interior angles are $5v$ and $2w$. The measures of a pair of same-side exterior angles are $10w$ and $5v$. What are the values of $w$ and $v$?

## PRACTICE

**Identify a pair of angles for each type.** SEE EXAMPLE 1

15. same-side interior

16. corresponding

17. alternate exterior

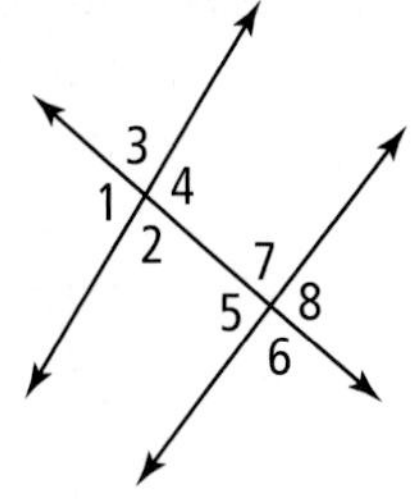


18. Which angles are supplementary to $\angle 1$? Which are congruent to $\angle 1$? SEE EXAMPLE 2

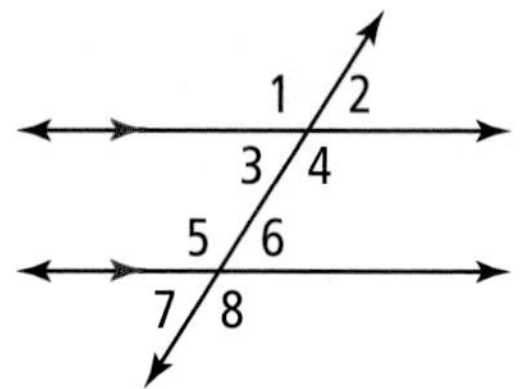


**Find each angle measure.** SEE EXAMPLE 3

19. $m\angle 1$

20. $m\angle 2$

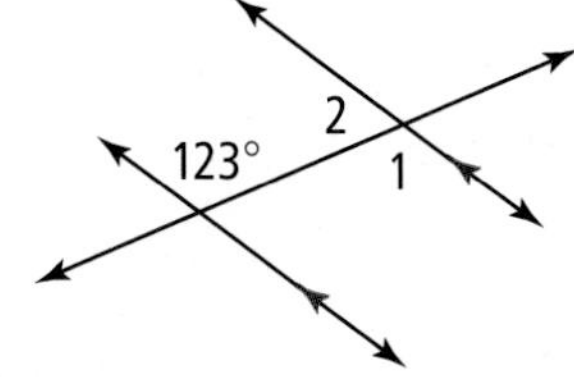


21. Opposite sides of a parallelogram are parallel. Prove that opposite angles of a parallelogram are congruent. SEE EXAMPLE 4

**Given:** $ABCD$ is a parallelogram

**Prove:** $\angle A \cong \angle C$, $\angle B \cong \angle D$

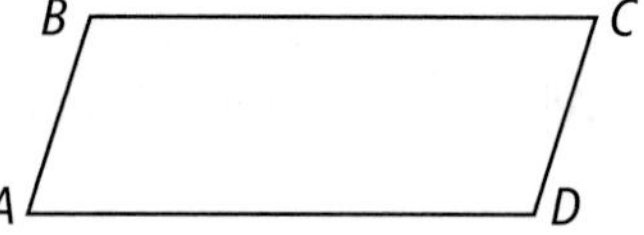


22. Three parallelograms are hinged at each vertex to create an arm that can extend and collapse for an exploratory spaceship robot. What is $m\angle 1$? Explain how you found the answer. SEE EXAMPLE 5

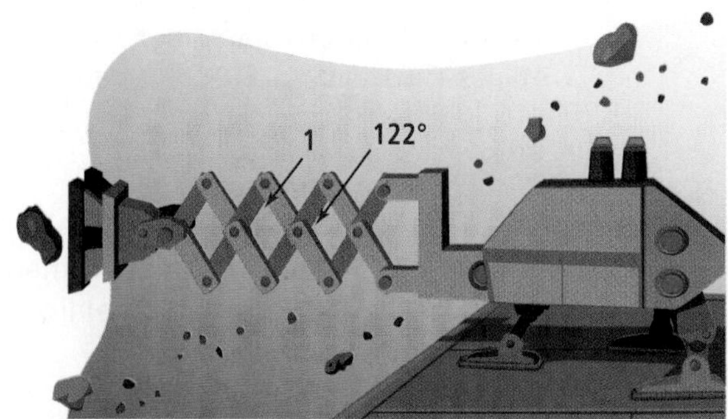

# PRACTICE & PROBLEM SOLVING

## APPLY

**23. Model With Mathematics** A glazier is setting supports in parallel segments to prevent glass breakage during storms. What are the values of $x$ and $y$? Justify your conclusions.

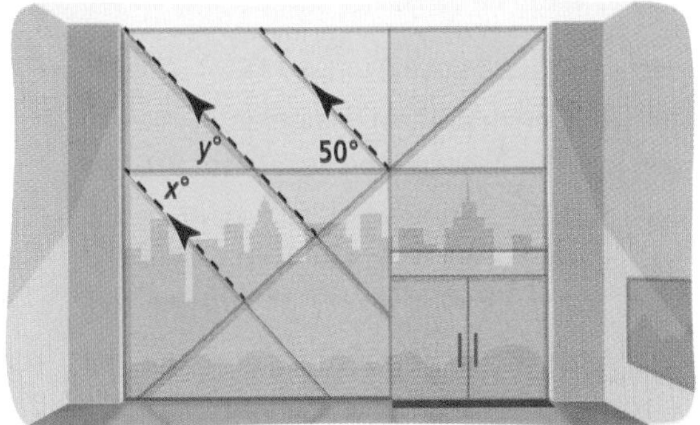


**24. Reason** In the parking lot shown, all of the lines for the parking spaces should be parallel. If $m\angle 3 = 61$, what should $m\angle 1$ and $m\angle 2$ be? Explain.

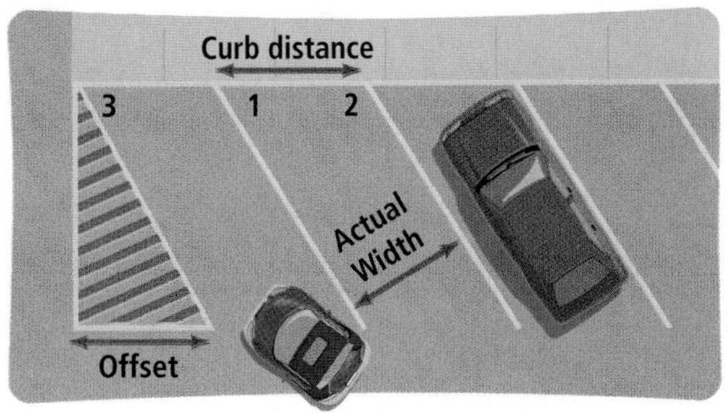


**25. Communicate Precisely** Margaret is in a boat traveling due west. She turned the boat 50° north of due west for a couple of minutes to get around a peninsula. Then she resumed due west again.

**a.** How many degrees would she turn the wheel to resume a due west course?

**b.** Name the pair of angles she used. Are the angles congruent or supplementary?

**26.** Parallel lines $m$ and $n$ intersect parallel lines $x$ and $y$, representing two sets of intersecting railroad tracks. At what angles do the tracks intersect?

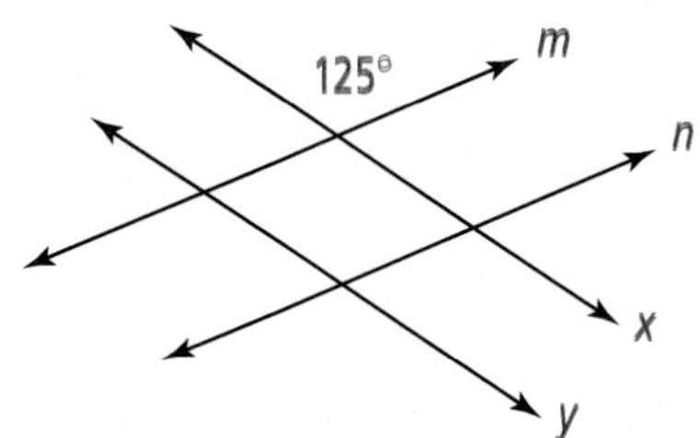


## ASSESSMENT PRACTICE

**27** Classify each angle as *congruent to* $\angle 1$ or *congruent to* $\angle 2$.

$\angle 3$ $\angle 4$

$\angle 5$ $\angle 6$

$\angle 7$ $\angle 8$

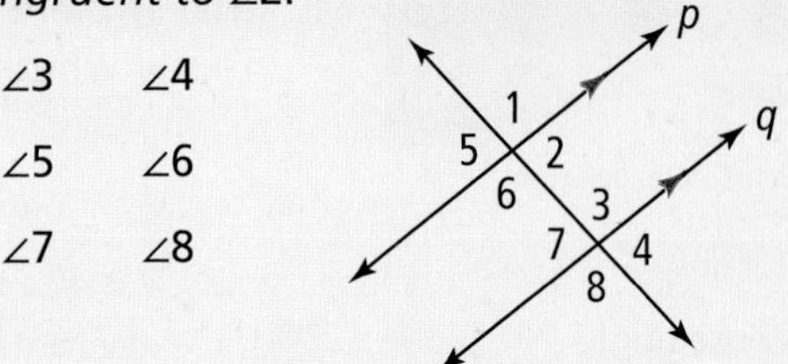


**28. SAT/ACT** In the diagram, $a \parallel b$. What is $m\angle 1$?

Ⓐ 28
Ⓑ 62
Ⓒ 90
Ⓓ 118

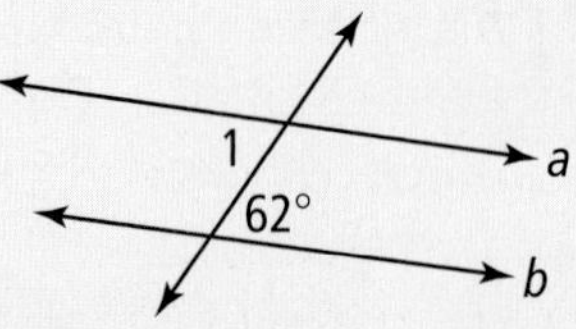


**29. Performance Task** Students on a scavenger hunt are given the map shown and several clues.

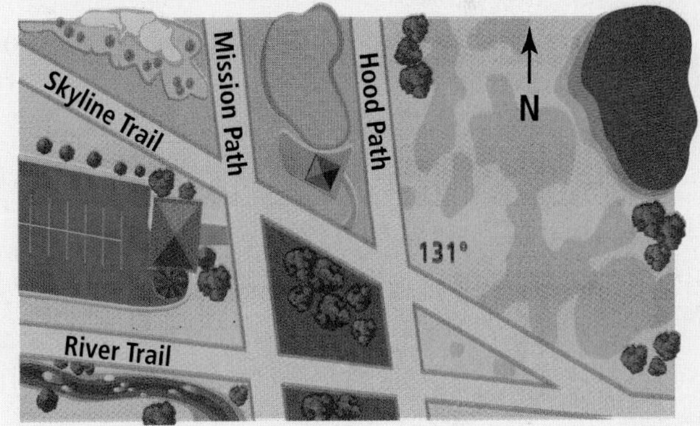


**Part A** The first clue states the following.

Skyline Trail forms a transversal with Hood Path and Mission Path. Go to the corners that form same side exterior angles north of Skyline Trail.

Which two corners does the clue mean? Use intersections and directions to explain.

**Part B** If the second clue states the following, what trail marker should they go to?

Hood and Mission Paths are parallel, and the northeast corner of Hood Path and Skyline Trail forms a 131° angle. The angle measure formed by the southwest corner of Skyline Trail and Mission Path is equal to the trail marker number on River Trail you must go to.

# 2-2 Proving Lines Parallel

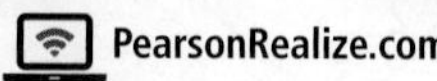
PearsonRealize.com

**I CAN…** use angle relationships to prove that lines are parallel.

**VOCABULARY**

- flow proof

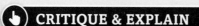

## CRITIQUE & EXPLAIN

**Juan analyzes the diagram to see if line $\ell$ is parallel to line $m$. His teacher asks if there is enough information to say whether the lines are parallel.**

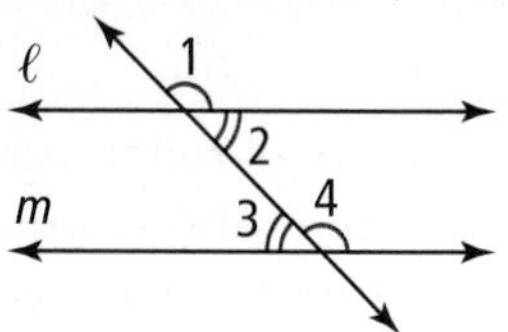


Yes, if a transversal intersects two parallel lines, then alternate interior angles are congruent and corresponding angles are congruent. I have both angle relationships here, so the lines are parallel.

**A. Make Sense and Persevere** Why is Juan's statement correct or incorrect?

**B.** Can you use the Alternate Exterior Angles Theorem to prove that the lines are not parallel?

## ESSENTIAL QUESTION

**What angle relationships can be used to prove that two lines intersected by a transversal are parallel?**

## EXAMPLE 1 Understand Angle Relationships

**Suppose two lines are not parallel. Can corresponding angles still be congruent?**

Draw two nonparallel lines $t$ and $m$ and a transversal $s$. Draw line $\ell$ parallel to $m$ that passes through the intersection of $s$ and $t$.

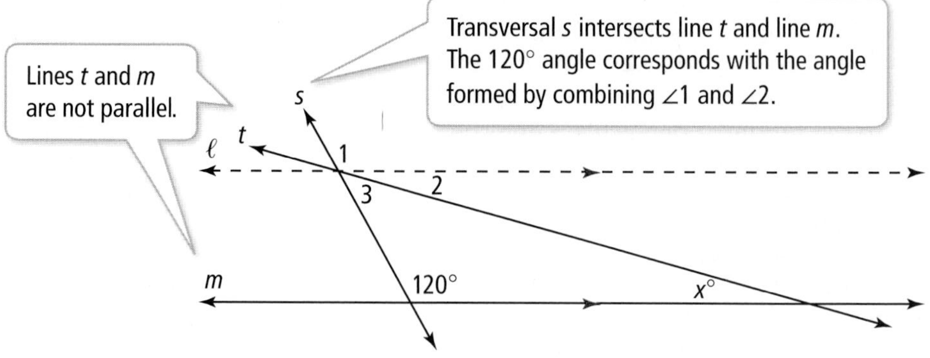


Since $\ell \parallel m$, $m\angle 1 = 120$ by the Corresponding Angles Theorem. By the Alternate Interior Angles Theorem, $m\angle 2 = x$. Since $m\angle 1 + m\angle 2 = 120 + x$, $m\angle 1 + m\angle 2 > 120$.

If two lines are not parallel, then corresponding angles are not congruent.

**COMMUNICATE PRECISELY**
Consider the conclusion in the example. What statement can you write that is logically equivalent to this statement?

**Try It!** **1.** Could $\angle 3$ be supplementary to a $120°$ angle? Explain.

## THEOREM 2-4 Converse of the Corresponding Angles Theorem

If two lines and a transversal form corresponding angles that are congruent, then the lines are parallel.

**PROOF: SEE EXERCISE 8.**

**If...**

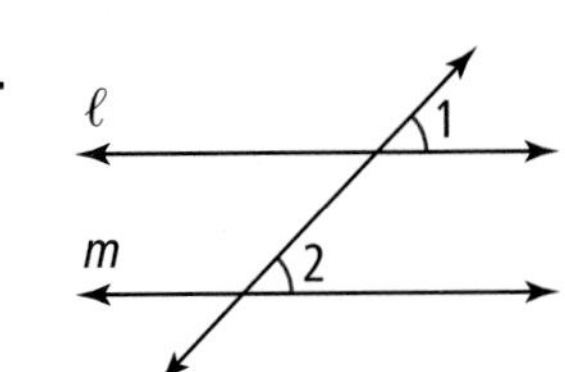


**Then...** $\ell \parallel m$

## THEOREM 2-5 Converse of the Alternate Interior Angles Theorem

If two lines and a transversal form alternate interior angles that are congruent, then the lines are parallel.

**PROOF: SEE EXAMPLE 2.**

**If...**

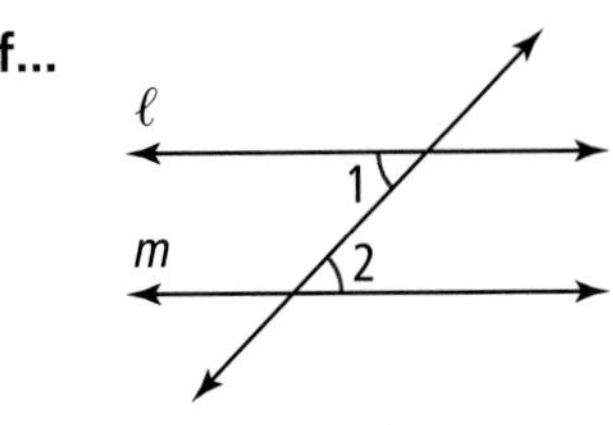


**Then...** $\ell \parallel m$

PROOF

## EXAMPLE 2 Write a Flow Proof of Theorem 2-5

**Write a flow proof to prove the Converse of the Alternate Interior Angles Theorem.**

In a **flow proof**, arrows show the logical connections between statements. Reasons are shown below the statements.

**Given:** $\angle 1 \cong \angle 2$

**Prove:** $\ell \parallel m$

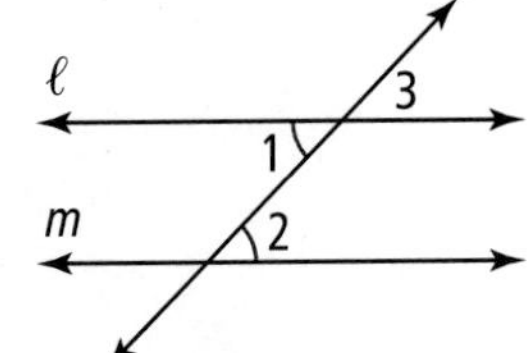


**Proof:**

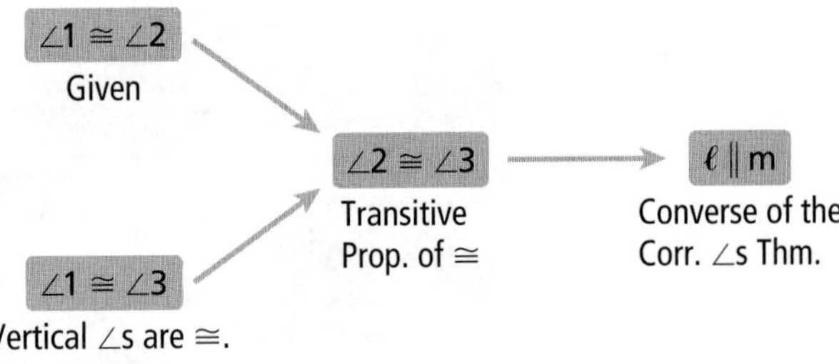

**COMMON ERROR**
You may incorrectly write all information along one line of the flow proof. Remember that you should have two separate arrows when two statements are needed to justify the next statement in a proof.

**Try It!** 2. Write a flow proof for Theorem 2-6, the Converse of the Same-Side Interior Angles Postulate.

## THEOREM 2-6 Converse of the Same-Side Interior Angles Postulate

If two lines and a transversal form same-side interior angles that are supplementary, then the lines are parallel.

PROOF: SEE EXAMPLE 2 TRY IT.

**If...** $m\angle 1 + m\angle 2 = 180$

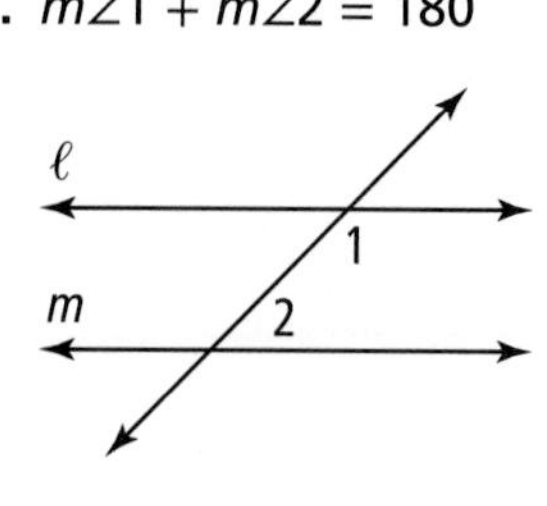


**Then...** $\ell \parallel m$

## THEOREM 2-7 Converse of the Alternate Exterior Angles Theorem

If two lines and a transversal form alternate exterior angles that are congruent, then the lines are parallel.

PROOF: SEE EXERCISE 16.

**If...**

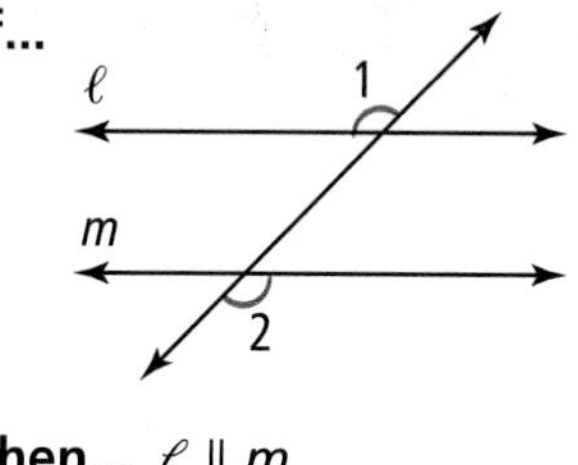


**Then...** $\ell \parallel m$

CONCEPTUAL UNDERSTANDING

## EXAMPLE 3 Determine Whether Lines Are Parallel

**The edges of a new sidewalk must be parallel in order to meet accessibility requirements. Concrete is poured between straight strings. How does an inspector know that the edges of the sidewalk are parallel?**

The inspector can first measure the angles of corners of the sidewalk.

Since the two 53° angles are congruent, he can apply the Converse of the Alternate Exterior Angles Theorem. The edges of the sidewalk are parallel.

**MAKE SENSE AND PERSEVERE** Think about what other theorems could be applied to determine parallel edges. What other measurements could the inspector make?

**Try It!** 3. What is $m\angle 1$? What should $\angle 2$ measure in order to guarantee that the sidewalk is parallel to Main Street? Explain.

### THEOREM 2-8

If two lines are parallel to the same line, then they are parallel to each other.

PROOF: SEE EXERCISE 17.

If...

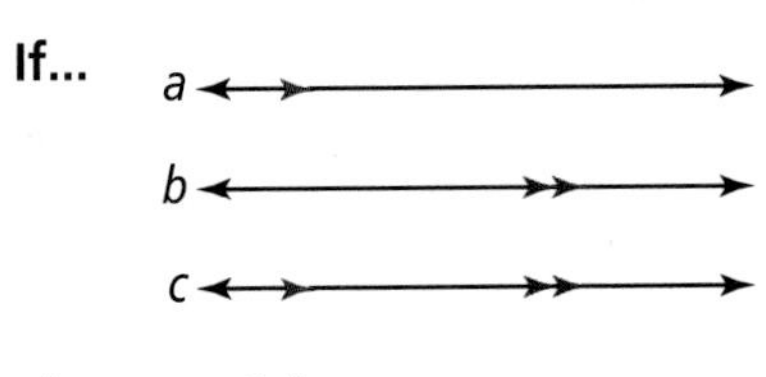


Then... $a \parallel b$

### THEOREM 2-9

If two lines are perpendicular to the same line, then they are parallel to each other.

PROOF: SEE EXERCISE 18.

If...

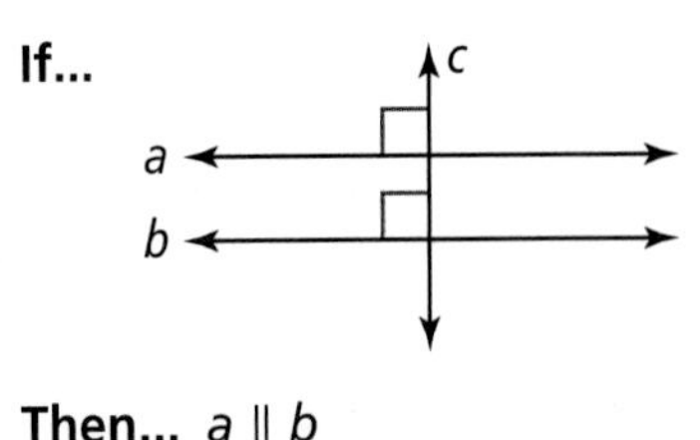


Then... $a \parallel b$

APPLICATION

## EXAMPLE 4 Solve a Problem With Parallel Lines

**A. When building a gate, how does Bailey know that the vertical boards *v* and *w* are parallel?**

**LOOK FOR RELATIONSHIPS**
Look for different ways that parts of a diagram are put together as a whole. How can you use the labeled parts to determine a strategy for solving a problem?

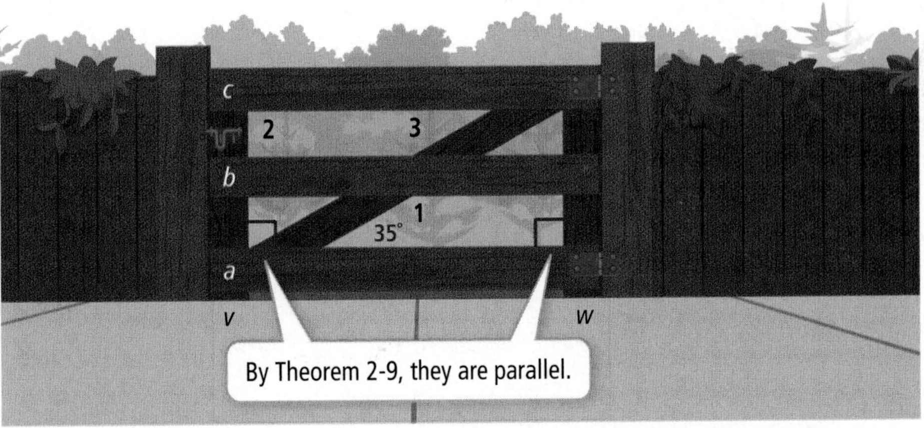


**B. What should $\angle 1$ measure to ensure board *b* is parallel to board *a*?**

Apply the Converse of the Same-Side Interior Angles Postulate.

$$35 + m\angle 1 = 180$$
$$m\angle 1 = 145$$

**Try It!** **4. a.** Bailey also needs board *c* to be parallel to board *a*. What should $\angle 2$ measure? Explain.

**b.** Is $b \parallel c$ ? Explain.

## CONCEPT SUMMARY Criteria for Parallel lines

DIAGRAM

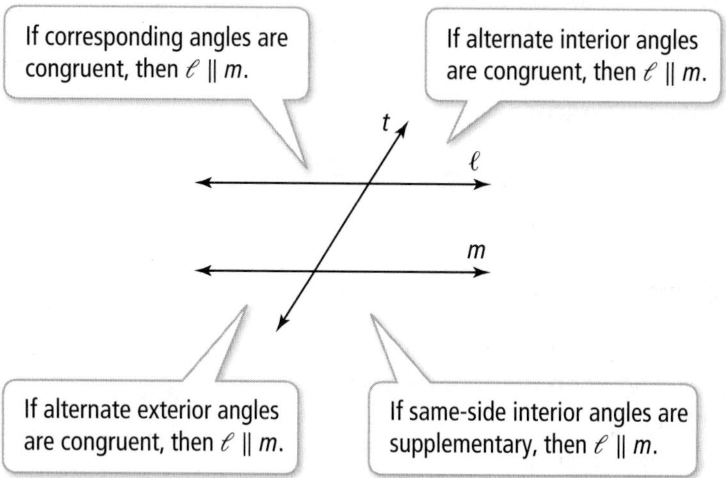

If corresponding angles are congruent, then ℓ ∥ m.
If alternate interior angles are congruent, then ℓ ∥ m.
t
ℓ
m
If alternate exterior angles are congruent, then ℓ ∥ m.
If same-side interior angles are supplementary, then ℓ ∥ m.


## Do You UNDERSTAND?

1. ESSENTIAL QUESTION What angle relationships can be used to prove that two lines intersected by a transversal are parallel?

2. **Error Analysis** Noemi wrote, "If $\angle 1 \cong \angle 2$, then by the Converse of the Same-Side Interior Angles Postulate, $\ell \parallel m$." Explain the error in Noemi's reasoning.

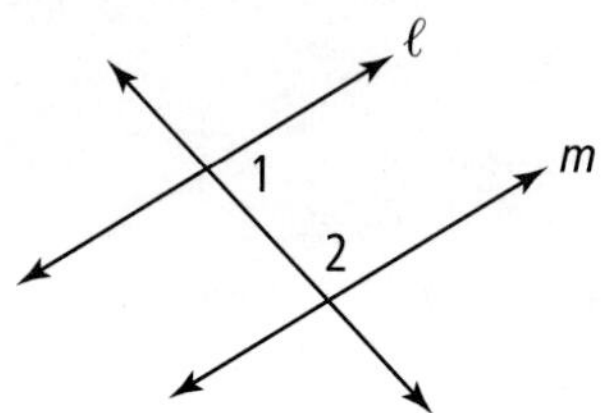


3. **Vocabulary** How does a *flow proof* show logical steps in the proof of a conditional statement?

4. **Reason** How is Theorem 2-9 a special case of the Converse of the Corresponding Angles Theorem?

## Do You KNOW HOW?

**Use the figure shown for Exercises 5 and 6.**

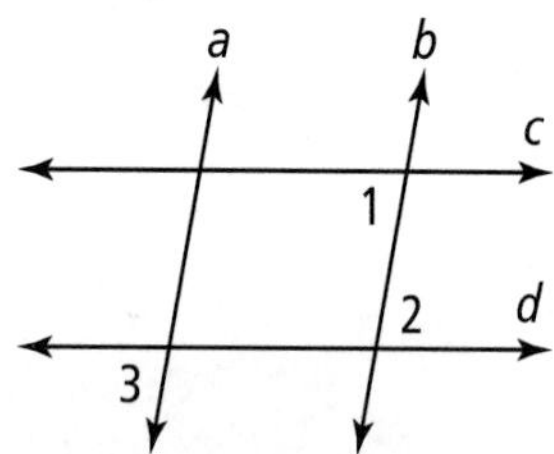


5. If $\angle 1 \cong \angle 2$, which theorem proves that $c \parallel d$?

6. If $m\angle 2 = 4x - 6$ and $m\angle 3 = 2x + 18$, for what value of $x$ is $a \parallel b$? Which theorem justifies your answer?

7. Using the Converse of the Same-Side Interior Angles Postulate, what equation shows that $g \parallel h$?

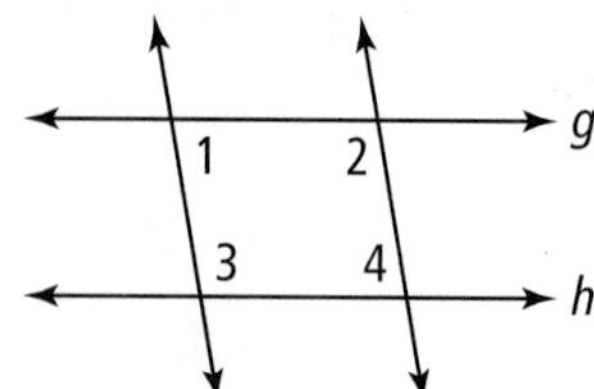

## PRACTICE & PROBLEM SOLVING

Scan for Multimedia

Additional Exercises Available Online

### UNDERSTAND

**8. Construct Arguments** Write an indirect proof of the Converse of the Corresponding Angles Theorem following the outline below.

**Given:** $\angle 1 \cong \angle 2$

**Prove:** $\ell \parallel m$

- Assume that lines $\ell$ and $m$ are not parallel.
- Draw line $n$ parallel to line $\ell$.
- Conclude that $m\angle 3 > 0$.
- Use the Same-Side Interior Angles Postulate to arrive at the contradiction that $m\angle 1 \neq m\angle 2$.

**Error Analysis** What is the student's error?

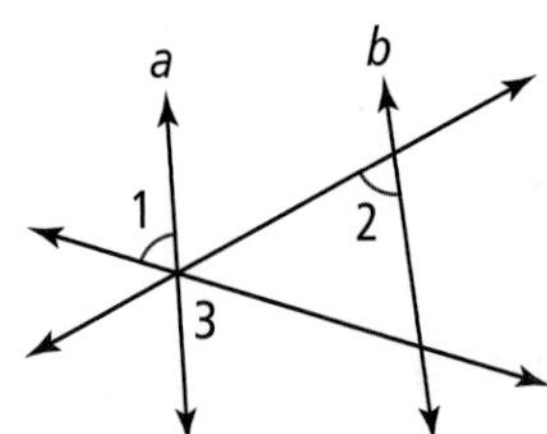


Given $\angle 1 \cong \angle 2$. By the Vertical Angles Thm., $\angle 1 \cong \angle 3$, so by the Transitive Property, $\angle 2 \cong \angle 3$. By the Converse of the Corresponding Angles Thm., $a \parallel b$.

**10. Mathematical Connections** Copy the figure below. Construct a line through $P$ parallel to $\ell$. (*Hint:* Copy either $\angle PCA$ or $\angle PCB$ so that one of the sides of the angle is parallel to $\ell$.) What theorem justifies your construction?

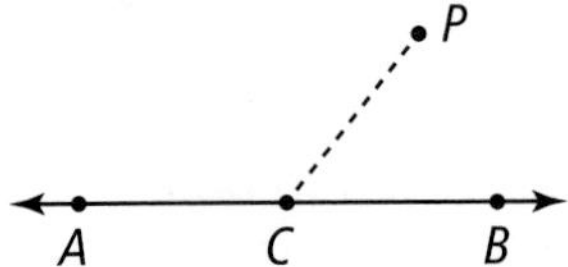


**11. Higher Order Thinking** The interior angles of a regular hexagon are congruent. Why are any pair of opposite sides parallel?

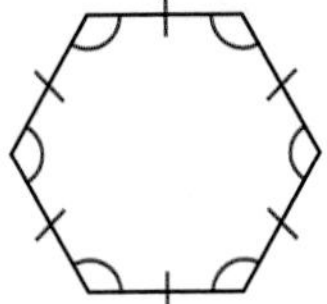

### PRACTICE

**For Exercises 12–15, use the given information. Which lines in the figure can you conclude are parallel? State the theorem that justifies each answer.** SEE EXAMPLES 1 AND 3

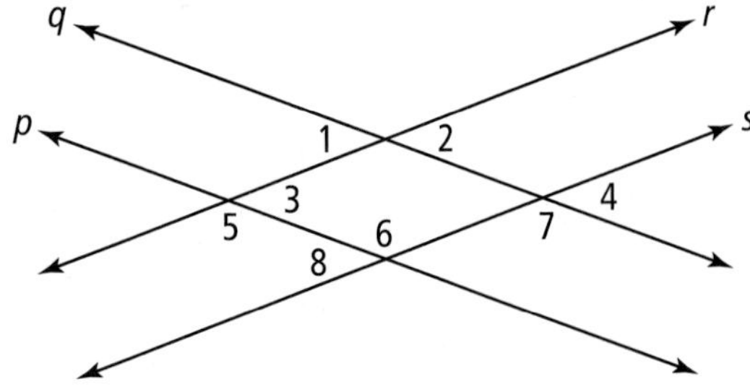


**12.** $\angle 2 \cong \angle 3$

**13.** $\angle 6 \cong \angle 7$

**14.** $\angle 1 \cong \angle 4$

**15.** $m\angle 5 + m\angle 8 = 180°$

**16.** Write a flow proof of the Converse of the Alternate Exterior Angles Theorem. SEE EXAMPLE 2

**Use the figure for Exercises 17 and 18.** SEE EXAMPLE 2

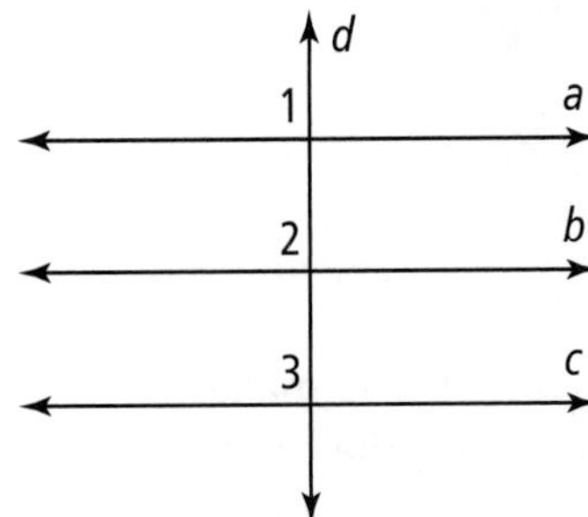


**17.** Given $a \parallel c$ and $b \parallel c$, write a flow proof of Theorem 2-8.

**18.** Given $a \perp d$ and $b \perp d$, write a flow proof of Theorem 2-9.

**19.** For what value of $x$ is $f \parallel g$? Which theorem justifies your answer? SEE EXAMPLE 4

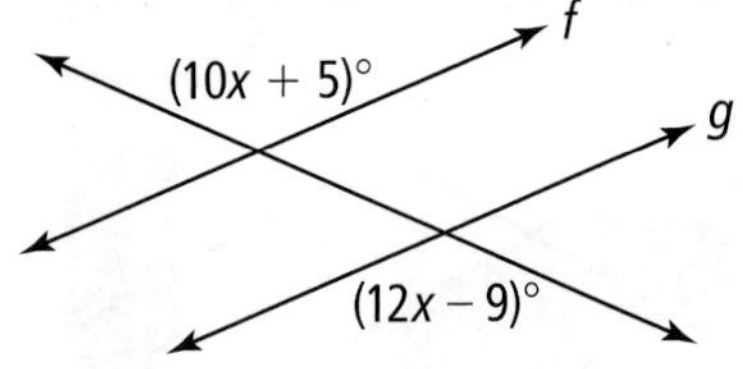

## PRACTICE & PROBLEM SOLVING

Practice Tutorial

Mixed Review Available Online

### APPLY

**20. Look for Relationships** To make a puzzle, Denzel draws lines *a* and *b* to cut along on a square piece of posterboard. He wants to draw line *c* so that it is parallel to line *b*. What should the measure of ∠1 be? Explain.

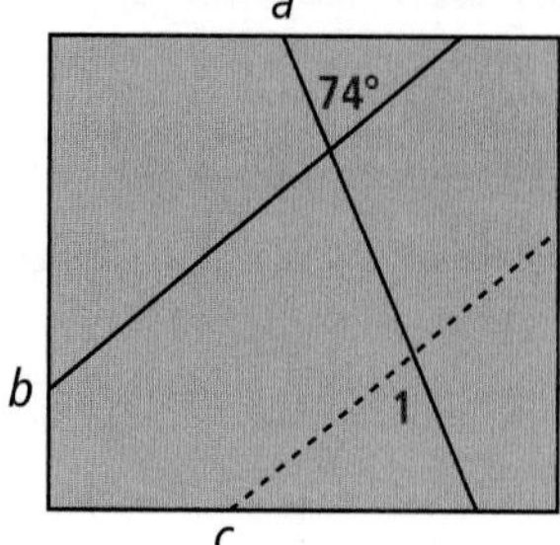


**21. Reason** A downhill skier is fastest when her skis are parallel. What should ∠1 be in order for the skier to maximize her speed through a gate? Which theorem justifies your answer?

**22. Make Sense and Persevere** Malia makes a fabric design by drawing diagonals between opposite corners. She wants to draw other lines parallel to one of the diagonal lines, as shown by the dashed lines.

**a.** What should ∠1 be in order for line *b* to be parallel to line *a*? Explain.

**b.** What should ∠2 be in order for line *c* to be parallel to line *b*? Explain.

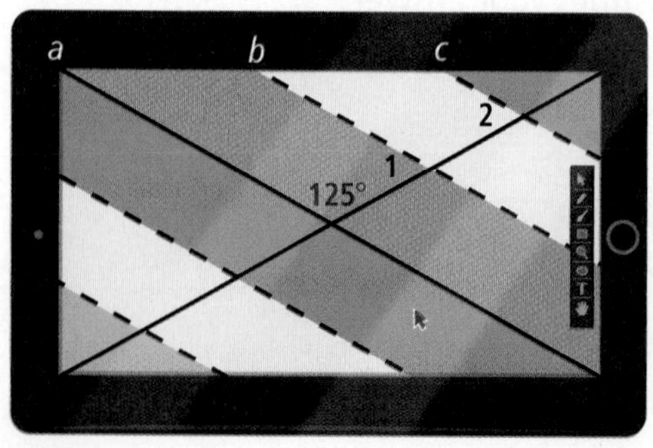


### ASSESSMENT PRACTICE

**23.** In order for $c \parallel d$, ∠2 and ∠7 must be __?__, and ∠3 and ∠5 must be __?__.

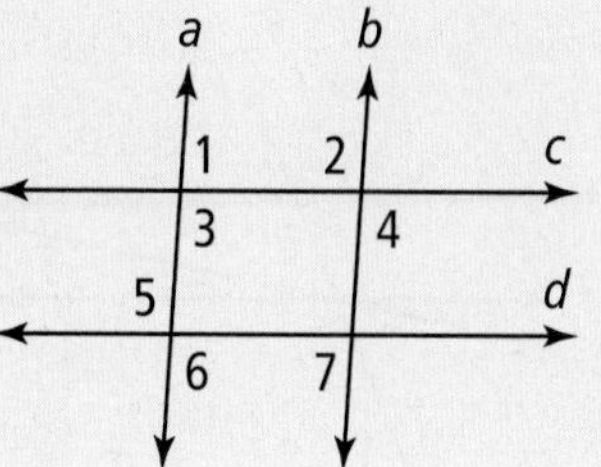


**24. SAT/ACT** Which statement must always be true?

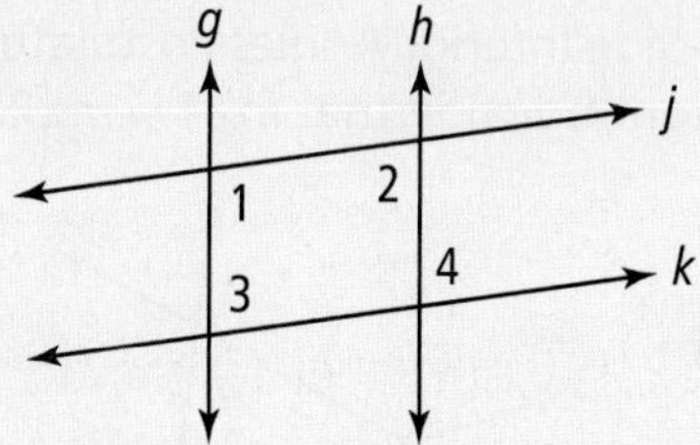


Ⓐ If ∠1 ≅ ∠2, then $g \parallel h$.

Ⓑ If ∠1 ≅ ∠3, then $g \parallel h$.

Ⓒ If ∠2 ≅ ∠4, then $j \parallel k$.

Ⓓ If ∠3 ≅ ∠4, then $j \parallel k$.

**25. Performance Task** The diagram shows part of a plan to arrange aisles in a store.

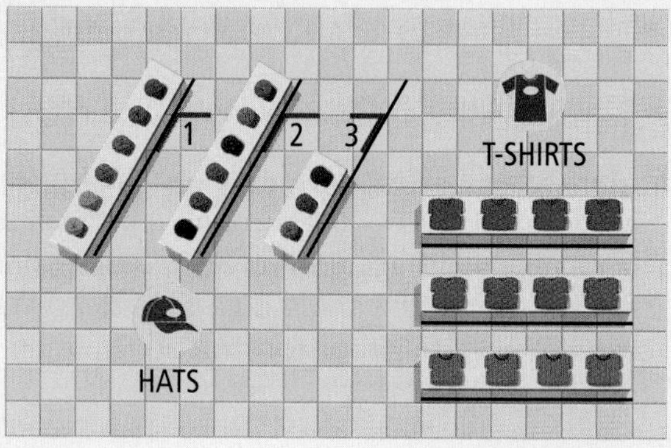


**Part A** The aisles are arranged so that $m\angle 1 = 125$. What should be the measures of the other labeled angles so that all three aisles will be parallel? Explain.

**Part B** Describe how theorems can be applied to make sure that the T-shirt aisles are parallel.

# 2-3 Parallel Lines and Triangle Angle Sums

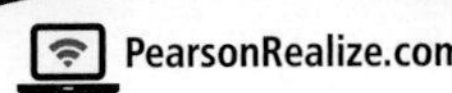
PearsonRealize.com

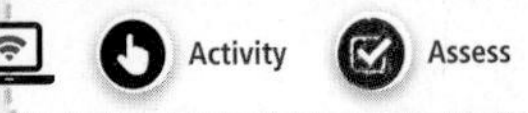
Activity
Assess

**I CAN…** solve problems using the measures of interior and exterior angles of triangles.

## EXPLORE & REASON

**Two parallel lines never intersect. But, can two lines that intersect ever be parallel to the same line?**

Draw point $P$. Then draw lines $a$ and $b$ that intersect at point $P$ as shown.

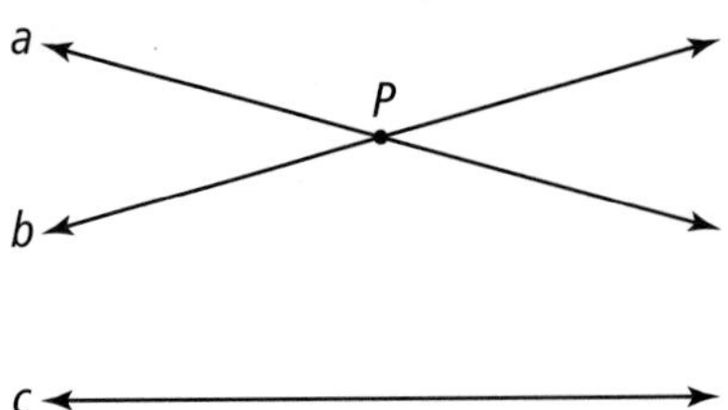


**A.** Place a pencil below the intersecting lines on your paper to represent line $c$. Rotate the pencil so that it is parallel to line $b$. Can you rotate the pencil so that it is parallel to line $a$ at the same time as line $b$?

**B. Look for Relationships** Can you adjust your drawing of the two intersecting lines so you can rotate the pencil to be parallel to both lines?

**ESSENTIAL QUESTION** What is true about the interior and exterior angle measures of a triangle?

CONCEPTUAL UNDERSTANDING

## EXAMPLE 1 Investigate the Measures of Triangle Angles

**What appears to be the relationship between the angle measures of a triangle?**

Using pencil and paper, or scissors and paper, construct several triangles of different types. Number the angles.

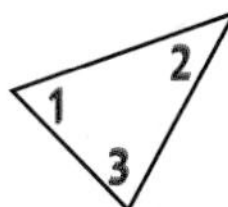


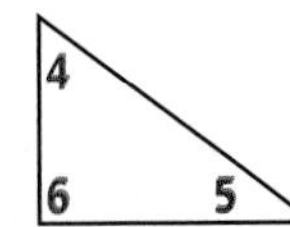


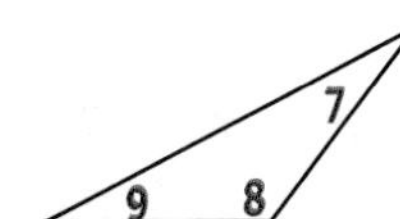


Trace the angles from each triangle and place the vertices together with the sides of the angles sharing a vertex and ray.

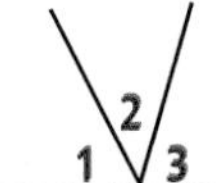


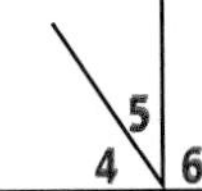

**USE APPROPRIATE TOOLS** What tools might you use to confirm that the angles sum to 180°?

For each triangle shown, the angles combine to form a straight angle.

So, the sum of the angle measures of a triangle appears to be 180.

**Try It!** 1. Given two angle measures in a triangle, can you find the measure of the third angle? Explain.

## THEOREM 2-10

Through a point not on a line, there is one and only one line parallel to the given line.

PROOF: SEE EXERCISE 10.

**If...**

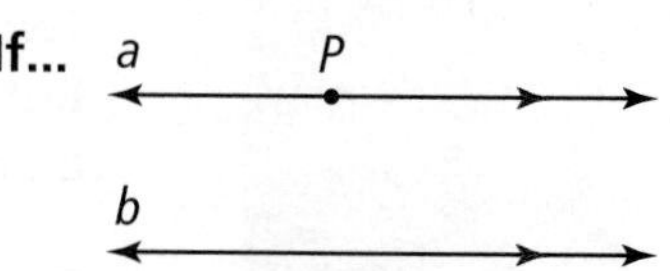


**Then...** line $a$ is the only line parallel to line $b$ through $P$.

## THEOREM 2-11 Triangle Angle-Sum Theorem

The sum of the measures of all the angles of a triangle is 180.

PROOF: SEE EXAMPLE 2.

**If...**

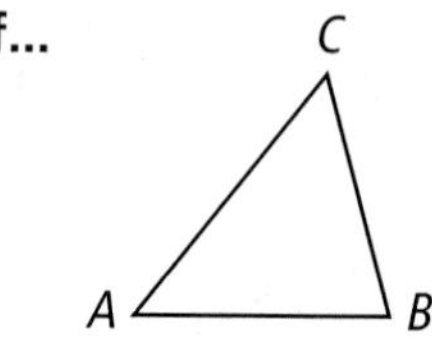


**Then...** $m\angle A + m\angle B + m\angle C = 180$

## EXAMPLE 2 Prove the Triangle Angle-Sum Theorem

**Prove the Triangle Angle-Sum Theorem.**

**Given:** $\triangle ABC$

**Prove:** $m\angle 1 + m\angle 2 + m\angle 3 = 180$

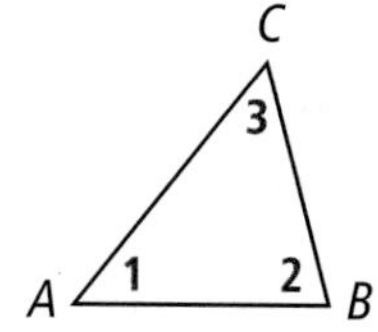


**STUDY TIP**
When using a geometric figure in a proof, you can construct additional parts to help with the proof, such as parallel lines, angle bisectors, and midpoints.

**Plan:** Draw a line through $C$, because a straight angle measures 180. This line should be parallel to the line containing $\overline{AB}$ so that an alternate interior angle relationship is formed.

**Proof:**

Use Theorem 2-10 to justify drawing a line through $C$ parallel to $\overleftrightarrow{AB}$.

By applying the Angle Addition Postulate, $m\angle 4 + m\angle 3 + m\angle 5 = 180°$.

By the Alternate Interior Angles Theorem, $\angle 1 \cong \angle 4$, so $m\angle 1 = m\angle 4$.

Also by the Alternate Interior Angles Theorem, $\angle 2 \cong \angle 5$, so $m\angle 2 = m\angle 5$.

By substitution, $m\angle 1 + m\angle 3 + m\angle 2 = 180$. Therefore, using the Commutative Property of Addition, $m\angle 1 + m\angle 2 + m\angle 3 = 180$.

**Try It!** 2. How does Theorem 2-10 justify the construction of the line through $C$ that is parallel to $\overleftrightarrow{AB}$?

## EXAMPLE 3 Use the Triangle Angle-Sum Theorem

**What are the values of $x$ and $y$?**

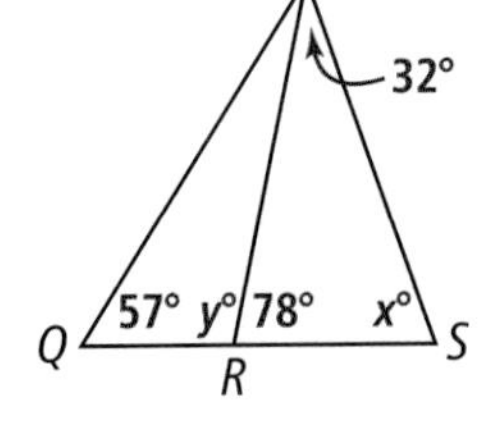


Write and solve an equation that relates the measures of the angles of $\triangle TRS$.

$$32 + 78 + x = 180$$
$$x = 70$$

Use the Triangle Angle-Sum Theorem.

To find the value of $y$, notice that $\angle QRS$ is a straight angle.

$$m\angle QRT + m\angle TRS = 180$$
$$y + 78 = 180$$
$$y = 102$$

Apply the Angle Addition Postulate.

The value of $x$ is 70 and the value of $y$ is 102.

 **Try It!** **3.** What are the values of $x$ and $y$ in each figure?

**a.**

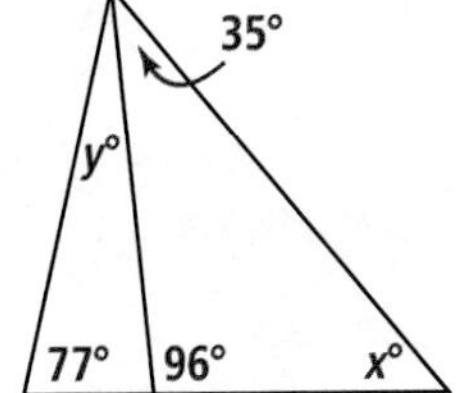


**b.**

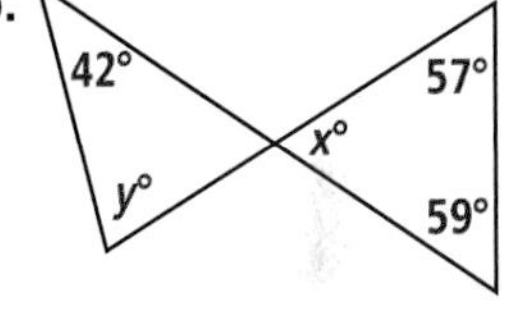


### THEOREM 2-12 Triangle Exterior Angle Theorem

The measure of each exterior angle of a triangle equals the sum of the measures of its two remote interior angles.

**PROOF: SEE EXERCISE 13.**

**If...**

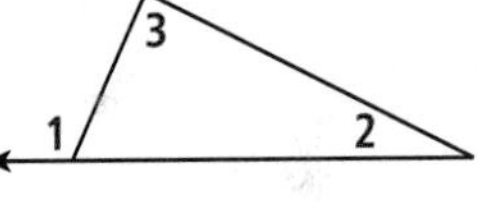


**Then...** $m\angle 1 = m\angle 2 + m\angle 3$

## EXAMPLE 4 Apply the Triangle Exterior Angle Theorem

**What is the missing angle measure in each figure?**

**A.**

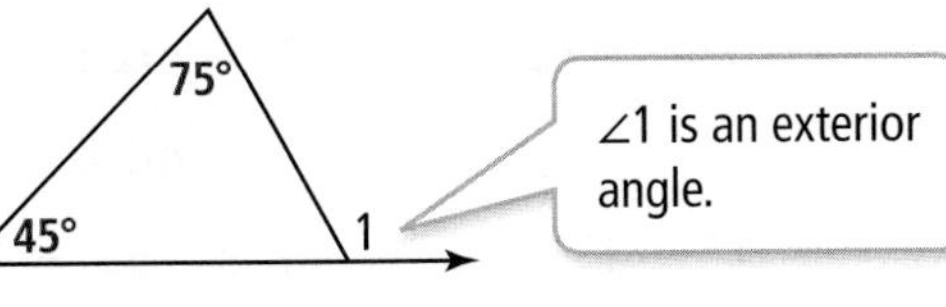


$$m\angle 1 = 45 + 75$$
$$m\angle 1 = 120$$

Use the Exterior Angles Theorem.

**B.**

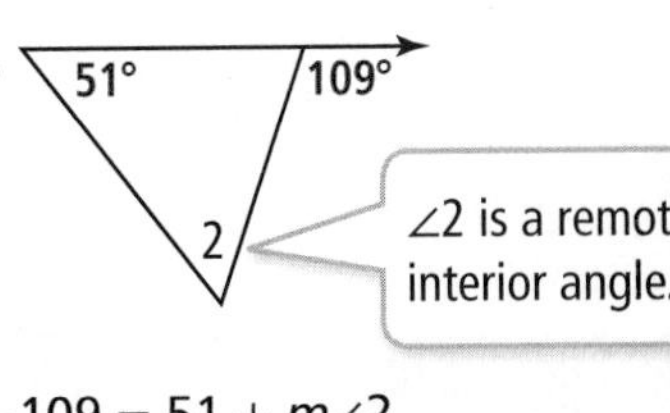


$$109 = 51 + m\angle 2$$
$$58 = m\angle 2$$

**COMMON ERROR**
Be careful when writing an equation to solve for the unknown angle measure. The unknown value can be an addend or the sum.

CONTINUED ON THE NEXT PAGE

**Try It!** **4.** What is the value of $x$ in each figure?

a. 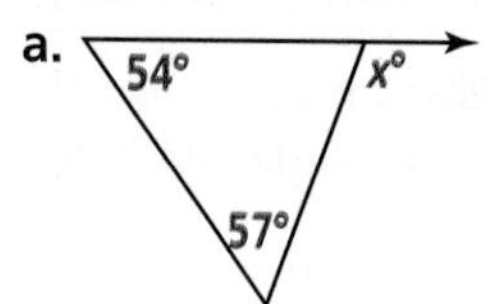


b. 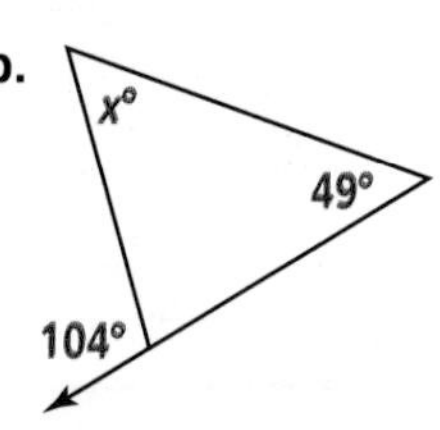


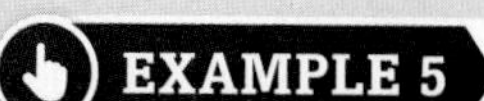


## EXAMPLE 5 Apply the Triangle Theorems

**Cheyenne built this display for her ornament collection. Each shelf is parallel to the base. She recalls only the angle measures shown in the diagram. Now she wants to build another just like it. What are the measures of ∠1, ∠2, and ∠3?**

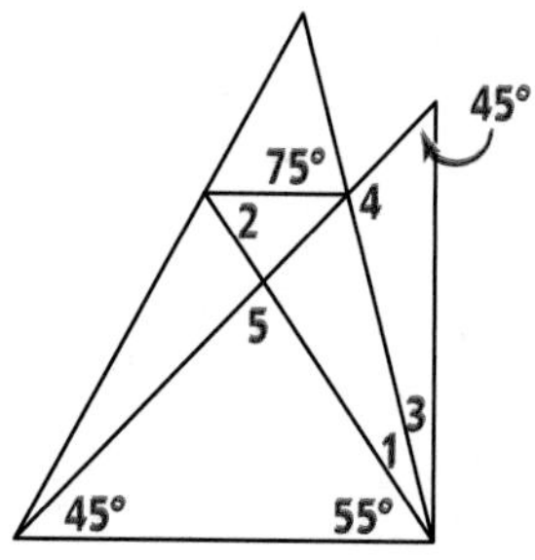


**Formulate** Begin by writing equations for the unknown angle measures. Since the bottom and top shelves are parallel, apply the Corresponding Angles Theorem.

$$55 + m\angle 1 = 75$$

Apply the Triangle Exterior Angle Theorem.

$$m\angle 1 + m\angle 2 = 75$$

Use the Triangle Angle-Sum Theorem.

$$45 + 45 + (m\angle 1 + m\angle 3 + 55) = 180$$

**Compute** Solve for $m\angle 1$, $m\angle 2$, and $m\angle 3$.

$$55 + m\angle 1 = 75 \qquad m\angle 1 + m\angle 2 = 75$$

$$m\angle 1 = 20 \qquad 20 + m\angle 2 = 75$$

$$m\angle 2 = 55$$

$$45 + 45 + (m\angle 1 + m\angle 3 + 55) = 180$$

$$45 + 45 + (20 + m\angle 3 + 55) = 180$$

$$m\angle 3 + 165 = 180$$

$$m\angle 3 = 15$$

**Interpret** The measures of the angles are $m\angle 1 = 20$, $m\angle 2 = 55$, and $m\angle 3 = 15$.

**Try It!** **5.** What are the measures of ∠4 and ∠5? Explain.

## CONCEPT SUMMARY Angle Measures of Triangles

**WORDS**

### Interior Angle Measures

The sum of the measures of all the angles of a triangle is 180.

### Exterior Angle Measure

The measure of each exterior angle of a triangle equals the sum of the measures of its two remote interior angles.

**DIAGRAM**

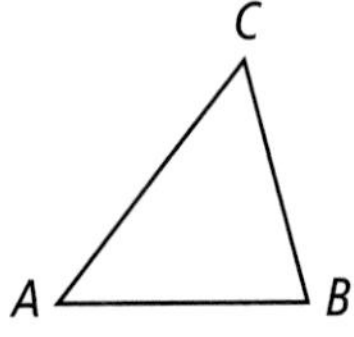


$m\angle A + m\angle B + m\angle C = 180$

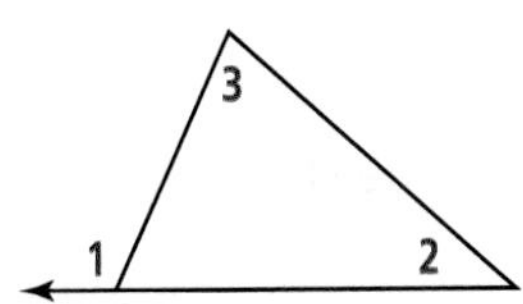


$m\angle 1 = m\angle 2 + m\angle 3$

## Do You UNDERSTAND?

1. **ESSENTIAL QUESTION** What is true about the interior and exterior angle measures of a triangle?

2. **Error Analysis** Chiang determined that the value of $x$ is 103 and the value of $y$ is 132 in the figure below. What mistake did Chiang make?

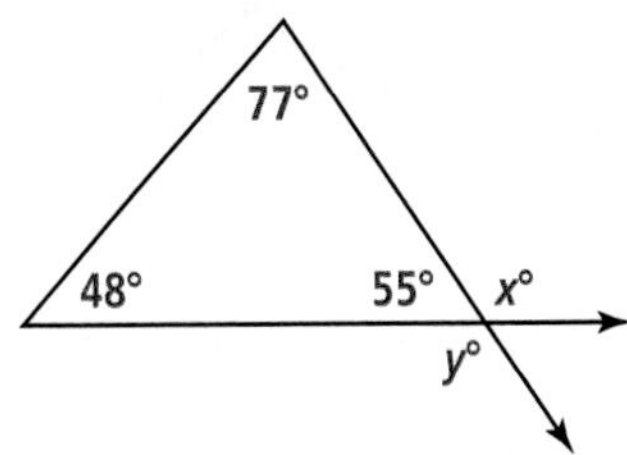


3. **Vocabulary** The word *remote* means distant or far apart. What parts of a figure are *remote interior angles* distant from?

4. **Look for Relationships** Use the Triangle Angle-Sum Theorem to answer the following questions. Explain your answers.

   a. What are the measures of each angle of an equiangular triangle?

   b. If one of the angle measures of an isosceles triangle is 90, what are the measures of the other two angles?

## Do You KNOW HOW?

**What is the value of $x$ in each figure?**

5. 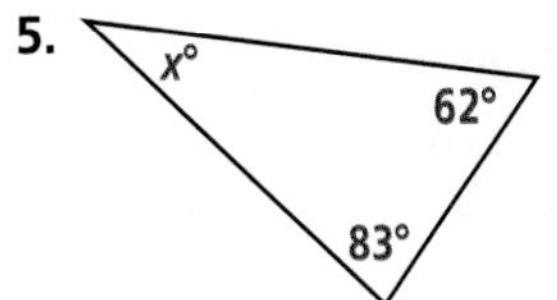


6. 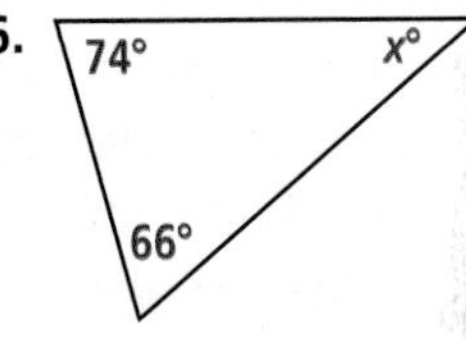


**What is the value of $x$ in each figure?**

7. 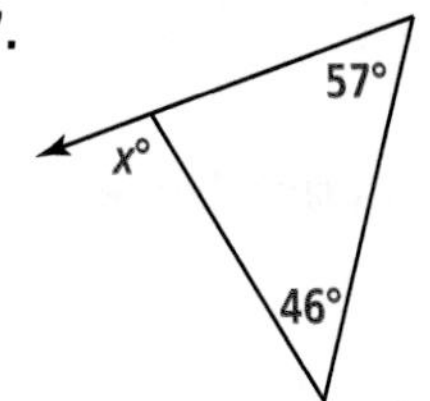


8. 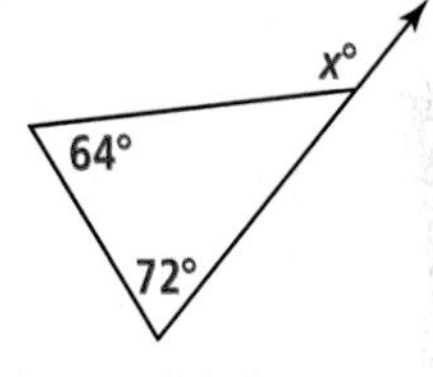


9. Write an equation relating the measures of $\angle 1$, $\angle 2$, and $\angle 3$. Write another equation relating the measures of $\angle 1$, $\angle 2$, and $\angle 4$.

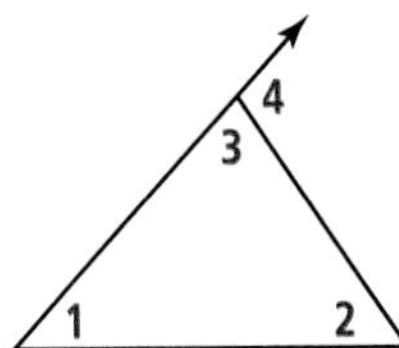

# PRACTICE & PROBLEM SOLVING

Scan for Multimedia

Practice | Tutorial

Additional Exercises Available Online

## UNDERSTAND

**10. Construct Arguments** Write a proof for Theorem 2-10.

**11. Higher Order Thinking** Marisol claims that each pair of remote interior angles in a triangle has two exterior angles. Do you agree? Use a diagram to support your answer.

**12. Error Analysis** A student was asked to find the value of $x$. What error did the student make?

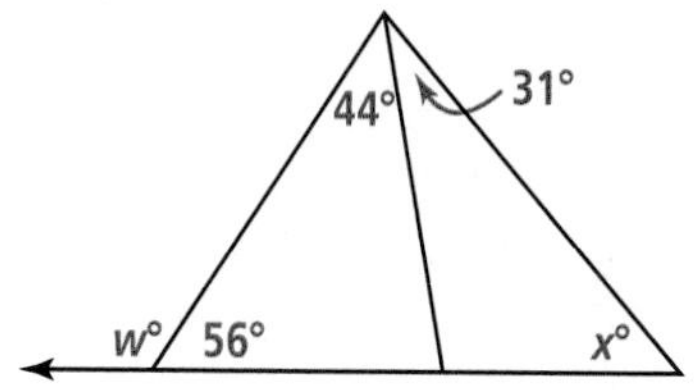


By the Linear Pairs Theorem,
$w + 56 = 180$, so $w = 124$.
By the Triangle Exterior Angle Theorem, $w = x + 31$, or
$124 = x + 31$, so $x = 93$.

**13. Reason** Prove the Triangle Exterior Angle Theorem.

**14. Mathematical Connections** What are the values of $x$, $y$, and $z$? Use theorems to justify each answer.

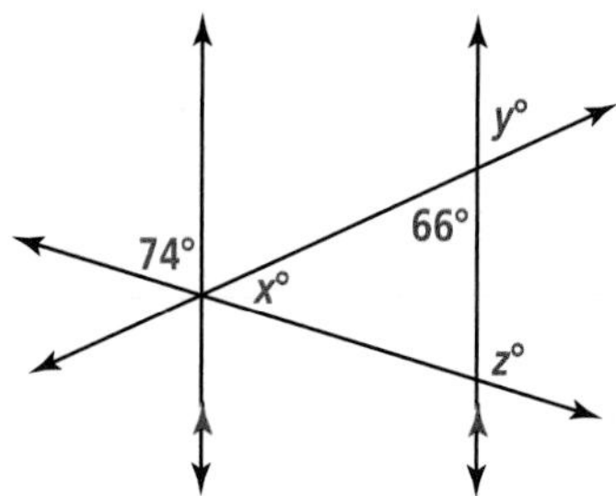


**15. Use Structure** Write and solve an equation to find the value of $x$. What is the measure of each labeled angle?

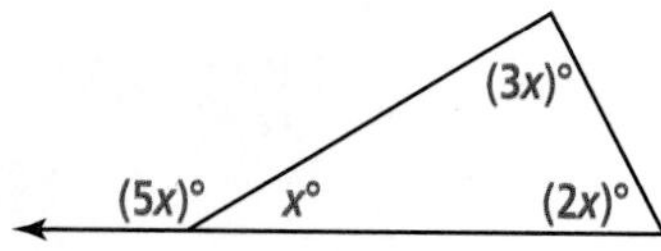


## PRACTICE

**What are the values of the variables in each figure?** SEE EXAMPLES 1–3

**16.**

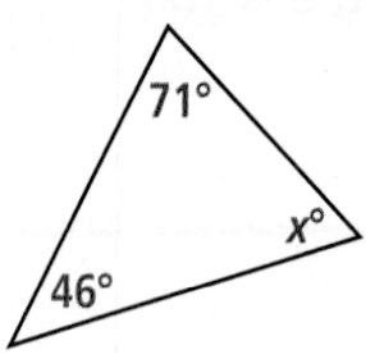


**17.**

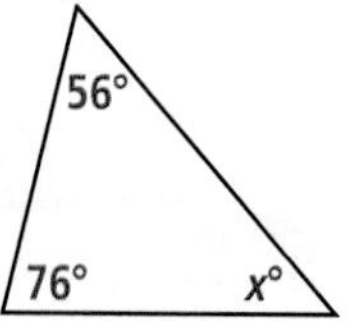


**18.**

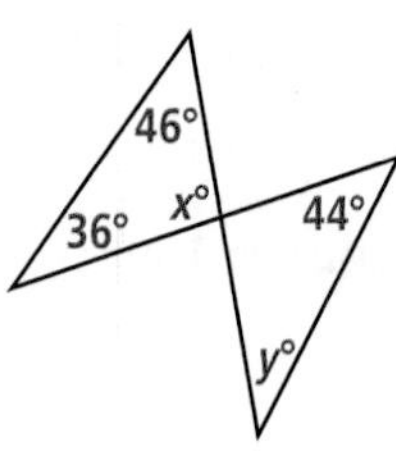


**19.**

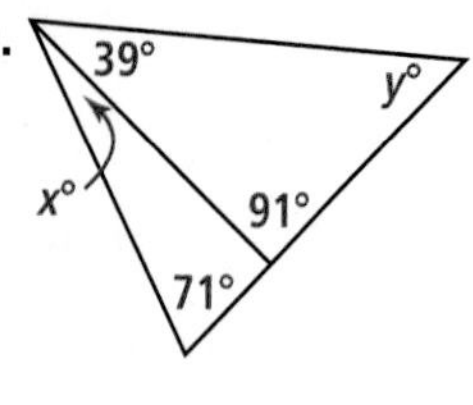


**What is the value of $x$ in each figure?** SEE EXAMPLE 4

**20.**

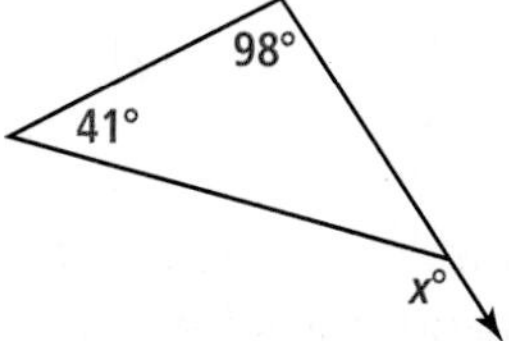


**21.**

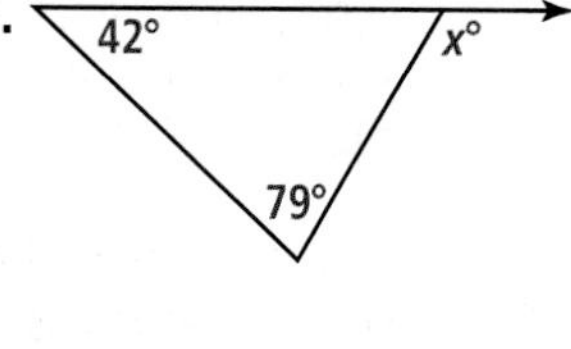


**22.**

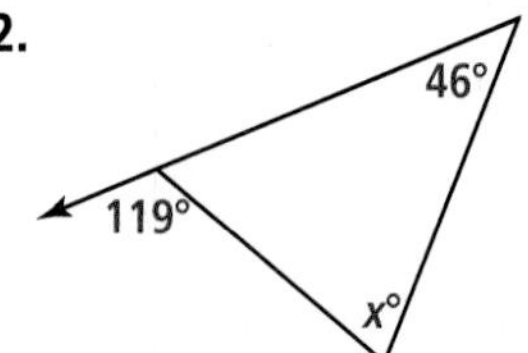


**23.**

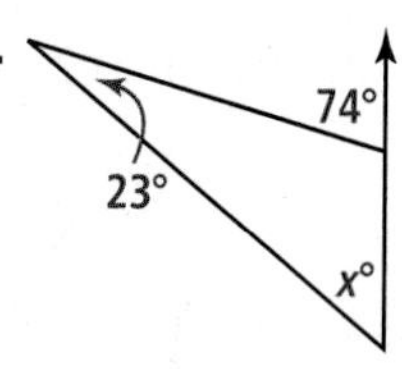


**For Exercises 24–27, find the measure of each angle.** SEE EXAMPLE 4

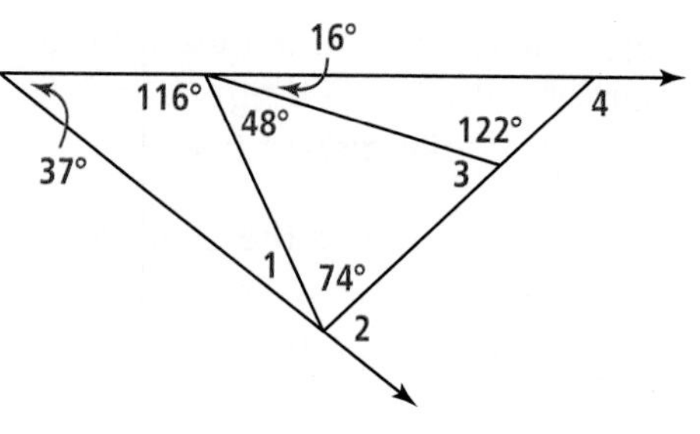


**24.** ∠1

**25.** ∠2

**26.** ∠3

**27.** ∠4

**28.** A pennant is in the shape of an isosceles triangle. One leg of the triangle is fastened to a stick. The stick forms an 84° angle with the other leg. What is the measure of each remote interior angle in the triangle?

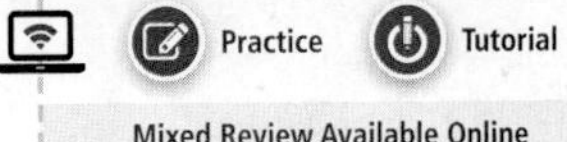


## PRACTICE & PROBLEM SOLVING

### APPLY

**29. Model With Mathematics** Pilar is making a replacement set of sails for a sailboat.

a. What equation can Pilar use that relates the values of $w$ and $x$?

b. What equation can Pilar use that relates the values of $y$ and $z$?

**30. Reason** An artist painting from a photo begins with a geometric sketch to match angle measures. What is the value of $z$?

**31. Look for Relationships** Use the figure shown.

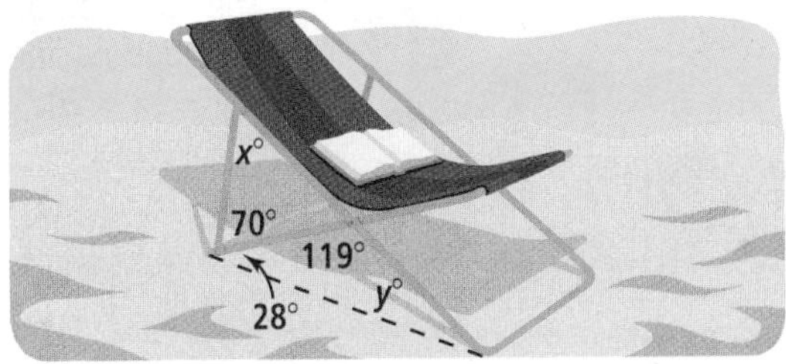


a. What is the value of $x$?

b. What is the value of $y$?

c. The chair can lay farther back so that the 70° angle changes to 86° and $x$° changes to 36°. How does this affect the 119° angle?

### ASSESSMENT PRACTICE

**32.** What are the values of $x$, $y$, and $z$?

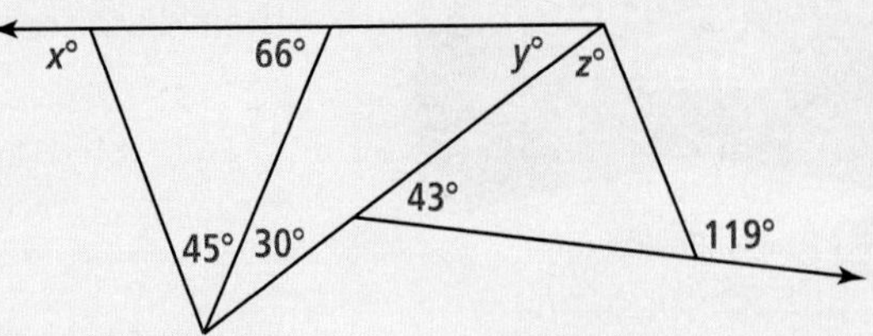


**33. SAT/ACT** What is the value of $x$?

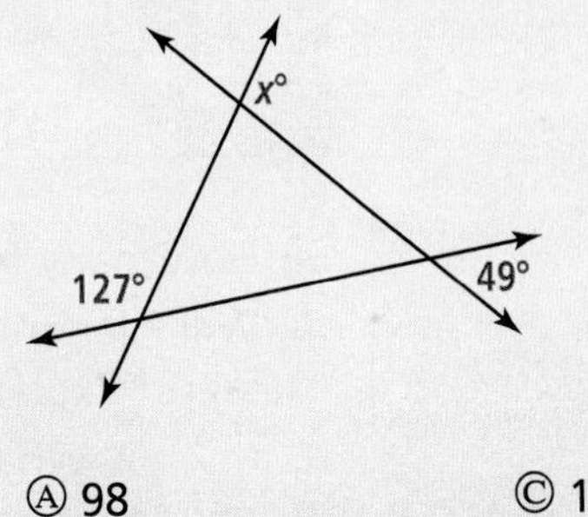


Ⓐ 98
Ⓑ 106
Ⓒ 102
Ⓓ 176

**34. Performance Task** A tablet case is supported at the back. The measure of the slant angle of the tablet can be changed, but $m\angle 2 = m\angle 3$ for any slant that is chosen.

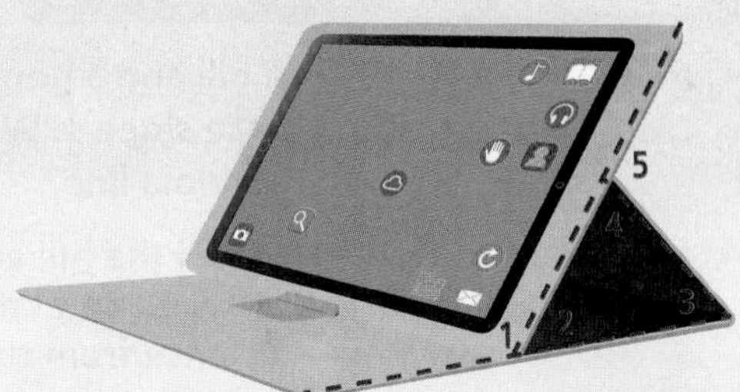


**Part A** A user adjusts the case so that $m\angle 2 = 42$. What are the measures of the other angles?

**Part B** Is it possible to slant the tablet case so that $m\angle 1 = m\angle 5$? If so, explain how. If not, explain why it is not possible.

**Part C** A user wants to slant the tablet case so that $m\angle 1 = 2(m\angle 5)$. What should the measure of each of the five angles be?

Activity Assess

# 2-4 Slopes of Parallel and Perpendicular Lines

PearsonRealize.com

**I CAN...** use slope to solve problems about parallel and perpendicular lines.

## MODEL & DISCUSS

**Pilar and Jake begin climbing to the top of a 100-ft monument at the same time along two different sets of steps at the same rate. The tables show their distances above ground level after a number of steps.**

$1\frac{1}{2}$ ft
$4\frac{1}{2}$ ft
Ground Level

| Pilar | | | | |
|---|---|---|---|---|
| Steps | 1 | 3 | 17 | 25 |
| Height (ft) | 2 | 3 | 10 | 14 |

| Jake | | | | |
|---|---|---|---|---|
| Steps | 1 | 7 | 15 | 29 |
| Height (ft) | 5 | 8 | 12 | 19 |

**A.** How many feet does each student climb after 10 steps? Explain.

**B.** Will Pilar and Jake be at the same height after the same number of steps? Explain.

**C. Reason** What would you expect the graphs of each to look like given your answers to parts A and B? Explain.

## ESSENTIAL QUESTION

**How do the slopes of lines that are parallel to each other compare? How do the slopes of lines that are perpendicular to each other compare?**

CONCEPTUAL UNDERSTANDING

## EXAMPLE 1 Slopes of Parallel Lines

**A hill and a gondola line 20 ft above the ground that goes up the hill both have slope $\frac{1}{2}$. What is the geometric relationship between the hill and the gondola line?**

Model the hill and gondola line on a coordinate plane where $x$ represents the horizontal distance from the base of the hill and $y$ represents the vertical distance from the base of the hill.

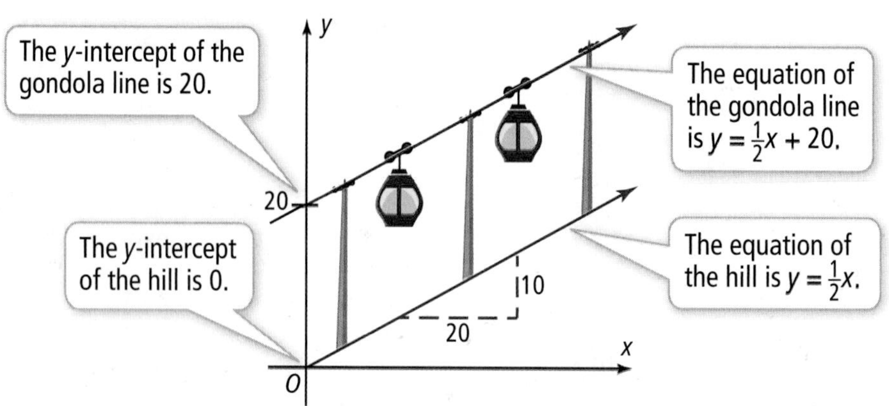

The $y$-intercept of the gondola line is 20.
The equation of the gondola line is $y = \frac{1}{2}x + 20$.
The $y$-intercept of the hill is 0.
The equation of the hill is $y = \frac{1}{2}x$.
y
x
O
20
10
20

Because the slope of the hill is $\frac{1}{2}$, the hill gains one foot of height for every two feet of horizontal distance. The same is true for the gondola. It never gets any closer or farther away from the hill.

**Conjecture:** If two linear equations have the same slope, then the graphs of the equations are parallel.

**MODEL WITH MATHEMATICS**
Would you describe a different relationship between the slopes of parallel lines if the $y$-intercept for the hill were not at (0, 0)?

CONTINUED ON THE NEXT PAGE

 **Try It!** **1.** Suppose another line for a chair lift is placed at a constant distance $c$ below the gondola line. What is an equation of the new line? Is the new line also parallel to the hill? Explain.

## THEOREM 2-13

Two non-vertical lines are parallel if and only if their slopes are equal.

Any two vertical lines are parallel.

PROOF: SEE LESSON 7-5.

**If...** $p$ and $q$ are both not vertical

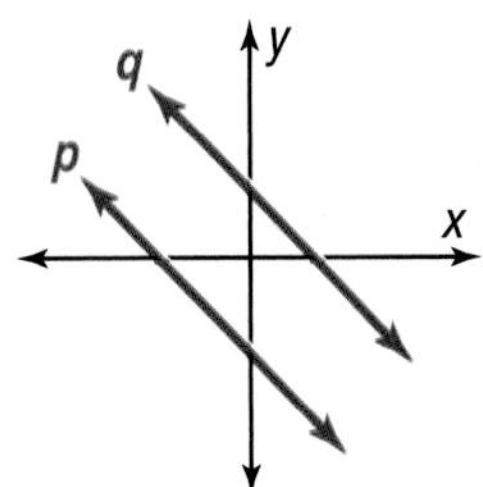


**Then...** $p \parallel q$ if and only if the slope of line $p$ = slope of line $q$

**If...** $p$ and $q$ are both vertical

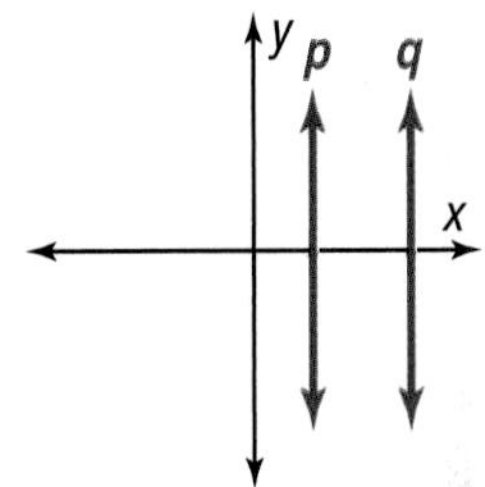


**Then...** $p \parallel q$

## EXAMPLE 2 Check Parallelism

**Are lines $k$ and $n$ parallel?**

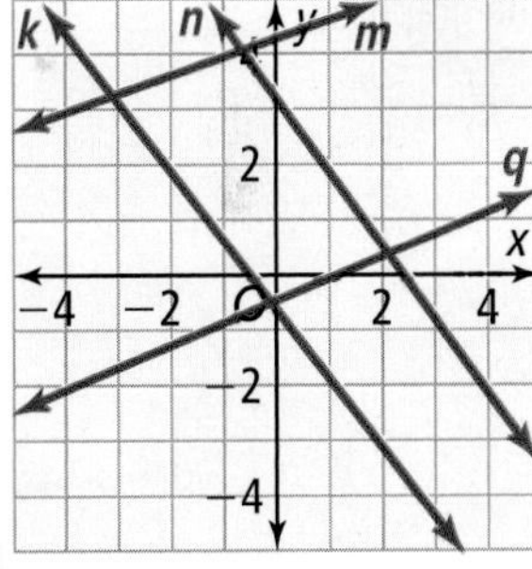


**Step 1** Find the slope of line $k$.

$$m = \frac{-3 - 2}{2 - (-2)} = -\frac{5}{4}$$

Line $k$ passes through (−2, 2) and (2, −3).

**COMMON ERROR**
Be sure that the first numbers in both subtraction expressions are the coordinates of the same point.

**Step 2** Find the slope of line $n$.

$$m = \frac{-2 - 2}{4 - 1} = -\frac{4}{3}$$

Line $n$ passes through (1, 2) and (4, −2).

**Step 3** Compare the slopes.

Parallel lines have equal slope, but $-\frac{5}{4} \neq -\frac{4}{3}$. Thus, lines $k$ and $n$ are not parallel.

 **Try It!** **2.** Are lines $m$ and $q$ parallel?

## THEOREM 2-14

Two non-vertical lines are perpendicular if and only if the product of their slopes is $-1$.

A vertical line and a horizontal line are perpendicular to each other.

PROOF: SEE LESSON 7-4.

**If...** $p$ and $q$ are both not vertical

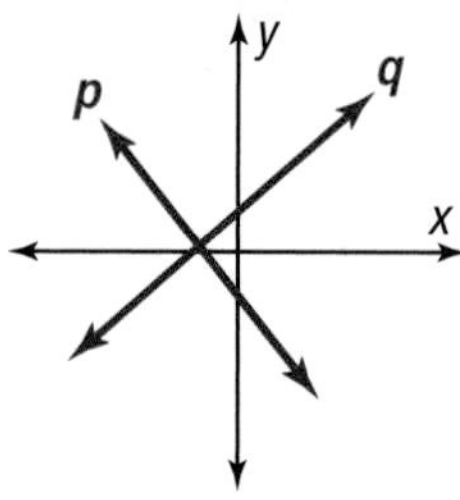


**Then...** $p \perp q$ if and only if the product of their slopes is $-1$

**If...** one of $p$ and $q$ is vertical and the other is horizontal

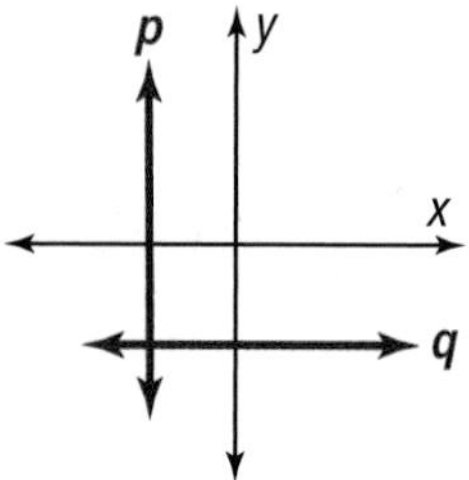


**Then...** $p \perp q$

## EXAMPLE 3 Check Perpendicularity

**STUDY TIP**
Look for two points on each line where you can easily read the coordinates of the points from the graph.

**Are lines $j$ and $k$ perpendicular?**

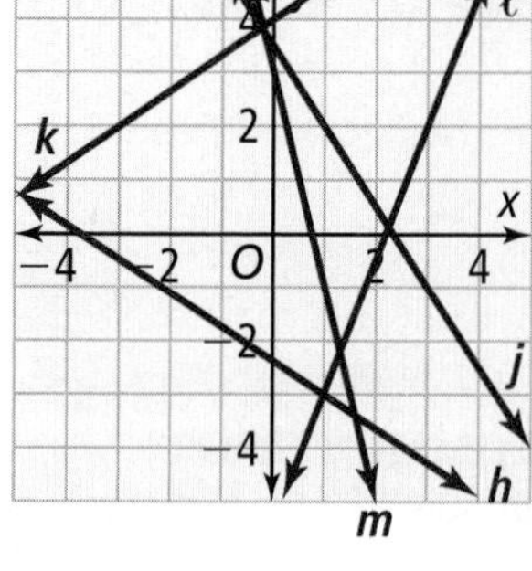


**Step 1** Find the slope of line $j$.

$$m = \frac{2 - 5}{1 - (-1)} = -\frac{3}{2}$$

Line $j$ passes through (−1, 5) and (1, 2).

**Step 2** Find the slope of line $k$.

$$m = \frac{4 - 2}{0 - (-3)} = \frac{2}{3}$$

Line $k$ passes through (−3, 2) and (0, 4).

**Step 3** Compare the slopes.

Perpendicular lines have slopes with a product of $-1$, and $-\frac{3}{2} \cdot \frac{2}{3} = -1$. Thus, lines $j$ and $k$ are perpendicular.

**Try It!** **3. a.** Are lines $h$ and $\ell$ perpendicular?

**b.** Are lines $k$ and $m$ perpendicular?

## EXAMPLE 4 Write Equations of Parallel and Perpendicular Lines

**A. What is an equation of the line through *P* that is parallel to $\ell$?**

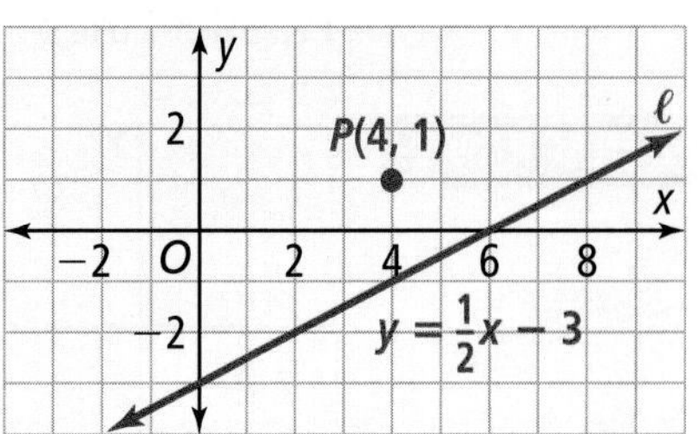


**Step 1** Identify the slope of the parallel line.

The slope of $\ell$ is $\frac{1}{2}$. Parallel lines have equal slope, so the slope of the parallel line is $\frac{1}{2}$.

**Step 2** Solve for the y-intercept of the parallel line.

$y = mx + b$

$1 = \frac{1}{2}(4) + b$ — Use the point (4, 1).

$b = -1$

**Step 3** Write an equation of the line.

$y = \frac{1}{2}x - 1$

The line parallel to $\ell$ passing through *P* is $y = \frac{1}{2}x - 1$.

**GENERALIZE**
If the slope of a line is $\frac{a}{b}$, what is the slope of any line perpendicular to it? How do you know?

**B. What is the equation of the line through *P* that is perpendicular to $\ell$?**

**Step 1** Identify the slope of the perpendicular line.

The slope of $\ell$ is $\frac{1}{2}$. Perpendicular lines have slopes with a product of −1, so the slope of the perpendicular line is −2.

**Step 2** Solve for the y-intercept of the perpendicular line.

$y = mx + b$

$1 = -2(4) + b$ — Use the point (4, 1).

$b = 9$

**Step 3** Write the equation of the line.

$y = -2x + 9$

The line perpendicular to $\ell$ passing through *P* is $y = -2x + 9$.

**Try It!** 4. What are equations of lines parallel and perpendicular to the given line *k* passing through point *T*?

**a.** $y = -3x + 2$; $T(3, 1)$

**b.** $y = \frac{3}{4}x - 5$; $T(12, -2)$

## CONCEPT SUMMARY Slopes of Parallel and Perpendicular Lines

| | Parallel Lines | Perpendicular Lines |
|---|---|---|
| DIAGRAMS | 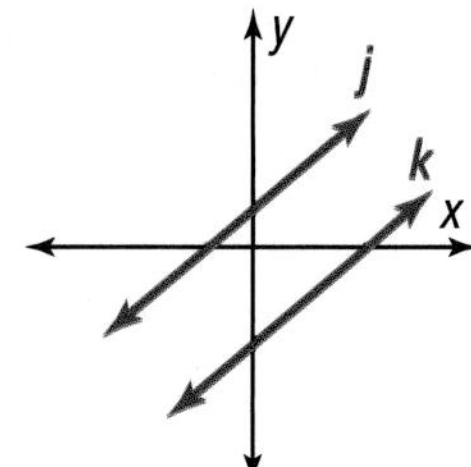 | 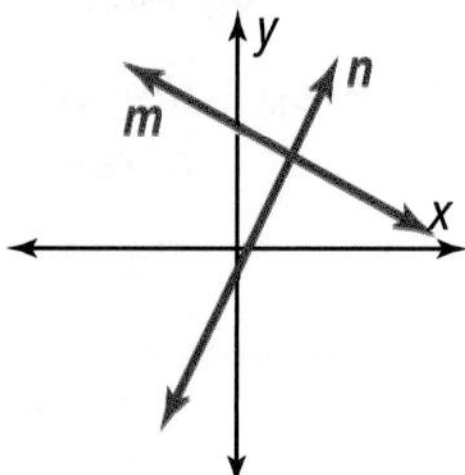 |
| SYMBOLS | $j \parallel k$ if and only if the slopes are the same. | $m \perp n$ if and only if the product of the two slopes is $-1$. |

## Do You UNDERSTAND?

1. ESSENTIAL QUESTION How do the slopes of lines that are parallel to each other compare? How do the slopes of lines that are perpendicular to each other compare?

2. **Error Analysis** Katrina said that the lines $y = -\frac{2}{3}x + 5$ and $y = -\frac{3}{2}x + 2$ are perpendicular. Explain Katrina's error.

3. **Reason** Give an equation for a line perpendicular to the line $y = 0$. Is there more than one such line? Explain.

4. **Communicate Precisely** What are two different if-then statements implied by Theorem 2-13?

5. **Error Analysis** Devin said that $\overleftrightarrow{AB}$ and $\overleftrightarrow{CD}$ for $A(-2, 0)$, $B(2, 3)$, $C(1, -1)$, and $D(5, -4)$ are parallel. Explain and correct Devin's error.

slope of $\overleftrightarrow{AB}$: $\frac{3-0}{2-(-2)} = \frac{3}{4}$

slope of $\overleftrightarrow{CD}$: $\frac{-1-(-4)}{5-1} = \frac{3}{4}$

slopes are equal, so $\overleftrightarrow{AB} \parallel \overleftrightarrow{CD}$ 

## Do You KNOW HOW?

**Use the diagram for Exercises 6–9.**

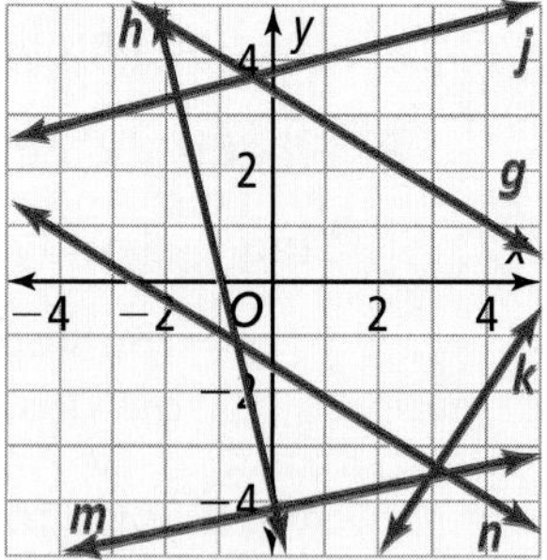


6. Are lines $g$ and $n$ parallel?

7. Are lines $j$ and $m$ parallel?

8. Are lines $n$ and $k$ perpendicular?

9. Are lines $h$ and $j$ perpendicular?

10. What is an equation for the line parallel to $y = -x + 7$ that passes through $(7, -2)$?

11. What is an equation for the line perpendicular to $y = 3x - 1$ that passes through $(-9, -2)$?

12. The graph of a roller coaster track goes in a straight line through coordinates (10, 54) and (42, 48), with coordinates in feet. A support beam runs parallel 12 feet below the track. What equation describes the support beam?

## UNDERSTAND

13. **Look for Relationships** What are the equations of lines *m* and *q*?

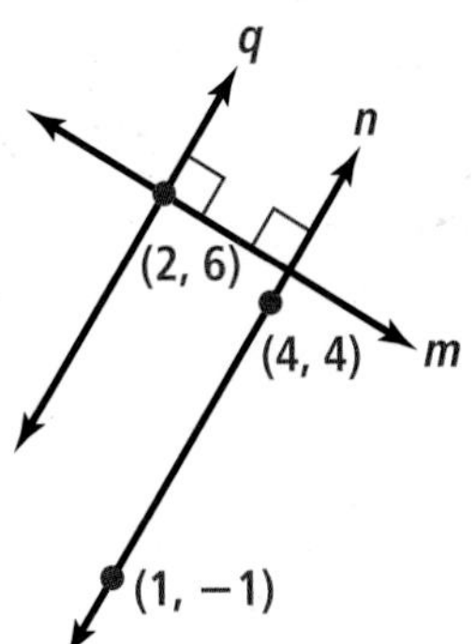


14. **Reason** Why can you not say that two vertical lines have equal slope? Why can you not say that the product of the slopes of a vertical and horizontal line is −1?

15. **Higher Order Thinking** Lines *k* and *n* intersect on the *y*-axis.

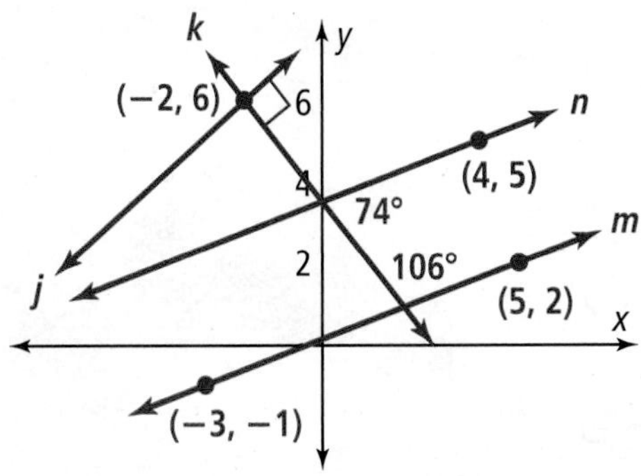


a. What is the equation of line *k* in slope-intercept form?

b. What is the equation of line *j* in slope-intercept form?

16. **Construct Arguments** Line *m* passes through points *X* and *Y*. Line *n* passes through points *X* and *Z*. If *m* and *n* have equal slope, what can you conclude about points *X*, *Y*, and *Z*? Explain.

17. **Error Analysis** Shannon says that the lines $y = -3x - 4$, $y = -\frac{1}{3}x + 6$, $y = -4x - 5$, and $y = \frac{1}{4}x - 5$ could represent the sides of a rectangle. Explain Shannon's error.

## PRACTICE

**Compare the slopes of the lines for $y = f(x)$ and $y = g(x)$ to determine if each pair of lines is parallel.**
SEE EXAMPLE 1

18.

| x | f(x) | g(x) |
|---|---|---|
| 0 | 20 | 22 |
| 1 | 35 | 37 |
| 2 | 50 | 52 |
| 3 | 65 | 67 |

19.

| x | f(x) | g(x) |
|---|---|---|
| 0 | 5 | 10 |
| 1 | 7 | 15 |
| 2 | 9 | 20 |
| 3 | 11 | 25 |

**Determine if each pair of lines is parallel.**
SEE EXAMPLE 2

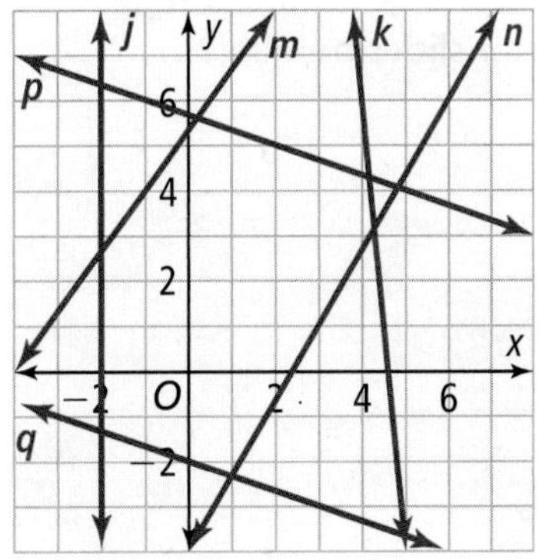


20. *j* and *k* 21. *m* and *n* 22. *p* and *q*

**Determine if each pair of lines is perpendicular.**
SEE EXAMPLE 3

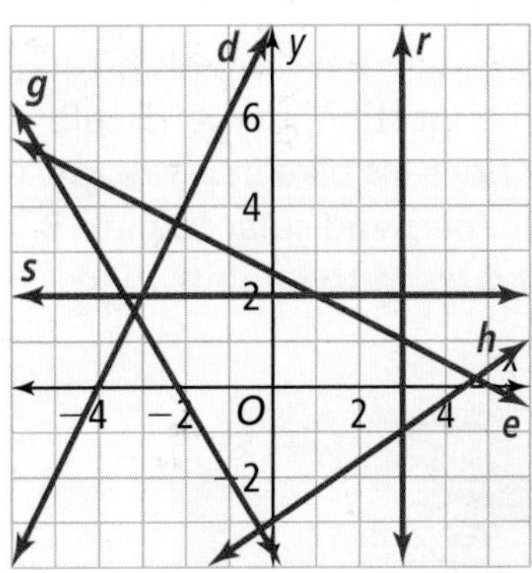


23. *d* and *e* 24. *g* and *h* 25. *r* and *s*

**Write the equations for the lines parallel and perpendicular to the given line *j* that passes through *Q*.** SEE EXAMPLE 4

26. $y = -4x + 1$; $Q(6, -1)$

27. $y = \frac{3}{2}x + 4$; $Q(-1, 1)$

# PRACTICE & PROBLEM SOLVING

## APPLY

**28. Model With Mathematics** The table shows locations of several sites at a high school campus. A landscaper wants to connect two sites with a path perpendicular to the path connecting the cafeteria and the library. Which two sites should he connect?

| Locations | |
|---|---|
| Cafeteria (5, 5) | Library (11, 14) |
| Office (4, 12) | Gym (15, 8) |
| Woodshop (11, 6) | Art Studio (3, 16) |

**29. Make Sense and Persevere** Are the steepest parts of the two water slides parallel? Explain.

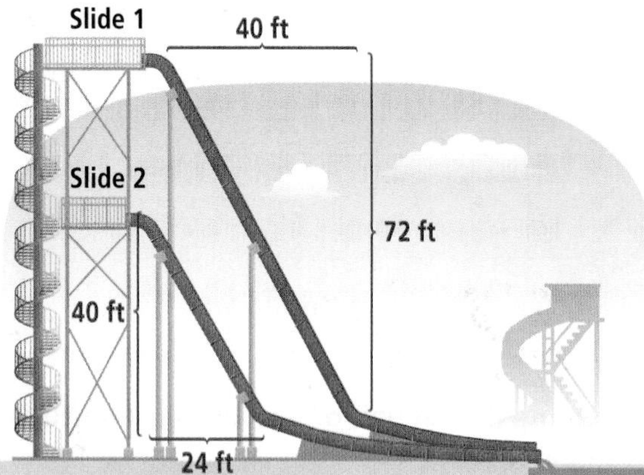


**30. Mathematical Connections** Teo rides his bike in a straight line from his location, perpendicular to path A, and Luke rides his bike in a straight line from his location, perpendicular to path B. What are the coordinates of the point where they meet?

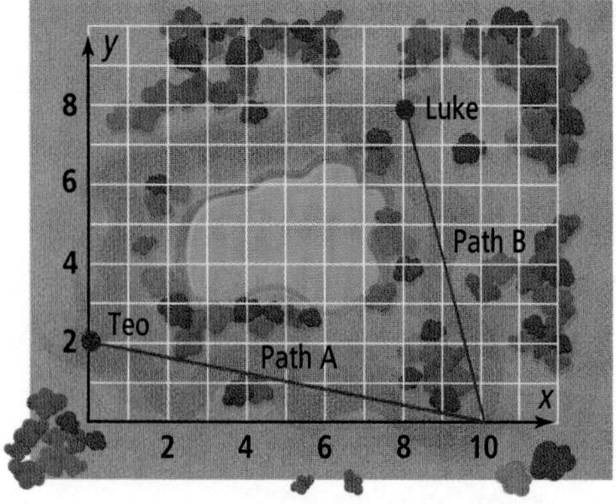


## ASSESSMENT PRACTICE

**31.** $\overleftrightarrow{AB} \perp \overleftrightarrow{BC}$ for $A(-3, 2)$ and $C(2, 7)$. Which of the following could be the coordinates of $B$? Select all that apply.

Ⓐ (8, 0)
Ⓑ (−2, 2)
Ⓒ (−4, 5)
Ⓓ (1, 3)
Ⓔ (−1, −1)
Ⓕ (−3, 7)

**32. SAT/ACT** Line $k$ passes through (2, −3) and (8, 1). Which equation represents a line that is parallel to $k$?

Ⓐ $y = -\frac{2}{3}x - \frac{5}{3}$
Ⓑ $y = \frac{2}{3}x - \frac{13}{3}$
Ⓒ $y = \frac{3}{2}x - 6$
Ⓓ $y = -\frac{3}{2}x$

**33. Performance Task** A knight travels in a straight line from the starting point to Token 1. The knight can only make right-angle turns to get to Tokens 2 and 3.

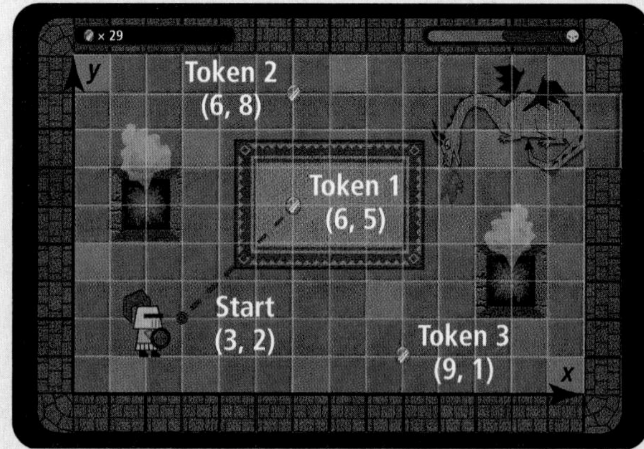


**Part A** Since the knight can only make right-angle turns, what are the slopes of the straight line paths the knight can travel?

**Part B** What equations describe a path that the knight can follow from the starting point to reach the tokens for the arrangement shown?

**Part C** What is the fewest number of turns that the knight can take in order to get all three tokens?

MATHEMATICAL MODELING IN 3 ACTS

PearsonRealize.com

Video

# Parallel Paving Company

Building roads consists of many different tasks. Once civil engineers have designed the road, they work with surveyors and construction crews to clear and level the land. Sometimes specialists have to blast away rock in order to clear the land. Once the land is leveled, the crews bring in asphalt pavers to smooth out the hot asphalt.

Sometimes construction crews will start work at both ends of the new road and meet in the middle. Think about this during the Mathematical Modeling in 3 Acts lesson.

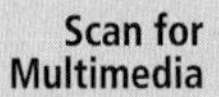

Scan for Multimedia

## ACT 1 Identify the Problem

1. What is the first question that comes to mind after watching the video?
2. Write down the main question you will answer about what you saw in the video.
3. Make an initial conjecture that answers this main question.
4. Explain how you arrived at your conjecture.
5. What information will be useful to know to answer the main question? How can you get it? How will you use that information?

## ACT 2 Develop a Model

6. Use the math that you have learned in this Topic to refine your conjecture.

## ACT 3 Interpret the Results

7. Did your refined conjecture match the actual answer exactly? If not, what might explain the difference?

TOPIC 2

# Topic Review

**TOPIC ESSENTIAL QUESTION**

1. What properties are specific to parallel lines and perpendicular lines?

## Vocabulary Review

**Choose the correct term to complete each sentence.**

2. Angles that are outside the space between parallel lines and that lie on the same side of a transversal are ________.
3. A ________ intersects coplanar lines at distinct points.
4. Two angles inside a triangle that correspond to the nonadjacent exterior angle are the ________.
5. ________ lie on the same side of a transversal of parallel lines and are in corresponding positions relative to the parallel lines.
6. Angles between parallel lines that are nonadjacent and that lie on opposite sides of a transversal are ________.
7. Angles between parallel lines that are on the same side of a transversal are ________.

- alternate exterior angles
- alternate interior angles
- corresponding angles
- exterior angle of a triangle
- remote interior angles
- same-side exterior angles
- same-side interior angles
- transversal

## Concepts & Skills Review

**LESSONS 2-1 & 2-2** Parallel Lines and Proving Lines Parallel

### Quick Review

When two **parallel lines** are intersected by a **transversal**, the angle pairs that are formed have special relationships. These angle pairs are either congruent or supplementary angles.

### Example

**Which angles are supplementary to $\angle 3$?**

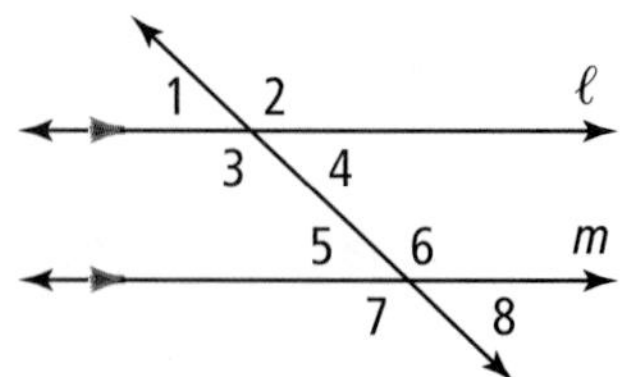


$\angle 1$, $\angle 4$, $\angle 5$, $\angle 8$

### Practice & Problem Solving

**Use the figure for Exercises 8–10.**

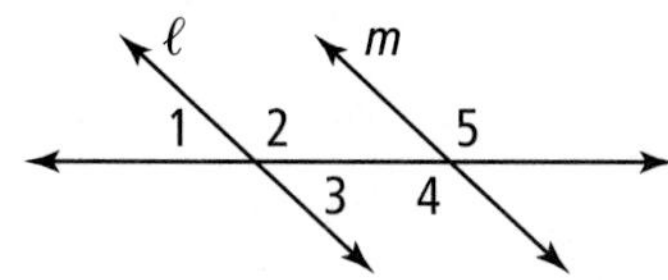


8. Suppose $\ell \parallel m$. What is the measure of each angle if $m\angle 2 = 138$?

   **a.** $m\angle 1$ **b.** $m\angle 3$ **c.** $m\angle 4$

9. If $m\angle 1 = 3x - 3$ and $m\angle 5 = 7x + 23$, for what value of $x$ is $\ell \parallel m$?

10. **Reason** The transversal that intersects two parallel lines forms corresponding angles with measures $m\angle 1 = 3x - 7$ and $m\angle 2 = 2x + 12$. What is the measure of each angle?

## LESSON 2-3 Parallel Lines and Triangle Angle Sums

### Quick Review

The interior and exterior angle measures of a triangle have the following properties.

- The sum of the interior angles of every triangle is 180°.
- The measure of each **exterior angle of a triangle** equals the sum of the measures of the two corresponding **remote interior angles.**

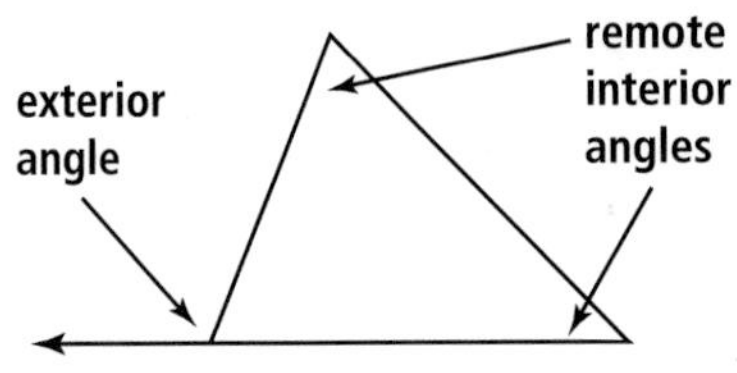


### Example

**What is $m\angle 1$?**

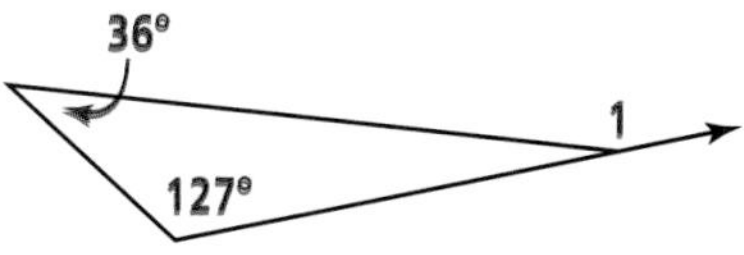


$m\angle 1 = 36 + 127$

$m\angle 1 = 163$

### Practice & Problem Solving

**What is the value of $x$ in each figure?**

11.

12.

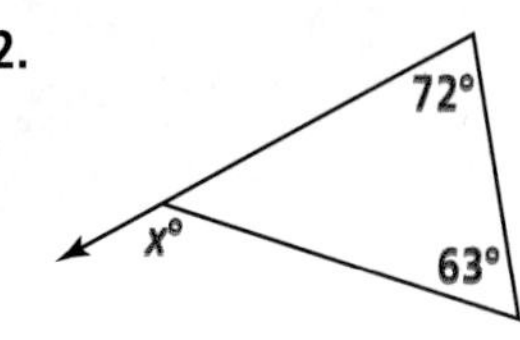


13.

14.

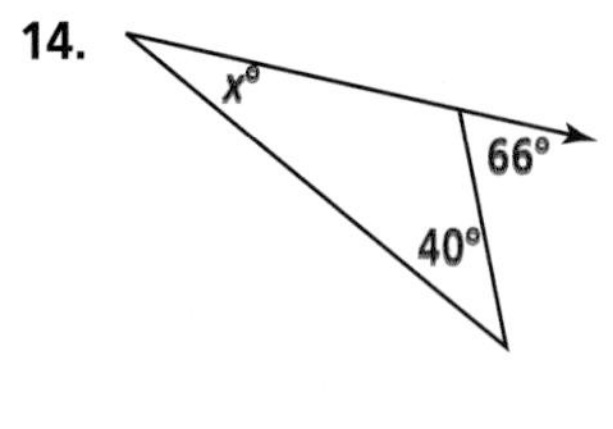


15. **Make Sense and Persevere** During a storm, a tree is blown against a building so that it forms a triangle with remote interior angles of 90° and 52°. What is the measure of the corresponding exterior angle formed by the leaning tree?



## LESSON 2-4 Slopes of Parallel and Perpendicular Lines

### Quick Review

Two non-vertical lines are parallel if they have the same slope. Two vertical lines are parallel to each other.

Two non-vertical lines are perpendicular if the product of the slopes is −1. A vertical line is perpendicular to a horizontal line.

### Example

**What is the equation of a line that is parallel to the line $y = 3x - 9$ and passes through (6, 12)?**

The slope of the line is 3.
Solve for the $y$-intercept of the parallel line:

$$y = mx + b$$
$$12 = (3)(6) + b$$
$$b = -6$$

The equation of the parallel line is $y = 3x - 6$.

### Practice & Problem Solving

**Use the figure for Exercises 16–17. Show the calculations you use to answer each question.**

16. Are lines $p$ and $q$ parallel?

17. Are lines $w$ and $t$ perpendicular?

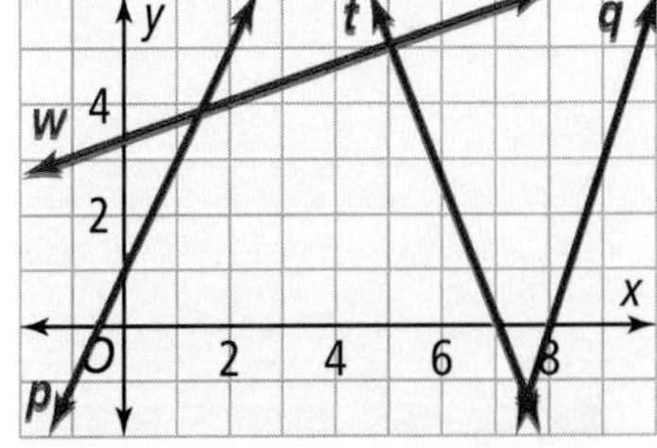


18. **Reason** Theorem 2-4 states that two non-vertical lines are perpendicular if and only if the product of their slopes is −1. Why are vertical lines excluded?

19. **Use Structure** Write an equation for each line that passes through (2, 7) and is parallel or perpendicular to the line $y = -3x - 6$.

TOPIC 3

# Transformations

TOPIC ESSENTIAL QUESTION

**What are properties of the four types of rigid motion?**

## Topic Overview

**enVision™ STEM Project**
Create an Animation

**3-1** Reflections

**3-2** Translations

**3-3** Rotations

**3-4** Classification of Rigid Motions

**3-5** Symmetry

**Mathematical Modeling in 3 Acts:**
The Perplexing Polygon

## Topic Vocabulary

- composition of rigid motions
- glide reflection
- point symmetry
- reflectional symmetry
- rigid motion
- rotational symmetry

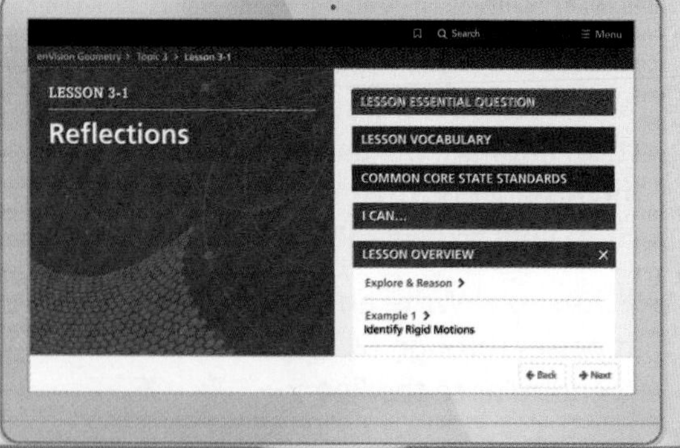

Go online | **PearsonRealize.com**

## Digital Experience

**INTERACTIVE STUDENT EDITION** Access online or offline.

**ACTIVITIES** Complete ***Explore & Reason, Model & Discuss***, and ***Critique & Explain*** activities. Interact with Examples and Try Its.

**ANIMATION** View and interact with real-world applications.

**PRACTICE** Practice what you've learned.

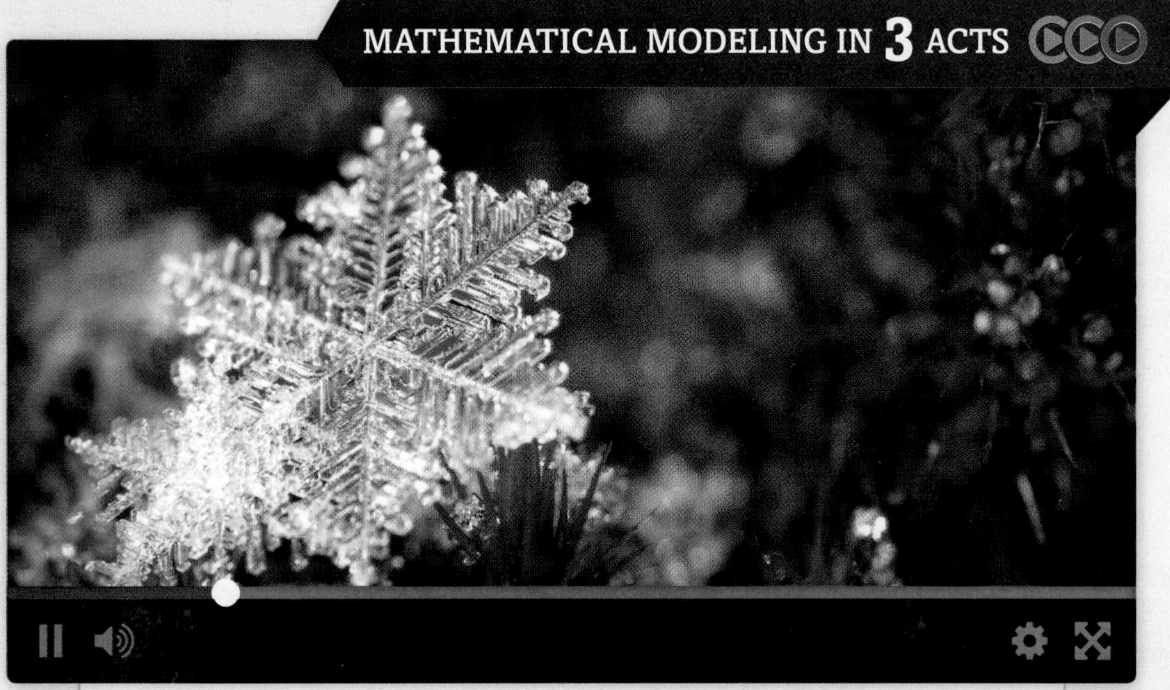


## The Perplexing Polygon

Look around and you will see shapes and patterns everywhere you look. The tiles on a floor are often all the same shape and fit together to form a pattern. The petals on a flower often make a repeating pattern around the center of the flower. When you look at snowflakes under a microscope, you can notice that they are made up of repeating three-dimensional crystals. Think about the patterns you have seen during the Mathematical Modeling in 3 Acts lesson.



**VIDEOS** Watch clips to support ***Mathematical Modeling in 3 Acts Lessons*** and **enVision™ *STEM Projects.***

**CONCEPT SUMMARY** Review key lesson content through multiple representations.

**ASSESSMENT** Show what you've learned.

**GLOSSARY** Read and listen to English and Spanish definitions.

**TUTORIALS** Get help from ***Virtual Nerd***, right when you need it.

**MATH TOOLS** Explore math with digital tools and manipulatives.

## Did You Know?

**Polygonal modeling** uses polygons to model the surfaces of three-dimensional objects. Animators use vertices and edges to define polygons (usually triangles or quadrilaterals), and they use multiple polygons to create more complex shapes.

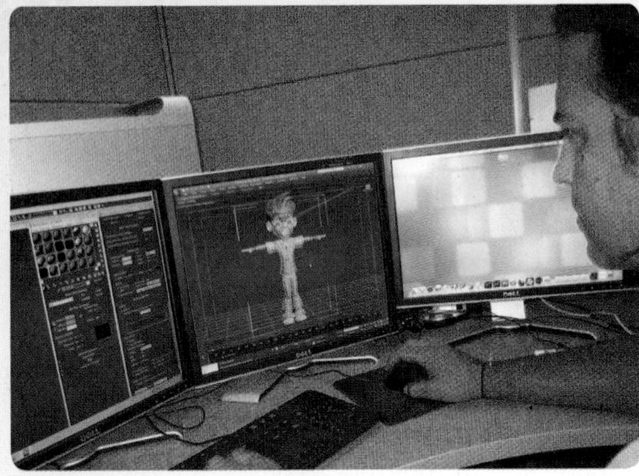

The phenakistoscope was invented nearly **200 years ago.** When the viewer looks through a slot, a sequence of images appears to show moving figures.

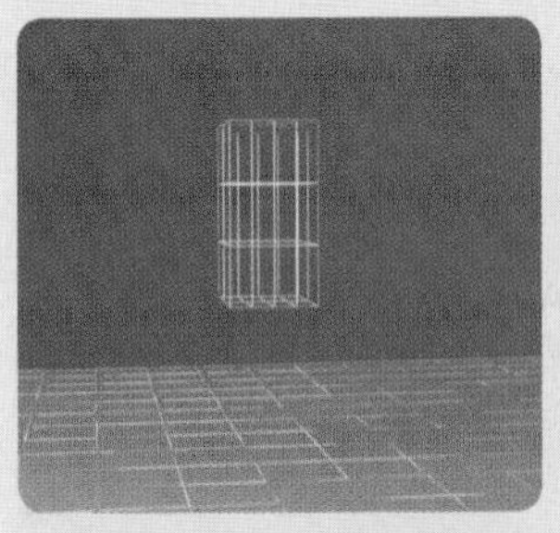
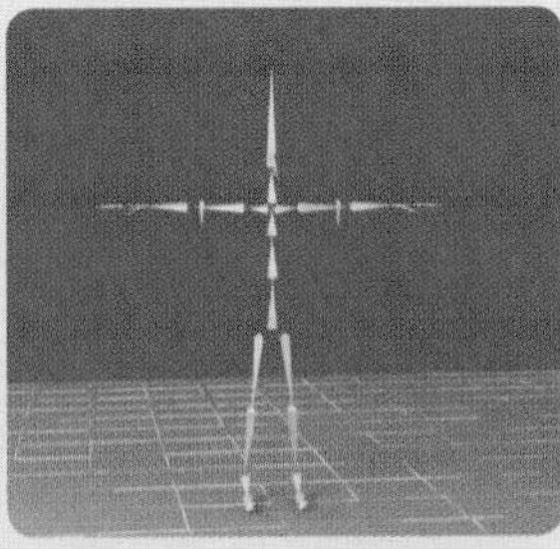
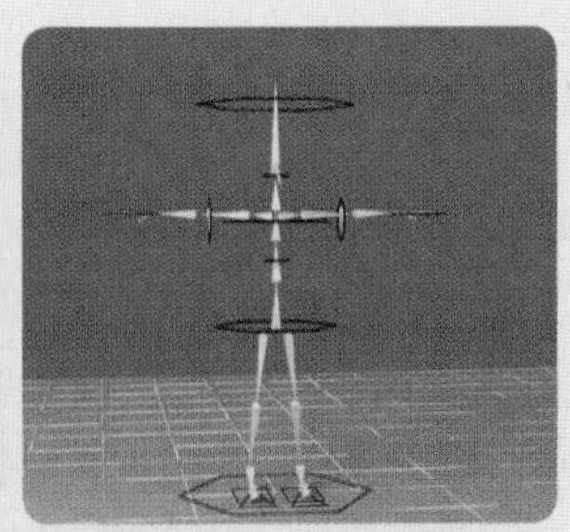

An animated character represents hundreds of hours of work. An animator builds a *mesh* of polygons connected through shared vertices and edges. A rigger links the mesh to a system of joints and control handles. To represent a curved surface in a realistic way, the animator uses a mesh of many small polygons. Then the animator programs the joints and handles so that the character moves realistically. Finally, an artist provides surface texture and shading.

## Your Task: Create an Animation

Starting with the pixels (points) of a simple geometric figure, you and your classmates will use translations and reflections to move the figure through a series of frames.

# 3-1 Reflections

PearsonRealize.com

**I CAN…** draw and describe the reflection of a figure across a line of reflection.

**VOCABULARY**

- rigid motion

## EXPLORE & REASON

**The illustration shows irregular pentagon-shaped tiles covering a floor.**

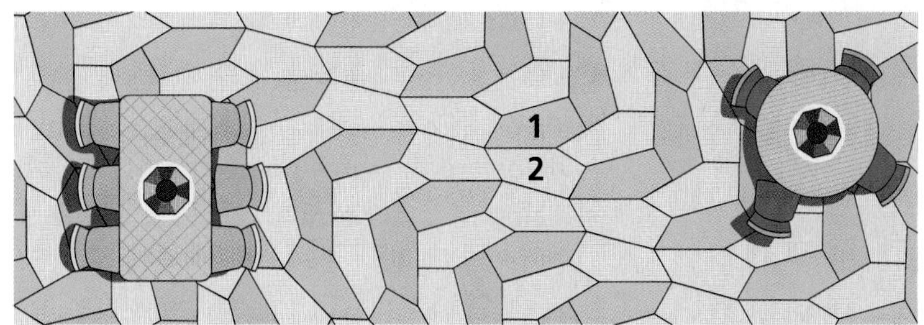


**A.** Which tiles are copies of tile 1. Explain.

**B. Communicate Precisely** If you were to move tile 1 from the design, what actions would you have to do so it completely covers tile 2?

**C.** Which tiles are *not* copies of tile 1? Explain.

## ESSENTIAL QUESTION

**How are the properties of reflection used to transform a figure?**

## EXAMPLE 1 Identify Rigid Motions

**A rigid motion is a transformation that preserves length and angle measure. Is the transformation a rigid motion? Explain.**

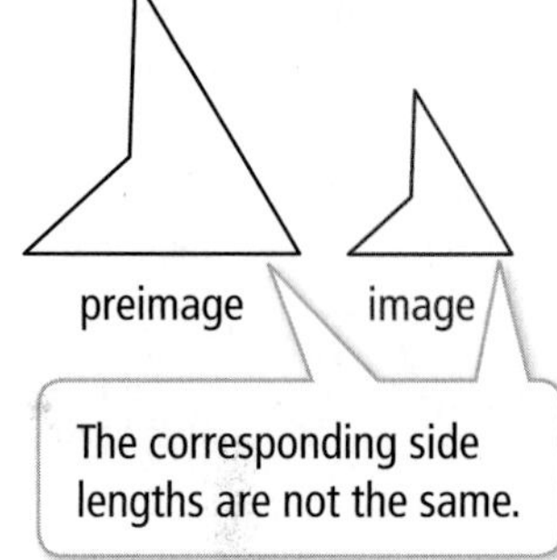


Although angle measure is preserved, the image is smaller than the preimage, so the transformation involves a change in length.

The transformation is not a rigid motion because the length is not preserved.

**STUDY TIP**

Recall that a transformation is a function that maps a given figure called the preimage onto the resulting figure, the image.

## Try It!

**1.** Is each transformation a rigid motion? Explain.

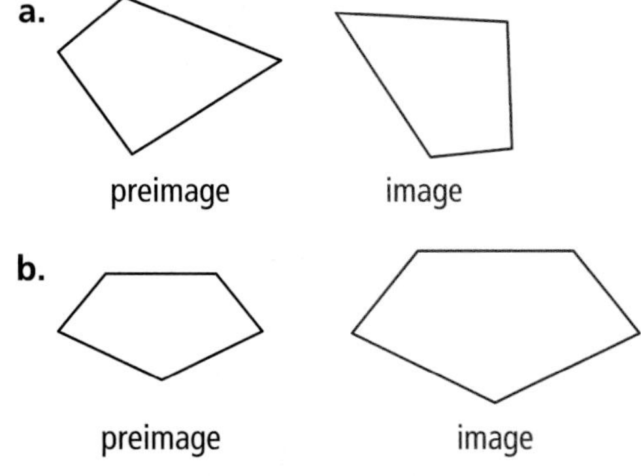

## CONCEPT Reflections

A reflection is a transformation that reflects each point in the preimage across a line of reflection.

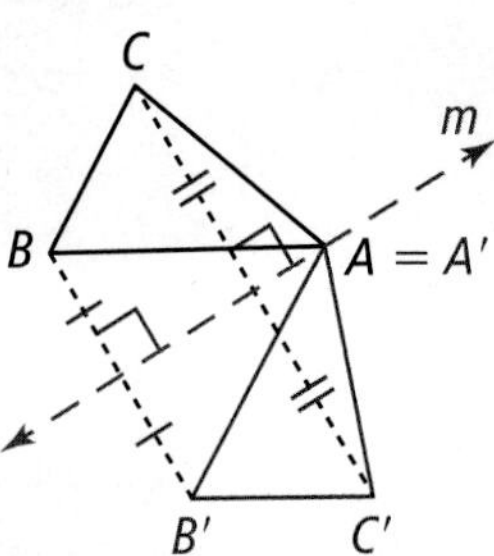


A reflection has these properties:

- If a point $A$ is on line $m$, then the point and its image are the same point (that is, $A' = A$).
- If a point $B$ is not on line $m$, line $m$ is the perpendicular bisector of $\overline{BB'}$.

The reflection of $\triangle ABC$ across line $m$ can be written as $R_m(\triangle ABC) = \triangle A'B'C'$.

A reflection is a rigid motion so length and angle measures are preserved.

CONCEPTUAL UNDERSTANDING

## EXAMPLE 2 Reflect a Figure Across a Line

**How can you reflect $\triangle FGH$ across line $\ell$?**

Use the properties of reflections to draw the image of $\triangle FGH$.

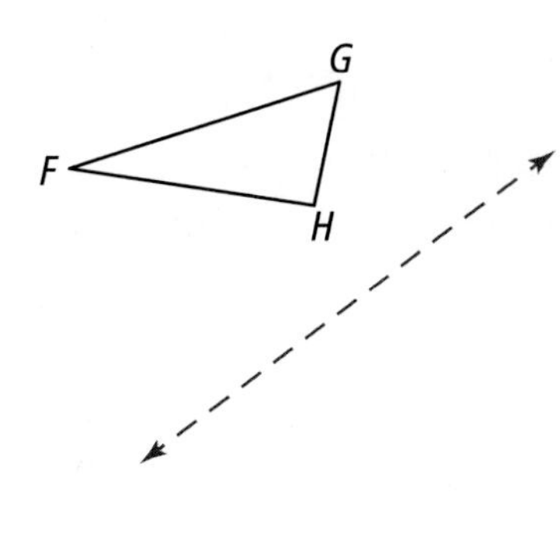


**MAKE SENSE AND PERSEVERE** For any point not on the line of reflection, the line of reflection is the perpendicular bisector of the segment between corresponding preimage and image points.

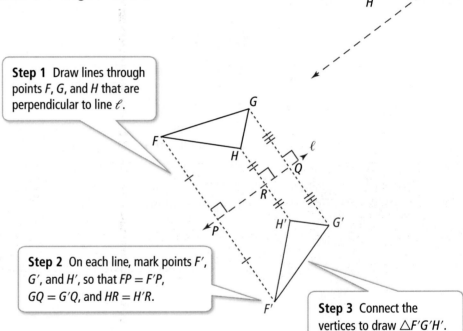

**Step 1** Draw lines through points $F$, $G$, and $H$ that are perpendicular to line $\ell$.

**Step 2** On each line, mark points $F'$, $G'$, and $H'$, so that $FP = F'P$, $GQ = G'Q$, and $HR = H'R$.

**Step 3** Connect the vertices to draw $\triangle F'G'H'$.

**Try It!** 2. What is the reflection of $\triangle LMN$ across line $n$?

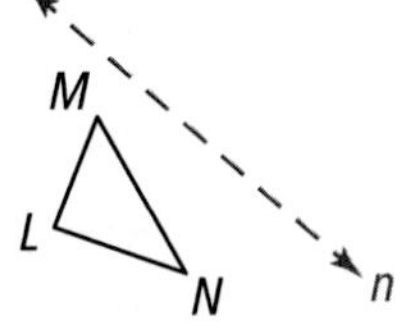

  Activity  Assess

## EXAMPLE 3 Reflect a Figure on a Coordinate Plane

**Quadrilateral *FGHJ* has coordinates *F*(0, 3), *G*(2, 4), *H*(4, 2), and *J*(−2, 0).**

**A. Graph and label *FGHJ* and $R_{x\text{-axis}}(FGHJ)$. What is a general rule for reflecting a point across the *x*-axis?**

**Step 1** Graph *FGHJ*.

**Step 2** Find *F′*, *G′*, *H′*, and *J′* and draw *F′G′H′J′*.

$R_{x\text{-axis}}(0, 3) = (0, -3)$

$R_{x\text{-axis}}(2, 4) = (2, -4)$

$R_{x\text{-axis}}(4, 2) = (4, -2)$

$R_{x\text{-axis}}(-2, 0) = (-2, 0)$

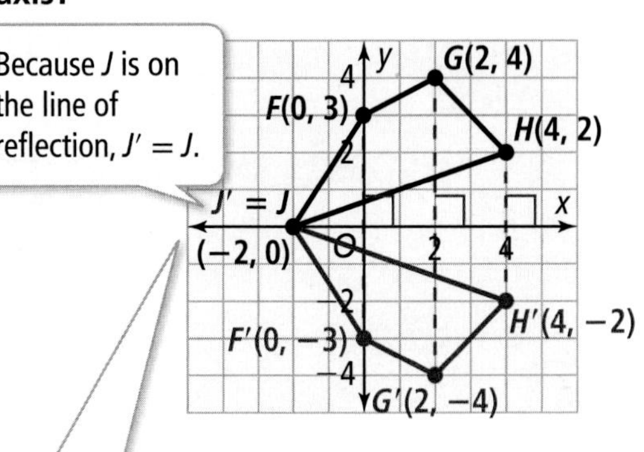


The reflection of any point (*x*, *y*) across the *x*-axis is the point (*x*, −*y*).

$R_{x\text{-axis}}(x, y) = (x, -y)$

**B. Graph and label *FGHJ* and $R_{y\text{-axis}}(FGHJ)$. What is a general rule for reflecting a point across the *y*-axis?**

**Step 1** Graph *FGHJ*.

**Step 2** Find *F′*, *G′*, *H′*, and *J′* and draw *F′G′H′J′*.

$R_{y\text{-axis}}(0, 3) = (0, 3)$

$R_{y\text{-axis}}(2, 4) = (-2, 4)$

$R_{y\text{-axis}}(4, 2) = (-4, 2)$

$R_{x\text{-axis}}(-2, 0) = (2, 0)$

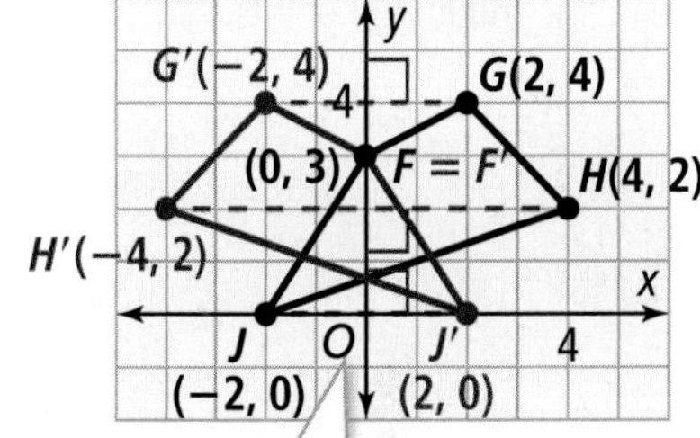


The reflection of any point (*x*, *y*) across the *y*-axis is the point (−*x*, *y*).

$R_{y\text{-axis}}(x, y) = (-x, y)$

**COMMON ERROR**
Remember, when the *y*-axis is the line of reflection, the image points must have the same distances from the *x*-axis and on a line perpendicular to the *y*-axis, so the *y*-coordinate stays the same and the *x*-coordinate is the opposite.

 **Try It!** 3. Triangle *ABC* has vertices *A*(−5, 6), *B*(1, −2), and *C*(−3, −4). What are the coordinates of the vertices of △*A′B′C′* for each reflection?

a. $R_{x\text{-axis}}$

b. $R_{y\text{-axis}}$

## CONCEPT Reflecting Points Across the $x$–axis and $y$-axis

When any point $P(x, y)$ on the coordinate plane is reflected across the $x$-axis, its image is $P'(x, -y)$.

When any point $P(x, y)$ on the coordinate plane is reflected across the $y$-axis, its image is $P'(-x, y)$.

## EXAMPLE 4 Describe a Reflection on the Coordinate Plane

**What reflection maps $\triangle KLM$ to its image?**

**Step 1** Write the coordinates of the preimage and the image.

$K(-3, 5)$ $L(1, 3)$ $M(-5, 1)$

$K'(5, -3)$ $L'(3, 1)$ $M'(1, -5)$

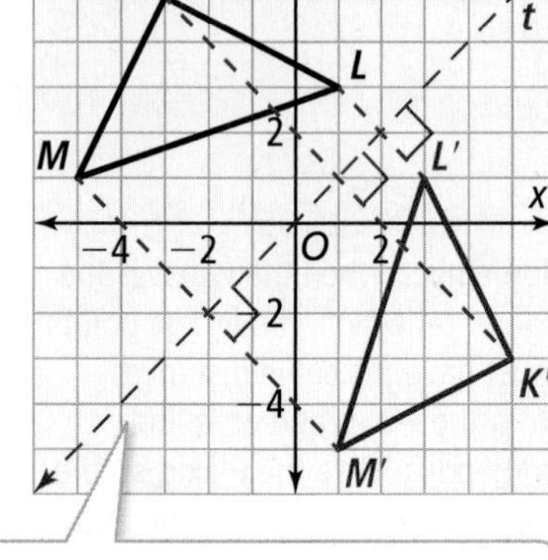


The line of reflection is the perpendicular bisector of the segments that connect corresponding vertices of the preimage and image.

**Step 2** Find the midpoints of the segments connecting two pairs of corresponding points.

Midpoint of $\overline{KK'}$:

$$\left(\frac{-3+5}{2}, \frac{5+(-3)}{2}\right) = (1, 1)$$

Midpoint of $\overline{MM'}$:

$$\left(\frac{-5+1}{2}, \frac{1+(-5)}{2}\right) = (-2, -2)$$

**STUDY TIP**
When providing a rule, you must clearly define the line of reflection. Be certain that the line of reflection is the perpendicular bisector of segments between preimage and image points.

**Step 3** Write the equation of the line through the midpoints.

Find the slope.

$$m = \frac{1-(-2)}{1-(-2)}$$
$$= 1$$

Use point slope form.

$$y - 1 = 1 \bullet (x - 1)$$
$$y = x$$

The transformation is a reflection across the line $y = x$.

**Try It!** **4.** What is a reflection rule that maps each triangle to its image?

**a.** $C(3, 8)$, $D(5, 12)$, $E(4, 6)$ and $C'(-8, -3)$, $D'(-12, -5)$, $E'(-6, -4)$

**b.** $F(7, 6)$, $G(0, -4)$, $H(-5, 0)$ and $F'(-5, 6)$, $G'(2, -4)$, $H'(7, 0)$

APPLICATION

## EXAMPLE 5 Use Reflections

**In a billiards game, a player must hit the white cue ball so that the cue ball hits the red ball without touching the yellow ball. Where should the cue ball bounce off the top rail so that it hits the red ball?**

Consider the top rail as a line of reflection and find the reflection of the red ball.

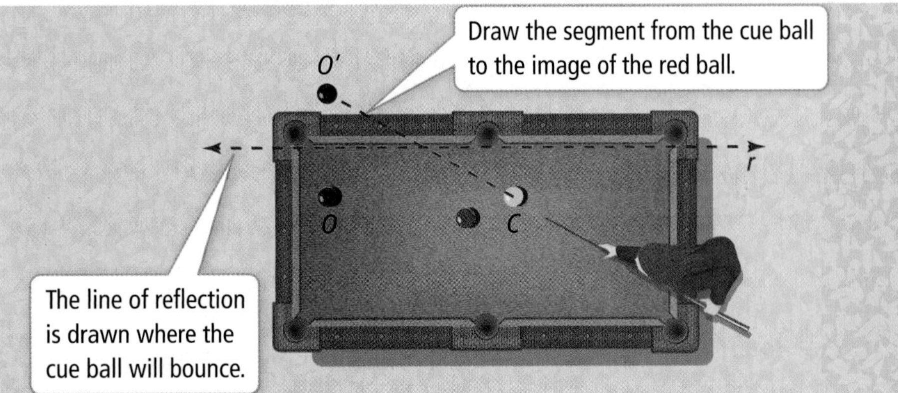
Draw the segment from the cue ball to the image of the red ball.
O′
r
O
C
The line of reflection is drawn where the cue ball will bounce.

Reflect the segment from the cue ball to the red ball across the line of reflection.

The player should aim at point *P*, where the two segments intersect.

r

P

O

C

**MAKE SENSE AND PERSEVERE** What do you notice about the angles formed by the line of reflection and the path of the cue ball? Which are congruent?

 **Try It!** **5.** Student *A* sees the reflected image across the mirror of another student who appears to be at *B*′. Trace the diagram and show the actual position of Student *B*.

B′

mirror

A

## CONCEPT SUMMARY Reflections

**WORDS** A reflection is a transformation that reflects each point in the preimage across a line of reflection.

**DIAGRAM**

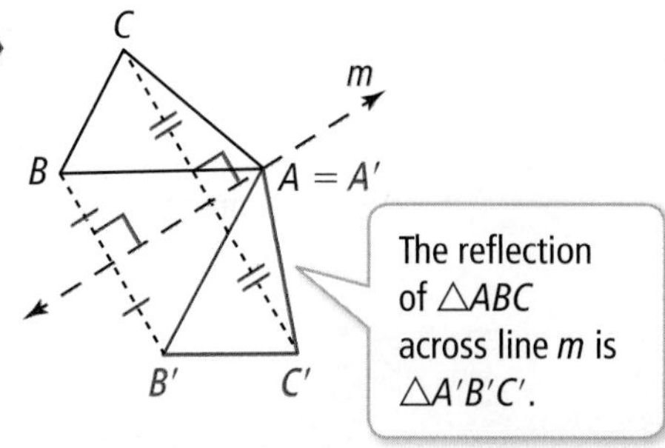


**SYMBOLS** $R_m(\triangle ABC) = \triangle A'B'C'$

$R_m(A) = A'$

Line $m$ is the perpendicular bisector of $\overline{BB'}$ and $\overline{CC'}$.

## Do You UNDERSTAND?

1. **ESSENTIAL QUESTION** How are the properties of reflection used to transform a figure?

2. **Error Analysis** Oscar drew the image of a triangle reflected across the line $y = -1$. What mistake did Oscar make?

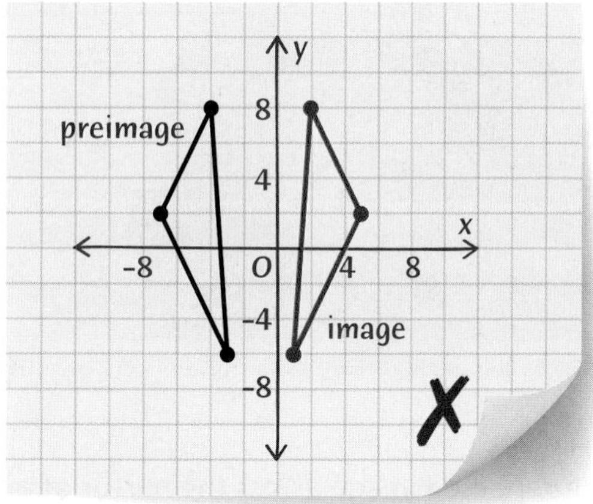


3. **Vocabulary** One meaning of the word *rigid* is "not bendable," and another is "unable to be changed." How do those meanings correspond to the definition of rigid motion?

4. **Communicate Precisely** How can you determine whether the transformation of a figure is a rigid motion?

5. **Generalize** Describe the steps you must take to identify the path an object will follow if it bounces off a surface and strikes another object.

## Do You KNOW HOW?

6. Does the transformation shown appear to be a rigid motion? Explain.

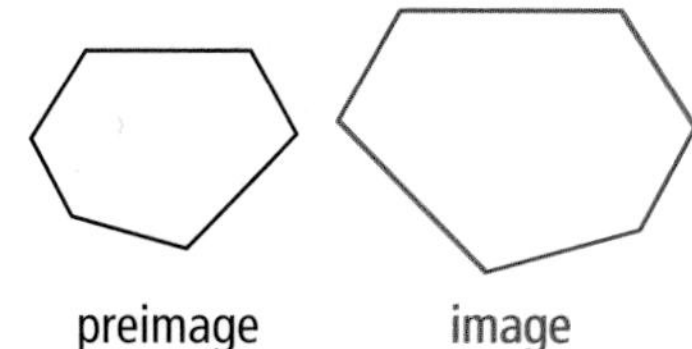


**What are the coordinates of each image?**

7. $R_{x\text{-axis}}(-5, 3)$

8. $R_{x\text{-axis}}(1, 6)$

9. Write a reflection rule that maps each triangle to its image.

   a. $J(1, 0)$, $K(-5, 2)$, $L(4, -4)$ and $J'(-9, 0)$, $K'(-3, 2)$, $L'(-12, -4)$

   b. $P(8, 6)$, $Q(-4, 12)$, $R(7, 7)$ and $P'(8, -20)$, $Q'(-4, -26)$, $R'(7, -21)$

10. Squash is a racket sport like tennis, except that the ball must bounce off a wall between returns. Trace the squash court. At what point on the front wall should player 1 aim in order to reach the rear wall as far from player 2 as possible?

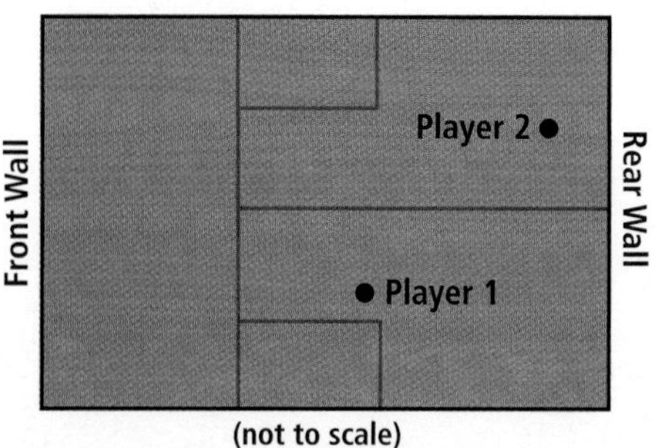

# PRACTICE & PROBLEM SOLVING

## UNDERSTAND

**11. Look for Relationships** Becky draws a triangle with vertices $A(6,7)$, $B(9,3)$, and $C(4, -2)$ on a coordinate grid. She reflects the triangle across the line $y = 4$ to get $\triangle A'B'C'$. She then reflects the image across the line $x = 3$ to get $\triangle A''B''C''$.

**a.** What are the coordinates of $\triangle A'B'C'$ and $\triangle A''B''C''$?

**b.** Write a rule for each reflection.

**12. Use Structure** Under a transformation, a preimage and its image are both squares with side length 3. The image, however, is rotated with respect to the preimage. Is the transformation a rigid motion? Explain.

**13. Error Analysis** Jacob is playing miniature golf. He states that he cannot hit the ball from the start, bounce it off the back wall once, and reach the hole in one shot. Is Jacob correct? Trace and label a diagram to support your answer.

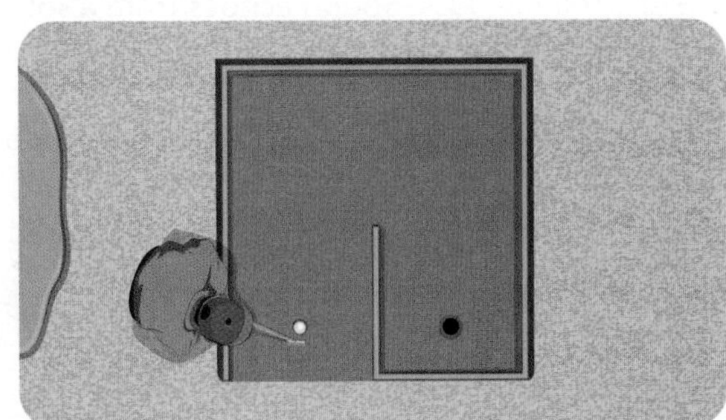

**14. Higher Order Thinking** For the miniature golf hole in Exercise 13, Jacob wants to bounce the ball off the back wall and then the right wall. Draw a diagram to show how Jacob can hit the ball so that it reaches the hole after two bounces.

**15. Mathematical Connection** Dana reflects point $A(2, 5)$ across line $\ell$ to get image point $A'(6, 1)$. What is an equation for line $\ell$?

**16. Look for Structure** Can a figure be reflected across three lines of reflection so the image is the original figure? Explain.

## PRACTICE

**For Exercises 17 and 18, does each transformation appear to be a rigid motion? Explain.** SEE EXAMPLE 1

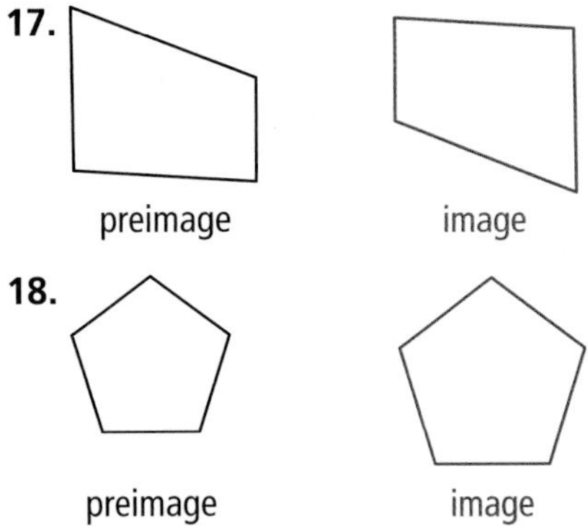


**For Exercises 19–24, suppose $m$ is the line with equation $x = -5$, line $n$ is the line with equation $y = 1$, line $g$ is the line with equation $y = x$, and line $h$ is the line with equation $y = -2$. Given $A(9, -3)$, $B(6, 4)$, and $C(-1, -5)$, what are the coordinates of the vertices of $\triangle A'B'C'$ for each reflection?** SEE EXAMPLES 2 AND 3

**19.** $R_{x\text{-axis}}$

**20.** $R_{y\text{-axis}}$

**21.** $R_m$

**22.** $R_n$

**23.** $R_g$

**24.** $R_h$

**For Exercises 25–28, what is a reflection rule that maps each triangle and its image?** SEE EXAMPLE 4

**25.** $D(3, 6)$, $E(-4, -3)$, $F(6, 1)$ and $D'(1, 6)$, $E'(8, -3)$, $F'(-2, 1)$

**26.** $G(9, 12)$, $H(-2, -15)$, $J(3, 8)$ and $G'(9, -2)$, $H'(-2, 25)$, $J'(3, 2)$

**27.** $K(7, -6)$, $L(9, -3)$, $M(-4, 6)$ and $K'(7, -4)$, $L'(9, -7)$, $M'(-4, -16)$

**28.**

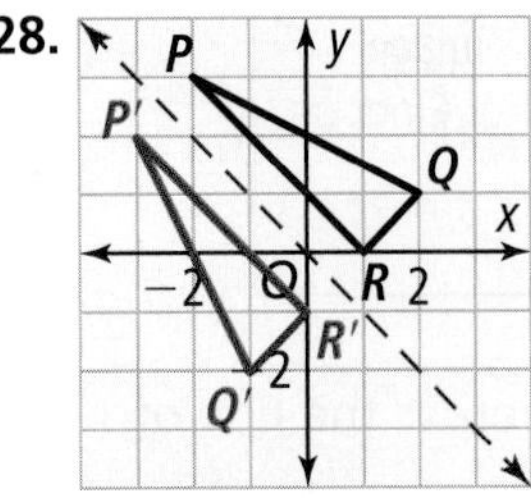


**29.** Trace the diagram below. Where does the shopper in a dressing room see her image in each mirror? SEE EXAMPLE 5

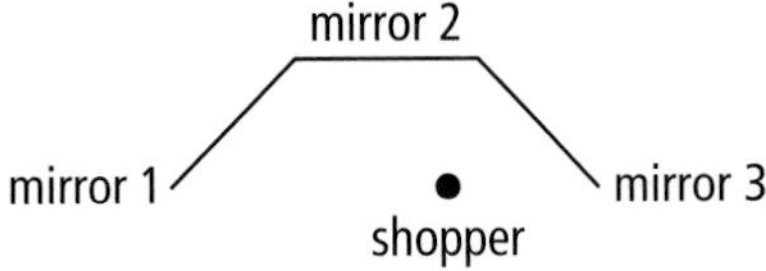

# PRACTICE & PROBLEM SOLVING



## APPLY

30. **Look for Relationships** Which of the numbered stones shown cannot be mapped to another with a rigid motion?

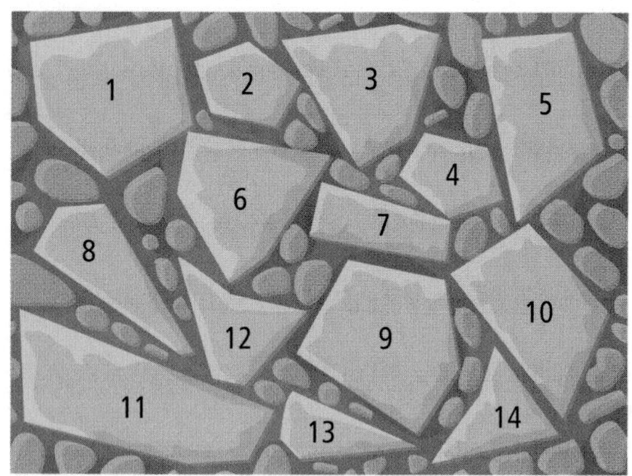


31. **Use Structure** Reese is inside a shop and sees the sign on the window from the back. Draw the letters as they would appear from the outside of the shop. Is the transformation a rigid motion?

32. **Make Sense and Persevere** Look at the floor plan below. Abdul sees the image of a clock in the mirror on the door.

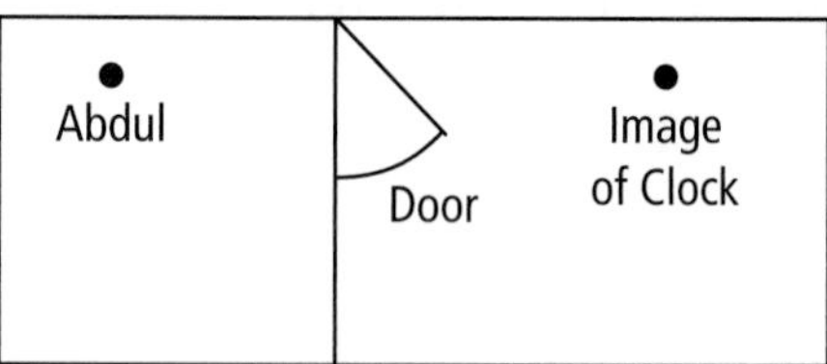


a. Trace the diagram. Where is the line of reflection? Explain.

b. Where is the clock located? Explain.

c. Find where Abdul's image is located relative to the line of reflection. Can Abdul see himself in the mirror? Explain.

## ASSESSMENT PRACTICE

33. Classify whether each pair of figures appears to be a *rigid motion* or *not a rigid motion*.

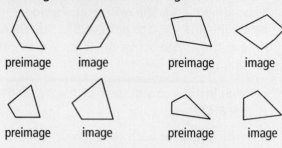

preimage image preimage image

preimage image preimage image

34. **SAT/ACT** Consider the following reflection.
Preimage: $A(3, 9)$, $B(2, -7)$, $C(6, 14)$
Image: $A'(-25, 9)$, $B'(-24, -7)$, $C'(-28, 14)$
Suppose $p$ is the line with equation $x = 11$, $q$ is the line with equation $x = 22$, $r$ is the line with equation $x = -11$, and s is the line with equation $x = -22$. What is the rule for the reflection?

Ⓐ $R_p(x, y)$
Ⓑ $R_q(x, y)$
Ⓒ $R_r(x, y)$
Ⓓ $R_s(x, y)$

35. **Performance Task** Sound echoes from a solid object in the same way that light reflects from a mirror. A hiker at point $A$ shouts the word *hello*. The hiker at point $B$ first hears the shout directly and later hears the echo.

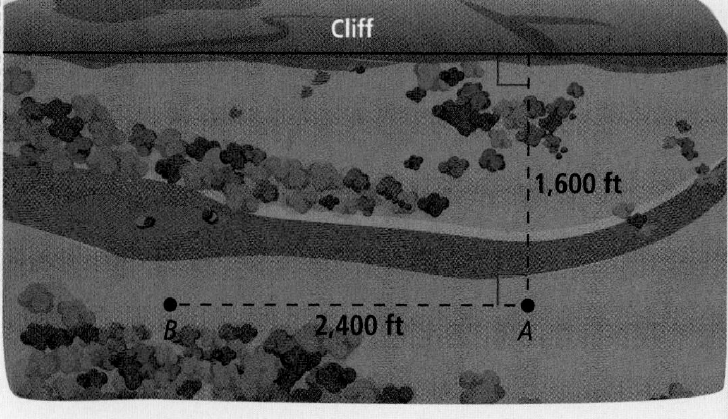


**Part A** Trace the diagram. Show the path taken by the sound the hiker at point $B$ hears echoing from the cliff.

**Part B** Sound travels at about 1,000 feet per second. After how long does the hiker at point $B$ hear the shout directly? After how long does he hear the echo? Show your work.

# 3-2 Translations

PearsonRealize.com

**I CAN…** describe the properties of a figure before and after translation.

**VOCABULARY**

- composition of rigid motions

## EXPLORE & REASON

**Draw a copy of *ABCD* on a grid. Using another color, draw a copy of *ABCD* on the grid in a different location with the same orientation, and label it *QRST*.**

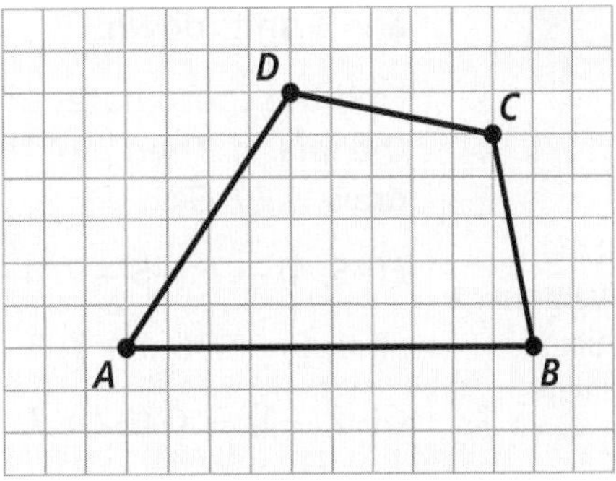


**A.** On another sheet of paper, write instructions that describe how to move *ABCD* to the location of *QRST*.

**B.** Exchange instructions with a partner. Follow your partner's instructions to draw a third shape *EFGH* in another color on the same grid. Compare your drawings. Do your drawings look the same? Explain.

**C. Communicate Precisely** What makes a set of instructions for this Explore & Reason a good set of instructions?

## ESSENTIAL QUESTION

**What are the properties of a translation?**

### CONCEPT Translations

A translation is a transformation in a plane that maps all points of a preimage the same distance and in the same direction.

The translation of $\triangle ABC$ by $x$ units along the $x$-axis and by $y$ units along the $y$-axis can be written as $T_{\langle x, y\rangle}(\triangle ABC) = \triangle A'B'C'$.

A translation has the following properties:

If $T_{\langle x, y\rangle}(\triangle ABC) = \triangle A'B'C'$, then

- $\overline{AA'} \parallel \overline{BB'} \parallel \overline{CC'}$.
- $\overline{AA'} \cong \overline{BB'} \cong \overline{CC'}$.
- $\triangle ABC$ and $\triangle A'B'C'$ have the same orientation.

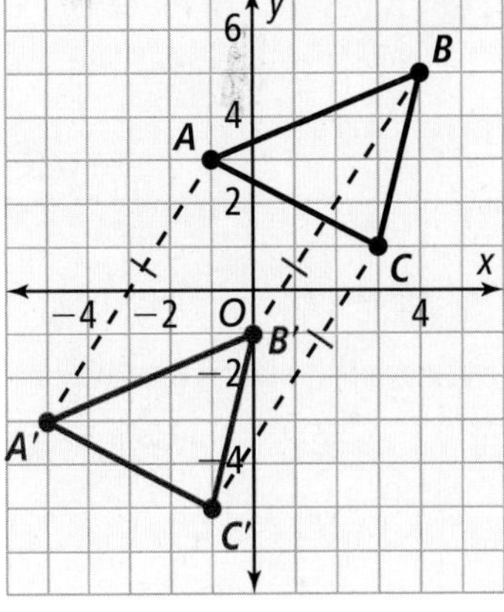


A translation is a rigid motion, so length and angle measure are preserved.

## EXAMPLE 1 Find the Image of a Translation

**What is the graph of $T_{\langle 7, -4 \rangle}(\triangle EFG) = \triangle E'F'G'$?**

The subscript $\langle 7, -4 \rangle$ indicates that each point of $\triangle EFG$ is translated 7 units right and 4 units down.

Find the coordinates of the vertices of the image. Then plot the points and draw $\triangle E'F'G'$.

$E(-5, 4) \rightarrow E'(-5 + 7, 4 - 4) = E'(2, 0)$

$F(-1, 5) \rightarrow F'(-1 + 7, 5 - 4) = F'(6, 1)$

$G(-2, -1) \rightarrow G'(-2 + 7, -1 - 4) = G'(5, -5)$

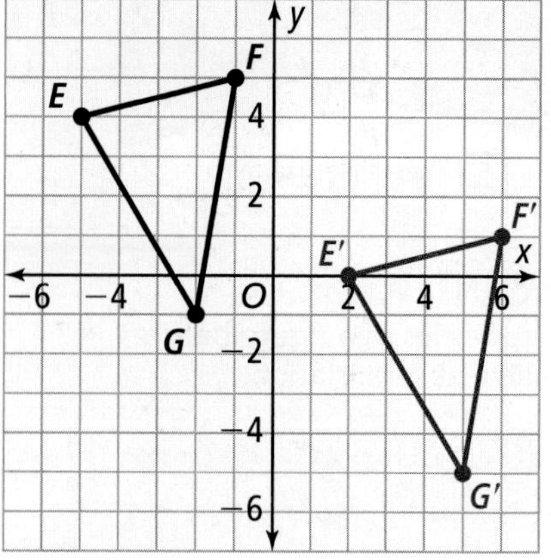


**COMMON ERROR**
Do not misunderstand that the translation only maps the vertices of the preimage to the vertices of the image. The translation maps $\triangle EFG$ onto $\triangle E'F'G'$.

**Try It!** **1.** What are the vertices of $\triangle E'F'G'$ for each translation?

**a.** $T_{\langle 6, -7 \rangle}(\triangle EFG) = \triangle E'F'G'$  **b.** $T_{\langle 11, 2 \rangle}(\triangle EFG) = \triangle E'F'G'$

## EXAMPLE 2 Write a Translation Rule

**What translation rule maps *STUV* onto *S'T'U'V'*?**

Use one pair of corresponding vertices to determine the change in the horizontal and vertical directions between the preimage to its image.

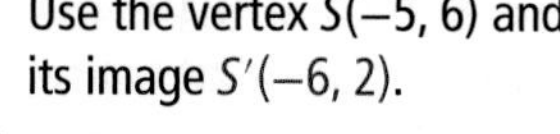

Use the vertex S(−5, 6) and its image S′(−6, 2).

Change in the horizontal direction $x$:

$-6 - (-5) = -1$

$x \rightarrow x - 1$

Change in the vertical direction y:

$2 - 6 = -4$

$y \rightarrow y - 4$

The translation maps every $(x, y)$ point to $(x - 1, y - 4)$, so this translation rule is $T_{\langle -1, -4 \rangle}$. You can verify the rule on the remaining vertices.

**Try It!** **2.** What translation rule maps $P(-3, 1)$ to its image $P'(2, 3)$?

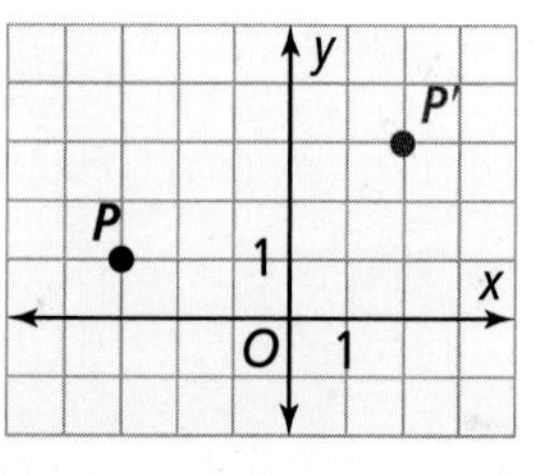

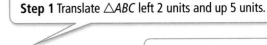

## CONCEPT Composition of Rigid Motions

A **composition of rigid motions** is a transformation with two or more rigid motions in which the second rigid motion is performed on the image of the first rigid motion.

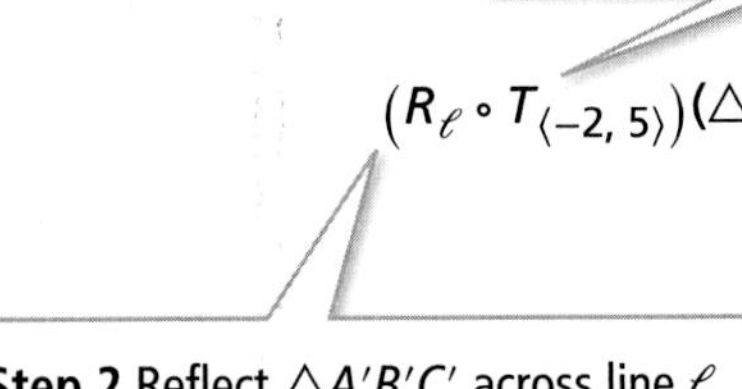

**Step 1** Translate $\triangle ABC$ left 2 units and up 5 units.

$(R_{\ell} \circ T_{\langle -2, 5\rangle})(\triangle ABC)$

This notation uses a small open circle to indicate a composition of rigid motions on $\triangle ABC$.

**Step 2** Reflect $\triangle A'B'C'$ across line $\ell$.

APPLICATION

## EXAMPLE 3 Compose Translations

**In learning a new dance, Kyle moves from position A to position B and then to position C. What single transformation describes Kyle's move from position A to position C?**

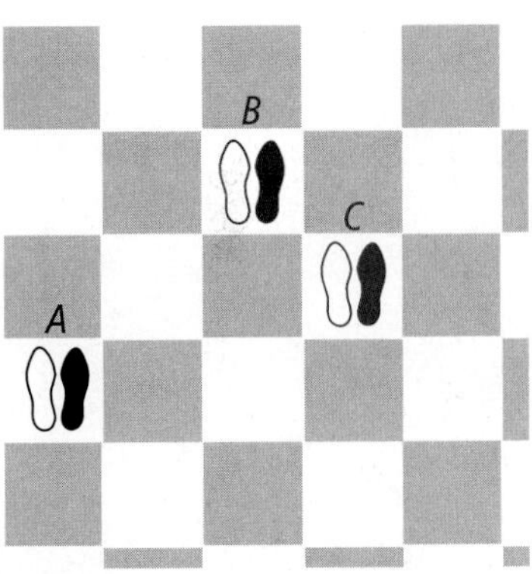


**Formulate** Let (0, 0) represent position A.
The translation from A to B is $T_{\langle 2, 2\rangle}(x, y)$.
The translation from B to C is $T_{\langle 1, -1\rangle}(x, y)$.
Kyle's final position is the composition of those two translations.

**Compute** Find $T_{\langle 1, -1\rangle} \circ T_{\langle 2, 2\rangle}(x, y)$.

$T_{\langle 2, 2\rangle}(x, y) = (x + 2, y + 2)$

$T_{\langle 1, -1\rangle}(x + 2, y + 2) = (x + 3, y + 1)$

First, apply $T_{\langle 2, 2\rangle}$. Then apply $T_{\langle 1, -1\rangle}$ to the result.

**Interpret** The translation $T_{\langle 3, 1\rangle}$(A) represents a single transformation that maps Kyle's move from position A to position C.

**Try It!** 3. What is the composition of the transformations written as one transformation?

a. $T_{\langle 3, -2\rangle} \circ T_{\langle 1, -1\rangle}$

b. $T_{\langle -4, 0\rangle} \circ T_{\langle -2, 5\rangle}$

CONCEPTUAL UNDERSTANDING

## EXAMPLE 4 Relate Translations and Reflections

**How is a composition of reflections across parallel lines related to a translation?**

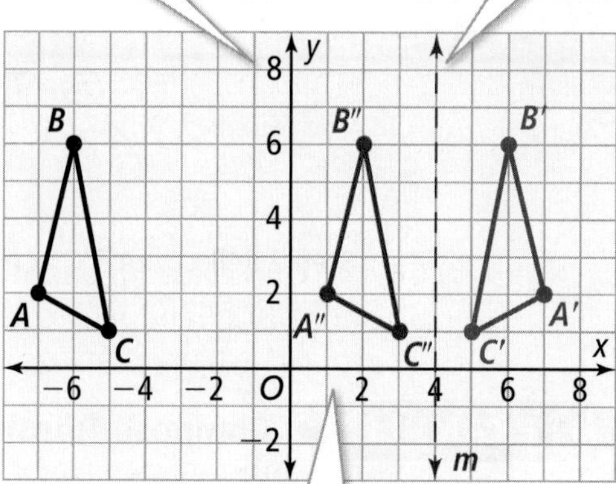


**STUDY TIP**
After the first reflection, the orientation of the figure is reversed. After the second reflection, the orientation of the figure returns to that of the preimage.

If $\triangle ABC$ is translated 8 units to the right, its image is also $\triangle A''B''C''$.

So, $(R_m \circ R_{y\text{-axis}})(\triangle ABC) = T_{\langle 8,\, 0\rangle}(\triangle ABC)$.

**Try It!** 4. Suppose $n$ is the line with equation $y = 1$. Given $\triangle DEF$ with vertices $D(0, 0)$, $E(0, 3)$, and $F(3, 0)$, what translation image is equivalent to $(R_n \circ R_{x\text{-axis}})(\triangle DEF)$?

### THEOREM 3-1

A translation is a composition of reflections across two parallel lines.

- Both reflection lines are perpendicular to the line containing a preimage point and its corresponding image point.
- The distance between the preimage and the image is twice the distance between the two reflection lines.

PROOF: SEE EXAMPLE 5.

**If...** $T(ABC) = A''B''C''$

$AA'' = BB'' = CC'' = 2d$

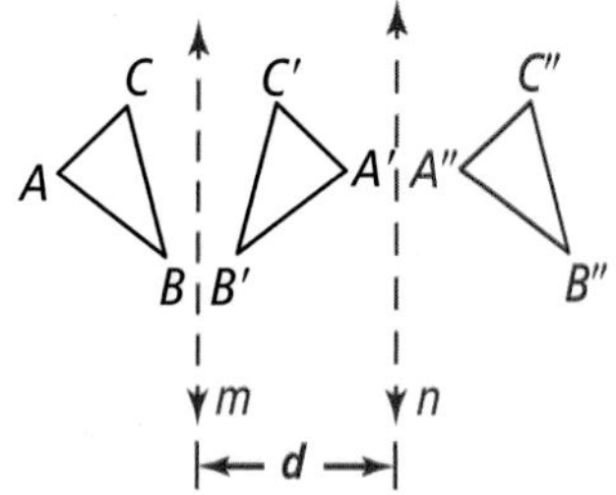


**Then...** $(R_n \circ R_m)(ABC) = A''B''C''$

## EXAMPLE 5 Prove Theorem 3-1

**Given:** A translation $T$, with $T(C) = C''$

**Prove:** There exist parallel lines $m$ and $n$ such that $T = R_n \circ R_m$.

**Plan:** The given information says the translation $T$ maps $C$ to $C''$. First find a composition of reflections that maps $C$ to $C''$. Then show that this composition of reflections is equivalent to the translation $T$ for *any* point. (There are several cases to consider. One case is shown below.)

**Proof:** Let $C'$ be the midpoint of $\overline{CC''}$, and let $CC' = C'C'' = d$. Let $m$ be the perpendicular bisector of $\overline{CC'}$ and $n$ be the perpendicular bisector of $\overline{C'C''}$.

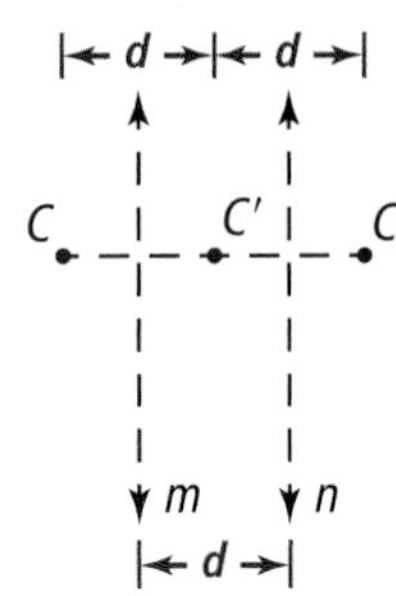


By the properties of reflections $R_m(C) = C'$ and $R_n(C') = C''$, so $(R_n \circ R_m)(C) = C''$. Also, the distance between $n$ and $m$ is $d$ and the distance between $C$ and $C''$ is $2d$.

Now pick another point $B$ and show that $(R_n \circ R_m)(B) = T(B)$. To do this, show that $BB'' = CC'' = 2d$, and $\overline{BB''} \parallel \overline{CC''}$.

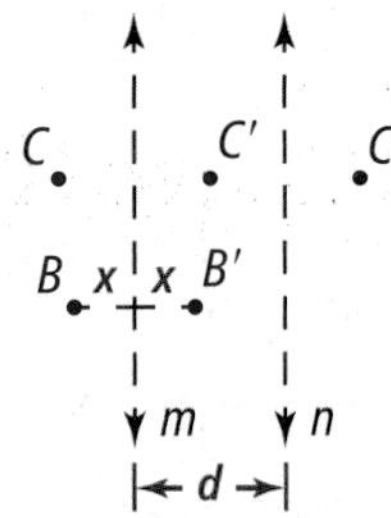


First reflect across $m$. Call the image $B'$. Let the distance from $B$ to $m$ and the distance from $m$ to $B'$ be $x$.

Now reflect $B'$ across $n$. Call the image $B''$. Since the distance between $m$ and $n$ is $d$, the distance between $B'$ and $n$ is $d - x$. By the properties of reflections, the distance between $n$ and $B''$ is also $d - x$.

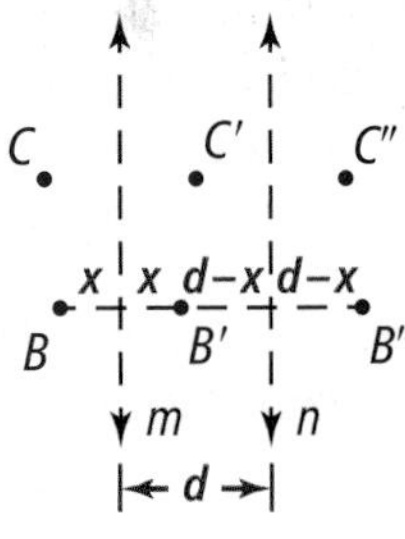


So $BB'' = x + x + (d - x) + (d - x) = 2d$.

Since $\overline{CC''}$ and $\overline{BB''}$ are both perpendicular to $m$ and $n$, they are parallel to each other.

Therefore $(R_n \circ R_m)(B) = T(B)$.

**CONSTRUCT ARGUMENTS**
The choice of $C$ and $C''$ were arbitrary. Why does this mean that this proof is valid for *any* translation?

**Try It!** 5. Suppose the point $B$ you chose in the Proof of Theorem 3-1 was between lines $m$ and $n$. How would that affect the proof? What are the possible cases you need to consider?

Concept Summary

## CONCEPT SUMMARY Translations and Compositions of Rigid Motions

**WORDS** A translation is a transformation that maps all points the same distance and in the same direction.

A composition of two reflections across parallel lines is a translation.

**GRAPH**

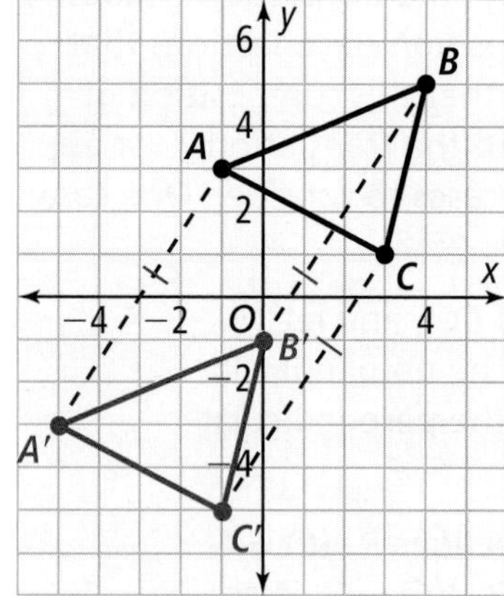


**DIAGRAM**

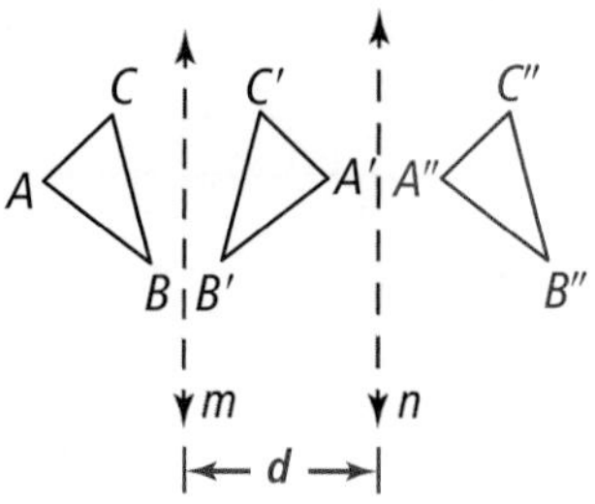


**SYMBOLS** $T_{\langle -4, -6\rangle}(\triangle ABC) = \triangle A'B'C'$

$\overline{AA'} \parallel \overline{BB'} \parallel \overline{CC'}$

$\overline{AA'} \cong \overline{BB'} \cong \overline{CC'}$

$T(ABC) = (R_n \circ R_m)(ABC)$

$AA'' = BB'' = CC'' = 2d$

## Do You UNDERSTAND?

1. **ESSENTIAL QUESTION** What are the properties of a translation?

2. **Error Analysis** Sasha says that for any $\triangle XYZ$, the reflection over the $y$-axis composed with the reflection over the $x$-axis is equivalent to a translation of $\triangle XYZ$. Explain Sasha's error.

3. **Vocabulary** Write an example of a composition of rigid motions for $\triangle PQR$.

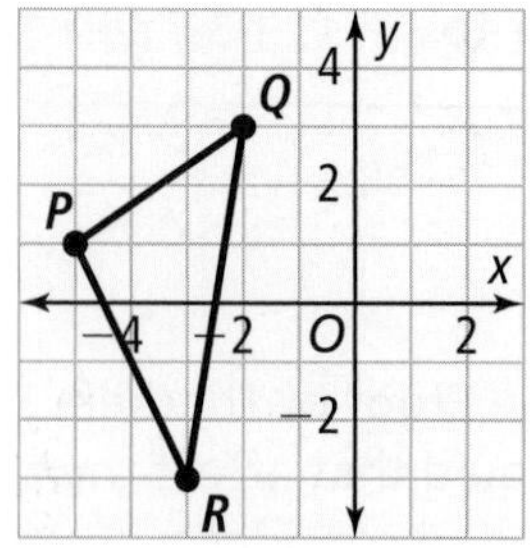


4. **Make Sense and Persevere** What are the values of $x$ and $y$ if $T_{\langle -2, 7\rangle}(x, y) = (3, -1)$?

## Do You KNOW HOW?

**For Exercises 5 and 6, the vertices of $\triangle XYZ$ are $X(1, -4)$, $Y(-2, -1)$, and $Z(3, 1)$. For each translation, give the vertices of $\triangle X'Y'Z'$.**

5. $T_{\langle -4, -3\rangle}(\triangle XYZ)$

6. $T_{\langle 5, -3\rangle}(\triangle XYZ)$

7. What is the rule for the translation shown?

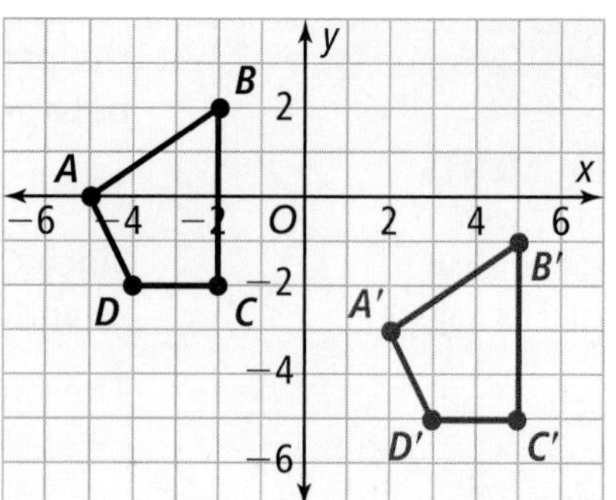


**For Exercises 8 and 9, write composition of translations as one translation.**

8. $T_{\langle 7, 8\rangle} \circ T_{\langle -3, -4\rangle}$

9. $T_{\langle 0, 3\rangle} \circ T_{\langle 4, 6\rangle}$

10. How far apart are two parallel lines $m$ and $n$ such that $T_{\langle 12, 0\rangle}(\triangle JKL) = (R_n \circ R_m)(\triangle JKL)$?

## PRACTICE & PROBLEM SOLVING

### UNDERSTAND

**11. Error Analysis** Hugo graphed $\triangle PQR$ and $(R_t \circ T_{\langle 3, 1\rangle})(\triangle PQR)$ where the equation of line $t$ is $y = 2$. His translation and reflection were both correct. What mistake did Hugo make?

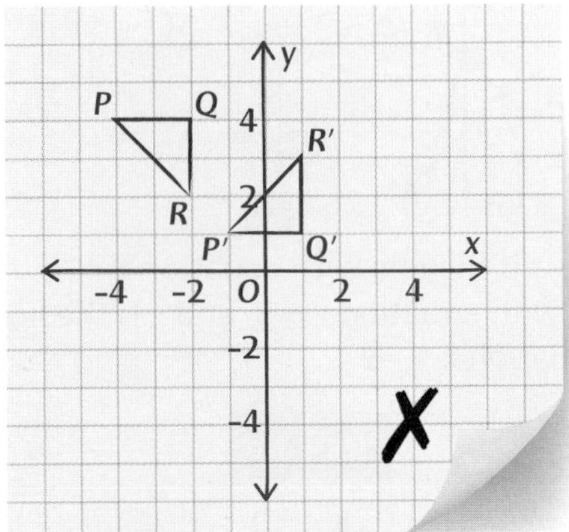


**12. Mathematical Connections** Suppose line $k$ has equation $x = 3$. Compare the areas of $ABCD$ and $A''B''C''D'' = (T_{\langle 1, 2\rangle} \circ R_k)(ABCD)$. Justify your answer.

**13. Make Sense and Persevere** A robot travels from position $A$ to $B$ to $C$ to $D$. What composition of rigid motions represents those moves?

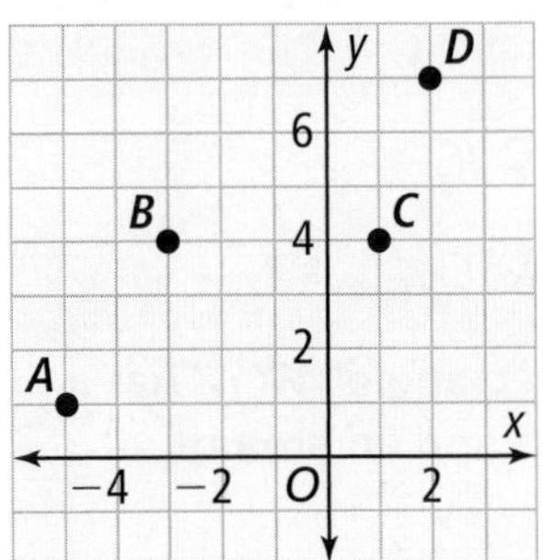


**14. Higher Order Thinking** How can you describe the complete transformation to a person who cannot see the transformations below?

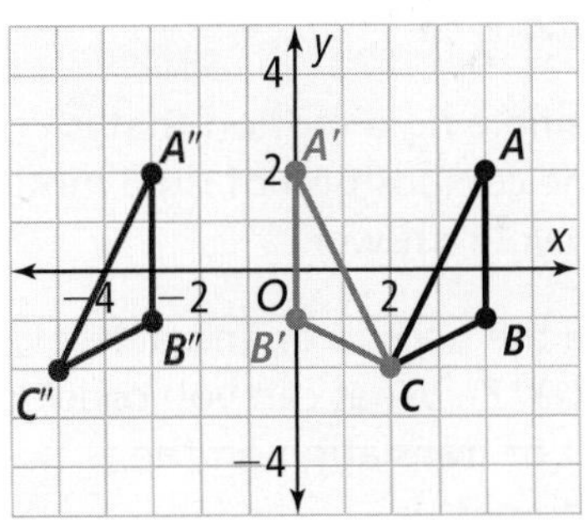


### PRACTICE

**For Exercises 15–17, give the coordinates of the image.** SEE EXAMPLE 1

15. $T_{\langle 3, -1\rangle}(\triangle ABC)$ for $A(5, 0)$, $B(-1, 2)$, $C(6, -3)$

16. $T_{\langle -4, 0\rangle}(\triangle DEF)$ for $D(3, 3)$, $E(-2, 3)$, $F(0, 2)$

17. $T_{\langle -10, -5\rangle}(\triangle GHJ)$ for $G(0, 0)$, $H(3, 6)$, $J(12, -1)$

18. What is the rule for the rigid motion?
SEE EXAMPLE 2

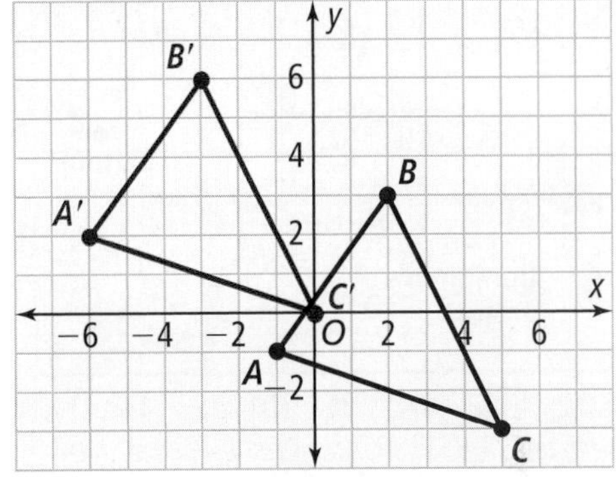


19. Write a composition of translations that is equivalent to $T_{\langle 8, -5\rangle}(x, y)$. SEE EXAMPLE 3

20. Given $\triangle XYZ$, line $n$ with equation $x = -2$, and line $p$ with equation $x = 2$, write a translation that is equivalent to $R_n \circ R_p$.
SEE EXAMPLE 4

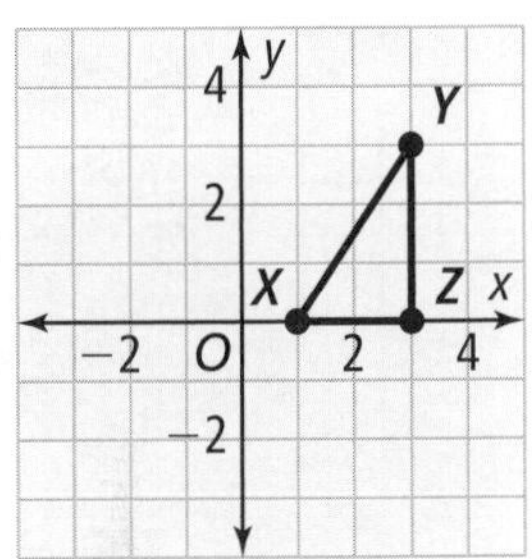


**For Exercises 21–24, write each composition of translations as one translation.** SEE EXAMPLE 3

21. $T_{\langle -3, 3\rangle} \circ T_{\langle -2, 4\rangle}$

22. $T_{\langle -4, -3\rangle} \circ T_{\langle 3, 1\rangle}$

23. $T_{\langle 5, -6\rangle} \circ T_{\langle -7, 5\rangle}$

24. $T_{\langle 8, -2\rangle} \circ T_{\langle -4, 9\rangle}$

**For Exericses 25–28, write each composition of reflections as one translation. Suppose $k$ is the line with equation $x = -3$, $\ell$ is the line with equation $x = -2$, $m$ is the line with equation $x = 1$, $n$ is the line with equation $x = -1$, $p$ is the line with equation $y = 1$, $q$ is the line with equation $y = 3$, $s$ is the line with equation $y = 2$, and $t$ is the line with equation $y = -4$.** SEE EXAMPLE 4

25. $R_k \circ R_\ell$

26. $R_m \circ R_n$

27. $R_p \circ R_q$

28. $R_s \circ R_t$

29. The distance between vertical lines $a$ and $b$ is 6 units and $a$ is left of $b$. If $T_{\langle x, 0\rangle}(\triangle JKL) = (R_b \circ R_a)(\triangle JKL)$, what is the value of $x$?
SEE EXAMPLE 5

# PRACTICE & PROBLEM SOLVING

Practice | Tutorial

Mixed Review Available Online

## APPLY

**30. Communicate Precisely** Benjamin walks from his house to Timothy's house and then to school. Describe Benjamin's walk as a composition of translations. If Benjamin walks from his house directly to school, what translation describes his walk?

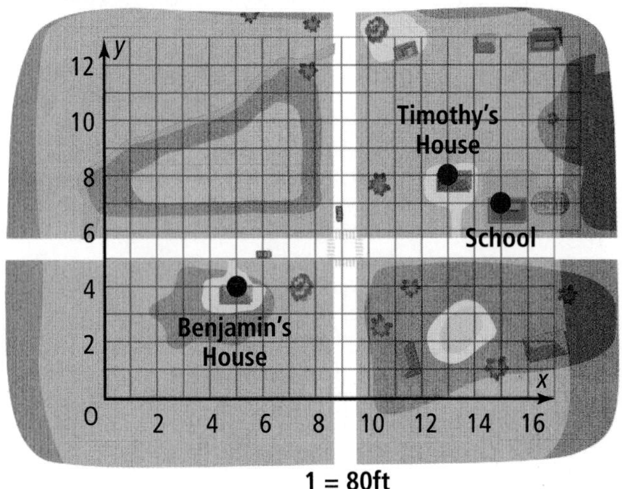


**Use the map for Exercises 31 and 32.**

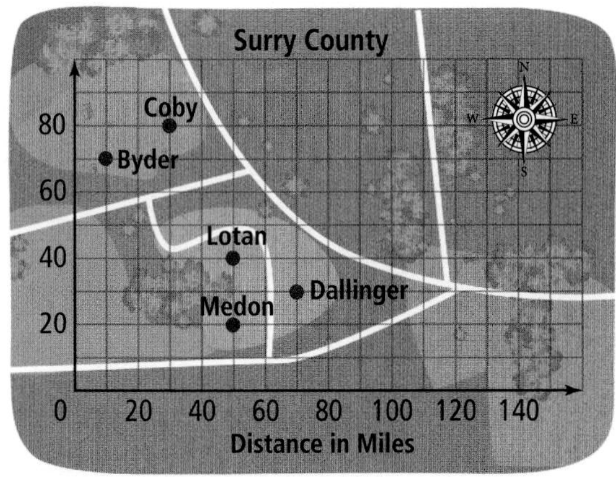


**31. Model With Mathematics** The Surry County sheriff's patrol route starts in Coby. The composition of rigid motions $T_{\langle -20,\ 10\rangle} \circ T_{\langle 40,\ -50\rangle}$ describes her route. How would you describe the sheriff's route in words?

**32. Reason** What composition of rigid motions describes a car trip starting in Medon, stopping in Dallinger, and then going on to Byder?

## ASSESSMENT PRACTICE

**33.** Does each of the rigid motions below result in $\triangle A''B''C''$? Select *Yes* or *No*.

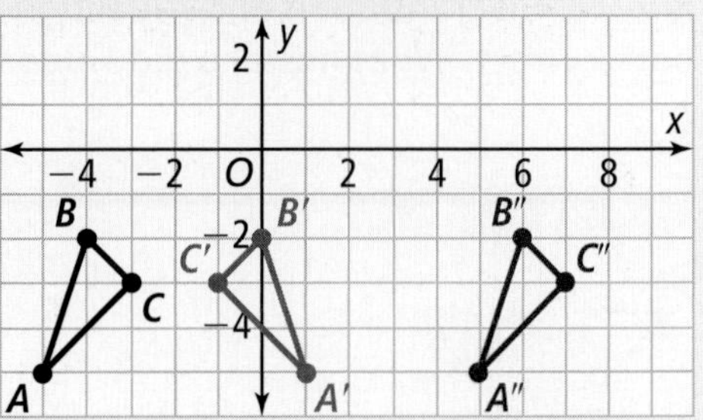

Suppose *a* is the line with equation $x = 6$, *b* is the line with equation $x = 3$, and *c* is the line with equation $x = -2$.

| | Yes | No |
|---|---|---|
| $T_{\langle 0,\ 10\rangle}(\triangle ABC)$ | ❑ | ❑ |
| $T_{\langle 10,\ 0\rangle}(\triangle ABC)$ | ❑ | ❑ |
| $(R_{y\text{-axis}} \circ R_a)(\triangle ABC)$ | ❑ | ❑ |
| $(R_b \circ R_c)(\triangle ABC)$ | ❑ | ❑ |

**34. SAT/ACT** Suppose the equation of line *m* is $x = -7$ and the equation of line *n* is $x = 7$. Which is the equivalent to the composition $T_{\langle -1,\ 3\rangle} \circ T_{\langle -6,\ 4\rangle}$?

Ⓐ $R_m$

Ⓑ $T_{\langle -7,\ 7\rangle}$

Ⓒ $R_n$

Ⓓ $T_{\langle -6,\ 4\rangle} \circ T_{\langle -1,\ 3\rangle}$

**35. Performance Task** Rectangle *WXYZ* has a perimeter of 16 units and an area of 15 square units.

**Part A** Graph *WXYZ* on a sheet of graph paper. Write a composition of rigid motions describing two reflections of *WXYZ* across parallel lines of your choosing. Graph and label the parallel lines $W'X'Y'Z'$ and $W''X''Y''Z''$.

**Part B** Write a single rigid motion that is equivalent to the composition of rigid motions in Part B. Justify your answer.

**Part C** Compare the perimeter and area of *WXYZ* and $W''X''Y''Z''$. What can you conclude about the effect of translation on the properties of figures?

# 3-3 Rotations

PearsonRealize.com

**I CAN…** draw and describe the rotation of a figure about a point of rotation for a given angle of rotation.

Activity Assess

## CRITIQUE & EXPLAIN

**Filipe says that the next time one of the hands of the clock points to 7 will be at 7:00 when the hour hand points to 7. Nadia says that it will be at 5:35 when the minute hand points to 7.**

**A.** Whose statement is correct? Explain.

**B. Communicate Precisely** Suppose the numbers on the clock face are removed. Write instructions that another person could follow to move the minute hand from 2 to 6.

## ESSENTIAL QUESTION

**What are the properties that identify a rotation?**

## EXAMPLE 1 Draw a Rotated Image

**How can you perform a 75° rotation of $\triangle XYZ$ about point $P$?**

To rotate $\triangle XYZ$ 75° about point $P$, each point in the triangle must rotate 75°. Then the measure of the angle formed by each preimage point, point $P$, and the corresponding image point is 75°.

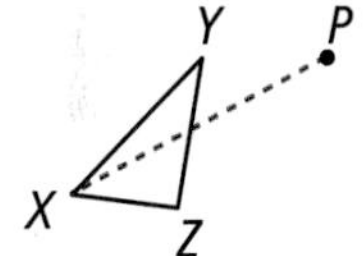


Use a ruler and protractor to draw 75° angles from each vertex on $\triangle XYZ$ with point $P$, and mark image points that are the same distance from $P$.

**STUDY TIP**
Unless otherwise stated, rotations are always performed counterclockwise.

**Step 1** To rotate $X$, draw $\overline{PX}$ to form one side of a 75° angle.

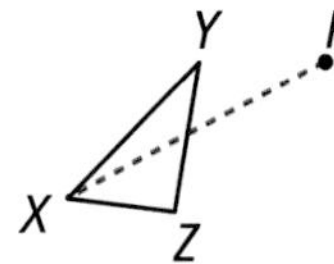


**Step 2** Measure the angle and draw the other side, $PX'$. Mark point $X'$ so $PX' = PX$.

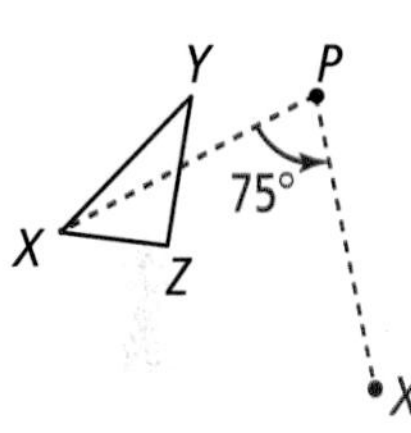


**Step 3** Repeat Step 1 and Step 2 for $Y$ and $Z$ in order to locate points $Y'$ and $Z'$.

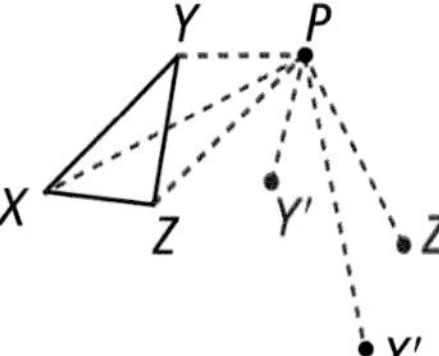


**Step 4** Connect the image points to form $\triangle X'Y'Z'$.

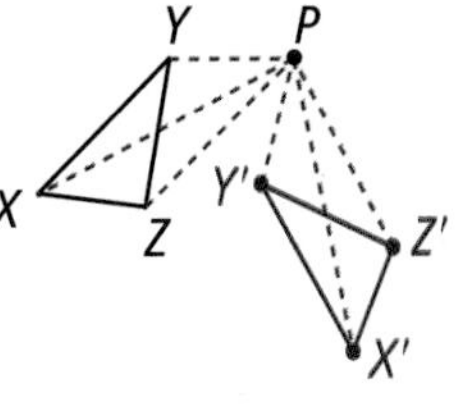


**Try It!** 1. Do you think a rotated image would ever coincide with the original figure? Explain.

## CONCEPT Rotations

A rotation $r_{(x°, P)}$ is a transformation that rotates each point in the preimage about a point $P$, called the center of rotation, by an angle measure of $x°$, called the angle of rotation. A rotation has these properties:

- The image of $P$ is $P'$ (that is, $P' = P$).
- For a preimage point $A$, $PA = PA'$ and $m\angle APA' = x°$.

A rotation is a rigid motion, so length and angle measure are preserved. Note that a rotation is counterclockwise for a positive angle measure.

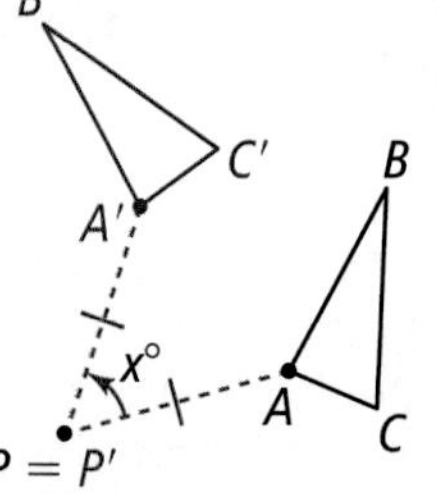


## CONCEPT Rotations in the Coordinate Plane

Rules can be used to rotate a figure 90°, 180°, and 270° about the origin $O$ in the coordinate plane.

$r_{(90°, O)}(x, y) = (-y, x)$ $r_{(180°, O)}(x, y) = (-x, -y)$ $r_{(270°, O)}(x, y) = (y, -x)$

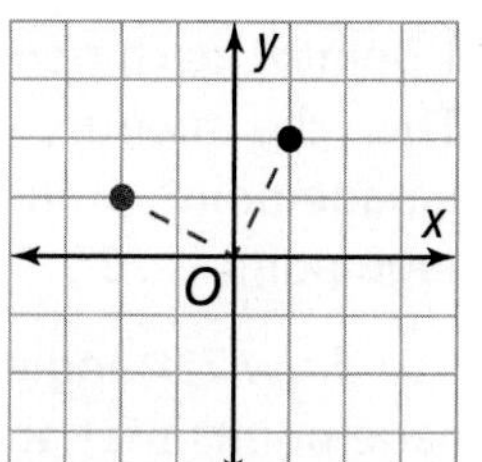


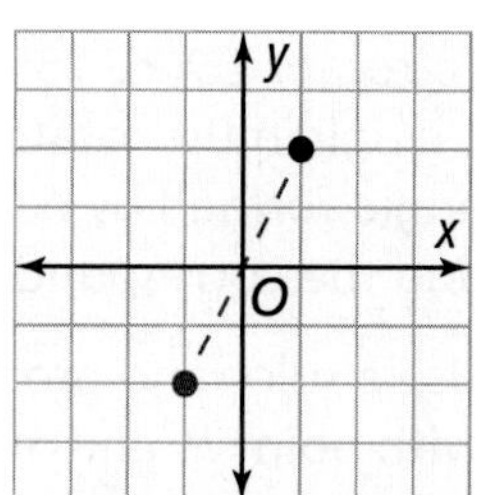


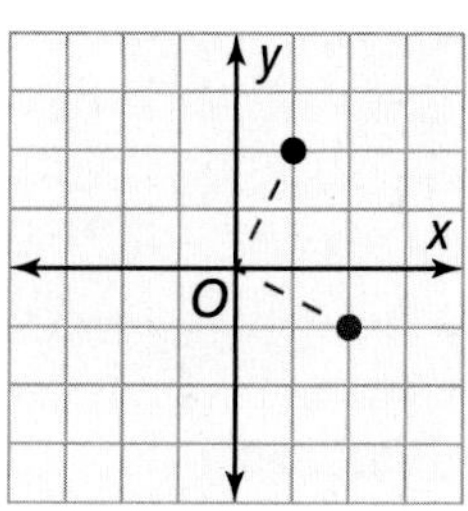


## EXAMPLE 2 Draw Rotations in the Coordinate Plane

**What is $r_{(90°, O)}ABCD$?**

A rotation of 90° about the origin follows the rule $(x, y) \rightarrow (-y, x)$.

Determine the vertices of the image.

$A(3, 5) \rightarrow A'(-5, 3)$

$B(1, 7) \rightarrow B'(-7, 1)$

$C(-2, 4) \rightarrow C'(-4, -2)$

$D(2, -1) \rightarrow D'(1, 2)$

Draw $A'B'C'D'$ on the coordinate plane.

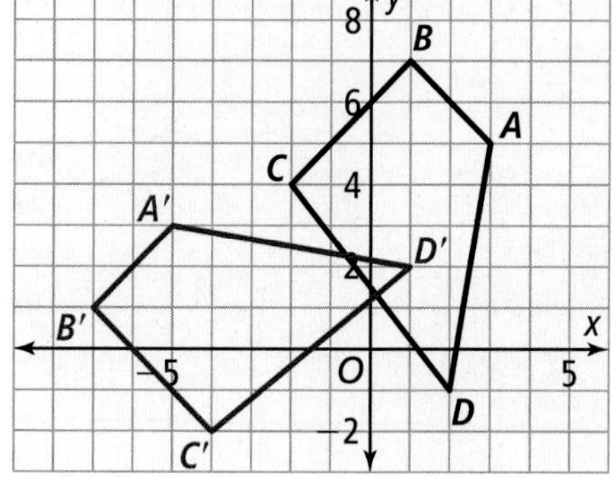


**LOOK FOR RELATIONSHIPS**
Compare the distance of each vertex from the origin for the preimage and image. What relationships must they have?

**Try It!** 2. The vertices of $\triangle XYZ$ are $X(-4, 7)$, $Y(0, 8)$, and $Z(2, -1)$.

a. What are the vertices of $r_{(180°, O)}(\triangle XYZ)$?

b. What are the vertices of $r_{(270°, O)}(\triangle XYZ)$?

APPLICATION

## EXAMPLE 3 Use Rotations

**The first drummer in a drumline is at the 20 yard line and the sixth drummer is at the 35 yard line. The drumline rotates counterclockwise 180° about the sixth drummer and then rotates 135° clockwise about the first drummer. Where does the sixth drummer stand after the rotations? Describe the change in position as a composition of rotations.**

Represent the first drummer as point $B$ and the sixth drummer as point $A$.

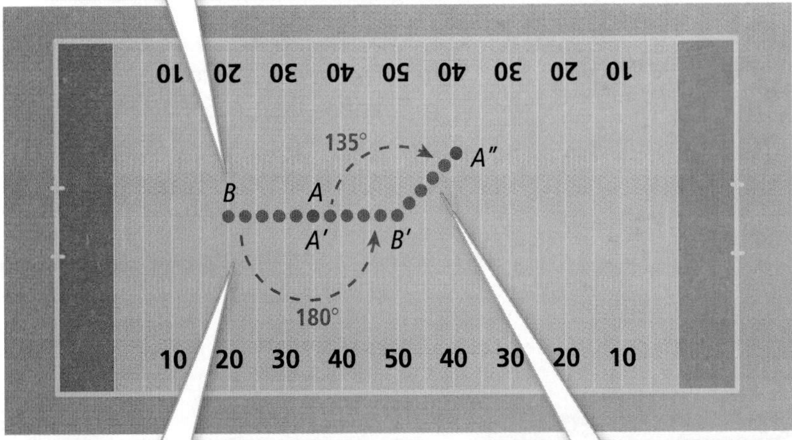


First, rotate the drumline 180° counterclockwise about point $A$.

Second, rotate the drumline 135° clockwise about point $B'$.

**COMMUNICATE PRECISELY**
Think about how the notation used represents the information shown. What information do you need to identify in order to use the notation?

The sixth drummer stands at the position labeled $A''$. The drumline is first transformed by the rotation $r_{(180°, A)}$ and then by the rotation $r_{(-135°, B')}$.

**Try It!** 3. a. Suppose the drumline instead turns counterclockwise about $B'$. How many degrees must it rotate so that the sixth drummer ends in the same position?

b. Can the composition of rotations be described by $r_{(45°, A)}$ since $180° - 135° = 45°$? Explain.

CONCEPTUAL UNDERSTANDING

## EXAMPLE 4 Investigate Reflections and Rotations

**LOOK FOR RELATIONSHIPS**
Consider how properties of the transformations are related. What properties would you consider in determining the number of reflections needed?

**Can you find a sequence of reflections that result in the same image as a rotation?**

The image of *JKLM* rotated about point *T* is *WXYZ*. Try to reflect *JKLM* one or more times so that the image aligns with *WXYZ*.

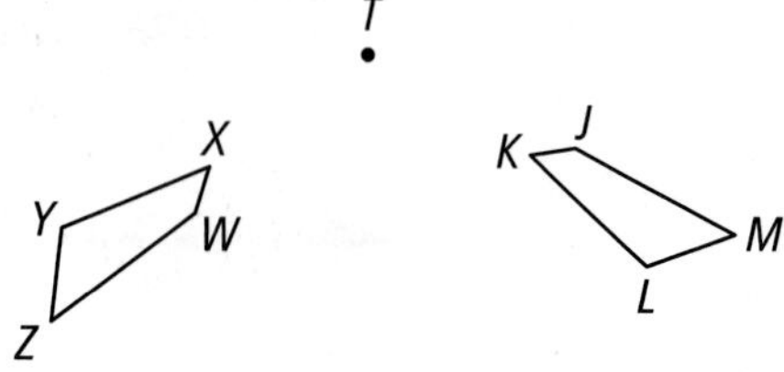


**Step 1** Draw line *p* through point *T* and reflect *JKLM* across *p* to form *J′K′L′M′*.

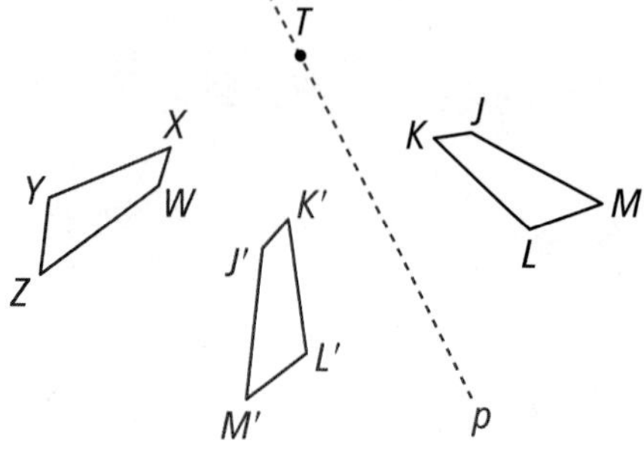


**Step 2** Think about how to reflect *J′K′L′M′* to form *WXYZ*. Connect corresponding points in *J′K′L′M′* and *WXYZ* and then find each midpoint.

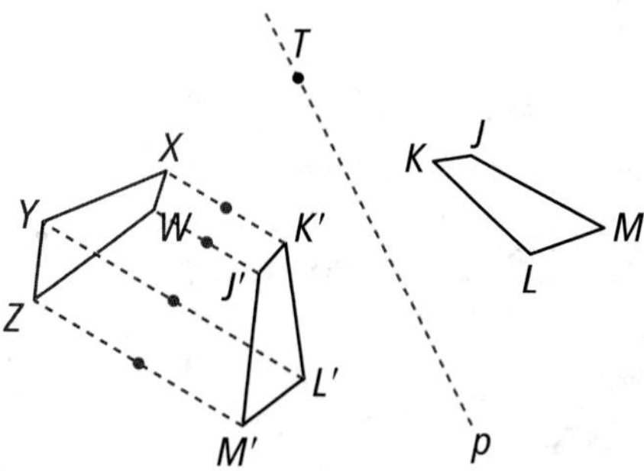


**Step 3** The midpoints appear to be collinear with *T*. Draw line *q* through the midpoints and *T*. The reflection of *J′K′L′M′* across *q* is *WXYZ*.

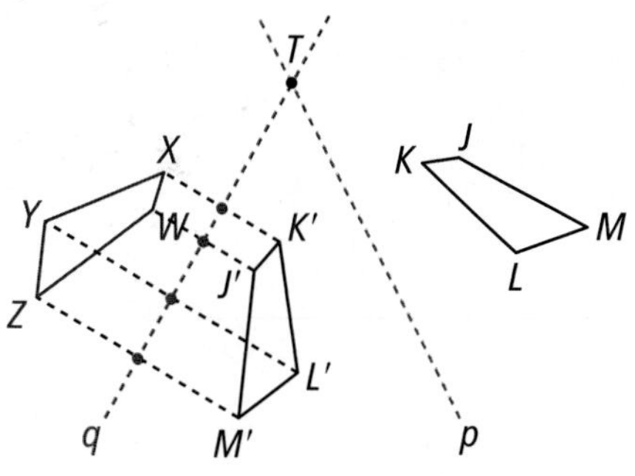


**Try It!** 4. Perform the same constructions shown, except draw line *p* so that it does not pass through *T*. Do you get the same results? Explain.

## THEOREM 3-2

Any rotation is a composition of reflections across two lines that intersect at the center of rotation.

The angle of rotation is twice the angle formed by the lines of reflection.

**If...**

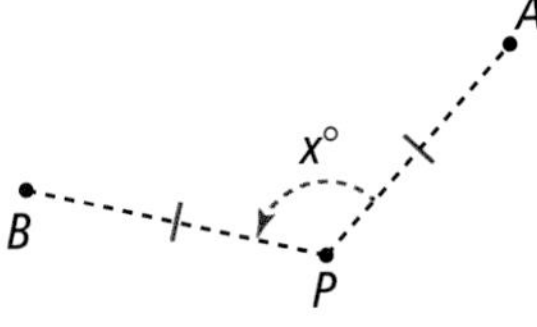


**Then...**

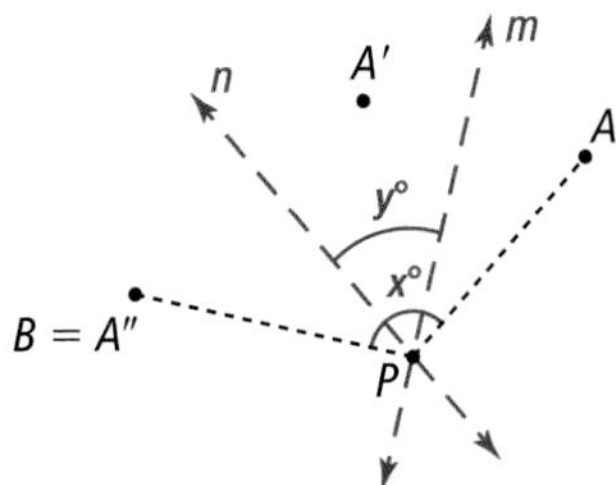


PROOF: SEE EXAMPLE 5.

$y = \frac{1}{2}x$

## EXAMPLE 5 Prove Theorem 3-2

**Prove Theorem 3-2.**

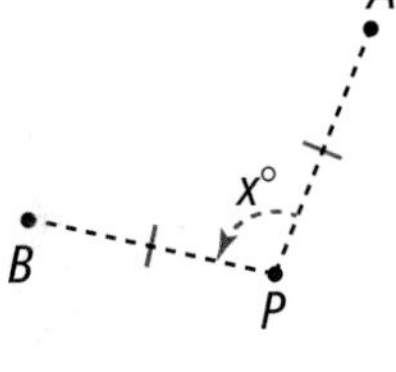


**Given:** $r_{(x°,\, P)}(A) = B$

**Prove:** There exist two lines $m$ and $n$ such that $(R_n \circ R_m)(A) = r_{(x°,\, P)}(A)$ equals $B$, and the measure of the angle formed by lines $m$ and $n$ is $\frac{1}{2}x$.

**Proof:**

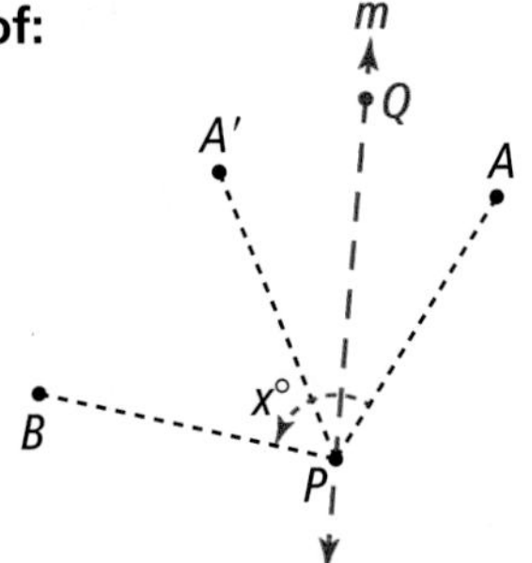


Mark a point $Q$ anywhere except on $\overrightarrow{PA}$. Then draw line $m$ through $Q$ and $P$. Reflect $A$ across $m$ to image $A'$. The reflection line is an angle bisector of $\angle APA'$. Let $m\angle APQ = m\angle A'PQ = a$.

Construct the angle bisector $n$ of $\angle BPA'$. Reflect $A'$ across $n$ to image $A''$. Since a reflection is rigid motion, $PA = PA' = PA'' = PB$. So $A'' = B$. The congruent angles formed measure $b$. Therefore, $r_{(x°,\, P)}(A) = (R_n \circ R_m)(A)$.

The angle of rotation $x°$ has a measure equal to $a + a + b + b$, or $2(a + b)$. The angle formed by lines $m$ and $n$ has a measure equal to $a + b$, or $\frac{1}{2}x$.

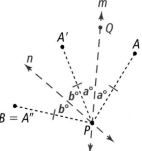

**LOOK FOR RELATIONSHIPS**
Think about how to construct lines to help you in the proof. What properties does the angle bisector preserve as a line of reflection?

**Try It!** 5. Suppose point $Q$ is closer to point $B$ or even outside of $\angle APB$. Does the relationship still hold for the angle between the reflection lines and the angle between the preimage and the image? Explain.

## CONCEPT SUMMARY Properties of Rotations

**WORDS**

A rotation is a transformation that rotates each point in the preimage about the center of rotation through the angle of rotation.

Any rotation is a composition of reflections across two intersecting lines.

**DIAGRAMS**

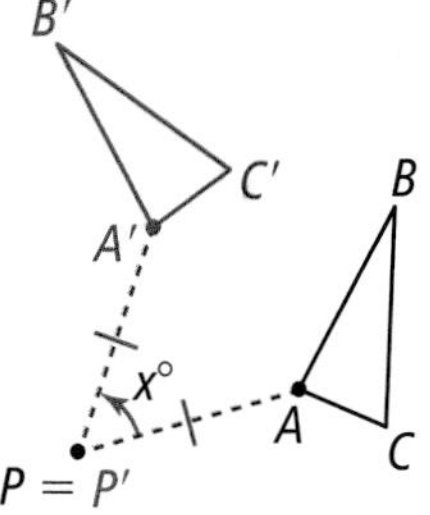


**SYMBOLS**

$r_{(x°,\ P)}(\triangle ABC) = \triangle A'B'C'$

$PA = PA',\ PB = PB',\ PC = PC'$

$m\angle APA' = m\angle BPB' = m\angle CPC' = x°$

$r_{(x°,\ P)}(A) = (R_n \circ R_m)(A) = B$

$y° = \frac{1}{2}x°$

## Do You UNDERSTAND?

1. **ESSENTIAL QUESTION** What are the properties that identify a rotation?

2. **Error Analysis** Isabel drew the diagram below to show the rotation of $\triangle DEF$ about point $T$. What is her error?

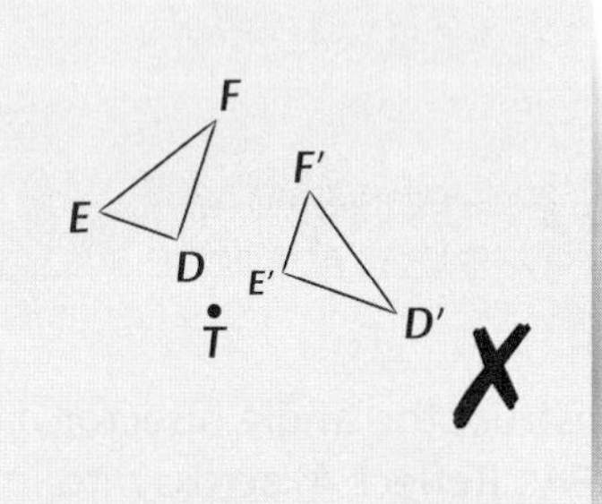


3. **Vocabulary** How is the *center of rotation* related to the *center of a circle*?

4. **Construct Arguments** In the diagram, $\triangle A''B''C''$ is the image of reflections of $\triangle ABC$ across lines $p$ and $q$. It is also the image of a rotation of $\triangle ABC$ about $R$. What is the angle of rotation? Explain.

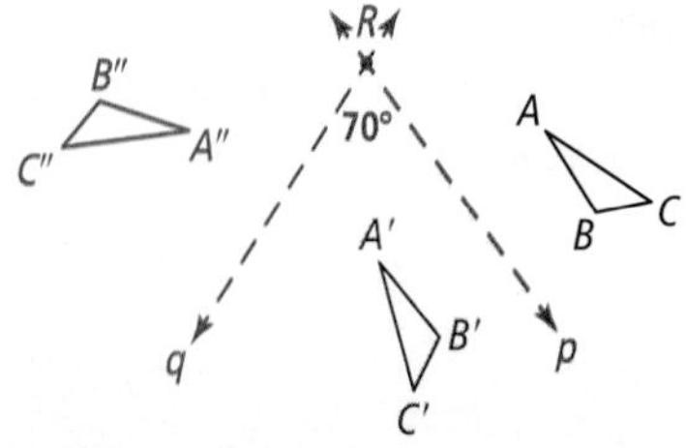


## Do You KNOW HOW?

**Trace each figure and draw its rotated image.**

5. $r_{(90°,\ P)}(\overline{MN})$

6. $r_{(120°,\ T)}(\triangle ABC)$

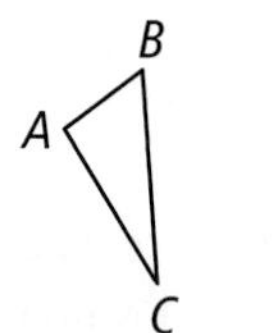


**Give the coordinates of each image.**

7. $r_{(180°,\ O)}(\overline{GH})$ for $G(2, -9)$, $H(-1, 3)$

8. $r_{(90°,\ O)}(\triangle XYZ)$ for $X(0, 3)$, $Y(1, -4)$, $Z(5, 2)$

**Trace each figure and construct two lines of reflection such that the composition of the reflections across the lines maps onto the image shown.**

9. Q

10.

J, K, L, M

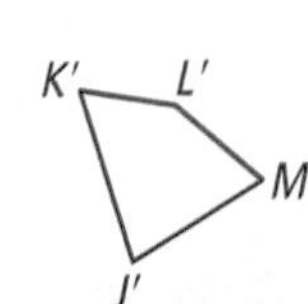

## PRACTICE & PROBLEM SOLVING

Scan for Multimedia

Practice | Tutorial

Additional Exercises Available Online

### UNDERSTAND

**11. Construct Arguments** When you rotate a figure, does every point move the same distance? Explain.

**12. Error Analysis** Shannon says that $\triangle X'Y'Z'$ is a rotation of $\triangle XYZ$ about $P$. What is the correct transformation from $\triangle XYZ$ to $\triangle X'Y'Z'$?

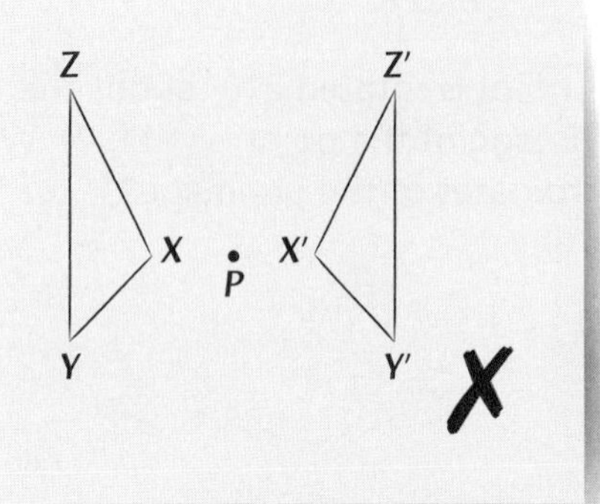


**13. Mathematical Connections** Points $A'$ and $B'$ are the images of points $A$ and $B$ after a 270° rotation about the origin. If the slope of $\overleftrightarrow{AB}$ is −3, what is the slope of $\overleftrightarrow{A'B'}$? Explain.

**14. Use Structure** The diagram shows $r_{(90°,\ O)}(ABCD)$. What are the coordinates of $ABCD$?

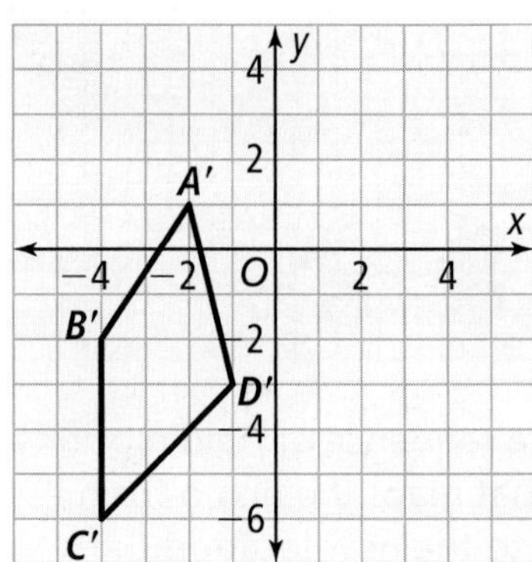


**15. Higher Order Thinking** In the diagram, $r_{(180°,\ O)}(\triangle ABC) = \triangle A'B'C'$. Describe a composition of a rotation and a translation that results in the same image.

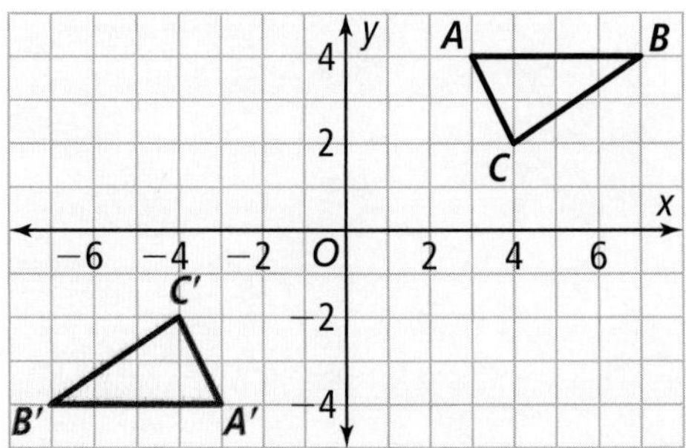


### PRACTICE

**For Exercises 16–18, trace each figure and draw its rotated image.** SEE EXAMPLES 1 AND 3

**16.** $r_{(80°,\ P)}(\triangle ABC)$

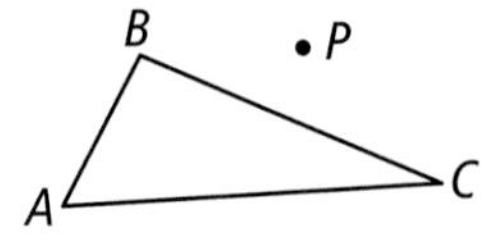


**17.** $r_{(110°,\ Q)}(\triangle DEFG)$

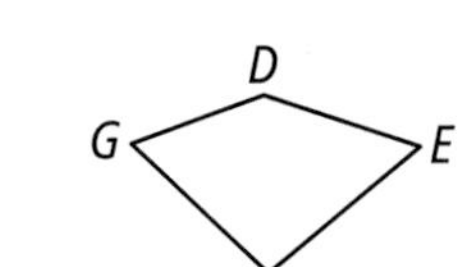


**18.** $r_{(175°,\ R)}(\triangle HJK)$

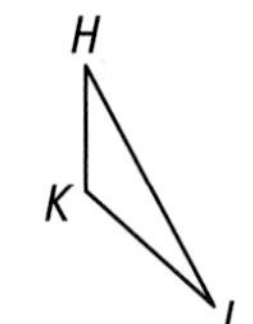


R

**For Exercises 19–22, give the coordinates of each image.** SEE EXAMPLE 2

**19.** $r_{(90°,\ O)}(\triangle DEF)$ for $D(0, 5)$, $E(-2, 8)$, $F(-3, -5)$

**20.** $r_{(270°,\ O)}(WXYZ)$ for $W(4, -2)$, $X(7, 3)$, $Y(1, 11)$, $Z(-4, 6)$

**21.** $r_{(180°,\ O)}(\triangle STU)$ for $S(-2, -6)$, $T(-5, 3)$, $U(1, 0)$

**22.** $r_{(360°,\ O)}(JKLM)$ for $J(-4, 7)$, $K(1, 5)$, $L(6, 1)$, $M(3, -9)$

**23.** Trace the point and triangle. Draw the image $r_{(160°,\ T)}(\triangle XYZ)$. Then draw two reflections that result in the same image. SEE EXAMPLES 4 AND 5

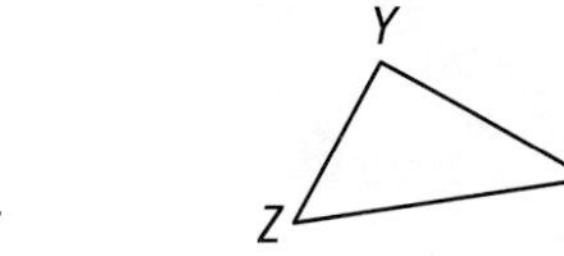


**24.** Find the angle of rotation for the rotation that is the composition $R_n \circ R_m$. Then trace the figure and draw the image.

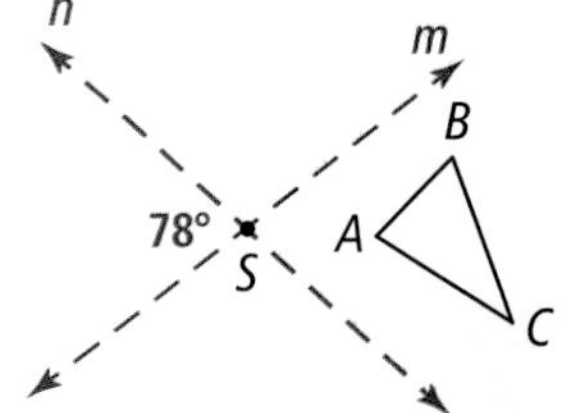

# PRACTICE & PROBLEM SOLVING

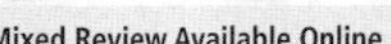


Mixed Review Available Online

## APPLY

**25. Make Sense and Persevere** What rotation must the driver gear make for gear A to rotate 90° clockwise? Explain how you found your answer.

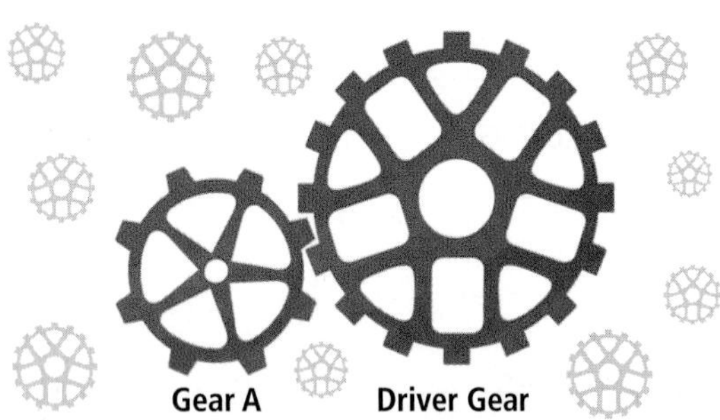


**26. Reason** Luis is programming an animation for a countdown timer where points flash in sequence, one at a time, around in a circle. He calculates that the coordinates of the first four points in his sequence are (6, 0), (5.5, 2.3), (4.2, 4.2), and (2.3, 5.5). He can find the rest of the coordinates by rotating the first four points by 90°, 180°, and 270°. What are the coordinates of the points that complete the sequence around in a circle?

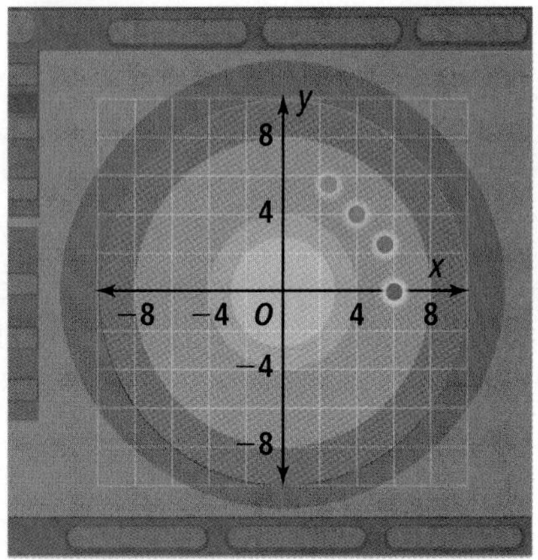


**27. Communicate Precisely** Lourdes created the design below by rotating $\triangle ABF$, quadrilateral $BCEF$, and $\triangle CDE$. Describe the rotations she used. How do you determine the angles of rotation?

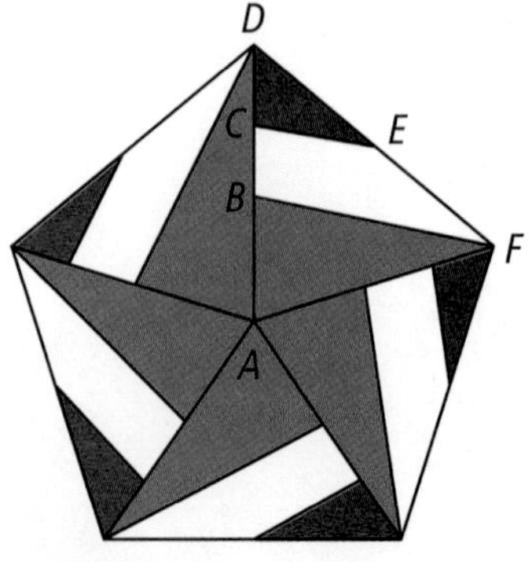


## ASSESSMENT PRACTICE

**28.** Quadrilateral $J'K'L'M'$ is the image of $JKLM$ rotated about point $P$. What completes each statement?

$KP$ ___?___ $K'P'$

$\overline{LM}$ ___?___ $\overline{L'M'}$

$\overline{JJ'}$ ___?___ $\overline{KK'}$

$m\angle KPK'$ ___?___ $m\angle LPL'$

**29. SAT/ACT** A point is rotated 270° about the origin. The image of the point is (−11, 7). What are the coordinates of the preimage?

Ⓐ (7, −11)

Ⓑ (−7, −11)

Ⓒ (7, 11)

Ⓓ (11, 7)

**30. Performance Task** Movers need to move the pianos as shown in the diagram.

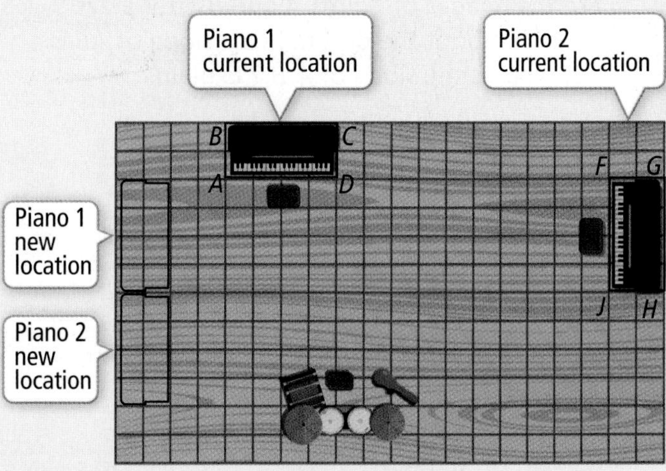


**Part A** Describe a sequence of rigid motions for each piano that maps the piano from its current location to the new location.

**Part B** Describe a single rotation for each piano that maps the piano from its current location to the new location. (*Hint*: You can find two reflections to determine the center of rotation.)

# 3-4 Classification of Rigid Motions

PearsonRealize.com

**I CAN…** identify different rigid motions used to transform two-dimensional shapes.

**VOCABULARY**

- glide reflection

## CRITIQUE & EXPLAIN

**Two students are trying to determine whether compositions of rigid motions are commutative. Paula translates a triangle and then reflects it across a line. When she reflects and then translates, she gets the same image. She concludes that compositions of rigid motions are commutative.**

Translate. Then reflect.

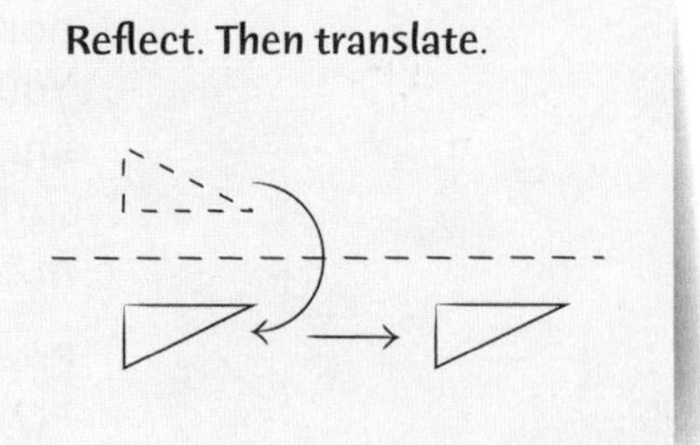


**Keenan rotates a triangle and then reflects it. When he changes the order of the rigid motions, he gets a different image. He concludes that compositions of rigid motions are not commutative.**

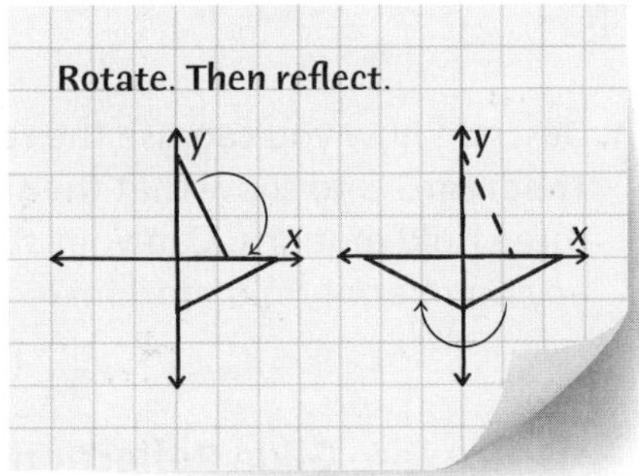


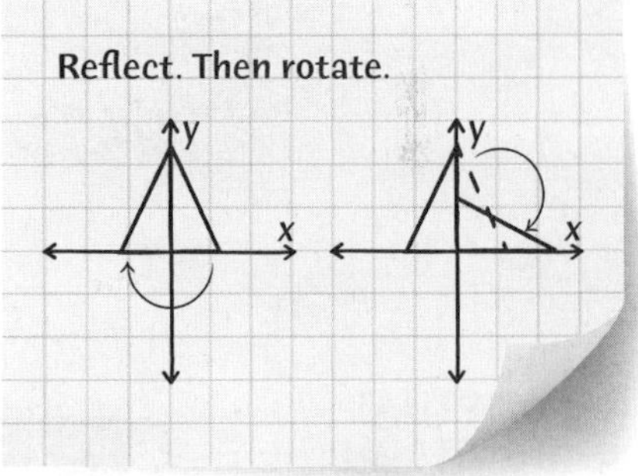


**A.** Should Paula have used grid paper? Explain.

**B. Communicate Precisely** Do you agree with Paula or with Keenan? Explain.

## ESSENTIAL QUESTION

**How can rigid motions be classified?**

### THEOREM 3-3

The composition of two or more rigid motions is a rigid motion.

**If...**

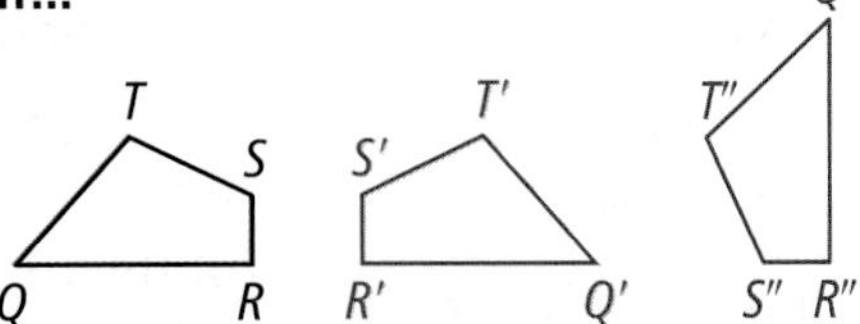


$M$: $QRST \to Q'R'S'T'$ and
$N$: $Q'R'S'T' \to Q''R''S''T''$ are rigid motions.

**Then...**

$(N \circ M)$: $QRST \to Q''R''S''T''$ is a rigid motion.

**PROOF: SEE EXAMPLE 1.**

PROOF

## EXAMPLE 1 Prove Theorem 3-3

**Write a paragraph proof of Theorem 3-3.**

**Given:** $T$ and $S$ are rigid motions.

**Prove:** $S \circ T$ is a rigid motion.

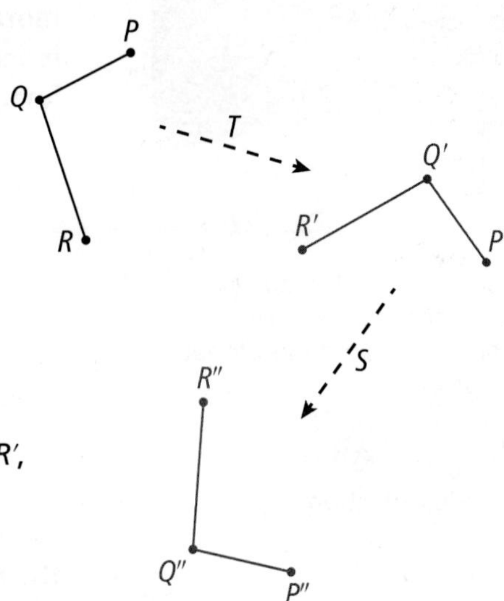


**Plan:** Let $P$, $Q$, and $R$ be any three noncollinear points in the preimage. You want to show that length and angle measure are preserved, so it is sufficient to show that $PQ = P''Q''$ and $m\angle PQR = m\angle P''Q''R''$.

**Proof:** Since $T$ and $S$ are rigid motions, $PQ = P'Q'$, $P'Q' = P''Q''$, $m\angle PQR = m\angle P'Q'R'$, and $m\angle P'Q'R' = m\angle P''Q''R''$.

By the Transitive Property of Equality, $PQ = P''Q''$ and $m\angle PQR = m\angle P''Q''R''$.

$S \circ T$ is a rigid motion because it preserves length and angle measure.

**Try It!** 1. Describe how you can use the reasoning used to prove Theorem 3-3 to show that the theorem is true when composing three rigid motions. Can your strategy be extended to include any number of rigid motions?

CONCEPTUAL UNDERSTANDING

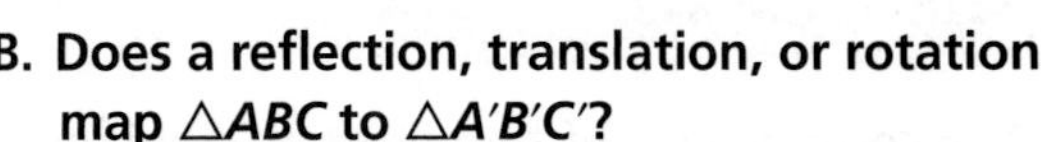

## EXAMPLE 2 Explore Glide Reflections

**A. Is there a rigid motion that maps $\triangle ABC$ to $\triangle A'B'C'$?**

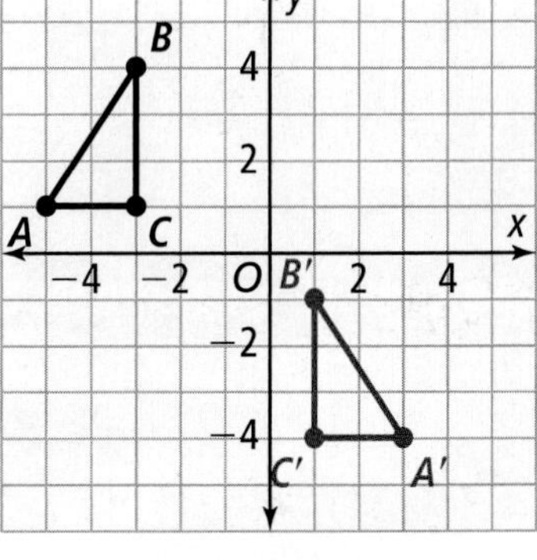


Observe that $m\angle A = m\angle A'$, $m\angle B = m\angle B'$, and $m\angle C = m\angle C'$.

Also, $AB = A'B'$, $AC = A'C'$, and $BC = B'C'$.

Length and angle measure are preserved, so the transformation is a rigid motion.

**B. Does a reflection, translation, or rotation map $\triangle ABC$ to $\triangle A'B'C'$?**

> **USE STRUCTURE**
> Each rigid motion has specific properties. What properties should you consider for each type?

Check whether a translation maps $\triangle ABC$ to $\triangle A'B'C'$.

Use the point $B(-3, 4)$ and its image $B'(1, -1)$ .

The translation rule that maps $B$ onto $B'$ is $T_{\langle 4, -5 \rangle}$. This rule does not map $A$ to $A'$.

The rigid motion is not a translation.

Check whether a rotation maps $\triangle ABC$ to $\triangle A'B'C'$.

Since orientation of the triangle is not preserved, the rigid motion is not a rotation.

Check whether a reflection maps $\triangle ABC$ to $\triangle A'B'C'$.

There is no line of reflection that produces the image, so the rigid motion is not a reflection.

CONTINUED ON THE NEXT PAGE

EXAMPLE 2 CONTINUED

**C. What composition of two rigid motions maps $\triangle ABC$ to $\triangle A'B'C'$?**

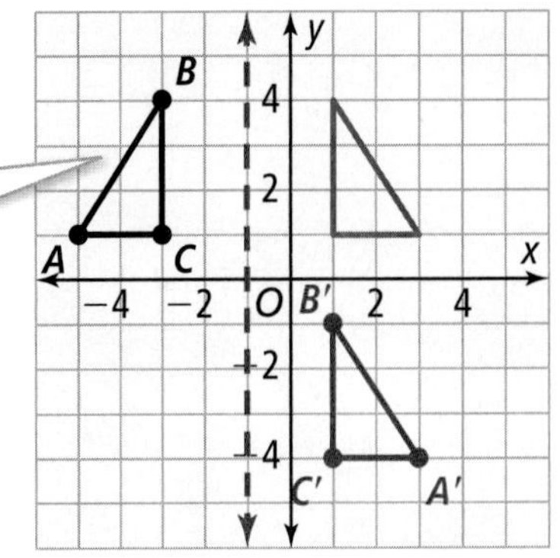


Because $\triangle ABC$ has a clockwise orientation and $\triangle A'B'C'$ has a counterclockwise orientation, orientation is not preserved. This means that one of the rigid motions must be a reflection.

Reflect $\triangle ABC$ across $k$, the line with equation $x = -1$.

Then translate the image down 5 units.

$$(T_{\langle 0,\,-5\rangle} \circ R_k)(\triangle ABC) = \triangle A'B'C'$$

The composition of a reflection followed by a translation in a direction parallel to the line of reflection is a rigid motion called a **glide reflection**.

**USE STRUCTURE**
Often there is more than one composition of rigid motions that maps a preimage to its image. What is another composition of rigid motions that maps $\triangle ABC$ to $\triangle A'B'C'$?

**Try It!** 2. Draw the perpendicular bisector of $\overline{BB'}$. Is that line also the perpendicular bisector of $\overline{AA'}$ and $\overline{CC'}$? Use your answer to explain why a reflection alone can or cannot map $\triangle ABC$ to $\triangle A'B'C'$.

## EXAMPLE 3 Find the Image of a Glide Reflection

**A digital artist is reproducing a tire tread pattern from a partial tire print from a crime scene by applying a glide reflection. She uses the rule $T_{\langle 0,\,0.1\rangle} \circ R_{y\text{-axis}}$ to generate a pattern. Confirm that her rule can be applied to the partial pattern that was taken from the crime scene.**

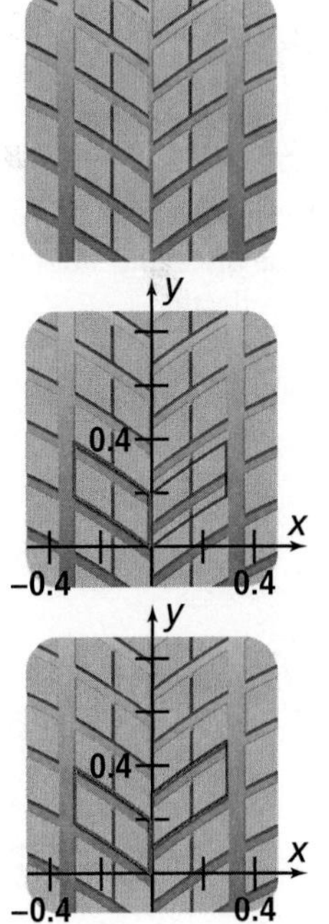


**Step 1** Apply the first rigid motion.

Reflect the outlined preimage across the line $x = 0$.

**Step 2** Apply the second rigid motion.

Translate the reflection 0.1 unit up.

The rule appears to map the pieces of the partial pattern onto itself.

**COMMON ERROR**
The notation tells you the order in which you should use the transformations. Remember that in the composition $T_{\langle 0,\,0.1\rangle} \circ R_{y\text{-axis}}$, the reflection is performed first.

**Try It!** 3. Quadrilateral $RSTV$ has vertices $R(-3, 2)$, $S(0, 5)$, $T(4, -4)$, and $V(0, -2)$. Use the rule $T_{\langle 1,\,0\rangle} \circ R_{x\text{-axis}}$ to graph and label the glide reflection of $RSTV$.

## THEOREM 3-4

Any rigid motion is either a translation, reflection, rotation, or glide reflection.

**If...** $M$ is a rigid motion

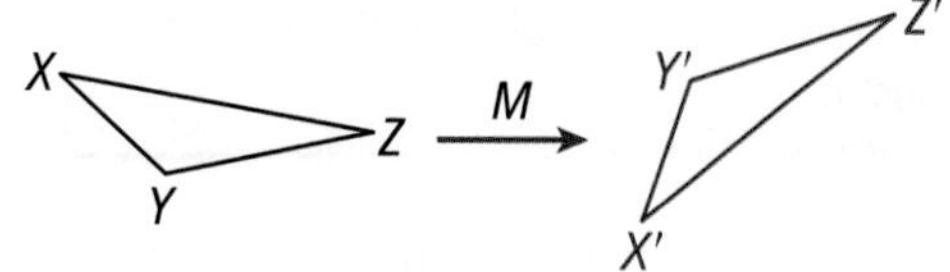


**Then...** $M = R_\ell$ or
$M = T_{\langle x, y \rangle}$ or
$M = r_{(n°, P)}$ or
$M = T_{\langle x, y \rangle} \circ R_\ell$

You will prove this in a more advanced course.

## COROLLARY TO THEOREM 3-4

Any rigid motion can be expressed as a composition of reflections.

**If...** $M$ is a rigid motion

**Then...** $M = R_\ell$ or $M = R_\ell \circ R_m$ or $M = R_\ell \circ R_m \circ R_n$

PROOF: SEE EXERCISE 11.

## EXAMPLE 4 Determine Any Glide Reflection

**What is the glide reflection that maps △JKL to △J″K″L″?**

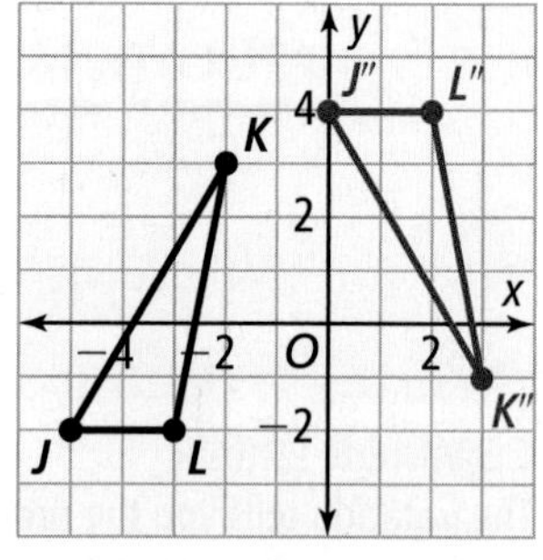


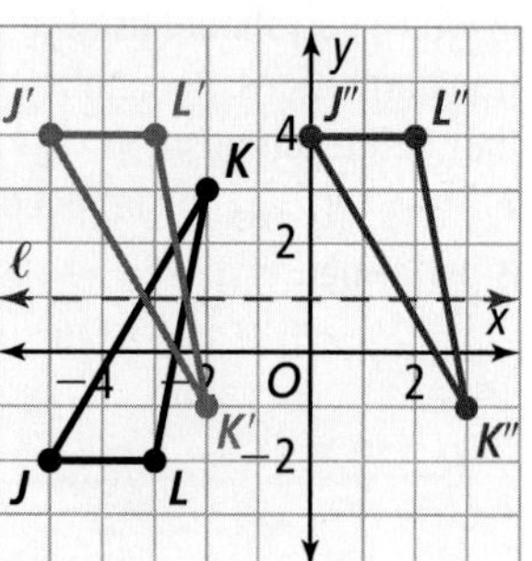


To determine the glide reflection, you can work backward.

**Step 1** Determine the translation.

First determine the translation that vertically aligns $J''$ with $J$ and $L''$ with $L$. It is 5 units horizontally and 0 units vertically.

**Step 2** Determine the line of reflection.

The vertices of an image and preimage are the same distance from the line $\ell$ with equation $y = 1$, so $\ell$ is the line of reflection. If you reflect △J′K′L′ across $\ell$, you map back to the original triangle, △JKL.

**Step 3** Write the complete glide reflection.

$$\left(T_{\langle 5, 0 \rangle} \circ R_\ell\right)(\triangle JKL) = (\triangle J'K'L'), \text{ where } \ell \text{ is the line } y = 1$$

STUDY TIP

The vertices of the preimage and of the image are equidistant from the line of reflection.

**Try It!** 4. What is the glide reflection that maps each of the following?

**a.** $\triangle ABC \to \triangle A'B'C'$ given $A(-3, 4)$, $B(-4, 2)$, $C(-1, 1)$, $A'(1, 1)$, $B'(2, -1)$, and $C'(-1, -2)$.

**b.** $\overline{RS} \to \overline{R'S'}$ given $R(-2, 4)$, $S(2, 6)$, $R'(0, -6)$, and $S'(2, -2)$.

  Concept Summary 

## CONCEPT SUMMARY Types of Rigid Motions

**REFLECTION**

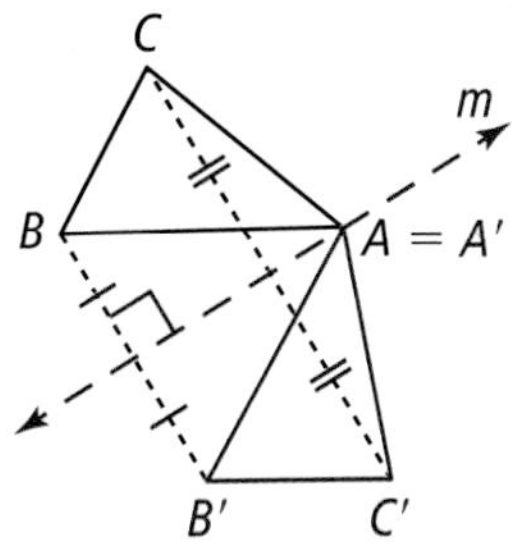


$R_m(\triangle ABC) = \triangle A'B'C'$

**TRANSLATION**

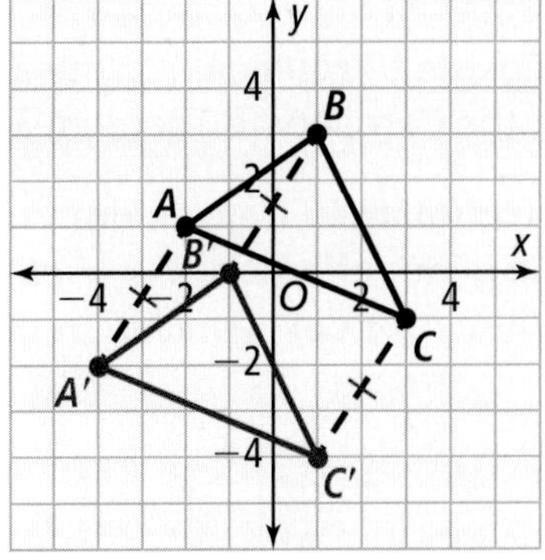


$T_{\langle -2, -3 \rangle}(\triangle ABC) = \triangle A'B'C'$

**ROTATION**

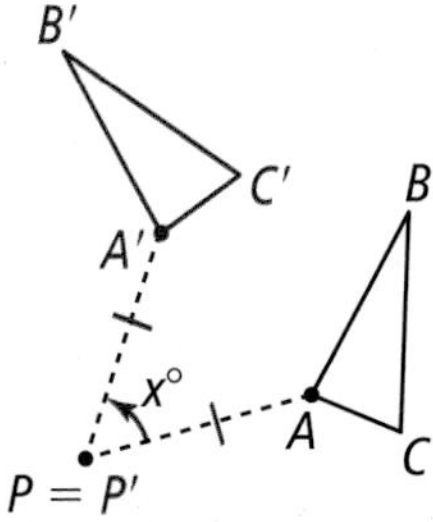


$r_{(x°, P)}(\triangle ABC) = \triangle A'B'C'$

**GLIDE REFLECTION**

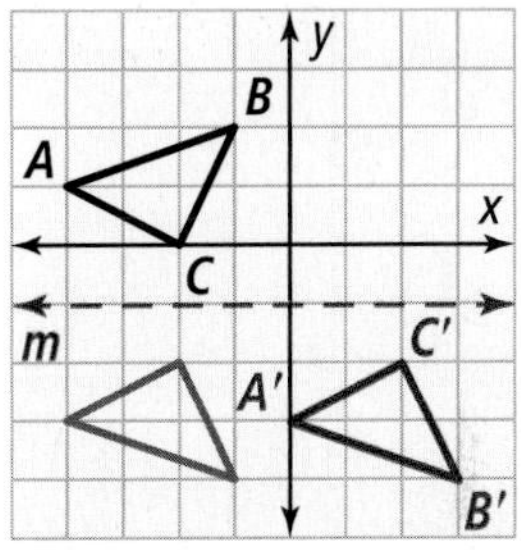


$(T_{\langle 4, 0 \rangle} \circ R_m)(\triangle ABC) = \triangle A'B'C'$

## Do You UNDERSTAND?

1. **ESSENTIAL QUESTION** How can rigid motions be classified?

2. **Vocabulary** Is it correct to say that the composition of a translation followed by a reflection is a glide reflection? Explain.

3. **Error Analysis** Tamika draws the following diagram as an example of a glide reflection. What error did she make?

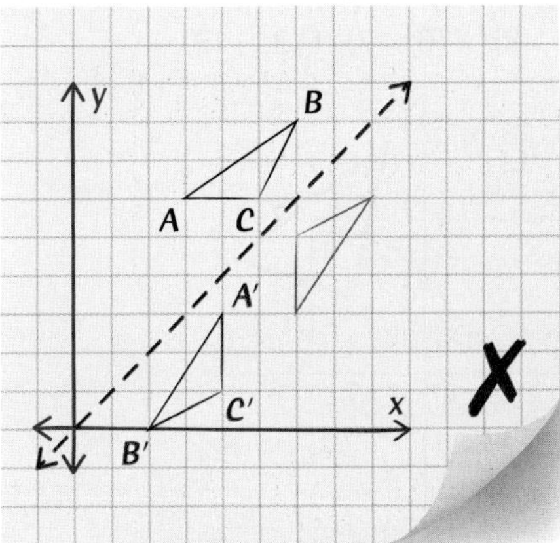


## Do You KNOW HOW?

**Use the figures for Exercises 4–7. Identify each rigid motion as a translation, a reflection, a rotation, or a glide reflection.**

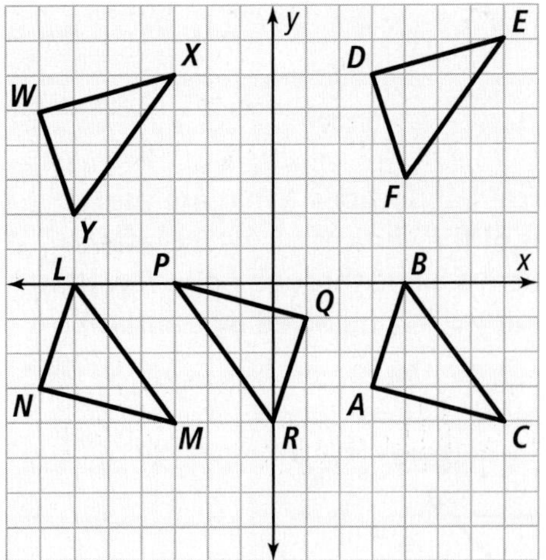


4. $\triangle WYX \to \triangle NLM$

5. $\triangle DFE \to \triangle WYX$

6. $\triangle WYX \to \triangle ABC$

7. $\triangle NLM \to \triangle QRP$

UNDERSTAND

8. **Construct Arguments** Write a paragraph proof of the Corollary to Theorem 3-4.

9. **Error Analysis** Damian draws the diagram for the glide reflection $(T_{\langle 7,\,0\rangle} \circ R_{y\text{-axis}})(ABCD)$. What error did he make?

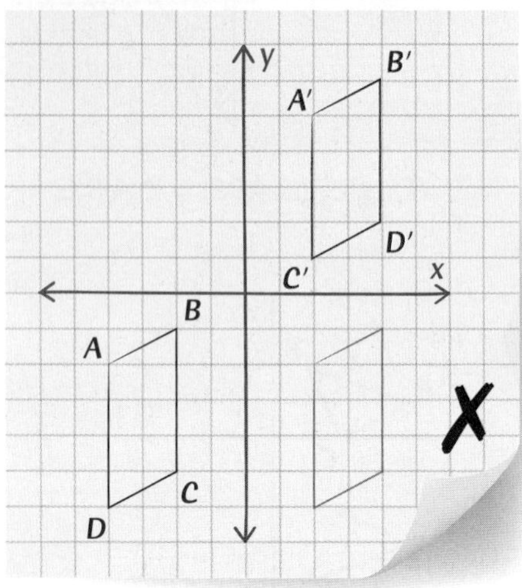


10. **Higher Order Thinking** What are the reflection and translation for the glide reflection shown? Sketch the intermediate image.

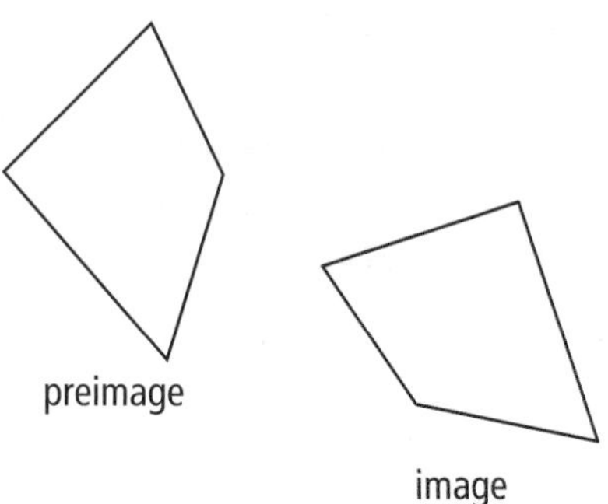


11. **Mathematical Connections** What are the coordinates of the vertices of $\triangle A'B'C'$ after a reflection across a line through point $P$ with a $y$-intercept at $y = -2$, followed by translation $T_{\langle 3,\,3\rangle}$?

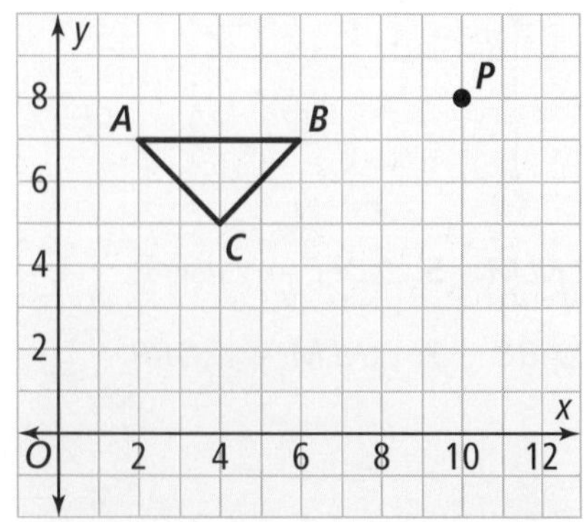


PRACTICE

12. What are two rigid motions with a composition that maps $\triangle JKL$ to $\triangle J'K'L'$? SEE EXAMPLES 1 AND 2

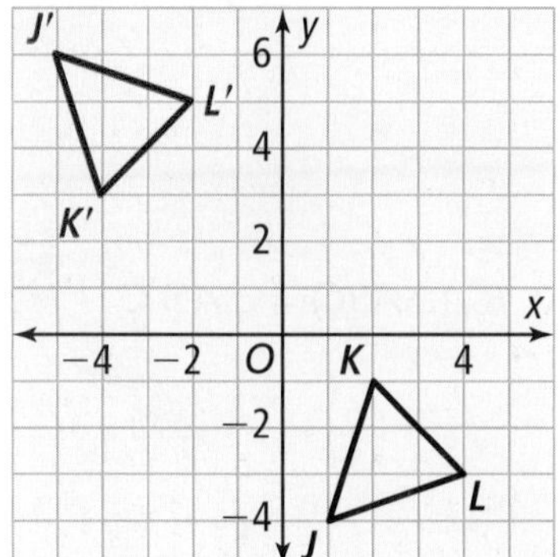


**For Exercises 13–17, given $A(6, -4)$, $B(3, 8)$, and $C(-7, 9)$, determine the coordinates of the vertices of $\triangle A'B'C'$ for each glide reflection. Suppose $p$ is the line with equation $x = -3$, $q$ is the line with equation $y = 9$, and $r$ is the line with equation $y = -2$.** SEE EXAMPLE 3

13. $(T_{\langle 0,\,-2\rangle} \circ R_{y\text{-axis}})(\triangle ABC) = \triangle A'B'C'$

14. $(T_{\langle 4,\,0\rangle} \circ R_{x\text{-axis}})(\triangle ABC) = \triangle A'B'C'$

15. $(T_{\langle 0,\,8\rangle} \circ R_{p})(\triangle ABC) = \triangle A'B'C'$

16. $(T_{\langle -5,\,0\rangle} \circ R_{q})(\triangle ABC) = \triangle A'B'C'$

17. $(T_{\langle 7,\,0\rangle} \circ R_{r})(\triangle ABC) = \triangle A'B'C'$

**For Exercises 18–21, write a rule for each glide reflection that maps $\triangle DEF$ to $\triangle D'E'F'$.** SEE EXAMPLE 4

18. $D(7, -2)$, $E(3, 9)$, $F(8, 6)$;
$D'(-5, 1)$, $E'(-1, 12)$, $F'(-6, 9)$

19. $D(-5, 8)$, $E(1, 4)$, $F(6, 3)$;
$D'(-3, 8)$, $E'(3, 12)$, $F'(8, 13)$

20. $D(0, 4)$, $E(6, 3)$, $F(9, 8)$;
$D'(-6, -8)$, $E'(0, -7)$, $F'(3, -12)$

21.

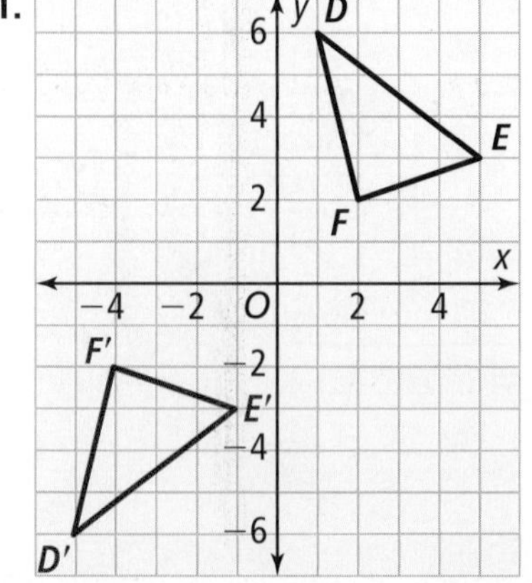

# PRACTICE & PROBLEM SOLVING

Practice  Tutorial

Mixed Review Available Online

## APPLY

**22. Look for Relationships** The diagram shows one section of concrete being stamped with a pattern. The design can be described by two glide reflections from triangle 1 to triangle 5. Write the rules for each glide reflection.

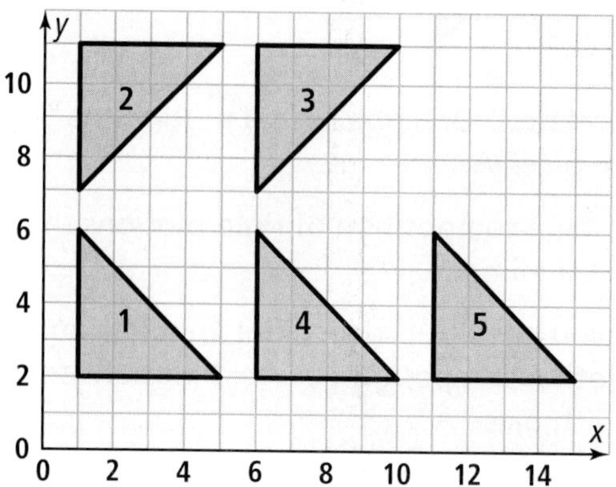

**23. Model With Mathematics** Each parking space in the figure can be the image of another parking space as a glide reflection. What is the rule that maps the parking space where the red car is parked to the parking space where the blue car is parked?

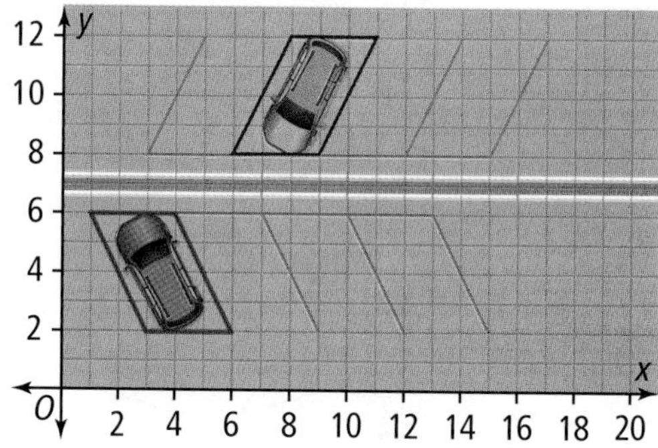

**24. Look for Relationships** Starting from tile 1, quadrilateral tiles are embedded into a wall following a pattern of glide reflections. If the pattern continues, what are the shapes and locations of the next two tiles the builder will place in the wall? Explain.

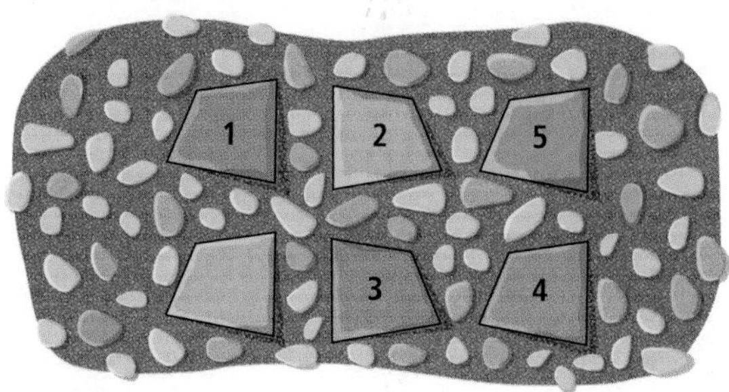


## ASSESSMENT PRACTICE

**25.** Match each rigid motion with its image.

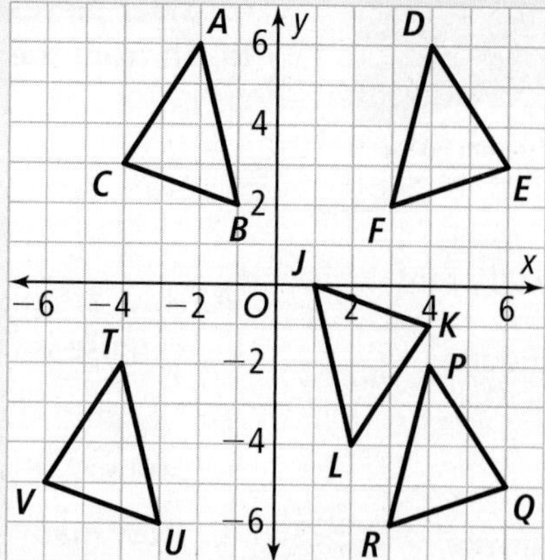

I. $r_{(180°, (0, 1))}(\triangle ABC)$ — A. $\triangle ABC$

II. $(T_{\langle 0, 8\rangle} \circ R_{y\text{-axis}})(\triangle TUV)$ — B. $\triangle DFE$

III. $(T_{\langle -2, 0\rangle} \circ R_{y\text{-axis}})(\triangle DFE)$ — C. $\triangle LJK$

IV. $R_{y\text{-axis}}(\triangle TUV)$ — D. $\triangle PRQ$

**26. SAT/ACT** Suppose $m$ is the line with equation $y = 3$. Given $A(7, 1)$, $B(2, 9)$, and $C(3, -5)$, what are the coordinates of the vertices of $\triangle A'B'C'$ for $(T_{\langle -4, 0\rangle} \circ R_m)(\triangle ABC) = \triangle A'B'C'$?

Ⓐ $A'(11, 4)$, $B'(6, 12)$, $C'(7, -2)$

Ⓑ $A'(11, 5)$, $B'(-6, -3)$, $C'(7, 11)$

Ⓒ $A'(3, 4)$, $B'(-2, 12)$, $C'(-1, -2)$

Ⓓ $A'(3, 5)$, $B'(-2, -3)$, $C'(-1, 11)$

**27. Performance Task** Glide reflections are used to print a design across a length of wrapping paper.

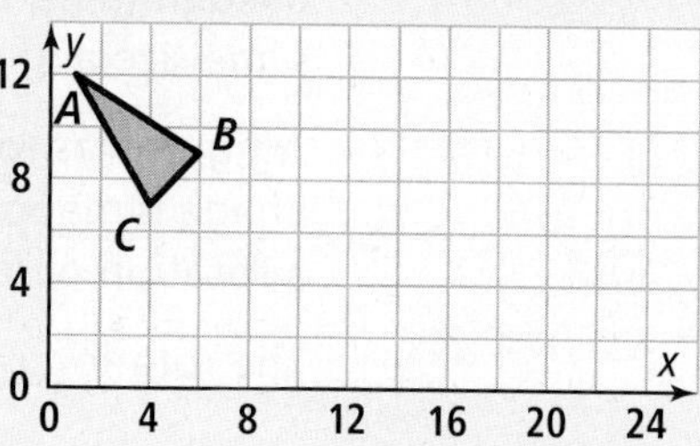

**Part A** The printer produces the second triangle $(T_{\langle 0, -2\rangle} \circ R_{\ell})(\triangle ABC)$, where $\ell$ is the line with equation $x = 5$. Copy the diagram and draw image $\triangle A'B'C'$.

**Part B** Translate $\triangle ABC$ to the right 7 units to $\triangle DEF$, and then translate $\triangle ABC$ to the right 14 units to $\triangle GHJ$. Draw and describe glide reflections that map $\triangle DEF$ and $\triangle GHJ$ to images $\triangle D'E'F'$ and $\triangle G'H'J'$ like those in Part A.

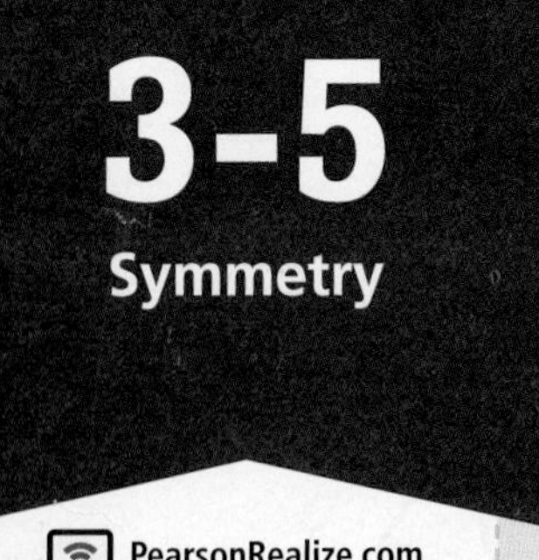

# 3-5 Symmetry

PearsonRealize.com

**I CAN…** identify different types of symmetry in two-dimensional figures.

## VOCABULARY

- point symmetry
- reflectional symmetry
- rotational symmetry

## EXPLORE & REASON

**Look at the kaleidoscope image shown. Then consider pieces A and B taken from the image.**

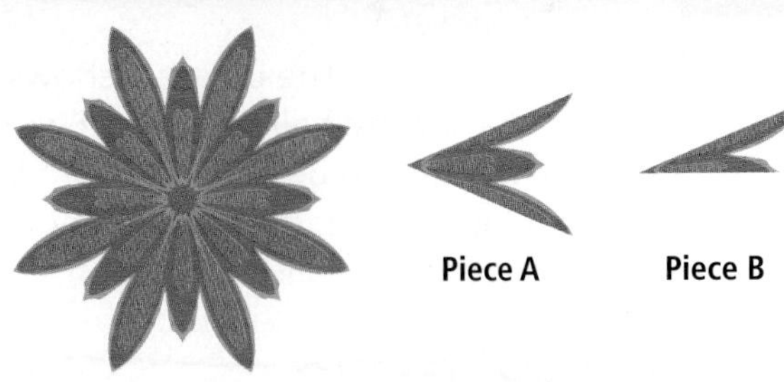


A. How are piece A and piece B related? Describe a rigid motion that you can use on piece B to produce piece A.

B. **Communicate Precisely** Describe a composition of rigid motions that you can use on piece A to produce the image.

C. How many rigid motions did you need to produce the image from piece A? Can you think of another composition of rigid motions to produce the image starting with piece A?

## ESSENTIAL QUESTION

**How can you tell whether a figure is symmetric?**

CONCEPTUAL UNDERSTANDING

## EXAMPLE 1 Identify Transformations for Symmetry

**What transformations can be used to map the figure onto itself? Why can some figures be mapped onto themselves?**

STUDY TIP
To identify reflectional symmetry, fold a figure so one half lines up with the other.

A figure has symmetry if a rigid motion can map the figure onto itself.

**Reflectional symmetry** is a symmetry for which a reflection maps the figure onto itself. The line of reflection for a reflection symmetry is called the line of symmetry.

The reflections $R_m$ and $R_n$ map the figure onto itself. Observe that lines $m$ and $n$ both divide the figure into two pieces with the same size and shape.

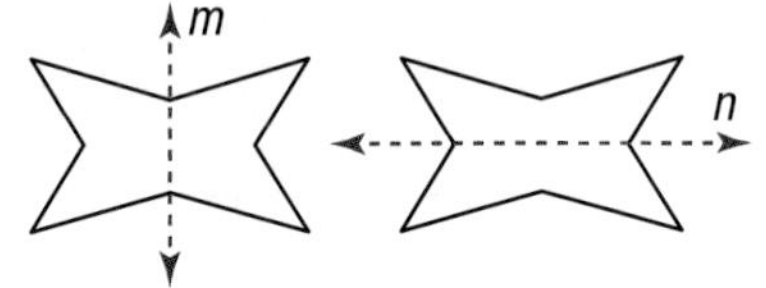


A figure has **rotational symmetry** if its image is mapped onto the preimage after a rotation of less than 360°.

The rotation $r_{(180°, P)}$ maps the figure onto itself.

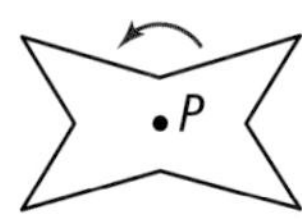


**Try It!** 1. What transformations map each figure onto itself?

a.

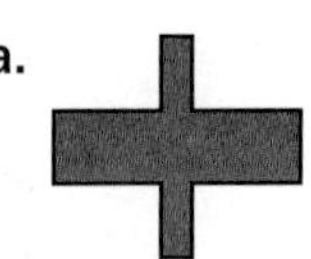

b.

## EXAMPLE 2 Identify Lines of Symmetry

**How many lines of symmetry does a regular hexagon have?**

Each line through opposite vertices creates equal halves.

Each line through midpoints of opposite sides creates equal halves.

A regular hexagon has six lines of symmetry.

**COMMON ERROR**
Remember that lines of symmetry are not necessarily horizontal or vertical lines.

**Try It!** 2. How many lines of symmetry does each figure have? How do you know whether you have found them all?

a. 

b.

## EXAMPLE 3 Identify Rotational Symmetry

**For what angles of rotation does the figure map onto itself?**

**A. an equilateral triangle**

Find the angles of rotation about the center that map $\triangle ABC$ onto itself.

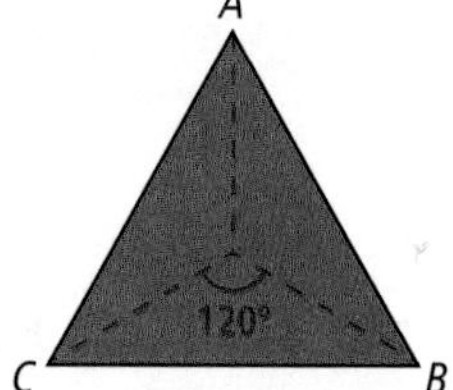


- A rotation of 120° creates an identical image with vertex $B$ at the top.
- A rotation of 240° creates an identical image with vertex $C$ at the top.

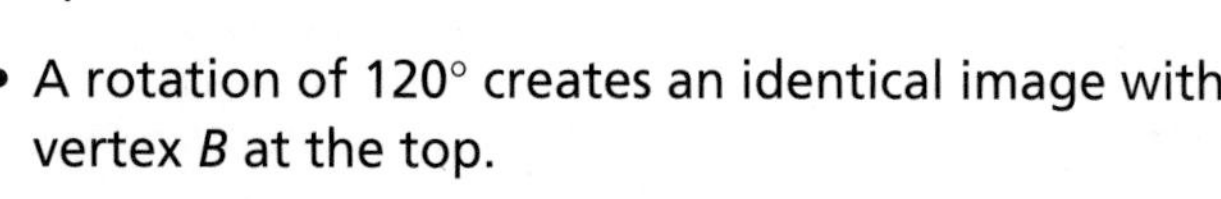

**USE STRUCTURE**
Think about how a regular polygon can be divided. How can you divide a regular polygon into pieces of the same size and shape?

**B. a parallelogram**

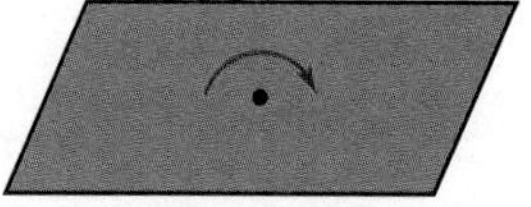

- Only a rotation of 180° maps the figure onto itself.

The type of symmetry for which there is rotation of 180° that maps a figure onto itself is called **point symmetry**. A parallelogram has 180° rotational symmetry, or point symmetry.

**Try It!** 3. What are the rotational symmetries for each figure? Does each figure have point symmetry?

a.  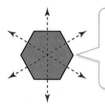 

b. 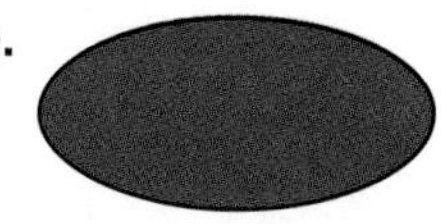

## EXAMPLE 4 Determine Symmetries

**What type(s) of symmetry does each figure have?**

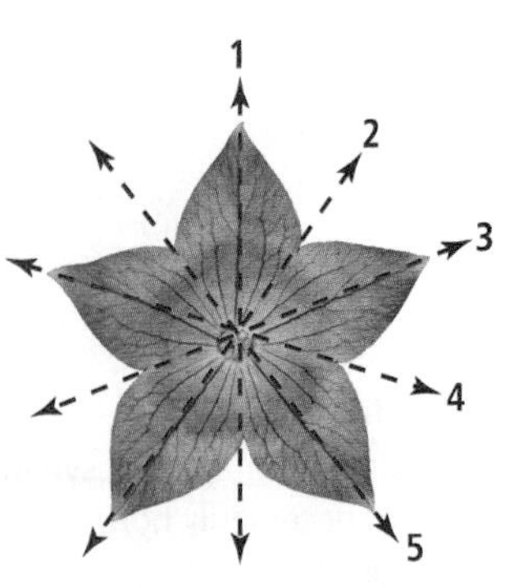


**A.** • A line through the center of a petal is a line of reflection. Since there are 5 petals, there are 5 lines of symmetry.

• Since $360° \div 5 = 72°$, there is rotational symmetry at multiples of 72°.

The flower has reflectional symmetry with 5 lines of symmetry and rotational symmetry for angles of 72°, 144°, 216°, and 288°.

COMMON ERROR
You may think a rectangular figure has reflectional symmetry along the diagonal. Recognize that a rectangular shape may only have horizontal or vertical lines of symmetry.

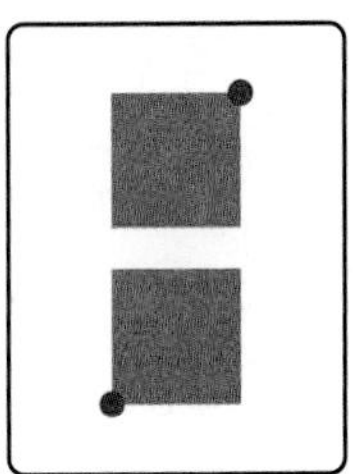

**B.** • No lines of symmetry can be drawn.

• Rotating the card 180° about its center creates an identical image.

The card has 180° rotational symmetry, or point symmetry.

**Try It!** **4.** What symmetries does a square have?

APPLICATION

## EXAMPLE 5 Use Symmetry

**A company CEO wants a new logo that looks the same for each rotation of 30° and uses the three company colors. What are some possible logo designs?**

**Formulate** Consider the different elements of the design.

Start with a polygon that has the specified rotational symmetry, which means a polygon that maps to itself at each 30° rotation.

The colors will have to be used carefully to achieve symmetry.

**Compute** To find the number of sides for the polygon, find the number of 30° rotations in a full circle.

$360° \div 30° = 12$

You need a regular 12-gon (dodecagon).

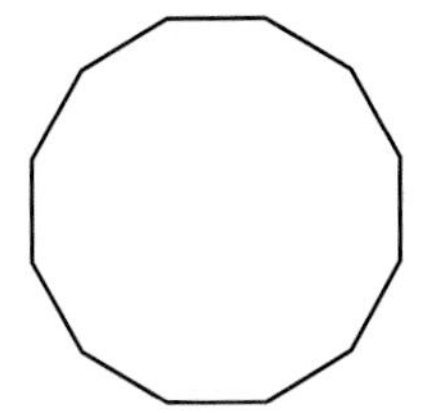

Then, consider how the colors can be used so that each section is the same.

**Interpret** Three possible designs are shown.

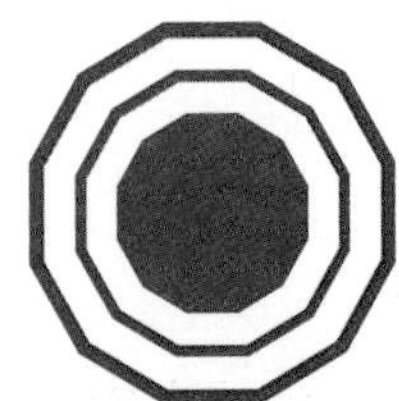

**Try It!** **5.** What is a possible design for a circular logo that looks the same for each 60° rotation and uses at least two colors?

## CONCEPT SUMMARY Symmetry

| | Reflectional Symmetry | Rotational Symmetry |
|---|---|---|
| WORDS | • A figure that maps onto itself when it is reflected over a line has reflectional symmetry.<br>• A line of symmetry is a line of reflection when a figure is reflected onto itself. | • A figure that maps onto itself when it is rotated about its center by an angle measuring less than 360° has **rotational symmetry**.<br>• A figure with 180° rotational symmetry has **point symmetry**. |
| DIAGRAM |  | 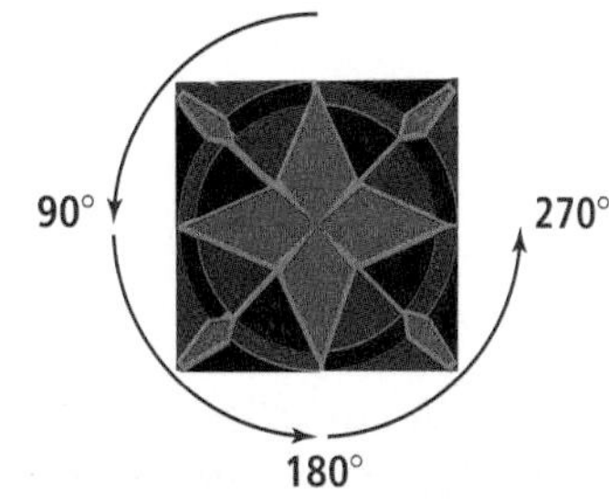 |

## Do You UNDERSTAND?

1. ESSENTIAL QUESTION How can you tell whether a figure is symmetric?

2. **Error Analysis** For the figure below, Adam was asked to draw all lines of reflection. His work is shown. What error did Adam make?

3. **Vocabulary** What type of symmetry does a figure have if it can be mapped onto itself by being flipped over a line?

4. **Communicate Precisely** What does it mean for a figure to have 60° rotational symmetry?

5. **Construct Arguments** Is it possible for a figure to have rotational symmetry and no reflectional symmetry? Explain or give examples.

## Do You KNOW HOW?

**Find the number of lines of symmetry for each figure.**

6. 

7. 

**Describe the rotational symmetry of each figure. State whether each has point symmetry.**

8. 

9. 

**Identify the types of symmetry of each figure. For each figure with reflectional symmetry, identify the lines of symmetry. For each figure with rotational symmetry, identify the angles of rotation that map the figure onto itself.**

10.  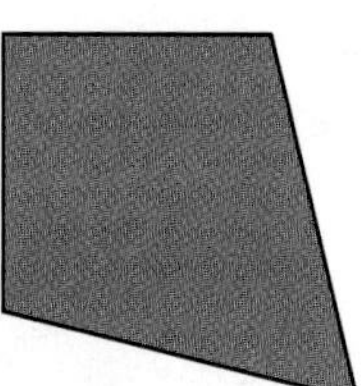

11. 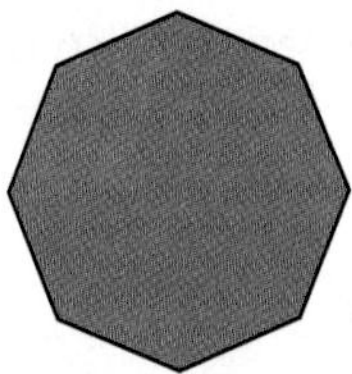

# PRACTICE & PROBLEM SOLVING

Scan for Multimedia

Practice  Tutorial

Additional Exercises Available Online

## UNDERSTAND

12. **Construct Arguments** Is it possible for a figure to have reflectional symmetry and no rotational symmetry? Explain or give examples.

13. **Reason** Explain how you would find the angles of rotational symmetry for the figure shown.

14. **Mathematical Connections** A figure that has 180° rotational symmetry also has point symmetry. Write a conditional to relate those facts. Then, write the converse, inverse, and contrapositive.

15. **Look for Relationships** If a figure has 90° rotational symmetry, what other symmetries must it have?

16. **Error Analysis** Yumiko's work is shown below. What error did she make?

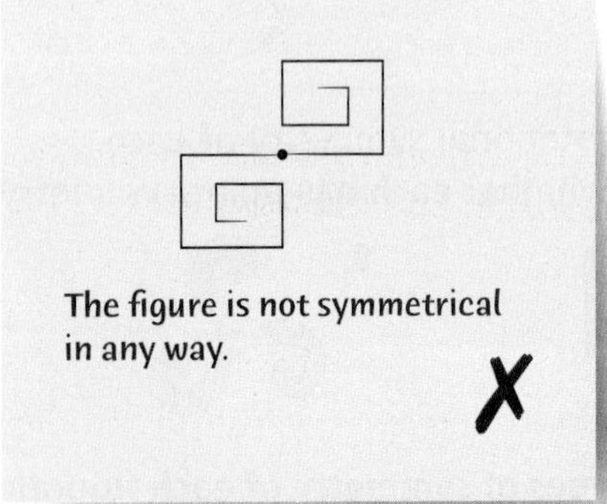

The figure is not symmetrical in any way.
✗


17. **Higher Order Thinking** Three types of rigid motion are translations, rotations, and reflections.

    A frieze pattern is a linear pattern that repeats, and it has translational symmetry. An example is shown below.

Find and name some occurrences of frieze patterns in the real world.

## PRACTICE

**For Exercises 18 and 19, find all transformations that can be used to map each figure onto itself.** SEE EXAMPLE 1

18. 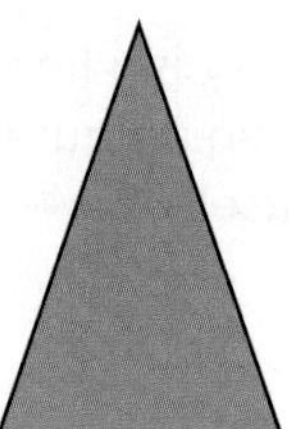

19. 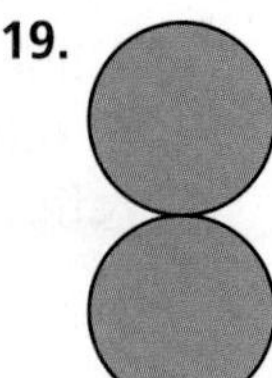

20. How many lines of symmetry does a regular five-pointed star have? SEE EXAMPLE 2

**For Exercises 21 and 22, describe the rotational symmetries of each figure.** SEE EXAMPLE 3

21. 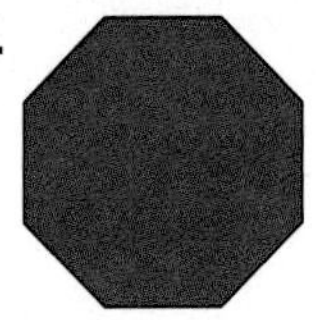

22. 

23. What types of symmetry does the figure have? Explain. SEE EXAMPLE 4

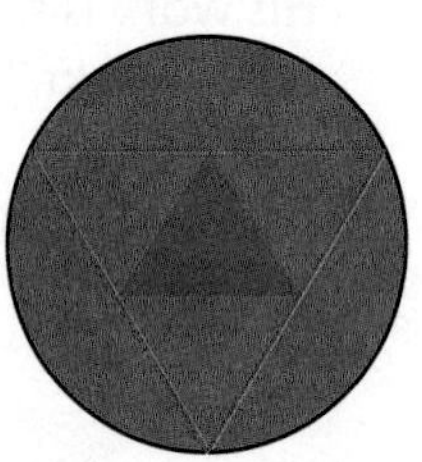

24. When drawn in the style shown, the number 808 has horizontal and vertical reflectional symmetry, as well as 180° rotational symmetry.

What are some other combinations of numbers or letters with symmetry? Find at least three other combinations, and identify the types of symmetry for each. SEE EXAMPLE 5

## PRACTICE & PROBLEM SOLVING

### APPLY

**25. Reason** How would you decide which flags show reflection symmetry? Rotational symmetry? No symmetry?

Canada

Sweden

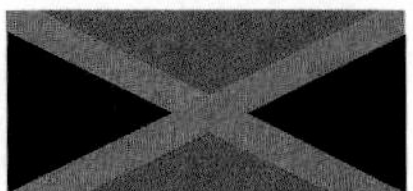
Jamaica

Saint Kitts and Nevis

**26. Look for Relationships** Make observations about the structure of each snowflake, and describe the types of symmetry that a snowflake can have.

**27. Make Sense and Persevere** Describe the symmetries of each molecule shown.

**a.** benzene

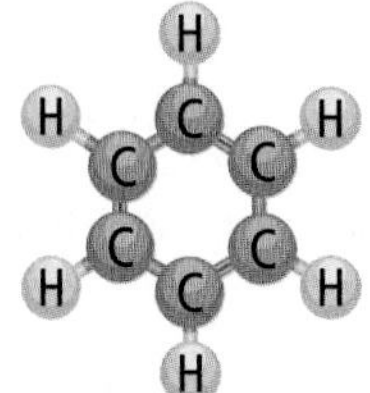


**b.** water

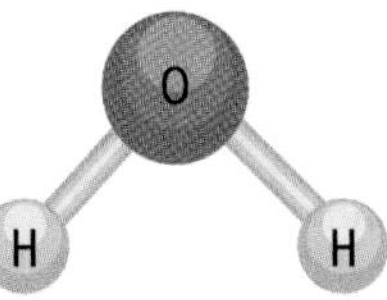


**c.** hydrogen peroxide

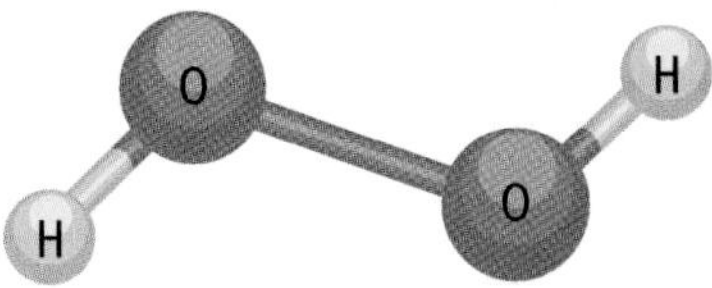


### ASSESSMENT PRACTICE

**28.** Which types of symmetry does the figure display? Select all that apply.

Ⓐ reflectional symmetry across a vertical line
Ⓑ reflectional symmetry across a horizontal line
Ⓒ 120° rotational symmetry
Ⓓ 180° rotational symmetry

**29. SAT/ACT** Which letter can be mapped onto itself by a 180° rotation about its center?

Ⓐ E

Ⓒ 

Ⓑ 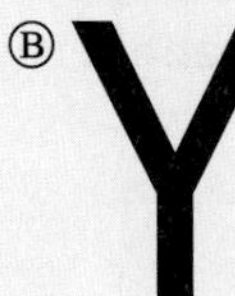

Ⓓ 

**30. Performance Task** A client wants a graphic designer to create an emblem that has rotational symmetry of 90° and 180°. The client needs the colors of the emblem to be red, yellow, and blue. The emblem should also include the first letter of the company name, X.

**Part A** The designer begins his design with a polygon. What polygons can he use?

**Part B** If a figure has rotational symmetry of 90° and 180°, what type of reflectional symmetry does the figure have?

**Part C** Create two possible designs for the client.

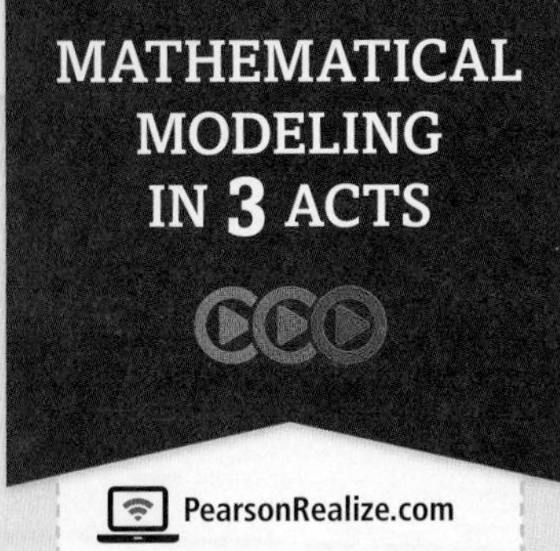


PearsonRealize.com

## The Perplexing Polygon

Look around and you will see shapes and patterns everywhere you look. The tiles on a floor are often all the same shape and fit together to form a pattern. The petals on a flower often make a repeating pattern around the center of the flower. When you look at snowflakes under a microscope, you'll notice that they are made up of repeating three-dimensional crystals. Think about this during the Mathematical Modeling in 3 Acts lesson.

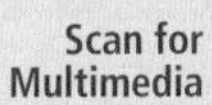

### ACT 1 Identify the Problem

1. What is the first question that comes to mind after watching the video?
2. Write down the main question you will answer about what you saw in the video.
3. Make an initial conjecture that answers this main question.
4. Explain how you arrived at your conjecture.
5. What information will be useful to know to answer the main question? How can you get it? How will you use that information?

### ACT 2 Develop a Model

6. Use the math that you have learned in this Topic to refine your conjecture.

### ACT 3 Interpret the Results

7. Did your refined conjecture match the actual answer exactly? If not, what might explain the difference?

TOPIC 3

# Topic Review

## TOPIC ESSENTIAL QUESTION

1. What are properties of the four types of rigid motion?

## Vocabulary Review

**Choose the correct term to complete each sentence.**

2. A(n) __________ is a transformation about a point with a given angle measure.
3. Reflections, translations, rotations, and glide reflections are the four types of __________.
4. A line that a figure is reflected across so that it maps onto itself is called a(n) __________.
5. The composition of a reflection and a translation is called a(n) __________.
6. The set of points that a transformation acts on is called the __________.
7. The result of a transformation is called the __________.

- composition of rigid motions
- glide reflection
- image
- line of reflection
- line of symmetry
- preimage
- rigid motion
- rotation
- translation

## Concepts & Skills Review

### LESSON 3-1 Reflections

#### Quick Review

A **rigid motion** is a transformation that preserves length and angle measure.

A reflection is a transformation that reflects a point across a line of reflection *m* such that the image of a point *A* on *m* is *A*, and for a point *B* not on *m*, line *m* is the perpendicular bisector $\overline{BB'}$.

A reflection is a rigid motion.

#### Example

**What is the reflection of $\triangle ABC$ across $\ell$?**

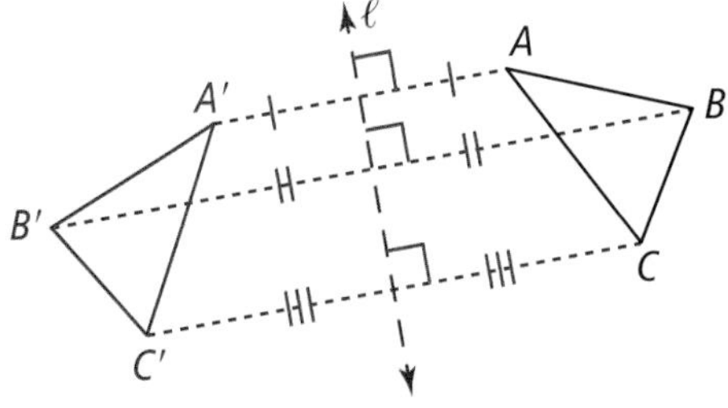


#### Practice & Problem Solving

8. Does the transformation appear to be a rigid motion?

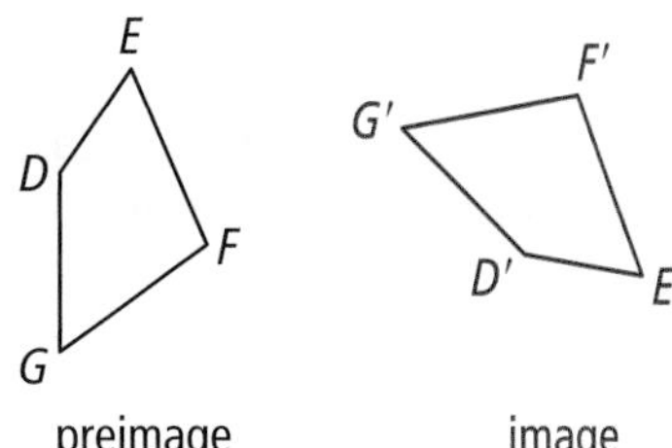


**For Exercises 9 and 10, the vertices of $\triangle HJK$ are $H(-3, 2)$, $J(-1, -3)$, and $K(4, 3)$. What are the coordinates of the vertices of $\triangle H'J'K'$ for each reflection?**

9. $R_{y\text{-axis}}$

10. $R_{x\text{-axis}}$

11. **Communicate Precisely** Given the coordinates of two points and the equation of a line, how can you check that one point is the image of the other point reflected across the line?

TOPIC 3 REVIEW

## LESSON 3-2 Translations

### Quick Review

A translation is a transformation that maps all points the same distance and in the same direction, so that for any two points $A$ and $B$, $AA' = BB'$.

A translation is a rigid motion. Any translation can be expressed as a composition of two reflections across two parallel lines.

### Example

**What is the graph of $T_{\langle 3, -2 \rangle}(\triangle LMN)$?**

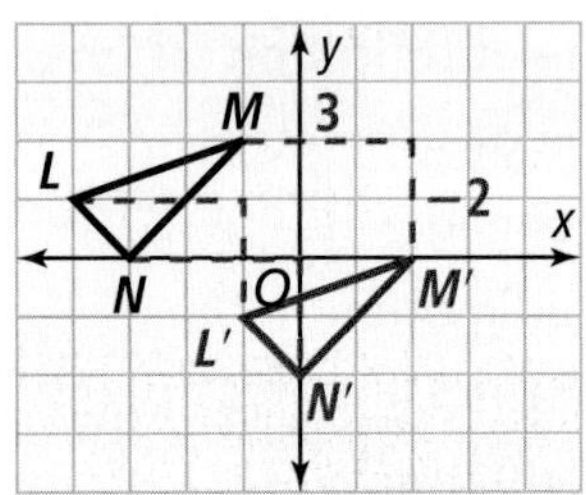


### Practice & Problem Solving

**For Exercises 12 and 13, the vertices of $\triangle PQR$ are $P(-4, 3)$, $Q(-2, 3)$, and $R(1, -3)$. What are the coordinates of the vertices of $\triangle P'Q'R'$ for each translation?**

**12.** $T_{\langle -3, 2 \rangle}$

**13.** $T_{\langle 4, -5 \rangle}$

**14.** What is the translation shown?

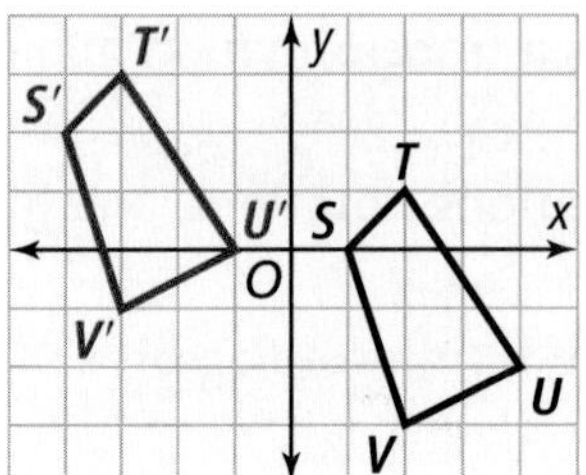


**15. Make Sense and Persevere** Given reflections $R_h$ and $R_k$, where $h$ is a line with equation $x = -3$ and $k$ is a line with equation $x = 2$, how can you determine the distance of the translation resulting from the composition $R_k \circ R_h$?

## LESSON 3-3 Rotations

### Quick Review

A rotation is a transformation that rotates a point about the center of rotation $P$ by the angle of rotation $x°$ such that the image of $P$ is $P$, $PA = PA'$, and $m\angle APA' = x$.

A rotation is a rigid motion. Any rotation can be expressed as a composition of reflections across two intersecting lines.

### Example

**What is the 150° rotation of $\overline{XY}$ about $P$?**

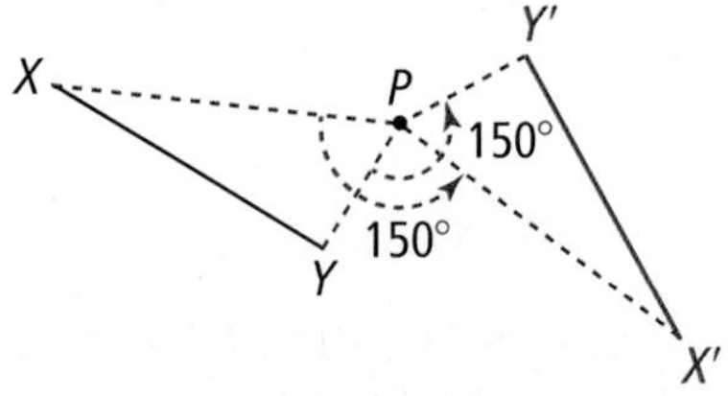


### Practice & Problem Solving

**For Exercise 16 and 17, the vertices of $\triangle ABC$ are $A(2, -2)$, $B(-3, -2)$, and $C(-1, 3)$. What are the coordinates of the vertices of $\triangle A'B'C'$ for each rotation?**

**16.** $r_{(90°, O)}$

**17.** $r_{(270°, O)}$

**18.** Draw two lines of reflection so the composition of the reflections across the lines is equivalent to the rotation shown.

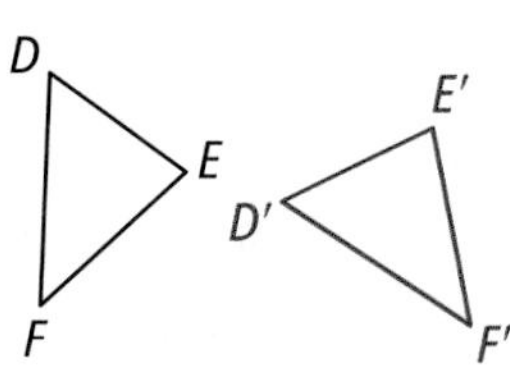


**19. Use Structure** If two lines intersect at a right angle at point $P$, what rotation is equivalent to the composition of the reflections across the two lines?

## LESSON 3-4 Classification of Rigid Motions

### Quick Review

A **glide reflection** is the composition of a reflection followed by a translation.

Any rigid motion is either a translation, reflection, rotation, or glide reflection. As a result, any rigid motion can be expressed as a combination of reflections.

### Example

**What is a glide reflection that maps $\triangle GHJ$ to $\triangle KLM$?**

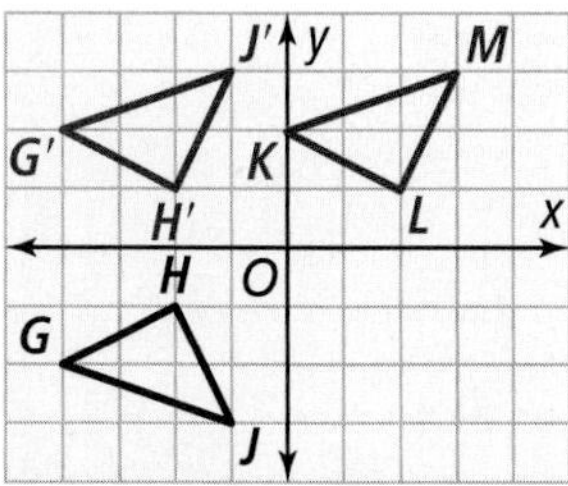


First reflect $\triangle GHJ$ across the $x$-axis to get $\triangle G'H'J'$. Then translate $\triangle G'H'J'$ by 4 units to the right to get $\triangle KLM$. The glide reflection is $T_{\langle 4,\ 0\rangle} \circ R_{x\text{-axis}}$.

### Practice & Problem Solving

**For Exercises 20 and 21, the vertices of $\triangle LMN$ are $L(-2, 4)$, $M(1, 2)$, and $N(-3, -5)$. Suppose $j$ is a line with equation $x = 3$ and $k$ is a line with equation $y = -2$. what are the coordinates of the vertices of $\triangle L'M'N'$ for each glide reflection?**

**20.** $T_{\langle -2,\ 4\rangle} \circ R_j$

**21.** $T_{\langle 2,\ -3\rangle} \circ R_k$

**22.** What is a glide reflection for the transformation shown?

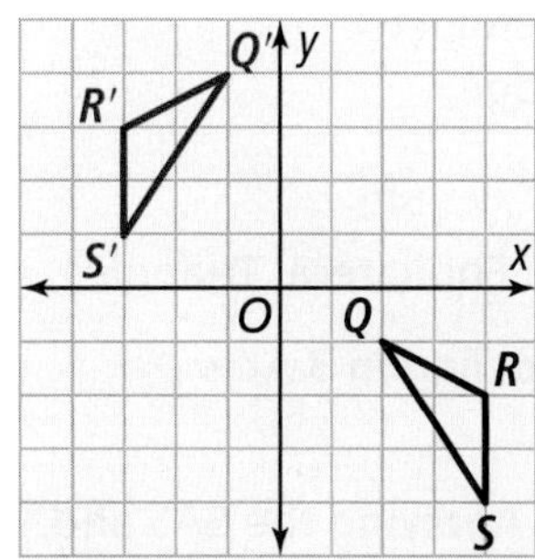


**23. Make Sense and Persevere** Is there more than one way to describe a glide reflection as a composition of a reflection and then a translation? Explain.

## LESSON 3-5 Symmetry

### Quick Review

A figure has **symmetry** if a rigid motion can map the figure to itself. If the rigid motion is a reflection, then the symmetry is **reflectional symmetry**. If the rigid motion is a rotation, then the symmetry is **rotational symmetry**.

When the angle of rotation is 180°, the rotational symmetry is called **point symmetry**.

### Example

**How many lines of symmetry does the figure have?**

You can draw a line of reflection through each vertex and the center of the star. There are six lines of symmetry.

### Practice & Problem Solving

**24.** Describe the transformations that can be used to map the figure onto itself.

**For Exercises 25 and 26, describe all the symmetries of each figure. If the figure has reflectional symmetry, identify all the lines of symmetry. If the figure has rotational symmetry, give the angles of rotation.**

**25.**

**26.**

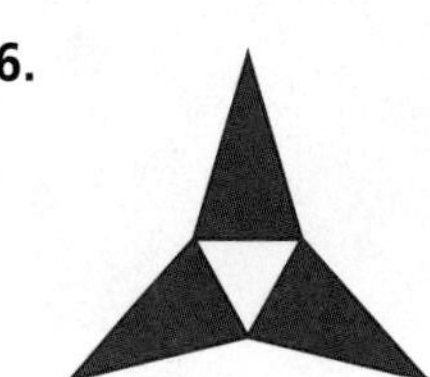

**27. Communicate Precisely** Suppose a figure has at least two lines of symmetry. Explain why the figure must have rotational symmetry.

TOPIC 4

# Triangle Congruence

## TOPIC ESSENTIAL QUESTION

**What relationships between sides and angles of triangles can be used to prove triangles congruent?**

## Topic Overview

**enVision™ STEM Project**
Design a Bridge

**4-1** Congruence

**4-2** Isosceles and Equilateral Triangles

**Mathematical Modeling in 3 Acts**
Check It Out!

**4-3** Proving and Applying the SAS and SSS Congruence Criteria

**4-4** Proving and Applying the ASA and AAS Congruence Criteria

**4-5** Congruence in Right Triangles

**4-6** Congruence in Overlapping Triangles

## Topic Vocabulary

- congruence transformation
- congruent

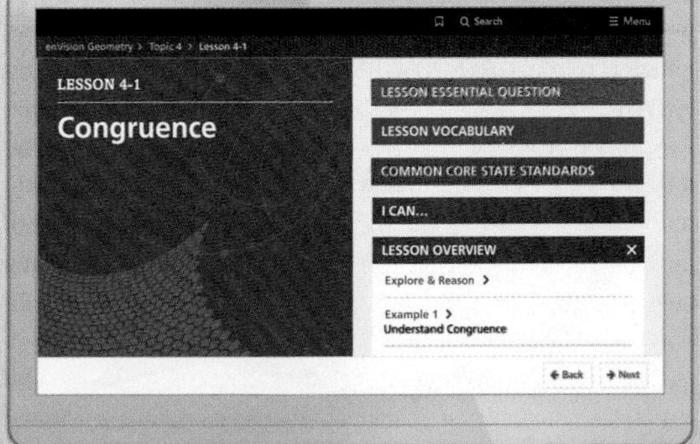

Go online | **PearsonRealize.com**

## Digital Experience

**INTERACTIVE STUDENT EDITION** Access online or offline.

**ACTIVITIES** Complete ***Explore & Reason, Model & Discuss***, and ***Critique & Explain*** activities. Interact with Examples and Try Its.

**ANIMATION** View and interact with real-world applications.

**PRACTICE** Practice what you've learned.

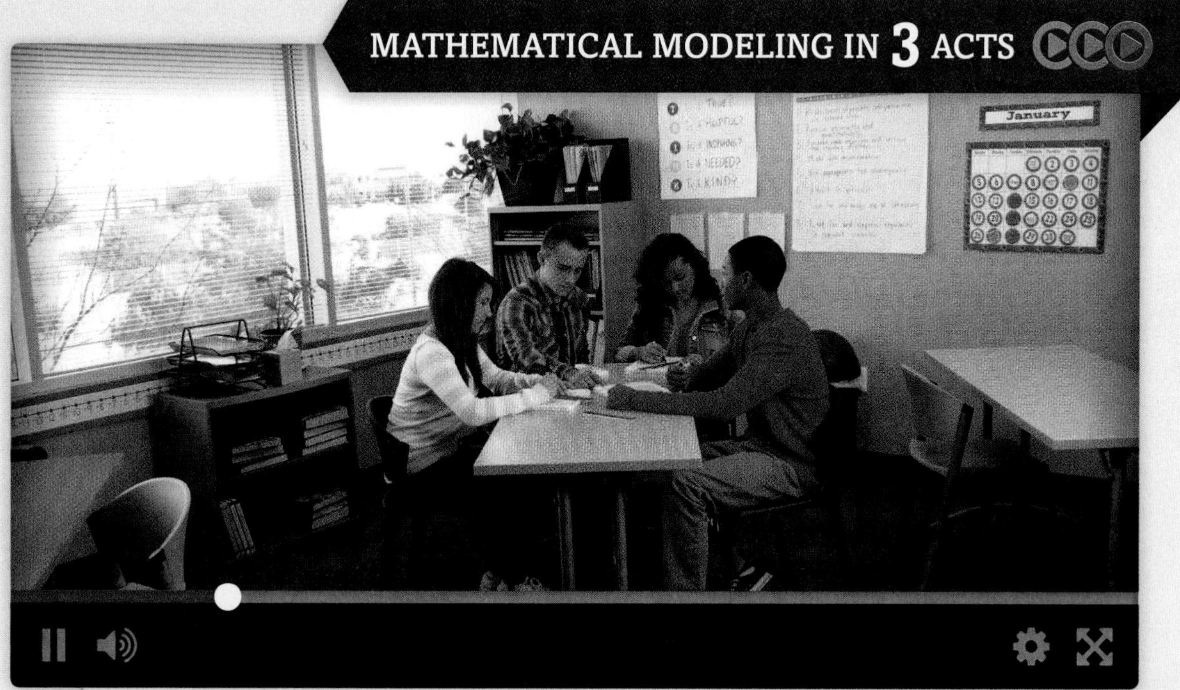


## Check It Out!

Maybe you've played this game before: you draw a picture. Then you try to get a classmate to draw the same picture by giving step-by-step directions but without showing your drawings.

Try it with a classmate. Draw a map of a room in your house or a place in your town. Then give directions to a classmate to draw the map that you drew. How similar are they? Think about your results during the Mathematical Modeling in 3 Acts lesson.

TOPIC 4

**VIDEOS** Watch clips to support ***Mathematical Modeling in 3 Acts Lessons*** and **enVision™ *STEM Projects.***

**CONCEPT SUMMARY** Review key lesson content through multiple representations.

**ASSESSMENT** Show what you've learned.

**GLOSSARY** Read and listen to English and Spanish definitions.

**TUTORIALS** Get help from *Virtual Nerd*, right when you need it.

**MATH TOOLS** Explore math with digital tools and manipulatives.

Video

## Did You Know?

The **Tacoma Narrows Bridge**, in Washington, collapsed in high winds a few months after it opened in 1940. The bridge was rebuilt in 1950 using a truss for stabilization.

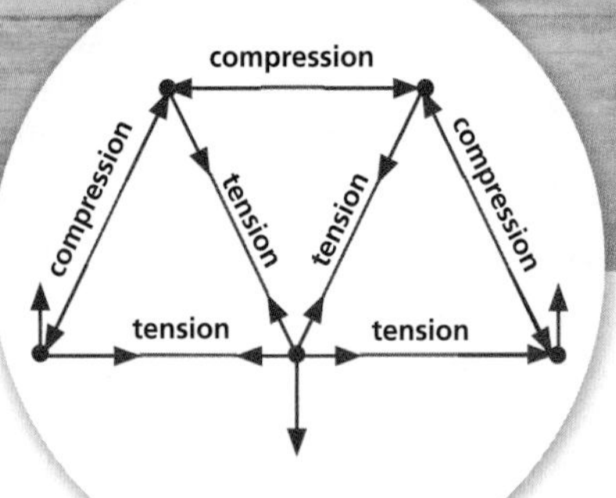


A bridge works by **balancing compression (pressing inward) and tension (pressing outward)**, distributing the load onto the bridge supports.

The design of a truss is based on the strength of a triangle. It distributes a load from a narrow point to a wider base.

Weight of **bridge** | Weight of **people** | Weight of **vehicles** | Weight of **precipitation**

## Your Task: Design a Bridge

You and your classmates will analyze different truss bridge designs and how congruent triangles are used in each construction. What type of truss would you use in a bridge design, and why?

# 4-1 Congruence

**I CAN…** use a composition of rigid motions to show that two objects are congruent.

**VOCABULARY**

- congruence transformation
- congruent

## EXPLORE & REASON

**Some corporate logos are distinctive because they make use of repeated shapes.**

A designer creates two versions of a new logo for the Bolt Company. Version 1 uses the original image shown at the right and a reflection of it. Version 2 uses reduced copies of the original image.

**A.** Make a sketch of each version.

**B. Communicate Precisely** The owner of the company says, "I like your designs, but it is important that the transformed image be the same size and shape as the original image." What would you do to comply with the owner's requirements?

**C.** What transformations can you apply to the original image that would produce logos acceptable to the owner? Explain.

**ESSENTIAL QUESTION** What is the relationship between rigid motions and congruence?

CONCEPTUAL UNDERSTANDING

## EXAMPLE 1 Understand Congruence

**Suppose there is a rigid motion that maps one figure to another. Why does that show that the two figures are congruent?**

Triangle *ABC* has the following lengths and angle measures, and $\triangle DEF$ is the image of $\triangle ABC$ after the rigid motion $T_{\langle 2,-5\rangle} \circ R_{\ell}$.

$AB = 4$ $\quad m\angle A = 90$

$BC = 5$ $\quad m\angle B = 37$

$AC = 3$ $\quad m\angle C = 53$

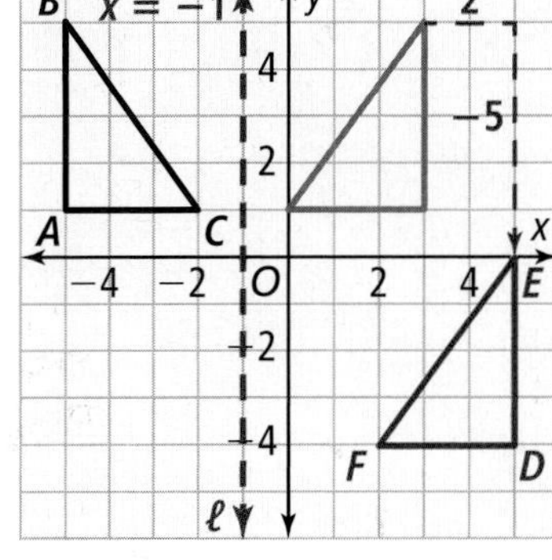


Because rigid motions preserve length and angle measure, $\triangle DEF$ has the following lengths and angle measures.

$DE = AB = 4$ $\quad m\angle D = m\angle A = 90$

$EF = BC = 5$ $\quad m\angle E = m\angle B = 37$

$DF = AC = 3$ $\quad m\angle F = m\angle C = 53$

Since rigid motions preserve measures of corresponding sides and angles, the two triangles are *congruent*.

**STUDY TIP**
Recall that angles with the same measure are congruent, and segments with the same length are congruent.

**Try It!** **1.** A 90° rotation about the origin maps $\triangle PQR$ to $\triangle LMN$. Are the triangles congruent? Explain.

## CONCEPT Congruence

Figures that have the same size and shape are said to be *congruent.* Two figures are **congruent** if there is a rigid motion that maps one figure to the other.

A rigid motion is sometimes called a **congruence transformation** because it maps a figure to a congruent figure.

Use the ≅ symbol to show that two figures are congruent. Since $R_m(\triangle ABC) = \triangle DEF$, $\triangle ABC \cong \triangle DEF$.

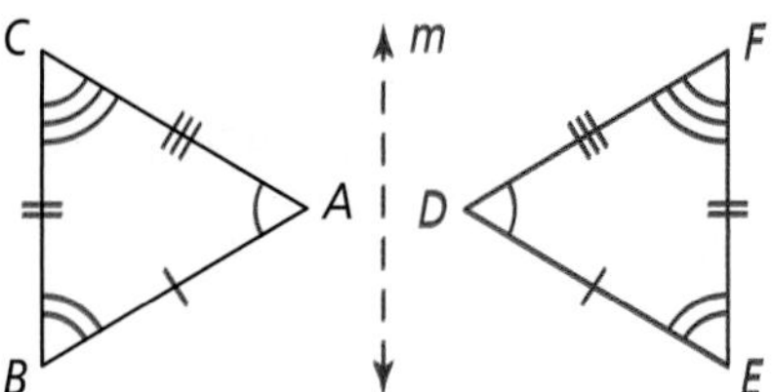


## EXAMPLE 2 Verify Congruence

**Given $\triangle XYZ \cong \triangle ABC$, what composition of rigid motions maps $\triangle XYZ$ to $\triangle ABC$?**

First rotate $\triangle XYZ$ 180° about point $Z$. Next translate the image three units to the right.

$$(T_{\langle 3, 0\rangle} \circ r_{(180°, Z)})(\triangle XYZ) = \triangle ABC$$

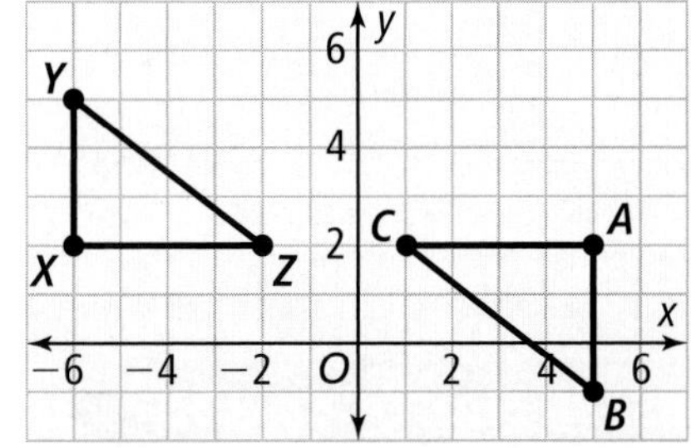


The composition $T_{\langle 3, 0\rangle} \circ r_{(180°, Z)}$ maps $\triangle XYZ$ to $\triangle ABC$.

**LOOK FOR RELATIONSHIPS**
Think of other solutions. Can you identify another composition of rigid motions that maps one triangle to the other?

## Try It! 2. Use the graph shown.

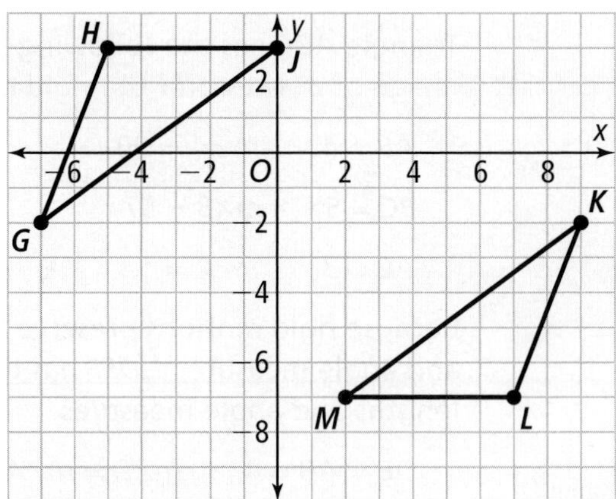


**a.** Given $\triangle GHJ \cong \triangle KLM$, what is one composition of rigid motions that maps $\triangle GHJ$ to $\triangle KLM$?

**b.** What is another composition of rigid motions that maps $\triangle GHJ$ to $\triangle KLM$?

## EXAMPLE 3 Identify Congruent Figures

**Given $\triangle ABC$, $\triangle EFG$, and $\triangle JKL$, which triangles are congruent?**

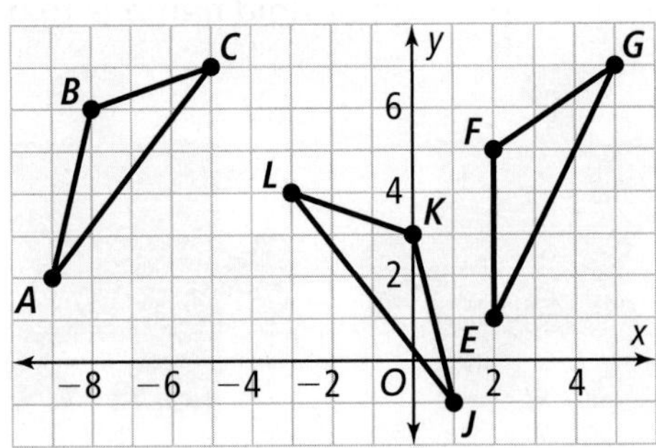

Find a composition of rigid motions to map $\triangle ABC$ to $\triangle JKL$.

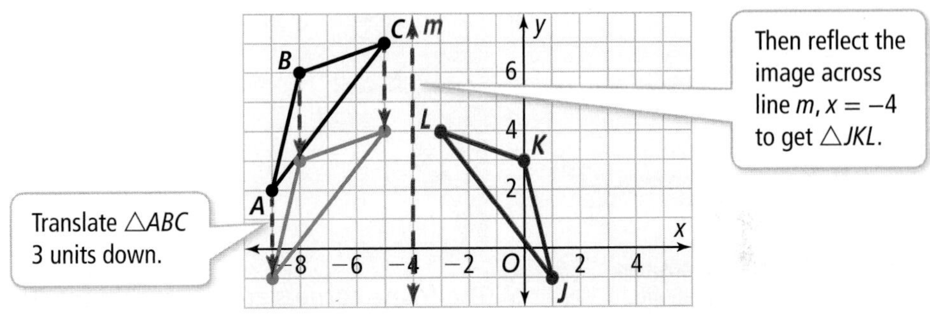

Translate △ABC 3 units down.
Then reflect the image across line m, x = −4 to get △JKL.


The composition of rigid motions $R_m \circ T_{\langle 0,\,-3\rangle}$ maps $\triangle ABC$ to $\triangle JKL$. Therefore, $\triangle ABC \cong \triangle JKL$.

Observe that $AC$ and $EG$ are the longest side in each corresponding triangle, and $AC \neq EG$, so there is no single rigid motion or composition of rigid motions that maps $\triangle ABC$ to $\triangle EFG$. Therefore, they are not congruent.

**STUDY TIP**
To show that two figures are not congruent, you only need to find one corresponding pair of sides or angles that do not have the same measure.

**Try It!** 3. Use the graph shown.

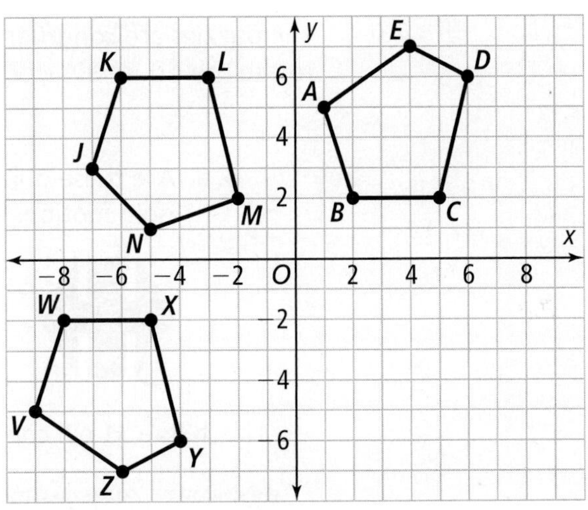

a. Are *ABCDE* and *JKLMN* congruent? If so, describe a composition of rigid motions that maps *ABCDE* to *JKLMN*. If not, explain.

b. Are *ABCDE* and *VWXYZ* congruent? If so, describe a composition of rigid motions that maps *ABCDE* to *VWXYZ*. If not, explain.

## EXAMPLE 4 Determine Congruence

**Which pairs of objects are congruent? If a pair of objects is congruent, describe a composition of rigid motions that maps one to the other.**

**A.**

The puzzle pieces are congruent. A reflection across a vertical line maps one puzzle piece to the other.

**B.**

The frame corners are not congruent. The diagonal segment at the corner of the left frame is longer than the diagonal segment at the corner of the right frame, so the two frame corners are not the same size.

**COMMON ERROR**
Remember that the composition of rigid motions must map *all* points from the preimage to the image for objects to be congruent.

**C.**

The puzzles are congruent. Translate the preimage puzzle on the left, rotate the figure 90° clockwise, and then reflect over a vertical line.

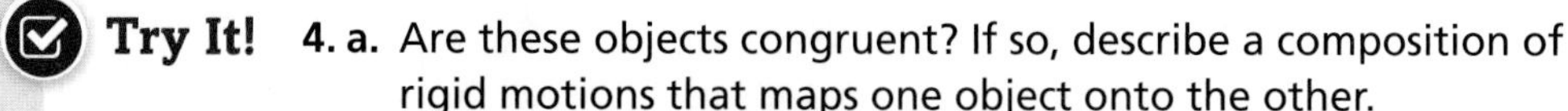

**Try It!** **4. a.** Are these objects congruent? If so, describe a composition of rigid motions that maps one object onto the other.

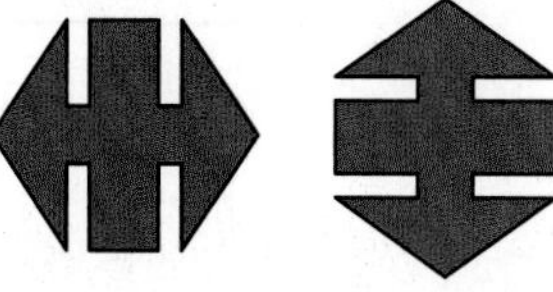

**b.** Is a \$1 bill congruent to a \$10 bill? Explain.

APPLICATION

## EXAMPLE 5 Apply Congruence

**A boat builder plans to connect two pieces of wood by using a puzzle joint as shown. For a successful joint, each unit must be congruent.**

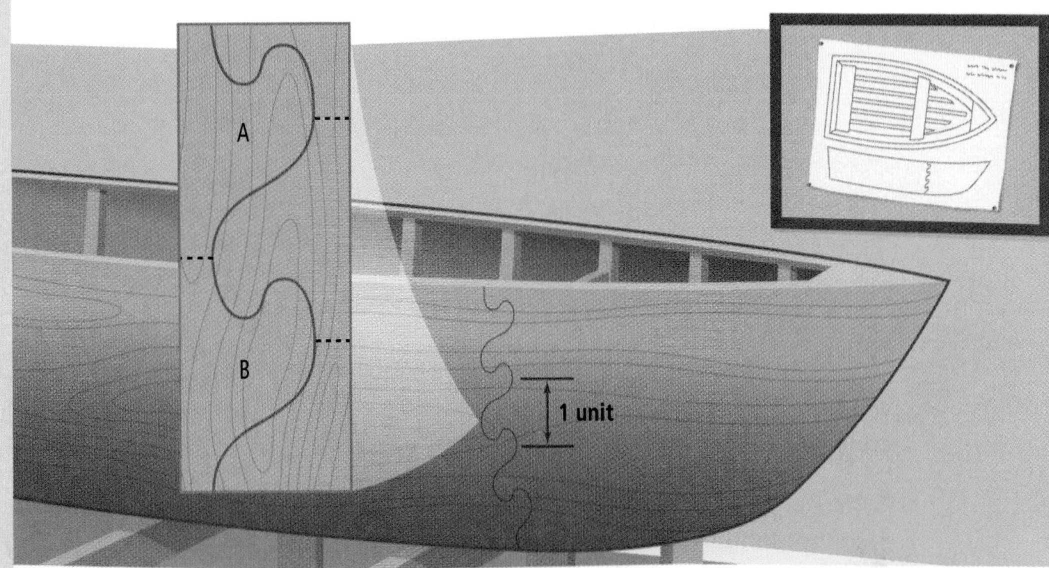


**STUDY TIP**
A composition of rigid motions can be one rigid motion as well as a composition of more than one rigid motion.

**Given Unit A, what composition of rigid motions maps Unit A to Unit B?**

Unit B is a translation of Unit A. Unit B has the same size, shape, and orientation as Unit A. The only difference is that it is farther down.

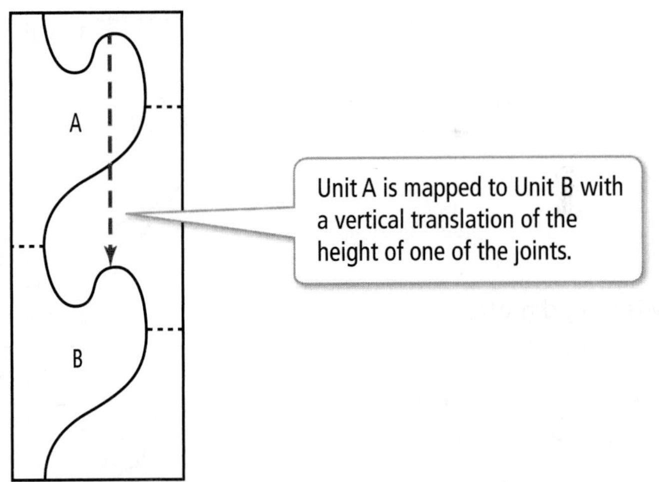

A
B
Unit A is mapped to Unit B with a vertical translation of the height of one of the joints.

**Try It!** 5. Is Unit C congruent to Unit A? If so, describe the sequence of rigid motions that maps Unit A to Unit C.

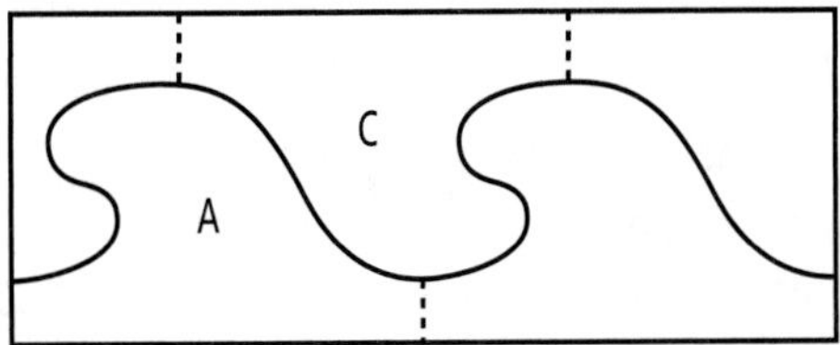

## CONCEPT SUMMARY Congruent Figures

**WORDS** If two figures are congruent, a composition of rigid motions maps one figure to another.

**DIAGRAM** Since $R_n(\triangle PQR) = \triangle P'Q'R'$, $\triangle PQR \cong \triangle P'Q'R'$.

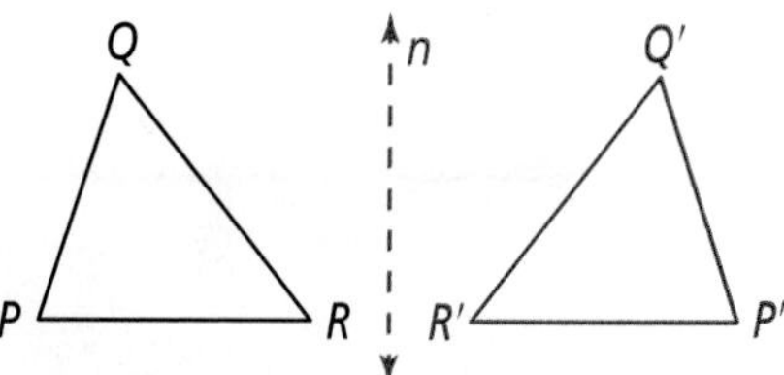


## Do You UNDERSTAND?

1. **ESSENTIAL QUESTION** What is the relationship between rigid motions and congruence?

2. **Error Analysis** Taylor says *ABCD* and *EFGH* are congruent because he can map *ABCD* to *EFGH* by multiplying each side length by 1.5 and translating the result to coincide with *EFGH*. What is Taylor's error?

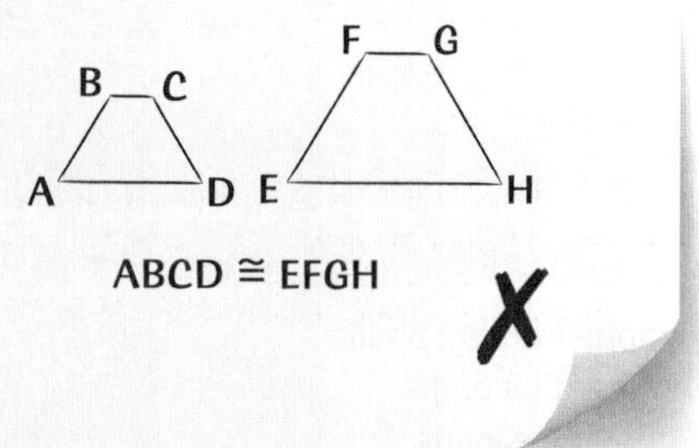


3. **Vocabulary** Why is a rigid motion also called a congruence transformation?

4. **Reason** For any two line segments that are congruent, what must be true about the lengths of the segments?

5. **Construct Arguments** A composition of rigid motions maps one figure to another figure. Is each intermediate image in the composition congruent to the original and final figures? Explain.

6. **Communicate Precisely** Describe how you can find a rigid motion or composition of rigid motions to map a segment to a congruent segment and an angle to a congruent angle.

## Do You KNOW HOW?

7. Given $ABCD \cong EFGH$, what is a composition of rigid motions that maps *ABCD* to *EFGH*?

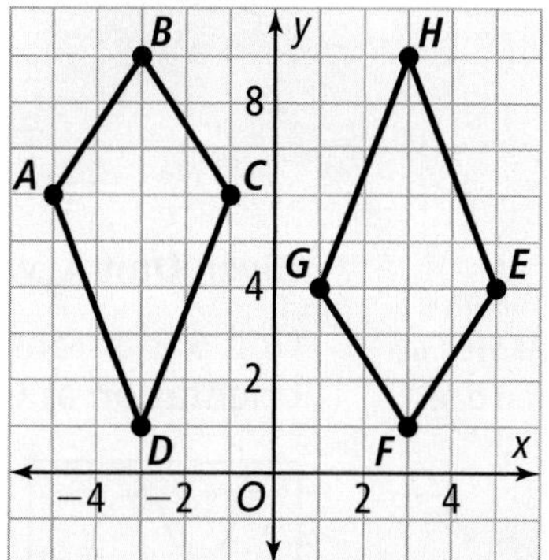


8. Which triangles are congruent?

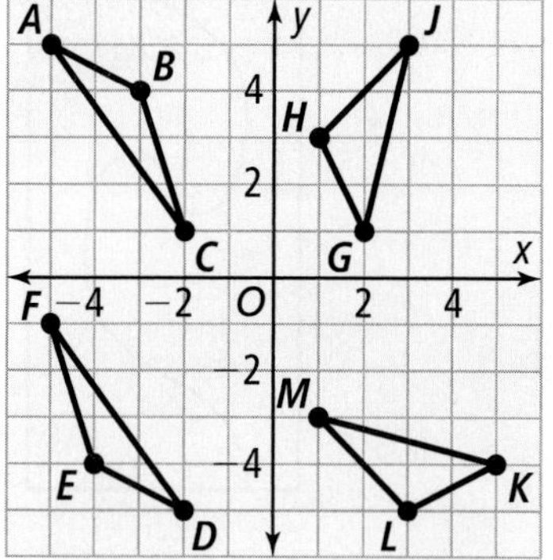


9. Are Figure A and Figure B congruent? If so, describe a composition of rigid motions that maps Figure A to Figure B. If not, explain.

Figure A

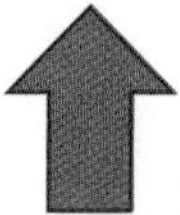
Figure B

# PRACTICE & PROBLEM SOLVING

Scan for Multimedia

Practice  Tutorial

Additional Exercises Available Online

## UNDERSTAND

10. **Reason** If $\triangle JKL \cong \triangle RST$, give the coordinates for possible vertices of $\triangle RST$. Justify your answer by describing a composition of rigid motions that maps $\triangle JKL$ to $\triangle RST$.

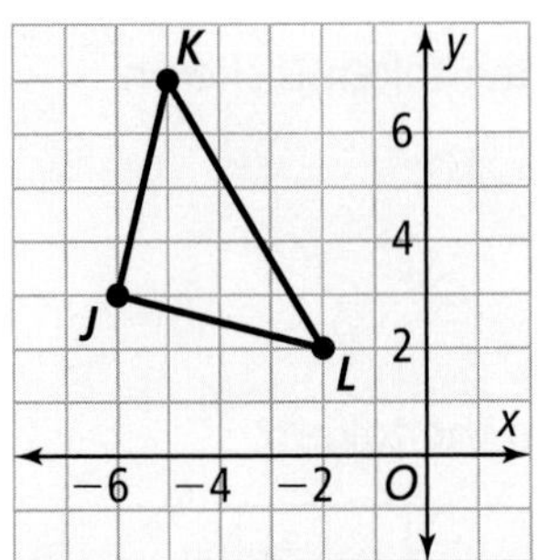


11. **Error Analysis** Yuki says that if all lines are congruent, then all line segments must be congruent. Is Yuki correct? Explain.

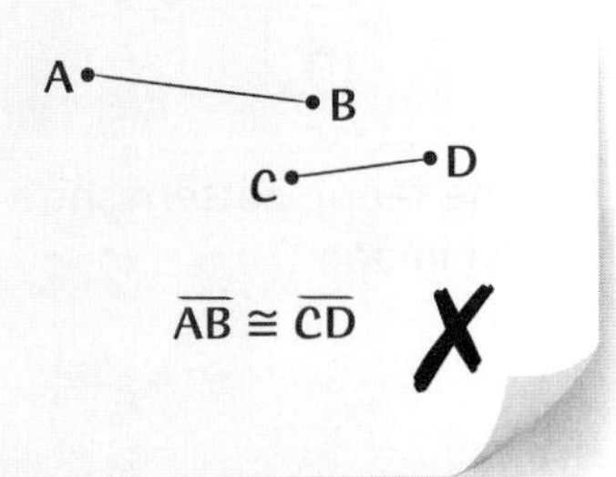


12. **Mathematical Connections** Given square $JKLM$ and $(T_{\langle -6, 4\rangle} \circ T_{\langle 1, 5\rangle})(JKLM) = RSTU$, what is the area of $RSTU$?

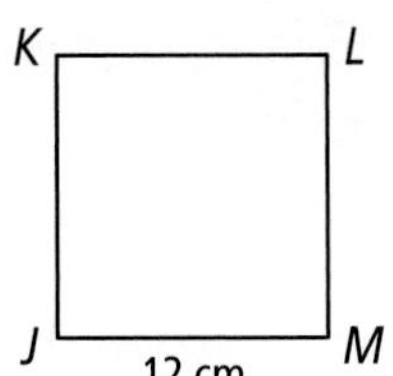


13. **Higher Order Thinking** Are $\overrightarrow{AB}$ and $\overrightarrow{CD}$ congruent? If so, describe a composition of rigid motions that maps any ray to any other ray. If not, explain. Are any two rays congruent? Explain.

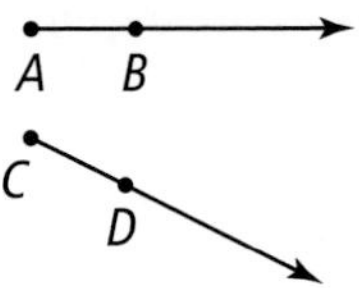


## PRACTICE

14. Given $R_m(\triangle PQR) = \triangle P'Q'R'$, do $\triangle P'Q'R'$ and $\triangle PQR$ have equal perimeters? Explain.
SEE EXAMPLE 1

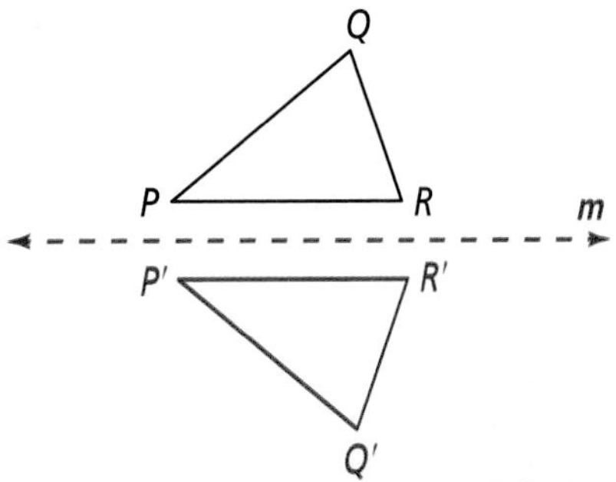


15. Given $WXYZ \cong WTUV$, describe a composition of rigid motions that maps $WXYZ$ to $WTUV$.
SEE EXAMPLE 2

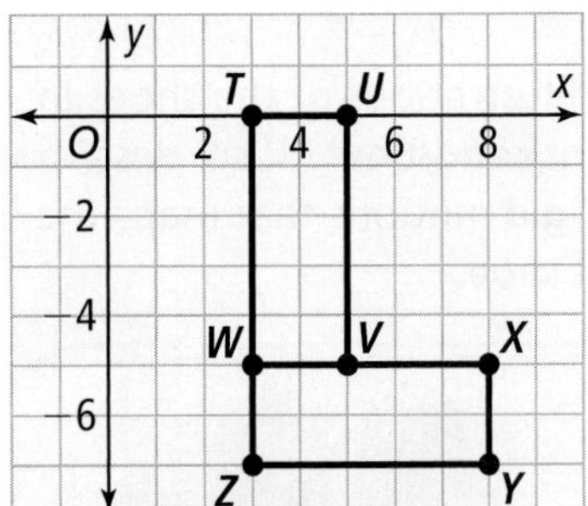


16. Are $ABCD$ and $EFGH$ congruent? If so, describe a composition of rigid motions that maps $ABCD$ to $EFGH$. If not, explain. SEE EXAMPLE 3

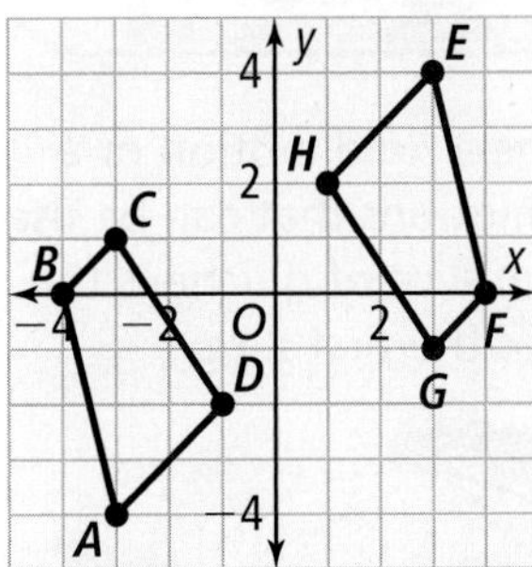


17. Which objects are congruent? For any congruent objects, describe a composition of rigid motions that maps the preimage to the image. SEE EXAMPLES 4 AND 5

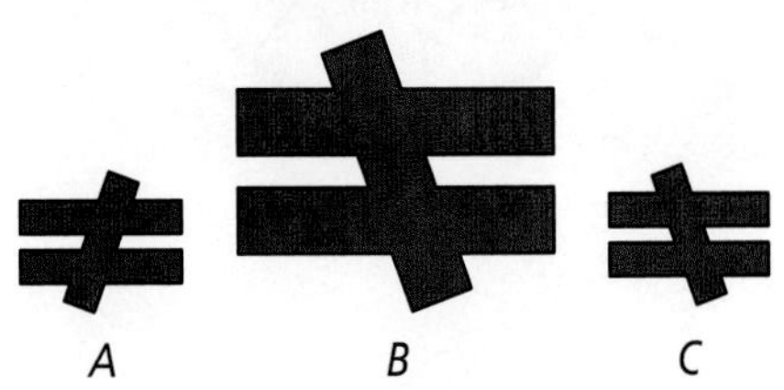

## PRACTICE & PROBLEM SOLVING

### APPLY

**18. Communicate Precisely** Using a 3D printer, Emery makes the chocolate mold shown by copying different shapes.

**a.** Which of the designs in the mold appear to be congruent?

**b.** Describe a composition of rigid motions that maps the congruent shapes.

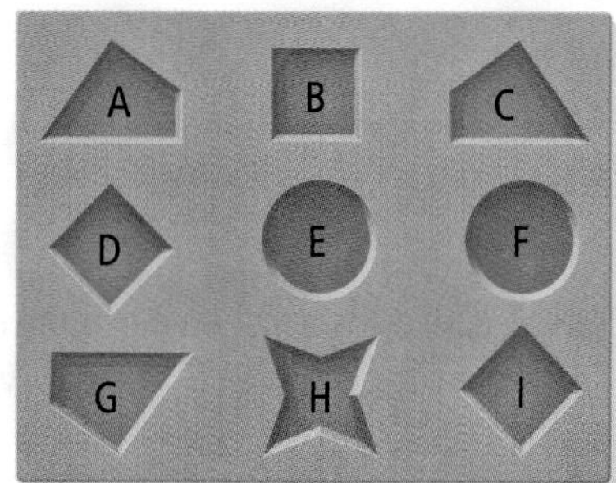

**19. Reason** Are the illustrations of the shoes in the advertisement congruent? If so, describe a composition of rigid motions that maps the left shoe to the right shoe.

**20. Use Structure** Describe a rigid motion or a composition of rigid motions that can be used to make sure that each slice of quiche is the same size and shape as the first slice.

### ASSESSMENT PRACTICE

**21.** The transformation $T_{\langle 3, 8\rangle} \circ r_{(90°, A)}$ maps $\triangle ABC$ to $\triangle DEF$.

Triangle $ABC$ is ___?___ to $\triangle DEF$ because $T_{\langle 3, 8\rangle} \circ r_{(90°, A)}$ is a ___?___.

**22. SAT/ACT** A board game token is shown.

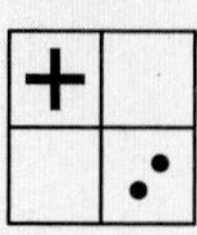

Which is congruent to the token?

Ⓐ 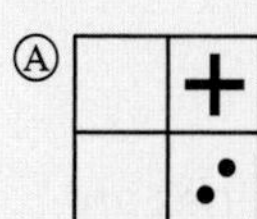

Ⓑ 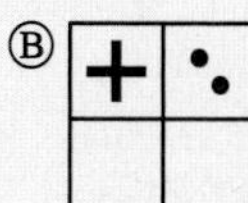

Ⓒ 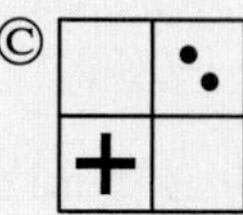

Ⓓ 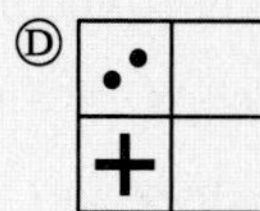

**23. Performance Task** The fabric pattern shown is based on the original image.

**Part A** Identify any images in the pattern that appear to be congruent to the original image.

**Part B** Describe a composition of rigid motions that maps the original image to each congruent image in the pattern.

**Part C** For any images in the pattern that are not congruent to the original image, explain how you know they are not congruent.

  Activity  Assess

# 4-2 Isosceles and Equilateral Triangles

PearsonRealize.com

**I CAN...** apply theorems about isosceles and equilateral triangles to solve problems.

## EXPLORE & REASON

**Cut out a triangle with two sides of equal length from a sheet of paper and label its angles 1, 2, and 3. Trace the outline of your triangle on another sheet of paper and label the angles.**

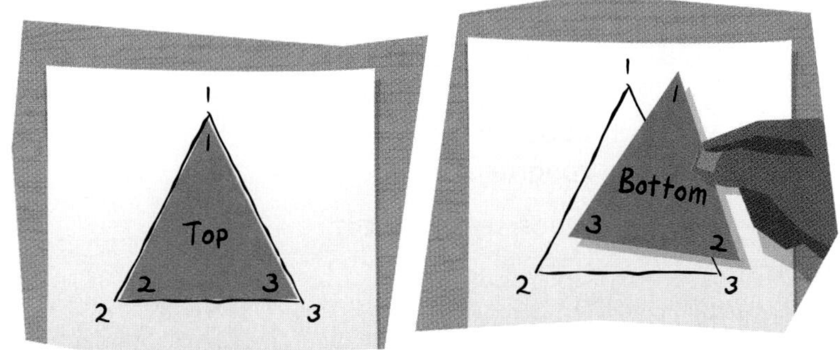


**A.** In how many different ways can you flip, slide, or turn the triangle so that it fits exactly on the outline?

**B.** **Look for Relationships** How do the angles and sides of the outline correspond to the angles and sides of the triangle?

**C.** How would your answer to Part A change if all three sides of the triangle were of equal length?

**ESSENTIAL QUESTION** **How are the side lengths and angle measures related in isosceles triangles and in equilateral triangles?**

CONCEPTUAL UNDERSTANDING

**STUDY TIP**
The rigid motion that maps $\overline{BC}$ to $\overline{BA}$ must map point $B$ to itself. A reflection across a line that contains point $B$ maps point $B$ to itself.

## EXAMPLE 1 Understand Angles of Isosceles Triangles

**How are the base angles of an isosceles triangle related?**

Draw isosceles triangle $ABC$.

Because $\overline{BC} \cong \overline{BA}$, there is a rigid motion that maps $\overline{BC}$ onto $\overline{BA}$. Draw the angle bisector $\overleftrightarrow{BD}$ of $\angle ABC$, so that $m\angle DBC = m\angle DBA$.

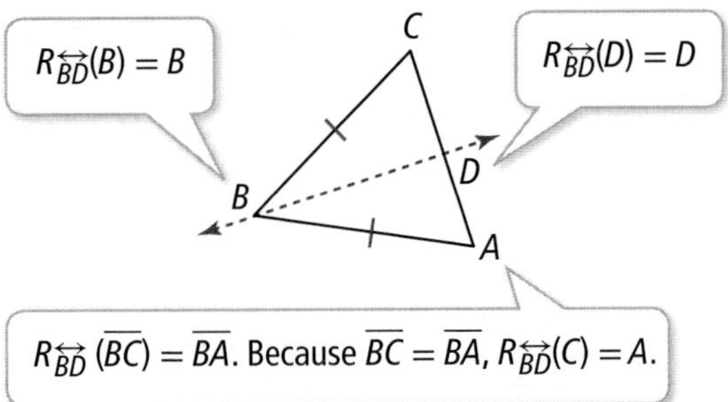


Since the reflection maps $\triangle BCD$ to $\triangle BAD$, $m\angle BCA = m\angle BAC$. Therefore, $\angle BCA \cong \angle BAC$.

**Try It!** **1.** Copy isosceles $\triangle ABC$. Reflect the triangle across line $BC$ to create the image $\triangle C'B'A'$. What rigid motion maps $\triangle C'B'A'$ onto $\triangle ABC$? Can you use this to show that $\angle A \cong \angle C$? Explain.

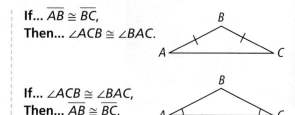

## THEOREM 4-1 Isosceles Triangle Theorem and the Converse

If two sides of a triangle are congruent, then the angles opposite those sides are congruent.

**If...** $\overline{AB} \cong \overline{BC}$,
**Then...** $\angle ACB \cong \angle BAC$.

If two angles of a triangle are congruent, then the sides opposite those angles are congruent.

**If...** $\angle ACB \cong \angle BAC$,
**Then...** $\overline{AB} \cong \overline{BC}$.

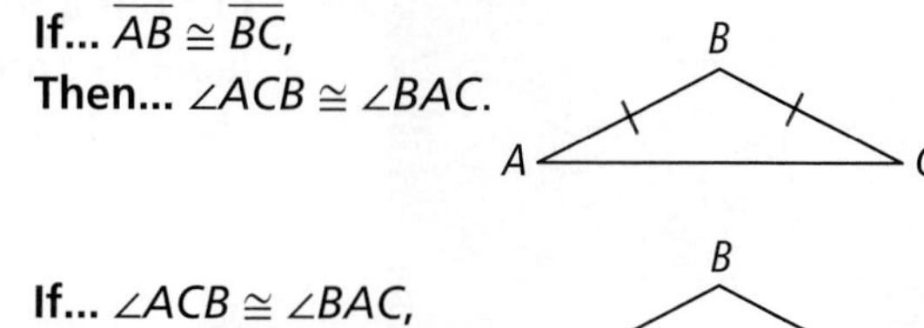


PROOF: SEE EXERCISE 17.

## EXAMPLE 2 Use the Isosceles Triangle Theorem

**An architect is designing a community park between N. First St and S. First St. The pathways on either side of the pool will be equal in length and will provide effective access and circulation around the pool. To protect the landscaping and to minimize erosion, the architect will place a triangular section of triangular cobblestones at the corners along Park Plaza. What angle measure should the architect specify for the corners in her design?**

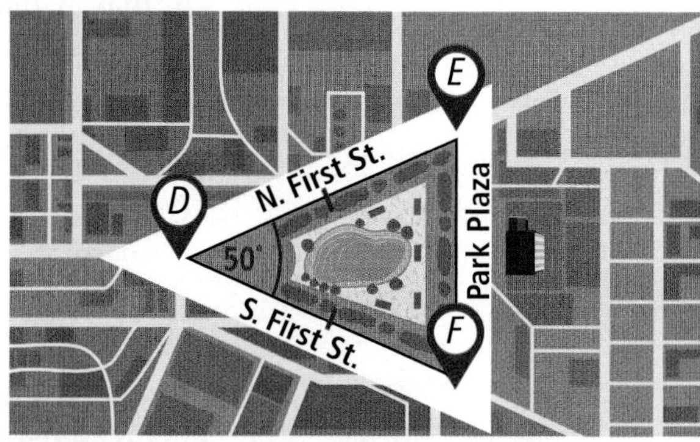


The park is in the shape of an isosceles triangle. Find $m\angle F$ and $m\angle E$.

$$m\angle D + m\angle E + m\angle F = 180$$

$$50^\circ + m\angle F + m\angle F = 180$$

$$m\angle F = 65$$

The base angles of the isosceles triangle are congruent by the Isosceles Triangle Theorem, so $m\angle E = m\angle F$.

**STUDY TIP**
Confirm your solution by using your original equation. In this example, the three angles of $\triangle ABC$ are $65^\circ$, $65^\circ$, and $50^\circ$, and the sum is $180^\circ$.

The landscape architect should specify that the angles at the corners measure $65^\circ$.

**Try It!** 2. What is the value of $x$?

a. $(5x + 9)^\circ$, $28^\circ$

b.

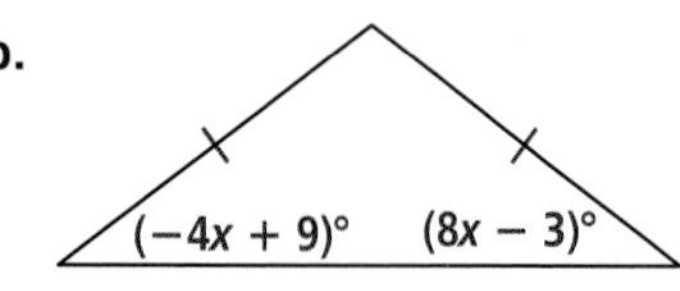

## EXAMPLE 3 Use the Converse of the Isosceles Triangle Theorem

**What are the lengths of all three sides of the triangle?**

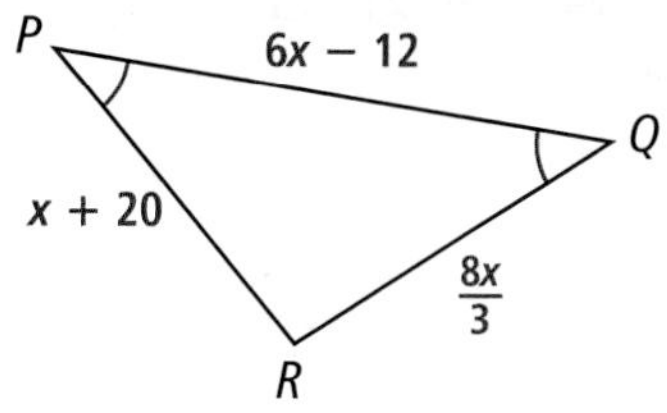


**COMMON ERROR**
Be careful not to set the expressions for the length of a leg and the length of the base equal to each other. Remember that the congruent legs are opposite the congruent base angles.

**Step 1** Find the value of $x$.

$$x + 20 = \frac{8x}{3}$$
$$3x + 60 = 8x$$
$$12 = x$$

Because $\angle P \cong \angle Q$, the sides opposite $\angle P$ and $\angle Q$ are also congruent.

**Step 2** Substitute 12 for $x$ to determine the side lengths.

$PR = x + 20$
$= 12 + 20$
$= 32$

$PQ = 6x - 12$
$= 6(12) - 12$
$= 60$

$QR = \frac{8x}{3}$
$= \frac{8(12)}{3}$
$= 32$

**Try It!** **3.** Use the figure shown.

**a.** What is the value of $x$?

**b.** What are the lengths of all three sides of the triangle?

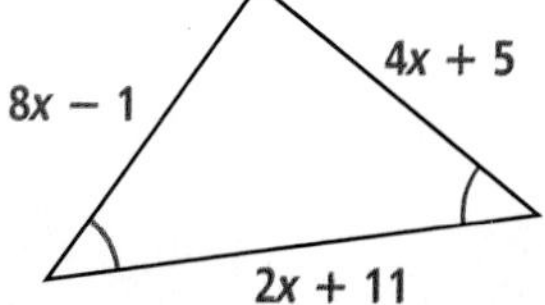

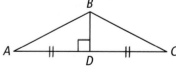

### THEOREM 4-2

If a line or line segment bisects the vertex angle of an isosceles triangle, then it is also the perpendicular bisector of the opposite side.

**If...**

B
A D C

$\overline{AB} \cong \overline{BC}$ and $m\angle ABD = m\angle CBD$

**Then...**

B
A D C

$\overline{BD} \perp \overline{AC}$ and $\overline{AD} \cong \overline{DC}$

PROOF: SEE EXERCISE 13.

APPLICATION

## EXAMPLE 4 Use Perpendicular Bisectors to Solve Problems

**A prefabricated house is delivered to a foundation in two symmetric halves that are assembled on-site. Along the planned route to the site, the truck must pass under a bridge that has a clearance height of 17 feet. Should the trucker plan a different route for delivering the house? Explain.**

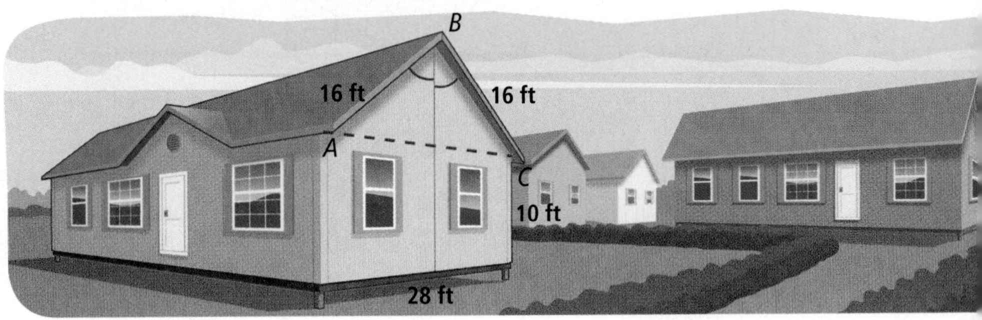


**CONSTRUCT ARGUMENTS**
Consider the information the figure provides about $\triangle ABC$. What other information given in the figure is needed?

Draw a diagram to represent the roof.

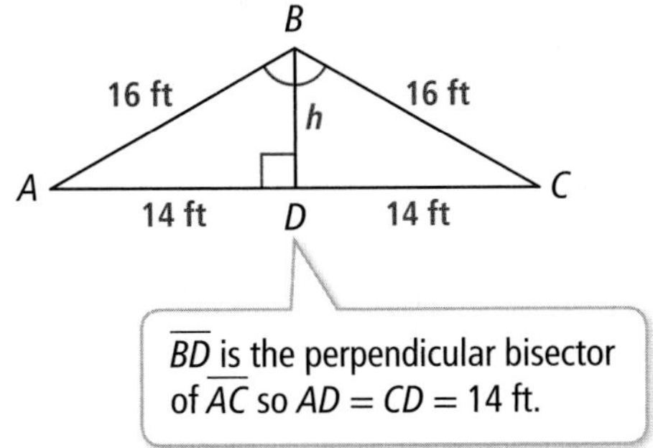


$\overline{BD}$ is the perpendicular bisector of $\overline{AC}$ so $AD = CD = 14$ ft.

Use the Pythagorean Theorem to find the height $h$.

$$h^2 + 14^2 = 16^2$$

$$h^2 = 60$$

$$h = \sqrt{60} \approx 7.7$$

The house is approximately 17.7 feet tall, so the total height that the truck must clear is greater than 17.7 ft. The trucker should plan a different route to the site.

**Try It!** **4.** Use the figure shown.

**a.** What is $m\angle RSQ$?

**b.** What is $PR$?

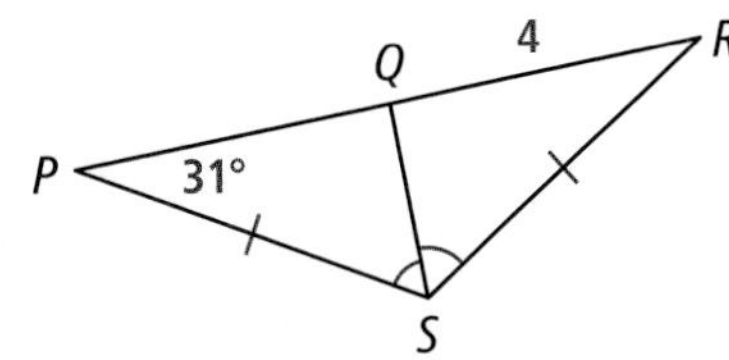

## CONCEPT Equilateral Triangles

An equilateral triangle is equiangular.

An equiangular triangle is equilateral.

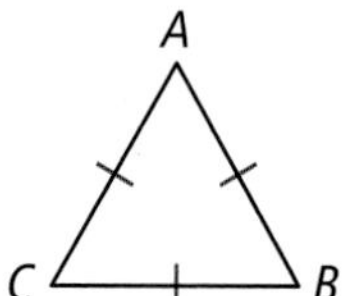


**If...** $\angle A \cong \angle B \cong \angle C$, **then...** $\overline{AB} \cong \overline{BC} \cong \overline{AC}$.

**If...** $\overline{AB} \cong \overline{BC} \cong \overline{AC}$, **then...** $\angle A \cong \angle B \cong \angle C$.

## EXAMPLE 5 Prove that Equilateral Triangles are Equiangular

**A. Prove that equilateral triangles are equiangular.**

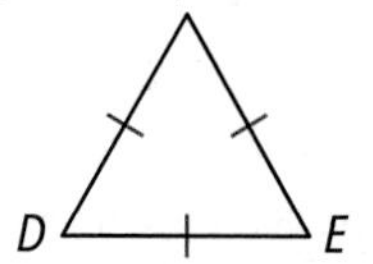


**Given:** $\overline{DE} \cong \overline{EF} \cong \overline{DF}$

**Prove:** $\angle D \cong \angle E \cong \angle F$

**Plan:** Use that an equilateral triangle is also an isosceles triangle to show that all three angles are congruent.

**Proof:**

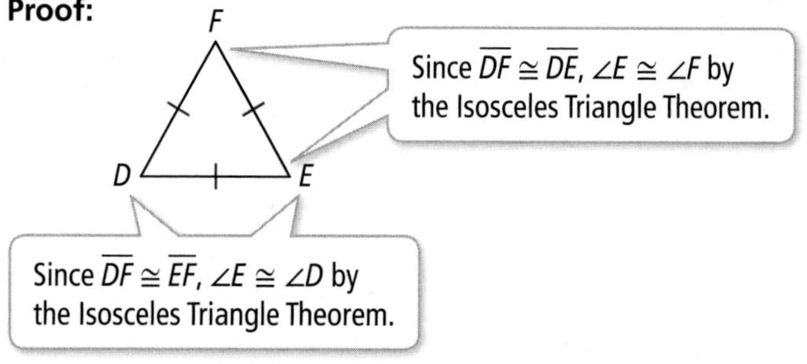

F
D
E
Since $\overline{DF} \cong \overline{DE}$, $\angle E \cong \angle F$ by the Isosceles Triangle Theorem.
Since $\overline{DF} \cong \overline{EF}$, $\angle E \cong \angle D$ by the Isosceles Triangle Theorem.


Since $\angle D \cong \angle E$ and $\angle E \cong \angle F$, $\angle D \cong \angle E \cong \angle F$.

**B. Prove that equiangular triangles are equilateral.**

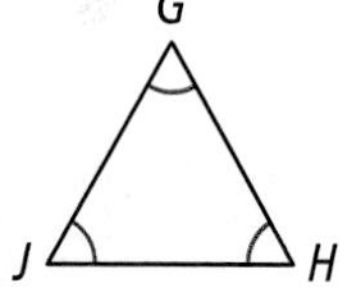


**Given:** $\angle G \cong \angle H \cong \angle J$

**Prove:** $\overline{GH} \cong \overline{HJ} \cong \overline{GJ}$

**Plan:** Use a strategy similar to the one in part A by applying the Converse of the Isosceles Triangle Theorem.

**Proof:**

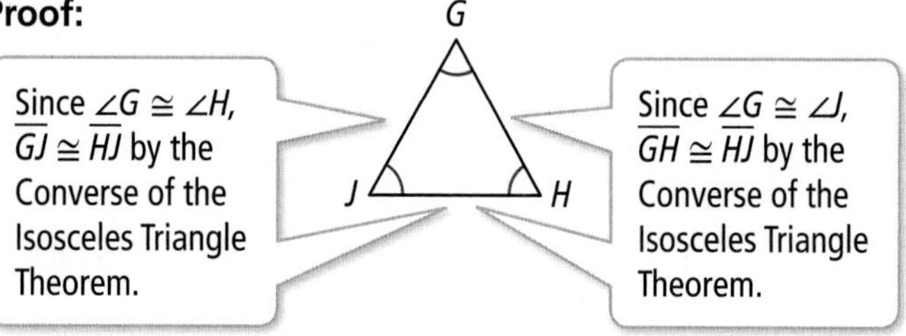


Since $\overline{GJ} \cong \overline{HJ}$ and $\overline{GH} \cong \overline{HJ}$, $\overline{GH} \cong \overline{HJ} \cong \overline{GJ}$.

**STUDY TIP**
When planning a proof, consider proofs that may be parallel in structure.

**Try It!** 5. What rotation can be used to show the angles of an equilateral triangle are congruent?

## Find Angle Measures in Isosceles and Equilateral Triangles

**A. If $m\angle CBD = 130$, what is $m\angle BAD$?**

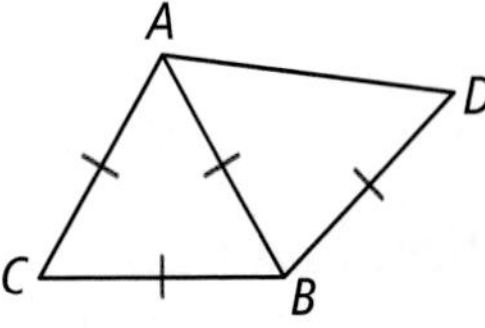


**Step 1** **Find $m\angle ABD$.**

$$m\angle ABC + m\angle ABD = m\angle CBD$$
$$60 + m\angle ABD = 130$$
$$m\angle ABD = 70$$

Since $\triangle ABC$ is equilateral, $m\angle ABC = 60$.

**COMMON ERROR**
You may think you have solved the problem after finding one angle measure. Make sure you provide the measure of the angle asked for in the question.

**Step 2** **Use the Isosceles Triangle Theorem to find $m\angle BAD$.**

$$m\angle ABD + m\angle BDA + m\angle BAD = 180$$
$$70 + m\angle BAD + m\angle BAD = 180$$
$$m\angle BAD = 55$$

Since $\triangle ABD$ is isosceles, $m\angle BDA = m\angle BAD$.

**B. What is $m\angle U$?**

**Step 1** Find $m\angle SVT$. Write an equation using the Triangle Angle-Sum Theorem.

$$m\angle S + m\angle STV + m\angle SVT = 180$$
$$72 + m\angle SVT + m\angle SVT = 180$$
$$2m\angle SVT = 108$$
$$m\angle SVT = 54$$

Since $\triangle STV$ is isosceles, $m\angle STV = m\angle SVT$.

**Step 2** Find $m\angle U$. Write an equation using the Triangle Exterior Angle Theorem.

$$m\angle SVT = m\angle VTU + m\angle U$$
$$54 = m\angle U + m\angle U$$
$$54 = 2m\angle U$$
$$m\angle U = 27$$

Since $\triangle VTU$ is isosceles, $m\angle VTU = m\angle U$.

**Try It!** 6. Find each angle measure in the figure.

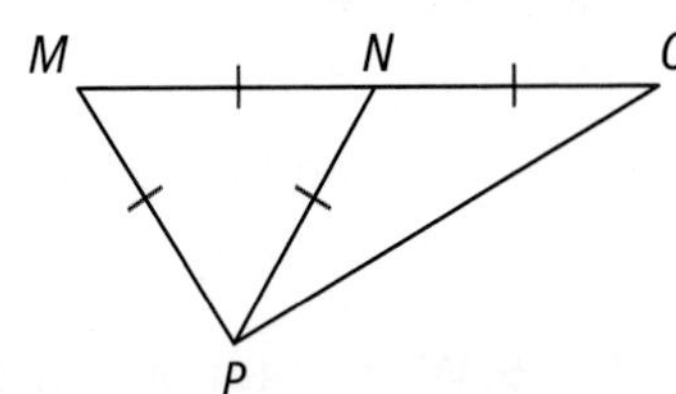


a. $m\angle PNO$

b. $m\angle NOP$

  Concept Summary  Assess

## CONCEPT SUMMARY Isosceles and Equilateral Triangles

### ISOSCELES TRIANGLES

If...

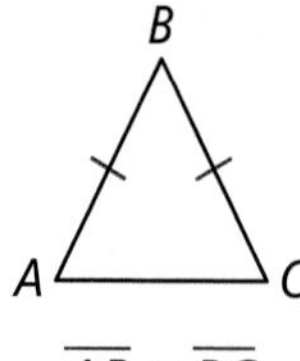

$\overline{AB} \cong \overline{BC}$

Then...

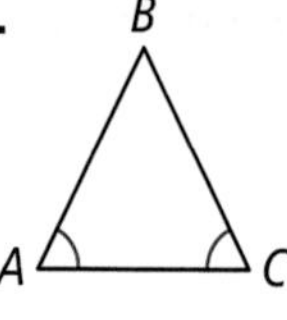

$\angle ACB \cong \angle BAC$

### PERPENDICULAR BISECTOR

If...

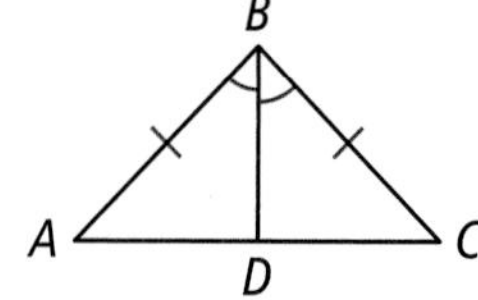

$\overline{AB} \cong \overline{BC}$ and $m\angle ABD = m\angle CBD$

Then...

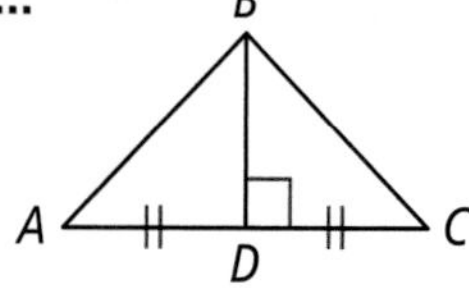

$\overline{BD} \perp \overline{AC}$ and $AD = DC$

### EQUILATERAL TRIANGLES

If...

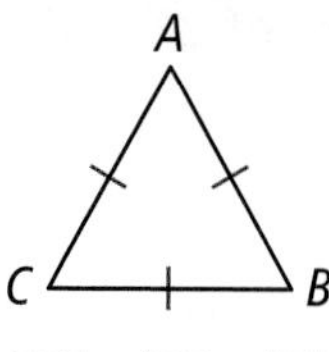

$\overline{AB} \cong \overline{BC} \cong \overline{AC}$

Then...

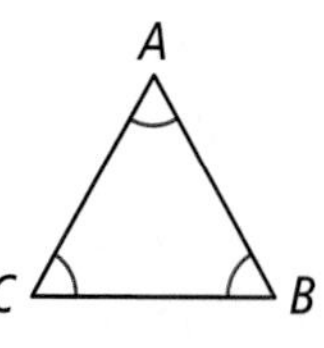

$\angle A \cong \angle B \cong \angle C$

## Do You UNDERSTAND?

1. ESSENTIAL QUESTION How are the side lengths and angle measures related in isosceles triangles and in equilateral triangles?

2. **Error Analysis** Nate drew the following diagram to represent an equilateral triangle and an isosceles triangle. What mistake did Nate make?

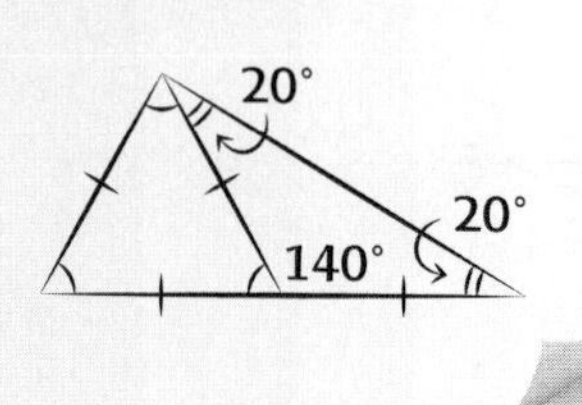


3. **Vocabulary** How can you distinguish the base of an isosceles triangle from a leg?

4. **Reason** Is it possible for the vertex of an isosceles triangle to be a right angle? Explain why or why not, and state the angle measures of the triangle, if possible.

5. **Communicate Precisely** Describe five rigid motions that map equilateral triangle $\triangle PQR$ onto itself.

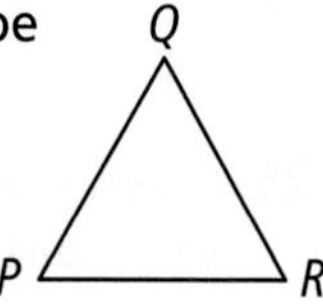

## Do You KNOW HOW?

**For Exercises 6 and 7, find the unknown angle measures.**

6. 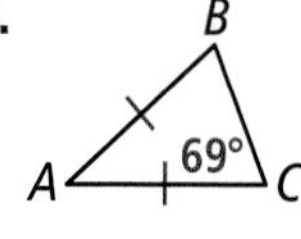

7. 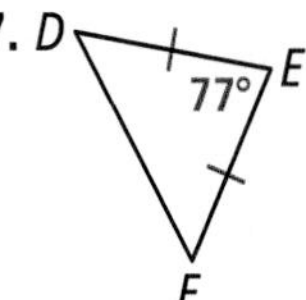

**For Exercises 8 and 9, find the lengths of all three sides of the triangle.**

8. 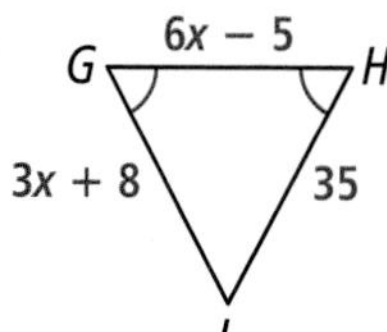


9. 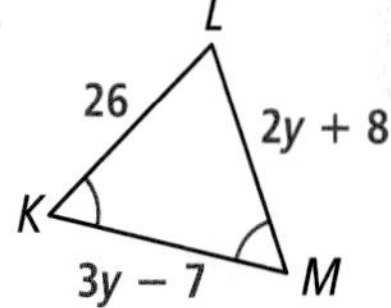


10. What is $m\angle ABD$ in the figure shown?

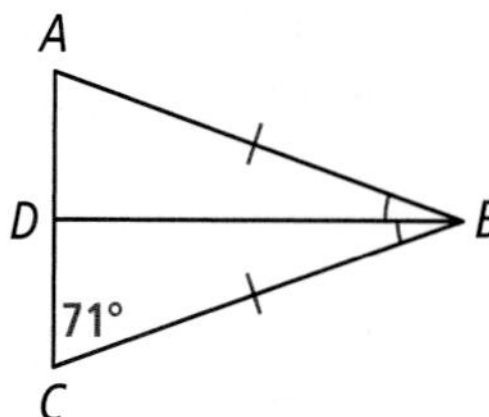

11. A light is suspended between two poles as shown. How far above the ground is the light? Round to the nearest tenth of a foot.

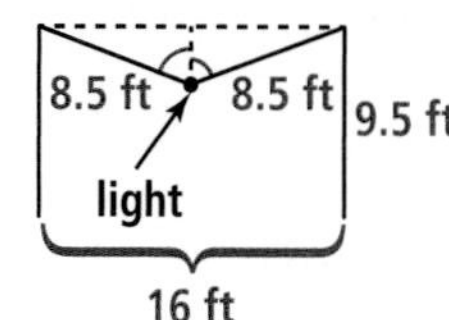

## UNDERSTAND

**12. Mathematical Connections** What are the measures of ∠1 and ∠2? Explain.

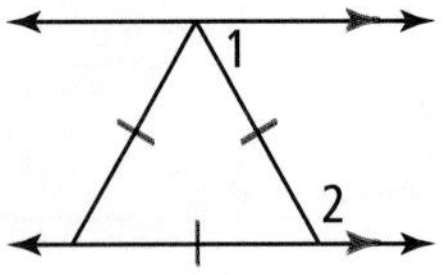


**13. Construct Arguments** Use the Isosceles Triangle Theorem and rigid motions to write a proof of Theorem 4-2.

**Given:** $\overline{PQ} \cong \overline{QR}$ and $m\angle PQS = m\angle RQS$

**Prove:** $\overline{QS} \perp \overline{PR}$ and $PS = SR$

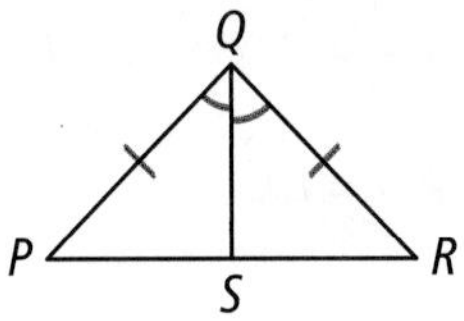


**14. Look for Relationships** Prove that $\angle BAD \cong \angle BCD$ and $\angle ABC \cong \angle CDA$.

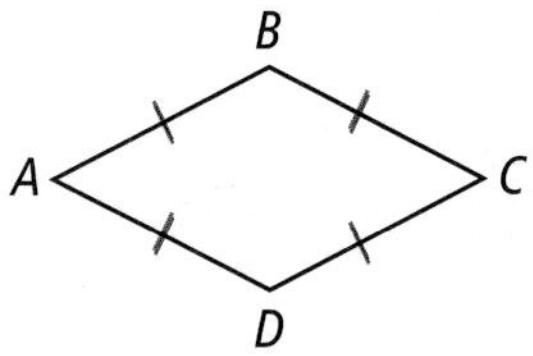


**15. Error Analysis** Amaya is asked to find the side lengths of the triangle shown. What is her error?

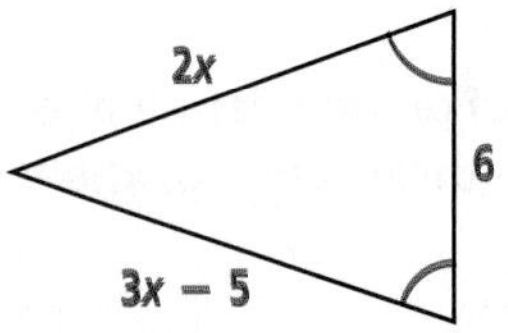


From the top leg and the base, 2x = 6, so x = 3. Substitute x into the expression for the bottom leg's length to get 3(3) − 5 = 4. ✗

**16. Higher Order Thinking** Deondra draws points at (1, 5) and (1, −1) on a coordinate plane. Each point will be a vertex of an isosceles right triangle. What are two possible points in the second quadrant that she can specify as a vertex of her triangle? Explain.

## PRACTICE

**17.** Use rigid motions to write a proof of the Converse of the Isosceles Triangle Theorem.
SEE EXAMPLE 1

**Given:** $\angle J \cong \angle L$

**Prove:** $JK \cong KL$

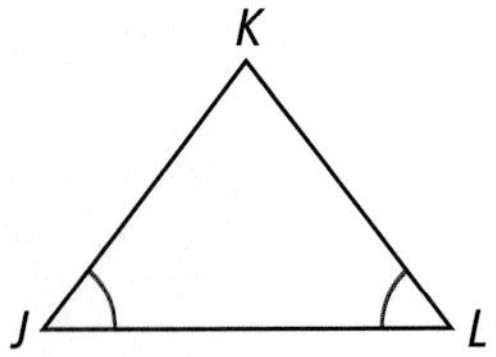


**Find the unknown angle measures in each triangle.**
SEE EXAMPLE 2

**18.**

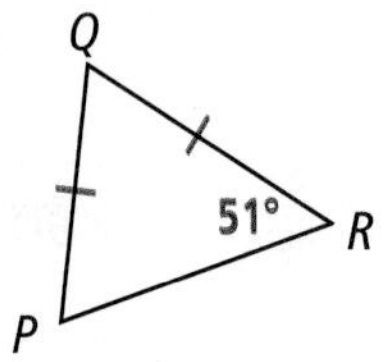


**19.**

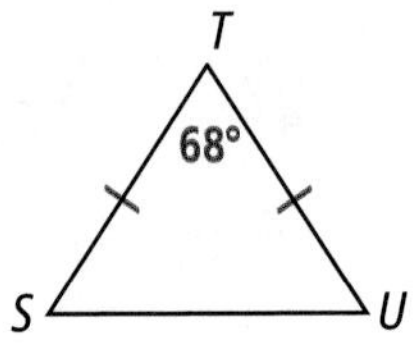


**Find the lengths of all three sides of each triangle.**
SEE EXAMPLE 3

**20.**

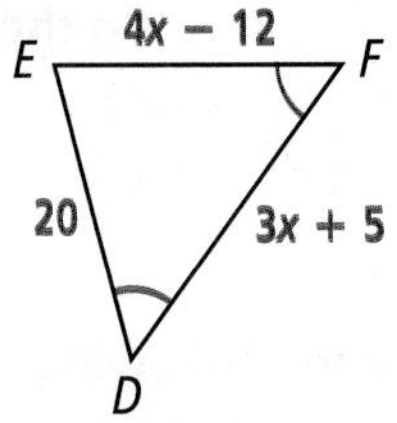


**21.**

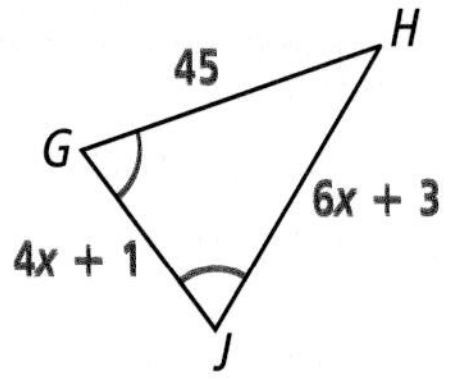


**Use the figure shown for Exercises 22 and 23.**
SEE EXAMPLE 4

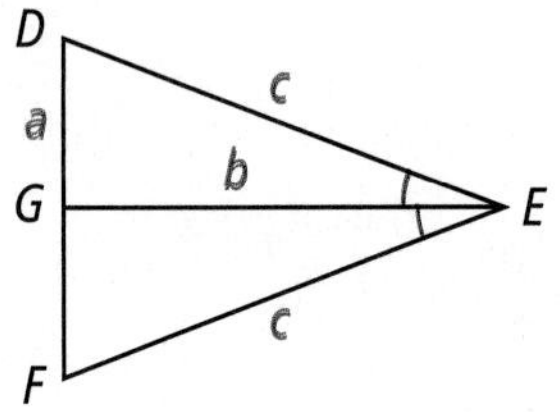


**22.** What is $m\angle DEG$ if $m\angle DFE = 70$?

**23.** What is the value of $b$ if $a = 8$ and $c = 24$?

**24.** Prove that ∠ABC is a right angle.
SEE EXAMPLE 5

**Given:** $\overline{AD} \cong \overline{BD} \cong \overline{CD}$

**Prove:** $m\angle ABC = 90$

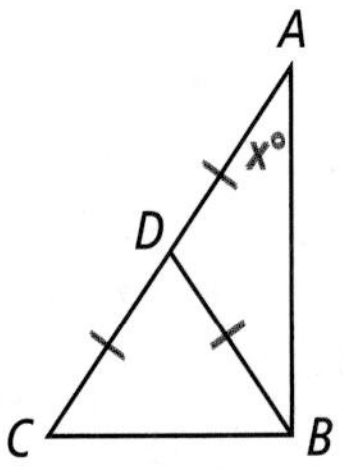


**25.** Given $m\angle PSR = 134$, what is the measure of ∠SQR?
SEE EXAMPLE 6

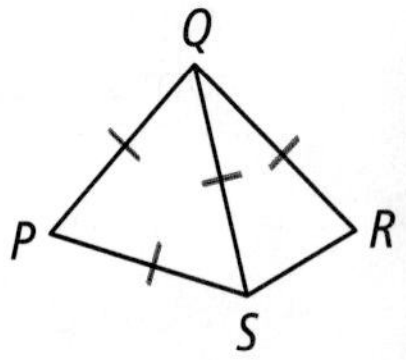

# PRACTICE & PROBLEM SOLVING



## APPLY

26. **Make Sense and Persevere** Each of the five points on a star produced for a flag is an isosceles triangle with leg length 6 cm and base length 4.2 cm. What is the total height $h$ of each star? Round to the nearest tenth of a centimeter.

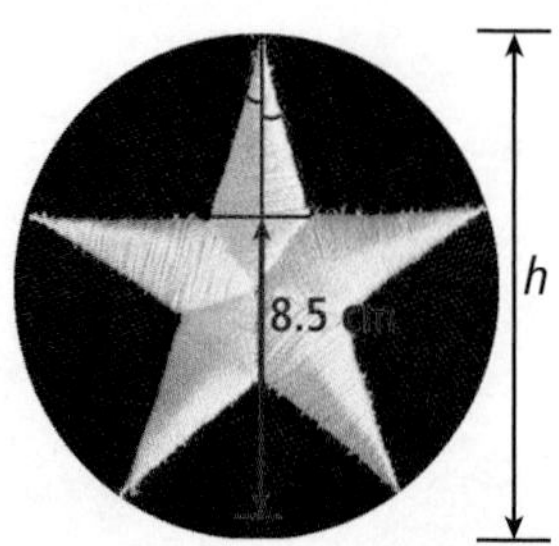


27. **Use Structure** The front of the tent below has the shape of an equilateral triangle.

    a. What is the side length of the triangle? Round to the nearest tenth of a foot.

    b. Explain the method you use to calculate the length.

28. **Look for Relationships** For a crane to lift the beam shown below, the beam and the two support cables must form an isosceles triangle with height $h$. If the distance between the cables along the beam is 18 ft and the height $h$ is 8 ft, what is the total length of the two cables? Round to the nearest tenth of a foot.

## ASSESSMENT PRACTICE

29. Consider the following triangle.

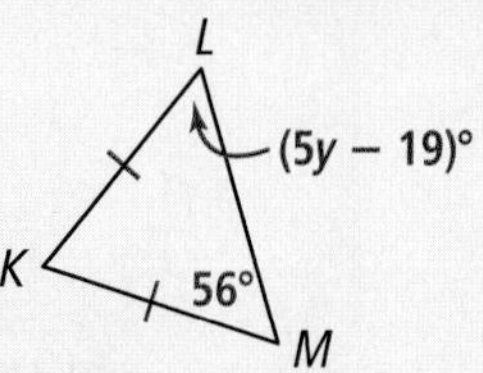


    a. Write an equation you can solve to find the value of $y$.

    b. What is $m\angle K$?

30. **SAT/ACT** Given $m\angle ABC = 114$, what is $m\angle BAD$?

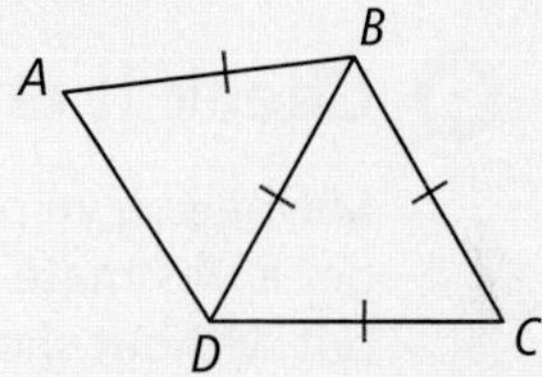


Ⓐ 54
Ⓑ 63
Ⓒ 60
Ⓓ 72

31. **Performance Task** Emaan designs the birdhouse shown below.

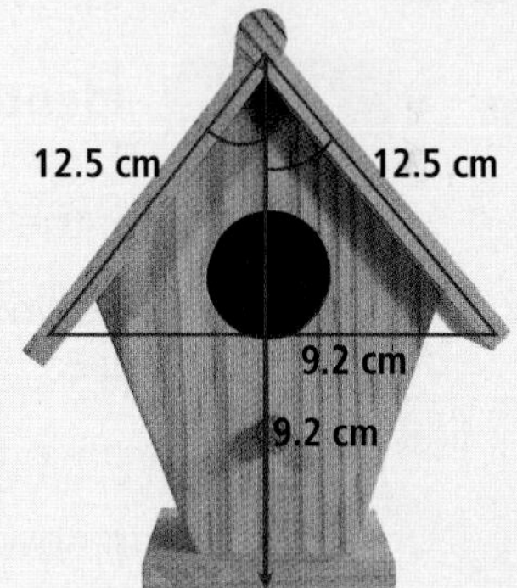


**Part A** What is the total height of the birdhouse? Show your work.

**Part B** If Emaan decides to change the design by increasing each side of the roof from 12.5 cm to 15.2 cm, what will be the new height of the birdhouse? All other labeled dimensions on the birdhouse will remain unchanged.

## Check It Out!

Maybe you've played this game before: you draw a picture. Then you try to get a classmate to draw the same picture by giving step-by-step directions but without showing your drawings.

Try it with a classmate. Draw a map of a room in your house or a place in your town. Then give directions to a classmate to draw the map that you drew. How similar are they? Think about this during the Mathematical Modeling in 3 Acts lesson.

### Identify the Problem

1. What is the first question that comes to mind after watching the video?
2. Write down the main question you will answer about what you saw in the video.
3. Make an initial conjecture that answers this main question.
4. Explain how you arrived at your conjecture.
5. What information will be useful to know in order to answer the main question? How can you get it? How will you use that information?

### ACT 2 Develop a Model

6. Use the math that you have learned in this Topic to refine your conjecture.

### ACT 3 Interpret the Results

7. Did your refined conjecture match the actual answer exactly? If not, what might explain the difference?

# 4-3 Proving and Applying the SAS and SSS Congruence Criteria

PearsonRealize.com

**I CAN...** use SAS and SSS to determine whether triangles are congruent.

Activity Assess

## EXPLORE & REASON

**Make five triangles that have a 5-inch side, a 6-inch side, and one 40° angle.**

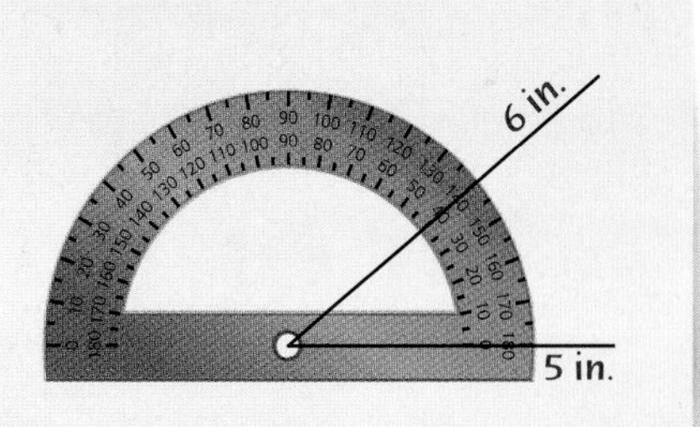


**A.** How many unique triangles can you make?

**B. Construct Arguments** How are the unique triangles different from the triangles you found that were not unique?

## ESSENTIAL QUESTION

**How are SAS and SSS used to show that two triangles are congruent?**

CONCEPTUAL UNDERSTANDING

## EXAMPLE 1 Explore the Side-Angle-Side (SAS) Congruence Criterion

**GENERALIZE**
Consider the relationship between corresponding parts of any pair of congruent triangles. How do the corresponding sides and angles compare to each other?

**Given two triangles with two pairs of sides congruent and the included angles congruent, verify that the triangles are congruent.**

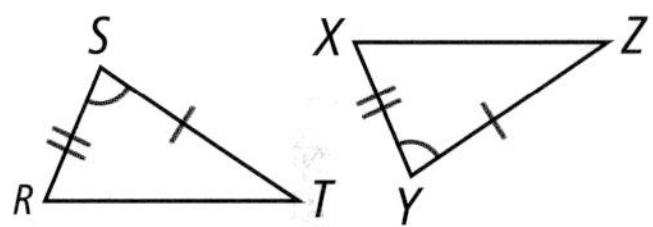


To prove that the triangles are congruent, show that a rigid motion maps $\triangle RST$ to $\triangle XYZ$.

Translate $\triangle RST$ so point $S$ maps to point $Y$.

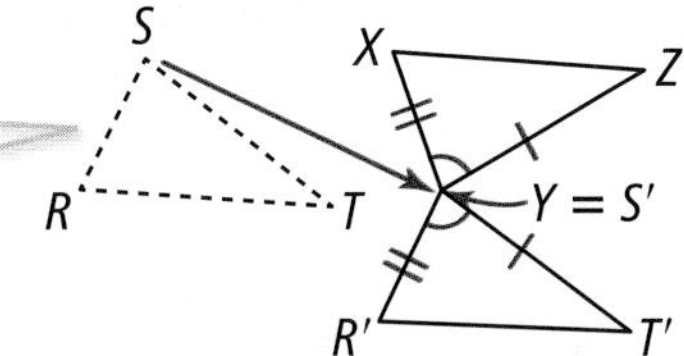


Since the translation maps $S$ to $Y$, $Y = S'$.

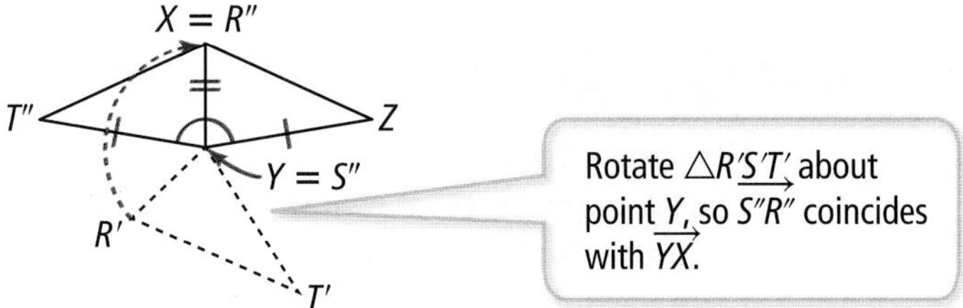


Rotate $\triangle R'S'T'$ about point $Y$, so $\overrightarrow{S''R''}$ coincides with $\overrightarrow{YX}$.

Since rotation preserves length, $R''S'' = RS = XY$, so $X = R''$.

Then reflect $\triangle R''S''T''$ across $\overleftrightarrow{XY}$.

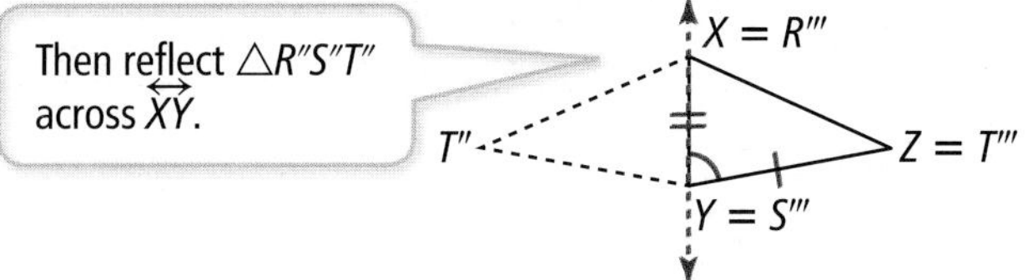


Since reflection preserves angle measure and length, $m\angle R'''S'''T''' = m\angle RST = m\angle XYZ$, so $\overrightarrow{S'''T'''}$ coincides with $\overrightarrow{YZ}$. Additionally, $S'''T''' = ST = YZ$, so $Z$ coincides with $T'''$.

Because the vertices of $\triangle R'''S'''T'''$ coincide with the vertices of $\triangle XYZ$, there exists a rigid motion that maps $\triangle RST$ to $\triangle XYZ$. By the definition of congruence, $\triangle RST \cong \triangle XYZ$.

CONTINUED ON THE NEXT PAGE

**Try It!** **1.** What rigid motion or composition of rigid motions shows that $\triangle UVW$ maps to $\triangle XYZ$?

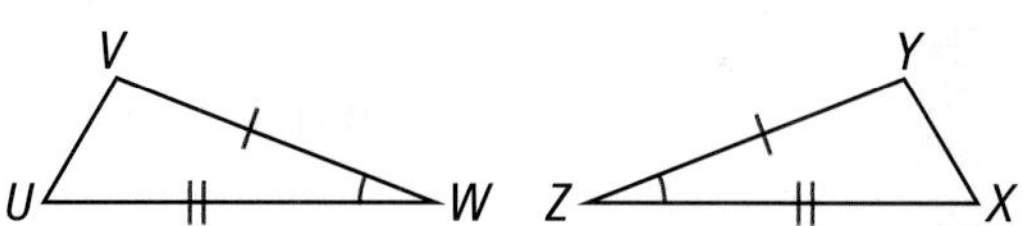


## THEOREM 4-3 Side-Angle-Side (SAS) Congruence Criterion

If two sides and the included angle of one triangle are congruent to two sides and the included angle of another triangle, then the two triangles are congruent.

PROOF: SEE EXAMPLE 1.

**If...**

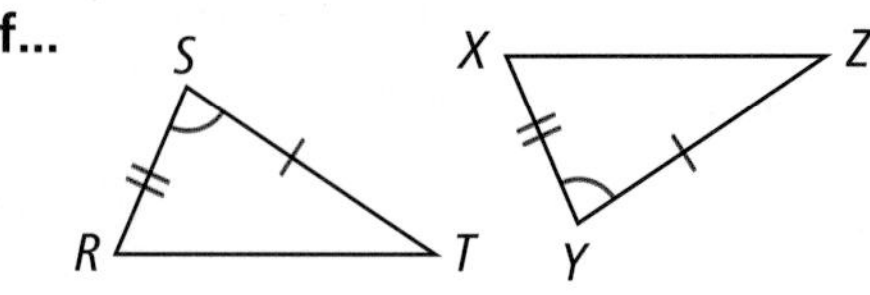


**Then...** $\triangle RST \cong \triangle XYZ$

## THEOREM 4-4 Corresponding Parts of Congruent Triangles are Congruent (CPCTC)

If two triangles are congruent, then each pair of corresponding sides is congruent and each pair of corresponding angles is congruent.

PROOF: SEE EXERCISE 13.

**If...** $\triangle ABC \cong \triangle XYZ$

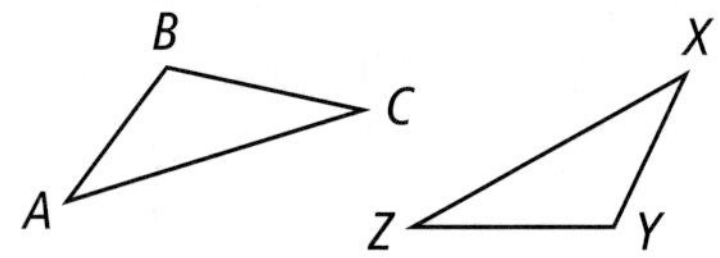


**Then...** $\overline{AB} \cong \overline{XY}$, $\overline{BC} \cong \overline{YZ}$, $\overline{AC} \cong \overline{XZ}$, $\angle A \cong \angle X$, $\angle B \cong \angle Y$, and $\angle C \cong \angle Z$.

APPLICATION

## EXAMPLE 2 Apply the SAS Congruence Criterion

**Allie cuts two triangles from a rectangular piece of metal along the dashed line to make earrings. How can Allie show that the earrings are the same size and shape?**

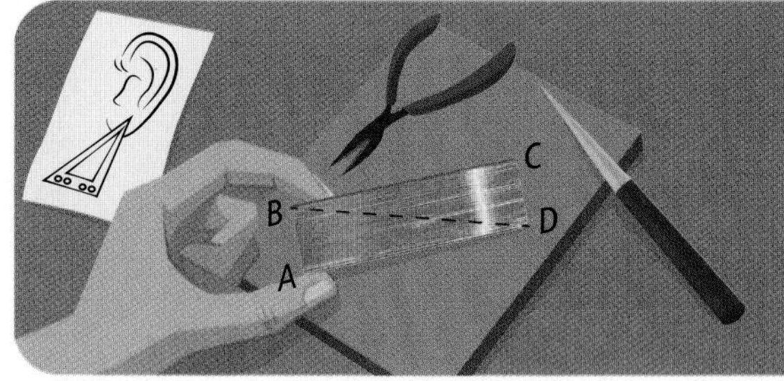


Draw diagrams to represent the earrings.

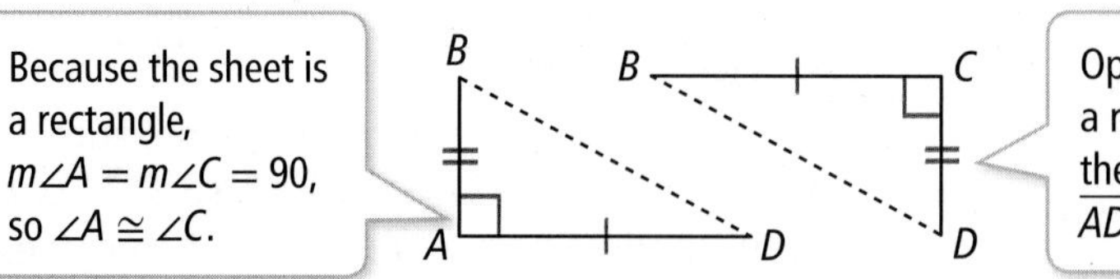

Because the sheet is a rectangle, $m\angle A = m\angle C = 90$, so $\angle A \cong \angle C$.
B
A
D
B
C
D
Opposite sides of a rectangle have the same length, so $\overline{AD} \cong \overline{BC}$ and $\overline{AB} \cong \overline{CD}$.


By SAS, $\triangle ABD \cong \triangle CDB$.

By CPCTC, all the corresponding sides and angles of the earrings are congruent, so the earrings are the same size and shape.

CONTINUED ON THE NEXT PAGE

**Try It!** 2. Given that $\overline{AB} \parallel \overline{CD}$ and $\overline{AB} \cong \overline{CD}$, how can you show that $\angle B \cong \angle D$?

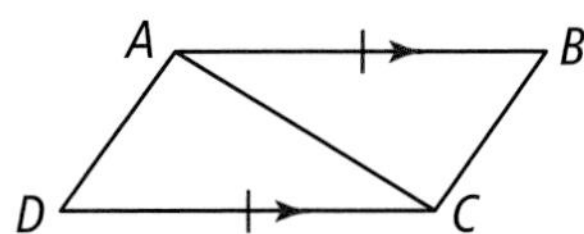


**THEOREM 4-5** Side-Side-Side (SSS) Congruence Criterion

If three sides of one triangle are congruent to three sides of another triangle, then the two triangles are congruent.

PROOF: SEE EXAMPLE 3.

**If...**

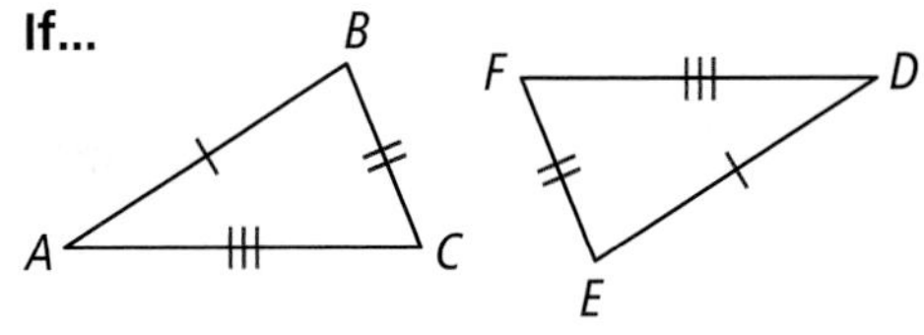


**Then...** $\triangle ABC \cong \triangle DEF$

PROOF

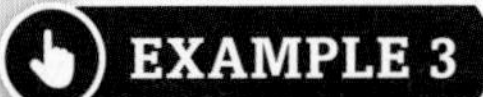


## Prove the Side-Side-Side (SSS) Congruence Criterion

**Prove the SSS Congruence Criterion.**

**Given:** $\overline{AB} \cong \overline{DE}$, $\overline{BC} \cong \overline{EF}$, $\overline{AC} \cong \overline{DF}$

**Prove:** $\triangle ABC \cong \triangle DEF$

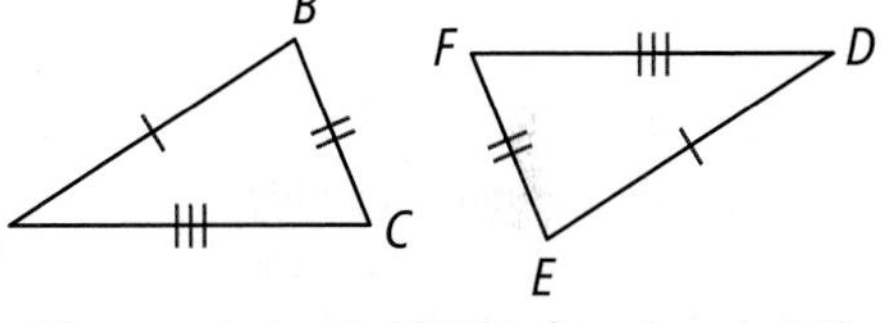


**Proof:** First, translate $\triangle ABC$ so point $B$ maps to point $E$. Since the translation maps $B$ to $E$, $E = B'$.

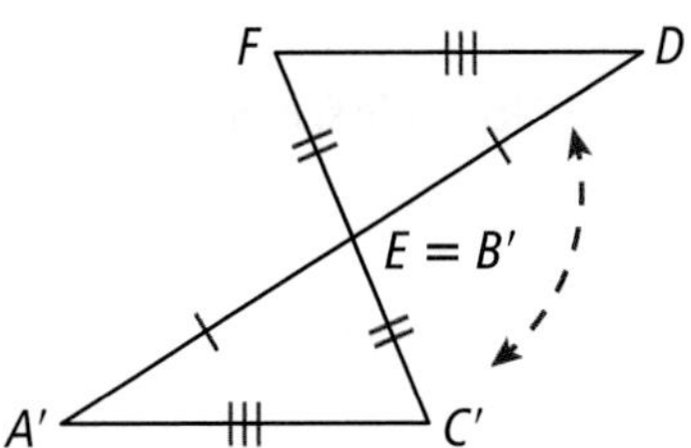


Then rotate $\triangle A'B'C'$ about point $E$ so the image $\overline{B''C''}$ coincides with $\overline{EF}$. It appears that $A''$ coincides with $D''$, but this needs to be proven.

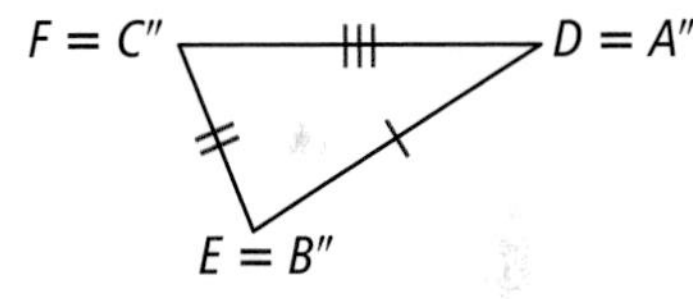


**STUDY TIP**
Use indirect reasoning to show that $A''$ must coincide with $D$.

To show that $A''$ does coincide with $D$, assume that $A''$ does not coincide.

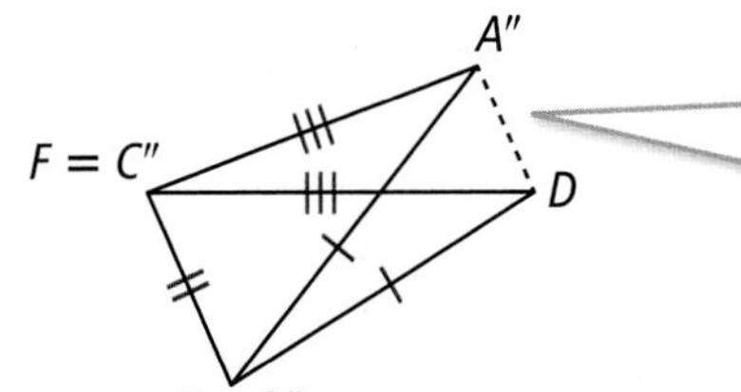

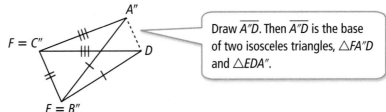

Draw $\overline{A''D}$. Then $\overline{A''D}$ is the base of two isosceles triangles, $\triangle FA''D$ and $\triangle EDA''$.

By the Isosceles Triangle Theorem, $\angle FA''D \cong \angle FDA''$ and $\angle EA''D \cong \angle EDA''$. From the diagram, observe that $m\angle FA''D > m\angle EA''D$ and $m\angle FDA'' < m\angle EDA''$.

$m\angle FA''D > m\angle EA''D$

$m\angle FDA'' > m\angle EA''D$

$m\angle FDA'' > m\angle EDA''$

Substitute $m\angle FDA''$ for $m\angle FA''D$, and substitute $m\angle EDA''$ for $m\angle EA''D$.

This contradicts the observation that $\angle FDA'' < \angle EDA''$. Therefore, $A''$ must coincide with $D$. Since $D = A''$, $E = B''$, and $F = C''$, there exists a rigid motion that maps $\triangle ABC$ to $\triangle DEF$, so $\triangle ABC \cong \triangle DEF$.

CONTINUED ON THE NEXT PAGE

**Try It!** **3.** Show that there is a rigid motion that maps $\triangle PQR$ to $\triangle STU$.
Hint: Be sure to consider a reflection when mapping $\triangle PQR$ to $\triangle STU$.

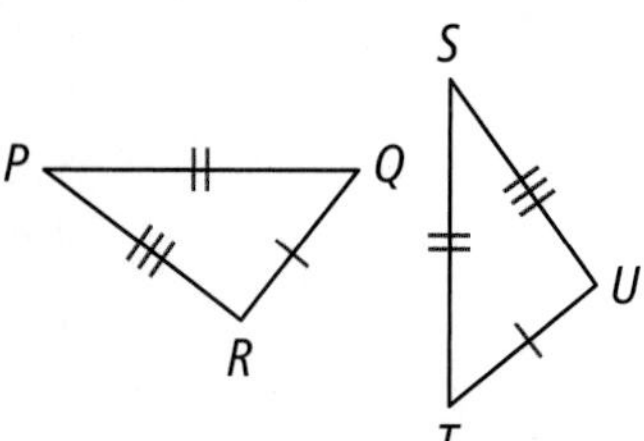


## EXAMPLE 4 Determine Congruent Triangles

**A. Which of the following pairs are congruent by SAS or SSS?**

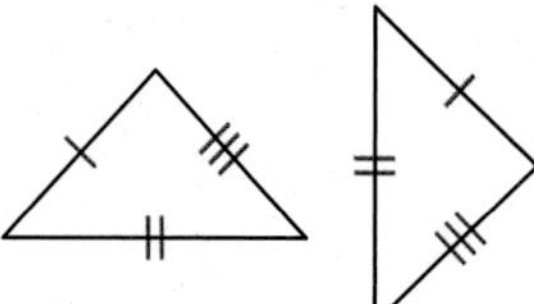

Congruent by SSS

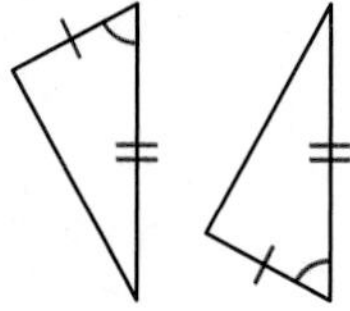

Congruent by SAS

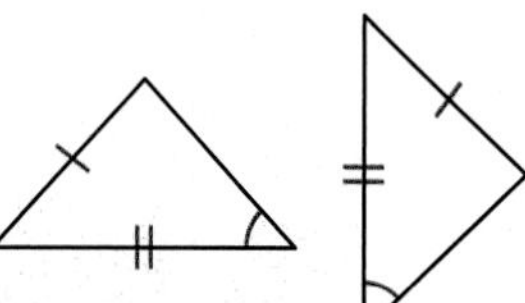

Cannot be determined

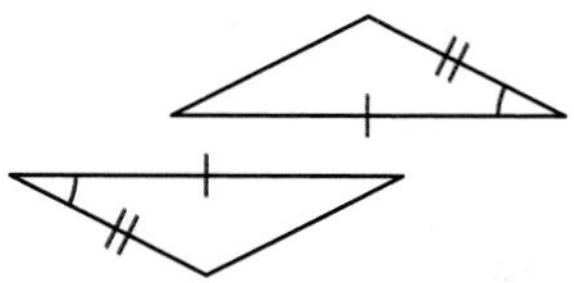

Congruent by SAS

COMMON ERROR
It may not be enough to identify two pairs of congruent sides and one pair of congruent angles. Recall that to apply SAS, the congruent angle pair must be the included angles.

**B. What additional information is needed to show $\triangle ABC \cong \triangle DEF$ by SAS? By SSS?**

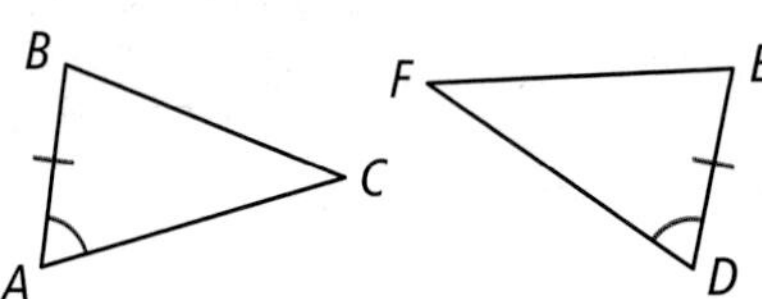


To show $\triangle ABC \cong \triangle DEF$ by SAS, you need $\overline{AC} \cong \overline{DF}$.

To show $\triangle ABC \cong \triangle DEF$ by SSS, you need $\overline{AC} \cong \overline{DF}$ and $\overline{BC} \cong \overline{EF}$.

**Try It!** **4. a.** Is $\triangle STU$ congruent to $\triangle XYZ$? Explain.

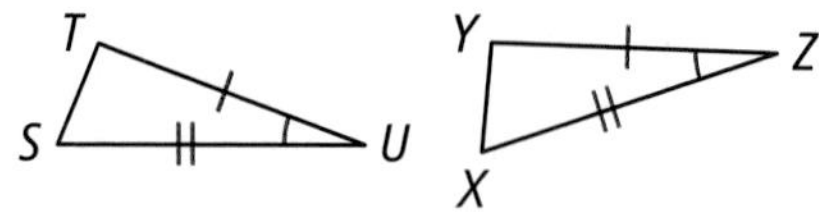


**b.** Is any additional information needed to show $\triangle DEF \cong \triangle GHJ$ by SAS? Explain.

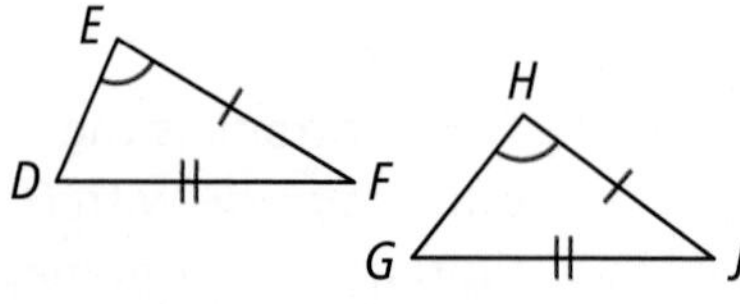

Concept Summary

Assess

## CONCEPT SUMMARY Triangle Congruence Criteria

**THEOREM 4-3** Side-Angle-Side (SAS)

If...

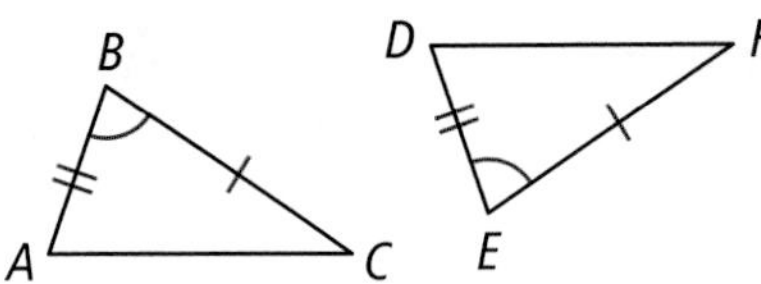


$\overline{AB} \cong \overline{DE}$, $\overline{BC} \cong \overline{EF}$, and $\angle B \cong \angle E$

Then... $\triangle ABC \cong \triangle DEF$

**THEOREM 4-5** Side-Side-Side (SSS)

If...

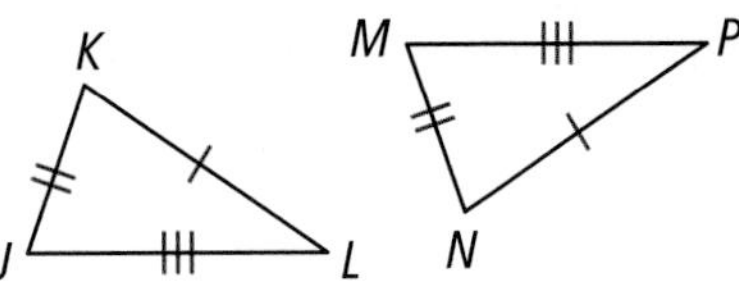


$\overline{JK} \cong \overline{MN}$, $\overline{JL} \cong \overline{MP}$, and $\overline{KL} \cong \overline{NP}$

Then... $\triangle JKL \cong \triangle MNP$

## Do You UNDERSTAND?

1. **ESSENTIAL QUESTION** How are SAS and SSS used to show that two triangles are congruent?

2. **Error Analysis** Elijah says $\triangle ABC$ and $\triangle DEF$ are congruent by SAS. Explain Elijah's error.

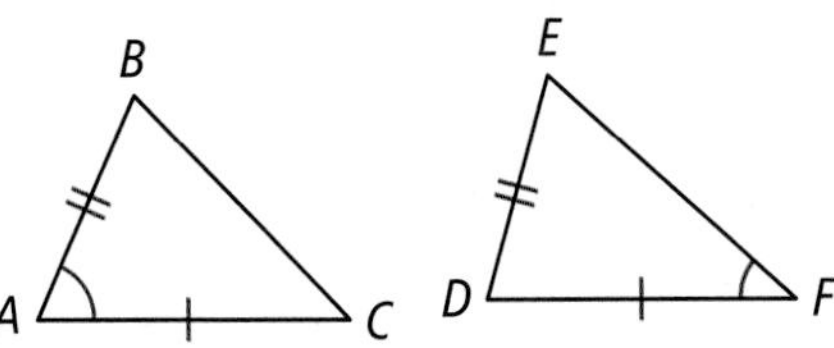


3. **Construct Arguments** Suppose $\overline{PR} \cong \overline{ST}$ and $\angle P \cong \angle S$. Ron wants to prove $\triangle PQR \cong \triangle STU$ by SAS. He says that all he needs to do is show $\overline{RQ} \cong \overline{SU}$. Will this work? Explain.

4. **Reason** How would you decide what theorem to use to prove $\angle JKL \cong \angle MNP$? Explain.

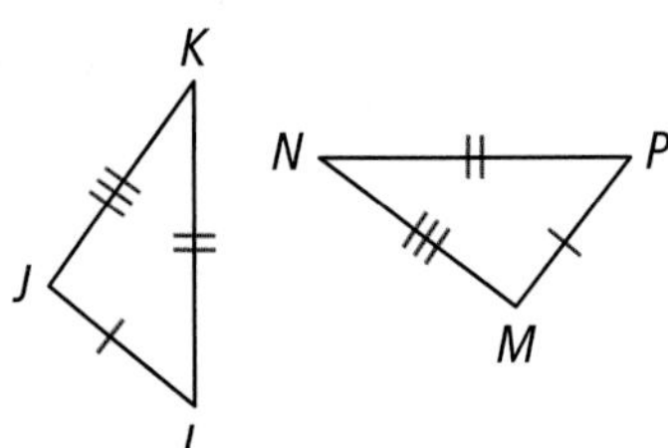


5. **Make Sense and Persevere** Suppose that $\overline{JK}$ and $\overline{LM}$ bisect each other. Is there enough information to show that $\triangle JPM \cong \triangle KPL$? Explain.

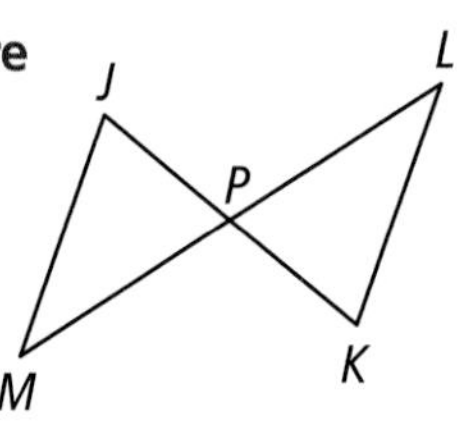


## Do You KNOW HOW?

**For Exercises 6–8, which pairs of triangles are congruent by SAS? By SSS?**

6.

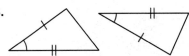

7.

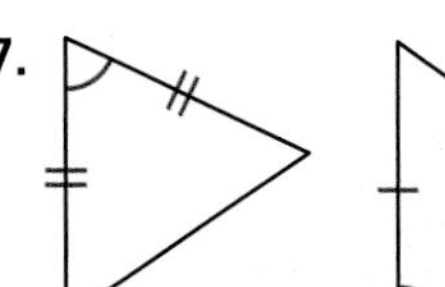

8.

**For Exercises 9–11, are the triangles congruent? Explain.**

9.

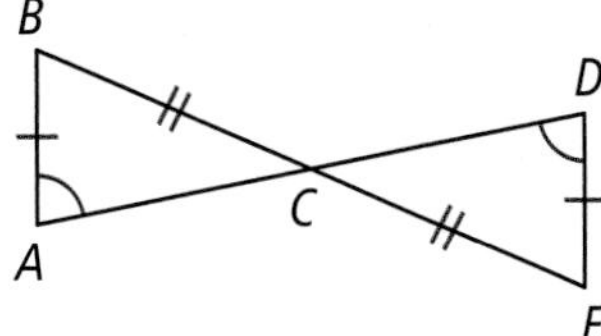


10.

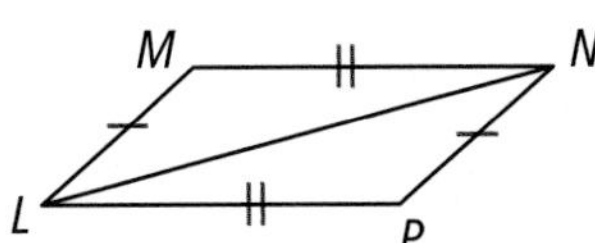


11.

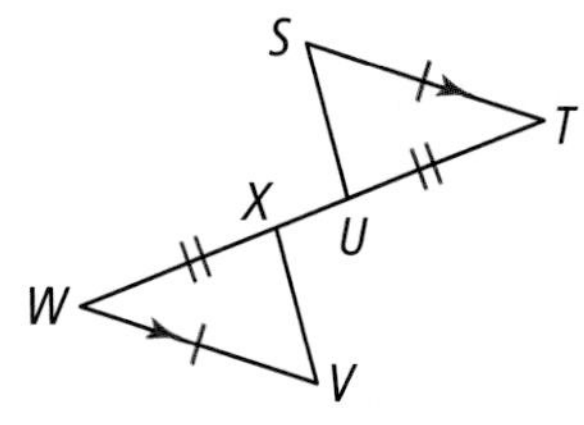

# PRACTICE & PROBLEM SOLVING

Scan for Multimedia

Practice Tutorial

Additional Exercises Available Online

## UNDERSTAND

**12. Error Analysis** Zhang says $\triangle ABC$ is congruent to $\triangle ADC$. Explain the error in Zhang's work.

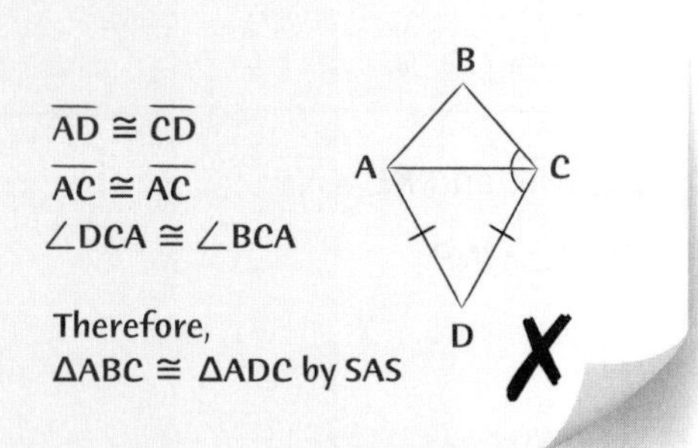


**13. Construct Arguments** Given $\triangle ABC \cong \triangle XYZ$, use a rigid motion to prove Theorem 4-4, Corresponding Parts of Congruent Triangles are Congruent.

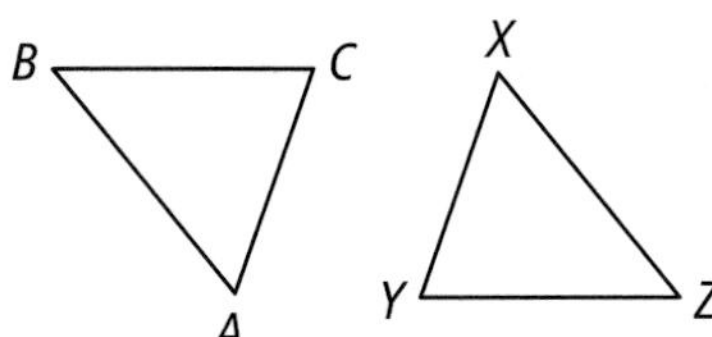


**14. Mathematical Connections** Is $\triangle JKL$ congruent to $\triangle MNL$? Explain.

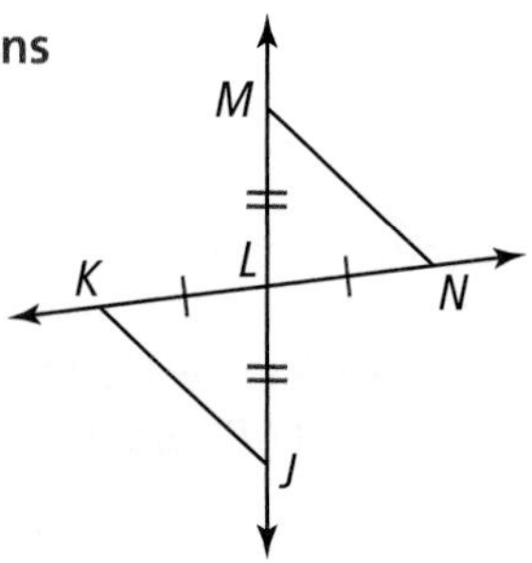


**15. Make Sense and Persevere** Why is $\triangle ABC \cong \triangle GHJ$?

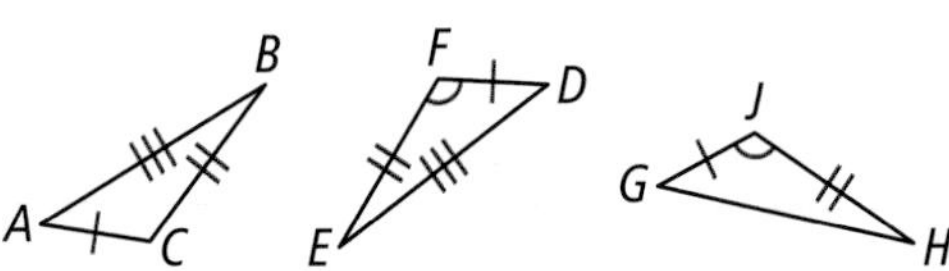


**16. Higher Order Thinking** Given quadrilaterals *ABCD* and *LMNO*, and $\overline{AC} \cong \overline{LN}$, how can you show that the corresponding angles of the quadrilaterals are congruent?

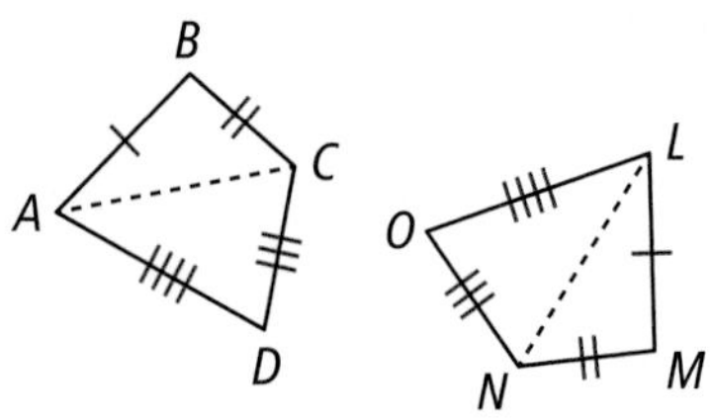


## PRACTICE

**17.** Prove $\triangle ACE$ is an isosceles triangle.
SEE EXAMPLES 1 AND 2

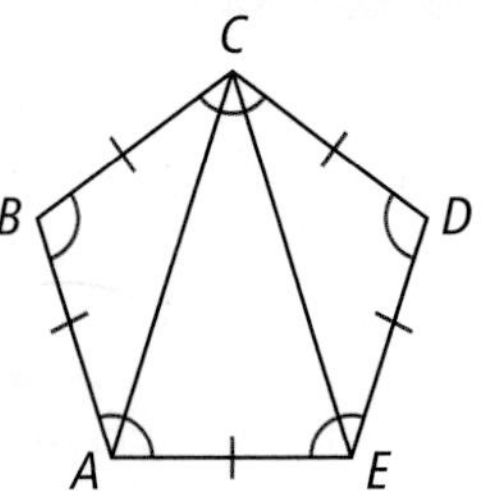


**18.** What is $m\angle RTS$? Justify your answer.
SEE EXAMPLES 1 AND 2

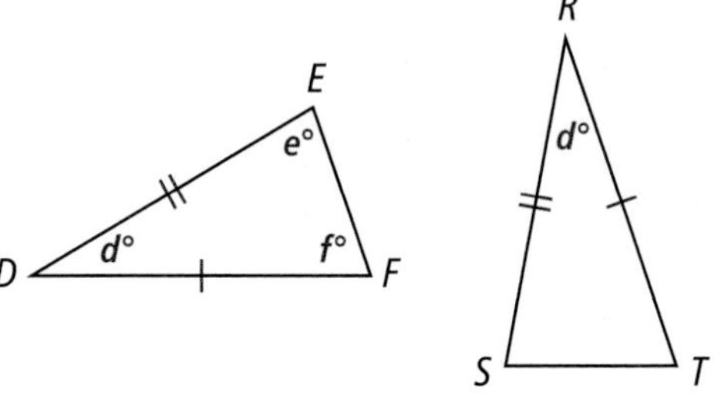


**19.** What additional information is needed to show that $\triangle PQR \cong \triangle STU$ by SSS? SEE EXAMPLE 3

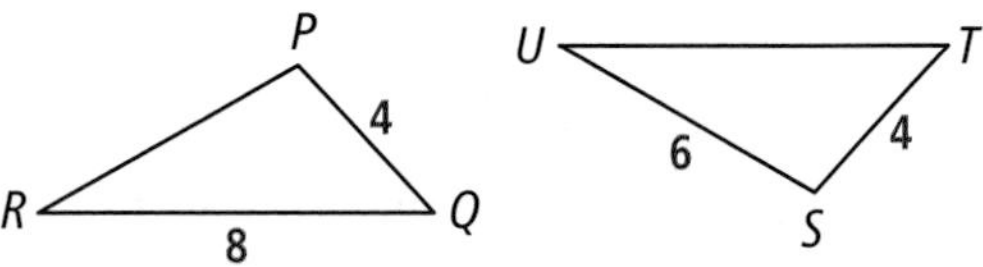


**20.** What additional information is needed to show that $\triangle ABC \cong \triangle DEF$? SEE EXAMPLE 3

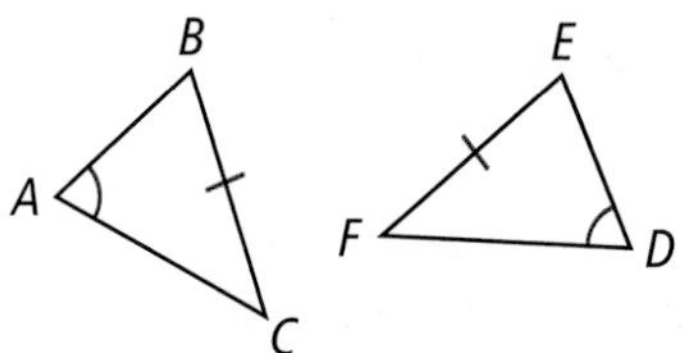


**21.** Is $\triangle RSV \cong \triangle UTV$? Explain.
SEE EXAMPLE 4

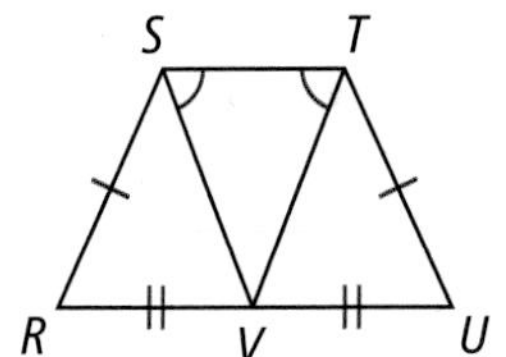


**22.** Is $\triangle PQR \cong \triangle PSR$? Explain.
SEE EXAMPLE 4

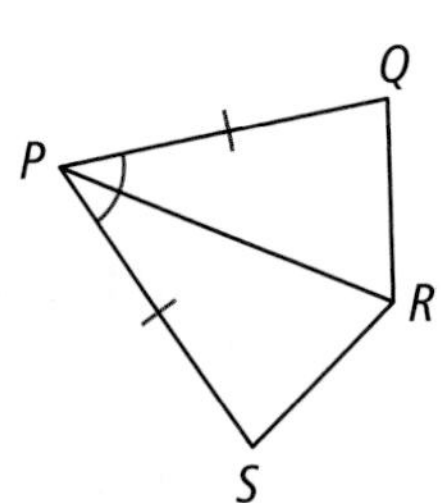

Practice Tutorial
Mixed Review Available Online

# PRACTICE & PROBLEM SOLVING

## APPLY

**23. Critique Reasoning** Kathryn runs from the northwest corner to the southeast corner of a rugby field and Mia runs from the northeast corner to the southwest corner. Mia says she ran farther. Is she correct? Explain.

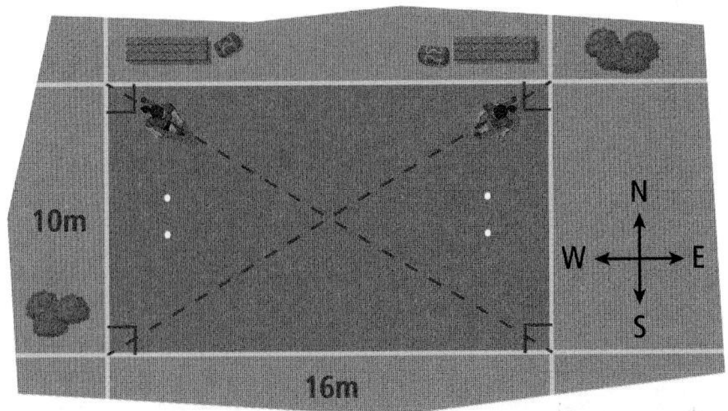


**24. Reason** Following the route shown, what is the total distance traveled by the architectural tour if it ends where it started? What properties and theorems did you use to find the distance?

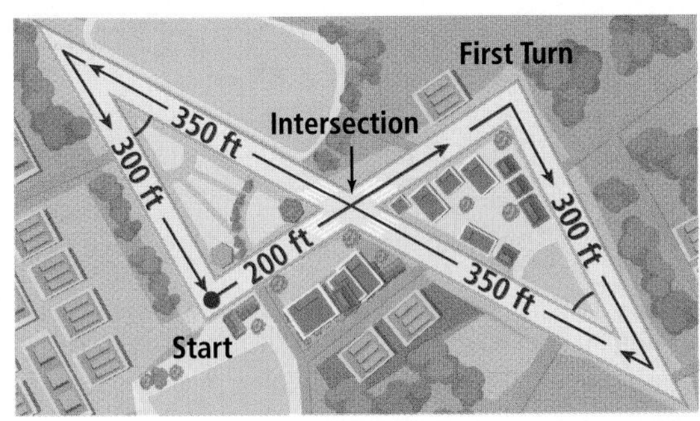


**25. Make Sense and Persevere** Justice and Leah both made a triangular scarf. Do the scarves have the same size and shape? What do you notice about the information that is given?

## ASSESSMENT PRACTICE

**26.** Which sets of congruent parts are sufficient to conclude that $\triangle FGH \cong \triangle JKL$? Select *Yes* or *No*.

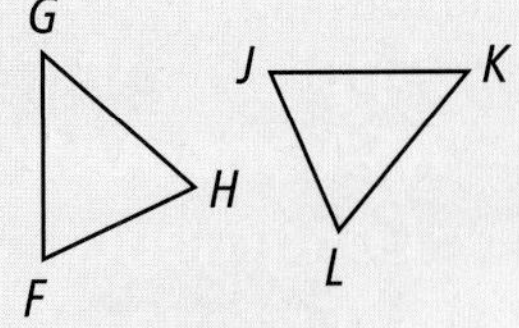


| | Yes | No |
|---|---|---|
| $\overline{FG} \cong \overline{JK}$, $\overline{GH} \cong \overline{KL}$, $\overline{FH} \cong \overline{JL}$ | | |
| $\overline{FG} \cong \overline{JK}$, $\overline{FH} \cong \overline{JL}$, $\angle FHG \cong \angle JLK$ | | |
| $\overline{GH} \cong \overline{KL}$, $\overline{FG} \cong \overline{JK}$, $\angle FGH \cong \angle JKL$ | | |
| $\overline{GH} \cong \overline{KL}$, $\overline{FH} \cong \overline{JL}$, $\angle FHG \cong \angle JLK$ | | |

**27. SAT/ACT** Consider $\triangle DEF$ and $\triangle PQR$. Which additional piece of information would allow you to conclude that $\triangle DEF \cong \triangle PQR$?

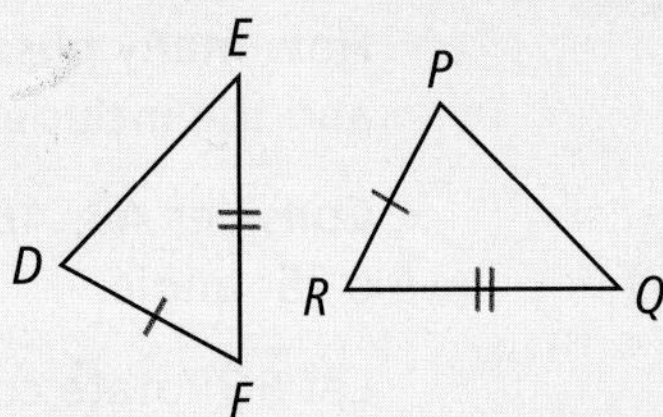


Ⓐ $\angle D \cong \angle P$
Ⓑ $\angle E \cong \angle Q$
Ⓒ $\angle D \cong \angle Q$
Ⓓ $\angle F \cong \angle R$

**28. Performance Task** In a marching band show, Kayden and Latoya start 10 yards apart. Kayden marches the path in blue and Latoya marches the path in green.

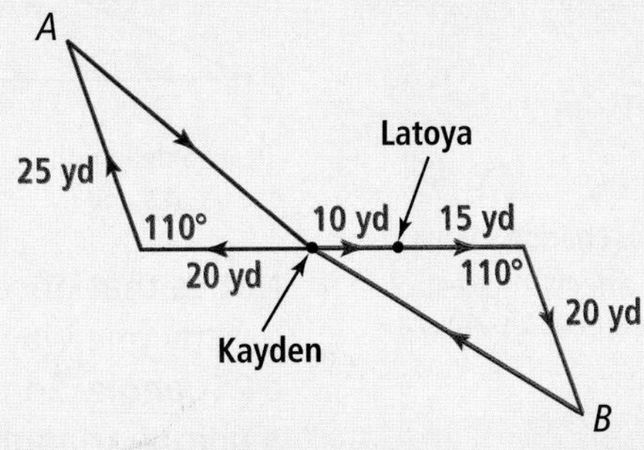


**Part A** Are the triangles formed by the paths congruent? Explain.

**Part B** Are the angle measures that Kayden and Latoya turn at points *A* and *B* the same? Explain.

# 4-4 Proving and Applying the ASA and AAS Congruence Criteria

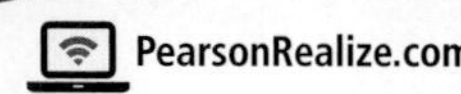


**I CAN…** determine congruent triangles by comparing two angles and one side.

## EXPLORE & REASON

**Are these triangles congruent?**

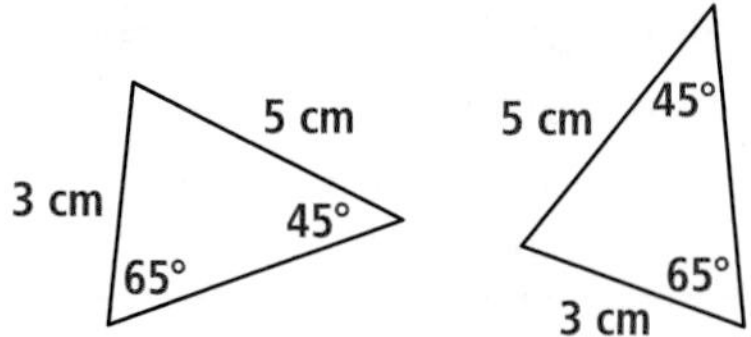


**A. Make Sense and Persevere** Assume the triangles are *not* congruent. What contradictions can you find to contradict your assumption? Explain.

**B.** Is it sufficient to say that the triangles are congruent because of the contradictions you found? Explain.

## ESSENTIAL QUESTION

**How are ASA and AAS used to show that triangles are congruent?**

CONCEPTUAL UNDERSTANDING

## EXAMPLE 1 Explore ASA Congruence Criteria

**How many possible triangles can you determine when given two angles and the included side of a triangle?**

Consider $\overline{AB}$, $\overrightarrow{AE}$, and $\overrightarrow{BG}$, where $\overline{AB}$ and $\overrightarrow{AE}$ form a 25° angle.

Let $\overrightarrow{BG}$ rotate counterclockwise about point $B$ to form a 68° angle, a 57° angle, and a 45° angle. The rays will intersect to form some triangles.

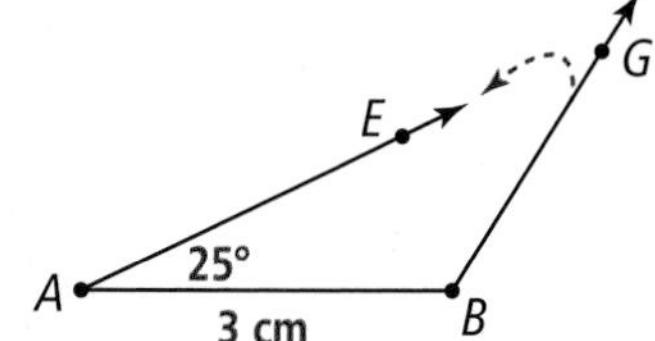


When $m\angle B$ changes, the second and third side lengths and third angle measure always change.

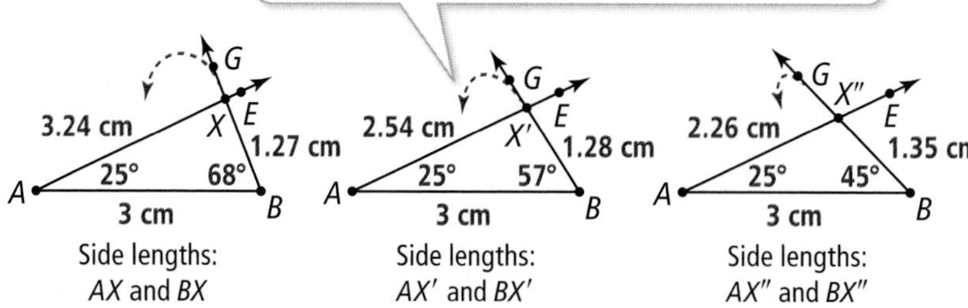


Side lengths: $AX$ and $BX$

Side lengths: $AX'$ and $BX'$

Side lengths: $AX''$ and $BX''$

**LOOK FOR RELATIONSHIPS**
Think about how change in one part of a figure affects the rest of the figure. Does the result follow a pattern?

Notice that once the 25° angle, and the side of length 3 cm are set, there is exactly one way to complete the triangle with a 68° angle, a 57° angle, or a 25° angle. So for each unique combination of $AB$, $m\angle A$, and $m\angle B$, there is a unique triangle.

**Try It!** 1. What is the relationship between $\triangle AXB$ and $\triangle AYB$?

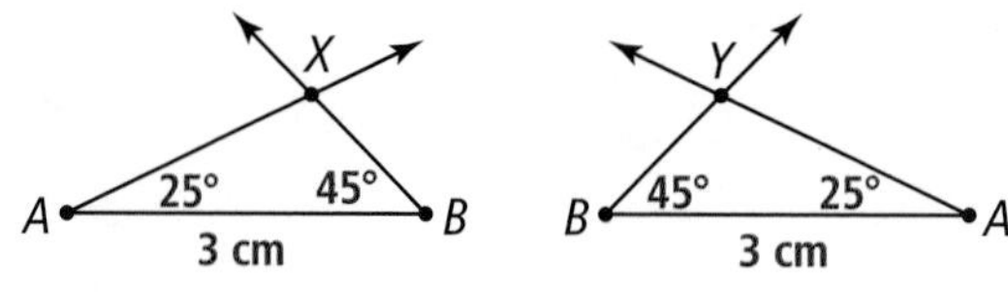

 Activity  Assess

## EXAMPLE 4 Investigate the Angle-Angle-Side (AAS) Congruence Criterion

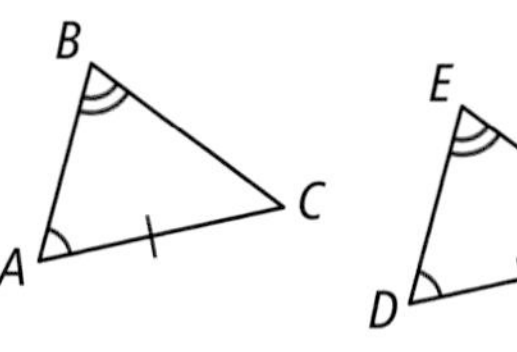

**Given $\triangle ABC$, is the triangle determined by $\angle A$, $\angle B$, and the non-included side $\overline{AC}$ unique?**

Assume that $\triangle ABC$ is not unique. Then there must exist $\triangle DEF$ such that $\triangle ABC \ncong \triangle DEF$, $\angle A \cong \angle D$, $\angle B \cong \angle E$, and $\overline{AC} \cong \overline{DF}$.

By the Triangle Angle-Sum Theorem, $m\angle C = 180 - m\angle A - m\angle B$ and $m\angle F = 180 - m\angle D - m\angle E$. Since $\angle A \cong \angle D$ and $\angle B \cong \angle E$, $m\angle C = 180 - m\angle D - m\angle E = m\angle F$, so $\angle C \cong \angle F$.

Therefore, by ASA, $\triangle ABC \cong \triangle DEF$, and the assumption is false. A unique triangle is determined by $\angle A$ and $\angle B$ and the non-included side $\overline{AC}$.

**Try It!** 4. Using the figures shown, describe a sequence of rigid motions that maps $\triangle JKL$ to $\triangle QRP$.

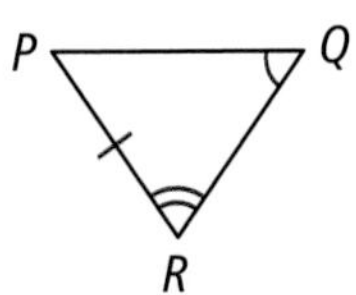

### THEOREM 4-7 Angle-Angle-Side (AAS) Congruence Criterion

If two angles and a nonincluded side of one triangle are congruent to two angles and a nonincluded side of another triangle, then the two triangles are congruent.

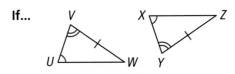

PROOF: SEE EXERCISE 16.

If...

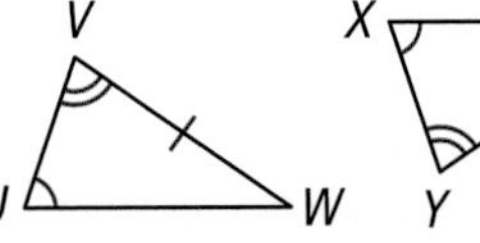

Then... $\triangle UVW \cong \triangle XYZ$

## EXAMPLE 5 Use Triangle Congruence Criteria

**A. State whether each pair of triangles is congruent by SAS, SSS, ASA, or AAS, or if the congruence cannot be determined.**

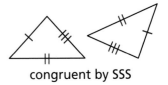

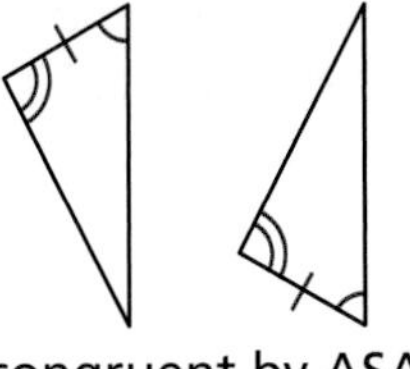

congruent by ASA

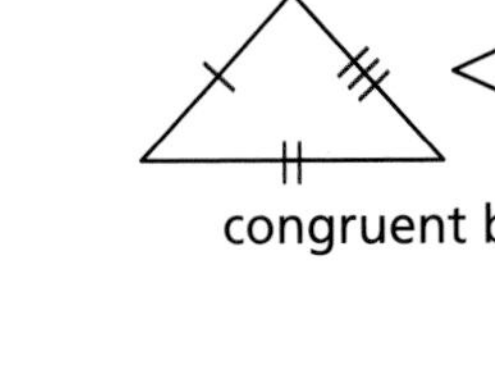

congruent by SSS

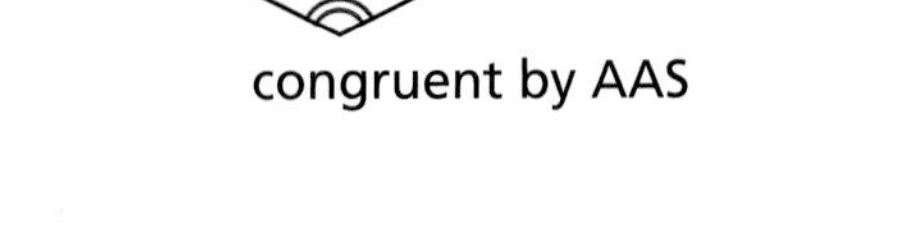

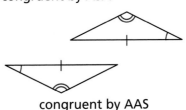

congruent by AAS

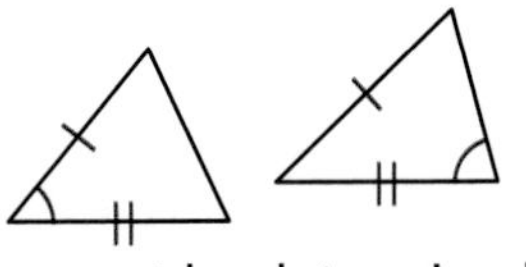

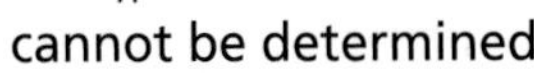

cannot be determined

**COMMON ERROR**
Be careful not to just assume that triangles are congruent when given two pairs of congruent angles and one pair of congruent sides. The congruent sides must be corresponding sides.

CONTINUED ON THE NEXT PAGE

EXAMPLE 5 CONTINUED

**B. Prove that $\overline{FH} \cong \overline{JL}$.**

**Given:** $\overline{GH} \cong \overline{KL}$, $\angle GFH \cong \angle KJL$, and $\angle FGH \cong \angle JKL$

**Prove:** $\overline{FH} \cong \overline{JL}$

| Statements | Reasons |
|---|---|
| 1) $\angle F \cong \angle J$, $\angle G \cong \angle K$, $\overline{GH} \cong \overline{KL}$ | 1) Given |
| 2) $\triangle FGH \cong \triangle JKL$ | 2) AAS |
| 3) $\overline{FH} \cong \overline{JL}$ | 3) CPCTC |

When triangle congruence applies, you can conclude the remaining sides and angles are congruent by CPCTC.

**Try It!** 5. a. What additional information is needed to show $\triangle ABC \cong \triangle DEF$ by ASA?

b. What additional information is needed to show $\triangle ABC \cong \triangle DEF$ by AAS?

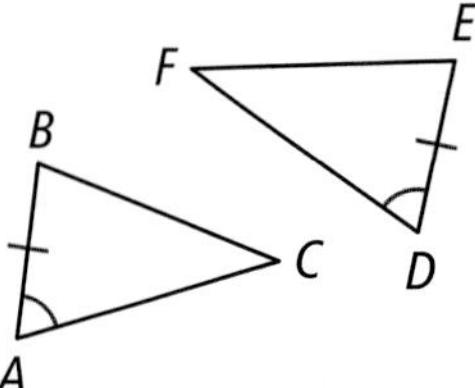

## EXAMPLE 6 Determine Congruent Polygons

**USE STRUCTURE**
Consider the diagonals of a polygon. Can any polygon be divided into a figure composed of triangles?

**All sides and angles of *ABCD* are congruent to the corresponding sides and angles of *A′B′C′D′*. Is *ABCD* congruent to *A′B′C′D′*?**

Each polygon can be divided into two triangles by the diagonals shown.

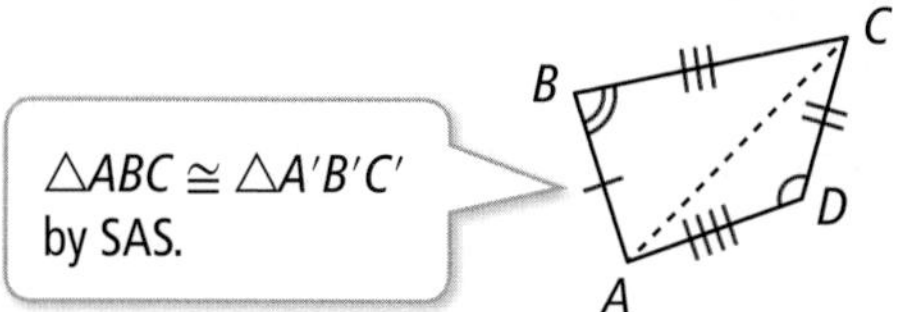


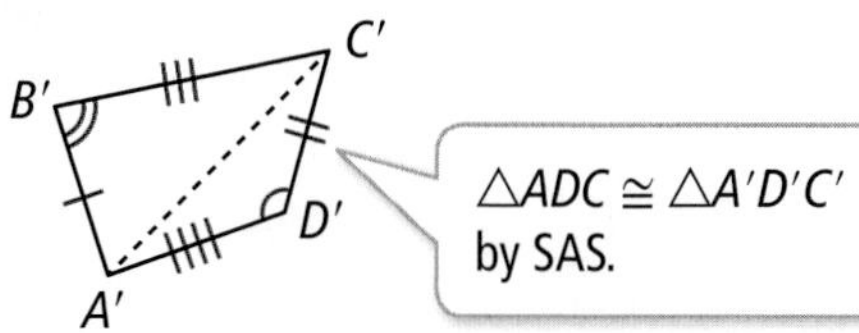


Since $\triangle ABC \cong \triangle A'B'C'$, there is a rigid motion that maps $\triangle ABC$ to $\triangle A'B'C'$. Consider this rigid motion applied to $\triangle ADC$. Side $\overline{AC}$ maps to $\overline{A'C'}$ since $\overline{AC}$ is shared by both $\triangle ABC$ and $\triangle ADC$.

Now suppose that this rigid motion maps *D* to some point other than *D′*. Call that point *E*. Since $\triangle A'D'C'$ and $\triangle A'EC'$ are congruent to $\triangle ADC$, $\triangle A'D'C' \cong \triangle A'EC'$. Since $\angle C'A'E \cong \angle C'A'D'$, *E* lies on $\overleftrightarrow{A'D'}$. By a similar argument, *E* lies on $\overleftrightarrow{C'D'}$. So *E* must be the point *D′*.

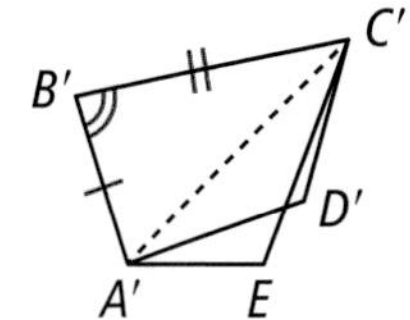


Since the rigid motion that maps $\triangle ABC$ to $\triangle A'B'C'$ also maps *ABCD* to *A′B′C′D′*, *ABCD* is congruent to *A′B′C′D′*.

**Try It!** 6. Given $ABCD \cong EFGH$, what is the value of *x*?

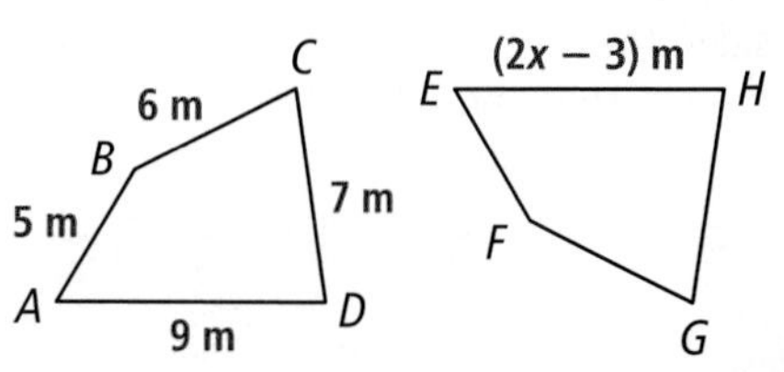

## CONCEPT SUMMARY Triangle Congruence

**THEOREM 4-6** **Angle-Side-Angle (ASA)**

**If...**

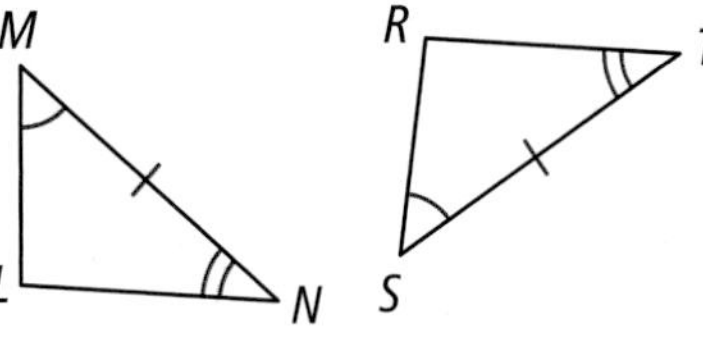


$\overline{MN} \cong \overline{ST}$, $\angle M \cong \angle S$, and $\angle N \cong \angle T$

**Then...** $\triangle MLN \cong \triangle SRT$

**THEOREM 4-7** **Angle-Angle-Side (AAS)**

**If...**

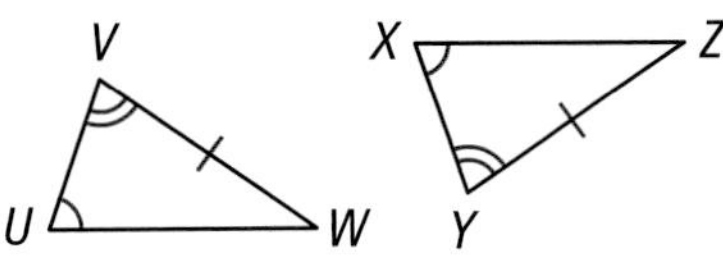


$\overline{VW} \cong \overline{YZ}$, $\angle U \cong \angle X$, and $\angle V \cong \angle Y$

**Then...** $\triangle UVW \cong \triangle XYZ$

## Do You UNDERSTAND?

1. **ESSENTIAL QUESTION** How are ASA and AAS used to show that triangles are congruent?

2. **Error Analysis** Why is Terrell's conclusion incorrect?

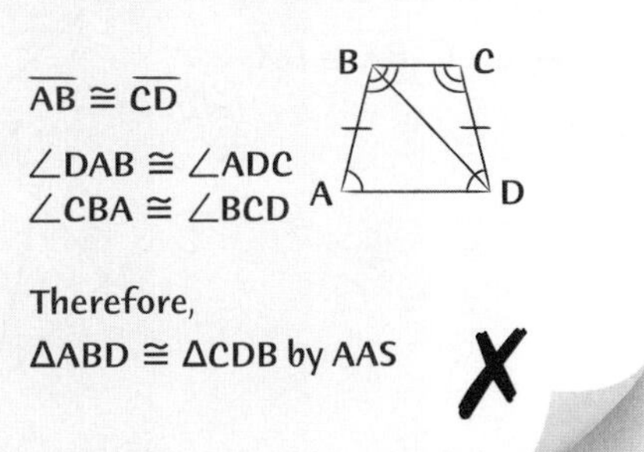

$\overline{AB} \cong \overline{CD}$
$\angle DAB \cong \angle ADC$
$\angle CBA \cong \angle BCD$
Therefore,
$\triangle ABD \cong \triangle CDB$ by AAS
B
C
A
D


3. **Reason** How can you tell which property of triangle congruence shows $\triangle RST \cong \triangle UVW$?

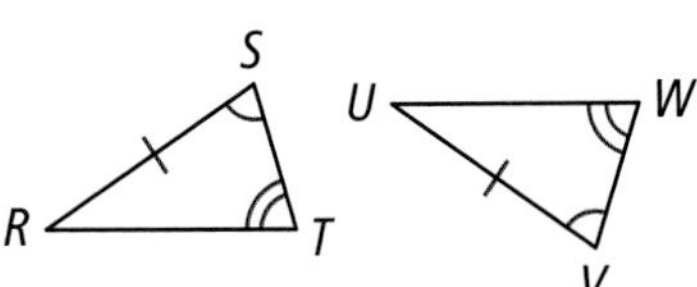


4. **Make Sense and Persevere** Is there a congruence relationship that is sufficient to show that $\triangle MNO \cong \triangle TUV$? Explain.

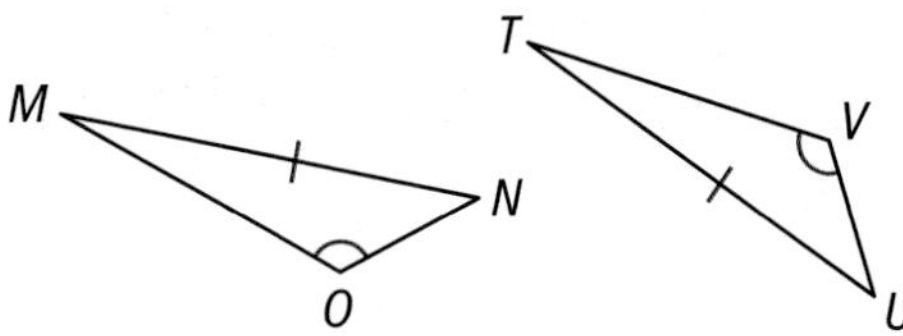


## Do You KNOW HOW?

**For Exercises 5 and 6, find the value of *x*.**

5.

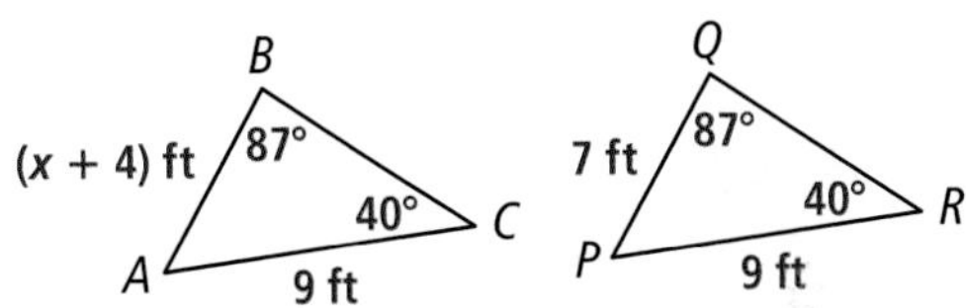


6.

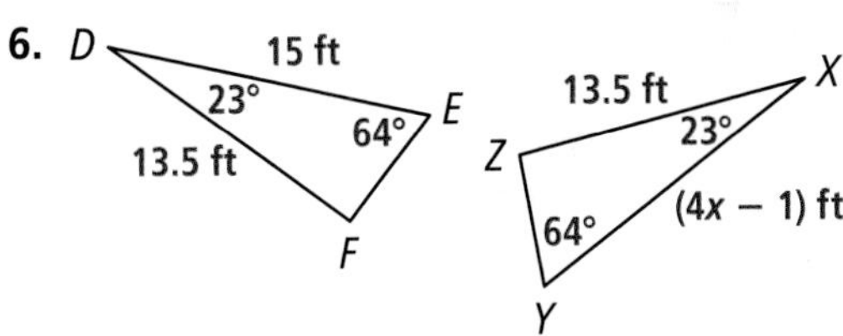


**For Exercises 7 and 8, state whether the triangles are congruent and by which theorem.**

7.

8.

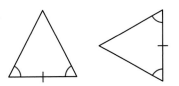

9. Why is $LMNO \cong PQRS$?

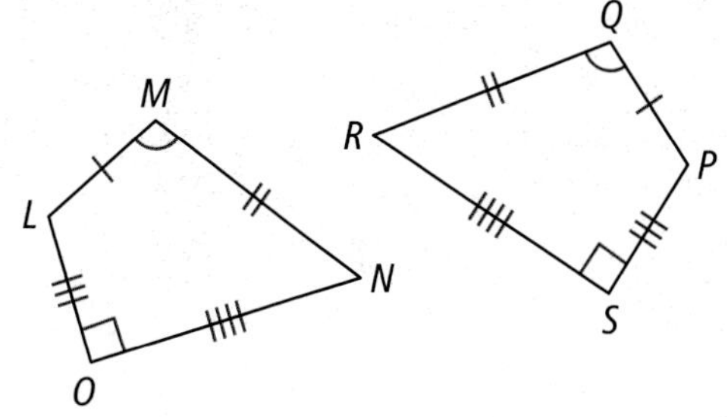

## UNDERSTAND

**10. Error Analysis** Stacy says there is not enough information to prove $\triangle ACX \cong \triangle BCX$. Explain why Stacy's statement is incorrect.

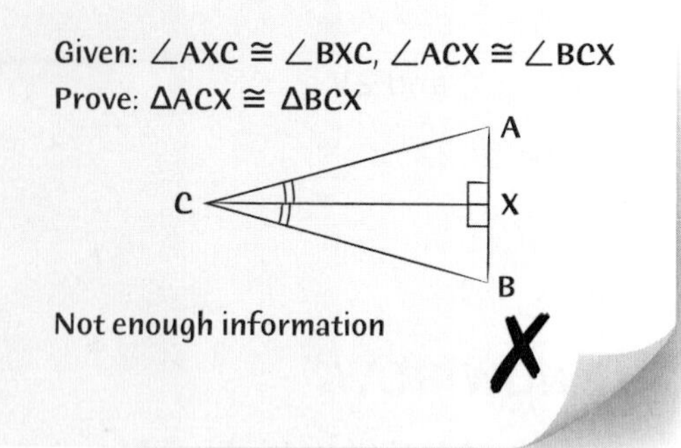

Given: $\angle AXC \cong \angle BXC$, $\angle ACX \cong \angle BCX$
Prove: $\Delta ACX \cong \Delta BCX$
A
C
X
B
Not enough information


**11. Mathematical Connections** Given $\overleftrightarrow{WZ} \parallel \overleftrightarrow{XY}$ and $\overleftrightarrow{WX} \parallel \overleftrightarrow{ZY}$, write a two-column proof to show $\overline{WX} \cong \overline{YZ}$.

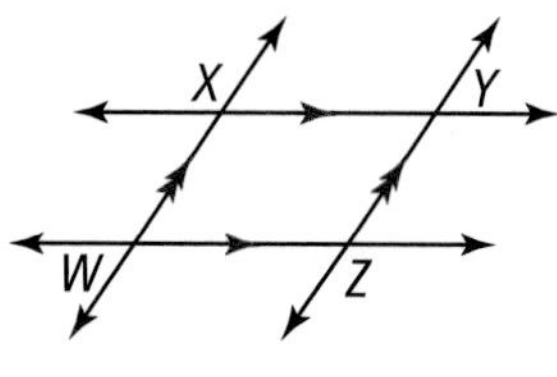


**12. Use Structure** Given the figure shown, write a two-column proof to prove $\angle CAE \cong \angle CEA$.

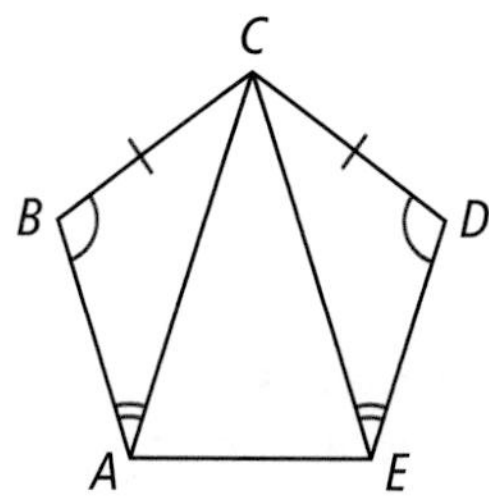


**13. Reason** How might you decide what additional piece of information you need to prove $\triangle JKL \cong \triangle NOM$?

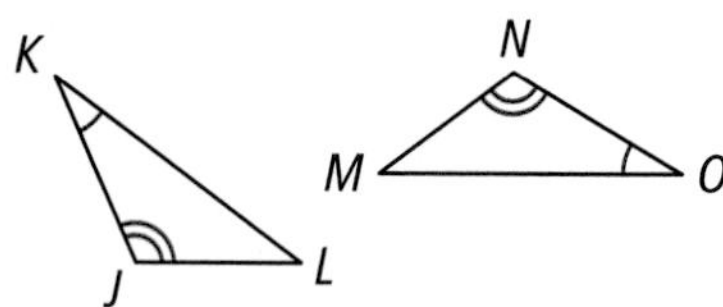


**14. Higher Order Thinking** Describe a composition of rigid motions that maps $\overline{DE}$ to $\overline{JK}$, $\overline{EF}$ to $\overline{KL}$, and $\angle D$ to $\angle J$. Why does this composition show that there is no angle-side-side congruence criterion?

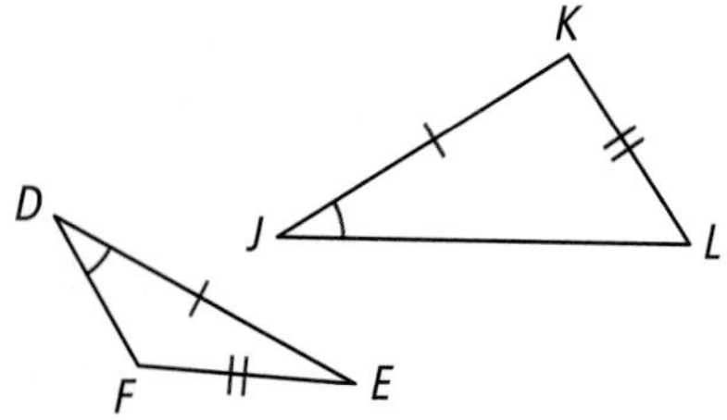


## PRACTICE

**15.** Carpenters build a set of triangular roof supports, each with the measurements shown. How can the carpenters be sure all the slanted beams are the same length? **SEE EXAMPLES 1–3**

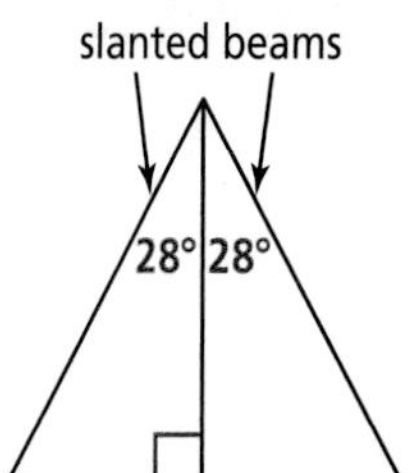


**16.** Prove the Angle-Angle-Side Congruence Criterion. **SEE EXAMPLE 4**

**Given:** $\angle P \cong \angle S$, $\angle Q \cong \angle T$, $\overline{QR} \cong \overline{TU}$

**Prove:** $\triangle PQR \cong \triangle STU$

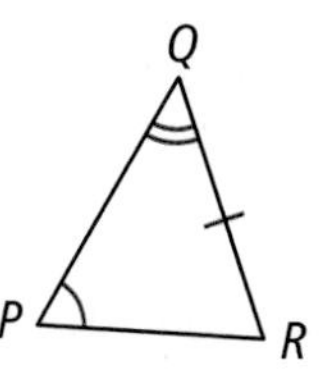


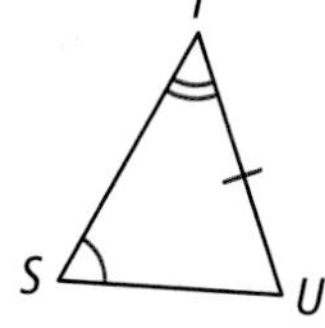


**17.** Write a proof. **SEE EXAMPLE 5**

**Given:** $\angle A \cong \angle C$, $\overline{BX} \cong \overline{DX}$

**Prove:** $\overline{AX} \cong \overline{CX}$

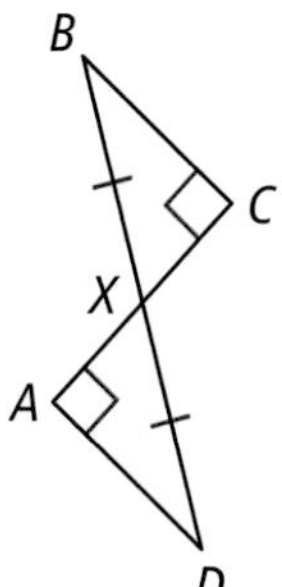


**18.** Is $ABCD \cong GHJK$? Explain. **SEE EXAMPLE 6**

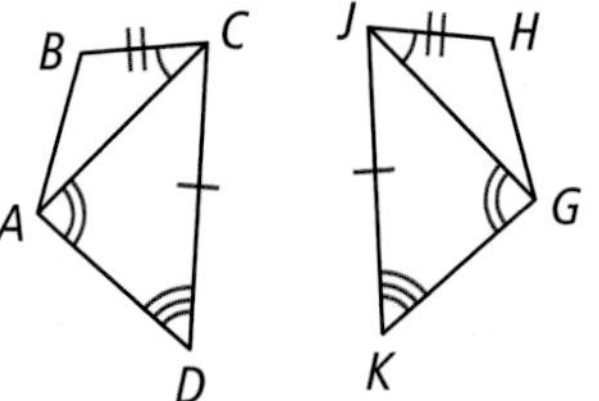


**19.** If $ABCD \cong EFGH$, are all corresponding parts congruent? Explain. **SEE EXAMPLE 6**

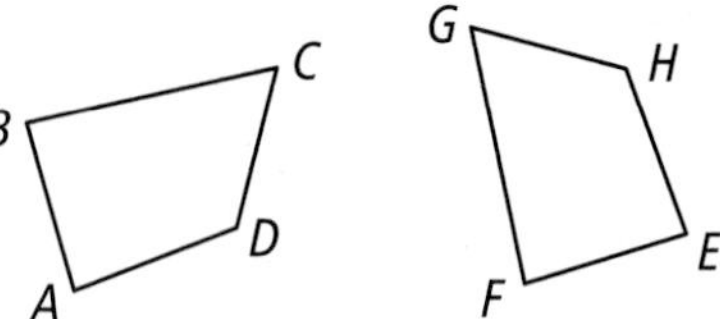

## PRACTICE & PROBLEM SOLVING

Practice Tutorial

Mixed Review Available Online

### APPLY

**20. Look for Relationships** Climbers want to determine a halfway point up a vertical cliff. If the top and bottom are parallel, why is point $P$, where the ropes intersect, halfway up the cliff?

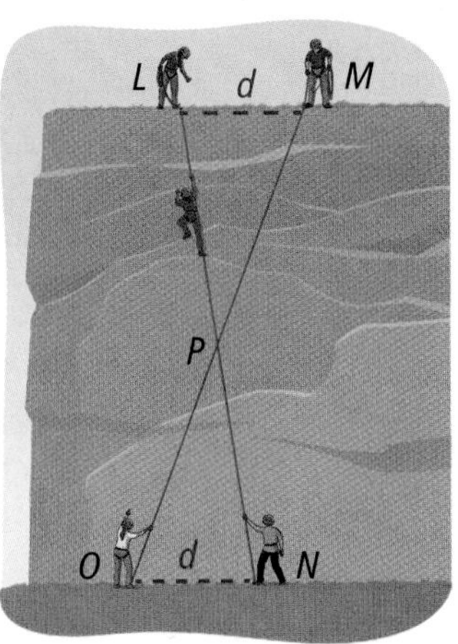


**21. Use Appropriate Tools** Keisha, Dwayne, and Lonzell are planning for a new bridge to replace the old bridge. The new bridge will start at point $B$, where Dwayne is standing, and end at point $C$, where Keisha is standing. Lonzell walks to point $D$ and then walks parallel to the river until he reaches point $E$, where he sees Dwayne and Keisha are aligned. Why is the distance from $E$ to $B$ the length of the new bridge?

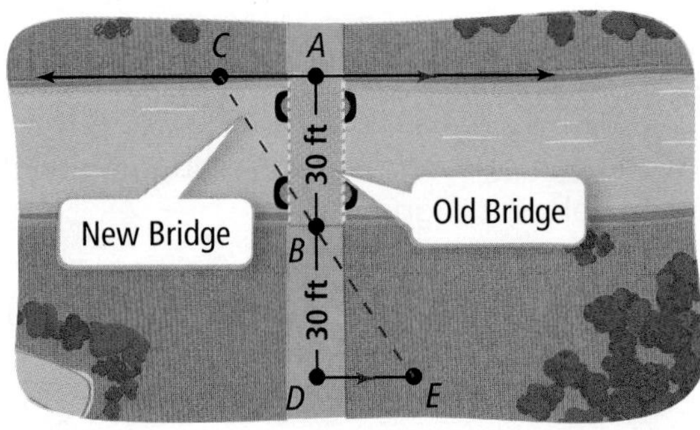


**22. Construct Arguments** The Robotics Club wants to divide their robot battle arena into two congruent arenas for a tournament. Paxton says that if they build a wall perpendicular to and bisecting $\overline{PO}$ from $M$, then the arenas will be congruent. Is Paxton correct? Explain.

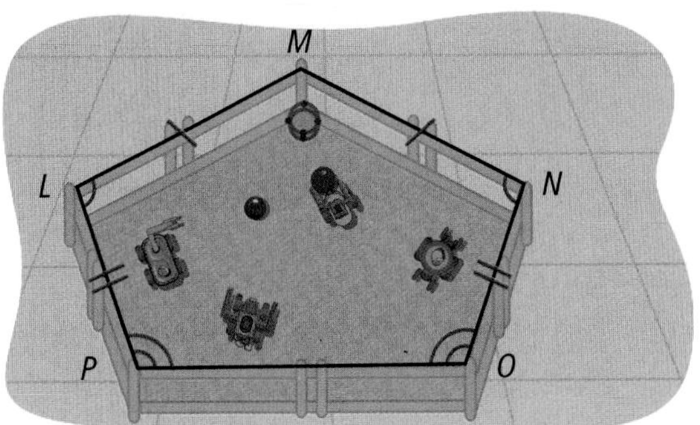


### ASSESSMENT PRACTICE

**23.** Given the figure shown, copy and complete the table to identify the congruent pairs.

| $\angle W$ | $\angle Y$ |
|---|---|
| | $\angle ZXY$ |
| $\angle WXZ$ | |
| | $\overline{XZ}$ |
| $\overline{WZ}$ | |

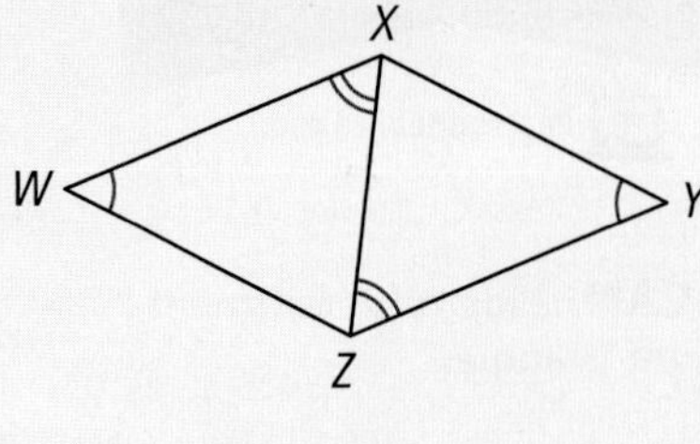


**24. SAT/ACT** Given $\triangle LMN \cong \triangle QRS$, what is the value of $x$?

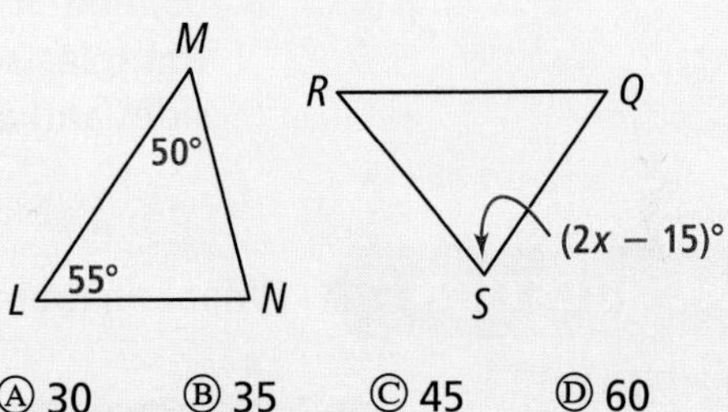


Ⓐ 30 Ⓑ 35 Ⓒ 45 Ⓓ 60

**25. Performance Task** Gregory wants to make four congruent triangular flags using as much of the rectangular canvas shown as possible.

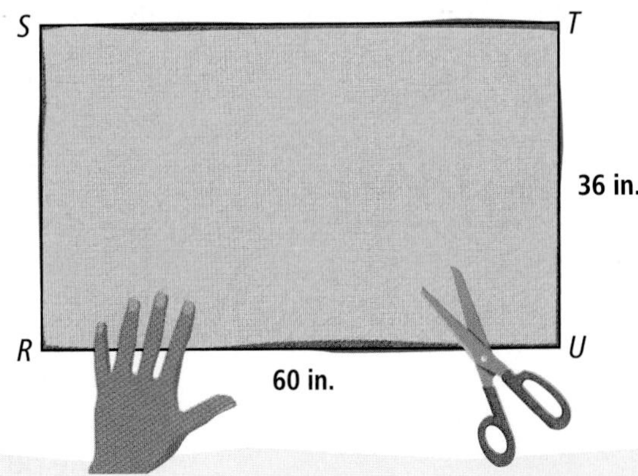


**Part A** Draw and label a diagram to show how Gregory should cut the fabric.

**Part B** Explain why the flags are congruent.

**Part C** Is there another way Gregory can cut the fabric to make 4 congruent triangular flags using the same amount of fabric? Explain.

# 4-5 Congruence in Right Triangles

PearsonRealize.com

**I CAN…** identify congruent right triangles.

## CRITIQUE & EXPLAIN

**Seth and Jae wrote the following explanations of why the two triangles are congruent.**

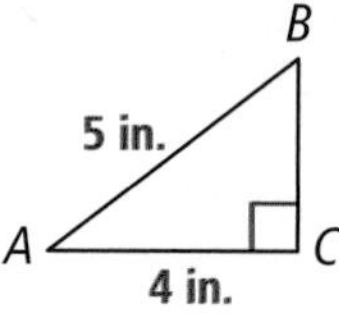


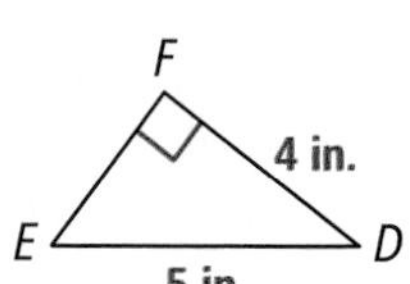


**Seth**

There are two pairs of congruent sides, $\overline{AB} \cong \overline{DE}$ and $\overline{AC} \cong \overline{DF}$, and a pair of congruent right angles, $\angle C \cong \angle F$. So $\Delta ABC \cong \Delta DEF$ by SSA.

**Jae**

The lengths of $\overline{BC}$ and $\overline{EF}$ are 3 in., since these are 3-4-5 right triangles. There are three pairs of congruent sides, $\overline{AB} \cong \overline{DE}$, $\overline{AC} \cong \overline{DF}$, and $\overline{BC} \cong \overline{EF}$. So $\Delta ABC \cong \Delta DEF$ by SSS.

**A.** Do you think either student is correct? Explain.

**B. Communicate Precisely** Describe when you can state that two right triangles are congruent if you are only given two pairs of congruent sides and a right angle in each triangle.

## ESSENTIAL QUESTION

**What minimum criteria are needed to show that right triangles are congruent?**

CONCEPTUAL UNDERSTANDING

## EXAMPLE 1 Investigate Right Triangle Congruence

**When any two pairs of corresponding sides are congruent, can you show that two right triangles $\triangle ABC$ and $\triangle DEF$ are congruent? Explain.**

Given that right triangles have one pair of congruent corresponding angles with right angles, look to see what else is congruent.

- If both pairs of corresponding legs are congruent, use SAS with $\overline{AC} \cong \overline{DF}$, $\angle C \cong \angle F$, and $\overline{BC} \cong \overline{EF}$.

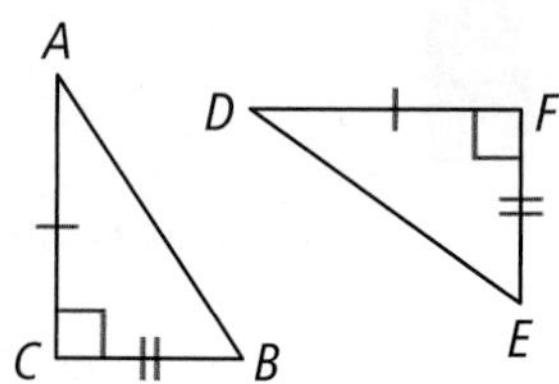


- If one pair of corresponding legs is congruent along with the hypotenuses, apply the Pythagorean Theorem to show that the other pair of corresponding legs is also congruent.

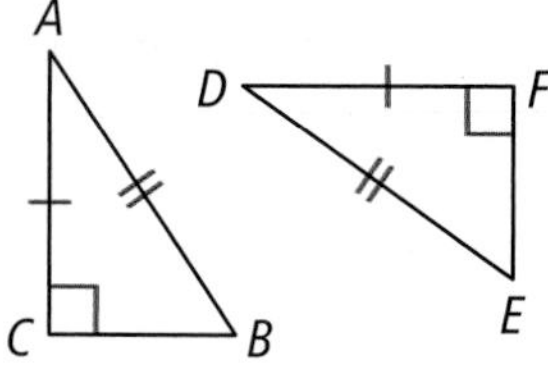


$$BC = \sqrt{AB^2 - AC^2} = \sqrt{DE^2 - DF^2} = EF$$

The right triangles are congruent by SSS.

**STUDY TIP**
To visualize congruent corresponding parts, draw copies of $\triangle ABC$ and $\triangle DEF$. Then mark the triangles to show the congruent relationships.

**Try It!** **1.** Can you show that two right triangles are congruent when any one pair of corresponding acute angles is congruent and any one pair of corresponding sides is congruent? Explain.

## THEOREM 4-8 Hypotenuse-Leg (HL) Theorem

If the hypotenuse and one leg of a right triangle are congruent to the hypotenuse and leg of another right triangle, then the triangles are congruent.

PROOF: SEE EXERCISE 9.

**If...**

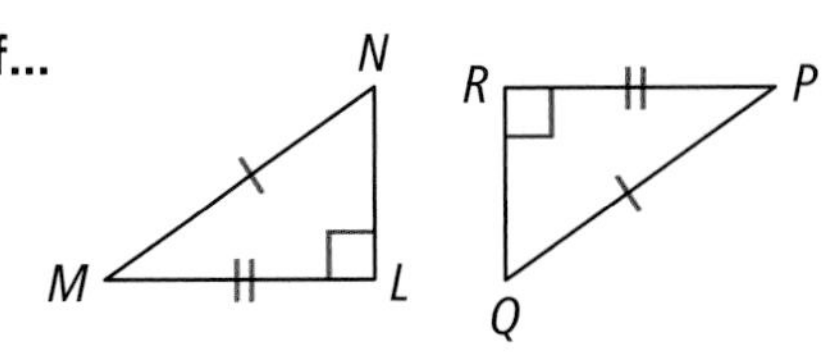


**Then...** $\triangle MNL \cong \triangle PQR$

APPLICATION

## EXAMPLE 2 Use the Hypotenuse-Leg (HL) Theorem

**Ashton is washing windows using a 10-foot ladder. For the first window, the ladder reaches the window when he places the base of the ladder at the rose bush. How can he determine where to place the ladder to be sure it reaches the last window?**

The ground, the ladder, and the side of the house form a right triangle, $\triangle RAH$. When Ashton moves the ladder, there will be another right triangle, $\triangle SBK$.

> **COMMON ERROR**
> Remember that the triangles must be right triangles in order to use the HL Theorem. Be sure the situation, like this one, describes right triangles.

Ashton wants $AH = BK$. If the two triangles are congruent, then he knows $\overline{AH} \cong \overline{BK}$ by CPCTC.

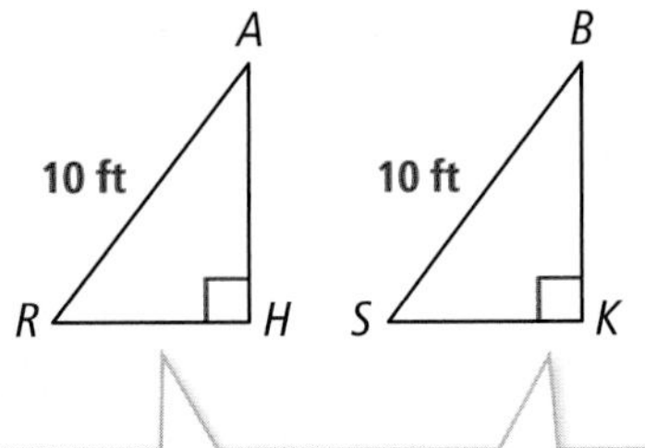


To make sure the triangles are congruent, Ashton can place the base of the ladder so that $RH = SK$.

If $RH = SK$, then $\triangle RAH \cong \triangle SBK$ by the HL Theorem.

Thus, by placing the base of the ladder the same distance away from the house as the rose bush, the ladder will reach the last window.

**Try It!** 2. What information is needed in order to apply the Hypotenuse-Leg (HL) Theorem?

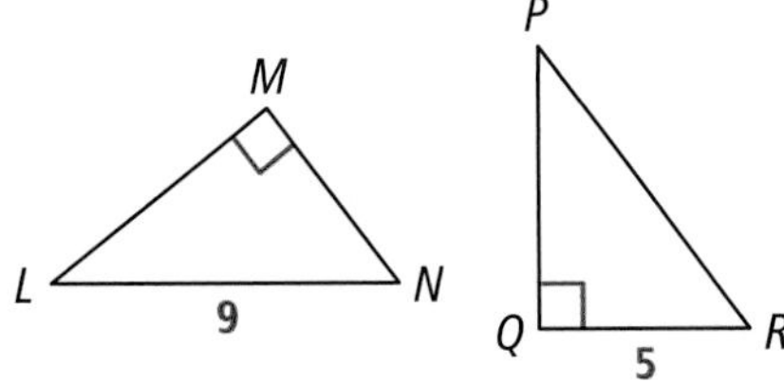

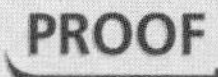

## EXAMPLE 3 Write a Proof Using the Hypotenuse-Leg (HL) Theorem

**Write a proof to show that a triangle is isosceles.**

**Given:** $\overline{FD} \perp \overline{AB}$, $\overline{FE} \perp \overline{AC}$, $\overline{AE} \cong \overline{AD}$, $\overline{FC} \cong \overline{FB}$

**Prove:** $\triangle ABC$ is isosceles.

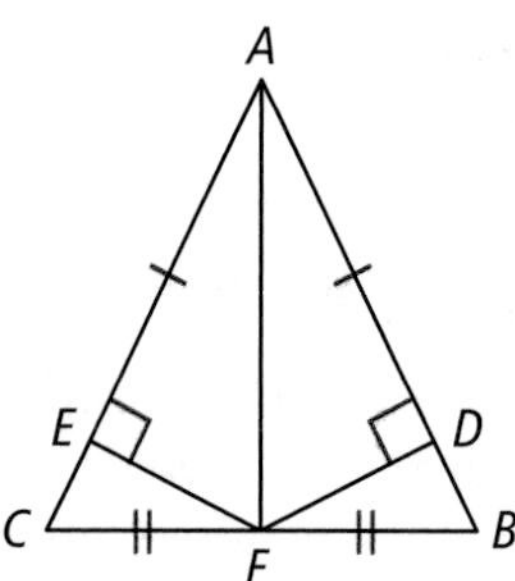


| Statement | Reason |
|---|---|
| **1)** $\overline{FD} \perp \overline{AB}$, $\overline{FE} \perp \overline{AC}$ | **1)** Given |
| **2)** $m\angle FDA = m\angle FDB = 90$, $m\angle FEA = m\angle FEC = 90$ | **2)** Def. of $\perp$ |
| **3)** $\triangle FEA$, $\triangle FDA$, $\triangle FEC$, and $\triangle FDB$ are rt. triangles | **3)** Def. of rt. triangle |
| **4)** $\overline{AE} \cong \overline{AD}$ | **4)** Given |
| **5)** $\overline{AF} \cong \overline{AF}$ | **5)** Refl. Prop. of Congruence |
| **6)** $\triangle FEA \cong \triangle FDA$ | **6)** HL Theorem |
| **7)** $\overline{EF} \cong \overline{DF}$ | **7)** CPCTC |
| **8)** $\overline{FC} \cong \overline{FB}$ | **8)** Given |
| **9)** $\triangle FDB \cong \triangle FEC$ | **9)** HL Theorem |
| **10)** $\angle ECF \cong \angle DBF$ | **10)** CPCTC |
| **11)** $\overline{AC} \cong \overline{AB}$ | **11)** Converse of Isosc. Triangle Thm. |
| **12)** $\triangle ABC$ is isosceles. | **12)** Def. of isosc. triangle |

**LOOK FOR RELATIONSHIPS**
Consider what properties can be used to identify congruent parts in two triangles. What property shows that a common side is congruent to itself?

**Try It!** **3.** Write a proof to show that two triangles are congruent.

**Given:** $\overline{JL} \perp \overline{KM}$, $\overline{JK} \cong \overline{LK}$

**Prove:** $\triangle JKM \cong \triangle LKM$

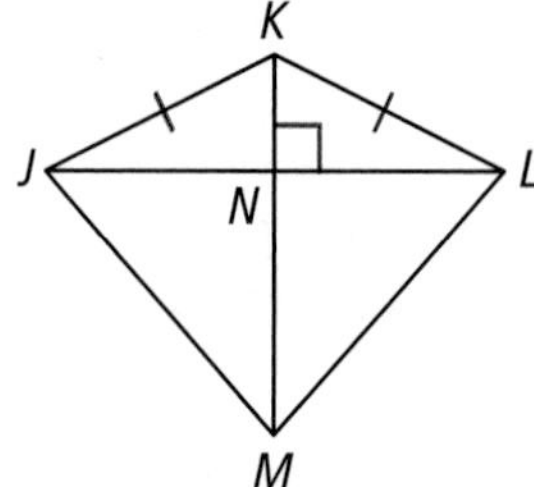

## CONCEPT SUMMARY Congruence of Right Triangles

Triangle congruence theorems apply to right triangles.

### THEOREM 4-3 Side-Angle-Side (SAS)

If...

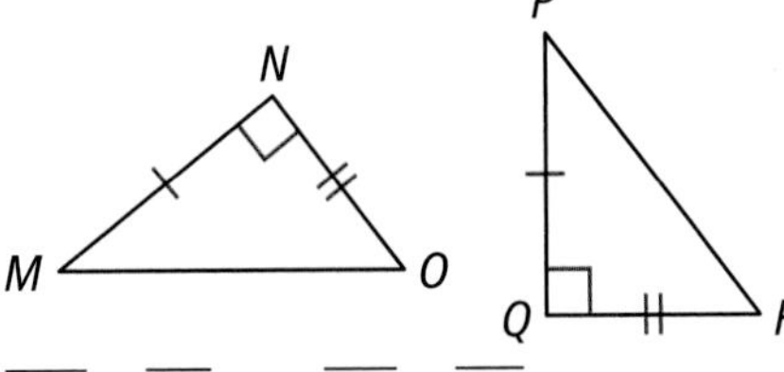


$\overline{MN} \cong \overline{PQ}$ and $\overline{NO} \cong \overline{QR}$

Then... $\triangle MNO \cong \triangle PQR$

### THEOREM 4-6 Angle-Side-Angle (ASA)

If...

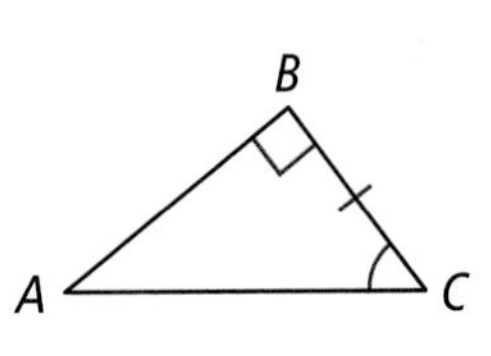


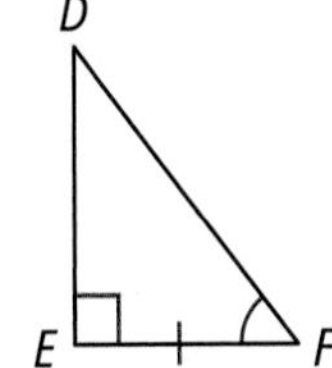


$\overline{BC} \cong \overline{EF}$ and $\angle C \cong \angle F$

Then... $\triangle ABC \cong \triangle DEF$

### THEOREM 4-7 Angle-Angle-Side (AAS)

If...

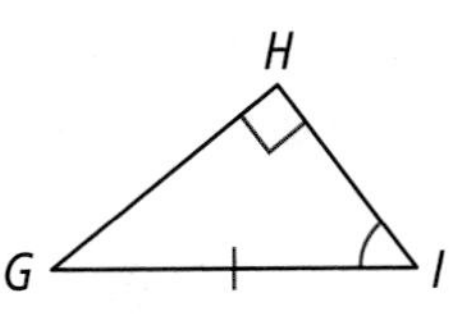


$\overline{GI} \cong \overline{JL}$ and $\angle I \cong \angle L$

Then... $\triangle GHI \cong \triangle JKL$

### THEOREM 4-8 Hypotenuse-Leg (HL) Theorem

If...

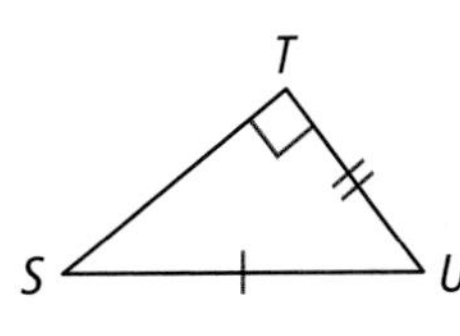


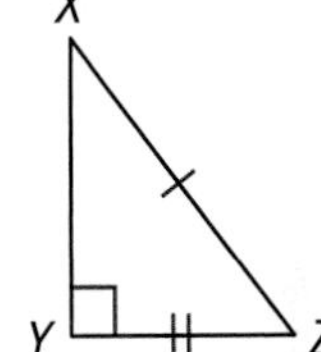


Then... $\triangle STU \cong \triangle XYZ$

## Do You UNDERSTAND?

1. **ESSENTIAL QUESTION** What minimum criteria are needed to show that right triangles are congruent?

2. **Error Analysis** Yama stated that $\triangle KLM \cong \triangle PLN$ by the HL Theorem. What mistake did Yama make?

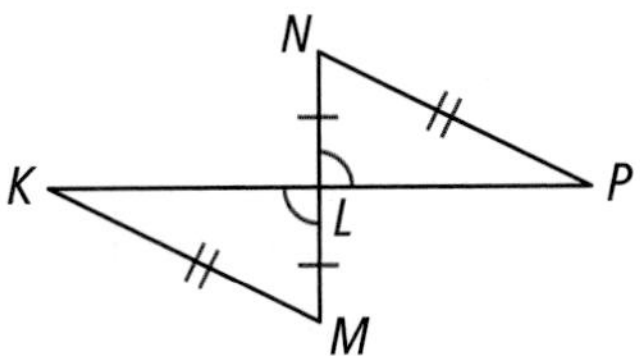


3. **Use Structure** What are the three conditions that two triangles must meet in order to apply the HL Theorem?

4. **Reason** The HL Theorem is a side-side-angle theorem for right triangles. Why does it prove congruence for two right triangles but not prove congruence for two acute triangles or for two obtuse triangles?

## Do You KNOW HOW?

**What information is needed to prove the triangles are congruent using the Hypotenuse-Leg (HL) Theorem?**

5.

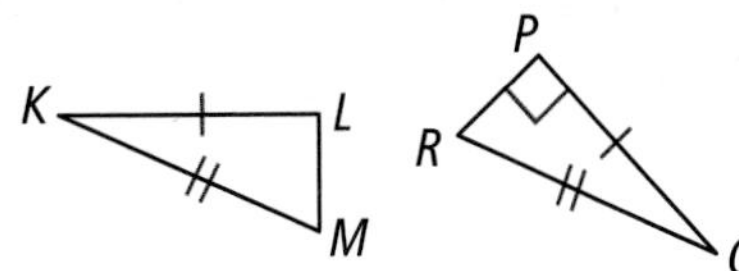


6.

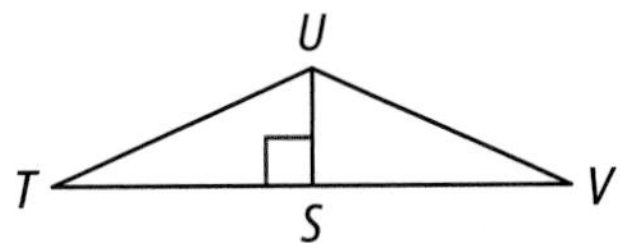


**What information would be sufficient to show the two triangles are congruent by the Hypotenuse-Leg (HL) Theorem?**

7.

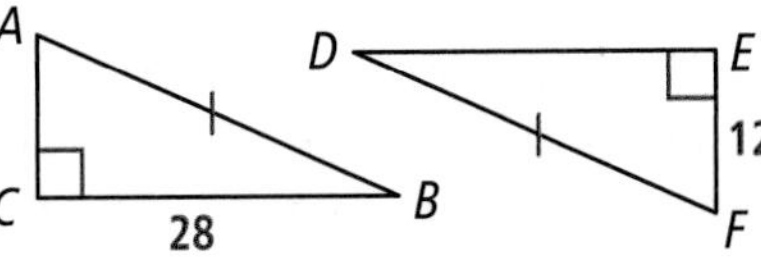


8.

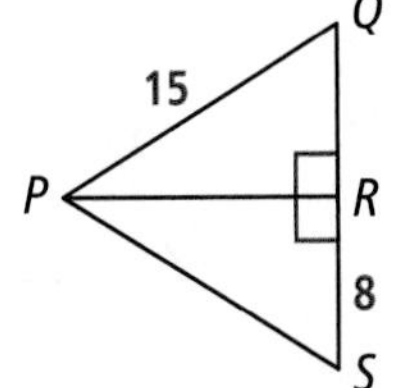

# PRACTICE & PROBLEM SOLVING

Scan for Multimedia

Practice Tutorial

Additional Exercises Available Online

## UNDERSTAND

9. **Construct Arguments** Follow the steps to prove the HL Theorem.

   **Given:** Right triangles $\triangle MNL$ and $\triangle PQR$, $\overline{MN} \cong \overline{PQ}$, $\overline{ML} \cong \overline{PR}$

   **Prove:** $\triangle MNL \cong \triangle PQR$

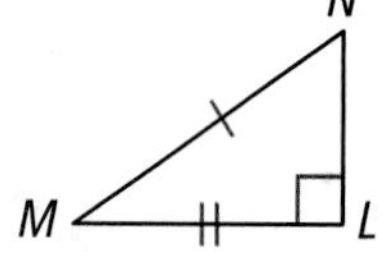


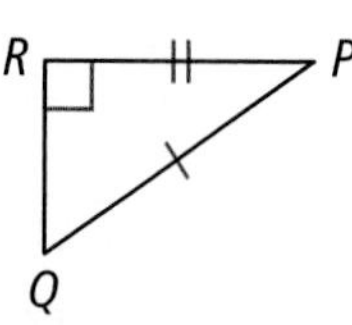


   - Show that there is a rigid motion that maps $L$ to $R$ and $M$ to $P$ so that $N'$ and $Q$ are on opposite sides of $\overleftrightarrow{PR}$.
   - Then show that $\triangle PQN'$ is isosceles.
   - Show that $\triangle M'N'L' \cong \triangle PQR$, so $\triangle MNL \cong \triangle PQR$.

10. **Mathematical Connections** Consider the figures.

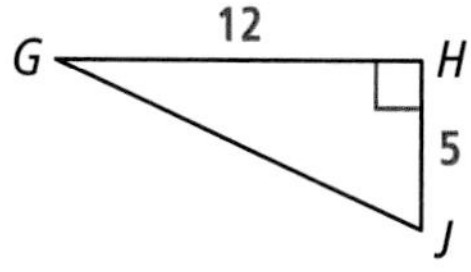


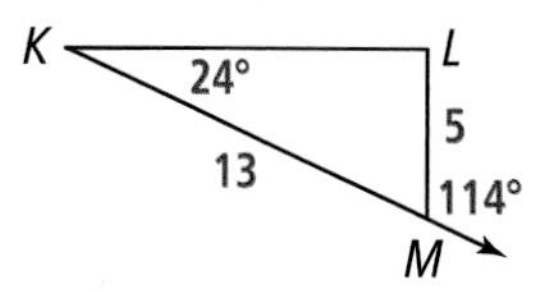


   Describe the steps you would have to take before you could use the HL Theorem to prove $\triangle GHJ \cong \triangle KLM$.

11. **Error Analysis** Mohamed wrote the paragraph proof to show that $\triangle DEG \cong \triangle EFG$. What mistake did he make?

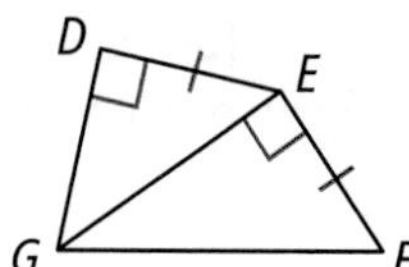


   ΔDEG and ΔEFG are right triangles. The figure shows $\overline{DE} \cong \overline{EF}$, AND $\overline{EG} \cong \overline{EG}$ by the Reflexive Property. Therefore, by the HL theorem, ΔDEG ≅ ΔEFG. ✗

12. **Higher Order Thinking** Suppose $\triangle ABC$ is an equilateral triangle. Use the HL Theorem to explain why any segment perpendicular to a side from the opposite vertex produces two congruent triangles. Would the same be true if $\triangle ABC$ were an isosceles triangle that was not equilateral? Explain.

## PRACTICE

**For Exercises 13–16, you are given a theorem and a congruence statement. What additional information is needed to prove that the triangles are congruent?** SEE EXAMPLE 1

13. By using ASA, given $\overline{AC} \cong \overline{EF}$

14. By using AAS, given $\angle B \cong \angle D$

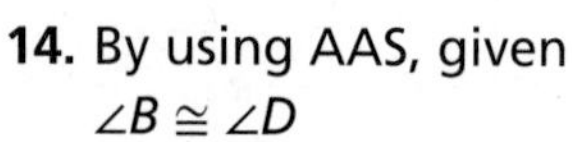

15. By using SAS, given $\overline{AB} \cong \overline{DE}$

16. By using HL, given $\overline{CB} \cong \overline{DF}$

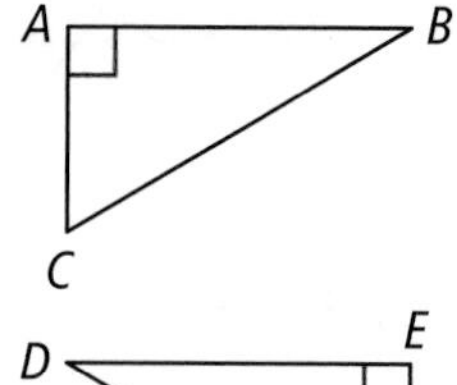


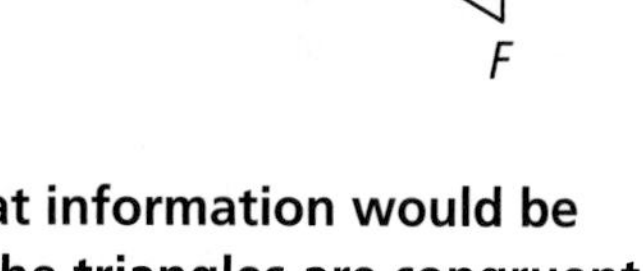


**For Exercises 17–18, what information would be sufficient to show that the triangles are congruent by the HL Theorem?** SEE EXAMPLE 2

17.

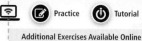

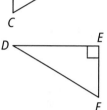

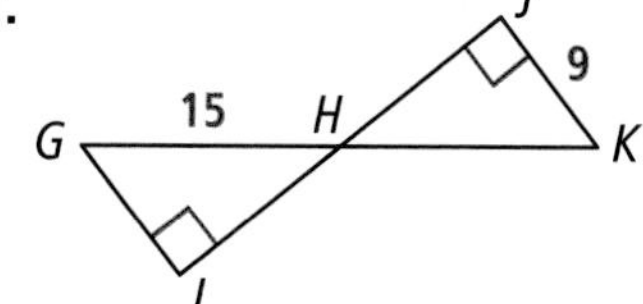


18.



**For Exercises 19–20, write a proof using the HL Theorem to show that the triangles are congruent.** SEE EXAMPLE 3

19. **Given:** $\overline{AB} \cong \overline{CB}$, $\overline{AC} \perp \overline{DB}$

   **Prove:** $\triangle ABD \cong \triangle CBD$

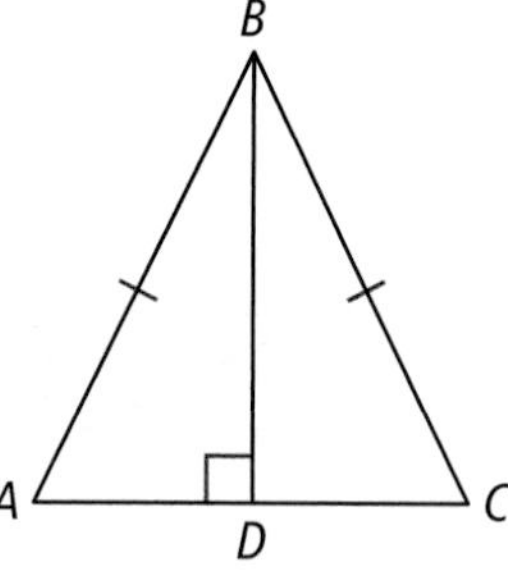


20. **Given:** $\overline{EF} \cong \overline{GH}$, $G$ is the midpoint of $\overline{EJ}$

   **Prove:** $\triangle EFG \cong \triangle GHJ$

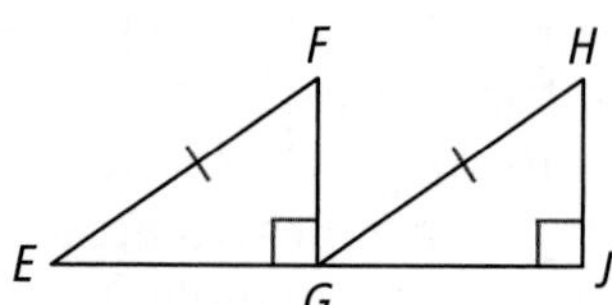

## PRACTICE & PROBLEM SOLVING

Practice Tutorial

Mixed Review Available Online

### APPLY

21. **Make Sense and Persevere** Part of a truss bridge consists of crossbeam $\overline{KM}$ and a perpendicular beam $\overline{LN}$. What beams could an engineer measure in order to show $\triangle KLN \cong \triangle MLN$ using the HL Theorem?

22. **Construct Arguments** Raul wants to verify that the steps built by a carpenter are uniform by checking that $\triangle ABC \cong \triangle CDE$. The carpenter assures him they are because $\overline{AB} \cong \overline{CD}$ and $\overline{BC} \cong \overline{DE}$.

    a. Explain why Raul cannot use the HL Theorem to prove $\triangle ABC \cong \triangle CDE$.

    b. Is there another theorem that Raul can apply to prove $\triangle ABC \cong \triangle CDE$? If so, state the theorem. If not, explain why not.

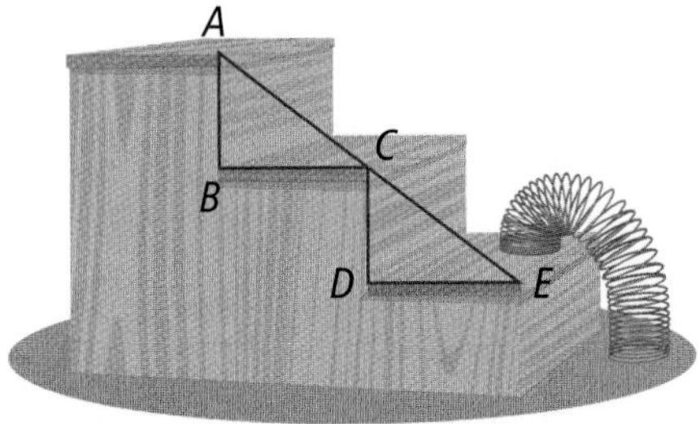


23. **Communicate Precisely** What are the fewest measurements that a homeowner could make to be certain that the front windows shown below are congruent?

### ASSESSMENT PRACTICE

24. Match each set of congruence statements with the theorem that can be used to prove that the two triangles are congruent.

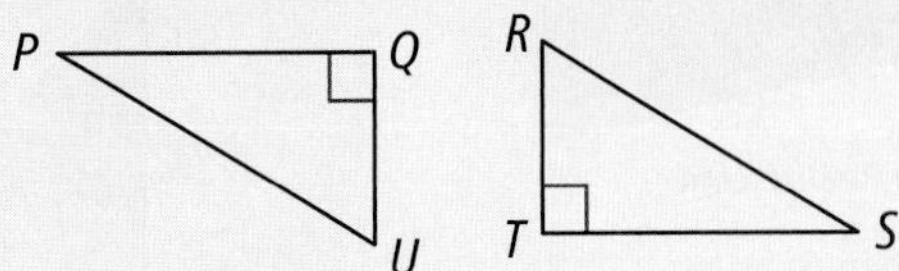


| | |
|---|---|
| I. $\overline{PQ} \cong \overline{ST}$ and $\overline{QU} \cong \overline{TR}$ | A. ASA |
| II. $\overline{PU} \cong \overline{SR}$ and $\overline{QU} \cong \overline{TR}$ | B. AAS |
| III. $\overline{QU} \cong \overline{TR}$ and $\angle U \cong \angle R$ | C. SAS |
| IV. $\overline{QU} \cong \overline{TR}$ and $\angle P \cong \angle S$ | D. HL |

25. **SAT/ACT** Which statement proves the triangles are congruent using the HL Theorem?

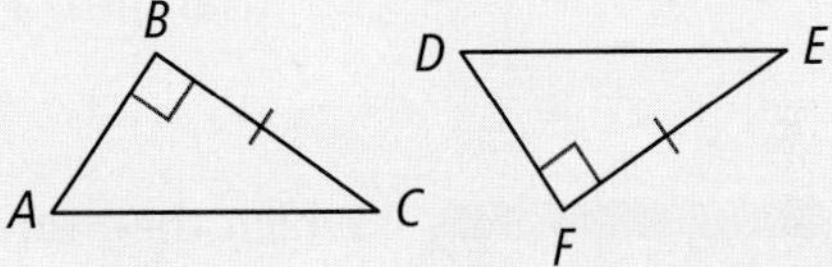


Ⓐ $\angle A \cong \angle D$

Ⓑ $\overline{AB} \cong \overline{DF}$

Ⓒ $\angle B \cong \angle F$

Ⓓ $\overline{AC} \cong \overline{DE}$

26. **Performance Task** Holly makes the origami figure shown. Assume that every angle that appears to be a right angle is a right angle.

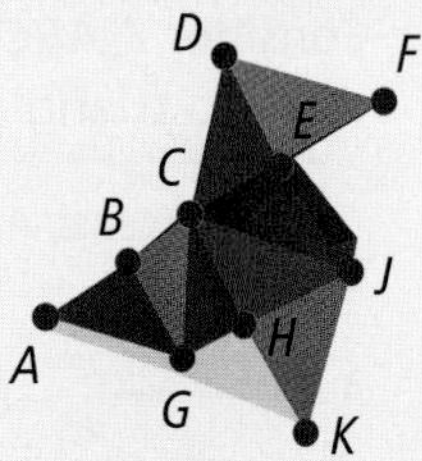


**Part A** What can Holly measure so that she can use the HL Theorem to prove that $\triangle ABG \cong \triangle CBG$?

**Part B** Holly measures to find that $HK = DE$ and $HJ = EC$. Is it possible for her to apply the HL Theorem to prove that $\triangle JHK \cong \triangle CED$? Explain.

**Part C** Choose two other triangles on the figure. Describe what Holly could measure to prove the triangles are congruent by using the HL Theorem.

Activity Assess

# 4-6 Congruence in Overlapping Triangles

PearsonRealize.com

**I CAN…** use triangle congruence to solve problems with overlapping triangles.

## EXPLORE & REASON

**Look at the painting shown.**

**A.** How many triangles can you find?

**B. Make Sense and Persevere** What strategy did you use to count the triangles? How well did your strategy work?

## ESSENTIAL QUESTION

**Which theorems can be used to prove that two overlapping triangles are congruent?**

CONCEPTUAL UNDERSTANDING

## EXAMPLE 1 Identify Corresponding Parts in Triangles

**Figure *ABCD* is a rectangle with diagonals $\overline{AC}$ and $\overline{BD}$. Why is it important to identify corresponding parts of overlapping triangles?**

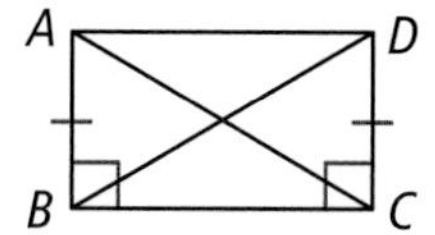
A
D
B
C

Consider $\triangle ABC$ and $\triangle DCB$. Identify the corresponding sides and angles in the two triangles by first determining congruent parts.

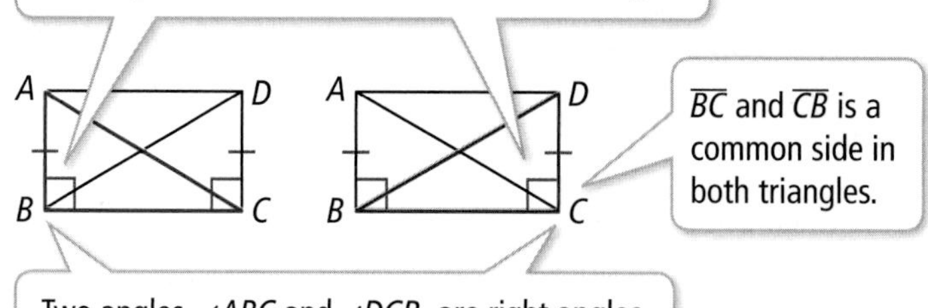
Two segments, $\overline{AB}$ and $\overline{DC}$, have the same length.
A
D
B
C
A
D
B
C
$\overline{BC}$ and $\overline{CB}$ is a common side in both triangles.
Two angles, $\angle ABC$ and $\angle DCB$, are right angles.

Use what you know about congruent parts to identify the corresponding vertices. Then use the corresponding vertices to identify the corresponding angles and sides.

| Corresponding angles: | Corresponding sides: |
|---|---|
| $\angle ACB$ and $\angle DBC$ | $\overline{AC}$ and $\overline{DB}$ |
| $\angle CBA$ and $\angle BCD$ | $\overline{CB}$ and $\overline{BC}$ |
| $\angle BAC$ and $\angle CDB$ | $\overline{BA}$ and $\overline{CD}$ |

Once you identify the corresponding angles and sides, you can determine if the triangles are congruent.

**COMMON ERROR**
Be careful to name corresponding segments correctly. While $\overline{BC}$ is congruent to itself, $\overline{BC}$ corresponds to $\overline{CB}$ in the two triangles.

CONTINUED ON THE NEXT PAGE

Activity

Assess

EXAMPLE 1 CONTINUED

**Try It!** **1.** What are the corresponding sides and angles in $\triangle FHJ$ and $\triangle KHG$?

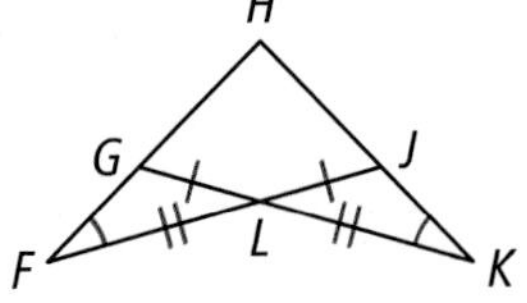


## EXAMPLE 2 Use Common Parts of Triangles

**Is $\angle EGD \cong \angle EFH$?**

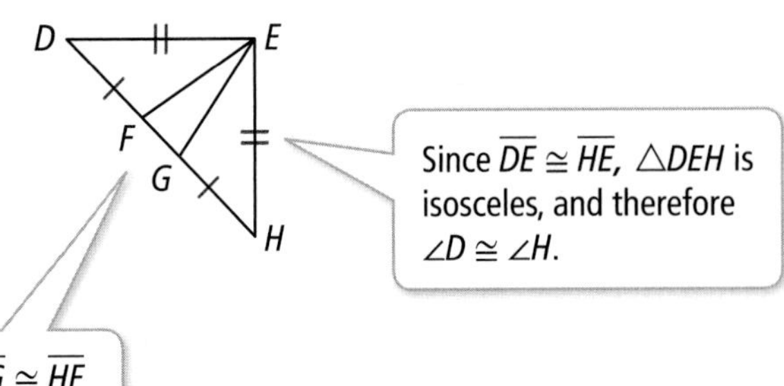

D
E
F
G
H
Since $\overline{DE} \cong \overline{HE}$, $\triangle DEH$ is isosceles, and therefore $\angle D \cong \angle H$.


Since $\overline{FG} \cong \overline{FG}$ and $\overline{DF} \cong \overline{HG}$, $\overline{DG} \cong \overline{HF}$ by the Segment Addition Postulate.

Because $\overline{DE} \cong \overline{HE}$, $\angle D \cong \angle H$, and $\overline{DG} \cong \overline{HF}$, $\triangle EDG \cong \triangle EHF$ by SAS. By CPCTC, $\angle EGD \cong \angle EFH$.

**Try It!** **2.** Are $\overline{VW}$ and $\overline{ZY}$ congruent? Explain.

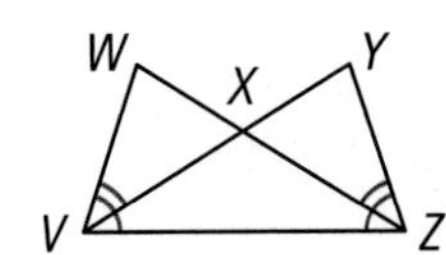


## EXAMPLE 3 Prove That Two Triangles Are Congruent

**Write a proof to show that $\triangle BFE$ is congruent to $\triangle CEF$.**

**Given:** $\overline{AB} \cong \overline{DC}$, $\overline{AF} \cong \overline{DE}$, and $\angle A \cong \angle D$

**Prove:** $\triangle BFE \cong \triangle CEF$

**Proof:** Given that $\overline{AF} \cong \overline{DE}$ and $\overline{FE} \cong \overline{FE}$, $\overline{AE} \cong \overline{DF}$ by the Segment Addition Postulate. Since $\overline{AB} \cong \overline{DC}$ and $\angle A \cong \angle D$, $\triangle ABE \cong \triangle DCF$ by SAS.

This means that by CPCTC, $\overline{BE} \cong \overline{CF}$ and $\angle BEA \cong \angle CFD$. Therefore, by SAS, $\triangle BFE \cong \triangle CEF$.

**MAKE SENSE AND PERSEVERE** There are often multiple ways to complete a proof. How could you use SSS triangle congruence in this proof?

**Try It!** **3.** Write a proof to show that $\triangle SRV \cong \triangle TUW$.

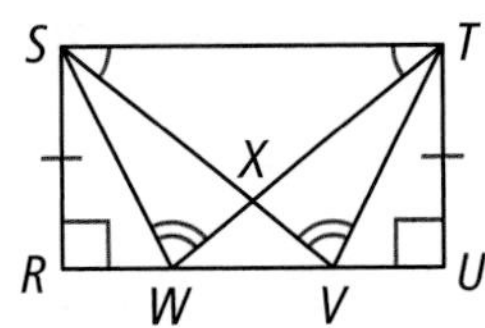

APPLICATION

## EXAMPLE 4 Separate Overlapping Triangles

**A city runs three triangular bus routes to various attractions. How can you draw a separate triangle for each route? Are any of the routes the same length?**

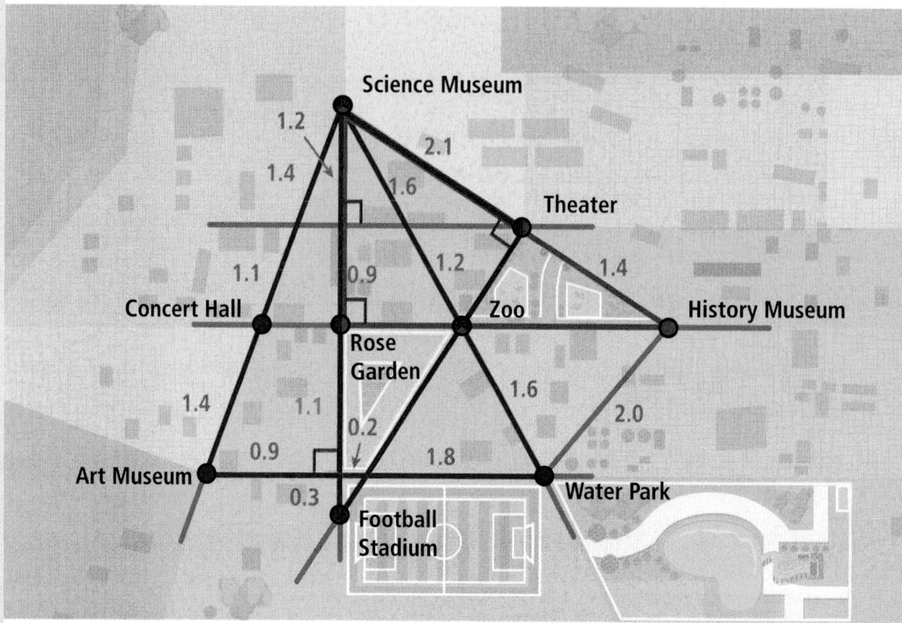


**Green Route Stops:**
- Science Museum
- Theater
- History Museum
- Zoo
- Rose Garden
- Science Museum

**Purple Route Stops:**
- Water Park
- Art Museum
- Concert Hall
- Science Museum
- Zoo
- Water Park

**Red Route**
- Football St
- Zoo
- Theater
- Science M
- Rose Gard
- Football St

Use the map and the list of locations for each route to help you draw the triangles. Add length and angle information to your diagrams.

STUDY TIP
When drawing each triangle, you might find it helpful to cover the parts of the diagram that you are not using.

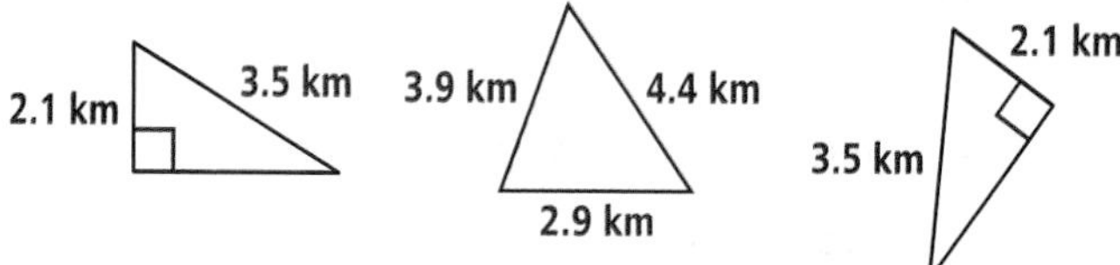


By HL, the triangles representing the green route and the red route are congruent. Therefore, the green route and the red route are the same length.

**Try It!** 4. A new route will stop at the History Museum, Water Park, Zoo, Science Museum, and Theater. Draw a triangle to represent the new route. Include any length or angle information that is given in the diagram.

## CONCEPT SUMMARY Congruence in Overlapping Triangles

All congruence criteria can be applied to overlapping triangles.

**THEOREM 4-5**

**Side-Side-Side (SSS)**

**If...**

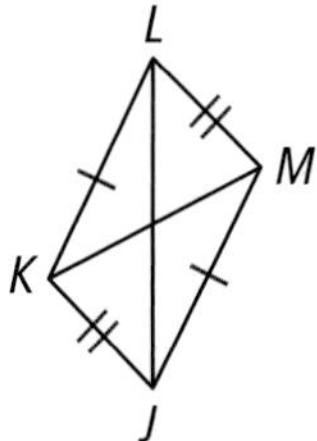


**Then...** $\triangle KLM \cong \triangle MJK$ and $\triangle LMJ \cong \triangle JKL$

**THEOREM 4-7**

**Angle-Angle-Side (AAS)**

**If...**

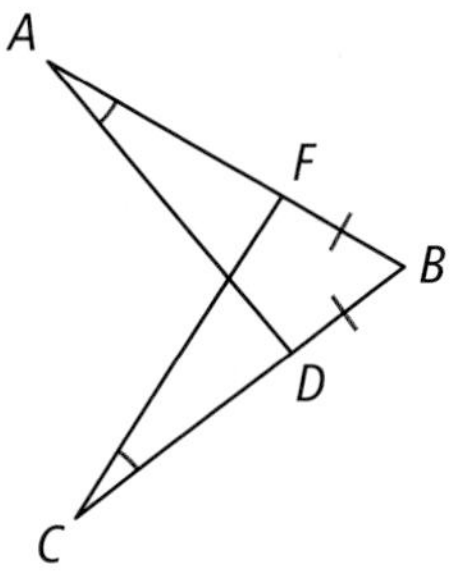


**Then...** $\triangle ABD \cong \triangle CBF$

**THEOREM 4-8**

**Hypotenuse-Leg (HL) Theorem**

**If...**

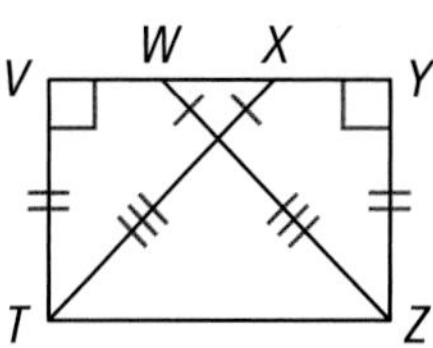


**Then...** $\triangle VXT \cong \triangle YWZ$

## Do You UNDERSTAND?

1. **ESSENTIAL QUESTION** Which theorems can be used to prove two overlapping triangles are congruent?

2. **Construct Arguments** How could you prove that $\triangle ACD \cong \triangle ECB$?

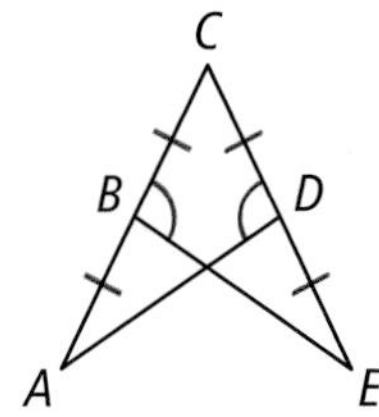


3. **Error Analysis** Nicholas wrote a proof to show that $\triangle EFD \cong \triangle DGE$. Explain Nicholas's error. Is it possible to prove the triangles congruent? Explain.

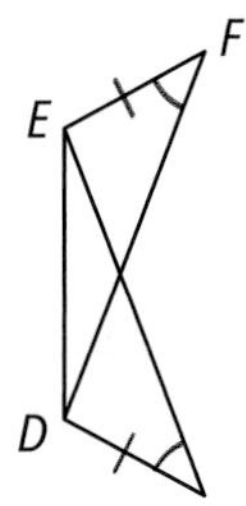


Since $\overline{EF} \cong \overline{DG}$, $\angle F \cong \angle G$, and $\overline{ED} \cong \overline{ED}$, by SAS, $\Delta EFD \cong \Delta DGE$.

4. **Use Structure** Quadrilateral *JKLM* is a rectangle. Which triangles are congruent to $\triangle JKL$? Explain.

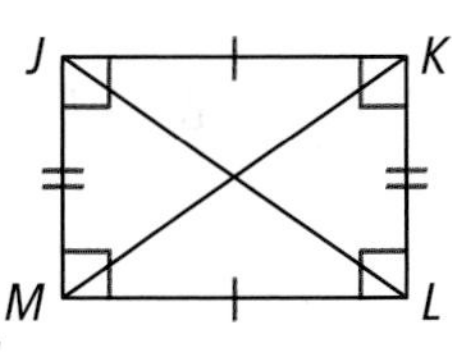


## Do You KNOW HOW?

5. What are the corresponding sides and angles in $\triangle WXV$ and $\triangle XWY$?

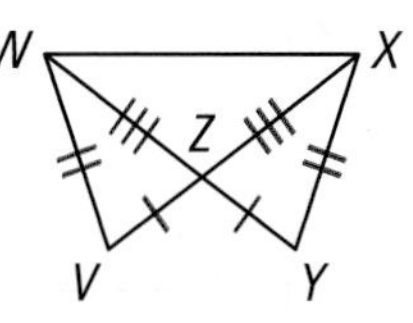


**In Exercises 6–9, name a side or angle congruent to each given side or angle.**

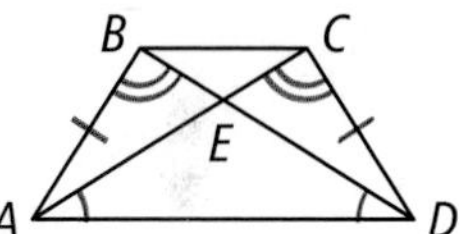


6. $\angle CDA$

7. $\overline{DB}$

8. $\angle FGH$

9. $\overline{HJ}$

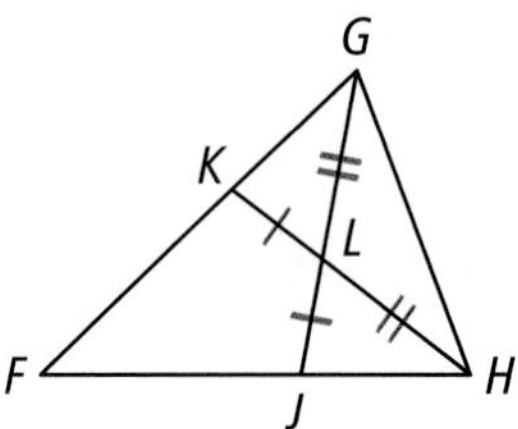


**For Exercises 10 and 11, name a theorem that can be used to prove that each pair of triangles is congruent.**

10. $\triangle GJL$ and $\triangle KHL$

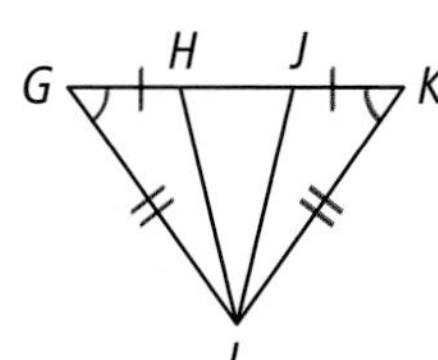


11. $\triangle NQM$ and $\triangle PMQ$

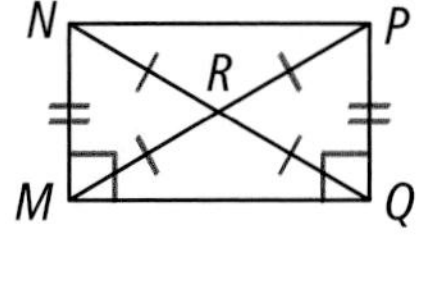

## PRACTICE & PROBLEM SOLVING

Scan for Multimedia

Practice Tutorial

Additional Exercises Available Online

### UNDERSTAND

**12. Construct Arguments** Write a proof to show that $\overline{AF} \cong \overline{GB}$.

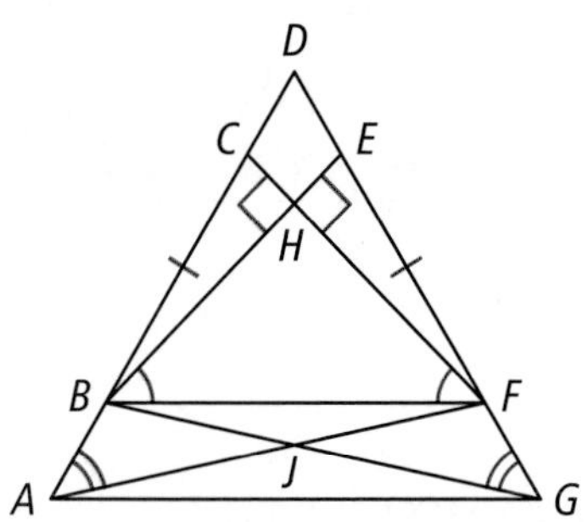

**13. Mathematical Connections** Explain why $\triangle ABF \cong \triangle GDE$.

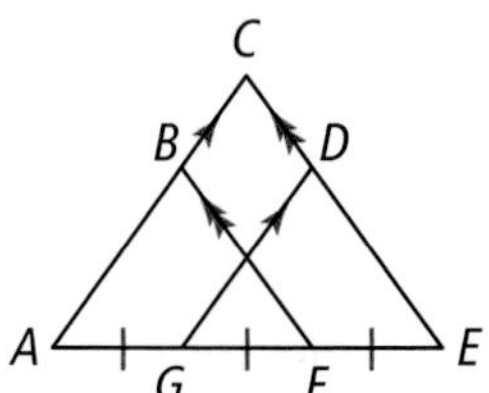

**14. Error Analysis** Dyani wrote a proof to show that $\angle XWY \cong \angle YZX$. What is her error?

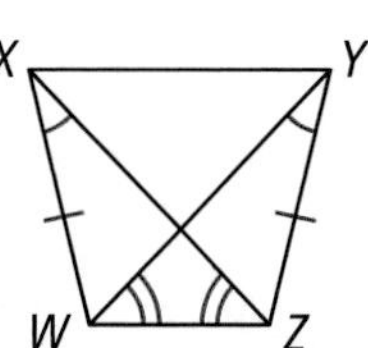

Since $\angle WXZ \cong \angle ZYW$, $\angle XZW \cong \angle YWX$, and $\overline{XW} \cong \overline{YZ}$, by AAS, $\Delta XWZ \cong \Delta YZW$. Therefore, by CPCTC, $\angle XWY \cong \angle YZX$. ✗

**15. Higher Order Thinking** Hexagon *ABCDEF* is a regular hexagon with all sides and angles congruent. List all sets of congruent triangles with vertices that are also vertices of the hexagon, and list all sets of congruent quadrilaterals with vertices that are also vertices of the hexagon.

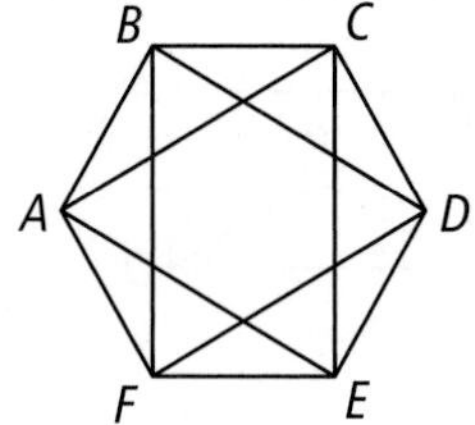

### PRACTICE

**16.** What are the corresponding parts of $\triangle CAE$ and $\triangle DAB$? SEE EXAMPLE 1

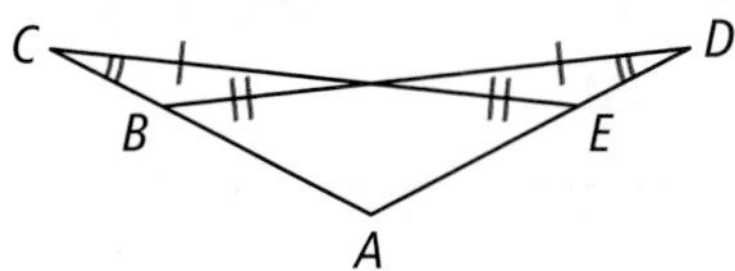

**For Exercises 17–20, identify which side or angle is congruent to each given part.** SEE EXAMPLE 2

**17.** $\angle JGK$

**18.** $\overline{HL}$

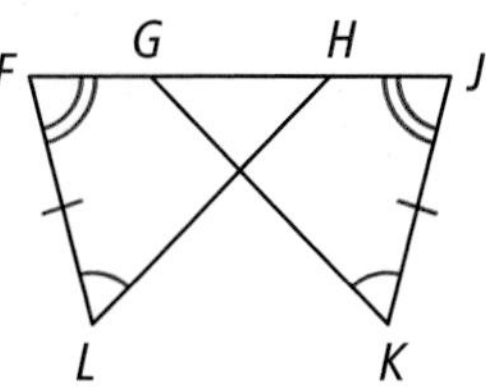

**19.** $\angle WYZ$

**20.** $\overline{XV}$

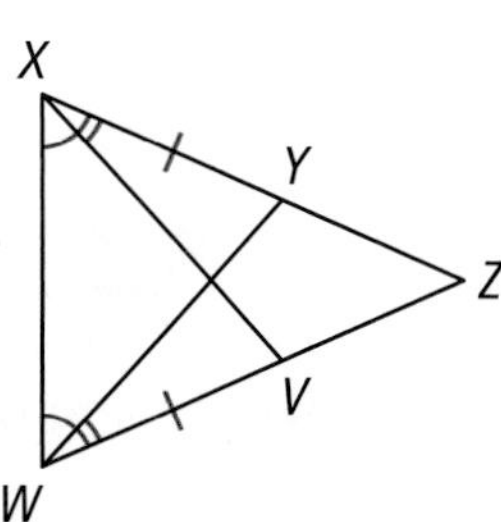

**21.** Write a proof to show triangles $\triangle MRO$ and $\triangle PQN$ are congruent. SEE EXAMPLE 3

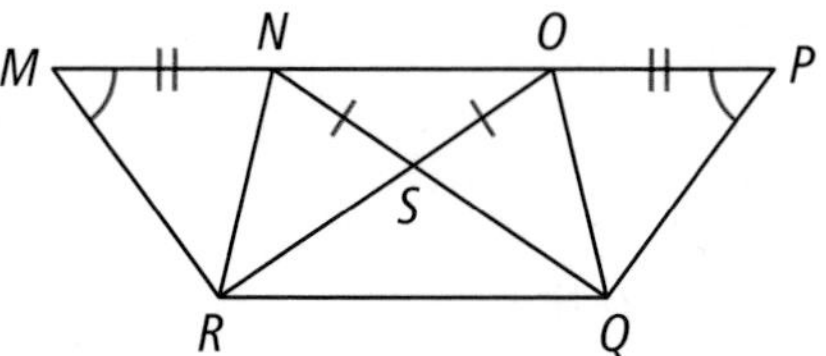

**22.** Write a proof to show that $\triangle BCE \cong \triangle CBD$. SEE EXAMPLE 3

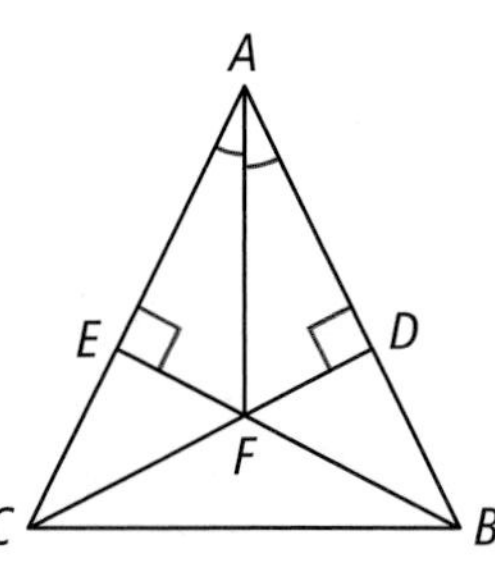

**23.** Draw separate diagrams showing $\triangle AEC$ and $\triangle DBG$. SEE EXAMPLE 4

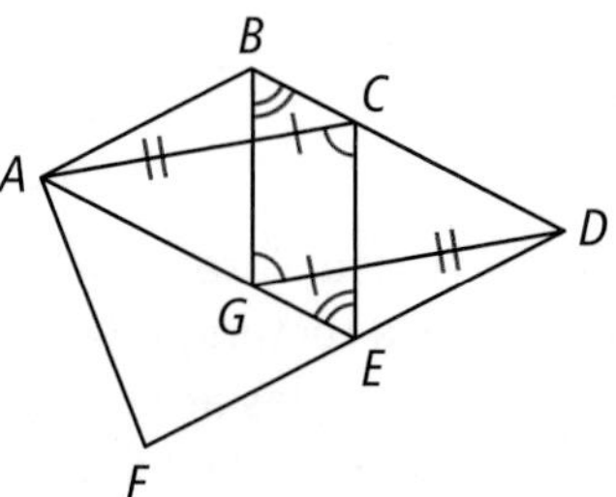

## APPLY

**24. Construct Arguments** Parker wants to place red trim along the seams, $\overline{AC}$ and $\overline{BD}$, of a patio umbrella. He assumes they are the same length. Is he correct? Explain.

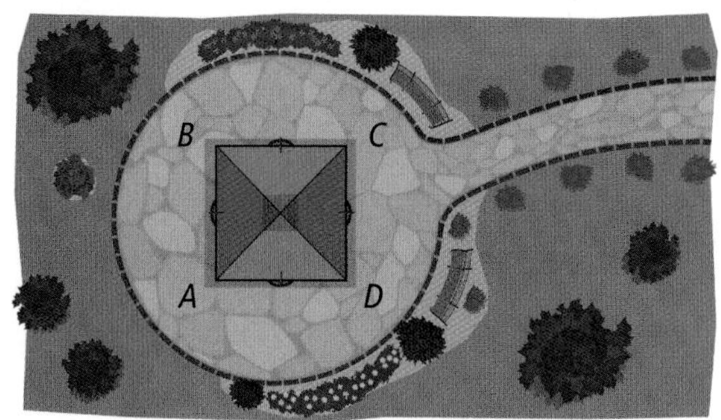


**25. Reason** A student is checking whether the design she drew is symmetric. Can she determine whether $\overline{MN}$ and $\overline{PN}$ are the same length? Explain.

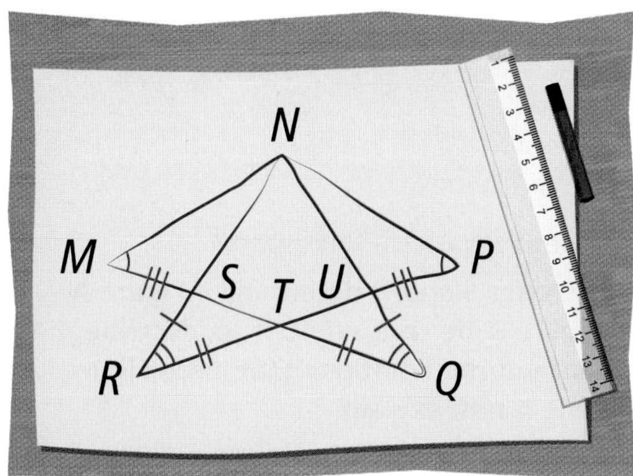


**26. Look for Relationships** The support for a drop tower ride is shown in the diagram. What is the width of the support? Round to the nearest hundredth.

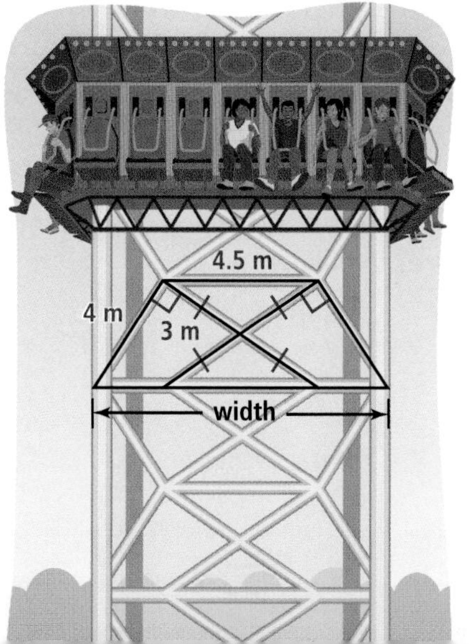


## ASSESSMENT PRACTICE

**27.** Which statements are true? Select all that apply.

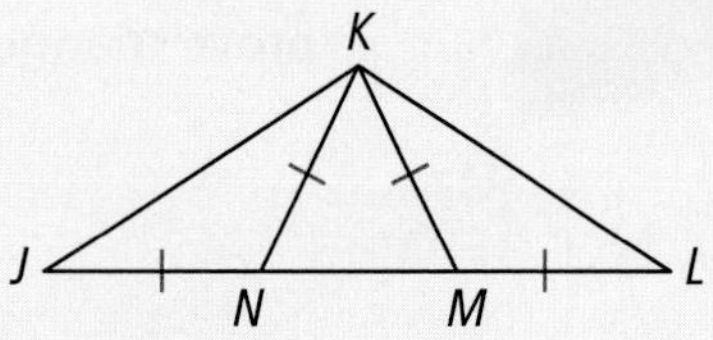


Ⓐ $\overline{KN} \cong \overline{KL}$

Ⓑ $\triangle KMJ \cong \triangle KNL$

Ⓒ $\angle KJN \cong \angle KLM$

Ⓓ $\overline{MJ} \cong \overline{NL}$

**28. SAT/ACT** Which theorem could you use to prove $\triangle ABD \cong \triangle DCA$?

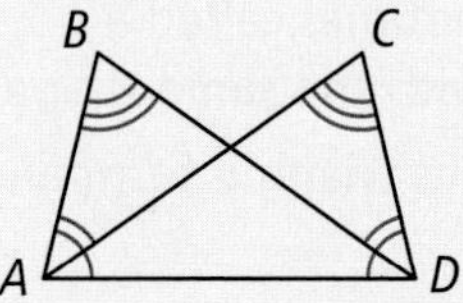


Ⓐ SAS

Ⓑ AAS

Ⓒ SSS

Ⓓ AAA

**29. Performance Task** The diagram shows running trails at a park.

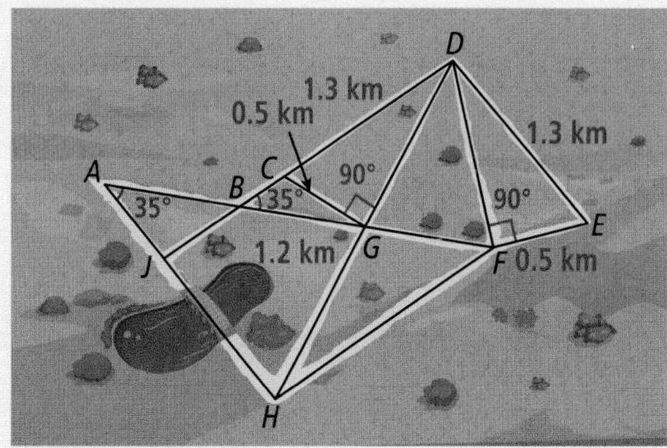


**Part A** Lucy ran the triangular route represented by $\triangle BDF$. Kaitlyn starts from point $H$ and wants to run the same distance as Lucy. What triangular route can Kaitlyn run? Explain.

**Part B** Draw separate triangles to represent the routes the two girls ran. Label as many side lengths and angle measures as you can determine.

**Part C** Can you determine the distances that the girls ran? Explain.

TOPIC 4

# Topic Review

## TOPIC ESSENTIAL QUESTION

1. What relationships between sides and angles of triangles can be used to prove triangles congruent?

## Vocabulary Review

**Choose the correct term to complete each sentence.**

- base
- base angle
- congruence transformation
- congruent
- leg
- vertex

2. Figures that have the same size and shape are said to be ________.
3. The side of an isosceles triangle that is opposite the vertex is called the ________.
4. A rigid motion is sometimes called a ________ because it maps a figure to a figure with the same shape and size.
5. The legs of an isosceles triangle form an angle called the ________.

## Concepts & Skills Review

### LESSON 4-1 Congruence

#### Quick Review

Two figures are **congruent** if there is a rigid motion, or sequence of rigid motions, that maps one figure to the other.

#### Example

**Figure 1 is translated right to form Figure 2. Are the figures congruent?**

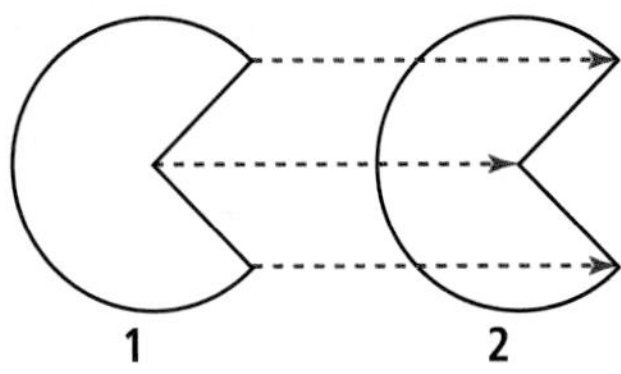


Yes, a translation is a congruence transformation.

#### Practice & Problem Solving

**For Exercises 6 and 7, determine if Figure A and Figure B are congruent. If so, describe the sequence of rigid motions that maps Figure A to Figure B. If not, explain.**

6.  

7. 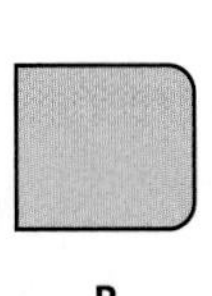


8. **Reason** If a figure is reflected across the same line twice, is the resulting image congruent to that figure? Explain.

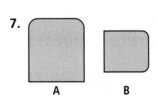

## LESSON 4-2 Isosceles and Equilateral Triangles

### Quick Review

Two sides of a triangle are congruent if and only if the angles opposite those sides are also congruent.

A line that bisects the **vertex** angle of an isosceles triangle is the perpendicular bisector of the opposite side.

### Example

**What is the measure of $\angle C$?**

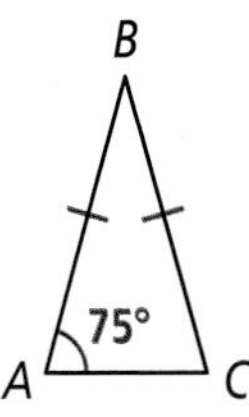


The sides opposite $\angle A$ and $\angle C$ are congruent, so $\angle A \cong \angle C$; $m\angle A$ is 75°, so $m\angle C$ is 75°.

### Practice & Problem Solving

**Find the unknown angle measures for each triangle.**

**9.**

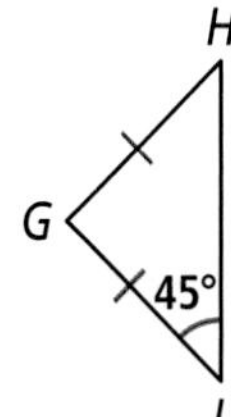


**10.**

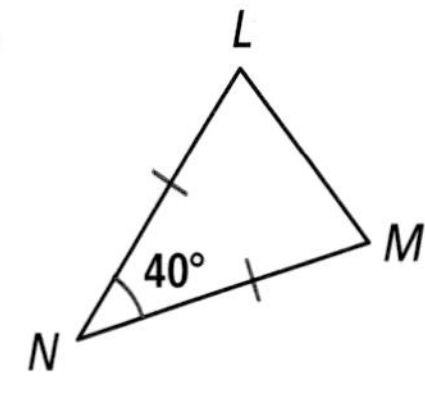


**11. Use Structure** A zipper bisects the vertex of the front of the tent, which is in the shape of an equilateral triangle, forming two triangles. What are the angle measures of the resulting triangles?

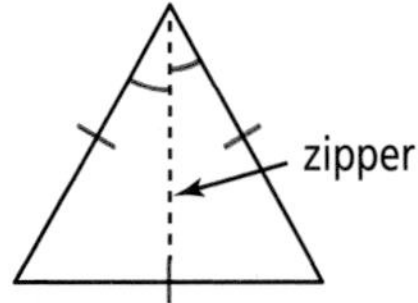


## LESSON 4-3 Proving and Applying the SAS and SSS Congruence Criteria

### Quick Review

Two triangles are congruent if two sides and the included angle of one triangle are congruent to two sides and the included angle of the other triangle (SAS).

Two triangles are congruent if three sides of one triangle are congruent to three sides of the other triangle (SSS).

Corresponding parts of congruent triangles are congruent (CPCTC).

### Example

**Are the two triangles congruent?**

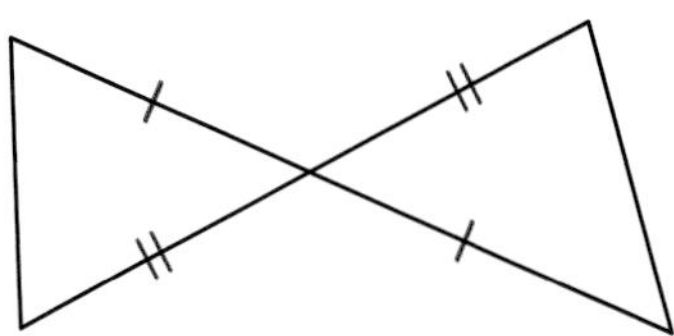

Yes, by SAS, two pairs of **congruent** sides are shown. The included angles are vertical angles and so are congruent.

### Practice & Problem Solving

**Which pairs of triangles are congruent by SAS or SSS? Explain.**

**12.**

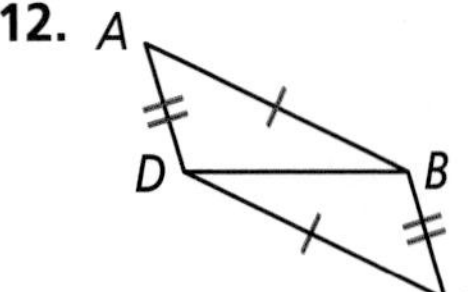


**13.**

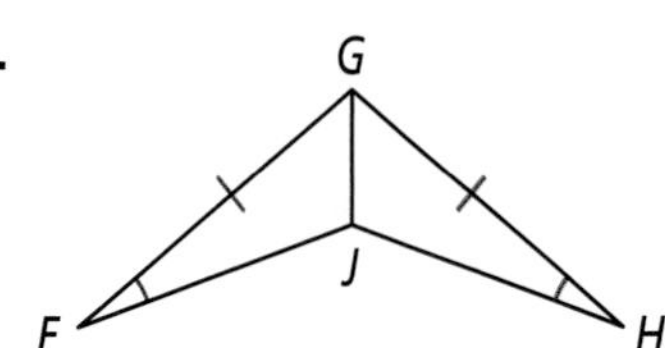


**14. Make Sense and Persevere** The paths of a ping-pong ball during two separate serves intersect at the center of the table. How many pairs of congruent triangles can you find?

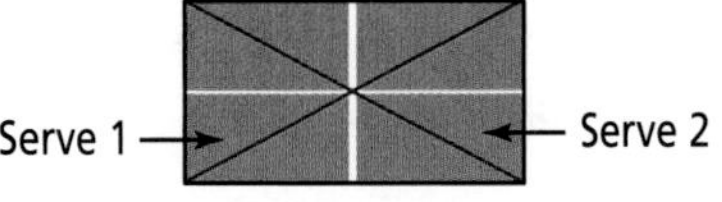

## LESSON 4-4 Proving and Applying the ASA and AAS Congruence Criteria

### Quick Review

Two triangles are congruent if two angles of one triangle and the included side are congruent to two angles and the included side of the other triangle (ASA).

Two triangles are congruent if two angles and a nonincluded side of one triangle are congruent to two angles and a nonincluded side of the other triangle (AAS).

### Example

**Show that the triangles are congruent.**

They are congruent by ASA because they have two pairs of congruent angles that have a congruent side between the angles.

### Practice & Problem Solving

**State whether each pair of triangles is congruent by SAS, SSS, ASA, AAS, or the congruence cannot be determined. Justify your answer.**

**15.**

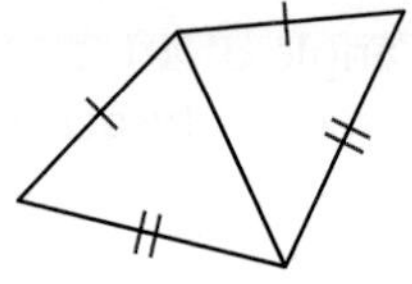

**16.**

**17. Generalize** Are two triangles with two pairs of congruent angles and one pair of congruent sides always congruent? Make a generalization based on your answer.

**18. Make Sense and Persevere** Are the triangles congruent? If they are, by which congruence criterion? Explain.

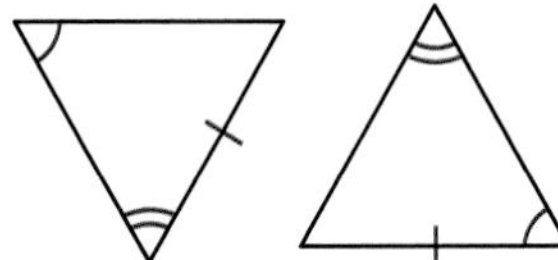

## LESSON 4-5 Congruence in Right Triangles

### Quick Review

If the hypotenuse and one leg of a right triangle are congruent to the hypotenuse and leg of another triangle, then the triangles are congruent (HL).

### Example

**Show that the triangles are congruent.**

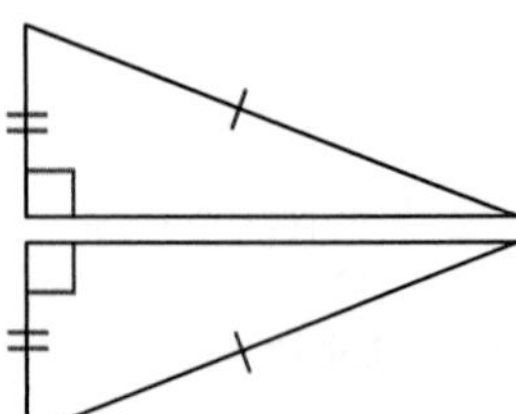

They are congruent by HL because the triangles are right triangles, and the hypotenuses and one pair of legs are congruent.

### Practice & Problem Solving

**Prove that each pair of triangles is congruent.**

**19.**

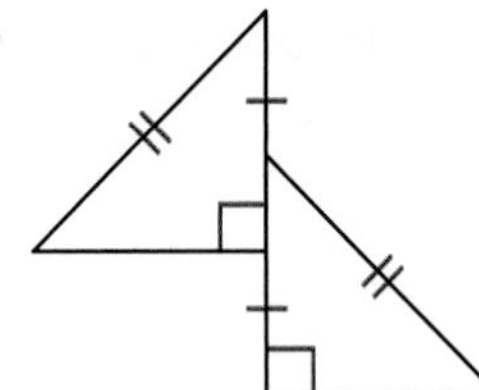

**20. Communicate Precisely** Triangle *ABC* is an isosceles triangle with the vertex bisected by a line segment. Draw the triangle and prove that the resulting triangles are congruent.

## LESSON 4-6 Congruence in Overlapping Triangles

### Quick Review

If two triangles are overlapping, all congruence criteria—AAS, ASA, HL, SAS, and SSS—can still be applied.

To identify congruent overlapping triangles, first identify the parts of each triangle. Then test if any of the congruence criteria hold.

### Example

**Given rectangle *ABCD*, how can you prove that $\angle ADB \cong \angle BCA$?**

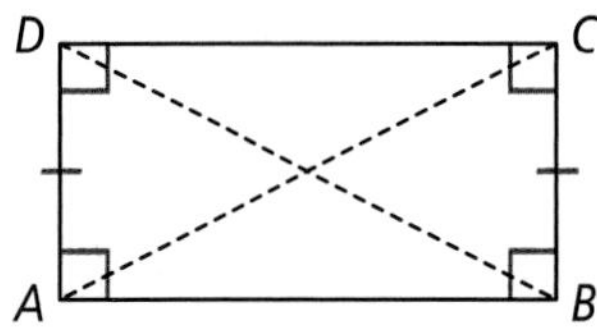


Opposite sides of a rectangle are congruent, so $\overline{AD} \cong \overline{BC}$. All right angles are congruent, so $\angle DAB \cong \angle CBA$. By the Reflexive Property, $\overline{AB} \cong \overline{BA}$. Thus, $\triangle ADB \cong \triangle BCA$ by SAS, and $\angle ADB \cong \angle BCA$ by CPCTC.

### Practice & Problem Solving

**Prove that each pair of triangles is congruent.**

21. 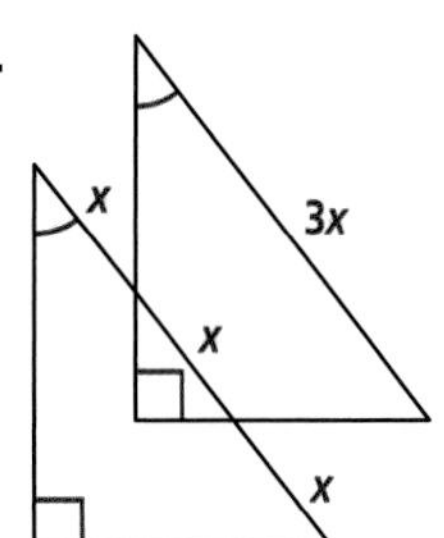


22. 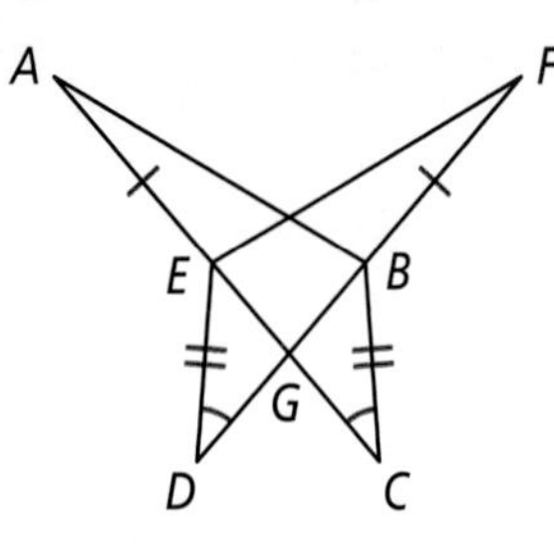


23. **Make Sense and Persevere** Describe where to place point $E$ along $\overline{AC}$ such that $\triangle ABD \cong \triangle CBE$. Then explain why the triangles are congruent.

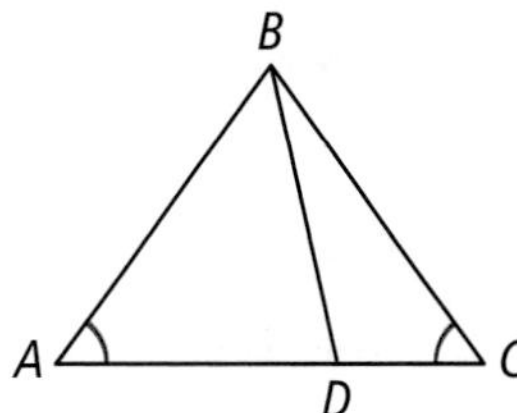


TOPIC 4 REVIEW

TOPIC 5

# Relationships in Triangles

**How are the sides, segments, and angles of triangles related?**

## Topic Overview

**enVision™ STEM Project**
Find the Center of Mass

**5-1** Perpendicular and Angle Bisectors

**5-2** Bisectors in Triangles

**Mathematical Modeling in 3 Acts:**
Making It Fair

**5-3** Medians and Altitudes

**5-4** Inequalities in One Triangle

**5-5** Inequalities in Two Triangles

## Topic Vocabulary

- altitude
- centroid
- circumcenter
- circumscribed
- concurrent
- equidistant
- incenter
- inscribed
- median
- orthocenter
- point of concurrency

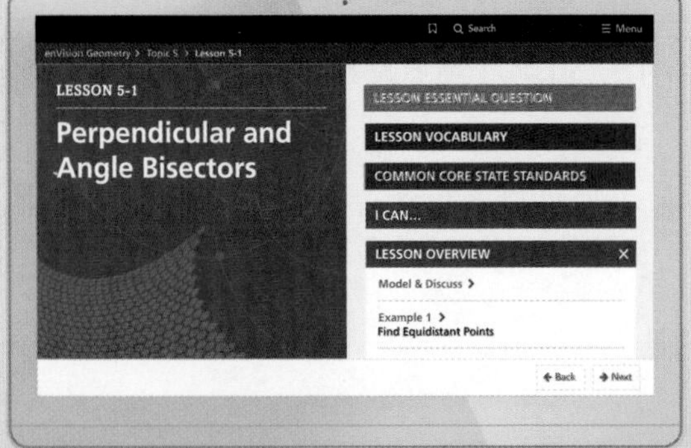

Go online | **PearsonRealize.com**

## Digital Experience

**INTERACTIVE STUDENT EDITION** Access online or offline.

**ACTIVITIES** Complete ***Explore & Reason, Model & Discuss***, and ***Critique & Explain*** activities. Interact with Examples and Try Its.

**ANIMATION** View and interact with real-world applications.

**PRACTICE** Practice what you've learned.

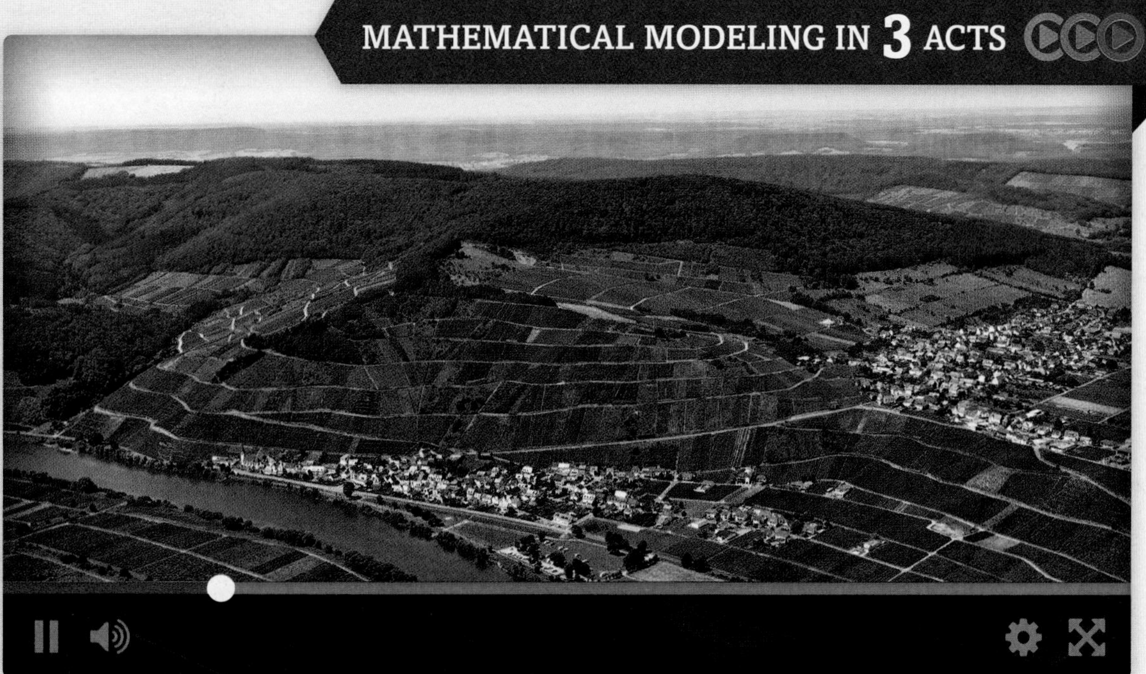


## Making it Fair

In rural areas, county planners often work with local officials from a number of small towns to establish a regional medical center to serve all of the nearby communities.

County planners might also establish regional medical evacuation centers to transport patients with serious trauma to larger medical centers. The locations of these regional centers are carefully planned. Think about this during the Mathematical Modeling in 3 Acts lesson.



**VIDEOS** Watch clips to support ***Mathematical Modeling in 3 Acts Lessons*** and **enVision™** ***STEM Projects.***

**CONCEPT SUMMARY** Review key lesson content through multiple representations.

**ASSESSMENT** Show what you've learned.

**GLOSSARY** Read and listen to English and Spanish definitions.

**TUTORIALS** Get help from ***Virtual Nerd***, right when you need it.

**MATH TOOLS** Explore math with digital tools and manipulatives.

Video

## Did You Know?

An object's **center of mass** is the single point at which its mass is evenly dispersed and the object is in balance.

When an object is moving within Earth's gravitational field, the object's center of mass is sometimes called its *center of gravity*.

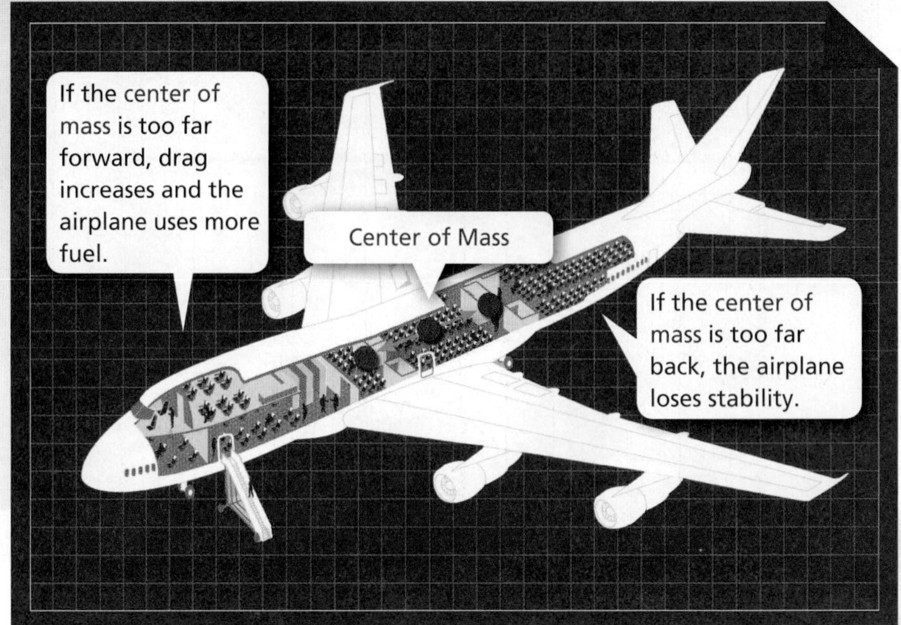
If the center of mass is too far forward, drag increases and the airplane uses more fuel.
Center of Mass
If the center of mass is too far back, the airplane loses stability.

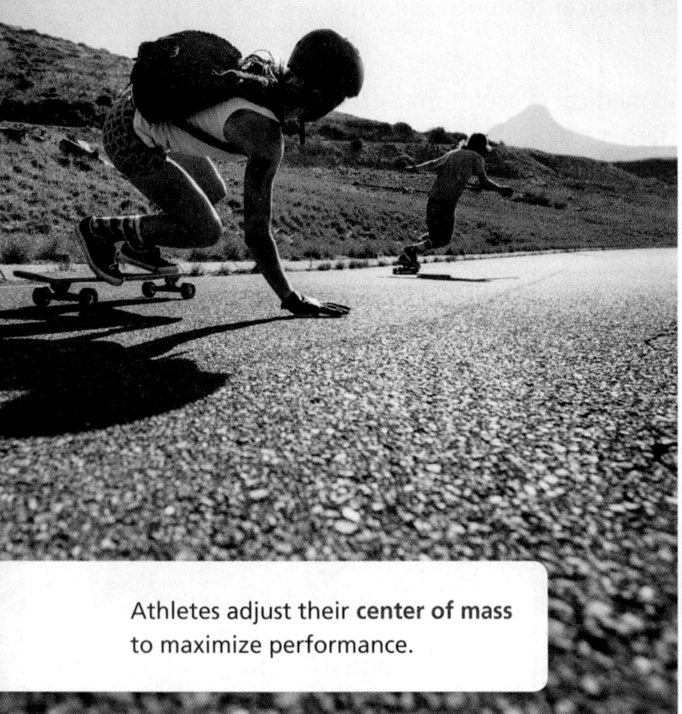

Athletes adjust their **center of mass** to maximize performance.

## Your Task: Find the Center of Mass

In this project, you and your classmates will find the center of mass for a triangular object using mathematics. You will also find the center of mass for an irregular object through experimentation.

# 5-1 Perpendicular and Angle Bisectors

PearsonRealize.com

**I CAN…** use perpendicular and angle bisectors to solve problems.

**VOCABULARY**

- equidistant

Activity

Assess

## MODEL & DISCUSS

**A new high school will be built for Brighton and Springfield. The location of the school must be the same distance from each middle school. The distance between the two middle schools is 18 miles.**

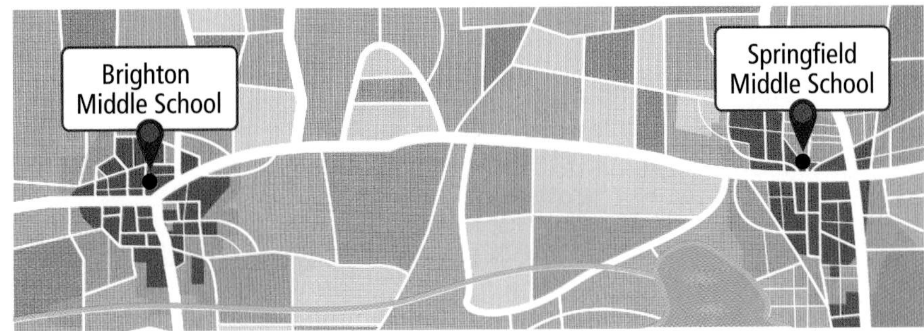


A. Trace the points for the schools on a piece of paper. Locate a new point that is 12 mi from each school. Compare your point with other students. Is there more than one location for the new high school? Explain.

B. **Reason** Can you find locations for the new high school that are the same distance from each middle school no matter what the given distance? Explain.

**ESSENTIAL QUESTION** What is the relationship between a segment and the points on its perpendicular bisector? Between an angle and the points on its bisector?

CONCEPTUAL UNDERSTANDING

## EXAMPLE 1 Find Equidistant Points

**How can you find points that are equidistant from the endpoints of $\overline{AB}$? What do you notice about these points and their relationship with $\overline{AB}$?**

A point that is the same distance from two points is **equidistant** from the points.

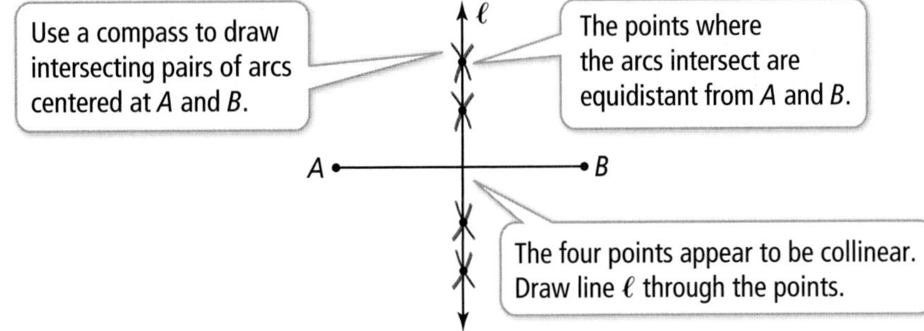

Use a compass to draw intersecting pairs of arcs centered at A and B.
The points where the arcs intersect are equidistant from A and B.
ℓ
A
B
The four points appear to be collinear. Draw line ℓ through the points.


**COMMON ERROR**
Be sure not to change the compass setting when drawing each pair of intersecting arcs from each endpoint.

The points that are equidistant from $A$ and $B$ appear to lie on line $\ell$. Line $\ell$ appears to bisect and be perpendicular to $\overline{AB}$. You can use a ruler and a protractor to support this hypothesis.

**Try It!** 1. Draw a pair of points, and find points that are equidistant from the two points. Draw a line through the set of points. Repeat this process for several pairs of points. What conjecture can you make about points that are the same distance from a given pair of points?

**THEOREM 5-1** Perpendicular Bisector Theorem

If a point is on the perpendicular bisector of a segment, then it is equidistant from the endpoints of the segment.

**If...**

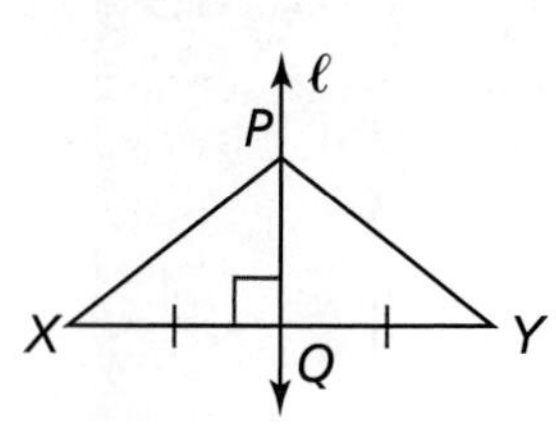


**Then...** $PX = PY$

PROOF: SEE EXAMPLE 2.

**THEOREM 5-2** Converse of the Perpendicular Bisector Theorem

If a point is equidistant from the endpoints of a segment, then it is on the perpendicular bisector of the segment.

**If...**

**Then...** $XQ = YQ$ and $\overleftrightarrow{PQ} \perp \overline{XY}$

PROOF: SEE EXAMPLE 2 TRY IT.

PROOF

## EXAMPLE 2 Prove the Perpendicular Bisector Theorem

**Prove the Perpendicular Bisector Theorem.**

**Given:** $\ell$ is the perpendicular bisector of $\overline{XY}$.

**Prove:** $PX = PY$

**Proof:**

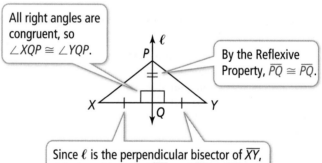

All right angles are congruent, so $\angle XQP \cong \angle YQP$.

By the Reflexive Property, $\overline{PQ} \cong \overline{PQ}$.

Since $\ell$ is the perpendicular bisector of $\overline{XY}$, $Q$ is the midpoint of $\overline{XY}$, and $\overline{XQ} \cong \overline{YQ}$.

By SAS, $\triangle XQP \cong \triangle YQP$. Therefore, $\overline{PX} \cong \overline{PY}$ by CPCTC, so $PX = PY$.

**STUDY TIP**

Remember that if a line is a perpendicular bisector of a segment, you can conclude two things: the line is perpendicular to the segment, and it bisects the segment.

**Try It!** **2.** Prove the Converse of the Perpendicular Bisector Theorem.

APPLICATION

## EXAMPLE 3 Use a Perpendicular Bisector

**Mr. Lee wants to park his ice cream cart on Main Street so that he is equidistant from the entrances of the amusement park and the zoo. Where should Mr. Lee park? How can he determine where to park?**

Mr. Lee can use the perpendicular bisector of the segment that connects the two entrances to find the location.

**Step 1** Label the entrances of the amusement park and zoo as points *A* and *Z*, and draw line *m* for Main Street.

**Step 2** Draw $\overline{AZ}$, and construct the perpendicular bisector.

**Step 3** Mark point *T* where the perpendicular bisector and line *m* intersect.

STUDY TIP
You may need to extend a line to find the point where it intersects with another line.

Mr. Lee should park his cart at point *T*, because it is equidistant from both entrances.

**Try It!** 3. The entrances are 40 feet apart. Mr. Lee decides to move his cart off Main Street. How can you find where Mr. Lee should park if he must be 30 feet from both entrances?

Activity Assess

## EXAMPLE 4 Apply the Perpendicular Bisector Theorem

**STUDY TIP**
Look for relationships in the diagram to help you solve a problem. For example, a right angle marker tells you that two line segments are perpendicular.

**What is the value of *AD*?**

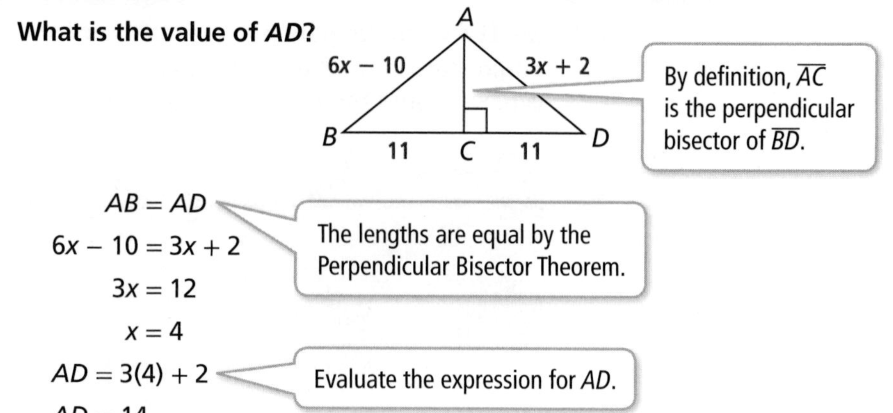


$AB = AD$

$6x - 10 = 3x + 2$

$3x = 12$

$x = 4$

$AD = 3(4) + 2$

$AD = 14$

The lengths are equal by the Perpendicular Bisector Theorem.

Evaluate the expression for *AD*.

**Try It!** **4. a.** What is the value of *WY*? **b.** What is the value of *OL*?

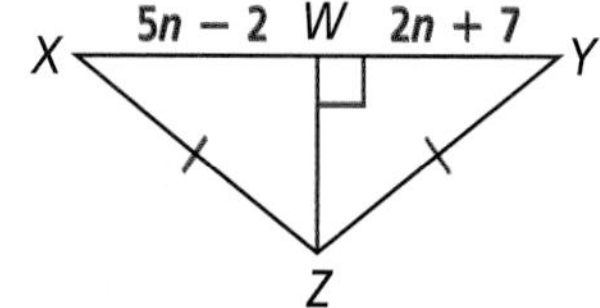


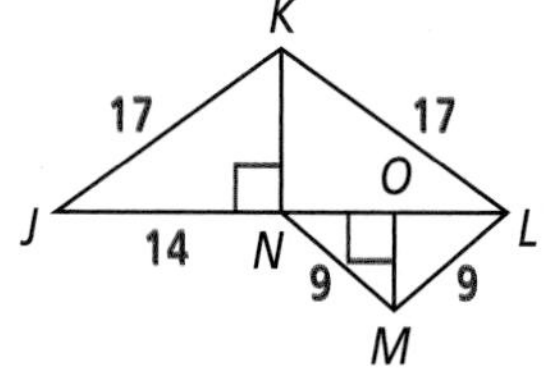


## EXAMPLE 5 Find Equidistant Points from the Sides of an Angle

**An airport baggage inspector needs to stand equidistant from two conveyor belts. How can the inspector determine where he should stand?**

Use pairs of corresponding points on each conveyor belt that are the same distance away from the vertex of the angle. To be equidistant from the conveyor belts, a point must have the same distance from corresponding points.

**USE APPROPRIATE TOOLS**
Think about the tools you can use to make sure that segments are perpendicular. What tool would you use?

Draw the lines perpendicular from each pair of corresponding points.

The distance between a point and a line is the length of the segment perpendicular from the line to the point.

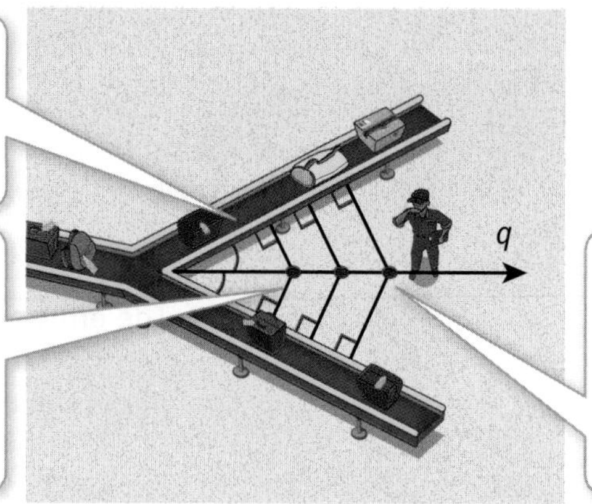


The points of intersection are equidistant from each belt and appear to be collinear.

Ray *q* appears to be the angle bisector. You can use a protractor to support this.

The inspector can determine where to stand by choosing a point on the angle bisector.

**Try It!** **5.** Consider two triangles that result from drawing perpendicular segments from where the inspector stands to the conveyor belts. How are the triangles related? Explain.

## THEOREM 5-3 Angle Bisector Theorem

If a point is on the bisector of an angle, then it is equidistant from the two sides of the angle.

**If...**

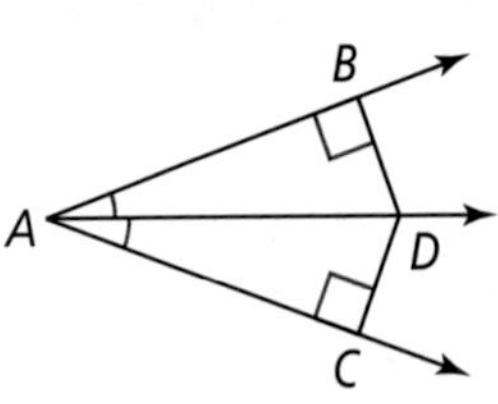


PROOF: SEE EXERCISE 9.

**Then...** $BD = CD$

## THEOREM 5-4 Converse of the Angle Bisector Theorem

If a point is equidistant from two sides of an angle, then it is on the angle bisector.

**If...**

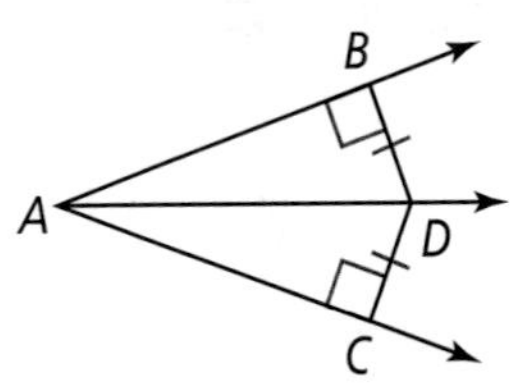


PROOF: SEE EXERCISE 10.

**Then...** $m\angle BAD = m\angle CAD$

## EXAMPLE 6 Apply the Angle Bisector Theorem

**What is the value of $KL$?**

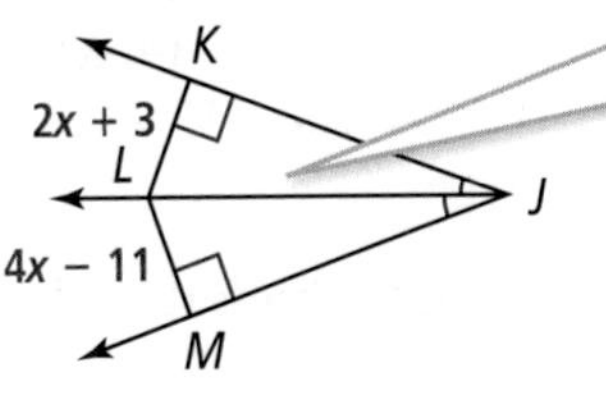


$\overrightarrow{JL}$ is the angle bisector of $\angle KJM$ since $m\angle KJL = m\angle MJL$.

$$KL = ML$$
$$2x + 3 = 4x - 11$$
$$2x = 14$$
$$x = 7$$
$$KL = 2(7) + 3$$
$$KL = 17$$

The lengths are equal by the Angle Bisector Theorem.

Evaluate the expression for $KL$.

**STUDY TIP**
To apply the Angle Bisector Theorem, be sure a diagram reflects the necessary conditions—angles are marked as congruent and right angles are marked to indicate that segments are perpendicular to the sides.

**Try It!** 6. Use the figure shown.

a. If $HI = 7$, $IJ = 7$, and $m\angle HGI = 25$, what is $m\angle IGJ$?

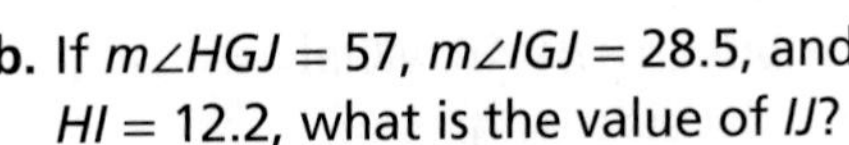

b. If $m\angle HGJ = 57$, $m\angle IGJ = 28.5$, and $HI = 12.2$, what is the value of $IJ$?

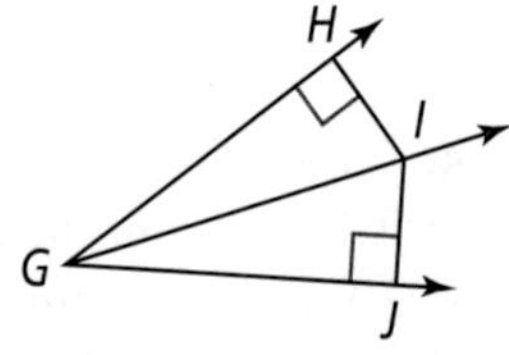

# CONCEPT SUMMARY Perpendicular and Angle Bisectors

## THEOREM 5-1 Perpendicular Bisector Theorem

**If...**

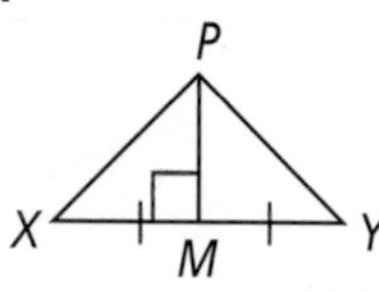


$XM = YM$ and $\overline{PM} \perp \overline{XY}$

**Then...**

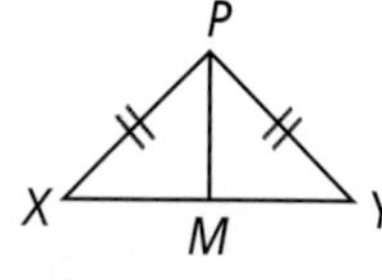


$PX = PY$

## THEOREM 5-2 Converse of Perpendicular Bisector Theorem

**If...**

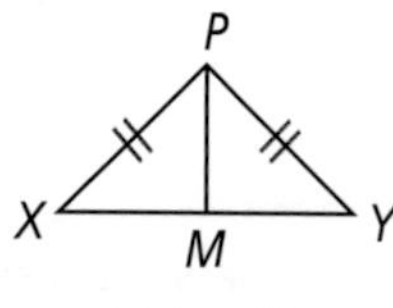


$PX = PY$

**Then...**

$XM = YM$ and $\overline{PM} \perp \overline{XY}$

## THEOREM 5-3 Angle Bisector Theorem

**If...**

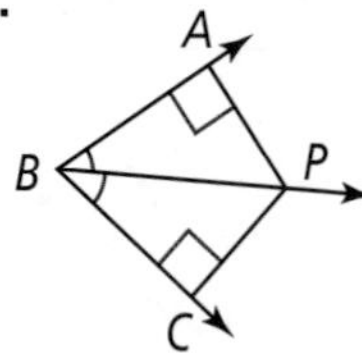


$\angle ABP \cong \angle CBP$

**Then...**

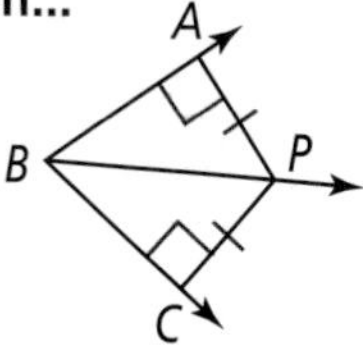


$AP = CP$

## THEOREM 5-4 Converse of Angle Bisector Theorem

**If...**

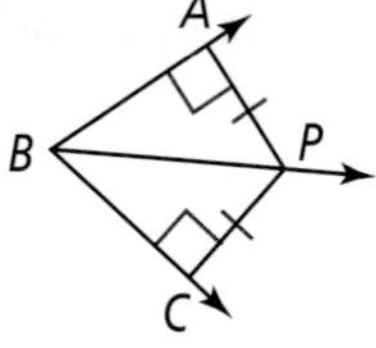


$AP = CP$

**Then...**

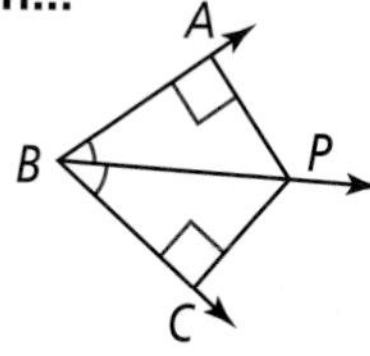


$\angle ABP \cong \angle CBP$

## Do You UNDERSTAND?

1. **ESSENTIAL QUESTION** What is the relationship between a segment and the points on its perpendicular bisector? Between an angle and the points on its bisector?

2. **Vocabulary** How can you determine if a point is *equidistant* from the sides of an angle?

3. **Error Analysis** River says that $\overrightarrow{KM}$ is the bisector of $\angle LKJ$ because $LM = MJ$. Explain the error in River's reasoning.

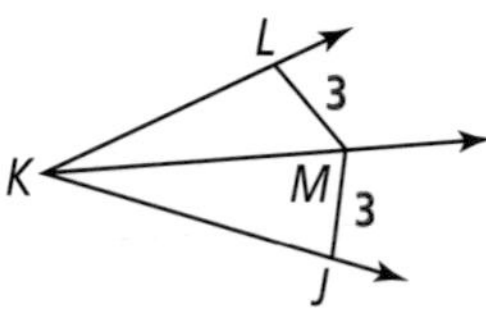


4. **Construct Arguments** You know that $\overline{AB}$ is the perpendicular bisector of $\overline{XY}$, and $\overline{XY}$ is the perpendicular bisector of $\overline{AB}$. What can you conclude about the side lengths of quadrilateral $AXBY$? Explain.

## Do You KNOW HOW?

5. If $JL = 14$, $KL = 10$, and $ML = 7$, what is $JK$?

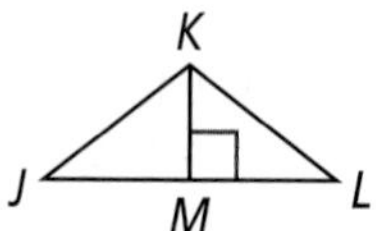


**Use the figure shown for Exercises 6 and 7.**

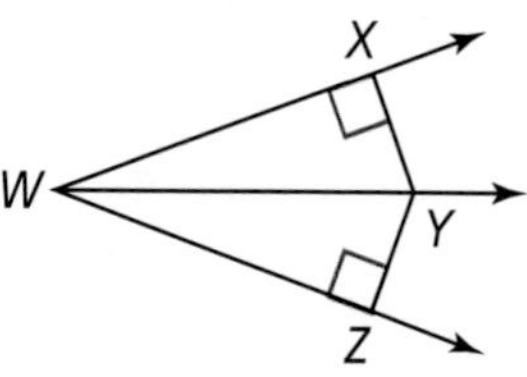


6. If $\angle XWY \cong \angle ZWY$ and $XY = 4$, what is $YZ$?

7. If $XY = ZY$ and $m\angle ZWY = 18$, what is $m\angle XWZ$?

8. What is an algebraic expression for the area of the square picture and frame?

## UNDERSTAND

9. **Construct Arguments** Write a two-column proof for the Angle Bisector Theorem.

10. **Construct Arguments** Write a paragraph proof for the Converse of the Angle Bisector Theorem.

11. **Reason** In the diagram below, $AB = BC$, $DF = EF$, and $m\angle BDF = m\angle BEF = 90°$. Is $\triangle ADF \cong \triangle CEF$? Justify your answer.

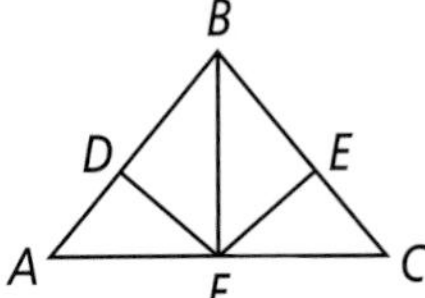


12. **Error Analysis** A student analyzed the diagram and incorrectly concluded that $AB = 2BC$. Explain the student's error.

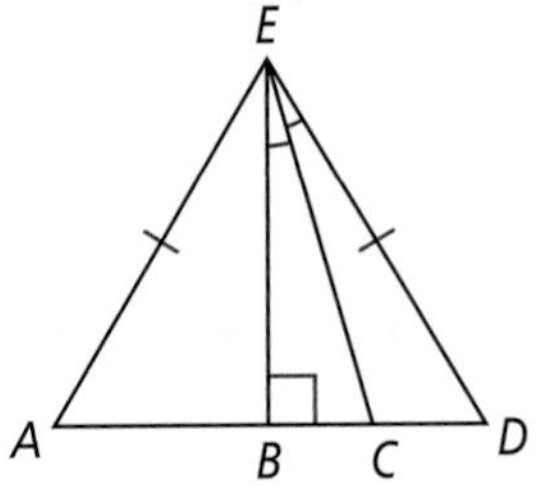


*$\overline{EB}$ is the perpendicular bisector of $\overline{AD}$,*
*so $AB = BD$.*
*$\angle BEC \cong \angle DEC$, so*
*$BC = CD$.*
*$BC + CD = BD = AB$, and*
*$BC + CD = BC + BC = 2BC$,*
*so $AB = 2BC$.*

13. **Higher Order Thinking** Describe the process of constructing the bisector of an angle. Draw a diagram and explain how this construction can be related to the Angle Bisector Theorem.

## PRACTICE

**Use the figure shown for Exercises 14 and 15.**

SEE EXAMPLES 1–3

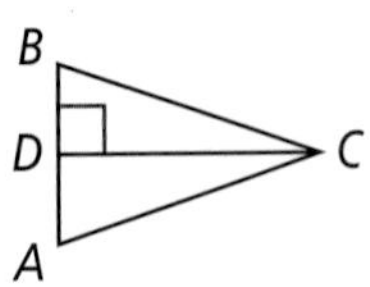


14. If $AD = 3$, $AC = 8$, and $BD = 3$, what is the perimeter of $\triangle ABC$?

15. If $BC = 10$, $AB = 7$, and the perimeter of $\triangle ABC$ is 27, what is the value of $BD$?

**Use the figure shown for Exercises 16 and 17.**

SEE EXAMPLE 4

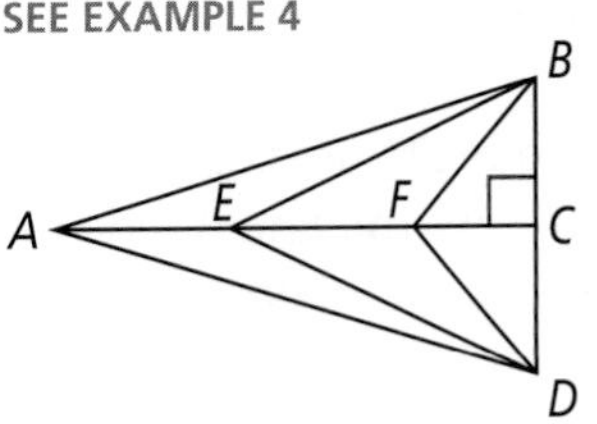


16. If $AD = 21$, $BF = 8$, and $DF = 8$, what is the value of $AB$?

17. If $EB = 6.2$, $CD = 3.3$, and $ED = 6.2$, what is the value of $BD$?

**Use the figure shown for Exercises 18 and 19.**

SEE EXAMPLES 5 AND 6

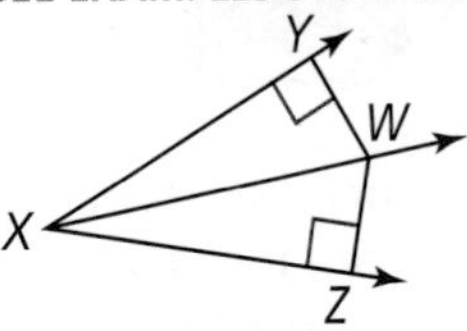


18. If $m\angle YXW = 21$, $YW = 5$, and $WZ = 5$, what is $m\angle ZXY$?

19. If $m\angle YXZ = 38$, $m\angle WXZ = 19$, and $WZ = 8.1$, what is the value of $YW$?

20. If $CD = 4$ and the perimeter of $\triangle ABC$ is 23, what is the perimeter of $\triangle ABE$?

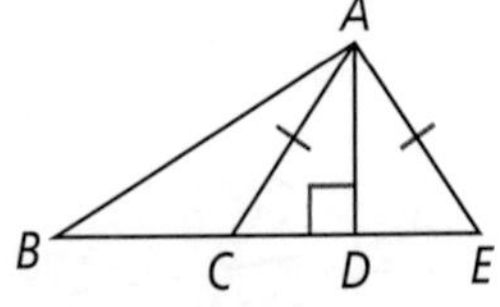


21. Given that $\angle ACF \cong \angle ECF$ and $m\angle ABF = m\angle EDF = 90$, write a two-column proof to show that $\triangle ABF \cong \triangle EDF$.

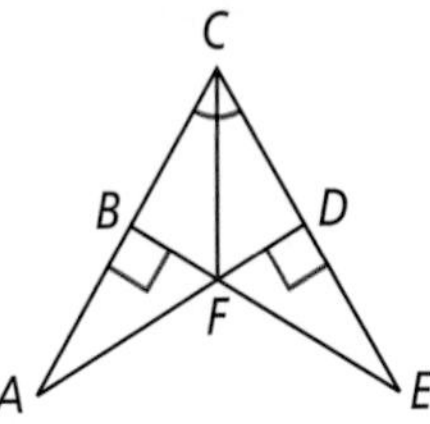

## PRACTICE & PROBLEM SOLVING

Practice Tutorial

Mixed Review Available Online

APPLY

22. **Make Sense and Persevere** A gardener wants to replace the fence along the perimeter of her garden. How much new fencing will be required?

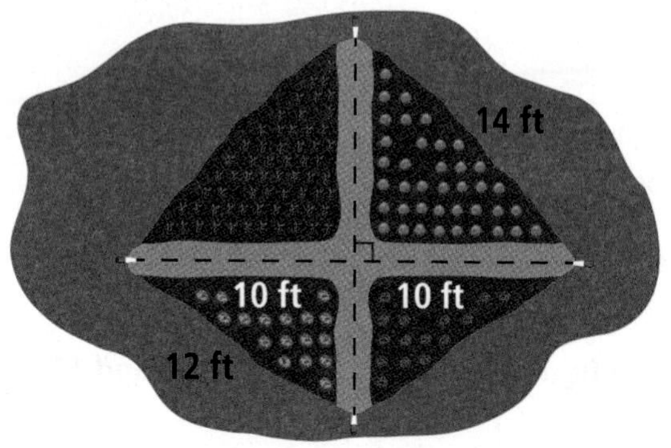


23. **Look for Relationships** An artist uses colored tape to divide sections of a mural. She needs to cut a piece of paper to cover $\triangle EFC$ while she works on other sections. What angles should she cut so she only covers the triangle?

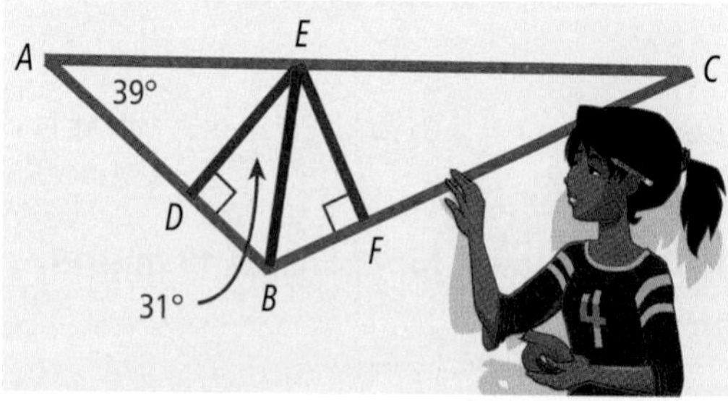


24. **Mathematical Connections** A surveyor took some measurements of a piece of land. The owner needs to know the area of the land to determine the value. What is the area of the piece of land?

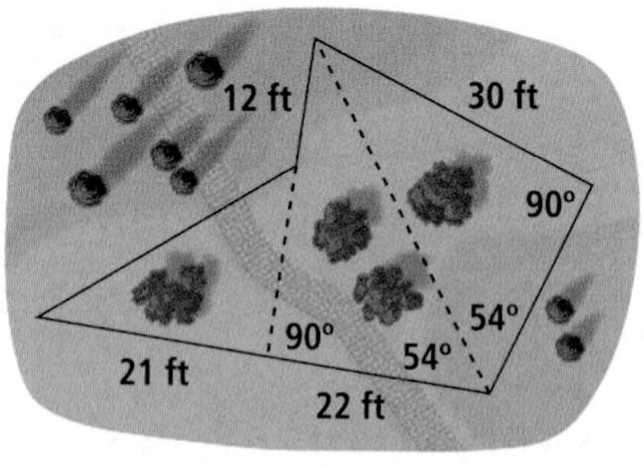


ASSESSMENT PRACTICE

25. $\overleftrightarrow{AB}$ is the perpendicular bisector of $\overline{XY}$. Point $P$ is the midpoint of $\overline{XY}$. Is each statement true? Select *Yes* or *No*.

| | Yes | No |
|---|---|---|
| $AP = XP$ | ❑ | ❑ |
| $AB = XY$ | ❑ | ❑ |
| $AP = BP$ | ❑ | ❑ |
| $XB = YB$ | ❑ | ❑ |
| $AY = XB$ | ❑ | ❑ |
| $XP = YP$ | ❑ | ❑ |

26. **SAT/ACT** Points $G$, $J$, and $K$ are not collinear, and $GJ = GK$. If $P$ is a point on $\overline{JK}$, which of the following conditions is sufficient to prove that $\overleftrightarrow{GP}$ is the perpendicular bisector of $\overline{JK}$?

Ⓐ $JG = PG$

Ⓑ $m\angle GPJ = 90$

Ⓒ $\angle GJK \cong \angle GKJ$

Ⓓ $PK = PG$

27. **Performance Task** A manufacturer makes roofing trusses in a variety of sizes. All of the trusses have the same shape with three supports, as shown.

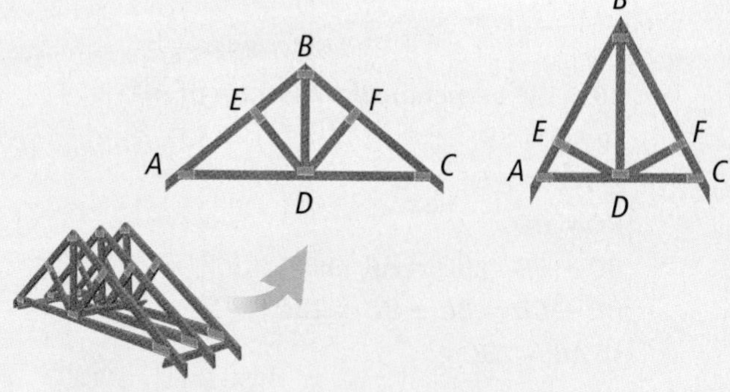


**Part A** One builder needs $\angle ABD$ and $\angle CBD$ to be congruent for a project. You need to check that a truss meets the builder's requirement. The only tools you have are a measuring tape and a steel square, which is a carpentry tool for measuring right angles. How can you use these tools to verify the angles are congruent?

**Part B** In addition to the requirement of the first builder, another builder also needs $\overline{AB}$ and $\overline{BC}$ to be congruent as well as $\overline{AD}$ and $\overline{DC}$. Using the same tools, how can you efficiently verify that all three pairs are congruent? Explain.

Activity Assess

# 5-2 Bisectors in Triangles

**I CAN…** use triangle bisectors to solve problems.

**VOCABULARY**

- circumcenter
- circumscribed
- concurrent
- incenter
- inscribed
- point of concurrency

## MODEL & DISCUSS

**A sporting goods company has three stores in three different towns. They want to build a distribution center so that the distance from each store to the distribution center is as close to equal as possible.**

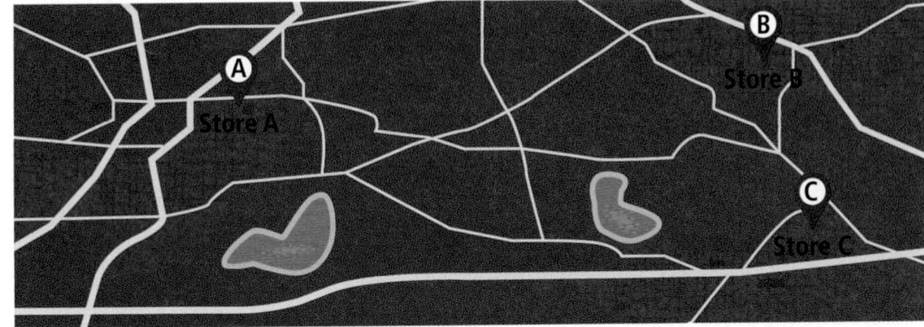


**A.** Points *A, B,* and *C* represent the locations of the three stores. Trace the points on a piece of paper. Locate a point *D* that appears to be the same distance from *A, B,* and *C* by sight only.

**B. Communicate Precisely** Measure the length from points *A, B,* and *C* to point *D* on your diagram. Are the lengths equal? If not, can you find a better location for point *D*? Explain.

**C.** What do you think is the quickest way to find the best point *D* in similar situations?

## ESSENTIAL QUESTION

**What are the properties of the perpendicular bisectors in a triangle? What are the properties of the angle bisectors in a triangle?**

The Concurrency of the Perpendicular Bisectors Theorem explains the relationship between the perpendicular bisectors of a triangle.

### THEOREM 5-5 Concurrency of Perpendicular Bisectors

The perpendicular bisectors of the sides of a triangle are concurrent at a point equidistant from the vertices.

**If...**

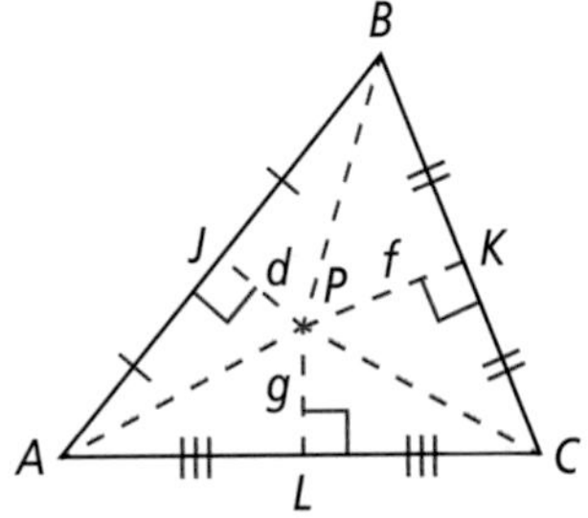


PROOF: SEE EXAMPLE 1.

**Then...** $d$, $f$, and $g$ intersect at $P$ and $PA = PB = PC$

PROOF

## EXAMPLE 1 Prove Theorem 5-5

**When three or more lines intersect at one point, the lines are concurrent. The point where the lines intersect is called the point of concurrency. How do you prove the Concurrency of Perpendicular Bisectors Theorem?**

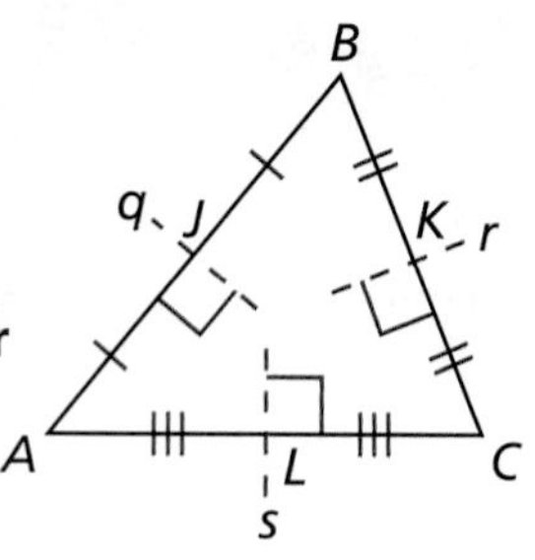


**Given:** $\triangle ABC$ with midpoints $J$, $K$, and $L$, and perpendicular bisectors $q$, $r$, and $s$.

**Prove:** Lines $q$, $r$, and $s$ are concurrent at a point that is equidistant from $A$, $B$, and $C$.

> **COMMON ERROR**
> Make sure that you prove everything required to complete the proof. For this proof, you need to show both that the lines are concurrent and that they are equidistant from the vertices.

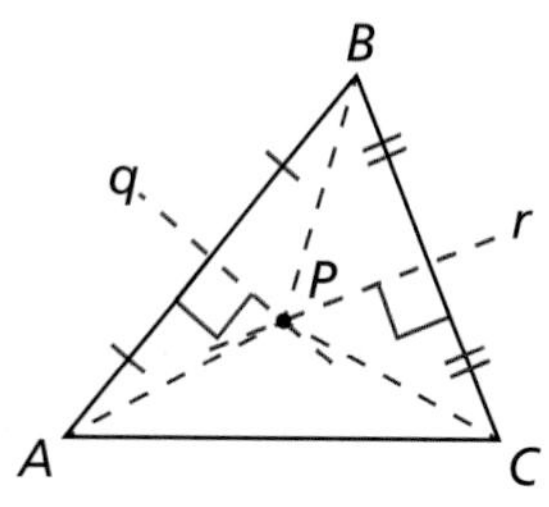


Let $P$ be the point of intersection of $q$ and $r$. By the Perpendicular Bisector Theorem, $PA = PB$, and $PB = PC$. Therefore $PA = PC$.

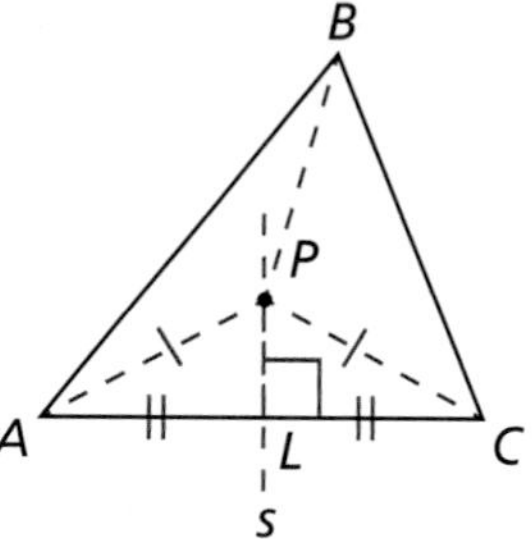


By the Converse of the Perpendicular Bisector Theorem, $P$ also lies on the perpendicular bisector of $\overline{AC}$.

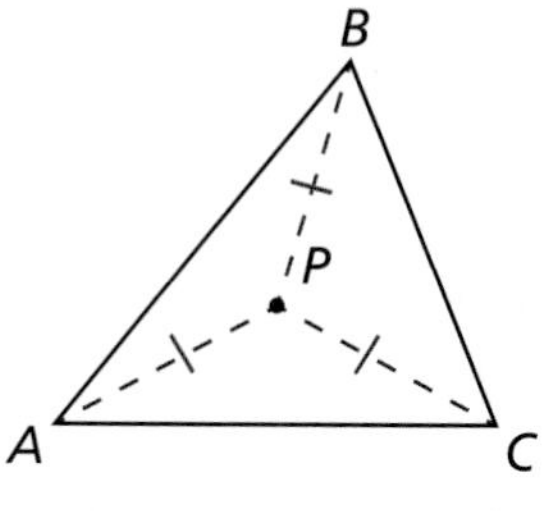


$P$ is the point of concurrency of $q$, $r$, and $s$. Since $PA = PB = PC$, point $P$ is equidistant from $A$, $B$, and $C$.

**Try It!** **1.** Verify the Concurrency of Perpendicular Bisectors Theorem on acute, right, and obtuse triangles using a straightedge and compass or geometry software.

CONCEPTUAL UNDERSTANDING

## EXAMPLE 2 Investigate Circumscribed Circles

**How can you construct a circle that contains the three vertices of a given triangle?**

The circle that contains all three vertices of a triangle is the circumscribed circle of the triangle.

All points on a circle are equidistant from the center of the circle.

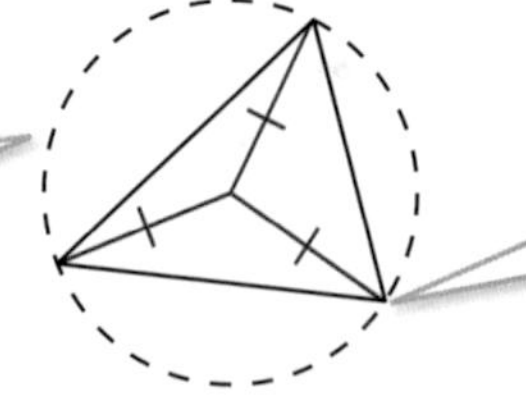

The vertices of the triangle must be equidistant from the center of the circle.

By the Concurrency of Perpendicular Bisectors Theorem, the perpendicular bisectors intersect at a point that is equidistant from the vertices.

CONTINUED ON THE NEXT PAGE

EXAMPLE 2 CONTINUED

The point of concurrency of the perpendicular bisectors of a triangle is the **circumcenter**, so the circumcenter is the center of the circumscribed circle of the triangle.

**COMMUNICATE PRECISELY**
When you are learning a new concept, think about how to explain it in your own words. How would you explain the circumcenter of a triangle to another student?

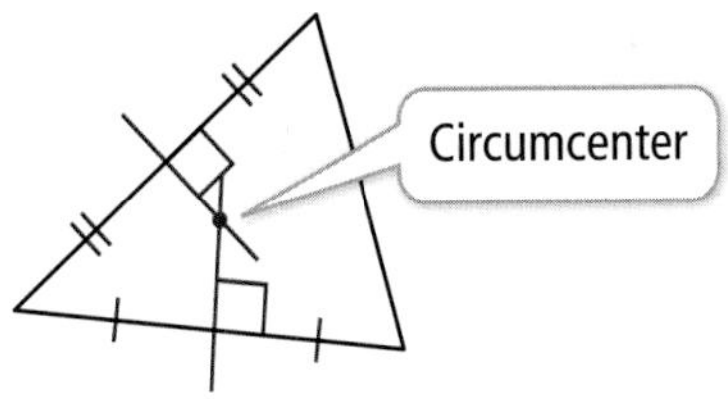


First, construct two perpendicular bisectors to find the circumcenter.

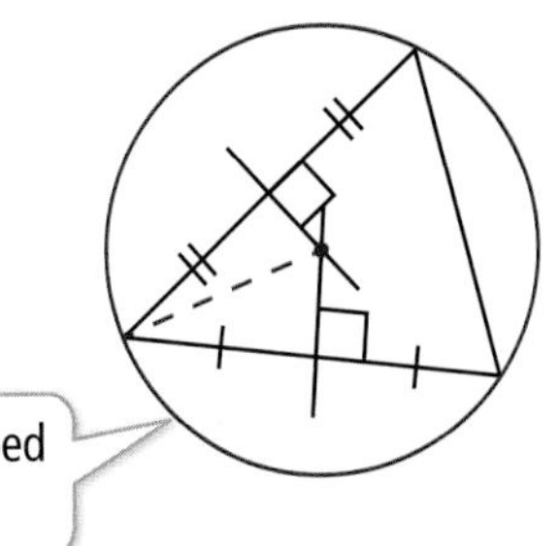


Then construct the circle centered on the circumcenter passing through any vertex.

**Try It!** 2. What conjecture can you make about the location of the circumcenter for acute, right, and obtuse triangles?

APPLICATION

## Use a Circumcenter

**A city manager wants to place a new emergency siren so that it is the same distance from the school, hospital, and recreation center. Where should the emergency siren be placed?**

**Step 1** Label *S* for the school, *H* for the hospital, and *R* for the recreation center. Connect the points to form a triangle.

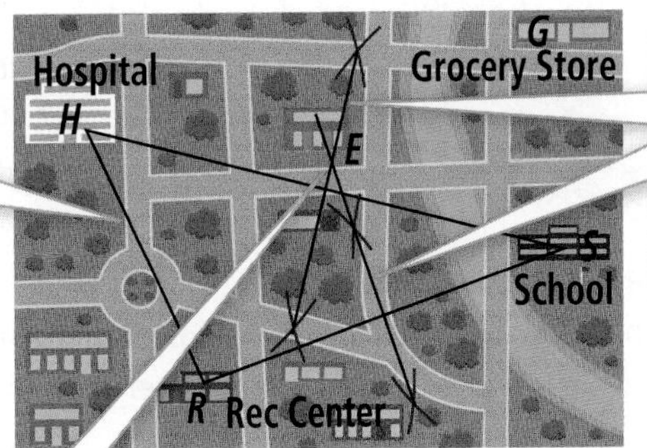


**Step 2** Construct the perpendicular bisectors of two of the sides.

**Step 3** Label point *E* where the perpendicular bisectors intersect.

The city manager should place the emergency siren at point E, because it is equidistant to the three locations.

**Try It!** 3. If the city manager decided to place the siren so that it is the same distance from the hospital, school, and grocery store, how can she find the location?

Activity
Assess

Another kind of special segment in a triangle is the angle bisector. Like the perpendicular bisectors of a triangle, the angle bisectors of a triangle also have a point of concurrency.

## THEOREM 5-6 Concurrency of Angle Bisectors

The angle bisectors of the angles of a triangle are concurrent at a point equidistant from the sides of the triangle.

PROOF: SEE EXERCISE 10.

**If...**

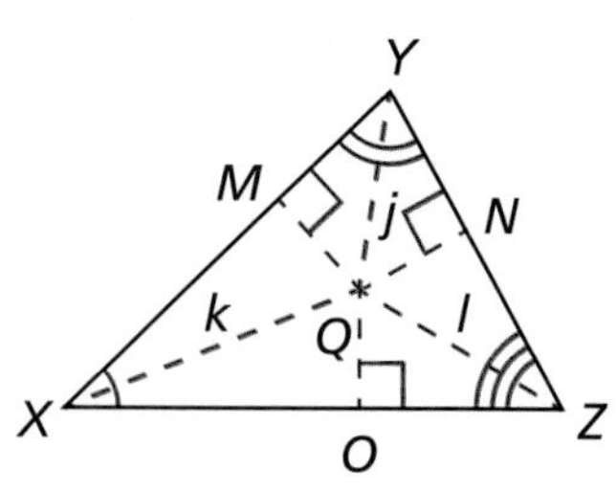

Y
M
j
N
k
Q
l
X
O
Z

**Then...** $j$, $k$, and $l$ intersect at $Q$ and $QM = QN = QO$

## EXAMPLE 4 Investigate Inscribed Circles

**How can you construct a circle that intersects each side of a given triangle in exactly one point?**

The circle that intersects each side of a triangle at exactly one point and has no points outside of the triangle is the **inscribed** circle of the triangle.

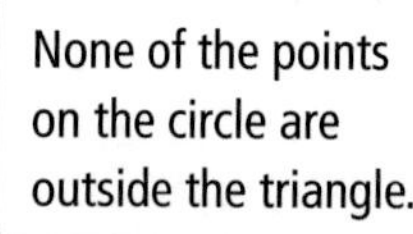

None of the points on the circle are outside the triangle.

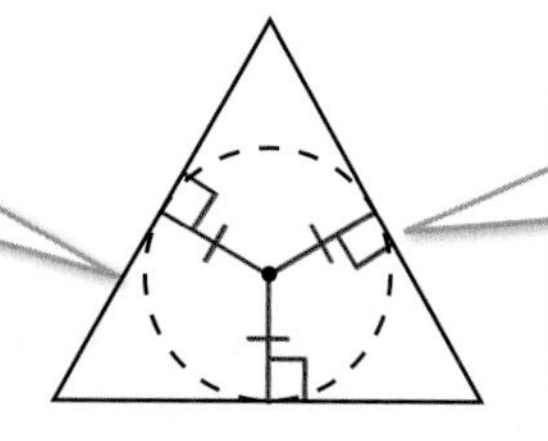

The sides of the triangle must be equidistant from the center of the circle.

**STUDY TIP**
The parts of the word *incenter* can help you remember what it means: it is the *center* of the circle that is *inside* the triangle.

By the Concurrency of Angle Bisectors Theorem, the angle bisectors of a triangle intersect at a point that is equidistant from the sides of the triangle. The point of concurrency of the angle bisectors of a triangle is the **incenter**, so the incenter is the center of the inscribed circle of the triangle.

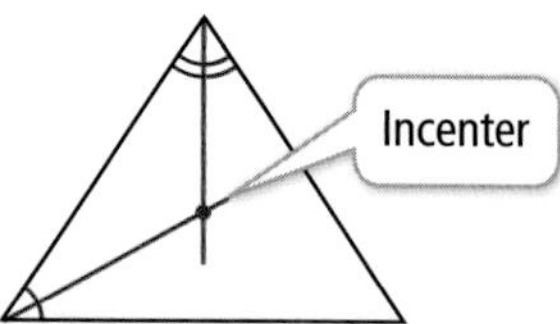

Incenter

First, construct two angle bisectors to find the incenter.

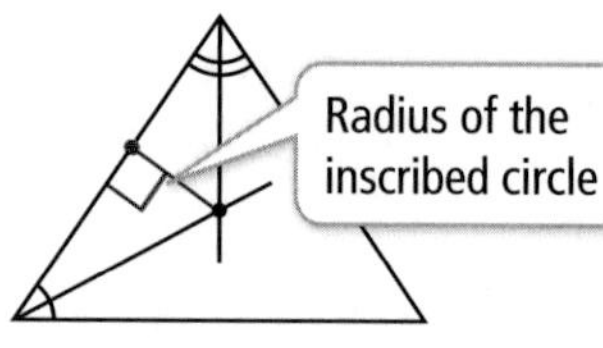

Radius of the inscribed circle

Next, construct a perpendicular segment from the incenter to any side.

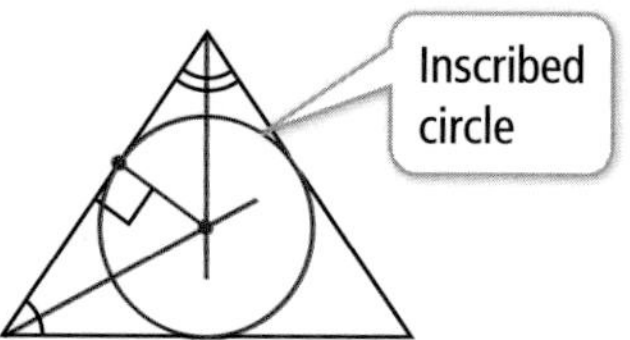

Inscribed circle

Finally, construct the circle centered on the incenter and passing through the point of intersection of the perpendicular segment and the side.

**Try It!** **4.** Do you think the incenter of a triangle can ever be located on a side of the triangle? Explain.

## EXAMPLE 5 Identify and Use the Incenter of a Triangle

**If $QP = 3(x + 1)$ and $RP = 5x - 3$, what is the radius of the inscribed circle of $\triangle JKL$?**

Since $\overline{KP}$ and $\overline{LP}$ are angle bisectors of $\triangle JKL$, $P$ is the incenter of $\triangle JKL$. Therefore, $\overline{QP} \cong \overline{RP}$.

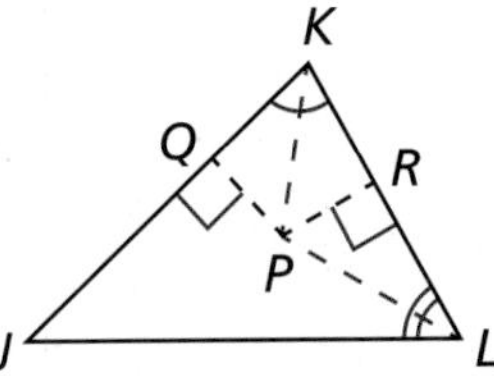


**STUDY TIP**
Remember that $QP = RP$, so evaluating either expression for $x = 3$ gives the value of the radius. Select the expression that is easier to evaluate.

**Step 1** Solve for $x$.

$$QP = RP$$ (Definition of congruent)

$$3(x + 1) = 5x - 3$$

$$3x + 3 = 5x - 3$$

$$6 = 2x$$

$$x = 3$$

**Step 2** Find the radius.

$$RP = 5x - 3$$ (The radius of the incircle is equal to $RP$.)

$$= 5(3) - 3$$

$$= 12$$

The radius of the inscribed circle is 12.

**Try It!** **5.** Use the figure shown.

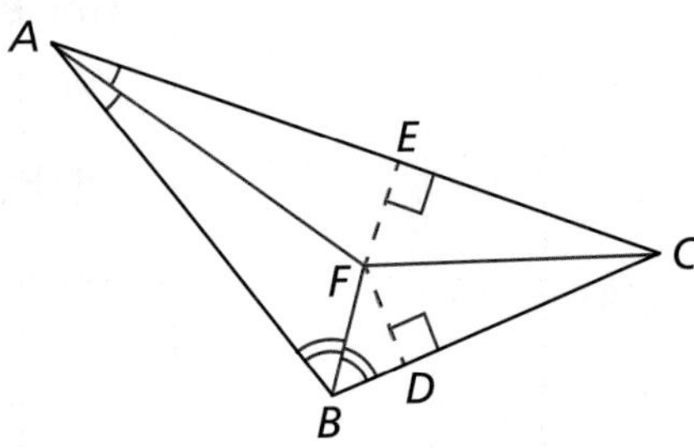


**a.** If $m\angle BAF = 15$ and $m\angle CBF = 52$, what is $m\angle ACF$?

**b.** If $EF = 3y - 5$ and $DF = 2y + 4$, what is the distance from $F$ to $AB$?

## CONCEPT SUMMARY Bisectors in Triangles

### PROPERTIES Perpendicular Bisectors

Perpendicular bisectors intersect at the circumcenter.

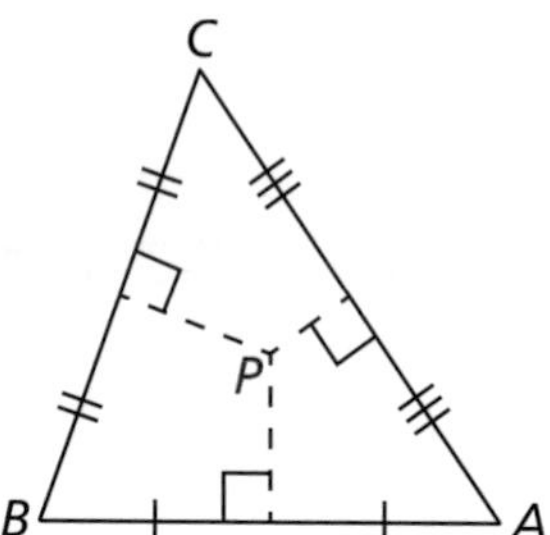


The circumcenter is equidistant from the vertices.

### PROPERTIES Angle Bisectors

Angle bisectors intersect at the incenter.

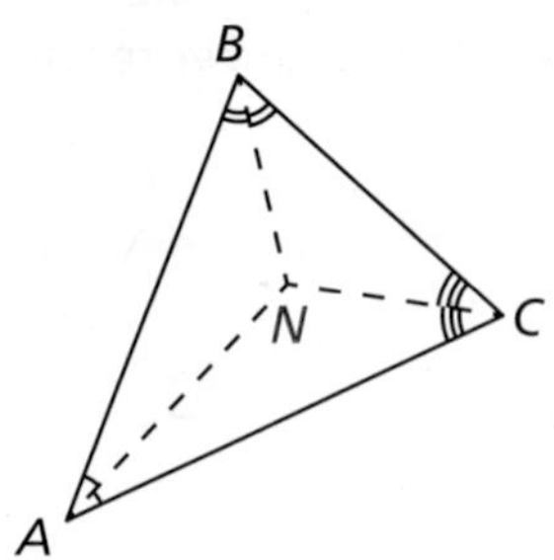


The incenter is equidistant from the sides.

## Do You UNDERSTAND?

1. **ESSENTIAL QUESTION** What are the properties of the perpendicular bisectors in a triangle? What are the properties of the angle bisectors in a triangle?

2. **Error Analysis** Terrence constructed the circumscribed circle for $\triangle XYZ$. Explain Terrence's error.

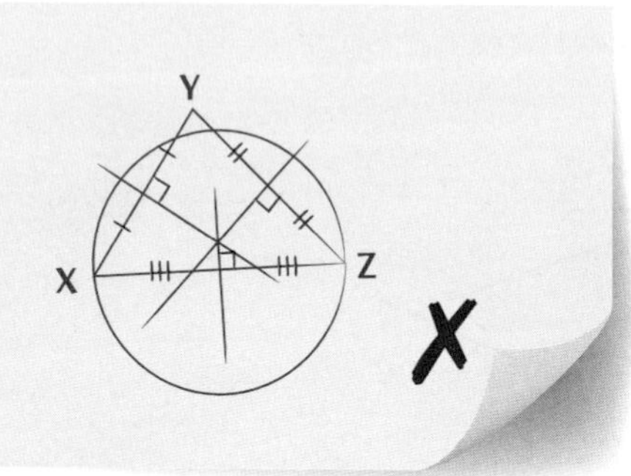


3. **Vocabulary** What parts of the triangle is the *circumcenter* equidistant from? What parts of the triangle is the *incenter* equidistant from?

4. **Reason** Is it possible for the circumscribed circle and the inscribed circle of a triangle to be the same? Explain your reasoning.

## Do You KNOW HOW?

**The perpendicular bisectors of $\triangle ABC$ are $\overline{PT}$, $\overline{QT}$, and $\overline{RT}$. Find each value.**

5. $AT$

6. $RC$

**Two of the angle bisectors of $\triangle ABC$ are $\overline{AP}$ and $\overline{BP}$. Find each value.**

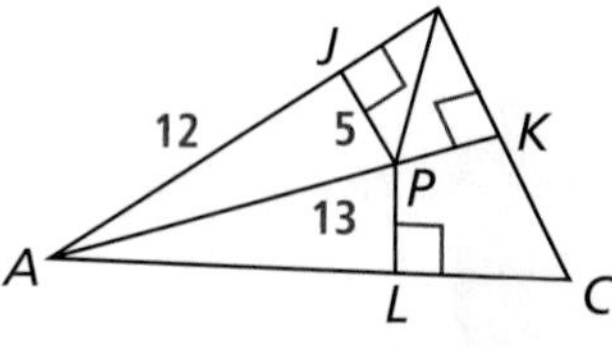


7. $PK$

8. Perimeter of $\triangle APL$

9. An artist will place a circular piece of stained glass inside the triangular frame so that the glass touches each side of the frame. What is the diameter of the stained glass? Round to the nearest tenth.

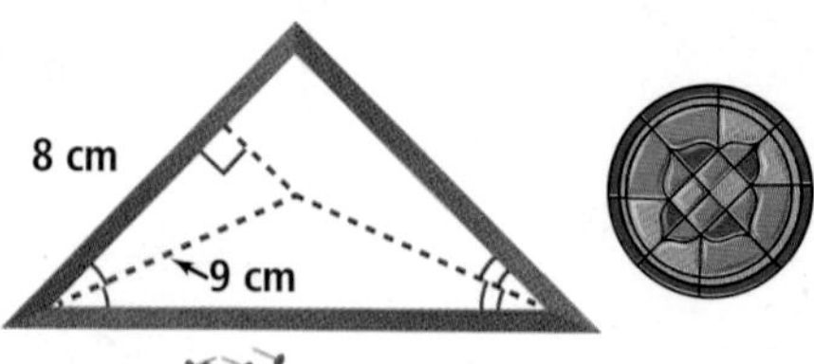

# PRACTICE & PROBLEM SOLVING

## UNDERSTAND

**10. Construct Arguments** Write a two-column proof of Theorem 5-6.

**11. Higher Order Thinking** A right triangle has vertices $X(0, 0)$, $Y(0, 2a)$, $Z(2b, 0)$. What is the circumcenter of the triangle? Make a conjecture about the diameter of a circle that is circumscribed about a right triangle.

**12. Error Analysis** What is the error that a student made in finding the perimeter of $\triangle DTM$? Correct the error.

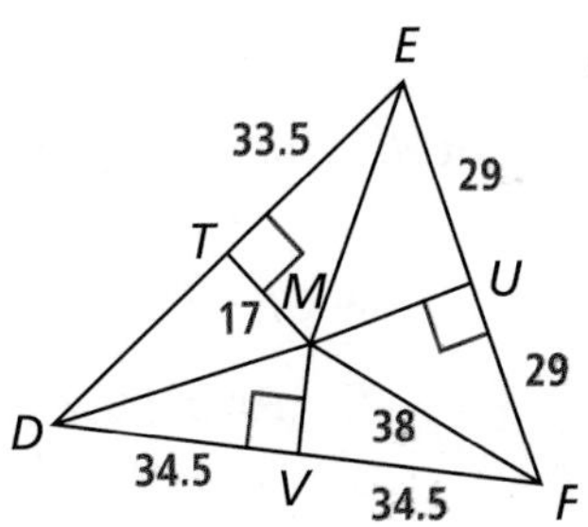


$DT = 34.5$, $TM = 17$, $DM = 34.5$.
The perimeter of $\Delta DTM$ is
$34.5 + 17 + 34.5 = 86$. ✗

**13. Mathematical Connections** A triangle with incenter $P$ has side lengths $x$, $y$, and $z$. The distance from $P$ to each side is $a$. Write an expression for the area of the triangle. Use the distributive property to factor your expression.

**14. Reason** In a right triangle with side lengths of 3, 4, and 5, what is the radius of the inscribed circle? Show your work. (Hint: Let $r$ be the radius. Label the lengths of each segment formed by the perpendiculars to the sides.)

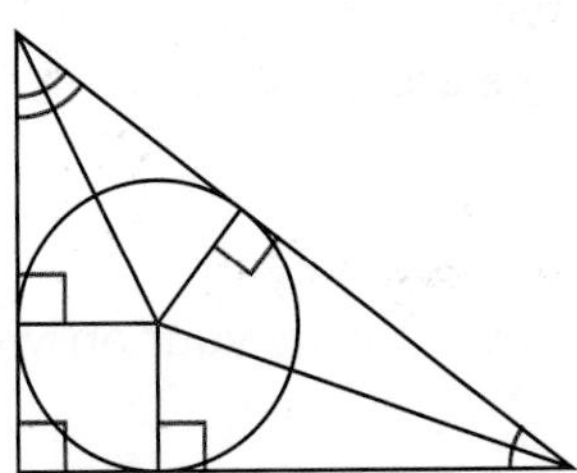

## PRACTICE

**15.** The perpendicular bisectors of $\triangle JKL$ are $\overline{PT}$, $\overline{QT}$, and $\overline{RT}$. Name three isosceles triangles. SEE EXAMPLE 1

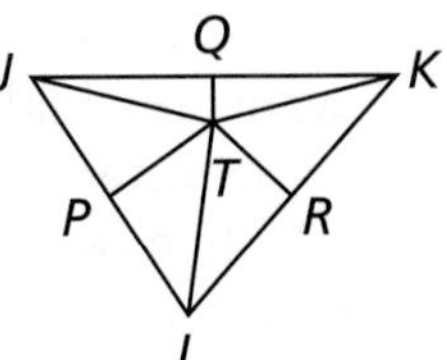


**Use the diagram below for Exercises 16–18. Points $D$, $E$, and $F$ are the midpoints of the sides of $\triangle ABC$.** SEE EXAMPLES 2 AND 4

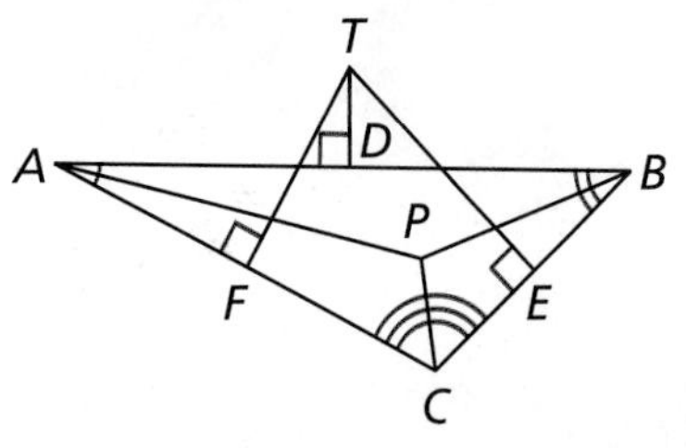


**16.** Which point is the center of a circle that contains $A$, $B$, and $C$?

**17.** Which point is the center of a circle that intersects each side of $\triangle ABC$ at exactly one point?

**18.** The perpendicular bisector of $\overline{AB}$ is $m$ and the perpendicular bisector of $\overline{BC}$ is $n$. Lines $m$ and $n$ intersect at $T$. If $TA = 8.2$, what is $TC$? SEE EXAMPLE 3

**Find the values.** SEE EXAMPLE 5

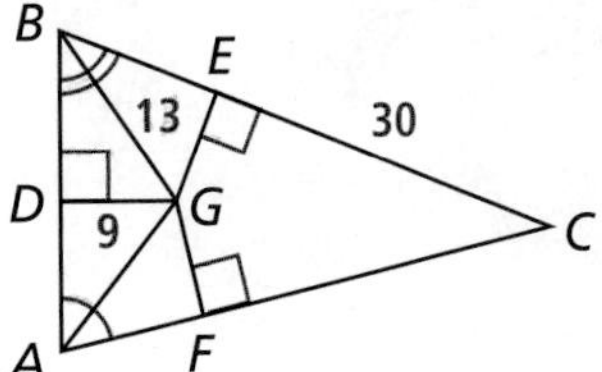


**19.** $EG$

**20.** $GF$

**If $XY = 24$, $XZ = 22$, and $JQ = 5$, find the values. Round to the nearest tenth.**

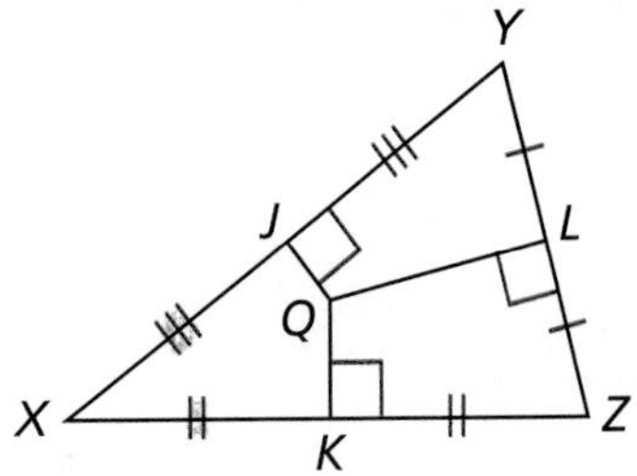


**21.** The radius of the circumscribed circle of $\triangle XYZ$

**22.** $QK$

APPLY

**23. Model With Mathematics** A maintenance crew wants to build a shed at a location that is the same distance from each path. Where should the shed be located? Justify your answer with a diagram.

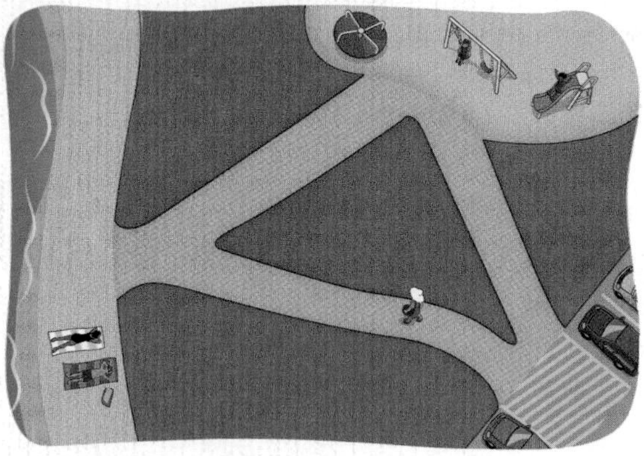

**24. Reason** What is the area of the patio **not** covered by the sunshade? Round to the nearest tenth, and explain how you found your answer.

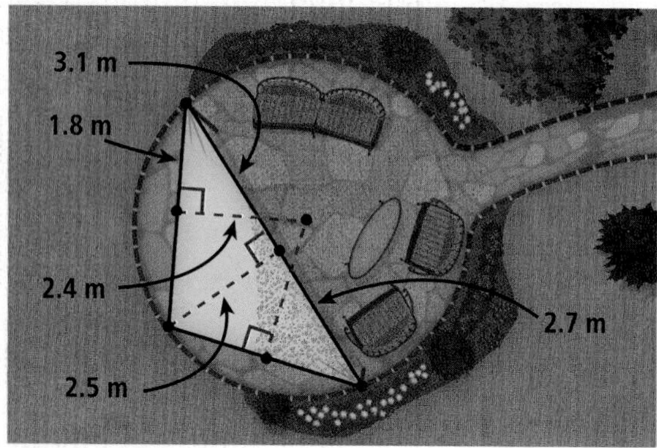


**25. Make Sense and Persevere** A ball manufacturer wants to stack three balls, each with an 8-centimeter diameter, in a box that is an equilateral triangular prism. The diagram shows the dimensions of the bases. Will the balls fit in the box? Explain how you know.

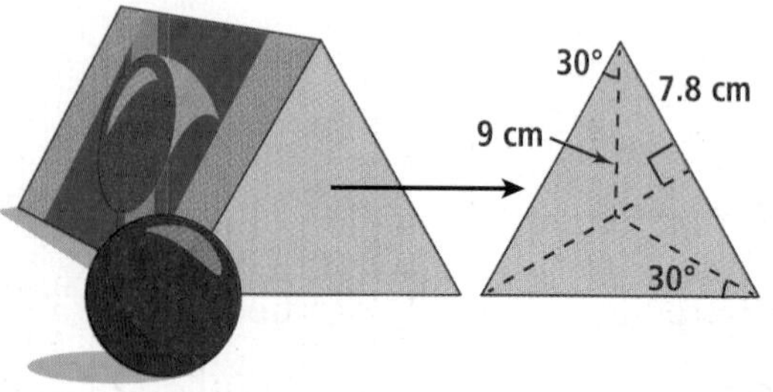


ASSESSMENT PRACTICE

**26.** In $\triangle ABC$, $\overline{AB}$ has midpoint $M$, and $\ell$ is the perpendicular bisector of $\overline{AB}$ and the angle bisector of $\angle ACB$. Which of the following must be true? Select all that apply.

Ⓐ The radius of the inscribed circle of $\triangle ABC$ is $AM$.

Ⓑ $AC = CB$

Ⓒ Both the circumcenter and incenter of $\triangle ABC$ are on $\ell$.

Ⓓ The circumcenter of $\triangle ABC$ is inside the triangle.

**27. SAT/ACT** Circle $O$ intersects $\overline{AB}$ only at $F$, $\overline{BC}$ only at $G$, and $\overline{AC}$ only at $H$. Which equation is true?

Ⓐ $AH = AC$

Ⓑ $m\angle OFB = 90$

Ⓒ $OB = OC$

Ⓓ $OF = OC$

Ⓔ $\angle BAO \cong \angle ABO$

**28. Performance Task** Edison High School is designing a new triangular pennant. The school mascot will be inside a circle, and the circle must touch each side of the pennant. The circle should fill as much of the pennant as possible.

**Part A** Using a straightedge and compass, draw at least 4 different types of triangles for the pennant. Construct an inscribed circle in each triangle.

**Part B** Make a table about your pennants. Include side lengths, type of triangle, circle radius and area, triangle area, and ratio of circle area to triangle area.

**Part C** What type of triangle do you recommend that they use? Justify your answer.

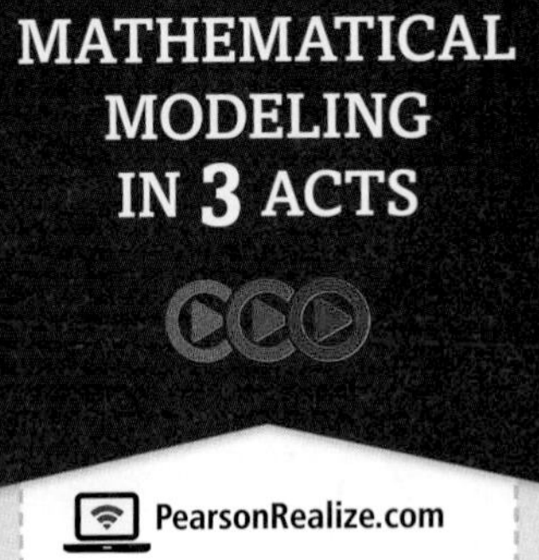


PearsonRealize.com

## Making It Fair

In rural areas, county planners often work with local officials from a number of small towns to establish a regional medical center to serve all of the nearby communities.

County planners might also establish regional medical evacuation centers to transport patients with serious trauma to larger medical centers. The locations of these regional centers are carefully planned. Think about this during the Mathematical Modeling in 3 Acts lesson.

### ACT 1 Identify the Problem

1. What is the first question that comes to mind after watching the video?
2. Write down the main question you will answer about what you saw in the video.
3. Make an initial conjecture that answers this main question.
4. Explain how you arrived at your conjecture.
5. What information will be useful to know to answer the main question? How can you get it? How will you use that information?

### ACT 2 Develop a Model

6. Use the math that you have learned in this Topic to refine your conjecture.

### ACT 3 Interpret the Results

7. Did your refined conjecture match the actual answer exactly? If not, what might explain the difference?

Activity | Assess

# 5-3 Medians and Altitudes

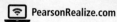

PearsonRealize.com

**I CAN…** find the points of concurrency for the medians of a triangle and the altitudes of a triangle.

**VOCABULARY**

- altitude
- centroid
- median
- orthocenter

## CRITIQUE & EXPLAIN

**Aisha wrote the following explanation of the relationships in the triangle.**

I can see that $\angle TVY \cong \angle YVU$, $\angle VUX \cong \angle XUT$, and $\angle UTZ \cong \angle ZTV$ because $\overline{TZ}$, $\overline{VY}$, and $\overline{UX}$ bisect the sides opposite each vertex. By the Concurrency of Angle Bisectors Theorem, $\overline{VY}$, $\overline{UX}$, and $\overline{TZ}$ are concurrent.

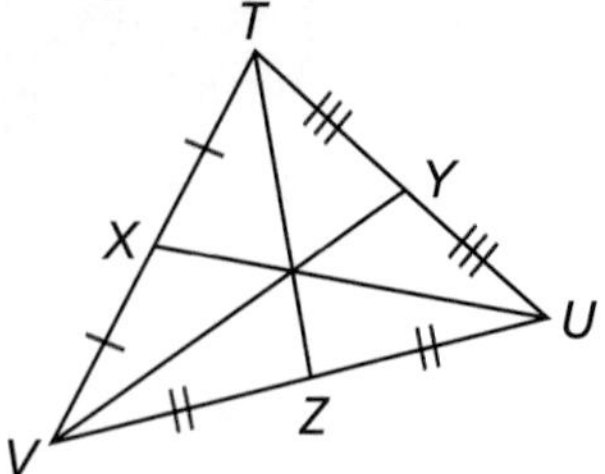


**A.** Why is Aisha's explanation not correct?

**B. Communicate Precisely** What can you do in the future to avoid Aisha's mistake?

## ESSENTIAL QUESTION

**What are the properties of the medians in a triangle? What are the properties of the altitudes in a triangle?**

## EXAMPLE 1 Identify Special Segments in Triangles

**What are the *altitude* and *median* that are shown in $\triangle ADC$?**

An **altitude** is a perpendicular segment from a vertex of a triangle to the line containing the side opposite the vertex. A **median** of a triangle is a segment that has endpoints at a vertex and the midpoint of the side opposite the vertex.

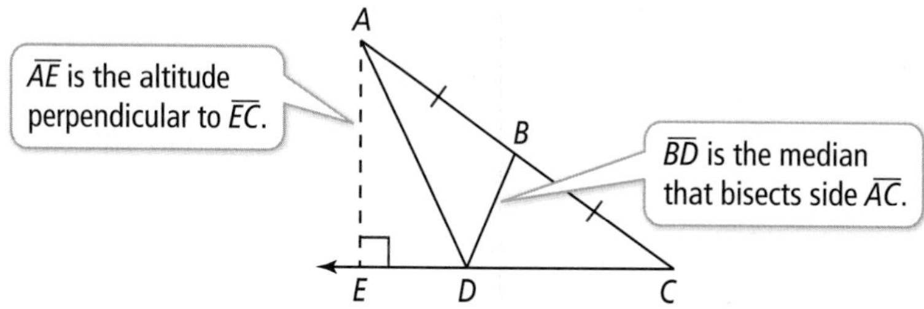


$\overline{AE}$ is the altitude perpendicular to $\overline{EC}$.

**STUDY TIP**
Recall that if congruency marks are not on a diagram, you cannot assume congruency.

**Try It!** 1. Use the figure shown.

a. What are the altitude and median that are shown in $\triangle ABC$?

b. Copy the triangle and draw the other altitudes and medians of the triangle.

$\overline{BD}$ is the median that bisects side $\overline{AC}$.

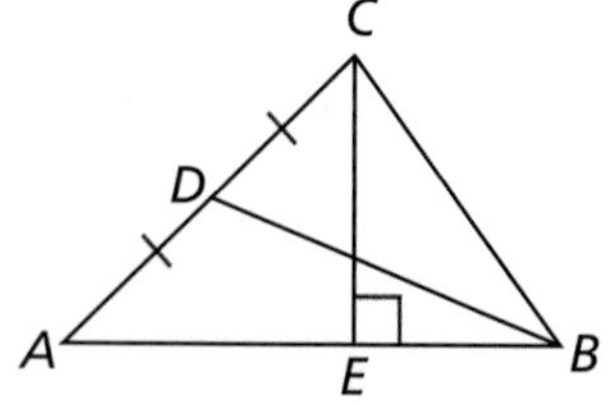

## THEOREM 5-7 Concurrency of Medians

The medians of a triangle are concurrent at a point that is two-thirds the distance from each vertex to the midpoint of the opposite side.

PROOF: SEE LESSON 9-2.

If...

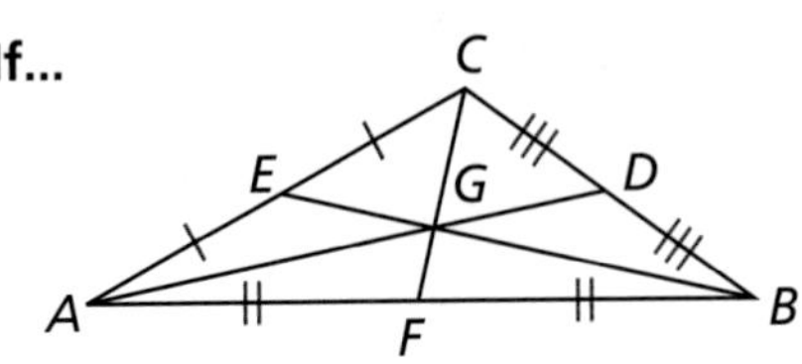


Then...

$AG = \frac{2}{3}AD \quad BG = \frac{2}{3}BE \quad CG = \frac{2}{3}CF$

## EXAMPLE 2 Find the Length of a Median

**What is the length of $\overline{JN}$ in the figure?**

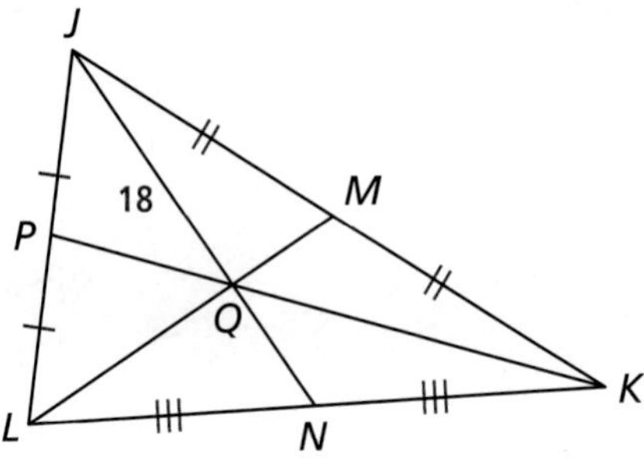


The medians of $\triangle JKL$ are $\overline{JN}$, $\overline{KP}$, and $\overline{LM}$. Point $Q$ is the point of concurrency of the medians. The point of concurrency of the medians of a triangle is called the **centroid**.

**COMMON ERROR**
Be careful not to confuse which part is $\frac{1}{3}$ of the length of the median and which part is $\frac{2}{3}$ of the length.

$\frac{2}{3}JN = JQ$ — Use the Concurrency of Medians Theorem.

$\frac{2}{3}JN = 18$

$JN = 27$

**Try It!** 2. Find $AD$ for each triangle.

a.

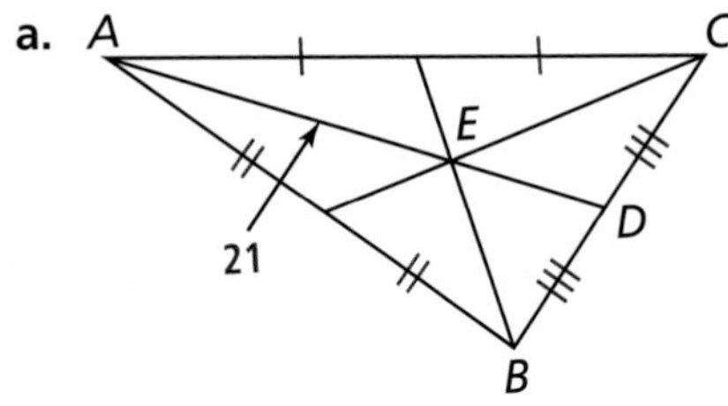


b.

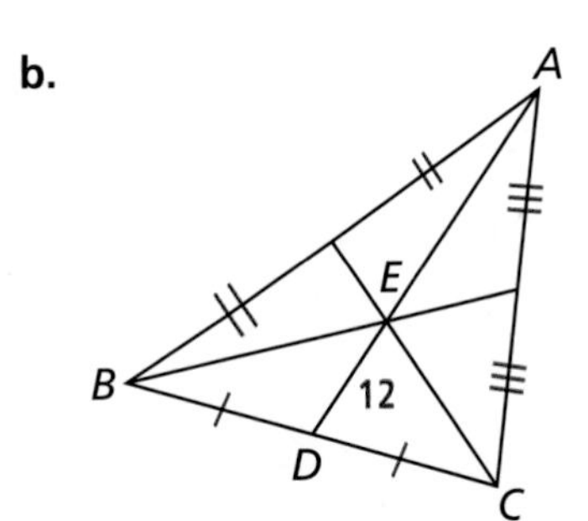

## EXAMPLE 3 Locate the Centroid

**An artist wants to balance a triangular piece of wood at a single point so that the triangle is parallel to the ground. Where should he balance the triangle?**

A triangle is balanced at its *center of gravity,* which is at the centroid of the triangle.

**USE APPROPRIATE TOOLS**
Think about what tools you can use to find the midpoint. What tool would you use?

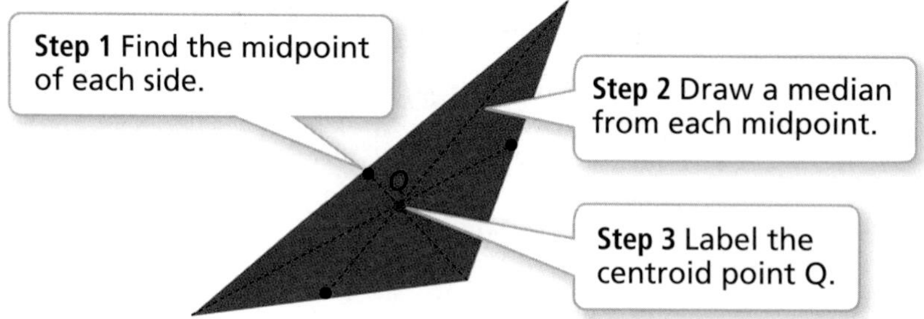
**Step 1** Find the midpoint of each side.
**Step 2** Draw a median from each midpoint.
**Step 3** Label the centroid point Q.
Q

The artist should balance the triangle at point $Q$.

**Try It!** 3. Copy the triangle shown.

a. Use the medians of the triangle to locate its centroid.

b. Use a ruler to verify the centroid is two-thirds the distance from each vertex to the midpoint of the opposite side.

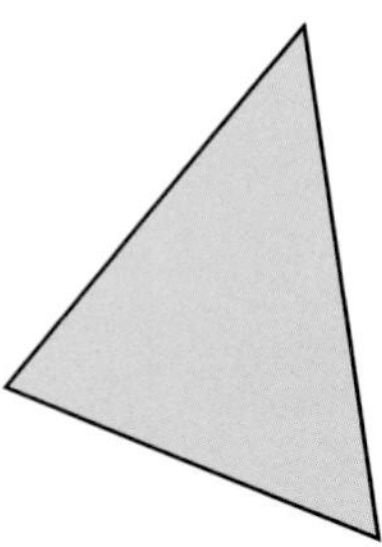

## THEOREM 5-8 Concurrency of Altitudes

The lines that contain the altitudes of a triangle are concurrent.

PROOF: SEE LESSON 9-2.

**If...**

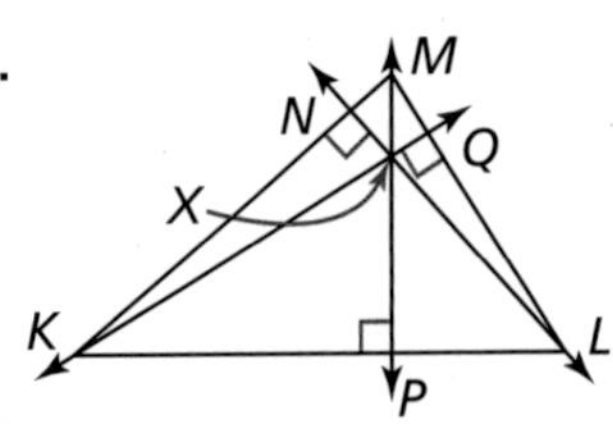


**Then...** $\overline{KQ}$, $\overline{LN}$, and $\overline{MP}$ are concurrent at $X$

CONCEPTUAL UNDERSTANDING

## EXAMPLE 4 Locate the Orthocenter

**The orthocenter is the point of concurrency of the lines containing the altitudes of a triangle. How does the type of triangle (obtuse, acute, right) relate to the location of its orthocenter?**

Draw at least two of each type of triangle. Describe any relationship you notice between the type of triangle and the location of its orthocenter.

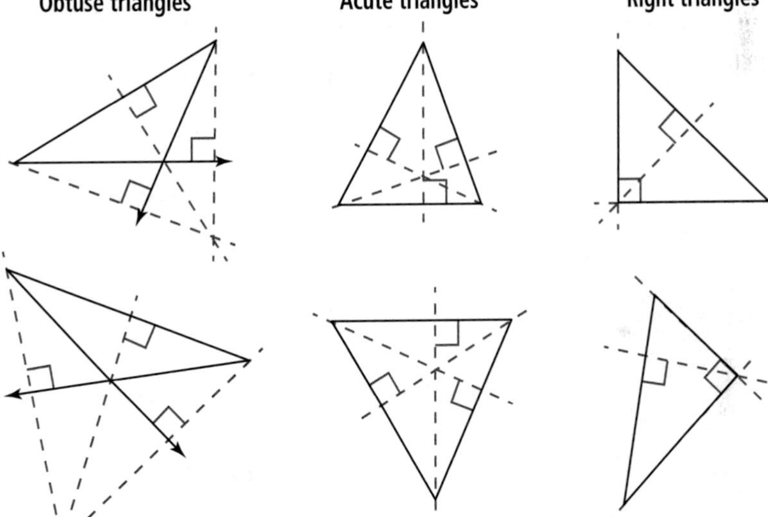


**STUDY TIP**
Recall that when you make a conjecture by observing a few examples, you are not actually proving the conjecture.

The orthocenter is outside an obtuse triangle and inside an acute triangle. For a right triangle, the orthocenter is at the vertex of the right angle.

 **Try It!** 4. What is the relationship between an isosceles triangle and the location of its orthocenter? Explain your answer.

## EXAMPLE 5 Find the Orthocenter of a Triangle

**Orthocenters can be found using constructions or coordinate geometry. Where is the orthocenter of $\triangle KLM$?**

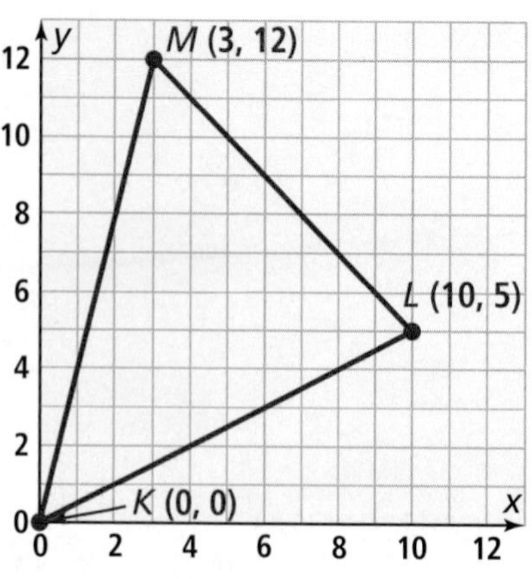


Since the orthocenter is the point of concurrency of the altitudes, find the equations for two altitudes, and solve for the point of intersection.

**Step 1** Find the slopes of two sides of the triangle.

$$\text{slope of } \overline{KL} = \frac{5-0}{10-0} = \frac{1}{2}$$

$$\text{slope of } \overline{LM} = \frac{12-5}{3-10} = -1$$

**STUDY TIP**

Remember that since an altitude is perpendicular to a side of the triangle, you must find the reciprocal and reverse the sign of the slope of a side to find the slope of an altitude.

**Step 2** Use the point slope form, $y - y_1 = m(x - x_1)$, to write the equations of the altitudes perpendicular to $\overline{KL}$ and $\overline{LM}$.

Equation of the altitude perpendicular to $\overline{KL}$:

$$y - 12 = -2(x - 3)$$
$$y = -2x + 6 + 12$$
$$y = -2x + 18$$

Point $M$ is the vertex opposite $\overline{KL}$, and the slope of a line perpendicular to $\overline{KL}$ is $-2$.

Equation of the altitude perpendicular to $\overline{LM}$:

$$y - 0 = 1(x - 0)$$
$$y = x$$

Point $K$ is the vertex opposite $\overline{LM}$, and the slope of a line perpendicular to $\overline{LM}$ is 1.

**Step 3** Solve the system of equations to determine the coordinates of the point of intersection.

$$y = -2x + 18$$
$$y = -2(y) + 18$$
$$y + 2y = 18$$
$$3y = 18$$
$$y = 6$$

Since $y = x$, substitute $y$ in the equation $y = -2x + 18$. Then solve for $y$.

Since $y = x$, $x = 6$.

Since all three altitudes intersect at the orthocenter, the intersection of two altitudes is sufficient to determine the orthocenter. The orthocenter of $\triangle KLM$ is (6, 6).

**Try It!** 5. Find the orthocenter of a triangle with vertices at each of the following sets of coordinates.

**a.** (0, 0), (10, 4), (8, 9) **b.** (0, 0), (6, 3), (8, 9)

## CONCEPT SUMMARY Medians and Altitudes

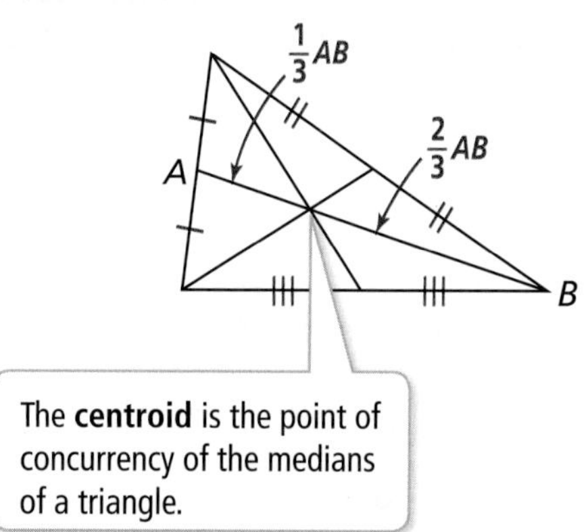


The **centroid** is the point of concurrency of the medians of a triangle.

ALTITUDES

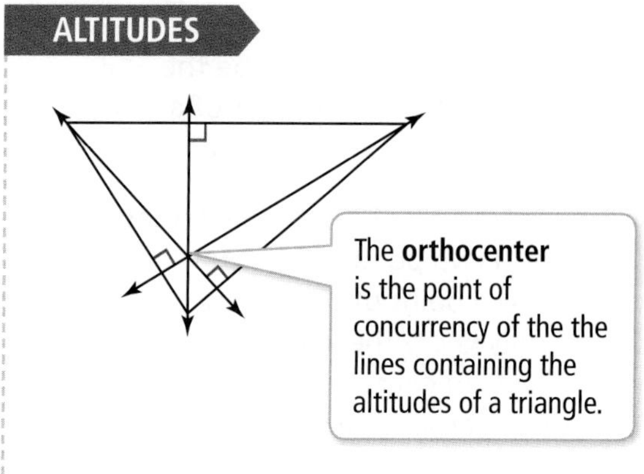

The **orthocenter** is the point of concurrency of the the lines containing the altitudes of a triangle.

## Do You UNDERSTAND?

1. ESSENTIAL QUESTION What are the properties of the medians in a triangle? What are the properties of the altitudes in a triangle?

2. **Vocabulary** The prefix *ortho-* means "upright" or "right." How can this meaning help you remember which segments of a triangle have a point of concurrency at the orthocenter?

3. **Error Analysis** A student labeled P as the centroid of the triangle. What error did the student make? Explain.

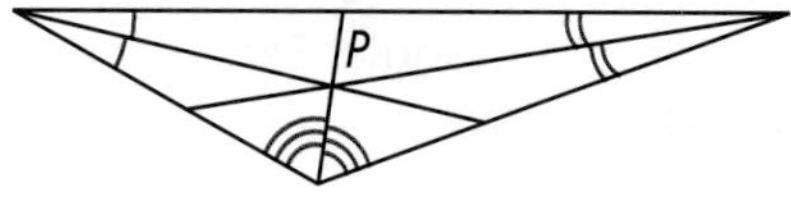


4. **Reason** Why is an orthocenter sometimes outside a triangle but a centroid is always inside?

5. **Look for Relationships** Consider the three types of triangles: acute, obtuse, and right. What is the relationship between the type of triangle and the location of the orthocenter? Does the type of triangle tell you anything about the location of the centroid?

6. **Generalize** For any right triangle, where is the orthocenter located?

## Do You KNOW HOW?

7. Find the length of each of the medians of the triangle.

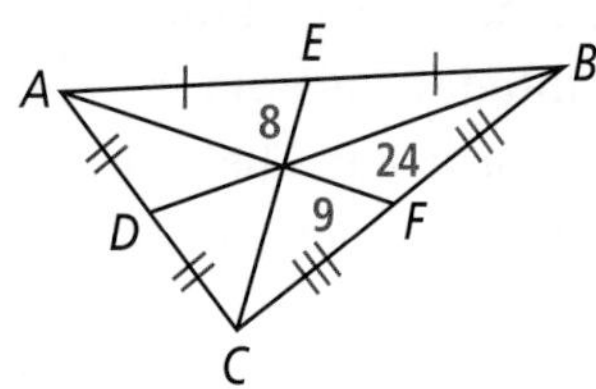


8. Where is the orthocenter of $\triangle ABC$?

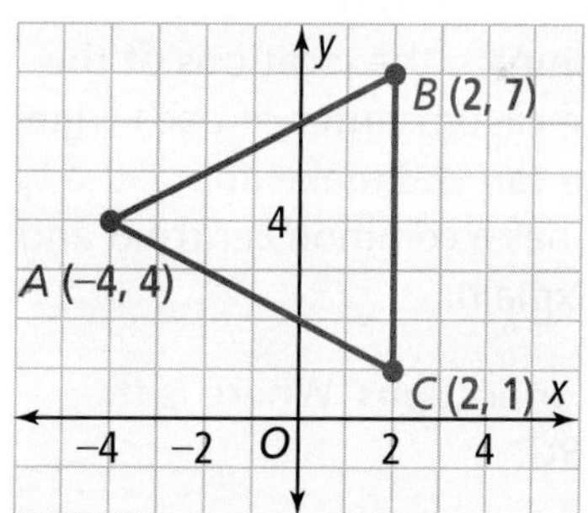


9. A crane operator needs to lift a large triangular piece of plywood. Copy the triangle and use its medians to locate the centroid.

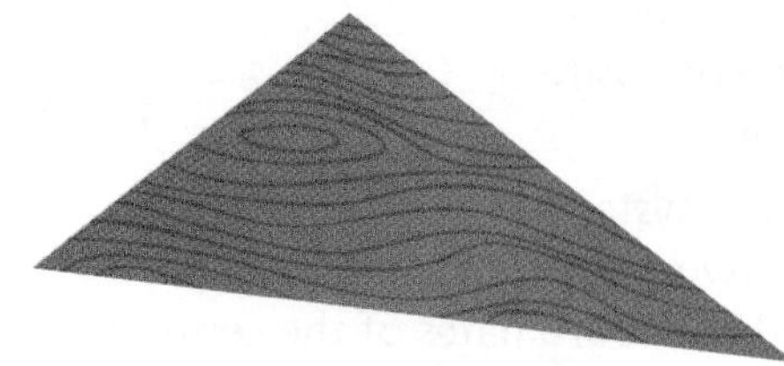

# PRACTICE & PROBLEM SOLVING

Scan for Multimedia

Practice | Tutorial

Additional Exercises Available Online

## UNDERSTAND

**10. Make Sense and Persevere** Describe the process for finding the orthocenter of a triangle that is on a coordinate plane.

**11. Look for Relationships** Given the midpoints of a triangle, which two points of concurrency can you locate? Which point of concurrency can you locate if you only know the angle bisectors? Which two points of concurrency can you locate by only drawing perpendicular segments?

**12. Error Analysis** A student uses the following explanation to identify the triangle's point of concurrency. Explain the student's error.

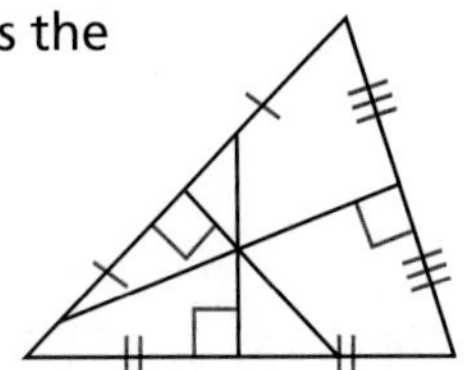

A perpendicular segment bisects each side of the triangle. According to the Concurrency of Altitudes Theorem, the segments are concurrent. The point of concurrency is the orthocenter. ✗

**13. Reason** Draw several different types of triangles and compare the locations of the centroid and the circumcenter of each triangle. What conjecture can you make about the type of triangle that has a common centroid and circumcenter? Explain.

**14. Mathematical Connections** Where is the centroid of $\triangle ABC$?

- Locate the midpoints of any two sides.
- Find the equations of two medians using the vertex and the opposite midpoint.
- Solve the system of the two equations to find the coordinates of the centroid.

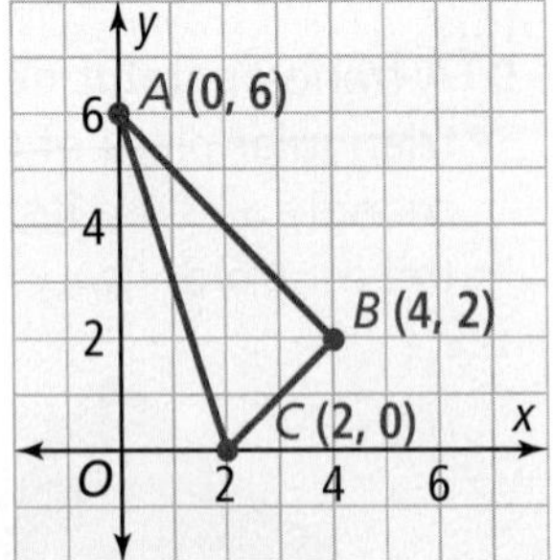


How can you verify that the coordinates you found are correct?

## PRACTICE

**15.** Identify whether each segment is an altitude, an angle bisector, a median, or a perpendicular bisector. SEE EXAMPLE 1

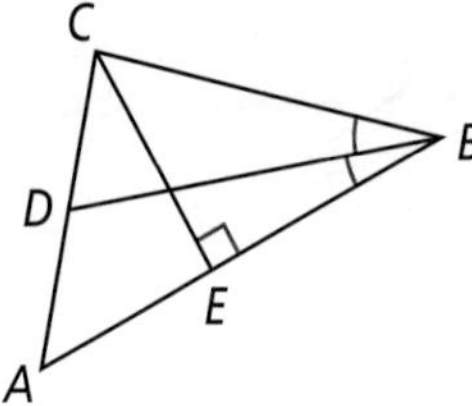


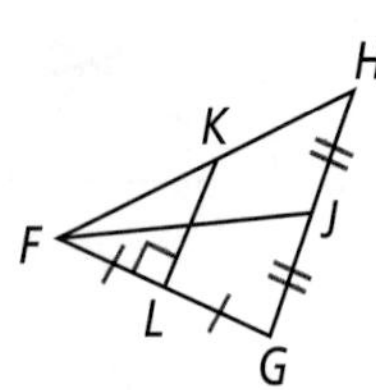


a. $\overline{BD}$ b. $\overline{FJ}$

c. $\overline{CE}$ d. $\overline{KL}$

**16.** What is the value of $KL$? SEE EXAMPLE 2

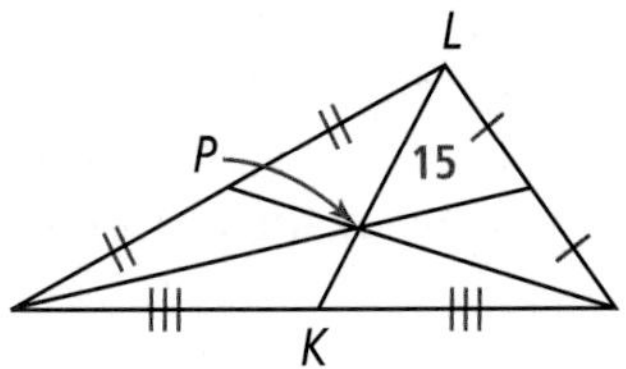


**17.** Copy the triangle and use its medians to locate the centroid. SEE EXAMPLE 3

**18.** State whether the orthocenter of each triangle is inside the triangle, outside the triangle, or on the triangle. Explain your reasoning. SEE EXAMPLE 4

a. 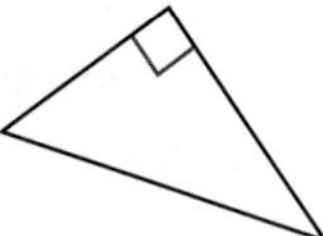

b. 

c. 

d. 

**19.** Find the coordinates of the orthocenter of a triangle with vertices at each set of points on a coordinate plane. SEE EXAMPLE 5

a. (0, 0), (8, 4), (4, 22)

b. (3, 1), (10, 8), (5, 13)

# PRACTICE & PROBLEM SOLVING

## APPLY

**20. Model With Mathematics** A large triangular-shaped table is supported by a single pole at the center of gravity. How far is vertex *C* from the center of gravity?

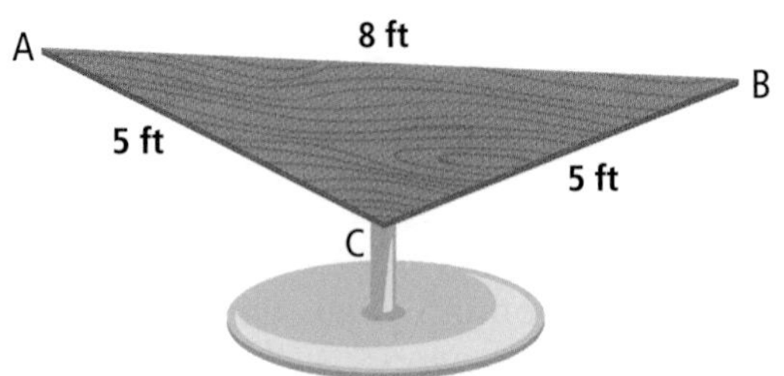


**21. Reason** To support a triangular kite, Hana attaches thin strips of wood from each vertex perpendicular to the opposite edge. She then attaches the kite's string at the point of concurrency. To calculate the point of concurrency, she determines the coordinates of each vertex on a coordinate plane. What are the coordinates where the wood strips cross? Round your answer to the nearest hundredth.

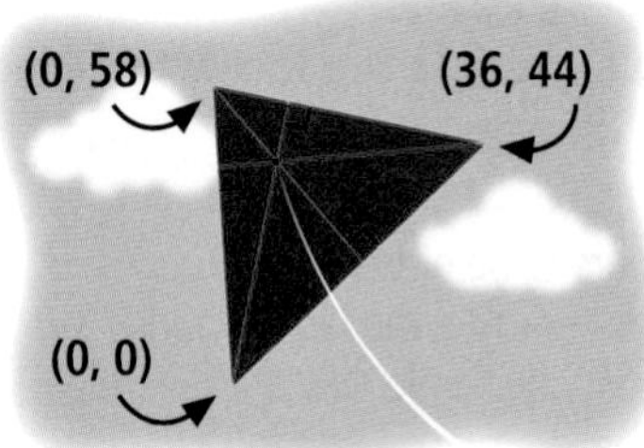


**22. Higher Order Thinking** A designer wants to place a fountain at the intersection of the shortest paths from each side to the opposite vertex. What mistake is made on her model? At what point of concurrency should the fountain be located?

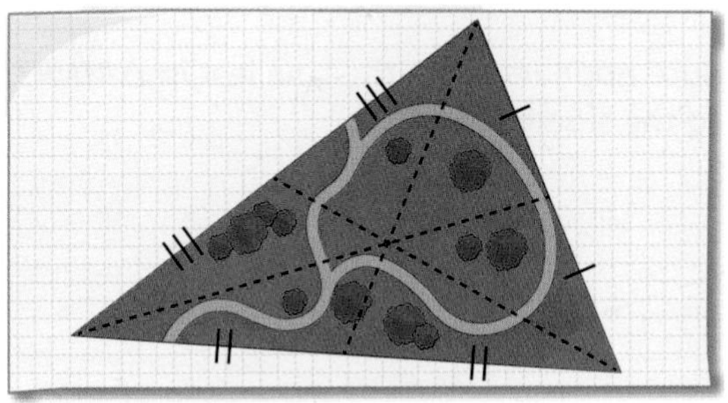

## ASSESSMENT PRACTICE

**23.** Identify the segments and point in $\triangle ABC$.

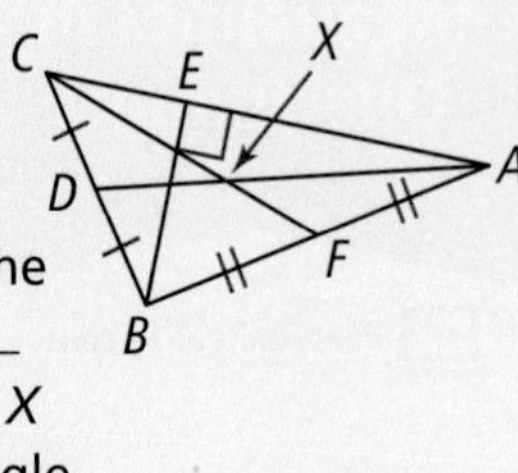


The segment $\overline{AD}$ is a(n) ___?___ of the triangle. The segment $\overline{BE}$ is a(n) ___?___ of the triangle. The point *X* is the ___?___ of the triangle.

**24. SAT/ACT** A triangle with vertices at (3, 4) and (9, 17) has a centroid at (8, 16). What are the coordinates of the third vertex?

Ⓐ (10, 4)
Ⓑ (10, 7)
Ⓒ (12, 14)
Ⓓ (12, 27)

**25. Performance Task** Steve is designing a mobile with triangular pieces of wood, where each piece attaches to a wire at the center of gravity and hangs parallel to the ground. The side lengths of the triangles will be between 4 cm and 8 cm.

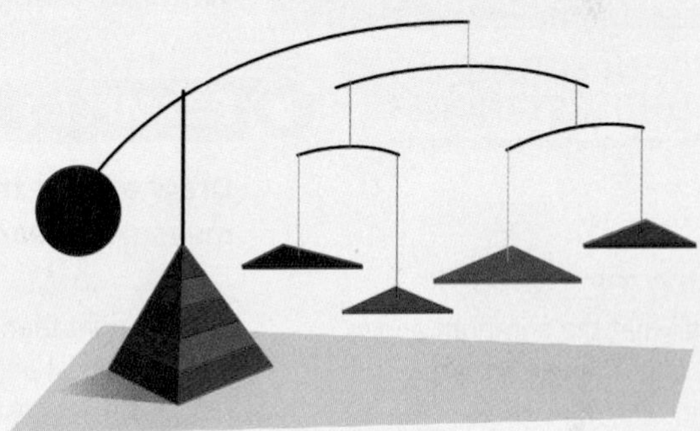

**Part A** Describe how Steve can find the center of gravity for any triangular piece. Then model this process by finding the center of gravity of a triangle with side lengths 5 cm, 5 cm, and 6 cm.

**Part B** Is it possible for a triangle attached at the orthocenter to hang so that it is parallel to the ground? If it is possible, describe the triangle. What are possible side lengths for such a triangle? If it is not possible, explain why not.

Activity Assess

# 5-4 Inequalities in One Triangle

PearsonRealize.com

**I CAN…** use theorems to compare the sides and angles of a triangle.

## EXPLORE & REASON

**Cut several drinking straws to the sizes shown.**

**A.** Take your two shortest straws and your longest straw. Can they form a triangle? Explain.

**B.** Try different combinations of three straws to form triangles. Which side length combinations work? Which combinations do not work?

**C. Look for Relationships** What do you notice about the relationship between the combined lengths of the two shorter sides and the length of the longest side?

## ESSENTIAL QUESTION

**What are some relationships between the sides and angles of any triangle?**

CONCEPTUAL UNDERSTANDING

## EXAMPLE 1 Investigate Side and Angle Relationships

**Draw a right triangle and a non-right triangle. How is the largest angle measure of each triangle related to the side lengths?**

STUDY TIP
Recall that the non-right angles in a right triangle are acute. This means the right angle is the largest angle.

In the right triangle, $\angle A$ is the largest angle and $\overline{BC}$ is the longest side.

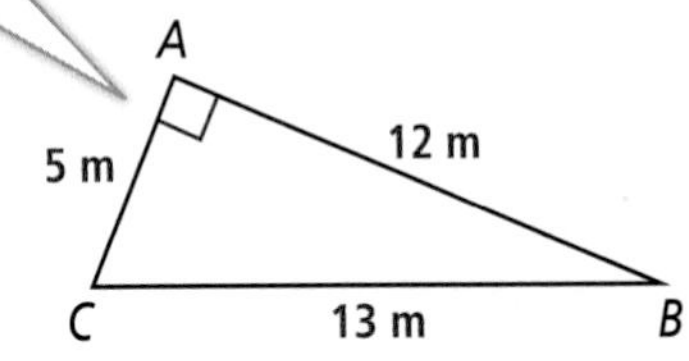


Angle $P$ appears to be obtuse, while $\angle Q$ and $\angle R$ appear to be acute. The largest angle $\angle P$ is across from longest side $\overline{QR}$.

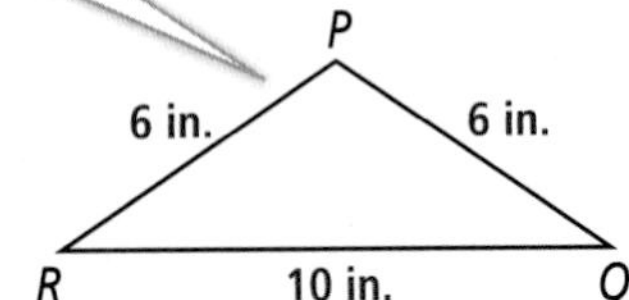


The largest angle appears to be opposite the longest side.

**Try It!** 1. Which angle measure appears to be the smallest in $\triangle MNP$? How is it related to the side lengths?

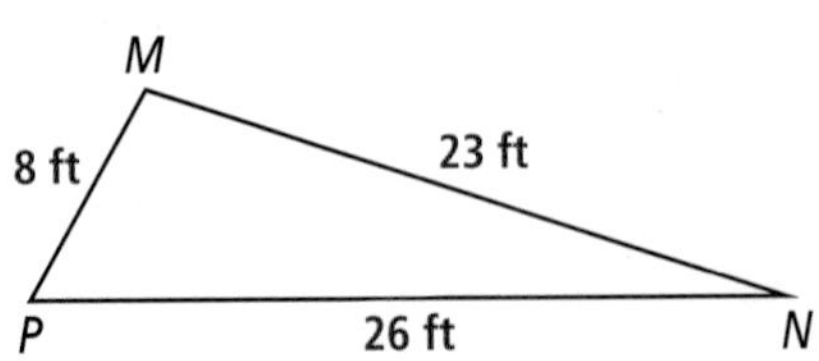

## THEOREM 5-9

If two sides of a triangle are not congruent, then the larger angle lies opposite the longer side.

**PROOF: SEE EXERCISE 13.**

**If...** $b > a$

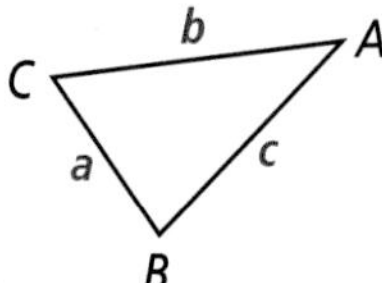


**Then...** $m\angle B > m\angle A$

## EXAMPLE 2 Use Theorem 5-9

**To support a triangular piece of a float, a brace is placed at the largest angle and a guide wire is placed at the smallest angle. Which angle is the largest? Which angle is the smallest?**

**REASON**
Think about the relationships between pairs of numbers. How can you use the relationships between pairs of numbers to order all the numbers?

Compare side lengths to find larger angle measures.

Since $12 > 10$, $m\angle A > m\angle B$.

Since $13 > 12$, $m\angle C > m\angle A$.

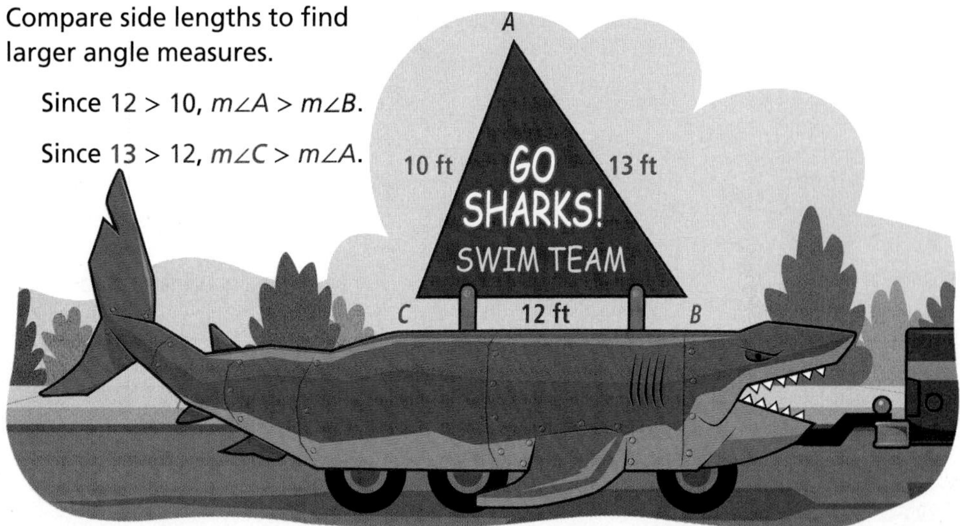


Combining the inequalities of the angle measures, $m\angle C > m\angle A > m\angle B$. Thus, the largest angle is $\angle C$ and the smallest angle is $\angle B$.

**Try It!** **2.** Lucas sketched a diagram for a garden box.

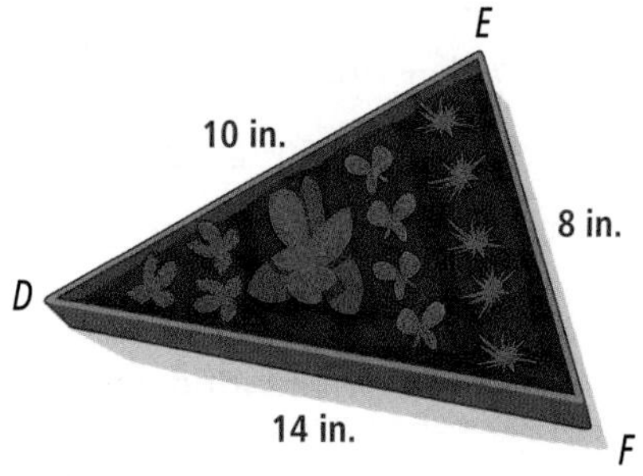


**a.** Which angle is the largest?

**b.** Which angle is the smallest?

**THEOREM 5-10** Converse of Theorem 5-9

If two angles of a triangle are not congruent, then the longer side lies opposite the larger angle.

PROOF: SEE EXAMPLE 3.

**If...** $m\angle B > m\angle A$

**Then...** $b > a$

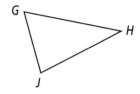

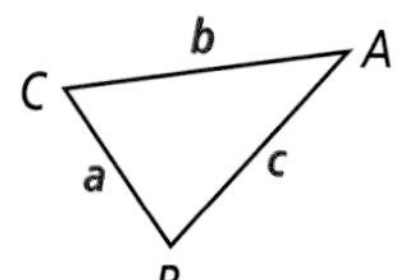


PROOF

## EXAMPLE 3 Prove Theorem 5-10

**STUDY TIP**
Recall that in an indirect proof, you assume the opposite of what you are trying to prove and then show that this leads to a contradiction.

**Use indirect reasoning to prove Theorem 5–10; assume that $GH \leq HJ$. This means that $GH = HJ$ or $GH < HJ$.**

**Given:** $m\angle J > m\angle G$

**Prove:** $GH > HJ$

First show that assuming $GH = HJ$ leads to a contradiction of the given condition that $m\angle J > m\angle G$.

$GH = HJ$ (Assumption) → $\overline{GH} \cong \overline{HJ}$ (Def. of congruent) → $\triangle GHJ$ is isosceles. (Def. of isosceles) → $m\angle J = m\angle G$ (Isosceles Triangle Thm.)

Because $m\angle J = m\angle G$ contradicts $m\angle J > m\angle G$, the assumption is false.

**Try It!** 3. To complete the proof of Theorem 5-10, show that assuming $GH < HJ$ leads to a contradiction of the given condition that $m\angle J > m\angle G$.

## EXAMPLE 4 Use Theorem 5-10

**Which side of $\triangle KLM$ is the longest?**

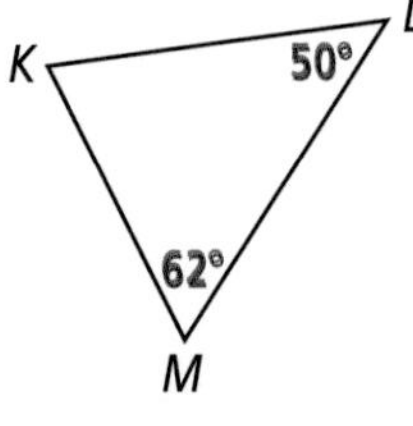


By Theorem 5-10, the longest side of the triangle is across from the largest angle. Find the unknown angle measure.

**STUDY TIP**
When needed information is missing from a diagram, you may need to apply properties and theorems to find the needed information.

$$m\angle K + m\angle L + m\angle M = 180$$

$$m\angle K + 50° + 62° = 180$$

$$m\angle K = 68$$

Apply Triangle Angle-Sum Theorem

The largest angle in the triangle is $\angle K$, so the longest side is the side opposite $\angle K$. The longest side is $LM$.

**Try It!** 4. Identify the sides of $\triangle NOP$.

**a.** Which side is the longest?

**b.** Which side is the shortest?

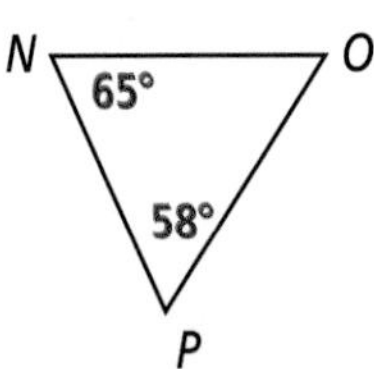

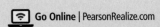

## THEOREM 5-11 Triangle Inequality Theorem

The sum of the lengths of any two sides of a triangle is greater than the length of the third side.

PROOF: SEE EXERCISE 14.

If...

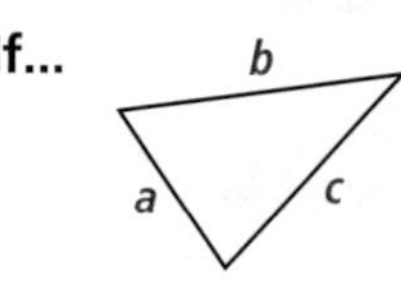


Then... $a + b > c$
$a + c > b$
$b + c > a$

## EXAMPLE 5 Use the Triangle Inequality Theorem

**A. Which of the following sets of segments could be the sides of a triangle?**

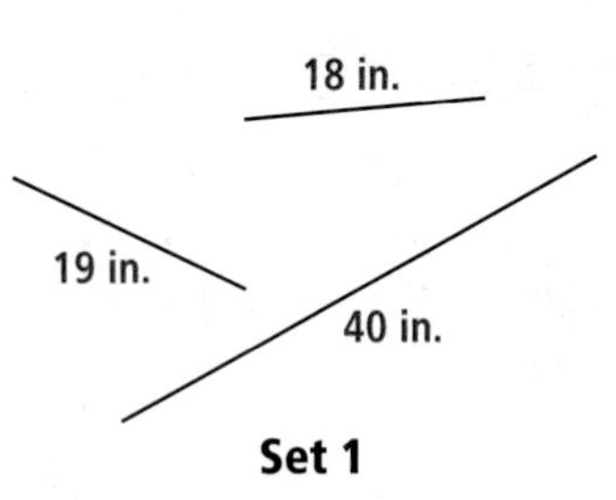


Set 1

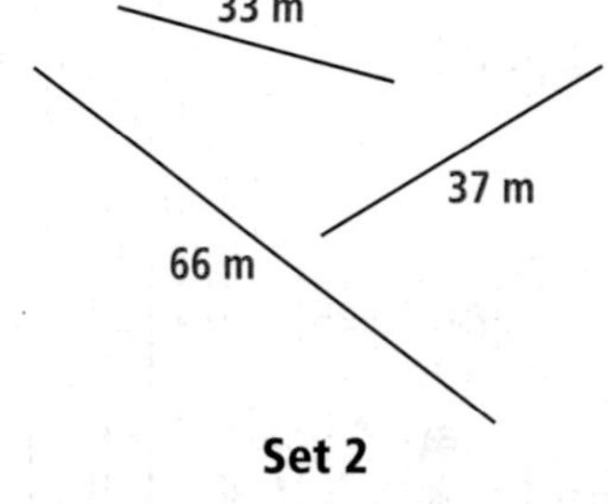


Set 2

Determine if the sum of the two shorter side lengths is longer than the longest side length.

$18 + 19 = 37$

Since $37 < 40$, the segments in Set 1 cannot form a triangle.

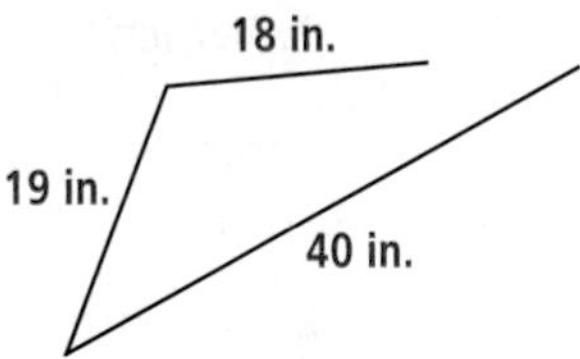


$33 + 37 = 70$

Since $70 > 66$, the segments in Set 2 can form a triangle.

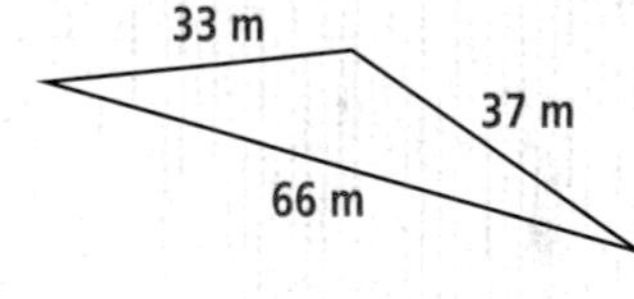


**COMMON ERROR**
You may compare any two sides to a third side, but you must compare the shorter two sides to the longest side to determine whether a triangle is possible.

**B. A triangle has sides that measure 11 cm and 16 cm. What are the possible lengths of the third side?**

Apply the Triangle Inequality Theorem.

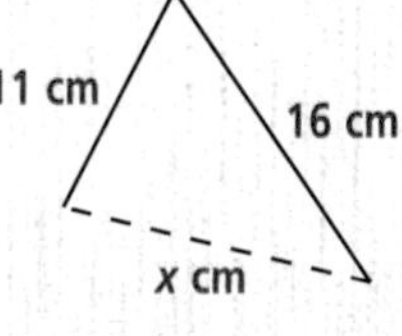


$x + 11 > 16$ $\quad$ $x + 16 > 11$ $\quad$ $11 + 16 > x$

- If $x + 11 > 16$, then $x > 5$. So, $x$ is greater than 5.
- The inequality $x + 16 > 11$ is true for all positive values of $x$, so this inequality only tells you that $x > 0$.
- If $11 + 16 > x$, then $27 > x$, so $x$ is less than 27.

Therefore, $5 < x < 27$.

The third side of the triangle could be between 5 cm and 27 cm long.

**Try It!** **5. a.** Could a triangle have side lengths 16 m, 39 m, and 28 m?

**b.** A triangle has side lengths that are 30 in. and 50 in. What are the possible lengths of the third side?

## CONCEPT SUMMARY Inequalities in One Triangle

**THEOREMS 5-9 AND 5-10**

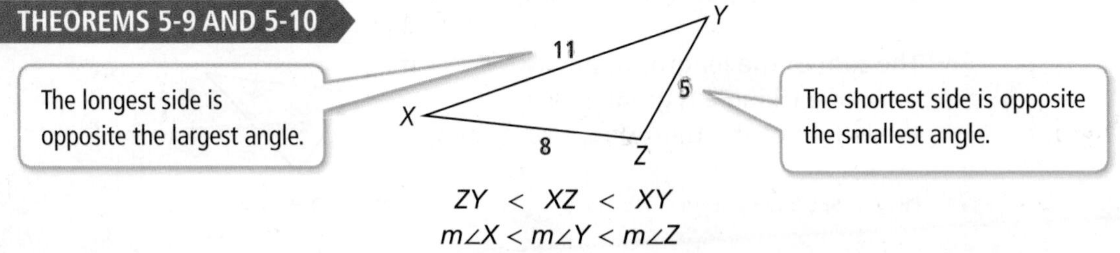


$ZY < XZ < XY$

$m\angle X < m\angle Y < m\angle Z$

**THEOREM 5-11** **Triangle Inequality Theorem**

The sum of the lengths of any two sides is greater than the length of the third side.

$5 + 8 > 11$
$5 + 11 > 8$
$8 + 11 > 5$

## Do You UNDERSTAND?

1. **ESSENTIAL QUESTION** What are some relationships between the sides and angles of any triangle?

2. **Reason** If a triangle has three different side lengths, what does that tell you about the measures of its angles?

3. **Error Analysis** Richard says that $\angle X$ must be the largest angle in $\triangle XYZ$. Explain his error.

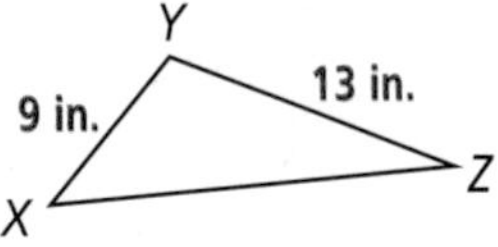


4. **Use Structure** An isosceles triangle has base angles that each measure 50. How could you determine whether *b* or *s* is greater?

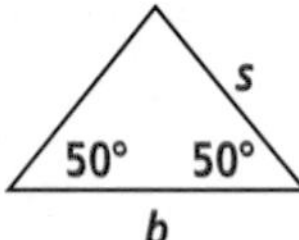


5. **Generalize** In $\triangle ABC$, $a < c < b$. List the angles in order from smallest to largest.

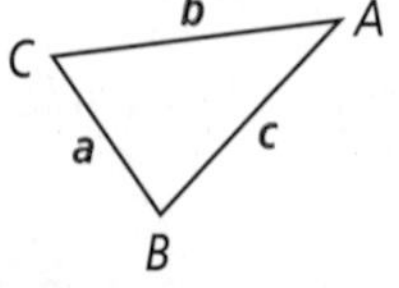


## Do You KNOW HOW?

**Identify the sides of $\triangle PQR$.**

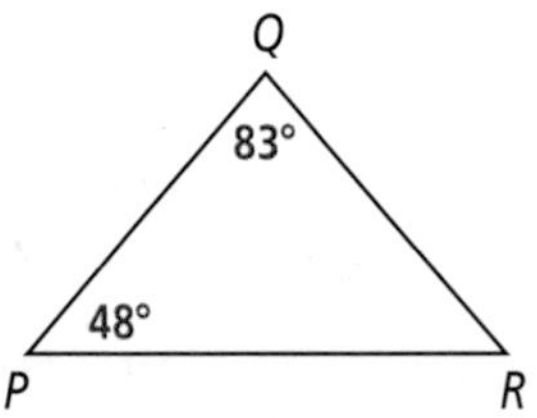


6. Which side is the longest?

7. Which side is the shortest?

**Determine whether each set of lengths could form a triangle.**

8. 5, 2, and 3

9. 55, 76, and 112

10. 102, 95, and 157

11. 17, 17, and 35

12. Kelsey is welding 3 metal rods to make a triangle. If the lengths of two of the rods are 15 in. and 22 in., what are the possible lengths of a third rod?

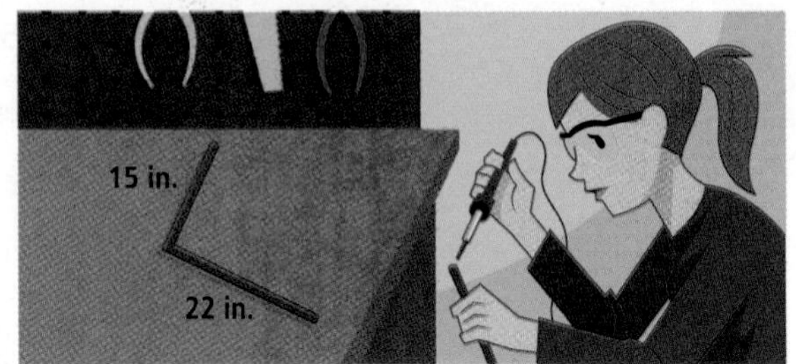

# PRACTICE & PROBLEM SOLVING

Scan for Multimedia    

Additional Exercises Available Online

## UNDERSTAND

**13. Construct Arguments** Fill in the missing reasons in the proof of Theorem 5-9. (Hint: The Comparison Property of Inequality states that if $a = b + c$ and $c > 0$, then $a > b$.)

**Given:** $AB > AC$, $\overline{AC} \cong \overline{AM}$

**Prove:** $m\angle ACB > m\angle B$

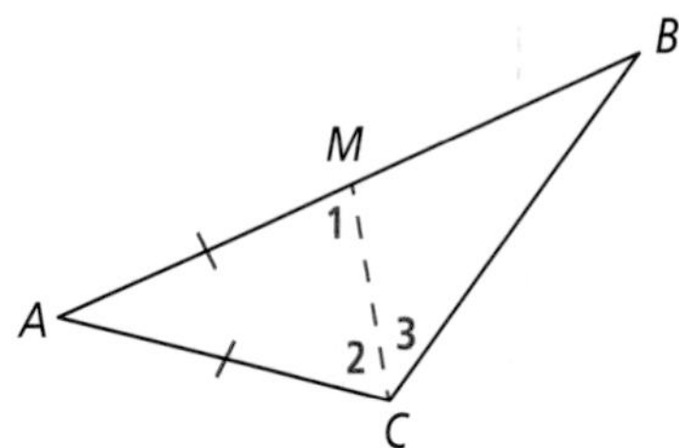


| Statements | Reasons |
|---|---|
| 1) $\overline{AC} \cong \overline{AM}$ | 1) Given |
| 2) $m\angle 1 = m\angle 2$ | 2) Isosc. Triangle Thm. |
| 3) $m\angle ACB = m\angle 2 + m\angle 3$ | 3) |
| 4) $m\angle ACB > m\angle 2$ | 4) |
| 5) $m\angle ACB > m\angle 1$ | 5) |
| 6) $m\angle 1 = m\angle B + m\angle 3$ | 6) Ext. Angles Thm. |
| 7) $m\angle 1 > m\angle B$ | 7) |
| 8) $m\angle ACB > m\angle B$ | 8) |

**14. Construct Arguments** Write a paragraph proof for Theorem 5-11. Use the figure shown and prove that $AB + CB > AC$.

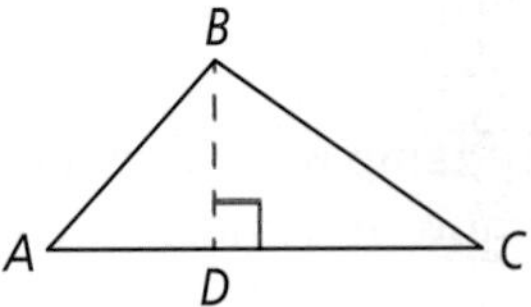


**15. Error Analysis** A student said that a triangle with side lengths of 3 ft and 4 ft could have a third side with a length of 7 ft. Explain why the student is incorrect. What is a correct statement about the third side of the triangle?

**16. Error Analysis** Tia says that $\angle Q$ must be the largest angle in $\triangle QRS$ because $150 > 70 > 1.7$. Explain Tia's error.

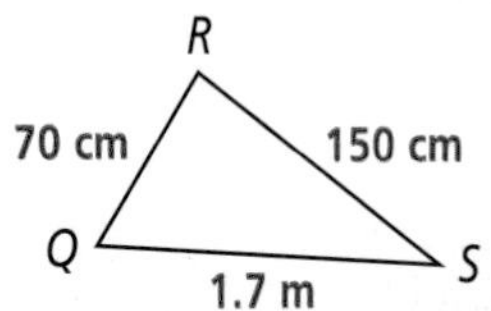


## PRACTICE

**17.** Which angle measure appears to be the smallest in $\triangle JKL$? What can you conclude about the side opposite that angle? SEE EXAMPLE 1.

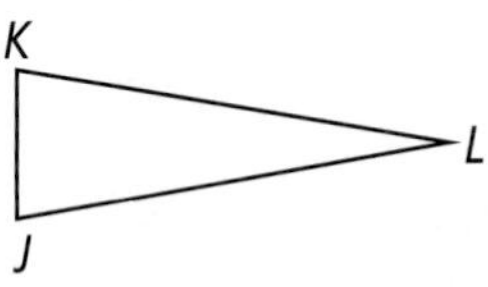


**Identify the angles of $\triangle FGH$.** SEE EXAMPLE 2.

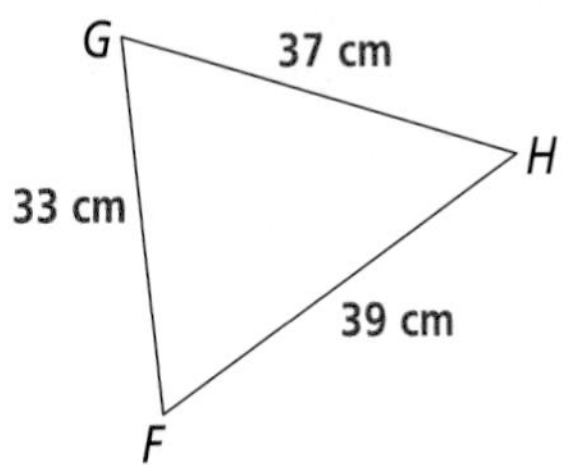


**18.** Which angle is the smallest?

**19.** Which angle is the largest?

**Identify the sides of $\triangle NOP$.** SEE EXAMPLES 3 AND 4.

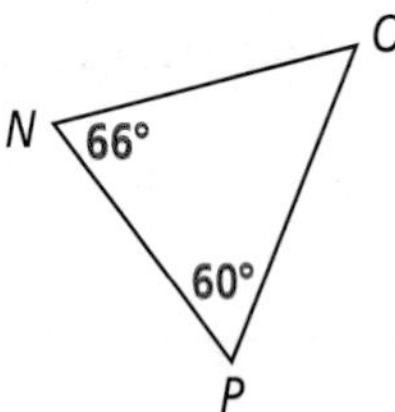


**20.** Which side is the longest?

**21.** Which side is the shortest?

**Determine whether the side lengths could form a triangle.** SEE EXAMPLE 5.

**22.** 13, 15, 9

**23.** 8, 15, 7

**24.** 35, 20, 11

**25.** 65, 32, 40

**Given two sides of a triangle, determine the range of possible lengths of the third side.** SEE EXAMPLE 5.

**26.** 10 in. and 12 in.

**27.** 5 ft and 10 ft

**28.** 200 m and 300 m

**29.** 90 km and 150 km

# PRACTICE & PROBLEM SOLVING

## APPLY

**30. Make Sense and Persevere** It took Ines 2 hours to bicycle the perimeter shown at a constant speed of 10 miles per hour. Which two roads form the largest angle?

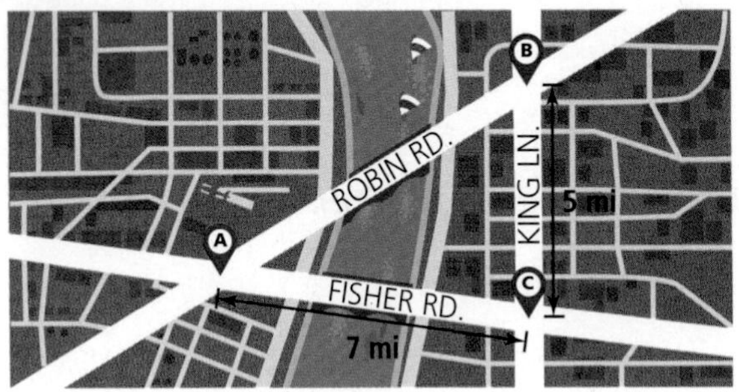


**31. Reason** A jewelry designer plans to make a triangular pendant out of gold wire. The wire costs $31.65 per centimeter. What is the possible range of costs for the wire?

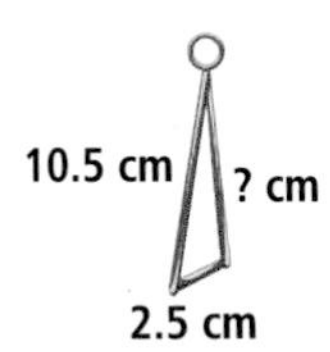


**32. Use Structure** A stage manager must use tape to outline a triangular platform on the set. Order the sides of the platform from longest to shortest.

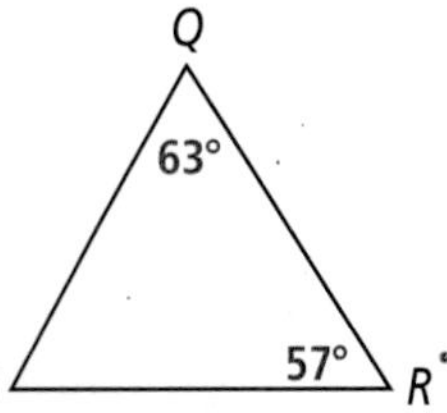


**33. Make Sense and Persevere** A dog running an agility course has difficulty making turns. The sharper the angle, the more difficult the turn. Which corner is most difficult for her to turn?

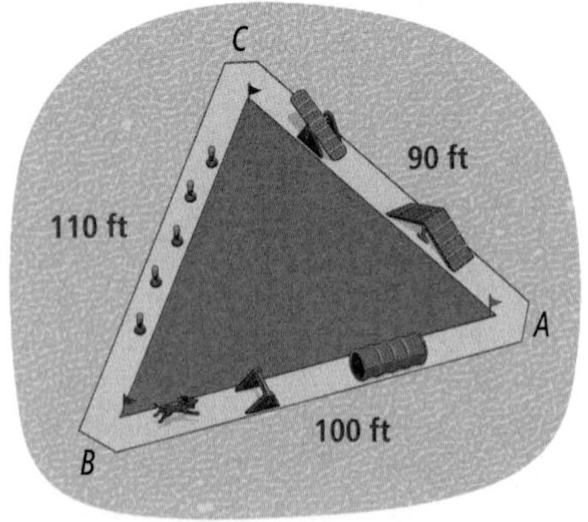


## ASSESSMENT PRACTICE

**34.** The lengths of two sides of a triangle are 13 and 20. What is the range of values for the length $x$ of the third side?

**35. SAT/ACT** Look at $\triangle RST$.

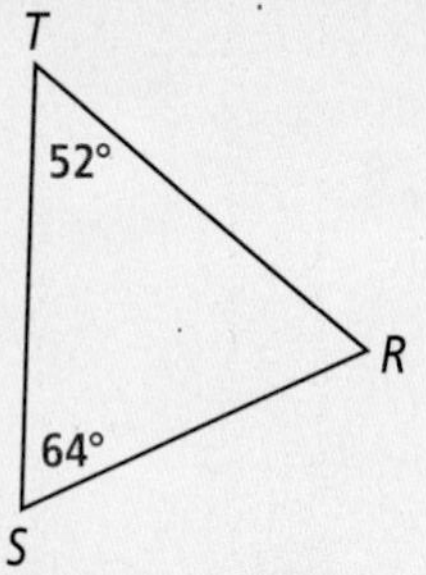


Which statement is false?

Ⓐ $TS = TR$

Ⓑ $m\angle STR < m\angle TRS$

Ⓒ $TR > SR$

Ⓓ $TS < SR$

Ⓔ $TS + TR > SR$

**36. Performance Task** Teo designed a skateboard ramp.

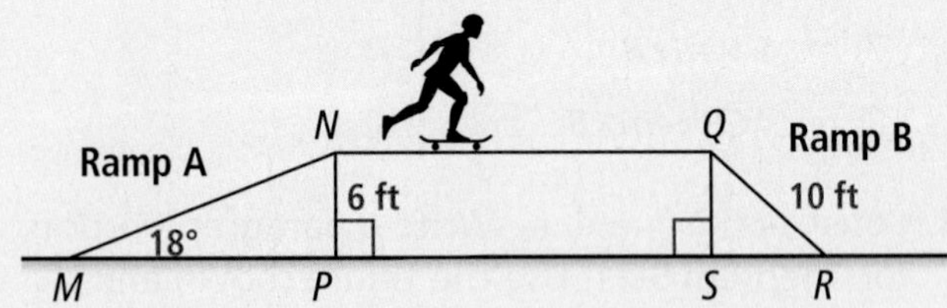


**Part A** List the sides of ramp A in order from shortest to longest.

**Part B** List the angles of ramp B from smallest to largest, and explain how you know.

**Part C** Ramp B cannot be steeper than 45°. Is it possible to build ramp B so that $\overline{SR}$ is shorter than 6 ft? Explain.

Activity Assess

# 5-5 Inequalities in Two Triangles

PearsonRealize.com

**I CAN...** compare a pair of sides of two triangles when the remaining pairs of sides are congruent.

## EXPLORE & REASON

**A woodworker uses a caliper to measure the widths of a bat to help him determine the widths for a new bat. The woodworker places the open tips of the caliper on the bat. The distance between the tips is a width of the bat.**

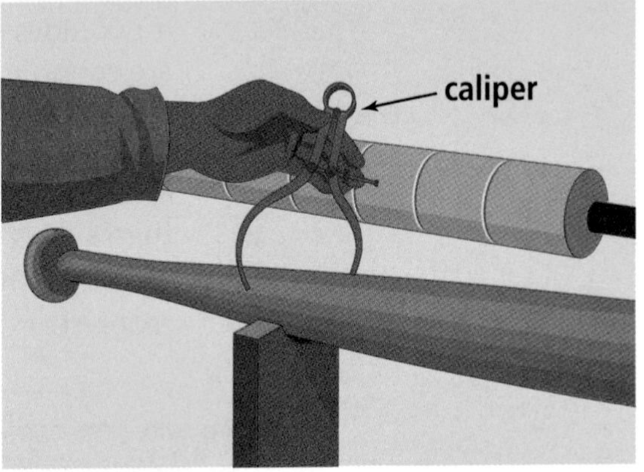


**A.** Suppose a caliper opens to an angle of 25° for one width of a bat and opens to an angle of 35° for another. What can you conclude about the widths of the bat?

**B. Look for Relationships** Next, suppose you use a caliper to measure the width of a narrow part of a bat and a wider part of the bat. What can you predict about the angle to which the caliper opens each time?

**ESSENTIAL QUESTION**

**When two triangles have two pairs of congruent sides, how are the third pair of sides and the pair of angles opposite the third pair of sides related?**

CONCEPTUAL UNDERSTANDING

## EXAMPLE 1 Investigate Side Lengths in Triangles

**As a rider pedals a unicycle, how do $\angle A$ and length $b$ change? What does this suggest about the change in the triangle?**

**LOOK FOR RELATIONSHIPS**
Consider how multiple diagrams are used to show the relationship between moving parts. What changes and what remains the same between diagrams?

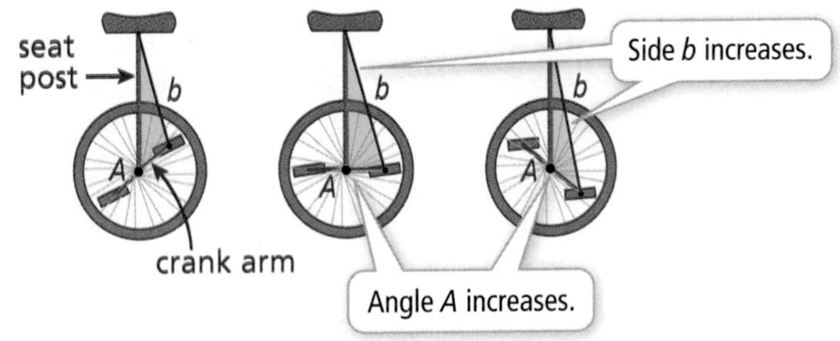


If two sides of a triangle stay the same, but the measure of the angle between them increases, the length of the third side also increases.

**Try It!** 1. Compare $\angle J$ and side length $k$ for the triangles.

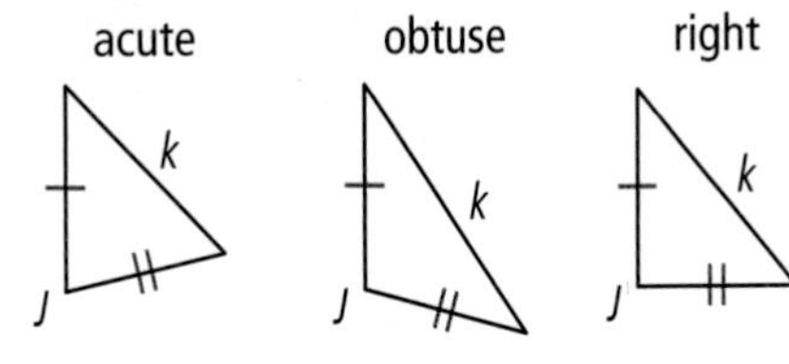

## THEOREM 5-12 Hinge Theorem

If two sides of one triangle are congruent to two sides of another triangle, and the included angles are not congruent, then the longer third side is opposite the larger included angle.

PROOF: SEE EXERCISE 9.

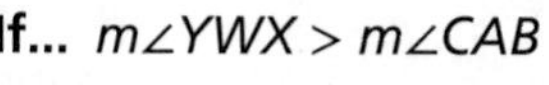

**If...** $m\angle YWX > m\angle CAB$

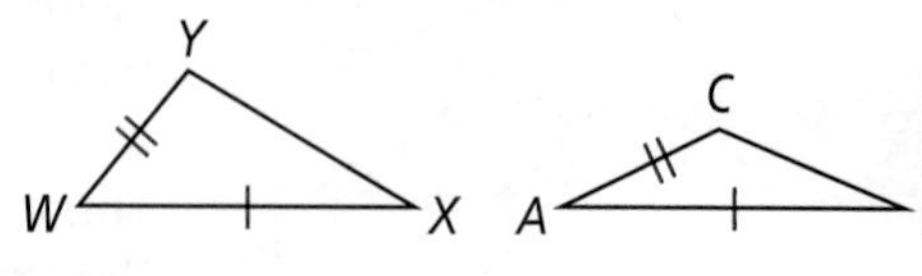

**Then...** $XY > BC$

APPLICATION

## EXAMPLE 2 Apply the Hinge Theorem

**The tension in the exercise band varies proportionally with the stretch distance. The tension *T* is described by the function $T(x) = kx$, where *k* is a constant that depends on the elasticity of the band and *x* is the stretch distance. Which position shown in the figures has a greater tension in the band?**

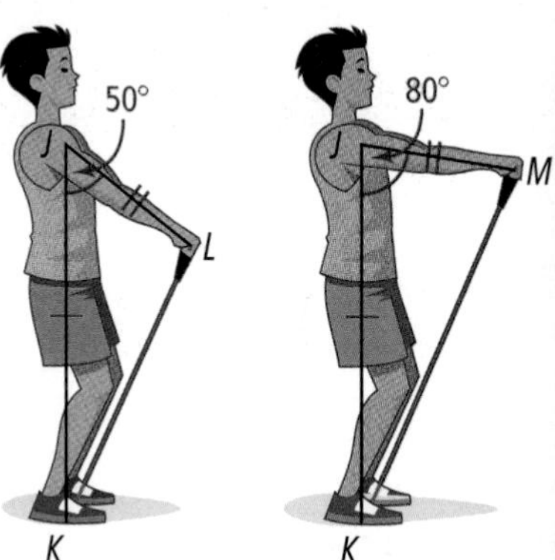


**Formulate** Model each figure with a triangle.

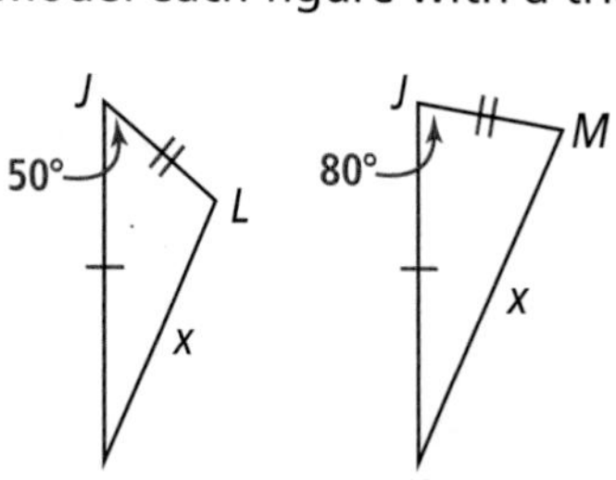


**Compute** $T(LK)$ is the tension when the angle is 50°, and $T(MK)$ is the tension when the angle is 80°. Since $m\angle MJK > m\angle LJK$, apply the Hinge Theorem.

$$MK > LK$$

$$\frac{T(MK)}{k} > \frac{T(LK)}{k}$$

Since the tension *T* is equal to the product of *k* and the stretch distance, we can substitute $\frac{T}{k}$ for each distance.

$$T(MK) > T(LK)$$

**Interpret** A larger angle corresponds to a larger distance from the man's hands to his feet. The larger distance corresponds to a higher tension.

The tension is greater when the man pulls higher on the tension band.

## Try It!

2. Suppose the distance the tension band is stretched does not change. Instead, the man bends his knees. How does $\angle L$ change as $JK$ changes?

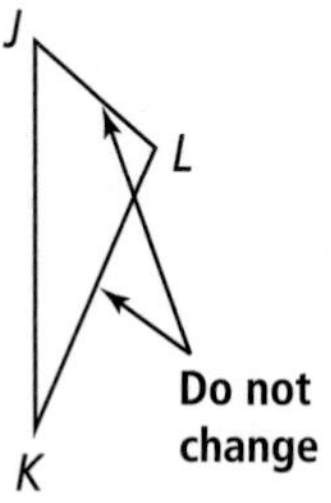

## THEOREM 5-13 Converse of the Hinge Theorem

If two sides of one triangle are congruent to two sides of another triangle, and the third sides are not congruent, then the larger included angle is opposite the longer third side.

**PROOF: SEE EXAMPLE 3.**

**If...** $EF > UV$

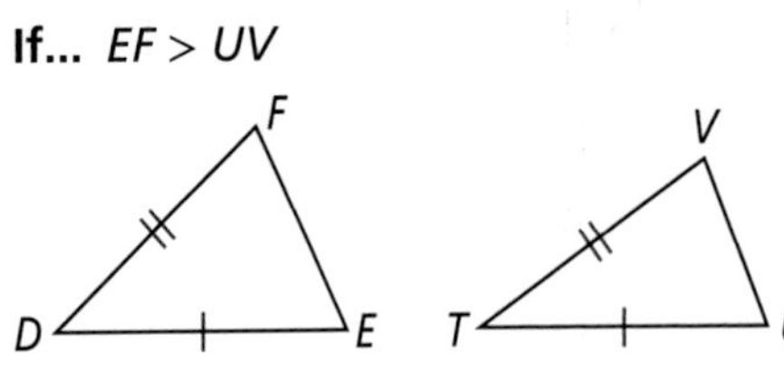


**Then...** $m\angle D > m\angle T$

## EXAMPLE 3 Prove the Converse of the Hinge Theorem

**Use indirect reasoning to prove the Converse of the Hinge Theorem. Assume that $m\angle FDE \not> m\angle VTU$. This means $m\angle FDE = m\angle VTU$ or $m\angle FDE < m\angle VTU$.**

**Given:** $\overline{DF} \cong \overline{TV}$; $\overline{DE} \cong \overline{TU}$; $EF > UV$

**Prove:** $m\angle FDE > m\angle VTU$

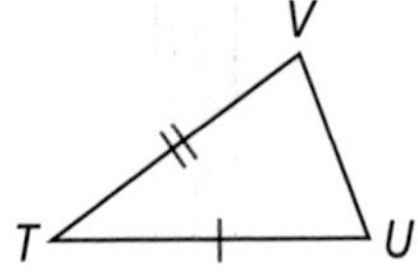


**STUDY TIP**
If you get stuck when writing a proof, make a list of things you know and what you want to prove.

First show that assuming $m\angle FDE = m\angle VTU$ leads to a contradiction of the given statement, $EF > UV$.

Assuming that $m\angle FDE = m\angle VTU$, $\angle FDE \cong \angle VTU$. Applying SAS, $\triangle DEF \cong \triangle TUV$, so by CPCTC, $\overline{EF} \cong \overline{UV}$ and $EF = UV$. But, this contradicts $EF > UV$.

**Try It!** **3.** To complete the proof of the Hinge Theorem, show that assuming $m\angle FDE < m\angle VTU$ leads to a contradiction of the given statement, $EF > UV$.

## EXAMPLE 4 Apply the Converse of the Hinge Theorem

**What are the possible values of $x$?**

Since $FG < CD$ and $CD < AB$, apply the Converse of the Hinge Theorem.

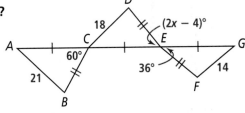

**COMMON ERROR**
Be careful to use the correct inequality sign when comparing triangles. After you write the inequality, check a second time to be sure it indicates that the larger angle is opposite the longer side.

$$m\angle FEG < m\angle CED < m\angle ACB$$
$$36 < 2x - 4 < 60$$
$$40 < 2x < 64$$
$$20 < x < 32$$

Use the Converse of the Hinge Theorem.

The possible values for $x$ are between 20 and 32.

**Try It!** **4.** What are the possible values of $x$ for each diagram?

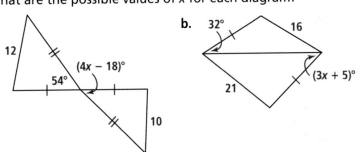

**a.**

**b.**

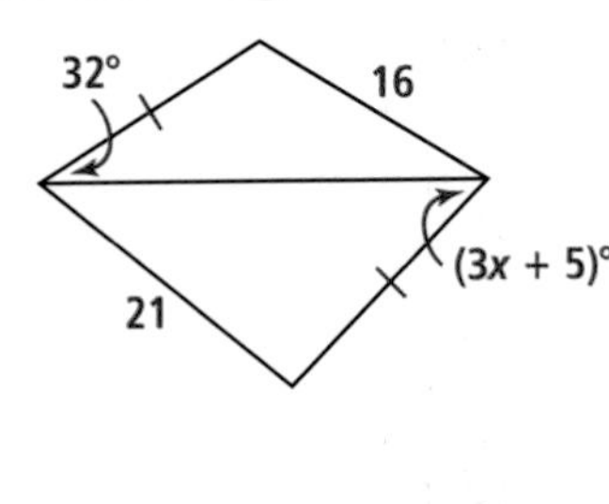

Concept Summary

Assess

## CONCEPT SUMMARY Inequalities in Two Triangles

**THEOREM 5-12** **Hinge Theorem**

**If...** $\overline{WX} \cong \overline{AB}$, $\overline{WY} \cong \overline{AC}$, and $m\angle W > m\angle A$

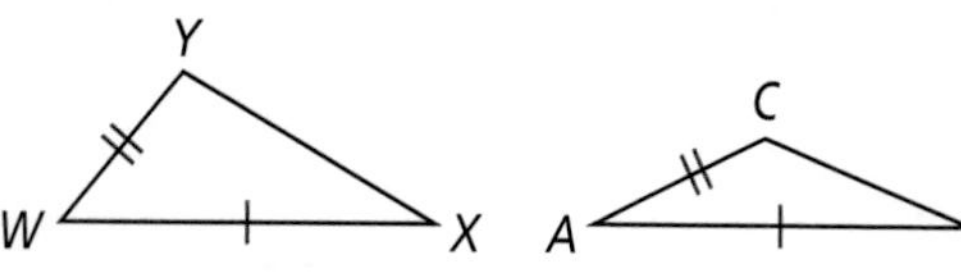


**Then...** $XY > BC$

**THEOREM 5-13** **Converse of the Hinge Theorem**

**If...** $\overline{DF} \cong \overline{TV}$, $\overline{DE} \cong \overline{TU}$, and $EF > UV$

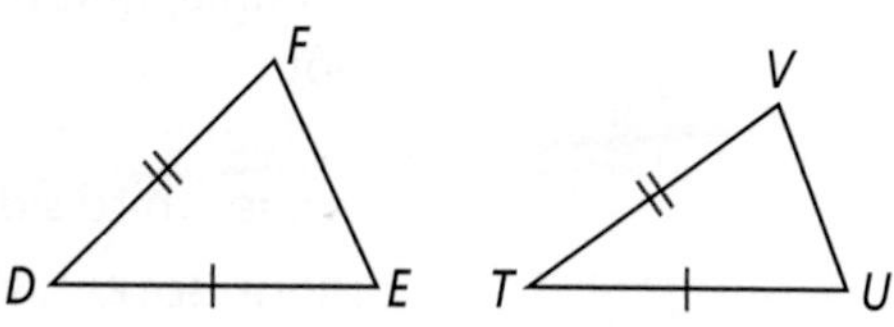


**Then...** $m\angle D > m\angle T$

## Do You UNDERSTAND?

1. **ESSENTIAL QUESTION** When two triangles have two pairs of congruent sides, how are the third pair of sides and the pair of angles opposite the third pair of sides related?

2. **Error Analysis** Venetta applies the Converse of the Hinge Theorem to conclude that $m\angle EKF > m\angle HKG$ for the triangles shown. Is Venetta correct? Explain your answer.

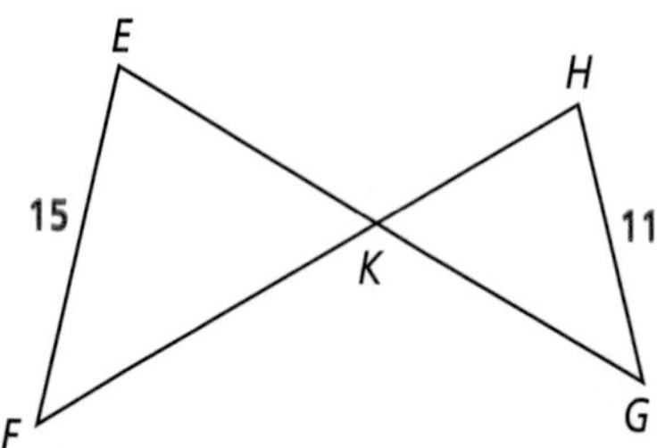


3. **Reason** Why must the angles described in the Hinge Theorem be between the congruent pairs of sides?

4. **Communicate Precisely** The Hinge Theorem is also known as the Side-Angle-Side Inequality Theorem or SAS Inequality Theorem. How are the requirements for applying the Hinge Theorem similar to the requirements for applying SAS? How are the requirements different?

## Do You KNOW HOW?

5. Order *AB*, *BC*, and *CD* from least to greatest.

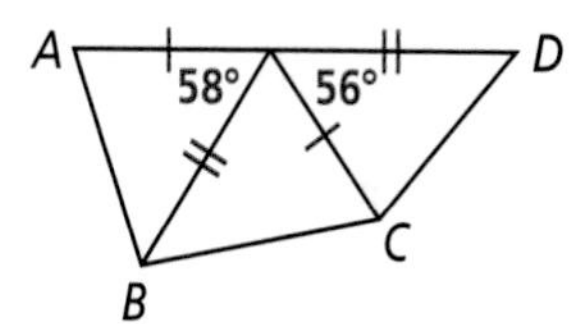


6. Order $\angle PTU$, $\angle SQT$, and $\angle QSR$ from least to greatest.

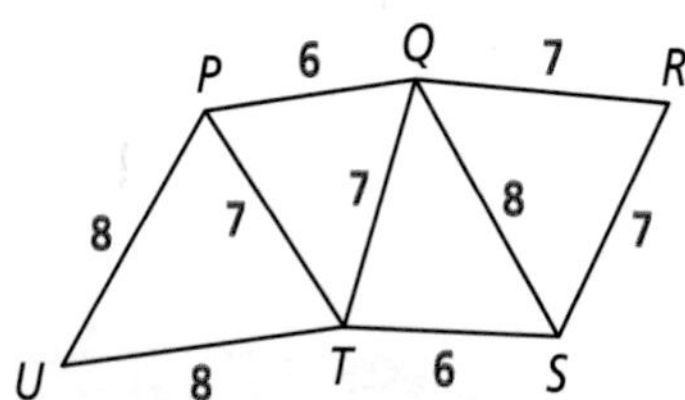


7. Kayak A and kayak B leave a dock as shown. Which kayak is closer to the dock?

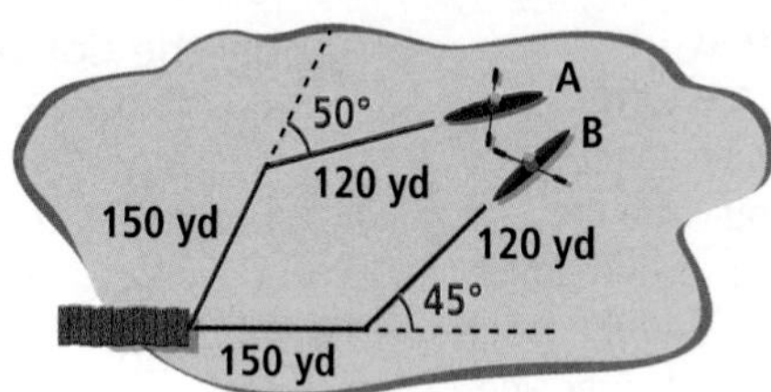

## UNDERSTAND

**8. Error Analysis** Tonya has the scissors shown.

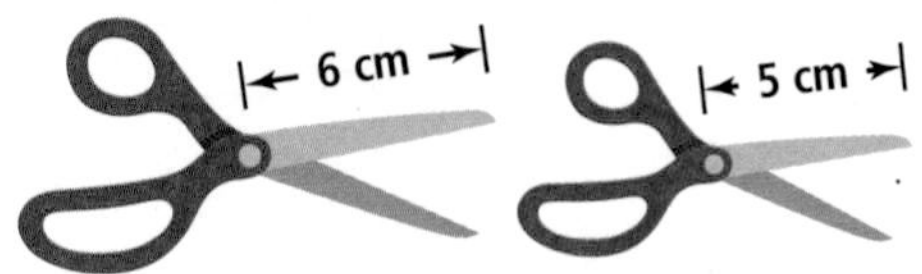


Tonya writes the following description of how she will use the Hinge Theorem with the scissors.

> If you open the right pair of scissors to an angle of 30° and open the left pair of scissors to an angle of 45°, then by the Hinge Theorem, the distance between the blade tips of the left pair of scissors will be larger. ✗

What is the mistake in her use of the Hinge Theorem?

**9. Construct Arguments** Write a paragraph proof of the Hinge Theorem.

**Given:** $\overline{WX} \cong \overline{AB}$, $\overline{WY} \cong \overline{AC}$, $m\angle W > m\angle A$

**Prove:** $XY > BC$

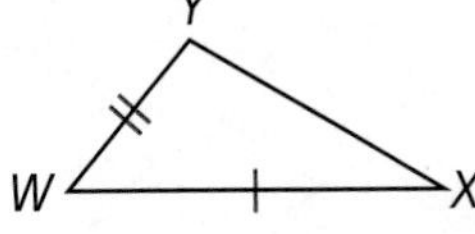


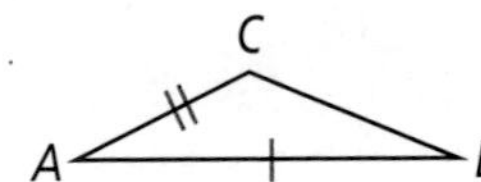


Use the following outline.

- Find a point $D$ outside $\triangle ABC$ so $\overline{AD} \cong \overline{WY}$ and $\angle DAB \cong \angle YWX$.
- Show that $\triangle WXY \cong \triangle ABD$.
- Construct the angle bisector of $\angle CAD$. Let point $E$ be the point where the angle bisector intersects $\overline{BD}$.

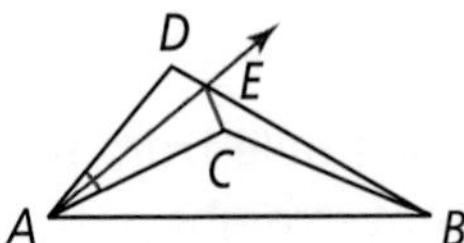


- Show that $\triangle ACE \cong \triangle ADE$ so $\overline{CE} \cong \overline{DE}$.
- Show that $DB = CE + EB$.
- Use the Triangle Inequality Theorem on $\triangle BCE$.

## PRACTICE

**10.** Write an inequality describing the range of $x$ for each pair of triangles. SEE EXAMPLES 1 AND 2.

**a.**

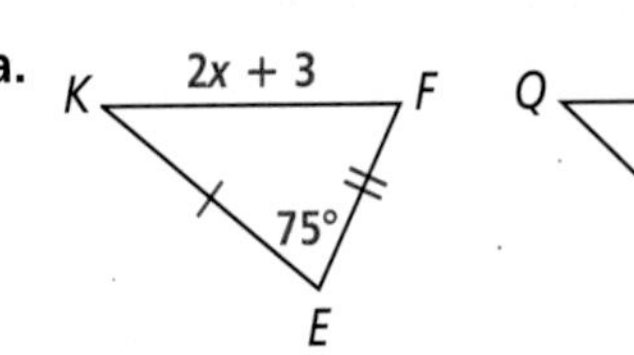


**b.**

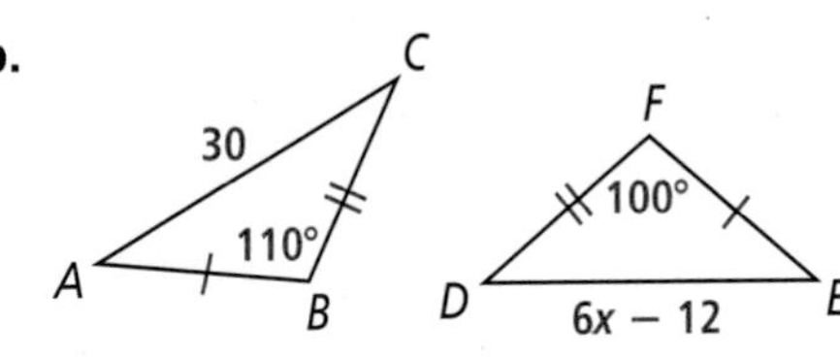


**11.** Write an inequality describing the possible values of $x$ for each pair of triangles.
SEE EXAMPLES 3 AND 4.

**a.**

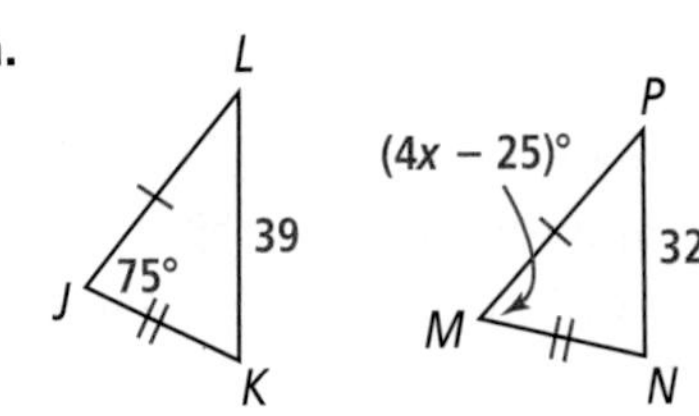


**b.**

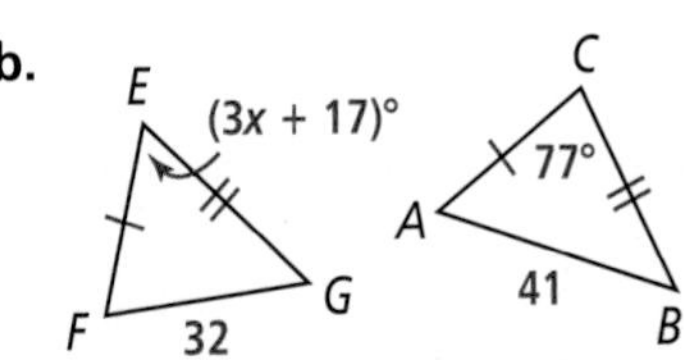


**12.** Write an inequality describing the possible values of $x$ for each diagram.

**a.**

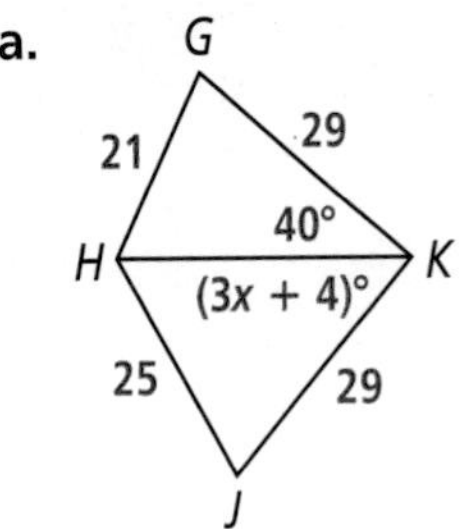


**b.**

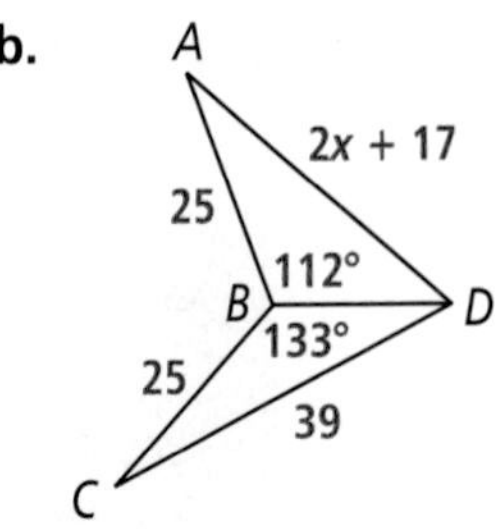

# PRACTICE & PROBLEM SOLVING

## APPLY

13. **Reason** Airplane A flies 300 miles due east of an airport and then flies 200 miles at 15° north of east. Airplane B flies 200 miles due north and then flies 300 miles at 20° west of north. Which airplane is closer to the airport? Explain how you know.

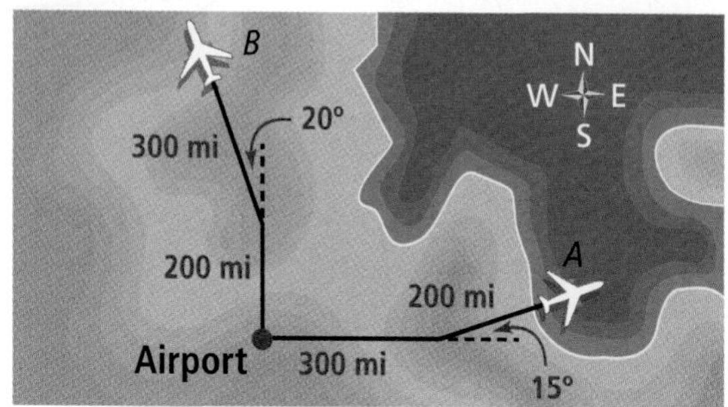


14. **Model With Mathematics** According to the Hinge Theorem, is the distance between the tips of the hands greater at 4:00 or at 7:00? Explain how the distance changes throughout a day.

15. **Mathematical Connections** Determine the shortest path from start to finish on the obstacle course.

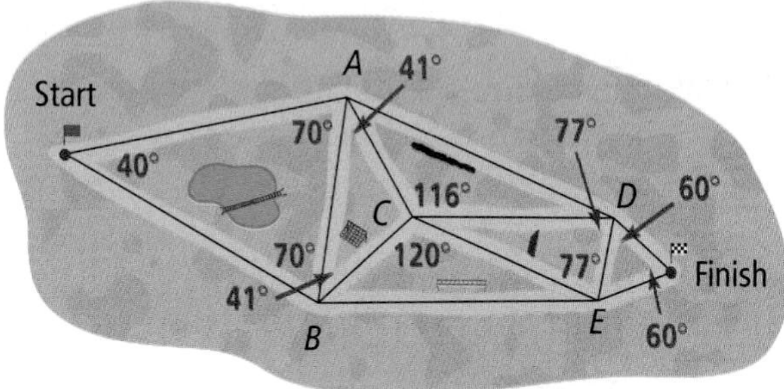


16. **Higher Order Thinking** When $m\angle 1 = 75$, $d = 43$ in., and when $m\angle 1 = 100$, $d = 54$ in. Neil wants to know how wide a sofa he can buy if he can open the door at most 85°. Using the Hinge Theorem or the Converse of the Hinge Theorem, can you determine the exact value of $d$ when $m\angle 1 = 85$? If you can, explain the method. If not, explain what you can determine about the distance.

## ASSESSMENT PRACTICE

17. Which of the following can you conclude from the diagram? Select all that apply.

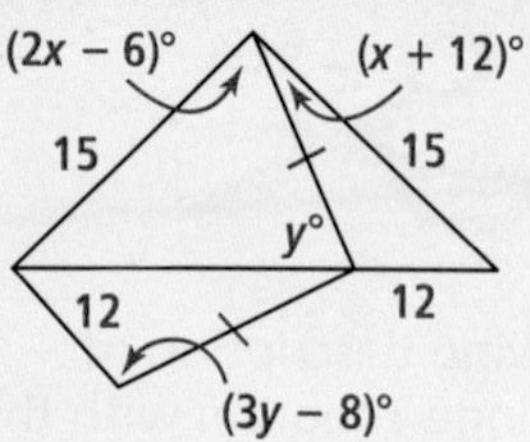


Ⓐ $x < 24$

Ⓑ $x > 18$

Ⓒ $y < 12$

Ⓓ $y > 4$

18. **SAT/ACT** Which of the following can you conclude from the diagram?

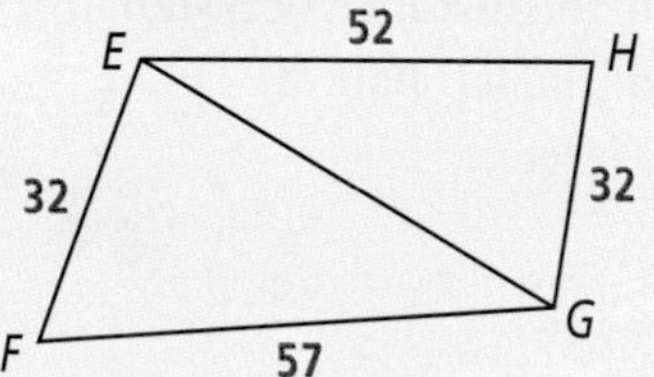


Ⓐ $m\angle EFG = m\angle GHE$

Ⓑ $m\angle FGE = m\angle HEG$

Ⓒ $m\angle GEF > m\angle EGH$

Ⓓ $m\angle FGE > m\angle EGH$

19. **Performance Task** Abby, Danielle, and Jacy walk from their campsite to get to the lake. The lake is located 3 miles away in the direction of 40° north of west.

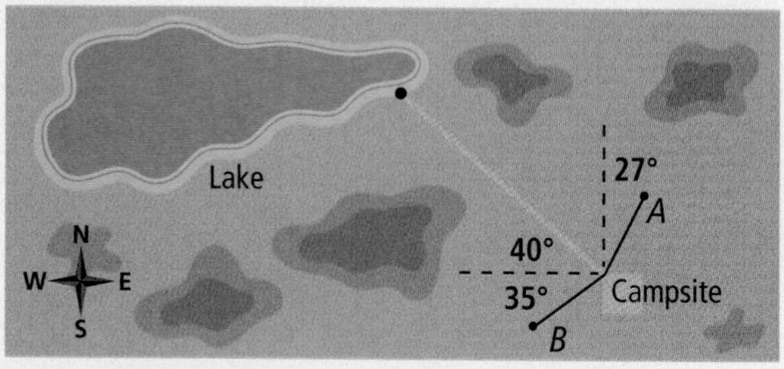


**Part A** Abby walks along a straight path in the direction of 27° east of north for 1 mile to point $A$. Using the Hinge Theorem, if Danielle walks along a straight path in the direction of 35° south of west for 1 mile to point $B$, who is closer to the lake?

**Part B** Jacy also walks for 1 mile from the campsite along a different straight path than Abby. Her straight-line distance to the lake is shorter than Abby's distance. What directions could Jacy have taken?

TOPIC 5

# Topic Review

## TOPIC ESSENTIAL QUESTION

1. How are the sides, segments, and angles of triangles related?

## Vocabulary Review

**Choose the correct term to complete each sentence.**

2. The ________ is the point of concurrency of the angle bisectors of a triangle.
3. Three or more lines that intersect at one point are ________.
4. The point of concurrency of the altitudes of a triangle is the ________.
5. A perpendicular segment from a vertex to the line containing the side opposite the vertex is a(n) ________ of a triangle.
6. A point that is the same distance from two points is ________ from the points.
7. A(n) ________ of a triangle has endpoints at a vertex and at the midpoint of the side opposite the vertex.

- altitude
- centroid
- circumcenter
- concurrent
- equidistant
- incenter
- median
- orthocenter

## Concepts & Skills Review

### LESSON 5-1 Perpendicular and Angle Bisectors

#### Quick Review

Perpendicular bisectors and angle bisectors are related to the segments or angles they bisect:

- Any point on the perpendicular bisector of a segment is **equidistant** from the endpoints of the segment.
- Any point on the bisector of an angle is equidistant from the two sides of the angle.

#### Example

**Find *AB*.**

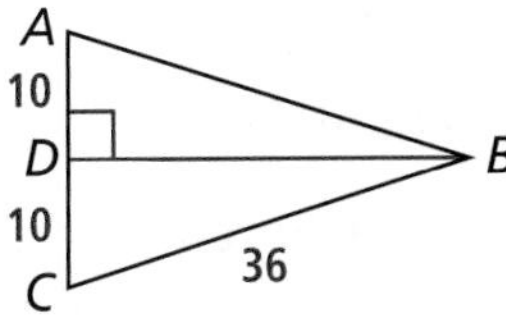


*DB* is the perpendicular bisector of $\overline{AC}$, so $AB = CB$. $AB = 36$.

#### Practice & Problem Solving

**Use the given values to find each unknown.**

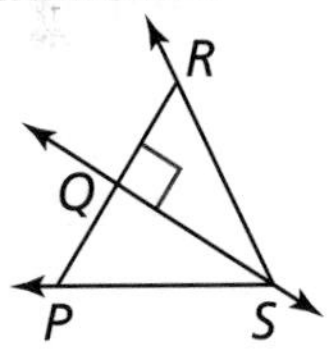


8. If $PS = 36$, $PQ = 3x + 5$, $QR = 6x - 10$, and $RS = 36$, then $PR = ■$.

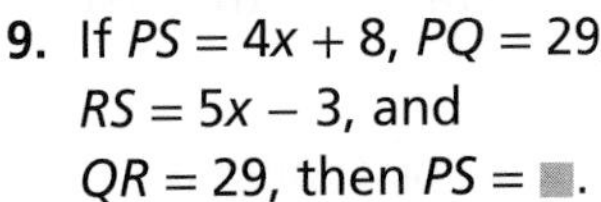

9. If $PS = 4x + 8$, $PQ = 29$, $RS = 5x - 3$, and $QR = 29$, then $PS = ■$.

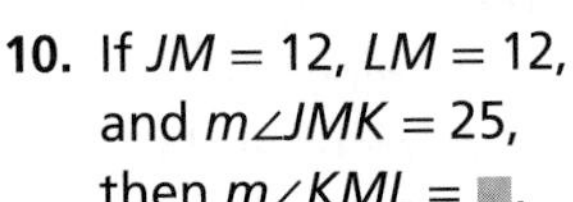

10. If $JM = 12$, $LM = 12$, and $m\angle JMK = 25$, then $m\angle KML = ■$.

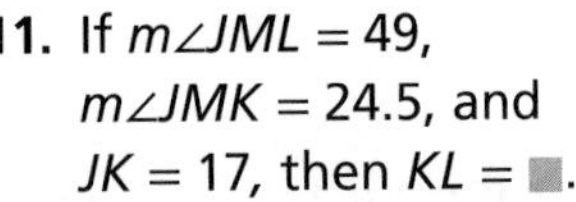

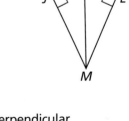

11. If $m\angle JML = 49$, $m\angle JMK = 24.5$, and $JK = 17$, then $KL = ■$.

12. **Reason** A point on a perpendicular bisector is 7 cm from each endpoint of the bisected segment and 5 cm from the point of intersection. What is the length of the segment?

## LESSON 5-2 Bisectors in Triangles

### Quick Review

The perpendicular bisectors of a triangle are concurrent at the point equidistant from the vertices of the triangle. This point is called the **circumcenter**.

The angle bisectors of a triangle are concurrent at a point equidistant from the sides of the triangle. This point is called the **incenter**.

### Example

**For $\triangle ABC$, what is the radius of the inscribed circle?**

$DF = EF$

$3x = 2x + 16$

$x = 16$

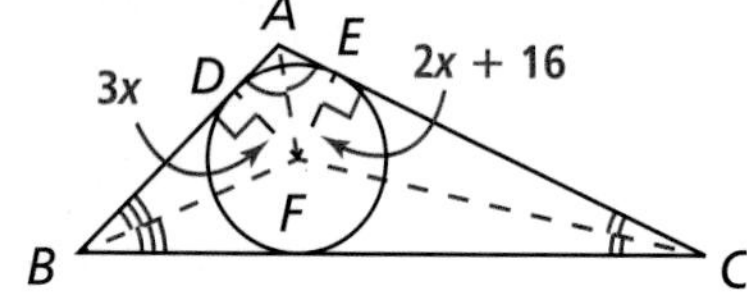


The radius is $DF = 3x = 3(16) = 48$.

### Practice & Problem Solving

**Identify each point of concurrency.**

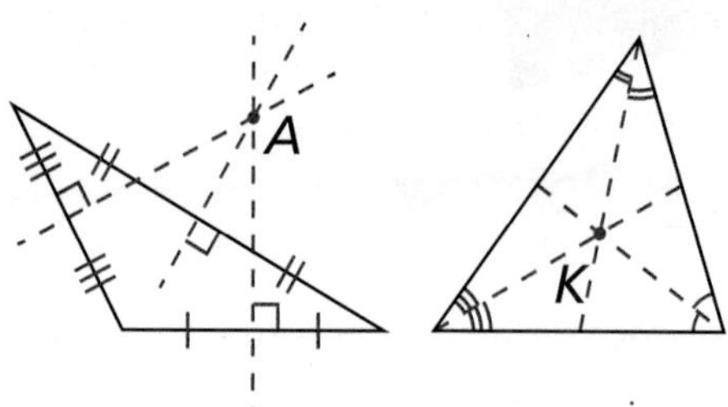


13. incenter

14. circumcenter

**Use the diagram to find each unknown quantity.**

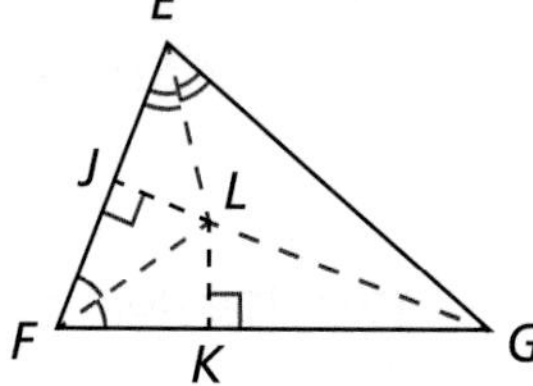


15. If $m\angle GFL = 34$, and $m\angle GEL = 36$, what is $m\angle FGL$?

16. If $JL = 5$, what is the measure of $KL$?

17. **Reason** The circumcenter of a triangle is on one side of the triangle. Explain how to find the area of the circumscribed circle of the triangle given the lengths of the sides.

## LESSON 5-3 Medians and Altitudes

### Quick Review

A **median** of a triangle is a line segment from the midpoint of one side to the opposite vertex. The medians of a triangle are concurrent at the **centroid**. The distance from a vertex to the centroid is two-thirds the distance of the median from that vertex.

An **altitude** of a triangle is a line segment perpendicular to one side and ending at the opposite vertex. The lines containing the altitudes of a triangle are concurrent at the **orthocenter**.

### Example

**$Q$ is the centroid of $\triangle XYZ$. If $DZ = 24$, what is $QZ$?**

$QZ = \frac{2}{3} DZ$

$QZ = \frac{2}{3}(24)$

$QZ = 16$

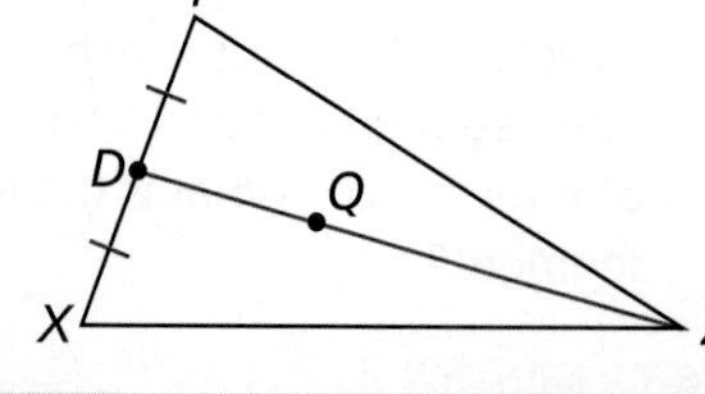


### Practice & Problem Solving

**Identify each segment type.**

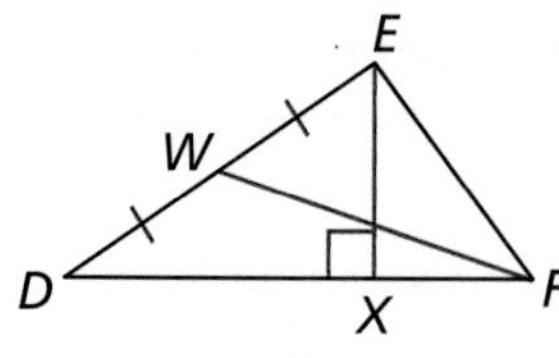


18. median

19. altitude

**Find the orthocenter of each triangle with the given set of vertices.**

20. (2, 0), (2, 12), (8, 6)

21. (7, 8), (9, 6), (5, 4)

22. **Reason** The orthocenter of $\triangle ABC$ is point $B$. What is the measure of $\angle ABC$?

23. A plastic triangle is suspended parallel to the ground by a string attached at the centroid. Copy the triangle and show where the string should be attached.

## LESSON 5-4 Inequalities in One Triangle

### Quick Review

In a triangle, if two sides are not congruent, then the larger angle is opposite the longer side. If two angles are not congruent, then the longer side is opposite the larger angle.

$XY > XZ > YZ$

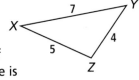

$m\angle Z > m\angle Y > m\angle X$

The sum of the lengths of any two sides of a triangle is greater than the length of the third side.

$4 + 5 > 7 \quad 4 + 7 > 5 \quad 5 + 7 > 4$

### Example

**Which side of $\triangle TUV$ is the longest?**

$m\angle T + m\angle U + m\angle V = 180$

$52 + 71 + m\angle V = 180$

$m\angle V = 57$

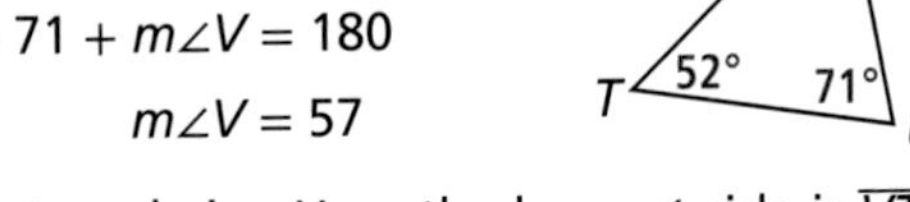

The largest angle is $\angle U$, so the longest side is $\overline{VT}$.

### Practice & Problem Solving

**Determine if the lengths can form a triangle.**

**24.** 14, 32, 18

**25.** 14, 25, 29

**26.** 37, 22, 56

**27.** 87, 35, 41

**Use the figure for Exercises 28 and 29.**

**28.** Which angle has the least measure?

**29.** Which angle has the greatest measure?

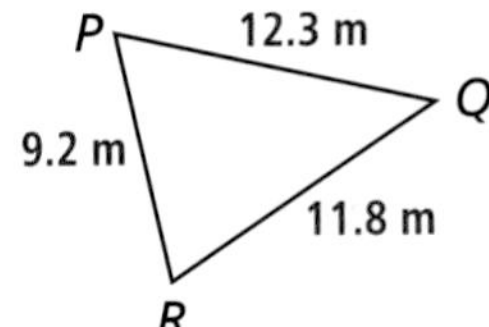


**30. Use Structure** Why must the sum of two sides of a triangle be greater than the third side?

**31. Reason** Two sides of a triangular garden are 6.4 m and 8.2 m. The gardener buys fencing for \$29.25 per meter. What is the range of total cost of the fencing?

## LESSON 5-5 Inequalities in Two Triangles

### Quick Review

The Hinge Theorem states that if two triangles have two congruent sides, and the included angles are not congruent, then the longer third side is opposite the larger included angle.

### Example

**Order *AC*, *DF*, and *GJ* from greatest to least.**

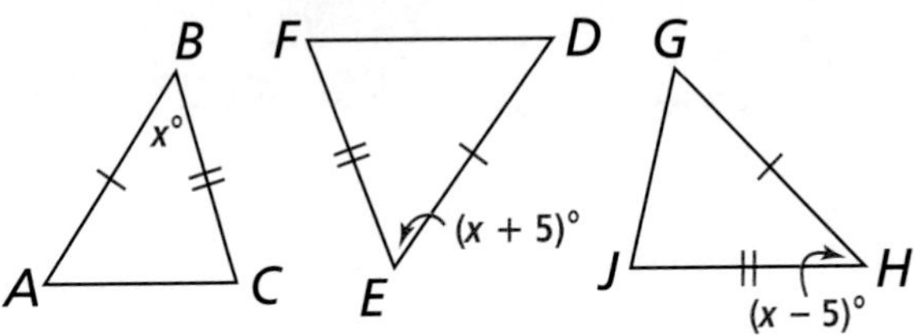


The triangles have two congruent sides.

$\overline{AB} \cong \overline{DE} \cong \overline{GH}$ and $\overline{BC} \cong \overline{EF} \cong \overline{HJ}$

The included angles are not congruent.

$(x + 5)° > x > (x - 5)°$

Therefore, $DF > AC > GJ$.

### Practice & Problem Solving

**32.** Write an inequality for the possible values of *x*.

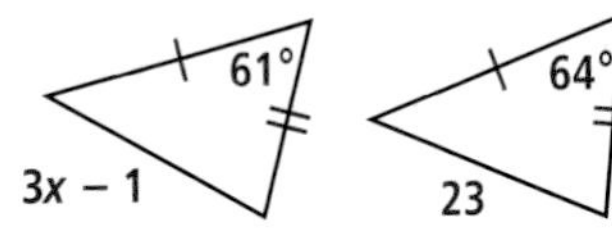


**33.** Write an inequality for the possible values of *x*.

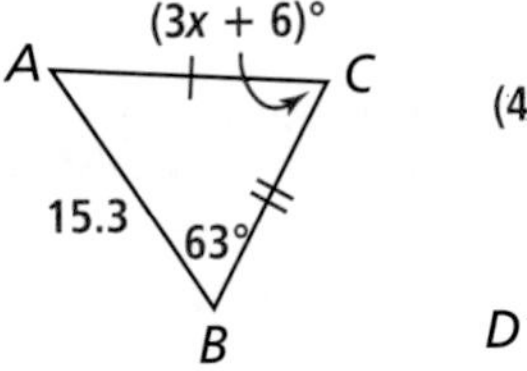


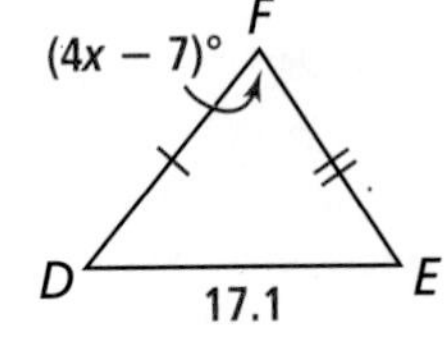


**34. Construct Arguments** Cameron incorrectly says the Converse of the Hinge Theorem proves that $m\angle S < m\angle W$. Explain his error.

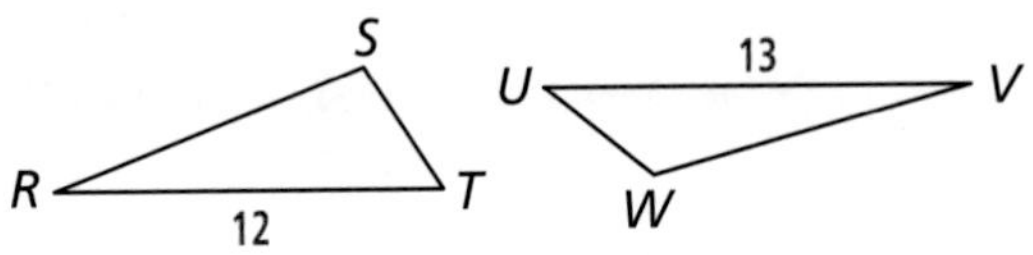


TOPIC 5 REVIEW

TOPIC 6

# Quadrilaterals and Other Polygons

## TOPIC ESSENTIAL QUESTION

**How are properties of parallelograms used to solve problems and to classify quadrilaterals?**

## Topic Overview

**enVision™ STEM Project:**
Design a Quadrilateral Lift

**6-1** The Polygon Angle-Sum Theorems

**Mathematical Modeling in 3 Acts:**
The Mystery Sides

**6-2** Kites and Trapezoids

**6-3** Properties of Parallelograms

**6-4** Proving a Quadrilateral Is a Parallelogram

**6-5** Properties of Special Parallelograms

**6-6** Conditions of Special Parallelograms

## Topic Vocabulary

- midsegment of a trapezoid

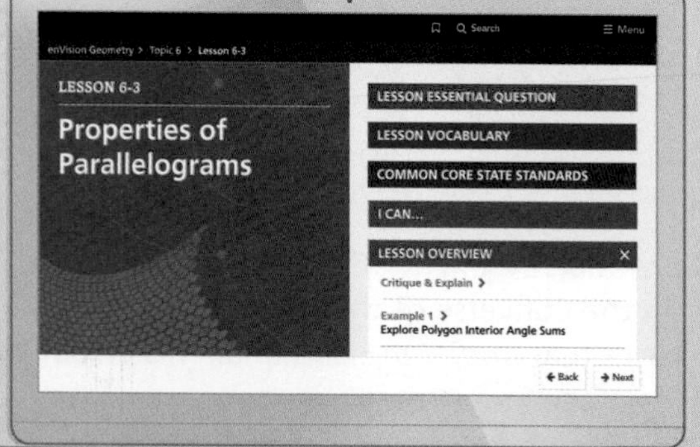

Go online | **PearsonRealize.com**

## Digital Experience

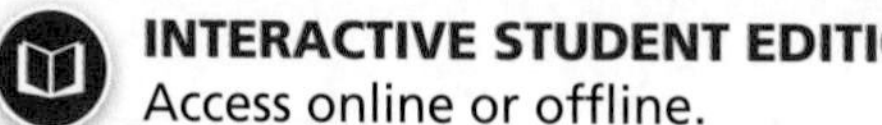

**INTERACTIVE STUDENT EDITION** Access online or offline.

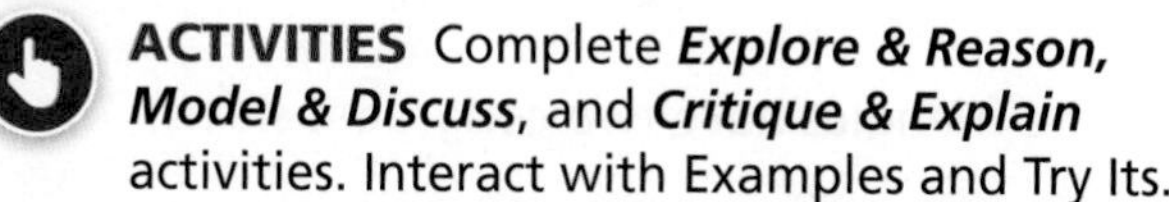

**ACTIVITIES** Complete ***Explore & Reason, Model & Discuss***, and ***Critique & Explain*** activities. Interact with Examples and Try Its.

**ANIMATION** View and interact with real-world applications.

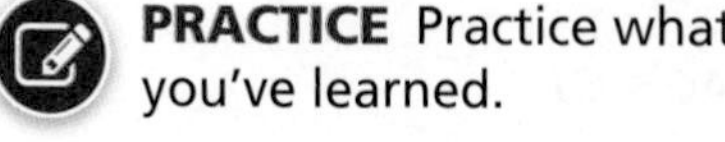

**PRACTICE** Practice what you've learned.

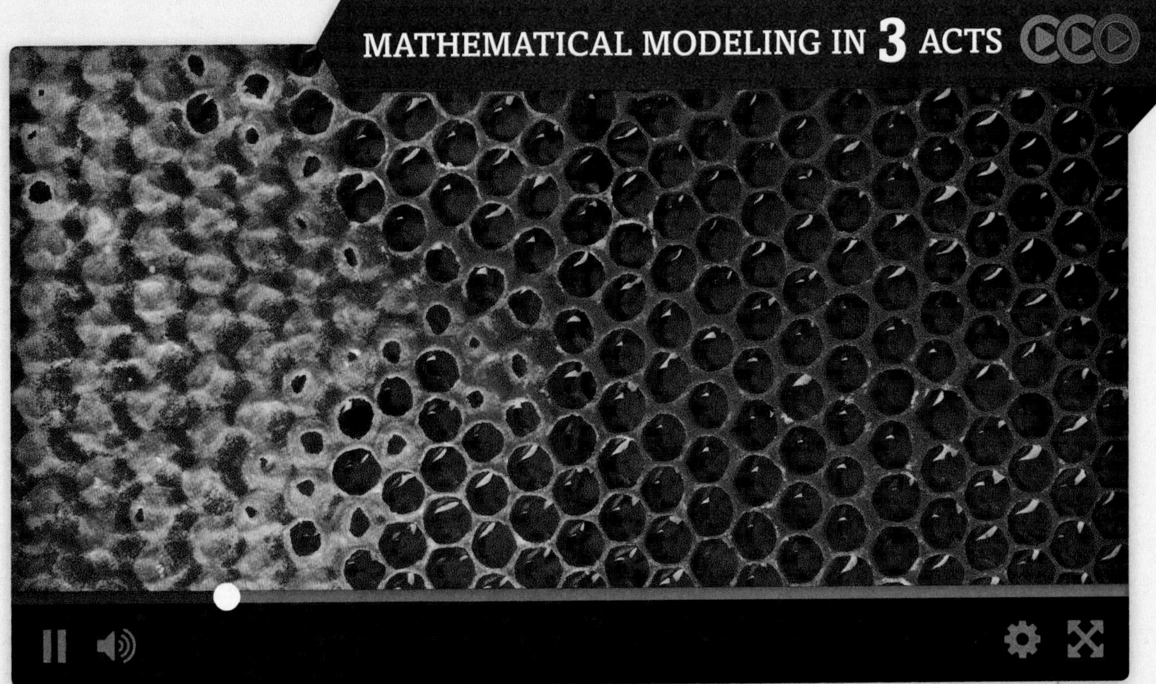


## The Mystery Sides

Have you ever looked closely at honeycombs? What shape are they? How do you know? Most often the cells in the honeycombs look like hexagons, but they might also look like circles. Scientists now believe that the bees make circular cells that become hexagonal due to the bees' body heat and natural physical forces.

What are some strategies you use to identify shapes? Think about this during the Mathematical Modeling in 3 Acts lesson.

TOPIC 6

**VIDEOS** Watch clips to support ***Mathematical Modeling in 3 Acts Lessons*** and **enVision™ *STEM Projects.***

**CONCEPT SUMMARY** Review key lesson content through multiple representations.

**ASSESSMENT** Show what you've learned.

**GLOSSARY** Read and listen to English and Spanish definitions.

**TUTORIALS** Get help from ***Virtual Nerd***, right when you need it.

**MATH TOOLS** Explore math with digital tools and manipulatives.

## Did You Know?

The rhinoceros beetle of Central and South America can lift up to **850 times** its own weight. That's equivalent to a 150-pound human lifting some 120,000 pounds, or **30 cars**.

Cargo bay

The world's largest cargo plane can carry more than half a million pounds. The cargo bay is 142 feet long, which is longer than the length of the first airplane *flight* by the Wright brothers, in 1903.

## Your Task: Design a Quadrilateral Lift

A 50,000-pound bus needs to be lifted 6 feet off the ground for engine repairs. You and your classmates will analyze quadrilaterals and design a hydraulic lift for a mechanic to use for those repairs.

# 6-1 The Polygon Angle-Sum Theorems

PearsonRealize.com

I CAN… find the sums of the measures of the exterior angles and interior angles of polygons.

## EXPLORE & REASON

**Start by drawing a pentagon. Then, for each side of the pentagon, draw the line that includes the side. An example is shown.**

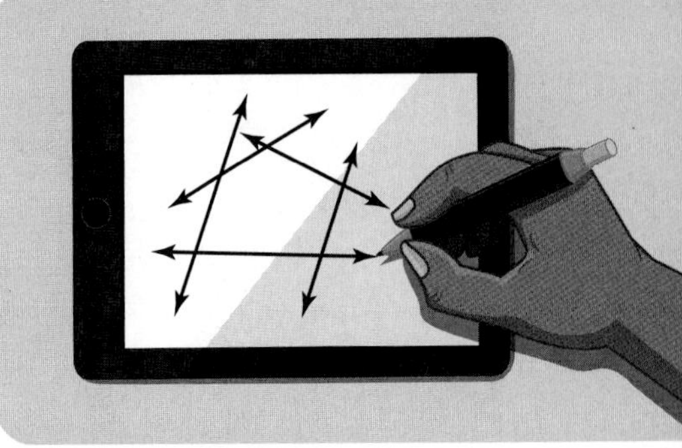

**A.** Choose one pair of lines that intersect at a vertex of the pentagon. Is each of the four angles formed at the vertex an interior angle or an exterior angle of the pentagon?

**B.** Are the relationships the same for the angles formed by the other pairs of intersecting lines?

**C. Make Sense and Persevere** If you drew a hexagon and the lines that included the sides of the hexagon, would the relationships between the angles at each vertex be the same as those in the pentagon?

## ESSENTIAL QUESTION

**How does the number of sides in convex polygons relate to the sums of the measures of the exterior and interior angles?**

CONCEPTUAL UNDERSTANDING

## EXAMPLE 1 Explore Polygon Interior Angle Sums

**How does the number of sides of a convex polygon, *n*, relate to the sum of measures of its interior angles?**

You know that the sum of the interior angle measures of a triangle is 180°. Decompose polygons into triangles and look for a pattern.

To decompose a convex polygon into triangles, construct all diagonals from one vertex.

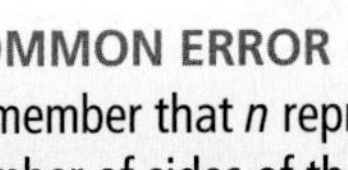

COMMON ERROR

Remember that $n$ represents the number of sides of the polygon, not the number of triangles.

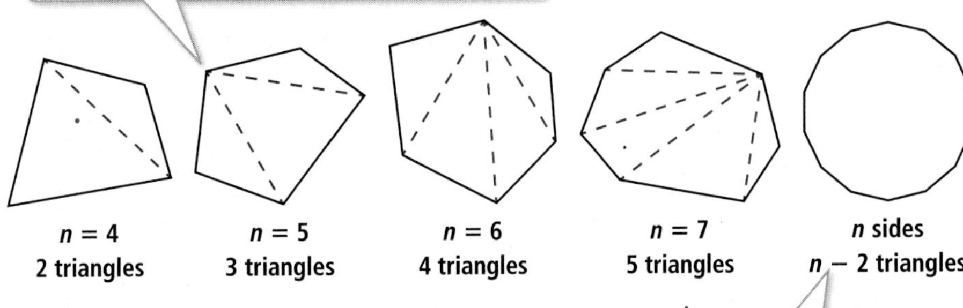

$n = 4$
**2 triangles**

$n = 5$
**3 triangles**

$n = 6$
**4 triangles**

$n = 7$
**5 triangles**

***n* sides**
**$n - 2$ triangles**

There are $n - 2$ triangles in every $n$-sided polygon. Each triangle has an angle sum of 180.

Interior angle sum of an $n$-sided polygon $= 180 \cdot (n - 2)$

**Try It!** **1. a.** How many triangles are formed by drawing diagonals from a vertex in a convex octagon?

**b.** What is the interior angle sum for a convex octagon?

**THEOREM 6-1** Polygon Interior Angle-Sum Theorem

The sum of the measures of the interior angles of a convex $n$-gon is $180 \cdot (n - 2)$.

PROOF: SEE EXERCISE 11.

**If...**

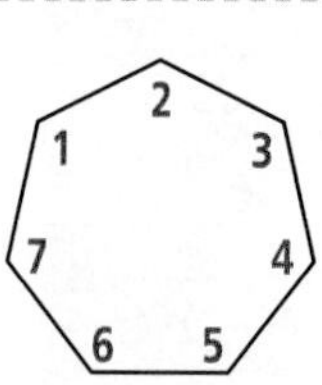


**Then...** $m\angle 1 + m\angle 2 + m\angle 3 + m\angle 4 + m\angle 5 + m\angle 6 + m\angle 7 = 180 \cdot (7 - 2) = 900$

**COROLLARY** to Theorem 6-1

The measure of an interior angle of a regular $n$-gon is $\frac{180 \cdot (n - 2)}{n}$.

**If...**

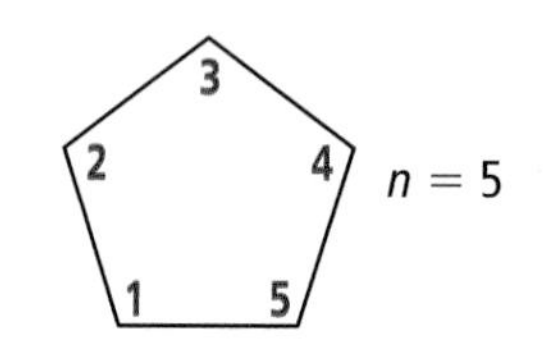


**Then...** $m\angle 1 = \frac{180 \cdot (5 - 2)}{5} = 108$

APPLICATION

## EXAMPLE 2 Apply the Polygon Interior Angle-Sum Theorem

**Jenna is building a corner cabinet to fit in a rectangular room. If she builds it with the angles shown, how can she determine whether the cabinet will fit?**

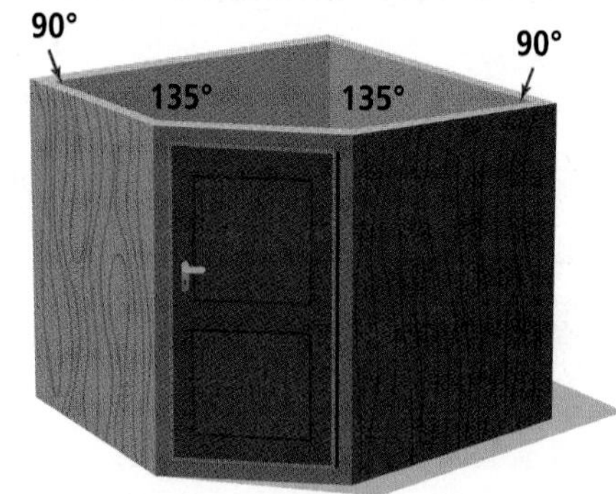


Formulate ◀ Draw a pentagon to represent the cabinet. Find the sum of interior angle measures of the pentagon and then subtract the known angle measures to determine whether the corner angle is a right angle.

To fit in the corner, this angle must be 90°.

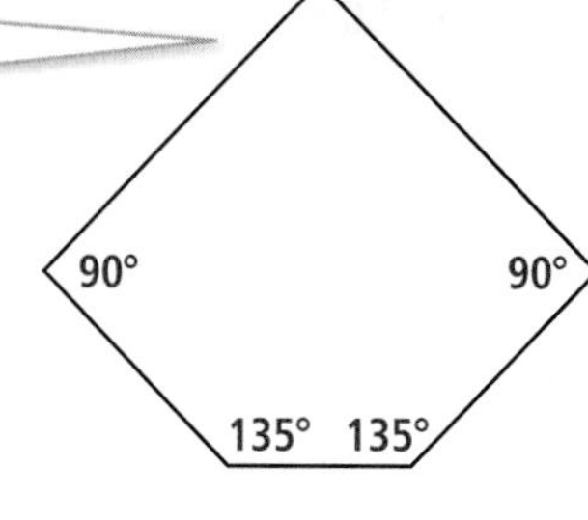


Compute ◀ **Step 1** Find the sum of the interior angles.

$$(n - 2) \cdot 180 = (5 - 2) \cdot 180$$
$$= 3 \cdot 180$$
$$= 540$$

**Step 2** Find the missing angle measure.

$$540 - (90 + 135 + 135 + 90) = 90$$

Interpret ◀ The angle is 90°, so the cabinet will fit in the corner.

CONTINUED ON THE NEXT PAGE

**Try It!** **2. a.** What is the interior angle sum of a 17-gon?

**b.** Each angle of a regular $n$-gon measures 172.8. How many sides does the $n$-gon have?

## EXAMPLE 3 Understand Exterior Angle Measures of a Polygon

**What is the sum of the exterior angle measures of a convex polygon?**

You can use what you know about the sum of the interior angle measures of convex polygons to find the sum of the exterior angle measures.

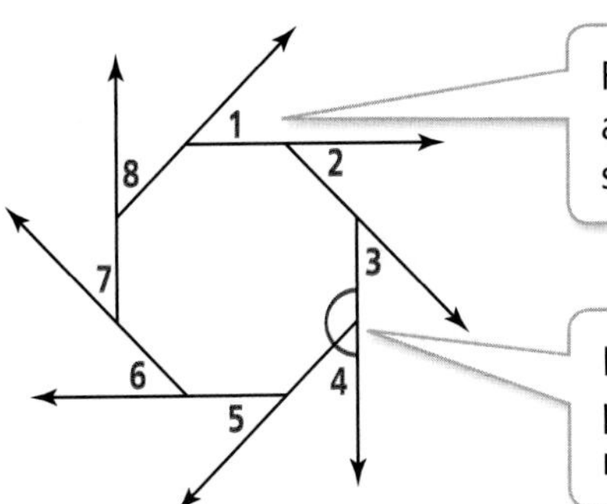


Remember, one side of the polygon and the extension of an adjacent side form an exterior angle.

Each interior and exterior angle pair forms a linear pair, which measures 180°.

**GENERALIZE**
How do you know that a polygon with $n$ sides has $n$ angle pairs?

The sum of the measures of $n$ interior and exterior angle pairs is $180 \cdot n$.

$$\text{sum of exterior angle measures} = \text{sum of interior and exterior angle measures} - \text{sum of interior angle measures}$$

$$= 180n - 180(n-2)$$

$$= 180n - 180n + 360$$

$$= 360$$

The sum of the exterior angle measures of any convex polygon is 360.

**Try It!** **3.** What is the sum of exterior angle measures of a convex 17-gon?

### THEOREM 6-2 Polygon Exterior Angle-Sum Theorem

The sum of the measures of the exterior angles of a convex polygon, one at each vertex, is 360.

**If...**

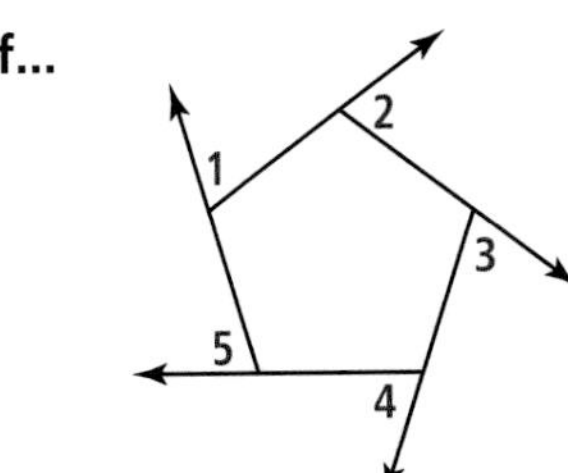


PROOF: SEE EXERCISE 15.

**Then...** $m\angle 1 + m\angle 2 + m\angle 3 + m\angle 4 + m\angle 5 = 360$

## EXAMPLE 4 Find an Exterior Angle Measure

**Suppose $\angle 1 \cong \angle 3$, $m\angle 1 = 3x$, and $m\angle 2 = 2x$. What is the measure of each exterior angle?**

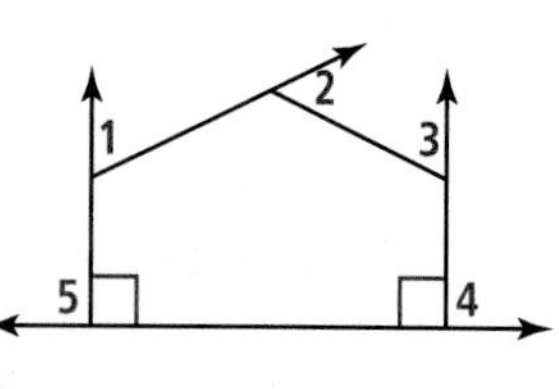


**Step 1** Find $x$.

$$m\angle 1 + m\angle 2 + m\angle 3 + m\angle 4 + m\angle 5 = 360$$
$$m\angle 1 + m\angle 2 + m\angle 1 + 90 + 90 = 360$$
$$3x + 2x + 3x + 180 = 360$$
$$8x = 180$$
$$x = 22.5$$

The exterior angle sum of a polygon is 360.

**MAKE SENSE AND PERSEVERE** Think about how to verify your answers. What must be true if your answers are correct?

**Step 2** Use the value of $x$ to determine the measure of each exterior angle.

| | | | |
|---|---|---|---|
| $m\angle 1 = 3x$ | $m\angle 2 = 2x$ | $m\angle 3 = m\angle 1$ | $m\angle 4 = 90$ |
| $m\angle 1 = 3(22.5)$ | $m\angle 2 = 2(22.5)$ | $m\angle 3 = 67.5$ | $m\angle 5 = 90$ |
| $m\angle 1 = 67.5$ | $m\angle 2 = 45$ | | |

**Try It!** 4. Suppose $\angle 1 \cong \angle 3 \cong \angle 4 \cong \angle 6$, $\angle 2 \cong \angle 5$, and $m\angle 3 = m\angle 2 + 30$. What is $m\angle 4$?

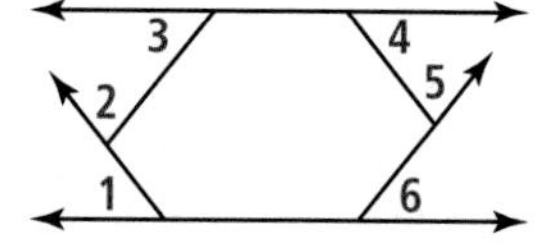


## EXAMPLE 5 Find the Measures of Interior Angles

**What are the measures of the interior angles of the pentagon shown?**

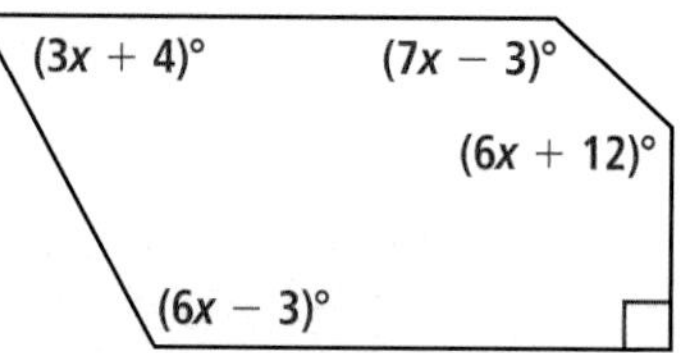


**Step 1** Apply the Polygon Interior Angle-Sum Theorem and solve for $x$.

$$90 + (6x - 3) + (3x + 4) + (7x - 3) + (6x + 12) = 180 \cdot (5 - 2)$$
$$90 + 22x + 10 = 540$$
$$22x = 440$$
$$x = 20$$

**Step 2** Substitute the value of $x$ to find each angle measure.

$$6x - 3 = 6(20) - 3 = 117 \qquad 3x + 4 = 3(20) + 4 = 64$$
$$7x - 3 = 7(20) - 3 = 137 \qquad 6x + 12 = 6(20) + 12 = 132$$

The measures of the interior angles are 90, 117, 64, 137, and 132.

**Try It!** 5. The measure of each interior angle of a regular 100-gon is $(3x + 26.4)$. What is the value of $x$?

## CONCEPT SUMMARY Polygon Angle Sums

### THEOREM 6-1 Polygon Interior Angle-Sum Theorem

The sum of the measures of the interior angles of a convex polygon is $180 \cdot (n - 2)$, where $n$ is the number of sides of the polygon.

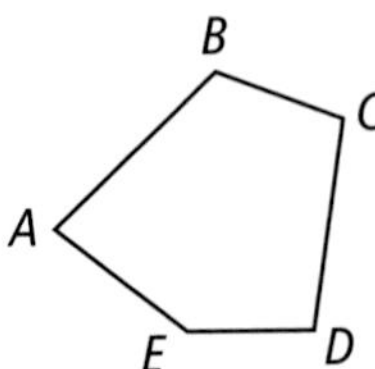


$$m\angle A + m\angle B + m\angle C + m\angle D + m\angle E = 180(5 - 2)$$
$$= 540$$

### THEOREM 6-2 Polygon Exterior Angle-Sum Theorem

The sum of the measures of the exterior angles of a convex polygon, one at each vertex, is 360.

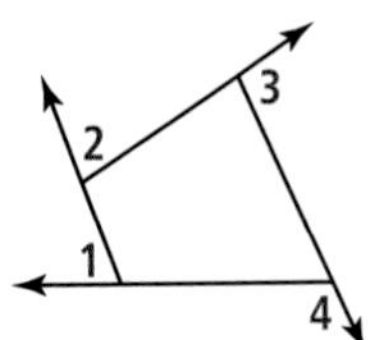


$$m\angle 1 + m\angle 2 + m\angle 3 + m\angle 4 = 360$$

## Do You UNDERSTAND?

1. **ESSENTIAL QUESTION** How does the number of sides in convex polygons relate to the sums of the measures of the exterior and interior angles?

2. **Error Analysis** In the calculation shown, what is Danielle's error?

The sum of the measures of the exterior angles of a 25-gon is $180 \cdot (25 - 2) = 4{,}140$.

3. **Make Sense and Persevere** What is the minimum amount of information needed to find the sum of the interior angles of a regular polygon?

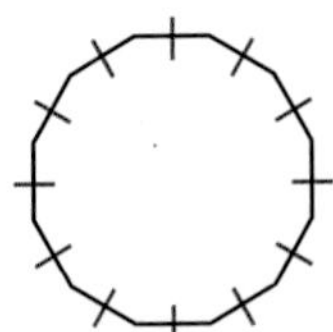

4. **Reason** A convex polygon can be decomposed into 47 triangles. How many sides does the polygon have? Explain.

## Do You KNOW HOW?

**Use polygon A for Exercises 5 and 6.**

5. What is the sum of the measures of the interior angles?

6. What is the sum of the measures of the exterior angles?

Polygon A

**Use polygon B for Exercises 7 and 8.**

7. What is the value of $y$?

8. What is the value of $x$?

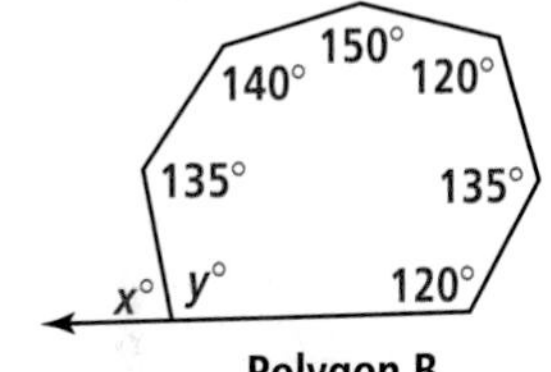


Polygon B

9. What are the measures of the exterior angles of the polygon shown?

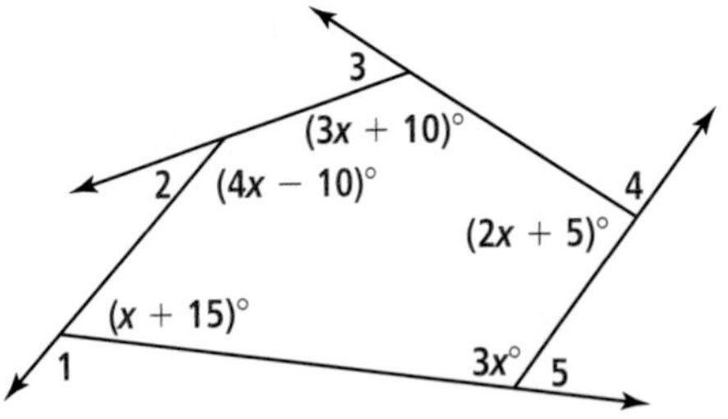


10. The sum of the interior angles of a regular $n$-gon is 6,120°. What is the measure of each interior angle?

## PRACTICE & PROBLEM SOLVING

Scan for Multimedia

Practice | Tutorial

Additional Exercises Available Online

### UNDERSTAND

**11. Construct Arguments** Write a proof of the Polygon Interior Angle-Sum Theorem.

**12. Make Sense and Persevere** What are the measures of the angles in the right triangles formed by the two regular pentagons shown?

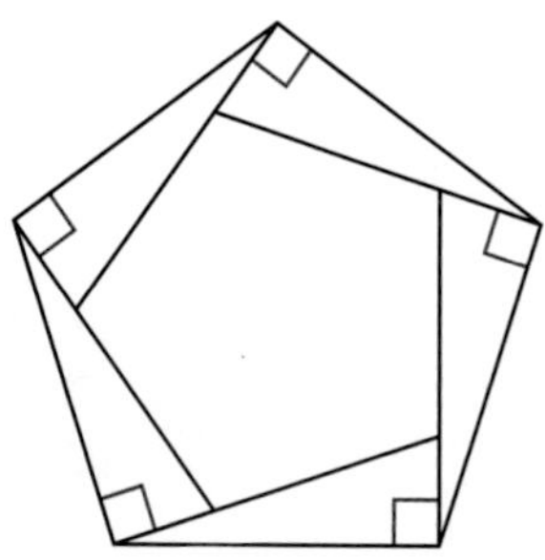

**13. Reason** Explain why a regular polygon cannot have an interior angle that is 40°.

**14. Error Analysis** Jayesh makes the calculation shown to find the measure of each interior angle of a regular nonagon. What is his error?

Sum of measure of exterior angles:
$180 \cdot 9 = 1{,}620$
Sum of measure of interior angles:
$1{,}620 \div 7 = 231$
✗

**15. Construct Arguments** Write a proof of the Polygon Exterior Angle-Sum Theorem.

**16. Higher Order Thinking** The star shown is constructed by extending each side of a regular pentagon. Explain why the surrounding triangles are isosceles and congruent.

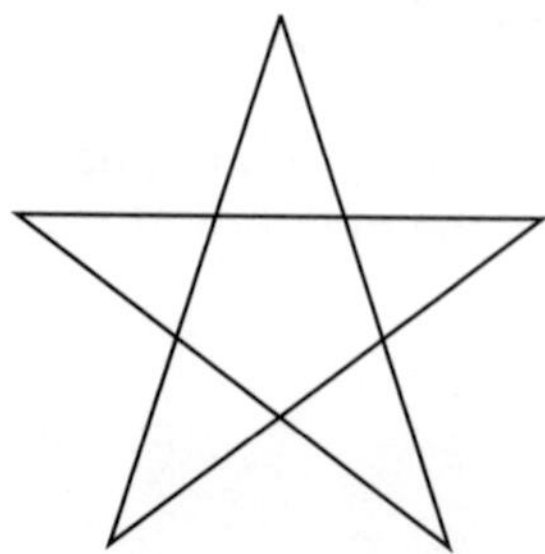

### PRACTICE

**For Exercises 17 and 18, find the sum of the interior angles and the measure of each angle for the given regular polygon.** SEE EXAMPLES 1 AND 2

**17.**

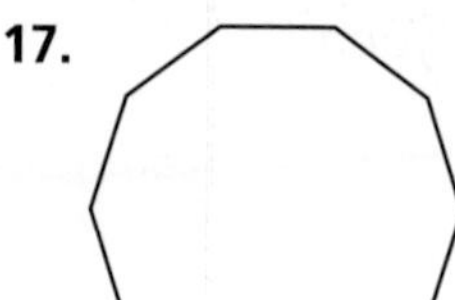

**18.**

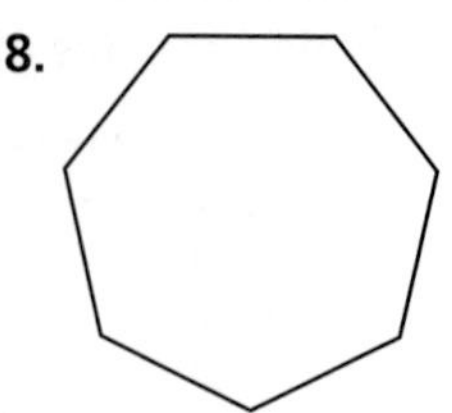

**19.** How many sides does a regular polygon have if the measure of each interior angle is 160°? SEE EXAMPLES 1 AND 2

**20.** What is the measure of each exterior angle of a regular polygon with 72 sides? SEE EXAMPLE 3

**21.** How many sides does a regular polygon with an exterior angle measure of 60° have? SEE EXAMPLE 3

**22.** What is the value of $x$? What is the measure of each exterior angle? SEE EXAMPLE 4

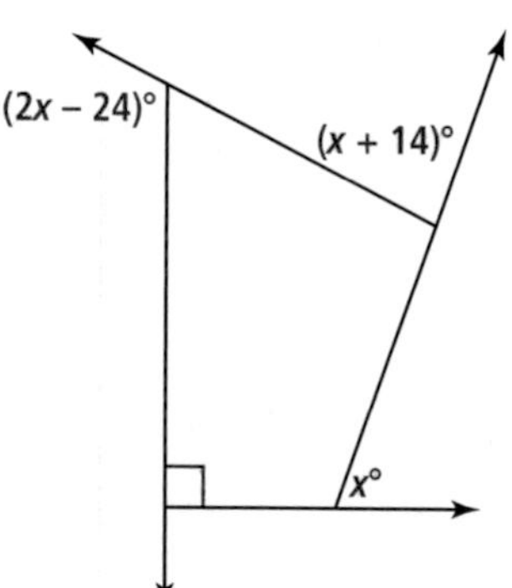


**For Exercises 23 and 24, find the value of $x$ and the measure of each interior angle.** SEE EXAMPLE 5

**23.**

$(4x - 80)°$ $(4x - 80)°$
$(2x + 50)°$ $(2x + 50)°$
$(2x + 50)°$ $(2x + 50)°$
$(4x - 80)°$ $(4x - 80)°$

**24.**

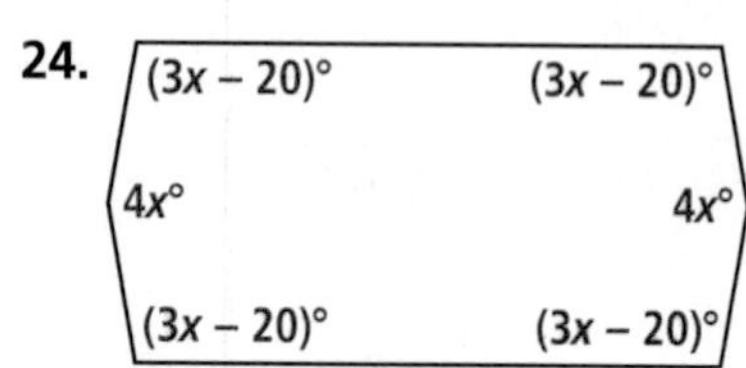

## PRACTICE & PROBLEM SOLVING

### APPLY

25. **Model With Mathematics** An airplane is navigating a polygon-shaped course. Each turn is labeled with the measure of the external angle at the striped post. What is $m\angle 1$?

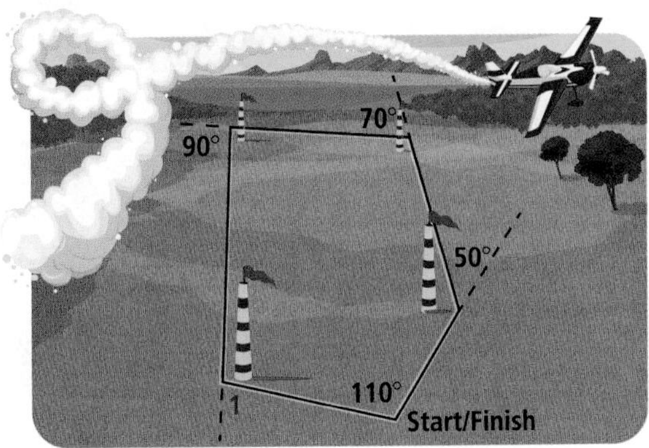


26. **Use Structure** A music producer needs to soundproof a wall with nonoverlapping foam panels consisting of regular polygons. When placed, there cannot be any space between the figures. Which of the regular polygons can she use? Explain.

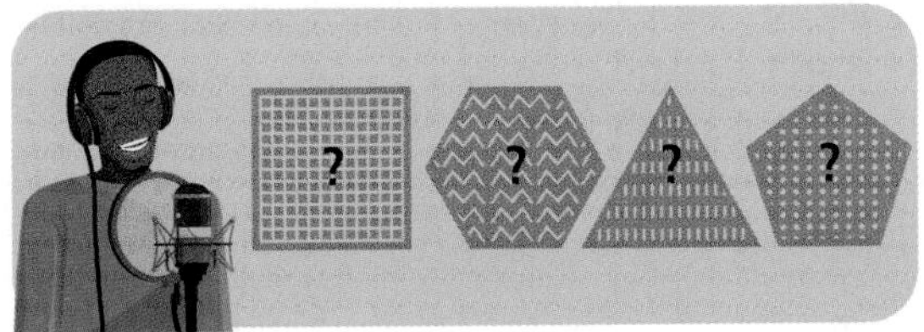


27. **Mathematical Connections** Ricardo wants to install two security cameras at point $A$ so the parking lot from side $\overline{AE}$ to side $\overline{AB}$ of the building can be monitored. Can he use two cameras, both with a field of view of 110°, installed at point $A$? Explain. If not, what is the minimum field of view that each camera should have?

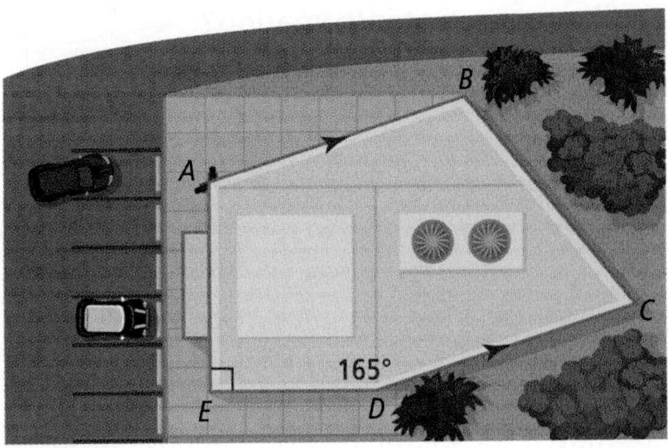


### ASSESSMENT PRACTICE

28. Match the number of sides of a regular polygon with the measure of each interior angle.

| | |
|---|---|
| I. 4 | A. 120 |
| II. 6 | B. 157.5 |
| III. 16 | C. 160 |
| VI. 18 | D. 90 |

29. **SAT/ACT** Suppose the figure below is a regular polygon. What is the value of $n$? Round to the nearest whole number.

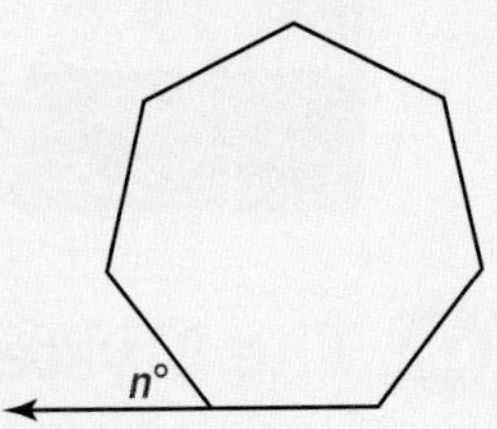


Ⓐ 45 Ⓑ 51 Ⓒ 129 Ⓓ 135

30. **Performance Task** The tables of a conference room are the same size, and all have the shape of a trapezoid. The conference coordinator wants to arrange the tables so they form a regular polygon.

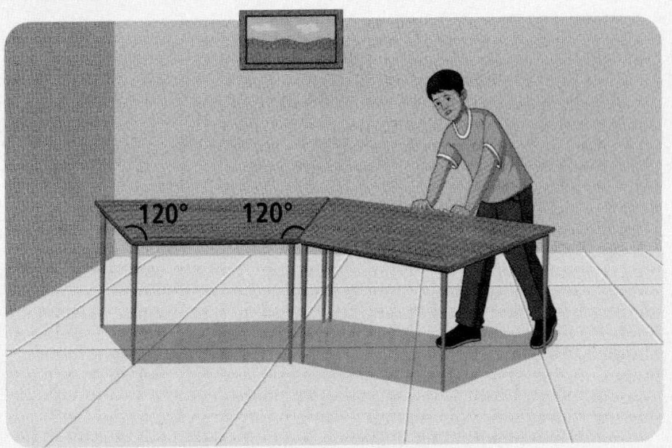


**Part A** Can the tables be arranged to form a regular polygon? Explain.

**Part B** If they can be arranged to form a regular polygon, how many tables are needed? If not, what should the measure of the 120° angle be changed to so that the tables can be arranged to form a regular polygon?

**Part C** What should the measures of the angles of the tables be if they can be arranged to form a regular pentagon?

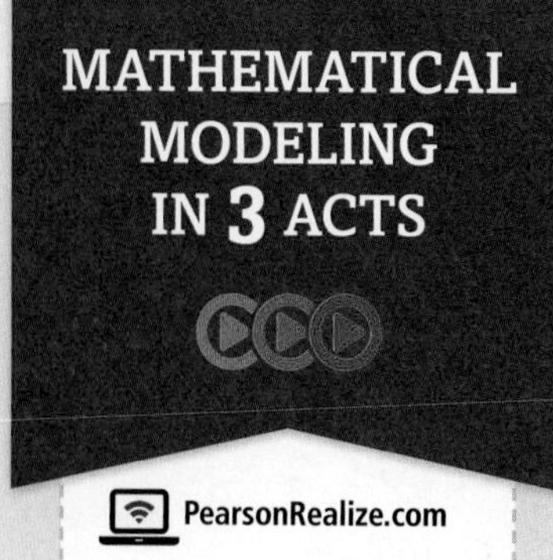


PearsonRealize.com

Video

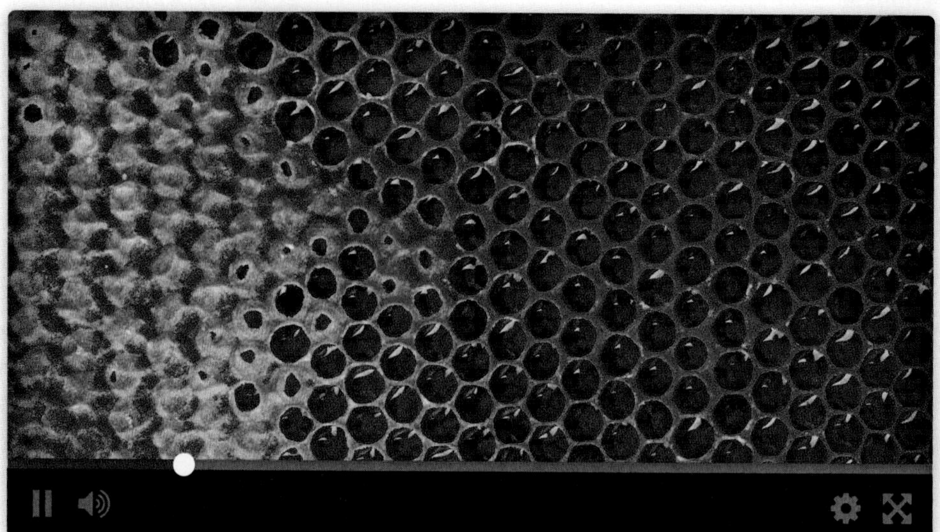

## The Mystery Sides

Have you ever looked closely at honeycombs? What shape are they? How do you know? Most often the cells in the honeycombs look like hexagons, but they might also look like circles. Scientists now believe that bees make circular cells that become hexagonal due to the bees' body heat and natural physical forces.

What are some strategies you use to identify shapes? Think about this during the Mathematical Modeling in 3 Acts lesson.

Scan for Multimedia 

### ACT 1 Identify the Problem

1. What is the first question that comes to mind after watching the video?
2. Write down the main question you will answer about what you saw in the video.
3. Make an initial conjecture that answers this main question.
4. Explain how you arrived at your conjecture.
5. What information will be useful to know to answer the main question? How can you get it? How will you use that information?

### ACT 2 Develop a Model

6. Use the math that you have learned in this Topic to refine your conjecture.

### ACT 3 Interpret the Results

7. Did your refined conjecture match the actual answer exactly? If not, how is it different? What might explain the difference?

# 6-2 Kites and Trapezoids

PearsonRealize.com

**I CAN...** use triangle congruence to understand kites and trapezoids.

**VOCABULARY**

- midsegment of a trapezoid

## CRITIQUE & EXPLAIN

**Manuel draws a diagram of kite *PQRS* with $\overleftrightarrow{QS}$ as the line of symmetry over a design of a kite-shaped key fob. He makes a list of conclusions based on the diagram.**

- $\overline{PR} \perp \overline{QS}$
- $\overline{QP} \cong \overline{QR}$
- $\overline{SP} \cong \overline{SR}$
- $\overline{PR}$ bisects $\overline{QS}$.
- $\Delta PQR$ is an equilateral triangle.
- $\Delta PSR$ is an isosceles triangle.

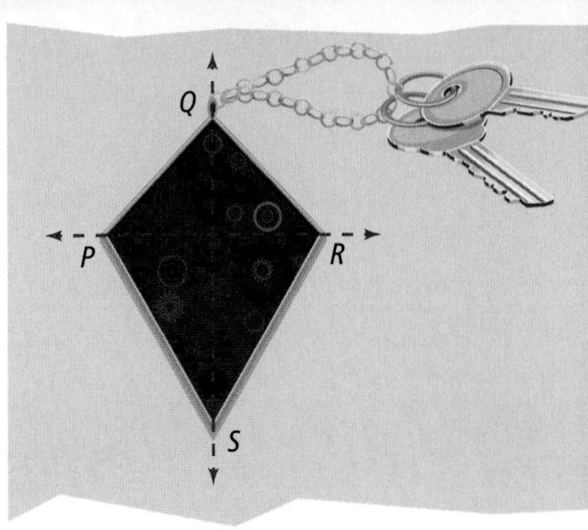
Q
P
R
S

**A.** Which of Manuel's conclusions do you agree with? Which do you disagree with? Explain.

**B. Use Structure** What other conclusions are supported by the diagram?

## ESSENTIAL QUESTION

**How are diagonals and angle measures related in kites and trapezoids?**

CONCEPTUAL UNDERSTANDING

## EXAMPLE 1 Investigate the Diagonals of a Kite

**How are the diagonals of a kite related?**

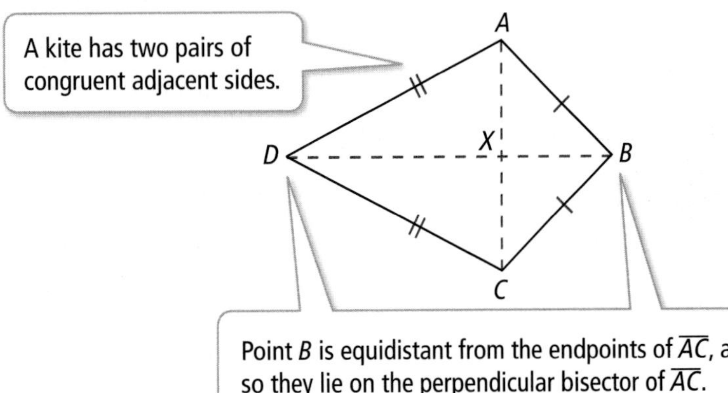
A kite has two pairs of congruent adjacent sides.
A
B
C
D
X
Point B is equidistant from the endpoints of AC, as is D, so they lie on the perpendicular bisector of AC.

The diagonals of a kite are perpendicular to each other. Exactly one diagonal bisects the other.

**STUDY TIP**
Remember that you must show that both *B* and *D* are on the perpendicular bisector in order to show that one diagonal is the perpendicular bisector of the other. It is not sufficient to show that only one is on the perpendicular bisector.

**Try It!** **1. a.** What is the measure of $\angle AXB$?

**b.** If $AX = 3.8$, what is $AC$?

**c.** If $BD = 10$, does $BX = 5$? Explain.

**THEOREM 6-3**

The diagonals of a kite are perpendicular.

**If...**

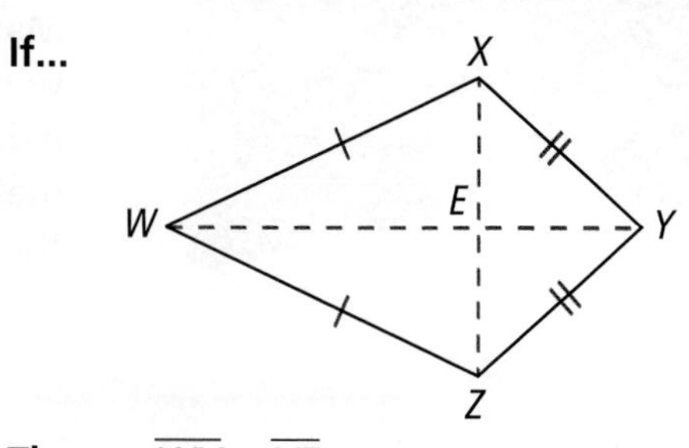


PROOF: SEE EXERCISE 12.

**Then...** $\overline{WY} \perp \overline{XZ}$

## EXAMPLE 2 Use the Diagonals of a Kite

**Quadrilateral *PQRS* is a kite with diagonals $\overline{QS}$ and $\overline{PR}$.**

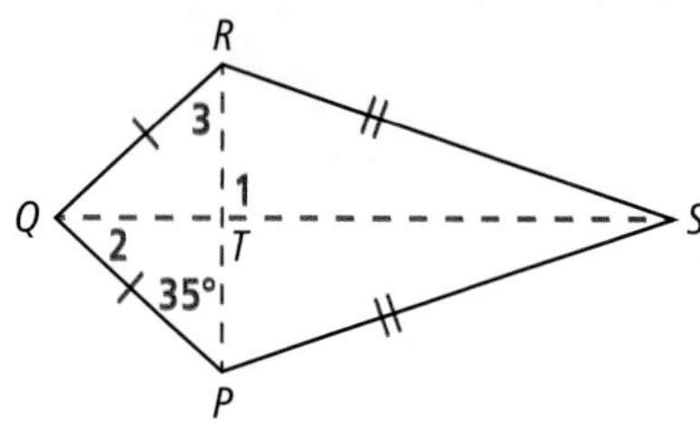


**A. What is $m\angle 1$?**

The diagonals of a kite are perpendicular, so $m\angle 1 = 90$.

**B. What is $m\angle 2$?**

The sum of the angles of $\triangle PQT$ is 180.

$$m\angle 2 + 35 + 90 = 180$$

$$m\angle 2 = 55$$

**C. What is $m\angle 3$?**

Since $\triangle PQR$ is an isosceles triangle, $m\angle 3 \cong m\angle QPT$.

So, $m\angle 3 = 35$.

**COMMON ERROR**
You may incorrectly assume angles are congruent just from their appearance. Always check that you can prove congruence first.

**Try It!** **2.** Quadrilateral *WXYZ* is a kite.

**a.** What is $m\angle 1$?

**b.** What is $m\angle 2$?

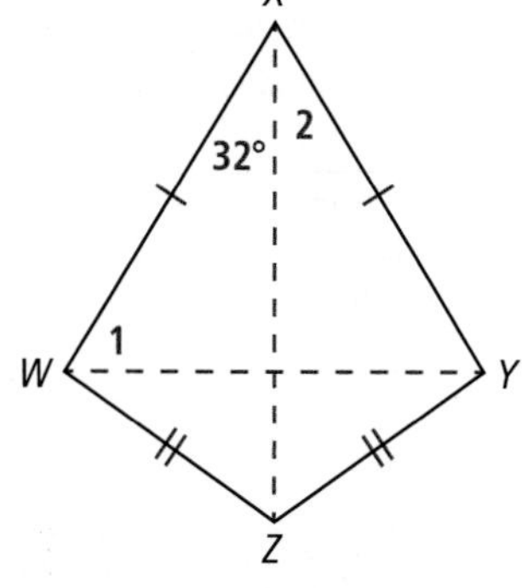

APPLICATION

## EXAMPLE 3 Explore Parts of an Isosceles Trapezoid

**Kiyo is designing a trapezoid-shaped roof. In order for the roof to be symmetric, the overlapping triangles $\triangle DAB$ and $\triangle ADC$ must be congruent. Will the roof be symmetric?**

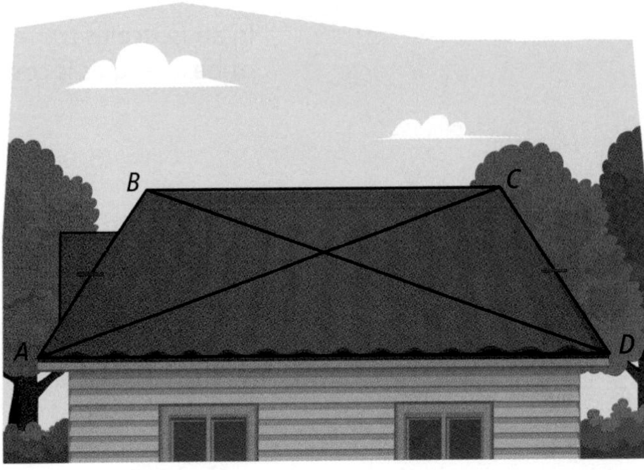


**Step 1** Show $\triangle ABE \cong \triangle DCF$.

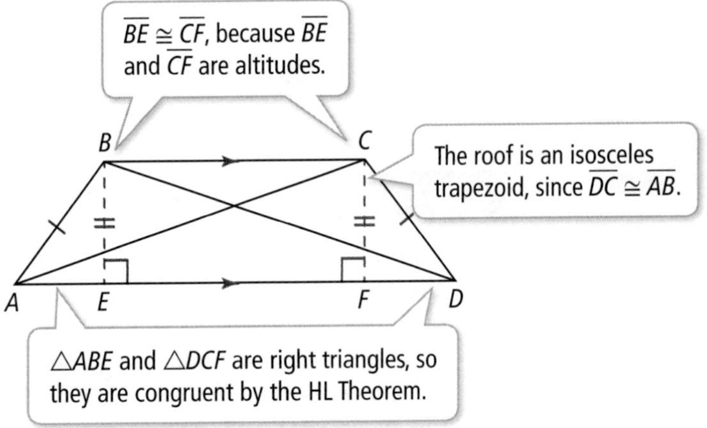

$\overline{BE} \cong \overline{CF}$, because $\overline{BE}$ and $\overline{CF}$ are altitudes.
The roof is an isosceles trapezoid, since $\overline{DC} \cong \overline{AB}$.
$\triangle ABE$ and $\triangle DCF$ are right triangles, so they are congruent by the HL Theorem.
B
C
A
E
F
D


**GENERALIZE**
How do the lengths of the diagonals and the way they intersect relate to the sides of a quadrilateral?

**Step 2** Show $\triangle DAB \cong \triangle ADC$.

By CPCTC, $\angle DAB \cong \angle ADC$. By the Reflexive Property of Congruency, $\overline{AD} \cong \overline{DA}$. So, $\triangle DAB \cong \triangle ADC$ by SAS.

The overlapping triangles are congruent, so the roof is symmetric.

**Try It!** **3. a.** Given isosceles trapezoid *PQRS*, what are $m\angle P$, $m\angle Q$, and $m\angle S$?

**b.** Given $\overline{ST} \parallel \overline{RU}$, what is the measure of $\angle TUR$?

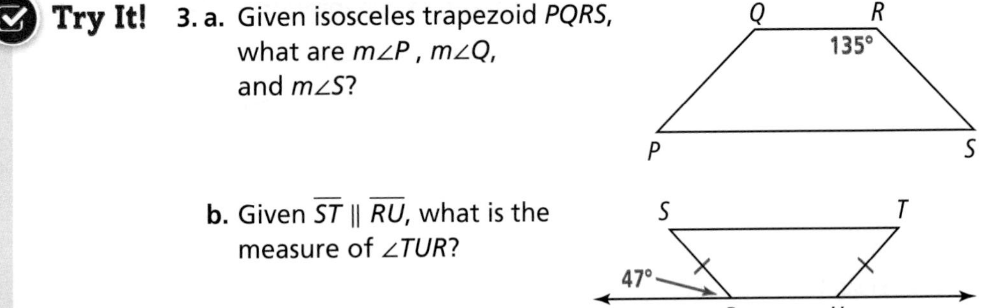

## THEOREM 6-4

In an isosceles trapezoid, each pair of base angles is congruent.

**If...**

**Then...** $\angle BAD \cong \angle CDA$, $\angle ABC \cong \angle DCB$

**PROOF: SEE EXERCISE 13.**

## THEOREM 6-5

The diagonals of an isosceles trapezoid are congruent.

**If...**

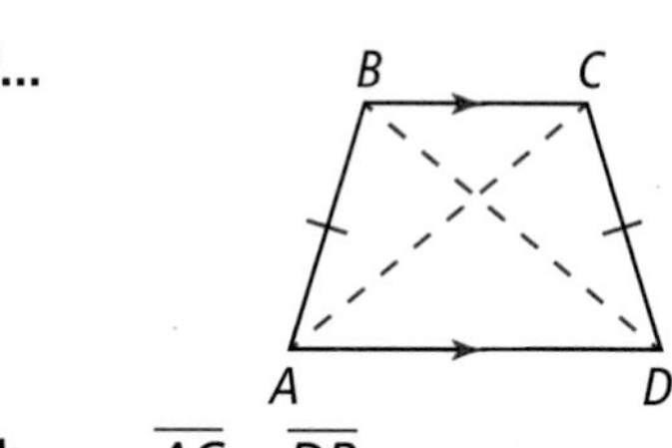


**Then...** $\overline{AC} \cong \overline{DB}$

**PROOF: SEE EXERCISE 18.**

## EXAMPLE 4 Solve Problems Involving Isosceles Trapezoids

**All horizontal beams of the high-voltage transmission tower are parallel to the ground.**

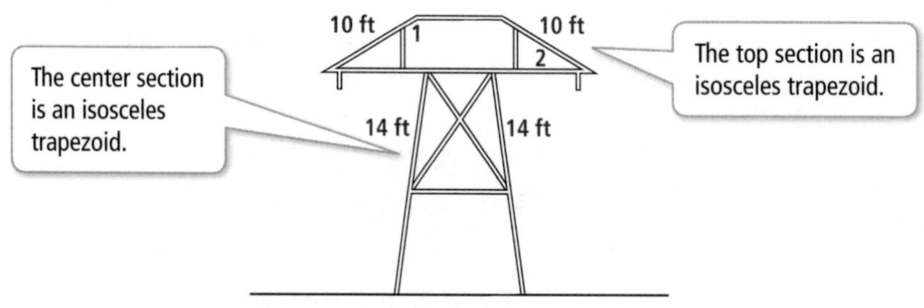


**A. If $m\angle 1 = 138$, what is $m\angle 2$?**

The sum of the interior angle measures of a quadrilateral is 360.

$$m\angle 1 + m\angle 1 + m\angle 2 + m\angle 2 = 360$$
$$138 + 138 + 2(m\angle 2) = 360$$
$$276 + 2(m\angle 2) = 360$$
$$2(m\angle 2) = 84$$
$$m\angle 2 = 42$$

The base angles are congruent.

The measure of $\angle 2$ is 42.

**MAKE SENSE AND PERSEVERE** What other strategy might you use to solve this problem?

CONTINUED ON THE NEXT PAGE

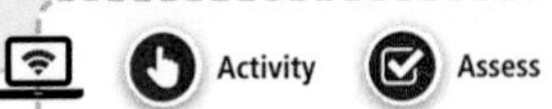


EXAMPLE 4 CONTINUED

**GENERALIZE**
Why might this strategy work for isosceles trapezoids but not for trapezoids with noncongruent legs?

**B. One cross support in the center of the tower measures $4c + 3$, and the other measures $6c - 5$. What is the length of each cross support?**

The cross supports are diagonals of an isosceles trapezoid, so they are congruent.

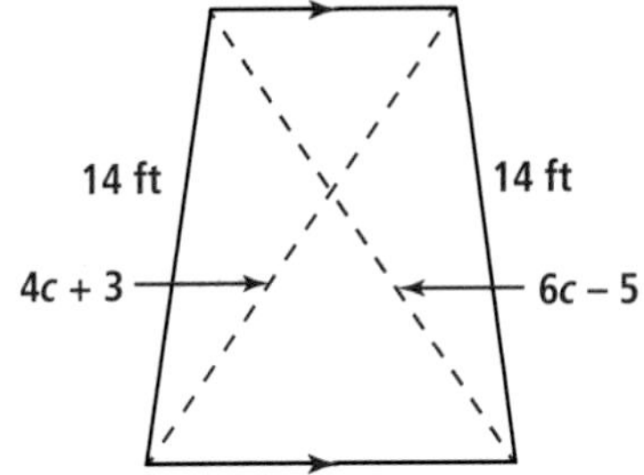


**Step 1** Find the value of $c$.

$$4c + 3 = 6c - 5$$
$$8 = 2c$$
$$4 = c$$

**Step 2** Find the lengths of the diagonals.

$$4c + 3 = 4(4) + 3$$
$$= 19$$
$$6c - 5 = 6(4) - 5$$
$$= 19$$

Each cross support measures 19 ft in length.

**Try It!** 4. Given isosceles trapezoid $MNOP$ where the given expressions represent the measures of the diagonals, what is the value of $a$?

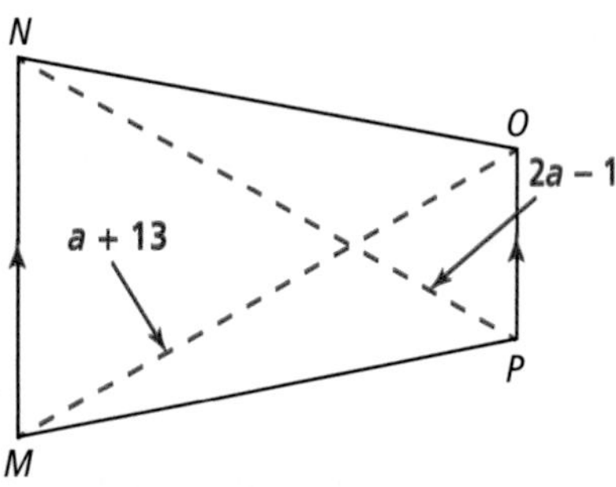


## THEOREM 6-6 Trapezoid Midsegment Theorem

In a trapezoid, the midsegment is parallel to the bases, and the length of the midsegment is half the sum of the lengths of the bases.

**If...**

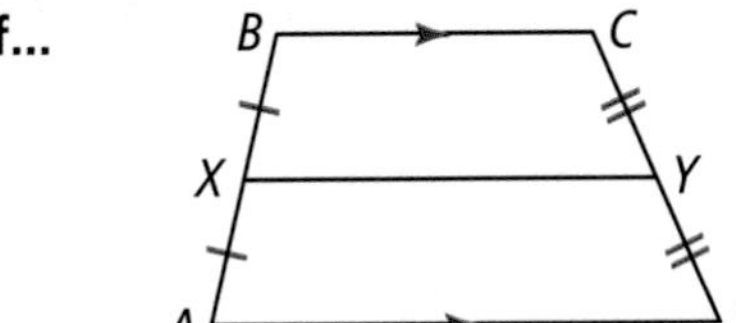


**Then...** $\overline{XY} \parallel \overline{AD}$, $\overline{XY} \parallel \overline{BC}$, and $XY = \frac{1}{2}(AD + BC)$

PROOF: SEE LESSON 9-2.

APPLICATION

## EXAMPLE 5 Apply the Trapezoid Midsegment Theorem

**Paxton makes trapezoidal handbags for her friends. She stiches decorative trim along the top, middle, and bottom on both sides of the handbags. How much trim does she need for three handbags? Explain.**

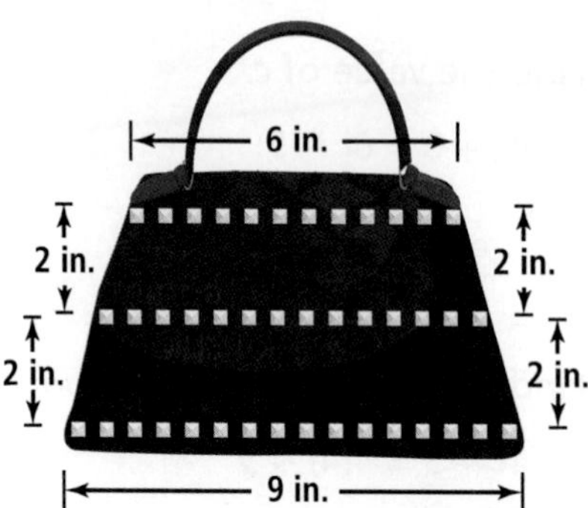


**Formulate** The top and bottom sides of the handbag are the bases of a trapezoid. The left and right sides are the legs. Since the middle segment divides both legs in half, it is the midsegment of the trapezoid. The **midsegment of a trapezoid** is the segment that connects the midpoints of the legs.

Let $x$ represent the length of the midsegment in inches.

**Compute** **Step 1** Find the value of $x$.

$$x = \frac{1}{2}(6 + 9)$$

Apply the Trapezoid Midsegment Theorem with the base lengths 6 and 9.

$$x = 7.5$$

The length of the midsegment is 7.5 in.

**Step 2** Find the amount of trim that she needs.

First, find the amount for one side.

$$6 + 9 + 7.5 = 22.5$$

Then, multiply by 2 for the number of sides per handbag and by 3 for the number of handbags.

$$22.5 \cdot 2 \cdot 3 = 135$$

**Interpret** Paxton needs 135 inches of trim.

**Try It!** 5. Given trapezoid *JKLM*, what is *KL*?

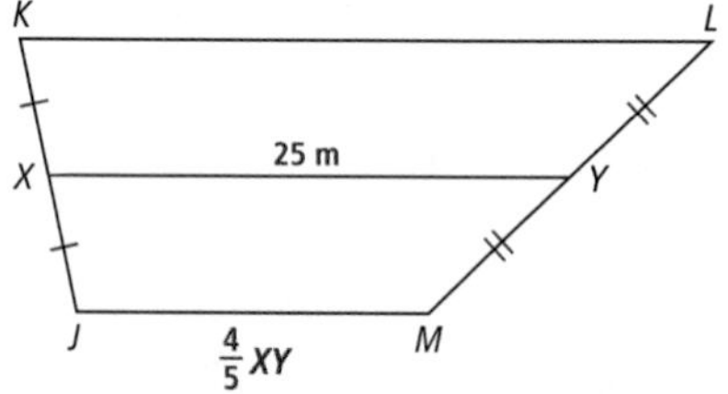

## CONCEPT SUMMARY Kites and Trapezoids

**WORDS**

### Kites

A kite is a quadrilateral with two pairs of adjacent sides congruent and no pairs of opposite sides congruent. Exactly one diagonal is a perpendicular bisector of the other.

### Trapezoids

A trapezoid is a quadrilateral with exactly one pair of parallel sides. The length of the midsegment is the average of the lengths of the two bases. A trapezoid with congruent legs is an isosceles trapezoid that has congruent base angles and congruent diagonals.

**DIAGRAMS**

Quadrilateral *ABCD* is a kite.

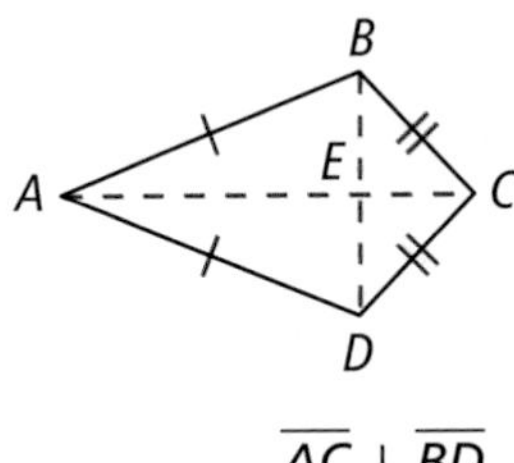


$\overline{AC} \perp \overline{BD}$

$BE = ED$

Quadrilateral *RSTU* is an isosceles trapezoid.

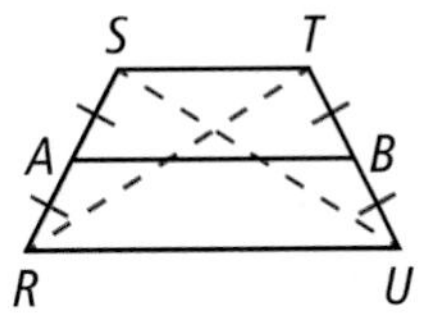


$\overline{SU} \cong \overline{TR}$

$AB = \frac{1}{2}(ST + RU)$

$\overline{AB} \parallel \overline{ST} \parallel \overline{RU}$

$m\angle S = m\angle T$

$m\angle R = m\angle U$

## Do You UNDERSTAND?

1. **ESSENTIAL QUESTION** How are diagonals and angle measures related in kites and trapezoids?

2. **Error Analysis** What is Reagan's error?

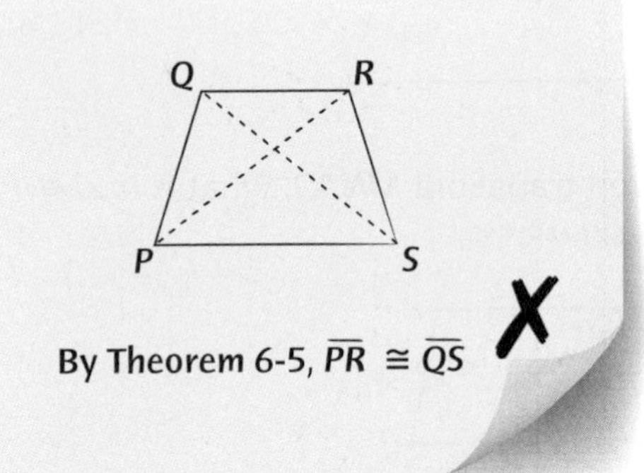


3. **Vocabulary** If $\overline{XY}$ is the midsegment of a trapezoid, what must be true about point *X* and point *Y*?

4. **Construct Arguments** Emaan says every kite is composed of 4 right triangles. Is he correct? Explain.

## Do You KNOW HOW?

**For Exercises 5–7, use kite *WXYZ* to find the measures.**

5. $m\angle XQY$

6. $m\angle YZQ$

7. $WY$

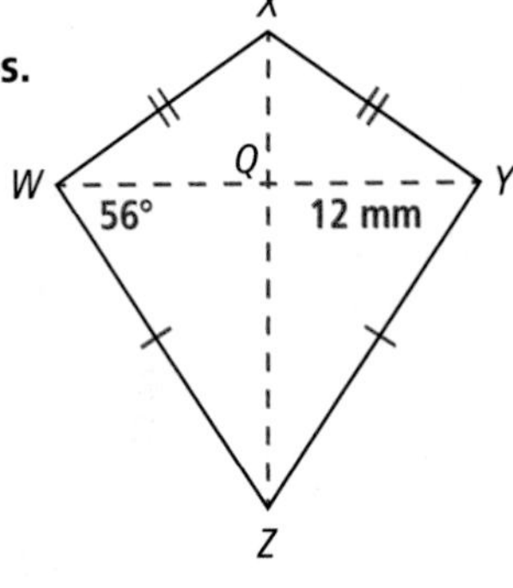


**For Exercises 8–10, use trapezoid *DEFG* with $EG = 21$ ft and $m\angle DGF = 77$ to find each measure.**

8. $ED$

9. $DF$

10. $m\angle DEF$

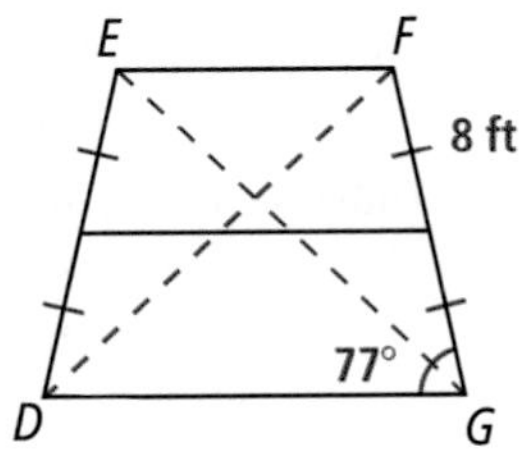


11. What is the length of $\overline{PQ}$?

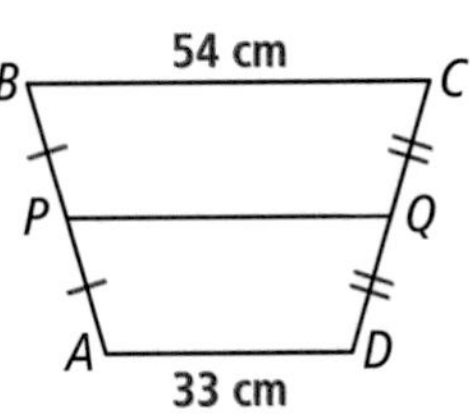

## UNDERSTAND

**12. Construct Arguments** Write a two-column proof to show that the diagonals of a kite are perpendicular.

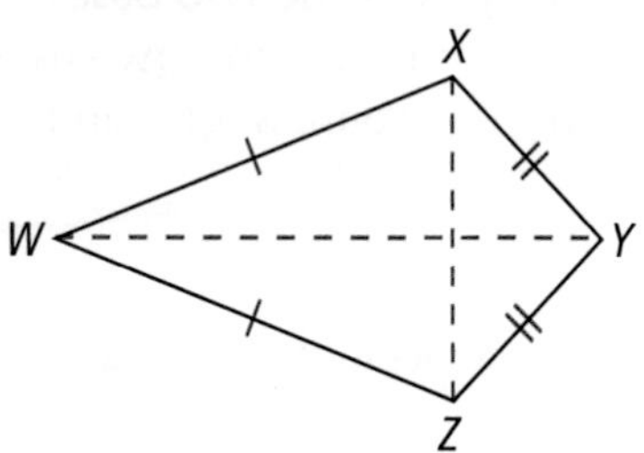


**13. Mathematical Connections** Write a paragraph proof to show that each pair of base angles in an isosceles trapezoid is congruent.

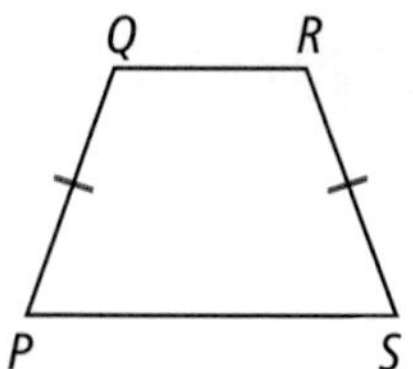


**14. Error Analysis** What is Emery's error?

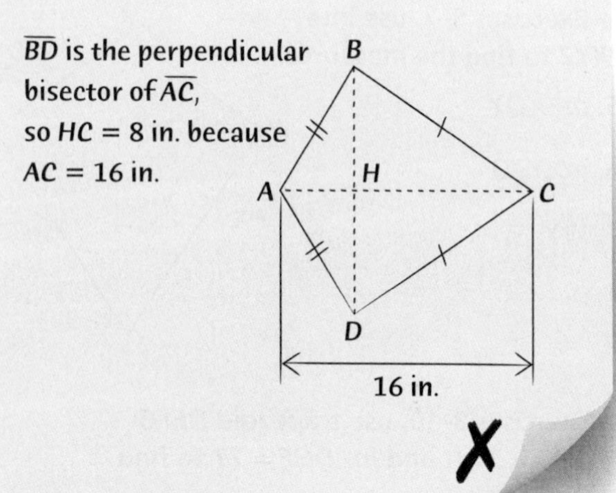

$\overline{BD}$ is the perpendicular bisector of $\overline{AC}$, so $HC = 8$ in. because $AC = 16$ in.
B
A
H
C
D
16 in.


**15. Higher Order Thinking** Given kite $JKLM$ with diagonal $\overline{KM}$, $JK < JM$, and $KL < LM$, prove that $\angle JMK$ is congruent to $\angle LMK$.

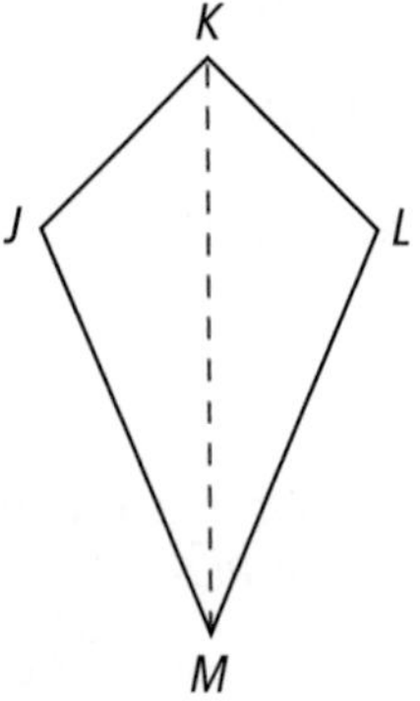


## PRACTICE

**16.** Given kite $ABCD$, in which $AN = 4.6$ m, what is $AC$? SEE EXAMPLE 1

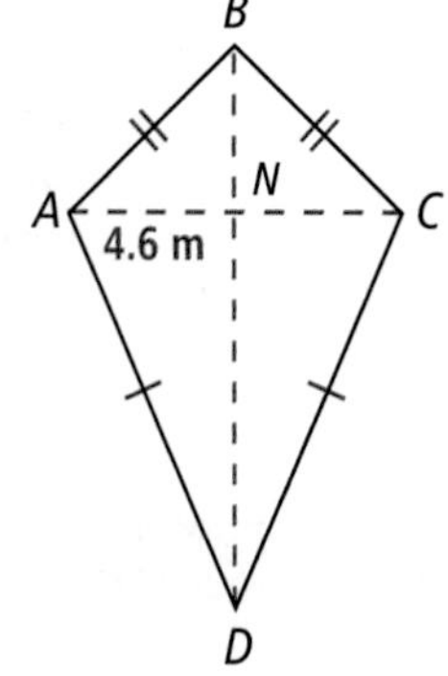


**17.** Given kite $RSTU$, what is $m\angle RUS$? SEE EXAMPLE 2

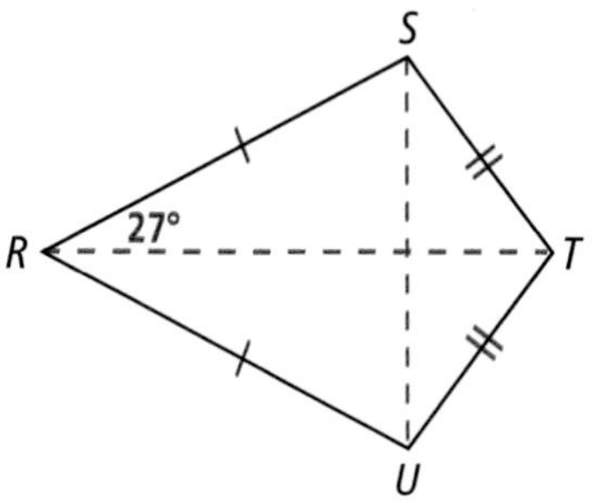


**18.** Write a two-column proof to show that the diagonals of an isosceles trapezoid are congruent. SEE EXAMPLES 3 AND 4

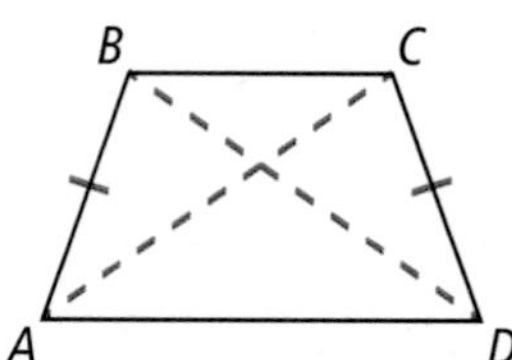


**19.** Given trapezoid $MNPQ$, what is $m\angle MNP$? SEE EXAMPLE 4

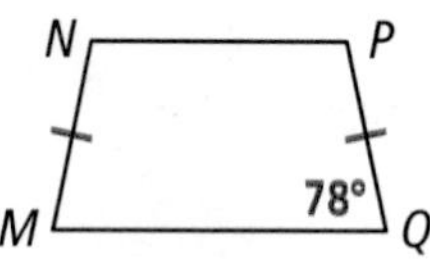


**20.** Given trapezoid $WXYZ$, what is $XY$? SEE EXAMPLE 5

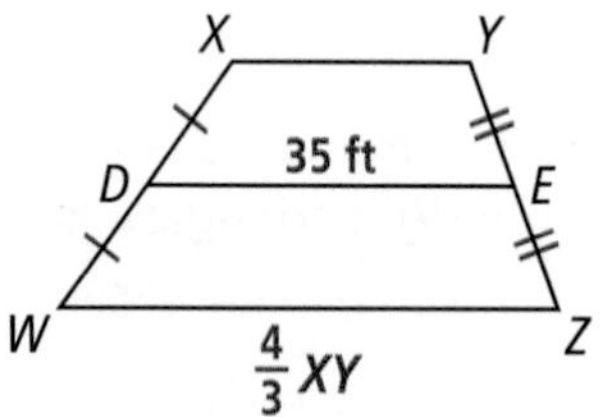

# PRACTICE & PROBLEM SOLVING

## APPLY

**21. Model With Mathematics** Gregory plans to make a kite like the one shown. He has 1,700 square inches of plastic sheeting. Does Gregory have enough plastic to make the kite? Explain.

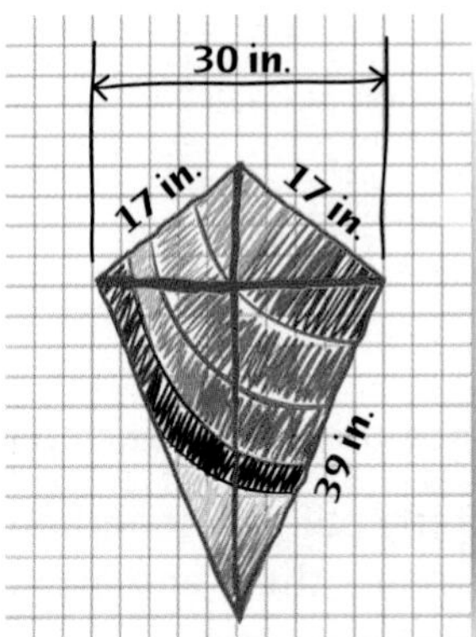


**22. Reason** Coach Murphy uses the map to plan a 2-mile run for the track team. How many times will the team run the route shown?

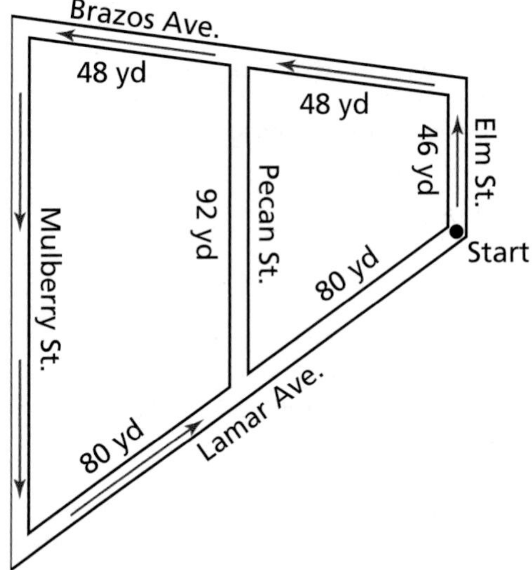


**23. Use Structure** Abby builds a bench with the seat parallel to the ground. She bends pipe to make the leg and seat supports. At what angles should she bend the pipe? Explain.

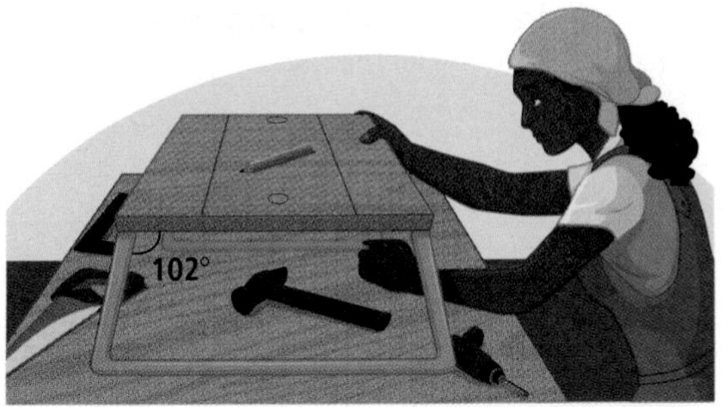


## ASSESSMENT PRACTICE

**24.** The ___?___ of a kite are always ___?___.

**25. SAT/ACT** Given trapezoid $ABCD$, what is the length of $\overline{XY}$?

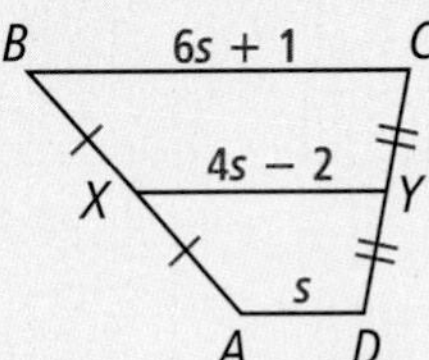


Ⓐ $3\frac{3}{5}$ Ⓑ $4\frac{2}{3}$ Ⓒ 5 Ⓓ 11 Ⓔ 18

**26. Performance Task** Cindy is a member of a volunteer group that built the play structure shown.

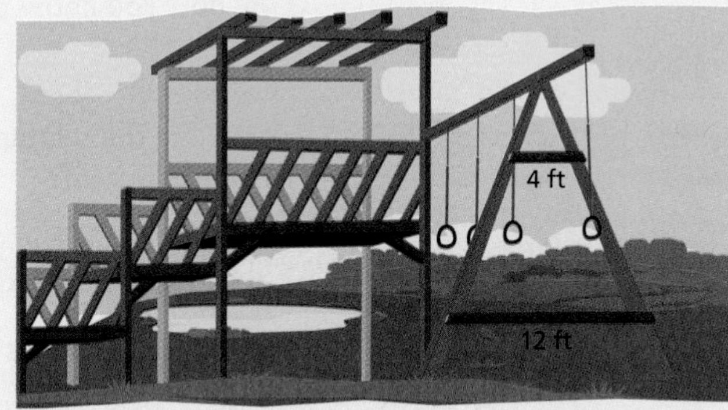


**Part A** Cindy wants to add three more trapezoid boards evenly spaced between the bottom and top boards of the triangular frame. Based on the average lengths of the top and bottom boards shown, what will be the average lengths of each of the three additional boards? Explain.

**Part B** The three boards will be trapezoids that have the same height as the top and bottom boards. How can Cindy use the lengths of the bases of the bottom board to determine the lengths of the bases of the three new boards?

**Part C** What other measurements should Cindy find to be certain that the boards will fit exactly onto the triangular frame?

Activity Assess

# 6-3 Properties of Parallelograms

PearsonRealize.com

**I CAN...** use the properties of parallel lines, diagonals, and triangles to investigate parallelograms.

## CRITIQUE & EXPLAIN

**Kennedy lists all the pairs of congruent triangles she finds in quadrilateral *ABCD*.**

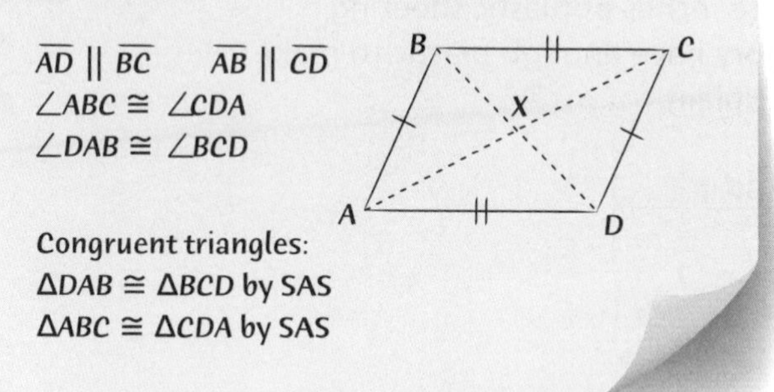

$\overline{AD} \parallel \overline{BC}$ $\overline{AB} \parallel \overline{CD}$
$\angle ABC \cong \angle CDA$
$\angle DAB \cong \angle BCD$
Congruent triangles:
$\triangle DAB \cong \triangle BCD$ by SAS
$\triangle ABC \cong \triangle CDA$ by SAS
B
C
X
A
D


**A.** Is Kennedy's justification for triangle congruence correct for each pair?

**B. Look for Relationships** Did Kennedy overlook any pairs of congruent triangles? If not, explain how you know. If so, name them and explain how you know they are congruent.

## ESSENTIAL QUESTION

**What are the relationships of the sides, the angles, and the diagonals of a parallelogram?**

CONCEPTUAL UNDERSTANDING

## EXAMPLE 1 Explore Opposite Sides of Parallelograms

**How do the lengths of the opposite sides of a parallelogram compare to each other?**

Quadrilateral *ABCD* is a parallelogram.

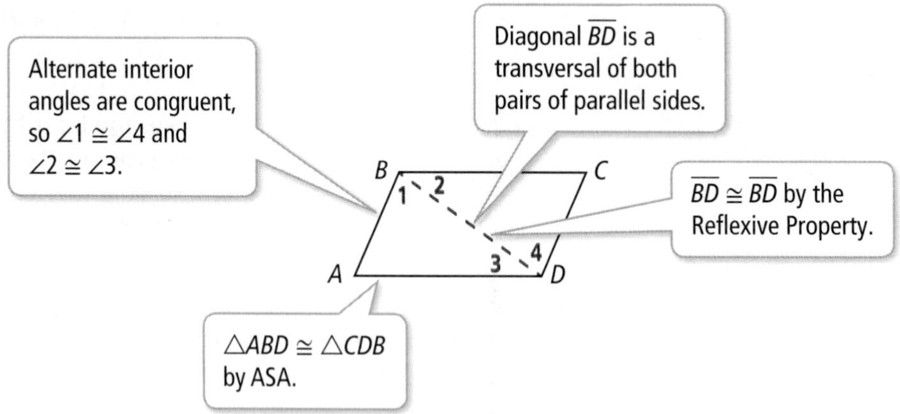

Alternate interior angles are congruent, so $\angle 1 \cong \angle 4$ and $\angle 2 \cong \angle 3$.
Diagonal $\overline{BD}$ is a transversal of both pairs of parallel sides.
$\overline{BD} \cong \overline{BD}$ by the Reflexive Property.
$\triangle ABD \cong \triangle CDB$ by ASA.
B
C
A
D
1
2
3
4


**USE STRUCTURE**
Can you use the same strategy to show other relationships in a parallelogram?

By CPCTC, $\overline{AD} \cong \overline{CB}$ and $\overline{AB} \cong \overline{CD}$, so the lengths of the opposite sides are congruent to each other.

**Try It!** 1. Given parallelogram *WXYZ*, what is *YZ*?

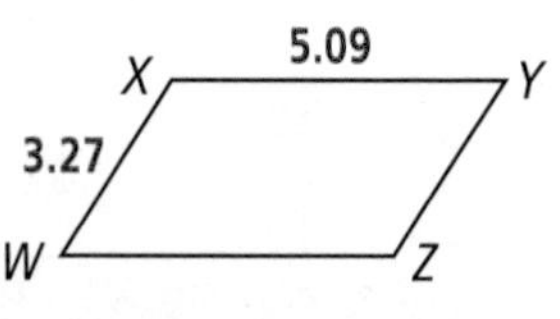

## THEOREM 6-7

If a quadrilateral is a parallelogram, then its opposite sides are congruent.

PROOF: SEE EXERCISE 13.

If...

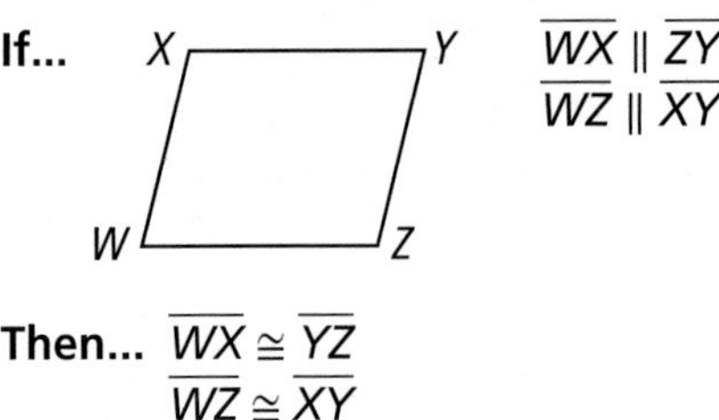


$\overline{WX} \parallel \overline{ZY}$
$\overline{WZ} \parallel \overline{XY}$

Then... $\overline{WX} \cong \overline{YZ}$
$\overline{WZ} \cong \overline{XY}$

## EXAMPLE 2 Use Opposite Sides of a Parallelogram

**Quadrilateral *PQRS* is a parallelogram.**

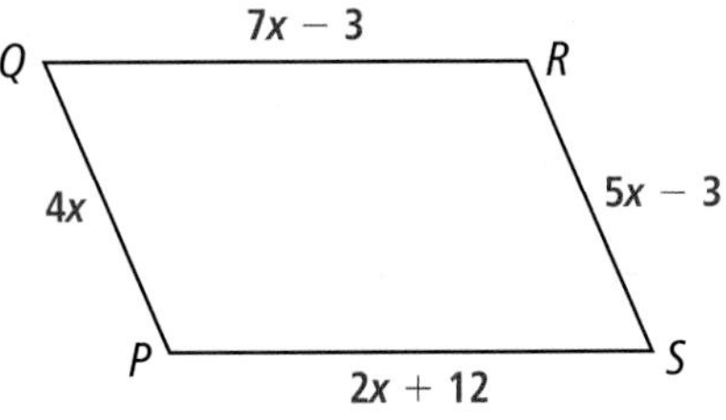


**STUDY TIP**
Remember there is often more than one way to solve a problem. You could also find the value of $x$ by solving the equation $4x = 5x - 3$, since $\overline{QP}$ and $\overline{RS}$ are also opposite sides of the parallelogram.

**A. What is the value of *x*?**

$7x - 3 = 2x + 12$

$\overline{QR} \cong \overline{PS}$ because they are opposite sides of a parallelogram.

$5x = 15$

$x = 3$

**B. What is the length of each side of *PQRS*?**

$PQ = 4x$
$= 4(3)$
$= 12$

$QR = 7x - 3$
$= 7(3) - 3$
$= 21 - 3$
$= 18$

$RS = 5x - 3$
$= 5(3) - 3$
$= 15 - 3$
$= 12$

$PS = 2x + 12$
$= 2(3) + 12$
$= 6 + 12$
$= 18$

**Try It!** 2. The 600-meter fence around City Park forms a parallelogram. The fence along Chaco Road is twice as long as the fence along Grover Lane. What is the length of the fence along Jones Road?

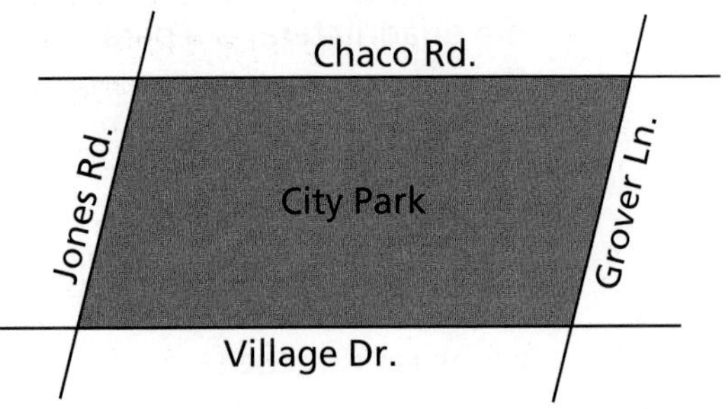

## EXAMPLE 3 Explore Angle Measures in Parallelograms

**A. How are consecutive angles in a parallelogram related?**

You can use what you know about angle relationships formed when parallel lines are cut by a transversal.

**STUDY TIP**
You can visualize a parallelogram as parallel lines intersected by transversals that are also parallel. This may help you determine how the angles are related.

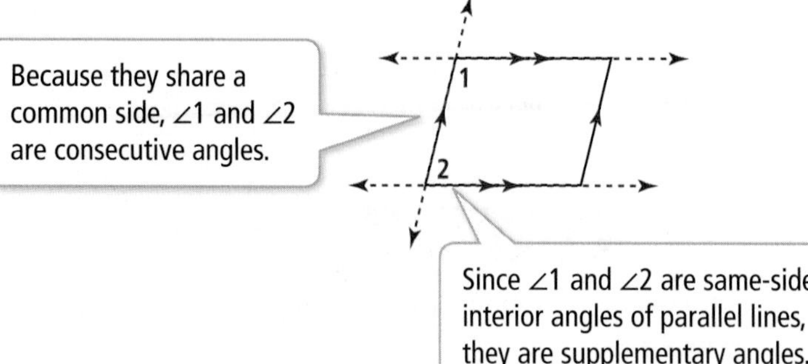

Because they share a common side, ∠1 and ∠2 are consecutive angles.
1
2
Since ∠1 and ∠2 are same-side interior angles of parallel lines, they are supplementary angles.


Consecutive angles $\angle 1$ and $\angle 2$ are supplementary.

**B. How are opposite angles in a parallelogram related?**

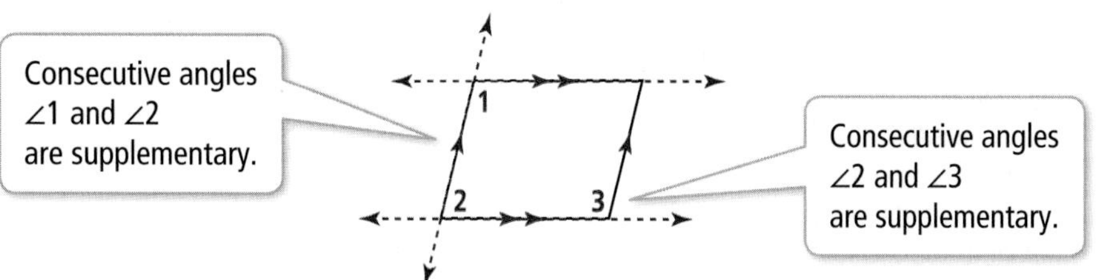


In the figure, $\angle 1$ and $\angle 3$ are opposite angles. Both angles are supplementary to $\angle 2$, so opposite angles in a parallelogram are congruent.

**Try It!** **3. a.** Given parallelogram *ABCD*, what are $m\angle A$ and $m\angle C$?

**b.** What is $m\angle B$?

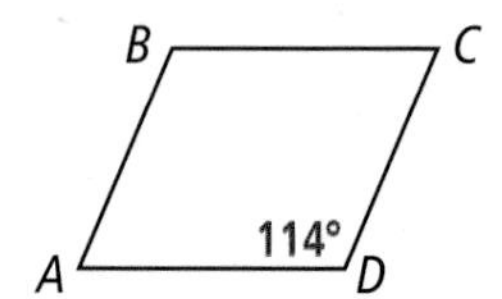


### THEOREM 6-8

If a quadrilateral is a parallelogram, then its consecutive angles are supplementary.

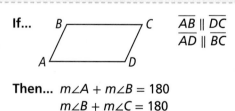

**If...** B C A D $\overline{AB} \parallel \overline{DC}$, $\overline{AD} \parallel \overline{BC}$

**Then...** $m\angle A + m\angle B = 180$
$m\angle B + m\angle C = 180$
$m\angle C + m\angle D = 180$
$m\angle D + m\angle A = 180$

PROOF: SEE EXERCISE 15.

## THEOREM 6-9

If a quadrilateral is parallelogram, then opposite angles are congruent.

PROOF: SEE EXERCISE 23.

If...

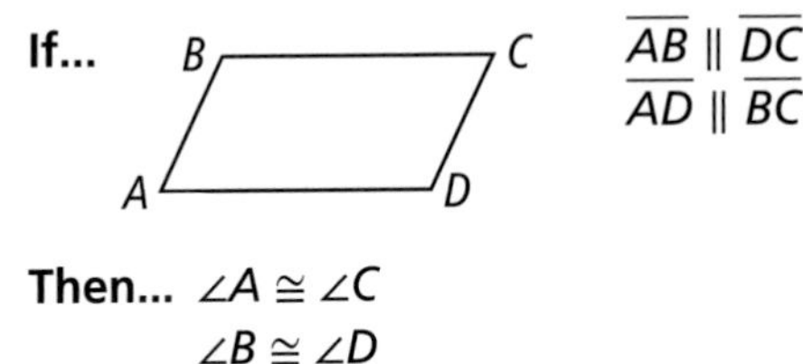
B
C
A
D

$\overline{AB} \parallel \overline{DC}$
$\overline{AD} \parallel \overline{BC}$

Then... $\angle A \cong \angle C$
$\angle B \cong \angle D$

## EXAMPLE 4 Use Angles of a Parallelogram

**The green shape in the fabric design is a parallelogram. The measure of $\angle 2$ is twice the measure of $\angle 1$. What are $m\angle 1$, $m\angle 2$, and $m\angle 3$?**

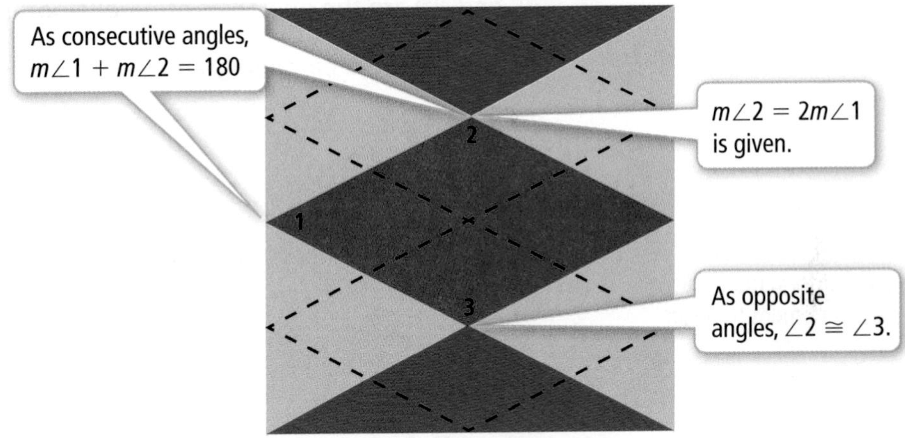
As consecutive angles, $m\angle 1 + m\angle 2 = 180$
$m\angle 2 = 2m\angle 1$ is given.
As opposite angles, $\angle 2 \cong \angle 3$.
1
2
3

**COMMON ERROR**
You may incorrectly write $m\angle 1 = 2m\angle 2$, but $m\angle 1 = 2m\angle 2$ means that $m\angle 1$ is twice $m\angle 2$.

Find $m\angle 1$.

$m\angle 1 + m\angle 2 = 180$

$m\angle 1 + 2m\angle 1 = 180$

$m\angle 1 = 60$

Find $m\angle 2$.

$m\angle 2 = 2m\angle 1$

$m\angle 2 = 2(60)$

$m\angle 2 = 120$

Find $m\angle 3$.

$m\angle 3 = m\angle 2$

$m\angle 3 = 120$

The measures of $\angle 1$, $\angle 2$, and $\angle 3$ are 60, 120, and 120, respectively.

## Try It!

4. Use the parallelogram shown.

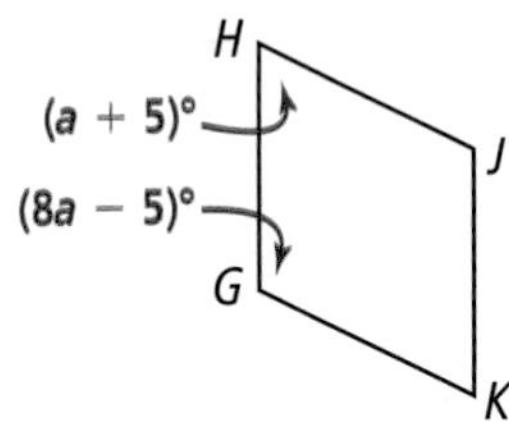
H
J
G
K
$(a + 5)°$
$(8a - 5)°$

a. Given parallelogram $GHJK$, what is the value of $a$?

b. What are $m\angle G$, $m\angle H$, $m\angle J$, and $m\angle K$?

## THEOREM 6-10

If a quadrilateral is a parallelogram, then its diagonals bisect each other.

PROOF: SEE EXAMPLE 5.

**If...**

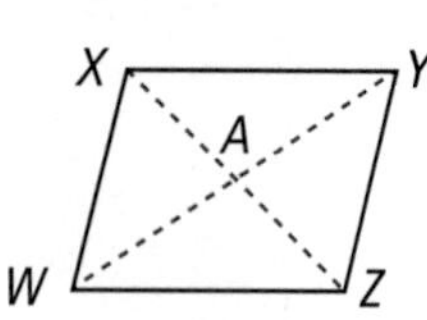


$\overline{WX} \parallel \overline{ZY}$
$\overline{WZ} \parallel \overline{XY}$

**Then...** $\overline{AW} \cong \overline{AY}$
$\overline{AX} \cong \overline{AZ}$

## EXAMPLE 5 Explore the Diagonals of a Parallelogram

**How are the diagonals of a parallelogram related?**

$\overline{AC}$ and $\overline{BD}$ are the diagonals of parallelogram *ABCD*.

**Given:** *ABCD* is a parallelogram.

**Prove:** $\overline{AQ} \cong \overline{CQ}$, $\overline{BQ} \cong \overline{DQ}$

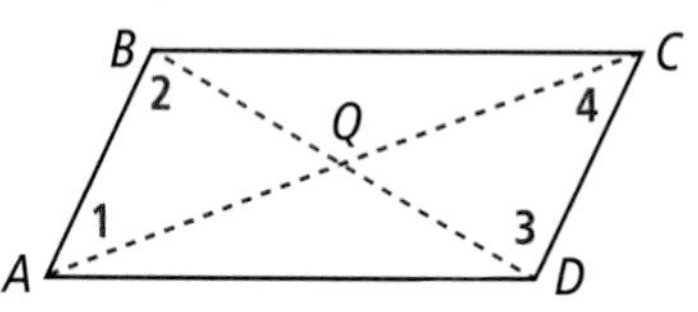


**Proof:**

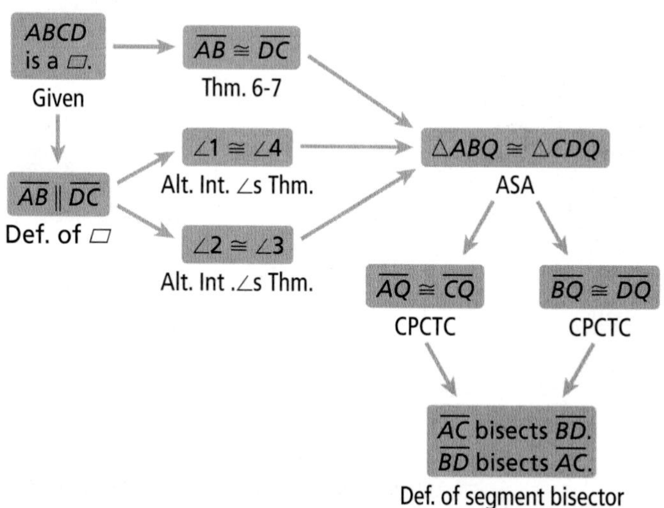


**STUDY TIP**
The given information is usually the best statement to begin a proof.

 **Try It!** 5. Use parallelogram *RSTU* with $SU = 35$ and $KT = 19$.

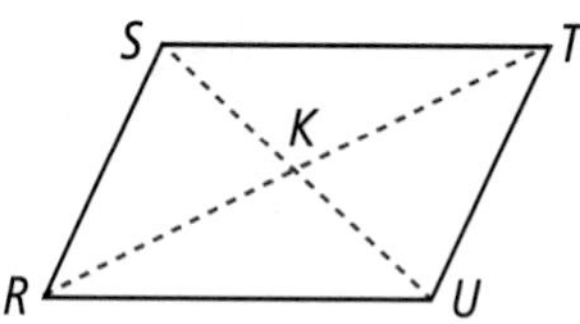


a. What is *SK*?

b. What is *RT*?

APPLICATION

## EXAMPLE 6 Find Unknown Lengths in a Parallelogram

**Corey stamps the orange and purple pattern shown on the front of a poster she is making. How many times will she need to stamp the design to make a row 60 cm wide along the dashed line?**

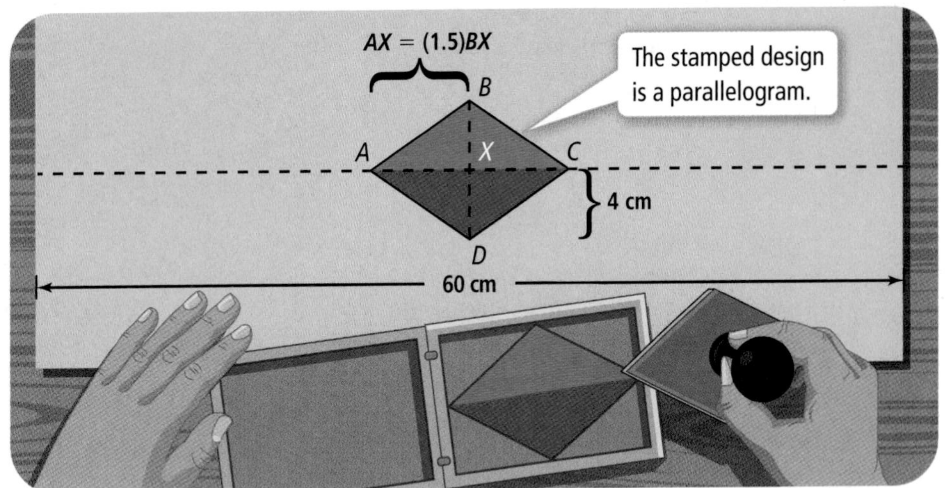


Formulate ◀ By Theorem 6-10, the diagonals $\overline{AC}$ and $\overline{BD}$ bisect each other. So $\overline{BX} \cong \overline{DX}$, and $\overline{AX} \cong \overline{CX}$.

Compute ◀ **Step 1** Determine the length of the diagonal, $\overline{AC}$.

$BX = DX$ (Diagonals bisect each other.)

$BX = 4$

$AX = 1.5\ BX$ (Given)

$AX = 1.5(4)$

$AX = 6$

$AC = 2(AX)$ (Diagonals bisect each other.)

$AC = 2(6)$

$AC = 12$

**Step 2** Find the number of times Corey needs to stamp.

$60 \div 12 = 5$

Interpret ◀ Corey will need to stamp the design 5 times to make a row 60 cm wide.

**Try It!** **6.** Given parallelogram $GHJK$, if $PK = 4$ and $HK = \frac{2}{3}(GJ)$, what is $GP$?

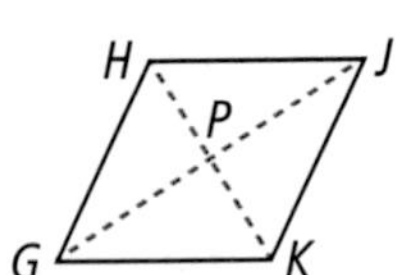

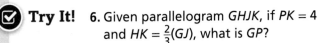

## CONCEPT SUMMARY Properties of Parallelograms

| | Angles of Parallelograms | Sides and Diagonals of Parallelograms |
|---|---|---|
| **WORDS** | Consecutive angles of a parallelogram are supplementary. Opposite angles of a parallelogram are congruent. | Opposite sides of a parallelogram are congruent. Diagonals of a parallelogram bisect each other. |
| **SYMBOLS** | **If...** $\overline{AD} \parallel \overline{CB}$, $\overline{AB} \parallel \overline{DC}$<br>**Then...** $m\angle A + m\angle B = 180$<br>$m\angle B + m\angle C = 180$<br>$m\angle C + m\angle D = 180$<br>$m\angle D + m\angle A = 180$<br>$m\angle A = m\angle C$<br>$m\angle B = m\angle D$ | **If...** $\overline{AD} \parallel \overline{CB}$, $\overline{AB} \parallel \overline{DC}$<br>**Then...** $AB = CD$<br>$AD = BC$<br>$AX = CX$<br>$BX = DX$ |

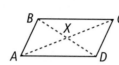

## Do You UNDERSTAND?

1. **ESSENTIAL QUESTION** What are the relationships of the sides, the angles, and the diagonals of a parallelogram?

2. **Error Analysis** What is Carla's error?

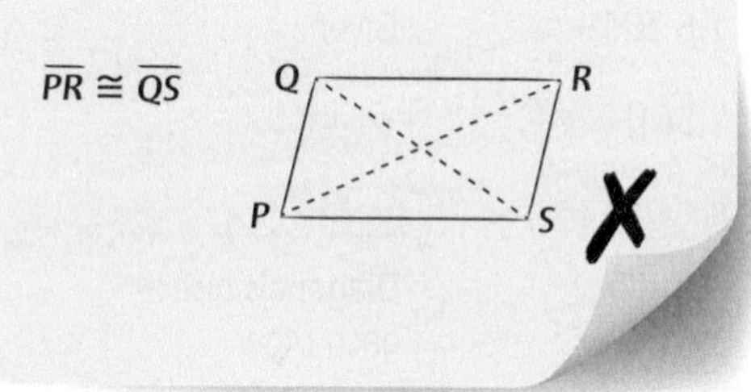


3. **Make Sense and Persevere** If you knew the length of $\overline{DF}$ in parallelogram *DEFG*, how would you find the length of $\overline{DK}$? Explain.

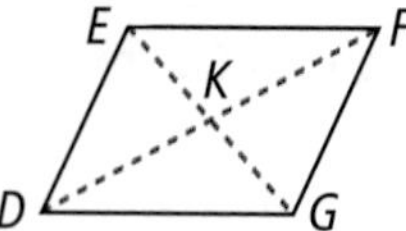


4. **Reason** Given parallelogram *JKLM*, what could the expression $180 - (3x + 8)$ represent? Explain.

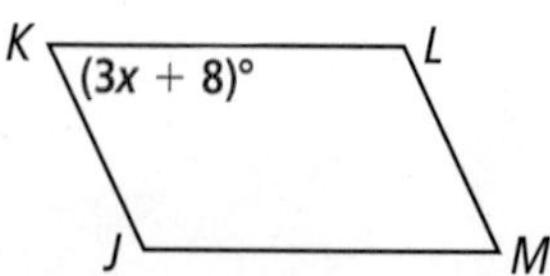


## Do You KNOW HOW?

**For Exercises 5 and 6, use parallelogram *ABCD* to find each length. The measure of $\overline{DE}$ is $x + 2$.**

5. *BC*

6. *BD*

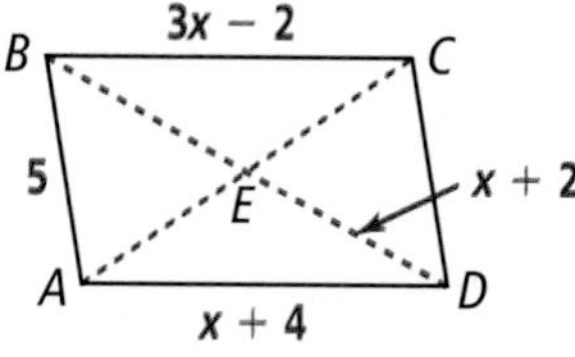


**For Exercises 7 and 8, use parallelogram *WXYZ* to find each angle measure.**

7. $m\angle WXY$

8. $m\angle XYZ$

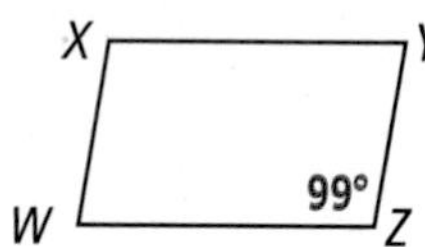


**For Exercises 9 and 10, use parallelogram *EFGH* to find each length.**

9. *EJ*

10. *FH*

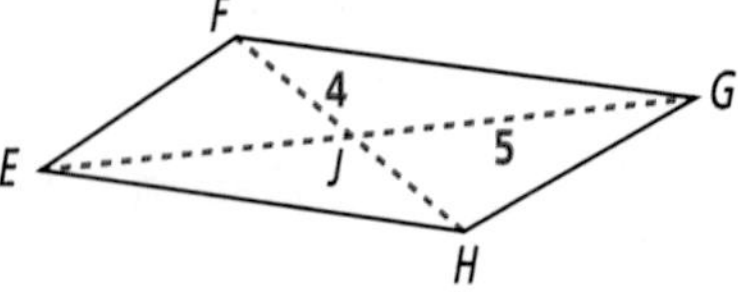


**For Exercises 11 and 12, use parallelogram *MNPQ* to find each angle measure.**

11. $m\angle NPQ$

12. $m\angle PQM$

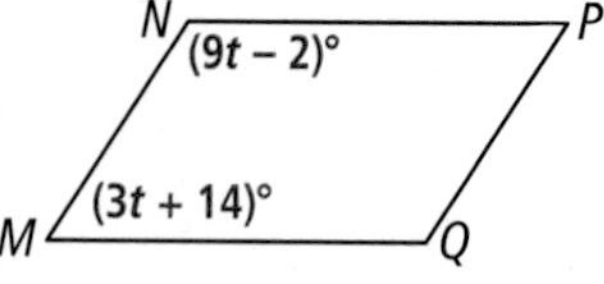

# PRACTICE & PROBLEM SOLVING

Scan for Multimedia

Additional Exercises Available Online

## UNDERSTAND

**13. Construct Arguments** Write a proof of Theorem 6-7.

**Given:** $\overline{WX} \parallel \overline{ZY}$, $\overline{WZ} \parallel \overline{XY}$

**Prove:** $\overline{WX} \cong \overline{ZY}$, $\overline{WZ} \cong \overline{XY}$

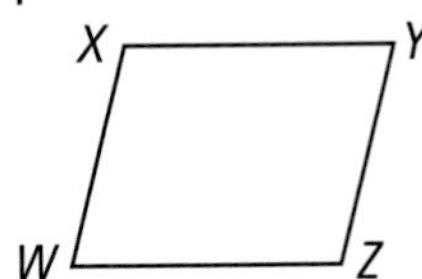


**14. Error Analysis** In the statements shown, explain the student's error. What shape is the quadrilateral?

$\overline{JK} \cong \overline{KL}$ and $\overline{LM} \cong \overline{MJ}$.
$\angle MJK \cong \angle KLM$

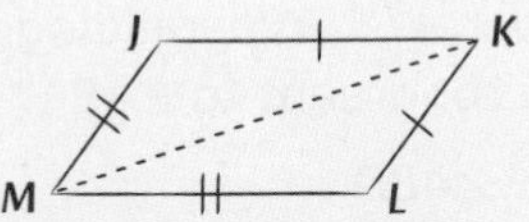


Therefore, $\triangle MJK \cong \triangle KLM$ by SAS. The triangular halves of $JKLM$ are congruent, so $JKLM$ must be a parallelogram.

✗

**15. Construct Arguments** Write a proof of Theorem 6-8.

**Given:** $\overline{AB} \parallel \overline{DC}$, $\overline{AD} \parallel \overline{BC}$

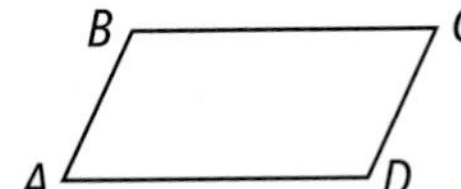


**Prove:** $m\angle A + m\angle B = 180$
$m\angle B + m\angle C = 180$
$m\angle C + m\angle D = 180$
$m\angle D + m\angle A = 180$

**16. Use Appropriate Tools** In a parallelogram, opposite sides are congruent, and opposite angles are congruent. If all sides in a parallelogram are congruent, are all angles congruent also? Draw a picture to explain your answer.

**17. Mathematical Connections** Only one pair of opposite vertices of parallelogram $RSTU$ is shown on the coordinate plane. Is there enough information to find the point where the diagonals of $RSTU$ intersect? Explain and find the point of intersection, if possible.

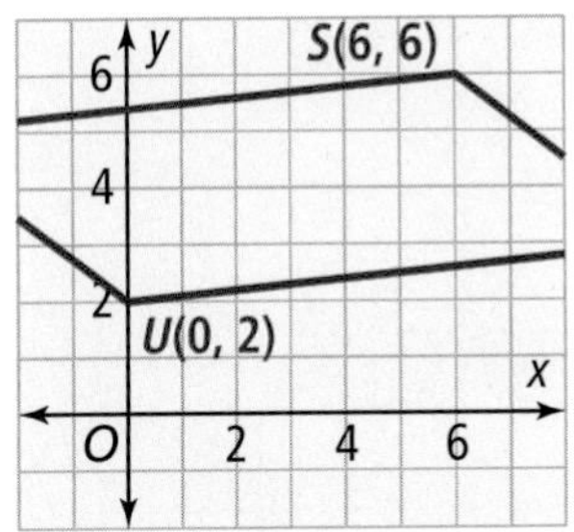


## PRACTICE

**18.** What are the values of $AB$ and $DE$ in parallelogram $ABCD$? SEE EXAMPLES 1 AND 2

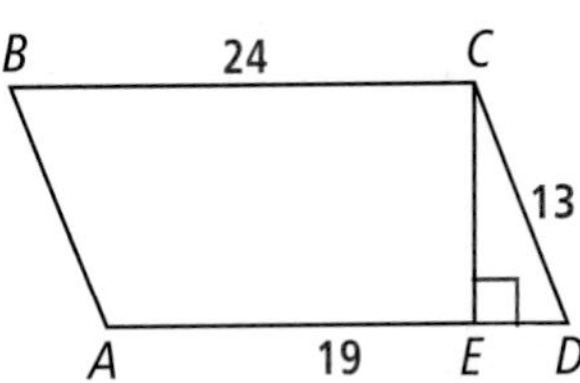


**19.** Quadrilateral $EFGH$ is a parallelogram. What is $m\angle F$? SEE EXAMPLES 3 AND 4

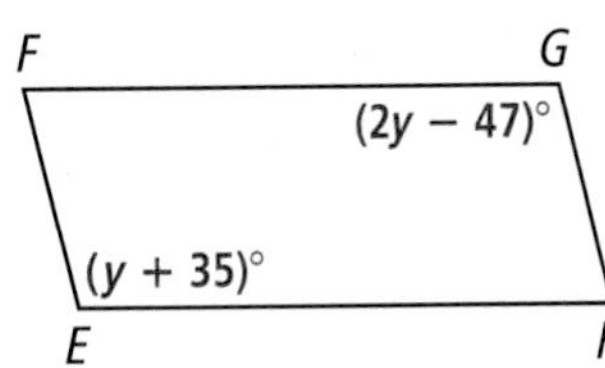


**20.** Quadrilateral $MNPQ$ is a parallelogram. What is $NQ$? SEE EXAMPLES 5 AND 6

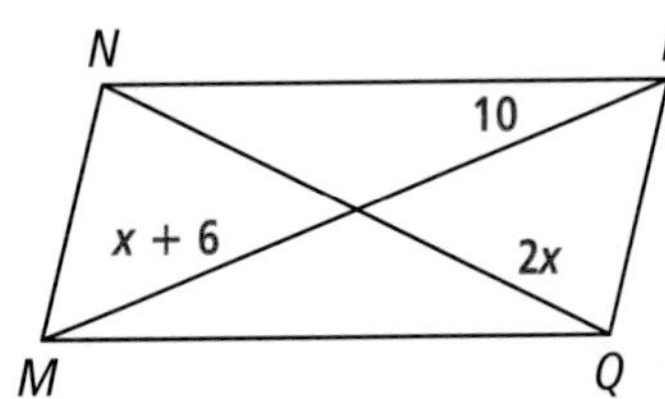


**21.** The figure below can be divided into two parallelograms. What is the angle measure of the point at the bottom?

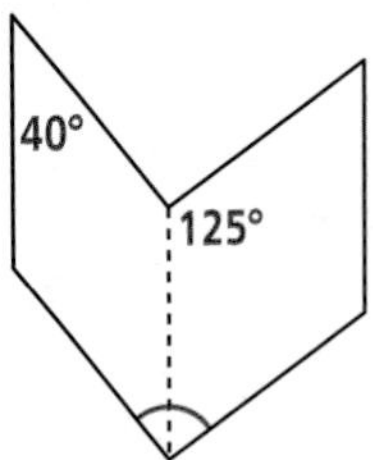


**22.** Find the perimeter of the parallelogram.

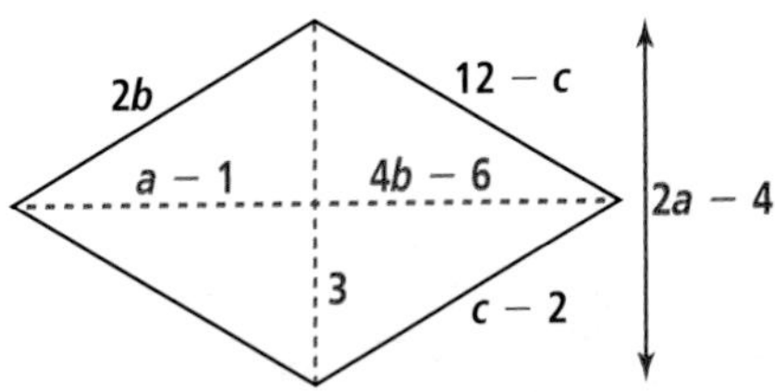


**23.** Write a proof of Theorem 6-9.

**Given:** $\overline{AB} \parallel \overline{DC}$, $\overline{AD} \parallel \overline{BC}$

**Prove:** $\angle A \cong \angle C$, $\angle B \cong \angle D$

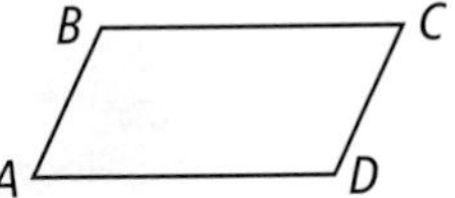

# PRACTICE & PROBLEM SOLVING

Practice | Tutorial

Mixed Review Available Online

## APPLY

24. **Model With Mathematics** All four arms of a mechanical jack are the same length, and they form a parallelogram. Turning the crank pulls the arms together, raising the top of the jack. How high is the top of the jack when the crank is 5 inches off the ground? Explain.

25. **Use Structure** The handrails for a steel staircase form a parallelogram *ABCD*. Additional bars are needed one third and two thirds of the way up the stairs. Explain why the additional bars must be the same length as the end bars.

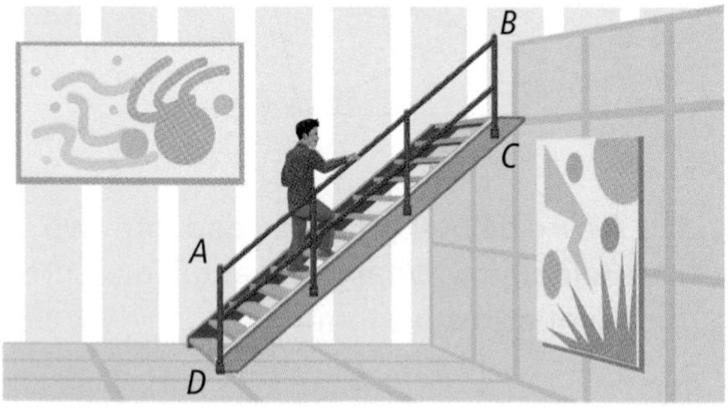


26. **Higher Order Thinking** Reagan designs a pattern consisting of large squares of the same size, small squares of the same size, and some parallelograms. She wants to replicate the pattern using tiles for her bathroom. Are the vertical and horizontal parallelograms congruent? Explain.

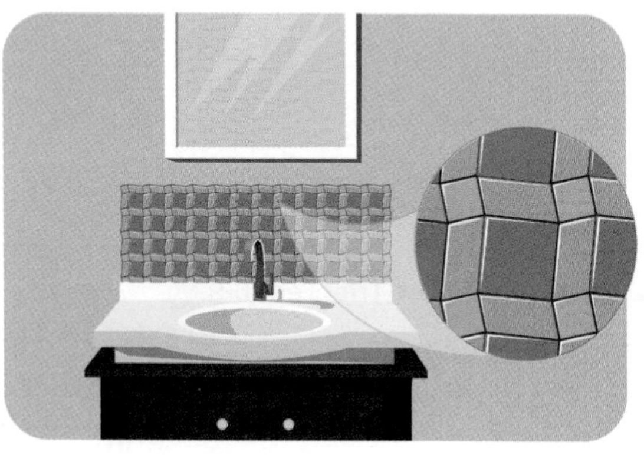

## ASSESSMENT PRACTICE

27. Find the values of *a*, *b*, and *c* in the parallelogram.

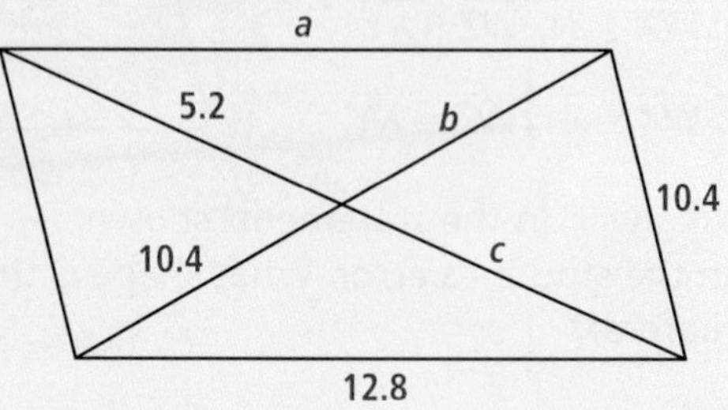


28. **SAT/ACT** In parallelogram *ABCD*, which angle is congruent to $\angle ABC$?

Ⓐ $\angle ABD$

Ⓑ $\angle CDA$

Ⓒ $\angle BCD$

Ⓓ $\angle DAB$

29. **Performance Task** A pipe at an amusement park sprays water onto visitors. A cross section of each pipe has the shape of a parallelogram.

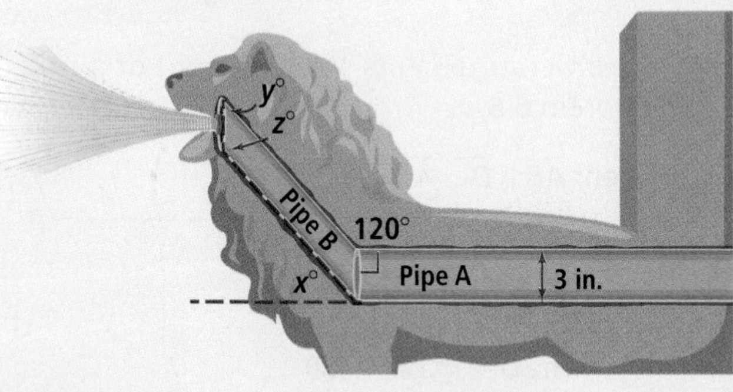


**Part A** Pipe A makes a 120° angle with Pipe B. What are the interior angles of parallelogram B? What is *x*, the measure of the angle that Pipe B makes with the horizontal? Explain.

**Part B** Park engineers fasten a circular cap onto the end of Pipe B. In the middle of the cap is a nozzle to turn the spray of water into a mist. If the diameter of Pipe A is 3 inches, what is the diameter of the circular cap? Explain.

**Part C** What are *x* and *y*, the angle measures that the cap makes with Pipe B? Explain.

# 6-4 Proving a Quadrilateral Is a Parallelogram

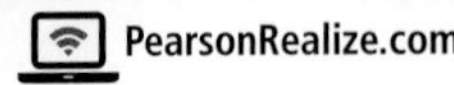
PearsonRealize.com

**I CAN...** use properties of sides, angles, and diagonals to identify a parallelogram.

## EXPLORE & REASON

**Sketch the quadrilaterals as described in the table. Include the diagonals.**

| | Parallel Sides | Congruent Sides |
|---|---|---|
| **Quadrilateral 1** | 0 pairs | 2 consecutive pairs |
| **Quadrilateral 2** | 1 pair | exactly 1 nonparallel pair |
| **Quadrilateral 3** | 2 pairs | 2 opposite pairs |

**A.** Measure the angles of each quadrilateral. How are the angle measures in Quadrilateral 1 related to each other? In Quadrilateral 2? In Quadrilateral 3?

**B.** Measure the diagonals of each quadrilateral. How are the diagonals in Quadrilateral 1 related to each other? In Quadrilateral 2? In Quadrilateral 3?

**C. Communicate Precisely** Compare the relationships among the angles and diagonals of Quadrilateral 3 to those of the other two quadrilaterals. Are there any relationships that make Quadrilateral 3 unique?

## ESSENTIAL QUESTION

**Which properties determine whether a quadrilateral is a parallelogram?**

## EXAMPLE 1 Investigate Sides to Confirm a Parallelogram

**In quadrilateral *ABCD*, $\overline{AC}$ is a diagonal, $\overline{AB} \cong \overline{CD}$, and $\overline{AD} \cong \overline{BC}$. Is *ABCD* a parallelogram? Explain.**

**STUDY TIP**
Recall that any segment is congruent to itself by the Reflexive Property of Congruence.

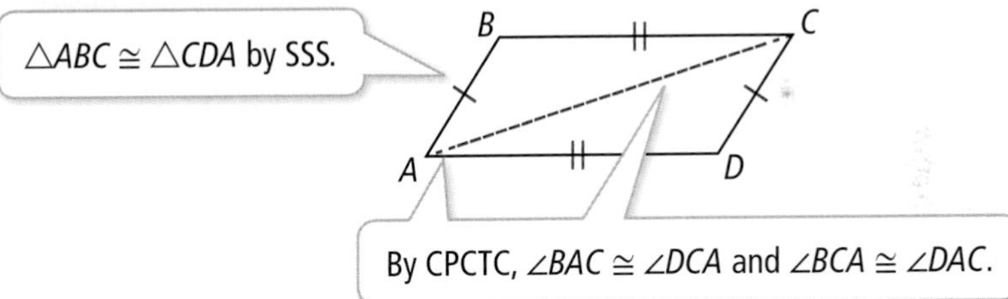


By the Converse of the Alternate Interior Angles Theorem, $\overline{AB} \parallel \overline{CD}$ and $\overline{AD} \parallel \overline{BC}$. By definition, quadrilateral *ABCD* is a parallelogram.

**Try It!** **1.** Explain why you cannot conclude that *ABCD* is a parallelogram.

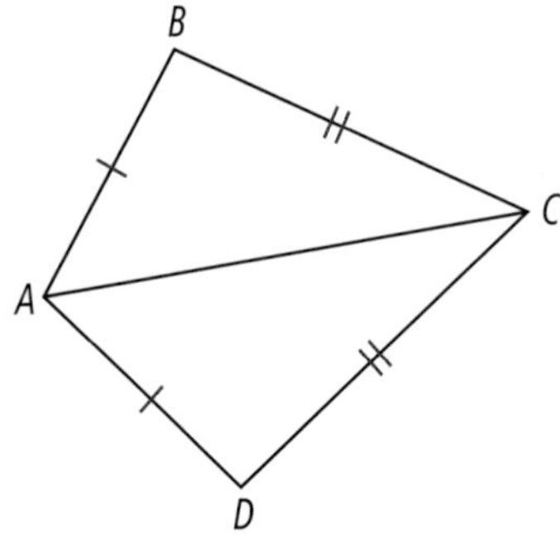

Activity Assess

**THEOREM 6-11** Converse of Theorem 6-7

If both pairs of opposite sides of a quadrilateral are congruent, then the quadrilateral is a parallelogram.

If... $\overline{AB} \cong \overline{CD}$, $\overline{AD} \cong \overline{BC}$

PROOF: SEE EXAMPLE 1.

Then... $ABCD$ is a parallelogram.

CONCEPTUAL UNDERSTANDING

## EXAMPLE 2 Explore Angle Measures to Confirm a Parallelogram

**A. Teo sketches a design of a parallelogram-shaped building. If ∠1 is supplementary to ∠2 and ∠4, is his design a parallelogram?**

**STUDY TIP**
By definition, opposite sides of a parallelogram are parallel. Use theorems about parallel lines to show that a quadrilateral is a parallelogram.

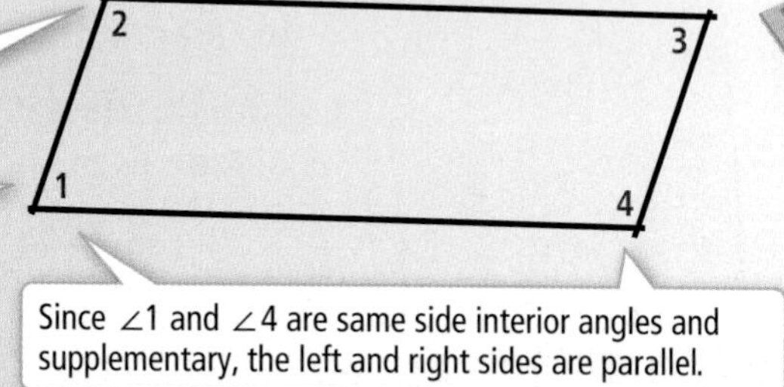


Since ∠1 and ∠2 are same-side interior angles and supplementary, the top and bottom sides are parallel.

Since ∠1 and ∠4 are same side interior angles and supplementary, the left and right sides are parallel.

The quadrilateral has two pairs of parallel sides, so it is a parallelogram. The design is a parallelogram.

**B. Teo sketches a second design in which ∠1 is congruent to ∠3, and ∠2 is congruent to ∠4. Is that design a parallelogram?**

The sum of interior angles is 360.

$$m\angle 1 + m\angle 2 + m\angle 3 + m\angle 4 = 360$$

$$m\angle 1 + m\angle 2 + m\angle 1 + m\angle 2 = 360$$

$$2(m\angle 1 + m\angle 2) = 360$$

$$m\angle 1 + m\angle 2 = 180$$

Since ∠1 ≅ ∠3 and ∠2 ≅ ∠4, substitute $m\angle 1$ for $m\angle 3$ and $m\angle 2$ for $m\angle 4$.

Substitute $m\angle 4$ for $m\angle 2$.

$$m\angle 1 + m\angle 4 = 180$$

Because the edges form a quadrilateral with one angle supplementary to both consecutive angles and from the result in part A, the second design is also a parallelogram.

**Try It!** **2. a.** Is *DEFG* a parallelogram? Explain.

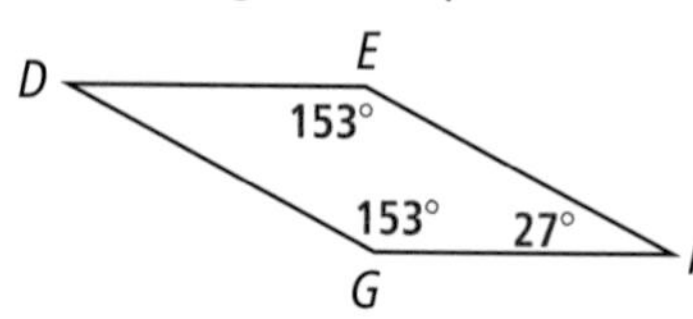


**b.** Is *LMNO* a parallelogram? Explain.

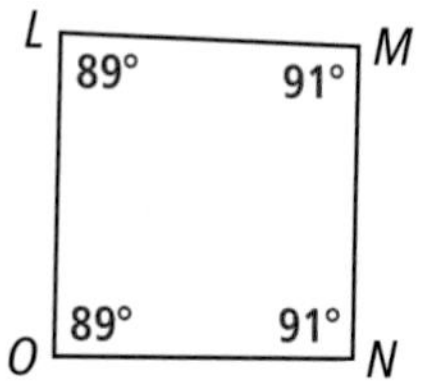

## THEOREM 6-12 Converse of Theorem 6-8

If an angle of a quadrilateral is supplementary to both of its consecutive angles, then the quadrilateral is a parallelogram.

**If...** B C A D

$m\angle A + m\angle B = 180$

$m\angle A + m\angle D = 180$

**Then...** *ABCD* is a parallelogram.

**PROOF: SEE EXERCISE 12.**

## THEOREM 6-13 Converse of Theorem 6-9

If both pairs of opposite angles of a quadrilateral are congruent, then the quadrilateral is a parallelogram.

**If...**

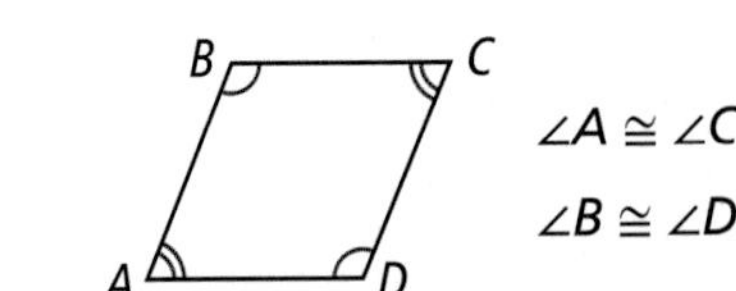


**Then...** *ABCD* is a parallelogram.

**PROOF: SEE EXERCISE 14.**

## EXAMPLE 3 Find Values to Make Parallelograms

**A. For what values of *r* and *s* is *WXYZ* a parallelogram?**

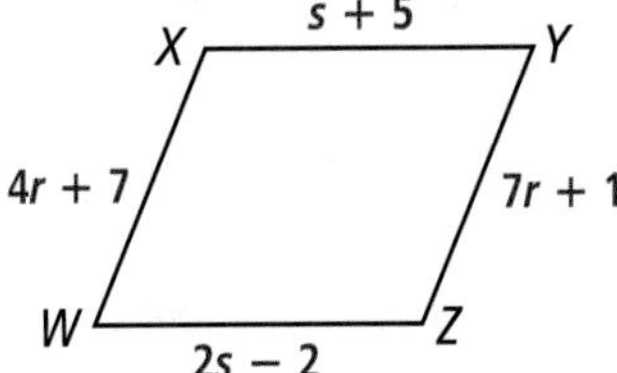


Quadrilateral *WXYZ* is a parallelogram if both pairs of opposite sides are congruent.

$7r + 1 = 4r + 7$ $\quad$ $2s - 2 = s + 5$

$r = 2$ $\quad$ $s = 7$

If $r = 2$ and $s = 7$, then *WX* and *ZY* are both 15, and *XY* and *WZ* are both 12. So *WXYZ* is a parallelogram.

**GENERALIZE**
Think about the properties of a parallelogram. What do you know about a quadrilateral that is a parallelogram?

**B. For what values of *a* and *b* is *RSTU* a parallelogram?**

S T R U: $5a°$, $(3b + 37)°$, $(4b + 1)°$, $(3a + 14)°$

Quadrilateral *RSTU* is a parallelogram if both pairs of opposite angles are congruent.

$5a = 3a + 14$ $\quad$ $4b + 1 = 3b + 37$

$2a = 14$ $\quad$ $b = 36$

$a = 7$

If $a = 7$ and $b = 36$, then angles *S* and *U* are both 35° and angles *T* and *R* are both 145°. So *RSTU* is a parallelogram.

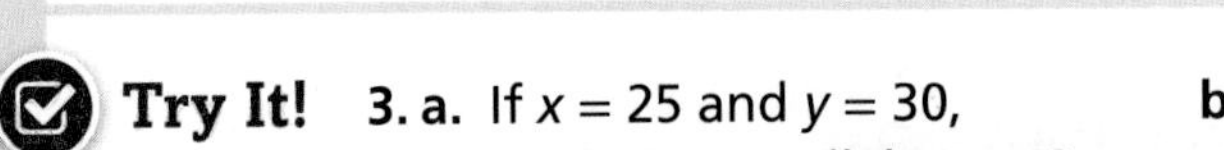

**Try It!** **3. a.** If $x = 25$ and $y = 30$, is *PQRS* a parallelogram?

Q R P S: $(5y - 10)°$, $(x + 15)°$, $(2x - 10)°$, $(3y + 50)°$

**b.** If $g = 14$ and $h = 5$, is *ABCD* a parallelogram?

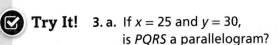

B C A D: $h + 1$, $2g - 11$, $g + 3$, $2h - 3$

### THEOREM 6-14 Converse of Theorem 6-10

If the diagonals of a quadrilateral bisect each other, then the quadrilateral is a parallelogram.

PROOF: SEE EXAMPLE 4.

**If...**

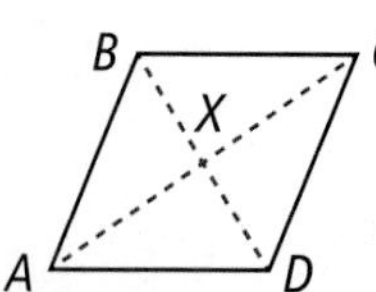


$\overline{AX} \cong \overline{CX}$

$\overline{BX} \cong \overline{DX}$

**Then...** *ABCD* is a parallelogram.

### THEOREM 6-15

If one pair of opposite sides of a quadrilateral is both congruent and parallel, then the quadrilateral is a parallelogram.

PROOF: SEE EXERCISE 20.

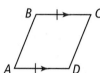

**If...**

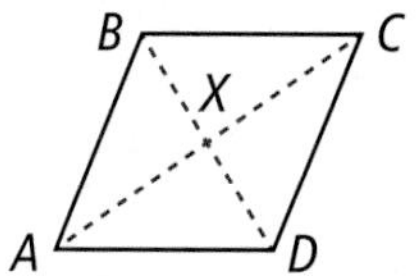


$\overline{AD} \cong \overline{BC}$

$\overline{AD} \parallel \overline{BC}$

**Then...** *ABCD* is a parallelogram.

## EXAMPLE 4 Investigate Diagonals to Confirm a Parallelogram

**Given:** $\overline{AX} \cong \overline{CX}$ and $\overline{BX} \cong \overline{DX}$

**Prove:** *ABCD* is a parallelogram

**Proof:**

| Statements | Reasons |
|---|---|
| **1)** $\overline{AX} \cong \overline{CX}$ and $\overline{BX} \cong \overline{DX}$ | **1)** Given |
| **2)** $\angle AXD \cong \angle CXB$ and $\angle AXB \cong \angle CXD$ | **2)** Vertical Angles Theorem |
| **3)** $\triangle AXD \cong \triangle CXB$ and $\triangle AXB \cong \triangle CXD$ | **3)** SAS |
| **4)** $\overline{AD} \cong \overline{CB}$ and $\overline{AB} \cong \overline{CD}$ | **4)** CPCTC |
| **5)** *ABCD* is a parallelogram. | **5)** Theorem 6-11 |

**COMMON ERROR**
Remember, noncongruent diagonals may bisect each other, just as congruent diagonals do.

**Try It!** **4.** For what values of *p* and *q* is *ABCD* a parallelogram?

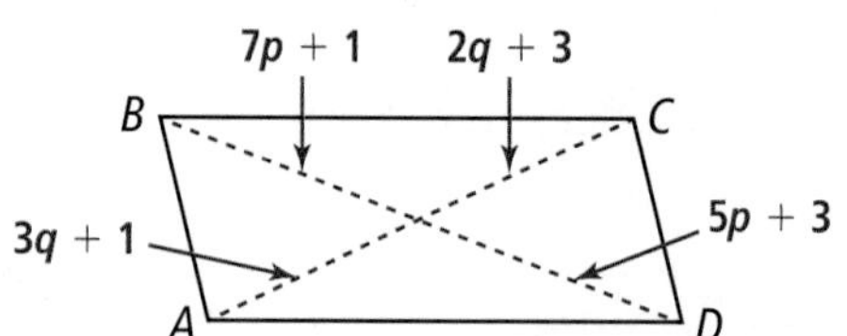


## EXAMPLE 5 Identify a Parallelogram

**A. Is *PQRS* a parallelogram? Explain.**

Same-side interior angles *Q* and *R* are supplementary, so $\overline{QP} \parallel \overline{RS}$.

*PQRS* is a parallelogram by Theorem 6-15.

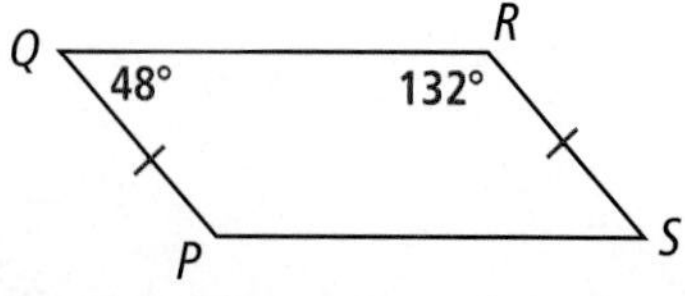


CONTINUED ON THE NEXT PAGE

**STUDY TIP**
After determining that there is not enough information, it is good practice to think about what additional information would be needed to show that the quadrilateral is a parallelogram and why.

EXAMPLE 1 CONTINUED

**B. Is *WXYZ* a parallelogram? Explain.**

Although diagonal $\overline{WY}$ bisects $\overline{XZ}$, diagonal $\overline{XZ}$ does not necessarily bisect $\overline{WY}$. Quadrilateral *WXYZ* does not meet the conditions of Theorem 6-14, and so it is not necessarily a parallelogram.

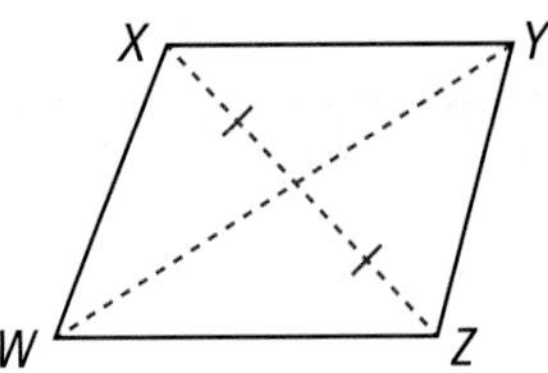

 **Try It!** **5. a.** Is *ABCD* a parallelogram? Explain.

**b.** Is *EFGH* a parallelogram? Explain.

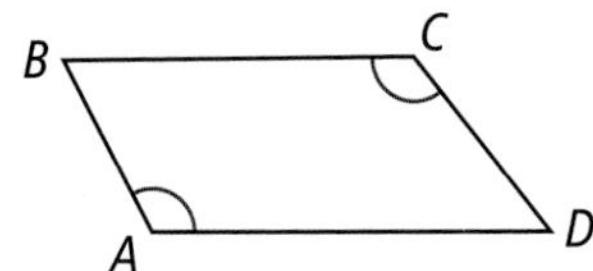


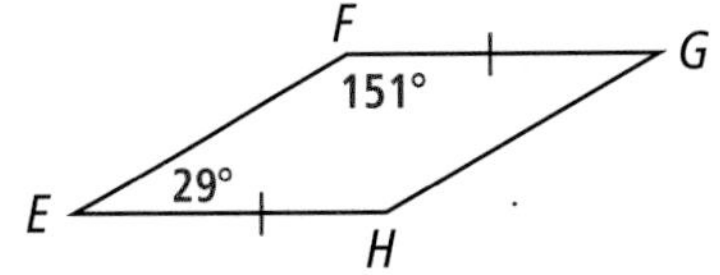


APPLICATION

## EXAMPLE 6 Verify a Parallelogram

**A mechanic raises a truck using a lift. For safety, the floor must be horizontal and the top of the lift must be parallel to the floor. Is the lift shown in a safe position? Explain.**

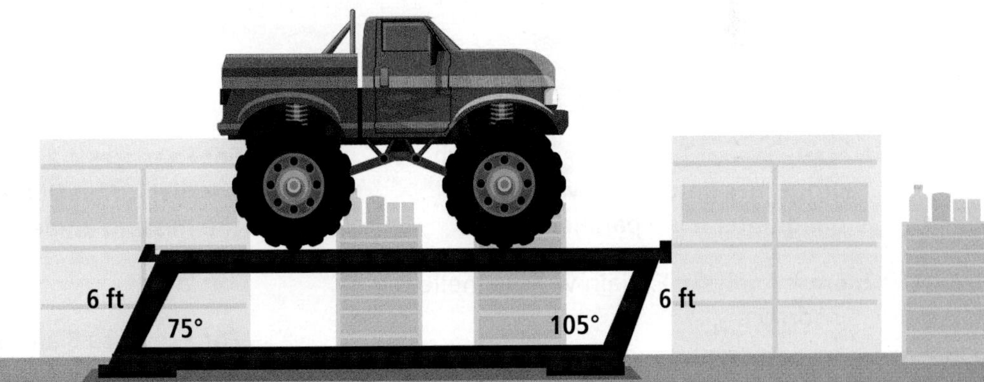


**Formulate** ◀ The lift and the floor form a quadrilateral. If the quadrilateral is a parallelogram, then the side holding the truck will be parallel to the floor and the lift will be safe.

**Compute** ◀ Find the sum of the given angles.

$105 + 75 = 180$

Since a pair of same-side alternate interior angles are supplementary, the 6-ft sides of the lift are parallel. The lift is a parallelogram by Theorem 6-15.

**Interpret** ◀ Opposite sides of a parallelogram are parallel, so the side of the lift holding the truck is parallel to the floor. The lift is in a safe position.

**Try It!** **6.** A carpenter builds the table shown. If the floor is level, how likely is it that a ball placed on the table will roll off?

10 in. 20 in. 20 in. 10 in.

## CONCEPT SUMMARY Identifying Quadrilaterals That Are Parallelograms

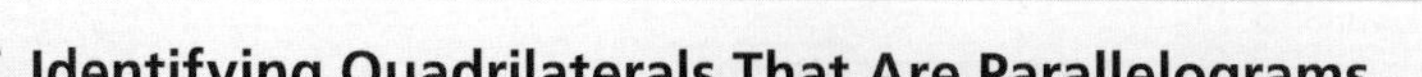

### SIDES AND DIAGONALS

A quadrilateral is a parallelogram if

- two pairs of opposite sides are congruent

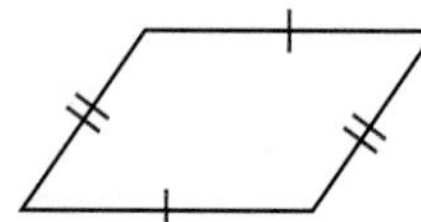

- one pair of opposite sides is congruent and parallel

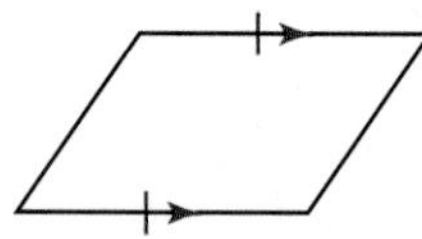

- the diagonals bisect each other

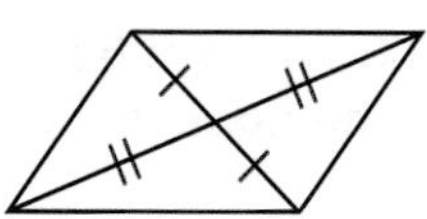

### ANGLES

A quadrilateral is a parallelogram if

- one angle is supplementary to both consecutive angles

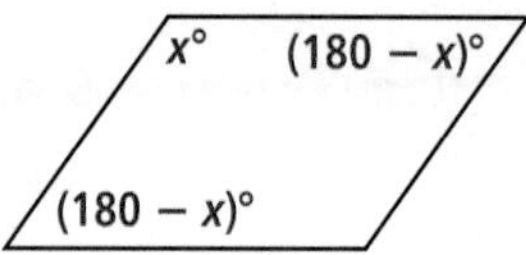


- two pairs of opposite angles are congruent

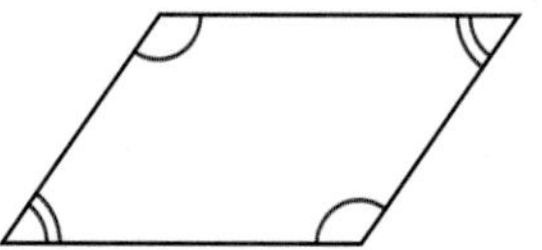

## Do You UNDERSTAND?

1. ESSENTIAL QUESTION Which properties determine whether a quadrilateral is a parallelogram?

2. **Error Analysis** Explain why Rochelle is incorrect.

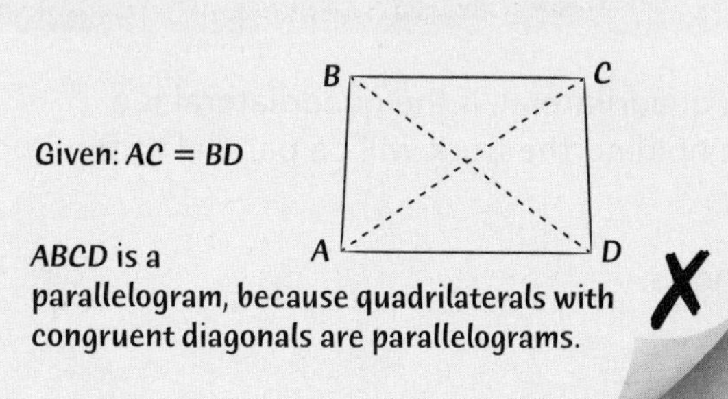

Given: AC = BD
B
C
A
D
ABCD is a parallelogram, because quadrilaterals with congruent diagonals are parallelograms.
X


3. **Make Sense and Persevere** Is the information in the diagram enough to show *WXYZ* is a parallelogram? Explain.

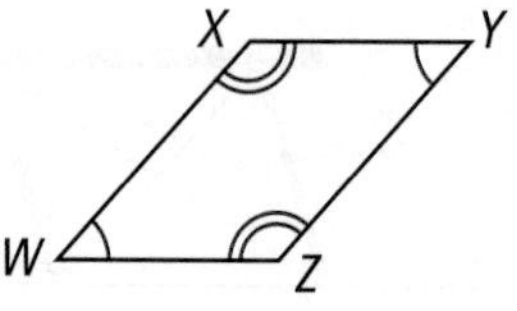


## Do You KNOW HOW?

**For Exercises 4 and 5, use parallelogram *DEFG* to find the missing angle measures.**

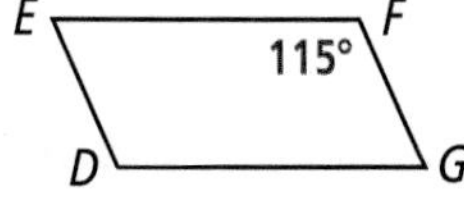


4. $m\angle D$

5. $m\angle E$

**For Exercises 6 and 7, use parallelogram *JKLM* to find the missing lengths.**

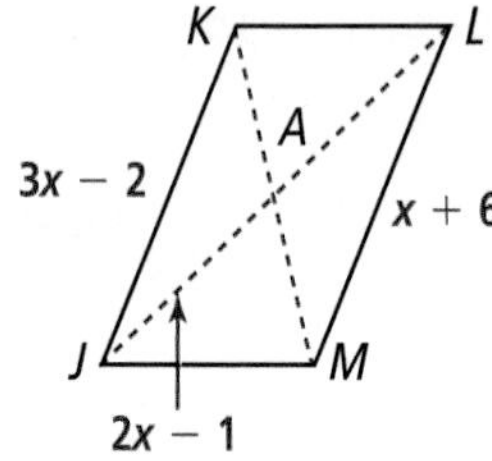


6. *JK*

7. *JL*

**Use the diagram for Exercises 8 and 9.**

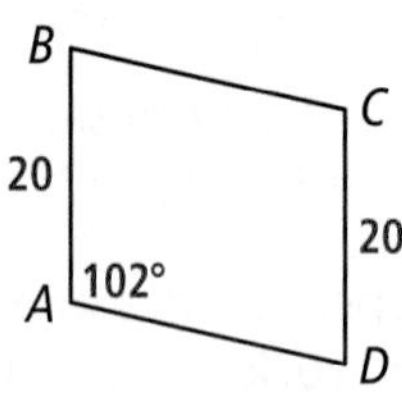


8. If $AB \parallel DC$, is *ABCD* a parallelogram? Explain.

9. If *ABCD* is a parallelogram, how does *AC* compare to *BD*? Explain.

# PRACTICE & PROBLEM SOLVING

Scan for Multimedia

Practice Tutorial

Additional Exercises Available Online

## UNDERSTAND

**10. Use Appropriate Tools** If you are given a drawing of a quadrilateral, how can you determine whether or not it is a parallelogram? What tool or tools can you use?

**11. Error Analysis** Ahmed uses the following explanation to prove that a figure is a parallelogram. What is Ahmed's error?

The quadrilateral has a pair of opposite sides congruent and a pair of opposite sides parallel. According to Theorem 6-15, the figure is a parallelogram.

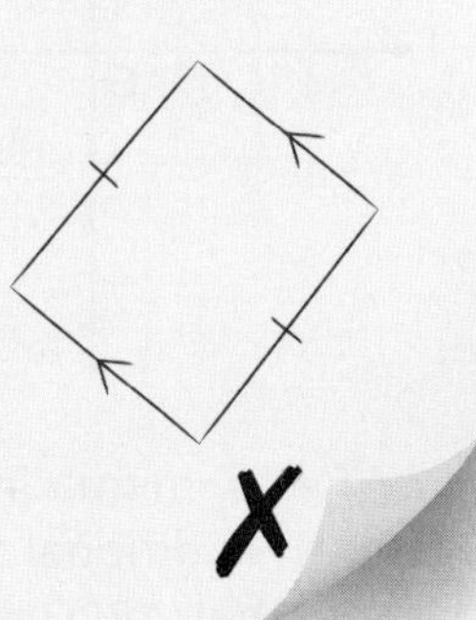

**12. Construct Arguments** Write a proof of Theorem 6-12.

**Given:** $m\angle F + m\angle G = 180$
$m\angle F + m\angle J = 180$

**Prove:** *FGHJ* is a parallelogram.

F G J H

**13. Mathematical Connections** A rectangle is defined as a quadrilateral with four right angles. Which theorem or theorems from the lesson explain why a rectangle is a parallelogram? Explain how the theorem or theorems apply.

**14. Construct Arguments** Write a proof of Theorem 6-13.

**Given:** $\angle L \cong \angle N$, $\angle M \cong \angle O$

**Prove:** *LMNO* is a parallelogram.

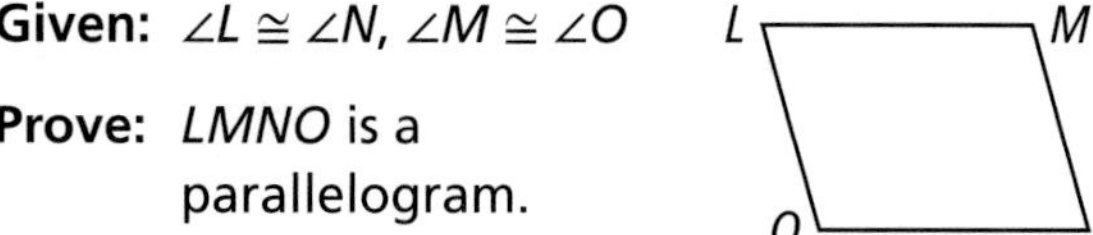


**15. Higher Order Thinking** Describe rigid motions you can apply to $\triangle PQR$ to construct three different parallelograms by combining the preimage and image. Explain why the resulting figures are parallelograms.

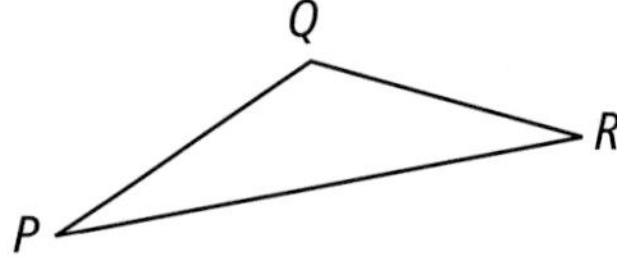


## PRACTICE

**16.** Is each quadrilateral a parallelogram? Explain.
SEE EXAMPLES 1 AND 2

a.

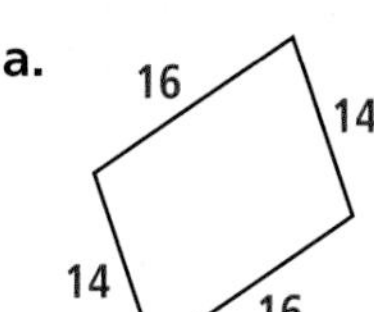


b.

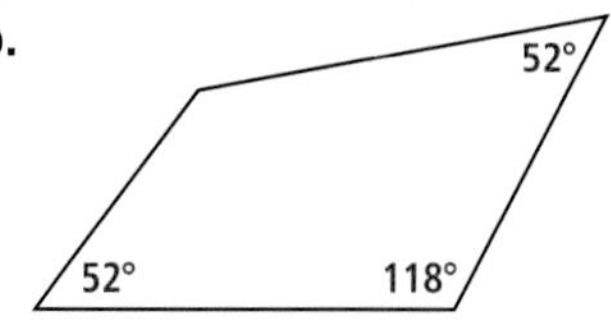


**17.** In each figure, for what values of *x* and *y* is the figure a parallelogram? SEE EXAMPLE 3

a.

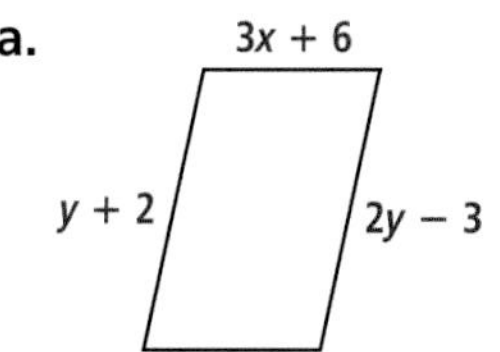


b.

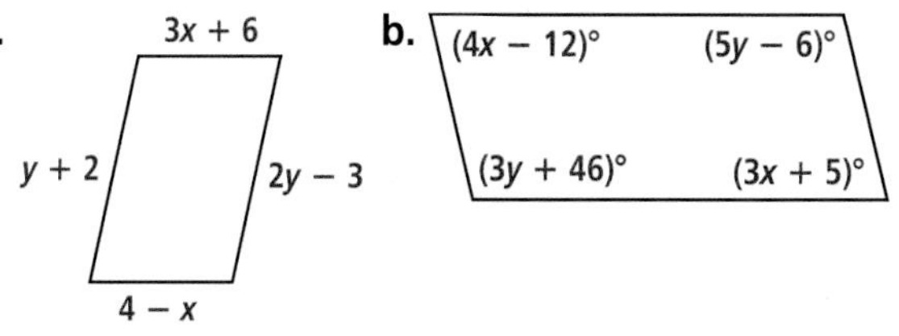


**18.** Given the lengths shown, for what values of *w* and *z* is the figure a parallelogram?
SEE EXAMPLE 4

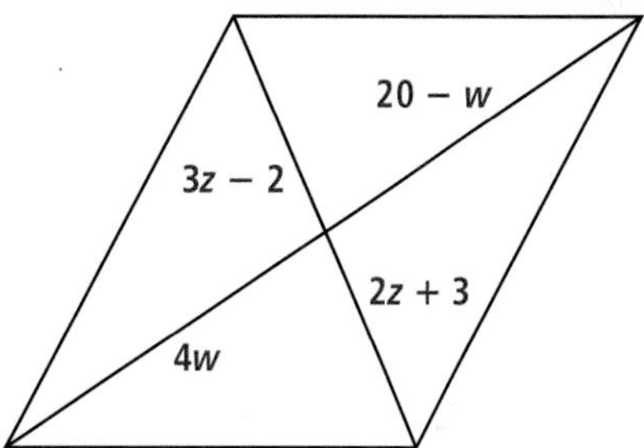


**19.** Is the figure below a parallelogram? Explain.
SEE EXAMPLES 5 AND 6

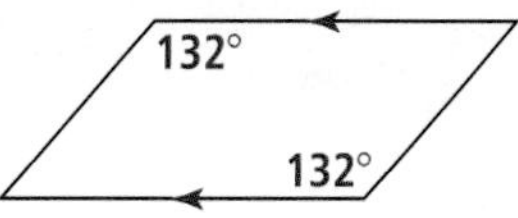


**20.** Write a proof of Theorem 6-15.

**Given:** $\overline{KL} \parallel \overline{JM}$, $\overline{KL} \cong \overline{JM}$

**Prove:** *JKLM* is a parallelogram.

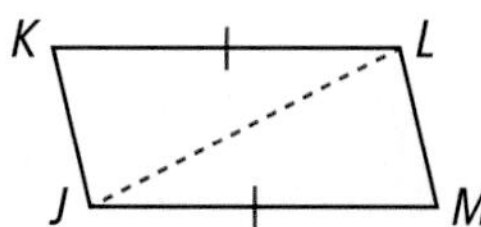


Hint: Construct diagonal $\overline{JL}$.

# PRACTICE & PROBLEM SOLVING

## APPLY

**21. Make Sense and Persevere** A lamp on a wall is suspended from an extendable arm that allows the lamp to slide up and down. When it expands, does the shape shown remain a parallelogram? Explain.

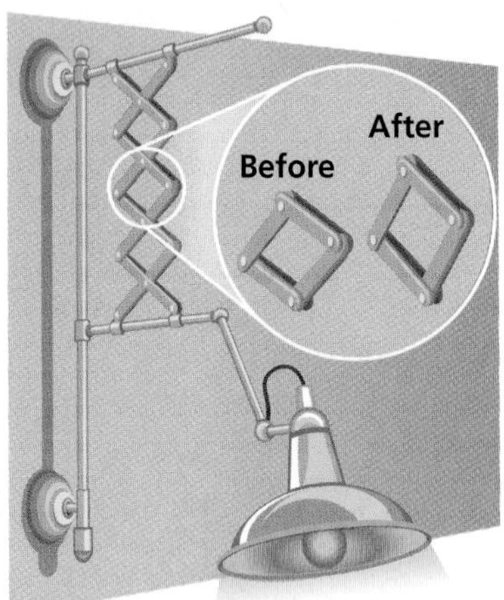


**22. Model With Mathematics** Simon wants to decorate a cake with a pattern of parallelograms. He first pipes two parallel lines that are 3 inches apart. He then makes a mark every $\frac{1}{2}$ inch along each line. He pipes a line from one mark to the next on the opposite side. Does this ensure that the lines will be parallel? Explain your answer.

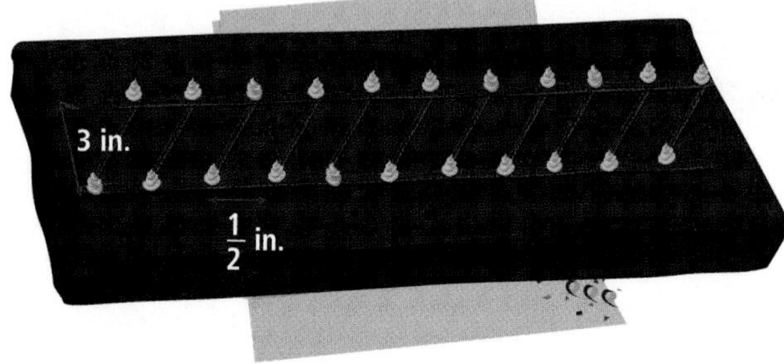


**23. Communicate Precisely** In the game shown, the arrangement of marbles on the board is called a *parallelogram formation*. Why is that name appropriate? Explain.

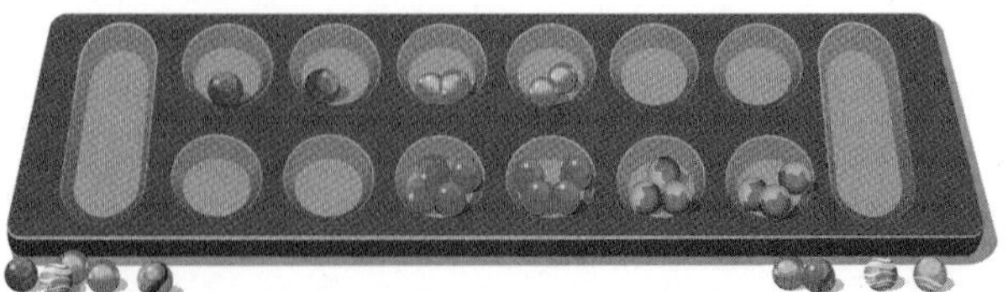

## ASSESSMENT PRACTICE

**24.** Copy the graph and plot all possible coordinate pairs for point *Q* on the coordinate plane so that points *P*, *Q*, *R*, and *S* form the vertices of a parallelogram.

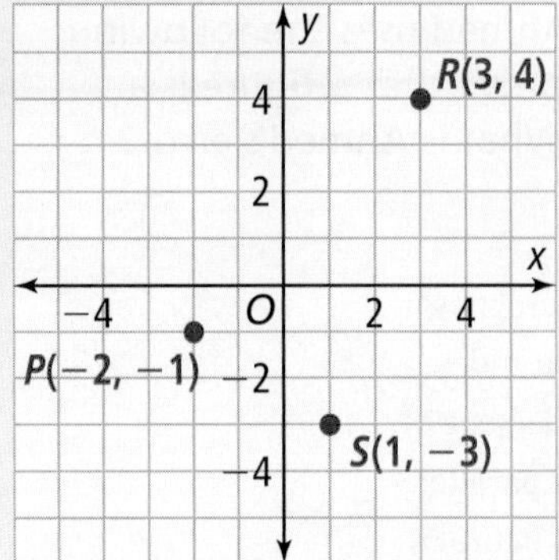


**25. SAT/ACT** In quadrilateral *ABCD*, $\angle A \cong \angle C$. Which additional statement can be used to show that *ABCD* is a parallelogram?

Ⓐ $m\angle A + m\angle C = 180$

Ⓑ $\overline{BD}$ bisects $\overline{AC}$

Ⓒ $m\angle B + m\angle D = 180$

Ⓓ $\angle B \cong \angle D$

**26. Performance Task** Margaret helps her sister build a baby gate that is built from dowels hinged at the top and bottom, so the gate can open up against the wall along the stairs. They call it the parallelogram gate.

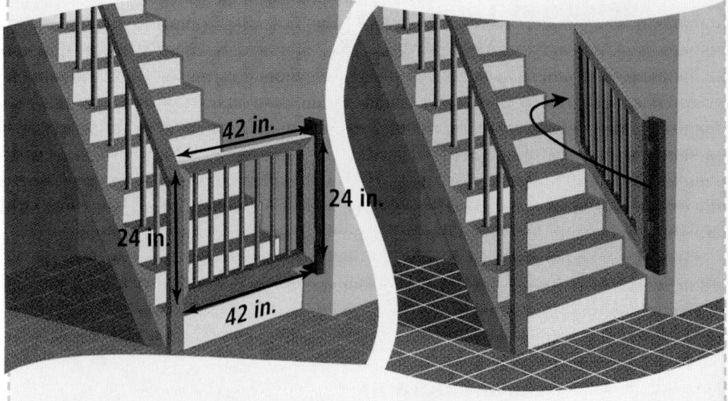


**Part A** Are they correct to call it a parallelogram gate? Explain.

**Part B** What are the measurements of the sides of the gate when the gate is open? Explain.

**Part C** Margaret's father suggests that they add two diagonal slats at the front of the baby gate. What would that do to the gate? Explain.

# 6-5 Properties of Special Parallelograms

PearsonRealize.com

**I CAN…** use the properties of rhombuses, rectangles, and squares to solve problems.

## EXPLORE & REASON

Consider these three figures.

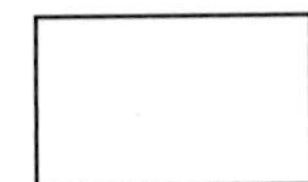
Figure 1

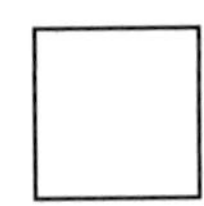
Figure 2

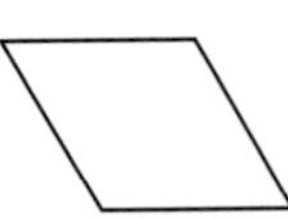
Figure 3

A. What questions would you ask to determine whether each figure is a parallelogram?

B. **Communicate Precisely** What questions would you ask to determine whether Figure 1 is a rectangle? What additional questions would you ask to determine whether Figure 2 is a square?

C. If all three figures are parallelograms, what is the most descriptive name for Figure 3? How do you know?

## ESSENTIAL QUESTION

**What properties of rhombuses, rectangles, and squares differentiate them from other parallelograms?**

CONCEPTUAL UNDERSTANDING

## EXAMPLE 1 Find the Diagonals of a Rhombus

**A. Parallelogram *ABCD* is a rhombus. What are the measures of ∠1, ∠2, ∠3, and ∠4?**

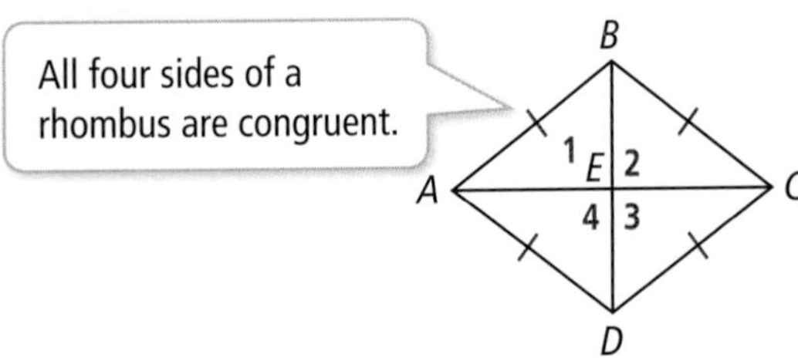


**STUDY TIP**
Recall that a rhombus is a parallelogram, so it has all the properties of parallelograms.

By the Converse of the Perpendicular Bisector Theorem, *B* and *D* are on the perpendicular bisector of $\overline{AC}$, so $\overline{AC} \perp \overline{BD}$.

All four angles formed by the intersection of the diagonals are right angles, so the measure of ∠1, ∠2, ∠3, and ∠4 is 90.

**B. Parallelogram *JKLM* is a rhombus. How are ∠1, ∠2, ∠3, and ∠4 related?**

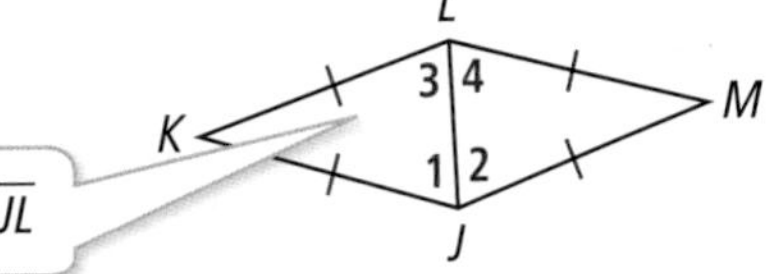


By SSS, $\triangle JKL \cong \triangle JML$, so ∠1 ≅ ∠2 and ∠3 ≅ ∠4.

The diagonals of a rhombus bisect the angles at each vertex.

**Try It!** 1. a. What is *WY*?  b. What is *m*∠*RPS*?

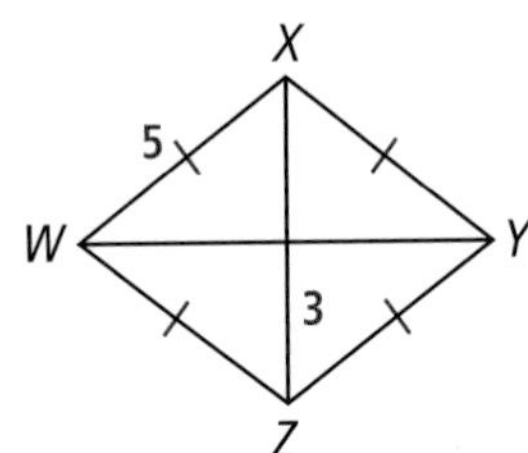


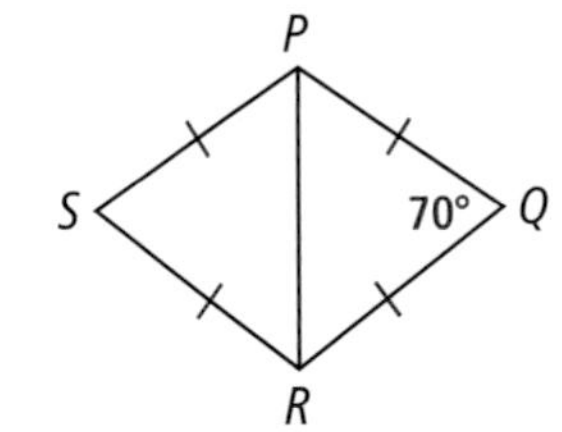

**THEOREM 6-16**

If a parallelogram is a rhombus, then its diagonals are perpendicular bisectors of each other.

PROOF: SEE EXERCISE 14.

**If...**

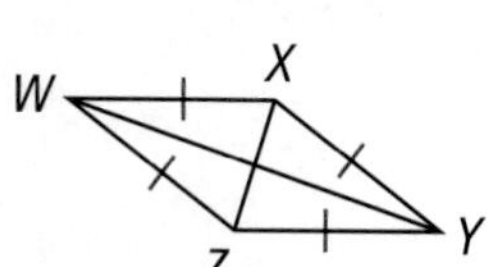


**Then...** $\overline{WY}$ and $\overline{XZ}$ are perpendicular bisectors of each other.

**THEOREM 6-17**

If a parallelogram is a rhombus, then each diagonal bisects a pair of opposite angles.

PROOF: SEE EXERCISE 17.

**If...**

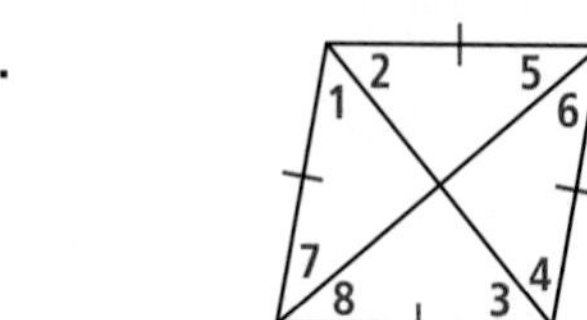


**Then...** $\angle 1 \cong \angle 2$, $\angle 3 \cong \angle 4$, $\angle 5 \cong \angle 6$, and $\angle 7 \cong \angle 8$.

## EXAMPLE 2 Find Lengths and Angle Measures in a Rhombus

**A. Quadrilateral *ABCD* is a rhombus. What is $m\angle ADE$?**

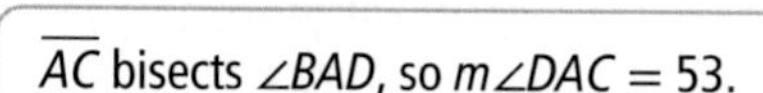


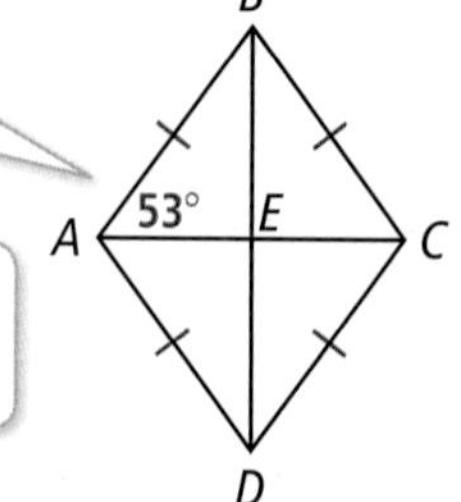


$$m\angle DAE + m\angle AED + m\angle ADE = 180$$

$$53 + 90 + m\angle ADE = 180$$

$$m\angle ADE = 37$$

$\overline{AC} \perp \overline{BD}$, so $m\angle AED = 90$.

**COMMON ERROR**
You may incorrectly state that $m\angle ADE = m\angle DAE$. Remember that consecutive angles are not necessarily congruent.

**B. Quadrilateral *GHJK* is a rhombus. What is *GH*?**

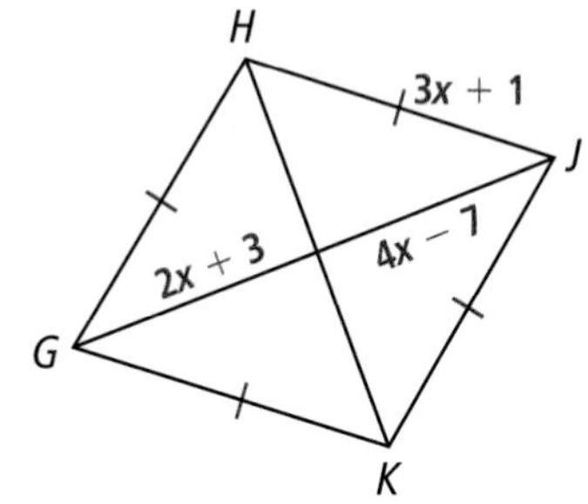


**Step 1** Find *x*.

$$2x + 3 = 4x - 7$$

$$2x = 10$$

$$x = 5$$

**Step 2** Use the value of *x* to find *GH*.

$$HJ = 3(5) + 1 = 16$$

$$GH = HJ$$

$$GH = 16$$

**Try It!** **2.** Each quadrilateral is a rhombus.

**a.** What is $m\angle MNO$?

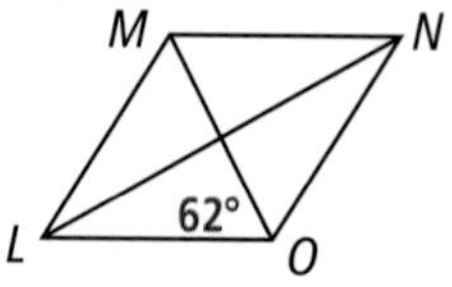


**b.** What is *QT*?

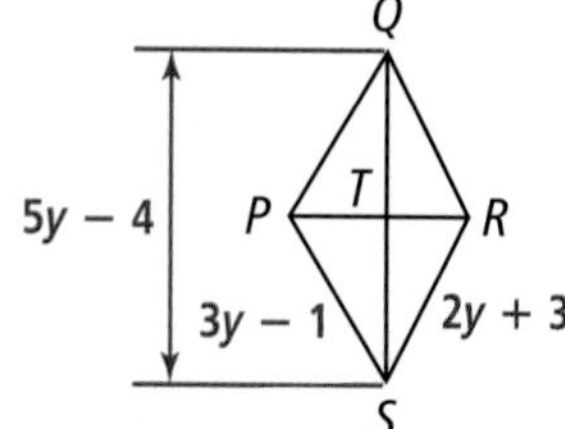

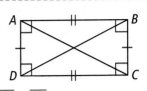

## THEOREM 6-18

If a parallelogram is a rectangle, then its diagonals are congruent.

**If...**

**Then...** $\overline{AC} \cong \overline{BD}$

PROOF: SEE EXAMPLE 3.

PROOF

## EXAMPLE 3 Prove Diagonals of a Rectangle Are Congruent

**Write a proof for Theorem 6-18.**

**Given:** *PQRS* is a rectangle.

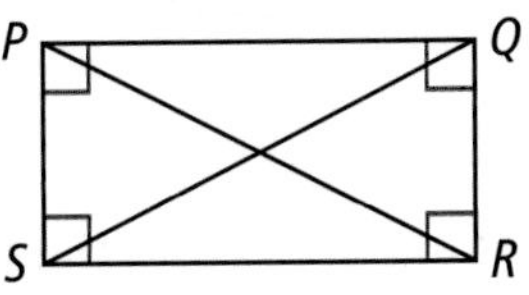


**Prove:** $\overline{PR} \cong \overline{QS}$

**Plan:** To show that the diagonals are congruent, find a pair of congruent triangles that each diagonal is a part of. Both $\triangle PSR$ and $\triangle QRS$ appear to be congruent. Think about how to use properties of rectangles to show they are congruent. Draw each triangle separately and label the congruent sides.

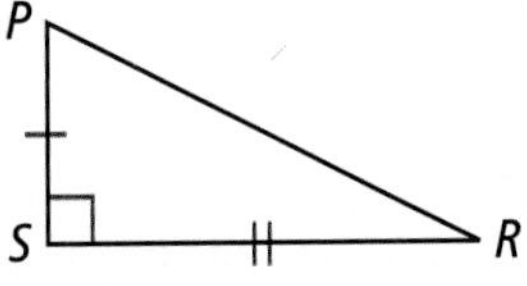


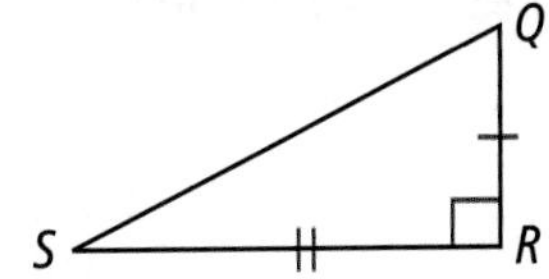


**Proof:**

| Statements | Reasons |
|---|---|
| 1) *PQRS* is a rectangle. | 1) Given |
| 2) *PQRS* is a parallelogram. | 2) Def. of rectangle |
| 3) $\overline{PS} \cong \overline{QR}$ | 3) Opposite sides of a parallelogram are congruent. |
| 4) $\angle PSR$ and $\angle QRS$ are right angles. | 4) Def. of rectangle |
| 5) $\angle PSR \cong \angle QRS$ | 5) All right angles are congruent. |
| 6) $\overline{SR} \cong \overline{RS}$ | 6) Reflexive Prop. of Equality |
| 7) $\triangle PSR \cong \triangle QRS$ | 7) SAS Triangle Congruence Thm. |
| 8) $\overline{PR} \cong \overline{QS}$ | 8) CPCTC |

**STUDY TIP**
When you see triangles in a diagram for a proof, you can often use congruent triangles and CPCTC to complete the proof.

**Try It!** 3. A carpenter needs to check the gate his apprentice built to be sure it is rectangular. The diagonals measure 52 inches and 53 inches. Is the gate rectangular? Explain.

APPLICATION

## EXAMPLE 4 Find Diagonal Lengths of a Rectangle

**Paul is training his horse to run the course at a pace of 4 meters per second or faster. Paul rides his horse from $D$ to $C$ to $E$ to $B$ in 1 minute 30 seconds. The figure $ABCD$ is a rectangle. Did he make his goal?**

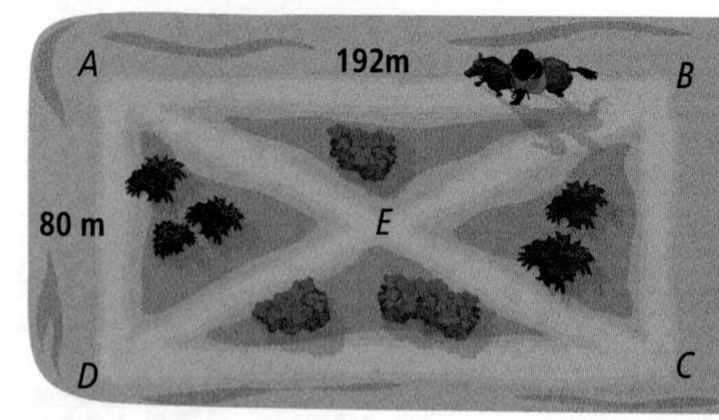


**Formulate** Use the Pythagorean Theorem to find $BD$. Then use properties of rectangles to find each segment length and the total distance. Finally, determine his speed.

**Compute**

$(BD)^2 = 80^2 + 192^2$

$(BD)^2 = 43{,}264$

$BD = 208$

Apply the Pythagorean Theorem.

Use the properties of rectangles to find the total distance.

$CE = EB = 104$

$DC + CE + EB = 192 + 104 + 104 = 400$

Diagonals are congruent and bisect each other.

Determine the pace.

$400 \div 90 \approx 4.4$

**Interpret** Paul's horse ran at a pace of about 4.4 m/s, so he made his goal.

**Try It!** 4. A rectangle with area 1,600 $m^2$ is 4 times as long as it is wide. What is the sum of the diagonals?

## EXAMPLE 5 Diagonals and Angle Measures of a Square

**Figure $WXYZ$ is a square. If $WY + XZ = 92$, what is the area of $\triangle WPZ$?**

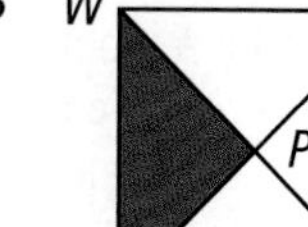


Since the figure is also a rhombus, $\overline{WY} \perp \overline{XZ}$ and $WP$ and $ZP$ are the base and height of $\triangle WPZ$.

**Step 1** Find the lengths of the diagonals.

$WY + XZ = 92$

$WY = XZ = 46$

$WXYZ$ is a rectangle, so $\overline{WY} \cong \overline{XZ}$.

**Step 2** Find $WP$ and $ZP$.

$WP = \frac{1}{2}(WY) = 23$

$ZP = \frac{1}{2}(XZ) = 23$

$WXYZ$ is a parallelogram, so $\overline{WY}$ and $\overline{XZ}$ bisect each other.

**Step 3** Find the area of $\triangle WPZ$.

$\text{area}(\triangle WPZ) = \frac{1}{2}(23)(23) = 264.5$

The area of $\triangle WPZ$ is 264.5 square units.

**USE STRUCTURE**
Consider the four triangles formed by the diagonals of a square. What observations do you make about these triangles?

**Try It!** 5. Square $ABCD$ has diagonals $\overline{AC}$ and $\overline{BD}$. What is $m\angle ABD$? Explain.

## CONCEPT SUMMARY Properties of Special Parallelograms

| | Rectangle | Rhombus | Square |
|---|---|---|---|
| WORDS | If a parallelogram is a rectangle, then the diagonals are congruent. | If a parallelogram is a rhombus, then the diagonals are perpendicular and bisect each pair of opposite angles. | If a parallelogram is a square, the properties of both a rectangle and a rhombus apply. |
| DIAGRAMS | 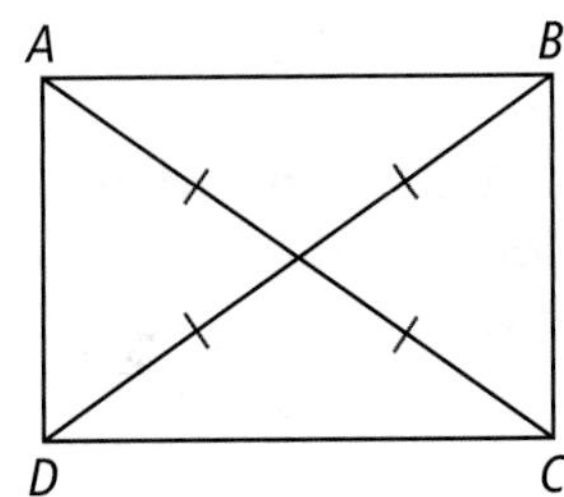 | 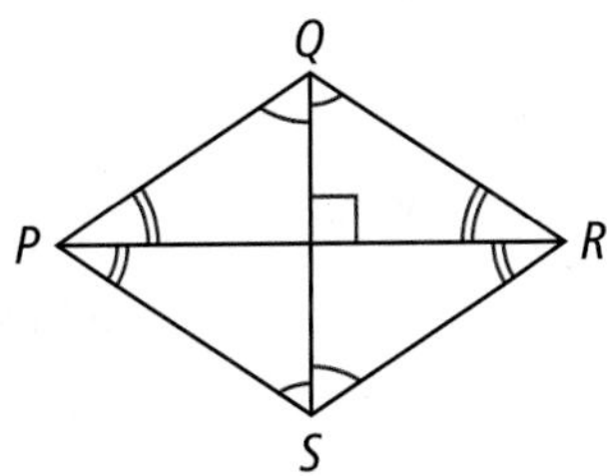 | 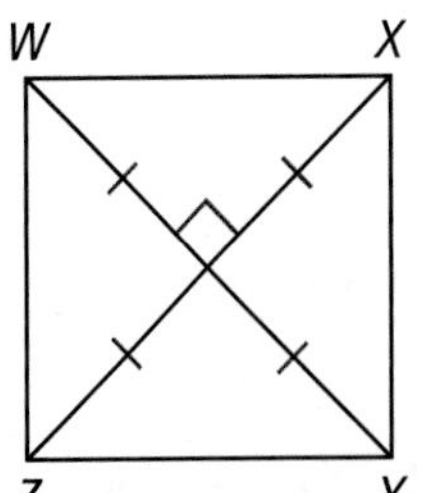 |
| SYMBOLS | $\overline{AC} \cong \overline{BD}$ | $\overline{PR} \perp \overline{QS}$ | $\overline{WY} \cong \overline{XZ}$<br>$\overline{WY} \perp \overline{XZ}$ |

## Do You UNDERSTAND?

1. ESSENTIAL QUESTION What properties of rhombuses, rectangles, and squares differentiate them from other parallelograms?

2. **Error Analysis** Figure $QRST$ is a rectangle. Ramona wants to show that the four interior triangles are congruent. What is Ramona's error?

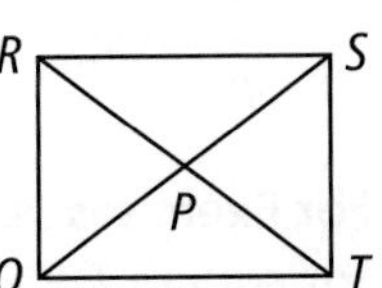

Diagonals of a rectangle are congruent and bisect each other, so $\overline{RP} \cong \overline{TP} \cong \overline{QP} \cong \overline{SP}$. Because the diagonals are perpendicular bisectors, $\angle RPS$, $\angle SPT$, $\angle TPQ$, and $\angle QPR$ are right angles. Therefore, by SAS,

$\triangle RPS \cong \triangle SPT \cong \triangle TPQ \cong \triangle PQR$.

3. **Construct Arguments** Is any quadrilateral with four congruent sides a rhombus? Explain.

## Do You KNOW HOW?

**Find each length and angle measure for rhombus *DEFG*. Round to the nearest tenth.**

4. $DF$

5. $m\angle DFG$

6. $EG$

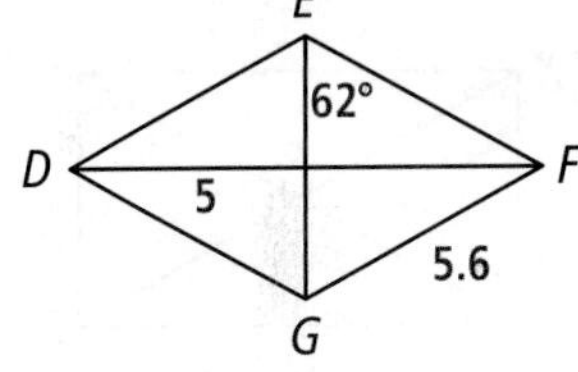

**Find each length for rectangle *MNPQ*. Round to the nearest tenth.**

7. $MP$

8. $MQ$

**Find each length and angle measure for square *WXYZ*.**

9. $m\angle YPZ$

10. $m\angle XWP$

11. $XZ$

12. What is the value of $x$?

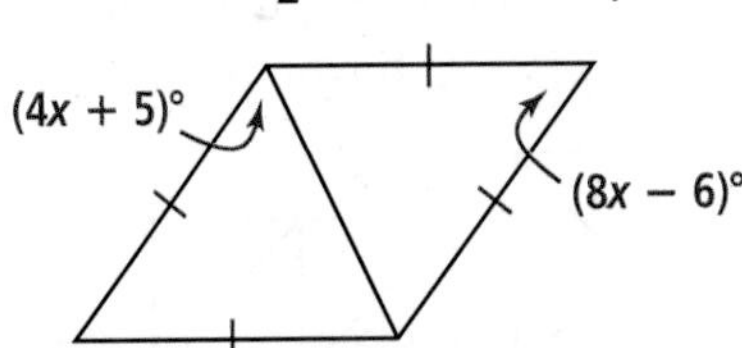

# PRACTICE & PROBLEM SOLVING



## UNDERSTAND

**13. Construct Arguments** Write a proof of Theorem 6-16.

**Given:** $WXYZ$ is a rhombus.

**Prove:** $\overline{WY}$ and $\overline{XZ}$ are perpendicular bisectors of each other.

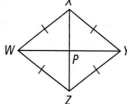

**14. Error Analysis** Figure $ABCD$ is a rhombus. What is Malcolm's error?

Since $ABCD$ is a rhombus, $\overline{AB} \cong \overline{CD}$. Since the diagonals of a rhombus bisect each other, $\overline{AE} \cong \overline{BE} \cong \overline{CE} \cong \overline{DE}$. So, by SSS, $\triangle ABE \cong \triangle CDE$.

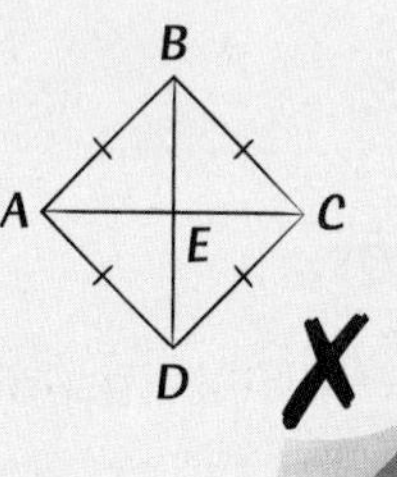


**15. Mathematical Connections** The area of rectangle $WXYZ$ is 115.5 in.$^2$. What is the perimeter of $\triangle XYZ$? Explain your work.

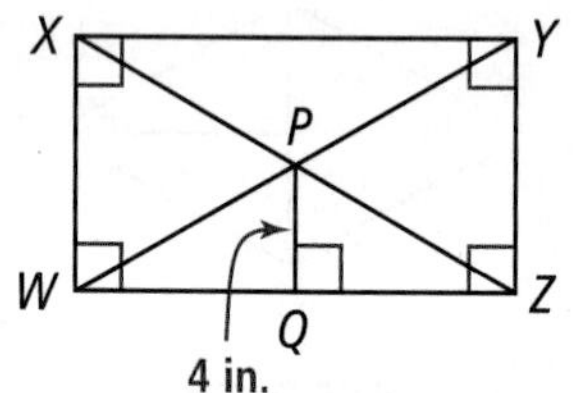


**16. Construct Arguments** Write a proof of Theorem 6-17.

**Given:** $ABCD$ is a rhombus.

**Prove:** $\angle 1 \cong \angle 2$, $\angle 3 \cong \angle 4$, $\angle 5 \cong 6$, $\angle 7 \cong \angle 8$

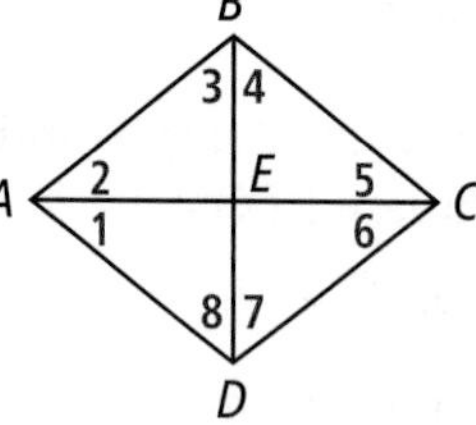


**17. Higher Order Thinking** A square is cut apart and reassembled into a rectangle as shown. Which figure has a greater perimeter? Explain.

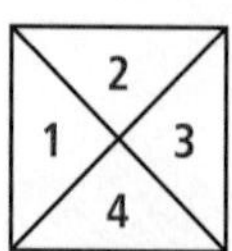


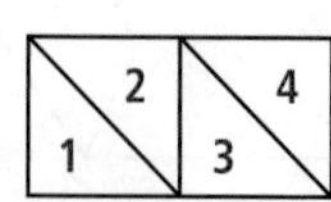


## PRACTICE

**For Exercises 18–20, find each angle measure for rhombus $ABCD$.** SEE EXAMPLES 1 AND 2

**18.** $m\angle ACD$

**19.** $m\angle ABC$

**20.** $m\angle BEA$

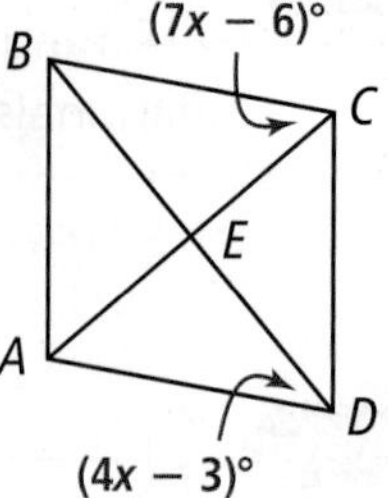


**For Exercises 21–23, find each length for rhombus $PQRS$. Round to the nearest tenth.** SEE EXAMPLES 1 AND 2

**21.** $TR$

**22.** $QS$

**23.** $PS$

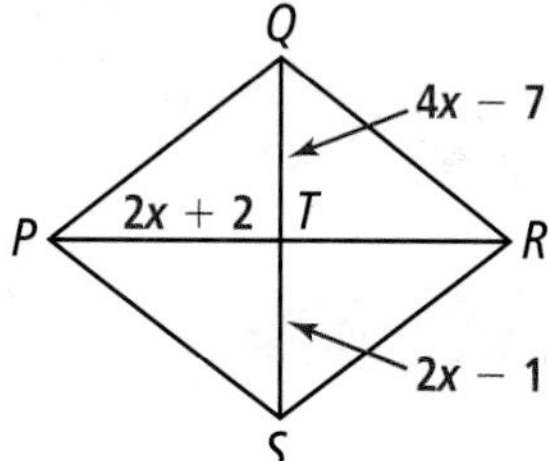


**For Exercises 24–27, find each length and angle measure for rectangle $GHJK$. Round to the nearest tenth.** SEE EXAMPLES 3 AND 4

**24.** $m\angle GHK$

**25.** $m\angle HLJ$

**26.** $GJ$

**27.** $HL$

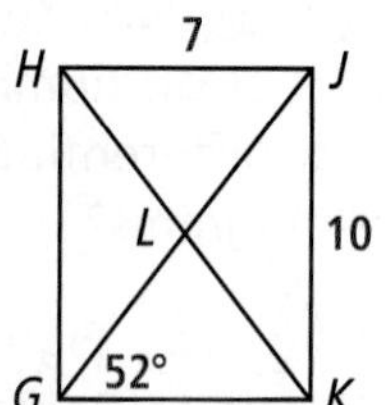


**For Exercises 28–30, find each length and value for square $QRST$. Round to the nearest tenth.** SEE EXAMPLE 5

**28.** $SV$

**29.** $RT$

**30.** perimeter of $\triangle RVS$

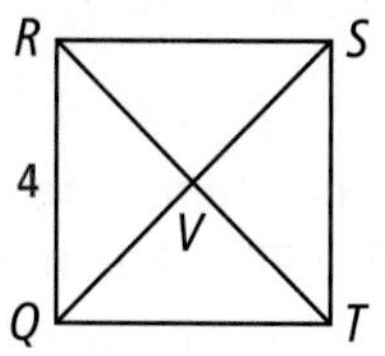


**31.** If $ABCD$ is a square, what is $GC$?

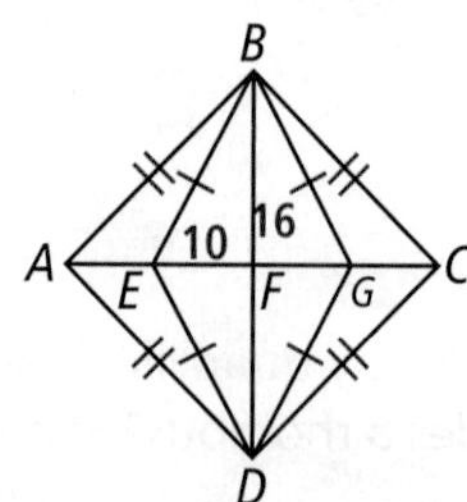

# PRACTICE & PROBLEM SOLVING

## APPLY

**32. Model With Mathematics** Jordan wants a collapsible puppy pen that gives his puppy at least 35 square feet of area and at least 10 feet of diagonal length. Should Jordan buy the pen shown? Explain.

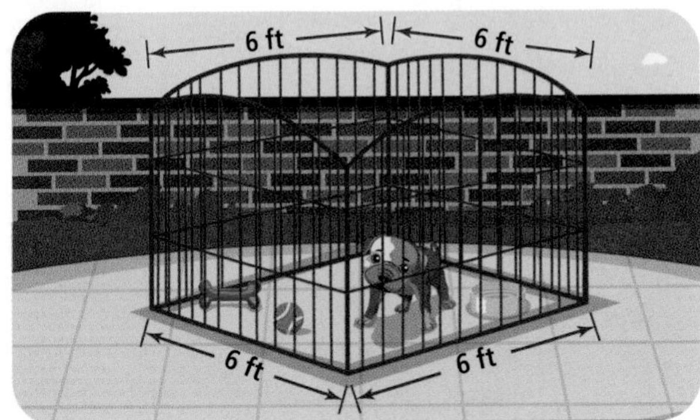


**33. Make Sense and Persevere** Luis is using different types of wood to make a rectangular inlay top for a chest with the pattern shown.

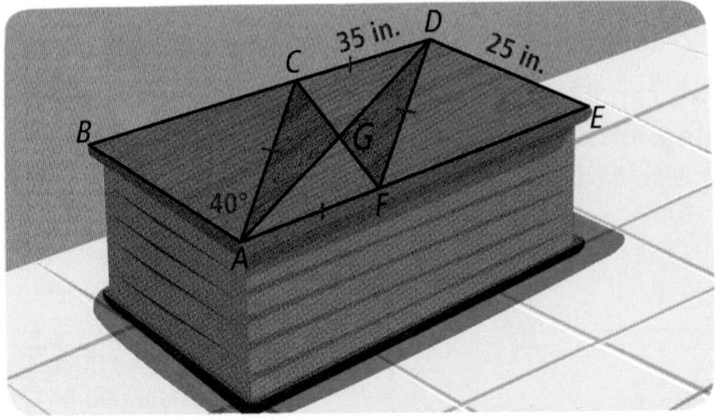


a. What angle should he cut for $\angle CDG$? Explain.

b. If he makes the table top correctly, what will the length of the completed top be?

**34. Look for Relationships** A carpenter is building a support for a stage. What should be the measures of $\angle 1$, $\angle 2$, $\angle 3$, and $\angle 4$? Explain your answers.

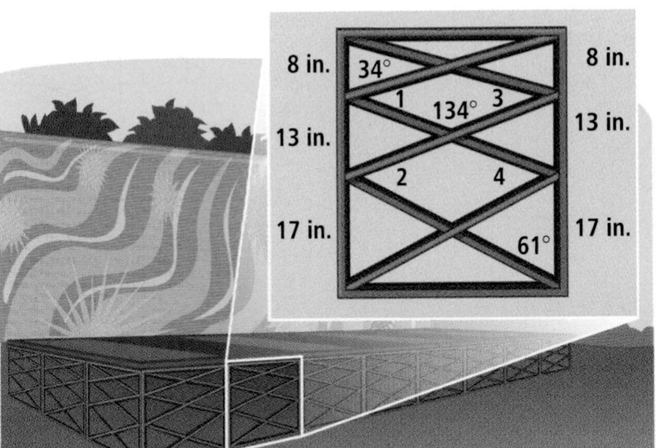


## ASSESSMENT PRACTICE

**35.** Which statements are true about all rectangles? Select all that apply.

Ⓐ Diagonals bisect each other.

Ⓑ Adjacent sides are perpendicular.

Ⓒ Diagonals are perpendicular.

Ⓓ Consecutive angles are supplementary.

**36. SAT/ACT** Which expression gives $m\angle DBC$?

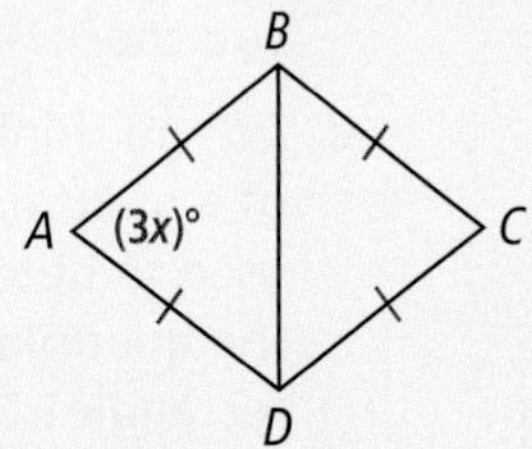


Ⓐ $\left(180 - \frac{3x}{2}\right)^\circ$

Ⓑ $(180 - 3x)^\circ$

Ⓒ $\left(\frac{180 - 3x}{2}\right)^\circ$

Ⓓ $\left(\frac{3x}{2} - 180\right)^\circ$

**37. Performance Task** At a carnival, the goal is to toss a disc into one of three zones to win a prize. Zone 1 is a square, zone 2 is a rhombus, and zone 3 is a rectangle. Some measurements have been provided.

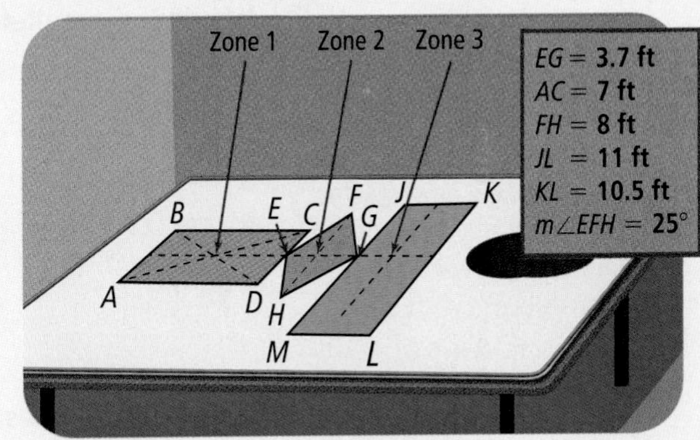


**Part A** What are the lengths of the sides of each zone?

**Part B** What are the angle measures of each zone?

**Part C** What is the area of each zone?

Activity Assess

# 6-6 Conditions of Special Parallelograms

PearsonRealize.com

I CAN… identify rhombuses, rectangles, and squares by the characteristics of their diagonals.

## MODEL & DISCUSS

**The sides of the lantern are identical quadrilaterals.**

**A. Construct Arguments** How could you check to see whether a side is a parallelogram? Justify your answer.

**B.** Does the side appear to be rectangular? How could you check?

**C.** Do you think that diagonals of a quadrilateral can be used to determine whether the quadrilateral is a rectangle? Explain.

## ESSENTIAL QUESTION

**Which properties of the diagonals of a parallelogram help you to classify a parallelogram?**

CONCEPTUAL UNDERSTANDING

## EXAMPLE 1 Use Diagonals to Identify Rhombuses

**Information about diagonals can help to classify a parallelogram. In parallelogram *ABCD*, $\overline{AC}$ is perpendicular to $\overline{BD}$. What else can you conclude about the parallelogram?**

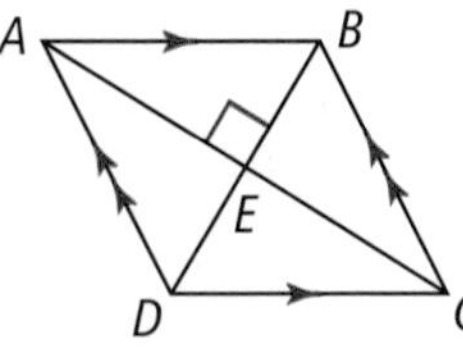


STUDY TIP
Parallelograms have several properties, and some properties may not help you solve a particular problem. Here, the fact that diagonals bisect each other allows the use of SAS.

The diagonals of a parallelogram bisect each other, so $\overline{AE} \cong \overline{CE}$ and $\overline{DE} \cong \overline{BE}$.

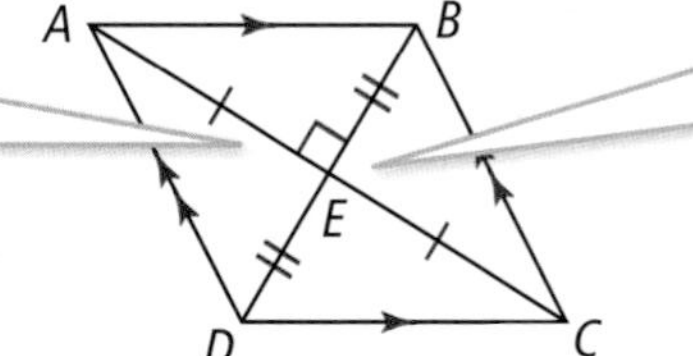


Any angle at *E* either forms a linear pair or is a vertical angle with $\angle AEB$, so all four angles are right angles.

The four triangles are congruent by SAS, so $\overline{AB} \cong \overline{CB} \cong \overline{CD} \cong \overline{AD}$.

Since *ABCD* is a parallelogram with four congruent sides, *ABCD* is a rhombus.

**Try It!** 1. If $\angle JHK$ and $\angle JGK$ are complementary, what else can you conclude about *GHJK*? Explain.

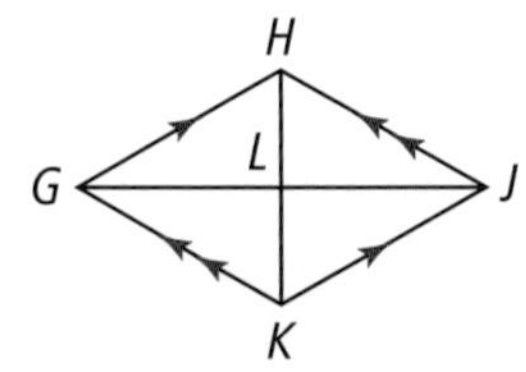

## THEOREM 6-19 Converse of Theorem 6-16

If the diagonals of a parallelogram are perpendicular, then the parallelogram is a rhombus.

PROOF: SEE EXERCISE 9.

If...

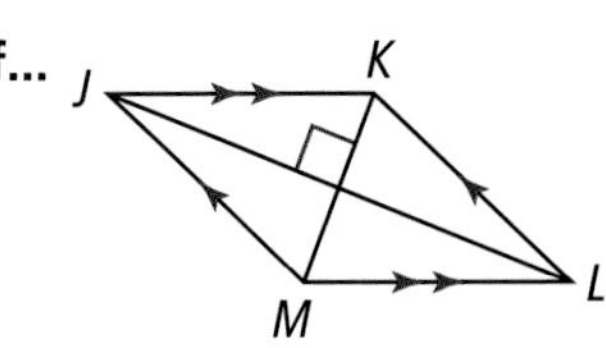


Then... $\overline{JK} \cong \overline{KL} \cong \overline{LM} \cong \overline{MJ}$

## THEOREM 6-20 Converse of Theorem 6-17

If a diagonal of a parallelogram bisects two angles of the parallelogram, then the parallelogram is a rhombus.

PROOF: SEE EXAMPLE 2.

If...

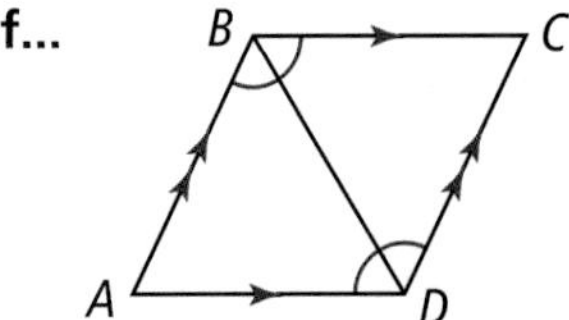


Then... $\overline{AB} \cong \overline{BC} \cong \overline{CD} \cong \overline{DA}$

PROOF

## EXAMPLE 2 Prove Theorem 6-20

**Write a proof of Theorem 6-20.**

**Given:** Parallelogram *FGHJ* with $\angle 1 \cong \angle 2$ and $\angle 3 \cong \angle 4$

**Prove:** *FGHJ* is a rhombus.

**Proof:**

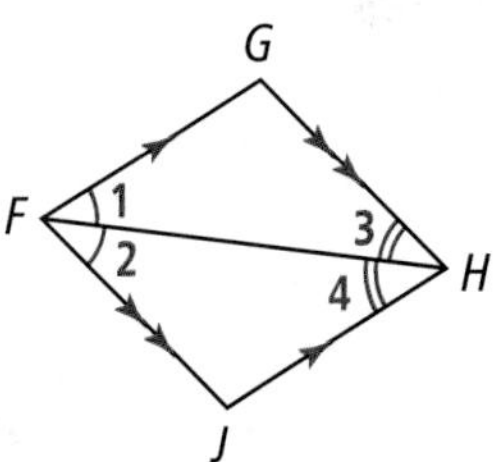


**STUDY TIP**
Drawing diagonals in parallelograms can help you see additional information that is useful in solving problems.

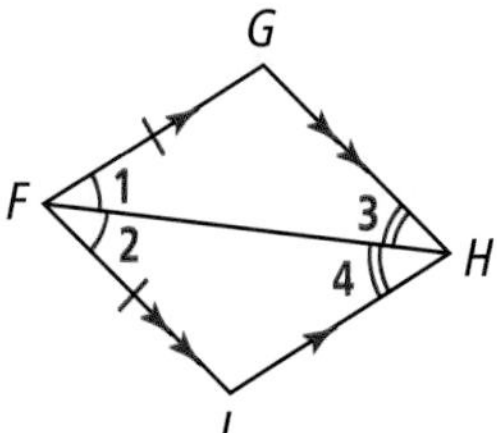


By ASA, $\triangle FHJ \cong \triangle FHG$. Thus, $\overline{FJ} \cong \overline{FG}$.

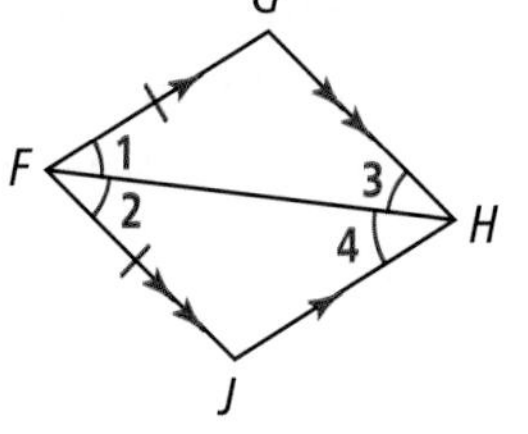


By the Alternate Interior Angles Theorem, $\angle 1 \cong \angle 4$, so $\angle 1 \cong \angle 2 \cong \angle 3 \cong \angle 4$.

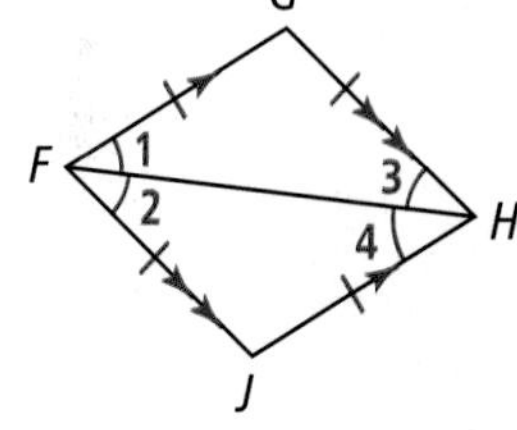


By the Converse of the Isosceles Triangle Theorem, $\overline{FG} \cong \overline{HG}$ and $\overline{FJ} \cong \overline{HJ}$.

Using the Transitive Property of Congruence, $\overline{FG} \cong \overline{HG} \cong \overline{FJ} \cong \overline{HJ}$. Since *FGHJ* is a parallelogram with congruent sides, it is a rhombus.

**Try It!** 2. Refer to the figure *FGHJ* in Example 2. Use properties of parallelograms to show that if $\angle 1 \cong \angle 2$ and $\angle 3 \cong \angle 4$, then the four angles are congruent.

## EXAMPLE 3 Use Diagonals to Identify Rectangles

**Ashton measures the diagonals for his deck frame and finds that they are congruent. Will the deck be rectangular?**

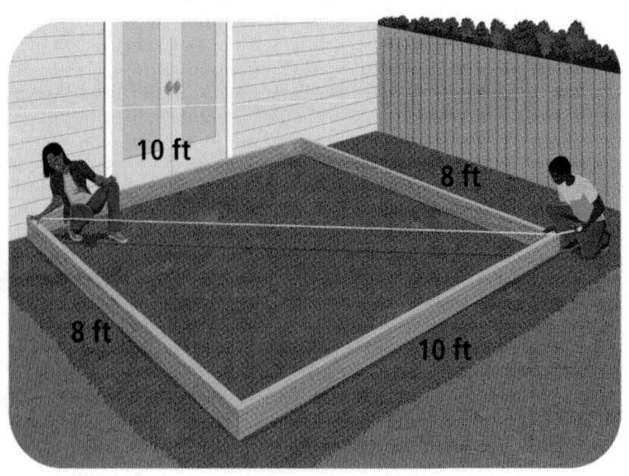


Since opposite sides are congruent, the supports form a parallelogram. To show that the structure is rectangular, show that the angles are right angles.

Opposite sides and the diagonals are congruent, so $\triangle ACD \cong \triangle BDC$ by SSS. Therefore, $\angle ADC \cong \angle BCD$.

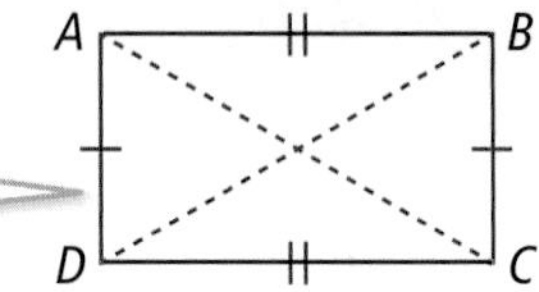


In a parallelogram, consecutive angles are supplementary. Angles that are congruent and supplementary are right angles. Similarly, $\angle DAB$ and $\angle CBA$ are also right angles.

The frame forms a parallelogram with four right angles, which is a rectangle.

 **Try It!** 3. If the diagonals of any quadrilateral are congruent, is the quadrilateral a rectangle? Justify your answer.

### THEOREM 6-21 Converse of Theorem 6-18

If the diagonals of a parallelogram are congruent, then the parallelogram is a rectangle.

**If...**

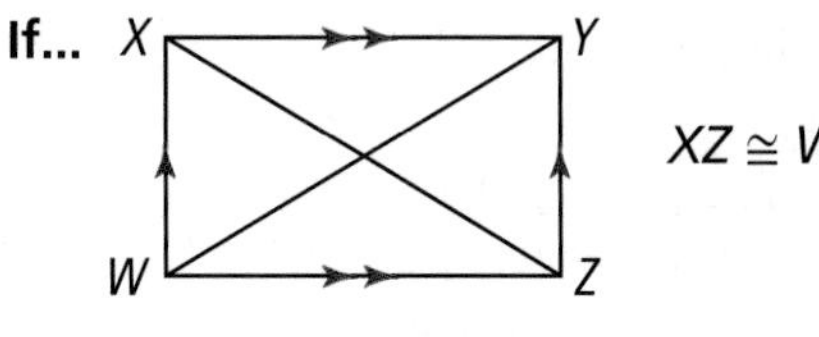


$XZ \cong WY$

**Then...** $\angle XWZ$, $\angle WZY$, $\angle XYZ$, and $\angle WXY$ are right angles

PROOF: SEE EXERCISE 11.

## EXAMPLE 4 Identify Special Parallelograms

**Can you conclude whether each parallelogram is a rhombus, a square, or a rectangle? Explain.**

**A. Parallelogram *ABCD***

By SAS, $\triangle ABD \cong \triangle CBD$.

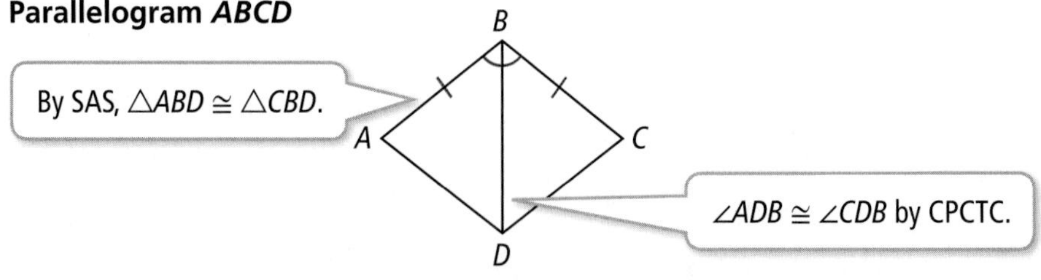


$\angle ADB \cong \angle CDB$ by CPCTC.

Diagonal $\overline{BD}$ bisects $\angle ABC$ and $\angle ADC$, so parallelogram *ABCD* is a rhombus.

**CONSTRUCT ARGUMENTS**
There are often multiple ways to prove something. How could you use properties of parallelograms to show the figure is a rhombus without the congruent angles shown?

CONTINUED ON THE NEXT PAGE

Activity

Assess

EXAMPLE 4 CONTINUED

**B. Parallelogram *PQRS***

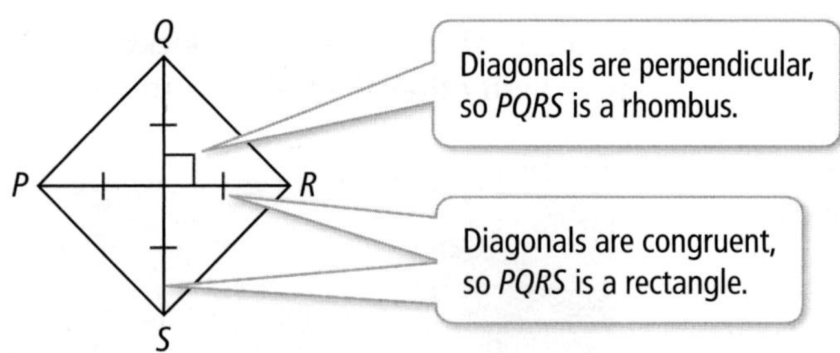


Since the parallelogram is a rhombus and a rectangle, it is a square.

**Try It!** **4.** Is each parallelogram a rhombus, a square, or a rectangle? Explain.

**a.**

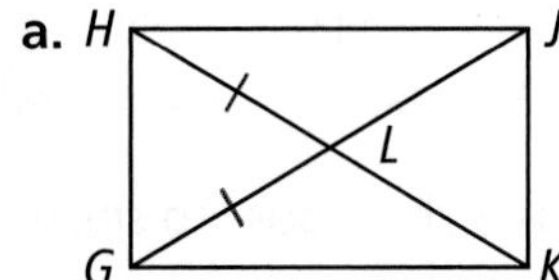


**b.**

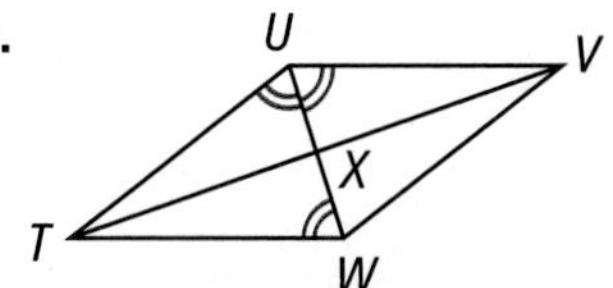


**EXAMPLE 5** **Use Properties of Special Parallelograms**

**MAKE SENSE AND PERSEVERE**
Consider the information given in the diagram. How can you determine whether $\overline{TV}$ bisects the angles?

**Quadrilateral *STUV* is a rhombus. What are the values of *x* and *y*?**

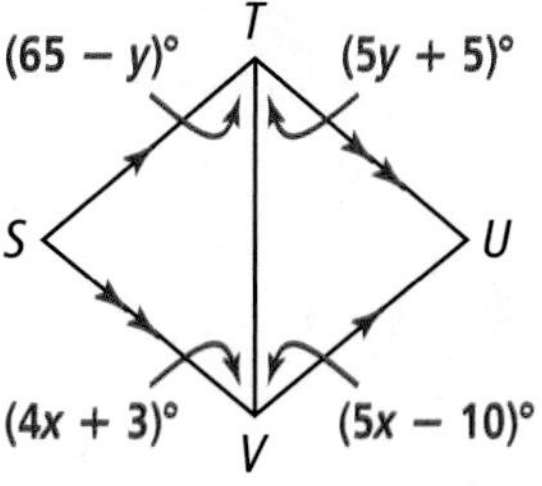


If a parallelogram is a rhombus then each diagonal bisects opposite angles. So, $\overline{TV}$ bisects $\angle SVU$ and $\angle STU$.

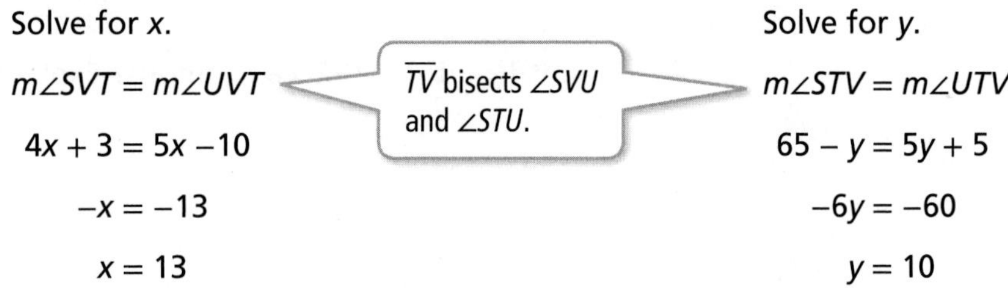

Solve for *x*.

$m\angle SVT = m\angle UVT$

$4x + 3 = 5x - 10$

$-x = -13$

$x = 13$

$\overline{TV}$ bisects $\angle SVU$ and $\angle STU$.

Solve for *y*.

$m\angle STV = m\angle UTV$

$65 - y = 5y + 5$

$-6y = -60$

$y = 10$

**Try It!** **5.** In parallelogram *ABCD*, $AC = 3w - 1$ and $BD = 2(w + 6)$. What must be true for *ABCD* to be a rectangle?

APPLICATION

## EXAMPLE 6 Apply Properties of Special Parallelograms

**COMMON ERROR**
The order in which the quadrilateral is identified matters. Be sure to first show that the quadrilateral is a parallelogram before applying the theorems to identify the quadrilateral as a rhombus or a rectangle.

**A group of friends set up a kickball field with bases 60 ft apart. How can they verify that the field is a square?**

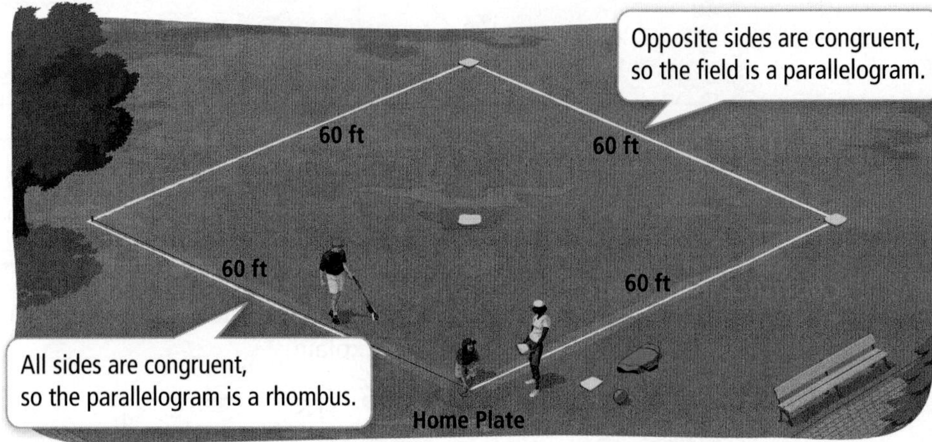

Opposite sides are congruent, so the field is a parallelogram.
60 ft
60 ft
60 ft
60 ft
All sides are congruent, so the parallelogram is a rhombus.
Home Plate

The field is a rhombus. To show that the rhombus is a square, show that it is also a rectangle.

A parallelogram is a rectangle if the diagonals are congruent.

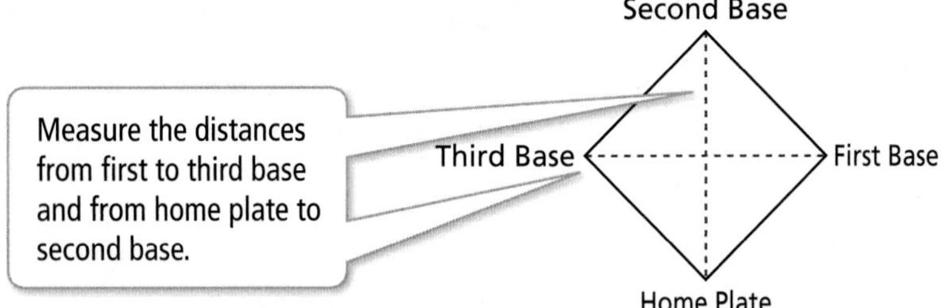

Second Base
Measure the distances from first to third base and from home plate to second base.
Third Base
First Base
Home Plate

The group of friends can verify the field is a square if they find that the distances from first base to third base and from second base to home plate are equal.

**Try It!** 6. Is *MNPQ* a rhombus? Explain.

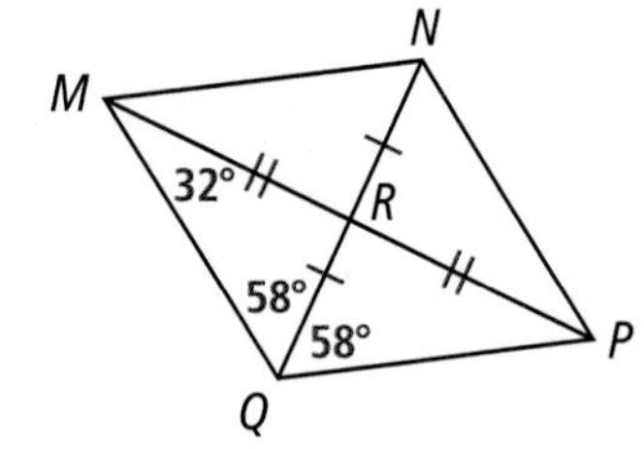

M
N
R
P
Q
32°
58°
58°

## CONCEPT SUMMARY Conditions of Special Parallelograms

**RHOMBUS**

A parallelogram is a rhombus if

- diagonals are perpendicular

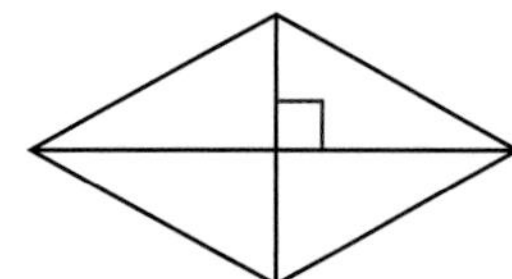

- a diagonal bisects angles

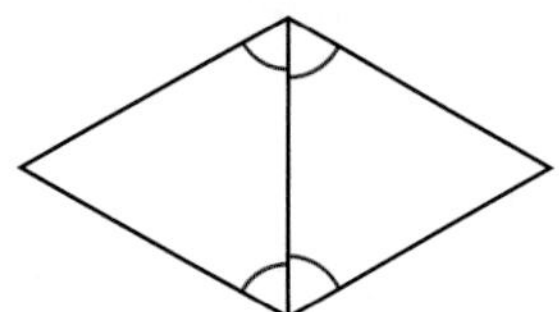

**RECTANGLE**

A parallelogram is a rectangle if

- diagonals are congruent

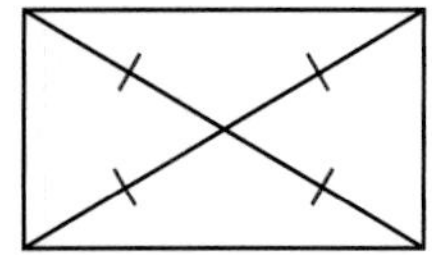

**SQUARE**

A parallelogram is a square if

- diagonals are perpendicular and congruent

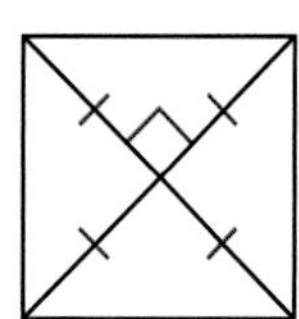

- a diagonal bisects angles and diagonals are congruent

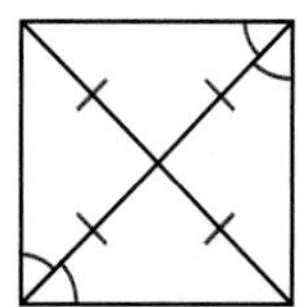

## Do You UNDERSTAND?

1. **ESSENTIAL QUESTION** Which properties of the diagonals of a parallelogram help you to classify a parallelogram?

2. **Error Analysis** Sage was asked to classify *DEFG*. What was Sage's error?

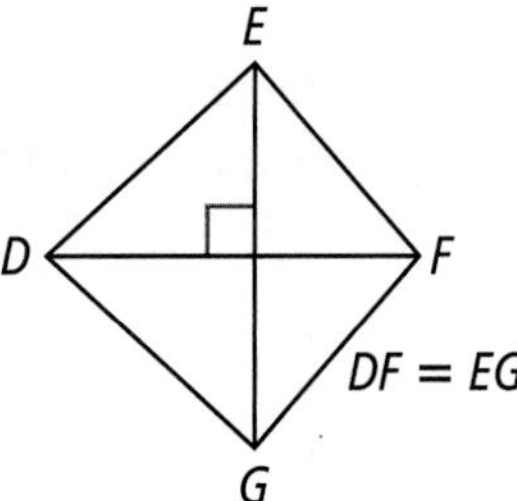


Since $DF = EG$, *DEFG* is a rectangle.
Since $\overline{EG} \perp \overline{DF}$, *DEFG* is also a rhombus.
Therefore, *DEFG* is a square.

X

3. **Construct Arguments** Write a biconditional statement about the diagonals of rectangles. What theorems justify your statement?

4. **Use Appropriate Tools** Make a concept map showing the relationships among quadrilaterals, parallelograms, trapezoids, isosceles trapezoids, kites, rectangles, squares, and rhombuses.

## Do You KNOW HOW?

**For Exercises 5–8, is the parallelogram a rhombus, a square, or a rectangle?**

5.

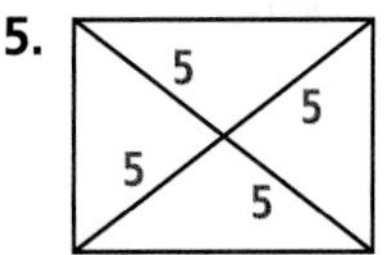


6.

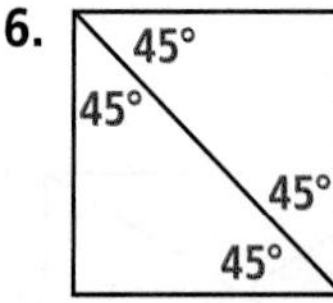


7.

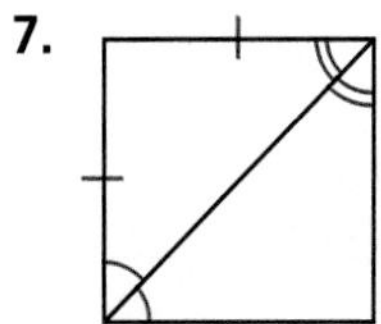

8.

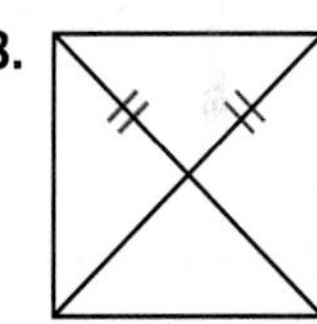

9. What value of *x* will make the parallelogram a rhombus?

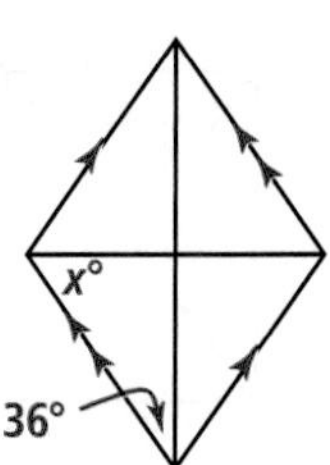


10. If $m\angle 1 = 36$ and $m\angle 2 = 54$, is *PQRS* a rhombus, a square, a rectangle, or none of these? Explain.

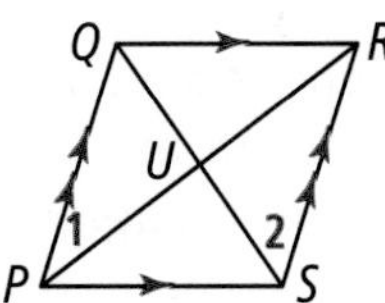

# PRACTICE & PROBLEM SOLVING



## UNDERSTAND

**11. Construct Arguments** Write a proof for Theorem 6-19 using the following diagram.

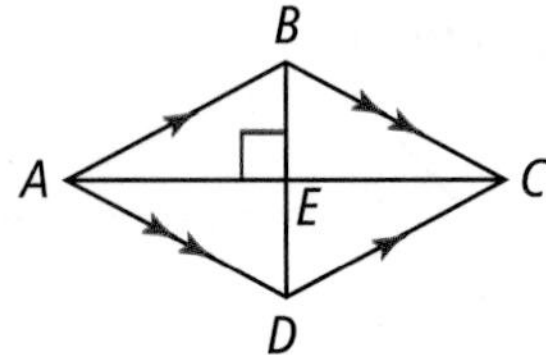


**12. Error Analysis** Becky is asked to classify *PQRS*. What is her error?

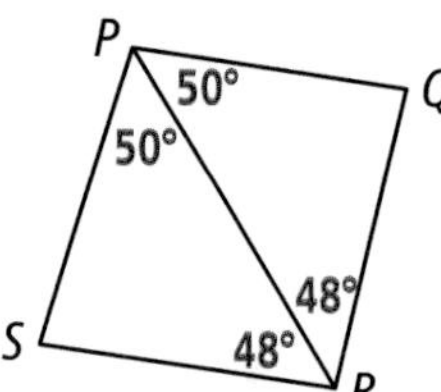


$\overline{PR}$ bisects opposite angles $\angle SPQ$ and $\angle QRS$, so *PQRS* must be a rhombus.

**13. Construct Arguments** Write a proof for Theorem 6-21 using the following diagram.

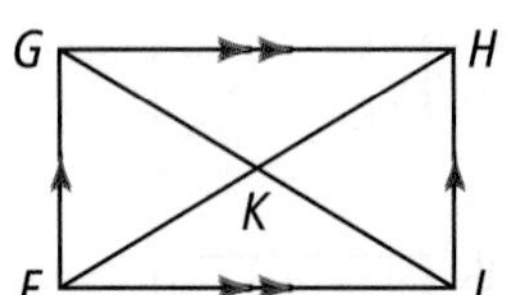


**14. Construct Arguments** Write a proof to show that if *ABCD* is a parallelogram and $\angle ABE \cong \angle BAE$, then *ABCD* is a rectangle.

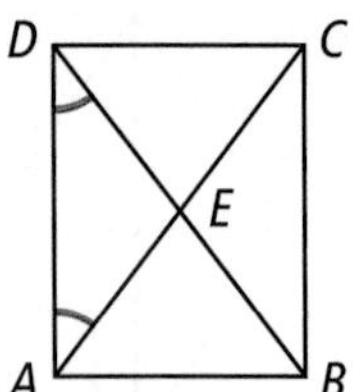


**15. Mathematical Connections** If *WXYZ* is a rhombus with $W(-1, 3)$ and $Y(9, 11)$, what must be an equation of $\overleftrightarrow{XZ}$ in order for *WXYZ* to be a rhombus? Explain how you found your answer.

**16. Higher Order Thinking** The longer diagonal of a rhombus is three times the length of the shorter diagonal. If the shorter diagonal is *x*, what expression gives the perimeter of the rhombus?

## PRACTICE

**For Exercises 17 and 18, determine whether each figure is a rhombus. Explain your answer.**
SEE EXAMPLES 1 AND 2

**17.**

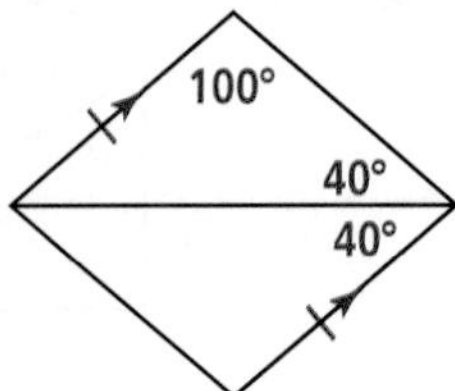


**18.**

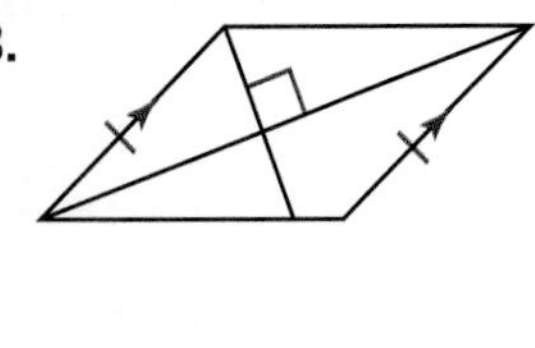

**19.** What is the perimeter of parallelogram *WXYZ*? SEE EXAMPLE 3

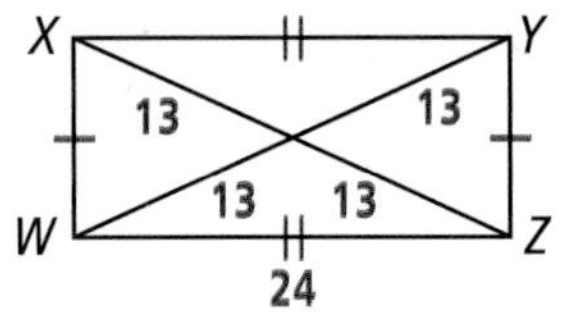


**For Exercises 20 and 21, determine the name that best describes each figure: parallelogram, rectangle, square, or rhombus.** SEE EXAMPLE 4

**20.**

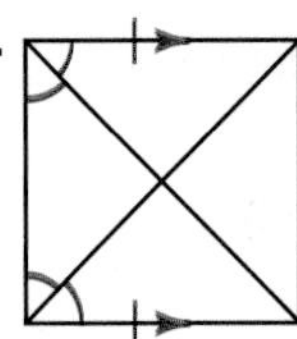

**21.**

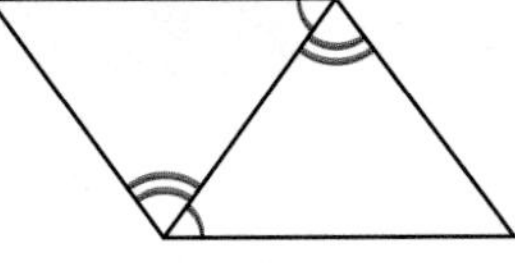

**For Exercises 22–24, give the condition required for each figure to be the specified shape.**
SEE EXAMPLES 5 AND 6

**22.** rectangle

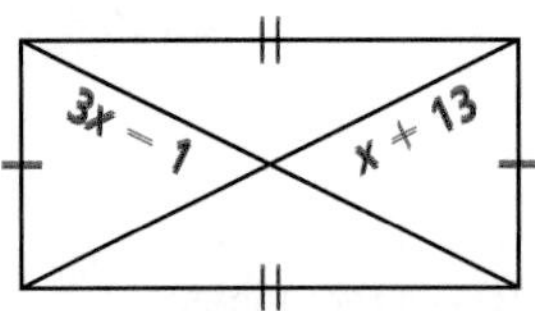


**23.** rhombus

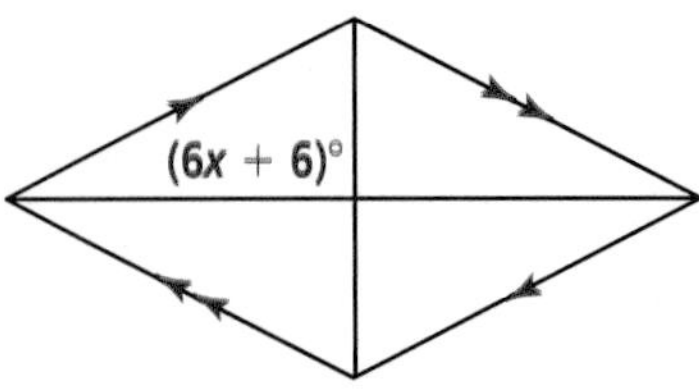


**24.** rhombus

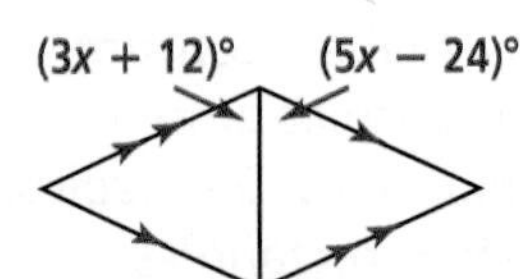

# PRACTICE & PROBLEM SOLVING



## APPLY

25. **Look for Relationships** Melissa charges \$1.50 per square meter for laying sod. She says she can compute the amount to charge for the pentagonal lawn by evaluating $1.50(12^2 + 0.25(12^2))$. Do you agree? Explain.

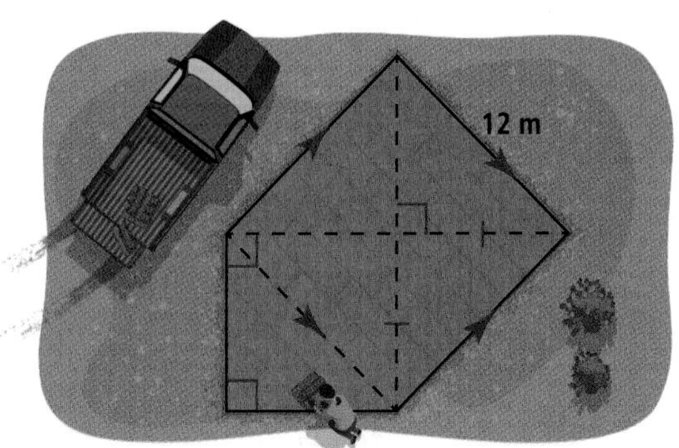


26. **Make Sense and Persevere** Jeffery is making a wall design with tape. How much tape does he need to put the design shown on his wall? Explain how you used the information in the diagram to find your answer.

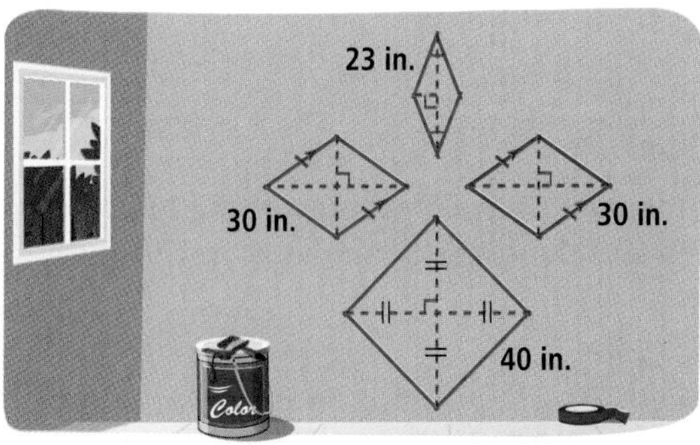


27. **Use Structure** After knitting a blanket, Monisha washes and stretches it out to the correct size and shape. Opposite sides line up with the edges of a rectangular table. She plans to sew a ribbon around the edge of the blanket. How much ribbon will she need?

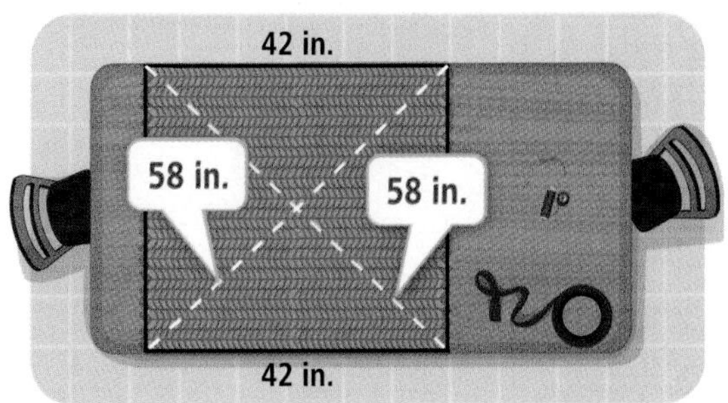


## ASSESSMENT PRACTICE

28. Are the terms below valid classifications for the figure? Select *Yes* or *No*.

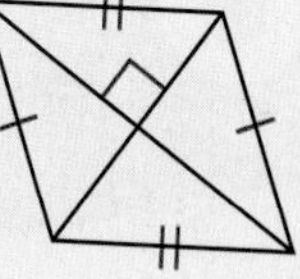

| | Yes | No |
|---|---|---|
| Square | ❑ | ❑ |
| Rhombus | ❑ | ❑ |
| Parallelogram | ❑ | ❑ |
| Rectangle | ❑ | ❑ |
| Trapezoid | ❑ | ❑ |

29. **SAT/ACT** Parallelogram $ABCD$ has diagonals with lengths $AC = 7x + 6$ and $BD = 9x - 2$. For which value of $x$ is $ABCD$ a rectangle?

Ⓐ 2 Ⓑ 4 Ⓒ 7 Ⓓ 9 Ⓔ 34

30. **Performance Task** Zachary is using the two segments shown as diagonals of quadrilaterals he is making for a decal design for the cover of his smart phone.

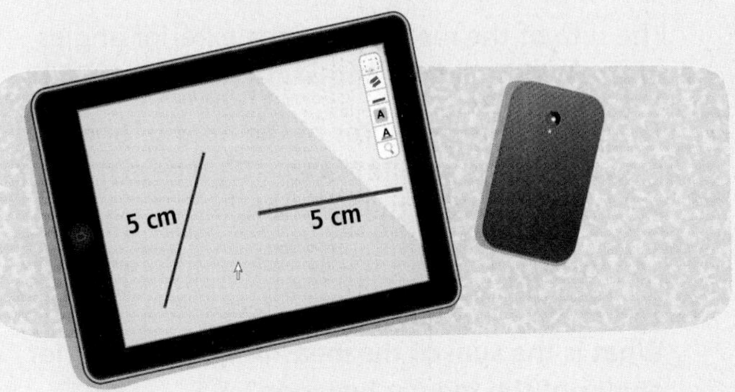


**Part A** Make a table showing at least four types of different quadrilaterals that Zachary can make using the segments as diagonals. For each type of quadrilateral, draw a diagram showing an example. Label angle measures where the diagonals intersect, and label segment lengths of the diagonals.

**Part B** Are some types of quadrilaterals not possible using these diagonals? Explain.

**Part C** Which has the greater area, a square or a rectangle? Explain.

TOPIC 6

# Topic Review

## TOPIC ESSENTIAL QUESTION

1. How are properties of parallelograms used to solve problems and to classify quadrilaterals?

## Vocabulary Review

**Choose the correct term to complete each sentence.**

2. A parallelogram is a(n) ________ if its diagonals are perpendicular and congruent.
3. A(n) ________ is a quadrilateral with two pairs of adjacent sides congruent and no pairs of opposite sides congruent.
4. The sum of the measures of the ________ angles of a convex polygon is $180° \cdot (n - 2)$, where $n$ is the number of sides of the polygon.
5. The length of the ________ is the average of its two bases.

- exterior
- interior
- kite
- midsegment of a trapezoid
- rectangle
- rhombus
- square

## Concepts & Skills Review

### LESSON 6-1 The Polygon Angle-Sum Theorems

#### Quick Review

The sum of the measures of the exterior angles of a convex polygon, one at each vertex, is 360°.

The sum of the measures of the interior angles of a convex polygon is $180° \cdot (n - 2)$, where $n$ is the number of sides of the polygon.

#### Example

**What is the sum of the measures of the interior angles of the regular hexagon?**

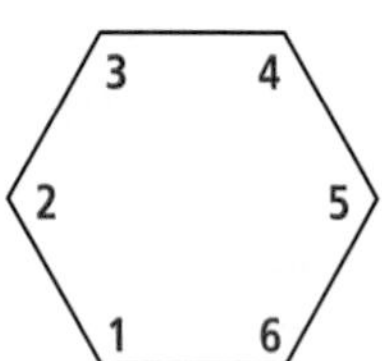


$180° \cdot (6 - 2) = 720°$

#### Practice & Problem Solving

**Find the sum of the measures of the interior angles and the exterior angles of each figure.**

6.

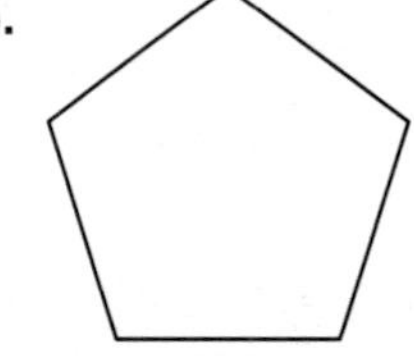

7.

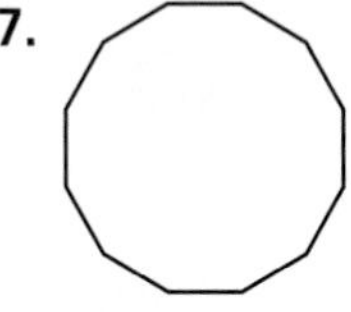

8. **Make Sense and Persevere** Is there enough information to determine the measures of the interior angles of the polygon shown? If so, find the measures. If not, explain.

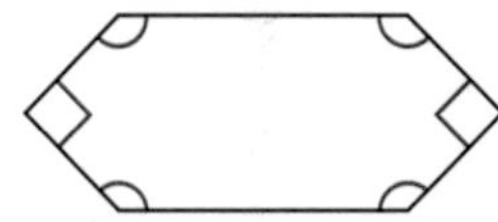

## LESSON 6-2 Kites and Trapezoids

### Quick Review

A kite is a quadrilateral with two pairs of adjacent sides congruent and no pairs of opposite sides congruent.

A trapezoid is a quadrilateral with exactly one pair of parallel sides. The length of the midsegment of a trapezoid is the average of the two bases.

### Example

**Given trapezoid *ABCD*, what is *EF*?**

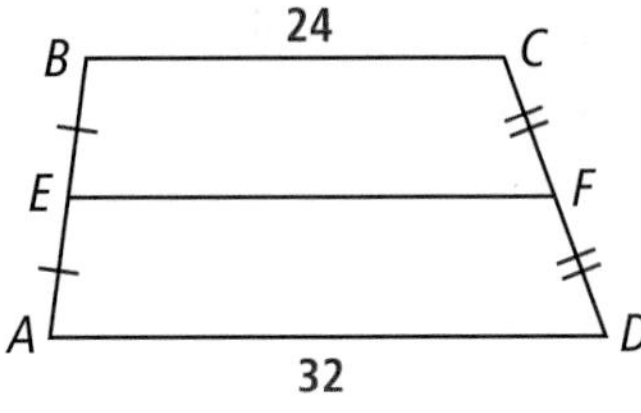


The midsegment of trapezoid *ABCD* is $\overline{EF}$, so $EF = \frac{1}{2}(24 + 32) = 28$.

### Practice & Problem Solving

**Find each measure.**

**9.** $m\angle 1$

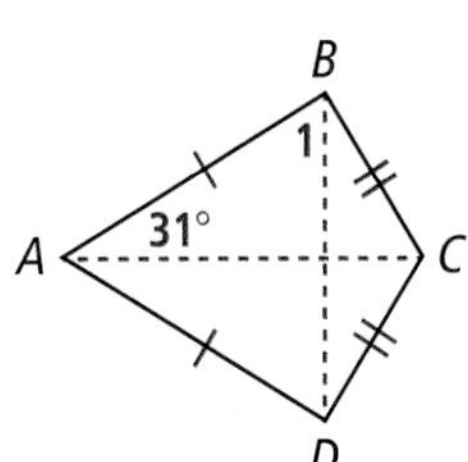


**10.** *BC*

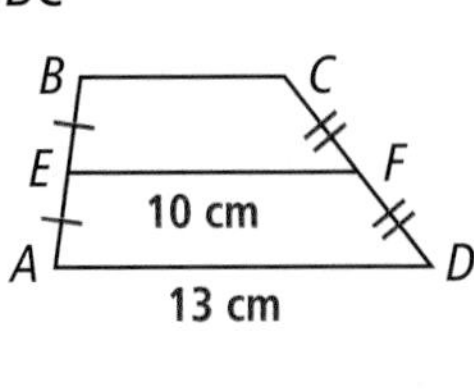


**11. Use Structure** Shannon wants to hang curtains using a tension rod across the top of the trapezoid-shaped window that is shown. Is a 36-inch tension rod long enough to go across the top of the window? Explain.

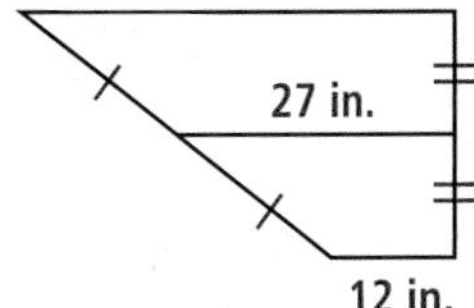


## LESSON 6-3 Properties of Parallelograms

### Quick Review

The sides, diagonals, and angles of parallelograms have special relationships.

- Opposite sides are congruent.
- Diagonals bisect each other.
- Consecutive angles are supplementary.
- Opposite angles are congruent.

### Example

**Given parallelogram *ABCD*, if $ED = 3$ and $BD = \frac{3}{4}(AC)$, what is *AC*?**

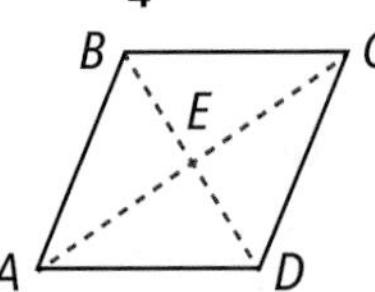


Since $ED = BE$, $BD = 6$. Substitute into $BD = \frac{3}{4}(AC)$ to get $6 = \frac{3}{4}(AC)$, and then solve to get $AC = 8$.

### Practice & Problem Solving

**Use the diagram to find each angle measure.**

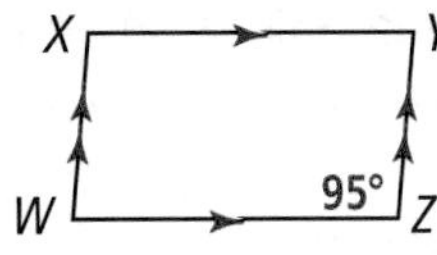


**12.** $m\angle W$

**13.** $m\angle X$

**14. Construct Arguments** The outline of a planned parking lot in the shape of a parallelogram is shown. Elijah says the north side of the lot is 130 ft and the west side of the lot is 240 ft. What is Elijah's mistake?

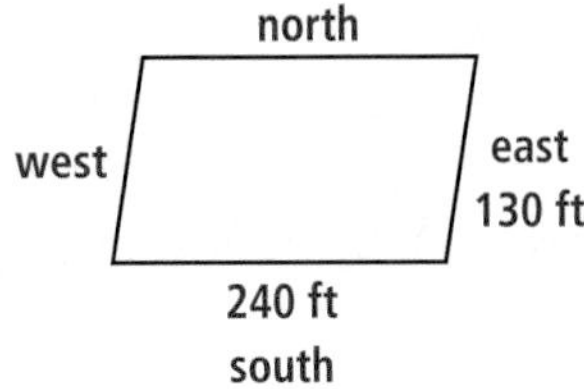


TOPIC 6 REVIEW

## LESSON 6-4 Proving a Quadrilateral is a Parallelogram

### Quick Review

A quadrilateral is a parallelogram if any of the following conditions is true.

- Both pairs of opposite sides are congruent.
- One pair of opposite sides is congruent and parallel.
- An angle is supplementary to both of its consecutive angles.
- Both pairs of opposite angles are congruent.
- The diagonals bisect each other.

### Example

**Explain why the quadrilateral is a parallelogram.**

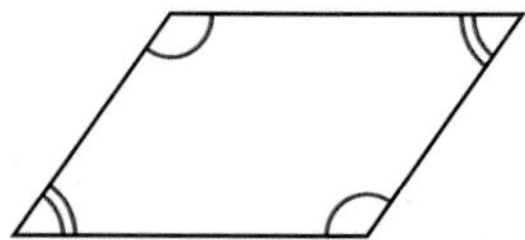

Two pairs of opposite angles are congruent, so the quadrilateral is a parallelogram.

### Practice & Problem Solving

**For what value of $x$ is each quadrilateral a parallelogram?**

**15.** **16.**

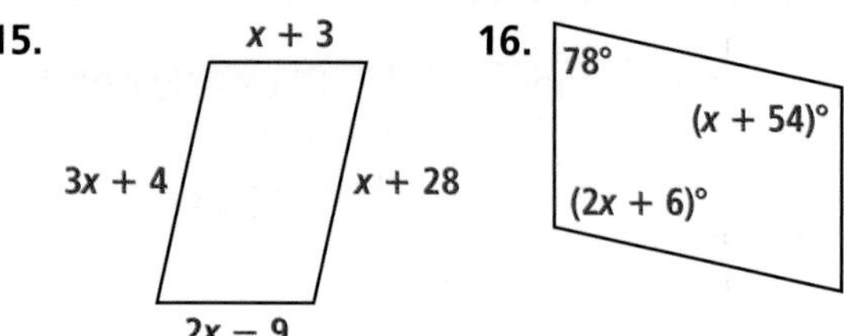


**17. Communicate Precisely** All the black lines in the pattern shown are vertical. What measurements can be used to show that each gray quadrilateral is a parallelogram? Explain.

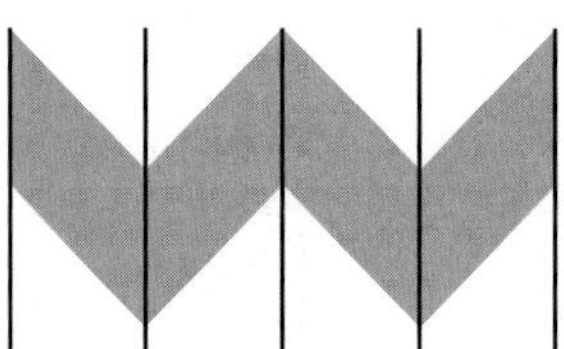

## LESSON 6-5 Properties of Special Parallelograms

### Quick Review

The diagonals of a rhombus are perpendicular bisectors of each other. The diagonals of a rectangle are congruent. The diagonals of a square are perpendicular bisectors of each other and congruent.

### Example

**Given that *WXYZ* is a rhombus, show that $\overline{PW} \cong \overline{PY}$.**

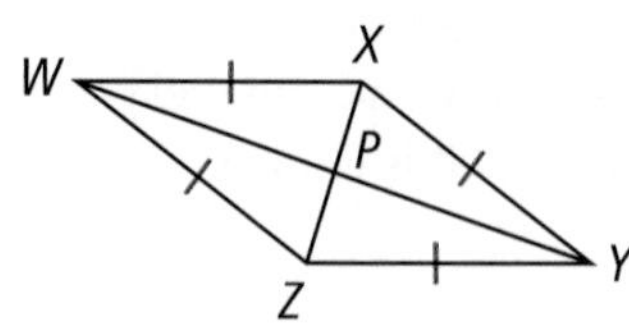


Quadrilateral *WXYZ* is a rhombus, so it is a parallelogram. Diagonals of parallelograms bisect each other, so $\overline{PW} \cong \overline{PY}$ by definition of bisect.

### Practice & Problem Solving

**18.** Given that *ABCD* is a rhombus, what is *BD*?

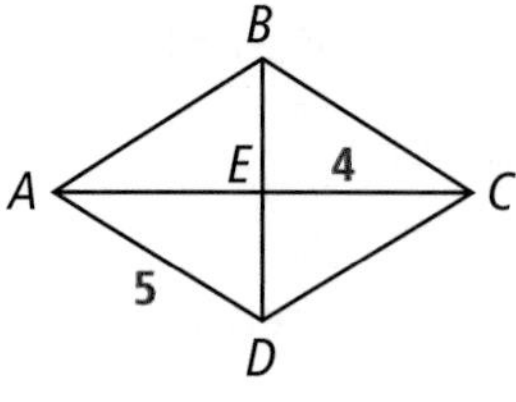


**19.** Given that *PQRS* is a rectangle, what is *QS*?

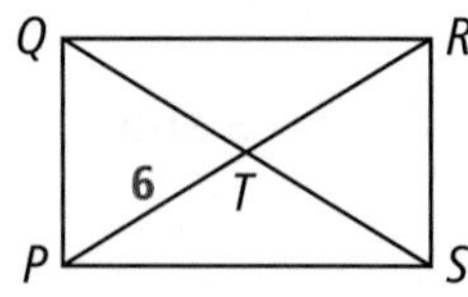


**20. Construct Arguments** Is any quadrilateral with four congruent sides a square? Explain.

## LESSON 6-6 Conditions of Special Parallelograms

### Quick Review

Suppose a figure is a parallelogram.

- If the diagonals are perpendicular, then the parallelogram is a rhombus.
- If the diagonals are congruent, then the parallelogram is a rectangle.
- If the diagonals are perpendicular and congruent, then the parallelogram is a square.

### Example

**Show that the parallelogram is a square.**

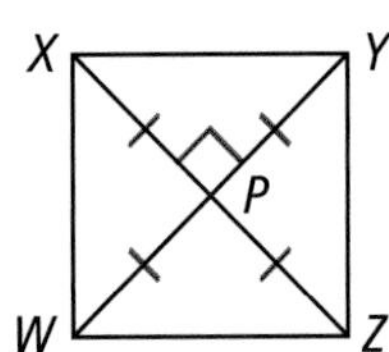


Since $XP = ZP = WP = YP$, $XZ = WY$, the diagonals are congruent. Since the diagonals are congruent, the parallelogram is a rectangle. The diagonals are also given to be perpendicular to each other, so the rectangle is a square.

### Practice & Problem Solving

**Is the parallelogram a rhombus, a rectangle, or a square?**

**21.**  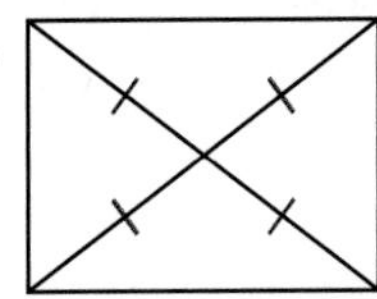

**22.** 

**23. Make Sense and Persevere** For what value of $x$ is $GHJK$ a rhombus? Explain.

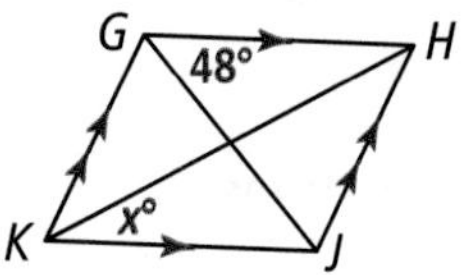


**24. Construct Arguments** Can Nora construct a kite with diagonals that bisect each other? Explain.

TOPIC 6 REVIEW

TOPIC

7

# Similarity

## TOPIC ESSENTIAL QUESTION

**How are properties of similar figures used to solve problems?**

## Topic Overview



## Topic Vocabulary

- center of dilation
- geometric mean
- similarity transformation

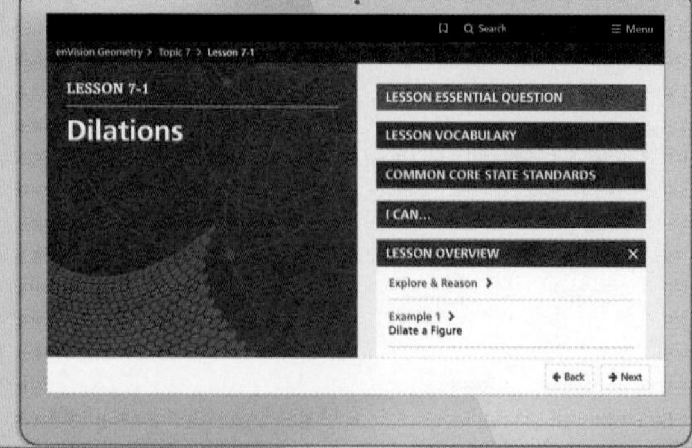

Go online | **PearsonRealize.com**

## Digital Experience

**INTERACTIVE STUDENT EDITION** Access online or offline.

**ACTIVITIES** Complete ***Explore & Reason, Model & Discuss***, and ***Critique & Explain*** activities. Interact with Examples and Try Its.

**ANIMATION** View and interact with real-world applications.

**PRACTICE** Practice what you've learned.

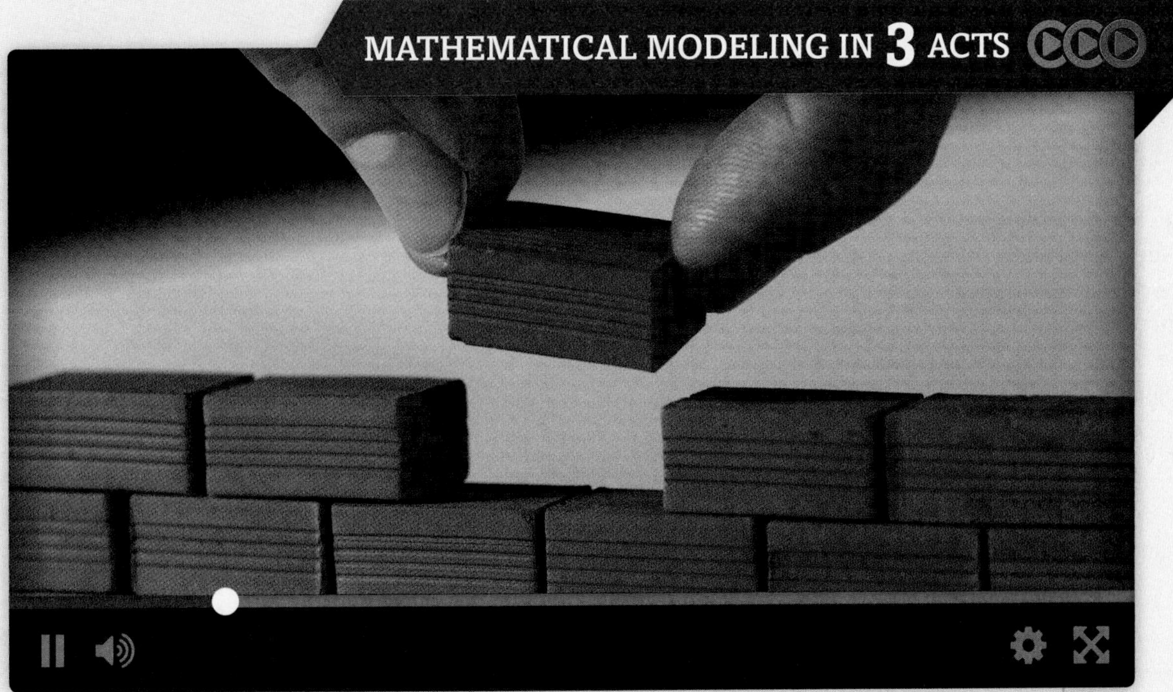


## Make It Right

Architects often make a scale physical model of a new building project. The scale model is usually a miniature version of the project it is representing.

When making a model, architects need to make sure that all of the parts of the model are the right size. Think about this during the Mathematical Modeling in 3 Acts lesson.

TOPIC 7

**VIDEOS** Watch clips to support ***Mathematical Modeling in 3 Acts Lessons*** and **enVision™** ***STEM Projects.***

**CONCEPT SUMMARY** Review key lesson content through multiple representations.

**ASSESSMENT** Show what you've learned.

**GLOSSARY** Read and listen to English and Spanish definitions.

**TUTORIALS** Get help from ***Virtual Nerd***, right when you need it.

**MATH TOOLS** Explore math with digital tools and manipulatives.

## Did You Know?

The **first 3-dimensional printer** was invented in **1983** by Colorado engineer Chuck Hull. Hull's idea was to "print" extremely thin layers of plastic, one atop the other, building up a 3-dimensional object.

3D printers make **toys, replacement parts for machines, and medical prosthetics**. They also make **architectural and scale models**.

Grecia, a toucan, eats and sings using a **3D-printed prosthetic** upper beak.

The **first printing press** was invented by Johannes Gutenberg around the year **1450**. To print a page, Gutenberg made individual letters from metal and arranged the letters **on a block**. Then he inked the letters and **stamped them** on paper.

## Your Task: Design With a 3D Printer

An engineer has built a scale model of a part for a rocket engine. Full-size, the part will be mass-produced using 3D printing. You and your classmates will use similarity to scale up the dimensions of the part. Then you'll describe and draw steps for the production of the part.

# 7-1 Dilations

PearsonRealize.com

**I CAN…** dilate figures and identify characteristics of dilations.

**VOCABULARY**

- center of dilation

## EXPLORE & REASON

**Roosevelt High School sells a sticker and a larger car decal with the school logo.**

Roosevelt High School
ROOSEVELT
R
HAWKS
ROOSEVELT
R
HAWKS
ROOSEVELT
R
HAWKS

A. **Look for Relationships** How are the sticker and the car decal alike? How are they different?

B. Suppose the sticker and decal are shown next to each other on a computer screen. If you zoom in to 125%, what would stay the same on the figures? What would be different?

**ESSENTIAL QUESTION** **How does a dilation affect the side lengths and angle measures of a figure?**

CONCEPTUAL UNDERSTANDING

## EXAMPLE 1 Dilate a Figure

**How can you draw a dilated image?**

A dilation produces an image that is a different size than the preimage.

**Method 1** The Ratio Method

Dilate $\triangle ABC$ by a scale factor of $\frac{1}{2}$ with fixed center $P$. This fixed center is called the **center of dilation**.

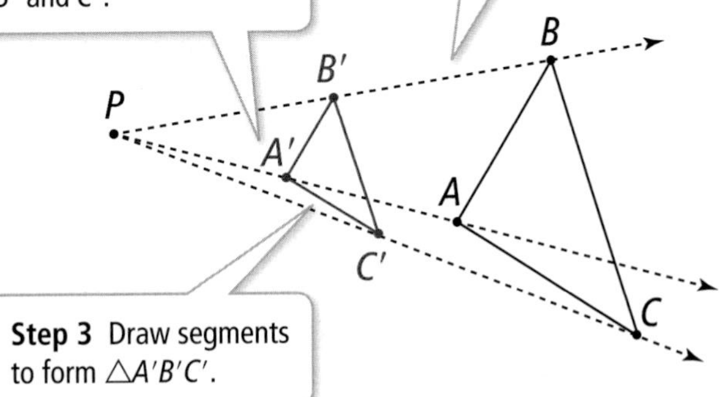
**Step 1** Draw rays from $P$ through each vertex of $\triangle ABC$.
**Step 2** Mark point $A'$ at a point that is half the distance from $P$ to $A$. Repeat for $B'$ and $C'$.
**Step 3** Draw segments to form $\triangle A'B'C'$.
P
A'
B'
C'
A
B
C

STUDY TIP

Recall that a dilation is a transformation in which a preimage is enlarged or reduced in size by a given scale factor.

So, $\triangle A'B'C'$ is a copy of $\triangle ABC$ with side lengths that are $\frac{1}{2}$ the length of the corresponding sides of $\triangle ABC$.

CONTINUED ON THE NEXT PAGE

EXAMPLE 1 CONTINUED

**Method 2** The Parallel Method

Dilate *WXYZ* by 2 with center of dilation *Q*.

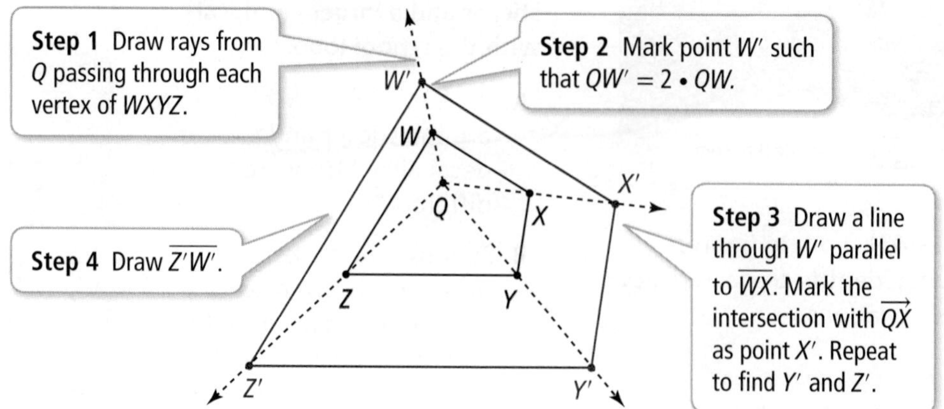

**Step 1** Draw rays from *Q* passing through each vertex of *WXYZ*.
**Step 2** Mark point *W′* such that *QW′* = 2 • *QW*.
**Step 3** Draw a line through *W′* parallel to $\overline{WX}$. Mark the intersection with $\overrightarrow{QX}$ as point *X′*. Repeat to find *Y′* and *Z′*.
**Step 4** Draw $\overline{Z'W'}$.
W′
W
Q
X
X′
Z
Y
Z′
Y′


**MAKE SENSE AND PERSEVERE**
Consider the two methods for dilating figures. How are they alike? How are they different?

Segment *W′Z′* is parallel to $\overline{WZ}$.

So, *W′X′Y′Z′* is a copy of *WXYZ* with side lengths that are twice the length of the corresponding sides of *WXYZ*.

 **Try It!**

**1. a.** Trace △*JKL* and point *R*. Use Method 1 to dilate △*JKL* by a scale factor of 3 with center of dilation *R*.

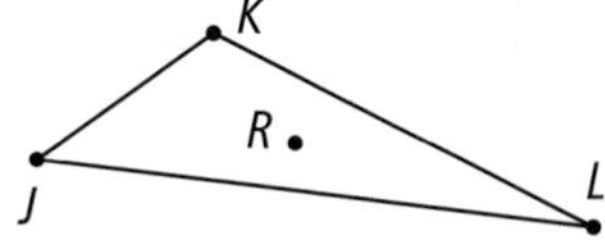


**b.** Trace △*PQR* and point *M*. Use Method 2 to dilate △*PQR* by a scale factor of $\frac{1}{3}$ with center of dilation *M*.

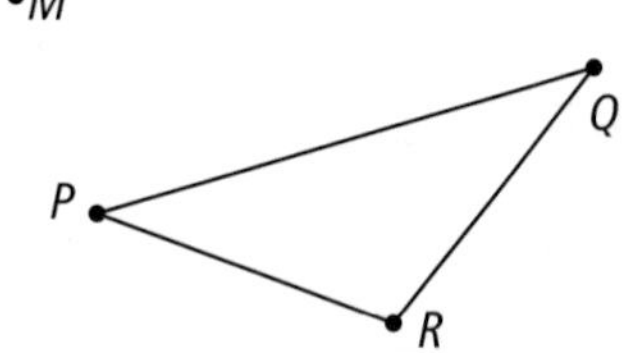


**CONCEPT** Dilations

A dilation $D_{(n,\, C)}$ is a transformation that has center of dilation *C* and scale factor *n*, where $n > 0$, with the following properties:

- Point *R* maps to *R′* in such a way that *R′* is on $\overrightarrow{CR}$ and $CR' = n \cdot CR$.
- Each length in the image is *n* times the corresponding length in the preimage (i.e., $X'R' = n \cdot XR$).

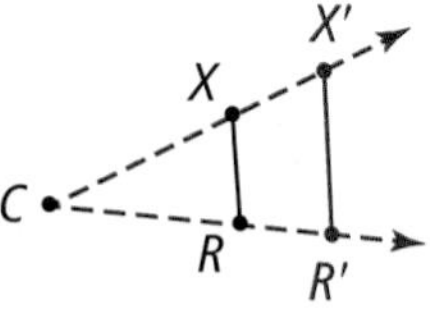


- The image of the center of dilation is the center itself (i.e., $C' = C$).
- If $n > 1$, the dilation is an *enlargement.*
- If $0 < n < 1$, the dilation is a *reduction.*
- Every angle is congruent to its image under the dilation.

On a coordinate plane, the notation $D_n$ describes the dilation with the origin as center of dilation.

## EXAMPLE 2 Analyze Dilations

**Rectangle $A'B'C'D'$ is a dilation with center $P$ of $ABCD$. How are the side lengths and angle measures of $ABCD$ related to those of $A'B'C'D'$?**

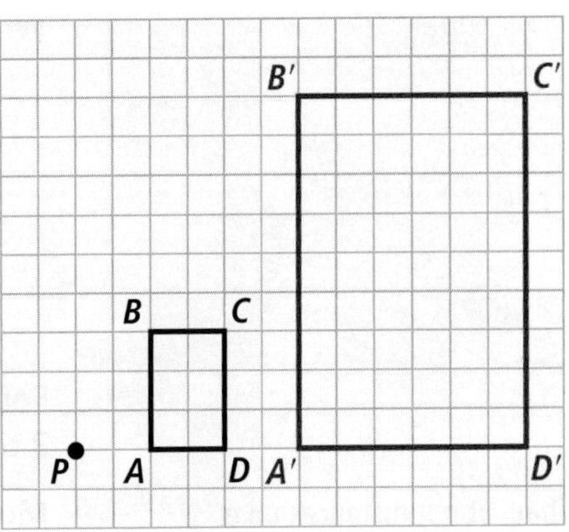


**Step 1** Compare the angles.

All angles of rectangles are right angles, so each angle in image $A'B'C'D'$ is congruent to the corresponding angle in $ABCD$.

**Step 2** Compare the side lengths.

Find the side lengths in the preimage and image.

$AB = 3$ $\quad BC = 2$ $\quad CD = 3$ $\quad DA = 2$

$A'B' = 9$ $\quad B'C' = 6$ $\quad C'D' = 9$ $\quad D'A' = 6$

Find the ratios of the corresponding side lengths.

$\frac{A'B'}{AB} = \frac{9}{3} = 3$ $\quad \frac{B'C'}{BC} = \frac{6}{2} = 3$ $\quad \frac{C'D'}{CD} = \frac{9}{3} = 3$ $\quad \frac{D'A'}{DA} = \frac{6}{2} = 3$

The ratios are equal, so the lengths of corresponding sides of the two figures are proportional.

**Try It!** 2. Rectangle $W'X'Y'Z'$ is a dilation with center $P$ of $WXYZ$. How are the side lengths and angle measures of the two figures related?

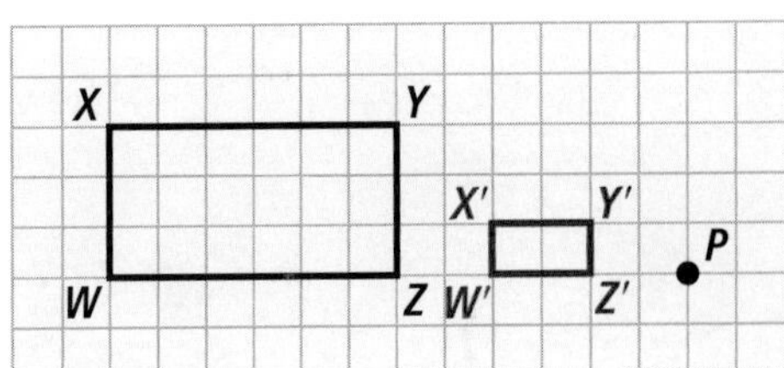


## EXAMPLE 3 Find a Scale Factor

**Quadrilateral $J'K'L'M'$ is a dilation of $JKLM$. What is the scale factor?**

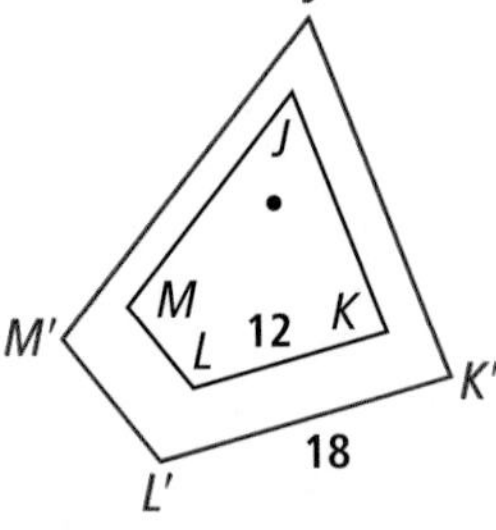


The scale factor is the ratio of side lengths in the image to the corresponding side lengths in the preimage.

$$\frac{K'L'}{KL} = \frac{18}{12} = \frac{3}{2}$$

The scale factor is $\frac{3}{2}$.

**COMMON ERROR**
Be careful to find the scale factor and not its reciprocal. Think about whether the dilation is an enlargement or reduction to see whether the scale factor makes sense.

**Try It!** 3. Consider the dilation shown.

a. Is the dilation an enlargement or a reduction?

b. What is the scale factor?

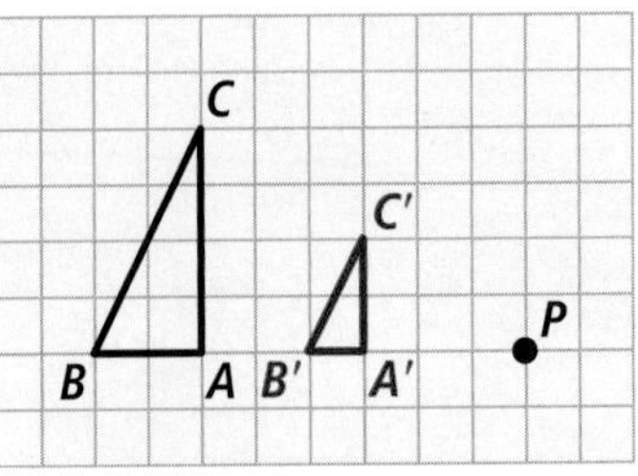

## EXAMPLE 4 Dilate a Figure With Center at the Origin

**What are the vertices of $D_3(\triangle ABC)$?**

The notation $D_3(\triangle ABC)$ means the image of $\triangle ABC$ after a dilation centered at the origin, with scale factor 3.

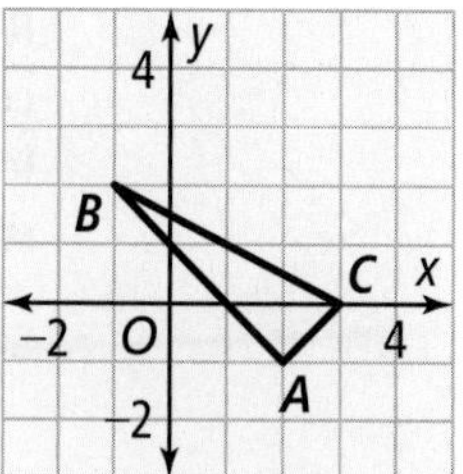


For a dilation with scale factor 3 centered at the origin, each image point is 3 times farther away from the origin than the corresponding preimage point.

**REASON**
Think about distances on a coordinate plane. How could you show algebraically that multiplying each coordinate by the scale factor $n$ produces a point that is $n$ times the distance from the origin?

Multiply each coordinate of each preimage point by 3 to find the coordinates of the image points.

$A(2, -1) \rightarrow A'(3 \cdot 2, 3 \cdot -1) = A'(6, -3)$

$B(-1, 2) \rightarrow B'(3 \cdot -1, 3 \cdot 2) = B'(-3, 6)$

$C(3, 0) \rightarrow C'(3 \cdot 3, 3 \cdot 0) = C'(9, 0)$

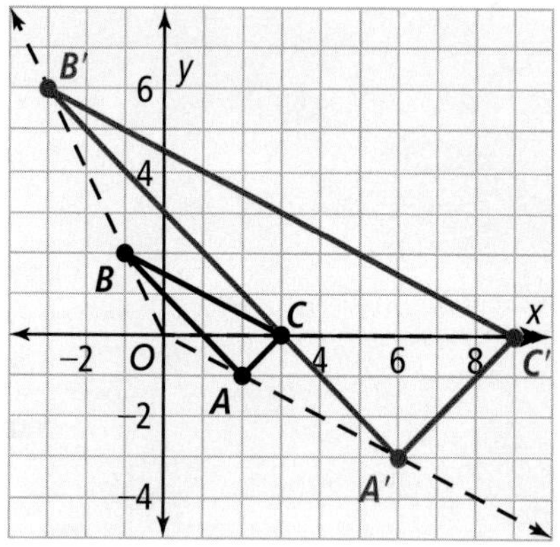


The vertices of $D_3(\triangle ABC)$ are $A'(6, -3)$, $B'(-3, 6)$, and $C'(9, 0)$.

## Try It!

4. Use $\triangle PQR$.

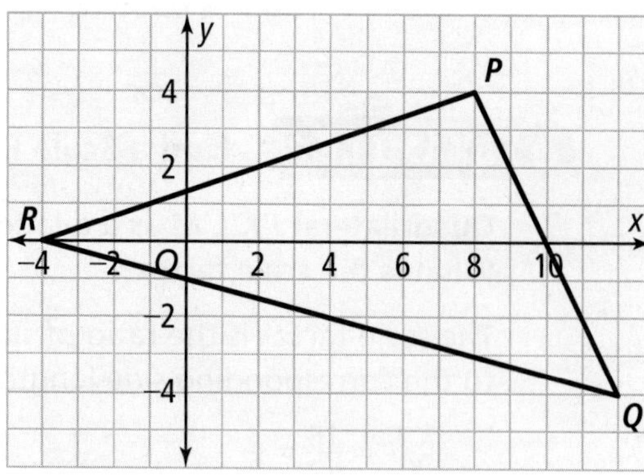


a. What are the vertices of $D_{\frac{1}{4}}(\triangle PQR)$?

b. How are the distances to the origin from each image point related to the distance to the origin from each corresponding preimage point?

## EXAMPLE 5 Dilate a Figure With Center Not at the Origin

**What are the vertices of $D_{\left(\frac{1}{2}, R\right)}(QRST)$?**

The dilation is centered at $R(-2, 7)$ with a scale factor of $\frac{1}{2}$. So each image point is half the distance from $R$ as the corresponding preimage point is. For each preimage point, multiply the horizontal and vertical distances from $R$ by $\frac{1}{2}$. Then add the distances to the coordinates of the center of dilation.

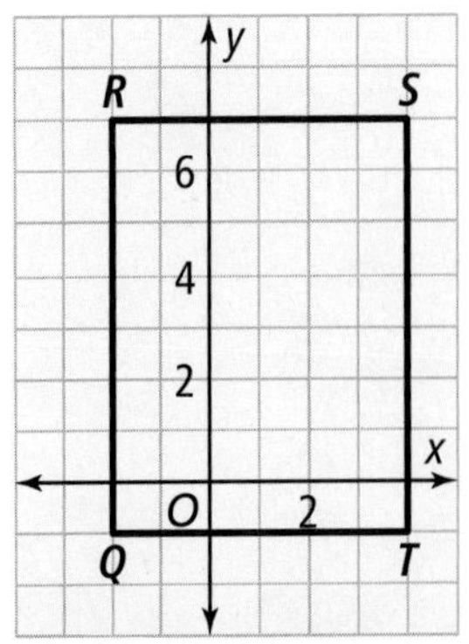


| Preimage Point | Distance From $R(-2, 7)$ | | Half-Distances From $R(-2, 7)$ | | Add to $R(-2, 7)$ | Image Point |
|---|---|---|---|---|---|---|
| | horiz. | vert. | horiz. | vert. | | |
| $Q(-2, -1)$ | 0 | −8 | 0 | −4 | $(-2 + 0, 7 - 4)$ | $Q'(-2, 3)$ |
| $S(4, 7)$ | 6 | 0 | 3 | 0 | $(-2 + 3, 7 + 0)$ | $S'(1, 7)$ |
| $T(4, -1)$ | 6 | −8 | 3 | −4 | $(-2 + 3, 7 - 4)$ | $T'(1, 3)$ |

Graph the preimage and image on the same coordinate plane.

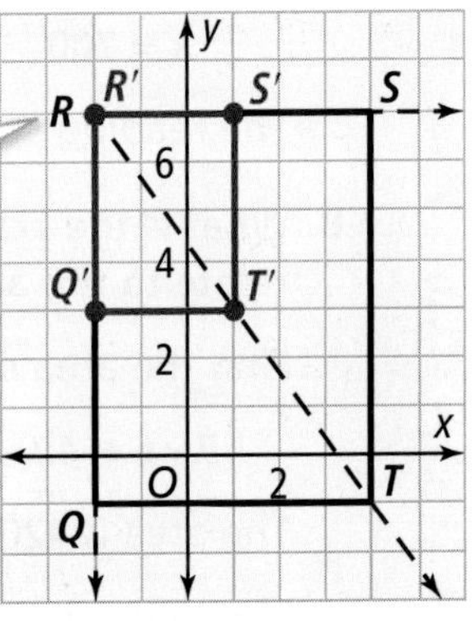


**STUDY TIP**
Remember to check your answers by measuring the distances between the center of dilation and the image and preimage vertices.

The vertices of $D_{\left(\frac{1}{2}, R\right)}(QRST)$ are $Q'(-2, 3)$, $R'(-2, 7)$, $S'(1, 7)$, and $T'(1, 3)$.

**Try It!** 5. A dilation of $\triangle ABC$ is shown.

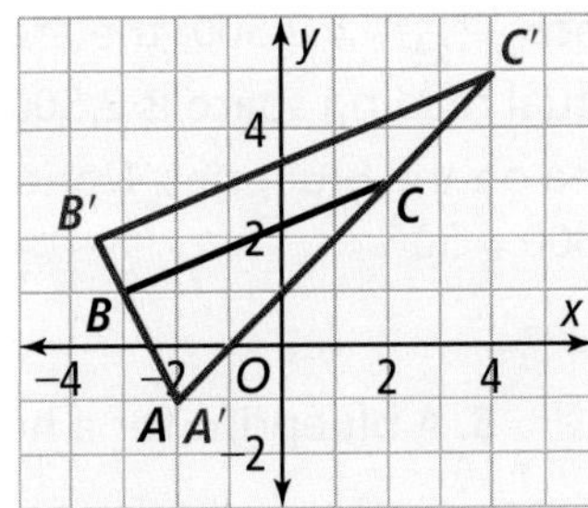


a. What is the center of dilation?

b. What is the scale factor?

APPLICATION

## EXAMPLE 6 Use a Scale Factor to Find Length and Area

**A blueprint for a new library uses a scale factor of $\frac{1}{50}$. Mr. Ayer measures the reading space on the blueprint to find the actual dimensions and area so he can order furniture.**

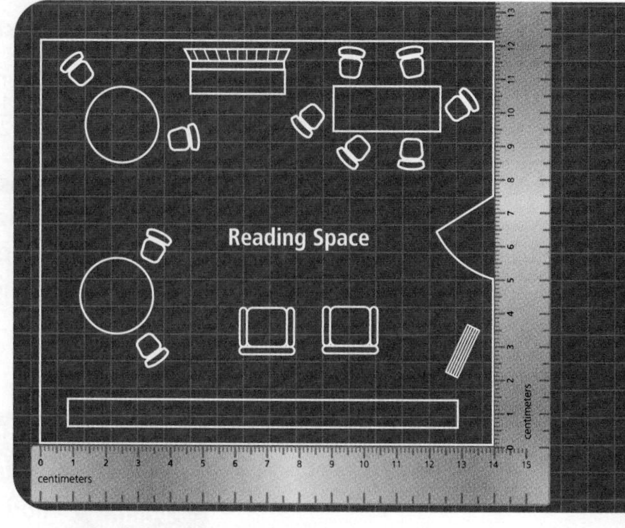


**A. What are the actual dimensions of the reading space?**

Let $x$ represent the length and $y$ represent the width.

$\frac{14}{x} = \frac{1}{50}$

$x = 14 \cdot 50$

$x = 700$

The ratio of image side length to actual side length is $\frac{1}{50}$.

$\frac{12}{y} = \frac{1}{50}$

$y = 12 \cdot 50$

$y = 600$

The reading space is 700 cm, or 7 m, long and 600 cm, or 6 m, wide.

**LOOK FOR RELATIONSHIPS**
Think about equivalent expressions to understand how quantities are related. How does writing $700 \times 600$ as $(50 \times 14) \times (50 \times 12)$ help you to understand the relationship between the areas?

**B. What is the actual area of the reading space? How does the actual area relate to the area on the blueprint?**

Find the area of the reading space.

$7 \cdot 6 = 42$, or $700 \cdot 600 = 420{,}000$

The area is 420,000 $cm^2$, or 42 $m^2$.

The actual area is more useful in square meters, but the actual area in square centimeters is needed to compare to the area on the blueprint.

Then find the area of the reading space on the blueprint.

$14 \cdot 12 = 168$

The area on the blueprint is 168 $cm^2$.

Since $\frac{420{,}000}{168} = 2{,}500$, the area of the actual reading space is 2,500 times the area on the blueprint. Notice that $2{,}500 = 50^2$.

In general, the ratio of the area of the image to the area of the preimage is the square of the scale factor.

 **Try It!** 6. A blueprint for a house uses a scale factor of $\frac{1}{20}$.

a. If the dimensions of the actual kitchen are 3.1 m by 3.4 m, what are the dimensions of the kitchen on the blueprint?

b. What is the relationship between the area of the actual kitchen and the area of the kitchen on the blueprint?

## CONCEPT SUMMARY Dilations

**WORDS** A dilation is a transformation that maps point $X$ to point $X'$ such that $X'$ lies on $\overrightarrow{CX}$ and $CX' = k \cdot CX$ for a center of dilation $C$ and a scale factor $k$. Dilations preserve angle measures.

**DIAGRAM**

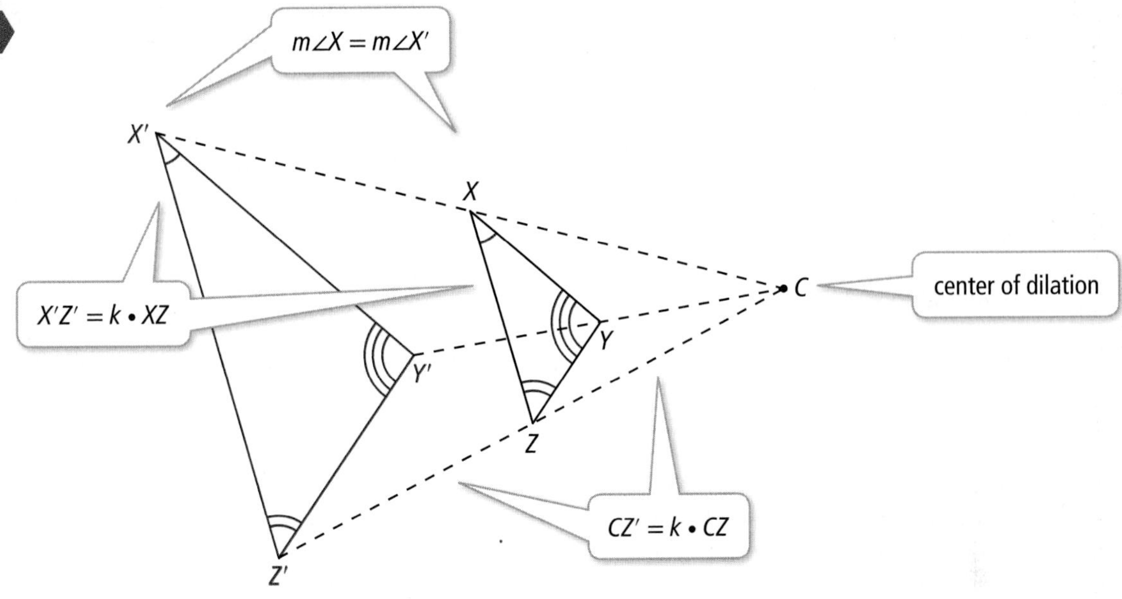


**NOTATION** Dilation centered at the origin: $D_k(X)$

Dilation centered at point $C$: $D_{(k,\ C)}(X)$

## Do You UNDERSTAND?

1. **ESSENTIAL QUESTION** How does a dilation affect the side lengths and angle measures of a figure?

2. **Error Analysis** Emilia was asked to find the coordinates of $D_2(\triangle ABC)$ for $A(2, 4)$, $B(0, 5)$, and $C(-2, 1)$. What is Emilia's error?

   $A(2, 4) \rightarrow A'(4, 6)$
   $B(0, 5) \rightarrow B'(2, 7)$
   $C(-2, 1) \rightarrow C'(0, 3)$ ✗

3. **Vocabulary** Why does it make sense that the point from where dilations are measured is called the *center* of dilation?

4. **Construct Arguments** Compare the vertices of $D_1(\triangle ABC)$ for any points $A$, $B$, and $C$. Justify your answer.

## Do You KNOW HOW?

5. Trace $\triangle JKL$ and point $P$. Draw the dilation of $\triangle JKL$ using scale factor 3 and $P$ as the center of dilation.

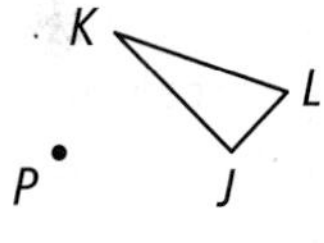


6. What is the scale factor for the dilation?

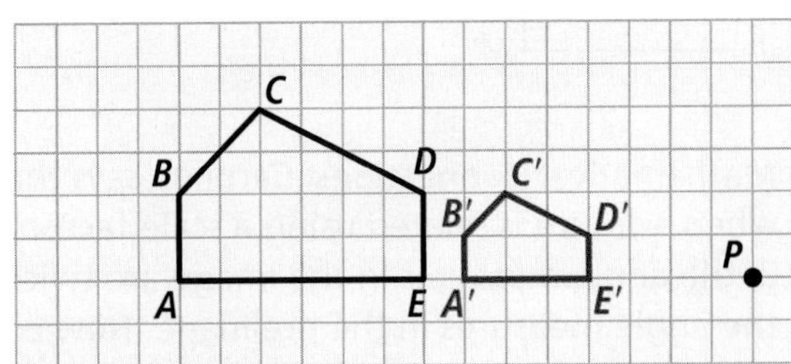


**Give the coordinates of the dilation.**

7. $D_5(\triangle PQR)$ for $P(1, -3)$, $Q(-5, -4)$, $R(6, 2)$

8. $D_{(3,\ B)}(\triangle ABC)$ for $A(0, 4)$, $B(0, 2)$, $C(-3, 2)$

9. $D_{(4,\ F)}(FGHJ)$ for $F(0, -1)$, $G(4, -1)$, $H(4, -3)$, $J(0, -3)$

# PRACTICE & PROBLEM SOLVING

Scan for Multimedia

Practice Tutorial

Additional Exercises Available Online

## UNDERSTAND

**10. Error Analysis** Kendall was asked to find the scale factor for the dilation. What is Kendall's error?

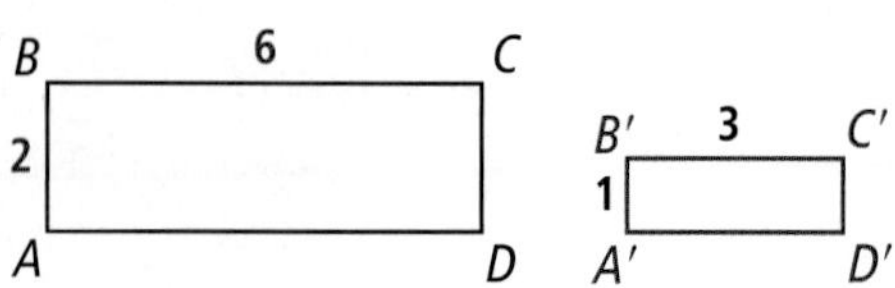


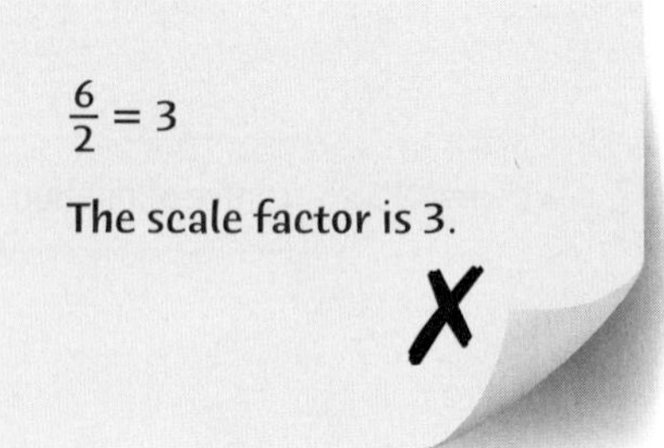


**11. Higher Order Thinking** Points $M(a, b)$ and $N(c, d)$ are dilated by scale factor $k$, with the origin as the center of dilation. Show algebraically that $\overleftrightarrow{MN} \parallel \overleftrightarrow{M'N'}$.

**12. Communicate Precisely** Suppose you want to dilate a figure on the coordinate plane with a center of dilation at point $(a, b)$ that is not the origin and with a scale factor $k$. Describe how you can use a composition of translations and a dilation centered at the origin to dilate the figure. Then write the transformation rule.

**13. Reason** Rectangle $J'K'L'M'$ is a dilation of $JKLM$ with scale factor $k$. What are the perimeter and area of $JKLM$?

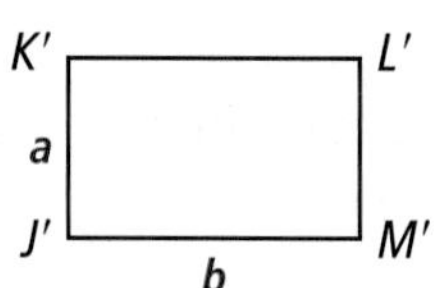


**14. Mathematical Connections** Carolina says that when a figure is dilated using a scale factor of 2, the angle measures in the image are twice the angle measures in the preimage. How could you use the Triangle Angle Sum Theorem to explain why this cannot be true?

**15. Generalize** Is it always true that $(D_m \circ D_n)(X) = D_{mn}(X)$? Explain.

## PRACTICE

**16.** Trace $ABCD$ and point $P$. Draw the dilation of $ABCD$ using $P$ as the center of dilation and sides that are two times as long. SEE EXAMPLE 1

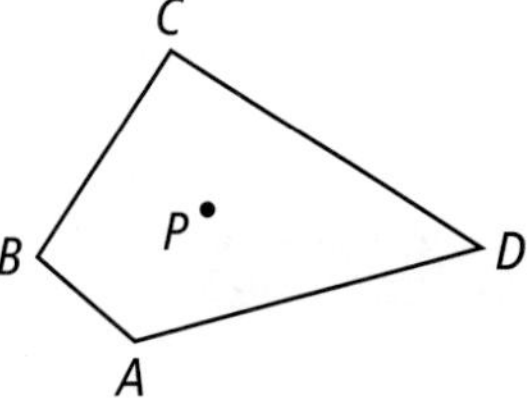


**17.** How are the side lengths of the preimage and dilated image related? SEE EXAMPLE 2

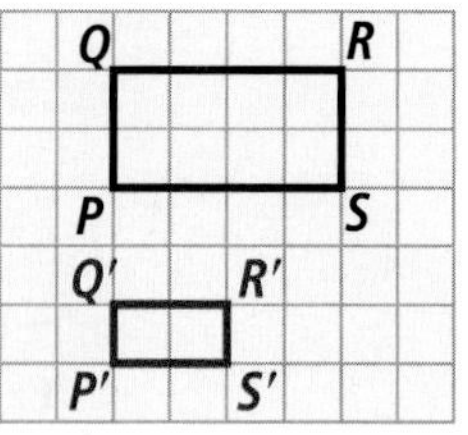


**18.** What is the scale factor of the dilation shown? SEE EXAMPLE 3

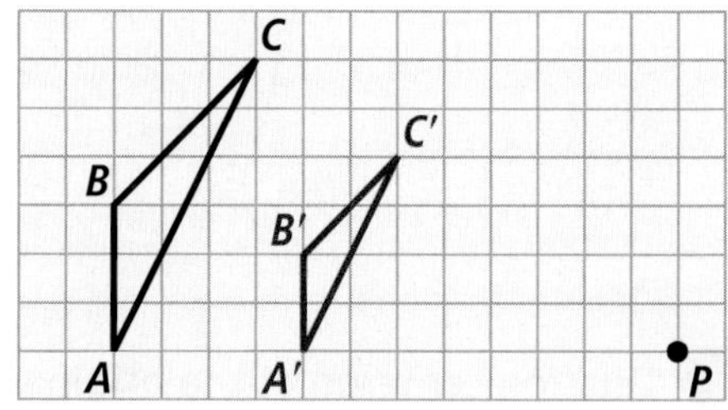


**19.** What are the coordinates of $D_{1.5}(ABCD)$ for $A(2, 0)$, $B(8, -4)$, $C(4, -6)$, and $D(-5, -10)$? SEE EXAMPLE 4

**20.** What are the coordinates of $D_{(2, X)}(\triangle XYZ)$ for $X(1, 1)$, $Y(2, 2)$, and $Z(3, 0)$? SEE EXAMPLE 5

**21.** A figure is dilated using a scale factor of 8. If the area of the image is 832 square units, what is the area of the preimage? SEE EXAMPLE 6

**22.** If $\triangle F'G'H'$ is a dilation of $\triangle FGH$ with a scale factor of 3, what are the values of $x$ and $y$?

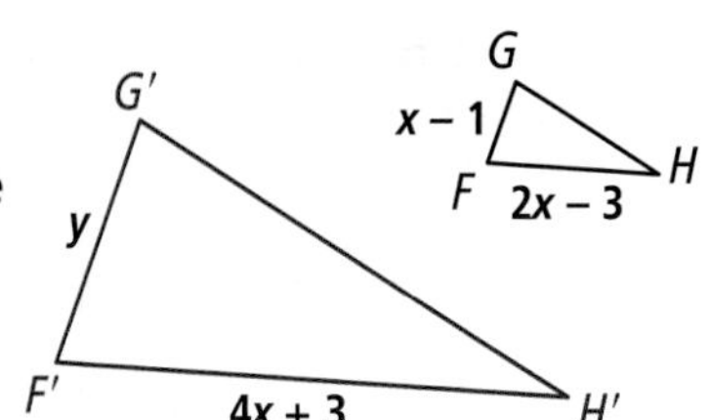


**23.** What are the coordinates of the center of dilation for the dilation shown?

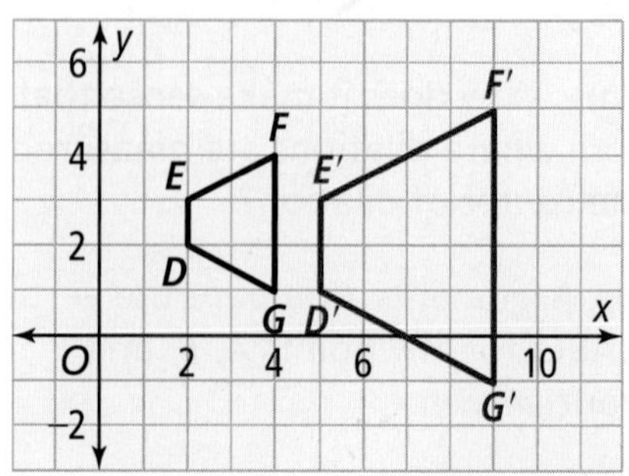

## PRACTICE & PROBLEM SOLVING



### APPLY

**24. Reason** The images on Henry's digital camera have a width-to-length ratio of 2 : 3. He wants to make an 8 in.-by-10 in. print of one of his photographs.

**a.** Is this possible? Explain.

**b.** How can Henry crop an image so that an 8 in.-by-10 in. print can be made?

**25. Model With Mathematics** Alex draws the scale model shown as a plan for a large wall mosaic.

**a.** The wall is 10 m wide and 7 m high. What are the dimensions of the largest mosaic he can make on that wall? Explain.

**b.** He will use 2-cm square tiles to make his mosaic. How many tiles will he need? Explain how you found your answer.

**26. Look for Relationships** How far from the screen should the light be placed in order for the shadow of the puppet to be 30 in. tall? Explain how you found your answer.

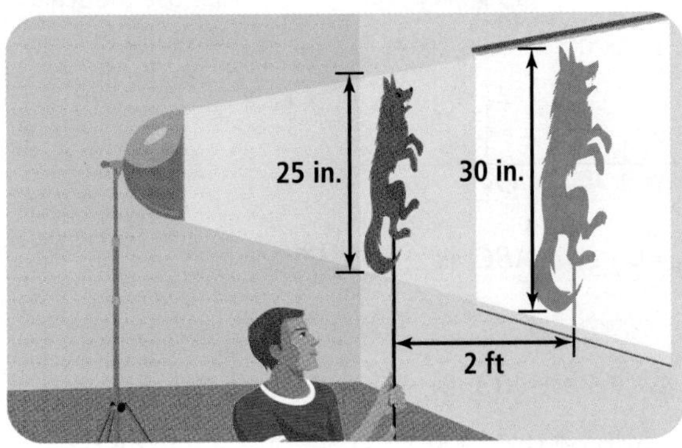


### ASSESSMENT PRACTICE

**27.** Copy and complete the table to show information about dilations centered at the origin.

| Preimage Coordinates | Scale Factor | Image Coordinates |
|---|---|---|
| (5, –2) | 4 | ■ |
| (9, 3) | ■ | (3, 1) |
| ■ | 1.5 | (–6, 0) |
| (–1, 2) | ■ | (–5, 10) |

**28. SAT/ACT** A dilation maps $\triangle ABC$ to $\triangle A'B'C'$. The area of $\triangle ABC$ is 13 square units, and the area of $\triangle A'B'C'$ is 52 square units. What is the scale factor?

Ⓐ 2
Ⓑ 13
Ⓒ 4
Ⓓ 26

**29. Performance Task** Alberto wants to make a scale model of the Wright brothers' glider.

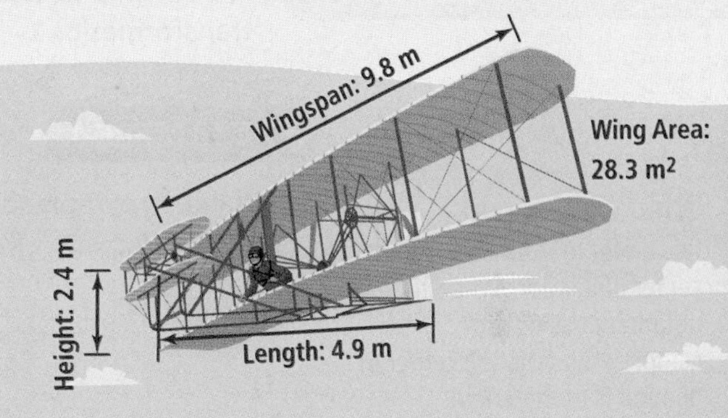


**Part A** The wingspan of the scale model must be between 15 cm and 18 cm. What scale factor should he use? Explain.

**Part B** What will be the length, wingspan, and height of the model glider?

**Part C** What will be the wing area of the model glider? If both wing sections are the same size, what will be the dimensions of each wing section?

Activity Assess

# 7-2 Similarity Transformations

I CAN... determine whether figures are similar.

**VOCABULARY**

- similarity transformation

## CRITIQUE & EXPLAIN

**Helena and Edwin were asked to apply a composition of transformations to *ABCD*.**

**Helena**

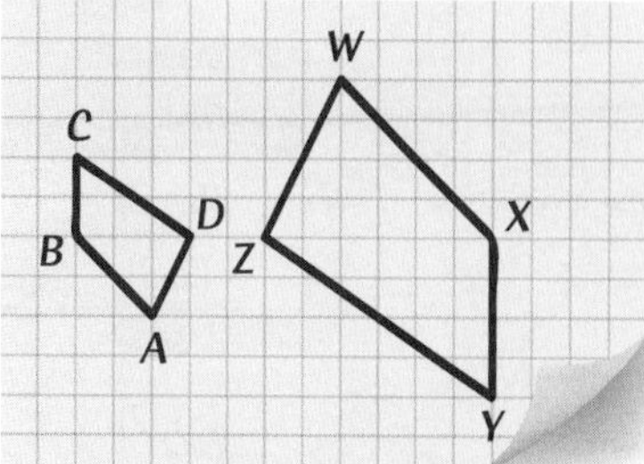


**Edwin**

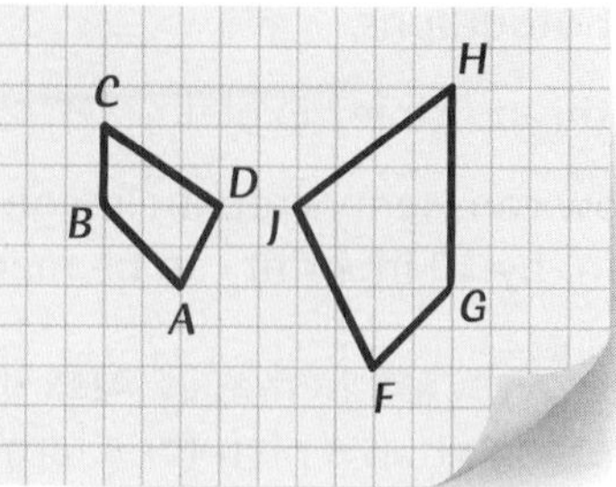


**A. Use Appropriate Tools** Is there a composition of transformations that maps *ABCD* to the second figure in each student's work? If so, what is it?

**B.** For each student whose work shows a composition of transformations, describe the relationship between the figures.

## ESSENTIAL QUESTION

**What makes a transformation a similarity transformation? What is the relationship between a preimage and the image resulting from a similarity transformation?**

## EXAMPLE 1 Graph a Composition of a Rigid Motion and a Dilation

**If line *m* is represented by the equation $x = -3$, what is a graph of the image $(R_m \circ D_{0.5})(\triangle ABC)$?**

**COMMON ERROR**
Be careful to use the correct center of dilation. When the notation does not specify the center of dilation, the center of dilation is at the origin.

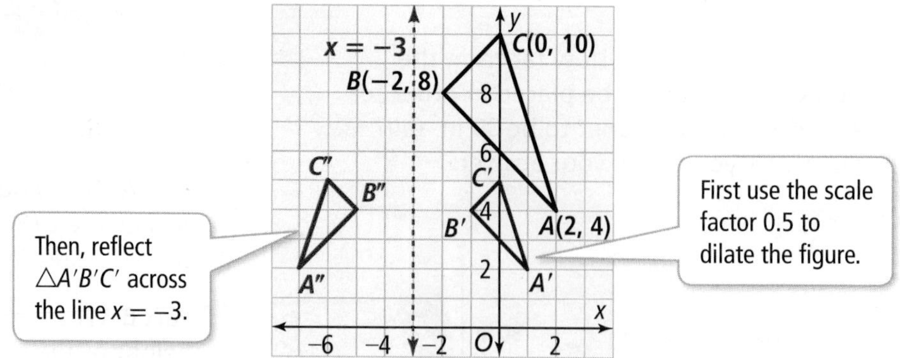


The graph of the image $(R_m \circ D_{0.5})(\triangle ABC)$ is $\triangle A''B''C''$.

**Try It!** 1. The vertices of $\triangle XYZ$ are $X(3, 5)$, $Y(-1, 4)$, and $Z(1, 7)$.

a. What is the graph of the image $(D_2 \circ T_{\langle 1, -2 \rangle})(\triangle XYZ)$?

b. What is the graph of the image $(D_3 \circ r_{(90^\circ, O)})(\triangle XYZ)$?

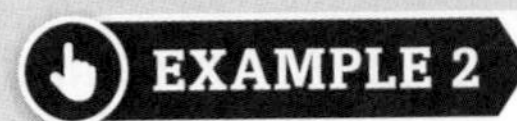

## EXAMPLE 2 Describe a Composition of a Rigid Motion and a Dilation

**Is there a composition of transformations that maps △*XYZ* to △*JKL*? Explain.**

**MAKE SENSE AND PERSEVERE**
Think about how you could use reflection, translation, or rotation to create an image of △*XYZ* with the orientation opposite of △*JKL*. Which rigid motion would you use?

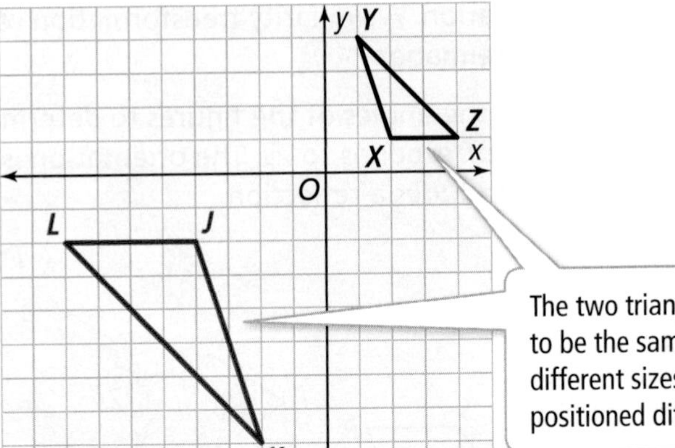


The two triangles appear to be the same shape but different sizes. They are also positioned differently.

Notice that *Y* in △*XYZ* is in the upper left of the first quadrant, but its corresponding vertex *K* in △*JKL* is in the lower right of the third quadrant, so it appears that △*XYZ* is rotated. Since △*JKL* is larger than △*XYZ*, it is also dilated.

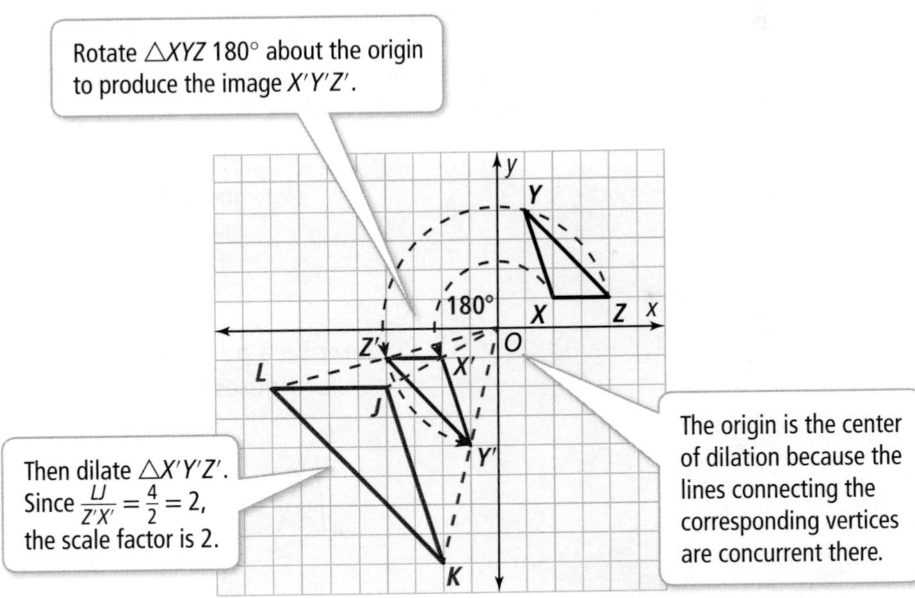

Rotate △XYZ 180° about the origin to produce the image X′Y′Z′.
y
Y
180°
X
Z
x
Z′
O
X′
L
J
Y′
K
Then dilate △X′Y′Z′. Since $\frac{LJ}{Z'X'} = \frac{4}{2} = 2$, the scale factor is 2.
The origin is the center of dilation because the lines connecting the corresponding vertices are concurrent there.


So, the composition of transformations $D_2 \circ r_{(180°, O)}$ maps △*XYZ* to △*JKL*.

**Try It!** 2. If the transformations in Example 2 are performed in the reverse order, are the results the same? Do you think your answer holds for all compositions of transformations? Explain.

CONCEPTUAL UNDERSTANDING

**STUDY TIP**

A similarity transformation is more precisely a rigid motion, a dilation, or a composition of a rigid motion and a dilation. Furthermore, the phrase "one or more rigid motions" is not necessary due to Theorem 3-3.

## EXAMPLE 3 Find Similarity Transformations

**Why is *PQRS* similar to *GHJK*?**

A **similarity transformation** is a composition of one or more rigid motions and a dilation. A similarity transformation results in an image that is similar to the preimage.

Measure the angles of the figures to determine that ∠*S* corresponds to ∠*H* and ∠*R* corresponds to ∠*J*. The orientation is reversed in *GHJK*, so the rigid motion includes a reflection.

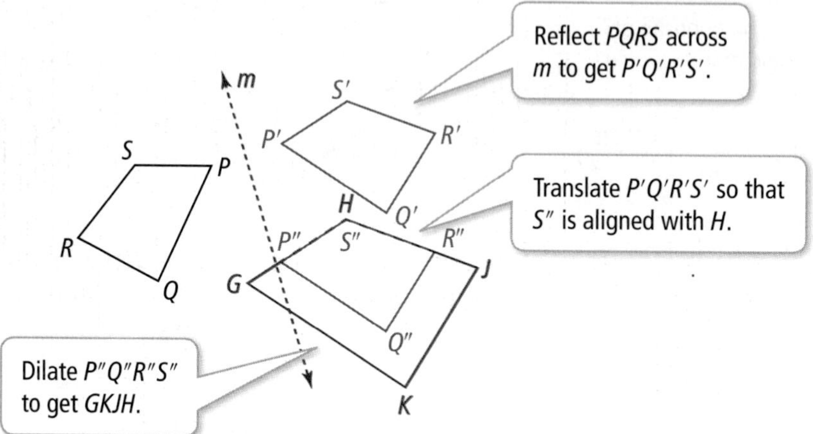

Dilate *P″Q″R″S″* to get *GKJH*.

A composition of a reflection, a translation, and a dilation maps *PQRS* to *GKJH*, so *PQRS* and *GKJH* are similar, or *PQRS* ~ *GKJH*.

The symbol ~ is used to indicate similarity.

**Try It!** 3. Describe a possible similarity transformation for each pair of similar figures shown, and then write a similarity statement.

**a.**

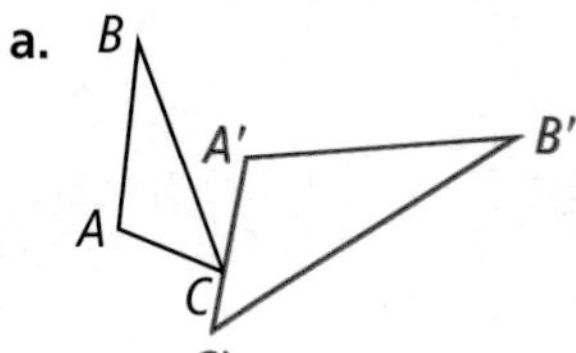


**b.**

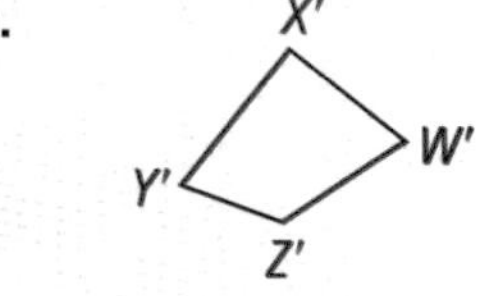


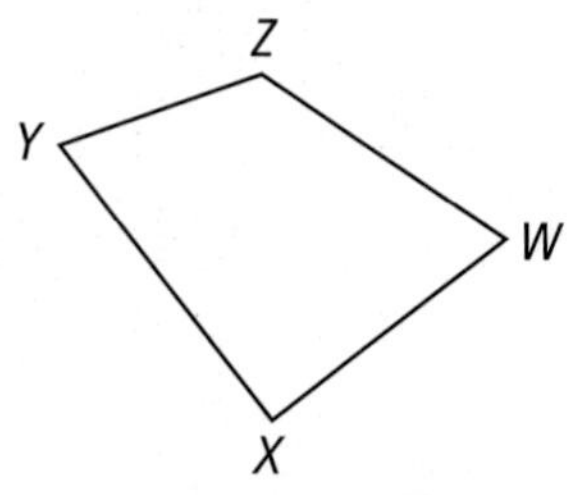

APPLICATION

## EXAMPLE 4 Determine Similarity

**Can an artist copy her sketch to cover an entire wall measuring 15 ft high by 20 ft wide so her wall mural is similar to her sketch? Explain.**

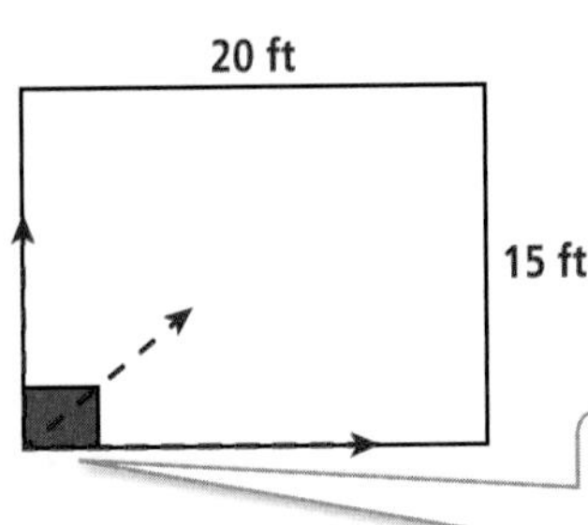


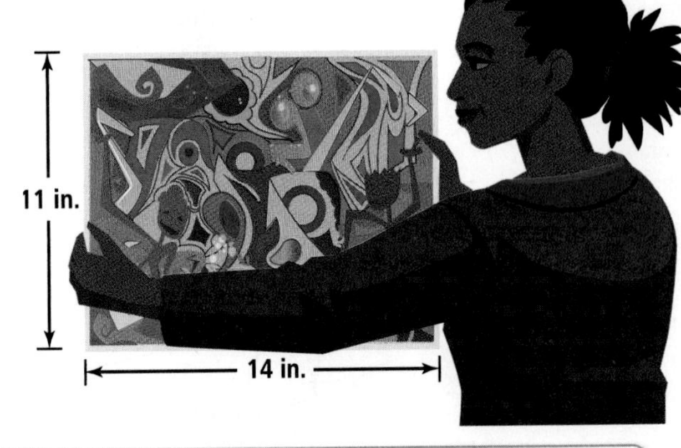


If the artist can map her sketch onto the wall, then she can place her sketch at the bottom left corner and dilate it.

**MAKE SENSE AND PERSEVERE**
Suppose you found the scale factor needed to map the width of the sketch to the width of the wall. Would the results be the same?

To determine the scale factor, convert the dimensions of the wall into inches.

$15 \cdot 12 = 180$ $\qquad$ $20 \cdot 12 = 240$

The dimensions of the wall are 180 in. high by 240 in. wide.

Divide the height of the wall by the height of the sketch to determine the scale factor needed to map the sketch to the height of the wall.

$180 \div 11 \approx 16.36$

Calculate to see whether the width of the sketch maps to the width of the wall.

$16.36 \cdot 14 \approx 229$

Since $229 < 240$, the sketch cannot be copied to cover the entire wall.

**Try It!** 4. Suppose the artist cuts 2 inches from the width of her sketch in Example 4. How much should she cut from the height so she can copy a similar image to cover the wall?

PROOF

## EXAMPLE 5 Identify Similar Circles

**Write a proof that any two circles are similar.**

**Given:** $\odot P$ with radius $r$, $\odot Q$ with radius $s$

**Prove:** $\odot P \sim \odot Q$

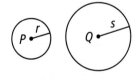

**Proof:** Translate $P$ to $Q$, so $P'$ coincides with $Q$. Then find a scale factor that dilates $\odot P'$ to the circle with radius $s$.

Let $k = \frac{s}{r}$. Then the translation followed by a dilation centered at $Q$ with scale factor $k$ maps $\odot P$ onto $\odot Q$. Since a similarity transformation exists, $\odot P \sim \odot Q$.

**Try It!** 5. Write a proof that any two squares are similar.

## CONCEPT SUMMARY Similarity

**WORDS**

- A similarity transformation is a composition of one or more rigid motions and a dilation.
- Two figures are similar if there is a similarity transformation that maps one to the other.
- All circles are similar to each other.

**DIAGRAMS**

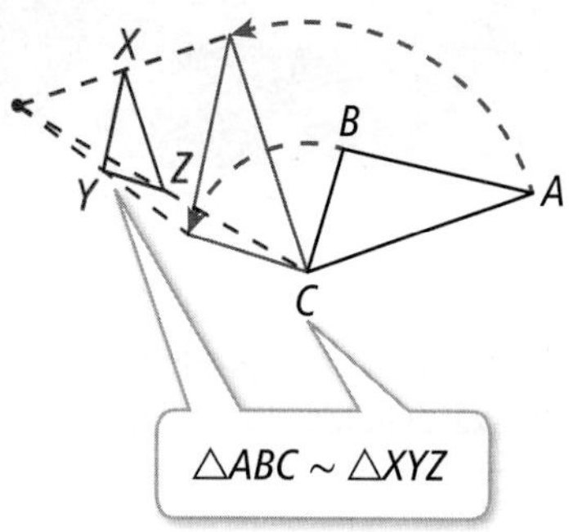


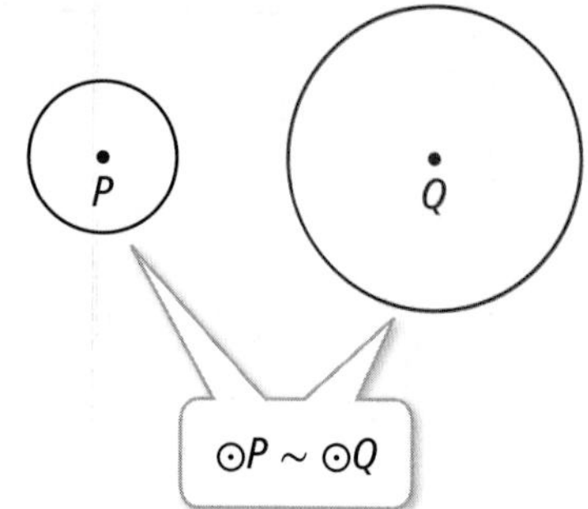


## Do You UNDERSTAND?

1. **ESSENTIAL QUESTION** What makes a transformation a similarity transformation? What is the relationship between a preimage and the image resulting from a similarity transformation?

2. **Error Analysis** Reese described the similarity transformation that maps △ABC to △XYZ. What is Reese's error?

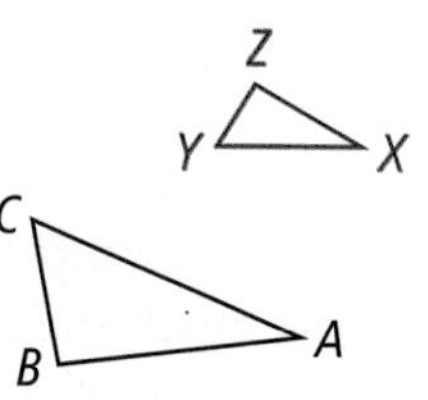


*△ABC is dilated and then rotated to produce the image △XYZ.* ✗

3. **Vocabulary** How are similarity transformations and congruence transformations alike? How are they different?

4. **Construct Arguments** A similarity transformation consisting of a reflection and a dilation is performed on a figure, and one point maps to itself. Explain how this can happen.

## Do You KNOW HOW?

**For Exercises 5 and 6, what are the vertices of each image?**

5. $r_{(90°, O)} \circ D_{0.5}(ABCD)$ for $A(5, 1)$, $B(-3, 4)$, $C(0, 2)$, $D(4, 6)$

6. $(D_3 \circ R_{x\text{-axis}})(\triangle GHJ)$ for $G(3, 5)$, $H(1, -2)$, $J(-1, 6)$

7. Describe a similarity transformation that maps △SQR to △DEF.

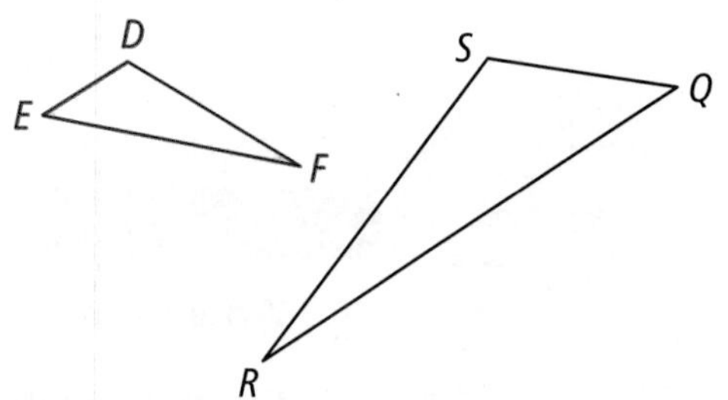


8. Do the two figures appear to be similar? Use transformations to explain.

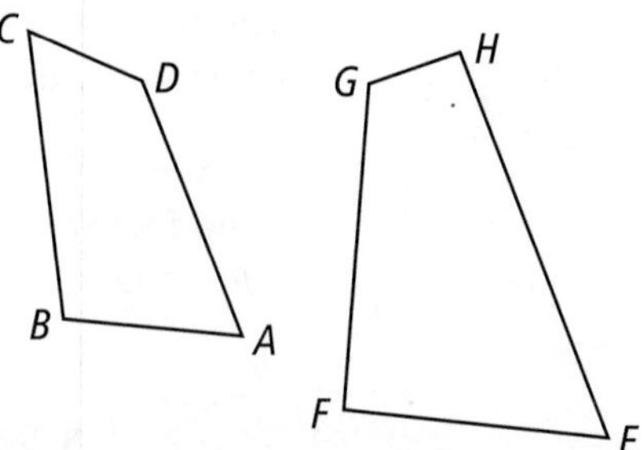

# PRACTICE & PROBLEM SOLVING

## UNDERSTAND

9. **Construct Arguments** Is it possible to use only translations and dilations to map one circle to another? Explain.

10. **Error Analysis** Keegan was asked to graph $(r_{90°} \circ D_2)(\triangle ABC)$. Explain Keegan's error.

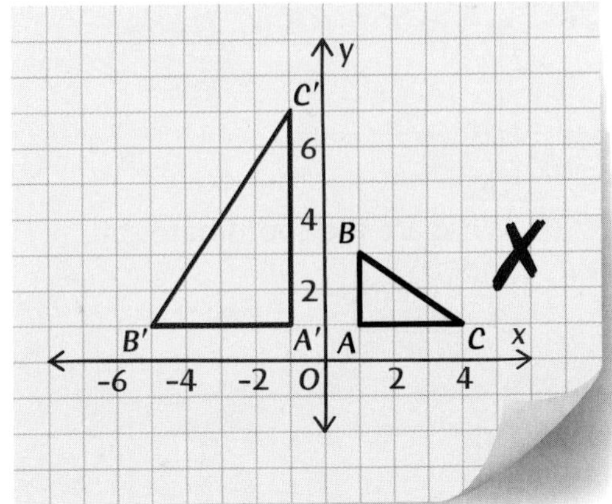


11. **Mathematical Connections** In the diagram, $ABCD \sim A'B'C'D'$. What are the angle measures of $A'B'C'D'$?

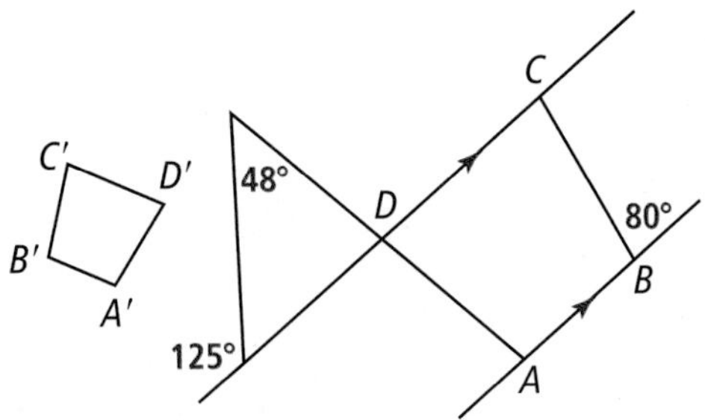


12. **Construct Arguments** Are all squares similar? Use transformations to explain.

13. **Generalize** Show whether a composition of a dilation and a translation can be performed in either order and result in the same image. (Hint: Test whether the equation $(D_k \circ T_{\langle a,\, b\rangle})(x, y) = (T_{\langle a,\, b\rangle} \circ D_k)(x, y)$ is true.)

14. **Higher Order Thinking** Point $D$ is the midpoint of $\overline{AB}$, $E$ is the midpoint of $\overline{BC}$, and $F$ is the midpoint of $\overline{CA}$.

    a. Write a similarity statement for $\triangle ABC$ and $\triangle DEF$, and explain why the triangles are similar.

    b. Describe the similarity transformation that maps one triangle to the other.

## PRACTICE

**What are the vertices of each image?** SEE EXAMPLE 1

15. $(T_{\langle 5,\, -4\rangle} \circ D_{1.5})(\triangle XYZ)$ for $X(6, -2)$, $Y(4, 1)$, $Z(-2, 3)$

16. $(R_{x\text{-axis}} \circ D_{0.5})(LMNP)$ for $L(2, 4)$, $M(4, 4)$, $N(4, -4)$, $P(2, -4)$

17. $(R_{y\text{-axis}} \circ D_2 \circ r_{270°})(\triangle PQR)$ for $P(1, 3)$, $Q(-4, 2)$, $R(0, 5)$

18. $(D_{0.25} \circ R_{x\text{-axis}})(ABCD)$ for $A(2, 6)$, $B(0, 0)$, $C(-5, 8)$, $D(-2, 10)$

**Describe the similarity transformation, and write a similarity statement.** SEE EXAMPLES 2 AND 3

19.

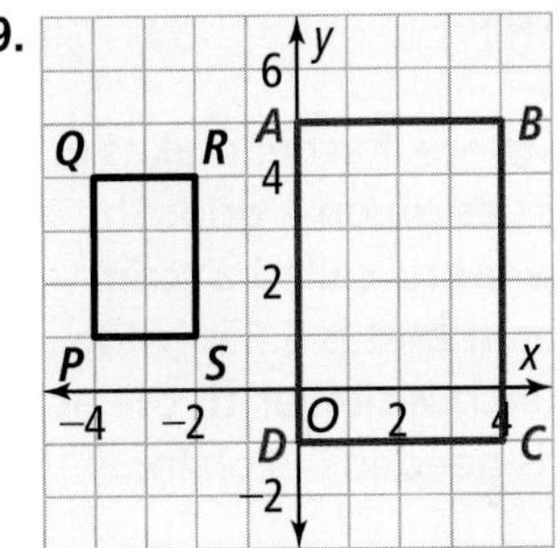


20.

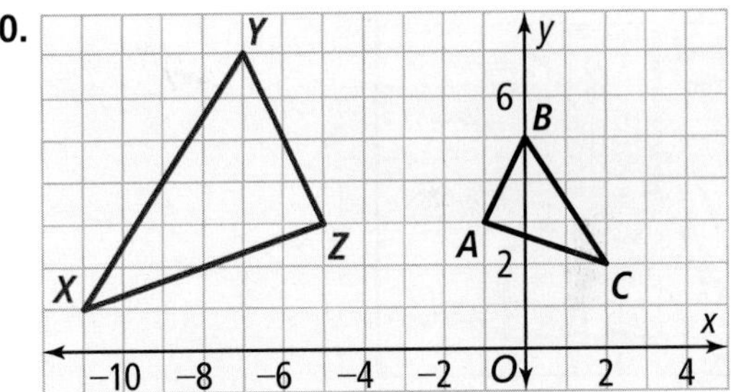


21.

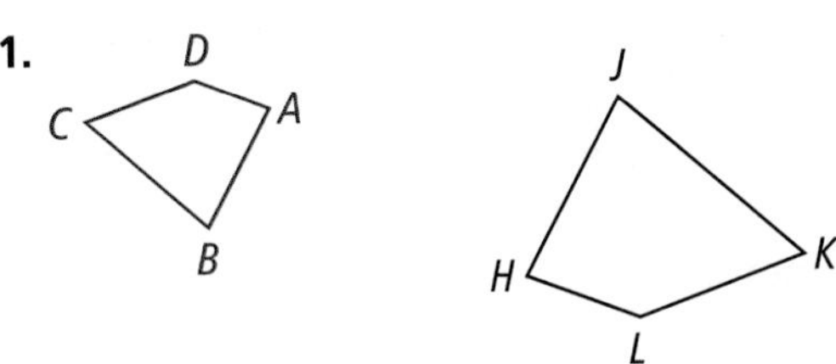


**Do the figures appear to be similar? Explain.**
SEE EXAMPLE 4

22.

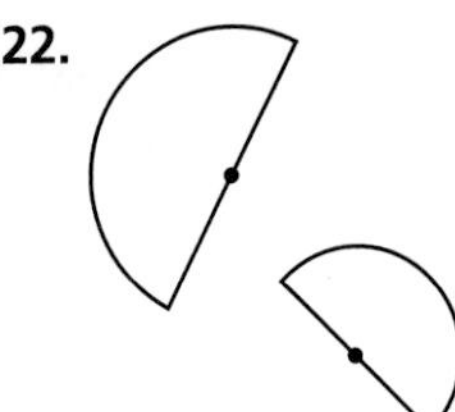

23.

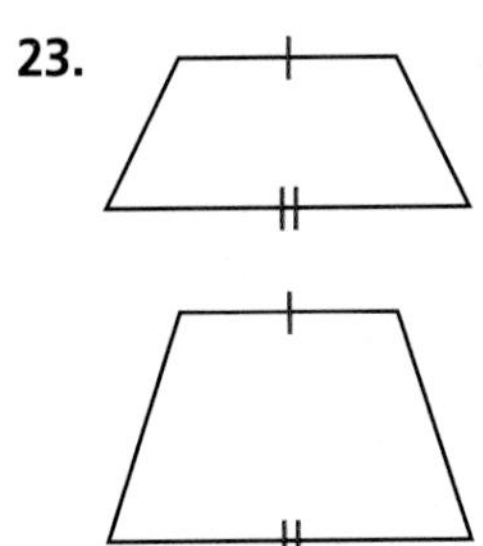

# PRACTICE & PROBLEM SOLVING

Practice | Tutorial

Mixed Review Available Online

## APPLY

**24. Reason** Can Ahmed use the larger sheets of paper shown to make paper cutouts similar to his original hummingbird cutout? If not, how can he trim the sheets of paper so he can use them? Justify your answer.

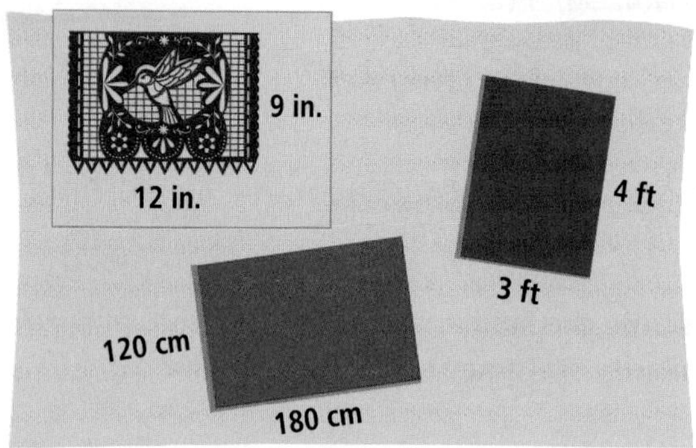


**25. Make Sense and Persevere** Rachel makes a sketch for a stage set design on a grid. She plans to have a gauze fabric called a scrim drop down from a beam that is 5.5 m wide. Assuming that her sketch is similar to the actual set, how much scrim is needed? Explain.

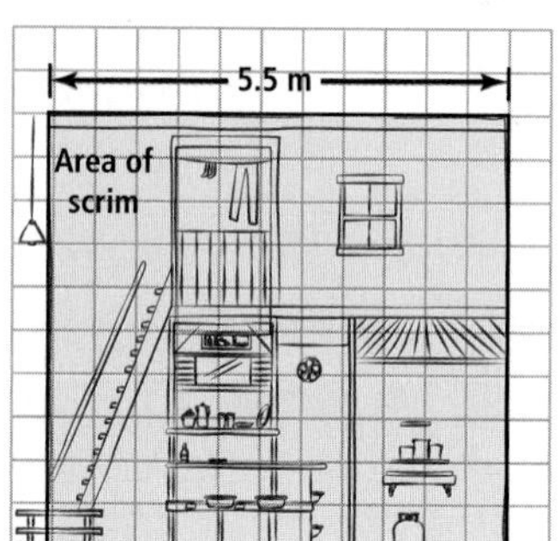


**26. Look for Relationships** Juanita wants to make a dollhouse following the pattern shown but with a reduced size so that the floor has an area of 25 in.$^2$. Make a sketch showing the dimensions of the pieces for the smaller dollhouse.

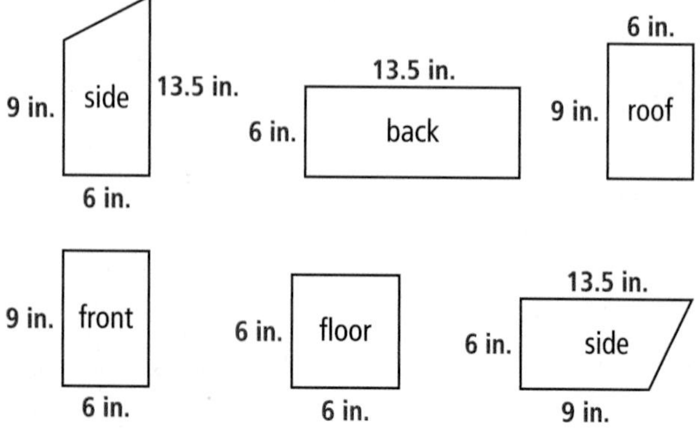


## ASSESSMENT PRACTICE

**27.** Graph the image of $(T_{\langle 1, -3 \rangle} \circ D_2)(\triangle ABC)$.

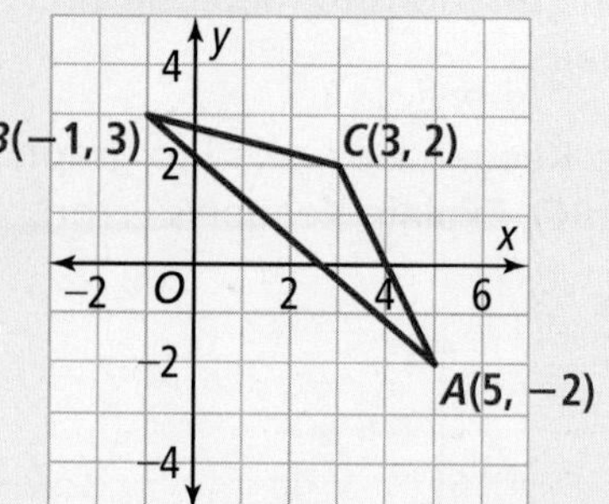


**28. SAT/ACT** What are the coordinates of $(D_4 \circ R_{x\text{-axis}})(8, 2)$?

Ⓐ (−32, 8)

Ⓑ (32, 8)

Ⓒ (−32, −8)

Ⓓ (32, −8)

**29. Performance Task** Lourdes makes sketches for her graphic novel using a repeating similar shape as a motif.

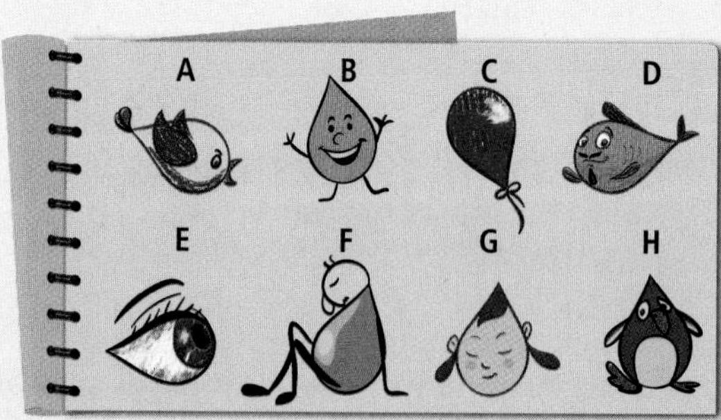


**Part A** On a separate sheet of paper, draw a small simple figure. Label it A.

**Part B** Use transformations, including similarity transformations, to create at least five images that are similar to figure A. Label the images B, C, D, E, and F.

**Part C** Is it possible to select any two of your figures and find a similarity transformation that maps one to the other? Explain.

Activity Assess

# 7-3 Proving Triangles Similar

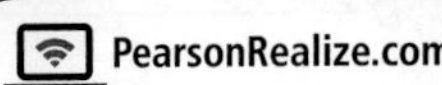

PearsonRealize.com

**I CAN…** use dilation and rigid motion to establish triangle similarity theorems.

## EXPLORE & REASON

**The measurements of two triangles are shown.**

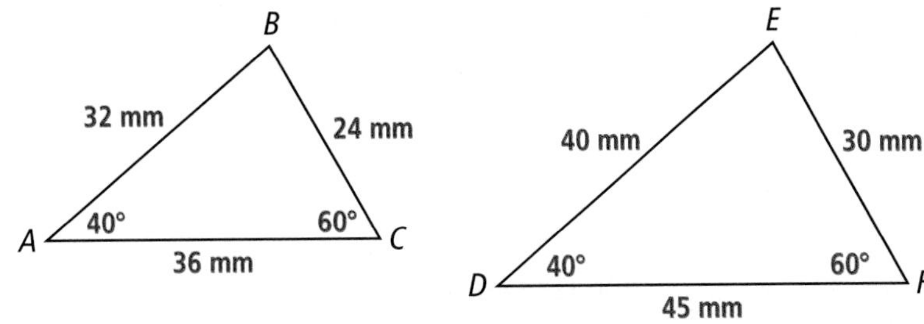


**A.** Are the triangles similar? Explain.

**B.** **Construct Arguments** Would any triangle with 40°- and 60°-angles be similar to $\triangle ABC$? Explain.

## ESSENTIAL QUESTION

**How do similarity transformations determine the angle and side length conditions necessary for triangle similarity?**

CONCEPTUAL UNDERSTANDING

## EXAMPLE 1 Establish the Angle-Angle Similarity (AA ~) Theorem

**If $\angle A \cong \angle R$ and $\angle B \cong \angle S$, is $\triangle ABC \sim \triangle RST$? Explain.**

To show that the triangles are similar, determine whether there is a similarity transformation that maps $\triangle ABC$ to $\triangle RST$.

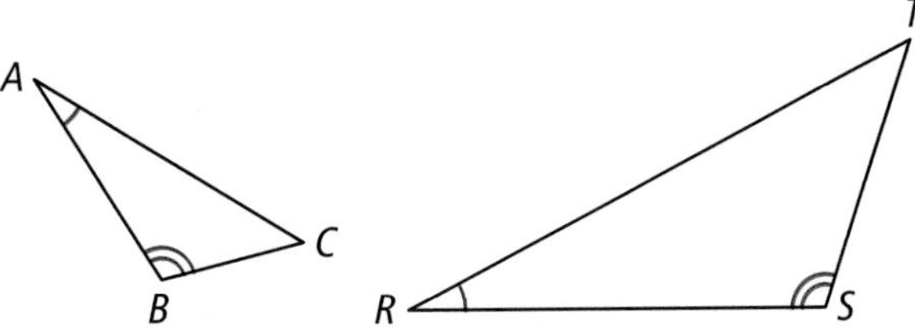


Determine the center of dilation and the scale factor that map $\triangle ABC$ to image $\triangle A'B'C'$ such that $A'B' = RS$.

Let the scale factor $k$ be $\frac{RS}{AB}$.

Then, $A'B' = k \bullet AB = RS$.

$A = A'$

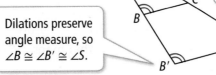

Use vertex $A$ as the center of dilation, so $A = A'$ and $\angle A \cong \angle A' \cong \angle R$.

Dilations preserve angle measure, so $\angle B \cong \angle B' \cong \angle S$.

**REASON**
Think about what it means for figures to be similar. Are congruent triangles similar to the same triangle?

The dilation $D_{(k,\ A)}$ maps $\triangle ABC$ to $\triangle A'B'C'$, and $\triangle A'B'C' \cong \triangle RST$ by ASA, so there is a rigid motion that maps $\triangle A'B'C'$ to $\triangle RST$. Thus, the composition is a similarity transformation that maps $\triangle ABC$ to $\triangle RST$. So, $\triangle ABC \sim \triangle RST$.

**Try It!** **1.** If $\angle A$ is congruent to $\angle R$, and $\angle C$ is congruent to $\angle T$, how would you prove the triangles are similar?

**THEOREM 7-1** Angle-Angle Similarity (AA ~) Theorem

If two angles of one triangle are congruent to two angles of another triangle, then the triangles are similar.

PROOF: SEE EXERCISE 10.

**If...**

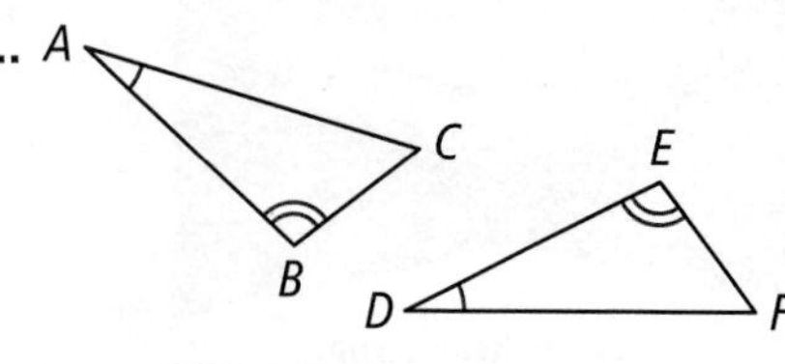


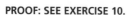

$\angle A \cong \angle D$ and $\angle B \cong \angle E$

**Then...** $\triangle ABC \sim \triangle DEF$

**EXAMPLE 2** **Establish the Side-Side-Side Similarity (SSS ~) Theorem**

**If $\frac{LM}{PQ} = \frac{MN}{QR} = \frac{LN}{PR}$, is there a similarity transformation that maps $\triangle PQR$ to $\triangle LMN$? Explain.**

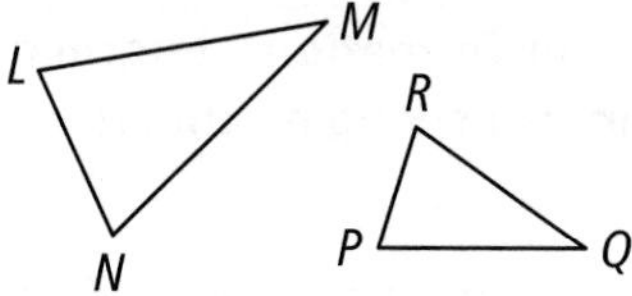


**STUDY TIP**
Remember, a similarity transformation must involve a dilation. The image that results from a similarity transformation is similar to the preimage.

Dilate $\triangle PQR$ by scale factor $k = \frac{LM}{PQ} = \frac{MN}{QR} = \frac{LN}{PR}$ to map $\triangle PQR$ to $\triangle P'Q'R'$.

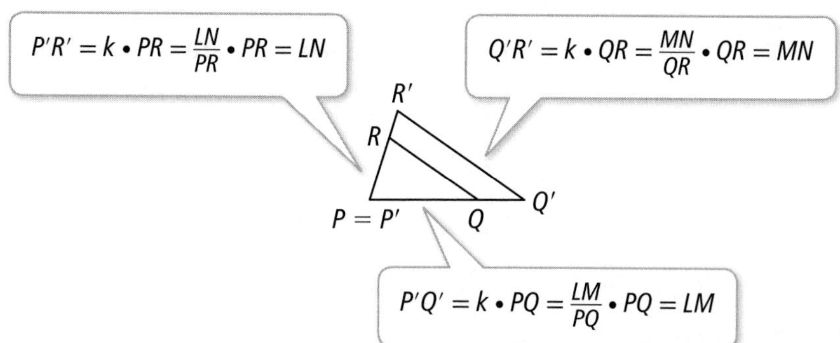

$P'R' = k \bullet PR = \frac{LN}{PR} \bullet PR = LN$
$Q'R' = k \bullet QR = \frac{MN}{QR} \bullet QR = MN$
R'
R
Q'
P = P'
Q
$P'Q' = k \bullet PQ = \frac{LM}{PQ} \bullet PQ = LM$


Because $P'R' = LN$, $P'Q' = LM$, and $Q'R' = MN$, $\triangle P'Q'R' \cong \triangle LMN$ by SSS. By the definition of congruence, there is a rigid motion that maps $\triangle P'Q'R'$ to $\triangle LMN$.

So, $\triangle PQR$ was mapped to $\triangle LMN$ by a similarity transformation and $\triangle PQR$ is similar to $\triangle LMN$.

**Try It!** 2. If $\frac{DF}{GJ} = \frac{EF}{HJ}$ and $\angle F \cong \angle J$, is there a similarity transformation that maps $\triangle DEF$ to $\triangle GHJ$? Explain.

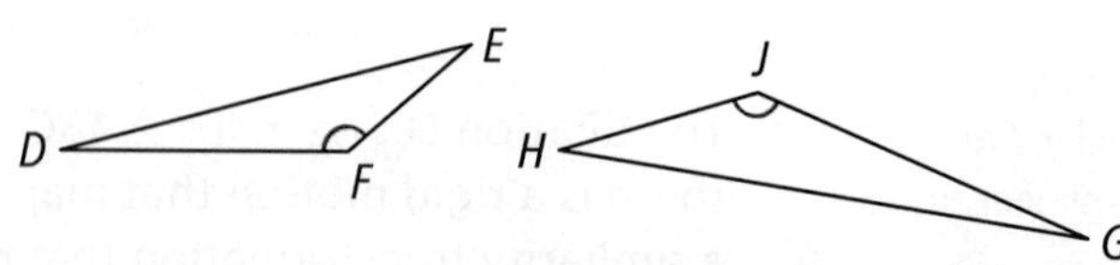

## THEOREM 7-2 Side-Side-Side Similarity (SSS ~) Theorem

If the corresponding sides of two triangles are proportional, then the triangles are similar.

If...

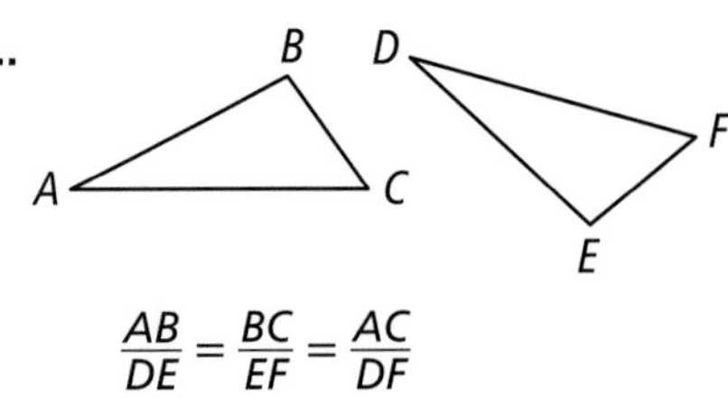


$$\frac{AB}{DE} = \frac{BC}{EF} = \frac{AC}{DF}$$

Then... $\triangle ABC \sim \triangle DEF$

PROOF: SEE EXERCISE 20.

## THEOREM 7-3 Side-Angle-Side Similarity (SAS ~) Theorem

If an angle of one triangle is congruent to an angle of a second triangle, and the sides that include the two angles are proportional, then the triangles are similar.

If...

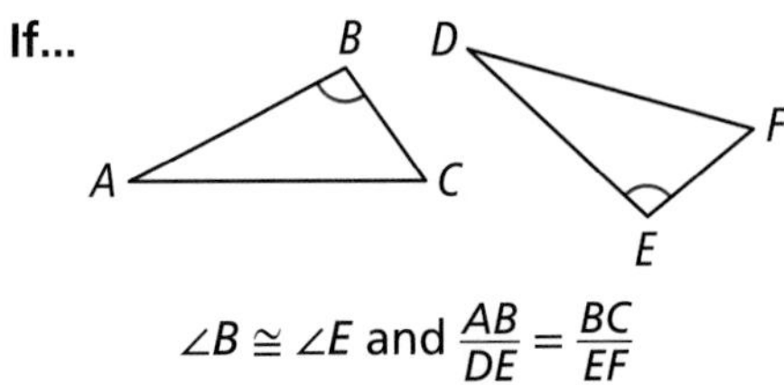


$\angle B \cong \angle E$ and $\frac{AB}{DE} = \frac{BC}{EF}$

Then... $\triangle ABC \sim \triangle DEF$

PROOF: SEE EXERCISE 13.

## EXAMPLE 3 Verify Triangle Similarity

**A. Are $\triangle ABC$ and $\triangle DEF$ similar?**

Determine whether the ratios of the corresponding side lengths are equal.

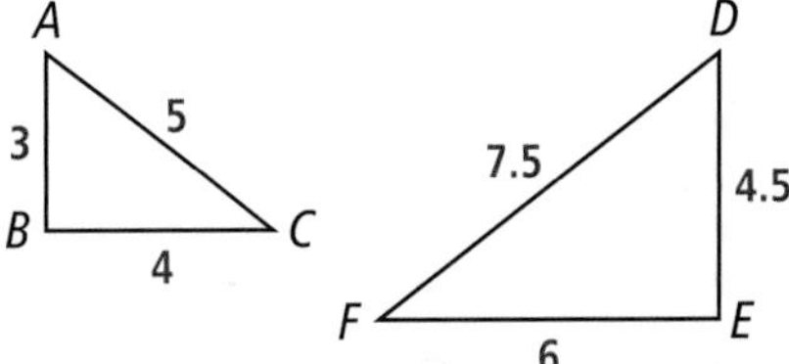


$$\frac{AB}{DE} = \frac{3}{4.5} = \frac{2}{3} \qquad \frac{BC}{EF} = \frac{4}{6} = \frac{2}{3} \qquad \frac{AC}{DF} = \frac{5}{7.5} = \frac{2}{3}$$

The ratios are equal, so the corresponding side lengths are proportional. $\triangle ABC \sim \triangle DEF$ by SSS ~.

**COMMON ERROR**
When setting up ratios to check if triangles are similar, be sure you place corresponding sides of the triangle in corresponding positions in the ratios.

**B. Are $\triangle PQS$ and $\triangle RQP$ similar?**

The two triangles share an included angle, $\angle Q$. Separate the triangles and see whether the lengths of the corresponding sides are in proportion.

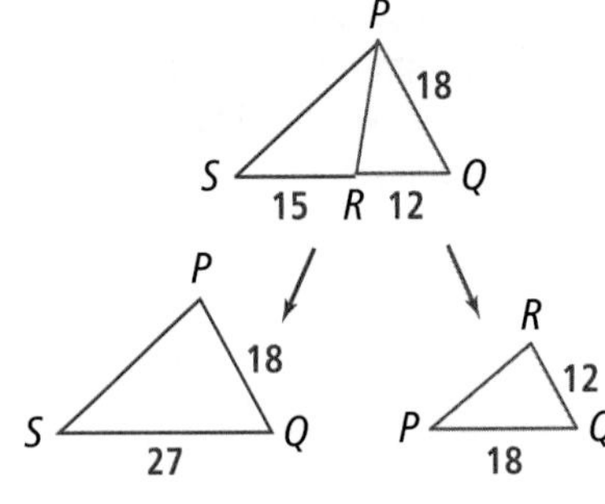


Since $\frac{SQ}{PQ} = \frac{27}{18} = \frac{3}{2}$ and $\frac{PQ}{RQ} = \frac{18}{12} = \frac{3}{2}$, the lengths of the sides that include $\angle Q$ are proportional. By SAS ~, $\triangle PQS \sim \triangle RQP$.

**Try It!** 3. a. Is $\triangle ADE \sim \triangle ABD$? Explain.

b. Is $\triangle ADE \sim \triangle BDC$? Explain.

Activity Assess

## EXAMPLE 4 Find Lengths in Similar Triangles

**What is *MN*?**

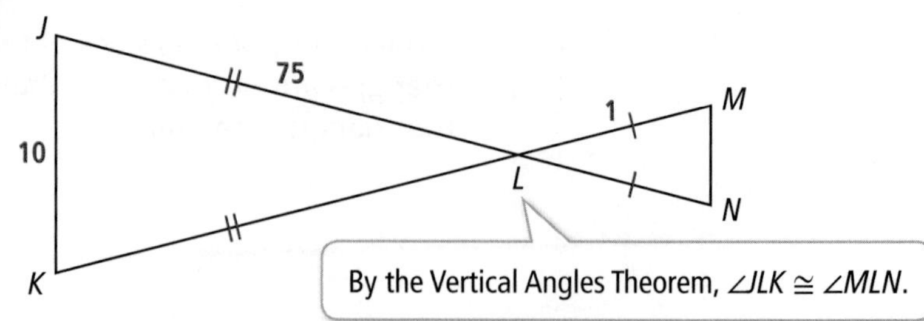
J
75
1
M
10
L
N
K
By the Vertical Angles Theorem, $\angle JLK \cong \angle MLN$.

**STUDY TIP**
The measures of the two corresponding pairs of legs of any two isosceles triangles will always be proportional, even if the triangles are not similar.

The sides that include $\angle JLK$ and $\angle MLN$ are proportional.

By SAS ~, $\triangle JLK \sim \triangle MLN$.

Write a proportion using corresponding sides, and solve for *MN*.

$$\frac{MN}{10} = \frac{1}{75}$$

$$MN = \frac{2}{15}$$

**Try It!** 4. a. In Example 4, if *JL* doubles and *JK* remains the same, how does the value of *MN* change?

b. In Example 4, if *JL* remains the same and *JK* doubles, how does the value of *MN* change?

APPLICATION

## EXAMPLE 5 Solve Problems Involving Similar Triangles

Avery puts up a radio antenna tower in his yard. Ella tells him that their city has a law limiting towers to 50 ft in height. How can Avery use the lengths of his shadow and the shadow of the tower to show that his tower is within the limit without directly measuring it?

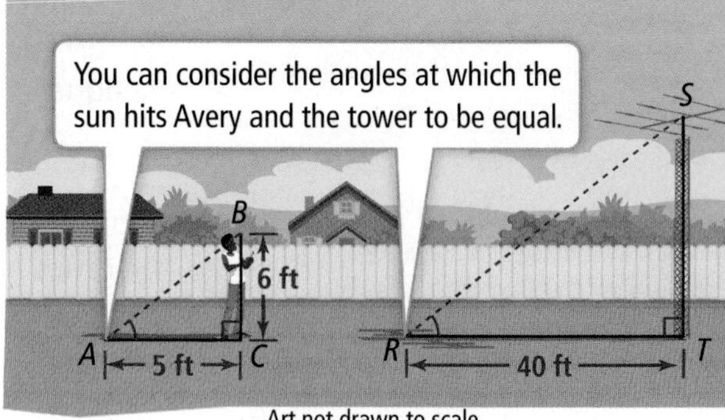
You can consider the angles at which the sun hits Avery and the tower to be equal.
S
B
6 ft
A
5 ft
C
R
40 ft
T
Art not drawn to scale.

**MODEL WITH MATHEMATICS**
Think about how the situation is modeled with triangles. What information do you need to be able to apply a similarity theorem?

Since $\angle BAC \cong \angle SRT$ and $\angle ACB \cong \angle RTS$, you can apply the AA ~ Theorem.

$$\frac{ST}{BC} = \frac{RT}{AC}$$

$$\frac{ST}{6} = \frac{40}{5}$$

$$ST = 48$$

Corresponding sides of $\triangle ABC$ and $\triangle RST$ are proportional.

The antenna tower is 48 ft high. Avery's tower is within the 50-ft limit.

**Try It!** 5. If the tower were 50 ft tall, how long would the shadow of the tower be?

## CONCEPT SUMMARY Triangle Similarity Theorems

**THEOREM 7-1**

### Angle-Angle Similarity

**If...**

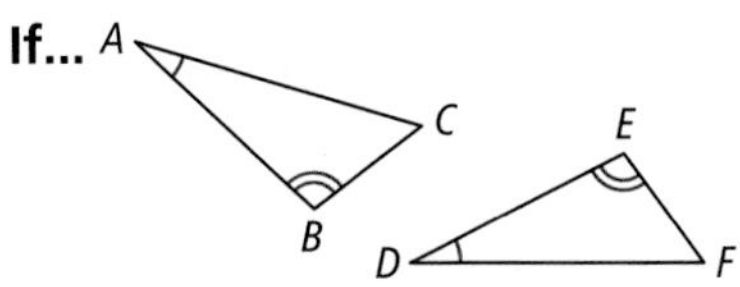


$\angle A \cong \angle D$ and $\angle B \cong \angle E$

**Then...** $\triangle ABC \sim \triangle DEF$

**THEOREM 7-2**

### Side-Side-Side Similarity

**If...**

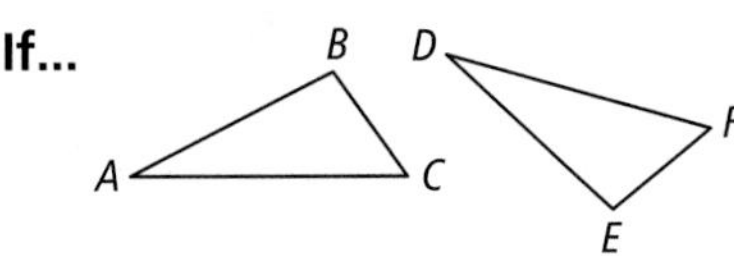


$\frac{AB}{DE} = \frac{BC}{EF} = \frac{AC}{DF}$

**Then...** $\triangle ABC \sim \triangle DEF$

**THEOREM 7-3**

### Side-Angle-Side Similarity

**If...**

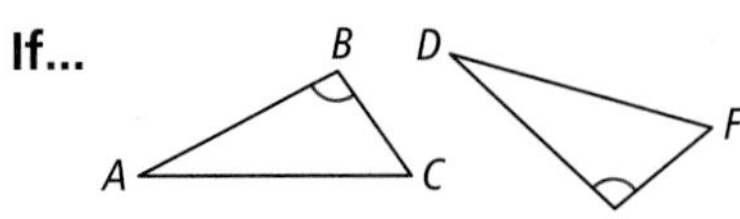


$\angle B \cong \angle E$ and $\frac{AB}{DE} = \frac{BC}{EF}$

**Then...** $\triangle ABC \sim \triangle DEF$

## Do You UNDERSTAND?

1. ESSENTIAL QUESTION How do similarity transformations determine the angle and side length conditions necessary for triangle similarity?

2. **Error Analysis** Allie says $\triangle JKL \sim \triangle XYZ$. What is Allie's error?

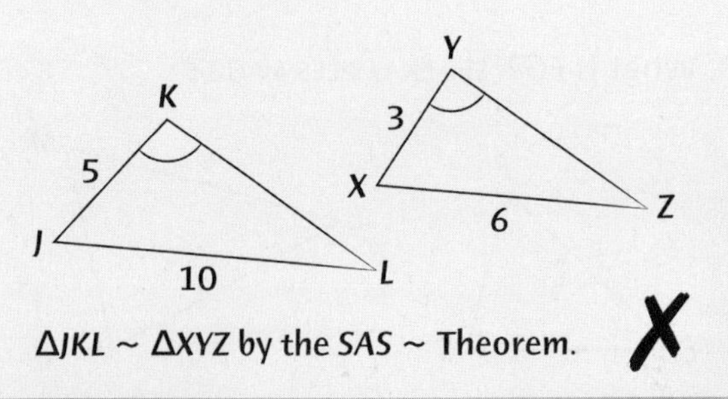


3. **Make Sense and Persevere** Is any additional information needed to show $\triangle DEF \sim \triangle RST$? Explain.

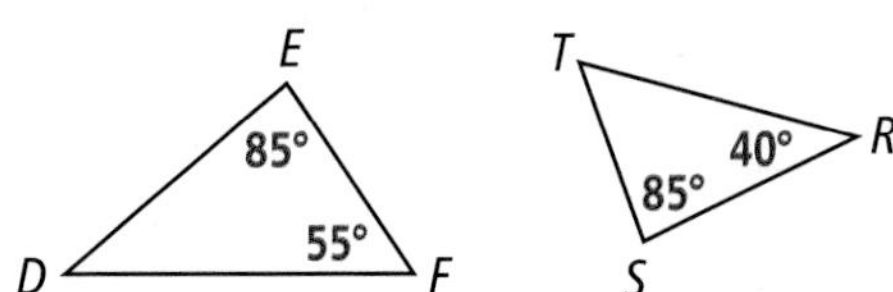


4. **Construct Arguments** Explain how you can use triangle similarity to show that $ABCD \sim WXYZ$.

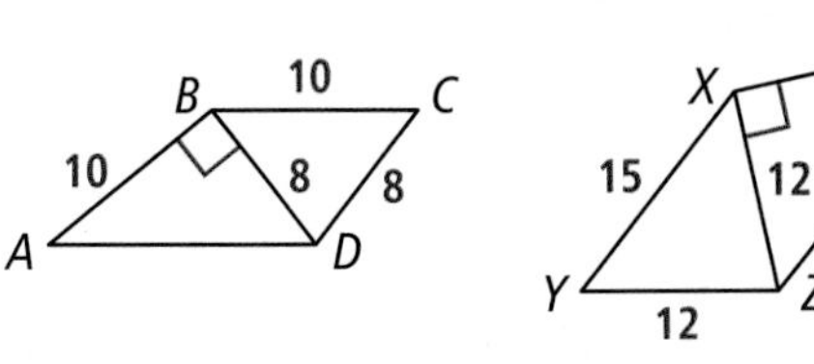


## Do You KNOW HOW?

**For Exercises 5 and 6, explain whether each pair of triangles is similar.**

5.

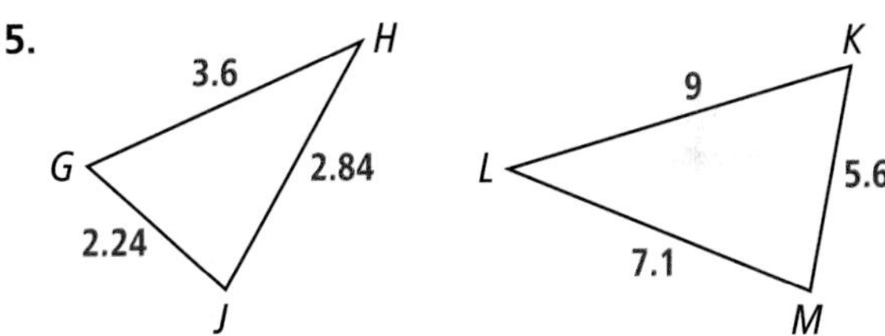


6.

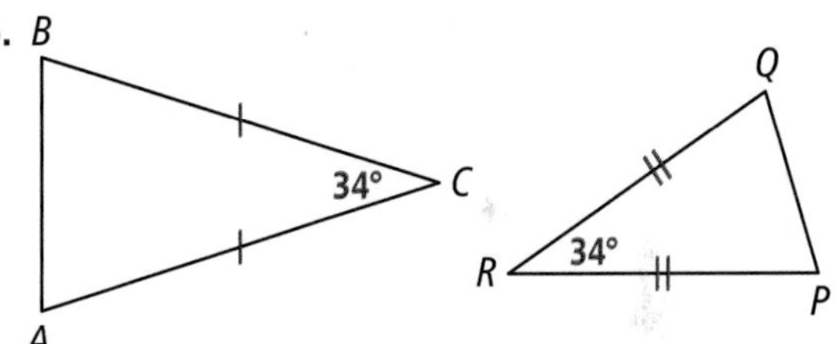


**For Exercises 7 and 8, find the value of each variable such that the triangles are similar.**

7. $a$

8. $b$

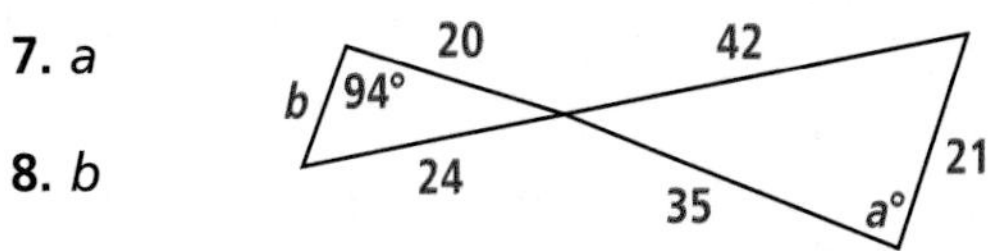


9. When Esteban looks at the puddle, he sees a reflection of the top of the cactus. How tall is the cactus?

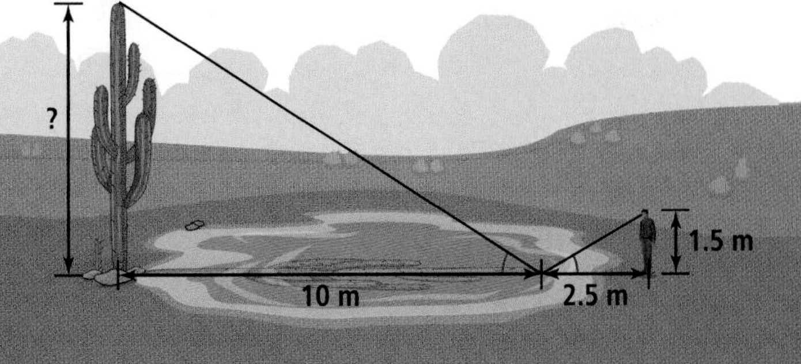

Scan for Multimedia

Practice Tutorial

Additional Exercises Available Online

## UNDERSTAND

**10. Construct Arguments** Write a proof of the Angle-Angle Similarity Theorem.

**Given:** $\angle T \cong \angle X$
$\angle U \cong \angle Y$

**Prove:** $\triangle TUV \sim \triangle XYZ$

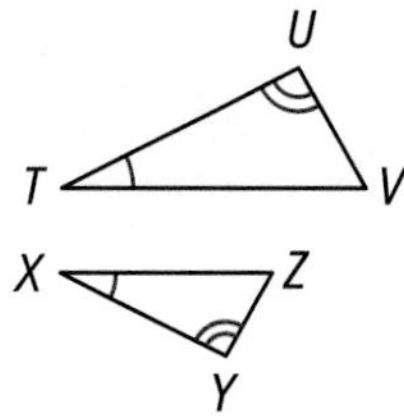




**11. Use Structure** For each triangle, name the triangle similar to $\triangle ABC$ and explain why it is similar.

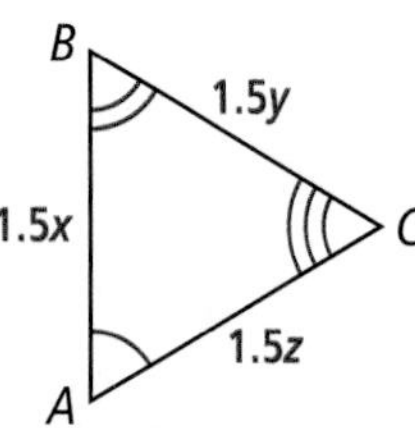


**a.**

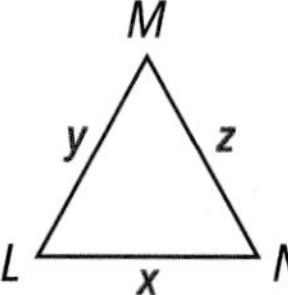


**b.**

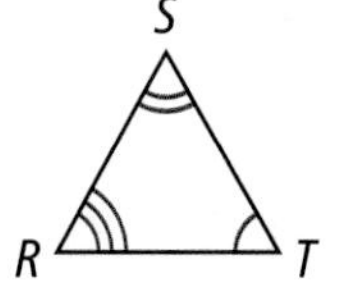


**12. Construct Arguments** If two triangles are congruent by ASA, are the triangles similar? Explain.

**13. Error Analysis** What is Russel's error?

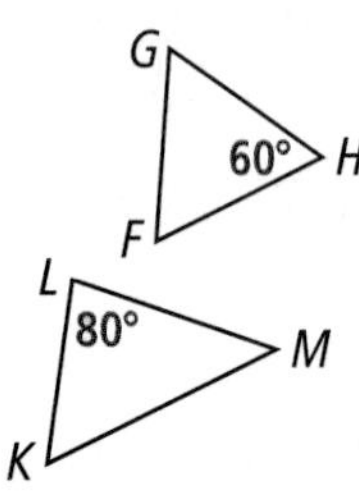


180 - 80 - 60 = 40,
so the unlabeled angle in each triangle is 40°. So, $m\angle M = 60$, and thus $\triangle FGH \sim \triangle KLM$ by AA ~.

**14. Construct Arguments** Write a proof of the Side-Angle-Side Similarity Theorem.

**Given:** $\frac{LM}{QR} = \frac{LN}{QS}$
$\angle L \cong \angle Q$

**Prove:** $\triangle LMN \sim \triangle QRS$

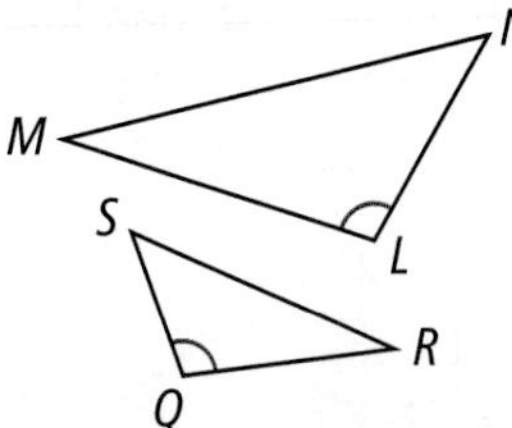


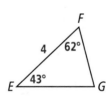

**15. Higher Order Thinking** Explain why there is no Side-Side-Angle Similarity Theorem.

## PRACTICE

**For Exercise 16–18, explain whether each pair of triangles is similar.** SEE EXAMPLES 1–3

**16.**

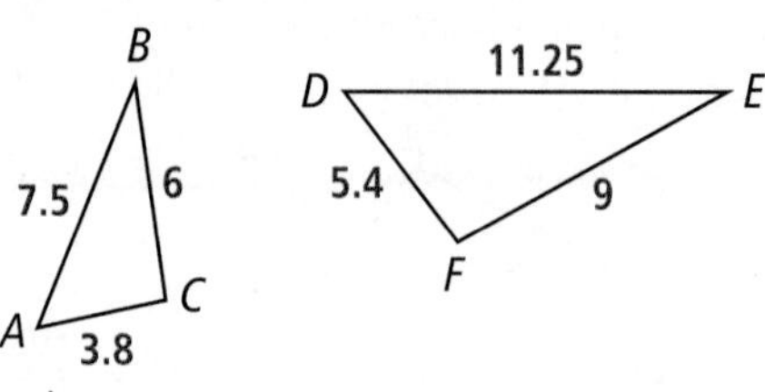


**17.**

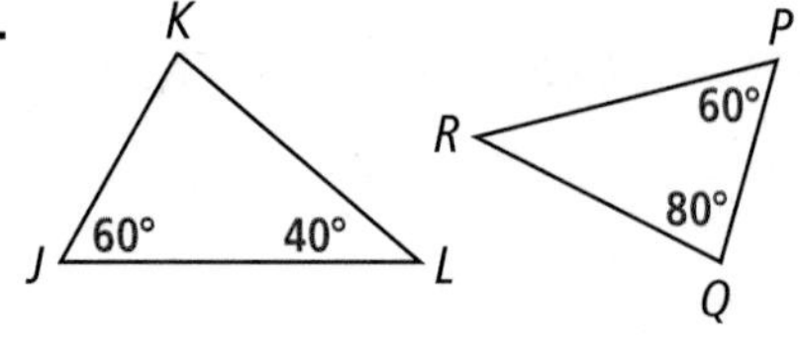


**18.**

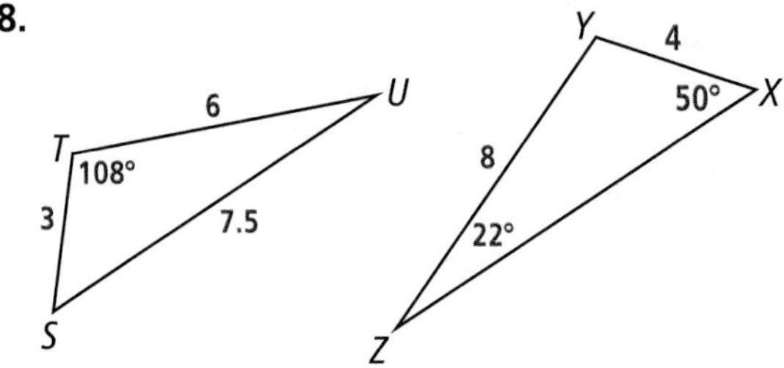


**19.** What is *FG*? SEE EXAMPLES 4 AND 5

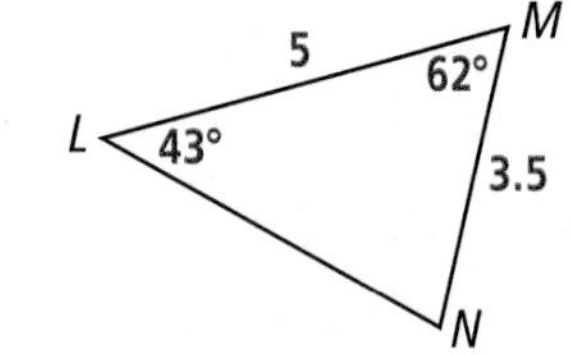

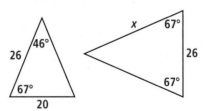


**20.** What is the value of *x*? SEE EXAMPLES 4 AND 5



**21.** Write a proof of the Side-Side-Side Similarity Theorem.

**Given:** $\frac{AB}{EF} = \frac{BC}{FG} = \frac{AC}{AG}$

**Prove:** $\triangle ABC \sim \triangle EFG$

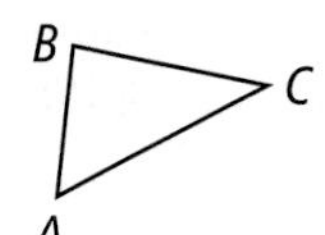


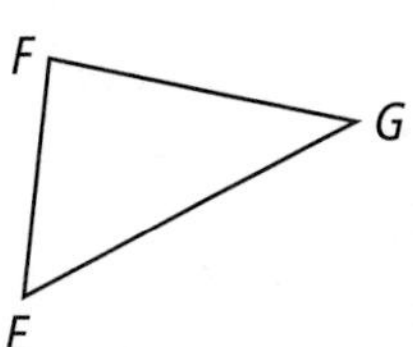




Go Online | PearsonRealize.com

# PRACTICE & PROBLEM SOLVING

## APPLY

**22. Communicate Precisely** A building manager needs to order 9 replacement panes that are all the same size, each similar to the window itself. At what angles should each pane be cut in order to fit in the window? What are the dimensions of each pane? Explain.

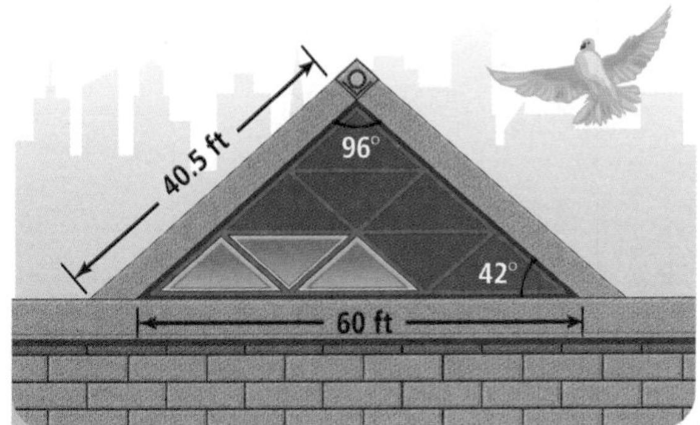


**23. Use Structure** The screen of a surveying device is 0.0026 m wide and is 0.1 m away from the lens. If the surveyor wants the image of the 2-m target to fit on the screen, what distance $d$ should the lens be from the target? Explain.

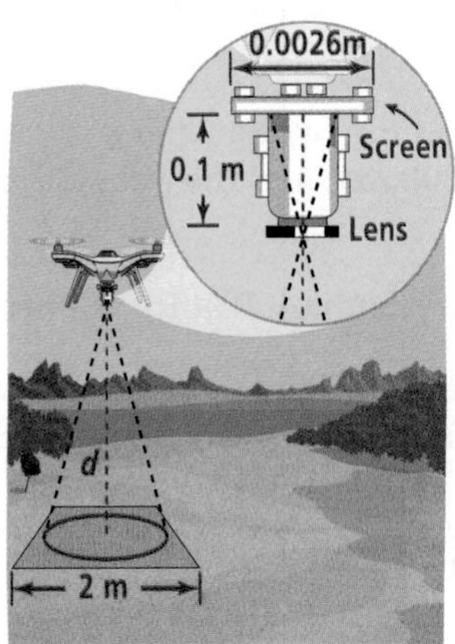


**24. Mathematical Connections** If a light beam strikes the inside of a fiber optic cable, it bounces off at the same angle. In a cable 1,200 micrometers (μm) long, if the beam strikes the wall after 720 μm what distance $x + y$ does the beam travel? Explain.

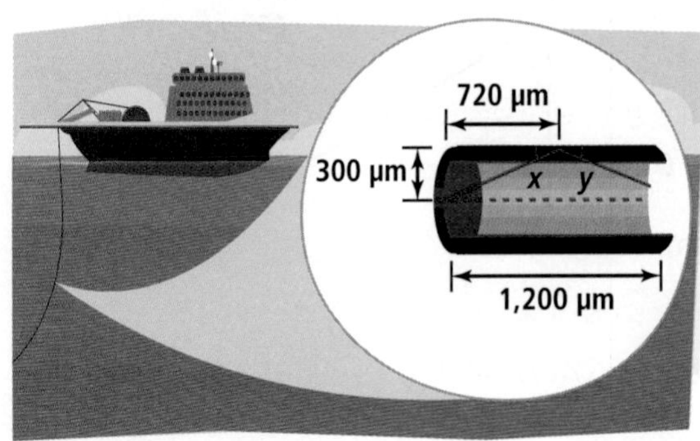


## ASSESSMENT PRACTICE

**25.** Which condition is sufficient to show that $\triangle ABC \sim \triangle QPR$? Select all that apply.

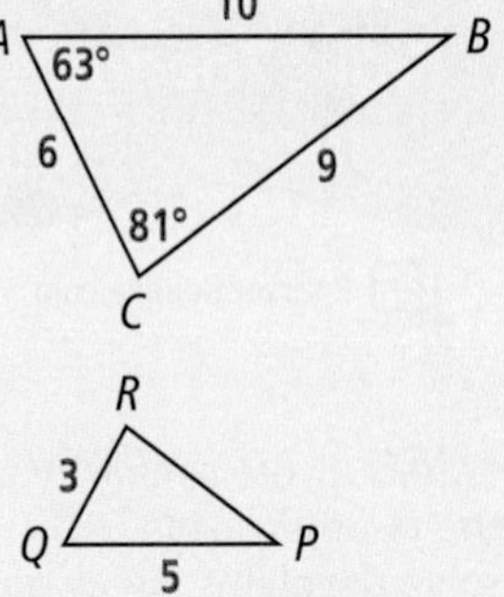


Ⓐ $RP = 4.5$

Ⓑ $m\angle Q = 63$

Ⓒ $m\angle P = 81$

Ⓓ $m\angle R = 81$

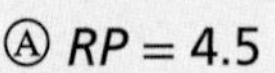

**26. SAT/ACT** For which value of $FJ$ must $\triangle FGJ$ be similar to $\triangle FHG$?

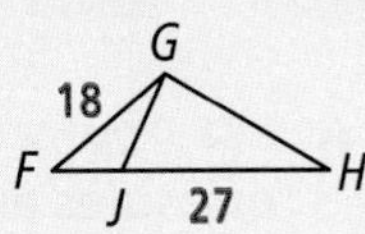


Ⓐ 6 Ⓑ 8 Ⓒ 9 Ⓓ 12

**27. Performance Task** A rescue helicopter hovering at an altitude of 3.5 km sights a campsite just over the peak of a mountain.

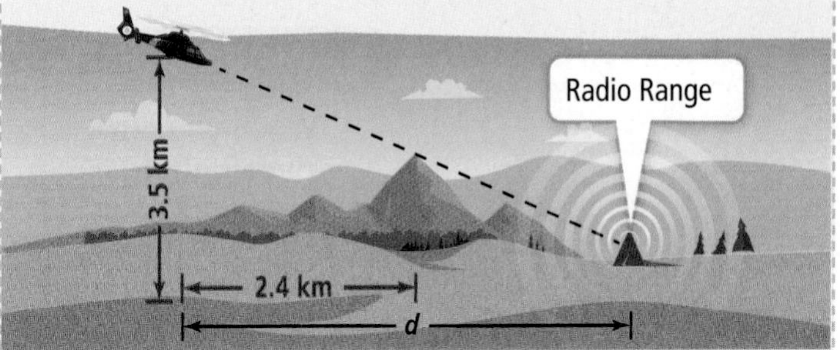


**Part A** The horizontal distance of the helicopter from the mountain is 2.4 km. If the height of the mountain is 2.8 km, what is the horizontal distance $d$ of the helicopter from the campsite? Explain.

**Part B** The groundspeed (horizontal speed) of the helicopter is 1.6 km/min. When will the helicopter reach the campsite? Explain.

**Part C** The radio at the campsite can only transmit to a distance of 5 km. If the helicopter begins immediately to descend toward the campsite (along the diagonal line), how far will the pilot be, horizontally, when he contacts the campsite?

# 7-4 Similarity in Right Triangles

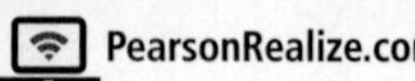

**I CAN…** use similarity and the geometric mean to solve problems involving right triangles.

**VOCABULARY**

- geometric mean

## EXPLORE & REASON

**Suppose you cut a rectangular sheet of paper to create three right triangles.**

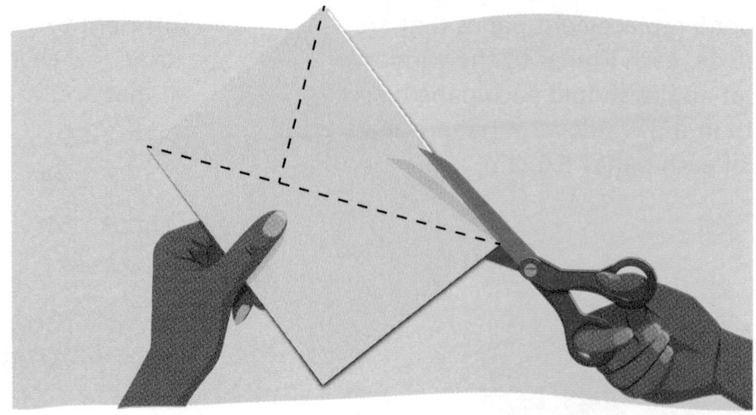

**A. Use Appropriate Tools** How can you compare leg lengths and angle measures among the triangles?

**B.** Are any of the triangles similar to each other? Explain.

**ESSENTIAL QUESTION** In a right triangle, what is the relationship between the altitude to the hypotenuse, triangle similarity, and the geometric mean?

CONCEPTUAL UNDERSTANDING

## EXAMPLE 1 Identify Similar Triangles Formed by an Altitude

**When you draw an altitude to the hypotenuse of a right triangle, you create three right triangles. How are the triangles related?**

**USE STRUCTURE**
Think about an altitude of a triangle. What type of angle does it form with the base?

The altitude $\overline{CD}$ divides $\triangle ABC$ into two right triangles, $\triangle ACD$ and $\triangle CBD$. Compare each triangle to $\triangle ABC$.

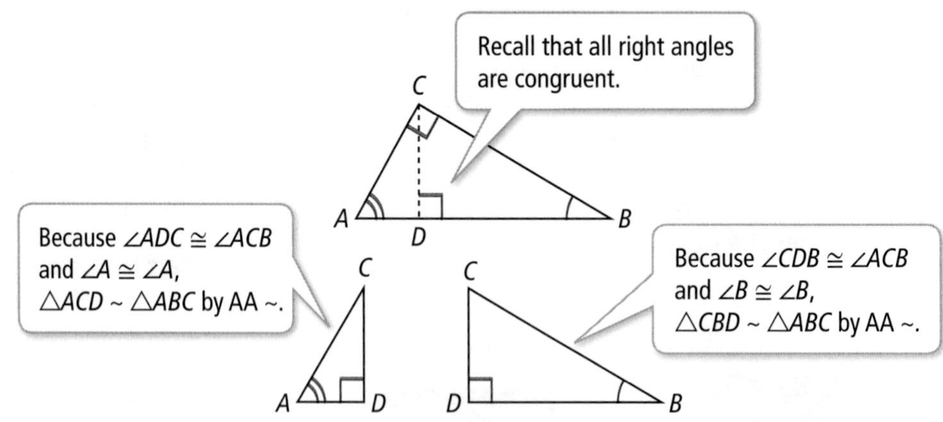

Recall that all right angles are congruent.
C
A
D
B
Because $\angle ADC \cong \angle ACB$ and $\angle A \cong \angle A$, $\triangle ACD \sim \triangle ABC$ by AA ~.
C
A
D
C
D
B
Because $\angle CDB \cong \angle ACB$ and $\angle B \cong \angle B$, $\triangle CBD \sim \triangle ABC$ by AA ~.


$\triangle ACD$ and $\triangle CBD$ are each similar to $\triangle ABD$.

**Try It!** 1. In Example 1, how is $\triangle ACD$ related to $\triangle CBD$? Explain.

  Activity  Assess

## THEOREM 7-4

The altitude to the hypotenuse of a right triangle divides the triangle into two triangles that are similar to the original triangle and to each other.

**If...**

**Then...** $\triangle CAB \sim \triangle DAC \sim \triangle DCB$

**PROOF: SEE EXERCISE 14.**

## EXAMPLE 2 Find Missing Lengths Within Right Triangles

**Given that $\triangle PQR \sim \triangle QSR$, what is $QS$?**

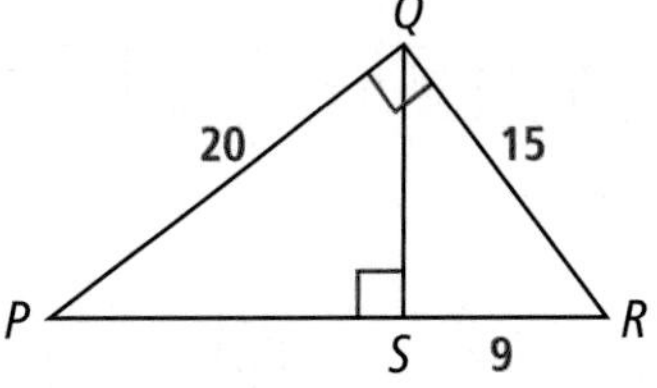


Draw $\triangle PQR$ and $\triangle QSR$.

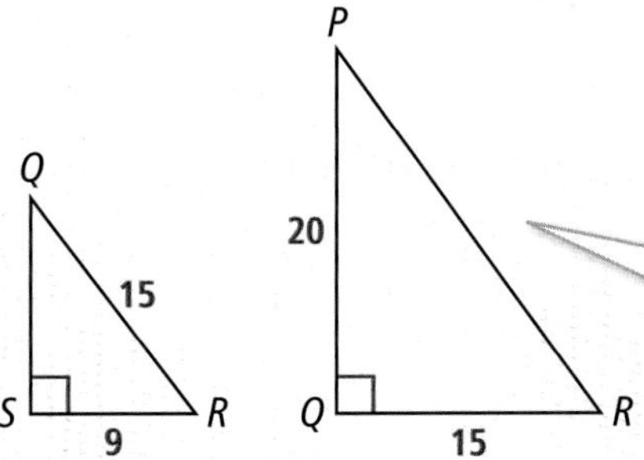


Because $\triangle QSR \sim \triangle PQR$, $\overline{QS}$ corresponds to $\overline{PQ}$, $\overline{SR}$ corresponds to $\overline{QR}$, and $\overline{QR}$ corresponds to $\overline{PR}$.

**COMMON ERROR**
Be careful to set up both ratios the same way when setting up the proportion to compare the corresponding sides. You may find it helpful to write the proportion in words, such as $\frac{\text{hypotenuse}}{\text{short leg}} = \frac{\text{hypotenuse}}{\text{short leg}}$.

To find $QS$, write a proportion using corresponding legs of $\triangle QSR$ and $\triangle PQR$.

$$\frac{QS}{PQ} = \frac{SR}{QR}$$

$$\frac{QS}{20} = \frac{9}{15}$$

$$QS = \frac{9}{15} \cdot 20$$

$$QS = 12$$

The length of altitude $\overline{QS}$ is 12.

 **Try It!** **2.** Refer to $\triangle PQR$ in Example 2.

**a.** Write a proportion that you can use to solve for $PS$.

**b.** What is $PS$?

## DEFINITION

The **geometric mean** is the number $x$ such that $\frac{a}{x} = \frac{x}{b}$, where $a$, $b$, and $x$ are positive numbers.

## EXAMPLE 3 Relate Altitude and Geometric Mean

**Given $\triangle ACB$, what is $CD$?**

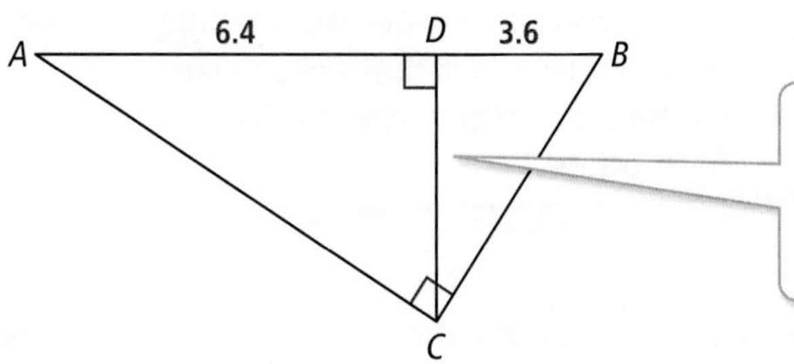

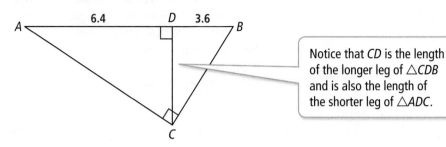

Notice that $CD$ is the length of the longer leg of $\triangle CDB$ and is also the length of the shorter leg of $\triangle ADC$.

**MODEL WITH MATHEMATICS**
What is another way to express the relationship of the geometric mean?

By Theorem 7-4, $\triangle ADC \sim \triangle CDB$. Use the properties of similar triangles to write a proportion.

$$\frac{AD}{CD} = \frac{CD}{BD}$$

$CD$ is the geometric mean of $AD$ and $BD$.

$$\frac{6.4}{CD} = \frac{CD}{3.6}$$

$$(CD)^2 = 23.04$$

$$CD = 4.8$$

The length of altitude $\overline{CD}$ is 4.8.

**Try It!** **3.** Use $\triangle ABC$.

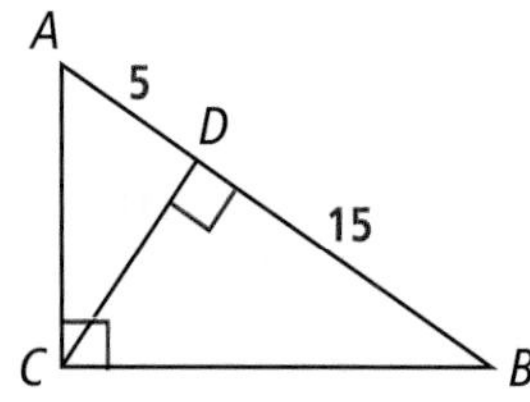


**a.** What is $CD$?

**b.** Describe how you can use the value you found for $CD$ to find $AC$ and $CB$.

### COROLLARY 1 TO THEOREM 7-4

The length of the altitude to the hypotenuse of a right triangle is the geometric mean of the lengths of the segments of the hypotenuse.

**If...**

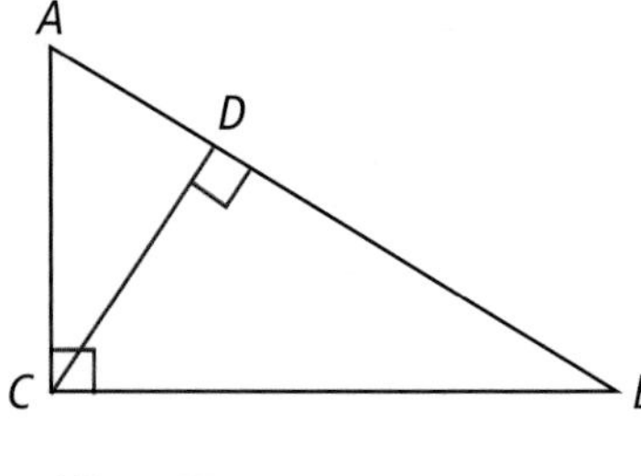


**Then...** $\frac{AD}{CD} = \frac{CD}{DB}$

**PROOF: SEE EXERCISE 14.**

## EXAMPLE 4 Relate Side Lengths and Geometric Mean

**Given $\triangle RST$, what is $RT$?**

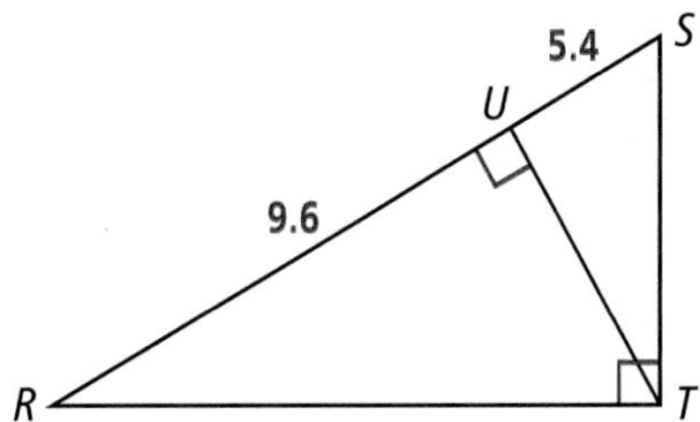


**STUDY TIP**
If you have difficulty identifying the similar triangles, remember that you can draw them separately as was done in Example 1.

By Theorem 7-4, $\triangle RST \sim \triangle RTU$. Use the properties of similar triangles to write a proportion.

$$\frac{RS}{RT} = \frac{RT}{RU}$$

$$\frac{15}{RT} = \frac{RT}{9.6}$$

$$(RT)^2 = 144$$

$$RT = 12$$

*RT* is the geometric mean of *RS* and *RU*.

The length of $\overline{RT}$ is 12.

## Try It!

**4.** Use triangle $\triangle JKL$.

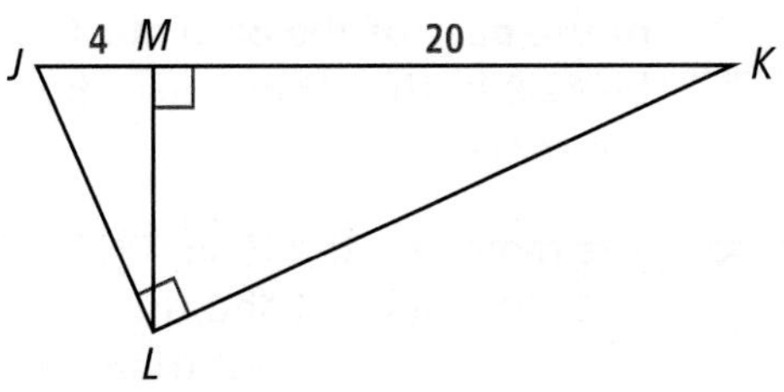


**a.** What is *JL*?

**b.** What is *KL*?

## COROLLARY 2 TO THEOREM 7-4

The altitude to the hypotenuse of a right triangle divides the hypotenuse so that the length of a given leg is the geometric mean of the length of the hypotenuse and the length of the segment of the hypotenuse that is adjacent to the leg.

**PROOF: SEE EXERCISE 14.**

**If...**

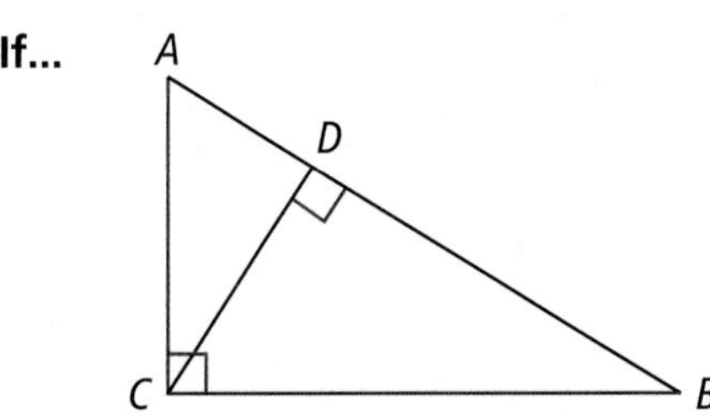


**Then...** $\frac{AB}{AC} = \frac{AC}{AD}$ and $\frac{AB}{CB} = \frac{CB}{DB}$

## EXAMPLE 5 Use the Geometric Mean to Solve Problems

**What is the value of *x*?**

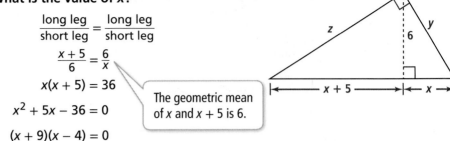

$$\frac{\text{long leg}}{\text{short leg}} = \frac{\text{long leg}}{\text{short leg}}$$

$$\frac{x+5}{6} = \frac{6}{x}$$

The geometric mean of $x$ and $x + 5$ is 6.

$$x(x+5) = 36$$

$$x^2 + 5x - 36 = 0$$

$$(x+9)(x-4) = 0$$

$$x = -9 \text{ or } x = 4$$

The value of $x$ is 4.

Length is always positive.

z, y, 6, $x + 5$, $x$

**STUDY TIP**
With right triangles, you can apply the Pythagorean Theorem to verify your results.

**Try It!** **5.** Use the geometric mean and Example 5 to find each unknown.

**a.** Find the value of $y$.

**b.** Find the value of $z$.

**APPLICATION**

## EXAMPLE 6 Apply Geometric Mean to Find a Distance

**Zhang is constructing a 4-ft high loading ramp. The length of the back of the base must be 12.8 ft. How long must the entire base be?**

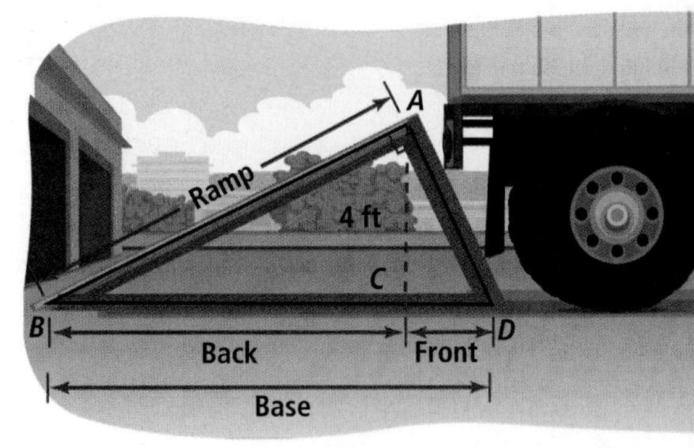


**Formulate** The ramp and the base form the long leg and the hypotenuse of a right triangle. The height of the ramp is the altitude of the triangle. The base of the ramp is composed of the front base $x$ and the back base 12.8.

**Compute** **Step 1** Find the length of the front base $x$.

$$\frac{\text{short leg}}{\text{long leg}} = \frac{\text{short leg}}{\text{long leg}}$$

$$\frac{x}{4} = \frac{4}{12.8}$$

The geometric mean of $x$ and 12.8 is 4.

$$12.8x = 16$$

$$x = 1.25$$

**Step 2** Find the length of the base.

$$12.8 + 1.25 = 14.05$$

**Interpret** The base is 14.05 feet long.

**Try It!** **6.** In Example 6, how long should Zhang make the ramp?

## CONCEPT SUMMARY Similarity in Right Triangles

**WORDS**

- The altitude to the hypotenuse of a right triangle divides the triangle into two triangles that are similar to the original triangle and to each other.
- The length of the altitude is the geometric mean of the lengths of the segments of the hypotenuse.
- The length of each leg is the geometric mean of the length of the hypotenuse and the length of the segment adjacent to the leg.

**DIAGRAMS**

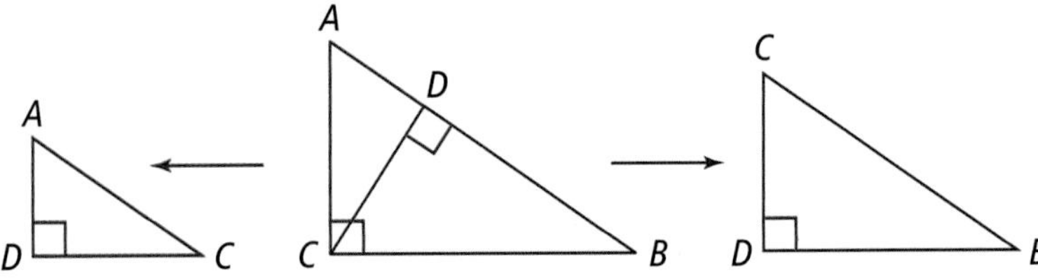


**SYMBOLS** $\triangle ACD \sim \triangle ABC \sim \triangle CBD$

$$\frac{AB}{AC} = \frac{AC}{AD}, \frac{AD}{CD} = \frac{CD}{DB}, \text{ and } \frac{AB}{CB} = \frac{CB}{DB}$$

## Do You UNDERSTAND?

1. **ESSENTIAL QUESTION** In a right triangle, what is the relationship between the altitude to the hypotenuse, triangle similarity, and the geometric mean?

2. **Error Analysis** Chris is asked to find a geometric mean in $\triangle JKL$. What is his error?

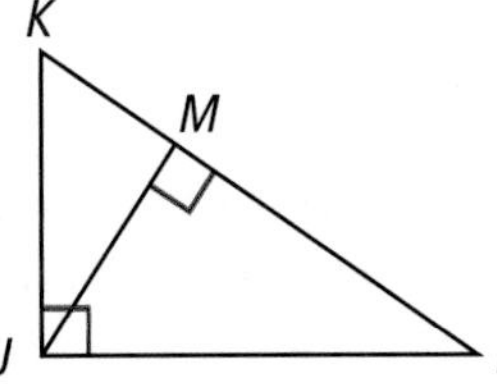


$\Delta JKL \sim \Delta MKJ$

$$\frac{\text{hypotenuse}}{\text{leg}} = \frac{\text{hypotenuse}}{\text{leg}}$$

$$\frac{KL}{JK} = \frac{JK}{JM}$$

✗

3. **Vocabulary** Recall that the arithmetic mean is the average of two numbers. How are the arithmetic mean and geometric mean alike? How are they different?

## Do You KNOW HOW?

**For Exercises 4–6, use $\triangle DEF$ to find the lengths.**

4. $ER$

5. $DF$

6. $DE$

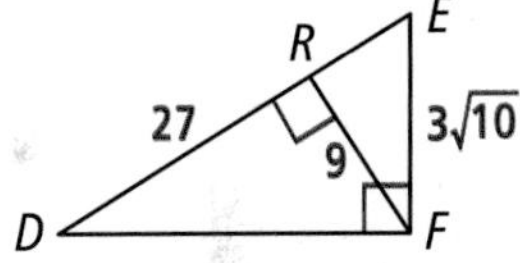


**For Exercises 7–9, use $\triangle PQR$ to find the lengths.**

7. $QA$

8. $PQ$

9. $QR$

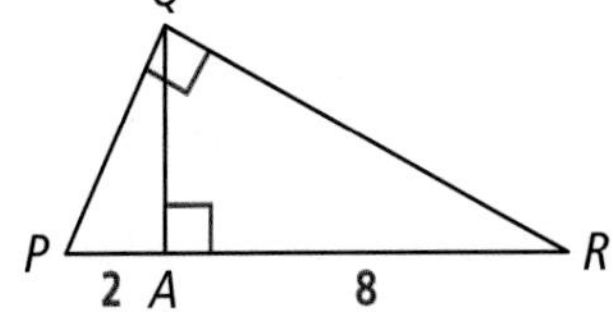


10. Deshawn installs a shelf bracket. What is the widest shelf that will fit without overhang? Explain.

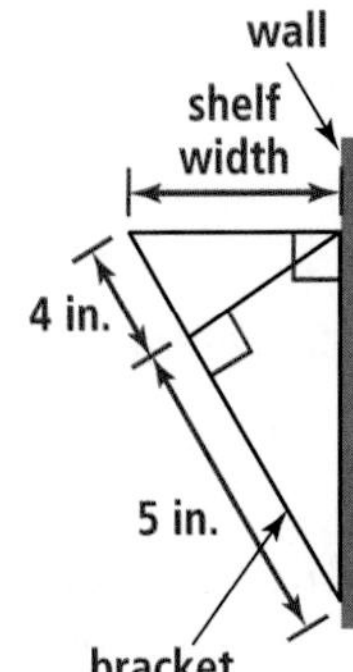

# PRACTICE & PROBLEM SOLVING

Scan for Multimedia 

Practice Tutorial

Additional Exercises Available Online

## UNDERSTAND

**11. Mathematical Connections** Consider $\triangle XYZ$ with altitude to the hypotenuse $\overline{ZW}$.

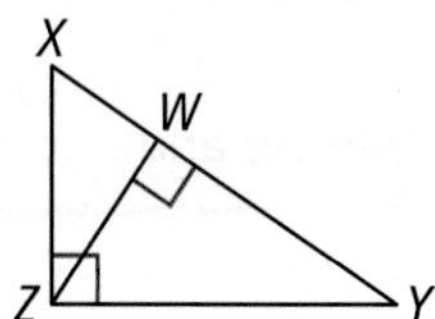


**a.** Describe a sequence of transformations that maps $\triangle XYZ$ to $\triangle XZW$.

**b.** Describe a sequence of transformations that maps $\triangle XYZ$ to $\triangle ZYW$.

**12. Error Analysis** Amaya was asked to find $DC$. What is Amaya's error?

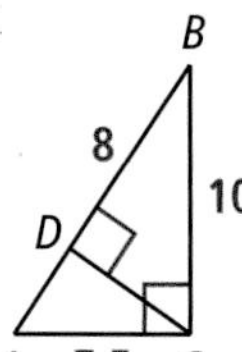


$\Delta ABC \sim \Delta ACD$ by Theorem 7-4.

$\frac{AC}{BC} = \frac{AC}{DC} \rightarrow \frac{7.5}{10} = \frac{7.5}{DC}$

$7.5 \times DC = 7.5 \times 10$,

so $DC = 10$.

**13. Make Sense and Persevere** Is $CD$ the geometric mean of $AD$ and $BD$? Explain.

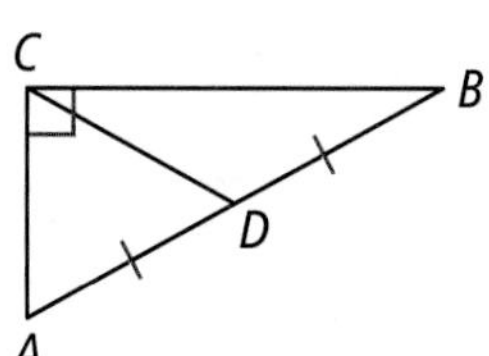


**14. Construct Arguments** Write proofs of Theorem 7-4 and its corollaries.

**a. Given:** $m\angle JLK = 90$ and $\overline{LM} \perp \overline{JK}$

**Prove:** $\triangle JKL \sim \triangle JLM \sim \triangle LKM$

**b. Given:** $\triangle JLM \sim \triangle LKM$

**Prove:** $\frac{JM}{LM} = \frac{LM}{KM}$

K
M
J
L

**c. Given:** $\triangle JKL \sim \triangle JLM \sim \triangle LKM$

**Prove:** $\frac{JK}{JL} = \frac{JL}{JM}$ and $\frac{JK}{LK} = \frac{LK}{MK}$

**15. Higher Order Thinking** Suppose the altitude to the hypotenuse of a right triangle also bisects the hypotenuse. What type of right triangle is it? Use the similarity of right triangles to explain your answer.

## PRACTICE

**16.** In the figure, what two smaller triangles are similar to $\triangle ABC$? Explain. SEE EXAMPLE 1

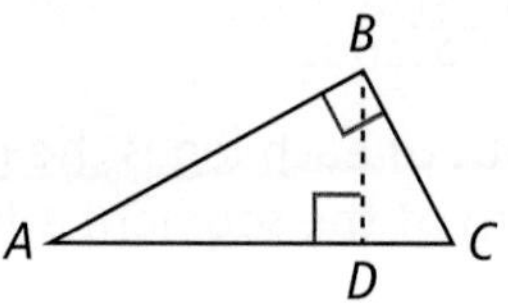


**17.** What are the values of $h$ and $x$ in the right triangle? Explain. SEE EXAMPLE 2

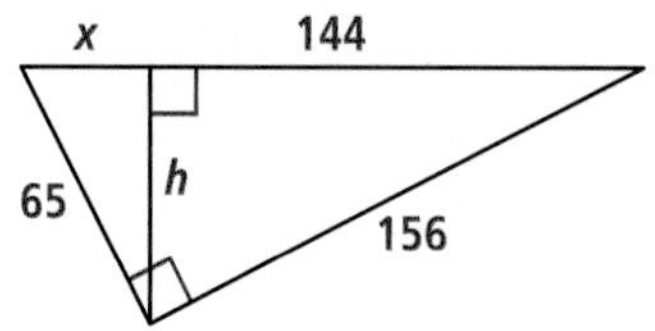


**18.** What is the value of $y$ in the right triangle? Explain. SEE EXAMPLE 3

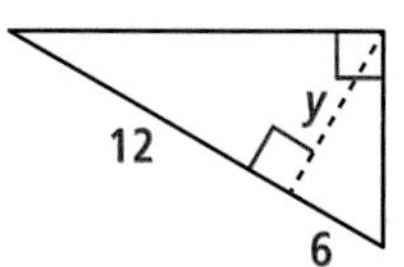


**19.** What are the values of $a$ and $b$ in each right triangle? Explain. SEE EXAMPLES 4 AND 6

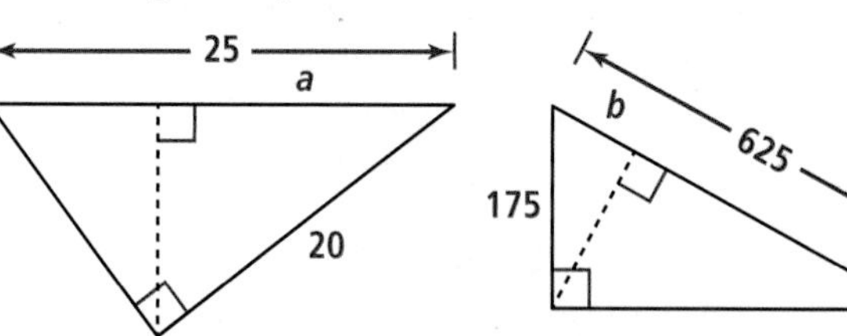


**20.** What are the values of $m$ and $n$ in each right triangle? Explain. SEE EXAMPLE 5

**a.**

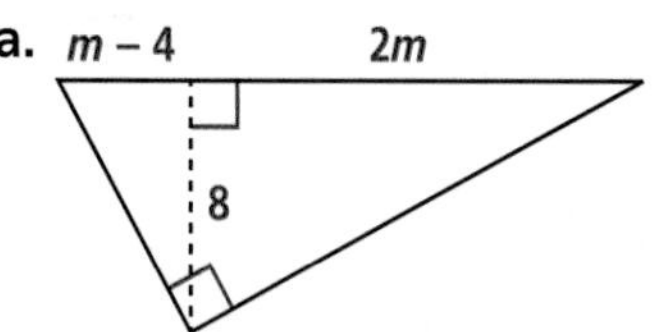


**b.**

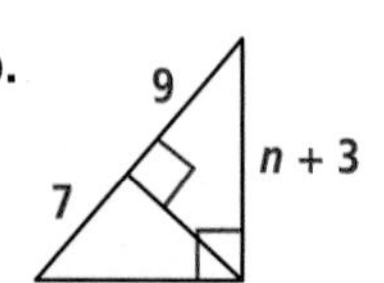


**21.** What is the value of $w$ in the right triangle? Explain.

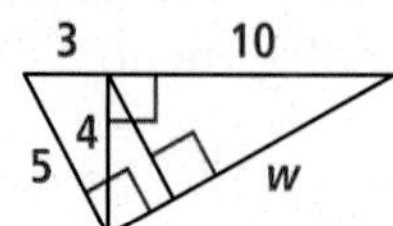

Practice Tutorial
Mixed Review Available Online

# PRACTICE & PROBLEM SOLVING

## APPLY

**22. Reason** Jake wants the profile of a hotel he is planning to be a right triangle with the dimensions shown. The city prohibits structures over 100 ft at the location where he would like to build. Can the hotel be located there? Explain.

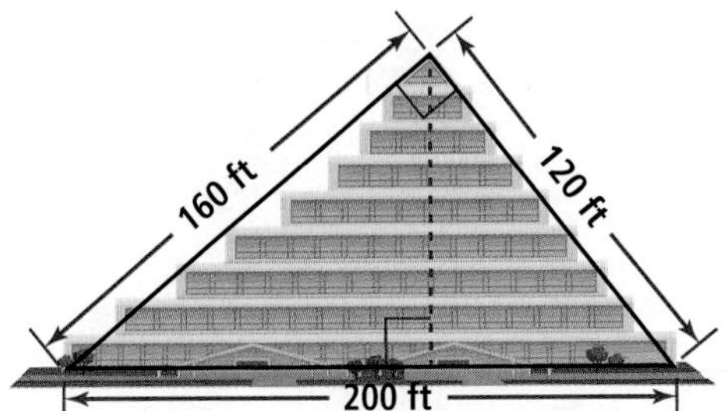


**23. Look for Relationships** Kiyo is repairing a wooden climbing tower.

**a.** He needs to cut two crossbars. What should the lengths of the two crossbars be? Explain.

**b.** Kiyo will make a notch in each crossbar in order to fit them together. Where should he make the notch on each crossbar? Explain.

**24. Higher Order Thinking** Write a proof for Theorem 2-14.

**Given:** Right $\triangle WXY$ with altitude $\overline{XZ}$ to hypotenuse $\overline{WY}$

**Prove:** The product of the slopes of perpendicular lines is $-1$.

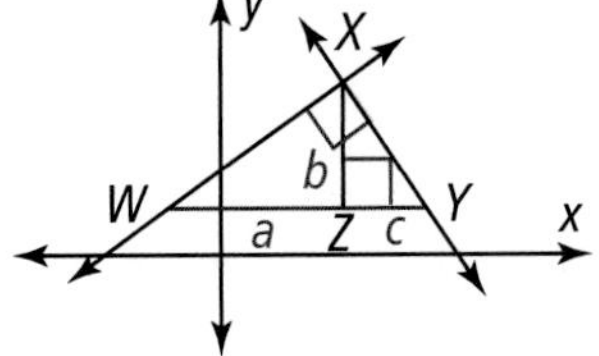


## ASSESSMENT PRACTICE

**25.** For each figure, write an equation that you could use to find the value of $x$.

**a.**

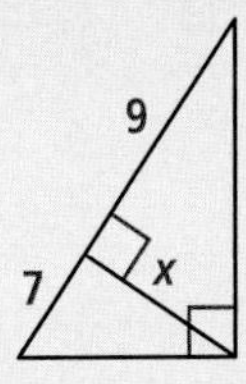


**b.**

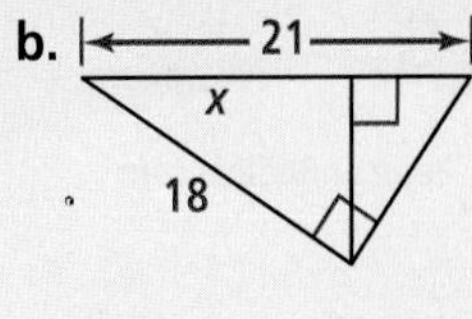


**26. SAT/ACT** Which triangle is similar to $\triangle ABC$?

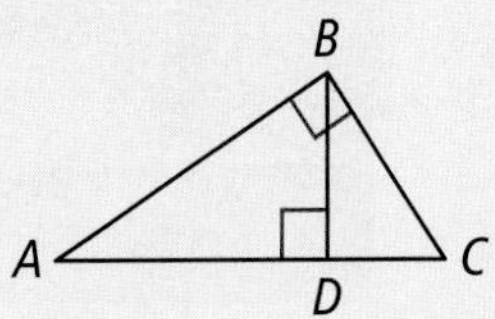


Ⓐ $\triangle CBA$

Ⓑ $\triangle ABD$

Ⓒ $\triangle CDB$

Ⓓ $\triangle BDC$

**27. Performance Task** To estimate the height of a tree, Tia and Felix walk away from the tree until the angle of sight with the top and bottom of the tree is a right angle. Let $h$ represent the height of a person's eyes and $d$ represent the distance away from the tree.

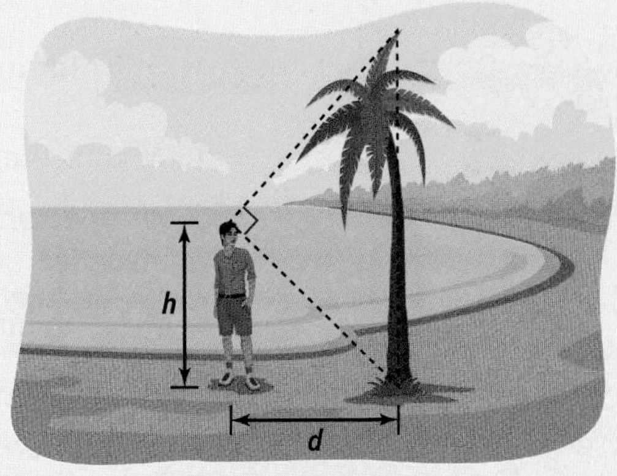


**Part A** If the height of Tia's eyes is 1.6 m and her distance away from the tree is 2.5 m, what is the height of the tree? Round to the nearest hundredth of a meter.

**Part B** If the height of Felix's eyes is 1.7 m, about how far from the tree is Felix if his angle of sight is a right angle? Round to the nearest hundredth of a meter.

**Part C** Suppose Tia and Felix stand the same distance away from another tree and their angles of sight are right angles, what is the height of the tree? Explain.

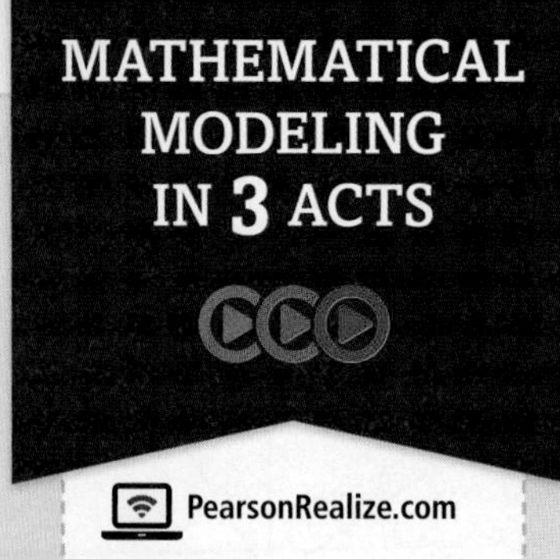


PearsonRealize.com

## Make It Right

Architects often make a scale physical model of a new building project. The scale model is usually a miniature version of the project it is representing.

When making a model, architects need to make sure that all of the parts of the model are the right size. Think about this during the Mathematical Modeling in 3 Acts lesson.

### ACT 1 Identify the Problem

1. What is the first question that comes to mind after watching the video?
2. Write down the main question you will answer about what you saw in the video.
3. Make an initial conjecture that answers this main question.
4. Explain how you arrived at your conjecture.
5. What information will be useful to know to answer the main question? How can you get it? How will you use that information?

### ACT 2 Develop a Model

6. Use the math that you have learned in this Topic to refine your conjecture.

### ACT 3 Interpret the Results

7. Did your refined conjecture match the actual answer exactly? If not, what might explain the difference?

# 7-5 Proportions in Triangles

PearsonRealize.com

**I CAN…** find the lengths of segments using proportional relationships in triangles resulting from parallel lines.

## EXPLORE & REASON

**Draw a triangle, like the one shown, by dividing one side into four congruent segments and drawing lines parallel to one of the other sides.**

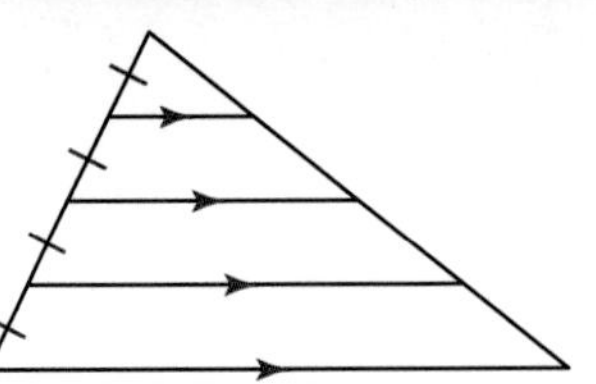

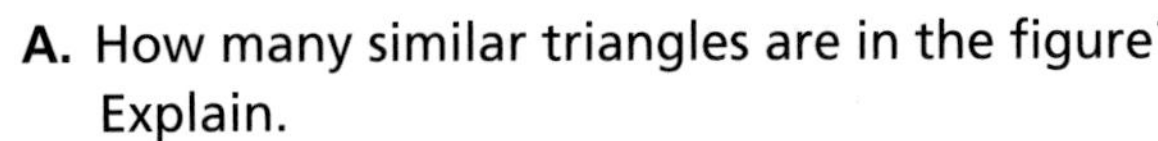

**A.** How many similar triangles are in the figure? Explain.

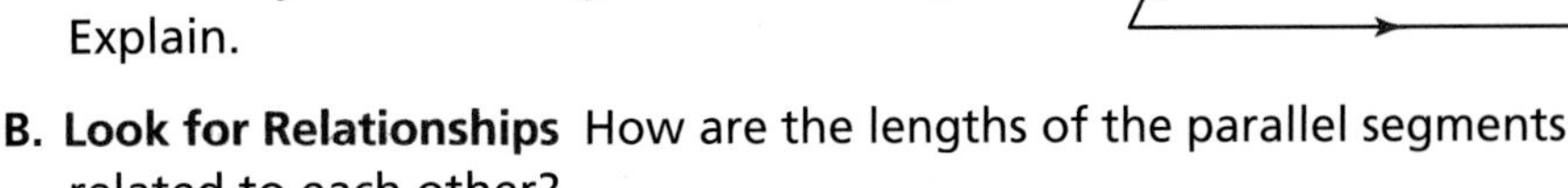

**B. Look for Relationships** How are the lengths of the parallel segments related to each other?

## ESSENTIAL QUESTION

**When parallel lines intersect two transversals, what are the relationships among the lengths of the segments formed?**

CONCEPTUAL UNDERSTANDING

## EXAMPLE 1 Explore Proportions from Parallel Lines

**In $\triangle JLN$, if $LN = 9.6$, what are $LM$ and $MN$? Are the sides divided into proportional segments? Explain.**

**Step 1** Determine how $\triangle JLN$ and $\triangle KLM$ are related.

The triangles share $\angle L$, and $\angle LJN \cong \angle LKM$ by the Corresponding Angles Theorem. Therefore, $\triangle JLN \sim \triangle KLM$ by AA ~.

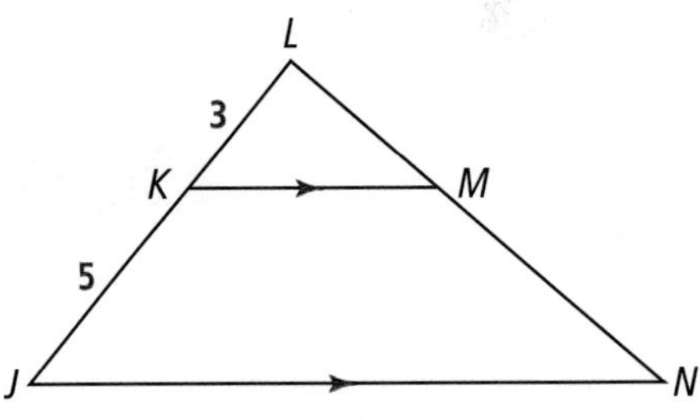


**Step 2** Write a proportion to relate the corresponding sides.

$$\frac{LK}{LJ} = \frac{LM}{LN}$$

**Step 3** Use the proportion to find $LM$ and $MN$.

$$\frac{3}{8} = \frac{LM}{9.6}$$

$$LM = 3.6$$

$LK = 3$, $LJ = LK + KJ = 3 + 5 = 8$, and $LN = 9.6$

Then $MN = LN - LM = 9.6 - 3.6 = 6$.

**LOOK FOR RELATIONSHIPS** Think about how the proportions are related to the scale factors for similar triangles. How can you use the scale factor to get the ratio between the sides?

**Step 4** Find the ratios of the corresponding segments in the sides divided by the parallel line.

$$\frac{LK}{KJ} = \frac{3}{5} = 0.6 \text{ and } \frac{LM}{MN} = \frac{3.6}{6} = 0.6$$

Since $\frac{LK}{KJ} = \frac{LM}{MN}$, $\overline{KM}$ divides $\overline{LJ}$ and $\overline{LN}$ proportionally.

**Try It!** **1.** Suppose $\overline{BD}$ bisects sides $\overline{AC}$ and $\overline{CE}$. Is $\overline{AE} \parallel \overline{BD}$? Explain.

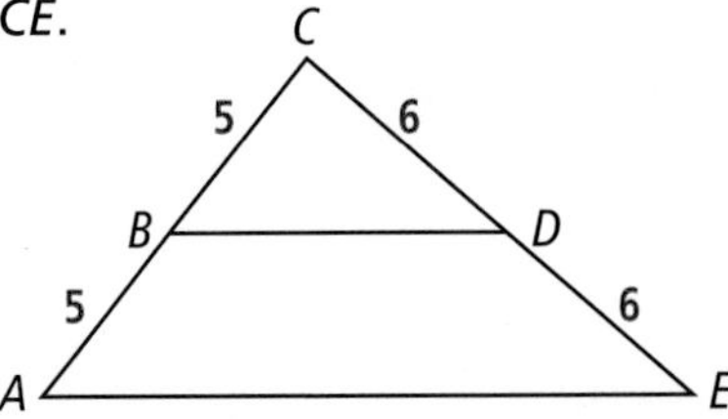

## THEOREM 7-5 Side-Splitter Theorem

If a line is parallel to one side of a triangle and intersects the other two sides, then it divides those sides proportionally.

PROOF: SEE EXERCISE 14.

**If...** $\overline{MN} \parallel \overline{AC}$

**Then...** $\frac{AM}{MB} = \frac{CN}{NB}$

## THEOREM 7-6 Triangle Midsegment Theorem

If a segment joins the midpoints of two sides of a triangle, then the segment is parallel to the third side and is half as long.

PROOF: SEE EXERCISE 24.

**If...** $\overline{DG} \cong \overline{GE}$ and $\overline{FH} \cong \overline{HE}$

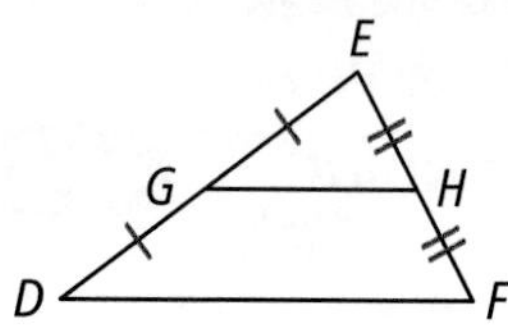


**Then...** $\overline{GH} \parallel \overline{DF}$ and $GH = \frac{1}{2}DF$

## EXAMPLE 2 Use the Side-Splitter Theorem

**MAKE SENSE AND PERSEVERE** Consider other strategies you can use. Can you use proportions of similar triangles?

**What is the value of $x$ in $\triangle PQR$?**

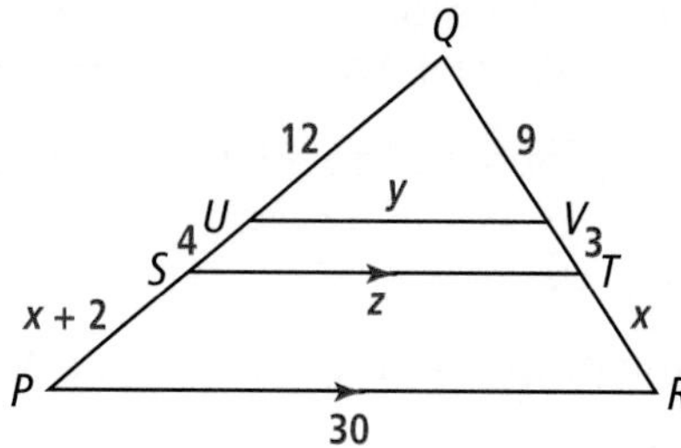


Since $\overline{ST} \parallel \overline{PR}$, $\frac{PS}{SQ} = \frac{RT}{TQ}$ by the Side-Splitter Theorem. Write a proportion in terms of $x$ and solve.

$$\frac{PS}{SQ} = \frac{RT}{TQ}$$

$SQ = 4 + 12 = 16$ and $TQ = 3 + 9 = 12$

$$\frac{x+2}{16} = \frac{x}{12}$$

$$48\left(\frac{x+2}{16}\right) = 48\left(\frac{x}{12}\right)$$

$$3x + 6 = 4x$$

$$x = 6$$

**Try It!** 2. Refer to $\triangle PQR$ in Example 2.

a. What is the value of $y$? Explain.

b. What is the value of $z$? Explain.

## COROLLARY TO THE SIDE-SPLITTER THEOREM

If three parallel lines intersect two transversals, then the segments intercepted on the transversals are proportional.

PROOF: SEE EXERCISE 25.

**If...** $\ell \parallel m \parallel n$

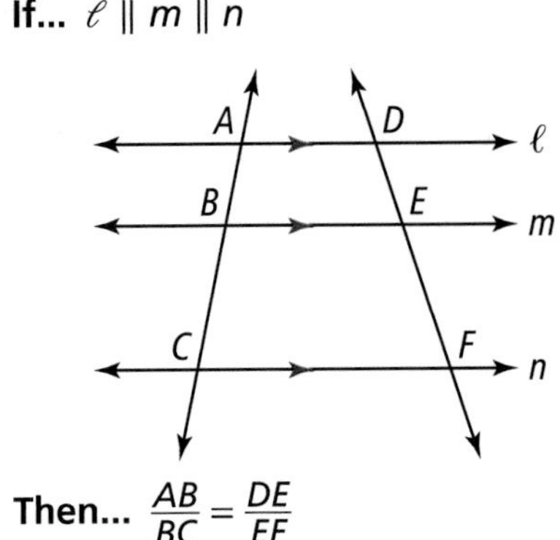


**Then...** $\frac{AB}{BC} = \frac{DE}{EF}$

APPLICATION

## EXAMPLE 3 Find a Length

**A reflecting pool is separated by walkways parallel to Lincoln St. and Jefferson St., which are parallel to each other. The city wants to add additional tiling around the pool. How much tiling does *x* ft represent?**

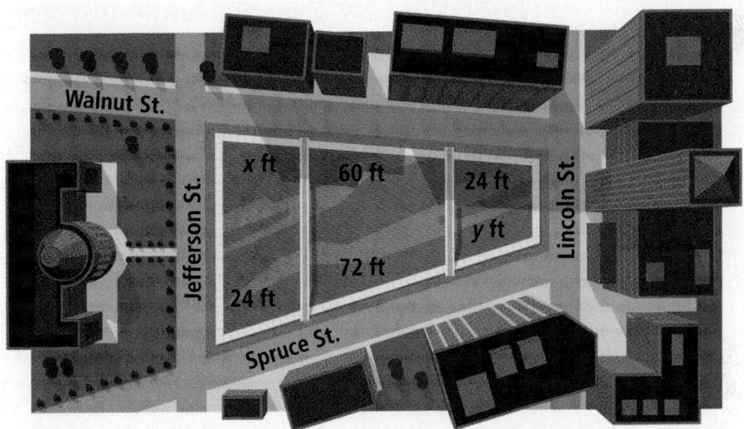


**Formulate** Walnut St. and Spruce St. are transversals of Jefferson St., Lincoln St., and the walkways that separate the pool.

**Compute** Write an equation with *x*.

$$\frac{x}{60} = \frac{24}{72}$$

Apply the Corollary to the Side-Splitter Theorem.

$$x = 60\left(\frac{24}{72}\right)$$

$$x = 20$$

**Interpret** The amount of tiling represented by *x* ft is 20 ft.

**Try It!** **3.** In Example 3, how much tiling does *y* ft represent?

## EXAMPLE 4 Investigate Proportionality with an Angle Bisector

**In $\triangle KLM$, $\overline{NL}$ bisects $\angle KLM$. Compare the ratios $\frac{KN}{MN}$ and $\frac{KL}{ML}$. Is $\triangle LKN \sim \triangle LMN$? Explain.**

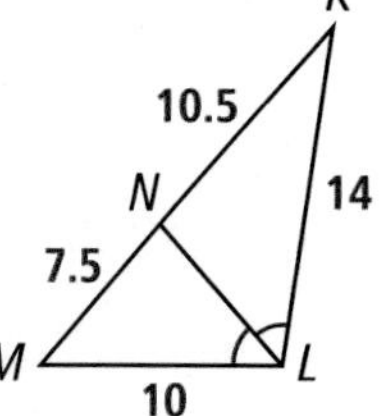


Compute the ratios of the corresponding sides for the given measures.

$\frac{KN}{MN} = \frac{10.5}{7.5} = 1.4$ $\qquad$ $\frac{KL}{ML} = \frac{14}{10} = 1.4$

The ratios $\frac{KN}{MN}$ and $\frac{KL}{ML}$ are equal. However, the third pair is $\overline{NL}$ and $\overline{NL}$, and that ratio is 1. So, the two triangles are not similar.

**Try It!** 4. Draw $\overrightarrow{ML}$ and a line through $K$ parallel to $\overline{NL}$. Let $P$ be the point of intersection.

a. Is $\triangle MNL \sim \triangle MKP$? Explain.

b. Is $\angle LKP \cong \angle LPK$? Explain.

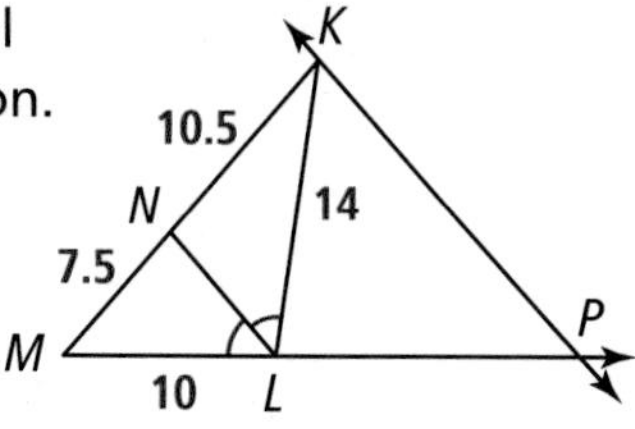


### THEOREM 7-7 Triangle-Angle-Bisector Theorem

If a ray bisects an angle of a triangle, then it divides the opposite side into two segments that are proportional to the other two sides of the triangle.

**PROOF: SEE EXERCISE 16.**

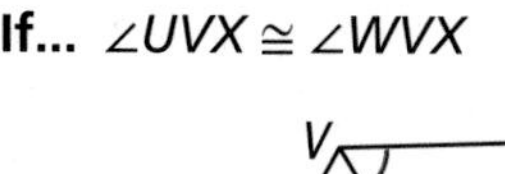

**If...** $\angle UVX \cong \angle WVX$

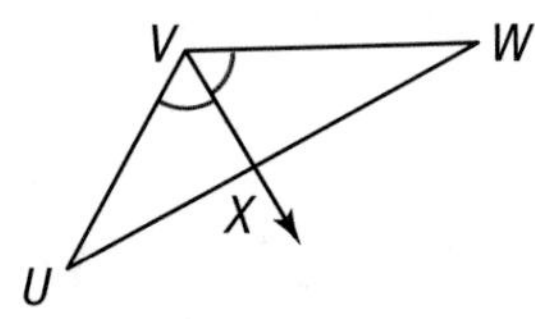


**Then...** $\frac{UX}{WX} = \frac{UV}{WV}$

## EXAMPLE 5 Use the Triangle-Angle-Bisector Theorem

**What are the values of $AD$ and $DC$?**

Since $\overline{BD}$ bisects $\angle ABC$, use the Triangle-Angle-Bisector Theorem to write a proportion.

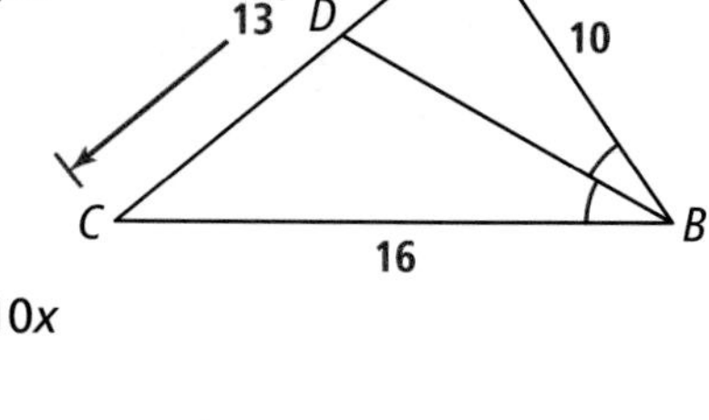


**COMMON ERROR**
You may incorrectly use 13 as the length of one of the shorter segments. Remember to correctly identify the lengths of all of the segments.

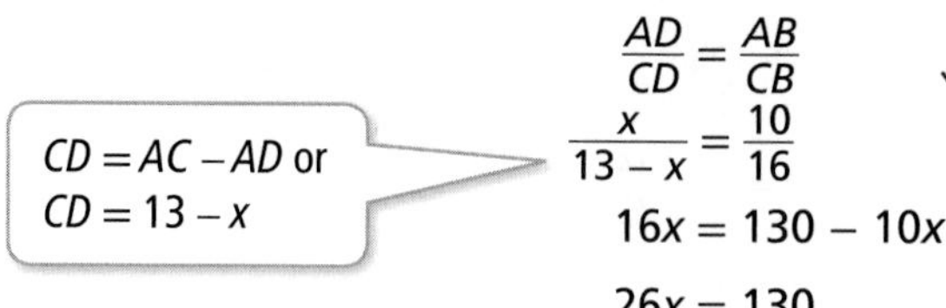

$$\frac{AD}{CD} = \frac{AB}{CB}$$

$$\frac{x}{13 - x} = \frac{10}{16}$$

$CD = AC - AD$ or $CD = 13 - x$

$$16x = 130 - 10x$$

$$26x = 130$$

$$x = 5$$

In the figure, $AD = 5$ and $CD = 13 - 5 = 8$.

**Try It!** 5. a. What is the value of $x$?

b. What are the values of $GH$ and $GK$?

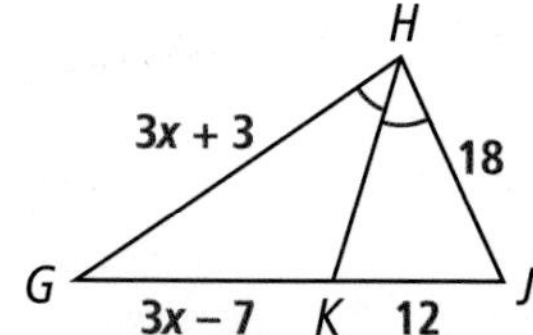

## CONCEPT SUMMARY Proportions in Triangles

**THEOREM 7-5**

**Side-Splitter Theorem**

**If...** $\overline{MN} \parallel \overline{AC}$

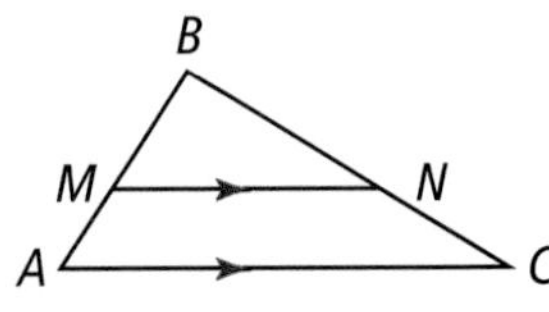


**Then...** $\frac{AM}{MB} = \frac{CN}{NB}$

**THEOREM 7-6**

**Triangle Midsegment Theorem**

**If...** $\overline{DG} \cong \overline{GE}$ and $\overline{FH} \cong \overline{HE}$

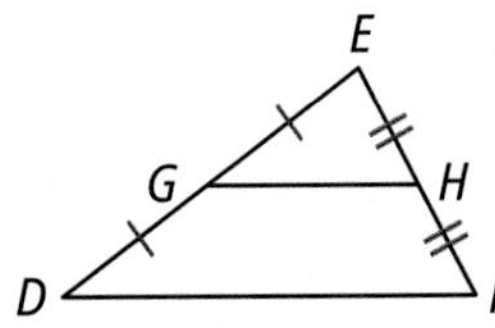


**Then...** $\overline{GH} \parallel \overline{DF}$ and $GH = \frac{1}{2}DF$

**THEOREM 7-7**

**Triangle-Angle-Bisector Theorem**

**If...** $\angle UVX \cong \angle WVX$

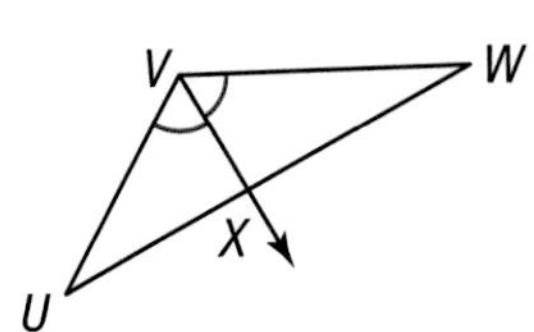


**Then...** $\frac{UX}{WX} = \frac{UV}{WV}$

## Do You UNDERSTAND?

1. **ESSENTIAL QUESTION** When parallel lines intersect two transversals, what are the relationships among the lengths of the segments formed?

2. **Error Analysis** Carmen thinks that $AD = BD$. What is Carmen's error?

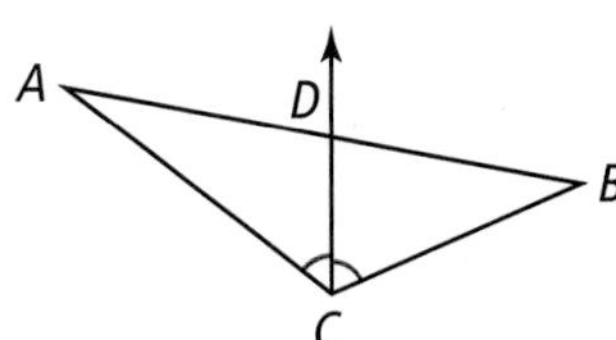


3. **Make Sense and Persevere** What information is needed to determine if $x$ is half of $y$?

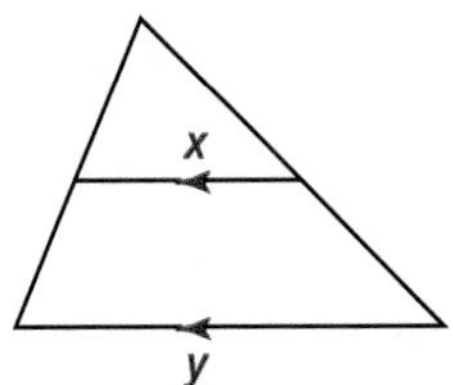


4. **Look for Relationships** If $\overline{RS} \cong \overline{QS}$, what type of triangle is $\triangle PQR$? Use the Triangle-Angle-Bisector Theorem to explain your reasoning.

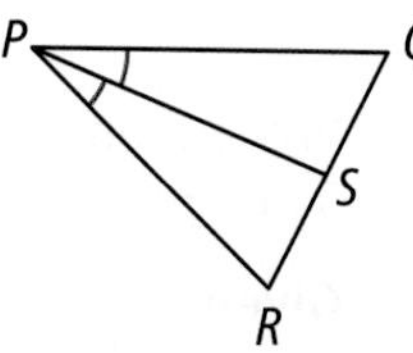


5. **Construct Arguments** Explain why $LP$ must be less than $LM$.

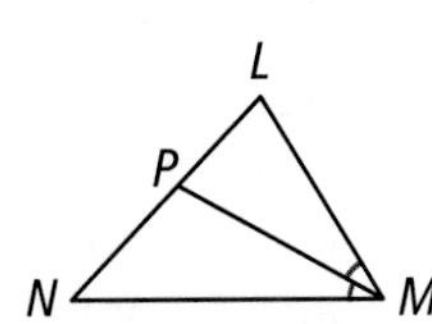


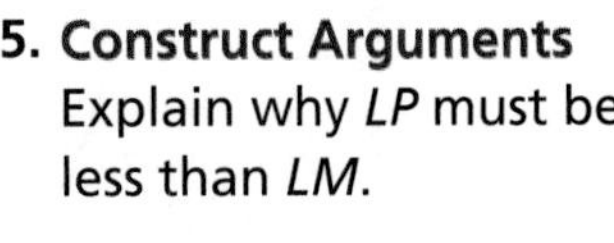

## Do You KNOW HOW?

**For Exercises 6–11, find each value of $x$.**

6.

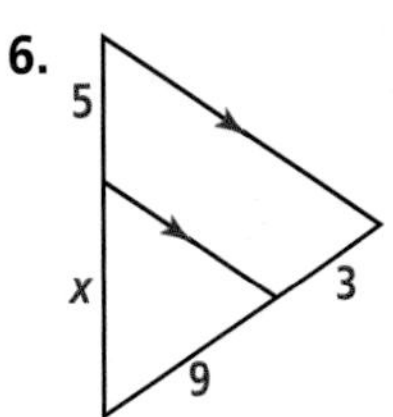


7.

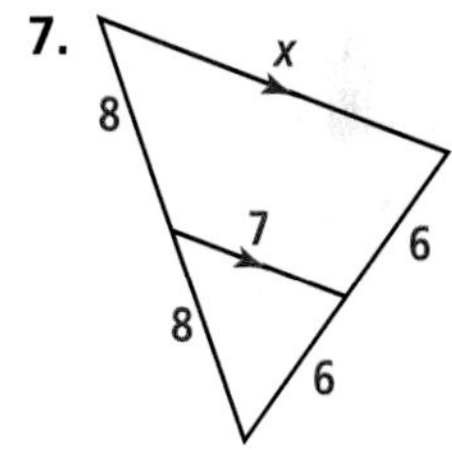


8.

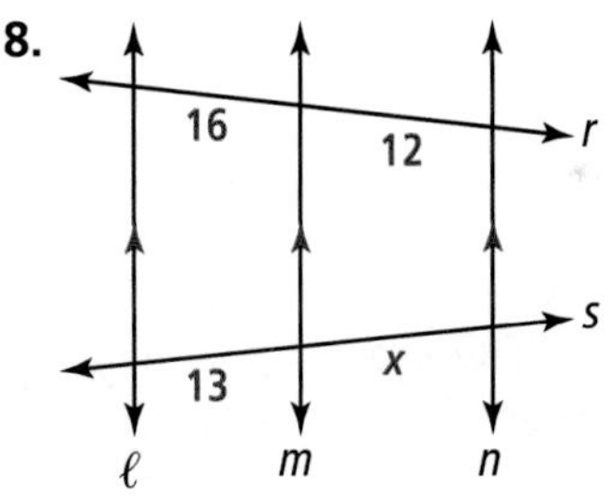


9.

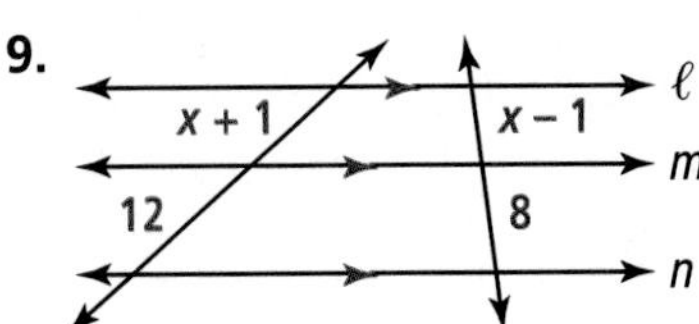


10.

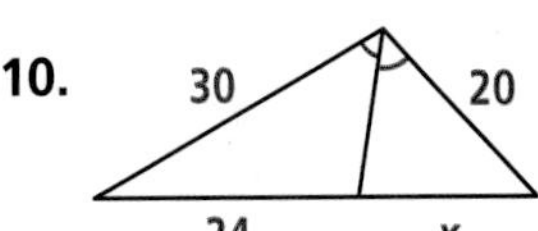


11.

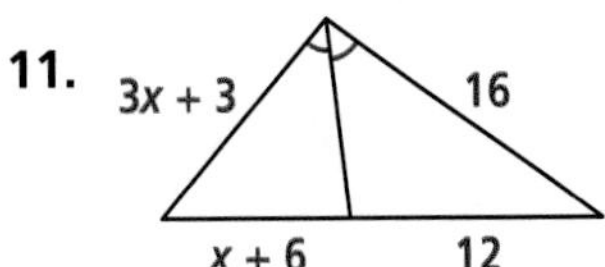

# PRACTICE & PROBLEM SOLVING

Scan for Multimedia

Practice Tutorial

Additional Exercises Available Online

## UNDERSTAND

12. **Error Analysis** What is Benson's error?

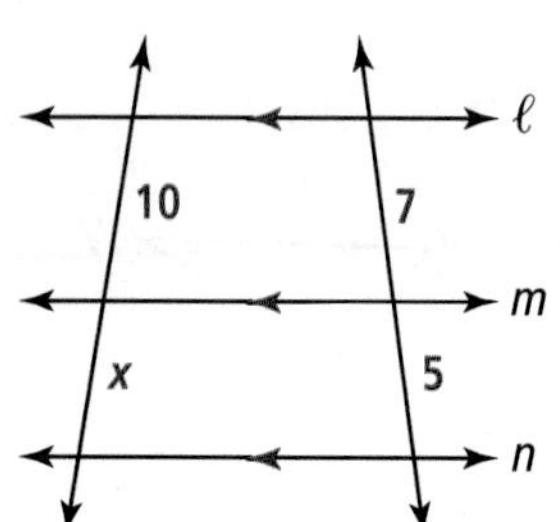


$$\frac{5}{10} = \frac{x}{7}$$

$$10x = 35$$

$$x = 3.5$$

13. **Mathematical Connections** What percent of the area of $\triangle PQR$ is the area of $\triangle QRS$? Explain.

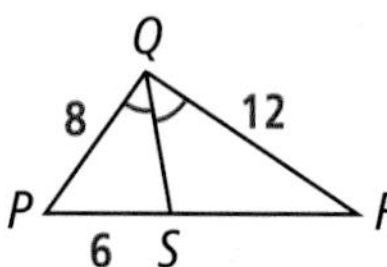


14. **Construct Arguments** Write a proof of the Side-Splitter Theorem.

**Given:** $\overline{MN} \parallel \overline{AC}$

**Prove:** $\frac{AM}{MB} = \frac{CN}{NB}$

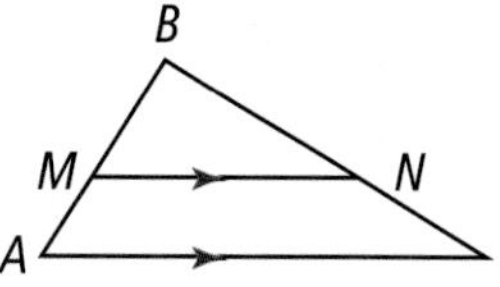


15. **Higher Order Thinking** Suppose $O$, $P$, and $Q$ are midpoints of the sides of $\triangle LMN$. Show that $\triangle LOQ$, $\triangle OMP$, $\triangle QPN$, and $\triangle PQO$ are congruent to each other.

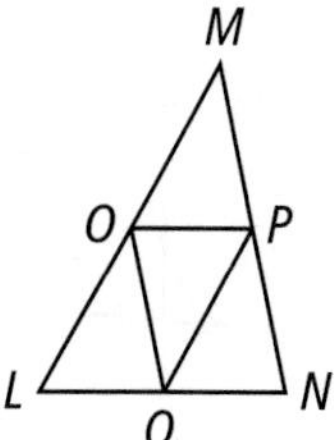


16. **Construct Arguments** Write a proof for the Triangle-Angle-Bisector Theorem.

**Given:** $\overrightarrow{AD}$ bisects $\angle A$.

**Prove:** $\frac{CA}{AB} = \frac{CD}{DB}$

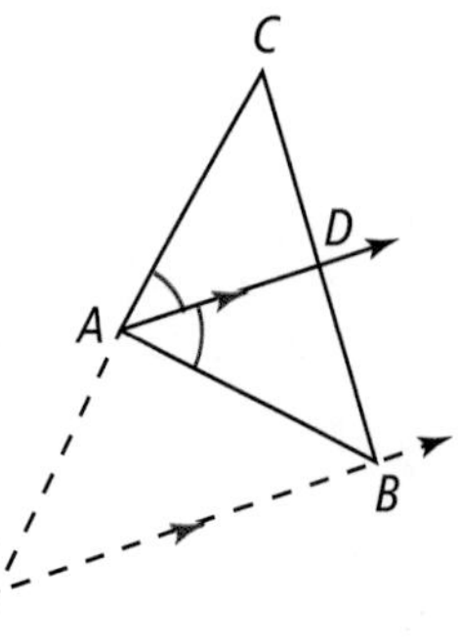


Use the following outline.

- Extend $\overrightarrow{CA}$ and draw a line through point $B$ parallel to $\overrightarrow{AD}$ that intersects $\overrightarrow{CA}$ at point $E$.
- Show that $\frac{CA}{AE} = \frac{CD}{DB}$.
- Then show that $\triangle AEB$ is isosceles.

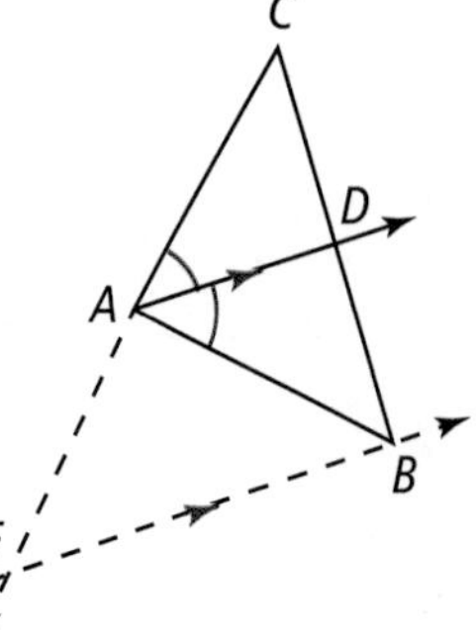


## PRACTICE

**For Exercises 17–19, find each value.**

SEE EXAMPLES 1 AND 2

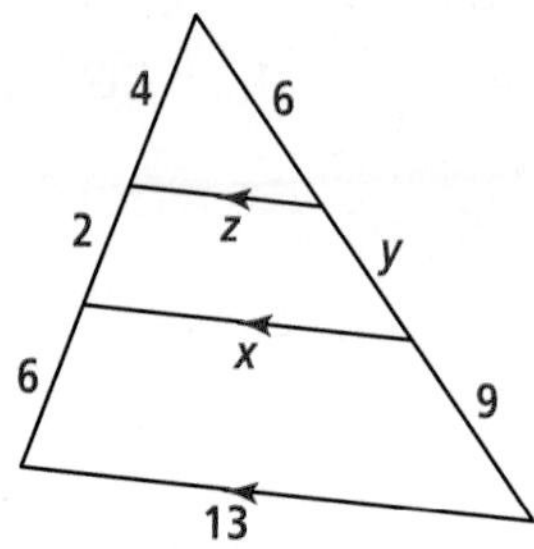


17. $x$

18. $y$

19. $z$

20. What is the value of $x$? SEE EXAMPLE 3

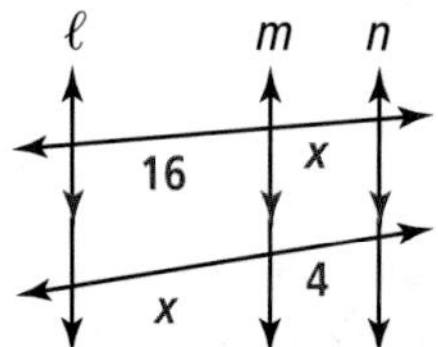


**For Exercises 21–23, find each value of $x$ for the given value of $y$. Round to the nearest tenth.**

SEE EXAMPLES 4 AND 5

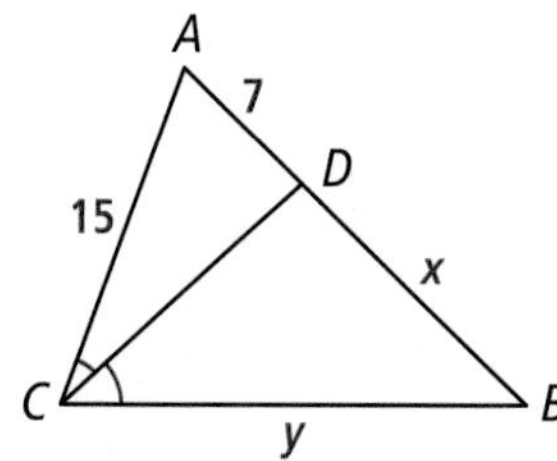


21. $y = 16$

22. $y = 20$

23. $y = 18$

24. Write a proof of the Triangle Midsegment Theorem.

**Given:** $\overline{DG} \cong \overline{GE}$, $\overline{FH} \cong \overline{HE}$

**Prove:** $\overline{GH} \parallel \overline{DF}$, $GH = \frac{1}{2}DF$

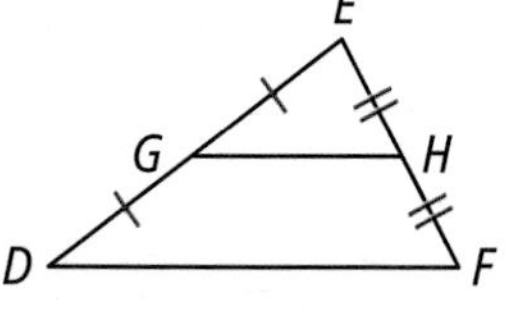


25. Write a proof of the Corollary to the Side-Splitter Theorem.

**Given:** $\ell \parallel m \parallel n$

**Prove:** $\frac{AB}{BC} = \frac{DE}{EF}$

*Hint:* Draw $\overline{AF}$. Label the intersection of $\overline{AF}$ and $\overleftrightarrow{BE}$ point $G$.

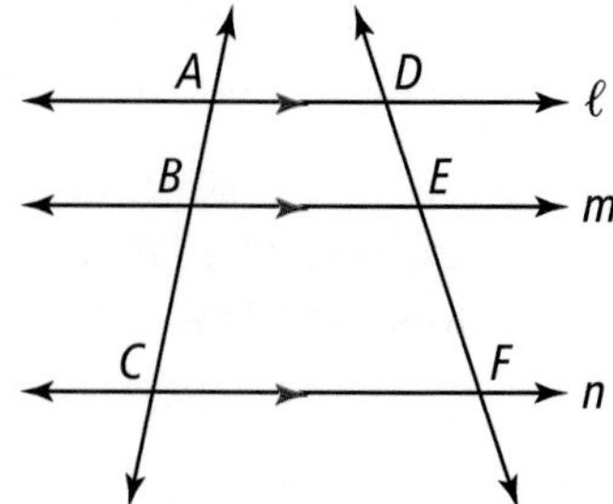

# PRACTICE & PROBLEM SOLVING

Practice Tutorial

Mixed Review Available Online

## APPLY

**26. Use Structure** A building in the shape of a pyramid needs to have supports repaired, and two parallel sections need to be reinforced. The face of the building is an equilateral triangle. What are the lengths of $\overline{KO}$ and $\overline{LN}$?

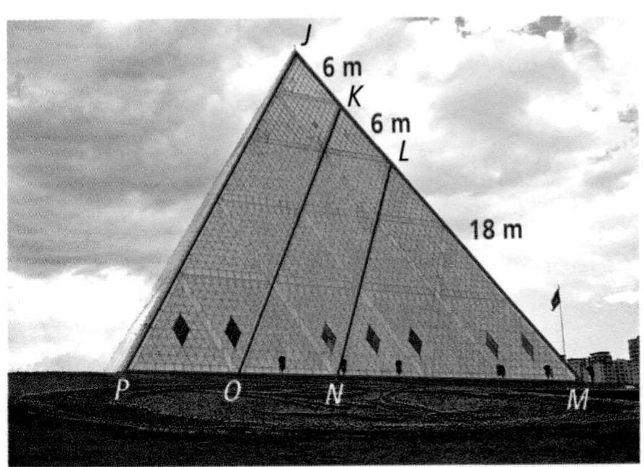


**27. Higher Order Thinking** Use the figure to prove Theorem 2-13: Two non-vertical lines are parallel if and only if they have the same slope.

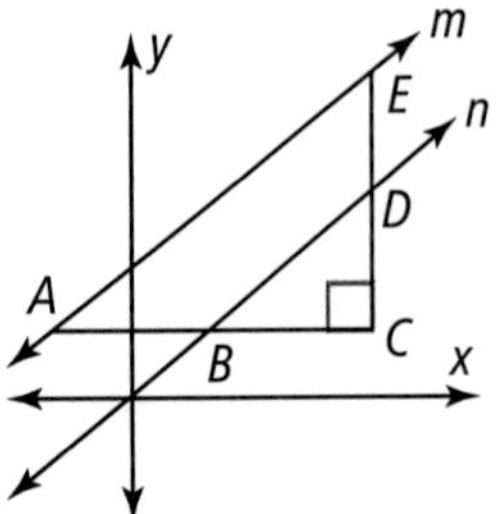


**a.** Assume the slopes of lines $m$ and $n$ are equal. Use proportions in $\triangle ACE$ and $\triangle BCD$ to show that $m \parallel n$.

**b.** Now assume that $m \parallel n$. Show that the slopes of $m$ and $n$ are equal.

**28. Use Structure** Aisha is building a roof and needs to determine the lengths of $\overline{CG}$ and $\overline{CF}$ from the design shown. How can she determine $CG$ and $CF$? What are $CG$ and $CF$?

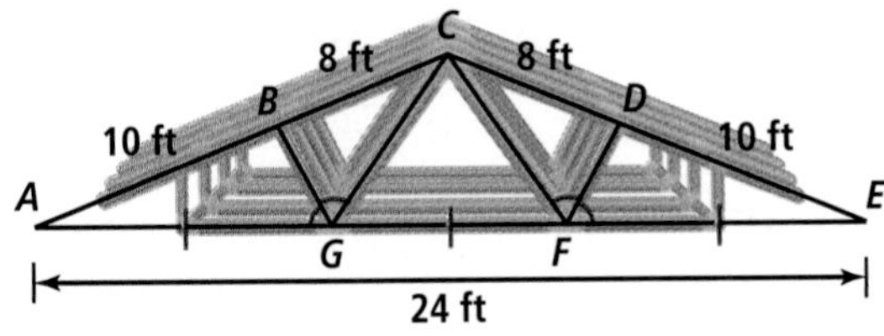


## ASSESSMENT PRACTICE

**29.** What is the value of $x$?

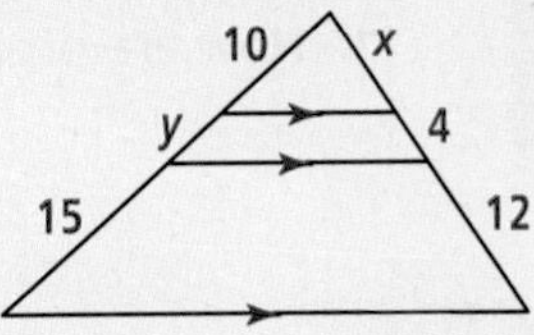


**30. SAT/ACT** What is the measure of side $CB$?

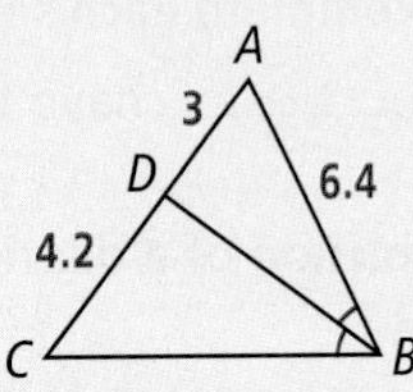


Ⓐ 4.57 Ⓑ 6.4 Ⓒ 8.96 Ⓓ 9.4

**31. Performance Task** Emma is determining measurements needed to simulate the distances in a shuffleboard computer game that she is programming.

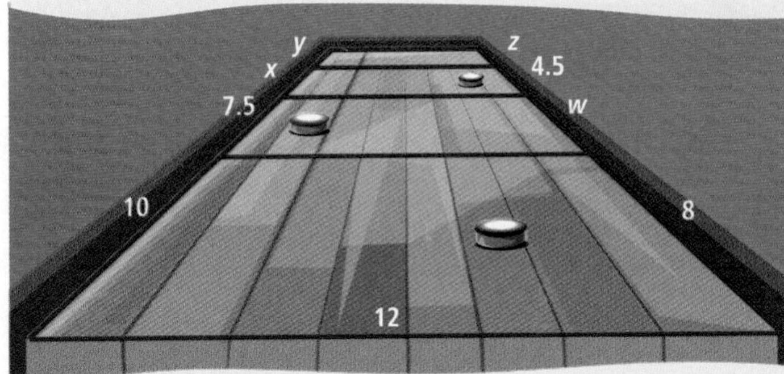


**Part A** The horizontal lines must be parallel and in proportion so that each zone of the shuffleboard appears to be the same length. What are the lengths $w$, $x$, and $y$?

**Part B** What is the length of each horizontal segment?

**Part C** Which horizontal segment is closest to the midsegment of the triangle that extends off of the screen? How do you know?

TOPIC 7

# Topic Review

## TOPIC ESSENTIAL QUESTION

1. How are properties of similar figures used to solve problems?

## Vocabulary Review

**Choose the correct term to complete each sentence.**

2. Two triangles that are __________ have two pairs of corresponding congruent angles.
3. A __________ is a composition of a dilation and one or more rigid motions.
4. A point that is its own image in a dilation is the __________.
5. As a result of a dilation, if $A'B' = n \cdot AB$, then $n$ is the __________.

- center of dilation
- dilation
- geometric mean
- scale factor
- similar
- similarity transformation

## Concepts & Skills Review

### LESSONS 7-1 & 7-2 Dilations and Similarity Transformations

**Quick Review**

A **dilation** is a transformation that maps a point $X$ to $X'$ such that $X'$ lies on $\overrightarrow{CX}$ and $CX' = k \cdot CX$, with **center of dilation** $C$ and **scale factor** $k$.

Two figures are **similar** if there is a **similarity transformation** that maps one figure onto the other.

**Example**

**Are $\triangle ABC$ and $\triangle DEF$ similar? Explain.**

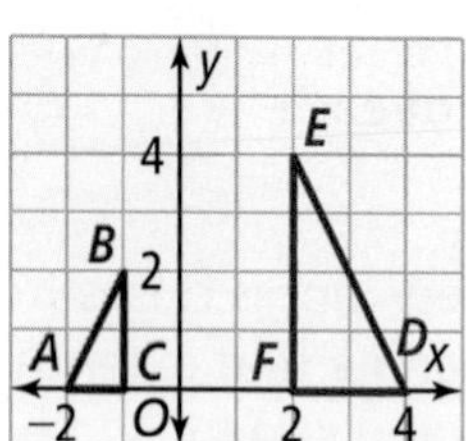


The reflection $R_{y\text{-axis}}$ maps $\triangle ABC$ to a triangle with vertices $A'(2, 0)$, $B'(1, 2)$ and $C'(1, 0)$. The dilation $D_2$ maps the image to $\triangle DEF$. Since the composition $D_2 \circ R_{y\text{-axis}}$ maps $\triangle ABC$ to $\triangle DEF$, the triangles are similar.

**Practice & Problem Solving**

**Give the coordinates of each image.**

6. $D_{\frac{1}{2}}(\triangle FGH)$ for $F(5, -2)$, $G(-2, -4)$, $H(0, 6)$
7. $D_{(3,\,K)}(\triangle KLM)$ for $K(0, 4)$, $L(3, 0)$, $M(-2, 4)$
8. What is a similarity transformation from $PQRS$ to $WXYZ$?

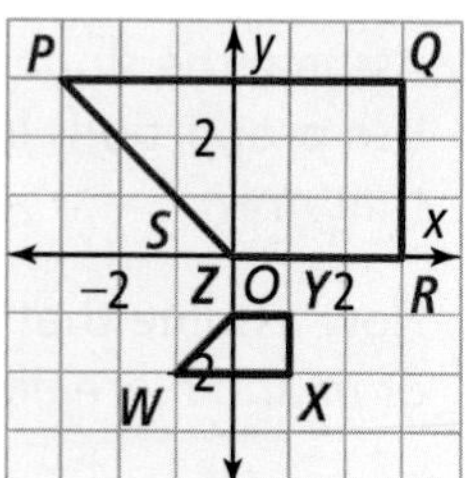


9. **Construct Arguments** Isabel says that the scale factor in the similarity transformation that maps $\triangle ABC$ to $\triangle PQR$ is 2. Is she correct? Explain.

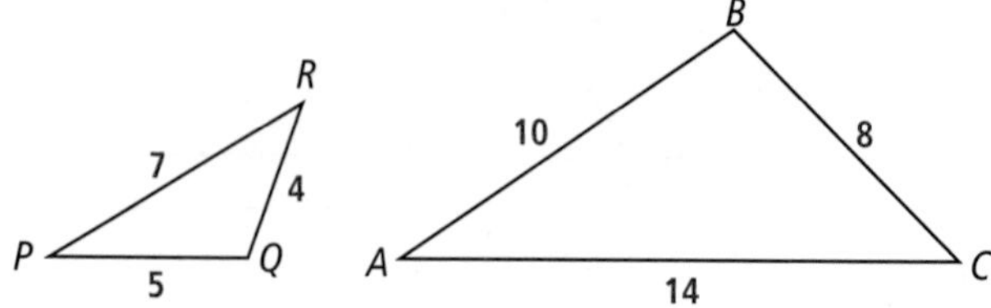

## LESSON 7-3 Proving Triangles Similar

### Quick Review

A pair of triangles can be shown to be similar by using the following criteria.

- Two pairs of corresponding angles are congruent.
- All corresponding sides are proportional.
- Two pairs of corresponding sides are proportional and the included angles are congruent.

### Example

**Explain whether $\triangle ABE$ and $\triangle DBC$ are similar.**

By the Alternate Interior Angles Theorem, $\angle A \cong \angle D$ and $\angle E \cong \angle C$. Since two pairs of corresponding angles are congruent, $\triangle ABE \sim \triangle DBC$.

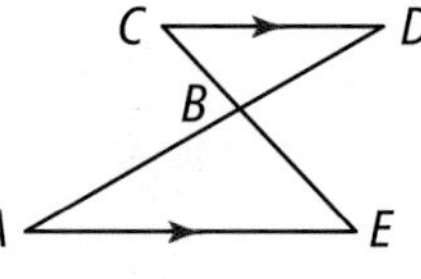


### Practice & Problem Solving

**For Exercises 10 and 11, explain whether each triangle similarity is true.**

**10.** $\triangle FGJ \sim \triangle JGH$

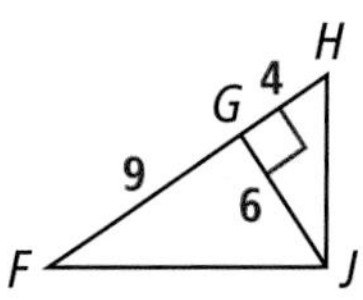


**11.** $\triangle KLN \sim \triangle NLM$

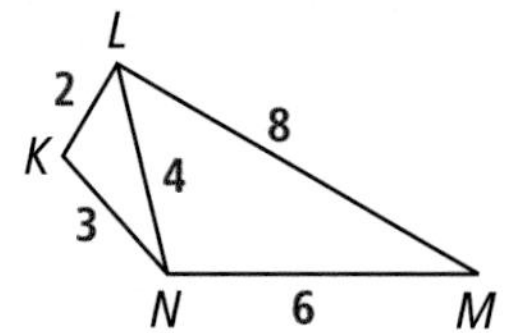


**12. Communicate Precisely** Explain what additional information is needed to use AA $\sim$ to show that $\triangle TUV \sim \triangle XZY$.

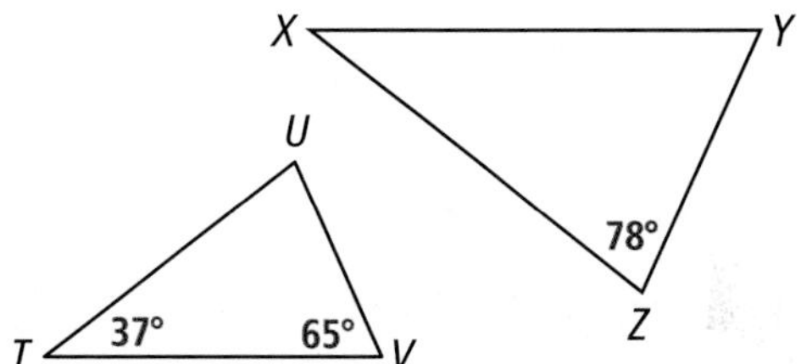


## LESSONS 7-4 & 7-5 Similarity in Right Triangles and Proportions in Triangles

### Quick Review

For right triangle $\triangle ABC$, $\triangle ABC \sim \triangle ACD \sim \triangle CBD$.

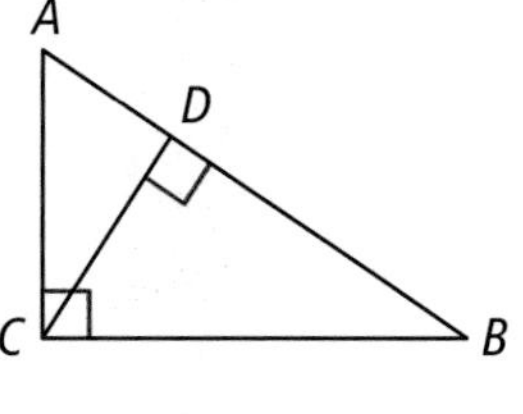


Also, $CD$ is the **geometric mean** of $AD$ and $BD$, $AC$ is the geometric mean of $AB$ and $AD$, and $CB$ is the geometric mean of $AB$ and $DB$.

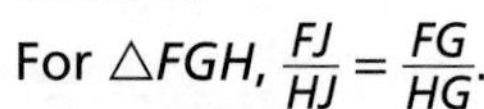

For $\triangle FGH$, $\frac{FJ}{HJ} = \frac{FG}{HG}$.

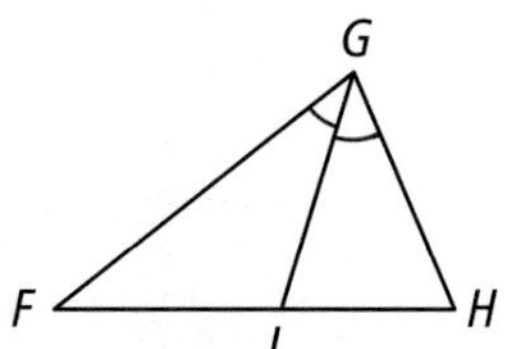


### Example

**For $\triangle LMN$, what is $x$?**

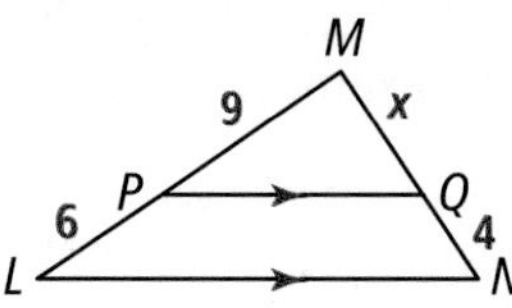


By the Side-Splitter Theorem, $\frac{LP}{PM} = \frac{NQ}{QM}$, so $\frac{6}{9} = \frac{4}{x}$. Solve for $x$ to get $x = \frac{9}{6}(4) = 6$.

### Practice & Problem Solving

**For Exercises 13–15, use $\triangle RST$ to find each length.**

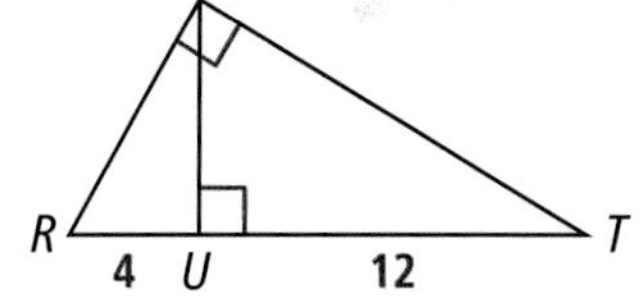


**13.** $RS$

**14.** $ST$

**15.** $SU$

**For Exercises 16–19, find the value of $x$.**

**16.**

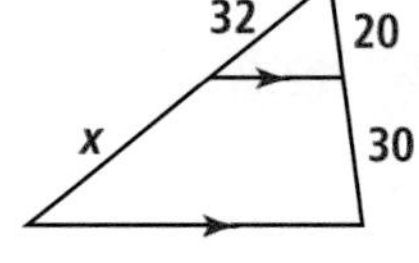


**17.**

**18.**

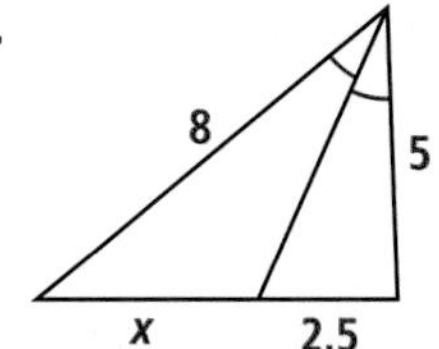


**19.**

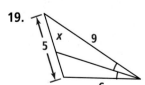

**20. Use Structure** Given right triangle $\triangle GHJ$ with $\overline{JK}$ the altitude to hypotenuse $\overline{GH}$, what is $GJ$ the geometric mean of? Explain.

# Right Triangles and Trigonometry

**How are the Pythagorean Theorem and trigonometry useful?**

## Topic Overview



## Topic Vocabulary

- angle of depression
- angle of elevation
- cosine
- Law of Cosines
- Law of Sines
- Pythagorean triple
- sine
- tangent
- trigonometric ratios

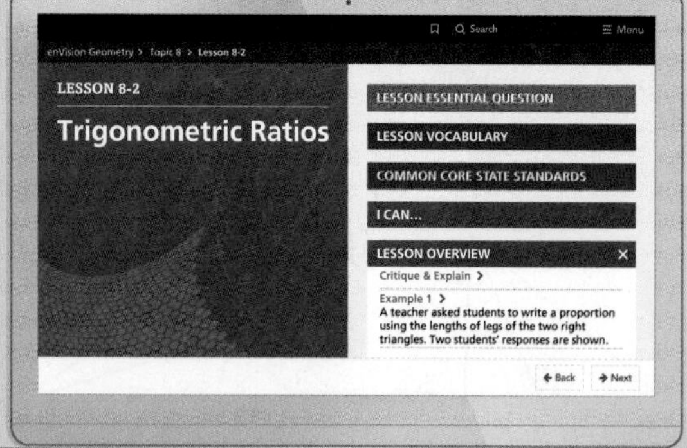

Go online | **PearsonRealize.com**

## Digital Experience

**INTERACTIVE STUDENT EDITION** Access online or offline.

**ACTIVITIES** Complete ***Explore & Reason, Model & Discuss***, and ***Critique & Explain*** activities. Interact with Examples and Try Its.

**ANIMATION** View and interact with real-world applications.

**PRACTICE** Practice what you've learned.

## The Impossible Measurement

Tall buildings are often some of the most recognizable structures of cities. The Empire State Building in New York City, the Transamerica Pyramid in San Francisco, and the JPMorgan Chase Tower in Houston are all famous landmarks in those cities.

Cities around the world compete for the tallest building bragging rights. Which city currently has the tallest building? This Mathematical Modeling in 3 Acts lesson will get you thinking about the height of structures, including tall buildings such as these.

TOPIC 8

**VIDEOS** Watch clips to support ***Mathematical Modeling in 3 Acts Lessons*** and **enVision™ *STEM Projects.***

**CONCEPT SUMMARY** Review key lesson content through multiple representations.

**ASSESSMENT** Show what you've learned.

**GLOSSARY** Read and listen to English and Spanish definitions.

**TUTORIALS** Get help from ***Virtual Nerd***, right when you need it.

**MATH TOOLS** Explore math with digital tools and manipulatives.

Video

## Did You Know?

A **laser rangefinder** measures the distance to an object indirectly. The instrument measures the time it takes a laser pulse to travel to the object and return, at a speed of approximately **186,000 miles per second**.

SONAR is used to measure distances underwater. The speed of sound in the ocean depends on the **temperature**, **pressure**, and **salt content** of the water. Once you know the speed of sound, you can bounce SONAR waves off an underwater object, measure the time it takes to return, and calculate the distance to the object.

In the 3rd Century B.C., the Greek mathematician **Eratosthenes** calculated the circumference of the Earth indirectly. He couldn't actually measure the distance foot by foot. So he used **geometry and the shadow of the sun** to make a determination of the circumference.

## Your Task: Measure a Distance

Trigonometry is a powerful tool for measuring lengths and distances indirectly. You and your classmates will use trigonometry and indirect measurement to find the height of an object that is too tall to measure directly.

# 8-1 Right Triangles and the Pythagorean Theorem

**I CAN...** prove the Pythagorean Theorem using similarity and establish the relationships in special right triangles.

**VOCABULARY**

- Pythagorean triple

## EXPLORE & REASON

**Consider $\triangle ABC$ with altitude $\overline{CD}$ as shown.**

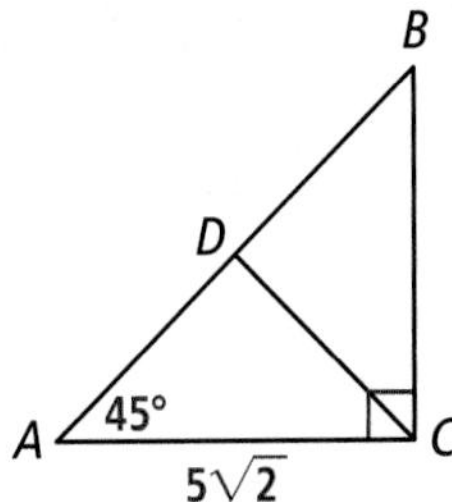


**A.** What is the area of $\triangle ABC$? Of $\triangle ACD$? Explain your answers.

**B.** Find the lengths of $\overline{AD}$ and $\overline{AB}$.

**C. Look for Relationships** Divide the length of the hypotenuse of $\triangle ABC$ by the length of one of its sides. Divide the length of the hypotenuse of $\triangle ACD$ by the length of one of its sides. Make a conjecture that explains the results.

## ESSENTIAL QUESTION

**How are similarity in right triangles and the Pythagorean Theorem related?**

Remember that the Pythagorean Theorem and its converse describe how the side lengths of right triangles are related.

### THEOREM 8-1 Pythagorean Theorem

If a triangle is a right triangle, then the sum of the squares of the lengths of the legs is equal to the square of the length of the hypotenuse.

**If...** $\triangle ABC$ is a right triangle.

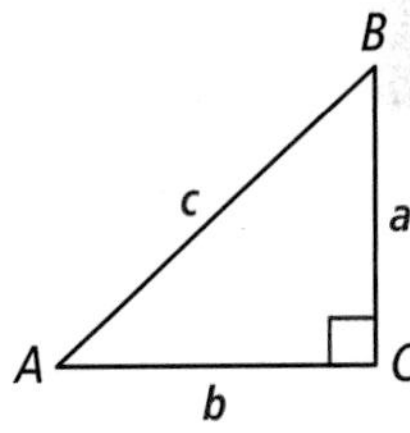


**Then...** $a^2 + b^2 = c^2$

PROOF: SEE EXAMPLE 1.

### THEOREM 8-2 Converse of the Pythagorean Theorem

If the sum of the squares of the lengths of two sides of a triangle is equal to the square of the length of the third side, then the triangle is a right triangle.

**If...** $a^2 + b^2 = c^2$

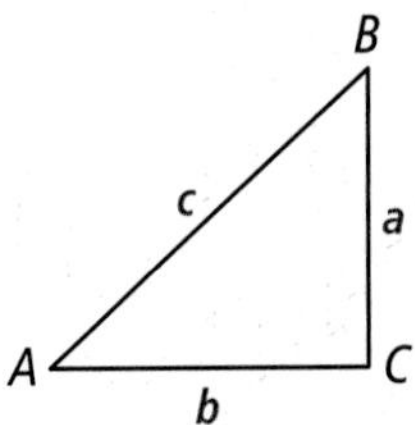


**Then...** $\triangle ABC$ is a right triangle.

PROOF: SEE EXERCISE 17.

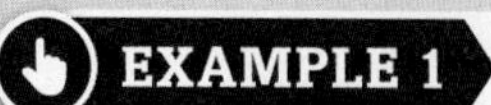


## Use Similarity to Prove the Pythagorean Theorem

**Use right triangle similarity to write a proof of the Pythagorean Theorem.**

**Given:** $\triangle XYZ$ is a right triangle.

**Prove:** $a^2 + b^2 = c^2$

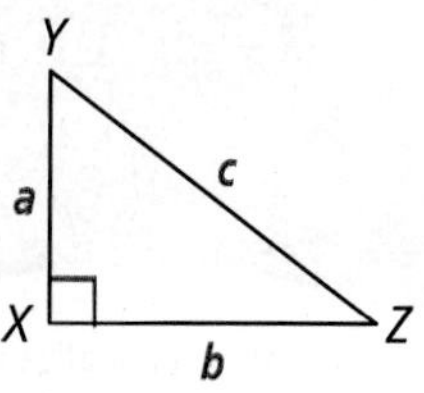


**Plan:** To prove the Pythagorean Theorem, draw the altitude to the hypotenuse. Then use the relationships in the resulting similar right triangles.

**Proof:**

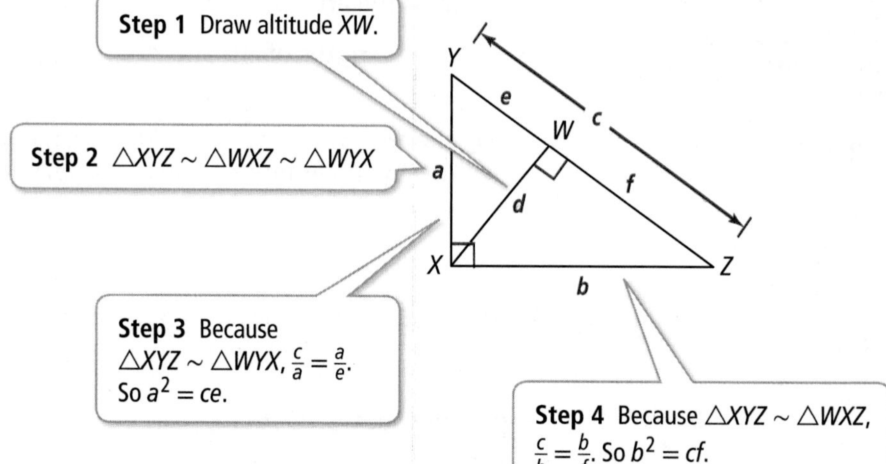

Step 1 Draw altitude $\overline{XW}$.
Step 2 $\triangle XYZ \sim \triangle WXZ \sim \triangle WYX$
Step 3 Because $\triangle XYZ \sim \triangle WYX$, $\frac{c}{a} = \frac{a}{e}$. So $a^2 = ce$.
Step 4 Because $\triangle XYZ \sim \triangle WXZ$, $\frac{c}{b} = \frac{b}{f}$. So $b^2 = cf$.
Y
e
W
c
a
f
d
X
Z
b


**LOOK FOR RELATIONSHIPS**
Think about how you can apply properties of similar triangles. What is the relationship between corresponding sides of similar triangles?

**Step 5** Write an equation that relates $a^2$ and $b^2$ to $ce$ and $cf$.

$$a^2 + b^2 = ce + cf$$

$$a^2 + b^2 = c(e + f)$$

$$a^2 + b^2 = c(c)$$

$$a^2 + b^2 = c^2$$

**Try It!** **1.** Find the unknown side length of each right triangle.

**a.** $AB$

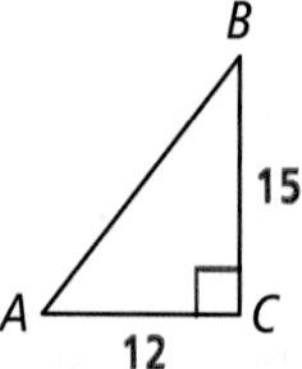


**b.** $EF$

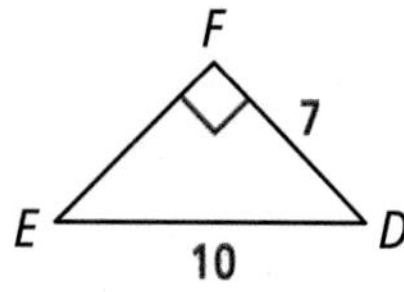

## EXAMPLE 2 Use the Pythagorean Theorem and Its Converse

**A. To satisfy safety regulations, the distance from the wall to the base of a ladder should be at least one-fourth the length of the ladder. Did Drew set up the ladder correctly?**

The floor, the wall, and the ladder form a right triangle.

**Step 1** Find the length of the ladder.

$$a^2 + b^2 = c^2$$
$$2.5^2 + 9^2 = c^2$$
$$87.25 = c^2$$
$$9.34 \approx c$$

Use the Pythagorean Theorem with $a = 2.5$ and $b = 9$.

**Step 2** Find $\frac{1}{4}$ the length of the ladder.

$$\frac{1}{4}c \approx \frac{1}{4}(9.34)$$
$$\approx 2.335$$

The length of the ladder is 9.34 ft.

Since $2.5 > 2.335$, Drew set up the ladder correctly.

**B. The length of each crosspiece of the fence is 10 ft. Why would a rancher build this fence with the measurements shown?**

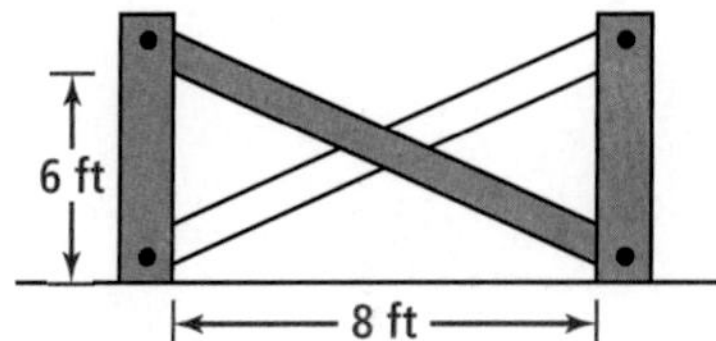


The numbers 6, 8, and 10 form a *Pythagorean triple*. A **Pythagorean triple** is a set of three nonzero whole numbers that satisfy the equation $a^2 + b^2 = c^2$.

Since $6^2 + 8^2 = 10^2$, the posts, the ground, and the crosspieces form right triangles.

By using those measurements, the rancher knows that the fence posts are perpendicular to the ground, which stabilizes the fence.

**STUDY TIP**
Learn and recognize common Pythagorean triples such as 3, 4, and 5; and 5, 12, and 13 to speed calculations.

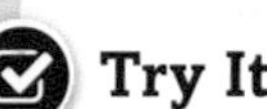

**Try It!** **2. a.** What is $KL$?

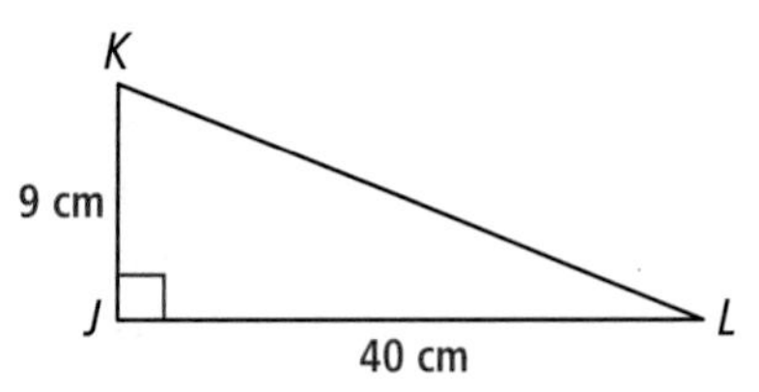


**b.** Is $\triangle MNO$ a right triangle? Explain.

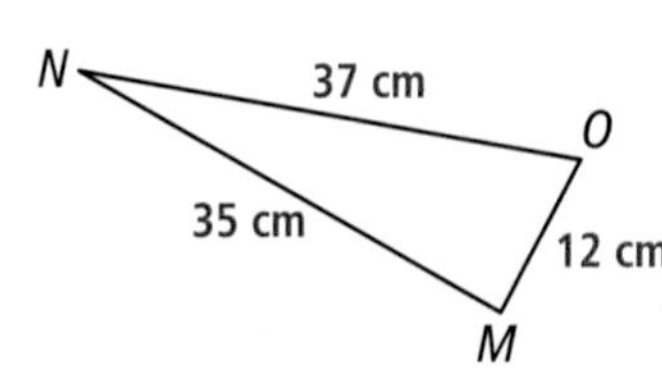

CONCEPTUAL UNDERSTANDING

## EXAMPLE 3 Investigate Side Lengths in 45°-45°-90° Triangles

**REASON**
Think about the properties of a triangle with two congruent angles. How do the properties of the triangle help you relate the side lengths?

**Is there a relationship between the lengths of $\overline{AB}$ and $\overline{AC}$ in $\triangle ABC$? Explain.**

Draw altitude $\overline{CD}$ to form similar right triangles $\triangle ABC$, $\triangle ACD$, and $\triangle CBD$.

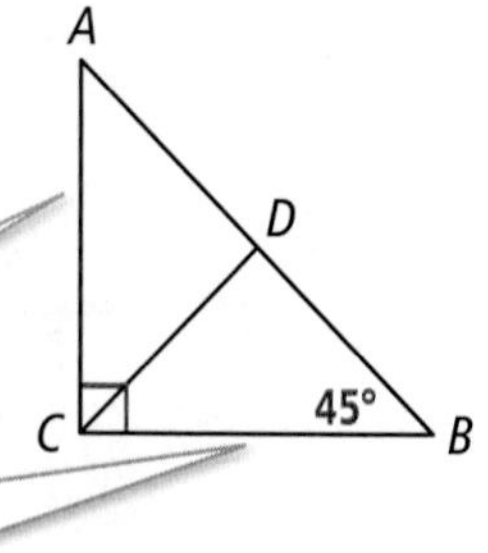


Notice that $\triangle ABC$ is a 45°-45°-90° triangle, and that $AC = BC$.

Use right-triangle similarity to write an equation.

$$\frac{AB}{AC} = \frac{AC}{AD}$$

Since $\triangle ABC \sim \triangle ACD$, $AC$ is the geometric mean of $AB$ and $AD$.

$$\frac{AB}{AC} = \frac{AC}{\frac{1}{2}AB}$$

Because $\triangle ABC$ is isosceles, $\overline{CD}$ bisects $\overline{AB}$.

$$\frac{1}{2}AB^2 = AC^2$$

$$AB^2 = 2AC^2$$

$$AB = \sqrt{2} \cdot AC$$

The length of $\overline{AB}$ is $\sqrt{2}$ times the length of $\overline{AC}$.

**Try It!** 3. Find the side lengths of each 45°-45°-90° triangle.

a. What are $XZ$ and $YZ$?

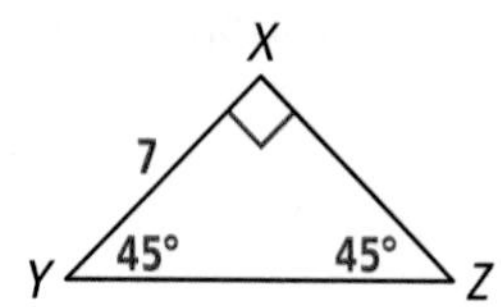


b. What are $JK$ and $LK$?

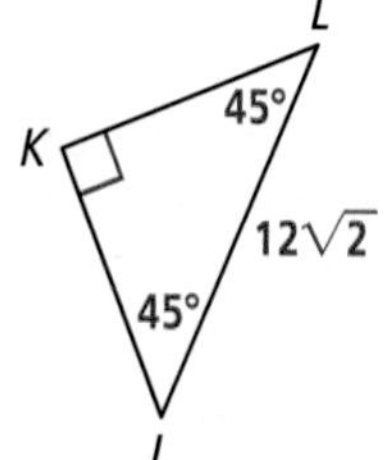


## THEOREM 8-3 45°-45°-90° Triangle Theorem

In a 45°-45°-90° triangle, the legs are congruent and the length of the hypotenuse is $\sqrt{2}$ times the length of a leg.

If... B, 45°, s, A, 45°, C, s

Then... $BC = s\sqrt{2}$

PROOF: SEE EXERCISE 18.

## EXAMPLE 4 Explore the Side Lengths of a 30°-60°-90° Triangle

**Using an equilateral triangle, show how the lengths of the short leg, the long leg, and the hypotenuse of a 30°-60°-90° triangle are related.**

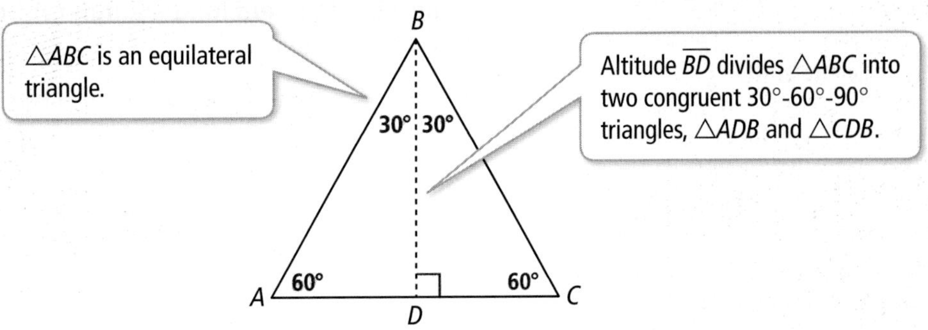

$\triangle ABC$ is an equilateral triangle.
Altitude $\overline{BD}$ divides $\triangle ABC$ into two congruent 30°-60°-90° triangles, $\triangle ADB$ and $\triangle CDB$.
B
30°
30°
A
60°
D
60°
C


**STUDY TIP**
Recall that an altitude of a triangle is perpendicular to a side. Think about what properties of the triangle result in the altitude also being a segment bisector.

Look at $\triangle ADB$. Let the length of the short leg $\overline{AD}$ be $s$.

Find the relationship between $AD$ and $AB$.

$AD = CD = s$ — $\overline{BD}$ bisects $\overline{AC}$.

$AC = AD + CD$

$AC = 2s$

$AB = 2s$ — $\triangle ABC$ is equilateral, so $AB = AC = 2s$.

Find the relationship between $AD$ and $BD$.

$AD^2 + BD^2 = AB^2$ — Use the Pythagorean Theorem.

$s^2 + BD^2 = (2s)^2$

$BD^2 = 3s^2$

$BD = s\sqrt{3}$

In $\triangle ADB$, the length of hypotenuse $\overline{AB}$ is twice the length of the short leg $\overline{AD}$. The length of the long leg $\overline{BD}$ is $\sqrt{3}$ times the length of the short leg.

**Try It!** **4. a.** What are $PQ$ and $PR$?

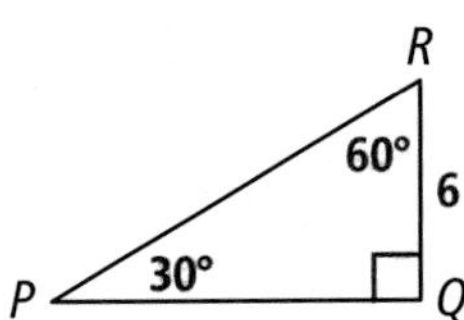


**b.** What are $UV$ and $TV$?

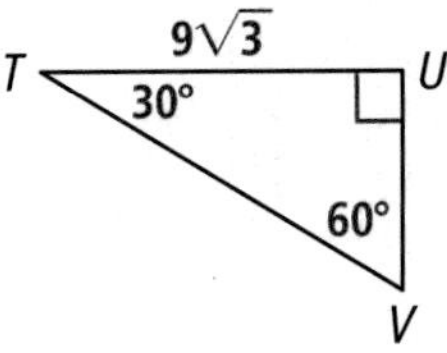


### THEOREM 8-4 30°-60°-90° Triangle Theorem

In a 30°-60°-90° triangle, the length of the hypotenuse is twice the length of the short leg. The length of the long leg is $\sqrt{3}$ times the length of the short leg.

**If...**

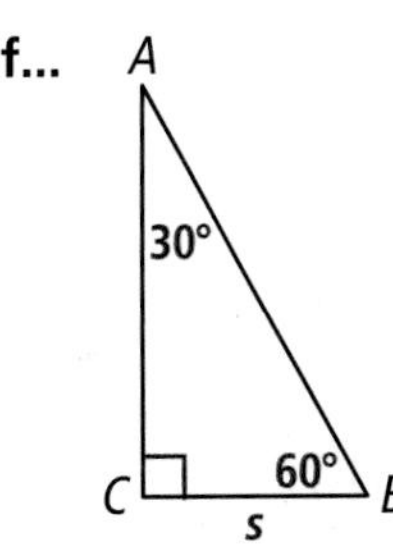


**Then...** $AC = s\sqrt{3}$, $AB = 2s$

PROOF: SEE EXERCISE 19.

## EXAMPLE 5 Apply Special Right Triangle Relationships

**A. Alejandro needs to make both the horizontal and vertical supports, $\overline{AC}$ and $\overline{AB}$, for the ramp. Is one 12-foot board long enough for both supports? Explain.**

B
60°
10 ft
30°
A
C

The ramp and supports form a 30°-60°-90° triangle.

| | |
|---|---|
| $BC = 2AB$ | $AC = AB\sqrt{3}$ |
| $10 = 2AB$ | $AC = 5\sqrt{3}$ ft |
| $AB = 5$ ft | |

**COMMON ERROR**
Be careful not to mix up the relationship of the shorter and longer legs. Remember that the longer leg is $\sqrt{3}$ times as long as the shorter leg, so the longer leg is between $1\frac{1}{2}$ and 2 times as long as the short leg.

Find the total length of the supports.

$$AB + AC = 5 + 5\sqrt{3}$$
$$\approx 13.66 \text{ ft}$$

Since $13.66 > 12$, the 12-foot board will not be long enough for Alejandro to make both supports.

**B. Olivia starts an origami paper crane by making the 200-mm diagonal fold. What are the side length and area of the paper square?**

**Step 1** Find the length of one side of the paper.

$$s\sqrt{2} = 200$$
$$s = \frac{200}{\sqrt{2}}$$
$$s \approx 141.4 \text{ mm}$$

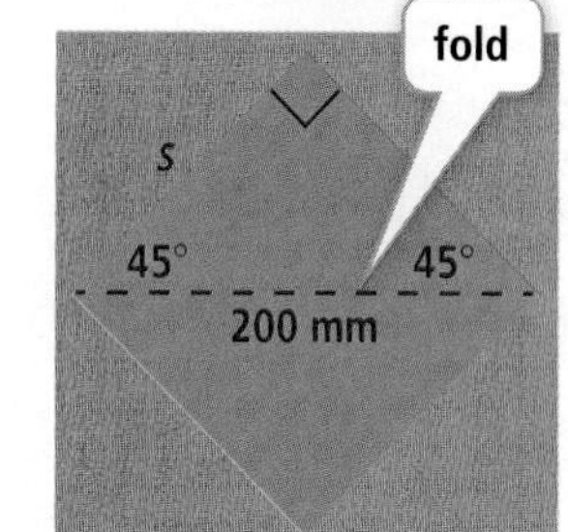


**Step 2** Find the area of the paper square.

$$A = s^2$$
$$A = (100\sqrt{2})^2$$
$$A = 20{,}000 \text{ mm}^2$$

The paper square has side length 141.4 mm and area 20,000 mm$^2$.

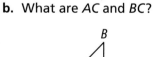

**Try It!** **5. a.** What are $AB$ and $BC$?

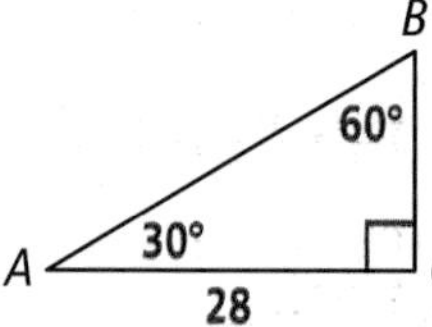


**b.** What are $AC$ and $BC$?

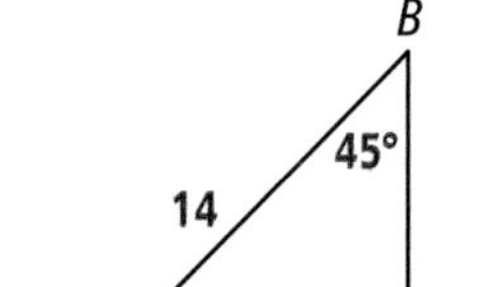
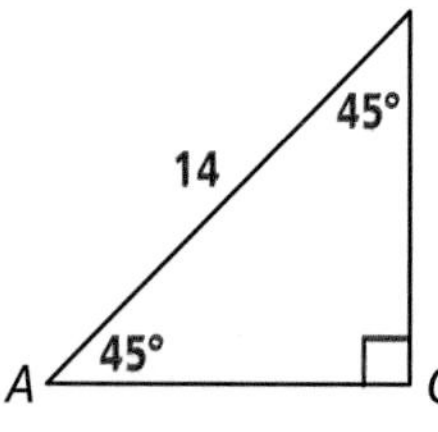

## CONCEPT SUMMARY The Pythagorean Theorem and Special Right Triangles

**THEOREM 8-1** **Pythagorean Theorem**

**If...** $\triangle ABC$ is a right triangle

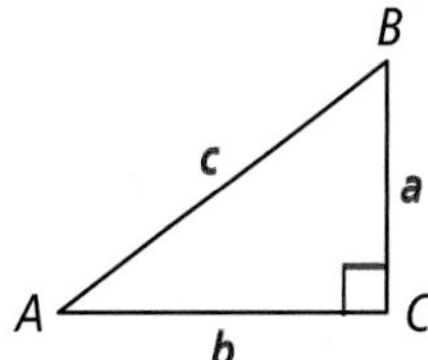


**Then...** $a^2 + b^2 = c^2$

**THEOREM 8-2** **Converse of the Pythagorean Theorem**

**If...** $a^2 + b^2 = c^2$

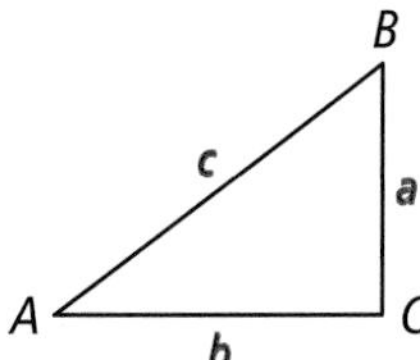


**Then...** $\triangle ABC$ is a right triangle.

**THEOREM 8-3** **45°-45°-90° Triangle Theorem**

**If...**

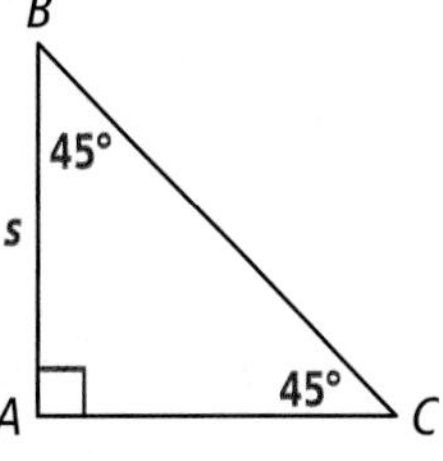


**Then...** $BC = s\sqrt{2}$

**THEOREM 8-4** **30°-60°-90° Triangle Theorem**

**If...**

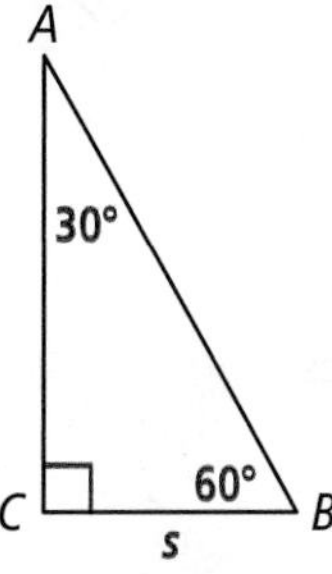


**Then...** $AC = s\sqrt{3}$, $AB = 2s$

## Do You UNDERSTAND?

1. **ESSENTIAL QUESTION** How are similarity in right triangles and the Pythagorean Theorem related?

2. **Error Analysis** Casey was asked to find $XY$. What is Casey's error?

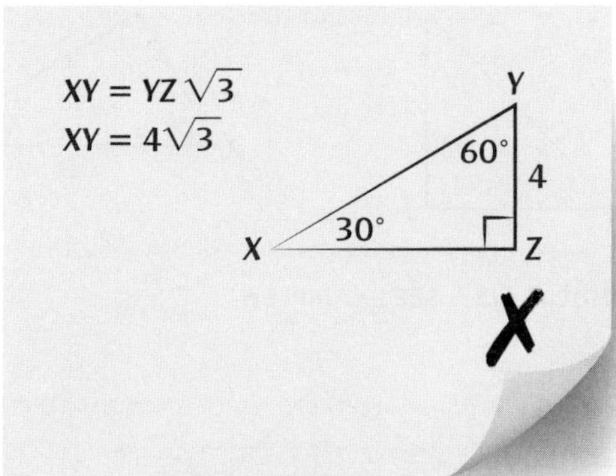


3. **Reason** A right triangle has leg lengths 4.5 and $4.5\sqrt{3}$. What are the measures of the angles? Explain.

## Do You KNOW HOW?

**For Exercises 4 and 5, find the value of *x*.**

4. 5.

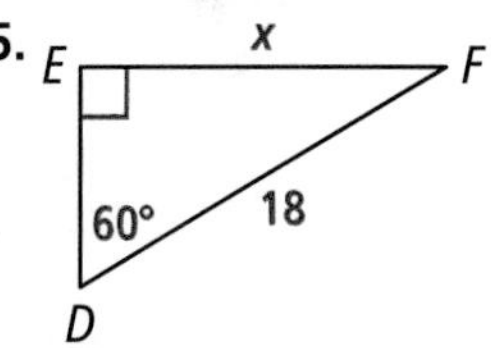


**For Exercises 6–8, is $\triangle RST$ a right triangle? Explain.**

6. $RS = 20$, $ST = 21$, $RT = 29$

7. $RS = 35$, $ST = 36$, $RT = 71$

8. $RS = 40$, $ST = 41$, $RT = 11$

9. Charles wants to hang the pennant shown vertically between two windows that are 19 inches apart. Will the pennant fit? Explain.

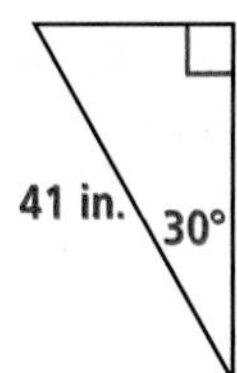

## UNDERSTAND

10. **Mathematical Connections** Which rectangular prism has the longer diagonal? Explain.

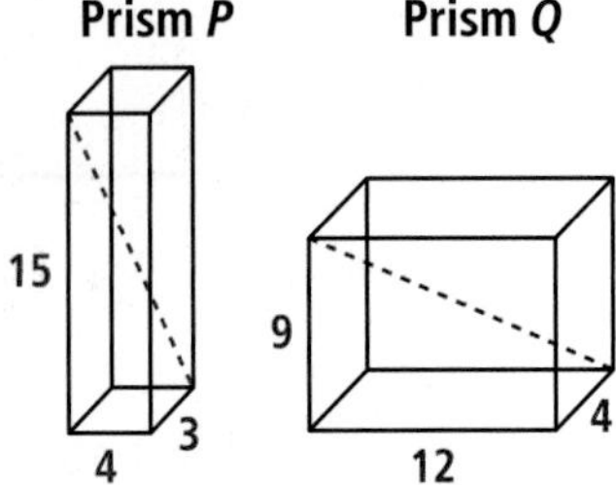


11. **Error Analysis** Dakota is asked to find *EF*. What is her error?

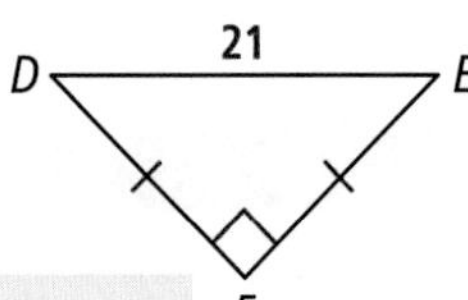


There is not enough information to find *EF* because you need to know either the length of $\overline{DF}$ or one of the other angle measures.

12. **Make Sense and Persevere** What are expressions for *MN* and *LN*? *Hint*: Construct the altitude from *M* to $\overline{LN}$.

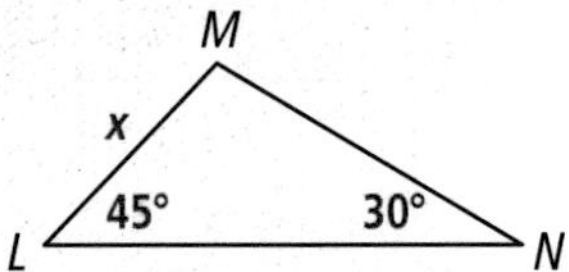


13. **Higher Order Thinking** Triangle *XYZ* is a right triangle. For what kind of triangle would $XZ^2 + XY^2 > YZ^2$? For what kind of triangle would $XZ^2 + XY^2 < YZ^2$? Explain.

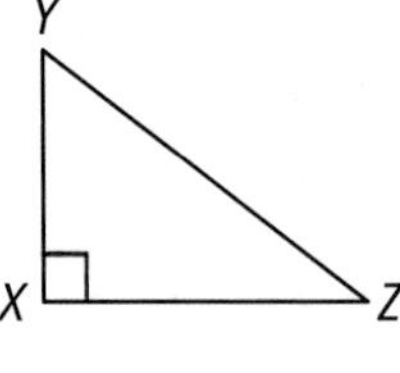


14. **Look for Relationships** Write an equation that represents the relationship between *JK* and *KL*.

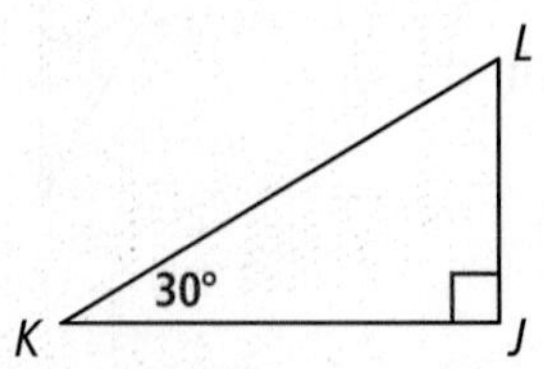


## PRACTICE

**For Exercises 15 and 16, find the unknown side length of each triangle.** SEE EXAMPLE 1

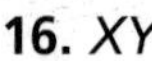

15. *RS*

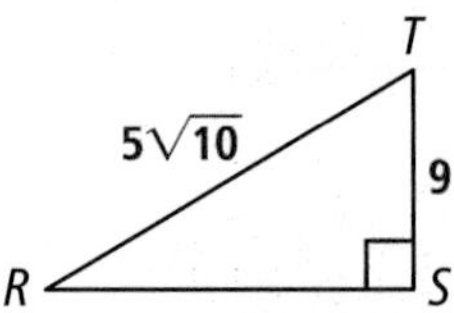


16. *XY*

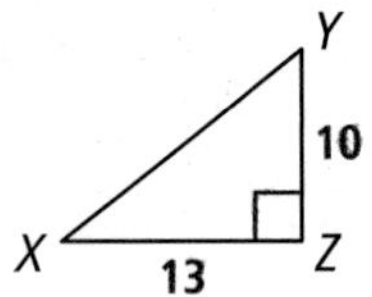


17. Given $\triangle ABC$ with $a^2 + b^2 = c^2$, write a paragraph proof of the Converse of the Pythagorean Theorem. SEE EXAMPLE 2

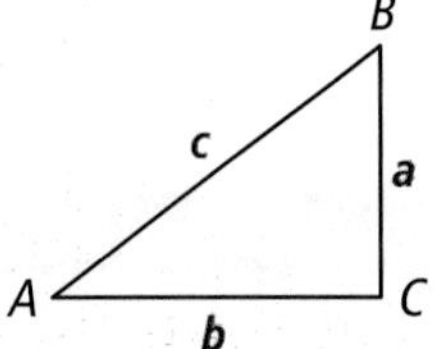


18. Write a two-column proof of the 45°-45°-90° Triangle Theorem. SEE EXAMPLE 3

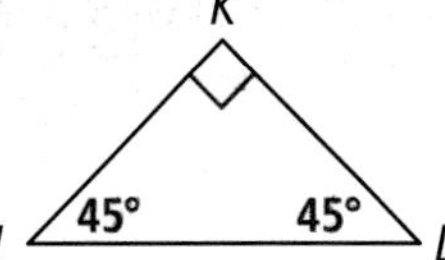


19. Write a paragraph proof of the 30°-60°-90° Triangle Theorem. SEE EXAMPLE 4

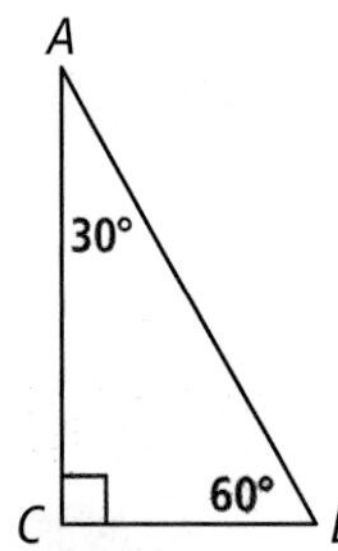


**For Exercise 20 and 21, find the side lengths of each triangle.** SEE EXAMPLES 3 AND 4

20. What are *GJ* and *HJ*?

21. What are *XY* and *YZ*?

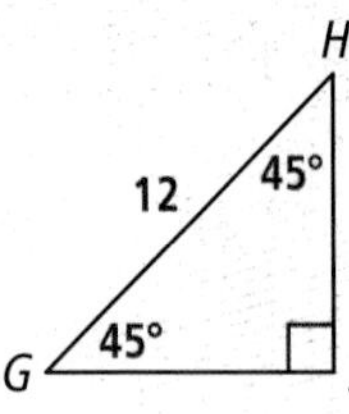


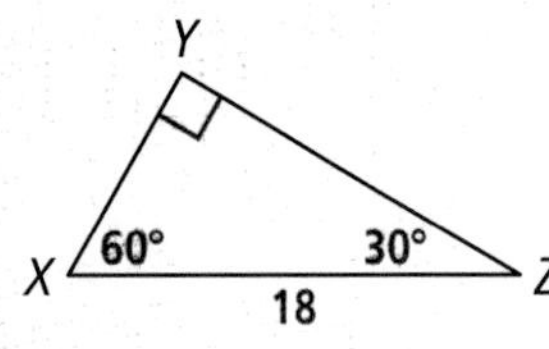


22. What is *QS*? SEE EXAMPLE 5

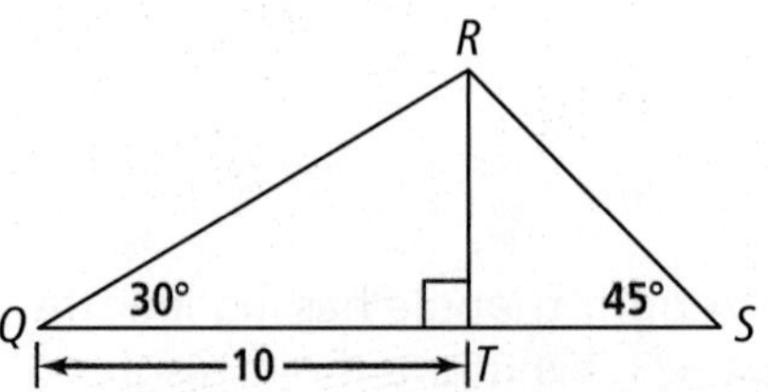

## PRACTICE & PROBLEM SOLVING

Practice Tutorial

Mixed Review Available Online

### APPLY

**23. Reason** Esteban wants marble bookends cut at a 60° angle, as shown. If Esteban wants his bookends to be between 7.5 in. and 8 in. tall, what length *d* should the marble cutter make the base of the bookends? Explain.

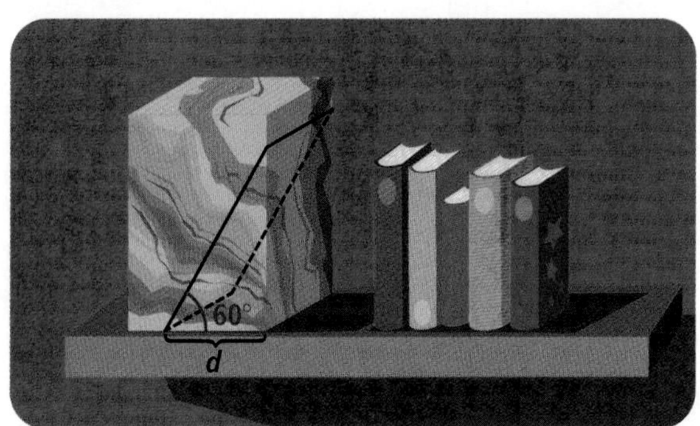


**24. Communicate Precisely** Sarah finds an antique dinner bell that appears to be in the shape of an isosceles right triangle, but the only measurement given is the longest side. Sarah wants to display the bell and wand in a 5.5-in. by 7.5-in. picture frame. Assuming that the bell is an isosceles right triangle, can Sarah display the bell and wand within the frame? Explain.

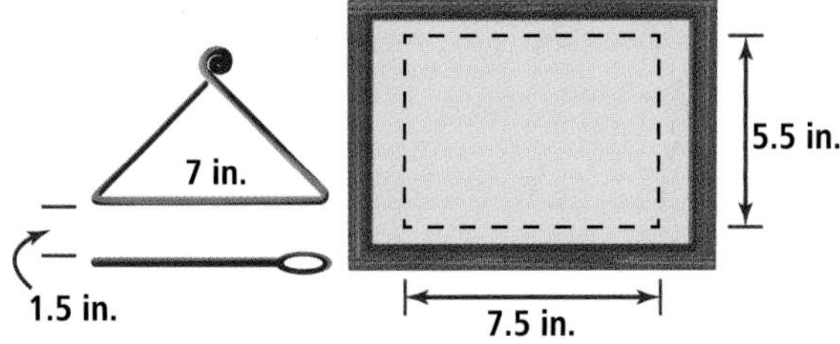


**25. Construct Arguments** When Carmen parks on a hill, she places chocks behind the wheels of her car. The height of the chocks must be at least one-fourth of the height of the wheels to hold the car securely in place. The chock shown has the shape of a right triangle. Is it safe for Carmen to use? Explain.

### ASSESSMENT PRACTICE

**26.** Match each set of triangle side lengths with the best description of the triangle.

| | |
|---|---|
| **I.** $\sqrt{2}, \sqrt{2}, \sqrt{3}$ | **A.** right triangle |
| **II.** $5, 3\sqrt{2}, \sqrt{43}$ | **B.** 30°-60°-90° triangle |
| **III.** $8, 8, 8\sqrt{2}$ | **C.** 45°-45°-90° triangle |
| **IV.** $11, 11\sqrt{3}, 22$ | **D.** not a right triangle |

**27. SAT/ACT** What is *GJ*?

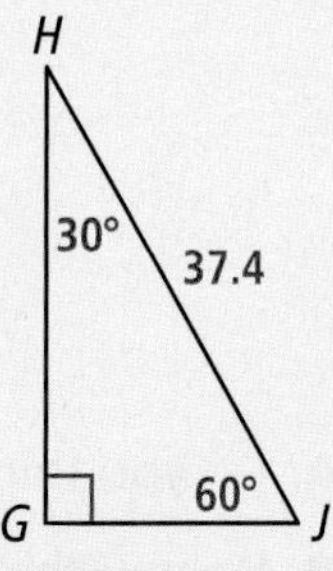


Ⓐ 18.7 Ⓒ $18.7\sqrt{3}$

Ⓑ $18.7\sqrt{2}$ Ⓓ 74.8

**28. Performance Task** Emma designed two triangular sails for a boat.

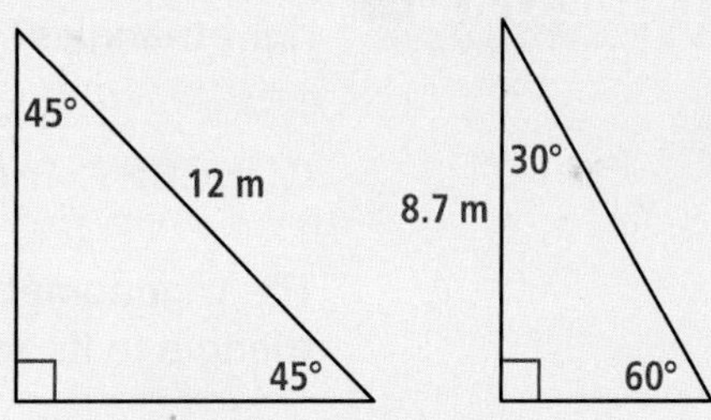


**Part A** What is the area of Sail A?

**Part B** What is the area of Sail B?

**Part C** Is it possible for Emma to cut both sails from one square of sailcloth with sides that are 9 meters in length? Draw a diagram to explain.

# 8-2 Trigonometric Ratios

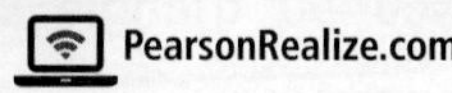


## I CAN...
use trigonometric ratios to find lengths and angle measures of right triangles.

## VOCABULARY
- cosine
- sine
- tangent
- trigonometric ratios

## CRITIQUE & EXPLAIN

**A teacher asked students to write a proportion using the lengths of the legs of the two right triangles.**

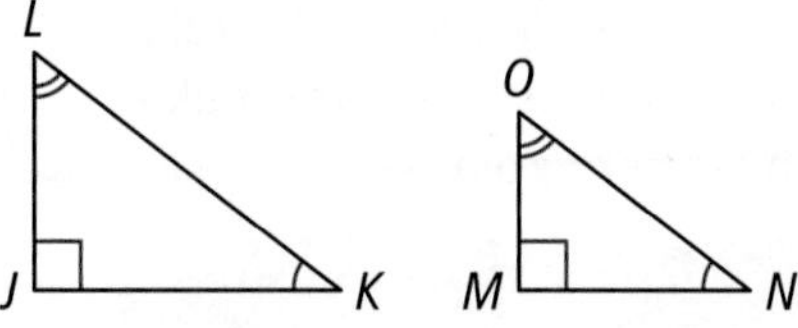


**Two students' responses are shown.**

**Diego**

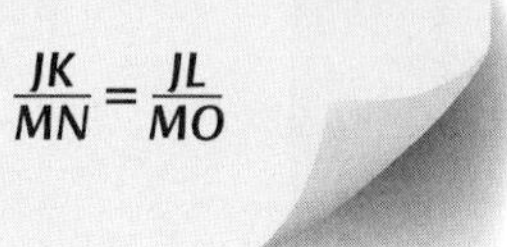


**Rebecca**

$$\frac{JK}{JL} = \frac{MN}{MO}$$

**A.** Do you think that the proportion that Diego wrote is correct? Explain.

**B.** Do you think that the proportion that Rebecca wrote is correct? Explain.

**C. Use Structure** If $\frac{a}{b} = \frac{c}{d}$, how can you get an equivalent equation such that the left side of the equation is $\frac{a}{c}$?

## ESSENTIAL QUESTION

**How do trigonometric ratios relate angle measures to side lengths of right triangles?**

### CONCEPT Trigonometric Ratios

The **trigonometric ratios**, or functions, relate the side lengths of a right triangle to its acute angles.

**sine** of $\angle A$

$$\sin A = \frac{\text{length of leg opposite } \angle A}{\text{length of hypotenuse}} = \frac{BC}{AB}$$

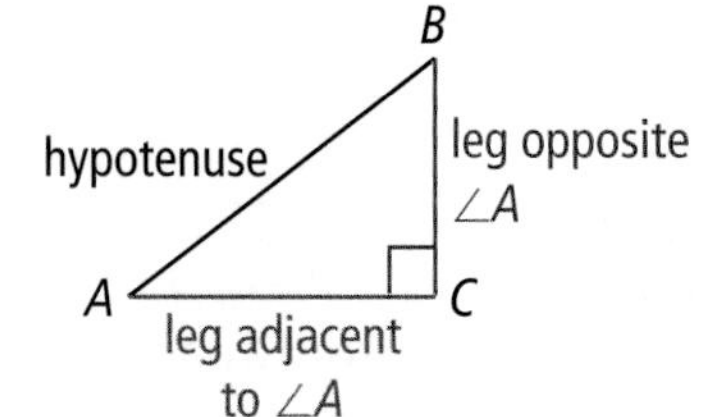


**cosine** of $\angle A$

$$\cos A = \frac{\text{length of leg adjacent to } \angle A}{\text{length of hypotenuse}} = \frac{AC}{AB}$$

**tangent** of $\angle A$

$$\tan A = \frac{\text{length of leg opposite } \angle A}{\text{length of leg adjacent to } \angle A} = \frac{BC}{AC}$$

CONCEPTUAL UNDERSTANDING

## EXAMPLE 1 Understand Trigonometric Ratios Using Similarity

**How are the sines of two different angles with the same measure related?**

Let $\triangle ABC$ and $\triangle DEF$ be right triangles with $m\angle B = m\angle E$.

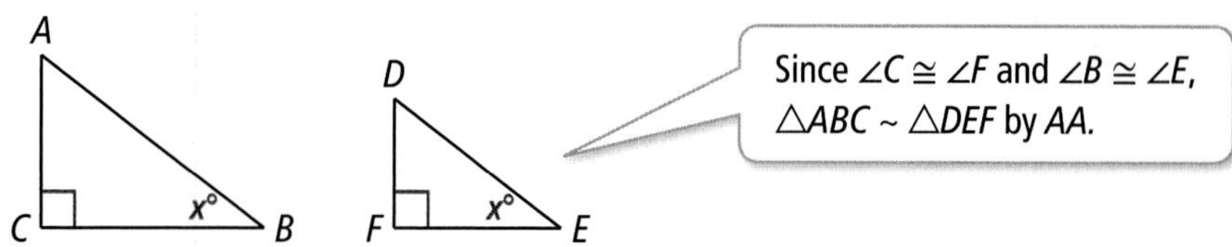


You can use properties of similarity to determine the relationship between sin $B$ and sin $E$.

**MAKE SENSE AND PERSEVERE**
There are many proportional relationships in similar triangles. Look for one that uses all the side lengths in the expressions for sin $B$ and sin $E$.

By the definition of the sine ratio, $\sin B = \frac{AC}{AB}$, and $\sin E = \frac{DF}{DE}$.

Because $\triangle ABC \sim \triangle DEF$, you know that corresponding side lengths are proportional. In particular, $\frac{AC}{DF} = \frac{AB}{DE}$. Rewrite this equation to compare the sides in $\triangle ABC$ to the sides in $\triangle DEF$.

$$\frac{AC}{DF} \cdot \frac{DF}{AB} = \frac{AB}{DE} \cdot \frac{DF}{AB}$$

$$\frac{AC}{AB} = \frac{DF}{DE}$$

Substitute sin $B$ for $\frac{AC}{AB}$ and sin $E$ for $\frac{DF}{DE}$.

$$\sin B = \sin E$$

Any two acute angles with the same measure have the same sine.

**Try It!** 1. Show that any two acute angles with the same measure have the same cosine.

## EXAMPLE 2 Write Trigonometric Ratios

**What are the sine, cosine, and tangent ratios for $\angle H$?**

**COMMON ERROR**
You may incorrectly assume the horizontal leg and vertical leg to be the adjacent and opposite legs. Remember that adjacent and opposite are relative to the angle.

Use the definitions of the trigonometric ratios.

$$\sin H = \frac{\text{length of leg opposite } \angle H}{\text{length of hypotenuse}} = \frac{12}{15}$$

$$\cos H = \frac{\text{length of leg adjacent } \angle H}{\text{length of hypotenuse}} = \frac{9}{15}$$

$$\tan H = \frac{\text{length of leg opposite } \angle H}{\text{length of leg adjacent } \angle H} = \frac{12}{9}$$

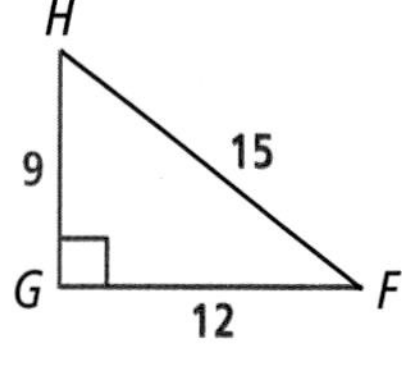


**Try It!** 2. In Example 2, what are the sine, cosine, and tangent ratios of $\angle F$?

## EXAMPLE 3 Trigonometric Ratios of Special Angles

**A. What are the sine, cosine, and tangent ratios for 30°, 45°, and 60° angles?**

You can use what you know about 45°-45°-90° and 30°-60°-90° right triangles to find the ratios.

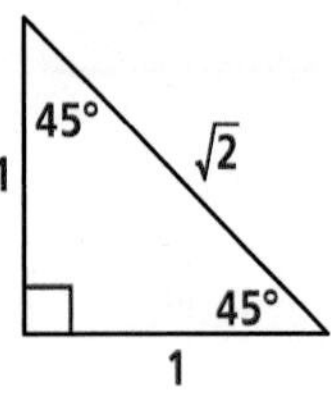


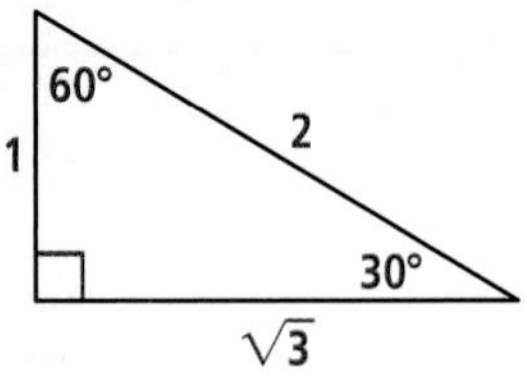


$\sin 45^\circ = \frac{1}{\sqrt{2}} = \frac{\sqrt{2}}{2}$ $\sin 30^\circ = \frac{1}{2}$ $\sin 60^\circ = \frac{\sqrt{3}}{2}$

$\cos 45^\circ = \frac{1}{\sqrt{2}} = \frac{\sqrt{2}}{2}$ $\cos 30^\circ = \frac{\sqrt{3}}{2}$ $\cos 60^\circ = \frac{1}{2}$

$\tan 45^\circ = \frac{1}{1} = 1$ $\tan 30^\circ = \frac{1}{\sqrt{3}} = \frac{\sqrt{3}}{3}$ $\tan 60^\circ = \frac{\sqrt{3}}{1} = \sqrt{3}$

**STUDY TIP**
You might find comparing irrational numbers is often easier if you rationalize the denominators.

**B.** Use trigonometric ratios to find the value of $x$ for each triangle.

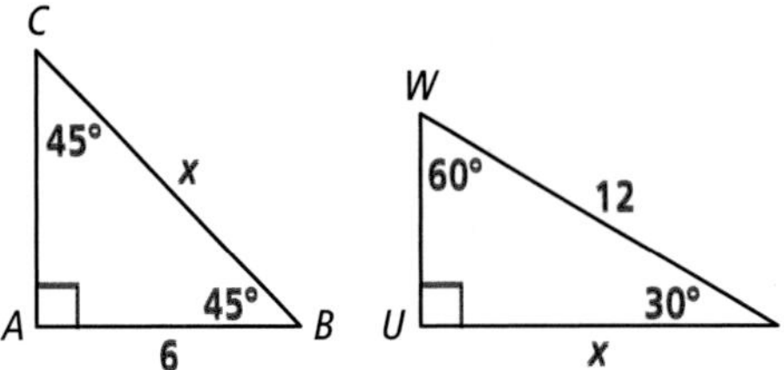


Choose an appropriate trigonometric ratio to write an equation, and then solve for $x$.

$\cos 45^\circ = \frac{6}{x}$

$\frac{1}{\sqrt{2}} = \frac{6}{x}$

$x = 6\sqrt{2}$

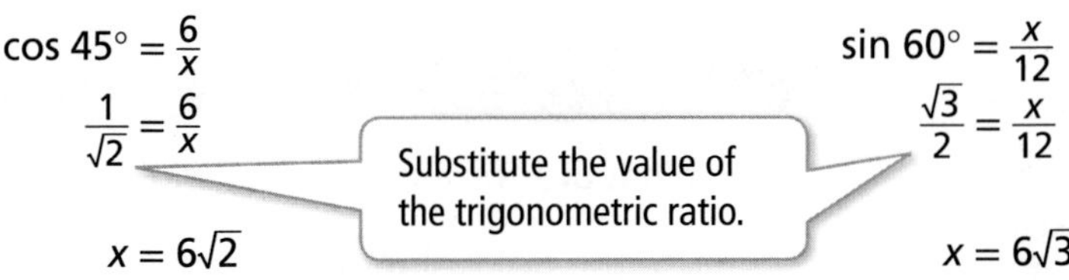


$\sin 60^\circ = \frac{x}{12}$

$\frac{\sqrt{3}}{2} = \frac{x}{12}$

$x = 6\sqrt{3}$

## Try It!

**3. a.** In $\triangle FGH$, what is the value of $y$?

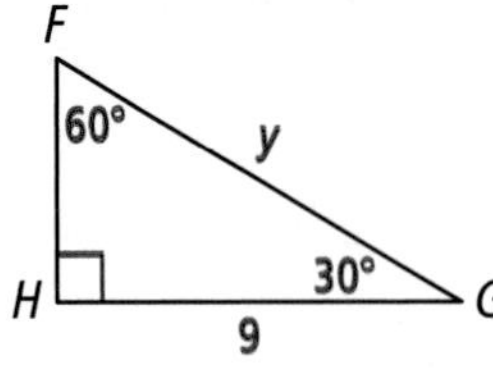


**b.** In $\triangle LMN$, what is the value of $z$?

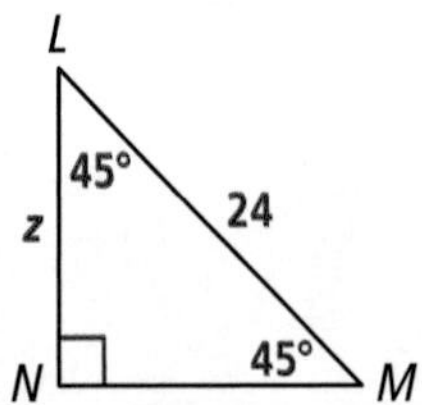

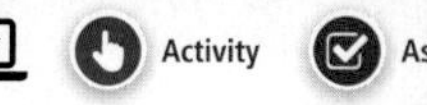


APPLICATION

## EXAMPLE 4 Use Trigonometric Ratios to Find Distances

**A plane takes off and climbs at a 12° angle. Is that angle sufficient enough to fly over an 11,088-foot mountain that is 12.5 miles from the runway or does the plane need to increase its angle of ascent?**

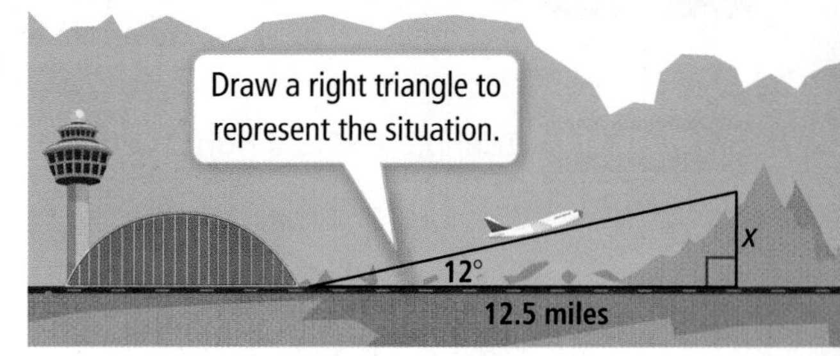


**STUDY TIP**
To choose the right trigonometric ratio, consider which side of the triangle you know and which side you need to find.

**Step 1** You know the length of the side adjacent to the 12° angle, so use the tangent ratio to find the altitude of the plane as it passes the mountain.

$$\tan 12^\circ = \frac{x}{12.5}$$

$$x = 12.5 \cdot \tan 12^\circ$$

$$\approx 2.66$$

Use a calculator.
12.5 TAN 12 ENTER

The altitude of the plane is about 2.66 miles.

**Step 2** Compare the altitude of the plane to the height of the mountain.

$$11{,}088 \text{ ft} \cdot \frac{1 \text{ mi}}{5{,}280 \text{ ft}} = 2.1 \text{ mi}$$

Write the height of the mountain in miles.

A 12° angle is sufficient because 2.1 mi < 2.66 mi.

**Try It!** **4.** If a plane climbs at 5° and flies 20 miles through the air as it climbs, what is the altitude of the airplane, to the nearest foot?

## EXAMPLE 5 Use Trigonometric Inverses to Find Angle Measures

**What are $m\angle A$ and $m\angle B$?**

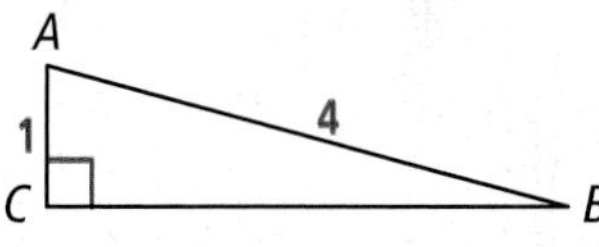


If you know the trigonometric ratio for an angle, you can use its inverse ($\sin^{-1}$, $\cos^{-1}$, or $\tan^{-1}$) to find the angle measure.

**USE APPROPRIATE TOOLS**
On many graphing calculators, you can use the 2nd key and the appropriate trigonometric function key to access the inverse functions.

Find $m\angle A$.

$$\cos A = \frac{1}{4}$$

$$\cos^{-1}(\cos A) = \cos^{-1}\left(\frac{1}{4}\right)$$

$$m\angle A = \cos^{-1}\left(\frac{1}{4}\right)$$

$$m\angle A \approx 75.5^\circ$$

Find $m\angle B$.

$$\sin B = \frac{1}{4}$$

$$\sin^{-1}(\sin B) = \sin^{-1}\left(\frac{1}{4}\right)$$

$$m\angle B = \sin^{-1}\left(\frac{1}{4}\right)$$

$$m\angle B \approx 14.5^\circ$$

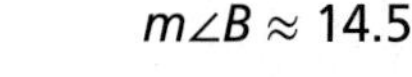

**Try It!** **5. a.** What is $m\angle P$?

**b.** What is $m\angle Q$?

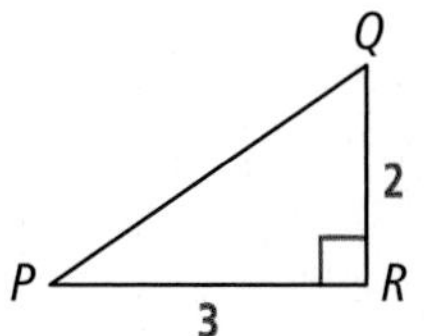

Concept Summary Assess

## CONCEPT SUMMARY Trigonometric Ratios

**WORDS** For a right triangle, **the trigonometric ratios sine, cosine,** and **tangent** relate the measure of an acute angle of the triangle to the lengths of the sides.

**DIAGRAM** Triangle $ABC$ is a right triangle.

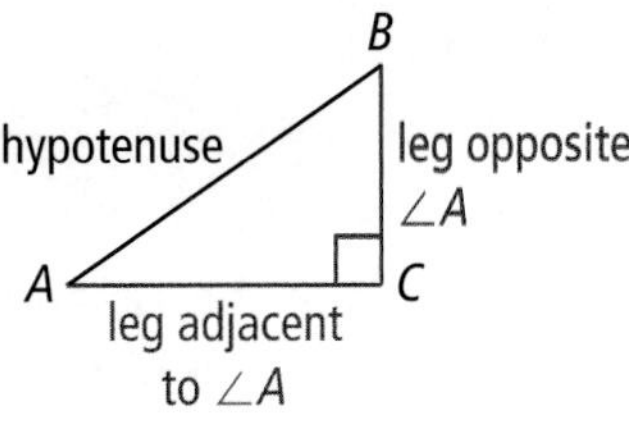


**SYMBOLS**

$$\sin A = \frac{\text{length of leg opposite } \angle A}{\text{length of hypotenuse}}$$

$$\cos A = \frac{\text{length of leg adjacent to } \angle A}{\text{length of hypotenuse}}$$

$$\tan A = \frac{\text{length of leg opposite } \angle A}{\text{length of leg adjacent to } \angle A}$$

## Do You UNDERSTAND?

1. **ESSENTIAL QUESTION** How do trigonometric ratios relate angle measures to side lengths of right triangles?

2. **Error Analysis** What is the error in this equation for a trigonometric ratio?

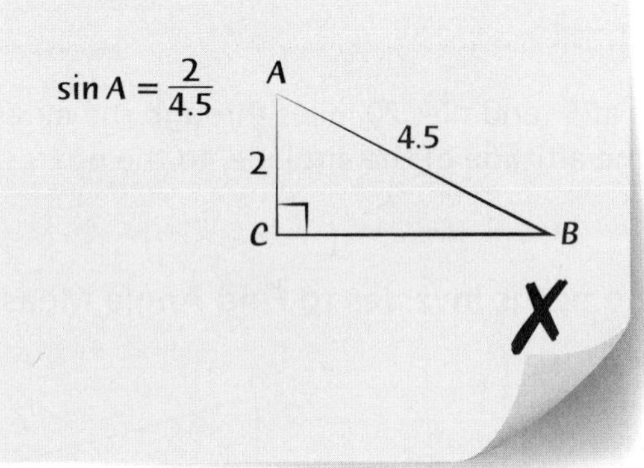


3. **Vocabulary** How are finding the inverses of trigonometric ratios similar to using inverse operations?

4. **Communicate Precisely** How is the sine ratio similar to the cosine ratio? How is it different?

5. **Look for Relationships** If $\sin A = \frac{a}{c}$, how could you use $a$ and $c$ to find $\cos A$?

6. **Reason** What is an expression for $d$ using $x°$, $y°$, and $h$?

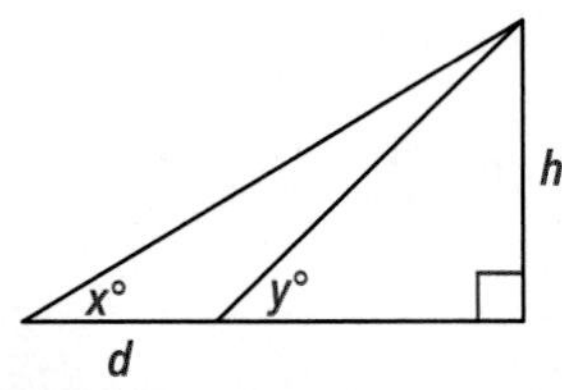


## Do You KNOW HOW?

**For Exercises 7–12, use △ABC to find each trigonometric ratio or angle measure.**

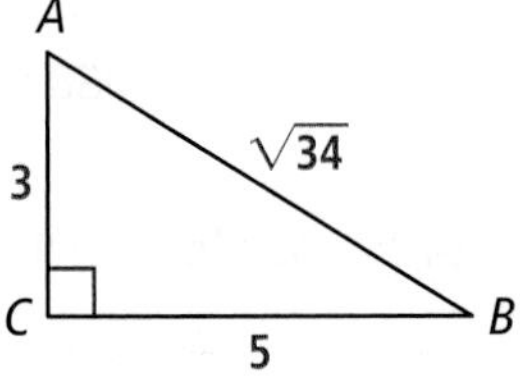


7. $\tan B$

8. $\cos B$

9. $\sin A$

10. $\tan A$

11. $m\angle B$

12. $m\angle A$

13. What are the sine and cosine of the smallest angle in the right triangle shown?

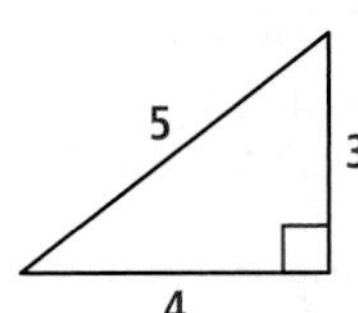


14. What is the measure of the largest acute angle in the right triangle shown?

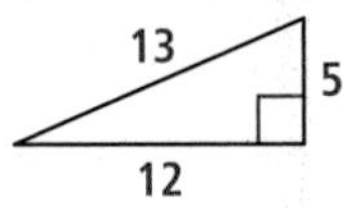


15. In the figure shown, what are $m\angle S$ and $m\angle T$?

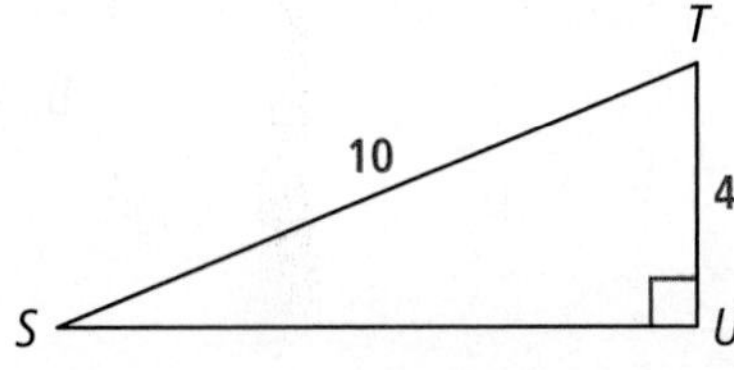

## PRACTICE & PROBLEM SOLVING

Scan for Multimedia

Practice Tutorial

Additional Exercises Available Online

### UNDERSTAND

16. **Error Analysis** Jacinta's teacher asks her to find the tangent of $\angle Y$. What is her error?

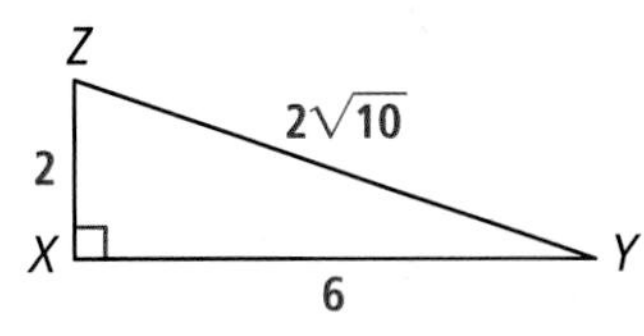


$\tan Y = \frac{XY}{XZ}$

$\tan Y = \frac{6}{2}$

$\tan Y = 3$

17. **Make Sense and Persevere** If $\sin B = 0.5$ in the triangle shown, what is an expression for $AB$?

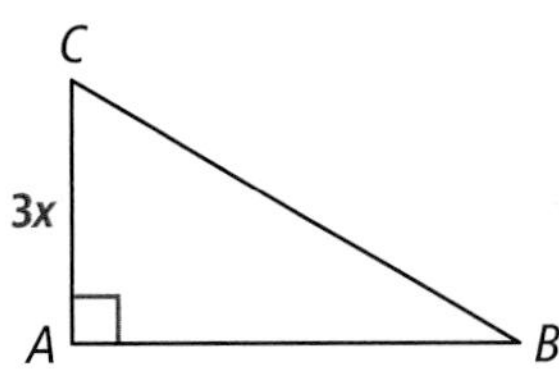


18. **Reason** Every tread of a staircase is 8 in. deep, and every riser is 6 in. high. How would you find the angle the staircase makes with the floor? Explain.

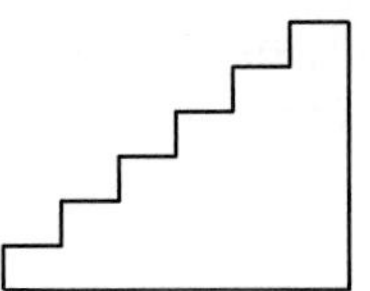

19. **Mathematical Connections** Find the values.

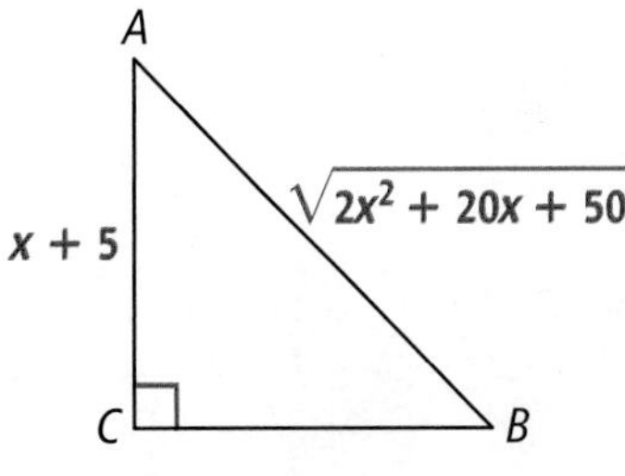


a. $\sin B$ b. $m\angle B$

20. **Higher Order Thinking** Why are the sine and cosine ratios of $x°$ never greater than one? Use the triangle below to explain your reasoning.

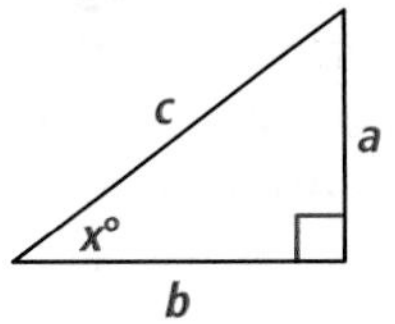


### PRACTICE

**For Exercises 21–23, write each ratio.** SEE EXAMPLE 1

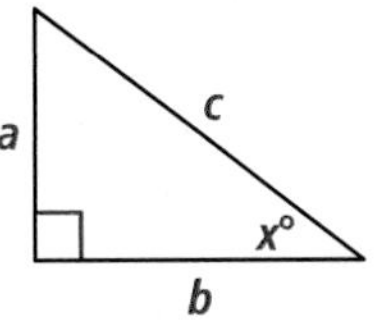


21. $\sin x°$ 22. $\cos x°$ 23. $\tan x°$

**For Exercises 24–29, find each value.** SEE EXAMPLE 2

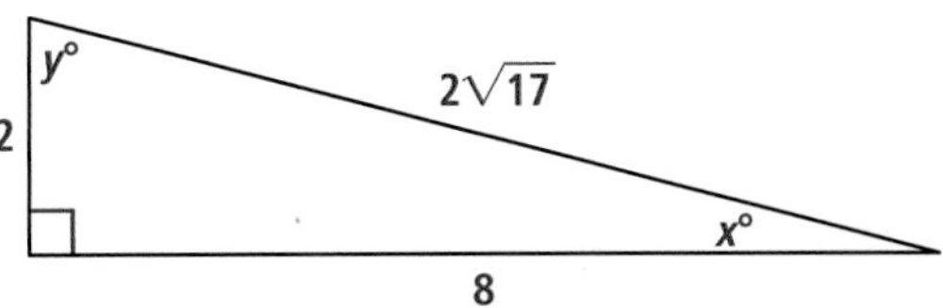


24. $\sin x°$ 25. $\cos x°$ 26. $\tan x°$

27. $\sin y°$ 28. $\cos y°$ 29. $\tan y°$

**For Exercises 30–35, find each value.** SEE EXAMPLE 3

30. $\sin 30°$ 31. $\cos 60°$ 32. $\sin 45°$

33. $\tan 45°$ 34. $\cos 30°$ 35. $\tan 60°$

**For Exercises 36 and 37, find each length.** SEE EXAMPLE 4

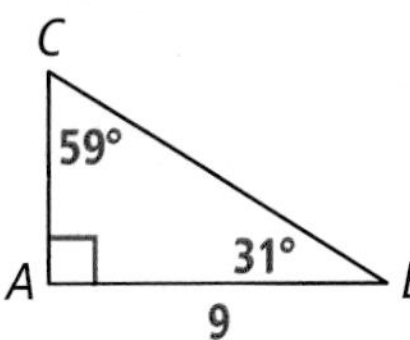


36. $AC$ 37. $BC$

**For Exercises 38–43, find the angle measures in each triangle.** SEE EXAMPLE 5

38. $m\angle B$

39. $m\angle C$

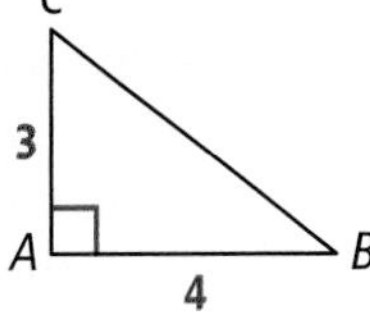


40. $m\angle E$

41. $m\angle F$

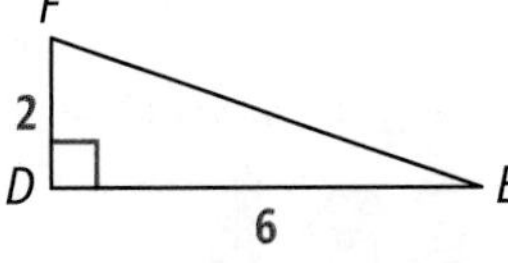


42. $m\angle K$

43. $m\angle L$

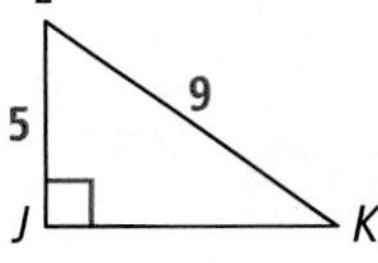

## APPLY

**44. Make Sense and Persevere** Workers need to make repairs on a building. A boom lift has maximum height of 60 ft at an angle of 48°. If the bottom of the boom is 60 ft from the building, can the boom reach the top of the building? Explain.

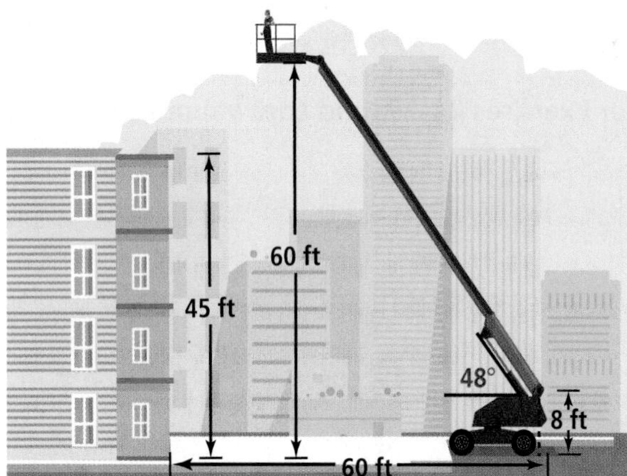


**45. Model With Mathematics** A coach draws up a play so a quarterback throws the football at the same time a receiver runs straight down the field. Suppose the quarterback throws the football at a speed of 20 ft/s and the receiver runs at a speed of 12 ft/s. At what angle $x°$ to the horizontal line must the quarterback throw the football in order for the receiver to catch it? Explain.

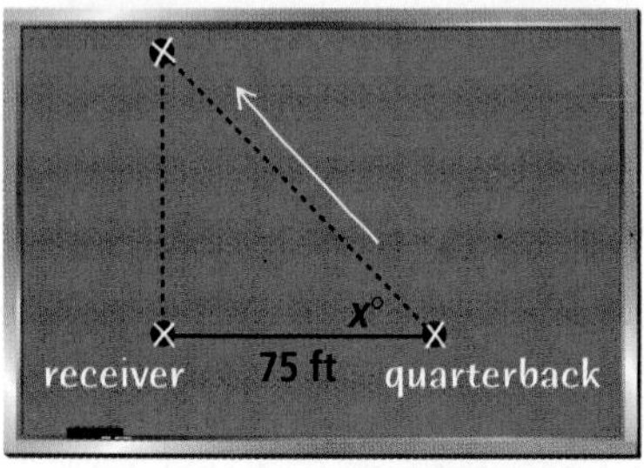


**46. Use Structure** Kelsey puts up an inflatable gorilla to advertise a sale. She realizes that she needs to secure the figure with rope. She estimates she needs to attach three pieces at the angles shown. How much rope does Kelsey need? Round to the nearest foot.

## ASSESSMENT PRACTICE

**47.** Match each expression to a trigonometric ratio.

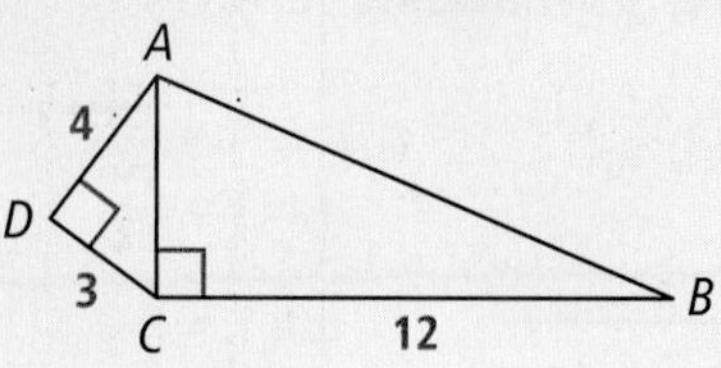


**I.** cos ∠$ACD$ **A.** $\frac{12}{13}$

**II.** tan ∠$ABC$ **B.** $\frac{4}{5}$

**III.** sin ∠$BAC$ **C.** $\frac{3}{5}$

**IV.** cos ∠$CAD$ **D.** $\frac{5}{12}$

**48. SAT/ACT** What is the value of cos $x°$?

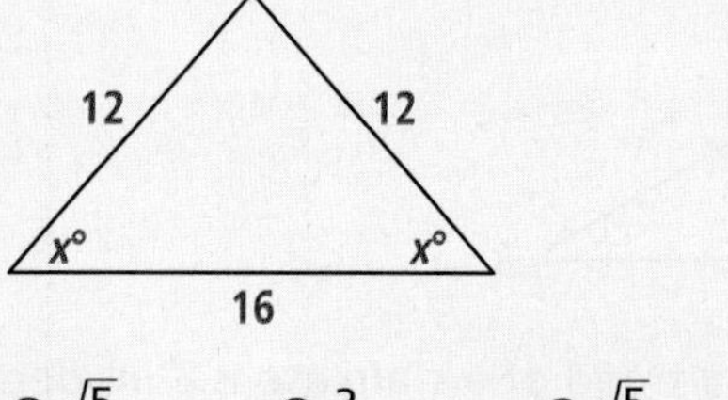


Ⓐ $\frac{\sqrt{5}}{2}$ Ⓑ $\frac{3}{2}$ Ⓒ $\frac{\sqrt{5}}{3}$ Ⓓ $\frac{2}{3}$

**49. Performance Task** Jacy anchors a retractable leash to a tree and attaches the leash to her dog's collar. When the dog fully extends the leash, the angle between the leash and the tree is 84°.

**Part A** If her neighbor's yard is 18 feet away from the tree, can Jacy's dog get into her neighbor's yard? If so, how far into the yard can the dog go? Round to nearest tenth of a foot.

**Part B** If Jacy wants to make sure her dog cannot get within 1 foot of her neighbor's yard, how high up the tree must she anchor the leash? Round to the nearest tenth of a foot.

# 8-3 The Law of Sines

I CAN… use the Law of Sines to solve problems.

VOCABULARY

- Law of Sines

## EXPLORE & REASON

**Consider the 30°-60°-90° triangle shown.**

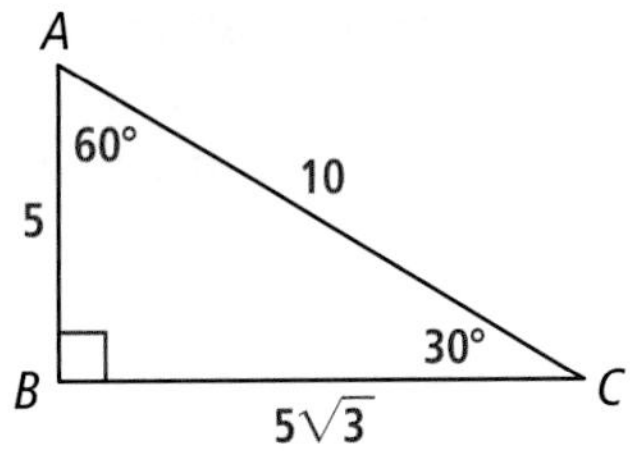


**A.** Calculate the values of the ratios $\frac{\sin A}{BC}$ and $\frac{\sin C}{AB}$. How are the values of the ratios related?

**B. Make Sense and Persevere** Do you think the ratios would have the same relationship in any 30°-60°-90° right triangle? Explain your answer.

## ESSENTIAL QUESTION

**How can the Law of Sines be used to determine side lengths and angle measures in acute and obtuse triangles?**

CONCEPTUAL UNDERSTANDING

## EXAMPLE 1 Explore the Sine Ratio

**How can you use the sine ratio to relate the lengths and angle measures in $\triangle ABC$?**

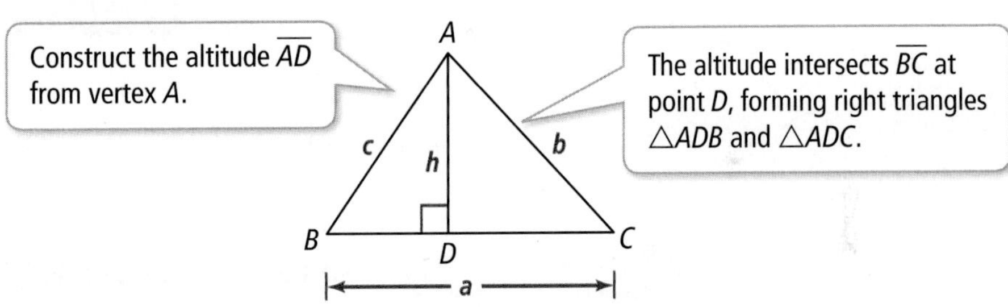

Construct the altitude $\overline{AD}$ from vertex $A$.
The altitude intersects $\overline{BC}$ at point $D$, forming right triangles $\triangle ADB$ and $\triangle ADC$.
A
c
h
b
B
D
C
a


Write equations for sin $B$ and sin $C$ using the right triangles.

$\sin B = \frac{h}{c}$ $\quad\quad$ $\sin C = \frac{h}{b}$

$c \sin B = h$ $\quad\quad$ $b \sin C = h$

Solve each equation for $h$.

**STUDY TIP**
Recall that the sine ratio relates the length of the opposite side to the length of the hypotenuse.

Set the two expressions for $h$ equal to each other.

$c \sin B = b \sin C$

$\frac{\sin B}{b} = \frac{\sin C}{c}$

The definition of the sine ratio only includes acute angles. For triangles with right and obtuse angles, you can extend the definition of sine and cosine to include these angles.

**Try It!** 1. For Example 1, show that $\frac{\sin A}{a} = \frac{\sin B}{b} = \frac{\sin C}{c}$.

## CONCEPT Law of Sines

For any $\triangle ABC$ with side lengths $a$, $b$, and $c$ opposite angles $A$, $B$, and $C$, respectively, the **Law of Sines** relates the sine of each angle to the length of the opposite side.

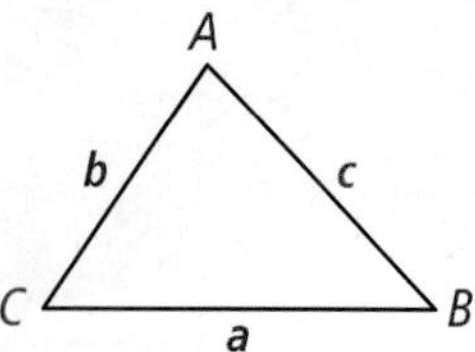


$$\frac{\sin A}{a} = \frac{\sin B}{b} = \frac{\sin C}{c}$$

## EXAMPLE 2 Use the Law of Sines to Find a Side Length

**For $\triangle XYZ$, what is $YZ$ to the nearest tenth?**

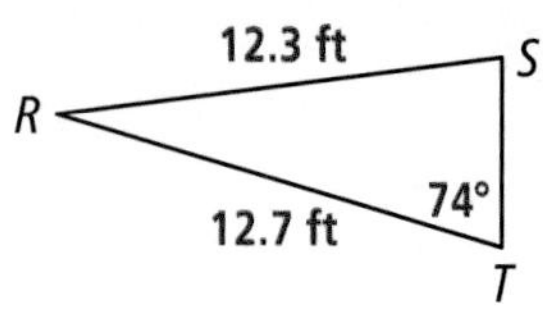


Identify pairs of known sides and angles.

- The measure of $\angle Z$ and the length of its opposite side $\overline{XY}$ are known.
- The measure of $\angle X$ is known. The length of $\overline{YZ}$ is the unknown quantity.

**COMMON ERROR**
Be careful to correctly write the ratio of the sine of an angle and its opposite side length. It may be helpful to draw an arrow from each angle that points to its opposite side.

Use the Law of Sines to write and solve an equation for $YZ$.

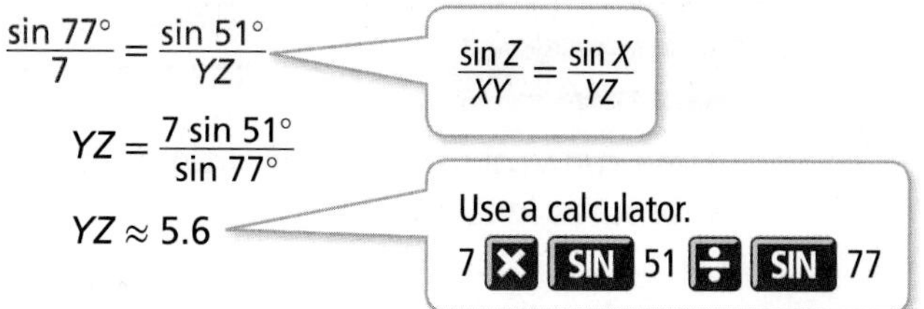

$$\frac{\sin 77^\circ}{7} = \frac{\sin 51^\circ}{YZ}$$

$\frac{\sin Z}{XY} = \frac{\sin X}{YZ}$

$$YZ = \frac{7 \sin 51^\circ}{\sin 77^\circ}$$

$$YZ \approx 5.6$$

Use a calculator.
7 × SIN 51 ÷ SIN 77

**Try It!** 2. In Example 2, what is $XZ$ to the nearest tenth?

## EXAMPLE 3 Use Law of Sines to Find the Measure of an Angle

**What are $m\angle R$ and $m\angle S$ in $\triangle RST$?**

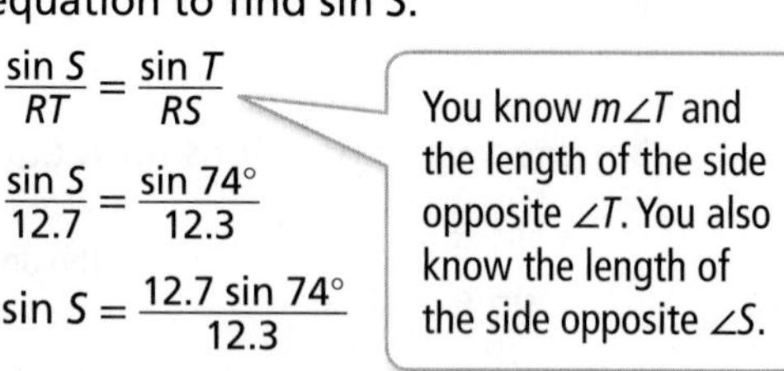


**Step 1** Use the Law of Sines to write and solve an equation to find sin $S$.

$$\frac{\sin S}{RT} = \frac{\sin T}{RS}$$

You know $m\angle T$ and the length of the side opposite $\angle T$. You also know the length of the side opposite $\angle S$.

$$\frac{\sin S}{12.7} = \frac{\sin 74^\circ}{12.3}$$

$$\sin S = \frac{12.7 \sin 74^\circ}{12.3}$$

$$\sin S \approx 0.9925$$

**Step 2** Use the inverse function $\sin^{-1}$ to find $m\angle S$.

$$\sin^{-1}(\sin S) = \sin^{-1}(0.9925)$$

$$m\angle S \approx 83$$

**Step 3** Find $m\angle R$.

$$m\angle R \approx 180 - 74 - 83$$

$$\approx 23$$

CONTINUED ON THE NEXT PAGE

**Try It!** **3. a.** What is $m\angle N$?

**b.** What is $m\angle O$?

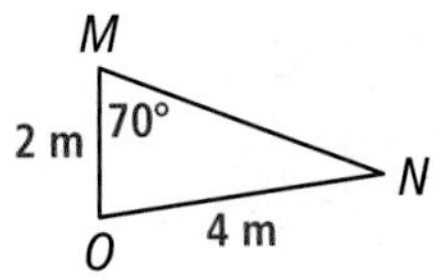

APPLICATION

## EXAMPLE 4 Apply the Law of Sines

**The map shows the path a pilot flew between Omaha and Chicago in order to avoid a thunderstorm. How much longer is this route than the direct route to Chicago?**

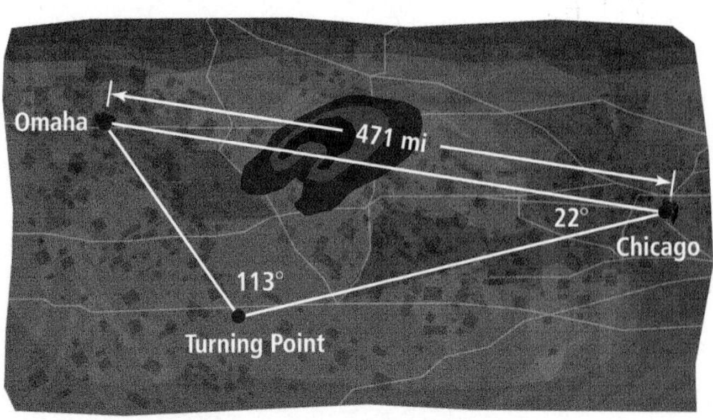


**MAKE SENSE AND PERSEVERE**
Think about what the problem is asking for. Which distances are you supposed to find?

**Step 1** Let $x$ represent the distance from the turning point to Omaha. Find $x$.

Use the Law of Sines.

$$\frac{\sin 113^\circ}{471} = \frac{\sin 22^\circ}{x}$$

$$x = \frac{471 \sin 22^\circ}{\sin 113^\circ}$$

$$x \approx 191.7$$

**Step 2** Let $y$ represent the distance from Chicago to the turning point. Find $y$.

First determine the measure of the angle opposite $y$.

$$180^\circ - 113^\circ - 22^\circ = 45^\circ$$

Then use the Law of Sines.

$$\frac{\sin 113^\circ}{471} = \frac{\sin 45^\circ}{y}$$

$$y = \frac{471 \sin 45^\circ}{\sin 113^\circ}$$

$$y \approx 361.8$$

**Step 3** Find the total distance the pilot flew.

$$191.7 \text{ mi} + 361.8 \text{ mi} = 553.5 \text{ mi}$$

The pilot flew 553.5 mi – 471 mi = 82.5 mi farther.

**Try It!** **4.** Suppose the pilot chose to fly north of the storm. How much farther is that route than the direct route?

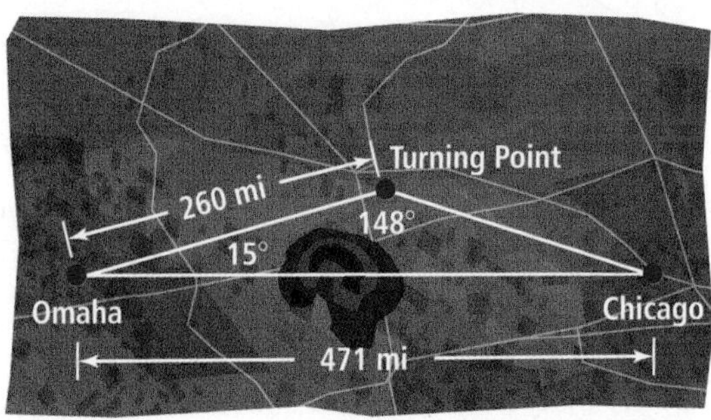

## CONCEPT SUMMARY Law of Sines

**WORDS** For any $\triangle ABC$ with side lengths $a$, $b$, and $c$ opposite angles $A$, $B$, and $C$, respectively, the Law of Sines relates the sine of each angle to the length of the opposite side.

**DIAGRAM**

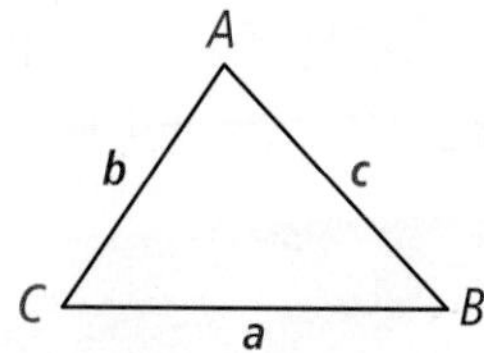


**SYMBOLS**

$$\frac{\sin A}{a} = \frac{\sin B}{b} = \frac{\sin C}{c}$$

## Do You UNDERSTAND?

1. **ESSENTIAL QUESTION** How can the Law of Sines be used to determine side lengths and angle measures in acute and obtuse triangles?

2. **Error Analysis** Amelia is asked to find a missing side length in $\triangle RST$. What is her error?

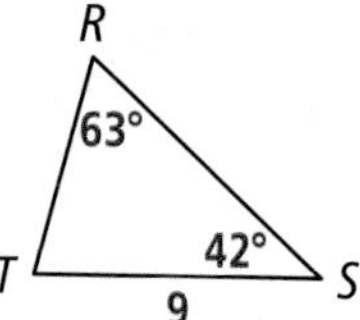


$$\frac{\sin R}{RT} = \frac{\sin S}{ST}$$

$$\frac{\sin 63°}{RT} = \frac{\sin 42°}{9}$$

$$RT = \frac{9 \sin 63°}{\sin 42°} \approx 12$$

3. **Vocabulary** What are the pairs of opposite angles and side lengths in $\triangle LMN$? What does the Law of Sines help you find?

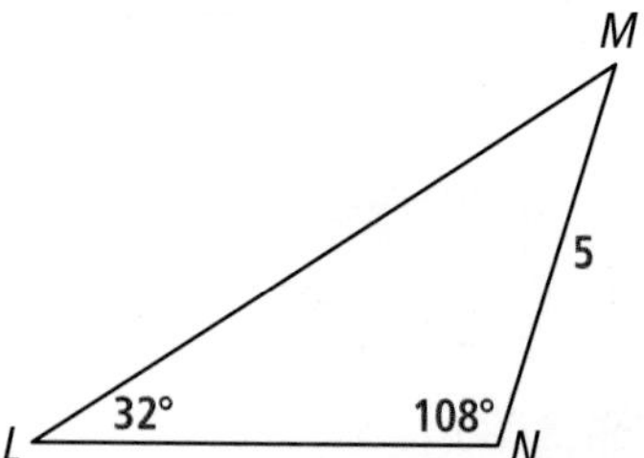


4. **Reason** Can you find all the missing parts of a triangle using the Law of Sines if you know the lengths of all three sides? Explain.

## Do You KNOW HOW?

**For Exercises 5 and 6, list the parts of each triangle you can determine using the Law of Sines.**

5.

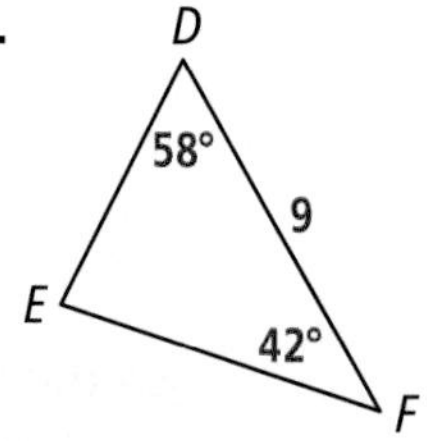


6.

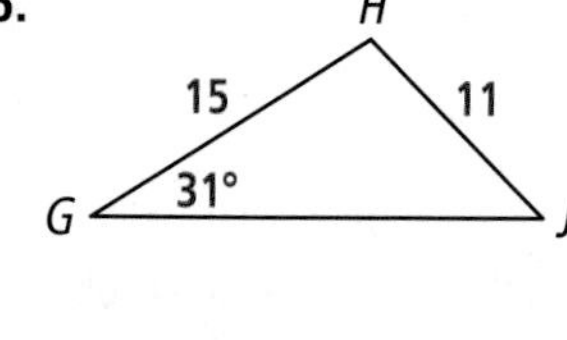


**For Exercises 7 and 8, use $\triangle QRS$.**

7. What are $m\angle Q$ and $m\angle R$?

8. What is the perimeter of $\triangle QRS$?

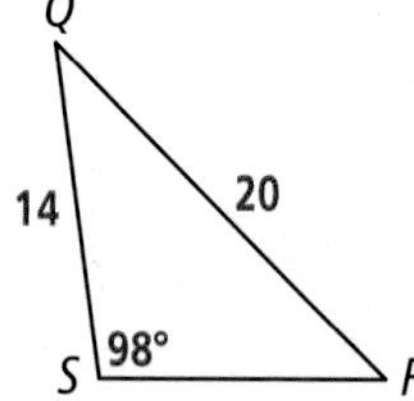


**For Exercises 9 and 10, use $\triangle XYZ$.**

9. What is $XY$?

10. What is $XZ$?

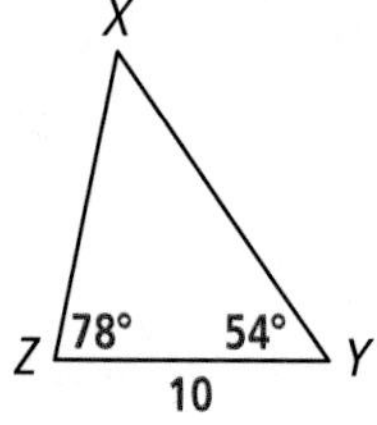


11. What are $AB$ and $BC$?

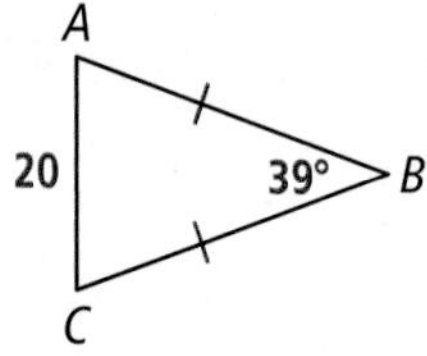


12. What is the perimeter of $\triangle TUV$?

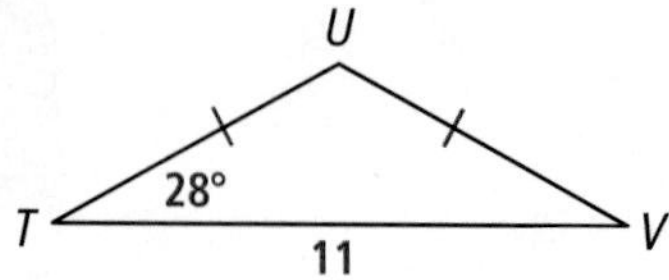

# PRACTICE & PROBLEM SOLVING

Scan for Multimedia

Practice | Tutorial

Additional Exercises Available Online

## UNDERSTAND

**13. Error Analysis** Kimberly is asked to find $m\angle M$. What is her error?

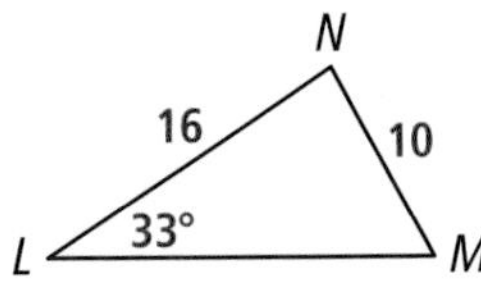


$$\frac{\sin M}{16} = \frac{\sin L}{10}$$

$$\sin M = \frac{16 \cdot \sin 33^\circ}{10}$$

$$m\angle M = 0.8714$$

✗

**14. Construct Arguments** Suppose you only know the lengths and angle measures of two triangles used to show they are congruent by SAS. Can you find the missing angle measures and side lengths of the triangles using the Law of Sines? Explain.

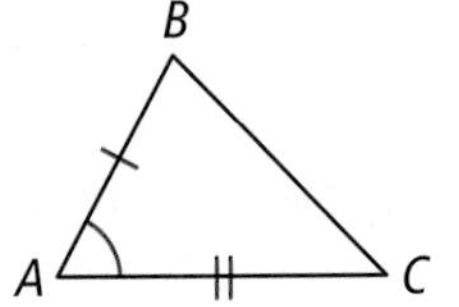


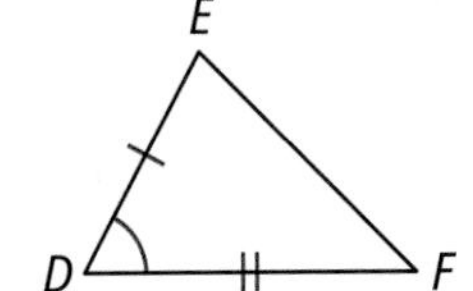


**15. Communicate Precisely** The measures of two angles are given along with the measure of the side opposite the third angle of a triangle. How can the Law of Sines be used to find missing angle measures and side lengths of the triangle? Explain.

**16. Mathematical Connections** What is $AC$? Use both the Distance Formula and the Law of Sines. How do the values compare? Explain.

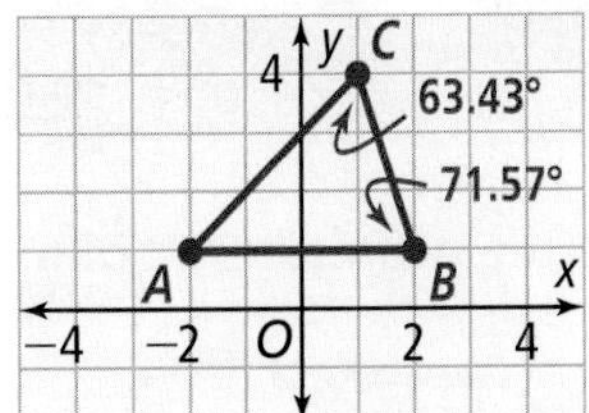


**17. Reason** Explain how to use the Law of Sines to find the perimeter of $\triangle PQR$. Then write an expression for the perimeter.

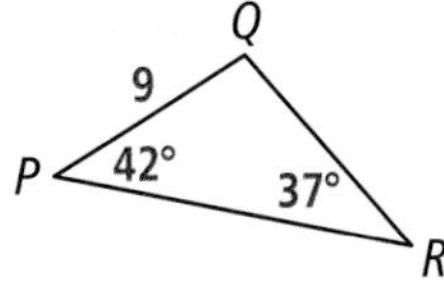


## PRACTICE

**For Exercises 18–23, find each length $x$. Round to the nearest tenth.** SEE EXAMPLES 1 AND 2

**18.**

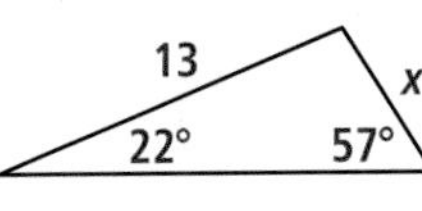


**19.**

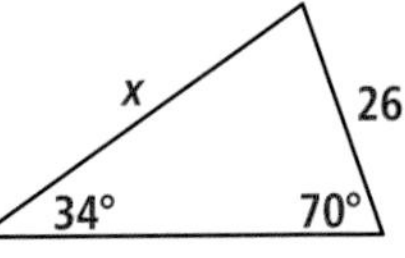


**20.**

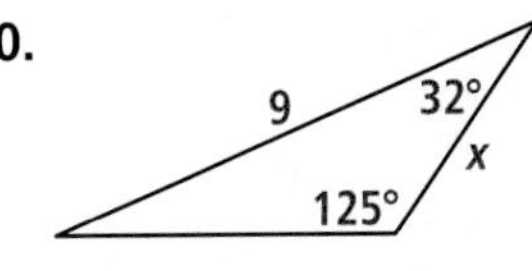


**21.**

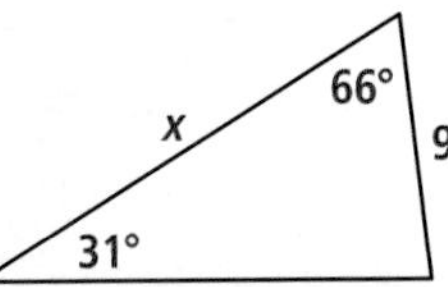


**22.**

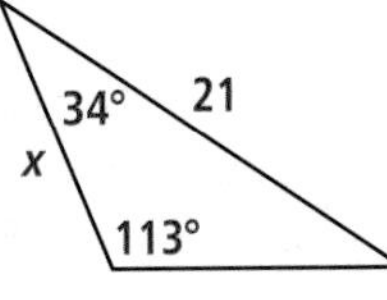


**23.**

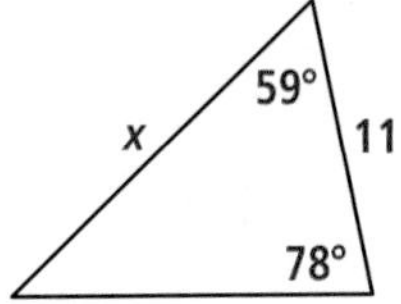


**For Exercises 24–29, find each angle measure $x°$. Round to the nearest tenth.** SEE EXAMPLE 3

**24.**

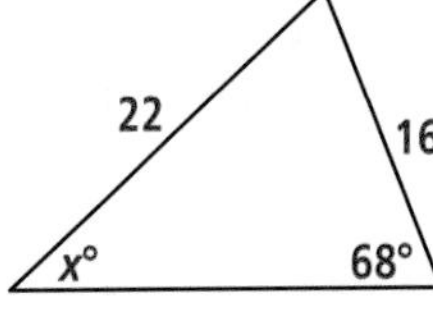


**25.**

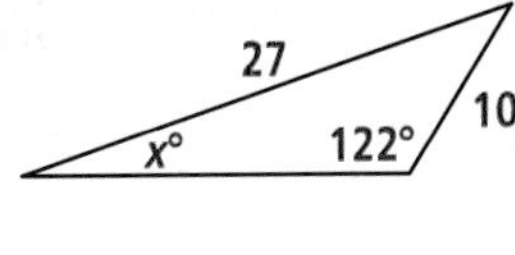


**26.**

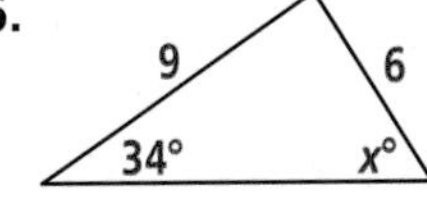


**27.**

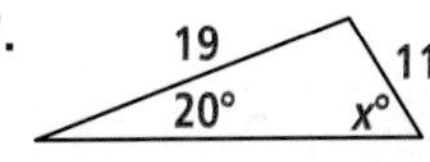


**28.**

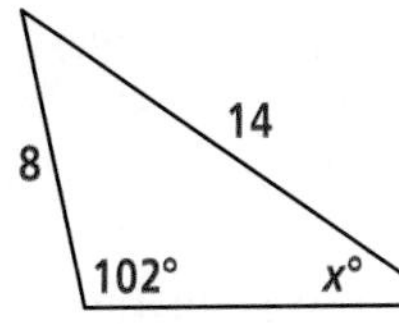


**29.**

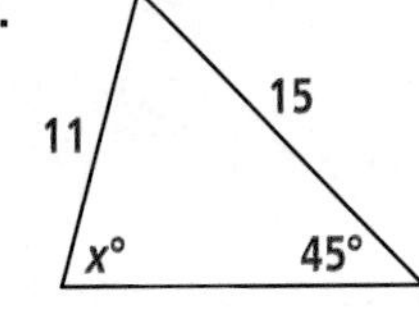


**For Exercises 30–33, find the perimeter of each triangle. Round to the nearest tenth.** SEE EXAMPLE 4

**30.**

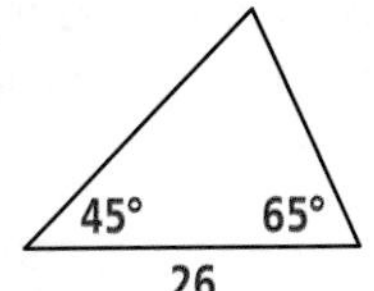


**31.**

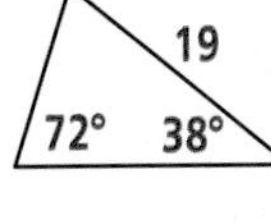


**32.**

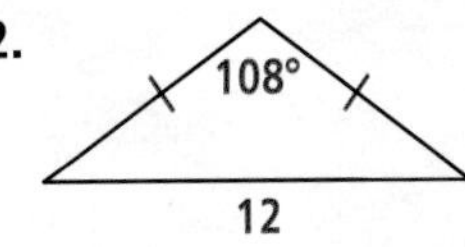


**33.**

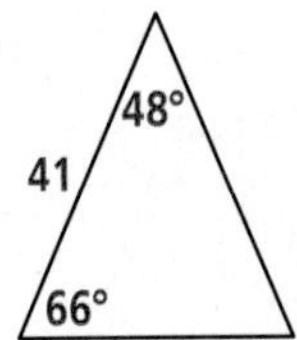

# PRACTICE & PROBLEM SOLVING

Practice Tutorial

Mixed Review Available Online

## APPLY

**34. Make Sense and Persevere** To find the height of a tree, a forester uses a clinometer to measure the angle to the top of the tree. She then measures again at a distance 8 feet farther away. What is the height of the tree? Round to the nearest foot.

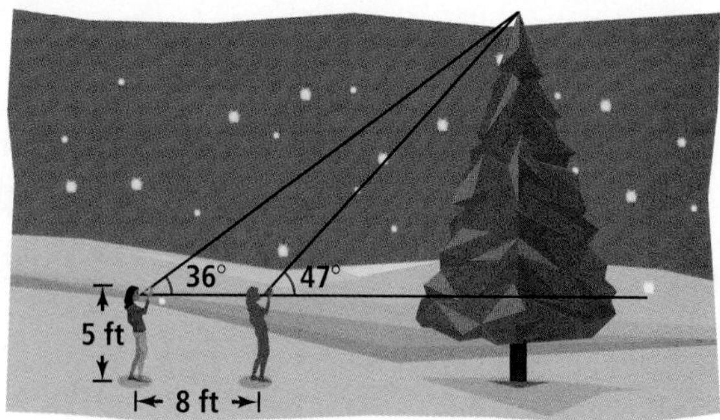


**35. Model With Mathematics** At point *A*, the pilot of a plane looks down at an angle of 7° at the landing strip. After flying up to point *B*, the pilot looks down at an angle of 9° to see the landing strip. What is the distance from point *B* to the landing strip if the distance from point *A* to point *B* is 1,100 ft? Round to the nearest foot.

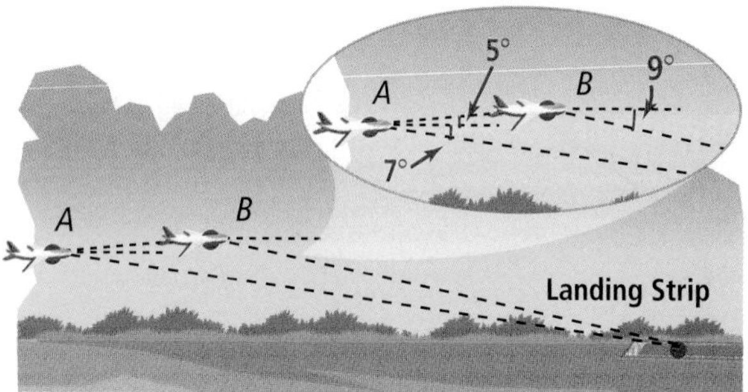


**36. Higher Order Thinking** A boat is cruising due east. At point *X*, the captain measures the angle east of north to a pier. At point *Y*, he again measures the angle east of north to the pier. A restricted area with radius 2.5 miles is centered at the end of the pier. Does the boat enter the restricted area? Explain.

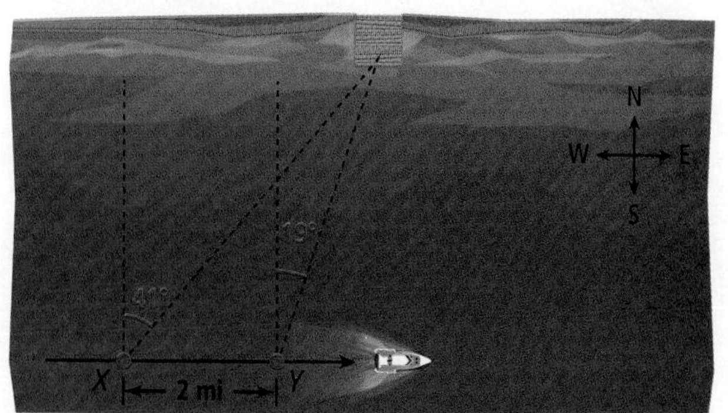


## ASSESSMENT PRACTICE

**37.** What is the value of *x*? Round to the nearest tenth.

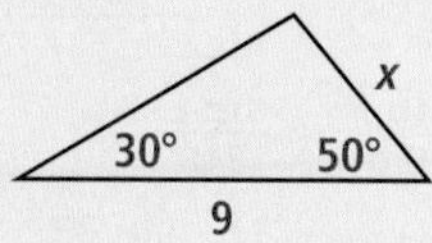


**38. SAT/ACT** What is the measure of the angle made by the roads at Bigville?

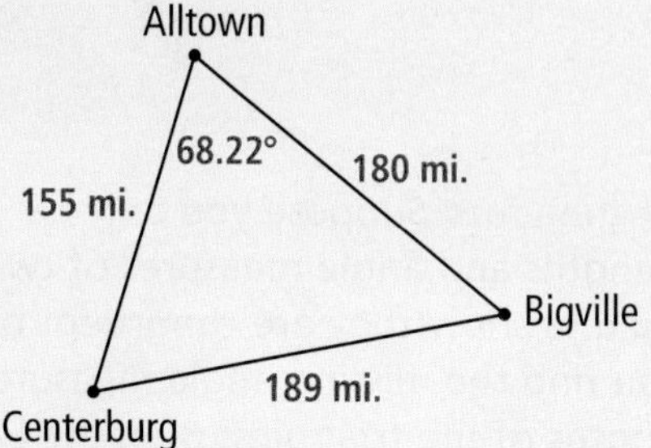


Ⓐ 55.10°

Ⓑ 72.28°

Ⓒ 49.60°

Ⓓ 40.40°

**39. Performance Task** An engineer is designing a walkway for an aquarium, but she only receives the partial information shown for the supports of the walkway. She must determine the lengths of the remaining supports to complete the design.

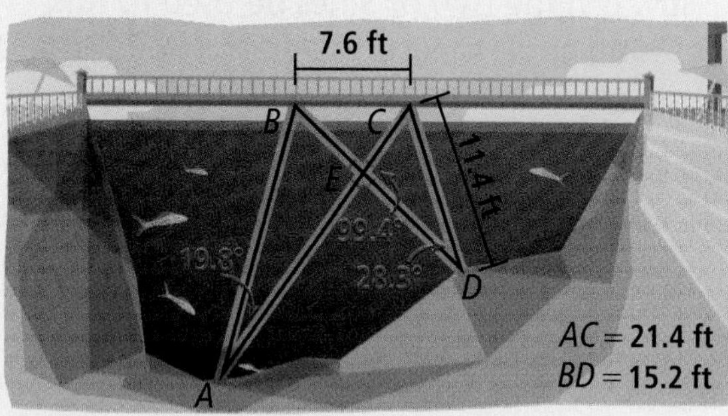


**Part A** What is *AB* to the nearest tenth of a foot?

**Part B** The engineer decides she wants beams from point *A* to the left end of the walkway and from point *D* to the right end of the walkway. Is there enough information given to find the lengths? If so, find the lengths. If not, explain what other information she needs.

Activity Assess

# 8-4 The Law of Cosines

**I CAN…** use the Law of Cosines to solve problems.

**VOCABULARY**

- Law of Cosines

## EXPLORE & REASON

**Use $\triangle ABC$ to answer the questions.**

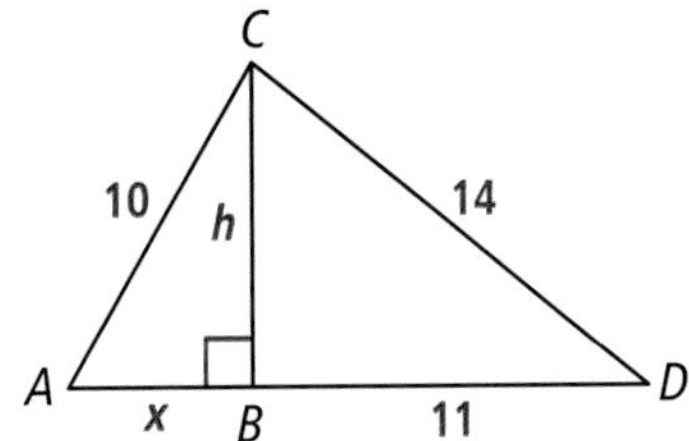


**A.** Write equations for the side lengths of $\triangle ABC$ and $\triangle CBD$ using the Pythagorean Theorem.

**B.** Use a system of equations to solve for $x$.

**C.** **Use Structure** How can you use the information you found to determine $m\angle A$?

## ESSENTIAL QUESTION

**How can the Law of Cosines be used to determine side lengths and angle measures of acute and obtuse triangles?**

CONCEPTUAL UNDERSTANDING

## EXAMPLE 1 Develop the Law of Cosines with Trigonometry

**Triangle $ABC$ is not a right triangle. How can you use a cosine ratio to write an equation relating the side lengths $a$, $b$, and $c$?**

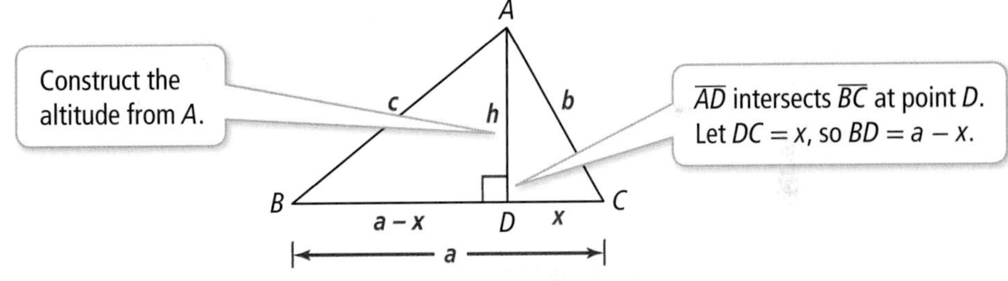


**USE STRUCTURE**
When constructing auxiliary lines, look for ones that result in right angles, right triangles, parallel lines, or other convenient geometric relationships.

Use the Pythagorean Theorem with $\triangle ABD$. Then distribute and combine like terms.

$$c^2 = (a - x)^2 + h^2$$

$$c^2 = a^2 - 2ax + x^2 + h^2$$

$$c^2 = a^2 - 2ax + b^2$$

$\triangle ACD$ is a right triangle, so $x^2 + h^2 = b^2$. Substitute $b^2$ for $x^2 + h^2$.

$$c^2 = a^2 - 2ab(\cos C) + b^2$$

Since $\cos C = \frac{x}{b}$, $x = b(\cos C)$. Substitute $b(\cos C)$ for $x$.

$$c^2 = a^2 + b^2 - 2ab \cos C$$

Thus, given side lengths $a$ and $b$ of a triangle and the included angle measure, you can find the length $c$ of the third side by taking the square root of the expression on the right side of the equation.

**Try It!** **1.** Use the same method as in Example 1 to write equations for $a^2$ using $\cos A$ and $b^2$ using $\cos B$.

## CONCEPT Law of Cosines

For any $\triangle ABC$, the **Law of Cosines** relates the cosine of each angle to the side lengths of the triangle.

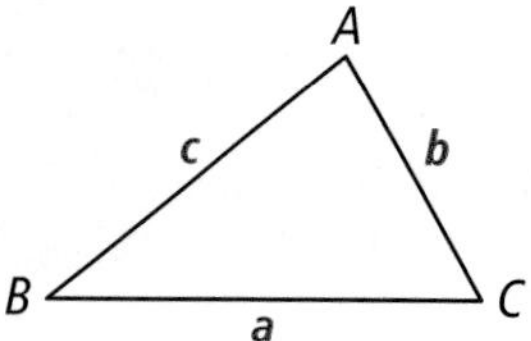


$$a^2 = b^2 + c^2 - 2bc \cos A$$

$$b^2 = a^2 + c^2 - 2ac \cos B$$

$$c^2 = a^2 + b^2 - 2ab \cos C$$

## EXAMPLE 2 Use the Law of Cosines to Find a Side Length

**What is $BC$ to the nearest tenth?**

The side length opposite $\angle A$ is unknown. You know two side lengths and the measure of their included angle, $\angle A$.

Use the Law of Cosines to write and solve an equation for $BC$.

$$BC^2 = AB^2 + AC^2 - 2(AB)(AC) \cos A$$

$$BC^2 \approx 8^2 + 10^2 - 2(8)(10)(0.5446)$$

$$BC^2 \approx 76.864$$

$$BC \approx 8.8$$

**USE STRUCTURE**
What information does the Law of Cosines provide that the Law of Sines does not?

 **Try It!** **2. a.** What is $DE$?

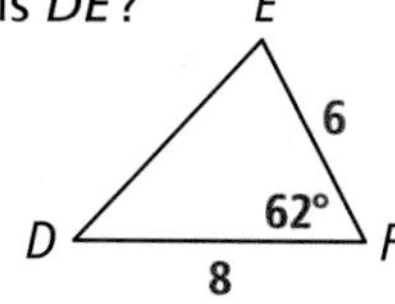


**b.** What is $GH$?

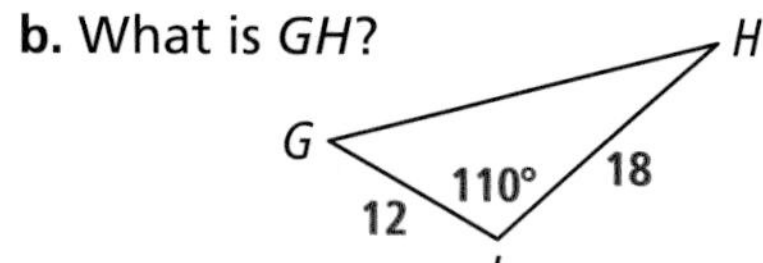


## EXAMPLE 3 Use the Law of Cosines to Find an Angle Measure

**The optimal tilt for Keenan's solar panel is between 58° and 60° to the horizontal. Has Keenan placed his solar panel at an optimal angle?**

Write an equation using the Law of Cosines. Then use the inverse cosine to find $m\angle P$.

$$QR^2 = PR^2 + PQ^2 - 2(PQ)(QR)\cos P$$

$$19^2 = 18^2 + 20^2 - 2(18)(20)\cos P$$

$$\cos P = \frac{-363}{-720}$$

$$\cos P \approx 0.5042$$

$$m\angle P \approx 59.72°$$

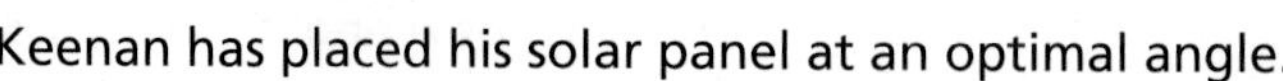

Keenan has placed his solar panel at an optimal angle.

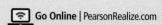

CONTINUED ON THE NEXT PAGE

**COMMON ERROR**
In applying the Law of Cosines, be sure to correctly place the included angle measure and the length of the side opposite the include angle on opposite sides of the equation.

 **Try It!** **3. a.** What is $m\angle X$?

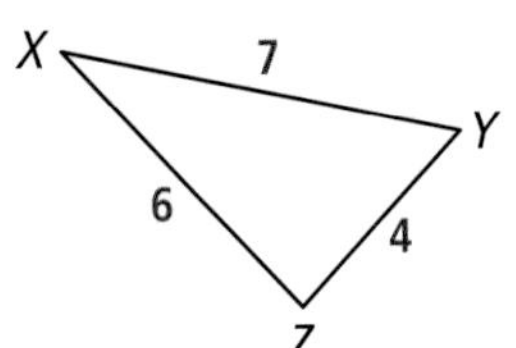


**b.** What is $m\angle P$?

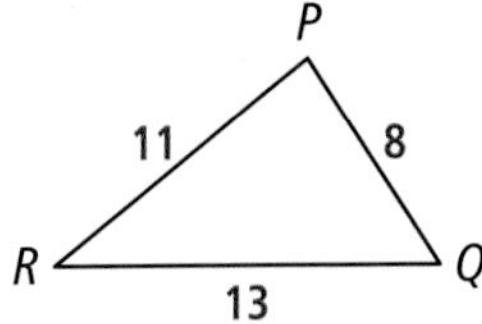


APPLICATION

## EXAMPLE 4 Use the Law of Cosines to Solve a Problem

**The district ranger wants to build a new ranger station at the location of the fire tower because it would be closer to Bald Mountain than the old station is. Is the district ranger correct? Explain.**

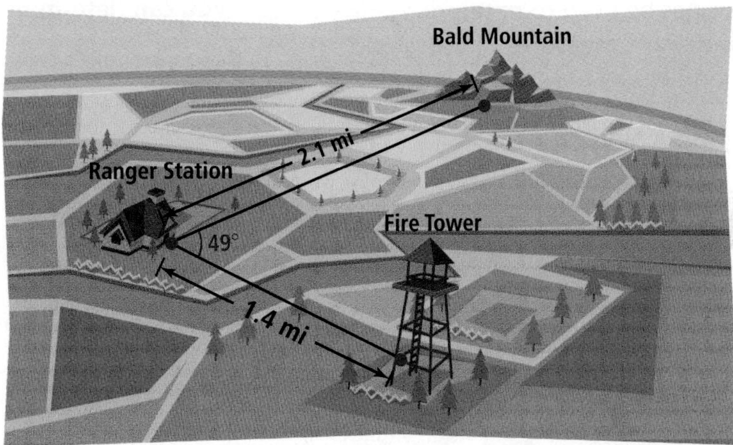


**Formulate** The ranger station, Bald Mountain, and the fire tower form the vertices of a triangle. Label the ranger station vertex $A$, Bald Mountain vertex $B$, and the fire tower vertex $C$. Draw the triangle.

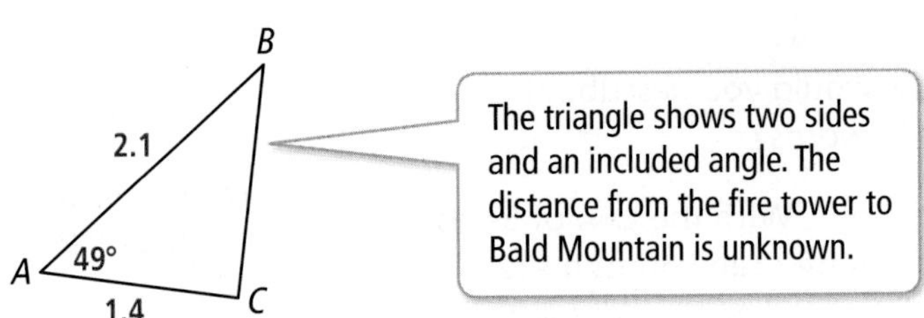


**Compute** Use the Law of Cosines to write an equation for the unknown.

$$BC^2 = AC^2 + AB^2 - 2(AC)(AB)\cos A$$

$$BC^2 = 1.4^2 + 2.1^2 - 2(1.4)(2.1)(\cos 49°)$$

Substitute the known values and solve.

$$BC^2 \approx 2.512$$

$$BC \approx 1.6$$

**Interpret** The distance from the fire tower to Bald Mountain is about 1.6 miles, so the district ranger is correct that a new station at the fire tower would be closer.

 **Try It!** **4.** In Example 4, what is the angle that the new path forms with the old path at Bald Mountain?

## CONCEPT SUMMARY Law of Cosines

**WORDS** For any $\triangle ABC$, the Law of Cosines relates the cosine of each angle to the side lengths of the triangle.

**SYMBOLS** $a^2 = b^2 + c^2 - 2bc \cos A$

$b^2 = a^2 + c^2 - 2ac \cos B$

$c^2 = a^2 + b^2 - 2ab \cos C$

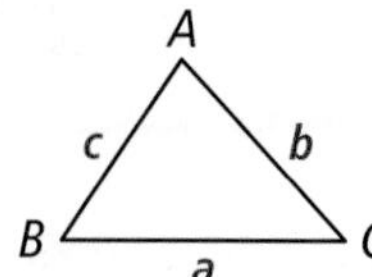


## Do You UNDERSTAND?

1. **ESSENTIAL QUESTION** How can the Law of Cosines be used to determine side lengths and angle measures of acute and obtuse triangles?

2. **Error Analysis** Cameron is asked to find $DE$. What is his error?

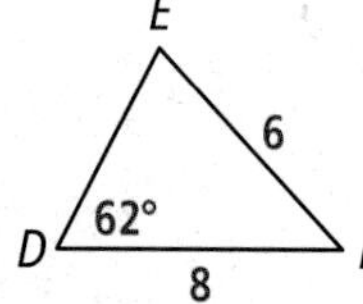


$DE^2 = DF^2 + EF^2 - 2(DF)(EF)\cos F$
$DE^2 = 8^2 + 6^2 - 2(8)(6)\cos 62°$
$DE^2 = 54.930\ldots$
$DE = 7.411\ldots$

3. **Vocabulary** How would you describe the Law of Cosines in words?

4. **Construct Arguments** With the Law of Sines and the Law of Cosines, can you find the missing side lengths and angle measures of any triangle for which you know any three parts? Explain.

5. **Reason** Use the Law of Cosines and the Pythagorean Theorem with $\triangle ABC$ to show that $\cos 90° = 0$.

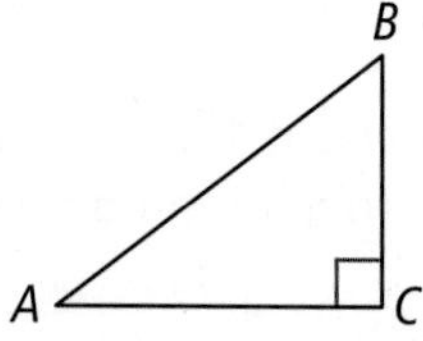


## Do You KNOW HOW?

**For Exercises 6–9, list the parts of each triangle you can determine using the Law of Cosines.**

6.

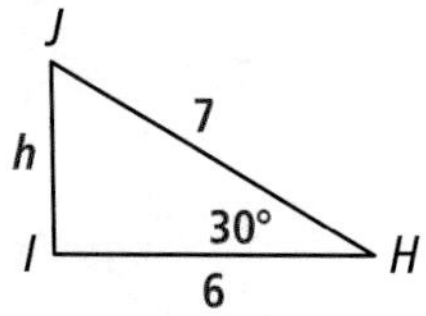

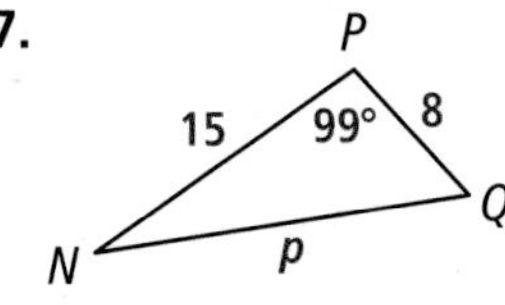


7.

8.

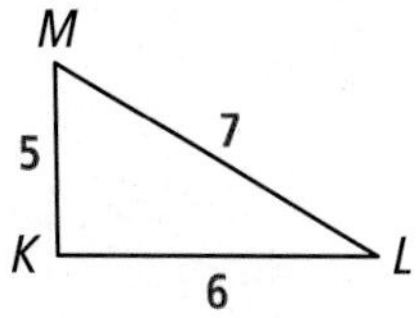

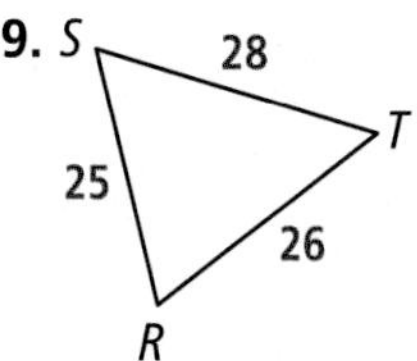


9.

10. What is $PR$ to the nearest tenth?

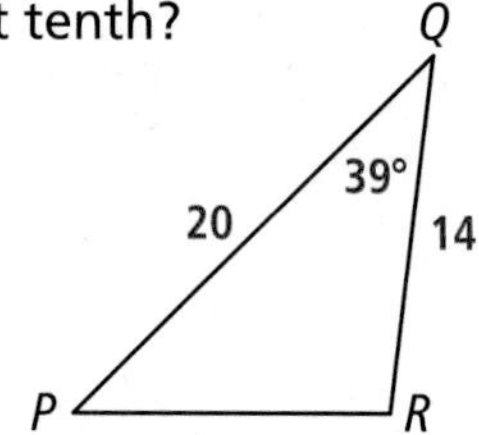


11. What is $m\angle B$ to the nearest tenth of a degree?

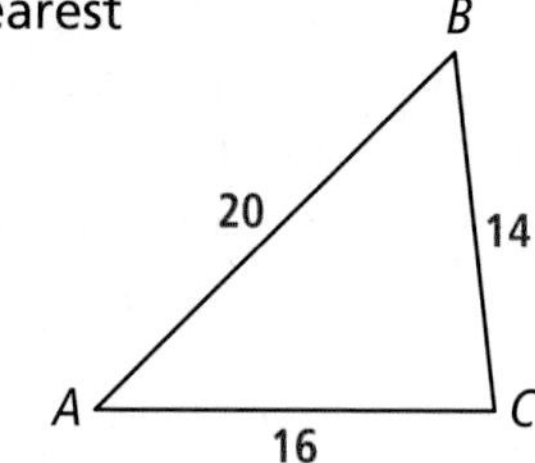

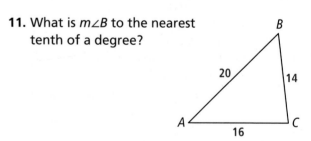

12. Use the Law of Cosines to find the diagonal of the parallelogram.

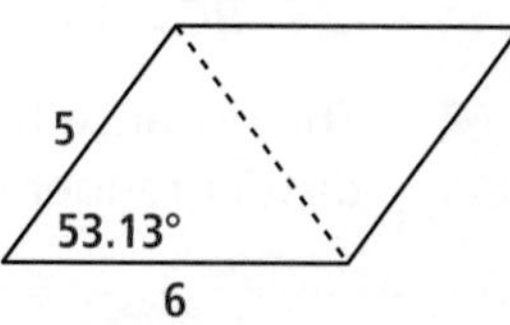

## PRACTICE & PROBLEM SOLVING

Scan for Multimedia

Practice Tutorial

Additional Exercises Available Online

### UNDERSTAND

**13. Construct Arguments** How is the Law of Cosines used to find missing angle measures if the side lengths of a triangle are given? Explain.

**14. Error Analysis** Tavon is asked to find *EF*. What error does Tavon make?

$EF^2 = DF^2 + DE^2 - 2(EF)(DE)\cos D$
$EF^2 = 8^2 + 10^2 - 2(8)(10)\cos 44^\circ$
$EF^2 \approx 64 + 100 - 160 \cdot 0.7193$
$EF \approx 48.91$

X

**15. Higher Order Thinking** Use the diagram to show that for acute angle $x^\circ$, $\cos(180 - x)^\circ = -\frac{a}{c}$. *Hint:* Apply the Law of Cosines to $\triangle ABD$ and write an equation involving $\cos(180 - x)^\circ$. Then, for $\triangle ABC$, use the relationship $a^2 + b^2 = c^2$.

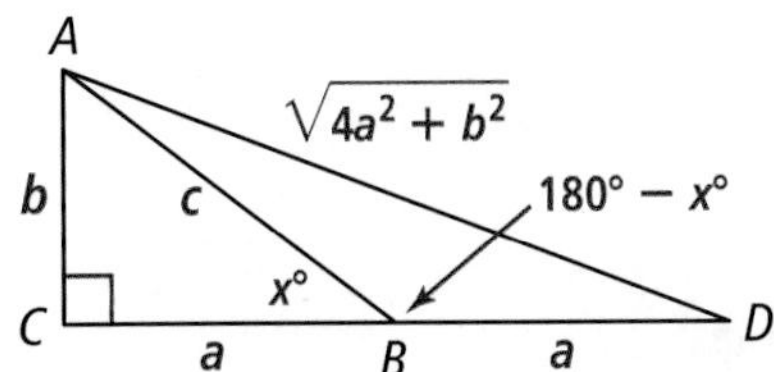


**16. Generalize** Suppose you know two of the side lengths of a triangle and the measure of one of the angles. How do you choose whether to find the third side length using the Law of Sines or the Law of Cosines? Explain.

**17. Look for Relationships** Consider $\triangle ABC$.

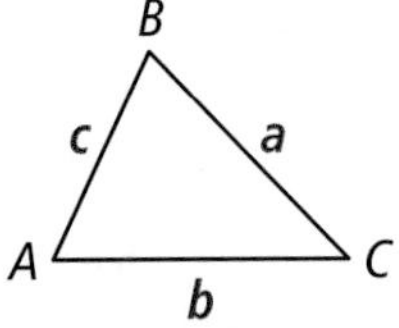


**a.** How would you find $m\angle A$ if you were given *a*, *b*, and *c*? Include an equation in your explanation.

**b.** How would you find *a* if you were given $m\angle A$, *b*, and *c*? Include an equation in your explanation.

### PRACTICE

**For Exercises 18 and 19, use $\triangle DEF$. Find an equation for each length.** SEE EXAMPLE 1

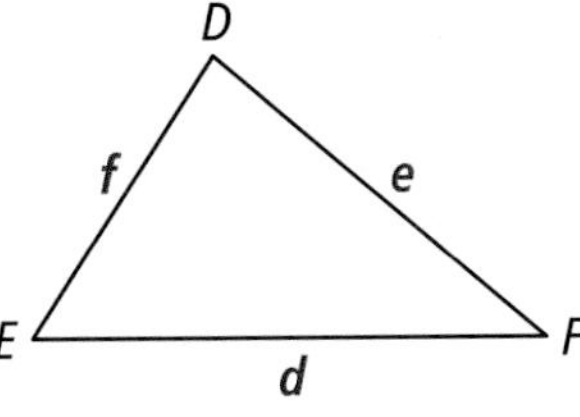


**18.** length *e*

**19.** length *f*

**For Exercises 20–23, find *x* to the nearest tenth.**
SEE EXAMPLE 2

**20.**

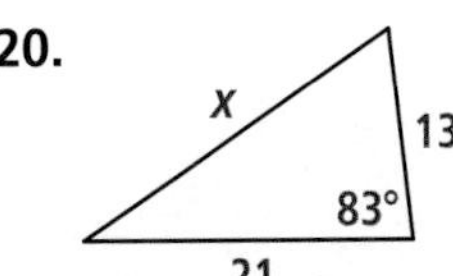


**21.**

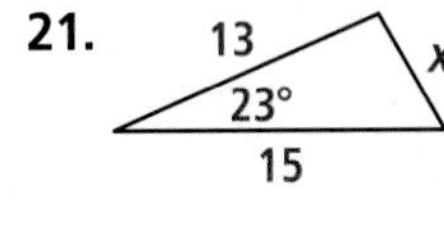


**22.**

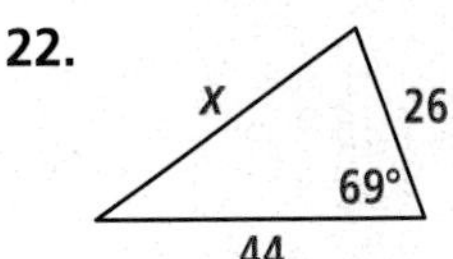


**23.**

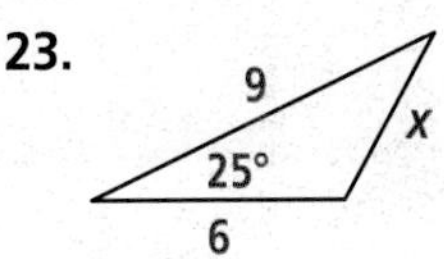


**For Exercises 24–27, find *x* to the nearest tenth.**
SEE EXAMPLE 3

**24.**

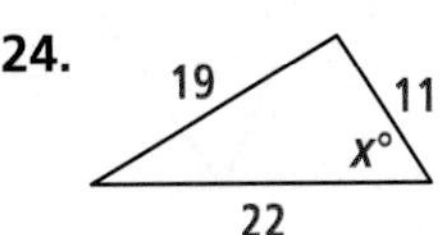


**25.**

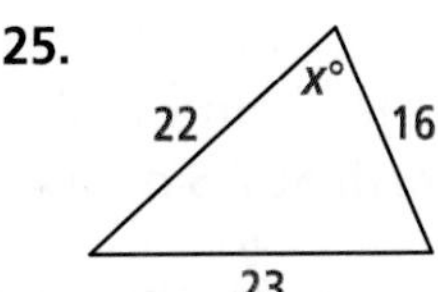


**26.**

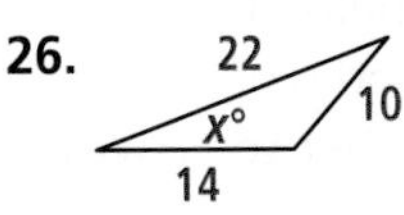


**27.**

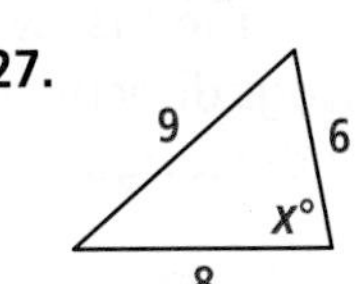


**28.** A golfer hits from the tee for a 300-yard hole. Her drive carries 275 yards but is 13° off line from the hole. How much farther must the golfer now hit the ball to reach the hole?
SEE EXAMPLE 4

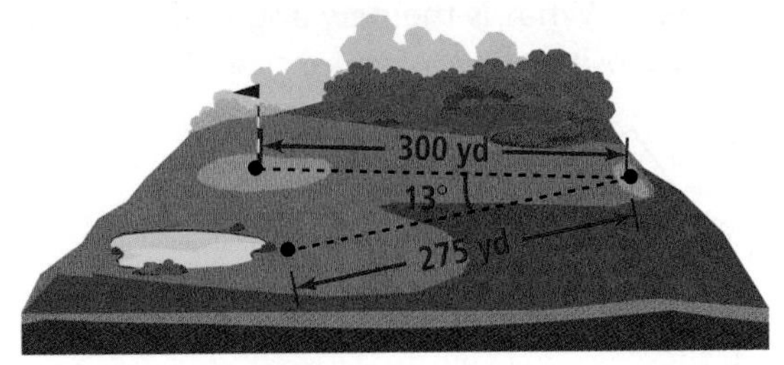

## APPLY

**29. Model With Mathematics** Alejandro, Camilla, and Damian are practicing for a game of ultimate, which is played on a field with a flying disc. Alejandro has the disc and Camilla is in the end zone, but Alejandro can only throw accurately for distances of 7.5 m or less. He throws the disc to Damian, because Damian can throw with accuracy up to 9.5 m. Is Camilla within Damian's range of accuracy? Explain.

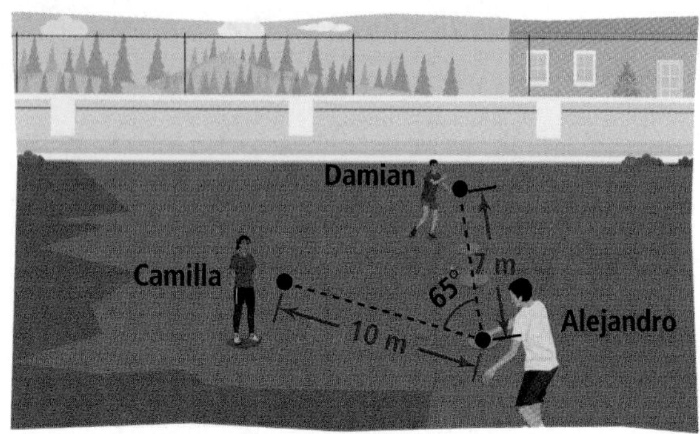


**30. Mathematical Connections** Two rescue workers leave at the same time to find an injured hiker. The first walks 25° west of north at 3.5 mi/h, and the second walks 36° east of north at 2.5 mi/h.

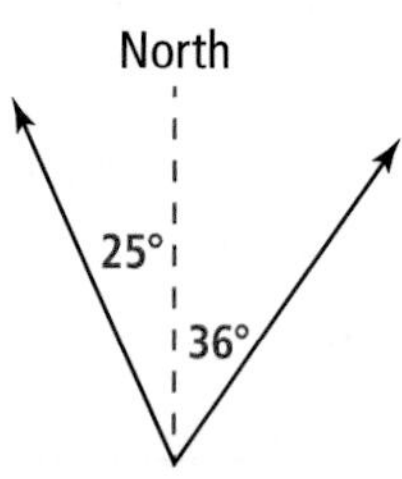


After 2 hours, the second worker finds the hiker and radios the first worker for help. If the first worker jogs directly to the second worker at 6 mi/h, how long will it take for her to arrive?

**31. Make Sense and Persevere** An architect proposes the plan shown for a new roof with a 40° incline on one side. The owner of the house thinks that 40° is not steep enough and wants the incline to be 50°. If the length of the adjacent side does not change, by how much does the length, $x$ ft, of the opposite side increase? What is the new angle of incline for the opposite side?

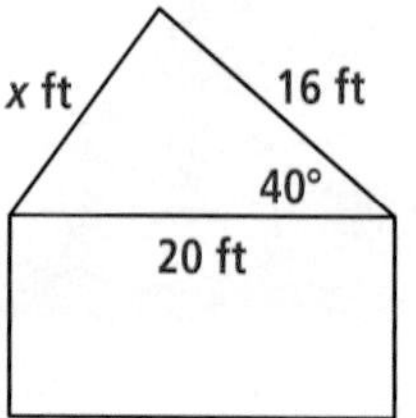


## ASSESSMENT PRACTICE

**32.** Which equation is true for the triangle shown? Select all that apply.

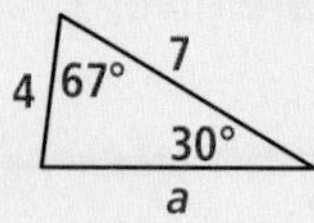


Ⓐ $a^2 = 16 + 49 - 28 \cos 30°$

Ⓑ $16 = a^2 + 49 - (14a)\cos 30°$

Ⓒ $49 = a^2 + 16 - (4a)\cos 67°$

Ⓓ $a^2 = 49 + 16 - 56 \cos 67°$

**33. SAT/ACT** A triangle has sides with lengths 12 cm and 15 cm. The measure of the included angle is 46°. What is the length of the third side, to the nearest tenth of a centimeter?

Ⓐ 24.9 cm　　Ⓒ 13.0 cm

Ⓑ 10.5 cm　　Ⓓ 10.9 cm

**34. Performance Task** A medical supply drone leaves Port A traveling 40 degrees east of north. After flying 32 mi on that course to point C, the drone turns 50° to the right to fly due east. It then flies another 8 mi, where it makes a drop at Island Port.

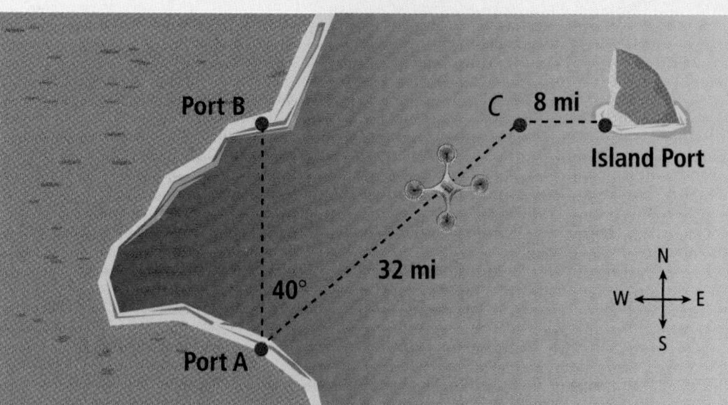


**Part A** The drone can fly a total distance of 75 miles before it needs to recharge. Can it fly directly back to Port A from Island Port? Explain.

**Part B** Port B is 24 miles due north of Port A. What is the distance from Island Port to Port B? Can the drone fly to Port B?

**Part C** Port B appears to be directly west of Island Port. Is it? If so, explain. If not, what direction is it from Island Port?

PearsonRealize.com

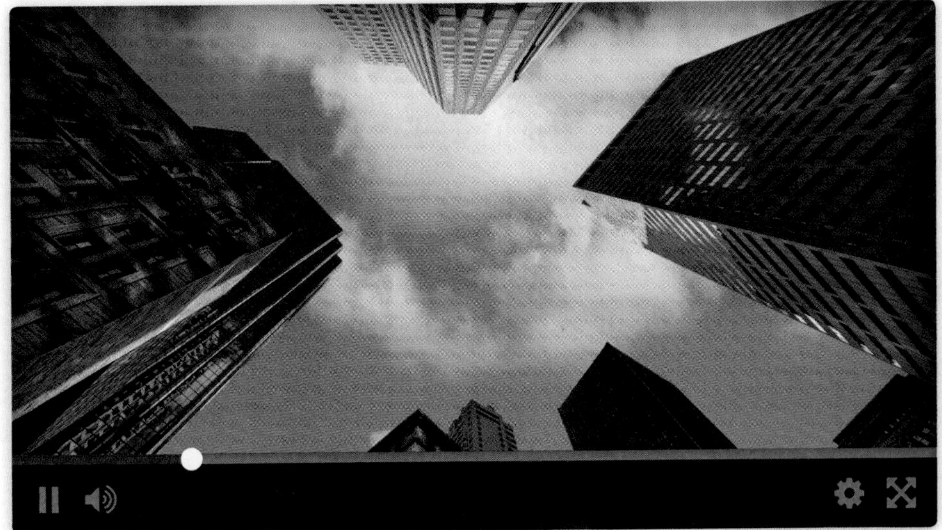

## The Impossible Measurement

Tall buildings are often some of the most recognizable structures of cities. The Empire State Building in New York City, the Transamerica Pyramid in San Francisco, and the JPMorgan Chase Tower in Houston are all famous landmarks in those cities.

Cities around the world compete for the tallest building bragging rights. Which city currently has the tallest building? This Mathematical Modeling in 3 Acts lesson will get you thinking about the height of structures, including tall buildings such as these.

### ACT 1 Identify the Problem

1. What is the first question that comes to mind after watching the video?
2. Write down the main question you will answer about what you saw in the video.
3. Make an initial conjecture that answers this main question.
4. Explain how you arrived at your conjecture.
5. What information will be useful to know to answer the main question? How can you get it? How will you use that information?

### ACT 2 Develop a Model

6. Use the math that you have learned in the topic to refine your conjecture.

### ACT 3 Interpret the Results

7. Did your refined conjecture match the actual answer exactly? If not, what might explain the difference?

# 8-5 Problem Solving With Trigonometry

**I CAN...** use trigonometry to solve problems.

**VOCABULARY**

- angle of depression
- angle of elevation

## MODEL & DISCUSS

**A search-and-rescue team is having a nighttime practice drill. Two members of the team are in a helicopter that is hovering at 2,000 feet above ground level.**

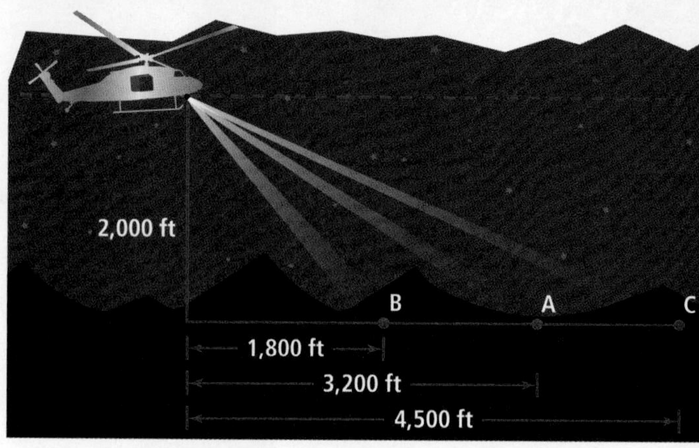


A. The team first tries to locate object A. At what angle from the horizontal line even with the helicopter should they position the spotlight so that it shines on object A?

B. Next, they shine the spotlight on object B. How does the angle of the spotlight from the horizontal line change?

C. **Use Structure** In general, how does the angle of the spotlight from the horizontal change as the light moves from object A to object B? From object A to object C?

## ESSENTIAL QUESTION

**How can trigonometry be used to solve real-world and mathematical problems?**

## EXAMPLE 1 Identify Angles of Elevation and Depression

**Identify ∠2 as an angle of elevation or an angle of depression. Do the same for ∠3. Explain your reasoning.**

**STUDY TIP**
When solving problems involving angle of elevation or angle of depression, use a diagram and look for right triangles.

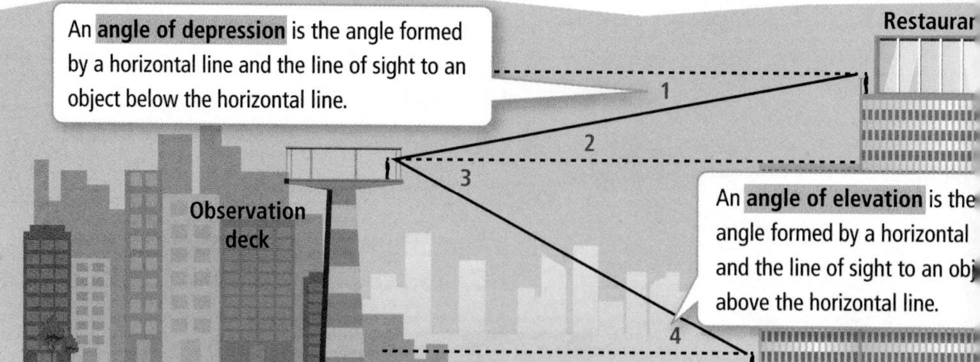


To see the person above, the person on the observation deck is looking up from the horizontal, so ∠2 is an angle of elevation.

To see the person below, the person on the observation deck is looking down from the horizontal, so ∠3 is an angle of depression.

**Try It!** **1.** In Example 1, how does the angle of depression, ∠1, compare with the angle of elevation, ∠2? Explain your reasoning.

Activity

Assess

APPLICATION

## EXAMPLE 2 Use Angles of Elevation and Depression

**For a reverse bungee ride, Reagan stands halfway between two vertical posts. Two bungee cords extend from the top of the posts to Reagan's waist at a height 1 m above the ground. How tall are the vertical posts?**

Write an equation to determine $x$ m, the vertical distance from the top of a post to a point 1 meter above the ground.

$$\tan 70^\circ = \frac{x}{4}$$

$$x = 4 \tan 70^\circ$$

$$x \approx 10.9899$$

The unknown length and the 4-m length are opposite and adjacent to a 70° angle. So use the tangent function.

**COMMON ERROR**
Be careful not to forget the distance between Reagan's waist and the ground.

Find the height of the vertical posts.

$$11 + 1 = 12$$

The vertical posts are about 12 meters tall.

**Try It!** 2. Nadeem sees the tour bus from the top of the tower. To the nearest foot, how far is the bus from the base of the tower?

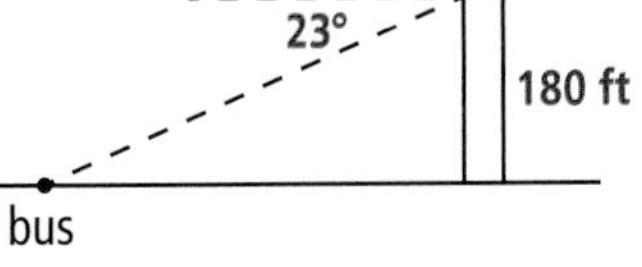


APPLICATION

## EXAMPLE 3 Use Trigonometry to Solve Problems

**An instructor holds a safety rope at point $C$ for a student to rappel from the anchor point $T$. The rope between them currently measures 61 ft. How much more rope should the instructor let out so the student can make it to a resting point at point $R$?**

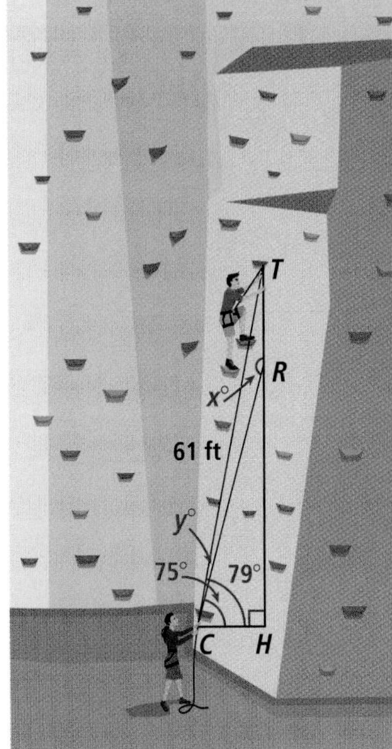


A side length and two angle measures are known for $\triangle TRC$. So, use the Law of Sines to solve for $TR$.

**Step 1** Write the Law of Sines in terms of the figure.

$$\frac{\sin x^\circ}{CT} = \frac{\sin y^\circ}{TR}$$

**Step 2** Find $y$ and $x$.

$$y = 79 - 75 = 4$$

$$m\angle CRH = 90 - 75 = 15$$

$$x = 180 - 15 = 165$$

**COMMUNICATE PRECISELY**
Think about how you could check the reasonableness of your answer. What theorems or definitions could you use?

**Step 3** Use the proportion to solve for $TR$.

$$\frac{\sin 165^\circ}{61} = \frac{\sin 4^\circ}{TR}$$

$$TR = \frac{61(\sin 4^\circ)}{\sin 165^\circ} \approx 16$$

The instructor should let out about 16 ft of rope.

CONTINUED ON THE NEXT PAGE

 **Try It!** 3. In Example 3, how far is the student from the instructor at the resting point?

CONCEPTUAL UNDERSTANDING

## EXAMPLE 4 Use Trigonometry to Find Triangle Area

**A. How can you use trigonometry to find the area of $\triangle ABC$?**

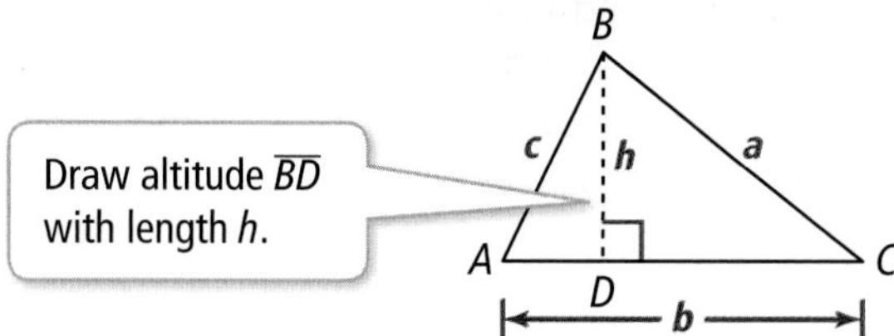


To write a formula with side lengths $b$ and $c$ and included $\angle A$, apply the area formula for a triangle.

$$\text{area} = \frac{1}{2}bh$$
$$= \frac{1}{2}b(c \sin A)$$
$$= \frac{1}{2}bc \sin A$$

In $\triangle ABD$, $\sin A = \frac{h}{c}$, so $h = c \sin A$.

You can apply the same reasoning to $\angle B$ and $\angle C$ to write the following area formulas.

$$\text{area} = \frac{1}{2}ac \sin B \qquad \text{area} = \frac{1}{2}ab \sin C$$

**B. What is the area of $\triangle FEG$?**

In the triangle, the lengths of sides $g$ and $f$ are 3 cm and 4 cm, respectively, and the measure of the included angle is 116°.

$$\text{area} = \frac{1}{2}gf \sin E$$
$$= \frac{1}{2}(3)(4) \sin 116^\circ$$
$$= 6 \sin 116^\circ$$
$$\approx 5.4$$

F, g, 116°, E, f, G

The area of the triangle is about 5.4 cm$^2$.

**STUDY TIP**
In order to use the formula area $= \frac{1}{2}bc \sin A$, you must know two side lengths and the measure of the included angle.

 **Try It!** 4. a. What is the area of $\triangle JKL$?

b. What is the area of $\triangle PQR$? *Hint:* First apply the Law of Cosines to find the measure of the angle included between $\overline{PQ}$ and $\overline{PR}$. Then apply the area formula with the sine of the angle measure.

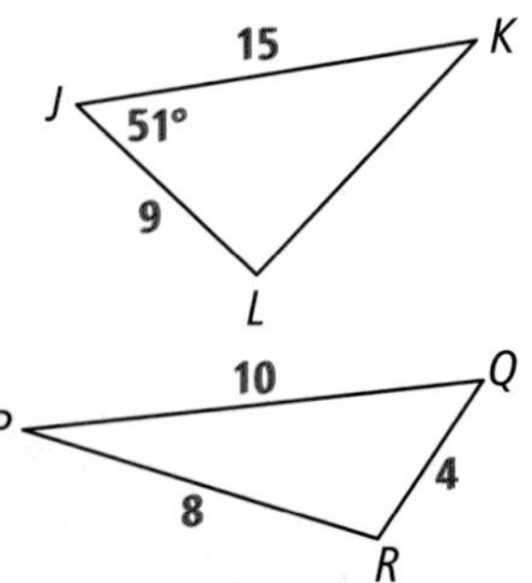

## CONCEPT SUMMARY Using Trigonometry to Solve Problems

| | Angles of Elevation or Depression | Area Formulas |
|---|---|---|
| **DIAGRAMS** | angle of elevation; object; $h$; 37°; 42°; 60 ft; 25 ft; $d$; angle of depression; object | 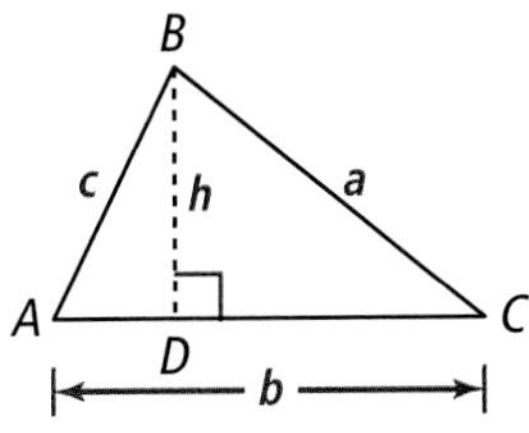 |
| **SYMBOLS** | $\tan 37^\circ = \frac{h}{60}$<br>$\sin 42^\circ = \frac{25}{d}$ | $\text{area} = \frac{1}{2}bc \sin A$<br>$\text{area} = \frac{1}{2}ac \sin B$<br>$\text{area} = \frac{1}{2}ab \sin C$ |



## Do You UNDERSTAND?

1. **ESSENTIAL QUESTION** How can trigonometry be used to solve real-world and mathematical problems?

2. **Error Analysis** What error does Jamie make in finding the area?

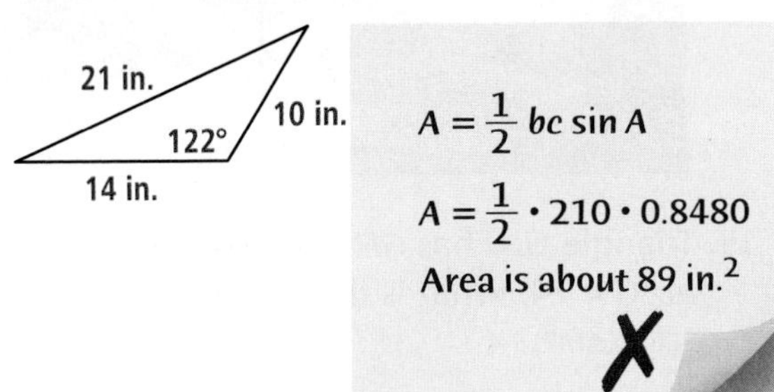

21 in.
10 in.
122°
14 in.
$A = \frac{1}{2} bc \sin A$
$A = \frac{1}{2} \cdot 210 \cdot 0.8480$
Area is about 89 in.$^2$
X


3. **Vocabulary** A person on a balcony and a person on a street look at each other. Draw a diagram to represent the situation and label the angles of elevation and depression.

4. **Make Sense and Persevere** How do you find the area of a triangle when given only the lengths of three sides?

## Do You KNOW HOW?

5. A person rides a glass elevator in a hotel lobby. As the elevator goes up, how does the angle of depression to a fixed point on the lobby floor change?

6. A person observes the top of a radio antenna at an angle of elevation of 5°. After getting 1 mile closer to the antenna, the angle of elevation is 10°. How tall is the antenna to the nearest tenth of a foot?

5° 10°
5,280 ft

7. Triangle $ABC$ has $AB = 13$, $AC = 15$, and $m\angle A = 59$. What is the area of the triangle to the nearest tenth?

8. Triangle $DEF$ has $DE = 13$, $DF = 15$, and $EF = 14$. What is the area of the triangle to the nearest tenth?

9. A temporary pen for cattle is built using 10-foot sections of fence arranged in a triangle. One side of the pen has 4 sections, one has 5 sections, and the last has 6 sections. What is the area enclosed by the pen?

## PRACTICE & PROBLEM SOLVING

Scan for Multimedia   Practice Tutorial

Additional Exercises Available Online

### UNDERSTAND

10. **Construct Arguments** How is the area of a triangle determined if the lengths of two sides and the measure of the included angle are given?

11. **Error Analysis** Leah is asked to find $AC$. What is her error?

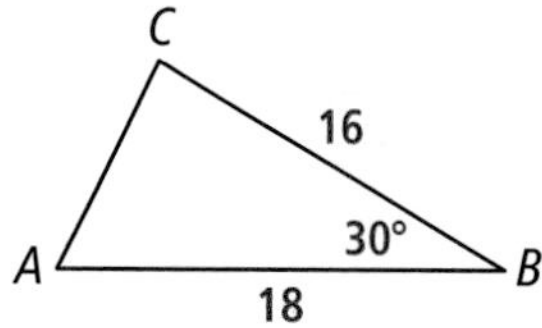


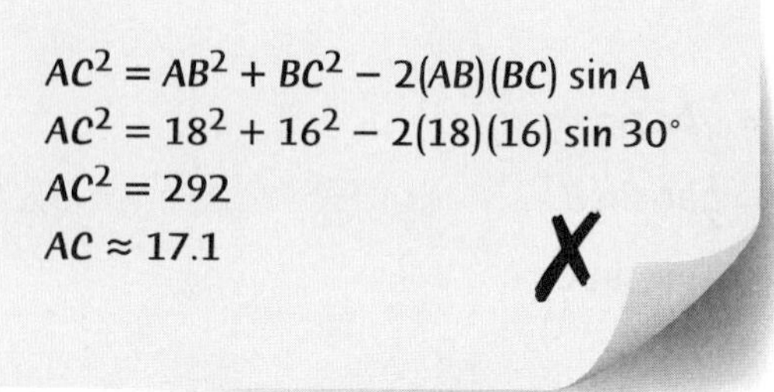

$AC^2 = AB^2 + BC^2 - 2(AB)(BC)\sin A$

$AC^2 = 18^2 + 16^2 - 2(18)(16)\sin 30°$

$AC^2 = 292$

$AC \approx 17.1$

✗

12. **Mathematical Connections** Find the length of the diagonal of the isosceles trapezoid. Then find the length of the fourth side.

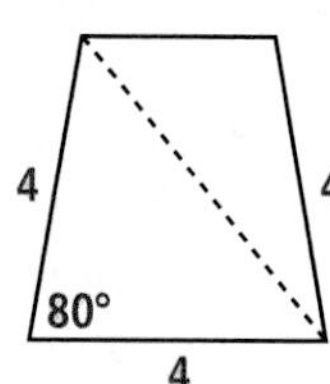


13. **Use Appropriate Tools** For each triangle, write an equation for $x$ using a trigonometric function.

a.

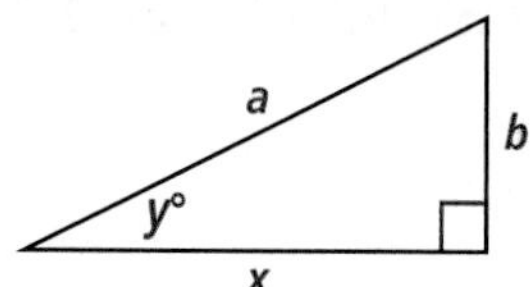


b.

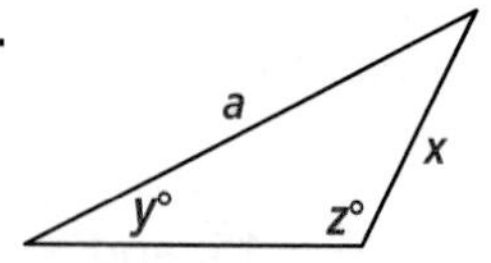


14. **Higher Order Thinking** What is a formula for the area of the parallelogram in the figure? Show your work.

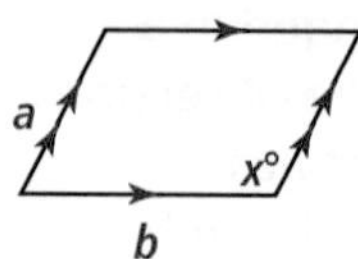


### PRACTICE

15. What is the angle of elevation to a building 1,000 m away that is 300 m high? SEE EXAMPLE 1

16. To what angle of depression should the security camera be adjusted in order to have the lens aimed at point $P$ on the ground? SEE EXAMPLE 2

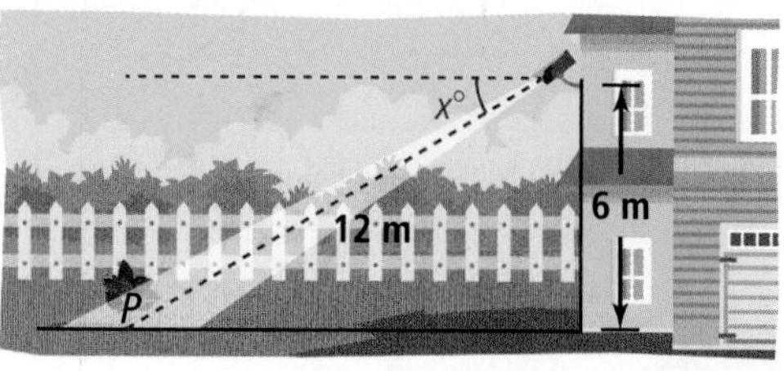


17. The angle of elevation to the sun is 21.5°. What is the length of the shadow cast by a person 5 ft 6 in. tall? SEE EXAMPLE 2

18. Libby's eyes are 5 ft above the ground, and the angle of elevation of her line of sight to the top of the monument is 74°. How far is she from the monument? SEE EXAMPLE 3

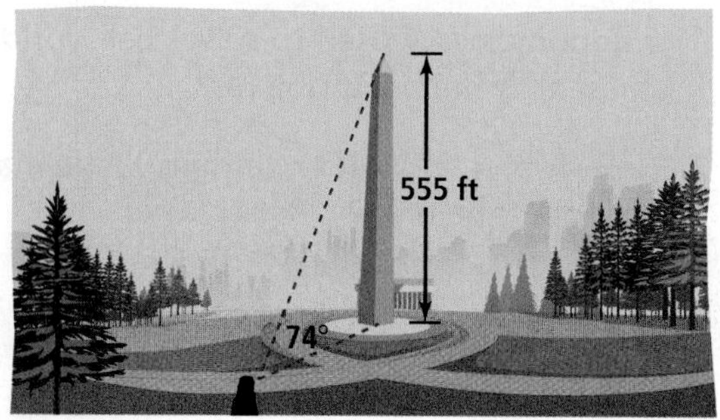


19. Triangle $GHJ$ has $GH = 13$, $GJ = 15$, and $m\angle G = 74$. What is the area of the triangle? SEE EXAMPLE 4

20. What is the area of the triangle? SEE EXAMPLE 4

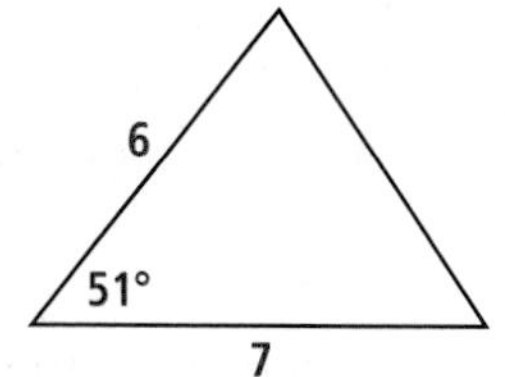


21. Triangle $KLM$ has $KL = 22$, $KM = 27$, and $LM = 29$. What is the area of the triangle? SEE EXAMPLE 4

22. What is the area of the triangle? SEE EXAMPLE 4

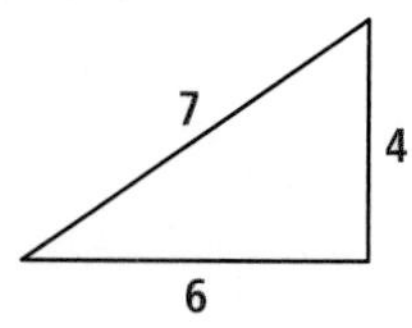

# PRACTICE & PROBLEM SOLVING

## APPLY

**23. Model With Mathematics** A research submarine dives at a speed of 100 ft/min directly toward the research lab. How long will it take the submarine to reach the lab from the surface of the ocean to the nearest tenth of a minute?

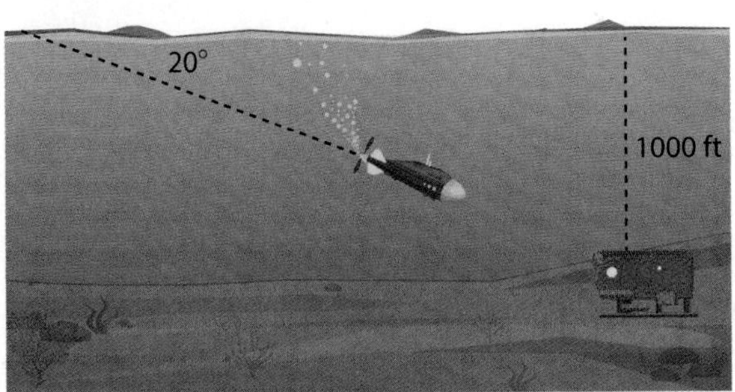


**24. Make Sense and Persevere** Benito aims for the center of the target from a distance of 70 meters. If Benito shoots an arrow at a 0.055° angle of depression below the center, will he hit the yellow circle? Explain.

**25. Reason** Ramona is climbing a hill with a 10° incline and wants to know the height of the rock formation. She walks 100 ft up the hill and uses a clinometer to measure the angle of elevation to the top of the formation. She then walks another 229.4 ft to the top of the hill. What is the height *h* of the rock formation?

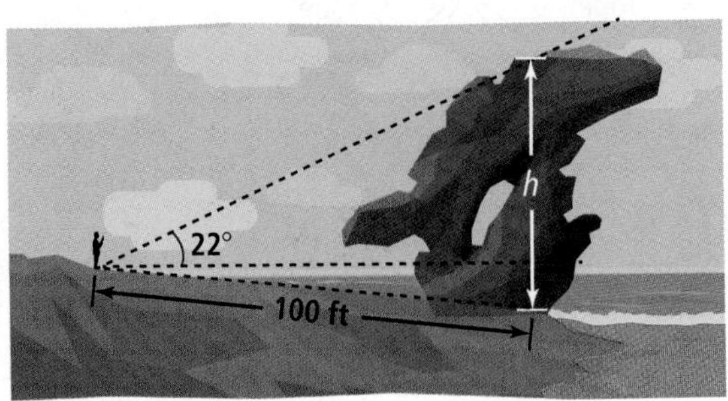


## ASSESSMENT PRACTICE

**26.** What is the area of the triangle? Round to the nearest one hundredth of a square unit.

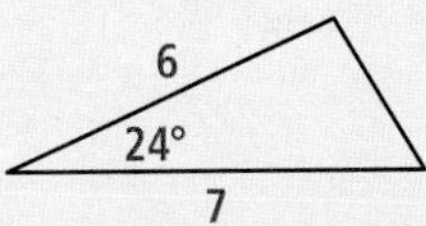


**27. SAT/ACT** Which of the following equations is true?

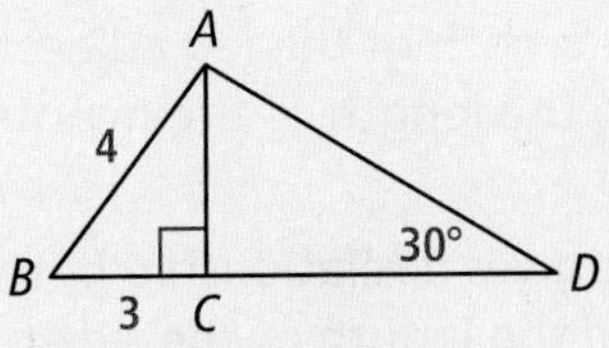


**I.** $\tan B = \frac{4}{3}$

**II.** $AD = 2\sqrt{7}$

**III.** $AB^2 = BD^2 + AD^2 - 2 \cdot (BD) \cdot (AD)\cos 30°$

Ⓐ I only
Ⓑ II only
Ⓒ III only
Ⓓ II and III only

**28. Performance Task** An amateur astronomer sets up his telescope in the center of a circular field. The field is surrounded by trees 20 m tall. The tripod holding the telescope pivots 1 m above the ground.

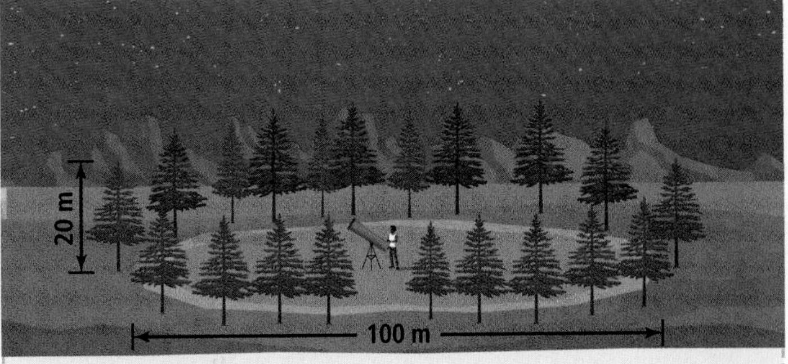


**Part A** What is the lowest angle of elevation at which the astronomer can observe a star?

**Part B** If the astronomer wants to observe a star 15° above the horizon to the east, how far west must the astronomer move the telescope to see the star?

**Part C** If the astronomer sets up the telescope in the center of the field on the bed of a truck 1.5 meters above the ground, what is the lowest angle at which he can observe?

TOPIC 8

# Topic Review

## ? TOPIC ESSENTIAL QUESTION

1. How are the Pythagorean Theorem and trigonometry useful?

## Vocabulary Review

**Choose the correct term to complete each sentence.**

2. The ratio of the length of the leg adjacent to an acute angle in a right triangle to the length of the hypotenuse is the ________ of the angle.
3. The ________ gives a relationship between the sine of each angle in a triangle and the length of the side opposite the angle.
4. The angle formed by a horizontal line and a line of sight to an object above the line is a(n) ________.
5. A(n) ________ is a set of three nonzero whole numbers that satisfies the equation $a^2 + b^2 = c^2$.

- angle of depression
- angle of elevation
- cosine
- Law of Cosines
- Law of Sines
- Pythagorean triple
- sine
- tangent
- trigonometric ratio

## Concepts & Skills Review

### LESSONS 8-1 & 8-2 Right Triangles and The Pythagorean Theorem, and Trigonometric Ratios

#### Quick Review

Given $\triangle ABC$, the Pythagorean Theorem states $a^2 + b^2 = c^2$.

The **trigonometric ratios** are

$\sin A = \frac{a}{c}$ $\cos A = \frac{b}{c}$ $\tan A = \frac{a}{b}$.

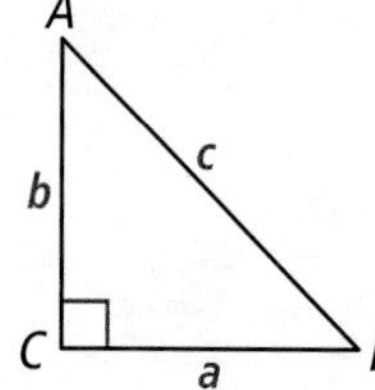


#### Example

**Given $\triangle DEF$, what is $\sin D$?**

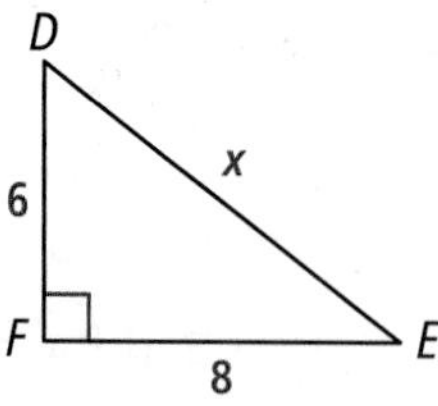


**Step 1** Use the Pythagorean Theorem to find $x$.

$8^2 + 6^2 = x^2$

$10 = x$

**Step 2** Use a trigonometric ratio to find $\sin D$.

$\sin D = \frac{8}{10} = \frac{4}{5}$

#### Practice & Problem Solving

**For Exercises 6–8, use $\triangle ABC$ to find each value.**

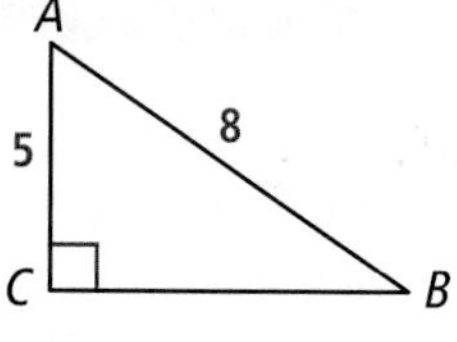


6. $BC$
7. $\cos B$
8. $m\angle A$ to the nearest tenth
9. Ines has 16 feet of rope to stake out the front part of her tent. Does she have enough rope? Explain.

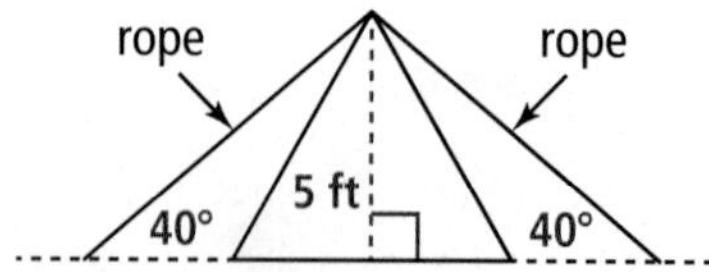


10. **Make Sense and Persevere** Given $\triangle XYZ$, what additional information do you need to find $YZ$? Explain.

## LESSONS 8-3 & 8-4 The Law of Sines and The Law of Cosines

### Quick Review

Given $\triangle ABC$, The **Law of Sines** states $\frac{(\sin A)}{a} = \frac{(\sin B)}{b} = \frac{(\sin C)}{c}$.

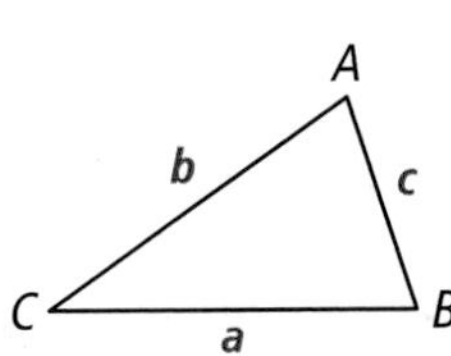


The **Law of Cosines** states

$a^2 = b^2 + c^2 - 2bc(\cos A)$

$b^2 = a^2 + c^2 - 2ac(\cos B)$

$c^2 = a^2 + b^2 - 2ab(\cos C)$.

### Example

**Given $\triangle DEF$, what is $EF$ to the nearest tenth?**

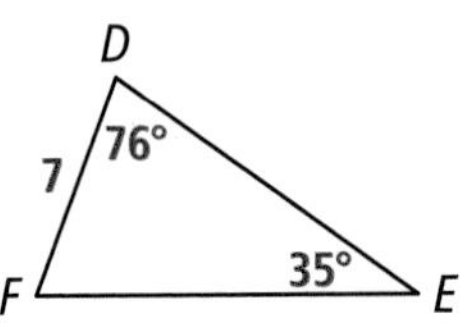


By the Law of Sines,

$$\frac{(\sin 35°)}{7} = \frac{(\sin 76°)}{EF}$$

$$EF = \frac{7(\sin 76°)}{(\sin 35°)}$$

$$EF \approx 11.8$$

### Practice & Problem Solving

**For Exercises 11 and 12, use $\triangle RST$ to find each measure to the nearest tenth.**

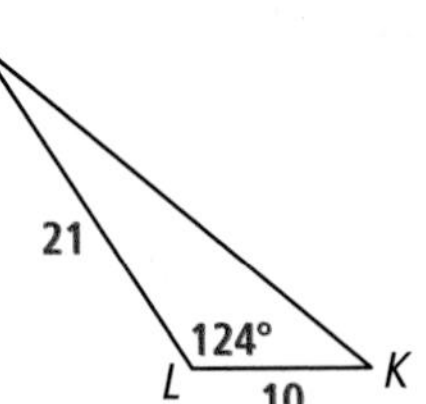


**11.** $m\angle T$ **12.** $RT$

**For Exercises 13 and 14, use $\triangle JKL$ to find each measure to the nearest tenth.**

J
21
124°
L
10
K

**13.** $JK$ **14.** $m\angle J$

**15.** How wide is the gate shown, to the nearest inch?

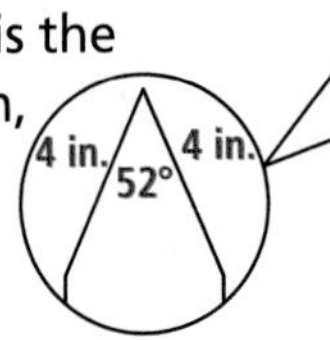


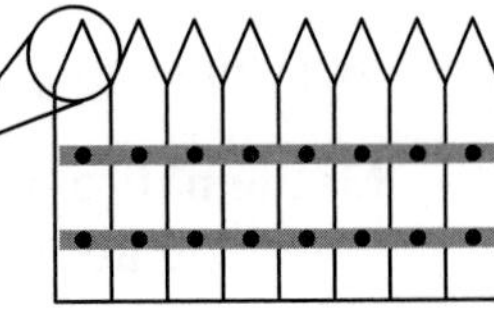

**16.** **Reason** How can the Law of Sines be applied to show that the expression is equivalent to the perimeter of $\triangle ABC$?

B
A
C

$$\frac{AB \sin A}{\sin C} + \frac{BC \sin B}{\sin A} + \frac{BC \sin C}{\sin A}$$

## LESSON 8-5 Problem Solving With Trigonometry

### Quick Review

Many problems, such as those with angles of elevation or depression, can be modeled with triangles.

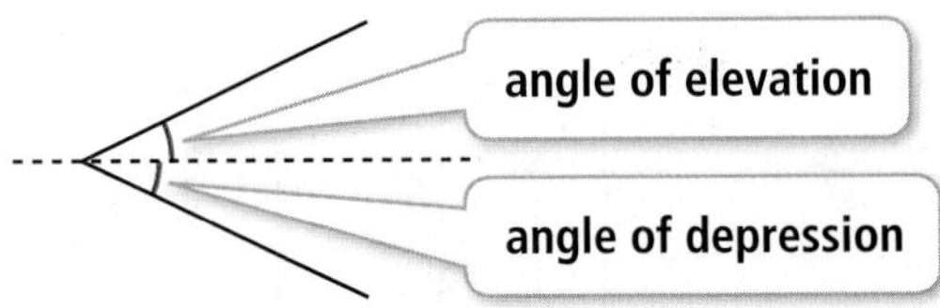


You can use trigonometric ratios, the Law of Sines, or the Law of Cosines to solve those problems.

### Example

**The angle of depression from the top to the bottom of a well is 62°. If the well is 4.5 feet in diameter, how deep is it?**

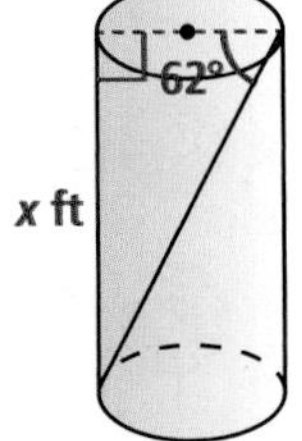


$$\tan 62° = \frac{x}{4.5 \text{ ft}}$$

$$x \approx 8.5 \text{ ft}$$

### Practice & Problem Solving

**For Exercises 17 and 18, find the area of each triangle.**

**17.**

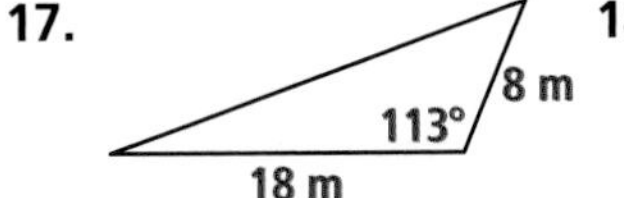


**18.**

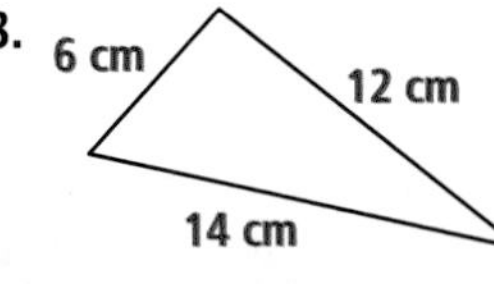


**19.**

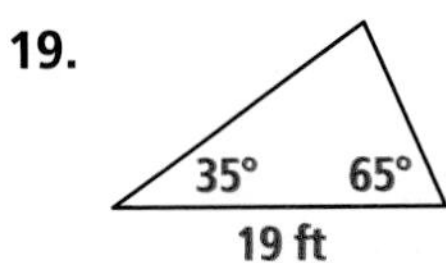


**20.**

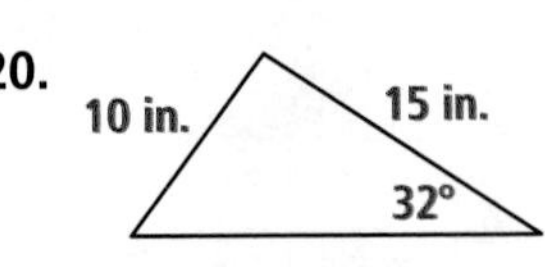


**21.** **Communicate Precisely** A hiker whose eyes are $5\frac{1}{2}$ feet above ground looks down at a kayaker on the far side of the river below. How could you find the approximate width of the river?

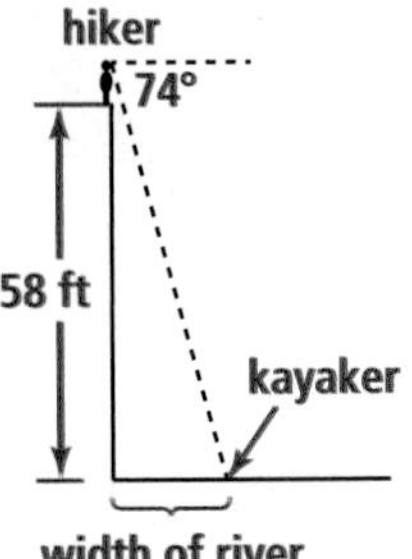


TOPIC 8 REVIEW

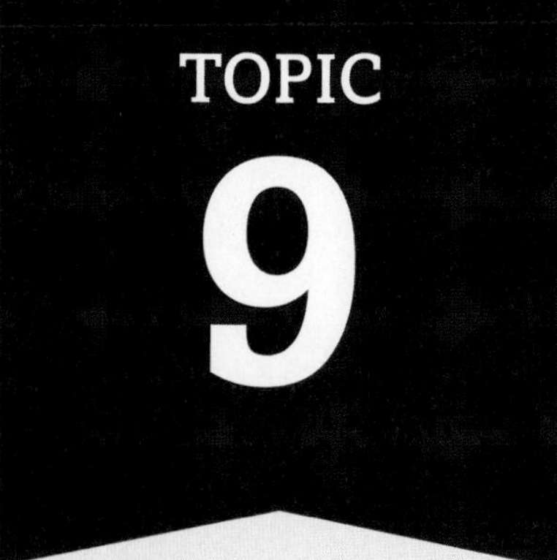


# Coordinate Geometry

## TOPIC ESSENTIAL QUESTION

**How can geometric relationships be proven by applying algebraic properties to geometric figures represented in the coordinate plane?**

## Topic Overview

**enVision™ STEM Project:**
Design a Solar Collector

**9-1** Polygons in the Coordinate Plane

**Mathematical Modeling in 3 Acts:**
You Be the Judge

**9-2** Proofs Using Coordinate Geometry

**9-3** Circles in the Coordinate Plane

**9-4** Parabolas in the Coordinate Plane

## Topic Vocabulary

- directrix
- focus
- parabola

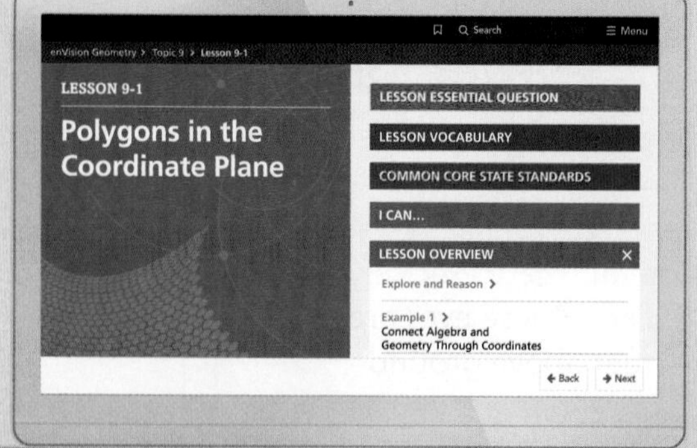

Go online | **PearsonRealize.com**

## Digital Experience

**INTERACTIVE STUDENT EDITION** Access online or offline.

**ACTIVITIES** Complete ***Explore & Reason, Model & Discuss***, and ***Critique & Explain*** activities. Interact with Examples and Try Its.

**ANIMATION** View and interact with real-world applications.

**PRACTICE** Practice what you've learned.

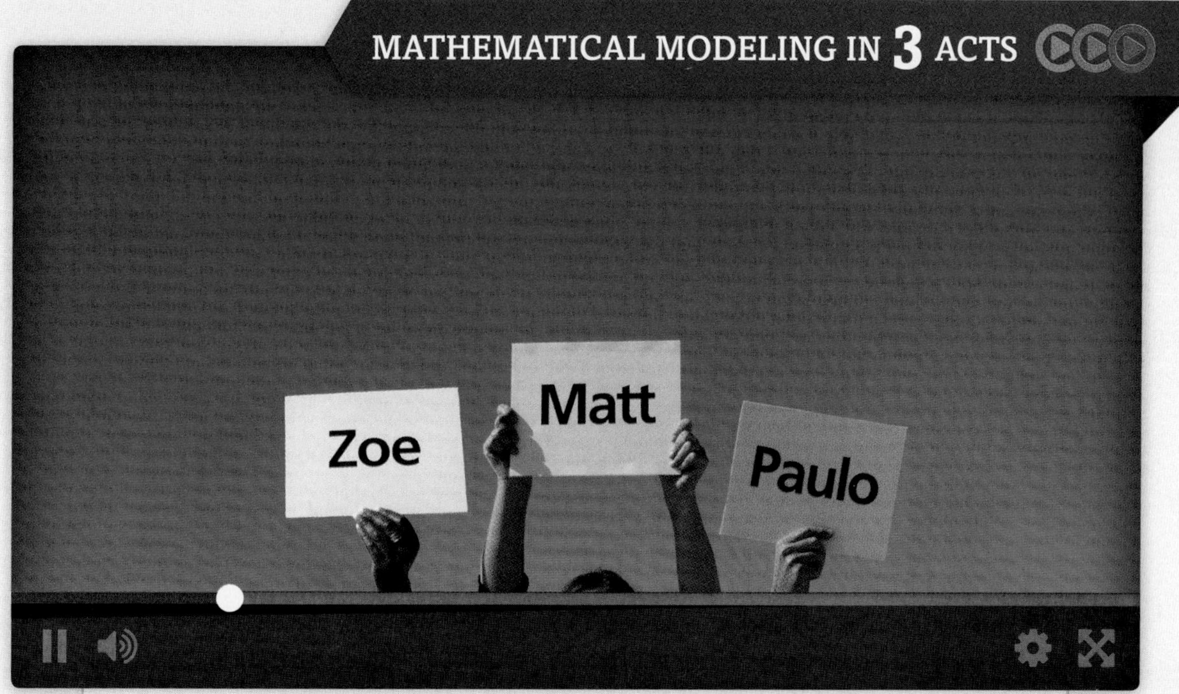


## You Be the Judge

Have you ever been a judge in a contest or competition? What criteria did you use to decide the winner? If you were one of many judges, did you all agree on who should win?

Often there is a set of criteria that judges use to help them score the performances of the contestants. Having criteria helps all of the judges be consistent regardless of the person they are rating. Think of this during the Mathematical Modeling in 3 Acts lesson.

TOPIC 9

**VIDEOS** Watch clips to support ***Mathematical Modeling in 3 Acts Lessons*** and **enVision™ *STEM Projects.***

**CONCEPT SUMMARY** Review key lesson content through multiple representations.

**ASSESSMENT** Show what you've learned.

**GLOSSARY** Read and listen to English and Spanish definitions.

**TUTORIALS** Get help from *Virtual Nerd*, right when you need it.

**MATH TOOLS** Explore math with digital tools and manipulatives.

## Did You Know?

Solar reflectors are made of mirrors or pieces of glass in many shapes and sizes. **Parabolic reflectors** collect the sun's rays from a wide area and **focus them on a small area**, concentrating the energy.

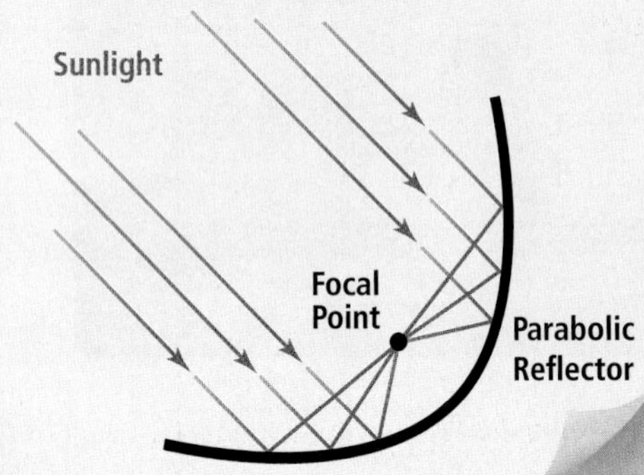


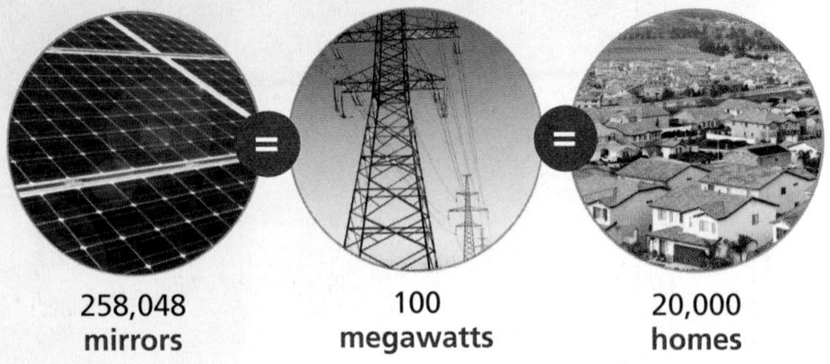


The world's largest power station, the SHAMS 1 in the United Arab Emirates, uses **258,048 mirrors**. That's enough to generate **100 megawatts** of electricity per day and power **20,000 homes**.

In 2016, the United States produced more than 40 billion kilowatt-hours of solar energy, 40 times more than it did a decade earlier.

## Your Task: Design a Solar Collector

Giant solar power plants are not the only place to see parabolic trough collectors—you might find a water purifier made from a single 6 ft-x-4 ft mirror in a neighbor's back yard! You and your classmates will analyze parabolas and design a solar collector for use in your school or community.

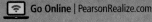

# 9-1 Polygons in the Coordinate Plane

PearsonRealize.com

**I CAN…** use the coordinate plane to analyze geometric figures.

## EXPLORE & REASON

**Players place game pieces on the board shown and earn points from the attributes of the piece placed on the board.**

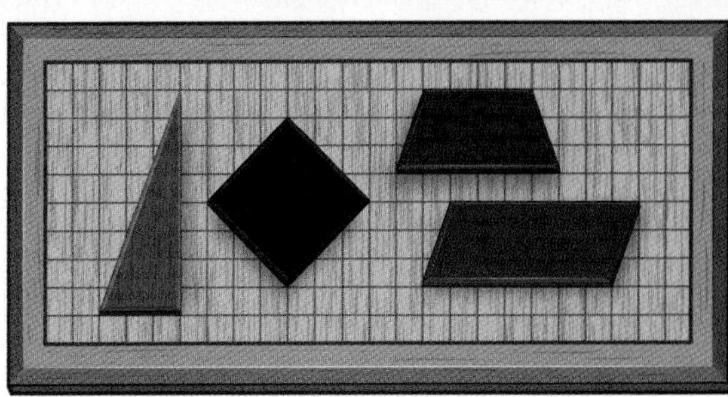

- 1 point for a right angle
- 2 points for a pair of parallel sides
- 3 points for the shortest perimeter

**A.** Which game piece is worth the greatest total points? Explain.

**B. Make Sense and Persevere** Describe a way to determine the perimeters that is different from the way you chose. Which method do you consider better? Explain.

**ESSENTIAL QUESTION** **How are properties of geometric figures represented in the coordinate plane?**

CONCEPTUAL UNDERSTANDING

## EXAMPLE 1 Connect Algebra and Geometry Through Coordinates

**What formulas can you use to identify properties of figures on the coordinate plane?**

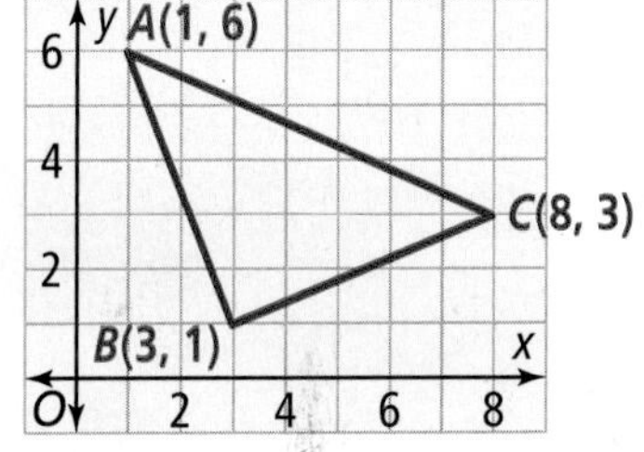


**A. Which formula can you use to find $AB$?**

Use the Distance Formula to find segment length.

$$AB = \sqrt{(3-1)^2 + (1-6)^2} = \sqrt{29}$$

**B. What point bisects $\overline{AB}$?**

Use the Midpoint Formula to find a segment bisector.

$$\text{midpoint of } \overline{AB} = \left(\frac{1+3}{2}, \frac{6+1}{2}\right) = \left(2, \frac{7}{2}\right)$$

**C. Why do slopes of $\overline{AB}$ and $\overline{BC}$ show that $m\angle ABC = 90°$?**

Use the slopes of the two segments to show that they are perpendicular.

$$\text{slope of } \overline{AB} = \frac{1-6}{3-1} = -\frac{5}{2}$$

$$\text{slope of } \overline{BC} = \frac{3-1}{8-3} = \frac{2}{5}$$

The product of the slopes is $-1$. So $\overline{AB} \perp \overline{BC}$, and $m\angle ABC = 90°$.

**COMMON ERROR**
Recall that the slope of a line is the ratio of the difference in the $y$-coordinates to the difference in the $x$-coordinates. Be careful not to reverse the ratio.

**Try It!** 1. Given $\triangle ABC$ in Example 1, what is the length of the line segment connecting the midpoints of $\overline{AC}$ and $\overline{BC}$?

## EXAMPLE 2 Classify a Triangle on the Coordinate Plane

**A. Is $\triangle XYZ$ equilateral, isosceles, or scalene?**

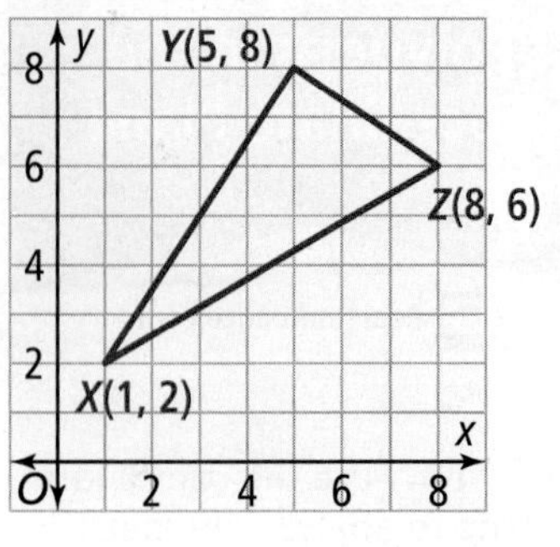


Find the length of each side.

$$XY = \sqrt{(5-1)^2 + (8-2)^2} = \sqrt{52}$$

$$YZ = \sqrt{(8-5)^2 + (6-8)^2} = \sqrt{13}$$

$$XZ = \sqrt{(8-1)^2 + (6-2)^2} = \sqrt{65}$$

No two sides are congruent. The triangle is scalene.

**B. Is $\triangle XYZ$ a right triangle?**

If $\triangle XYZ$ is a right triangle, then $\overline{XZ}$ is the hypotenuse because it is the longest side, and $XY$, $YZ$, and $XZ$ satisfy the Pythagorean Theorem.

$$(\sqrt{52})^2 + (\sqrt{13})^2 \stackrel{?}{=} (\sqrt{65})^2$$

$$65 = 65 \checkmark$$

Triangle $XYZ$ is a right triangle.

**Try It!** 2. The vertices of $\triangle PQR$ are $P(4, 1)$, $Q(2, 7)$, and $R(8, 5)$.

a. Is $\triangle PQR$ equilateral, isosceles, or scalene? Explain.

b. Is $\triangle PQR$ a right triangle? Explain.

## EXAMPLE 3 Classify a Parallelogram on the Coordinate Plane

**What type of parallelogram is *RSTU*?**

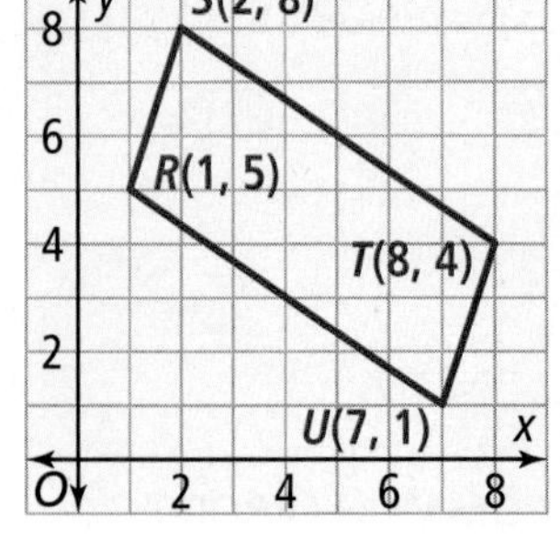


Determine whether *RSTU* is a rhombus, a rectangle, or a square. First calculate *ST* and *SR*:

$$ST = \sqrt{(2-8)^2 + (8-4)^2} = \sqrt{52}$$

$$RS = \sqrt{(2-1)^2 + (8-5)^2} = \sqrt{10}$$

Since not all side lengths are equal, *RSTU* is not a rhombus or a square.

Check for right angles by finding the slopes.

$$\text{slope of } \overline{ST} = \frac{4-8}{8-2} = -\frac{2}{3}$$

$$\text{slope of } \overline{RS} = \frac{8-5}{2-1} = 3$$

The product of the slopes is not −1, so $\overline{ST}$ and $\overline{RS}$ are not perpendicular. At least one angle is not a right angle, and *RSTU* is not a rectangle. Therefore, quadrilateral *RSTU* is a parallelogram that is neither a square, nor a rhombus, nor a rectangle.

**MAKE SENSE AND PERSEVERE**
Consider other formulas you use on the coordinate plane. What are some ways to show that a quadrilateral is not a rectangle or a rhombus?

**Try It!** 3. The vertices of a parallelogram are $A(-2, 2)$, $B(4, 6)$, $C(6, 3)$, and $D(0, -1)$.

a. Is *ABCD* a rhombus? Explain.

b. Is *ABCD* a rectangle? Explain.

## EXAMPLE 4 Classify Quadrilaterals as Trapezoids and Kites on the Coordinate Plane

**A. Is *ABCD* a trapezoid?**

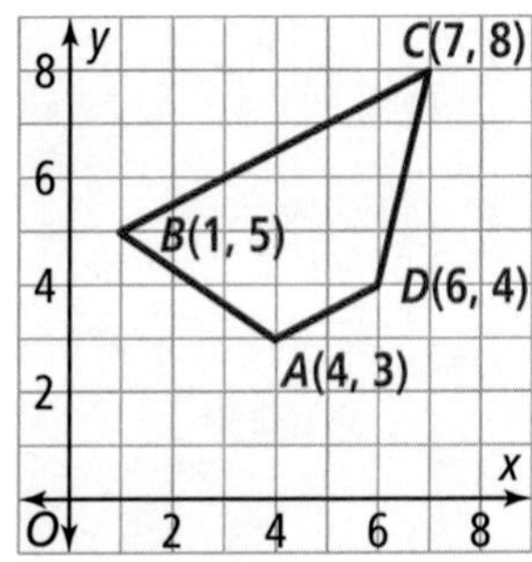


A trapezoid has exactly one pair of parallel sides. Use the slope formula to determine if only one pair of opposite sides is parallel.

slope of $\overline{AB} = \frac{5-3}{1-4} = -\frac{2}{3}$

slope of $\overline{BC} = \frac{8-5}{7-1} = \frac{1}{2}$

slope of $\overline{CD} = \frac{4-8}{6-7} = \frac{4}{1}$

slope of $\overline{AD} = \frac{4-3}{6-4} = \frac{1}{2}$

Since only the slopes of $\overline{BC}$ and $\overline{AD}$ are equal, $\overline{BC} \parallel \overline{AD}$, and only one pair of opposite sides is parallel. Therefore, quadrilateral *ABCD* is a trapezoid.

**COMMUNICATE PRECISELY**
Think about the properties of a trapezoid. Why do you need to find the slopes for all four sides?

**B. Is *JKLM* a kite?**

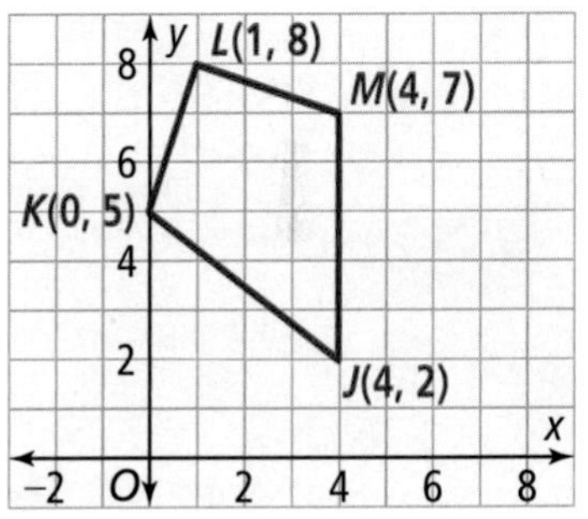


A kite has two pairs of consecutive congruent sides and no opposite sides congruent. Use the Distance Formula to find the lengths of the sides.

$JK = \sqrt{(0-4)^2 + (5-2)^2} = 5$

$KL = \sqrt{(1-0)^2 + (8-5)^2} = \sqrt{10}$

$LM = \sqrt{(4-1)^2 + (7-8)^2} = \sqrt{10}$

$MJ = \sqrt{(4-4)^2 + (2-7)^2} = 5$

Consecutive pair $\overline{KL}$ and $\overline{LM}$ and consecutive pair $\overline{JK}$ and $\overline{MJ}$ are congruent. No opposite pair is congruent, so *JKLM* is a kite.

**Try It!** 4. Is each quadrilateral a kite, trapezoid, or neither?

a.

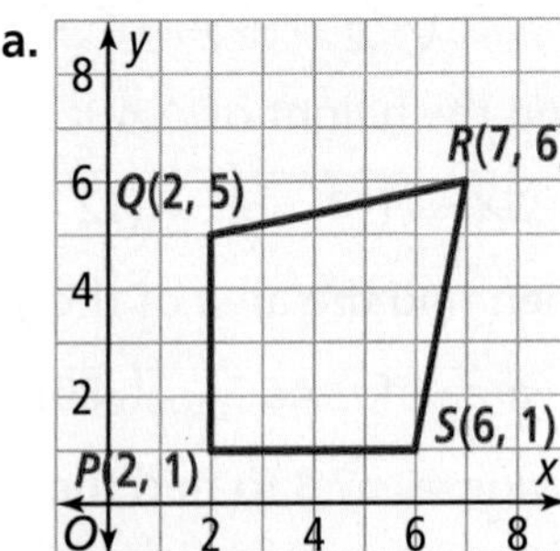


b.

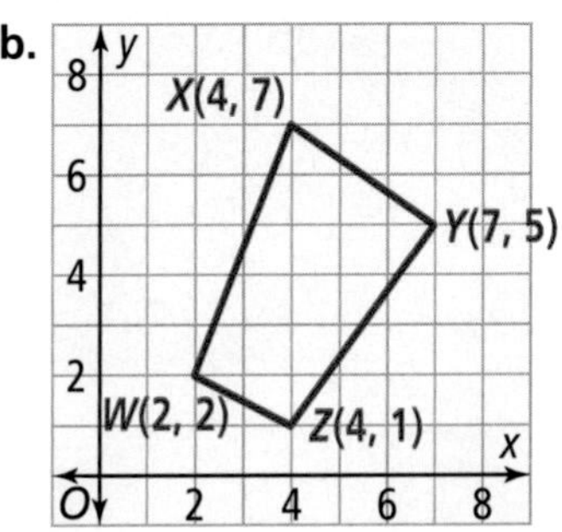

APPLICATION

## EXAMPLE 5 Find Perimeter and Area

**Dylan draws up a plan to fence in a yard for his chickens. The distance between grid lines is 1 foot.**

**A. Is 30 feet of fencing enough to enclose the yard?**

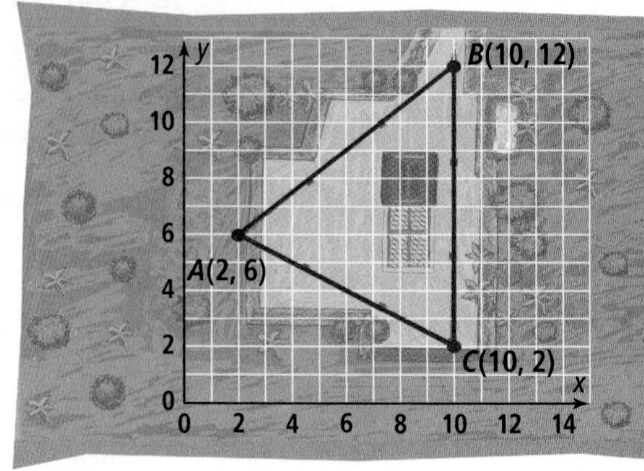


Find the lengths of the sides.

$AB = \sqrt{(2 - 10)^2 + (6 - 12)^2} = 10$ ft

$BC = \sqrt{(10 - 10)^2 + (12 - 2)^2} = 10$ ft

$AC = \sqrt{(2 - 10)^2 + (6 - 2)^2} = \sqrt{80}$ ft

Find the perimeter of the yard.

$P = 10 + 10 + \sqrt{80}$

$\approx 28.9$ ft

The perimeter is about 28.9 feet, which is less than 30 feet. Dylan has enough fencing material.

**CONSTRUCT ARGUMENTS**
Consider the properties of an isosceles triangle. What property of an isosceles triangle justifies that $\overline{BX}$ is a height of the triangle?

**B. For a healthy flock, each chicken needs at least 8 square feet of space. What is the maximum number of chickens Dylan can put in the yard?**

The yard is an isosceles triangle. To find the area, you need the height of the triangle. The height of $\triangle ABC$ is $BX$, where $X$ is the midpoint of $\overline{AC}$.

Find the midpoint of $\overline{AC}$.

$X = \left(\frac{2 + 10}{2}, \frac{6 + 2}{2}\right) = (6, 4)$

Find the height of $\triangle ABC$.

$BX = \sqrt{(10 - 6)^2 + (12 - 4)^2} = \sqrt{80}$ ft

Then find the area of the yard.

area of $\triangle ABC = \frac{1}{2}(\sqrt{80})(\sqrt{80}) = 40$ ft$^2$

Divide 40 by 8 to find the number of chickens.

$40 \div 8 = 5$

Dylan can keep as many as 5 chickens in the yard.

**Try It!** 5. The vertices of $WXYZ$ are $W(5, 4)$, $X(2, 9)$, $Y(9, 9)$, and $Z(8, 4)$.

a. What is the perimeter of $WXYZ$?

b. What is the area of $WXYZ$?

## CONCEPT SUMMARY Connecting Algebra and Geometry

You can use algebra to determine properties of and to classify geometric figures on the coordinate plane.

**WORDS**

Use the Distance Formula to find the lengths of segments to classify figures.

Use the Slope Formula to determine whether two lines or segments are parallel or perpendicular.

Use the Midpoint Formula to determine if a point bisects a segment.

**GRAPH**

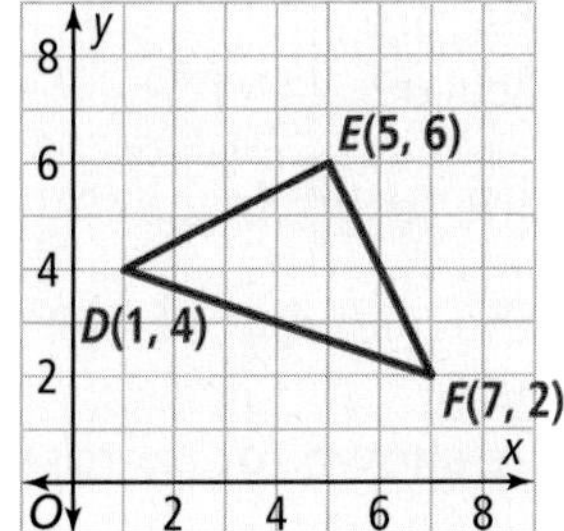


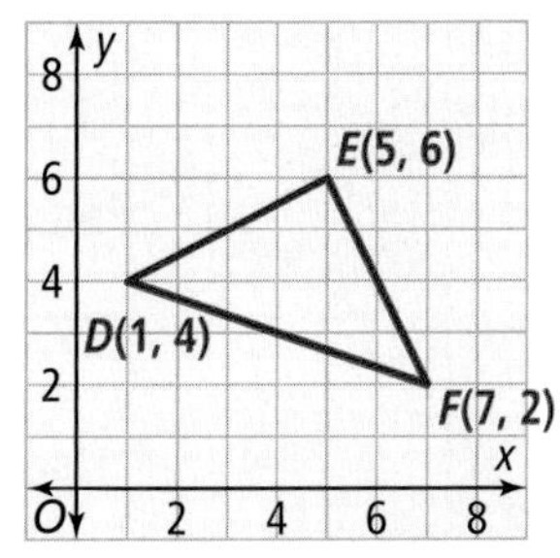


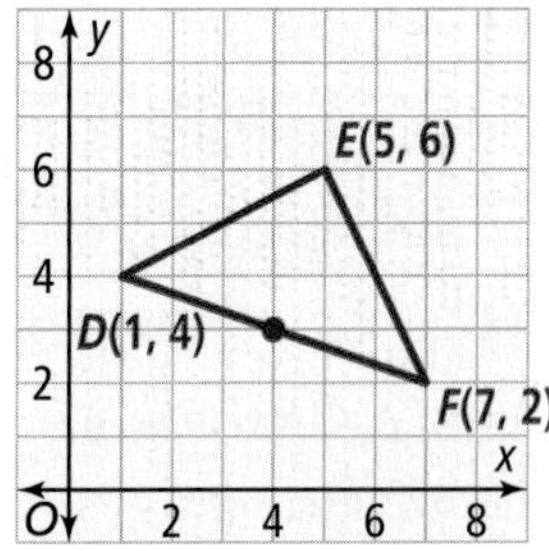


**NUMBERS**

$DE = \sqrt{(5 - 1)^2 + (6 - 4)^2}$

$= \sqrt{20}$

slope of $\overline{DE} = \frac{6 - 4}{5 - 1}$

$= \frac{1}{2}$

midpoint of $\overline{DF}$

$= \left(\frac{1 + 7}{2}, \frac{4 + 2}{2}\right) = (4, 3)$

## Do You UNDERSTAND?

1. ESSENTIAL QUESTION How are properties of geometric figures represented in the coordinate plane?

2. **Error Analysis** Chen is asked to describe two methods to find *BC*. Why is Chen incorrect?

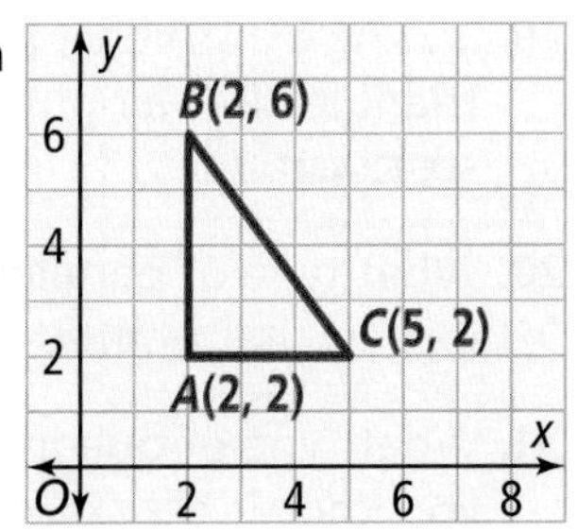


The only possible method is to use the Distance Formula because you only know the endpoints of $\overline{BC}$.

3. **Communicate Precisely** Describe three ways you can determine whether a quadrilateral is a parallelogram given the coordinates of the vertices.

## Do You KNOW HOW?

**Use *JKLM* for Exercises 4–6.**

4. What is the perimeter of *JKLM*?

5. What is the relationship between $\overline{JL}$ and $\overline{KM}$? Explain.

6. What type of quadrilateral is *JKLM*? Explain.

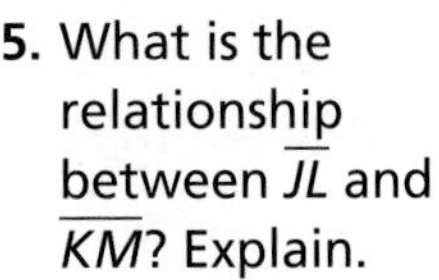

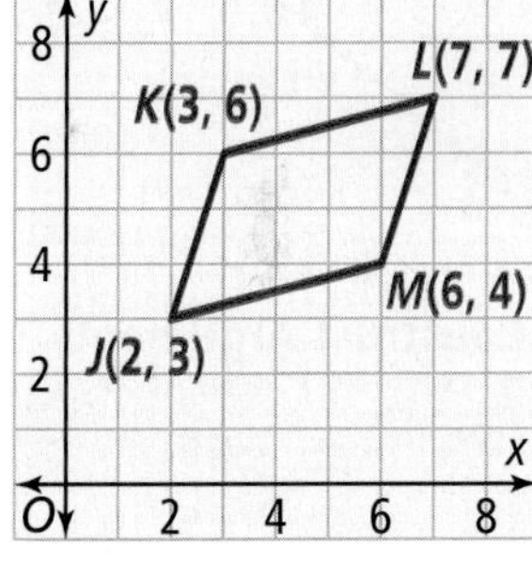


**Use △*PQR* for Exercises 7 and 8.**

7. What kind of triangle is *PQR*? Explain.

8. What is the area of *PQR*?

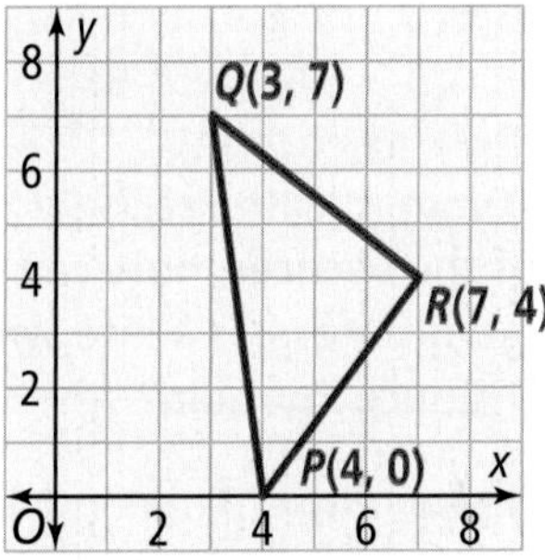

## UNDERSTAND

**9. Error Analysis** What error did Kelley make in finding the area of $\triangle PQR$?

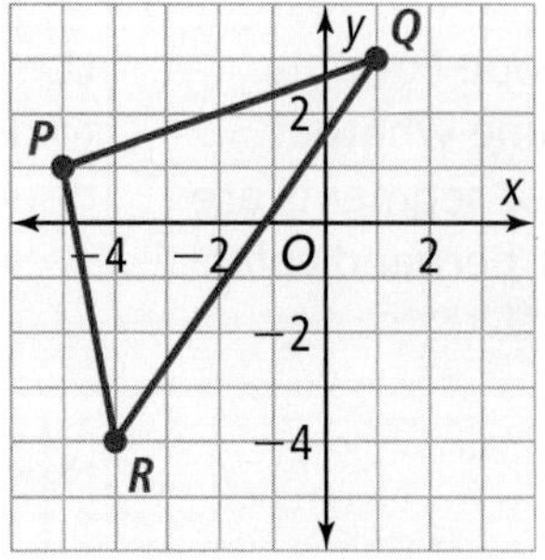


Area $= \frac{1}{2}bh = \frac{1}{2}(PR)(PQ) = \frac{1}{2}\sqrt{26}\sqrt{40}$

The area of $\Delta PQR$ is about 16.12 square units.

✗

**10. Mathematical Connections** Find the equation of the line that passes through point $R$ and is perpendicular to line $m$.

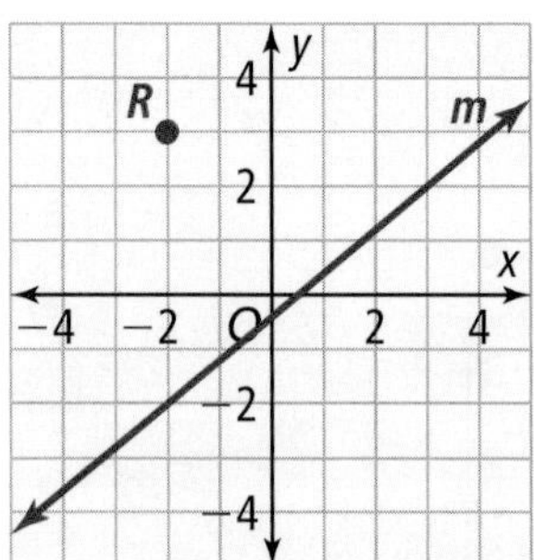


**11. Construct Arguments** Prove $\triangle ABC \cong \triangle DEF$.

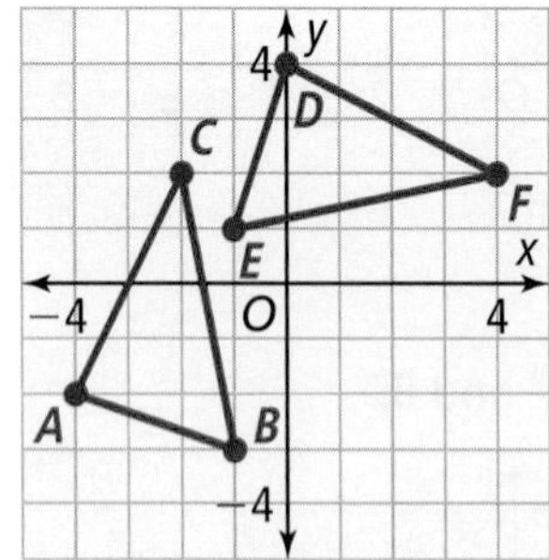


**12. Communicate Precisely** Given the coordinates of the vertices, how can you show that a quadrilateral is a kite without using the Distance Formula?

**13. Higher Order Thinking** Let line $p$ be the perpendicular bisector of $\overline{AB}$ that has endpoints and $A(x_1, y_1)$ and $B(x_2, y_2)$. Describe the process for writing a general equation in slope-intercept form for line $p$.

## PRACTICE

**Use the figure shown for Exercises 14–17.**

SEE EXAMPLE 1

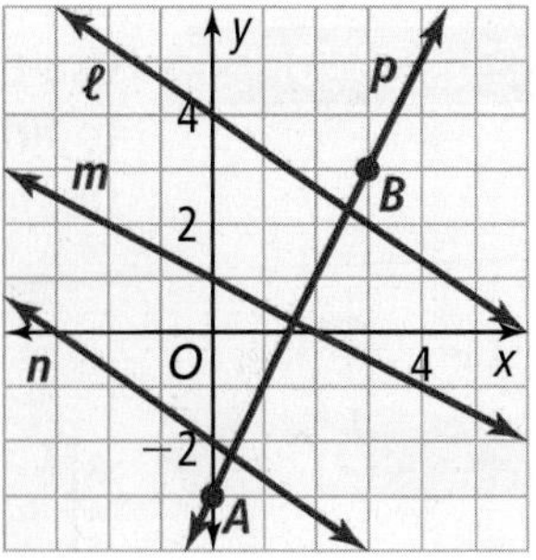


**14.** Which lines are parallel?

**15.** Which lines are perpendicular?

**16.** What is the length of $\overline{AB}$?

**17.** What is the midpoint of $\overline{AB}$?

**Use the figure shown for Exercises 18–23.**

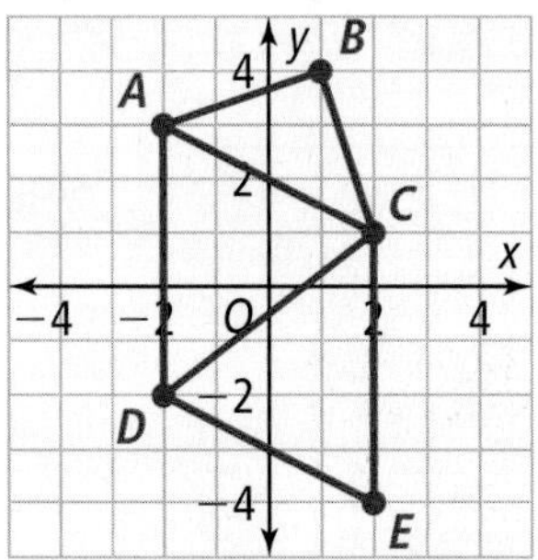


**18.** Is $\triangle ABC$ a scalene, isosceles, or equilateral triangle? Is it a right triangle? Explain.
SEE EXAMPLE 2

**19.** Is $\triangle ADC$ a scalene, isosceles, or equilateral triangle? Is it a right triangle? Explain.
SEE EXAMPLE 2

**20.** What type of parallelogram is $ACED$? Explain. SEE EXAMPLE 3

**21.** What type of quadrilateral is $ABCD$? How do you know? SEE EXAMPLE 4

**22.** Find the area and perimeter of $\triangle ABC$.
SEE EXAMPLE 5

**23.** Find the area and perimeter of $ABCD$.
SEE EXAMPLE 6

**Three vertices of a quadrilateral are $P(-2, 3)$, $Q(2, 4)$, and $R(1, 0)$.** SEE EXAMPLE 3

**24.** Suppose $PQRS$ is a parallelogram. What are the coordinates of vertex $S$? What type of parallelogram is $PQRS$?

**25.** Suppose $PQSR$ is a parallelogram. What are the coordinates of vertex $S$? What type of parallelogram is $PQSR$?

# PRACTICE & PROBLEM SOLVING

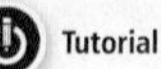

Practice Tutorial

Mixed Review Available Online

## APPLY

**26. Use Appropriate Tools** An architect overlays a coordinate grid on her plans for attaching a greenhouse to the side of a house. She wants to locate point $D$ so that $ABCD$ is a trapezoid and $\overline{CD}$ is perpendicular to the house. What are the coordinates for point $D$?

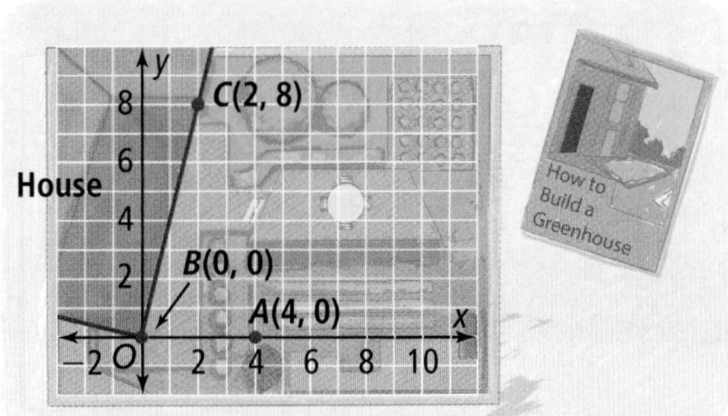


**27. Model With Mathematics** Yuson thinks the design she made is symmetric across the dashed line she drew. How can she use coordinates to show that her design is symmetric?

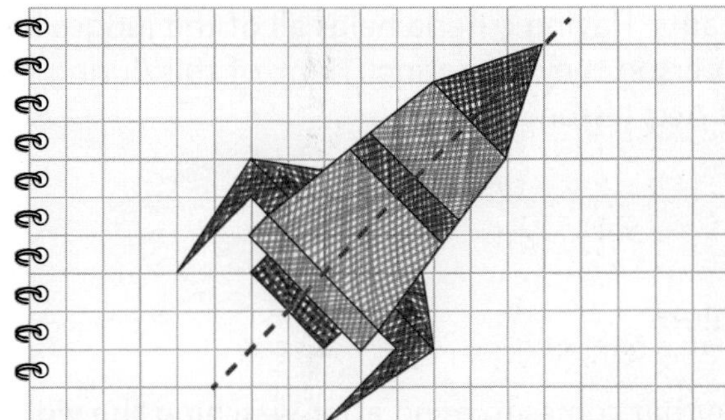

**28. Construct Arguments** The map shows the regions that Anna and Richard have explored. Each claims to have explored the greater area. Who is correct? Explain.

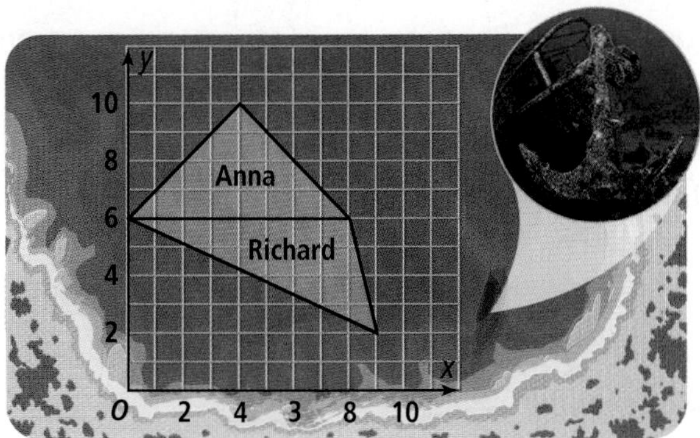


## ASSESSMENT PRACTICE

**29.** Triangle $ABC$ has vertices $A(2, 5)$, $B(6, 8)$, and $C(5, 1)$. Determine whether each statement about $\triangle ABC$ is true. Select *Yes* or *No*.

| | Yes | No |
|---|---|---|
| $\overline{AB} \cong \overline{AC}$ | ❑ | ❑ |
| $BC = AB\sqrt{2}$ | ❑ | ❑ |
| The midpoint of $BC$ is (5.5, 4). | ❑ | ❑ |
| The perimeter is 12.5 units. | ❑ | ❑ |

**30. SAT/ACT** Quadrilateral $JKLM$ has vertices $J(1, -2)$, $K(7, 1)$, $L(8, -1)$, and $M(2, -4)$. Which is the most precise classification of $JKLM$?

Ⓐ rectangle

Ⓑ rhombus

Ⓒ trapezoid

Ⓓ kite

**31. Performance Task** Dana draws the side view of a TV stand that has slanted legs. Each unit in his plan equals half of a foot.

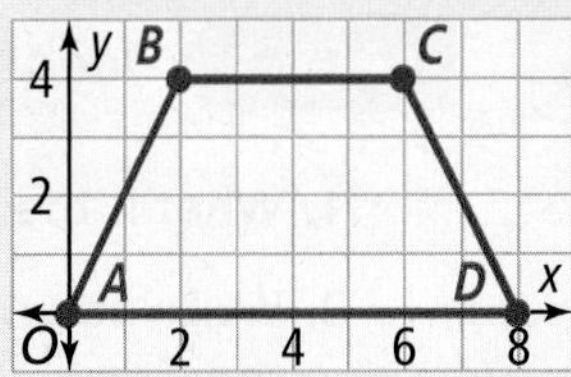


**Part A** Dana thinks his TV stand is in the shape of isosceles trapezoid. Is he correct? Explain.

**Part B** Dana adds an additional support by connecting the midpoints of the legs. How long is the support?

**Part C** Dana decides he wants to make the TV stand a half foot higher by placing $B$ at (2, 5) and $C$ at (6, 5). How much longer will the legs and support connecting the midpoints be?

## You Be the Judge

Have you ever been a judge in a contest or competition? What criteria did you use to decide the winner? If you were one of many judges, did you all agree on who should win?

Often there is a set of criteria that judges use to help them score the performances of the contestants. Having criteria helps all of the judges be consistent regardless of the person they are rating. Think of this during the Mathematical Modeling in 3 Acts lesson.

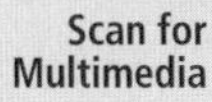

### ACT 1 Identify the Problem

1. What is the first question that comes to mind after watching the video?
2. Write down the main question you will answer about what you saw in the video.
3. Make an initial conjecture that answers this main question.
4. Explain how you arrived at your conjecture.
5. What information will be useful to know to answer the main question? How can you get it? How will you use that information?

### ACT 2 Develop a Model

6. Use the math that you have learned in this Topic to refine your conjecture.

### ACT 3 Interpret the Results

7. Did your refined conjecture match the actual answer exactly? If not, what might explain the difference?

Activity

Assess

# 9-2 Proofs Using Coordinate Geometry

PearsonRealize.com

**I CAN…** prove geometric theorems using algebra and the coordinate plane.

## CRITIQUE & EXPLAIN

**Dakota and Jung are trying to show that $\triangle ABC$ is a right triangle. Each student uses a different method.**

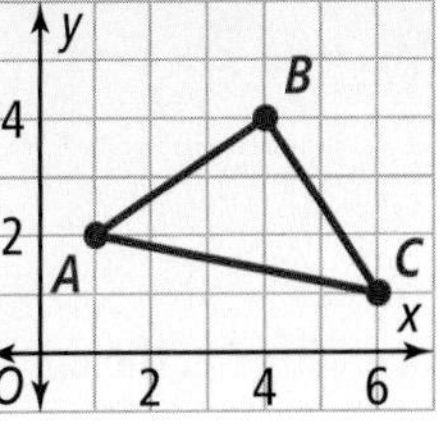


**Dakota**

slope of $\overline{AB} = \frac{2}{3}$, slope of $\overline{BC} = -\frac{3}{2}$

slope of $\overline{AB}$ • slope of $\overline{BC} = -1$

Triangle $ABC$ is a right triangle.

**Jung**

$AB = BC = \sqrt{13}$, $AC = \sqrt{26}$

$(\sqrt{13})^2 + (\sqrt{13})^2 = (\sqrt{26})^2$

Triangle $ABC$ is a right triangle.

**A.** Did Dakota and Jung both show $\triangle ABC$ is a right triangle? Explain.

**B. Reason** If the coordinates of $\triangle ABC$ were changed to (2, 3), (5, 5), and (7, 2), how would each student's method change? Explain.

## ESSENTIAL QUESTION

**How can geometric relationships be proven algebraically in the coordinate plane?**

CONCEPTUAL UNDERSTANDING

## EXAMPLE 1 Plan a Coordinate Proof

**How can you use coordinates to prove geometric relationships algebraically? Plan a proof for the Trapezoid Midsegment Theorem.**

Draw and label a diagram that names all points to be used in the proof.

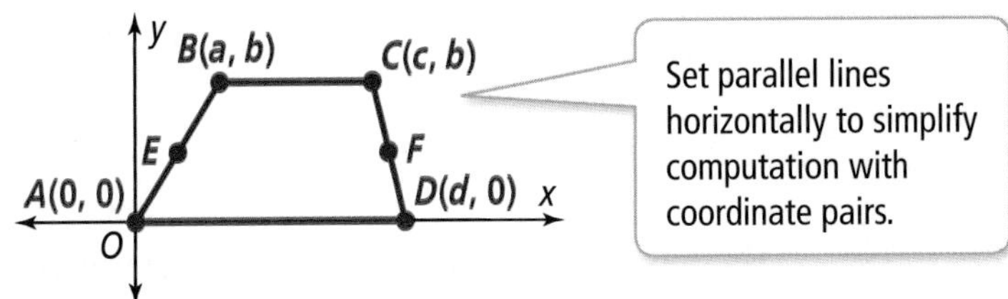


Restate the Trapezoid Midsegment Theorem so the statement can be proved using algebra on the coordinate plane.

**Theorem:** The midsegment of a trapezoid is parallel to each base and its length is one half the sum of the lengths of the bases.

**Restatement:** If $\overline{EF}$ is the midsegment of trapezoid $ABCD$, then slope $\overline{EF}$ = slope $\overline{AD}$ = slope $\overline{BC}$ and $EF = \frac{AD + BC}{2}$.

**Plan:** To show that the midsegment is parallel to the bases, show that their slopes are equal. Then show that the mean of the base lengths is the length of the midsegment.

**USE STRUCTURE**
Variables are used according to the properties of trapezoids. Why is the proof valid for all trapezoids?

**Try It!** 1. Plan a proof to show that the diagonals of a square are congruent and perpendicular.

PROOF

## EXAMPLE 2 Write a Coordinate Proof

**Write a coordinate proof of the Trapezoid Midsegment Theorem. Use the conditional statement from Example 1 to decide what is given and what is to be proved.**

**STUDY TIP**
Placing one vertex at the origin makes calculations of slopes and distances easier. If a figure is symmetrical, align the line of symmetry along one of the axes to simplify calculations.

**Given:** Trapezoid *ABCD*, with midpoints *E* and *F*

**Prove:** $\overline{EF} \parallel \overline{AD} \parallel \overline{BC}$ and $EF = \frac{AD + BC}{2}$

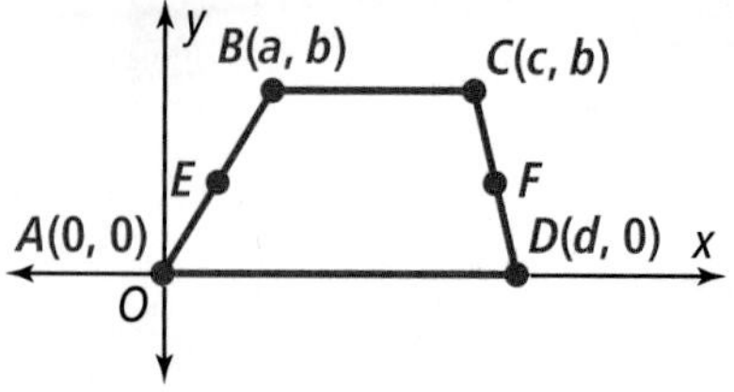


**Plan:** Apply the plan and diagram from Example 1. Use the coordinates in the diagram to show that slope $\overline{EF}$ = slope $\overline{AD}$ = slope $\overline{BC}$, and $EF = \frac{AD + BC}{2}$.

**Proof:**

**Step 1** Use the Midpoint Formula to find the coordinates of points *E* and *F*.

$$E = \left(\frac{0 + a}{2}, \frac{0 + b}{2}\right) = \left(\frac{a}{2}, \frac{b}{2}\right) \qquad F = \left(\frac{c + d}{2}, \frac{b + 0}{2}\right) = \left(\frac{c + d}{2}, \frac{b}{2}\right)$$

**Step 2** The slopes of $\overline{AD}$, $\overline{BC}$, and $\overline{EF}$ all equal zero, because the segments are horizontal.

Therefore, $\overline{EF} \parallel \overline{AD} \parallel \overline{BC}$.

**Step 3** Determine *AD*, *BC*, and *EF*.

Since the segments are horizontal lines, the lengths are differences of the *x*-coordinates.

$$AD = d - 0 = d \qquad BC = c - a \qquad EF = \frac{c + d}{2} - \frac{a}{2} = \frac{c + d - a}{2}$$

**Step 4** Use algebra to show that $\frac{AD + BC}{2} = EF$.

$$\frac{AD + BC}{2} = \frac{d + (c - a)}{2} = \frac{c + d - a}{2} = EF$$

The bases and the midsegment are parallel, and the length of the midsegment is equal to the mean of the base lengths.

Therefore, $\overline{EF} \parallel \overline{AD} \parallel \overline{BC}$ and $EF = \frac{AD + BC}{2}$.

**Try It!** 2. Use coordinate geometry to prove that the diagonals of a rectangle are congruent.

PROOF

## EXAMPLE 3 Plan and Write a Coordinate Proof

**Write a coordinate proof of the Concurrency of Medians Theorem.**

**Given:** $\triangle ABC$ with medians $\overline{AD}$, $\overline{BE}$, and $\overline{CF}$

**Prove:** The medians are concurrent at point $P$ such that

$$AP = \frac{2}{3}AD,\ BP = \frac{2}{3}BE, \text{ and } CP = \frac{2}{3}CF.$$

**Plan:** Draw and label a triangle in the coordinate plane. Then use the Midpoint Formula to locate the midpoints. Draw two medians and locate the point of intersection $P$. Use algebra to determine that the medians are concurrent at $P$. Finally, find the distance from $P$ to each vertex.

**Proof:** Draw the triangle with the coordinates shown.

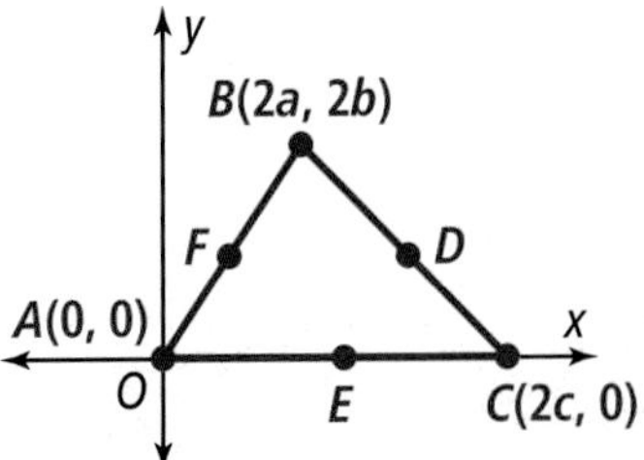


Find the coordinates of $D$, $E$, and $F$ using the Midpoint Formula.

$D = (a + c, b)$ $\quad E = (c, 0)$ $\quad F = (a, b)$

Then find the slopes of the lines containing the medians $\overline{AD}$ and $\overline{CF}$.

$$\text{slope of } \overline{AD} = \frac{b - 0}{a + c - 0} = \frac{b}{a + c} \qquad \text{slope of } \overline{CF} = \frac{b - 0}{a - 2c} = \frac{b}{a - 2c}$$

Write equations for $\overleftrightarrow{AD}$ and $\overleftrightarrow{CF}$ using point-slope form.

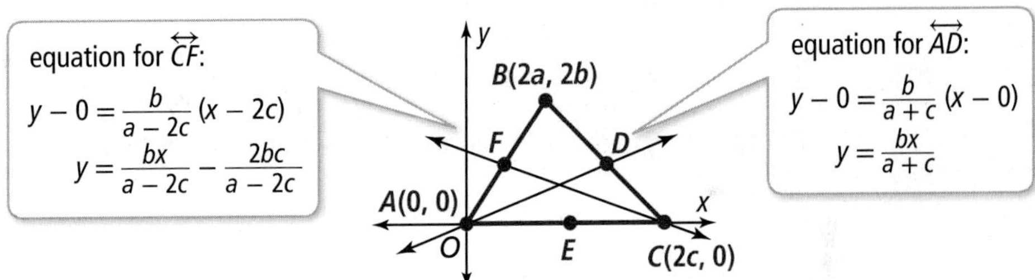


Set the expressions for $y$ equal to each other. Solve for $x$ to get $x = \frac{2(a + c)}{3}$. Then substitute the expression for $x$ into $y = \frac{bx}{a + c}$ to get $y = \frac{2b}{3}$. Let point $P$ be $\left(\frac{2(a + c)}{3}, \frac{2b}{3}\right)$.

To show that point $P$ is on $\overline{BE}$, find an equation for the line containing $\overline{BE}$. Start by finding the slope of $\overline{BE}$.

$$\text{slope of } \overline{BE} = \frac{0 - 2b}{c - 2a} = -\frac{2b}{c - 2a}$$

Then, using point-slope form, an equation for $\overleftrightarrow{BE}$ is $y = -\frac{2bx}{c - 2a} + \frac{2bc}{c - 2a}$.

Substituting $\frac{2(a + c)}{3}$ for $x$ into the equation results in $y = \frac{2b}{3}$, so point $P$ is on $\overline{BE}$. The three medians are concurrent at $P$.

To complete the proof in the Try It, use the Distance Formula to show that $AP = \frac{2}{3}AD$, $BP = \frac{2}{3}BE$, and $CP = \frac{2}{3}CF$.

CONTINUED ON THE NEXT PAGE

**COMMON ERROR**
Do not confuse the Midpoint and Distance Formulas. The $x$-coordinate of a midpoint is the average of the $x$-coordinates of the endpoints and the $y$-coordinate is the average of the $y$-coordinates.

**Try It!** **3.** To complete the proof in Example 3, use the coordinates to show that $AP = \frac{2}{3}AD$, $BP = \frac{2}{3}BE$, and $CP = \frac{2}{3}CF$.

APPLICATION

## EXAMPLE 4 Use Coordinate Proofs to Solve Problems

**An interior designer wants the center of a circular fountain to be equidistant from the corners of a triangular lobby. Where should he place the center of the fountain?**

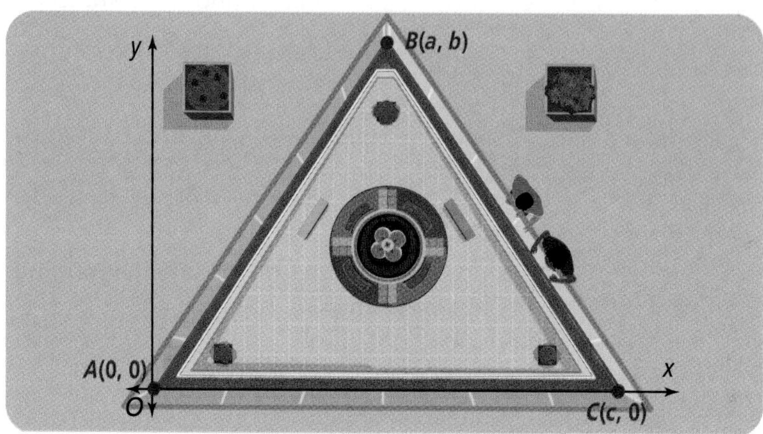


**Formulate** The center of the fountain must be at the circumcenter of the triangle. Find the point of intersection of the perpendicular bisectors of two sides of the triangle.

**Compute** Determine the intersection of the perpendicular bisectors of $\overline{AC}$ and $\overline{AB}$.

An equation of the perpendicular bisector of $\overline{AC}$ is $x = \frac{c}{2}$.

The perpendicular bisector of $\overline{AB}$ contains the point $\left(\frac{a}{2}, \frac{b}{2}\right)$ and has slope $-\frac{a}{b}$. Its point-slope equation is $y - \frac{b}{2} = -\frac{a}{b}\left(x - \frac{a}{2}\right)$, which simplifies to $y = -\frac{a}{b}x + \frac{a^2 + b^2}{2b}$.

Calculate the intersection of the two lines.

$$y = -\frac{a}{b}x + \frac{a^2 + b^2}{2b}$$

$$y = -\frac{a}{b} \cdot \frac{c}{2} + \frac{a^2 + b^2}{2b}$$

$$y = \frac{a^2 - ac + b^2}{2b}$$

Substitute $\frac{c}{2}$ for $x$, and then solve for $y$.

**Interpret** The center of the fountain should be at the point $\left(\frac{c}{2}, \frac{a^2 - ac + b^2}{2b}\right)$.

**Try It!** **4.** A table in the corner of a restaurant is a right triangle whose legs have lengths $a$ and $b$. The salt and pepper shakers should be placed equidistant from the sides of the table. Plan a coordinate geometry proof to find their location.

## CONCEPT SUMMARY Writing a Coordinate Proof

**WORDS**

- Determine which numerical relationships you must calculate to show the statement is true.
- Draw and label a figure on a coordinate plane. Choose coordinates that simplify computations.
- Calculate the numerical values needed to prove a statement or solve a problem.

**DIAGRAMS**

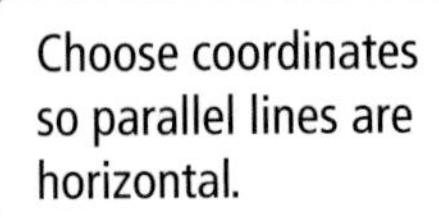


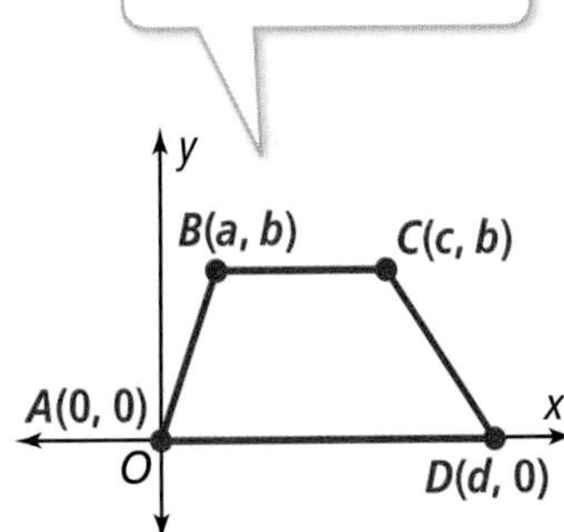


Choose coordinates so the line of symmetry is the $y$-axis.

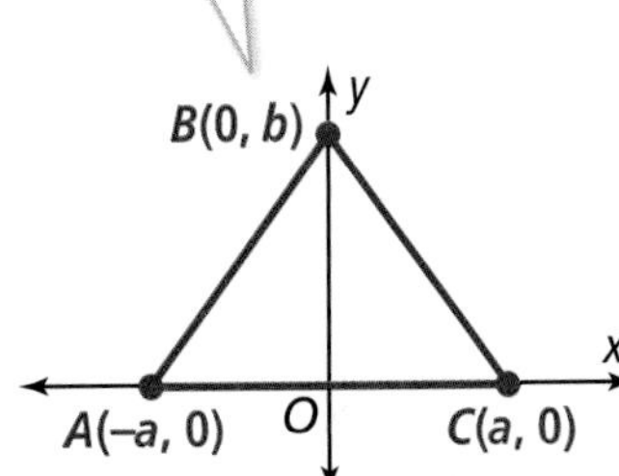


Choose coordinates so the coordinates of midpoints are convenient.

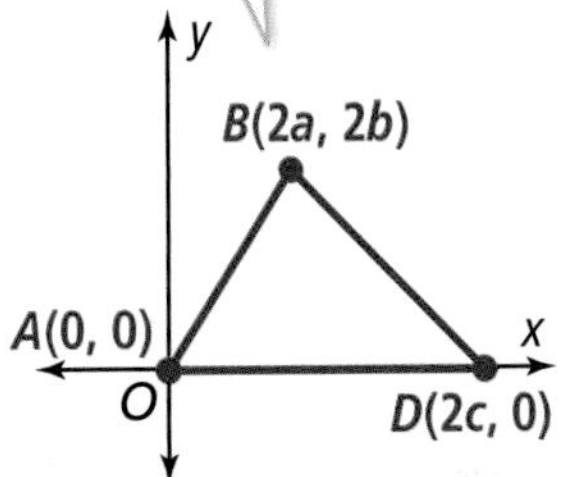


## Do You UNDERSTAND?

1. **ESSENTIAL QUESTION** How can geometric relationships be proven algebraically in the coordinate plane?

2. **Error Analysis** Venetta tried to find the slope of $\overline{AB}$. What is her error?

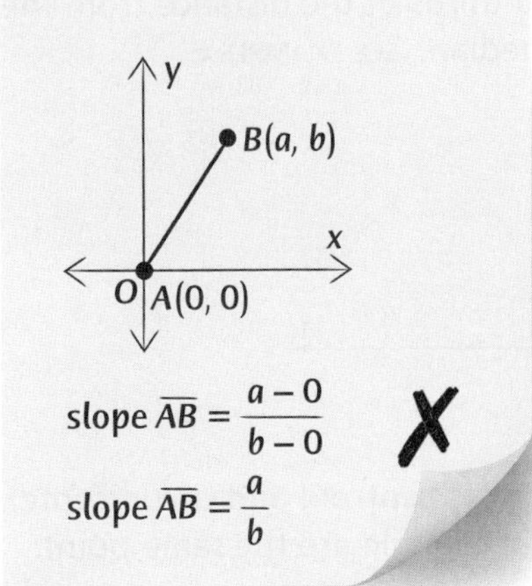


3. **Communicate Precisely** What is a coordinate geometry proof?

4. **Reason** Describe why it is important to plan a coordinate proof.

5. **Use Structure** What coordinates would you use to describe an isosceles triangle on a coordinate plane? Explain.

## Do You KNOW HOW?

**For Exercises 6–8, write a plan for a coordinate proof.**

6. The diagonals of a rhombus are perpendicular.

7. The area of a triangle with vertices $A(0, 0)$, $B(0, a)$ and $C(b, c)$ is $\frac{ac}{2}$.

8. The lines that contain the altitudes of a triangle are concurrent.

**For Exercises 9–11, plan and write a coordinate proof.**

9. A point on the perpendicular bisector of a segment is equidistant from the endpoints.

10. The diagonals of a kite are perpendicular.

11. All squares are similar.

12. Show that the diagonals of an isosceles trapezoid are congruent.

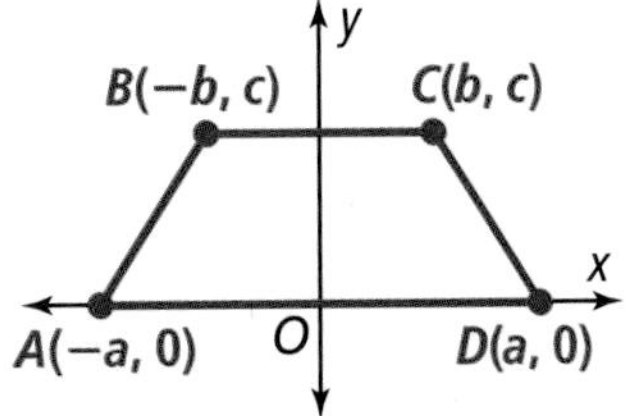

## UNDERSTAND

**13. Communicate Precisely** What coordinates would you use to describe an equilateral triangle in the coordinate plane? Explain.

**14. Error Analysis** Tonya drew a diagram to prove the Perpendicular Bisector Theorem using coordinate geometry. What coordinates should she use for point *C*?

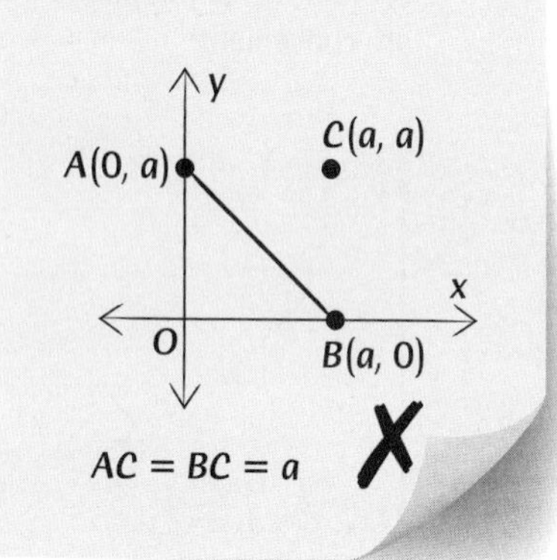


**For Exercises 15 and 16, use the graph.**

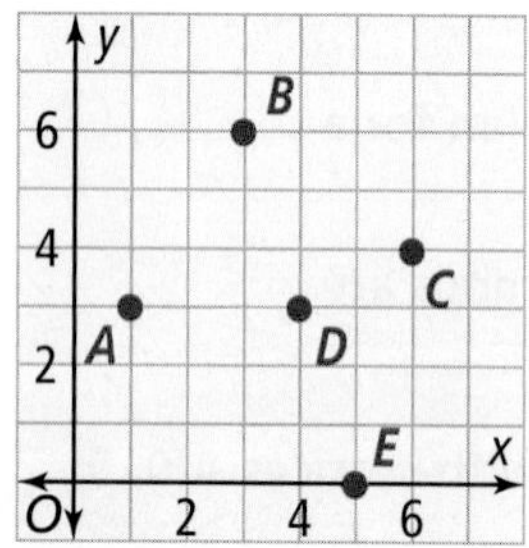


**15. Make Sense and Persevere** How would you plan a proof to show that $\triangle ABC$ is a right triangle?

**16. Make Sense and Persevere** Describe how you would prove points *B*, *D*, and *E* are collinear.

**17. Mathematical Connections** What is the equation of the line containing the perpendicular bisector of $\overline{AB}$?

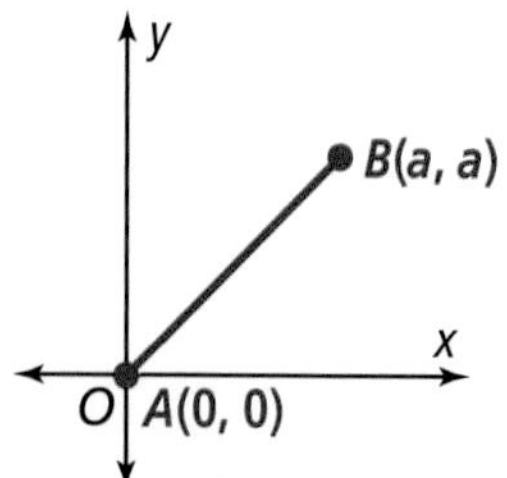


## PRACTICE

**For Exercises 18–21, write a plan for a coordinate proof.** SEE EXAMPLE 1

**18.** The diagonals of a parallelogram that is not a rectangle are not congruent.

**19.** The length of a diameter of a circle is twice that of its radius.

**20.** The diagonals of a parallelogram bisect each other.

**21.** The area of $\triangle XYZ$ is twice the area of $\triangle XWZ$, where *W* is the midpoint of $\overline{YZ}$.

**For Exercises 22–25, plan and write a coordinate proof.** SEE EXAMPLES 2 AND 3

**22.** The length of a diagonal of a rectangle is the square root of the sum of the squares of the lengths of two adjacent sides.

**23.** All right triangles with one acute angle measuring 30° are similar.

**24.** One and only one diagonal of a kite bisects the other.

**25.** The length of the median to the hypotenuse of a right triangle is half the length of the hypotenuse.

**26.** Find the centroid of the triangle by finding the point two thirds of the distance from the vertex on one median. SEE EXAMPLE 4

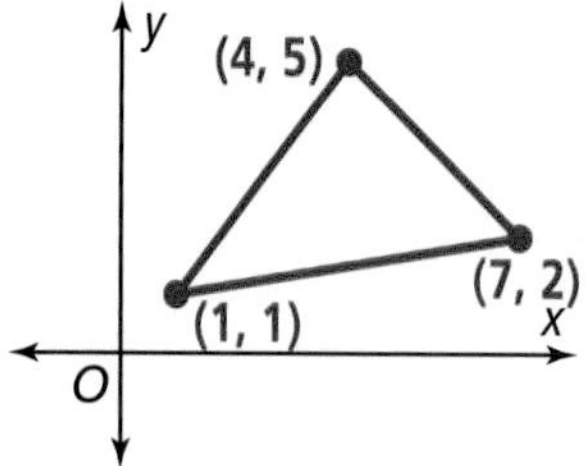


**27.** Show that the centroid and circumcenter of an equilateral triangle are the same point.

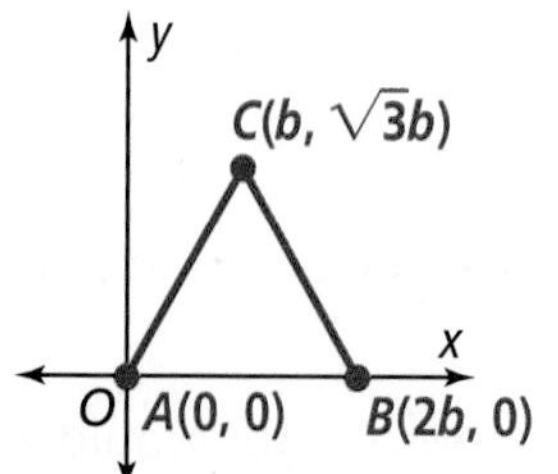

## APPLY

28. **Model With Mathematics** Each student in a woodworking class inlays brass wire along the lines connecting the midpoints of adjacent sides of a trivet. A trivet is six inches square. If the wire costs \$0.54 per inch, what is the cost of the wire for making 12 trivets?

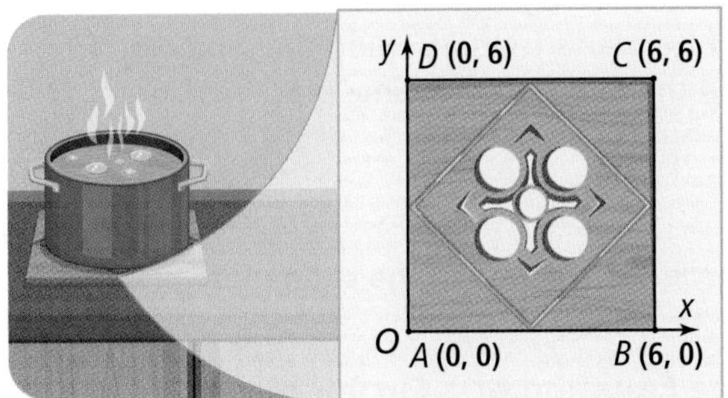


29. **Make Sense and Persevere** The owner of an animal park wants a quadrilateral trail that connects the four sides of the iscosceles-trapezoid-shaped park, with all sides of the trail the same length. Deon says that if the trail connects the midpoint of each side to the midpoints of the adjacent sides, the trail will be a rhombus. Write a coordinate proof to show that Deon is correct.

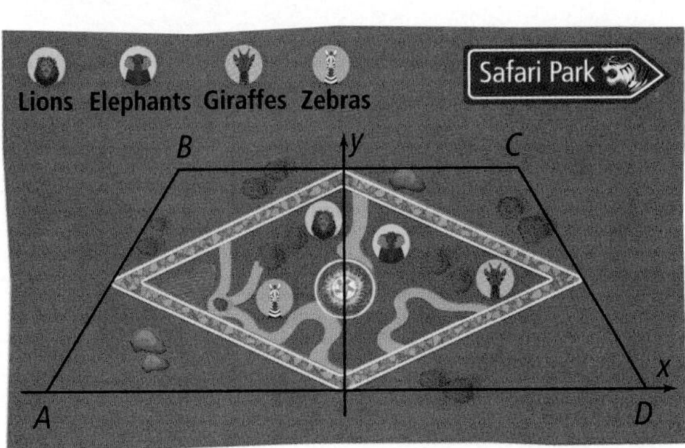


30. **Higher Order Thinking** The front of a sculpture is symmetric about the y-axis. Point A is located at (–3, 0), and $\overline{AC}$ is the longest side of $\triangle ABC$. The perimeter of $\triangle ABC$ is 16. What is the value of a?

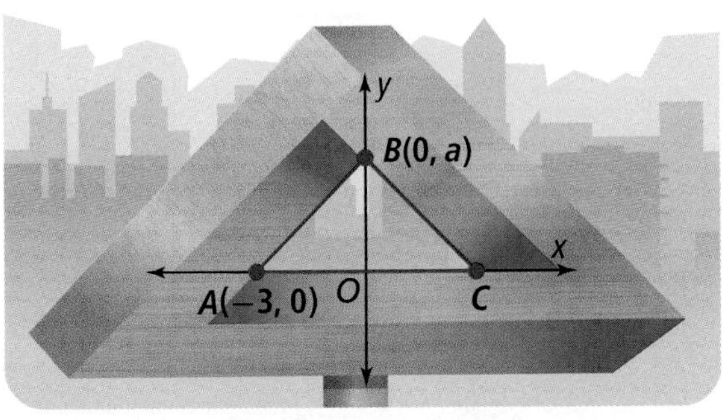


## ASSESSMENT PRACTICE

31. A coordinate proof requires a ___?___ and then uses ___?___ on the ___?___ of the points in the diagram to complete the proof.

32. **SAT/ACT** Which statements are true?

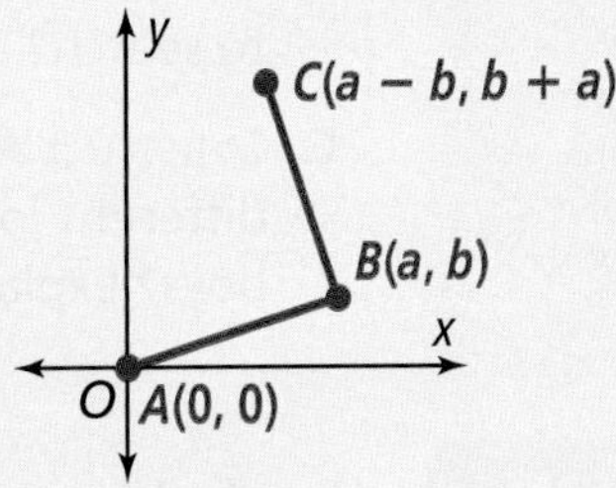


I. $AB = BC$

II. $\overline{AB} \perp \overline{BC}$

III. $AC = 2a^2 + 2b^2$

Ⓐ I only
Ⓑ II only
Ⓒ I and II only
Ⓓ I, II, and III

33. **Performance Task** Consider $\triangle ABC$ on the coordinate plane. Points D, E, and F are the midpoints of the sides.

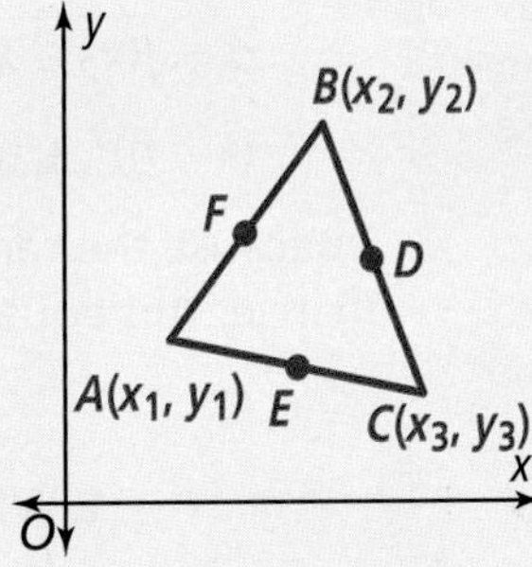


**Part A** What are the coordinates of D, E, and F?

**Part B** Prove that the coordinates of the point of concurrency of the medians is the average of the x and y coordinates of the vertices.

$$\left(\frac{x_1 + x_2 + x_3}{3}, \frac{y_1 + y_2 + y_3}{3}\right)$$

*Hint:* Apply the Concurrency of Medians Theorem and find the point $\frac{2}{3}$ of the way from A to D.

**Part C** Explain why it does not make sense to place one of the coordinates at the origin for this proof.

Activity Assess

# 9-3 Circles in the Coordinate Plane

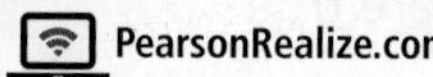
PearsonRealize.com

**I CAN…** use the equations and graphs of circles to solve problems.

## MODEL & DISCUSS

**Damian uses an app to find all pizza restaurants within a certain distance of his current location.**

**A.** What is the shape of the region that the app uses to search for pizza restaurants? Explain how you know.

**B.** What information do you think the app needs to determine the area to search?

**C. Construct Arguments** If Damian's friend is using the same app from a different location, could the app find the same pizza restaurant for both boys? Explain.

## ESSENTIAL QUESTION

**How is the equation of a circle determined in the coordinate plane?**

CONCEPTUAL UNDERSTANDING

## EXAMPLE 1 Derive the Equation of a Circle

**What equation defines a circle in the coordinate plane?**

Draw a circle with point $(h, k)$ as the center of the circle. Then select any point $(x, y)$ on the circle.

Use the Distance Formula to find the distance $r$ between the two points.

Use variables that can apply to any circle on the coordinate plane.

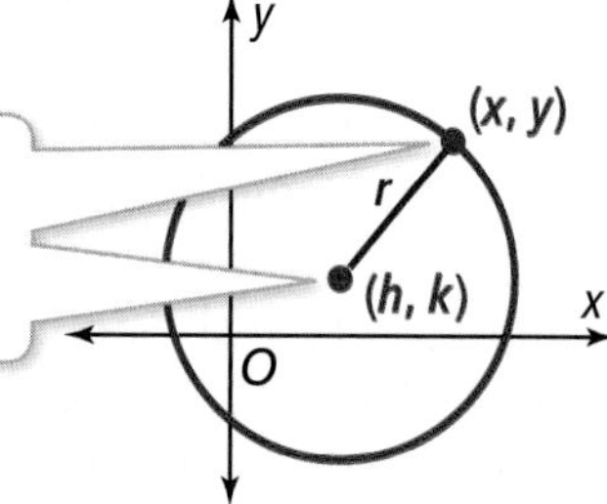


$$d = \sqrt{(x_2 - x_1)^2 + (y_2 - y_1)^2}$$

$$(x - h)^2 + (y - k)^2 = r^2$$

Because the radius is the same from the center to any point $(x, y)$ on the circle, this equation satisfies all points of the circle.

**GENERALIZE**
What other formula or formulas compares the sum of two squares to a third square? How do these formulas relate?

**Try It!** 1. What are the radius and center of the circle with the equation $(x - 2)^2 + (y - 3)^2 = 25$?

## THEOREM 9-1 Equation of a Circle

An equation of a circle with center $(h, k)$ and radius $r$ is $(x - h)^2 + (y - k)^2 = r^2$.

PROOF: SEE EXERCISE 13.

**If...**

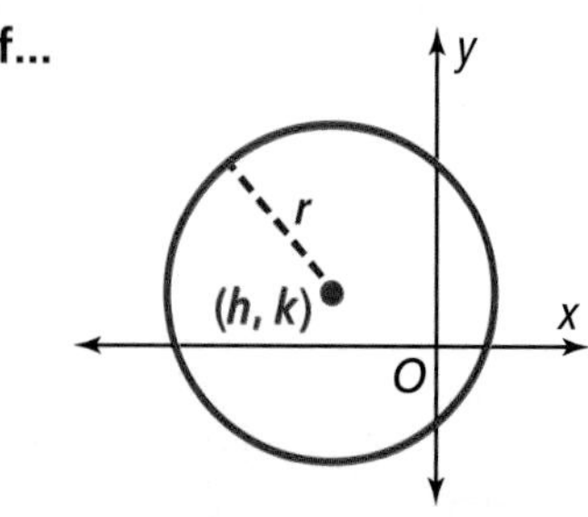


**Then...** $(x - h)^2 + (y - k)^2 = r^2$

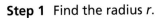

## EXAMPLE 2 Write the Equation of a Circle

**What is the equation for ⊙$A$?**

The notation ⊙$A$ means a circle with center at point $A$.

**Step 1** Find the radius $r$.

The radius is the distance from $P$ to $A$.

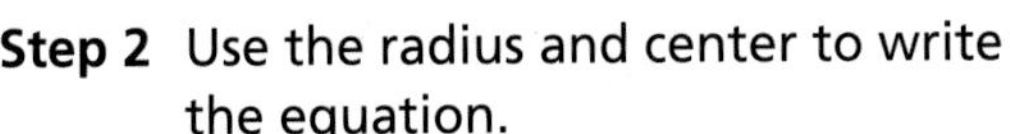

$$r = \sqrt{(-1-1)^2 + (2-5)^2} = \sqrt{13}$$

The radius of the circle is $\sqrt{13}$.

**Step 2** Use the radius and center to write the equation.

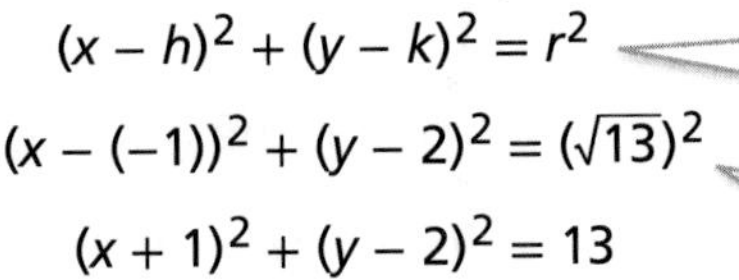

$$(x-h)^2 + (y-k)^2 = r^2$$

Use the equation of a circle.

$$(x-(-1))^2 + (y-2)^2 = (\sqrt{13})^2$$

Substitute values for $h$, $k$, and $r$.

$$(x+1)^2 + (y-2)^2 = 13$$

The equation for ⊙$A$ is $(x+1)^2 + (y-2)^2 = 13$.

**COMMON ERROR**
Be careful with the signs of coordinates. Coordinates of the center are subtracted, so if a coordinate is negative, the expression will convert to addition.

**Try It!** 2. What is the equation for each circle?

a.

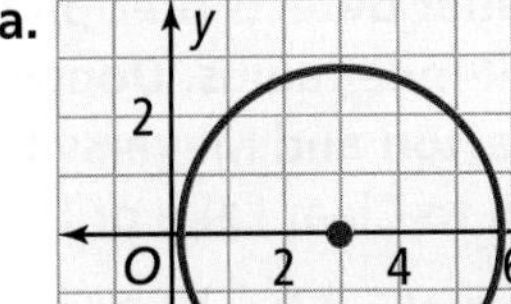

b.

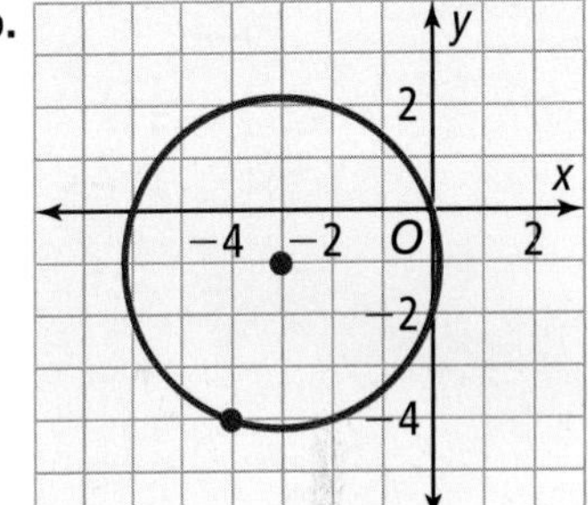

## EXAMPLE 3 Determine Whether a Point Lies on a Circle

**Circle $Q$ has radius 7 and is centered at the origin. Does the point $(-3\sqrt{2}, 5)$ lie on ⊙$Q$?**

**Step 1** Write the equation for ⊙$Q$.

$$(x-h)^2 + (y-k)^2 = r^2$$
$$(x-0)^2 + (y-0)^2 = 7^2$$
$$x^2 + y^2 = 49$$

**Step 2** Test the point $(-3\sqrt{2}, 5)$ in the equation.

$$(-3\sqrt{2})^2 + 5^2 \stackrel{?}{=} 49$$
$$18 + 25 \stackrel{?}{=} 49$$
$$43 \neq 49$$

The point $(-3\sqrt{2}, 5)$ does not lie on ⊙$Q$.

**STUDY TIP**
Remember that to square an expression $a\sqrt{b}$, you square both factors: $(a\sqrt{b})^2 = a^2(\sqrt{b})^2$.

**Try It!** 3. Determine whether each point lies on the given circle.

a. $(-3, \sqrt{11})$; circle with center at the origin and radius $2\sqrt{5}$

b. $(6, 3)$; circle with center at $(2, 4)$ and radius $3\sqrt{3}$

## EXAMPLE 4 Graph a Circle from Its Equation

**What is the graph of $(x - 3)^2 + (y + 4)^2 = 9$?**

Write the equation in the form $(x - h)^2 + (y - k)^2 = r^2$ to identify the center and radius.

$(x - 3)^2 + (y - (-4))^2 = 3^2$

center $(h, k) = (3, -4)$

radius $r = 3$

Plot the point (3, −4).

Plot points 3 units above, below, left, and right of the center. Use the points as a guide to draw the circle.

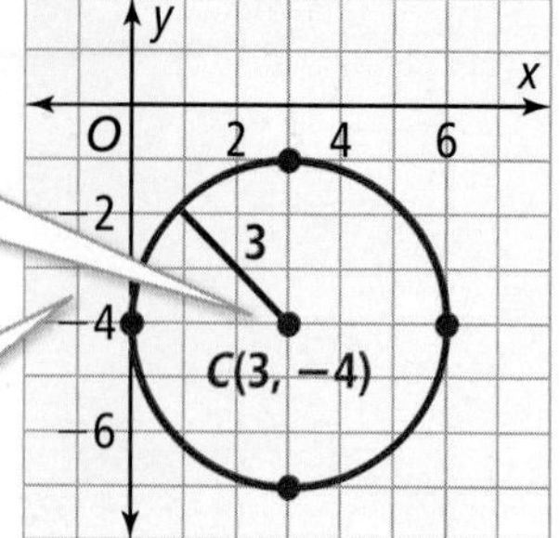

**Try It!** **4.** What is the graph of each circle?

**a.** $(x + 2)^2 + y^2 = 25$

**b.** $(x + 1)^2 + (y - 2)^2 = 1$

APPLICATION

## EXAMPLE 5 Use the Graph and Equation of a Circle to Solve Problems

**Doppler radar detects precipitation within a 90-mile radius. Doppler radar gear in Grafton and Meyersville does not extend to Clear Lake or Davis.**

**Where can a third Doppler station be placed so all towns are covered?**

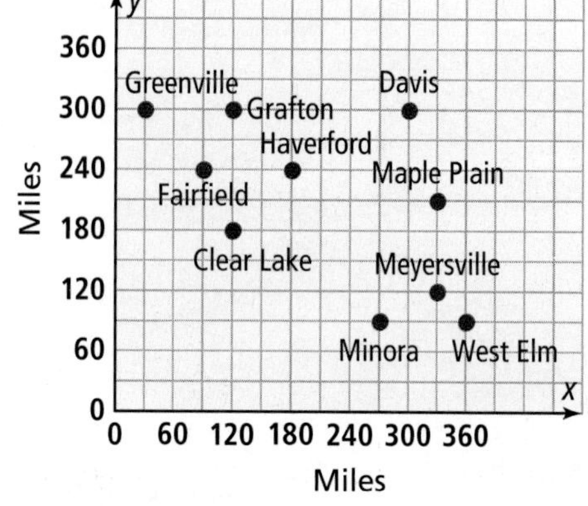


Draw circles with a 90-mile radius with centers at Grafton and Meyersville.

A circle with a 90-mile radius has a diameter of 180 miles, so 180 miles is the farthest distance between two locations covered by the same radar.

**REASON**
Think about the parts of the equation for a circle. How could you write an inequality to determine whether a point is within a circle?

Use the Distance Formula to find the distance between Clear Lake and Davis.

$$\sqrt{(300 - 180)^2 + (300 - 120)^2} \approx 216$$

The towns are more than 180 miles apart. Adding one more Doppler radar will not cover all the towns.

**Try It!** **5.** If one or both of the existing radar stations could be moved to another town, would three radar stations be sufficient to cover all the towns? Explain.

  Concept Summary 

## CONCEPT SUMMARY Equations and Graphs of Circles

**WORDS** A circle is the set of points equidistant from a fixed point. The fixed point is the center.

**ALGEBRA** $(x - h)^2 + (y - k)^2 = r^2$ where $(h, k)$ is the center and $r$ is the radius.

**GRAPH**

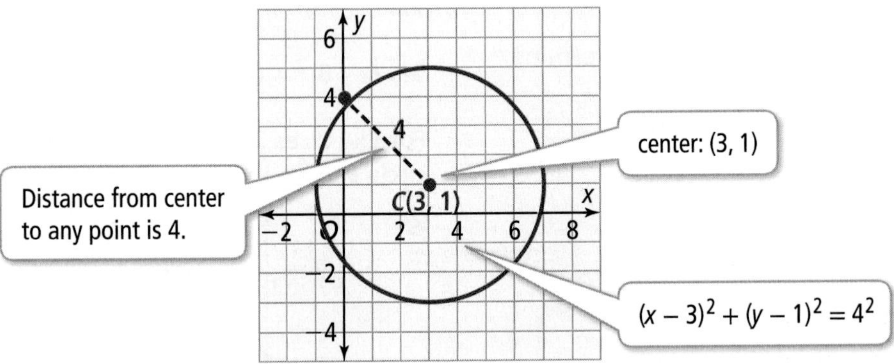


## Do You UNDERSTAND?

1. **ESSENTIAL QUESTION** How is the equation of a circle determined in the coordinate plane?

2. **Error Analysis** Leo says that the equation for the circle is $(x - 1)^2 + (y - 2)^2 = 3$. What is his error?

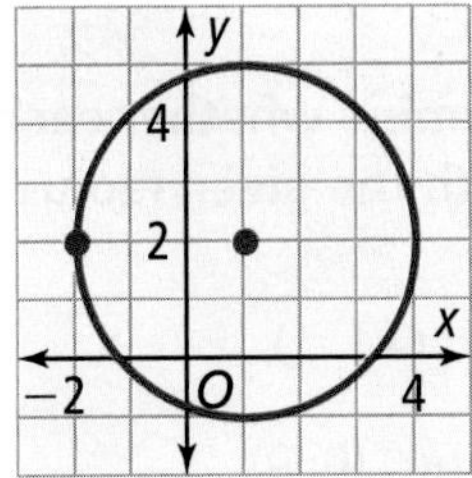

3. **Construct Arguments** If you are given the coordinates of the center and one point on a circle, can you determine the equation of the circle? Explain.

4. **Make Sense and Persevere** How could you write the equation of a circle given only the coordinates of the endpoints of its diameter?

## Do You KNOW HOW?

5. What are the center and radius of the circle with equation $(x - 4)^2 + (y - 9)^2 = 1$?

6. What is the equation for the circle with center (6, 2) and radius 8?

7. What are the center and radius of the circle with equation $(x + 7)^2 + (y - 1)^2 = 9$?

8. What is the equation for the circle with center (–9, 5) and radius 4?

**For Exercises 9 and 10, write an equation for each circle shown.**

9. 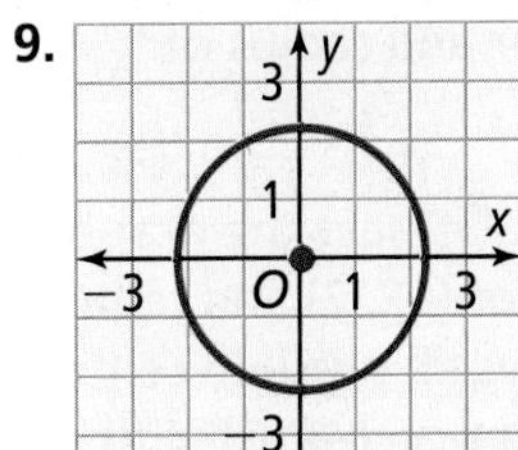

10. 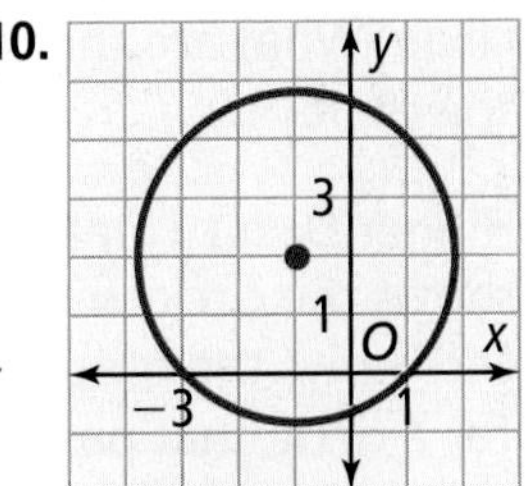

11. Is point (5, –2) on the circle with radius 5 and center (8, 2)?

12. What is the equation for the circle with center (5, 11) that passes through (9, –2)?

## PRACTICE & PROBLEM SOLVING

Scan for Multimedia | Practice | Tutorial | Additional Exercises Available Online

### UNDERSTAND

**13. Construct Arguments** Write a proof of Theorem 9-1.

**14. Mathematical Connections** What are the point(s) of intersection of $x^2 + y^2 = 25$ and $y = 2x - 5$? Graph both equations to check your answer.

**15. Error Analysis** LaTanya was asked to determine if $(3\sqrt{5}, 4)$ lies on the circle with radius 7 centered at $(0, -2)$. What is her error?

$$x^2 + (y - 2)^2 = 49$$
$$(3\sqrt{5})^2 + (4 - 2)^2 \stackrel{?}{=} 49$$
$$45 + 4 = 49$$

The point $(3\sqrt{5}, 4)$ lies on the circle with radius 7 and center $(0, -2)$. ✗

**16. Communicate Precisely** Describe the graph of $(x - a)^2 + (y - b)^2 = 0$.

**17. Reason** If the area of square $ABCD$ is 50, what is the equation for $\odot R$?

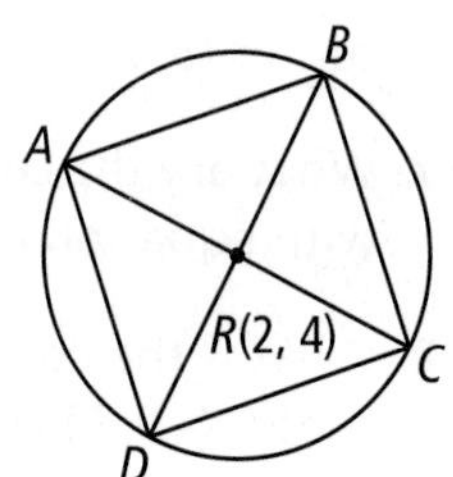


**18. Construct Arguments** The points $(a, b)$ and $(c, d)$ are the endpoints of a diameter of a circle. What are the center and radius of the circle?

**19. Higher Order Thinking** Isabel says the graph shows the circle with center $(-2, 2)$ and radius 3. Nicky says the graph shows all possible centers for a circle that passes through $(-2, 2)$ with radius 3. Which student is correct? Explain.

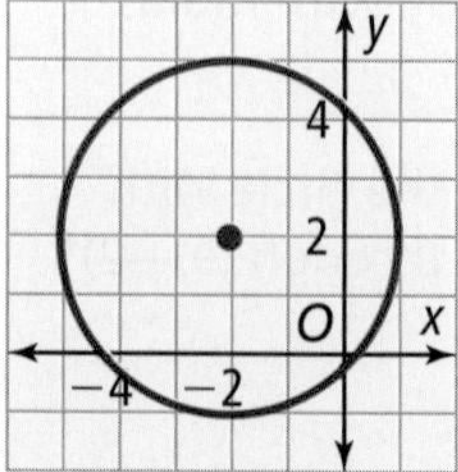


### PRACTICE

**For Exercises 20–23, find the center and radius for each equation of a circle.** SEE EXAMPLE 1

**20.** $(x - 4)^2 + (y + 3)^2 = 64$

**21.** $(x + 2)^2 + y^2 = 13$

**22.** $(x + 5)^2 + (y + 11)^2 = 32$

**23.** $(x - 8)^2 + (y - 12)^2 = 96$

**For Exercises 24 and 25, write the equation for the circle shown in each graph.** SEE EXAMPLE 2

**24.**

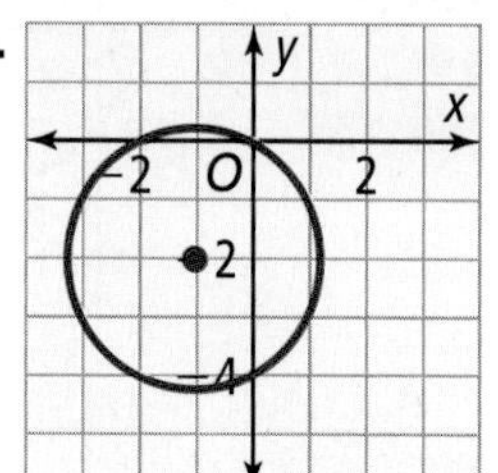


**25.**

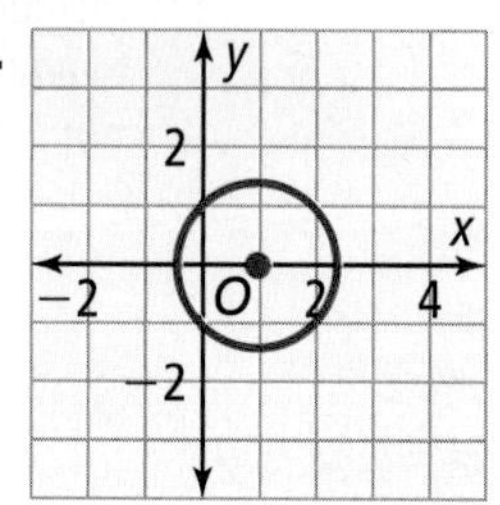


**For Exercises 26–29, write the equation for each circle with the given radius and center.** SEE EXAMPLE 2

**26.** radius: 4, center: $(5, 1)$

**27.** radius: 9, center: $(-3, 8)$

**28.** radius: $5\sqrt{5}$, center: $(2, -4)$

**29.** radius: $\sqrt{13}$, center: $(-5, -9)$

**For Exercises 30–32, determine whether each given point lies on the circle with the given radius and center.** SEE EXAMPLE 3

**30.** $(2, 4)$; radius: 4, center: $(-1, 1)$

**31.** $(\sqrt{17}, 8)$; radius: 9, center: $(0, 0)$

**32.** $(2, 0)$; radius: $\sqrt{10}$, center: $(3, -9)$

**For Exercises 33–35, graph each equation.**
SEE EXAMPLES 4 AND 5

**33.** $(x - 5)^2 + (y + 1)^2 = 4$

**34.** $x^2 + (y - 1)^2 = 16$

**35.** $(x + 3)^2 + (y + 4)^2 = 9$

**36.** The point $(2, b)$ lies on the circle with radius 5 and center $(-1, -1)$. What are the possible values of $b$?

**37.** Is $(7, 2)$ inside, outside, or on the circle $(x - 4)^2 + y^2 = 25$? Explain.

# PRACTICE & PROBLEM SOLVING

## APPLY

**38. Model With Mathematics** After an earthquake, a circle-shaped tsunami travels outward from the epicenter at an average speed of 420 miles per hour. If the earthquake with the epicenter shown occurred at 5:48 A.M., at what time will the tsunami reach Port Charles? Justify your answer.

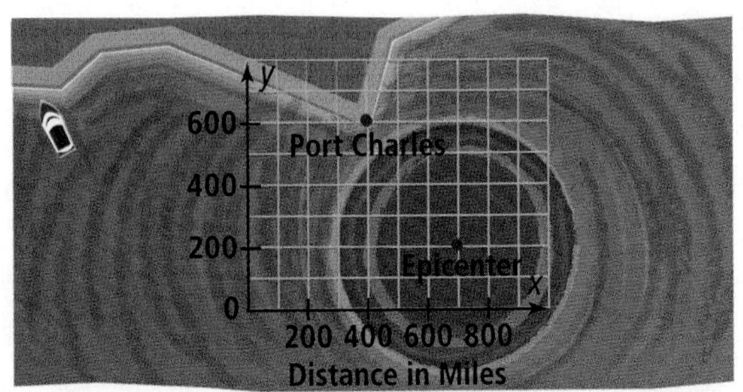


**39. Make Sense and Persevere** A cell phone tower is attached to the ground as shown. A circular security fence must be placed around the tower 10 feet from where the guy wires are attached to the ground. Can a cell phone tower be placed in the location shown? If so, what are possible coordinates of the tower?

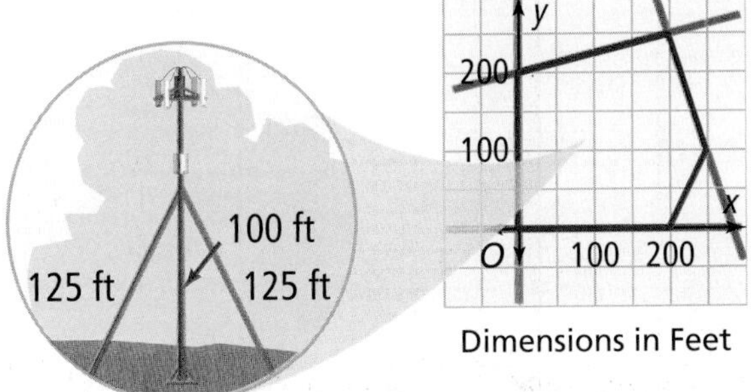


**40. Reason** Semitrailer trucks can be up to 14 feet tall. Should they be allowed in the outer lanes of the semicircular tunnel? Explain.

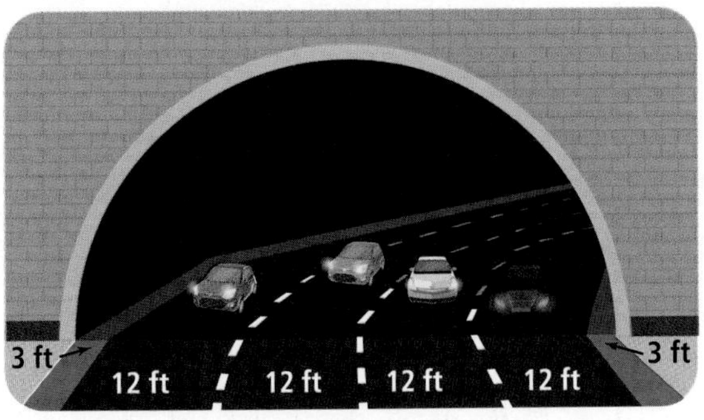


## ASSESSMENT PRACTICE

**41.** A circle has center (0, 0) and passes through the point (−5, 2). Which other points lie on the circle? Select all that apply.

Ⓐ (0, 6)
Ⓑ $(\sqrt{11}, 3\sqrt{2})$
Ⓒ (2, 5)
Ⓓ (−5, −2)
Ⓔ $(4, -\sqrt{13})$
Ⓕ $(-\sqrt{29}, 0)$

**42. SAT/ACT** Which equation represents the circle with center (−3, 7) and radius 9?

Ⓐ $(x + 3)^2 + (y - 7)^2 = 3^2$
Ⓑ $(x - 3)^2 + (y + 7)^2 = 9^2$
Ⓒ $(x - 7)^2 + (y + 3)^2 = 9^2$
Ⓓ $(x + 3)^2 + (y - 7)^2 = 9^2$
Ⓔ $(x + 7)^2 + (y - 3)^2 = 3^2$

**43. Performance Task** A farmer can use up to four rotating sprinklers for the field shown. He has ten 50-meter sections that can be combined to form rotating arms with lengths from 50 m to 500 m. The irrigation circles cannot overlap and must not extend beyond the edges of the field. The distance between grid lines is 50 m.

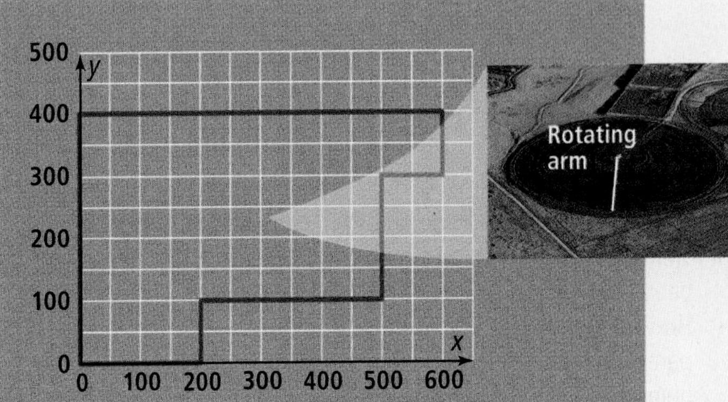


**Part A** Design an irrigation system for the field that irrigates as much of the field as possible. Draw a sketch of your system. For each sprinkler, give the coordinates of the center of the sprinkler, the radius, and the equation.

**Part B** What is the total area of the field? What is the total area irrigated by your system? What percent of the field does your system irrigate?

Activity
Assess

# 9-4 Parabolas in the Coordinate Plane

PearsonRealize.com

**I CAN...** use the equations and graphs of parabolas to solve problems.

**VOCABULARY**
- directrix
- focus
- parabola

## EXPLORE & REASON

**Consider two points and two intersecting lines.**

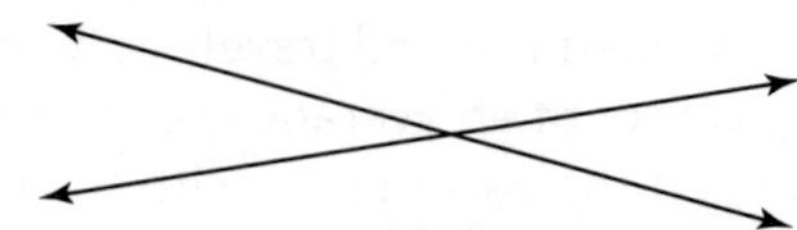

**A.** Describe the set of points that is equidistant from two points. Draw a diagram to support your answer.

**B.** Describe the set of points that is equidistant from each of two intersecting lines. Draw a diagram to support your answer.

**C. Look for Relationships** What do you think a set of points that is equidistant from a line and a point would look like? Draw a diagram to support your answer.

## ESSENTIAL QUESTION

**How does the geometric description of a parabola relate to its equation?**

CONCEPTUAL UNDERSTANDING

## EXAMPLE 1 Explore the Graph of a Parabola

**What is the set of points that are equidistant from the graph of the equation $y = -2$ and the point (0, 2)?**

Graph the line and the point.

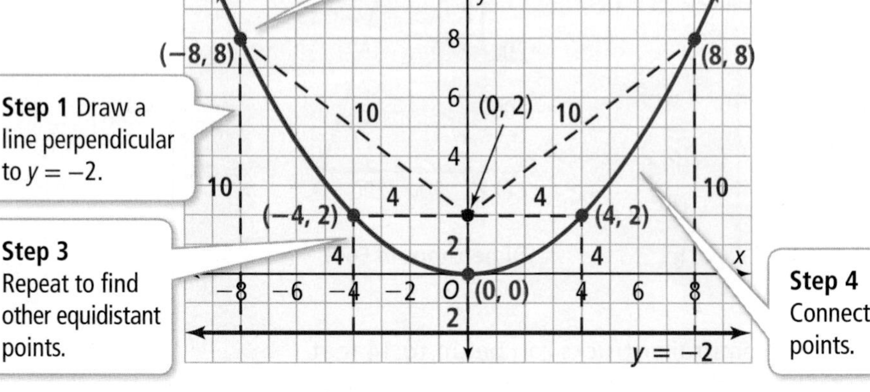
Step 2 Find a point on the perpendicular that is equidistant from (0, 2) and y = −2.
Step 1 Draw a line perpendicular to y = −2.
Step 3 Repeat to find other equidistant points.
Step 4 Connect the points.
(−8, 8)
(8, 8)
(0, 2)
(−4, 2)
(4, 2)
(0, 0)
10
4
2
y = −2
x
y
O

**MAKE SENSE AND PERSEVERE**
Think about the relationship between the point and line. How would the shape of the parabola change if the line and point were closer together or farther apart?

The set of points equidistant from (0, 2) and $y = -2$ is a curve called a *parabola*.

**Try It!** 1. The set of points equidistant from (3, 5) and the line $y = 9$ is also a parabola.

**a.** What is the vertex of the parabola?

**b.** Describe the graph of the parabola.

## EXAMPLE 2 Derive the Equation of a Parabola

**What is the equation of a parabola?**

A **parabola** is the set of all points in a plane that are the same distance from a fixed point $F$, the **focus**, as they are from a line $d$, the **directrix**.

**STUDY TIP**
The focus is $p$ units above the vertex, so the directrix must be $p$ units below the vertex.

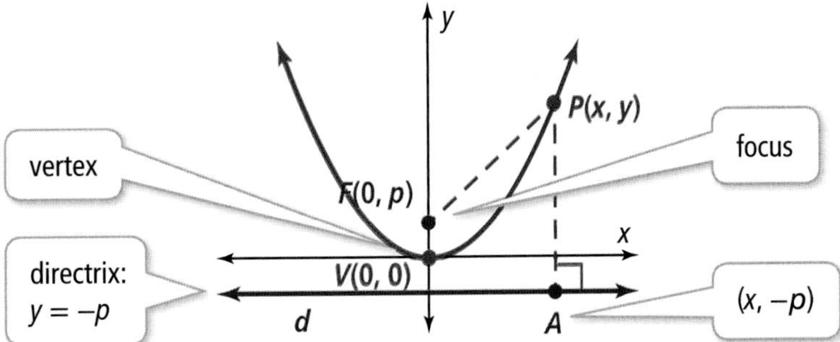


Every point on the parabola is equidistant from $F$ and line $d$.

$$PF = PA$$

$$\sqrt{(x-0)^2 + (y-p)^2} = \sqrt{(x-x)^2 + (y-(-p))^2} \quad \text{Distance Formula}$$

$$\sqrt{x^2 + (y-p)^2} = \sqrt{(y+p)^2} \quad \text{Simplify.}$$

$$x^2 + (y-p)^2 = (y+p)^2 \quad \text{Square each side.}$$

$$x^2 + y^2 - 2py + p^2 = y^2 + 2py + p^2 \quad \text{Simplify.}$$

$$x^2 - 2py = 2py$$

$$x^2 = 4py$$

$$y = \frac{1}{4p}x^2 \quad \text{Solve for } y.$$

The equation for a parabola with vertex at the origin is $y = \frac{1}{4p}x^2$.

If the vertex is at $(h, k)$, then the parabola is translated $h$ units horizontally and $k$ units vertically, and the equation is $y - k = \frac{1}{4p}(x-h)^2$.

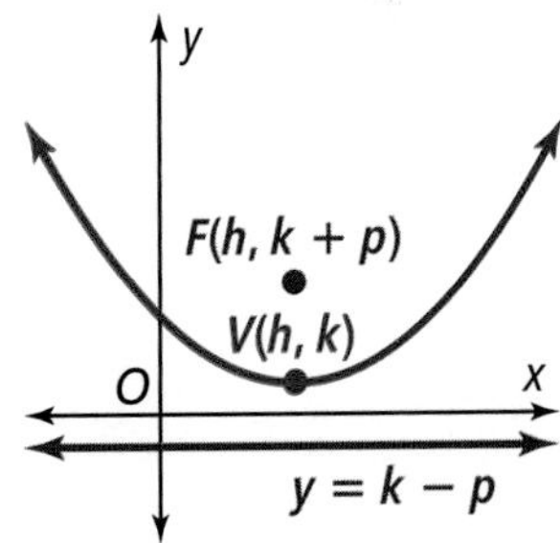

**Try It!** 2. What expression represents the distance between the focus and the directrix?

## CONCEPT Equation of a Parabola

Vertex at origin:

$$y = \frac{1}{4p}x^2$$

Vertex at $(h, k)$:

$$y - k = \frac{1}{4p}(x - h)^2$$

The variable $p$ represents the distance between the focus and the vertex.

## EXAMPLE 3 Write the Equation of a Parabola

**A. What equation represents the parabola with focus (5, 5) and directrix $y = 1$?**

Graph the focus and directrix to determine the vertex and $p$.

The vertex is the midpoint of the segment connecting the focus and the directrix.

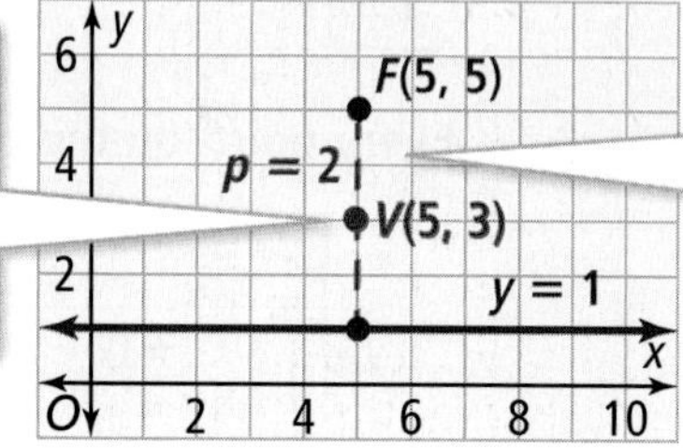


The value of $p$ is the distance between the focus and the vertex.

Write the equation for the parabola with vertex (5, 3) and $p = 2$.

$$y - k = \frac{1}{4p}(x - h)^2$$

Write the formula for a parabola with vertex $(h, k)$.

$$y - 3 = \frac{1}{4(2)}(x - 5)^2$$

$$y = \frac{1}{8}(x - 5)^2 + 3$$

**COMMON ERROR**
When substituting values into the equation of a parabola, be sure to use the coordinates of the vertex, not the coordinates of the focus.

**B. Graph the parabola from part A.**

Use the equation to make a table of values to help you sketch the graph.

| $x$ | $y$ | $(x, y)$ |
|---|---|---|
| 1 | $\frac{1}{8}(1 - 5)^2 + 3$ | (1, 5) |
| 3 | $\frac{1}{8}(3 - 5)^2 + 3$ | $\left(3, 3\frac{1}{2}\right)$ |
| 8 | $\frac{1}{8}(8 - 5)^2 + 3$ | $\left(8, 4\frac{1}{8}\right)$ |

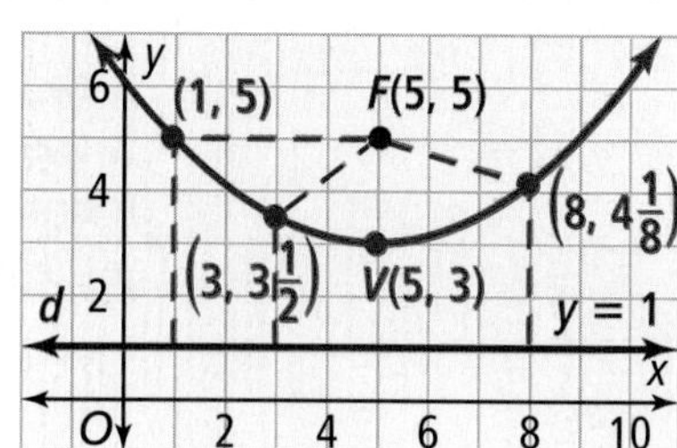

**Try It!** 3. a. What equation represents the parabola with focus (−1, 4) and directrix $y = -2$?

b. What equation represents the parabola with focus (3, 5) and vertex (3, −1)?

APPLICATION

## EXAMPLE 4 Apply the Equation of a Parabola

**The cross section of a satellite dish is a parabola, with the feed horn at the focus. How long do the braces holding the feed horn need to be?**

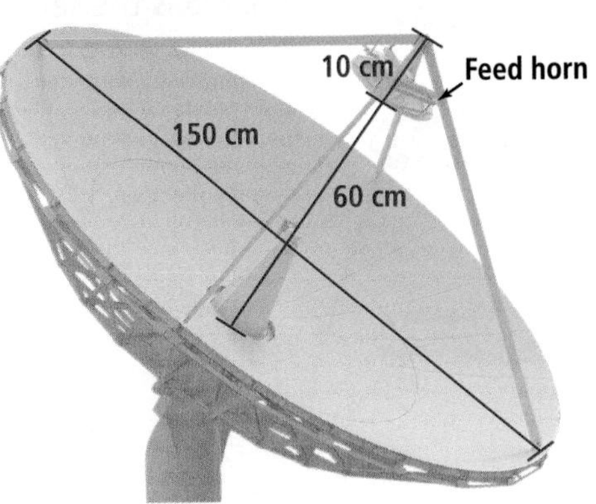


**Formulate** Place the parabola on a coordinate plane. Parabolas are symmetric, so computations are easier for a parabola with its vertex at the origin.

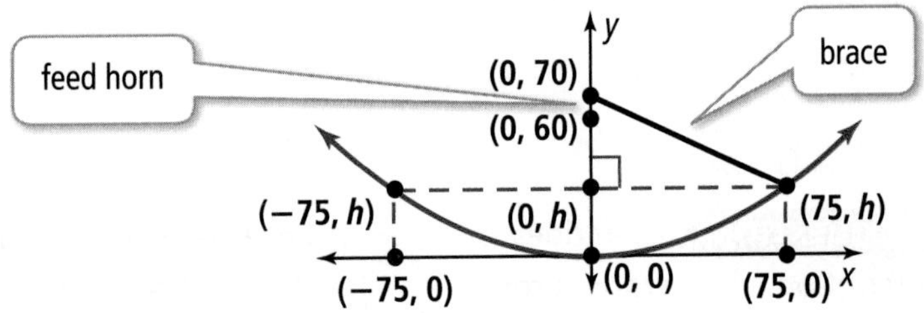


Write an equation for the parabola, and then use the equation to find the height $h$ of the dish. Finally, use the Pythagorean Theorem to find the length of the brace.

**Compute** **Step 1** Write the equation.

$$y = \frac{1}{4p}x^2$$

Write the equation for a parabola with vertex at the origin, where $p$ is the distance between the focus and the vertex.

$$y = \frac{1}{4(60)}x^2$$

Substitute 60 for $p$.

$$y = \frac{1}{240}x^2$$

**Step 2** Evaluate for $x = 75$ to find the height $h$ of the dish.

$$h = \frac{1}{240}(75)^2 \approx 23.4 \text{ cm}$$

**Step 3** Use the Pythagorean Theorem to find the length of the brace.

$$(70 - 23.4)^2 + 75^2 = b^2$$

$$7{,}796.56 = b^2$$

$$b \approx 88.3$$

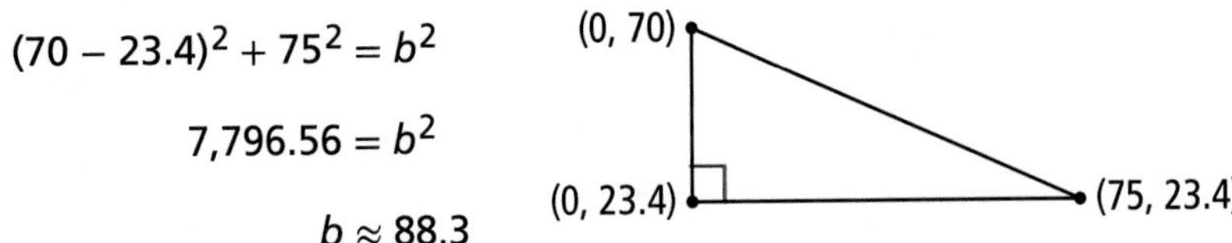


**Interpret** The braces need to be 88.3 cm long.

**Try It!** **4.** On a different satellite dish, the feed horn is 38 inches above the vertex. If the height of the dish is 22 inches, what is its width?

## CONCEPT SUMMARY Parabolas

**WORDS** A parabola is the set of points equidistant from a focus and a directrix.

**ALGEBRA** $y - k = \frac{1}{4p}(x - h)^2$

where $(h, k)$ is the vertex and $p$ is the distance from the vertex to the focus

**GRAPH**

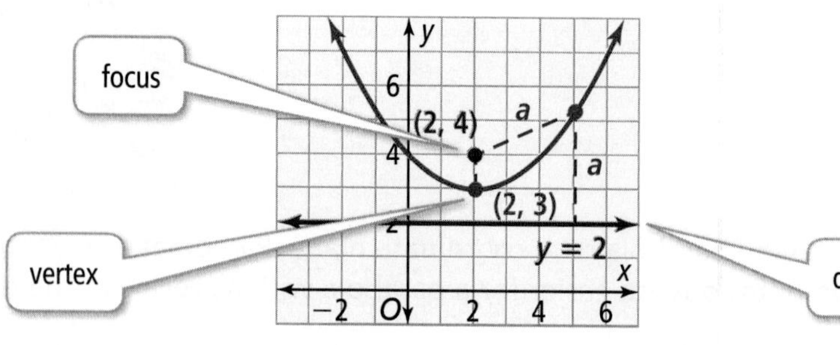


## Do You UNDERSTAND?

1. **ESSENTIAL QUESTION** How does the geometric description of a parabola relate to its equation?

2. **Error Analysis** Arthur says that an equation of the parabola with directrix $y = 0$ and focus $= (0, 6)$ is $y - 3 = \frac{1}{24}x^2$. What is his error?

3. **Vocabulary** How could the word *direction* help you remember that the directrix is a line?

4. **Reason** What are the coordinates of point $P$? Show your work.

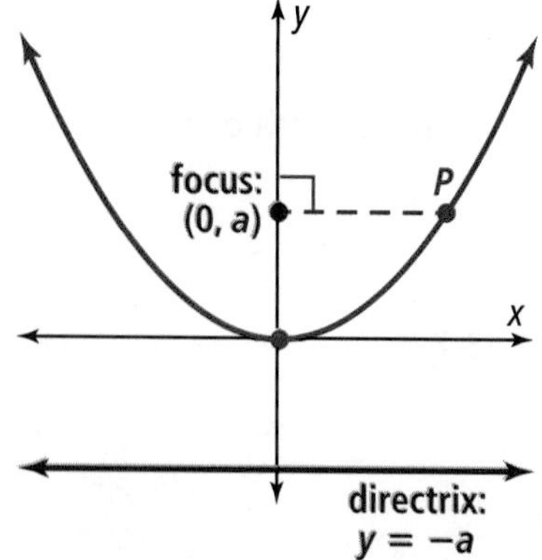


5. **Communicate Precisely** Given vertex $(a, b)$ and focus $(a, c)$, describe how you would write an equation for the parabola.

## Do You KNOW HOW?

**For Exercises 6–9, write an equation of each parabola with the given focus and directrix.**

6. focus: (0, 4); directrix: $y = -4$

7. focus: (5, 1); directrix: $y = -5$

8. focus: (4, 0); directrix: $y = -4$

9. focus: (2, −1); directrix: $y = -4$

**For Exercises 10–13, give the vertex, focus, and directrix of each parabola.**

10. $y = \frac{1}{8}x^2$

11. $y - 2 = \frac{1}{6}x^2$

12. $y - 6 = \frac{1}{4}(x - 1)^2$

13. $y + 3 = \frac{1}{20}(x - 9)^2$

**For Exercises 14–17, write an equation of each parabola with the given focus and vertex.**

14. focus: (6, 2); vertex: (6, −4)

15. focus: (−1, 8); vertex: (−1, 7)

16. focus: (4, 0); vertex: (4, −2)

17. focus: (−3, −1); vertex: (−3, −4)

18. Consider the parabola $y = \frac{1}{36}x^2$.

   a. What are the focus and directrix?

   b. The parabola passes through (12, 4). Show that this point is equidistant from the focus and the directrix.

# PRACTICE & PROBLEM SOLVING

Scan for Multimedia

Practice Tutorial

Additional Exercises Available Online

## UNDERSTAND

19. **Communicate Precisely** Use the graph to answer the questions. Line $m$ is the directrix of the parabola.

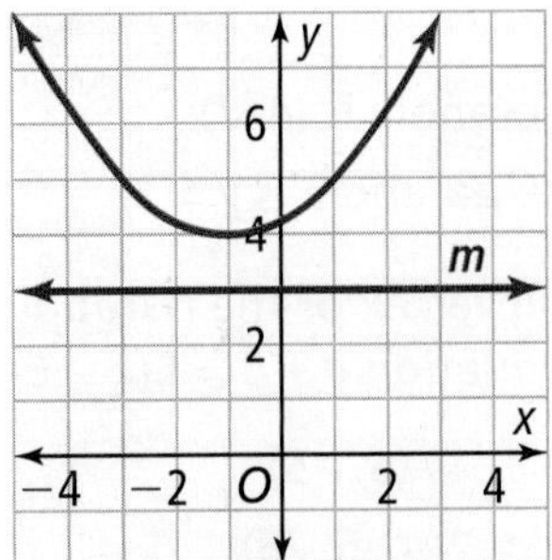


a. How would you find the vertex of the parabola? Explain.

b. How would you find the focus of the parabola? Explain.

c. How would you find an equation of the parabola? Explain.

20. **Communicate Precisely** Define a parabola as a set of points. What is the relationship of the points to the lines and points associated with the parabola?

21. **Mathematical Connections** The general form of the equation of a parabola is $y = x^2 - 6x + 9$. What are the focus, vertex, and directrix of the parabola?

22. **Reason** How does changing the distance from the focus to the directrix change the shape of a parabola in the coordinate plane? Explain.

23. **Construct Arguments** The parabola has its focus at $\left(0, \frac{1}{4}\right)$ and vertex at (0, 0). How would you find the equation of the parabola?

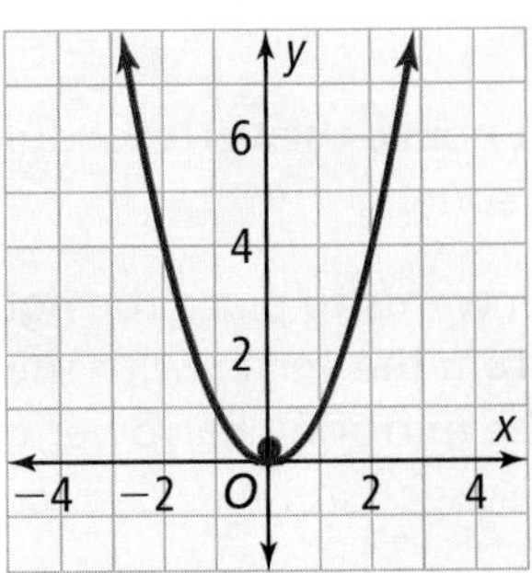


## PRACTICE

**For Exercises 24–27, find the vertex of each parabola.** SEE EXAMPLE 1

24. focus: (3, 7); directrix: $y = -1$

25. focus: (6, 2); directrix: $y = -4$

26. focus: (−4, 3); directrix: $y = 0$

27. focus: (−2, −1); directrix: $y = -6$

**For Exercises 28–31, find the vertex, focus and directrix of each parabola.** SEE EXAMPLE 2

28. $y - 7 = \frac{1}{8}(x - 3)$

29. $y + 4 = \frac{1}{36}(x - 1)$

30. $y - 3 = \frac{1}{16}(x + 6)$

31. $y + 5 = \frac{1}{2}(x - 10)$

**For Exercises 32–34, write an equation of each parabola with the given focus and directrix.** SEE EXAMPLE 3

32. focus: (0, 4); directrix: $y = 0$

33. focus: (5, 1); directrix: $y = -9$

34. focus: (−4, 5); directrix: $y = 2$

**For Exercises 35–37, write an equation of each parabola with the given focus and vertex.** SEE EXAMPLE 3

35. focus: (4, 5); vertex: (4, −1)

36. focus: (−4, 9); vertex: (−4, 5)

37. focus: (2, 4); vertex: (2, 0)

**For Exercises 38–40, use the graph of the parabola shown to answer each question.** SEE EXAMPLE 4

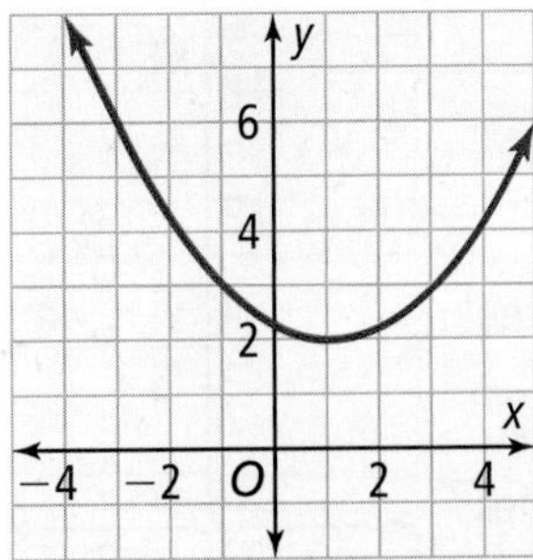


38. What is the vertex of the parabola?

39. Using a point on the parabola and the equation $y - k = \frac{1}{4p}(x - h)^2$, what is $p$?

40. What is the focus of the parabola?

# PRACTICE & PROBLEM SOLVING



## APPLY

**41. Reason** Henry is building a model of the Clifton Suspension Bridge using a scale factor of 100 ft : 1 in. The cables between the towers are in the shape of a parabola. He writes an equation of the parabola to describe the model he is building and uses the equation to determine the distances from the cable to the deck of the bridge. Suppose the deck is the $x$-axis and the vertex lies on the $y$-axis. What is the equation that Henry writes?

**42. Model With Mathematics** Devin builds a solar hot dog cooker for the science fair. Suppose the base of the cooker is the $x$-axis and the hot dog is on the $y$-axis at the focus. What is the equation of the parabola that models the cooker?

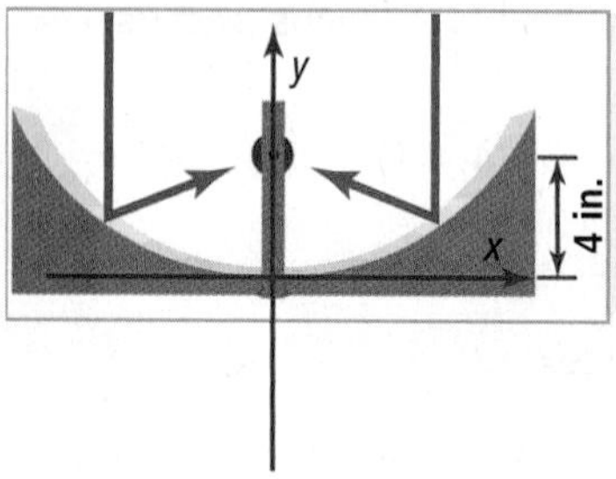

**43. Higher Order Thinking** An engineer is making an impact analysis on a car bumper. He graphs the kinetic energy of a 2-kg steel ball as a function of the velocity of the ball. Kinetic energy is measured in joules (J) and velocity is measured in meters per second.

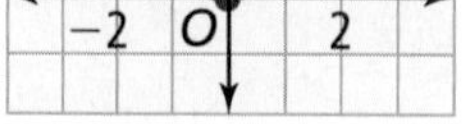


**a.** What are the vertex, focus, and directrix of the parabola?

**b.** The car bumper has to withstand an impact of 25 J from the 2-kg steel ball without any damage. How fast is the ball moving when it strikes the bumper with that amount of energy?

## ASSESSMENT PRACTICE

**44.** An equation of a parabola is $y - 5 = \frac{1}{8}(x - 4)$. Select all that apply.

Ⓐ The vertex of the parabola is (5, 4).

Ⓑ $p = 2$

Ⓒ The focus of the parabola is (4, 7).

Ⓓ The directrix of the parabola is $y = 3$.

**45. SAT/ACT** Which is the vertex of the parabola represented by the equation $y + 5 = 6(x - 6)^2$?

Ⓐ (6, 5)

Ⓑ (−6, −5)

Ⓒ (6, −5)

Ⓓ (−6, 25)

**46. Performance Task** Some flashlights are designed so that a parabolic mirror reflects light forward from a light source.

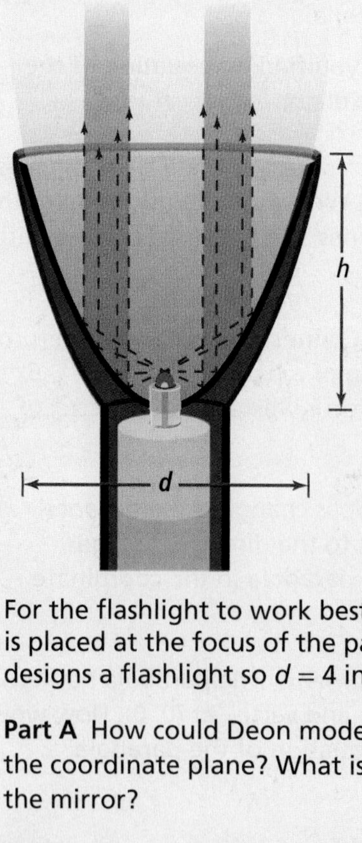


For the flashlight to work best, the light source is placed at the focus of the parabola. Deon designs a flashlight so $d = 4$ in. and $h = 3$ in.

**Part A** How could Deon model the mirror on the coordinate plane? What is an equation for the mirror?

**Part B** At what point above the vertex would Deon place the light source?

**Part C** Suppose Deon wants to place the light source $\frac{1}{2}$ in. farther from the vertex with the same $h = 3$ in. Will the mirror be narrower or wider? Explain.

TOPIC 9

# Topic Review

## TOPIC ESSENTIAL QUESTION

1. How can geometric relationships be proven by applying algebraic properties to geometric figures represented in the coordinate plane?

## Vocabulary Review

**Choose the correct term to complete each sentence.**

2. All the points on a parabola are the same distance from a fixed point, the ________ as they are from a line, the ________.
3. A ________ is a set of points equidistant from a point.
4. A ________ is the highest or lowest point on the graph of a function.

- circle
- directrix
- focus
- parabola
- radius
- vertex

## Concepts & Skills Review

### LESSON 9-1 Polygons in the Coordinate Plane

#### Quick Review

When a geometric figure is represented in a coordinate plane, you can use slope, distance, and midpoints to analyze properties of the figure.

#### Example

**Is $\triangle ABC$ an isosceles triangle? Explain.**

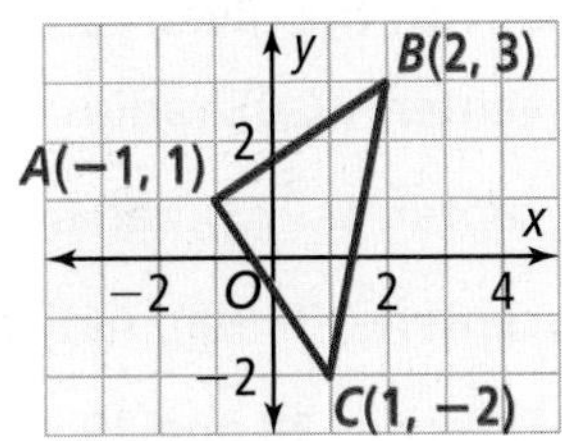


A triangle is isosceles if two sides are congruent. Use the Distance Formula to find the side lengths.

$AB = \sqrt{(2-(-1))^2 + (3-1)^2} = \sqrt{13}$

$BC = \sqrt{(1-2)^2 + (-2-3)^2} = \sqrt{26}$

$CA = \sqrt{(1-(-1))^2 + (-2-1)^2} = \sqrt{13}$

Since $AB = CA$, $\triangle ABC$ is isosceles.

#### Practice & Problem Solving

**For Exercises 5–8, determine whether each figure is the given type of figure.**

5. $F(-2, 4)$, $G(0, 0)$, $H(3, 1)$; right triangle
6. $A(7, 2)$, $B(3, -1)$, $C(3, 4)$; equilateral triangle
7. $J(-4, -4)$, $K(-7, 0)$, $L(-4, 4)$, $M(-1, 0)$; rhombus
8. What are the area and perimeter of $PQRS$?

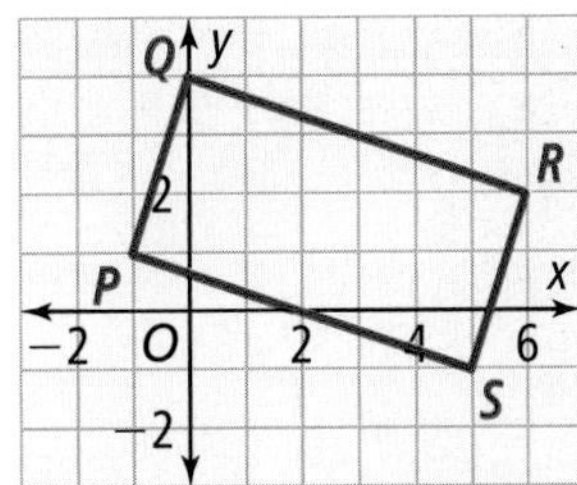


9. **Make Sense and Persevere** Parallelogram $WXYZ$ has coordinates $W(a, b)$, $X(c, d)$, $Y(f, g)$, and $Z(h, j)$. What equation can you use to determine whether $WXYZ$ is a rhombus? Explain.

TOPIC 9 REVIEW

## LESSON 9-2 Proofs Using Coordinate Geometry

### Quick Review

To prove theorems using coordinate geometry, place the figure on the coordinate plane. Use slope, midpoint, and distance to write an algebraic proof.

### Example

**Prove that the diagonals of a rectangle are congruent.**

Place a rectangle on a coordinate plane with one vertex at the origin and two sides along the axes.

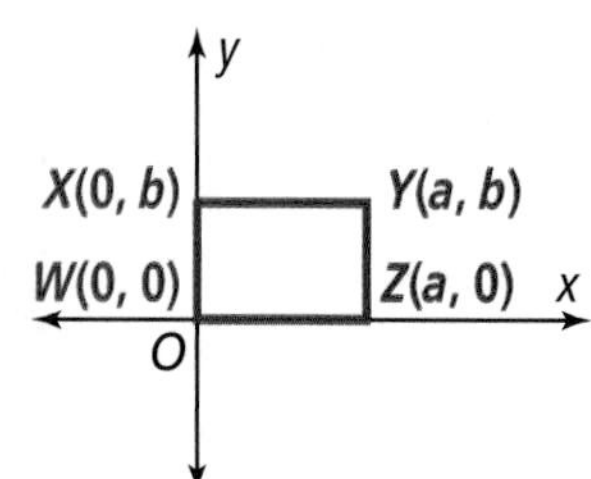


$$WY = \sqrt{(a - 0)^2 + (b - 0)^2} = \sqrt{a^2 + b^2}$$

$$XZ = \sqrt{(a - 0)^2 + (0 - b)^2} = \sqrt{a^2 + b^2}$$

Since $WY = XZ$, the diagonals of a rectangle are congruent.

### Practice & Problem Solving

**For Exercises 10–12, give the coordinates of each missing vertex.**

**10.** *ABCD* is a parallelogram; $A(0, 0)$, $B(p, q)$, $D(t, 0)$

**11.** *JKLM* is a kite; $J(0, 0)$, $K(a, b)$, $L(0, c)$

**12.** *WXYZ* is a rhombus; $W(0, 0)$, $Y(0, h)$, $Z(j, k)$

**13. Communicate Precisely** If you are given the coordinates of a quadrilateral, how can you prove that the quadrilateral is an isosceles trapezoid?

**14.** The diagram shows a fenced garden area, where $PX = PY$. The gardener is dividing the garden with a fence from *P* to the midpoint of $\overline{XY}$. Will the new fence be perpendicular to $\overline{XY}$? Use coordinate geometry to explain.

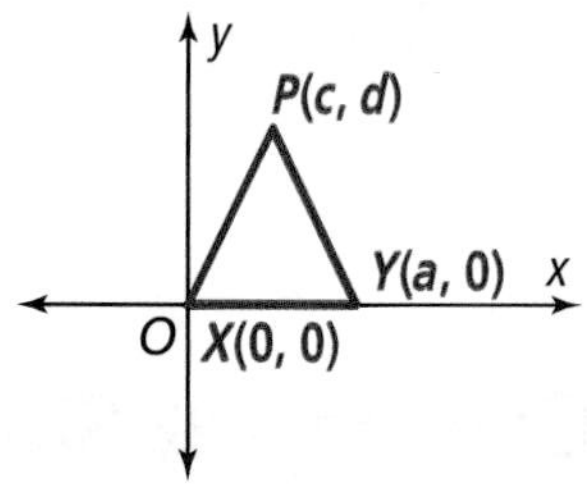


## LESSON 9-3 Circles in the Coordinate Plane

### Quick Review

The equation of a circle in the coordinate plane is

$$(x - h)^2 + (y - k)^2 = r^2$$

where $(h, k)$ is the center of the circle and $r$ is the radius.

### Example

**What is the equation of ⊙*Q*?**

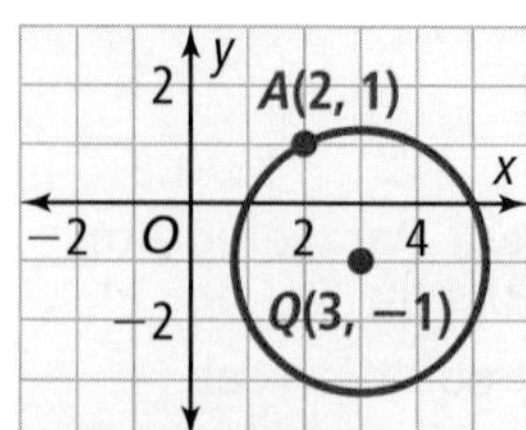


The center of the circle is $(3, -1)$, and the radius is *QA*.

$$QA = \sqrt{(2 - 3)^2 + (1 - (-1))^2} = \sqrt{5}$$

So, the equation of ⊙*Q* is $(x - 3)^2 + (y + 1)^2 = 5$.

### Practice & Problem Solving

**For Exercises 15–17, write the equation for the circle with the given center and radius.**

**15.** center: $(0, 0)$, radius: 9

**16.** center: $(-2, 3)$, radius: 5

**17.** center: $(-5, -8)$, radius: $\sqrt{13}$

**For Exercises 18 and 19, determine whether the given point lies on the circle with the given center and radius.**

**18.** $(-3, 0)$; center: $(-5, 2)$, radius: $2\sqrt{2}$

**19.** $(11, -1)$; center: $(4, 4)$, radius: $6\sqrt{2}$

**20.** Suppose that $\overline{AB}$, with $A(1, 15)$ and $B(13, -1)$, and $\overline{CD}$, with $C(15, 13)$ and $D(-1, 1)$, are diameters of ⊙*T*. What is the equation of ⊙*T*?

**21. Construct Arguments** Is it possible to write the equation of a circle given only two points on the circle? Explain.

## LESSON 9-4 Parabolas in the Coordinate Plane

### Quick Review

A **parabola** is the set of points that are equidistant from a fixed point, the **focus**, and a line, the **directrix**. The equation for a parabola in the coordinate plane is

$$y - k = \frac{1}{4p}(x - h)^2$$

where $(h, k)$ is the vertex and $p$ is the distance between the vertex and focus.

### Example

**What is the equation of the parabola with focus (4, 2) and directrix $y = 0$?**

The vertex is the midpoint of the segment connecting the focus and the directrix, so the vertex is (4, 1). Since $p$ is the distance between the focus and the vertex, $p = 1$. So, the equation of the parabola is

$$y - 1 = \frac{1}{4}(x - 4)^2.$$

### Practice & Problem Solving

**For Exercises 22 and 23, write the equation for the parabola with the given focus and directrix.**

**22.** focus: (0, 0), directrix: $y = -6$

**23.** focus: (−1, −3), directrix: $y = -4$

**24. Reason** Point $F$ is the focus and $y = -p$ is the directrix of the parabola shown. What is $AB$? Explain how you found your answer.

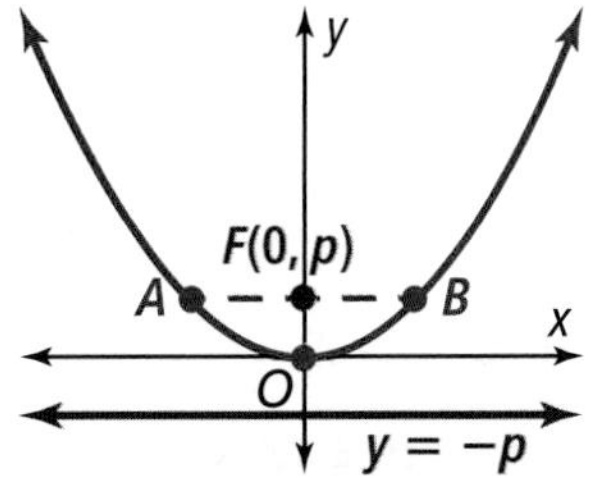


**25.** The cables for a suspension bridge are parabolic. The support towers are 40 m tall and 100 m apart. At its lowest point, the cable is 15 m above the bridge deck. If the bridge deck represents the $x$-axis and the vertex is on the $y$-axis, what equation represents the bridge cables?

TOPIC 9 REVIEW

# TOPIC 10

# Circles

## TOPIC ESSENTIAL QUESTION

**How are the figures formed related to the radius, circumference, and area of a circle when a line or lines intersect a circle?**

## Topic Overview



## Topic Vocabulary

- arc length
- central angle
- chord
- inscribed angle
- intercepted arc
- major arc
- minor arc
- point of tangency
- radian
- secant
- sector of a circle
- segment of a circle
- tangent to a circle

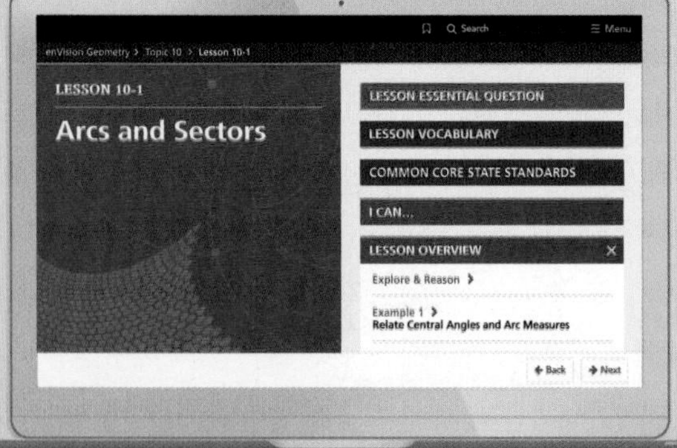

Go online | **PearsonRealize.com**

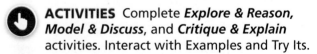

## Digital Experience

**INTERACTIVE STUDENT EDITION** Access online or offline.

**ACTIVITIES** Complete ***Explore & Reason, Model & Discuss***, and ***Critique & Explain*** activities. Interact with Examples and Try Its.

**ANIMATION** View and interact with real-world applications.

**PRACTICE** Practice what you've learned.

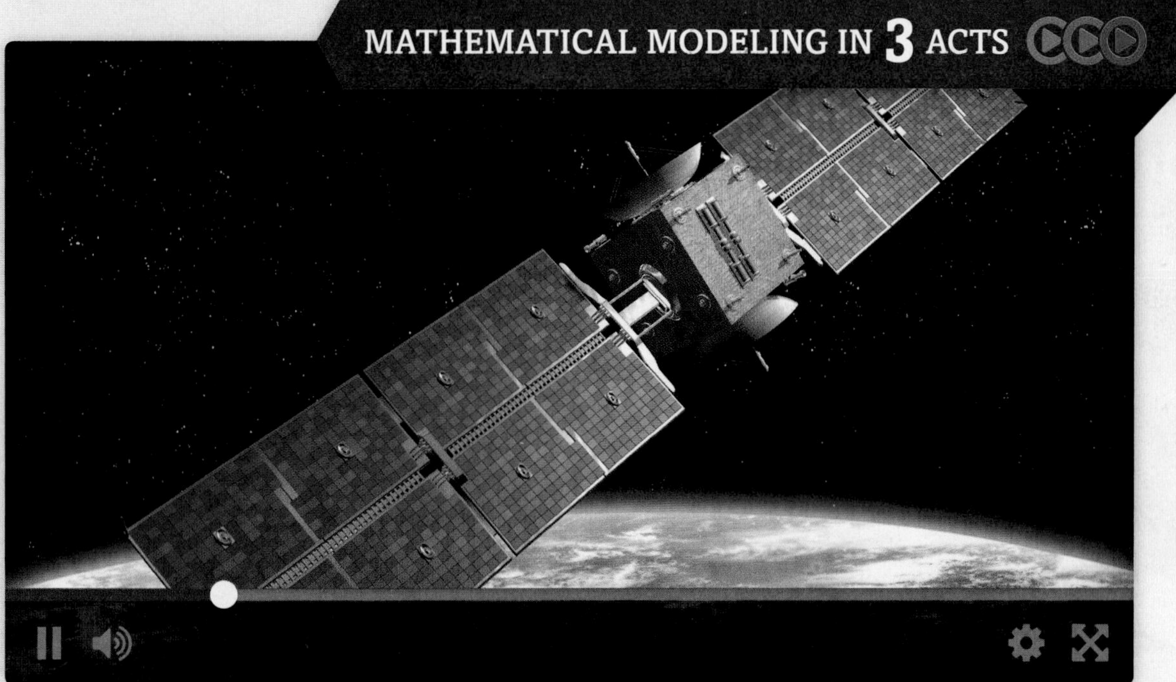


## Earth Watch

Scientists estimate that there are currently about 3,000 operational man-made satellites orbiting Earth. These satellites serve different purposes, from communication to navigation and global positioning. Some are weather satellites that collect environmental information.

The International Space Station is the largest man-made satellite that orbits Earth. It serves as a space environment research facility, and it also offers amazing views of Earth. Think about this during the Mathematical Modeling in 3 Acts lesson.

TOPIC 10

**VIDEOS** Watch clips to support ***Mathematical Modeling in 3 Acts Lessons*** and **enVision™** ***STEM Projects.***

**CONCEPT SUMMARY** Review key lesson content through multiple representations.

**ASSESSMENT** Show what you've learned.

**GLOSSARY** Read and listen to English and Spanish definitions.

**TUTORIALS** Get help from *Virtual Nerd*, right when you need it.

**MATH TOOLS** Explore math with digital tools and manipulatives.

## Did You Know?

Astronauts, six at a time, have lived and worked in the International Space Station (ISS) since 2000. Residents of 17 countries have visited the ISS.

The size of a football field, ISS circles the Earth every 90 minutes at an **altitude of 248 miles** and a speed of about **17,500 miles per hour.**

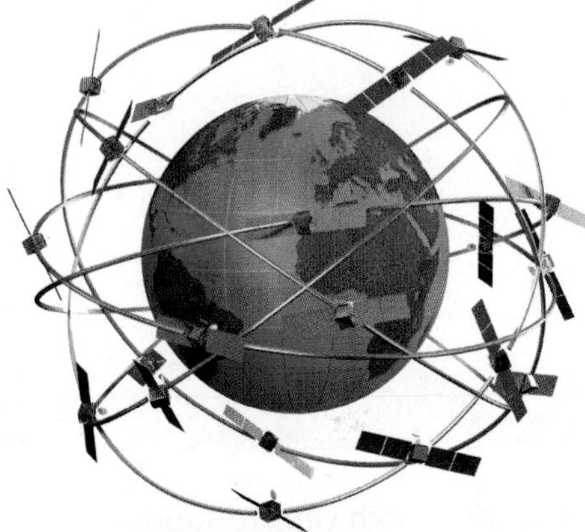

At its closest, the planet Mars is **150 times as far from Earth** as the Moon is. Despite the distance, the United States and Russia have been landing spacecraft and scientific instruments on Mars for several decades.

## Your Task: Design Space Cities

Suppose it's 500 years in the future. Space stations the size of small cities are journeying through space. Use trigonometry and the geometry of circles to calculate the measurements of two of these stations, then design, measure, and describe a group of three "space cities."

# 10-1 Arcs and Sectors

**I CAN…** find arc length and sector area of a circle and use them to solve problems.

**VOCABULARY**

- arc length
- central angle
- intercepted arc
- major arc
- minor arc
- radian
- sector of a circle
- segment of a circle

## EXPLORE & REASON

**Darren bends a piece of wire using a circular disc to make the shape as shown.**

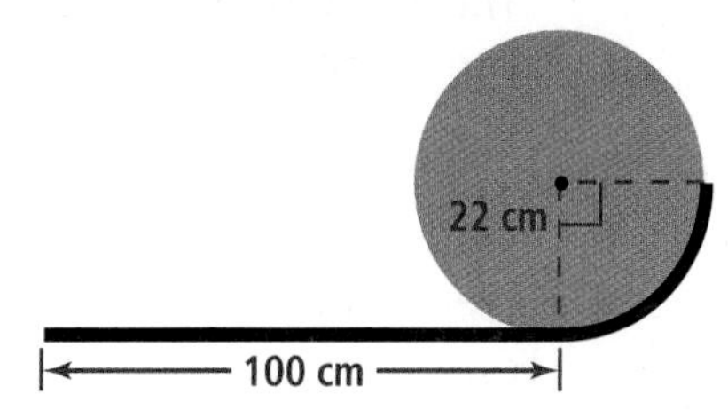


**A.** How long does the piece of wire need to be to make the shape? Explain.

**B. Construct Arguments** What information do you think is needed to find part of the circumference of a circle? Justify your answer.

## ESSENTIAL QUESTION

**How are arc length and sector area related to circumference and area of a circle?**

## EXAMPLE 1 Relate Central Angles and Arc Measures

**What are $m\widehat{AB}$ and $m\widehat{ACB}$?**

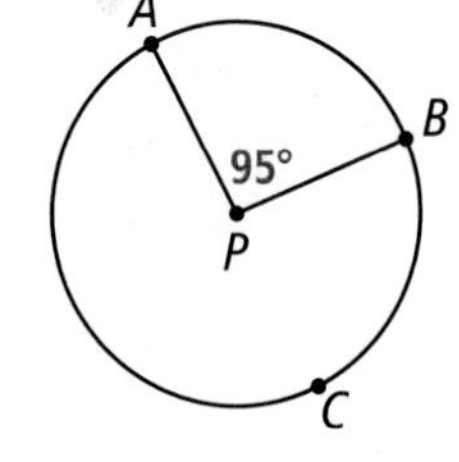


A **central angle** of a circle is an angle formed by two radii with the vertex at the center of the circle. Angle $APB$ is a central angle.

A central angle creates two intercepted arcs. An **intercepted arc** is the part of a circle that lies between two segments, rays, or lines that intersect the circle.

A central angle and its intercepted minor arc have equal measure.

**STUDY TIP**

A minor arc may be written with just two letters, as in $\widehat{AB}$. Use the third point between the endpoints of an arc to name a major arc, as in $\widehat{ABC}$.

$\angle APB$ is a central angle, and $\widehat{AB}$ is its corresponding intercepted arc.

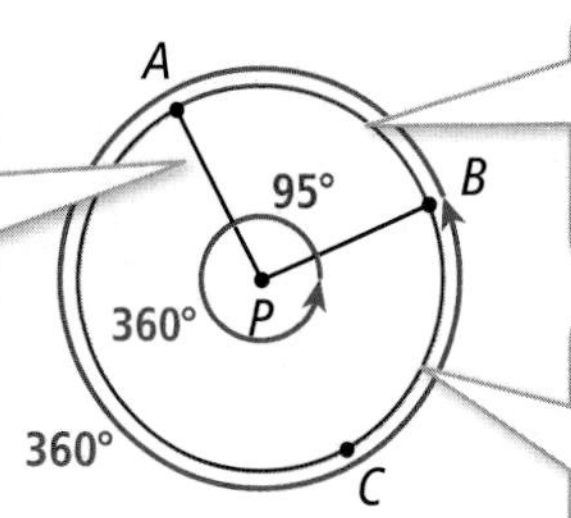


A **minor arc** of a circle is an arc that is smaller than a semicircle. $\widehat{AB}$ is a minor arc.

A **major arc** of a circle is an arc that is larger than a semicircle. $\widehat{ACB}$ is a major arc.

Find $m\widehat{AB}$.

$m\widehat{AB} = m\angle APB = 95$

The degree measure of $\widehat{AB}$ is equal to the measure of its corresponding central angle $\angle APB$.

Find $m\widehat{ACB}$.

$m\widehat{ACB} = 360 - 95 = 265$

**Try It!** **1.** Use $\odot W$.

**a.** What is $m\widehat{XZ}$?

**b.** What is $m\widehat{XYZ}$?

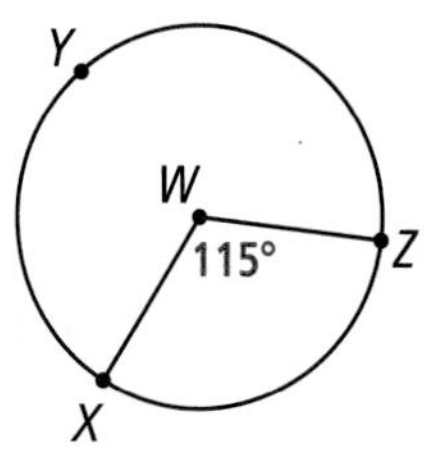

## CONCEPT Arc Measure

The measure of an arc is equal to the measure of its corresponding central angle.

$m\widehat{JM} = m\angle JPM$

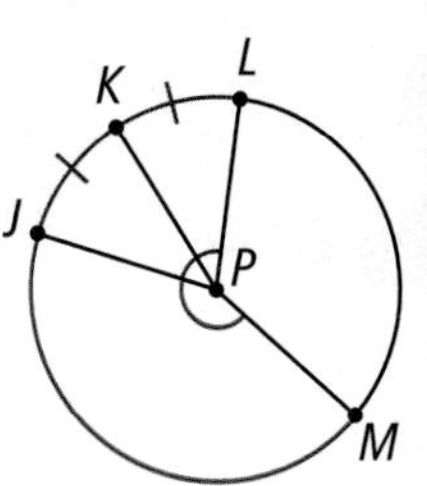

K
L
J
P
M

Congruent central angles intercept congruent arcs, and congruent arcs are intercepted by congruent central angles.

$\angle JPK \cong \angle KPL$ $\qquad$ $\widehat{JK} \cong \widehat{KL}$

CONCEPTUAL UNDERSTANDING

## EXAMPLE 2 Relate Arc Length to Circumference

**A. How do you find the length *s* of an arc measured in degrees?**

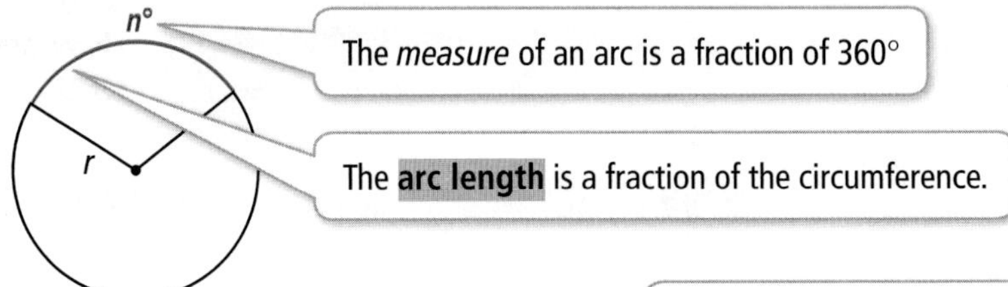

n°
r
The *measure* of an arc is a fraction of 360°
The **arc length** is a fraction of the circumference.

$$\frac{\text{arc length}}{\text{circumference}} = \frac{\text{arc measure}}{360}$$

$$\frac{s}{2\pi r} = \frac{n}{360}$$

$$s = \frac{n}{360} \cdot 2\pi r$$

Use a proportion to represent the relationship between arc length *s*, radius *r*, and arc measure *n*.

The formula to find the length of an arc is $s = \frac{n}{360} \cdot 2\pi r$.

**B. How do you find the length *s* of an arc measured in radians?**

Besides degrees, angle measures can be expressed in *radians*.

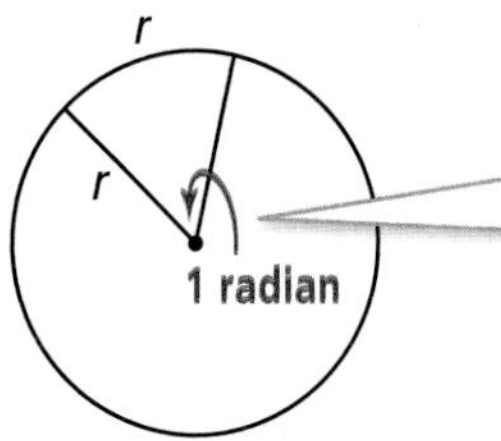

r
r
1 radian

A **radian** is equal to the measure of a central angle that intercepts an arc with length equal to the radius of the circle.

Circumference is $2\pi r$, which is $2\pi$ arcs of length $r$. Since each arc of length $r$ corresponds to 1 radian, there are $2\pi$ radians in a circle. So, $2\pi$ radians is equivalent to 360°.

To find the arc length, use the following proportion.

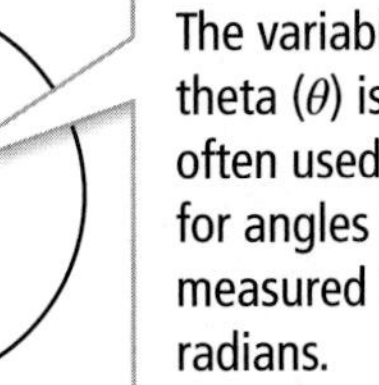

s
θ
r

The variable theta ($\theta$) is often used for angles measured in radians.

$$\frac{\text{arc length}}{\text{circumference}} = \frac{\text{arc measure (radians)}}{2\pi}$$

$$\frac{s}{2\pi r} = \frac{\theta}{2\pi}$$

$$s = \frac{\theta}{2\pi} \cdot 2\pi r = \theta r$$

Arc length is proportional to radius, with $\theta$ as the constant of proportionality.

To find the length of an arc measured in radians, use the formula $s = \theta r$.

**STUDY TIP**

Remember that the circumference measures the distance around all of the circle and the arc length is the distance around part of the circle.

CONTINUED ON THE NEXT PAGE

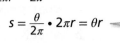

**Try It!** **2. a.** In a circle with radius 4, what is the length of an arc that has a measure of 80? Round to the nearest tenth.

**b.** In a circle with radius 6, what is the length of an arc that has a measure of $\pi$ radians? Round to the nearest tenth.

## CONCEPT Arc Length

The length $s$ of an arc of a circle is the product of the ratio relating the measure of the central angle in degrees to 360 and the circumference of the circle. The length of the arc is also the product of the radius and the central angle measure in radians.

Central angle in degrees:

$$s = \frac{n}{360} \cdot 2\pi r$$

Central angle in radians:

$$s = \theta r$$

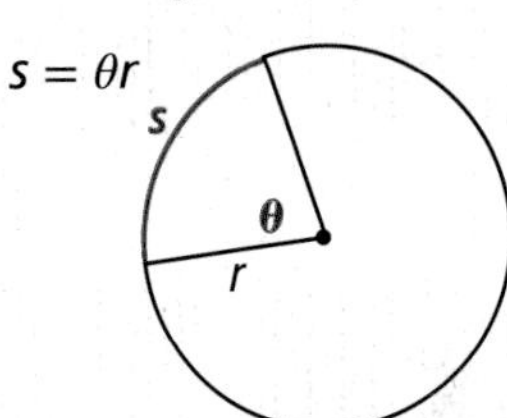


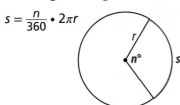

## EXAMPLE 3 Apply Arc Length

**What is the length of $\widehat{AD}$? Express the answer in terms of $\pi$.**

**Step 1** Find the arc measure.

$$m\widehat{AD} = 360 - m\widehat{AB} - m\widehat{BC} - m\widehat{CD}$$
$$= 360 - 73 - 43 - 104$$
$$= 140$$

Each arc measure is equal to the measure of the corresponding central angle.

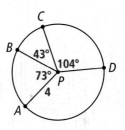

**MAKE SENSE AND PERSEVERE** Think about when you should express arc lengths in terms of $\pi$ and when you should give approximate answers. How would you decide?

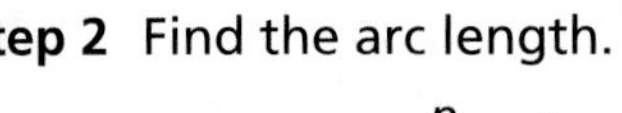

**Step 2** Find the arc length.

$$s = \frac{n}{360} \cdot 2\pi r$$
$$= \frac{140}{360} \cdot 2\pi(4) = \frac{28}{9}\pi$$

Use the formula for arc length for angles given in degrees.

The length of $\widehat{AD}$ is $\frac{28}{9}\pi$.

**Try It!** **3.** Use $\odot Q$. Express answers in terms of $\pi$.

**a.** What is the length of $\widehat{JK}$?

**b.** What is the length of $\widehat{HK}$?

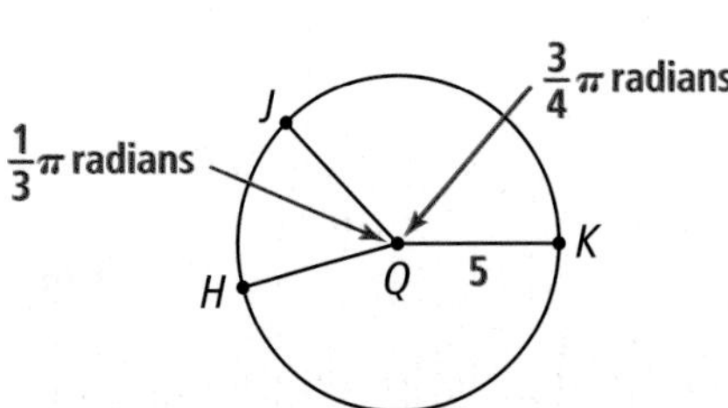

## EXAMPLE 4 Relate the Area of a Circle to the Area of a Sector

**A sector of a circle is the region bounded by two radii and the intercepted arc. What is the area of sector *MQN*?**

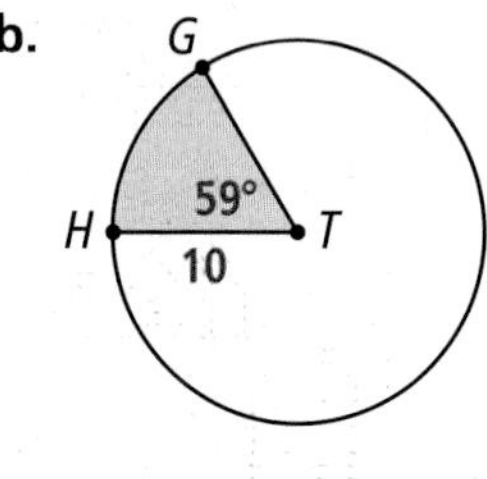


**GENERALIZE**
Compare the formulas for arc length and sector area. What relationships do you see between the arc length and sector area for any given arc?

To find the area of the sector, find $\frac{78}{360}$ of the area of the circle.

$$A = \frac{78}{360} \cdot \pi r^2$$

$$= \frac{78}{360} \cdot \pi(10)^2 = \frac{65}{3}\pi$$

In general, the area of a sector is $A = \frac{n}{360} \cdot \pi r^2$, where $n°$ is the measure of the intercepted arc and $r$ is the radius of the circle.

The area of sector *MQN* is $\frac{65}{3}\pi$ cm$^2$.

**Try It!** 4. What is the area of each sector?

a.

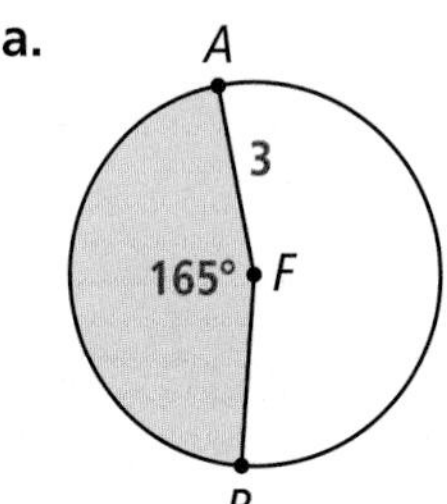

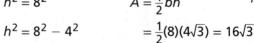

b.



## EXAMPLE 5 Find the Area of a Segment of a Circle

**A segment of a circle is the part of a circle bounded by an arc and the segment joining its endpoints. What is the area of the shaded region?**

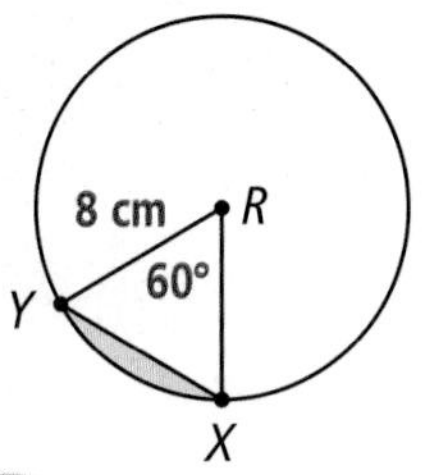


To find the area of the segment, subtract the area of the triangle from the area of the sector.

**Step 1** Find the area of the sector.

$$A = \frac{n}{360} \cdot \pi r^2 = \frac{32}{3}\pi$$

Use the formula for area of a sector.

**STUDY TIP**
To find areas of triangles in circles, you may need to apply trigonometric ratios to find the base and height.

**Step 2** Find the area of the triangle.

Since $\overline{RX}$ and $\overline{RY}$ are both radii and the angle between them is 60°, $\triangle RYX$ is equilateral.

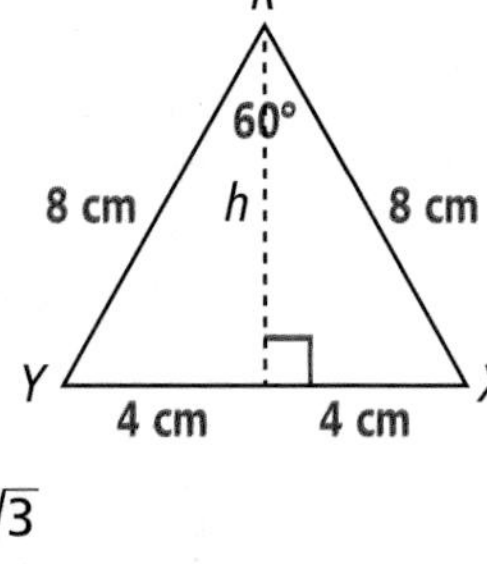


Use the Pythagorean Theorem to find $h$.

$$4^2 + h^2 = 8^2$$

$$h^2 = 8^2 - 4^2$$

$$h = \sqrt{48} = 4\sqrt{3}$$

Find the area of the triangle.

$$A = \frac{1}{2}bh$$

$$= \frac{1}{2}(8)(4\sqrt{3}) = 16\sqrt{3}$$

**Step 3** Find the area of the segment.

area of segment = area of sector − area of triangle

$$= \frac{32}{3}\pi - 16\sqrt{3} \approx 5.8$$

The area of the shaded region is about 5.8 cm$^2$.

CONTINUED ON THE NEXT PAGE

 **Try It!** **5.** What is the area of each segment?

**a.**

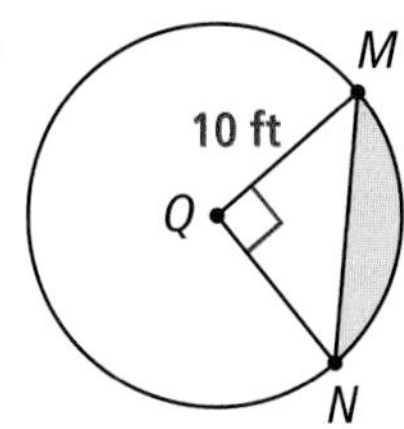


**b.**

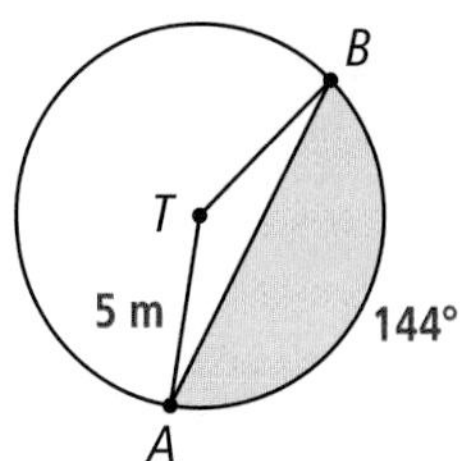


APPLICATION

## EXAMPLE 6 Solve Problems Involving Circles

**Chen uses circular corkboards to make 18 watermelon coasters to sell at a craft fair.**

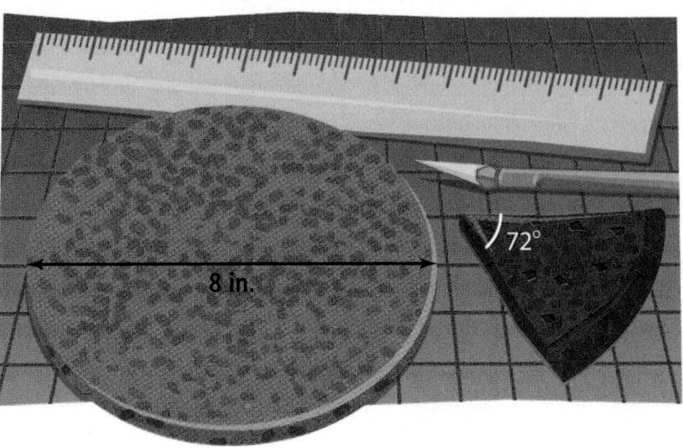


> **COMMON ERROR**
> Be careful not to confuse the formula for the area of a sector with the formula for arc length. Remember that the area of a sector is proportional to the area of the circle, and the arc length is proportional to the circumference.

**A. He paints one side of each coaster with special paint. Each jar of paint covers 200 in.$^2$. Will one jar of paint be enough to paint all the coasters?**

Find the area of one watermelon coaster. Use 3.14 for $\pi$.

$$A = \frac{n}{360} \cdot \pi r^2$$

Use the formula for area of a sector.

$$= \frac{72}{360} \cdot \pi(4)^2$$

$$\approx 10.0$$

The area of one watermelon coaster is about 10 in.$^2$.

Chen can paint $200 \div 10 = 20$ coasters with one jar of paint, so he has enough paint for 18 coasters.

**B. He puts decorative tape around the edge of each coaster. How much tape does he need for each coaster?**

The perimeter of the coaster consists of two radii and an arc.

$$P = r + r + \frac{n}{360} \cdot 2\pi r$$

$$= 4 + 4 + \frac{72}{360} \cdot 2\pi(4)$$

$$\approx 13.0$$

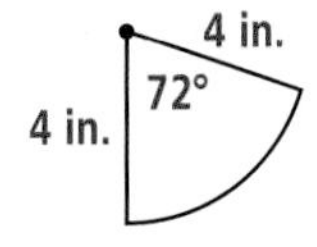


Chen needs about 13 inches of tape for each coaster.

 **Try It!** **6.** What is the area and perimeter of sector *QNR*? Round to the nearest tenth.

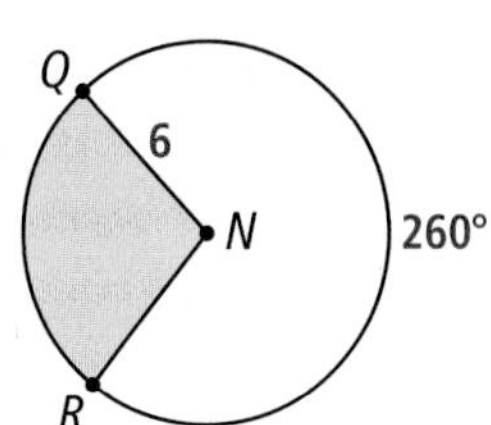

## CONCEPT SUMMARY Arc Length and Sector Area

**WORDS** | **DIAGRAMS**

### Arc Length

The arc length is a fraction of the circumference.

**Degrees**

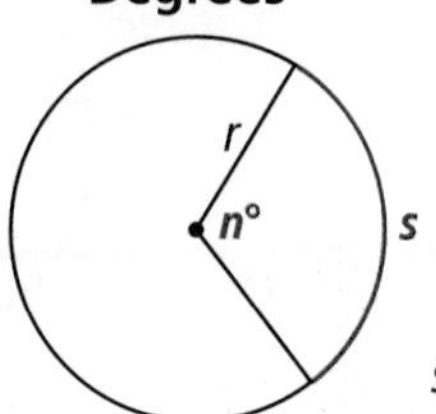


$s = \frac{n}{360} \cdot 2\pi r$

**Radians**

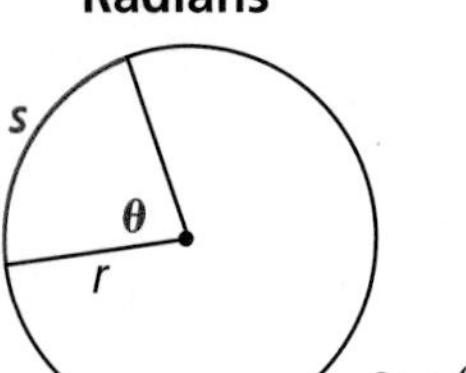


$s = \theta r$

### Sector

A sector of a circle is the region bounded by two radii and the intercepted arc.

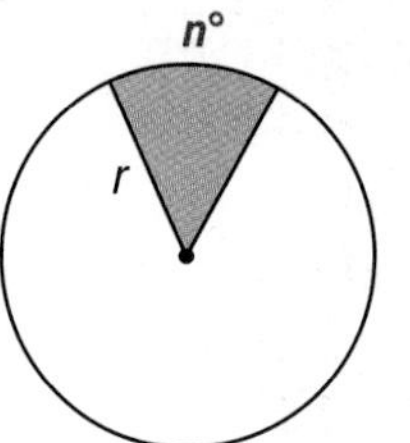


$A = \frac{n}{360} \cdot \pi r^2$

### Segment

A segment of a circle is the part of a circle bounded by an arc and the segment joining its endpoints.

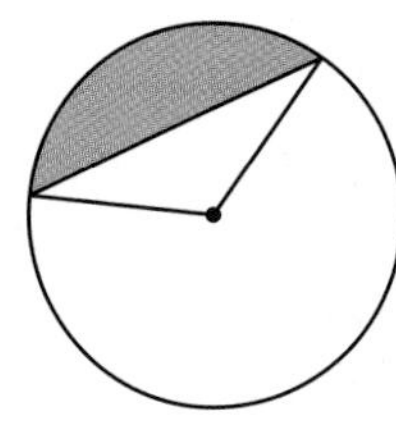

segment area = sector area − triangle area

## Do You UNDERSTAND?

1. **ESSENTIAL QUESTION** How are arc length and sector area related to circumference and area of a circle?

2. **Error Analysis** Luke was asked to compute the length of $\widehat{AB}$. What is Luke's error?

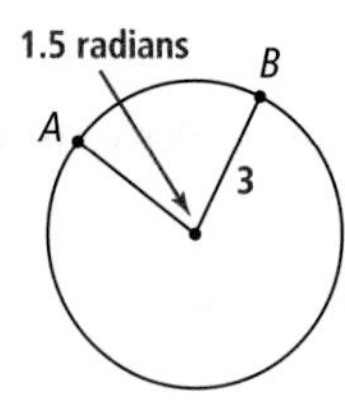


$$S = \frac{n}{360} \cdot 2\pi r$$
$$= \frac{1.5}{360} \cdot 2\pi(3)$$
$$= 0.0785$$

✗

3. **Vocabulary** How can the word *segment* help you remember what a *segment of a circle* is?

4. **Reason** Mercedes says that she can find the area of a quarter of a circle using the formula $A = \frac{1}{4}\pi r^2$. Using the formula for the area of a sector, explain why Mercedes is correct.

## Do You KNOW HOW?

**For Exercises 5 and 6, find the measures and lengths of each arc. Express the answers in terms of $\pi$.**

51°, B, A, 4, 83°, C

5.  $\widehat{BC}$

6.  $\widehat{ABC}$

7. Circle $P$ has radius 8. Points $Q$ and $R$ lie on circle $P$, and the length of $\widehat{QR}$ is $4\pi$. What is $m\angle QPR$ in radians?

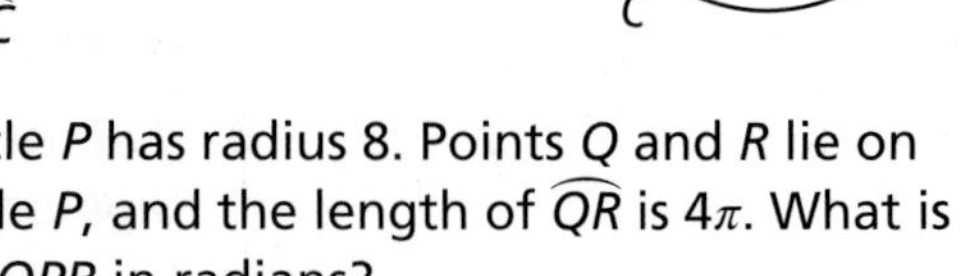

8. What is the area of sector $EFG$? Express the answer in terms of $\pi$.

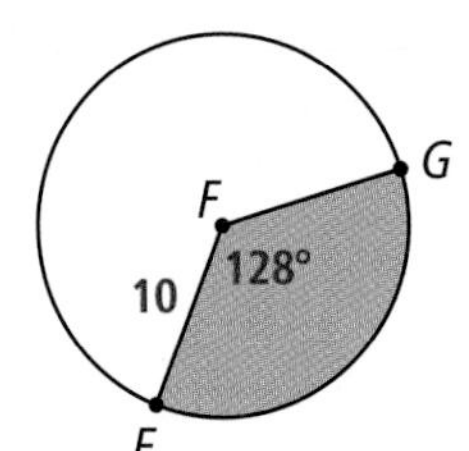

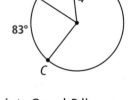

9. What is the area of the segment? Express the answer in terms of $\pi$.

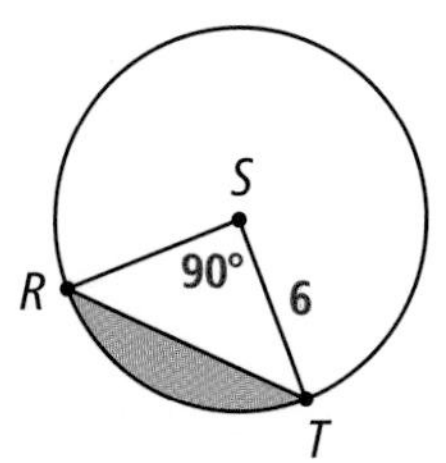

## PRACTICE & PROBLEM SOLVING

Scan for Multimedia

Practice Tutorial

Additional Exercises Available Online

### UNDERSTAND

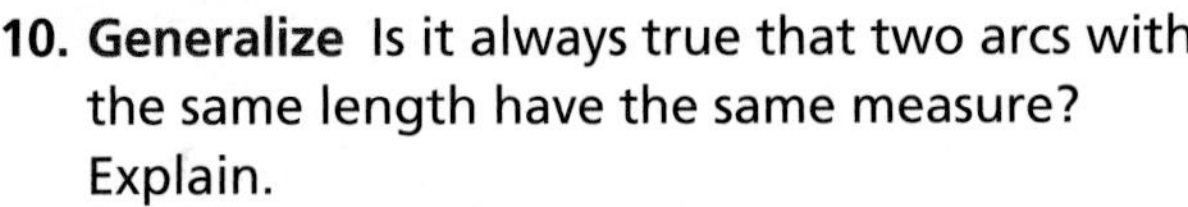

**10. Generalize** Is it always true that two arcs with the same length have the same measure? Explain.

**11. Error Analysis** Steve is asked to compute the area of the shaded region. What is his error?

C 3 S D

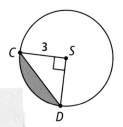

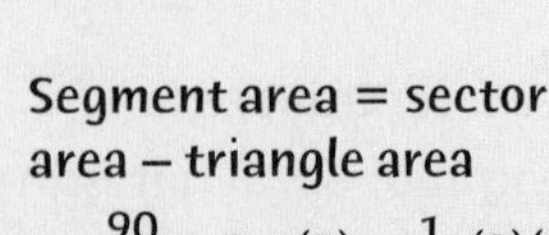
Segment area = sector area – triangle area

$= \frac{90}{360} \cdot 2\pi(3) - \frac{1}{2}(3)(3)$

$\approx 0.21$

**12. Mathematical Connections** The equation $(x - 2)^2 + (y - 3)^2 = 25$ represents $\odot T$. Points $X(-2, 6)$ and $Y(-1, -1)$ lie on $\odot T$. What is $m\overset{\frown}{XY}$? Explain how you know.

**13. Reason** Figure $GHJKL$ is a regular pentagon. Rounded to the nearest tenth, what percent of the area of $\odot T$ is not part of the area of $GHJKL$? Explain.

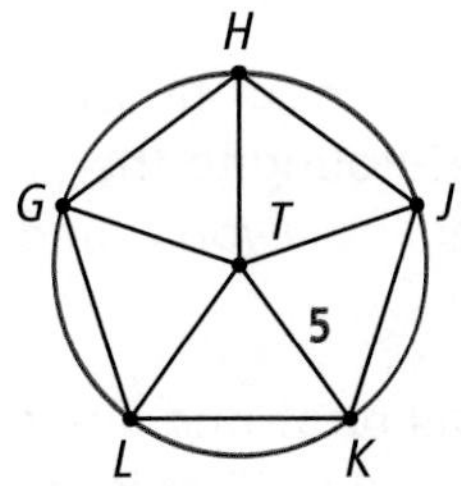


**14. Use Structure** Explain why the length of an arc with arc measure $a°$ is proportional to the radius of the circle.

**15. Higher Order Thinking** The areas of sectors $ACB$ and $DEF$ are equal. What expression gives the value of $x$? Show your work.

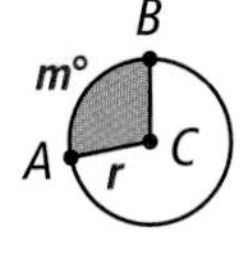


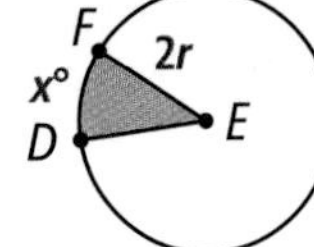


### PRACTICE

**For Exercises 16–19, find each arc measure.** SEE EXAMPLE 1

16. $m\overset{\frown}{FE}$

17. $m\overset{\frown}{BC}$

18. $m\overset{\frown}{CE}$

19. $m\overset{\frown}{CFE}$

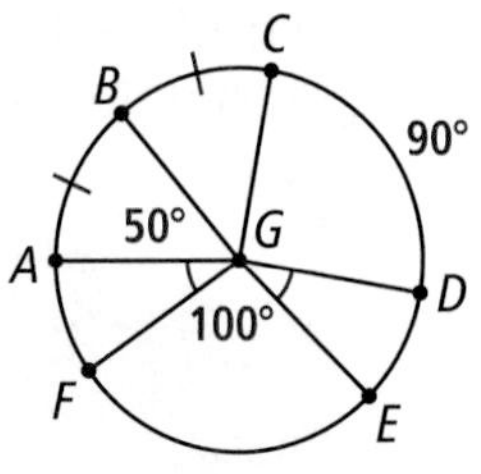


**For Exercises 20 and 21, find each arc length in terms of $\pi$.** SEE EXAMPLES 2 AND 3

20. length of $\overset{\frown}{JK}$

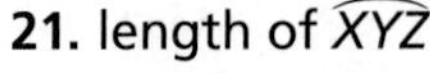

21. length of $\overset{\frown}{XYZ}$

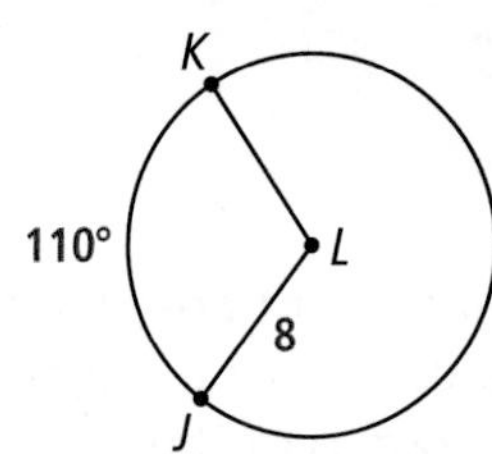


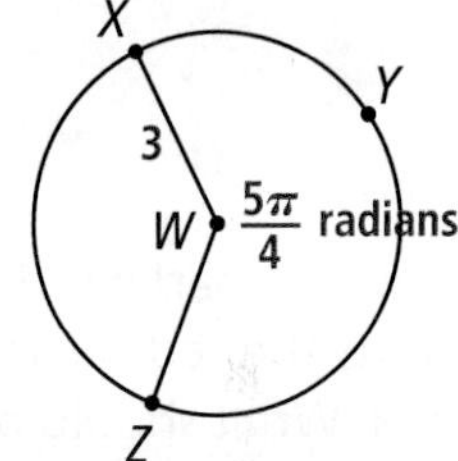


**For Exercises 22 and 23, find the area of each sector. Round to the nearest tenth.** SEE EXAMPLES 4 AND 6

22. sector $DEF$

23. sector $GHJ$

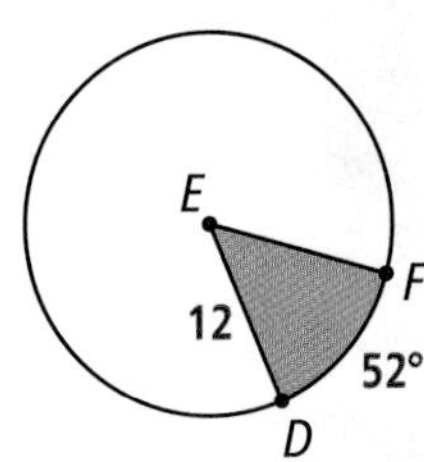


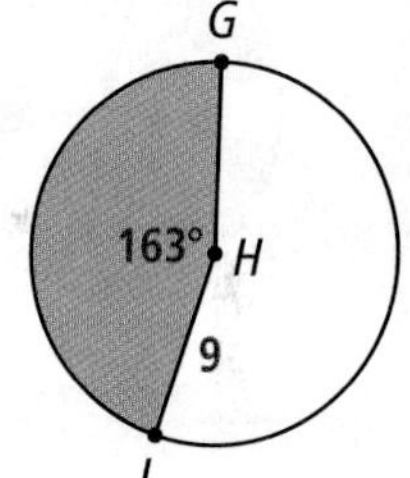


**For Exercises 24 and 25, find the area of each segment. Round to the nearest tenth.** SEE EXAMPLE 5

24.

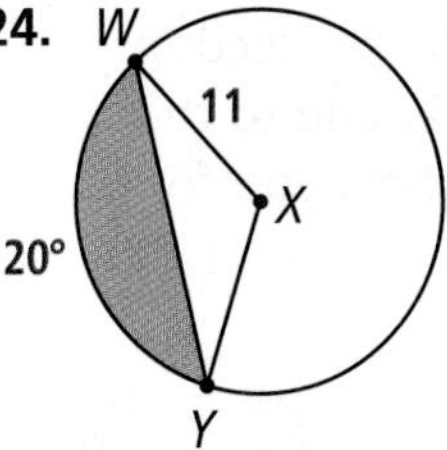


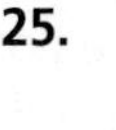

25.

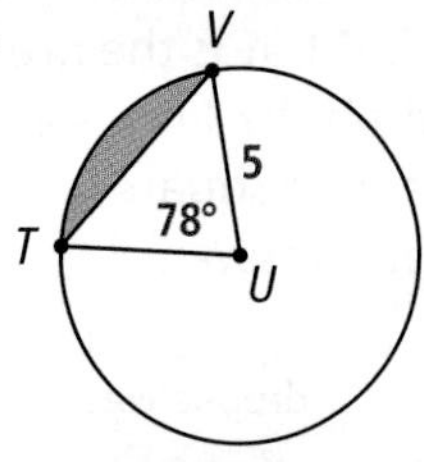


26. The length of $\overset{\frown}{ABC}$ is 110 ft. What is the radius of $\odot D$? Round to the nearest tenth.

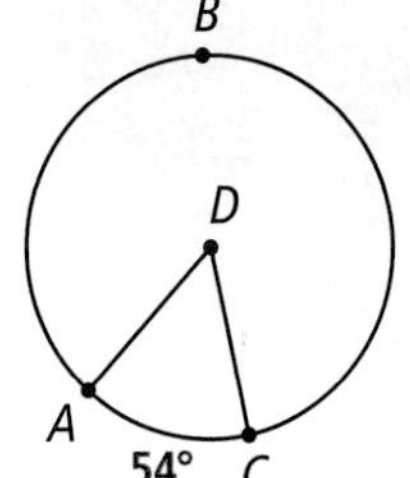

# PRACTICE & PROBLEM SOLVING

## APPLY

**27. Make Sense and Persevere** Aubrey and Fatima will each run 150 m on the two inside lanes of the track, so the end markers need to be placed correctly. To the nearest hundredth, what are $x$ and $y$?

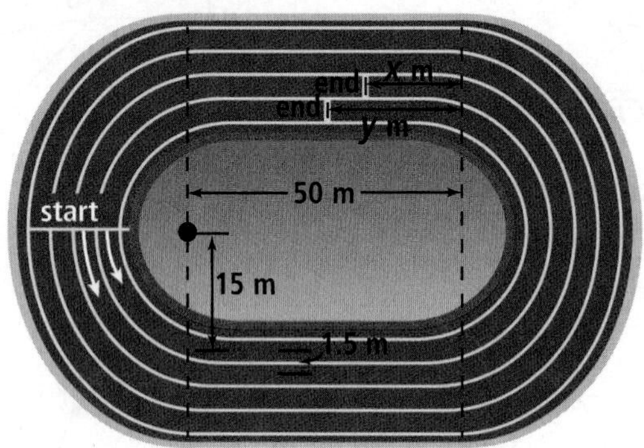


**28. Reason** Charlie is designing a dart board and wants the red sections to be 25% of the total area. What should be the radius of the inner circle? Round to the nearest tenth.

**29. Look for Relationships** Enrique is selling the drop-leaf table and wants to include the area of the table when the leaves are down in his ad. What is the area of the center section when the leaves are down? Round to the nearest square inch. Explain how you found your answer.

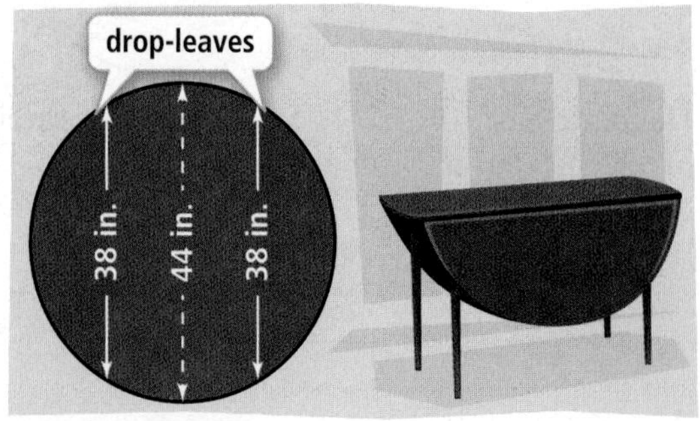


## ASSESSMENT PRACTICE

**30.** What is the diameter of $\odot T$?

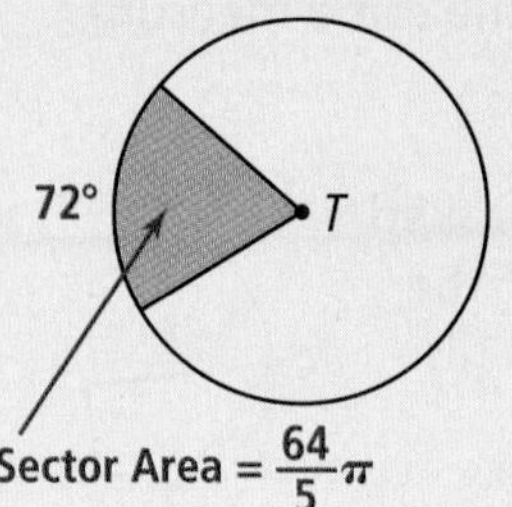


**31. SAT/ACT** An arc has a central angle of $\frac{2}{5}\pi$ radians and a length of $6\pi$. What is the circumference of the circle?

Ⓐ $12\pi$ Ⓑ $15\pi$ Ⓒ $30\pi$ Ⓓ $36\pi$

**32. Performance Task** A carpenter is constructing the stage for a concert.

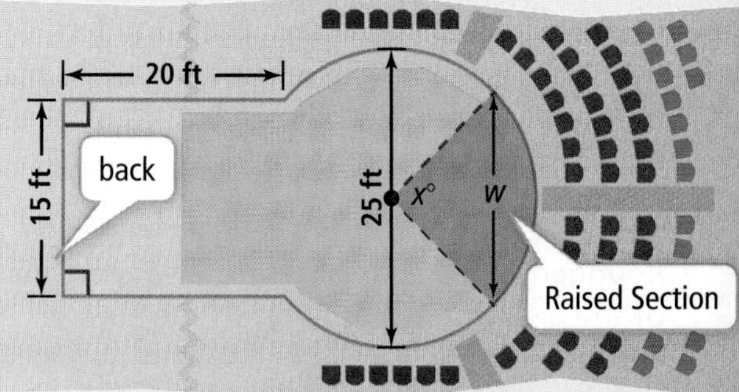


**Part A** What is the total amount of flooring needed to cover the stage? Round to the nearest square foot. Explain how you found your answer.

**Part B** A string of lights will be strung along the sides and front of the stage. What is the total length of light string needed? Show your work.

**Part C** One portion of the stage can be raised during the concert. The lift mechanism can lift a maximum area of 180 ft$^2$, but the band needs the width $w$ of the raised area to be at least 20 ft. What could be the value of $x$? Justify your answer.

# 10-2 Lines Tangent to a Circle

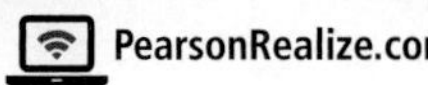

PearsonRealize.com

Activity | Assess

**I CAN...** use properties of tangent lines to solve problems.

## VOCABULARY

- point of tangency
- tangent to a circle

## CRITIQUE & EXPLAIN

**Alicia and Renaldo made conjectures about the lines that intersect a circle only once.**

**Alicia**

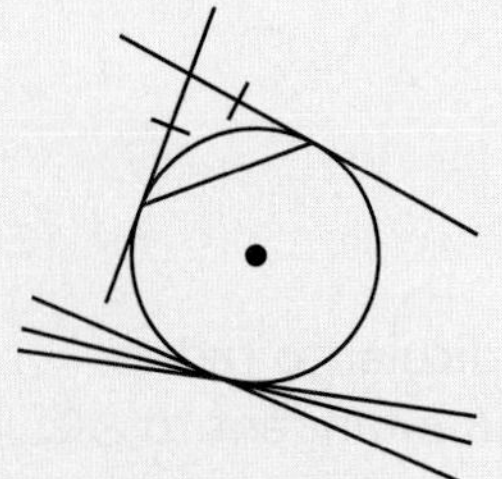

- Many lines intersect the circle once at the same point.
- Two lines that intersect the circle once and the segment connecting the points form an isosceles triangle.

**Renaldo**

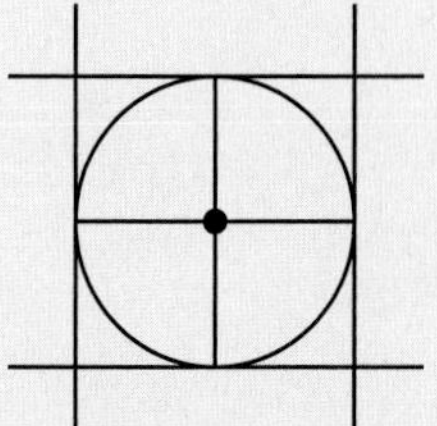

- Parallel lines intersect the circle at opposite ends of the same diameter.
- The lines intersecting the circle at one point are perpendicular to a diameter of the circle.

**A. Use Appropriate Tools** Which of the four conjectures do you agree with? Which do you disagree with? Draw sketches to support your answers.

**B.** What other conjectures can you make about lines that intersect a circle at one point?

**ESSENTIAL QUESTION** How is a tangent line related to the radius of a circle at the point of tangency?

CONCEPTUAL UNDERSTANDING

## EXAMPLE 1 Understand Tangents to a Circle

**What is the relationship between a circle and a tangent to the circle?**

A **tangent to a circle** is a line in the plane of the circle that intersects the circle in exactly one point. That point is the **point of tangency**.

Circle $C$ has tangent line $m$ with point of tangency $X$. Point $Y$ is any other point on $m$.

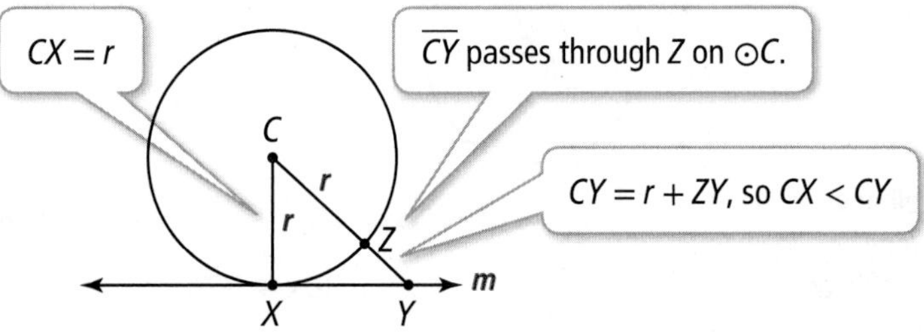


So, $\overline{CX}$ is the shortest segment from $C$ to line $m$. Since the shortest segment from a point to a line is perpendicular to the line, $\overline{CX} \perp m$.

**GENERALIZE**
Point $Y$ represents any point other than the point of tangency. Would the result be true no matter where point $Y$ is located on $m$?

**Try It!** **1.** Does Example 1 support Renaldo's conjecture that parallel lines intersect the circle at opposite ends of the same diameter? Explain.

## THEOREM 10-1 AND THE CONVERSE

**Theorem**

If $\overleftrightarrow{AB}$ is tangent to $\odot C$ at $P$, then $\overleftrightarrow{AB}$ is perpendicular to $\overline{CP}$.

**If...**

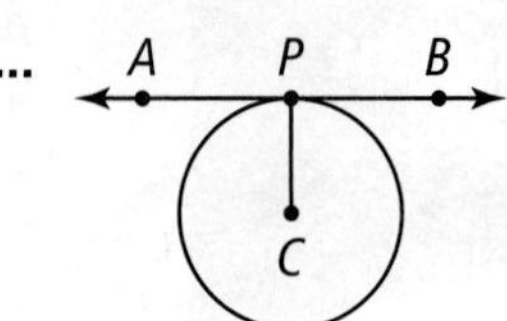


**Then...** $\overleftrightarrow{AB} \perp \overline{CP}$

**Converse**

If $\overleftrightarrow{AB}$ is perpendicular to radius $\overline{CP}$ at $P$, then $\overleftrightarrow{AB}$ is tangent to $\odot C$.

**If...**

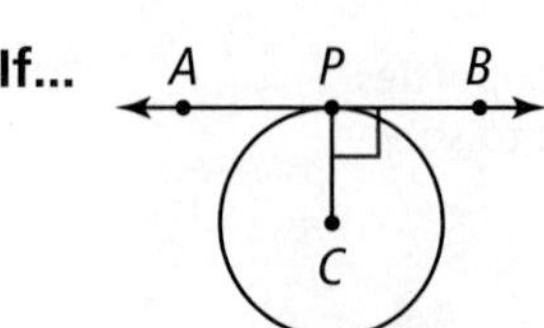


**Then...** $\overleftrightarrow{AB}$ is tangent to $\odot C$.

PROOF: SEE EXERCISES 12 AND 13.

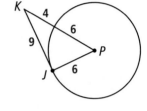

## EXAMPLE 2 Use Tangents to Solve Problems

**A. Is $\overline{KJ}$ tangent to $\odot P$ at $J$?**

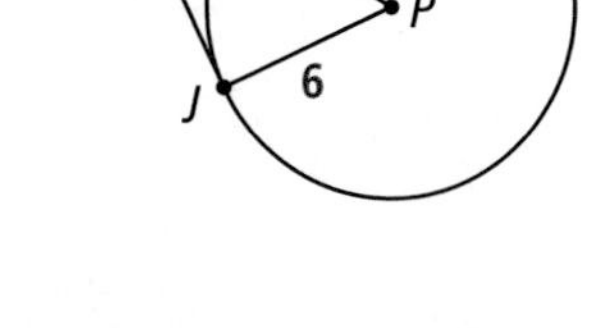


A segment or ray that intersects a circle in one point is tangent to the circle if it is part of a tangent line.

If $\overline{KJ}$ is part of a line that is tangent to $\odot P$ at $J$, then $\overline{PJ} \perp \overline{JK}$ and $\triangle PJK$ is a right triangle.

$$9^2 + 6^2 \stackrel{?}{=} (4 + 6)^2$$
$$117 \neq 100$$

Use the Converse of the Pythagorean Theorem to determine whether $\triangle PJK$ is a right triangle.

So, $\overline{PJ}$ is not perpendicular to $\overline{KJ}$.

Therefore, $\overline{KJ}$ is not tangent to $\odot P$ at $J$.

**B. Segment $ST$ is tangent to $\odot R$. What is the radius of $\odot R$?**

Since $\overline{ST}$ is tangent to $\odot R$, $\triangle RST$ is a right triangle.

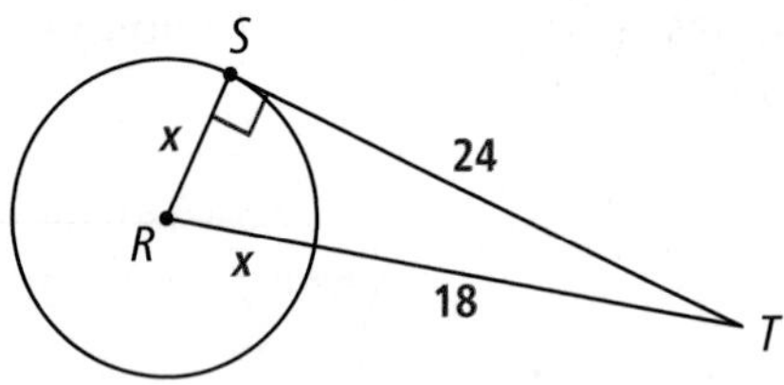


$$x^2 + 24^2 = (x + 18)^2$$
$$x^2 + 576 = x^2 + 36x + 324$$
$$252 = 36x$$
$$7 = x$$

Use the Pythagorean Theorem with length of the hypotenuse $x + 18$.

The radius of $\odot R$ is 7.

**COMMON ERROR**

You may incorrectly square just the terms $x$ and 18. Recall how to square a binomial. It may be helpful to first write $(x + 18)^2$ as $(x + 18)(x + 18)$ and multiply.

CONTINUED ON THE NEXT PAGE

EXAMPLE 2 CONTINUED

**C. Line *m* is tangent to ⊙*T* at *B*, and line *n* is tangent to ⊙*T* at *C*. What is the value of *x*?**

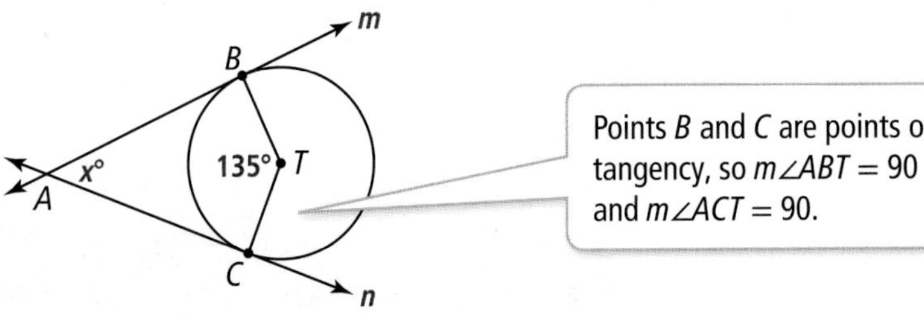


**STUDY TIP**
Remember that for any convex polygon, the sum of the interior angles is $(n - 2)180°$, where $n$ is the number of sides.

Use the Polygon Angle-Sum Theorem to find $x$.

$$m\angle BAC + m\angle ACT + m\angle CTB + m\angle TBA = 360$$
$$x + 90 + 135 + 90 = 360$$
$$x = 45$$

 **Try It!** 2. Use ⊙$N$.

a. Is $\overleftrightarrow{MP}$ tangent to ⊙$N$? Explain.

b. If $\overline{LK}$ is tangent to ⊙$N$ at $L$, what is $KN$?

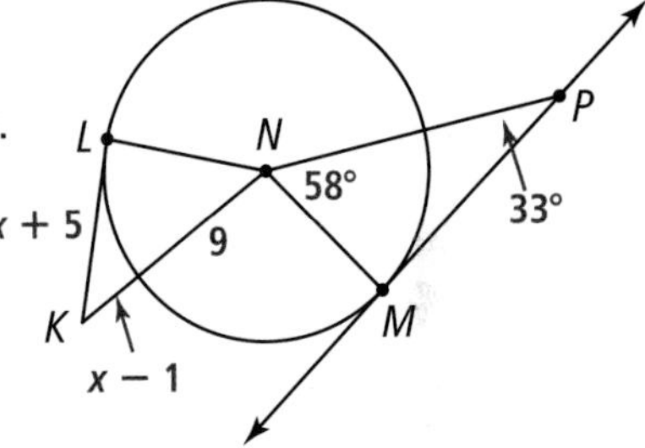

 **EXAMPLE 3** Find Lengths of Segments Tangent to a Circle

**What is the relationship between $\overline{YZ}$ and $\overline{XZ}$?**

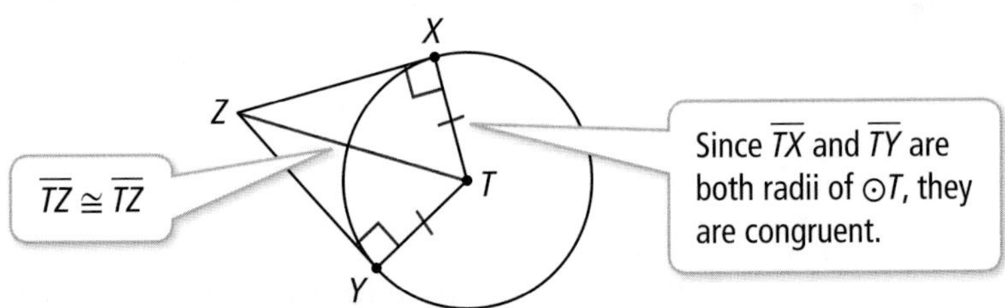


By HL, $\triangle TXZ \cong \triangle TYZ$, so $\overline{YZ} \cong \overline{XZ}$ by CPCTC.

 **Try It!** 3. If $TX = 12$ and $TZ = 20$, what are $XZ$ and $YZ$?

**THEOREM 10-2** Segments Tangent to a Circle Theorem

If two segments with a common endpoint exterior to a circle are tangent to the circle, then the segments are congruent.

**If...** (Figure: A, B, P, C)

**Then...** $\overline{AB} \cong \overline{AC}$

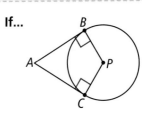

PROOF: SEE EXERCISE 14.

APPLICATION

## EXAMPLE 4 Find Measures Involving Tangent Lines

**A satellite requires a line of sight for communication. Between the ground stations farthest from the satellite, what is the amount of time needed for a signal to go from one station up to the satellite, and then down to the other station?**

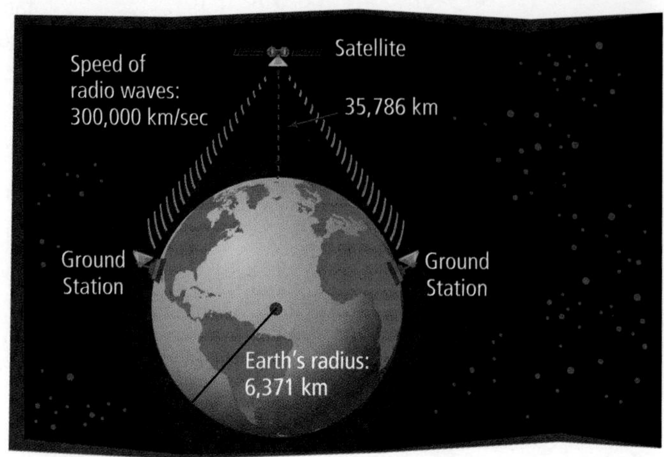


**Formulate** The lines from the satellite to the farthest ground stations are tangent to Earth's surface.

Use the Pythagorean Theorem to compute the distance to the ground stations. Then compute the time for radio waves to travel twice this distance.

**Compute** **Step 1** Find the distance from the farthest ground stations to the satellite.

$$x^2 + 6{,}371^2 = (6{,}371 + 35{,}786)^2$$

$$x^2 + 40{,}589{,}641 = 1{,}777{,}212{,}649$$

$$x^2 = 1{,}736{,}623{,}008$$

$$x \approx 41{,}673$$

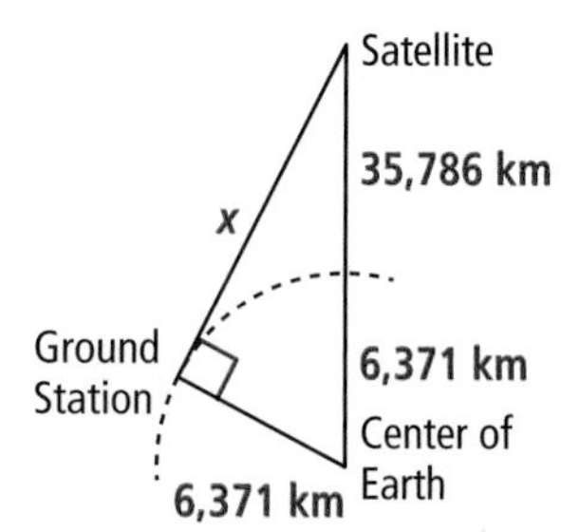


**Step 2** Find the time for radio waves to travel this distance twice.

$$(41{,}673 \times 2) \text{ km} \div 300{,}000 \text{ km/sec} \approx 0.28 \text{ sec}$$

**Interpret** The amount of time for a signal to travel from one of the farthest ground stations to the satellite and back to the other ground station is about 0.28 second.

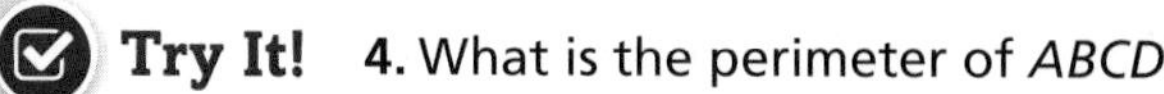

**Try It!** **4.** What is the perimeter of *ABCD*?

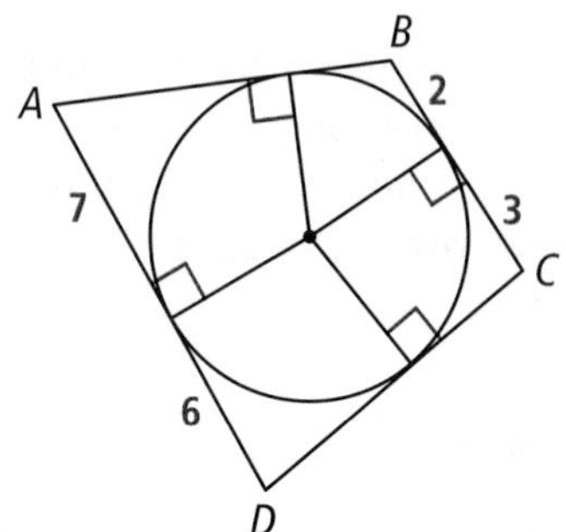

## EXAMPLE 5 Construct Tangent Lines

**How do you construct a tangent to ⊙$P$ passing through point $T$?**

**Step 1** Use a straightedge to draw $\overline{PT}$. Label point $A$ where $\overline{PT}$ intersects the circle.

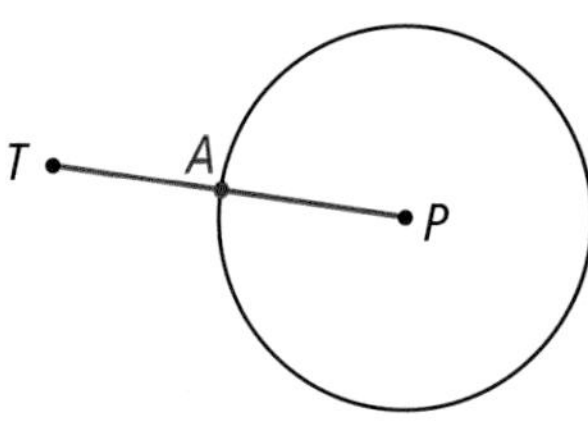


**Step 2** Use a compass to construct a circle with center $P$ and passing through $T$. Construct a perpendicular to $\overline{PT}$ at $A$. Label point $B$ where the perpendicular intersects the outer circle.

**COMMON ERROR**
You may think that $A$ is the midpoint of $\overline{PT}$. However, the construction of a perpendicular line here is different from constructing the perpendicular bisector of $\overline{PT}$.

**Step 3** Use a straightedge to construct $\overline{BP}$. Label point $C$ where $\overline{BP}$ intersects the inner circle.

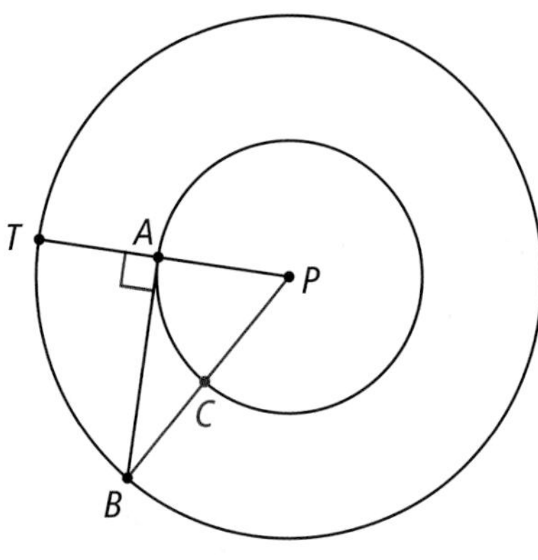


**Step 4** Use a straightedge to construct $\overline{TC}$.

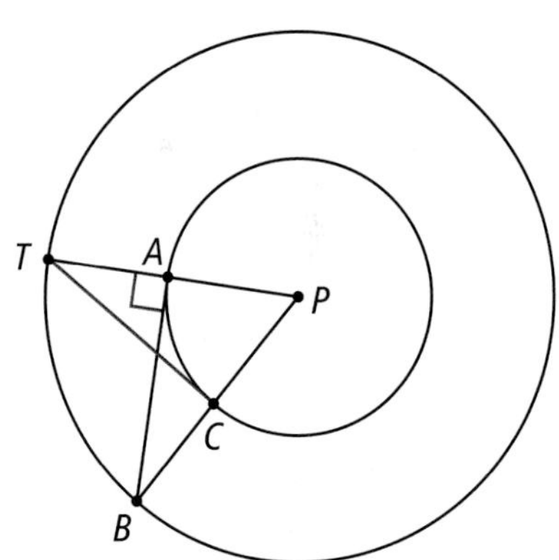


The tangent to ⊙$P$ passing through $T$ is $\overline{TC}$.

**Try It!** **5.** Prove that $\overline{TC}$ is tangent to ⊙$P$.

**Given:** Concentric circles with center $P$, points $A$ and $C$ on the smaller circle, points $T$ and $B$ on the larger circle, $\overline{AB} \perp \overline{PT}$

**Prove:** $\overline{TC}$ is tangent to ⊙$P$ at $C$.

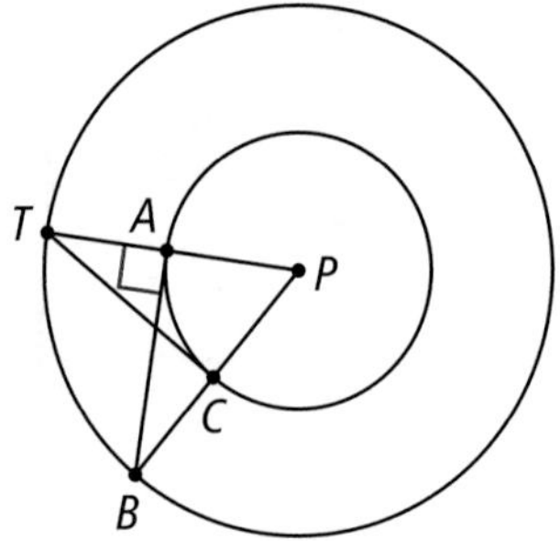

## CONCEPT SUMMARY Tangents to a Circle

**WORDS** A tangent to a circle intersects the circle at exactly one point. The radius that contains the point of tangency is perpendicular to the tangent.

**DIAGRAM**

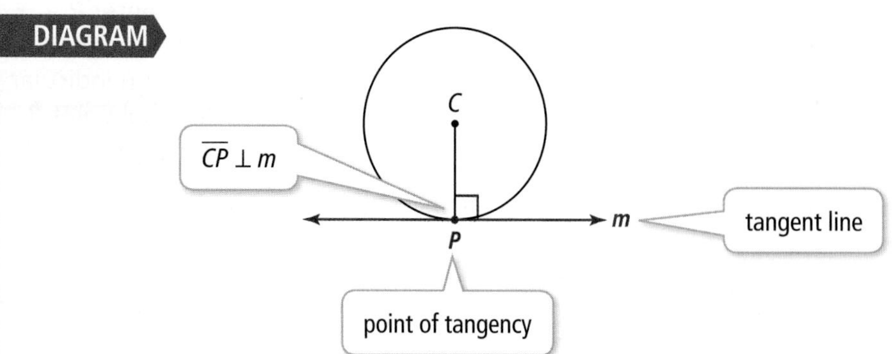


## Do You UNDERSTAND?

1. **ESSENTIAL QUESTION** How is a tangent line related to the radius of a circle at the point of tangency?

2. **Error Analysis** Kona looked at the figure shown and said that $\overline{AB}$ is tangent to $\odot G$ at $A$ because it intersects $\odot G$ only at $A$. What was Kona's error?

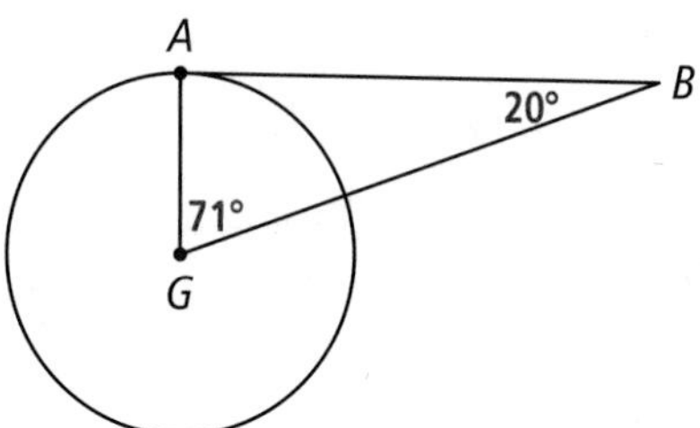


3. **Vocabulary** Can any point on a circle be a *point of tangency*? Explain.

4. **Reason** Lines $m$ and $n$ are tangent to circles $A$ and $B$. What are the relationships between $\angle PAS$, $\angle PQS$, $\angle RQS$, and $\angle RBS$? Explain.

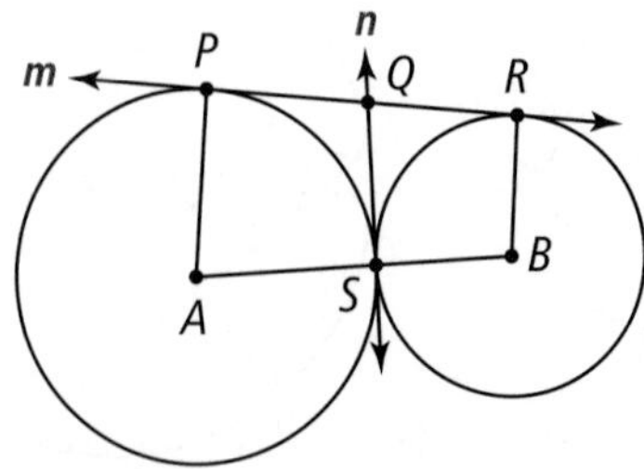


## Do You KNOW HOW?

**Tell whether each line or segment is a tangent to $\odot B$.**

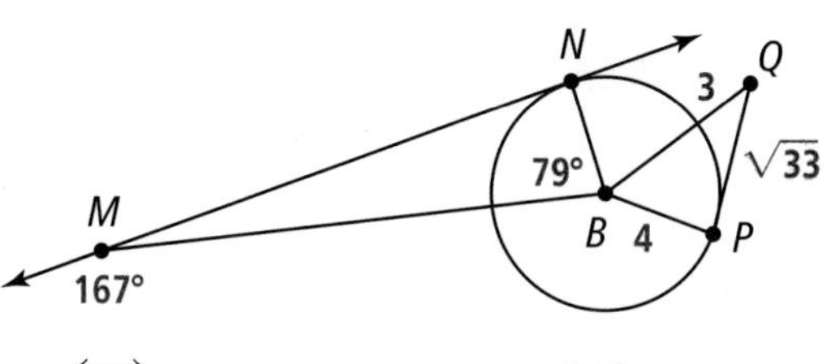


5. $\overleftrightarrow{MN}$

6. $\overline{QP}$

**Segment $AC$ is tangent to $\odot D$ at $B$. Find each value.**

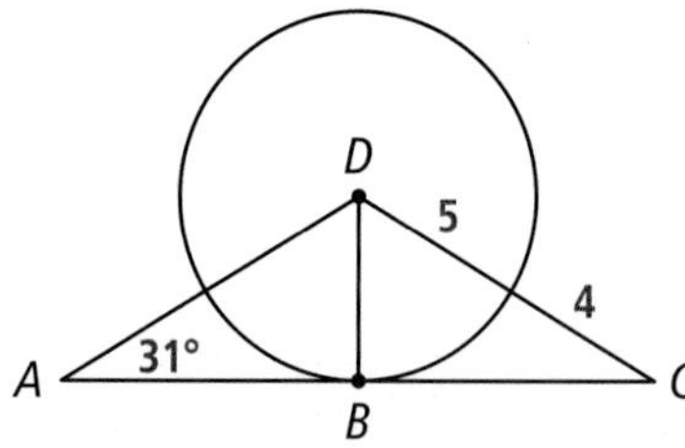


7. $m\angle ADB$

8. $BC$

**Segment $FG$ is tangent to $\odot K$ at $F$ and $\overline{HG}$ is tangent to $\odot K$ at $H$. Find each value.**

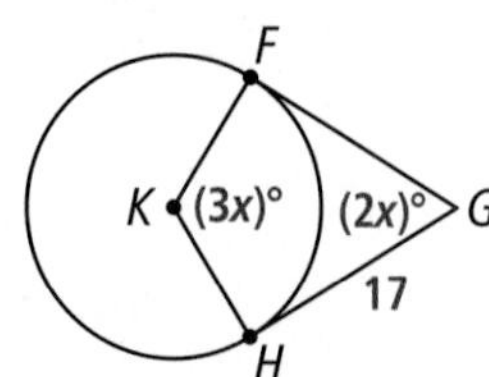


9. $FG$

10. $m\angle FGH$

# PRACTICE & PROBLEM SOLVING

Scan for Multimedia   

Additional Exercises Available Online

## UNDERSTAND

**11. Error Analysis** Segments $\overline{DF}$, $\overline{DH}$, and $\overline{GF}$ are tangent to the circle. Andrew was asked to find *DF*. Explain Andrew's error.

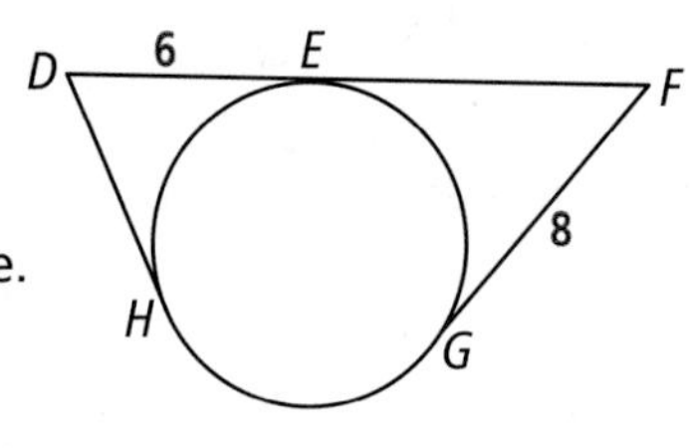


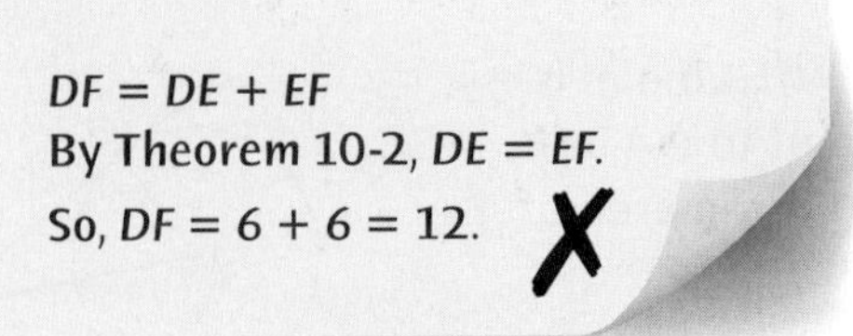

$DF = DE + EF$

By Theorem 10-2, $DE = EF$.

So, $DF = 6 + 6 = 12$. ✗

**12. Construct Arguments** Use the following outline to write an indirect proof of Theorem 10-1.

**Given:** Line *m* is tangent to ⊙*T* at *G*.

**Prove:** $\overline{GT} \perp m$

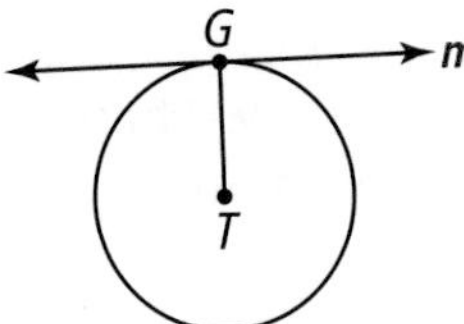


- Assume that $\overline{GT}$ is not perpendicular to *m*.
- Draw $\overline{HT}$ such that $\overline{HT} \perp m$.

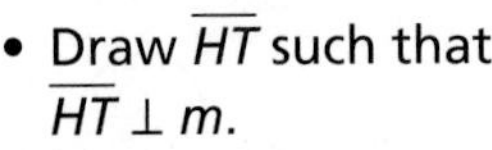

- Use triangles to show that $GT > HT$.
- Show that this is a contradiction, since *H* is in the exterior of ⊙*T*.

**13. Construct Arguments** Prove the Converse of Theorem 10-1.

**Given:** $\overline{QR} \perp n$

**Prove:** *n* is tangent to ⊙*Q* at *R*

*Hint:* Select any other point *S* on line *n*. Show that $\overline{QS}$ is the hypotenuse of $\triangle QRS$, so $QS > QR$ and therefore *S* lies outside ⊙*Q*.

**14. Construct Arguments** Prove Theorem 10-2.

**Given:** $\overline{DE}$ and $\overline{DF}$ are tangent to ⊙*T*.

**Prove:** $\overline{DE} \cong \overline{DF}$

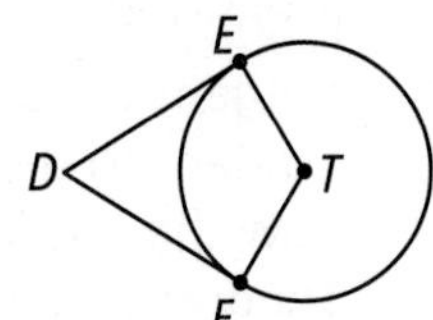


**15. Higher Order Thinking** If $AC = x$, what is the perimeter of $\triangle BCE$? Explain.

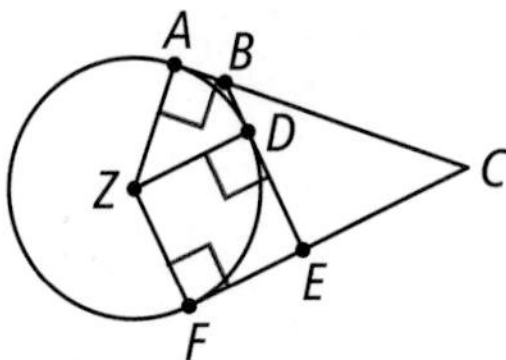


## PRACTICE

**The segments $\overline{AB}$ and $\overline{CD}$ are tangent to ⊙*T*. Find each value.** SEE EXAMPLES 1 AND 2

**16.** *AB*

**17.** $m\angle TDC$

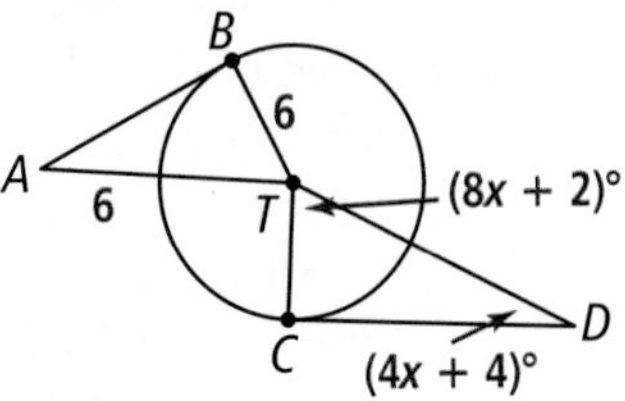


**For Exercises 18–20, the segments are tangent to the circle. Find each value.** SEE EXAMPLES 3 AND 4

**18.** *DG*

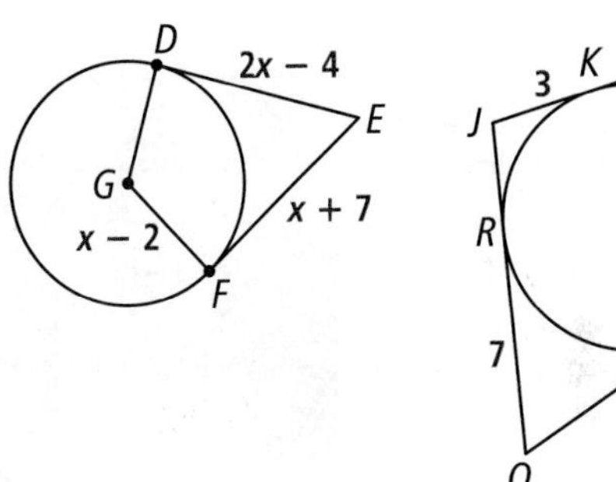


**19.** Perimeter of *JLNQ*

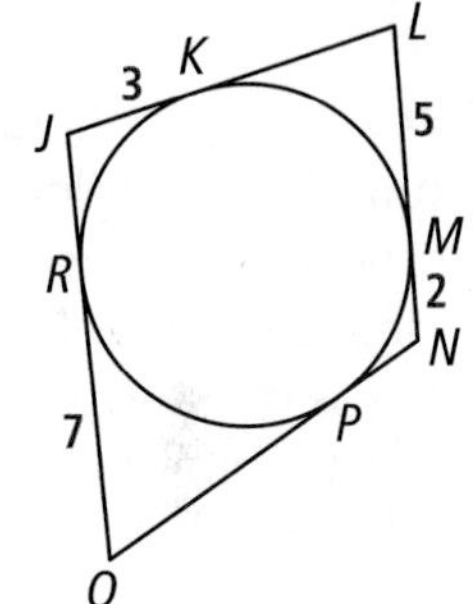


**20.** *AC*

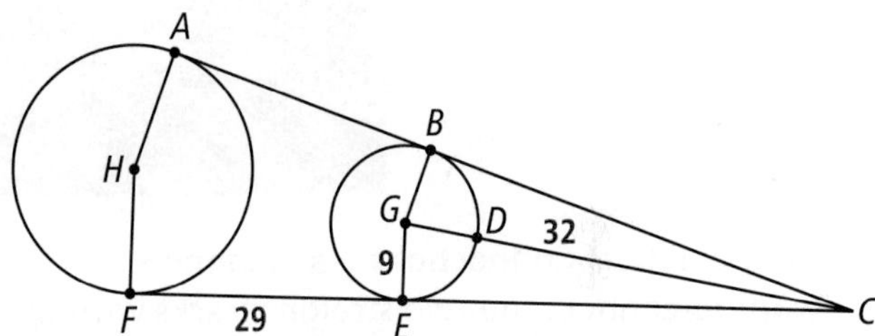


**21.** Trace ⊙*P* and point *A*. Construct a tangent to ⊙*P* that passes through *A*. SEE EXAMPLE 5

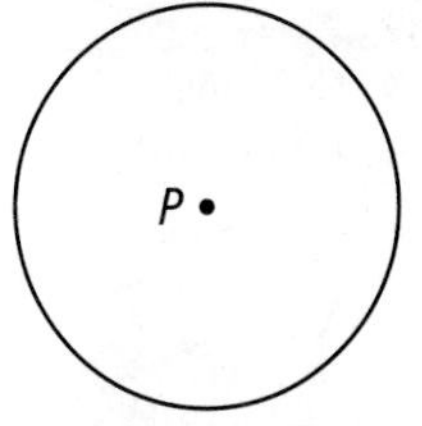


**22.** The diameter of ⊙*F* is 8; $AB = 10$; and $\overline{AB}$, $\overline{BC}$, and $\overline{AC}$ are tangent to ⊙*F*. What is the perimeter of $\triangle ABC$?

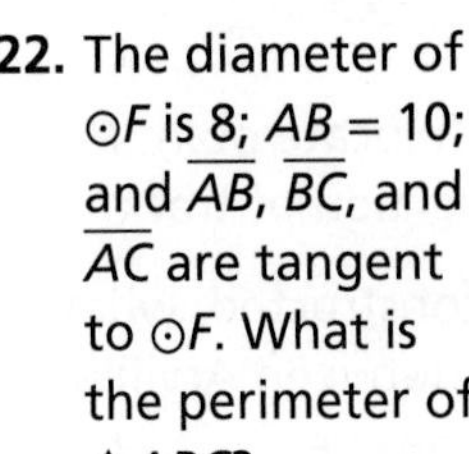

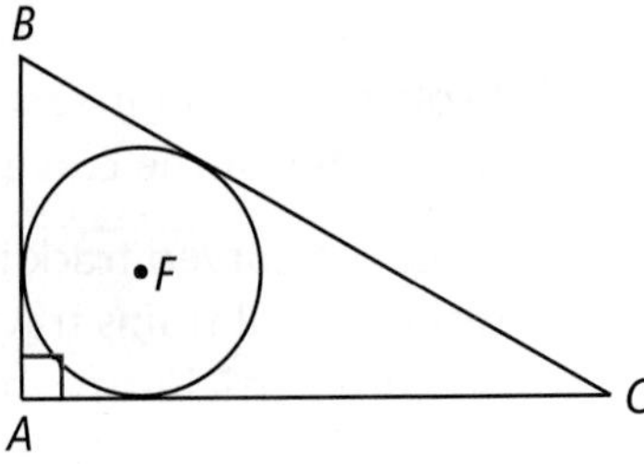

## APPLY

**23. Make Sense and Persevere** Yumiko is shopping for a stand for a decorative glass ball with an 8-inch diameter. She is considering the stand shown and wants to know the height $h$ of the portion of the ball that will be visible if the sides of the stand are tangent to the sphere. What is the value of $h$?

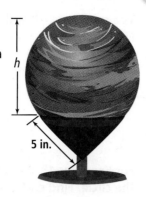

**24. Use Structure** Samantha is looking out from the 103rd floor of the Willis Tower on a clear day. How far away is the horizon? Earth's radius is about 6,400 km.

**25. Mathematical Connections** Rail planners want to connect the two straight tracks with a curved track as shown. Any curves must have a radius of at least 450 m.

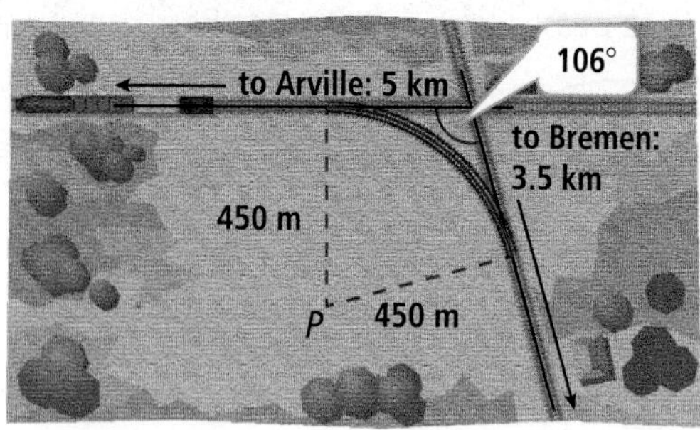


a. Explain how engineers can locate point $P$, the center of the curved section of track.

b. Once the curved track is constructed, what distance will trains travel between Arvillle and Bremen? Justify your answer.

## ASSESSMENT PRACTICE

**26.** Circle $P$ is described by the equation $(x + 3)^2 + (y - 2)^2 = 25$. Which of the following lines are tangent to $\odot P$? Select all that apply.

Ⓐ $y = x + 3$

Ⓑ $y = 5$

Ⓒ $y = x$

Ⓓ $x = 2$

Ⓔ $y = -3$

Ⓕ $y = x - 3$

**27. SAT/ACT** Line $m$ is tangent to $\odot A$ at $B$. What is the area of $\triangle ABC$?

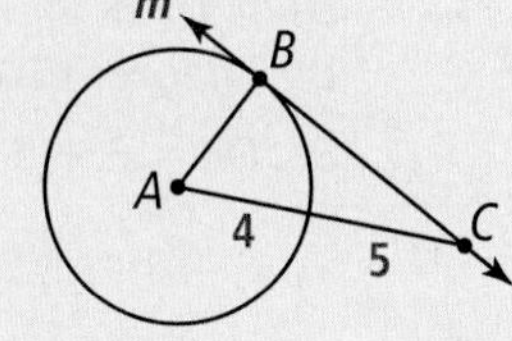


Ⓐ 10

Ⓑ 18

Ⓒ $2\sqrt{65}$

Ⓓ $\frac{5\sqrt{65}}{2}$

**28. Performance Task** The African art design below is based on circles that are tangent to each other.

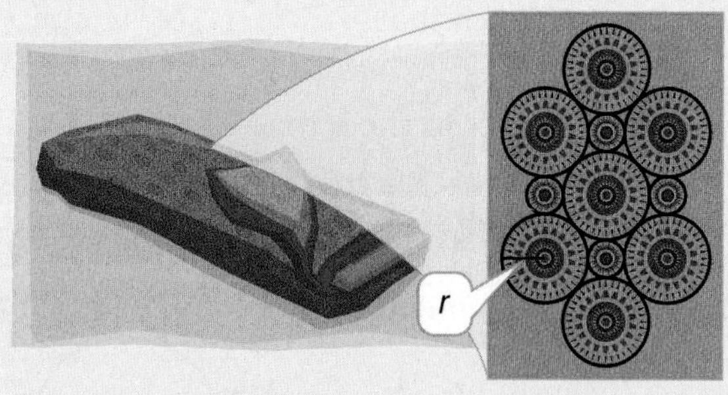


**Part A** If the radius of the larger circles is $r$, what is the radius of the smaller circles?

**Part B** Choose a value for the larger radius and draw the pattern. Measure the radii of the small and large circles. Are the values related in the way you described in Part A?

**Part C** In your diagram for Part B, mark the points where the small and large circles are tangent to each other. Add lines that are tangent to the circles at these points. Describe how the tangent lines you drew illustrate Theorems 10-1 and 10-2.

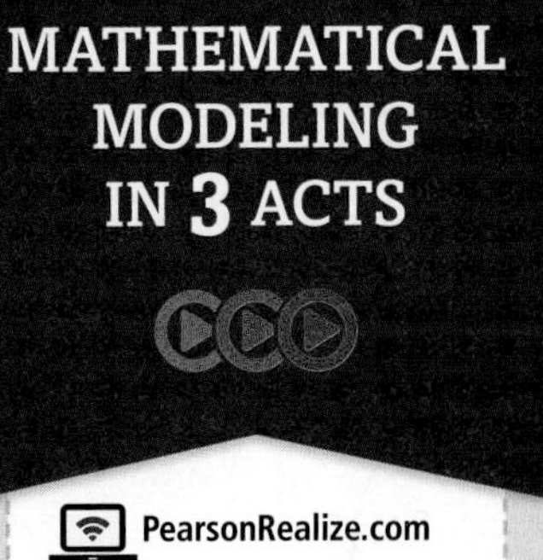


PearsonRealize.com

## Earth Watch

Scientists estimate that there are currently about 3,000 operational man-made satellites orbiting Earth. These satellites serve different purposes, from communication to navigation and global positioning. Some are weather satellites that collect environmental information.

The International Space Station is the largest man-made satellite that orbits Earth. It serves as a space environment research facility, and it also offers amazing views of Earth. Think about this during the Mathematical Modeling in 3 Acts lesson.

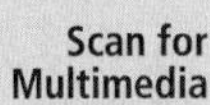

### ACT 1 Identify the Problem

1. What is the first question that comes to mind after watching the video?
2. Write down the main question you will answer about what you saw in the video.
3. Make an initial conjecture that answers this main question.
4. Explain how you arrived at your conjecture.
5. What information will be useful to know to answer the main question? How can you get it? How will you use that information?

### ACT 2 Develop a Model

6. Use the math that you have learned in this Topic to refine your conjecture.

### ACT 3 Interpret the Results

7. Did your refined conjecture match the actual answer exactly? If not, what might explain the difference?

# 10-3 Chords

PearsonRealize.com

**I CAN…** relate the length of a chord to its central angle and the arc it intercepts.

**VOCABULARY**

- chord

## EXPLORE & REASON

**Use the diagram to answer the questions.**

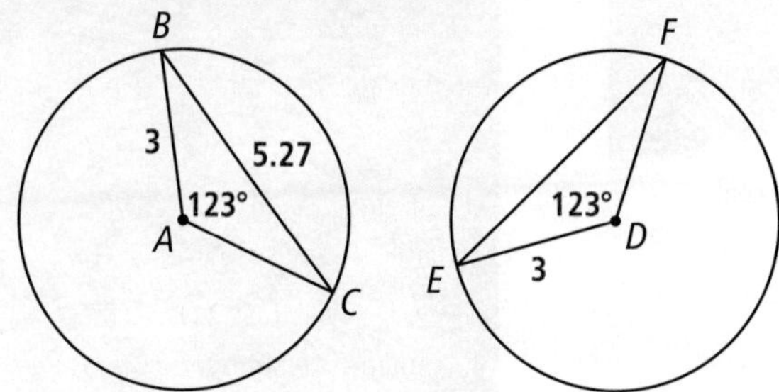


**A.** What figures in the diagram are congruent? Explain.

**B. Look for Relationships** How can you find $EF$?

## ESSENTIAL QUESTION

**How are chords related to their central angles and intercepted arcs?**

CONCEPTUAL UNDERSTANDING

## EXAMPLE 1 Relate Central Angles and Chords

**A chord is a segment whose endpoints are on a circle. Why is $\overline{RS} \cong \overline{UT}$?**

**STUDY TIP**
Refer to the diagram as you read the proof. Note which parts of the triangles are congruent.

$\angle RQS \cong \angle UQT$ because they are vertical angles.

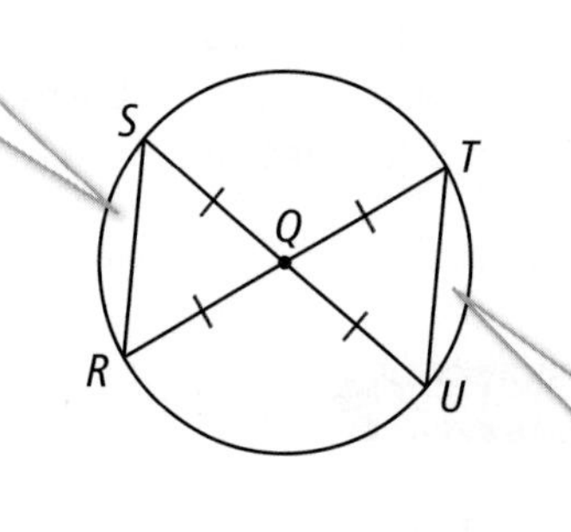

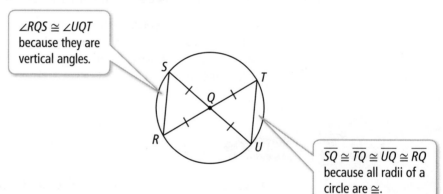

$\overline{SQ} \cong \overline{TQ} \cong \overline{UQ} \cong \overline{RQ}$ because all radii of a circle are $\cong$.

By the SAS Congruence Theorem, $\triangle QRS \cong \triangle QUT$. Therefore $\overline{RS} \cong \overline{UT}$ because they are corresponding parts of congruent triangles.

**Try It!** **1.** Why is $\angle BAC \cong \angle DAE$?

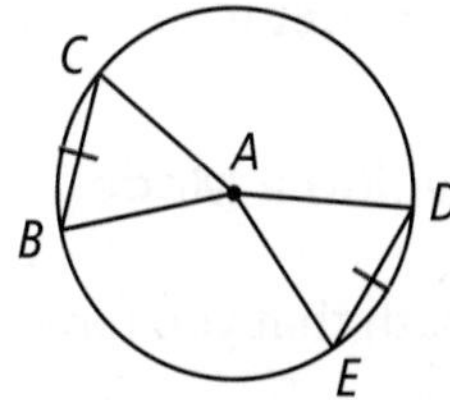

## THEOREM 10-3 AND THE CONVERSE

**Theorem**

If two chords in a circle or in congruent circles are congruent, then their central angles are congruent.

**Converse**

If two central angles in a circle or in congruent circles are congruent, then their chords are congruent.

PROOF: SEE EXERCISES 12 AND 13.

**If...** $\overline{MN} \cong \overline{PQ}$
**Then...** $\angle MTN \cong \angle PTQ$

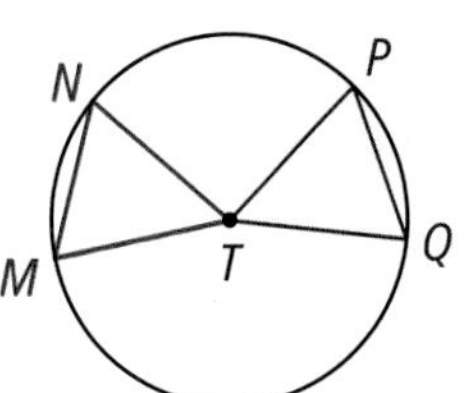


**If...** $\angle MTN \cong \angle PTQ$
**Then...** $\overline{MN} \cong \overline{PQ}$

## THEOREM 10-4 AND THE CONVERSE

**Theorem**

If two arcs in a circle or in congruent circles are congruent, then their chords are congruent.

**Converse**

If two chords in a circle or in congruent circles are congruent, then their arcs are congruent.

PROOF: SEE EXAMPLE 2 AND EXAMPLE 2 TRY IT.

**If...** $\widehat{MN} \cong \widehat{PQ}$
**Then...** $\overline{MN} \cong \overline{PQ}$

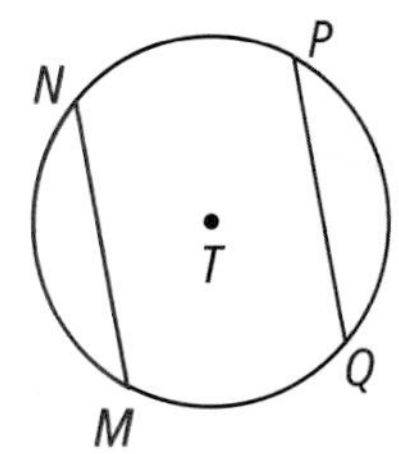


**If...** $\overline{MN} \cong \overline{PQ}$
**Then...** $\widehat{MN} \cong \widehat{PQ}$

PROOF

## EXAMPLE 2 Relate Arcs and Chords

**Write a proof of Theorem 10-4.**

**Given:** $\widehat{AB} \cong \widehat{CD}$

**Prove:** $\overline{AB} \cong \overline{CD}$

**Plan:** Use the relationship between central angles and arcs by drawing the radii $\overline{PA}$, $\overline{PB}$, $\overline{PC}$, and $\overline{PD}$.

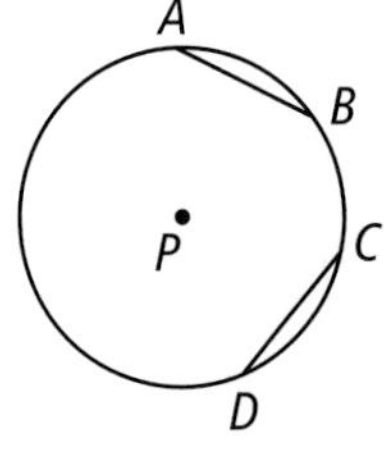


**MAKE SENSE AND PERSEVERE**
Think about other strategies you can use. How could you use congruent triangles to prove the relationship?

**Proof:** Since $\widehat{AB} \cong \widehat{CD}$, you know that $m\widehat{AB} = m\widehat{CD}$. And since the measure of a central angle is equal to the measure of its arc, $m\angle APB = m\widehat{AB}$ and $m\angle CPD = m\widehat{CD}$. Using the given, $m\angle APB = m\angle CPD$ and $\angle APB \cong \angle CPD$. So, by the Converse of Theorem 10-3, $\overline{AB} \cong \overline{CD}$.

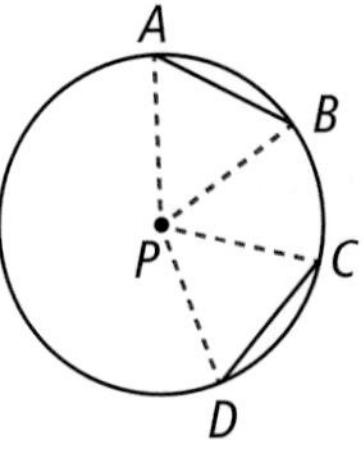

 **Try It!** **2.** Write a flow proof of the Converse of Theorem 10-4.

## THEOREM 10-5 AND THE CONVERSE

**Theorem**

If chords are equidistant from the center of a circle or the centers of congruent circles, then they are congruent.

**Converse**

If chords in a circle or in congruent circles are congruent, then they are equidistant from the center or centers.

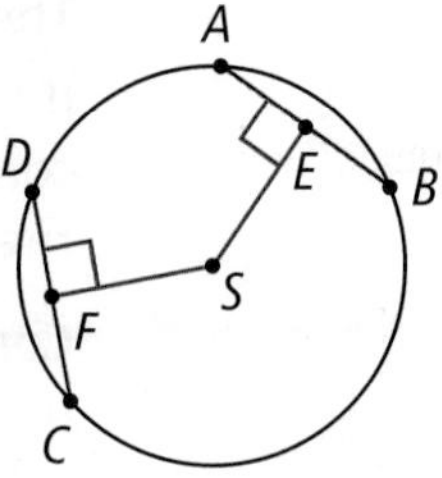

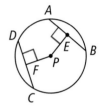


**If...** $\overline{SE} \cong \overline{SF}$, **Then...** $\overline{AB} \cong \overline{CD}$

**If...** $\overline{AB} \cong \overline{CD}$, **Then...** $\overline{SE} \cong \overline{SF}$

PROOF: SEE EXAMPLE 3 AND EXAMPLE 3 TRY IT.

## EXAMPLE 3 Relate Chords Equidistant from the Center

**COMMON ERROR**
Be sure to construct the triangles with corresponding parts that yield the desired conclusion.

**Write a proof of Theorem 10-5.**

**Given:** $\odot P$ with $\overline{AB} \perp \overline{PE}$, $\overline{CD} \perp \overline{PF}$, $\overline{PE} \cong \overline{PF}$

**Prove:** $\overline{AB} \cong \overline{CD}$

**Plan:** Construct triangles by drawing the radii $\overline{PA}$, $\overline{PB}$, $\overline{PC}$, and $\overline{PD}$. Then show that the triangles are congruent in order to apply CPCTC.

**Proof:**

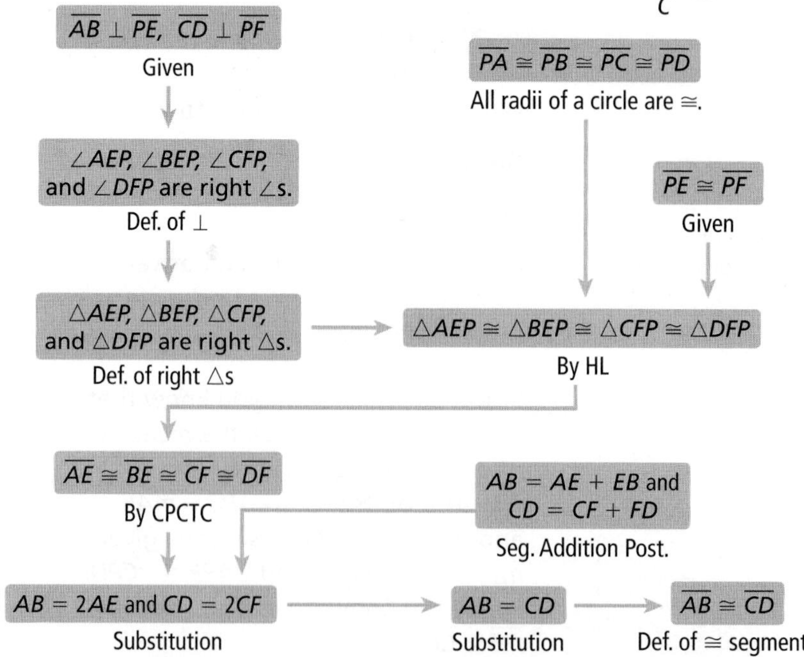

**Try It!** **3.** Write a flow proof of the Converse of Theorem 10-5.

## EXAMPLE 4 Construct a Regular Hexagon Inscribed in a Circle

**STUDY TIP**

Remember, a regular polygon is both equilateral and equiangular.

**How do you draw a regular hexagon inscribed in ⊙*P*?**

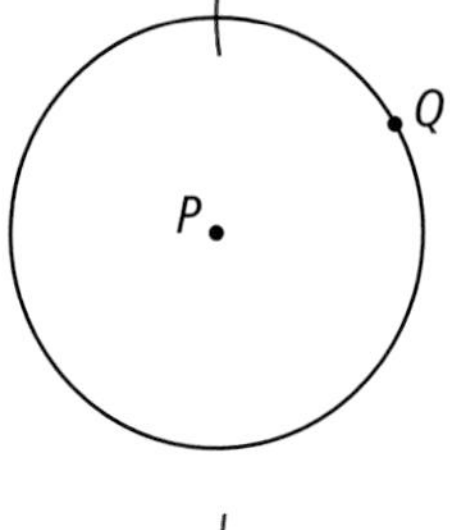


**Step 1** Mark point *Q* on the circle.

**Step 2** Set the compass the radius of the circle. Place the compass point at *Q* and draw an arc through the circle.

**Step 3** Keep the compass setting. Move the compass point to the intersection of the arc and the circle. Draw another arc through the circle. Each point of intersection is a vertex of the hexagon. Continue this way until you have five arcs.

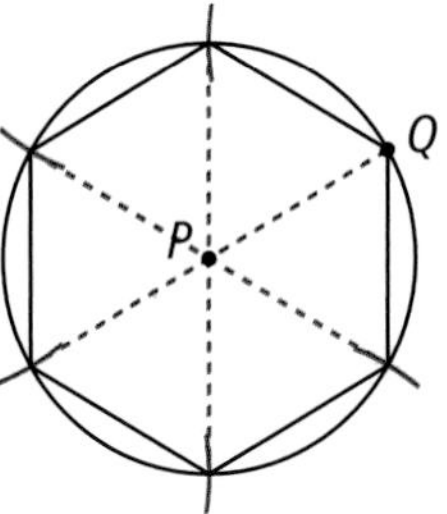


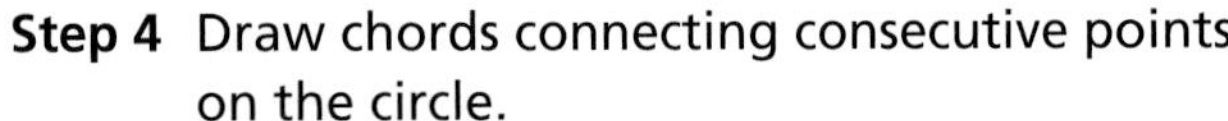

**Step 4** Draw chords connecting consecutive points on the circle.

The side lengths of the resulting figure are all congruent because they have the same length as the radius of the circle.

Connecting the center of the circle with the six vertices of the inscribed polygon forms six equilateral triangles, so each angle measures 120. The figure is a regular hexagon.

**Try It!** **4.** Construct an equilateral triangle inscribed in a circle.

### THEOREM 10-6 AND THE CONVERSE

**Theorem**

If a diameter is perpendicular to a chord, then it bisects the chord.

**Converse**

If a diameter bisects a chord (that is not a diameter), then it is perpendicular to the chord.

PROOF: SEE EXERCISES 15 AND 16.

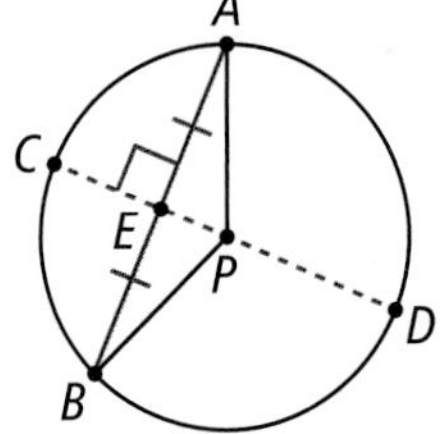


**If...** $\overline{CD}$ is a diameter, $\overline{AB} \perp \overline{CD}$
**Then...** $\overline{AE} \cong \overline{BE}$

**If...** $\overline{CD}$ is a diameter, $\overline{AE} \cong \overline{BE}$
**Then...** $\overline{AB} \perp \overline{CD}$

### THEOREM 10-7

The perpendicular bisector of a chord contains the center of the circle.

PROOF: SEE EXERCISE 27.

**If...**

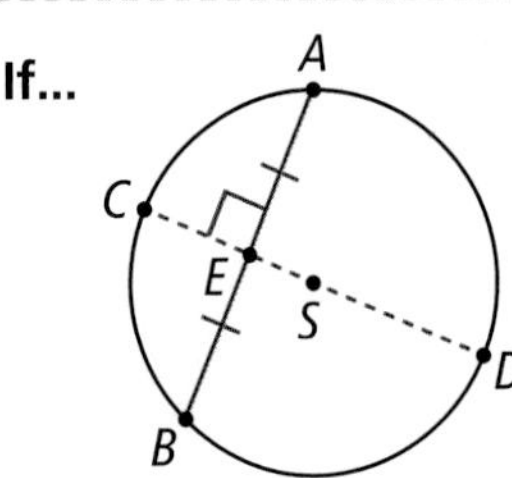


**Then...** $S$ is on $\overline{CD}$

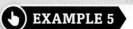

APPLICATION

## EXAMPLE 5 Solve Problems Involving Chords of Circles

**An engineer is designing a service tunnel to accommodate two trucks simultaneously. If the tunnel can accommodate a width of 18 ft, what is the greatest truck height that the tunnel can accommodate? Subtract 0.5 ft to account for fluctuations in pavement.**

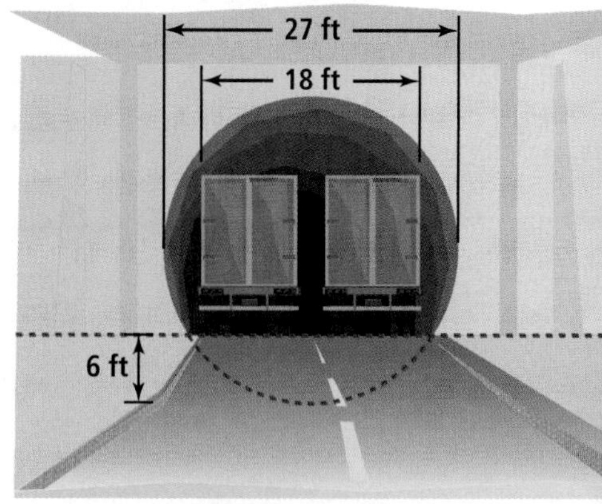


Formulate ◀ Draw and label a sketch to help solve the problem.

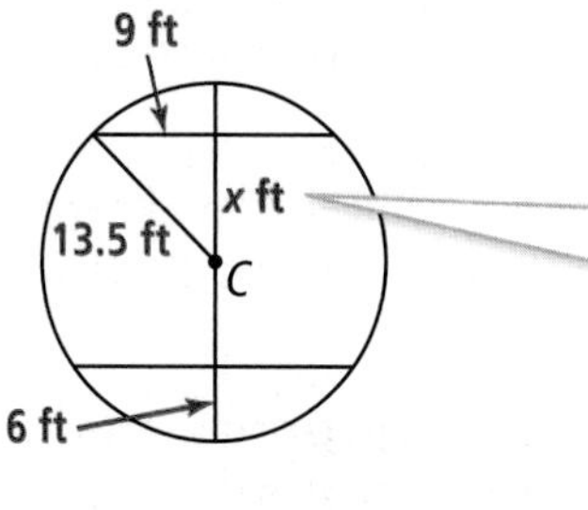


Let $x$ be the distance from the center to the greatest height. The radius is 13.5 ft.

Compute ◀ Write and solve an equation for $x$.

$$9^2 + x^2 = 13.5^2$$

Use the Pythagorean Theorem.

$$x^2 = 13.5^2 - 9^2$$

$$x = \sqrt{13.5^2 - 9^2}$$

$$x \approx 10.06$$

Add the distance from the ground to the center $13.5 - 6 = 7.5$ to $x$ and subtract 0.5 ft to account for fluctuations in pavement.

$$7.5 + 10.06 - 0.5 = 17.06$$

Interpret ◀ The greatest height that the tunnel can accommodate is about 17.06 ft.

**Try It!** 5. Fresh cut flowers need to be in at least 4 inches of water. A spherical vase is filled until the surface of the water is a circle 5 inches in diameter. Is the water deep enough for the flowers? Explain.

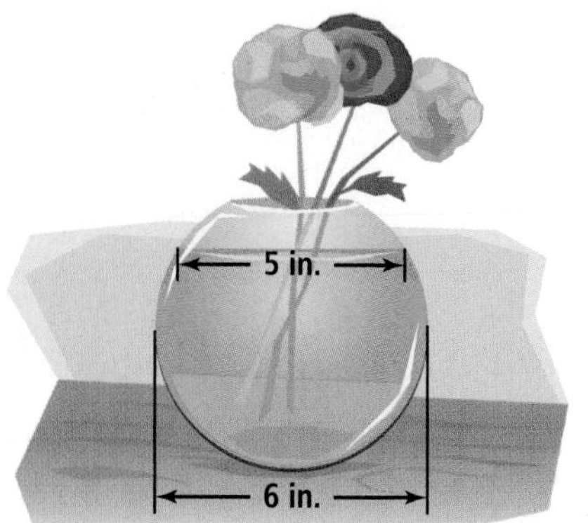

# PRACTICE & PROBLEM SOLVING

## APPLY

**29. Mathematical Connections** Nadia designs a water ride and wants to use a half-cylindrical pipe in the construction. If she wants the waterway to be 8 ft wide when the water is 2 ft deep, what is the diameter of the pipe?

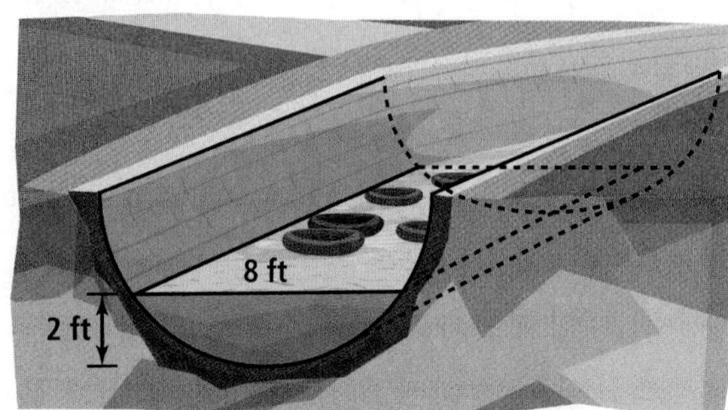


**30. Model With Mathematics** A bike trail has holes up to 20 in. wide and 5 in. deep. If the diameter of the wheels of Anna's bike is 26 in., can she ride her bike without the wheels hitting the bottom of the holes? Explain.

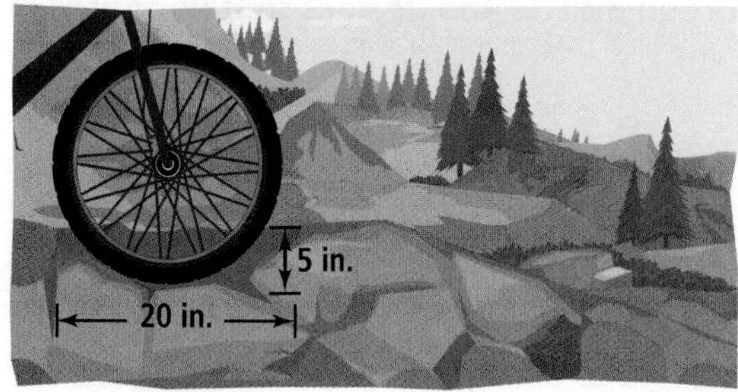


**31. Make Sense and Persevere** The bottom of a hemispherical cake has diameter 8 in.

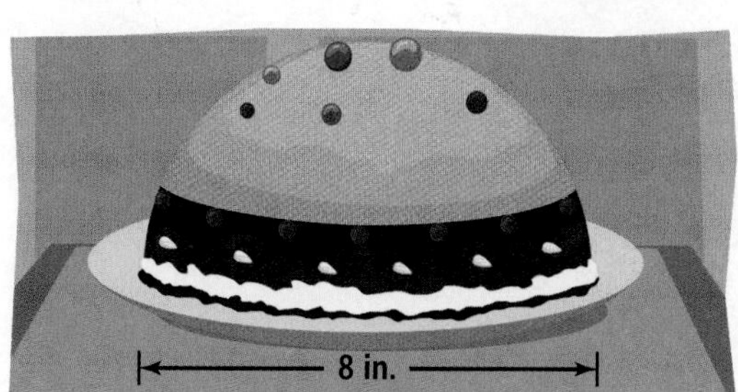


a. If the cake is sliced horizontally in half so each piece has the same height, would the top half fit on a plate with diameter 6 in.? Explain.

b. If the cake is sliced horizontally in thirds so each piece has the same height, would the top third fit on a plate with diameter 5 in.? Explain.

## ASSESSMENT PRACTICE

**32.** Which must be true? Selec

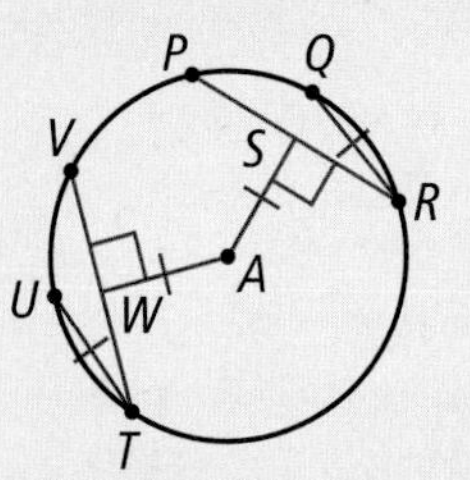


Ⓐ $\overset{\frown}{QR} \cong \overline{TU}$ Ⓒ

Ⓑ $PR = TV$ Ⓓ

**33. SAT/ACT** The radius of the $CD = \frac{3}{4} \cdot AB$. What is the di chord to the diameter?

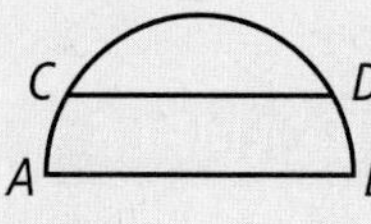


Ⓐ $\frac{5}{4}r$ Ⓑ $\frac{\sqrt{7}}{4}r$ Ⓒ

**34. Performance Task** The radiu radar is 50 miles. At 1:00 P.M radar screen flying due nort aircraft is due east of the rad aircraft leaves the screen. Th 8 miles per minute.

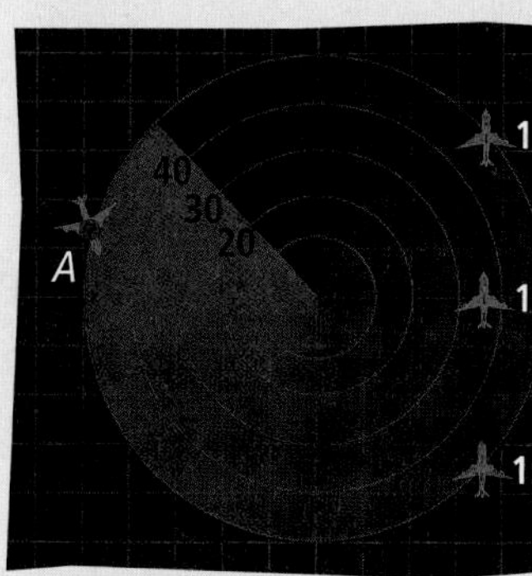


**Part A** What distance does controller's screen?

**Part B** What is the distance the radar at 1:04 P.M.?

**Part C** Another plane enter A at 1:12 P.M. and flies in a s 9 miles per minute. If it gets 40 miles from the radar, at w leave the screen? Explain.

# CONCEPT SUMMARY Chords

| | Chords and Central Angles | Chords and Arcs |
|---|---|---|
| WORDS | Two chords in a circle or in congruent circles are congruent if and only if the central angles of the chords are congruent. | Two chords in a circle or in congruent circles are congruent if and only if the chords intercept congruent arcs. |
| DIAGRAMS | 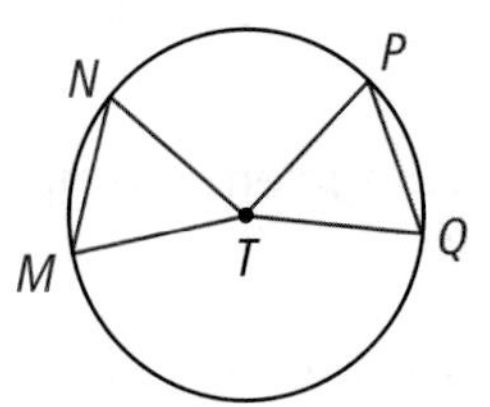 $\angle MTN \cong \angle PTQ$ if and only if $\overline{MN} \cong \overline{PQ}$. | 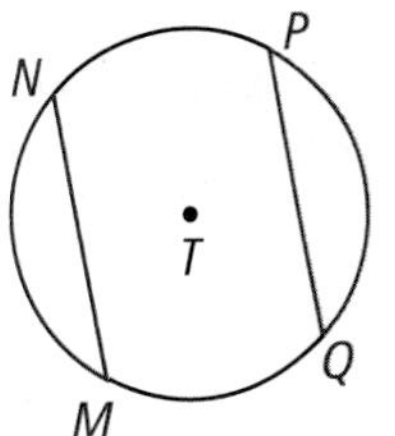 $\overset{\frown}{MN} \cong \overset{\frown}{PQ}$ if and only if $\overline{MN} \cong \overline{PQ}$. |

## Do You UNDERSTAND?

1. **ESSENTIAL QUESTION** How are chords related to their central angles and intercepted arcs?

2. **Error Analysis** Sasha writes a proof to show that two chords are congruent. What is her error?

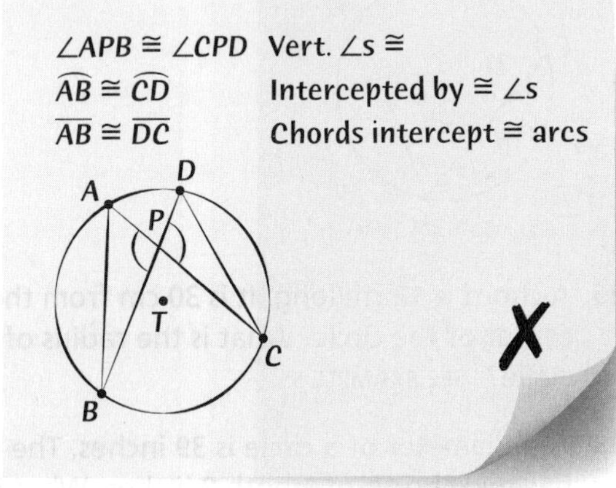


3. **Vocabulary** Explain why all diameters of circles are also chords of the circles.

4. **Reason** Given $\overset{\frown}{RS} \cong \overset{\frown}{UT}$, how can you find $UT$?

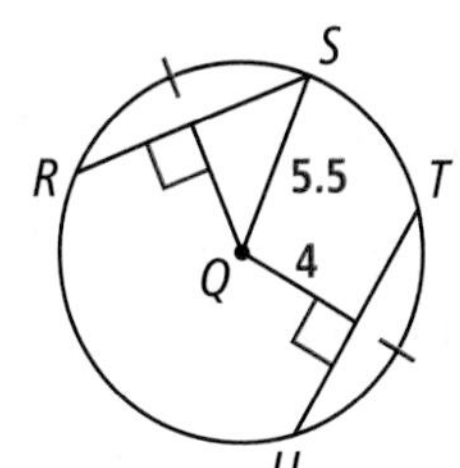


## Do You KNOW HOW?

**For Exercises 5–10, in ⊙$P$, $m\overset{\frown}{AB} = 43°$, and $AC = DF$. Find each measure.**

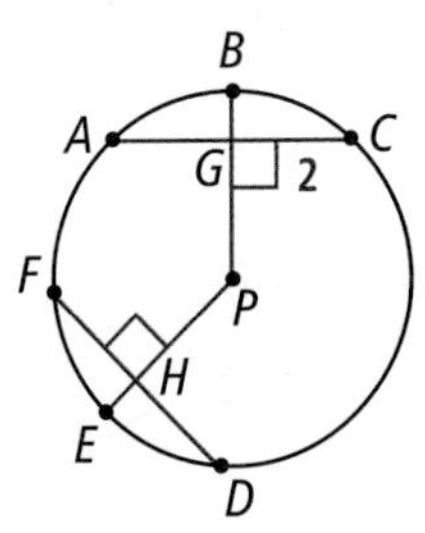


5. $DF$

6. $m\overset{\frown}{AC}$

7. $FH$

8. $m\overset{\frown}{DE}$

9. $AC$

10. $m\overset{\frown}{DF}$

11. For the corporate headquarters, an executive wants to place a company logo that is six feet in diameter with the sides of the H five feet tall on the front wall. What is the width $x$ of the crossbar for the H?

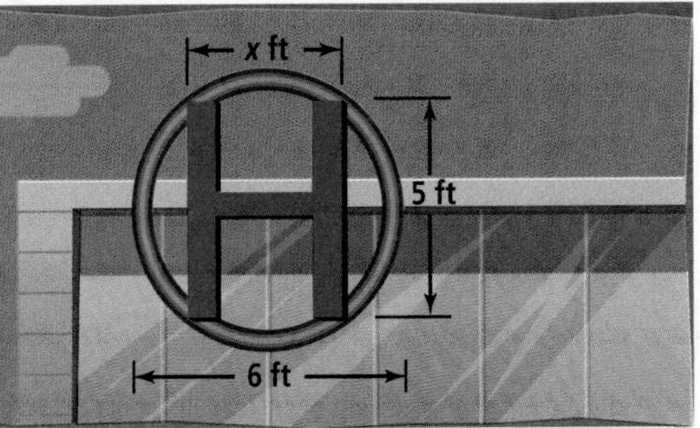

## PRACTICE & PROBLEM SOLVING

Scan for Multimedia 

### UNDERSTAND

**12. Construct Arguments** Write a paragraph proof of Theorem 10-3.

**Given:** $\overline{AB} \cong \overline{CD}$

**Prove:** $\angle AEB \cong \angle CED$

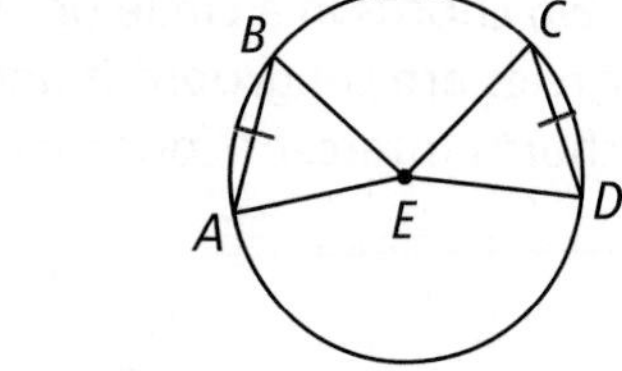


**13. Construct Arguments** Write a two-column proof of the Converse of Theorem 10-3.

**Given:** $\angle AEB \cong \angle CED$

**Prove:** $\overline{AB} \cong \overline{CD}$

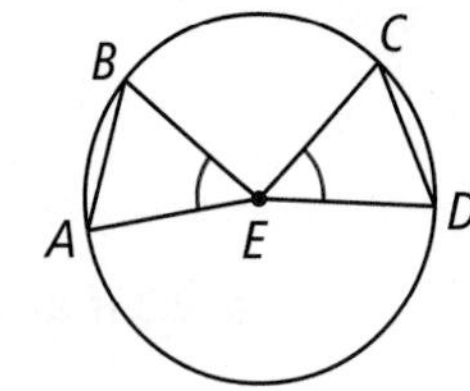


**14. Error Analysis** What is Ashton's error?

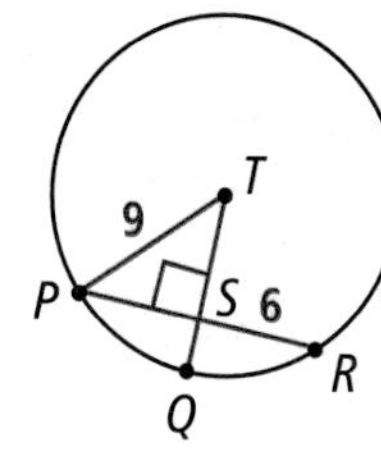


$TS = \sqrt{PR^2 - PS^2}$
$= \sqrt{12^2 - 9^2}$
$\approx 7.9$
✗

**15. Construct Arguments** Write a proof of Theorem 10-6.

**Given:** $\overline{LN}$ is a diameter of $\odot Q$; $\overline{LN} \perp \overline{KM}$

**Prove:** $\overline{KP} \cong \overline{MP}$

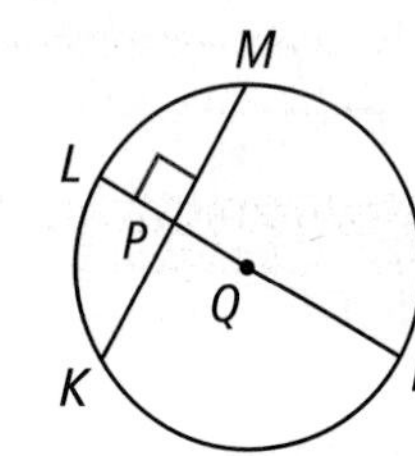


**16. Construct Arguments** Write a proof of the Converse of Theorem 10-6.

**Given:** $\overline{LN}$ is a diameter of $\odot Q$; $\overline{KP} \cong \overline{MP}$

**Prove:** $\overline{LN} \perp \overline{KM}$

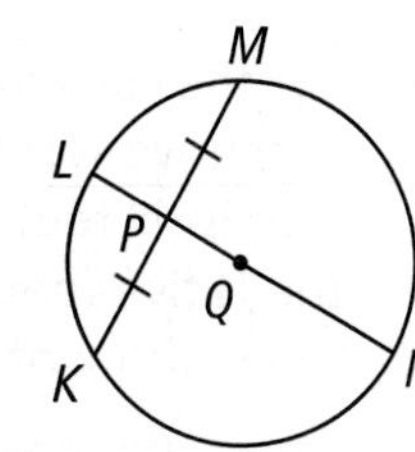


**17. Higher Order Thinking** $\triangle ABP \sim \triangle CDE$. How do you show that $\widehat{AB} \cong \widehat{CD}$?

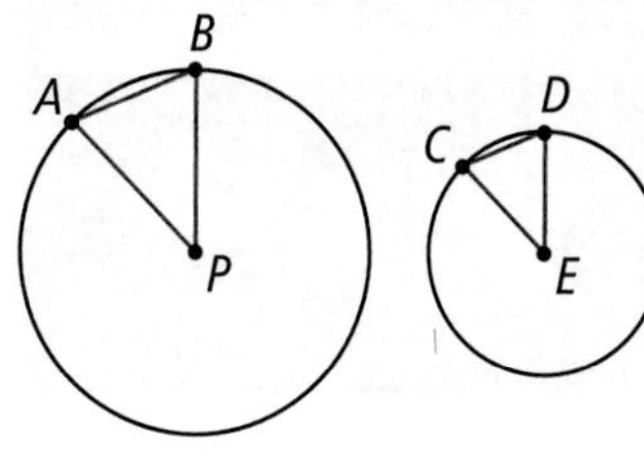


### PRACTICE

**For Exercises 18–21, in ⊙B and $QR = TU$.** SEE EXAMPLE

**18.** Find $m\angle PBR$.

**19.** Find $m\widehat{TV}$.

**20.** Which angle is congru to $\angle QBR$?

**21.** Which segment is con to $\overline{TV}$?

**22.** Construct a square ins is drawing an inscribe drawing an inscribed SEE EXAMPLE 4

**23.** Find $CD$. SEE EXAMPLE 3

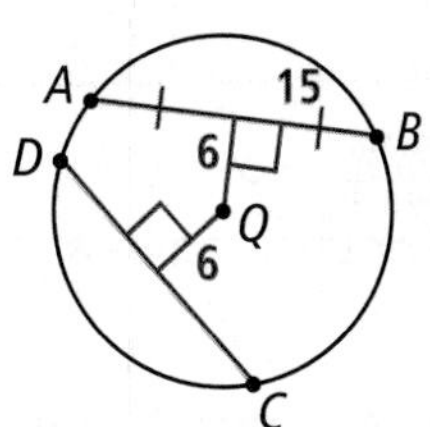


**24.** Find $FG$. SEE EXAMPLE 3

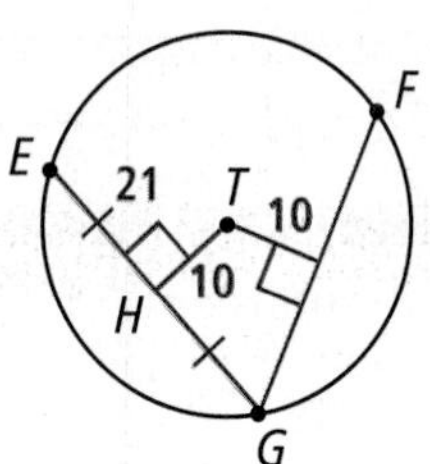


**25.** A chord is 12 cm long. center of the circle. Wh circle? SEE EXAMPLE 5

**26.** The diameter of a circl has two chords of leng the distance from each the circle?

**27.** A chord is 4 units from The radius of the circle length of the chord?

**28.** Write a proof of Theor

**Given:** $\overline{QR}$ is a chord in $\overline{AB}$ is the perper bisector of $\overline{QR}$.

**Prove:** $\overline{AB}$ contains $P$.





# 10-4 Inscribed Angles

PearsonRealize.com

**I CAN…** use the relationships between angles and arcs in circles to find their measures.

**VOCABULARY**

- inscribed angle

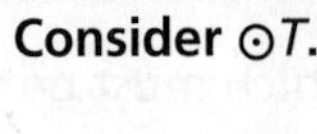

## EXPLORE & REASON

Consider $\odot T$.

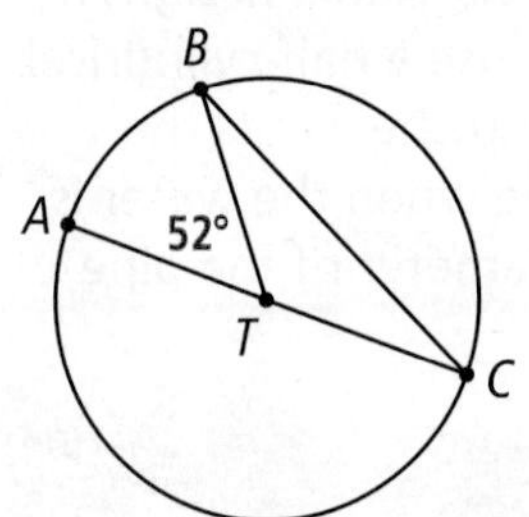


**A. Make Sense and Persevere** List at least seven things you can conclude about the figure.

**B.** How is $\angle ACB$ related to $\angle ATB$? Explain.

**ESSENTIAL QUESTION** How is the measure of an inscribed angle related to its intercepted arc?

CONCEPTUAL UNDERSTANDING

## EXAMPLE 1 Relate Inscribed Angles to Intercepted Arcs

**What is the relationship between $\widehat{AB}$ and $\angle ACB$?**

An **inscribed angle** has its vertex on a circle and its sides contain chords of the circle.

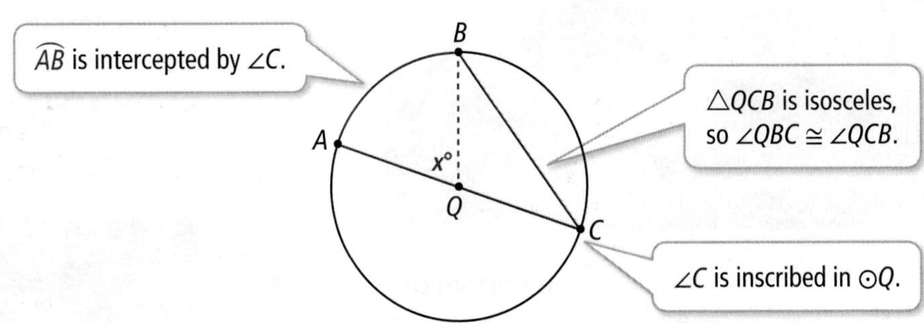


Draw radius $\overline{QB}$ to form $\triangle QCB$ and central angle $\angle AQB$.

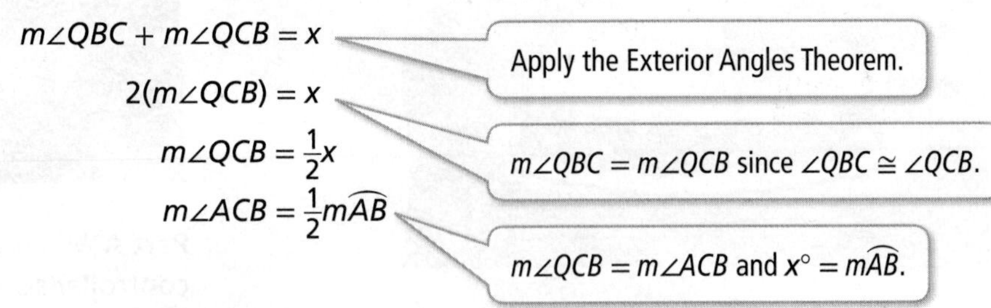

$m\angle QBC + m\angle QCB = x$ — Apply the Exterior Angles Theorem.

$2(m\angle QCB) = x$ — $m\angle QBC = m\angle QCB$ since $\angle QBC \cong \angle QCB$.

$m\angle QCB = \frac{1}{2}x$

$m\angle ACB = \frac{1}{2}m\widehat{AB}$ — $m\angle QCB = m\angle ACB$ and $x° = m\widehat{AB}$.

**STUDY TIP**
There are an infinite number of inscribed angles that intercept the arc. These inscribed angles all have the same angle measure.

The measure of an inscribed angle $\angle ACB$ is half the measure of the intercepted arc $\widehat{AB}$.

**Try It!** **1.** Given $\odot P$ with inscribed angle $\angle S$, if $m\widehat{RT} = 47$, what is $m\angle S$?

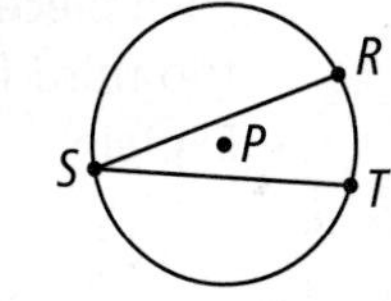

## THEOREM 10-8 Inscribed Angles Theorem

The measure of an inscribed angle is half the measure of its intercepted arc.

**Case 1**

The center is on one side of the angle.

**If...**

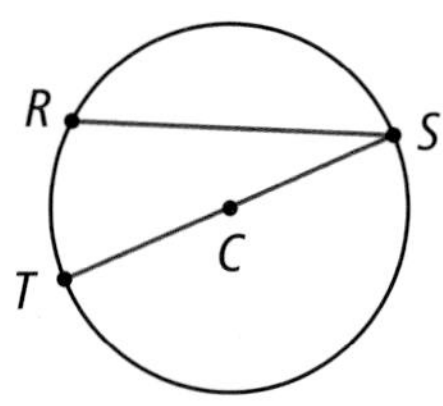


**Then...** $m\angle S = \frac{1}{2}m\widehat{RT}$

**Case 2**

The center is inside the angle.

**If...**

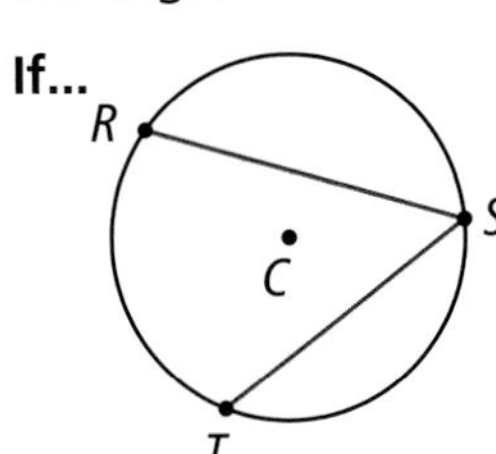


**Then...** $m\angle S = \frac{1}{2}m\widehat{RT}$

**Case 3**

The center is outside the angle.

**If...**

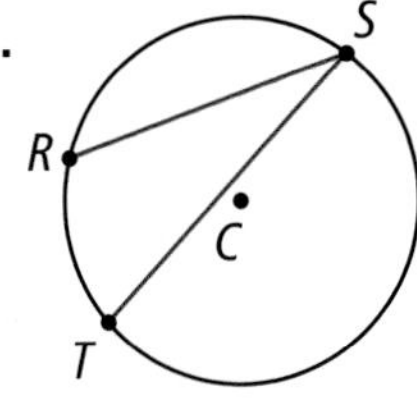


**Then...** $m\angle S = \frac{1}{2}m\widehat{RT}$

**PROOF: SEE EXERCISES 19, 32, AND 33.**

## EXAMPLE 2 Use the Inscribed Angles Theorem

**A. If $m\widehat{DG} = 45.6$, what are $m\angle E$ and $m\angle F$?**

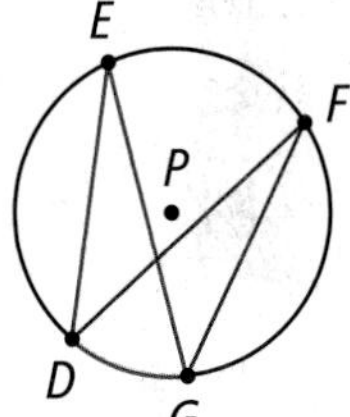


$m\angle E = \frac{1}{2}m\widehat{DG}$

$= \frac{1}{2}(45.6) = 22.8$

$m\angle F = \frac{1}{2}m\widehat{DG}$

$= \frac{1}{2}(45.6) = 22.8$

**LOOK FOR RELATIONSHIPS**
The diameter of a circle is a straight angle. What is the measure of the arc intercepted by a diameter?

**B. If $\widehat{RT}$ is a semicircle, what is $m\angle RST$?**

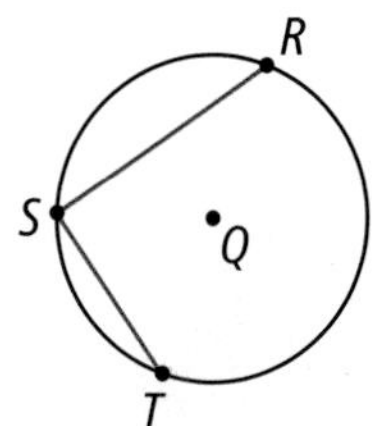


$m\angle S = \frac{1}{2}m\widehat{RT}$

$= \frac{1}{2}(180) = 90$

**C. If $m\widehat{ABC} = 184$ and $m\widehat{BCD} = 242$, what are the measures of the angles of quadrilateral $ABCD$?**

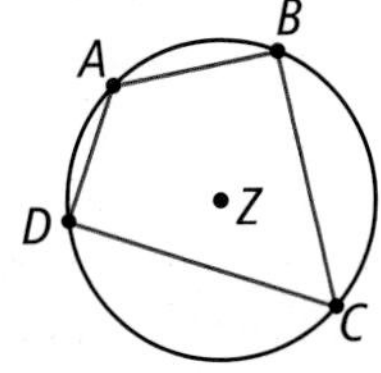
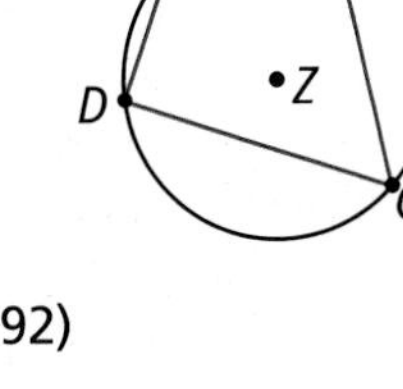


$m\angle A = \frac{1}{2}m\widehat{BCD}$

$= \frac{1}{2}(242) = 121$

$m\angle B = \frac{1}{2}m\widehat{ADC}$

$= \frac{1}{2}(360 - 184) = 88$

$m\angle D = \frac{1}{2}m\widehat{ABC}$

$= \frac{1}{2}(184) = 92$

$m\angle C = 360 - (121 + 88 + 92)$

$= 59$

**Try It!** **2. a.** If $m\widehat{RST} = 164$, what is $m\angle RVT$?

**b.** If $m\angle SPU = 79$, what is $m\widehat{STU}$?

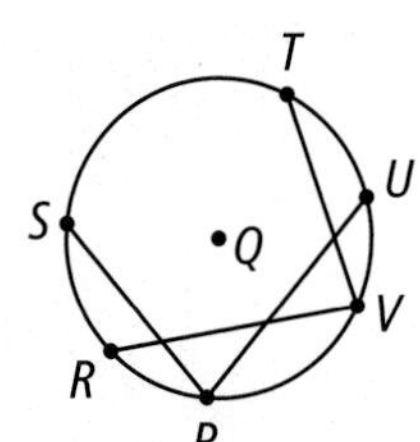

## COROLLARIES TO THE INSCRIBED ANGLES THEOREM

**Corollary 1**

Two inscribed angles that intercept the same arc are congruent.

**If...**

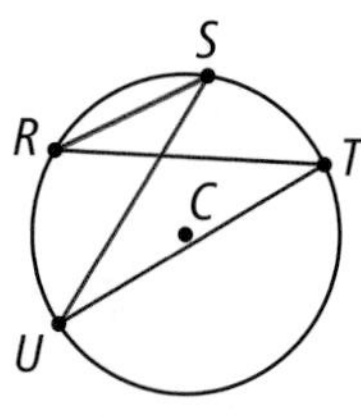


**Then...** $\angle S \cong \angle T$

**Corollary 2**

An angle inscribed in a semicircle is a right angle.

**If...** $m\widehat{RS} = 180$

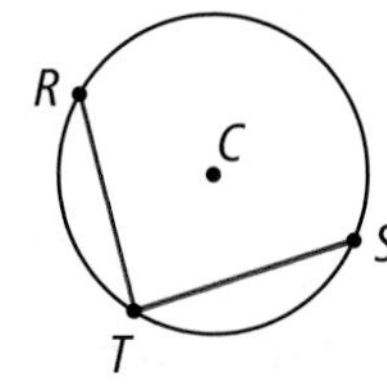


**Then...** $m\angle T = 90$

**Corollary 3**

The opposite angles of an inscribed quadrilateral are supplementary.

**If...**

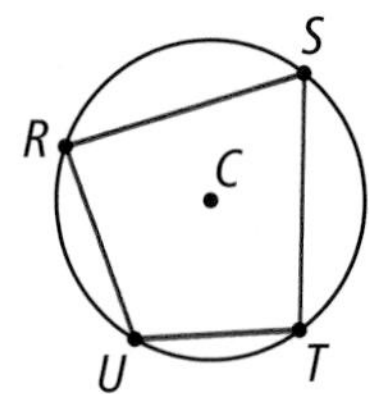


**Then...**

$m\angle R + m\angle T = 180$

$m\angle S + m\angle U = 180$

## EXAMPLE 3 Explore Angles Formed by a Tangent and a Chord

**Given chord $\overline{FH}$ and $\overleftrightarrow{HJ}$ tangent to $\odot E$ at point $H$, what is the relationship between $\angle FHJ$ and $\widehat{FGH}$?**

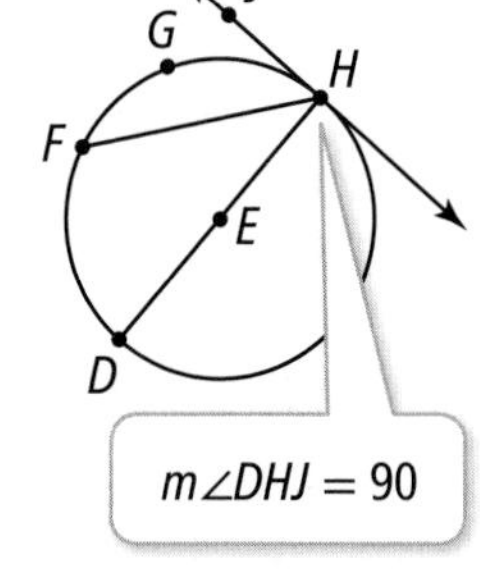


Consider the angles and arcs formed by the chord, tangent line, and diameter.

Let $m\angle FHJ = x$, so $m\angle FHD = 90 - x$.

$$m\angle FHD = \frac{1}{2}m\widehat{DF}$$

Use the Inscribed Angles Theorem.

$$90 - x = \frac{1}{2}m\widehat{DF}$$

$$m\widehat{DF} = 180 - 2x$$

**COMMON ERROR**
Be careful not to assume arc measure relationships such as assuming $m\widehat{DF} = m\widehat{FH}$. Think about concepts and theorems you can apply when writing mathematical statements.

Since $\overline{DH}$ is a diameter, $m\widehat{DFH} = 180$.

$$m\widehat{DF} + m\widehat{FGH} = m\widehat{DFH}$$

$$180 - 2x + m\widehat{FGH} = 180$$

$$m\widehat{FGH} = 2x$$

$$m\widehat{FGH} = 2m\angle FHJ$$

$$m\angle FHJ = \frac{1}{2}m\widehat{FGH}$$

**Try It!** 3. a. Given $\overleftrightarrow{BD}$ tangent to $\odot P$ at point $C$, if $m\widehat{AC} = 88$, what is $m\angle ACB$?

b. Given $\overleftrightarrow{EG}$ tangent to $\odot P$ at point $F$, if $m\angle GFC = 115$, what is $m\widehat{FAC}$?

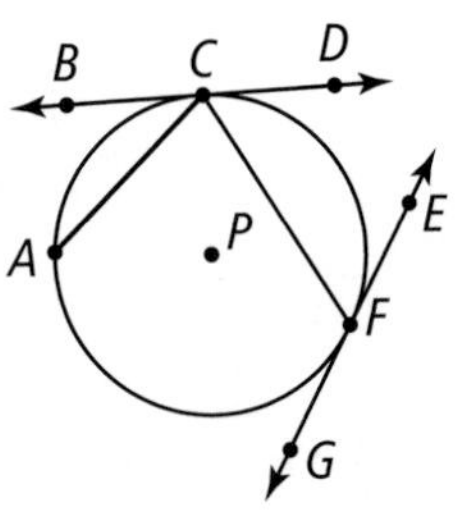

## THEOREM 10-9

The measure of an angle formed by a tangent and a chord is half the measure of its intercepted arc.

PROOF: SEE EXERCISE 34.

**If...**

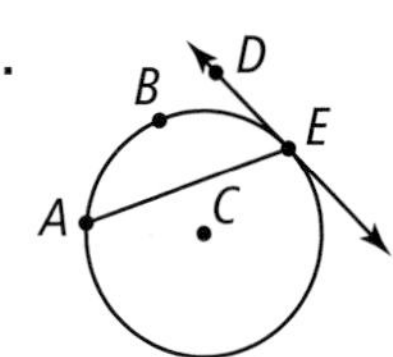


**Then...** $m\angle AED = \frac{1}{2}m\widehat{ABE}$

APPLICATION

## EXAMPLE 4 Use Arc Measure to Solve a Problem

**A director wants to position two cameras to capture an entire circular backdrop behind two newscasters. Where should he position the cameras?**

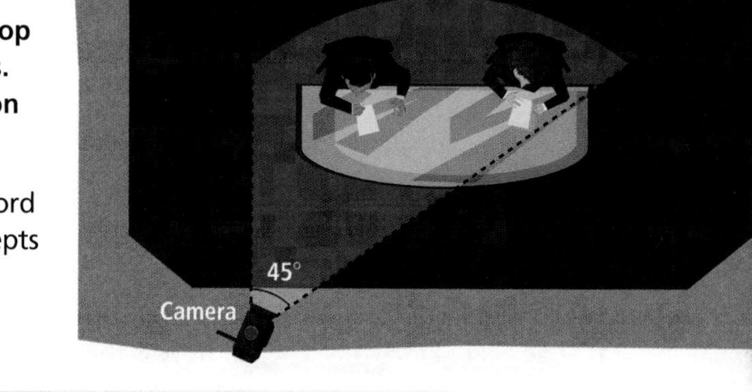


**Formulate** Represent the set as a chord $\overline{AB}$ of a circle that intercepts an arc measuring 90°.

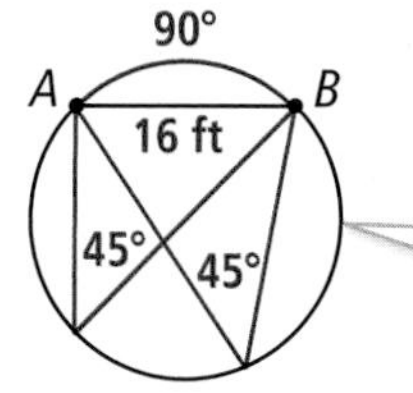


Any point on the major arc $\widehat{AB}$ is the vertex of a 45° angle that intercepts arc $\widehat{AB}$.

To find the size of the circle, find the radius of the circle.

**Compute** Let $P$ be the center of the circle.

$m\angle APB = m\widehat{AB} = 90$

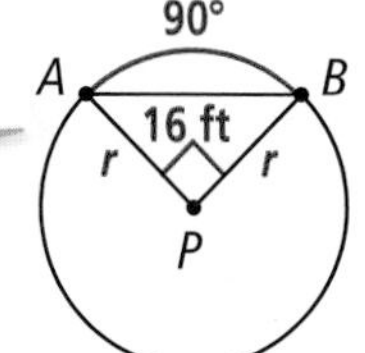


Find $r$.

$$\sqrt{2} \cdot r = 16$$

$$r = \frac{16}{\sqrt{2}}$$

$$r = 8\sqrt{2}$$

$\triangle APB$ is a 45°-45°-90° triangle, and the length of the hypotenuse is 16.

Center $P$ is on the perpendicular bisector of $\overline{AB}$, so $P$ is 8 ft from the midpoint of $\overline{AB}$.

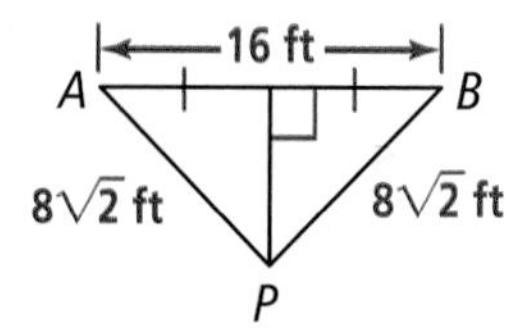


**Interpret** Position a camera on any point of circle with radius $8\sqrt{2}$ ft and center 8 ft from the midpoint of the set.

**Try It!** **4. a.** Given $\overleftrightarrow{WY}$ tangent to $\odot C$ at point $X$, what is $m\widehat{XZ}$?

**b.** What is $m\angle VXW$?

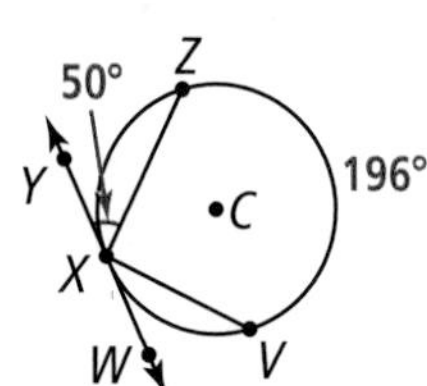

## CONCEPT SUMMARY Inscribed Angles and Intercepted Arcs

| | Inscribed Angles | Angles Formed by a Tangent and a Chord |
|---|---|---|
| WORDS | The measure of an inscribed angle is one-half the measure of its intercepted arc. | The measure of an angle formed by a tangent and a chord is one-half the measure of its intercepted arc. |
| DIAGRAMS | 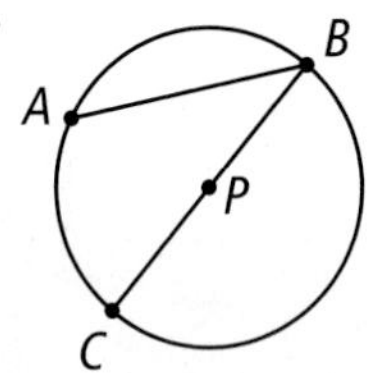 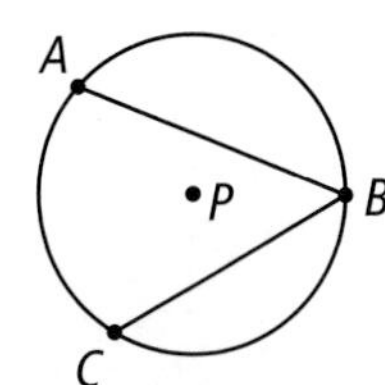 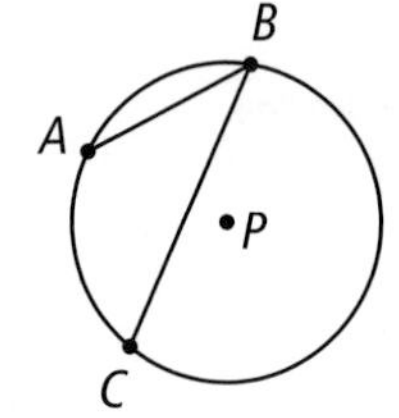 | 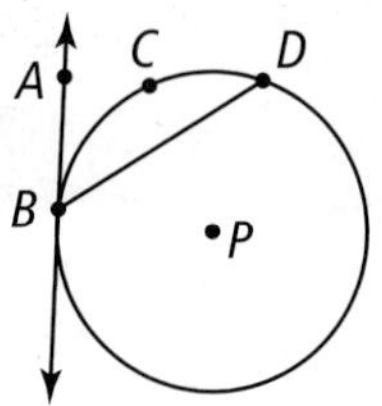 |
| SYMBOLS | $m\angle ABC = \frac{1}{2} m\widehat{AC}$ | $m\angle ABD = \frac{1}{2} m\widehat{BCD}$ |

## Do You UNDERSTAND?

1. **ESSENTIAL QUESTION** How is the measure of an inscribed angle related to its intercepted arc?

2. **Error Analysis** Darren is asked to find $m\widehat{XZ}$. What is his error?

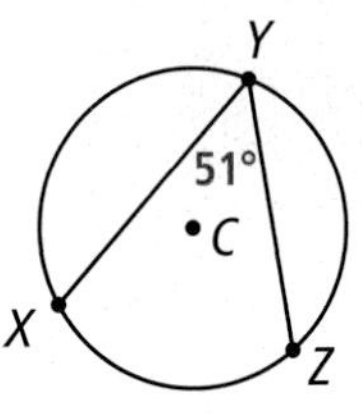


$m\widehat{XZ} = \frac{1}{2} m\angle XYZ$
$= \frac{1}{2}(51)$ ✗
$= 25.5$

3. **Reason** Can the measure of an inscribed angle be greater than the measure of the intercepted arc? Explain.

4. **Make Sense and Persevere** Is there enough information in the diagram to find $m\widehat{RST}$? Explain.

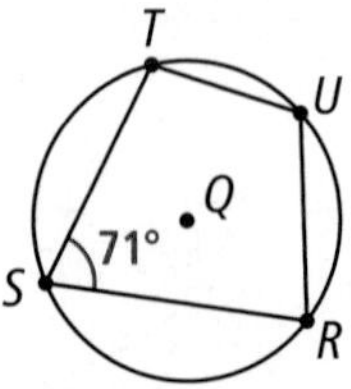


## Do You KNOW HOW?

**For Exercises 5–8, find each measure in ⊙*Q*.**

5. $m\widehat{JL}$

6. $m\widehat{MJ}$

7. $m\angle KJM$

8. $m\angle KLM$

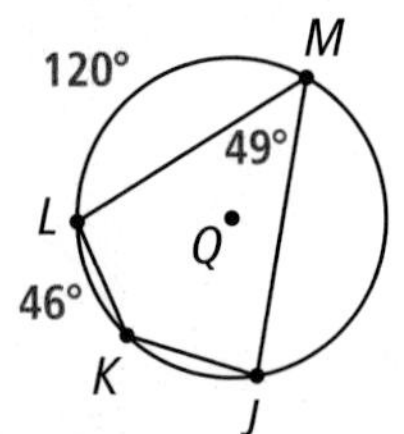


**For Exercises 9–12, $\overleftrightarrow{DF}$ is tangent to ⊙*Q* at point *E*. Find each measure.**

9. $m\widehat{EH}$

10. $m\widehat{EJ}$

11. $m\angle HEJ$

12. $m\angle DEJ$

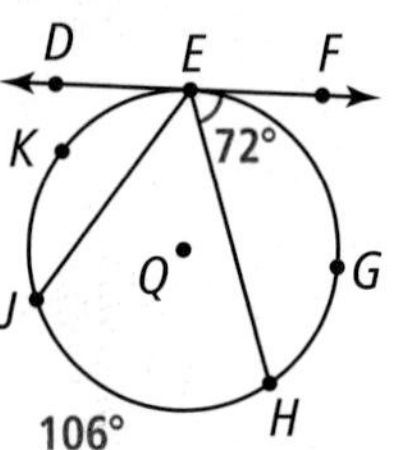


**For Exercises 13–16, find each measure in ⊙*M*.**

13. $m\angle PRQ$

14. $m\angle PTR$

15. $m\angle RST$

16. $m\angle SRT$

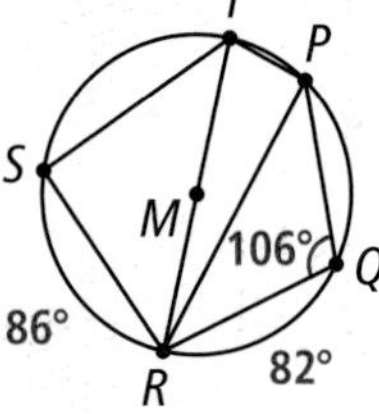

# PRACTICE & PROBLEM SOLVING

Practice Tutorial

Additional Exercises Available Online

## UNDERSTAND

**17. Mathematical Connections** Given $m\overset{\frown}{ABC} = x$, what is an expression for $m\overset{\frown}{DAB}$ in terms of $x$? Explain.

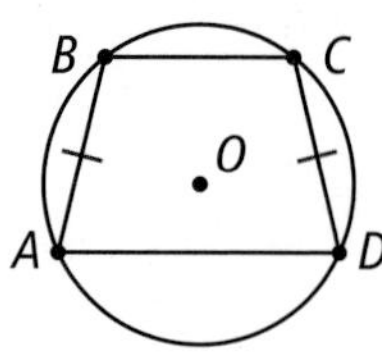


**18. Error Analysis** Casey is asked to find $m\overset{\frown}{WVZ}$. What is Casey's error?

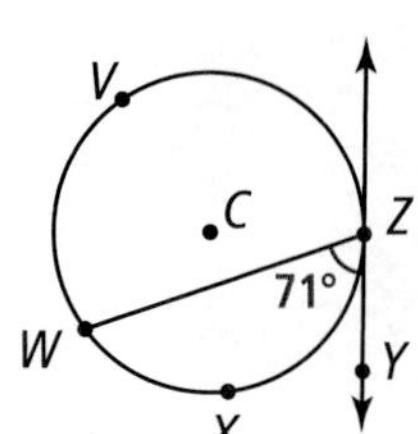


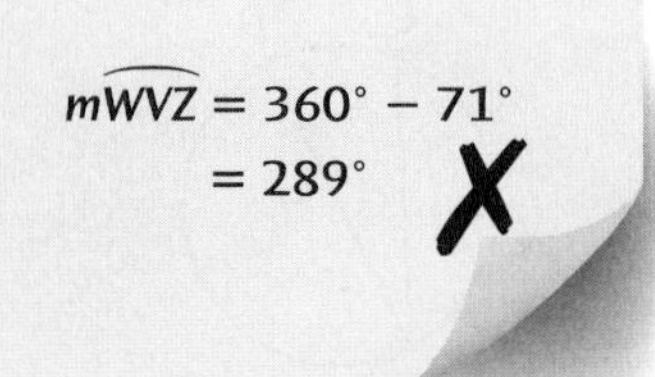


**19. Higher Order Thinking** Write a proof of the Inscribed Angles Theorem, Case 2.

**Given:** Center $C$ is inside $\angle RST$.

**Prove:** $m\angle RST = \frac{1}{2}m\overset{\frown}{RT}$

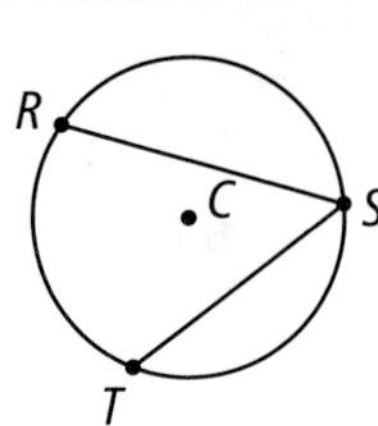


**20. Construct Arguments** Margaret measures $\angle HGK$ with a protractor and says that it is 98°. Is Margaret's answer reasonable? Explain.

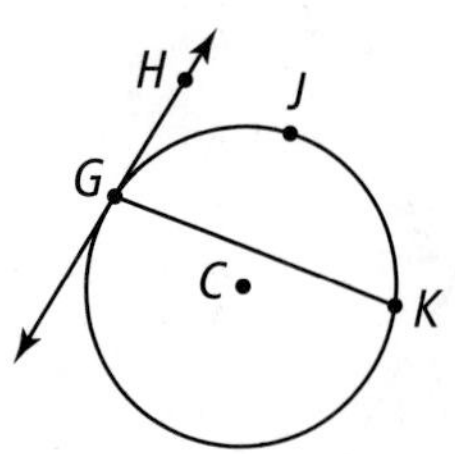


**21. Use Structure** Given $\odot Q$ with diameter $\overline{AC}$, if point $B$ is located on $\odot Q$, can $\angle ABC$ ever be less than 90°? Can it ever be greater than 90°? Explain.

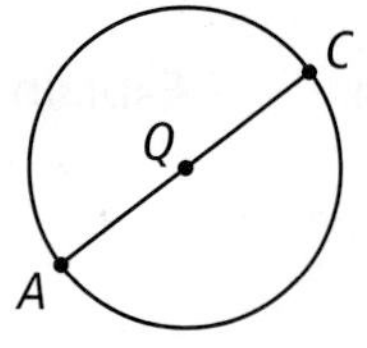


## PRACTICE

**For Exercises 22–25, find each measure in $\odot P$.** SEE EXAMPLES 1 AND 2

**22.** $m\overset{\frown}{AD}$

**23.** $m\overset{\frown}{BDC}$

**24.** $m\angle ADC$

**25.** $m\angle BAD$

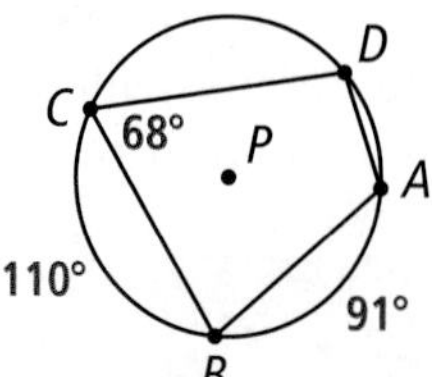


**For Exercises 26–28, $\overleftrightarrow{SU}$ is tangent to $\odot P$ at point $T$. Find each measure.** SEE EXAMPLES 2 AND 3

**26.** $m\overset{\frown}{TW}$

**27.** $m\angle TWX$

**28.** $m\angle TWV$

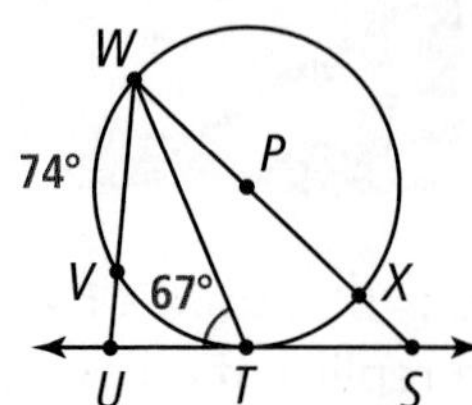


**For Exercises 29–31, $\overleftrightarrow{HK}$ is tangent to $\odot C$ at point $J$. Find each measure.** SEE EXAMPLES 3 AND 4

**29.** $m\angle KJM$

**30.** $m\angle MJN$

**31.** $m\angle HJN$

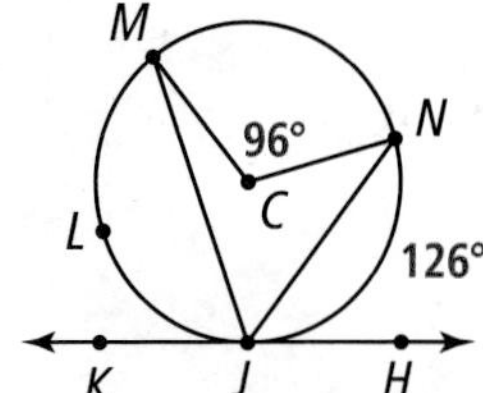


**32.** Write a proof of the Inscribed Angles Theorem, Case 1.

**Given:** Center $C$ is on $\overline{ST}$.

**Prove:** $m\angle RST = \frac{1}{2}m\overset{\frown}{RT}$

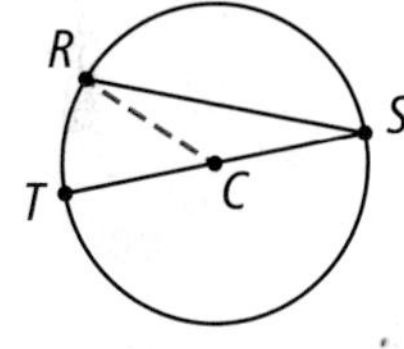


**33.** Write a proof of the Inscribed Angles Theorem, Case 3.

**Given:** Center $C$ is outside $\angle RST$.

**Prove:** $m\angle RST = \frac{1}{2}m\overset{\frown}{RT}$

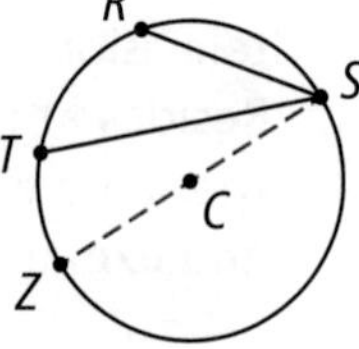


**34.** Write a two-column proof of Theorem 10-9.

**Given:** $\overleftrightarrow{AB}$ tangent to $\odot P$ at point $B$.

**Prove:** $m\angle ABD = \frac{1}{2}m\overset{\frown}{BCD}$

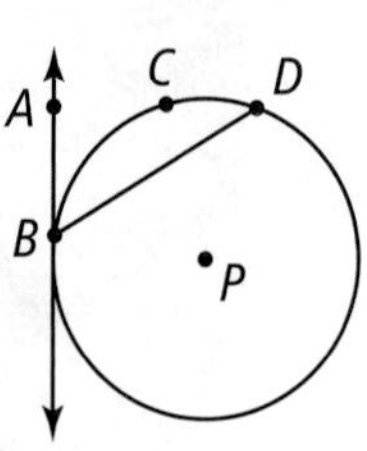

# PRACTICE & PROBLEM SOLVING

## APPLY

**35. Construct Arguments** Deondra needs to know the angle measure for each notch in the 16-notch socket wrench she is designing. The notches will be the same size. What is the angle measure?

**36. Use Structure** Cheyenne wants to make a replica of an antique sundial using the fragment of the sundial she acquired. Is there enough information for her to determine the diameter of the sundial? Explain.

**37. Use Appropriate Tools** Malcom sets up chairs for a home theater showing on his television. His optimal viewing angle is 50°. Besides at chair A, where else could he sit with the same viewing angle? Draw a diagram and explain.

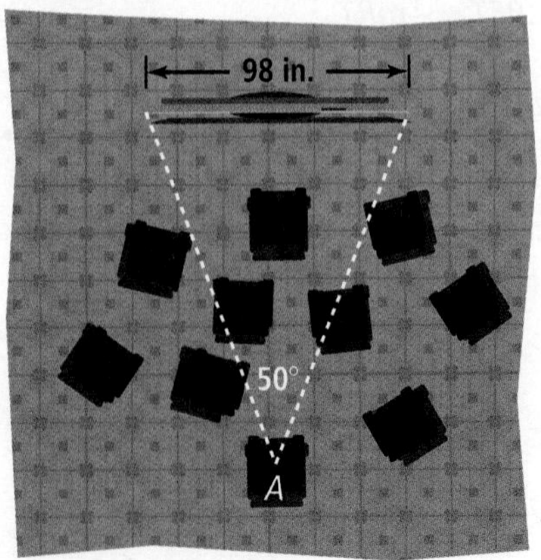


## ASSESSMENT PRACTICE

**38.** Write an expression that represents $m\angle DGF$.

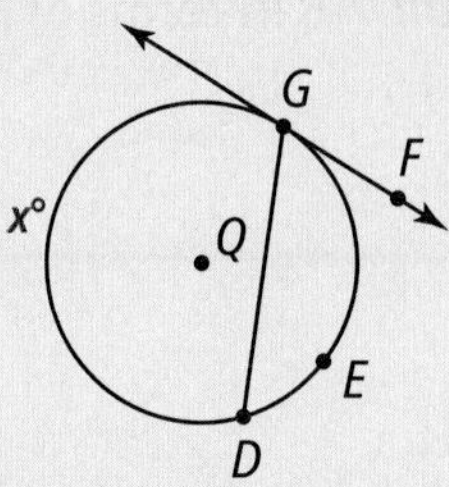


**39. SAT/ACT** Segment $AB$ is tangent to $\odot M$ at Point $A$. What is $m\angle DAC$?

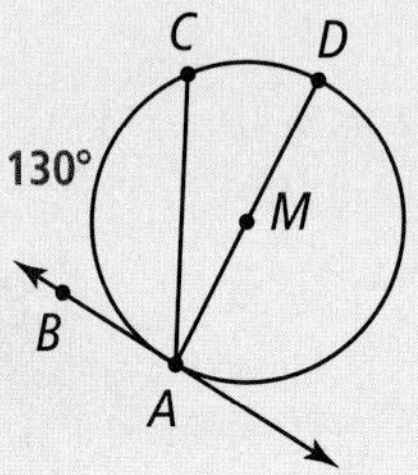


Ⓐ 25

Ⓑ 65

Ⓒ 50

Ⓓ 90

Ⓔ 100

**40. Performance Task** Triangle $DEF$ is inscribed in $\odot G$, and $\overline{AB}$, $\overline{BC}$, and $\overline{AC}$ are tangent to $\odot G$.

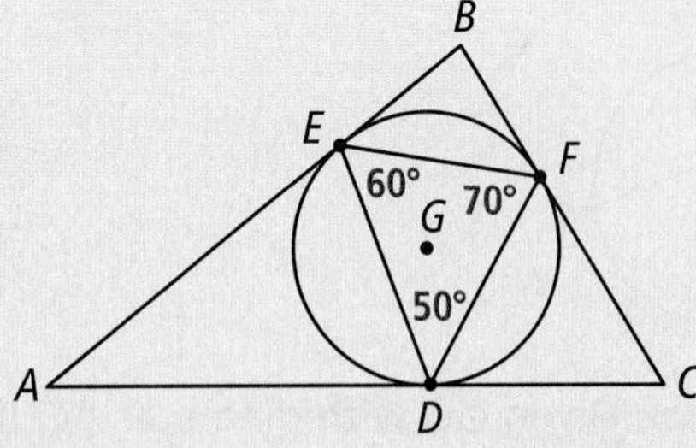


**Part A** Are there any isosceles triangles in the diagram? If so, explain why the triangles are isosceles. If not, explain why not.

**Part B** Are $\triangle ABC$ and $\triangle DEF$ similar? Explain.

# 10-5

## Secant Lines and Segments

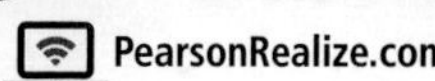

PearsonRealize.com

**I CAN…** use angle measures and segment lengths formed by intersecting lines and circles to solve problems.

**VOCABULARY**

- secant

Activity Assess

## EXPLORE & REASON

**Skyler made the design shown. Points *A*, *B*, *C*, and *D* are spaced evenly around the circle.**

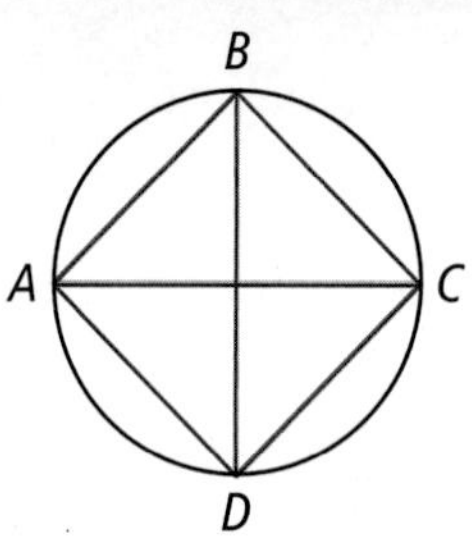


**A.** Using points *A*, *B*, *C*, and *D* as vertices, what congruent angles can you find? How can you justify that they are congruent?

**B. Make Sense and Persevere** What strategy did you use to make sure you found all congruent angles?

## ESSENTIAL QUESTION

**How are the measures of angles, arcs, and segments formed by intersecting secant lines related?**

CONCEPTUAL UNDERSTANDING

## EXAMPLE 1 Relate Secants and Angle Measures

**A secant is a line, ray, or segment that intersects a circle at two points. Secants $\overleftrightarrow{AC}$ and $\overleftrightarrow{BD}$ intersect to form $\angle 1$. How can you use arc measures to find $m\angle 1$?**

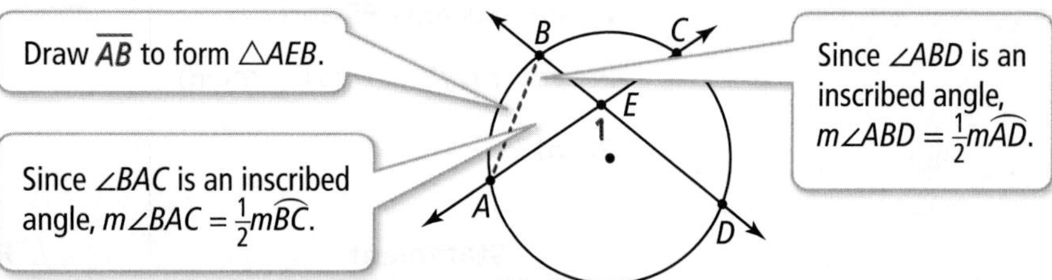

Draw $\overline{AB}$ to form $\triangle AEB$.
Since $\angle BAC$ is an inscribed angle, $m\angle BAC = \frac{1}{2}m\widehat{BC}$.
Since $\angle ABD$ is an inscribed angle, $m\angle ABD = \frac{1}{2}m\widehat{AD}$.
B
C
E
1
A
D


Apply the Triangle Exterior Angle Theorem.

$$m\angle 1 = m\angle ABD + m\angle BAC$$
$$= \frac{1}{2}m\widehat{AD} + \frac{1}{2}m\widehat{BC}$$

So the measure of the angle is half the sum of the measures of the two intercepted arcs.

**MAKE SENSE AND PERSEVERE** Consider other relationships in the diagram. What is an alternate plan you could use to solve the problem?

**Try It!** **1.** If $m\widehat{AD} = 155$ and $m\widehat{BC} = 61$, what is $m\angle 1$?

## THEOREM 10-10

The measure of an angle formed by two secant lines that intersect inside a circle is half the sum of the measures of the intercepted arcs.

**If...**

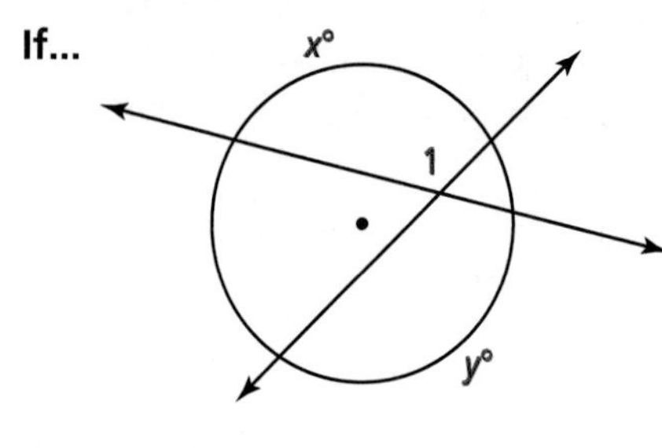


**Then...** $m\angle 1 = \frac{1}{2}(x + y)$

PROOF: SEE EXERCISE 16.

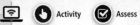

## THEOREM 10-11

The measure of an angle formed by two lines that intersect outside a circle is half the difference of the measures of the intercepted arcs.

| | Case 1 | Case 2 | Case 3 |
|---|---|---|---|
| If... | 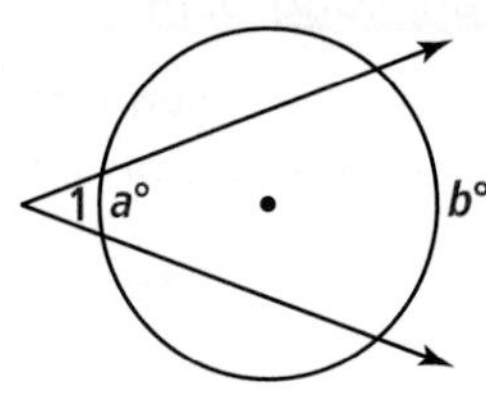 | 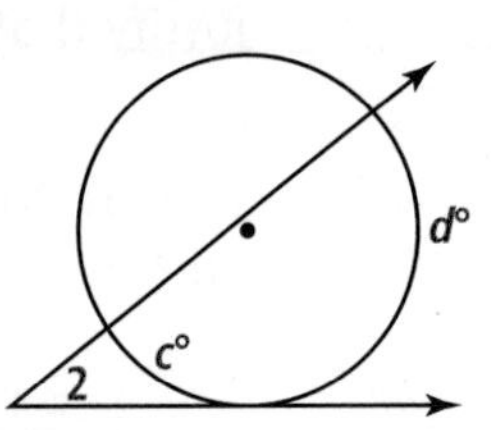 | 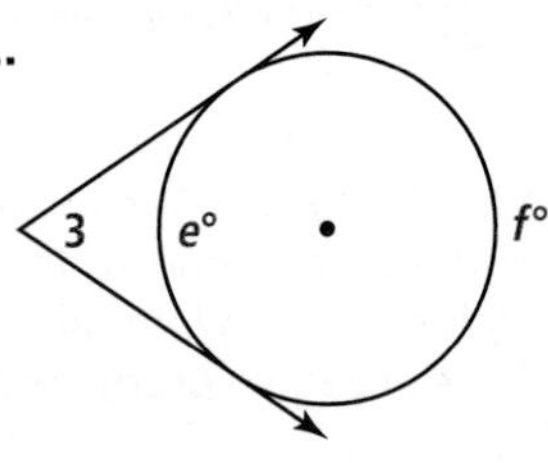 |
| Then... | $m\angle 1 = \frac{1}{2}(b - a)$ | $m\angle 2 = \frac{1}{2}(d - c)$ | $m\angle 3 = \frac{1}{2}(f - e)$ |

PROOF: SEE EXAMPLE 2, TRY IT 2, AND EXERCISE 18.

## EXAMPLE 2 Prove Theorem 10-11, Case 1

**Write a proof for Theorem 10-11, Case 1.**

**Given:** Secants $\overrightarrow{PS}$ and $\overrightarrow{PT}$

**Prove:** $m\angle P = \frac{1}{2}(m\widehat{ST} - m\widehat{QR})$

**Proof:**

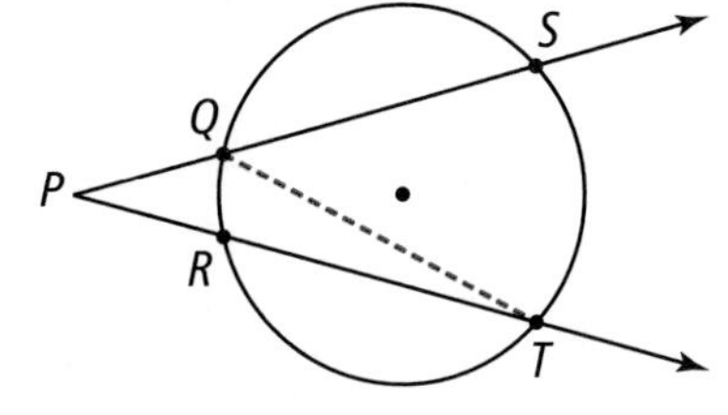


| Statement | Reason |
|---|---|
| **1)** $\overrightarrow{PS}$ and $\overrightarrow{PT}$ are secants. | **1)** Given |
| **2)** Draw $\overline{QT}$. | **2)** Two points determine a segment. |
| **3)** $m\angle QTP = \frac{1}{2}m\widehat{QR}$ | **3)** Inscribed Angles Theorem |
| **4)** $m\angle SQT = \frac{1}{2}m\widehat{ST}$ | **4)** Inscribed Angles Theorem |
| **5)** $m\angle SQT = m\angle P + m\angle QTP$ | **5)** Triangle Exterior Angle Theorem |
| **6)** $m\angle P = m\angle SQT - m\angle QTP$ | **6)** Subtraction Property of Equality |
| **7)** $m\angle P = \frac{1}{2}m\widehat{ST} - \frac{1}{2}m\widehat{QR}$ | **7)** Substitution |
| **8)** $m\angle P = \frac{1}{2}(m\widehat{ST} - m\widehat{QR})$ | **8)** Distributive Property |

**STUDY TIP**
Remember to look for helpful relationships that you can draw on the given figure when completing a proof. Drawing $\overline{QT}$ forms inscribed angles, which are needed for this proof.

 **Try It!** 2. Prove Theorem 10-11, Case 2.

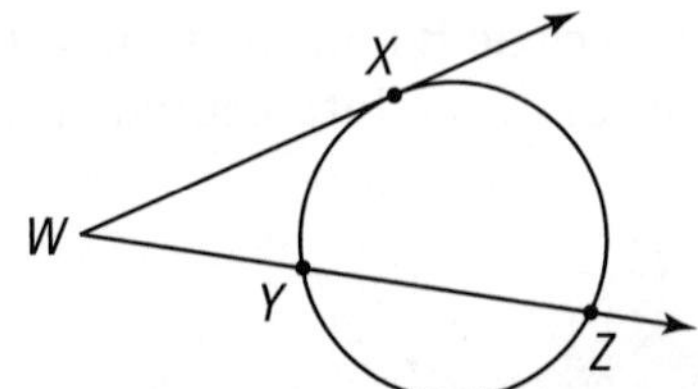

  Activity  Assess

## EXAMPLE 3 Use Secants and Tangents to Solve Problems

**A. What is $m\angle ABD$?**

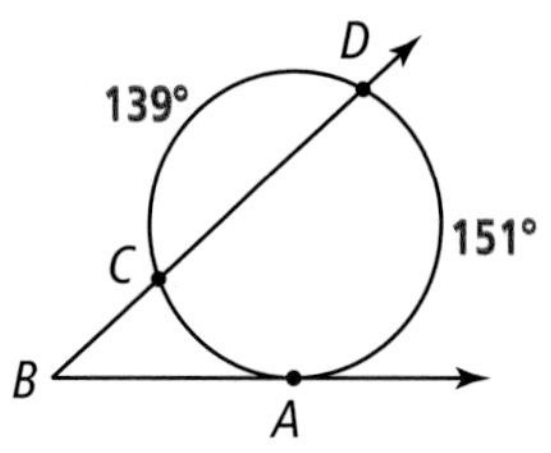


**Step 1** Find $m\widehat{AC}$.

$$m\widehat{AC} = 360 - m\widehat{AD} - m\widehat{CD}$$
$$= 360 - 151 - 139$$
$$= 70$$

**Step 2** Find $m\angle ABD$.

$$m\angle ABD = \frac{1}{2}(m\widehat{AD} - m\widehat{AC})$$
$$= \frac{1}{2}(151 - 70)$$
$$= 40.5$$

Since the angle is formed outside the circle by a secant and a tangent, apply Theorem 10-11, Case 2.

**B. What is $m\widehat{LM}$?**

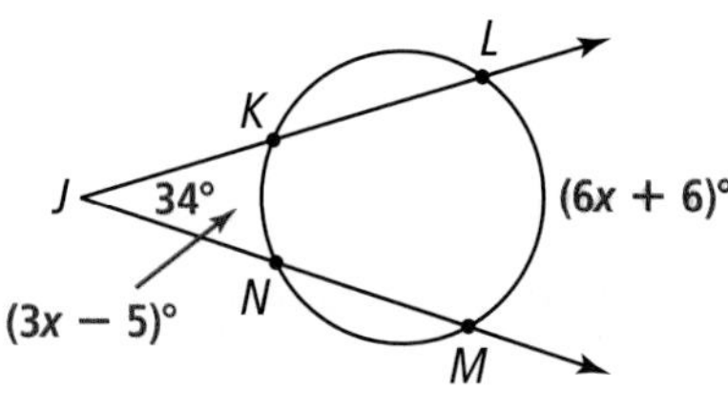

**COMMON ERROR**
Remember to add the arc measures when the vertex is inside the circle and to subtract them when it is outside the circle.

**Step 1** Find $x$.

$$m\angle LJM = \frac{1}{2}(m\widehat{LM} - m\widehat{KN})$$
$$34 = \frac{1}{2}((6x + 6) - (3x - 5))$$
$$34 = \frac{1}{2}(3x + 11)$$
$$68 = 3x + 11$$
$$19 = x$$

Since the angle is formed outside the circle by two secants, apply Theorem 10-11, Case 1.

**Step 2** Find $m\widehat{LM}$.

$$m\widehat{LM} = 6x + 6$$
$$= 6(19) + 6$$
$$= 120$$

Substitute the value of $x$ found in Step 1.

**Try It!** **3. a.** What is $m\widehat{WX}$?

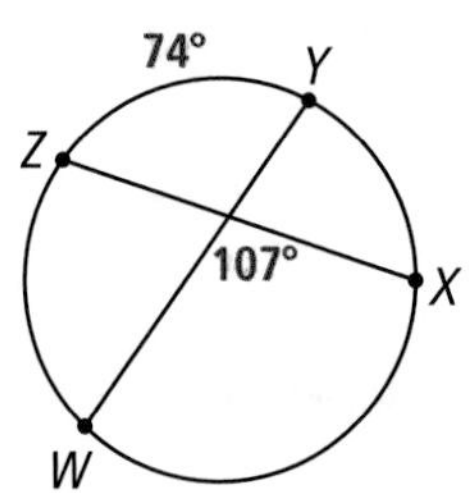


**b.** What is $m\angle PSQ$?

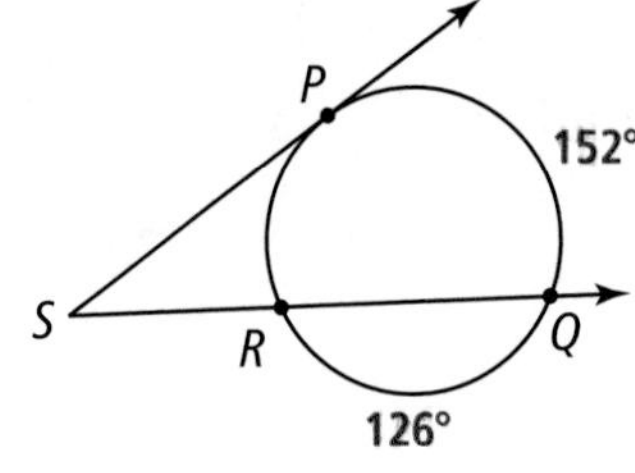

## EXAMPLE 4 Develop Chord Length Relationships

**What is the value of *x*?**

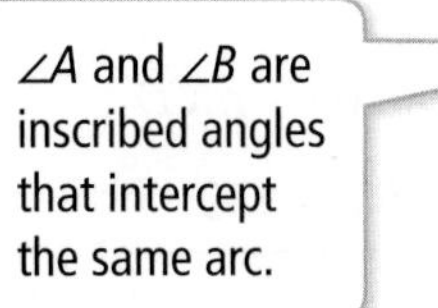


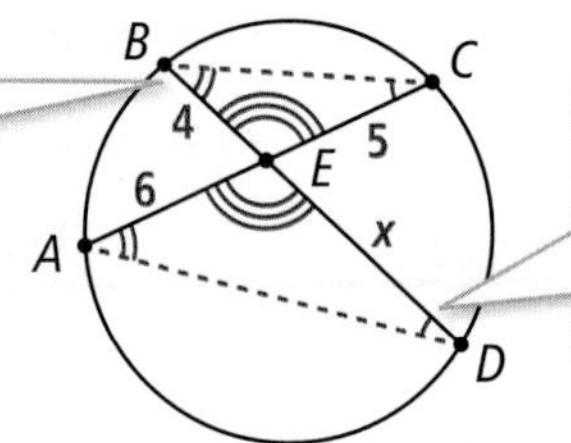


∠C and ∠D are inscribed angles that intercept the same arc.

By the Angle-Angle Similarity Theorem, $\triangle AED \sim \triangle BEC$.

$$\frac{ED}{EC} = \frac{EA}{EB}$$

The ratios of corresponding sides of similar triangles are equal.

$$\frac{x}{5} = \frac{6}{4}$$

$$4 \bullet x = 6 \bullet 5$$

$$x = 7.5$$

The value of $x$ is 7.5.

**COMMON ERROR**
Be careful to correctly identify corresponding sides in similar triangles. The sides opposite congruent angles are the corresponding sides.

**Try It!** **4.** What is the value of $y$?

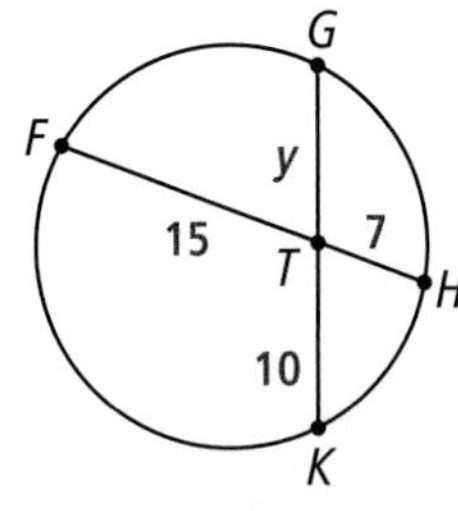


### THEOREM 10-12

For a given point and circle, the product of the lengths of the two segments from the point to the circle is constant along any line through the point and circle.

**Case 1**

**If...**

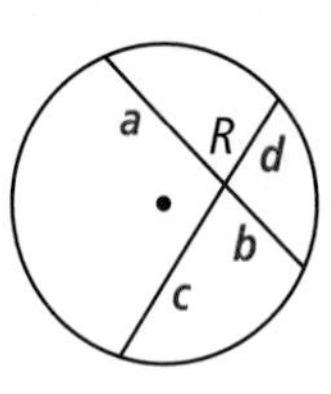


**Then...**

$ab = cd$

**Case 2**

**If...**

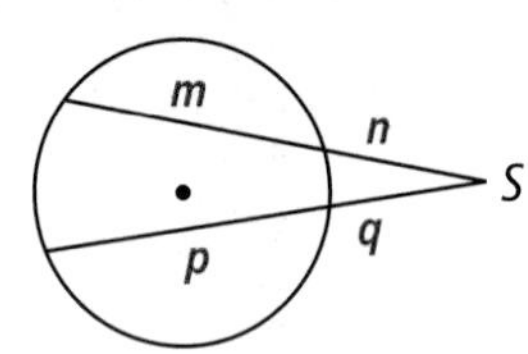


**Then...**

$(n + m)n = (q + p)q$

**Case 3**

**If...**

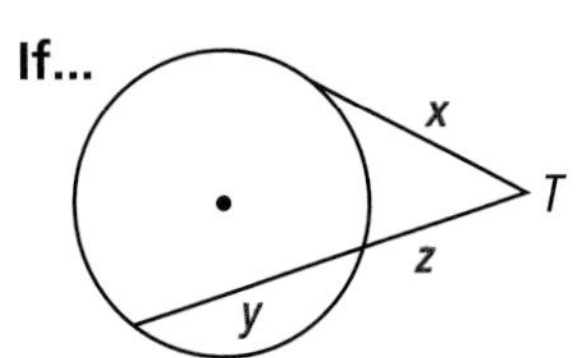


**Then...**

$x^2 = (z + y)z$

**PROOF: SEE EXERCISES 11, 23, and 24.**

APPLICATION

## EXAMPLE 5 Use Segment Relationships to Find Lengths

**Archaeologists found part of the circular wall that surrounds an ancient city. They measure the distances shown. The 272-m segment lies on a line through the center of the circular wall. What was the diameter of the circular wall?**

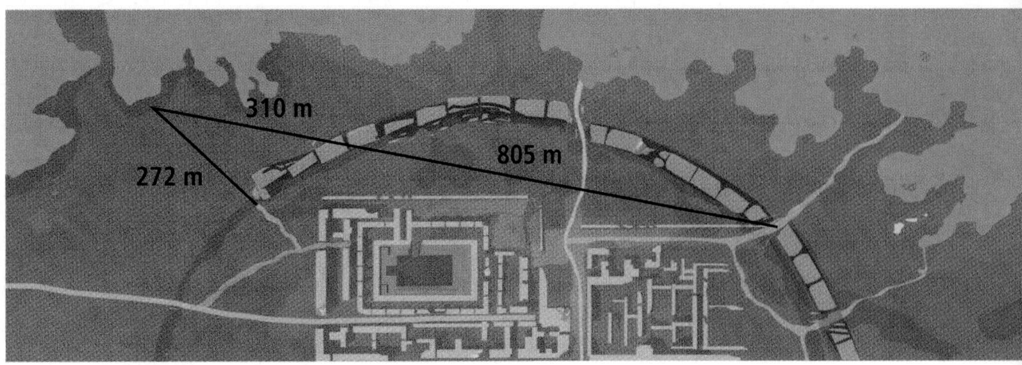


Draw a diagram to represent the situation.

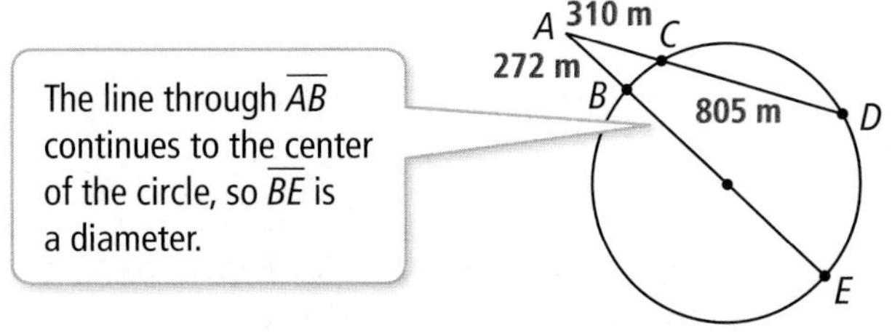


The line through $\overline{AB}$ continues to the center of the circle, so $\overline{BE}$ is a diameter.

**MAKE SENSE AND PERSEVERE** Are there other measurements that archaeologists could have taken to help find the diameter using another method?

Write an equation to relate the segment lengths.

$$(AB + BE)AB = (AC + CD)AC$$

$$(272 + BE)(272) = (310 + 805)(310)$$

$$73{,}984 + 272 \cdot BE = 345{,}650$$

$$272 \cdot BE = 271{,}666$$

$$BE \approx 998.8$$

Apply Theorem 10-12 and substitute known segment lengths.

The diameter of the circular wall was about 998.8 meters.

**Try It!** **5. a.** What is the value of $a$?

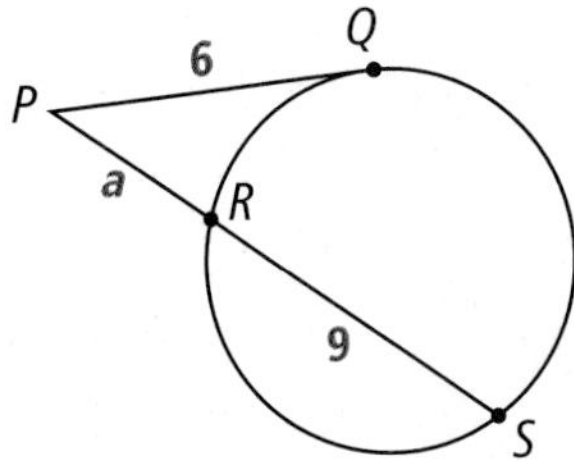


**b.** What is $EC$?

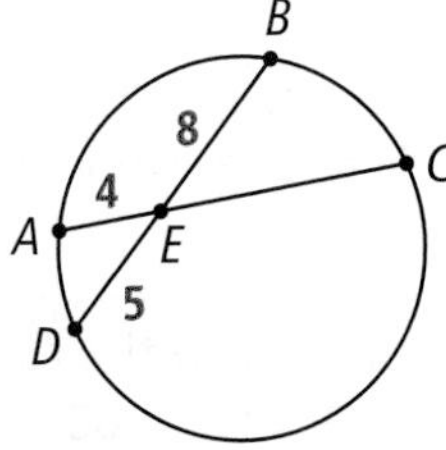

## CONCEPT SUMMARY Angle and Segment Relationships in a Circle

| | Vertex Inside the Circle | Vertex Outside the Circle |
|---|---|---|
| **ANGLES** | 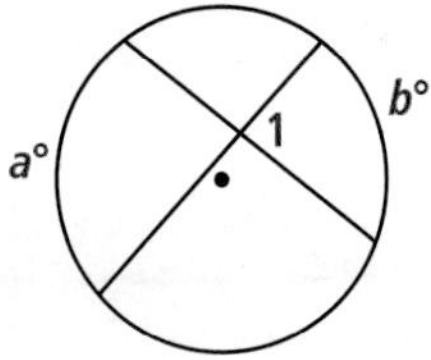 $m\angle 1 = \frac{1}{2}(a + b)$ | 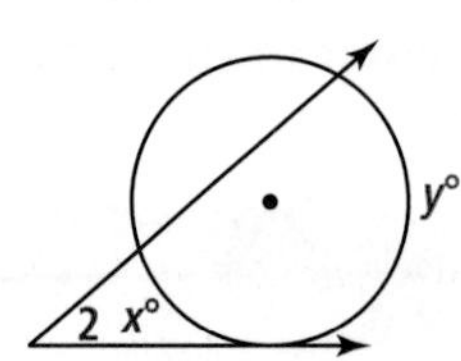 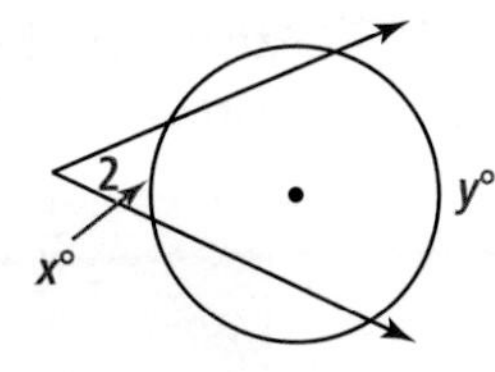 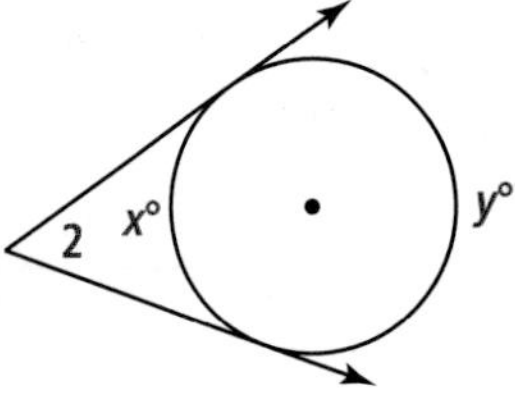 $m\angle 2 = \frac{1}{2}(y - x)$ |
| **SEGMENTS** | 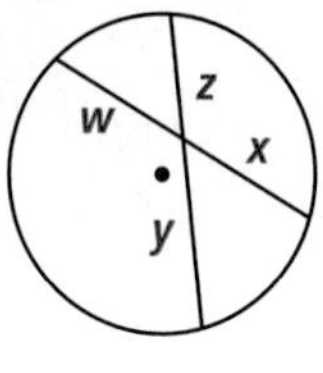 $wx = yz$ | 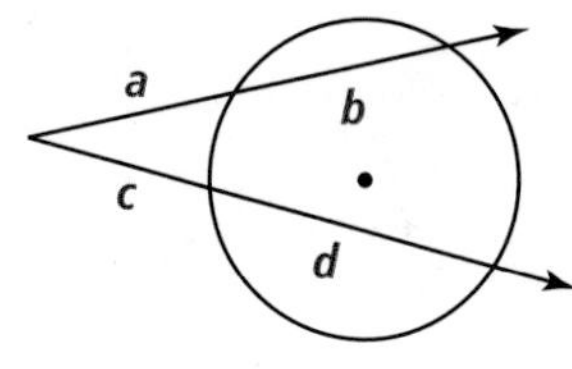 $(a + b)a = (c + d)c$ 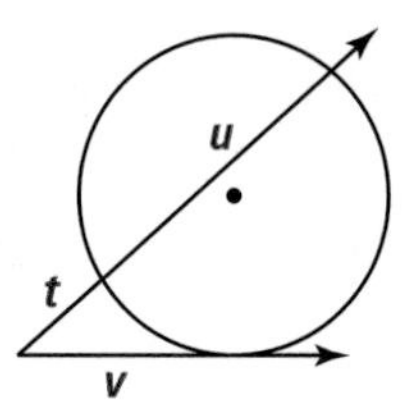 $(t + u)t = v^2$ |

## Do You UNDERSTAND?

1. **ESSENTIAL QUESTION** How are the measures of angles, arcs, and segments formed by intersecting secant lines related?

2. **Error Analysis** Derek is asked to find the value of $x$. What is his error?

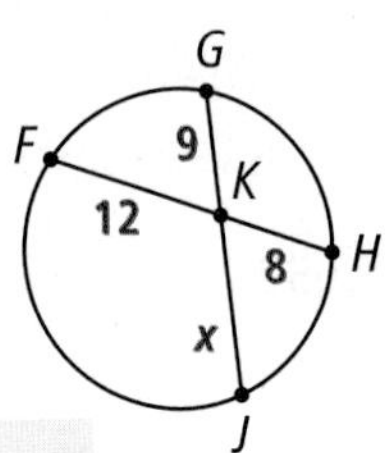


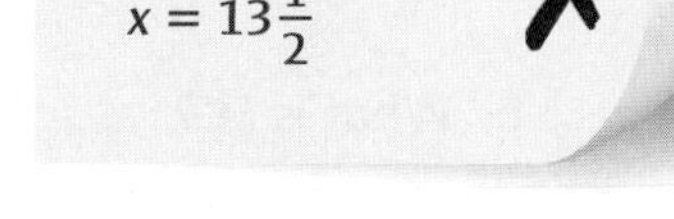

$GK \cdot FK = HK \cdot JK$
$12 \cdot 9 = 8 \cdot x$
$x = 13\frac{1}{2}$

✗

3. **Vocabulary** How are *secants* and *tangents* to a circle alike and different?

4. **Construct Arguments** The rays shown are tangent to the circle. Show that $m\angle 1 = (x - 180)$.

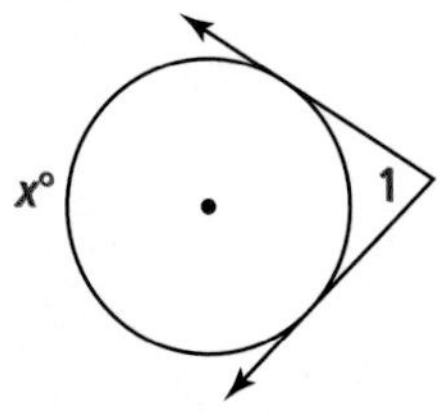


## Do You KNOW HOW?

**For Exercises 5 and 6, find each angle measure. Rays *QP* and *QR* are tangent to the circle in Exercise 6.**

5. $m\angle BEC$

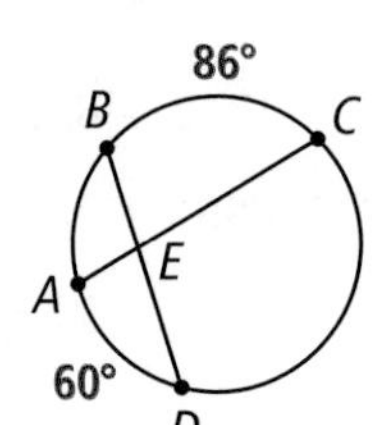


6. $m\angle PQR$

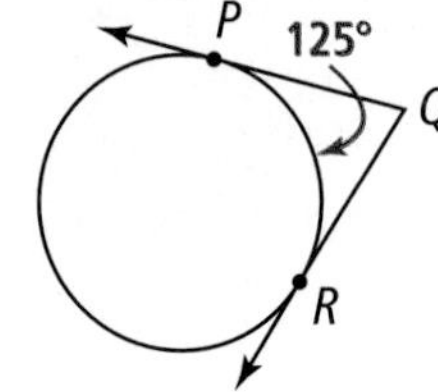


**For Exercises 7 and 8, find each length. Ray *HJ* is tangent to the circle in Exercise 7.**

7. $GF$

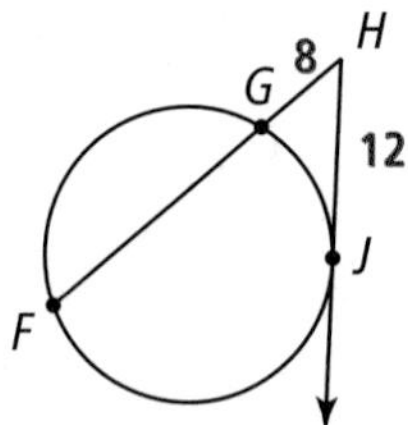


8. $LM$

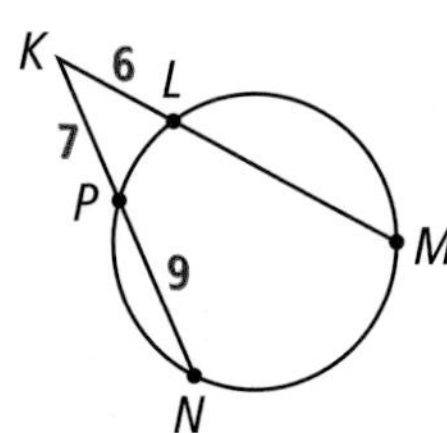


**For Exercises 9 and 10, $\overline{AE}$ is tangent to $\odot P$. Find each length.**

9. $BC$

10. $EF$

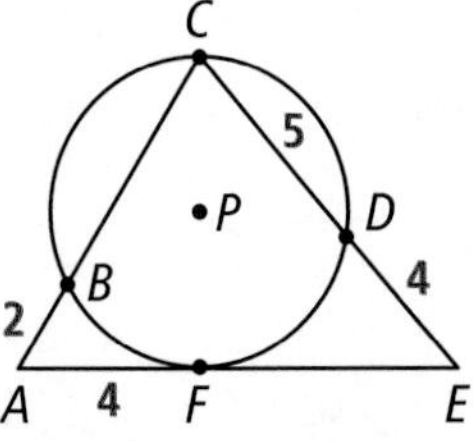

# PRACTICE & PROBLEM SOLVING

Scan for Multimedia

Practice Tutorial

Additional Exercises Available Online

## UNDERSTAND

11. **Construct Arguments** Given ⊙$X$, write a two-column proof of Theorem 10-12, Case 2.

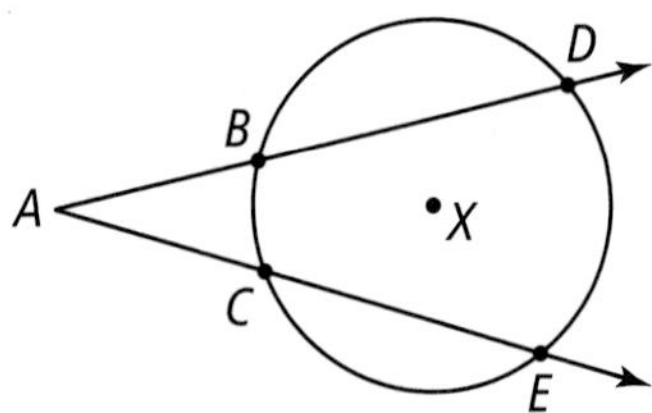

12. **Error Analysis** Cindy is asked to find $m\angle VXZ$. What is her error?

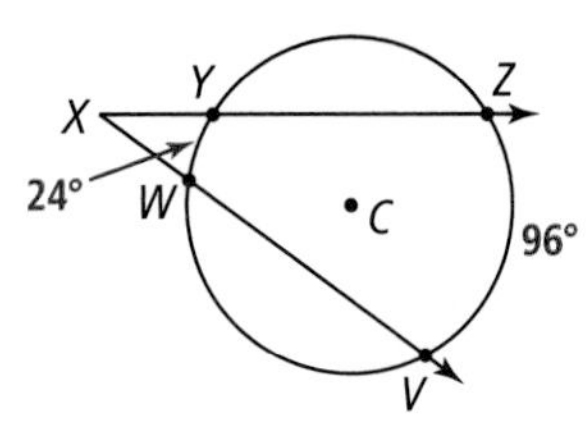

$$m\angle VXZ = \frac{1}{2}(m\widehat{WY} + m\widehat{VZ})$$
$$= \frac{1}{2}(24 + 96)$$
$$= 60$$

✗

13. **Mathematical Connections** Given ⊙$P$, secant $\overrightarrow{CA}$, and tangent $\overrightarrow{CD}$, what is the area of ⊙$P$?

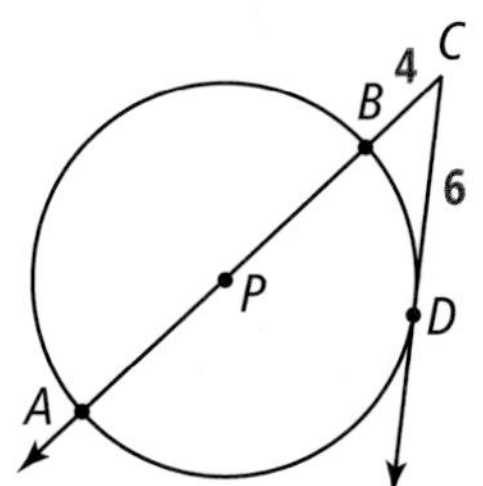

14. **Higher Order Thinking** Given ⊙$T$, and tangents $\overline{AD}$ and $\overline{CD}$, what is the measure of $\angle ADC$?

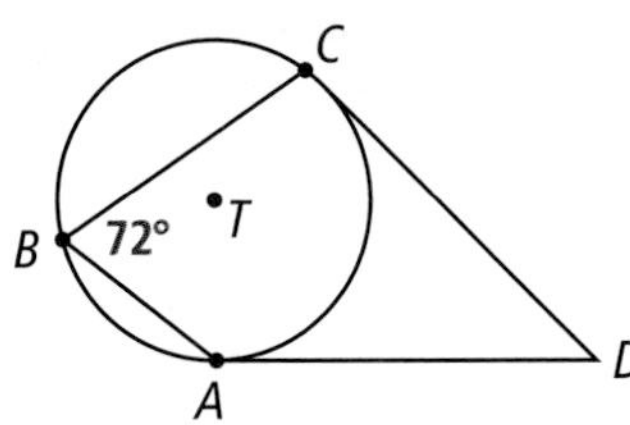

15. **Communicate Precisely** How would you describe each case of Theorem 10-11?

## PRACTICE

**For Exercises 16 and 17, find each measure.**

SEE EXERCISE 1

16. $m\angle 1$

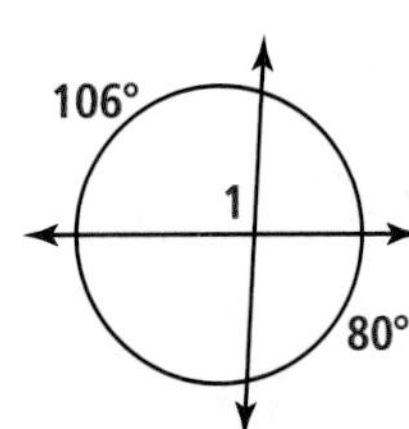

17. $x$

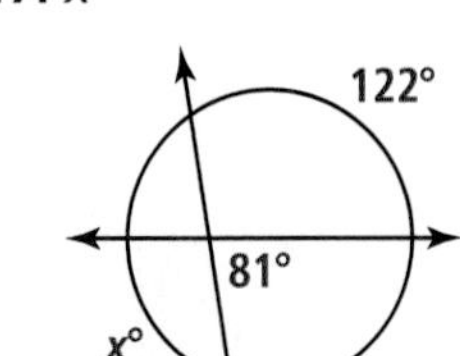

18. Given ⊙$A$ and secants $\overline{PR}$ and $\overline{QS}$, write a paragraph proof of Theorem 10-10. SEE EXAMPLE 1

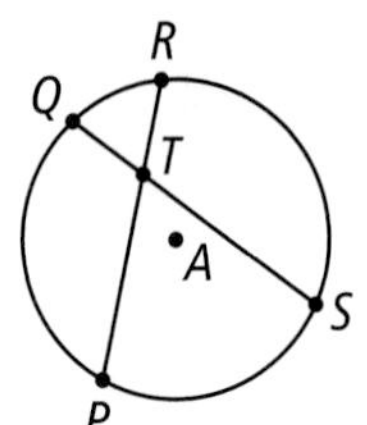

19. Given ⊙$Q$ and tangents $\overrightarrow{AB}$ and $\overrightarrow{AC}$, write a two-column proof of Theorem 10-11, Case 3.

SEE EXAMPLE 2

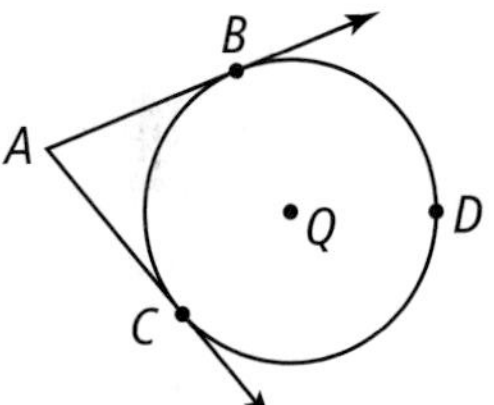

20. Given ⊙$C$, inscribed angle $\angle RWV$, and secants $\overrightarrow{TR}$ and $\overrightarrow{TV}$, what is the measure of $\angle RTV$?

SEE EXAMPLE 3

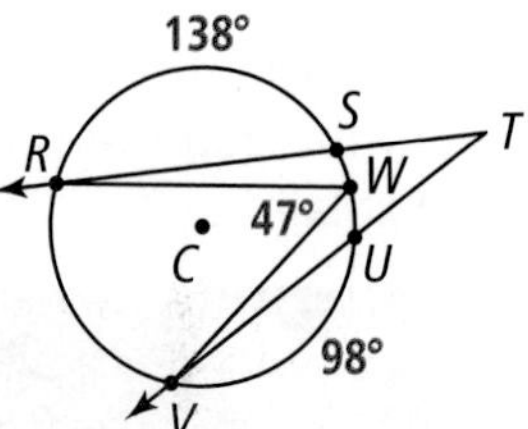

**For Exercises 21 and 22, find each length.**

SEE EXERCISE 4

21. $a$

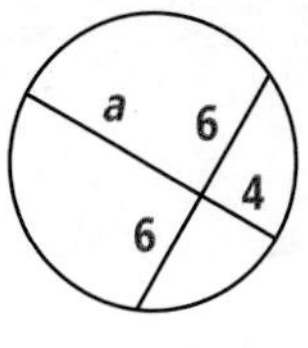

22. $b$

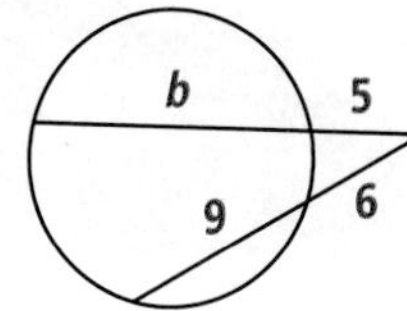

23. Given ⊙$T$ and secants $\overline{JK}$ and $\overline{LM}$ intersecting at point $N$, write a paragraph proof of Theorem 10-12, Case 1.

SEE EXAMPLE 4

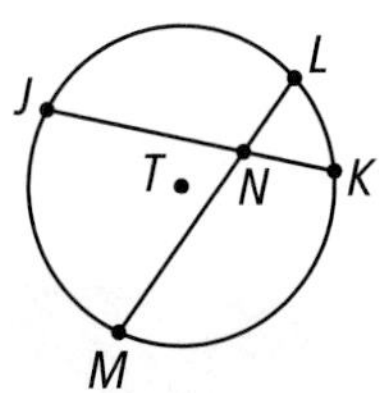

24. Given ⊙$C$, secant $\overrightarrow{QS}$ and tangent $\overline{PQ}$, write a two-column proof of Theorem 10–12, Case 3.

SEE EXAMPLE 5

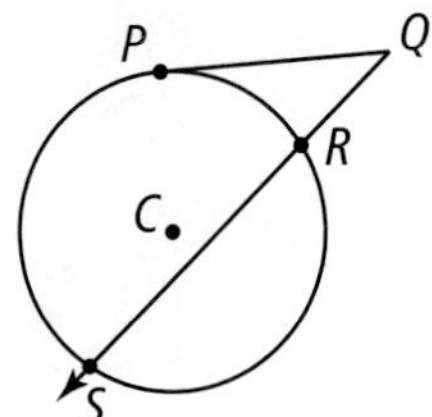

# PRACTICE & PROBLEM SOLVING

## APPLY

**25. Use Structure** Chris stands in the position shown to take a picture of a sculpture with a circular base.

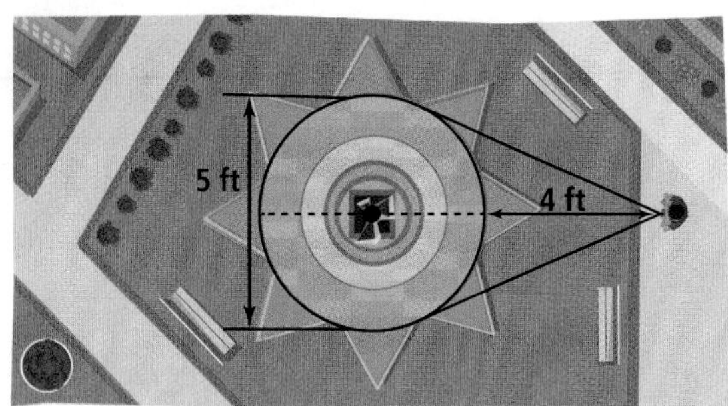


a. Chris is deciding on which lens to use. What is the minimum view angle from where he stands so he can get as much of the base as possible in his picture?

b. If Chris uses a lens with a view angle of 40°, what is the shortest distance he could stand from the sculpture?

**26. Reason** A satellite orbits above the equator of Mars as shown and transmits images back to a scientist in the control room. What percent of the equator is the scientist able to see? Explain.

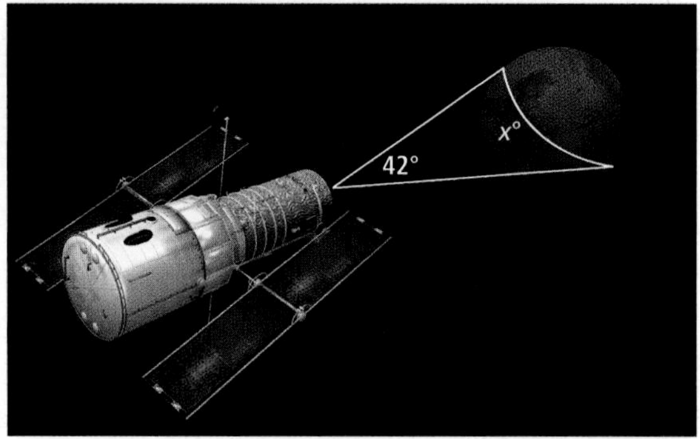


**27. Use Structure** Carolina wants to etch the design shown onto a circular piece of glass. At what measure should she cut ∠1? Explain.

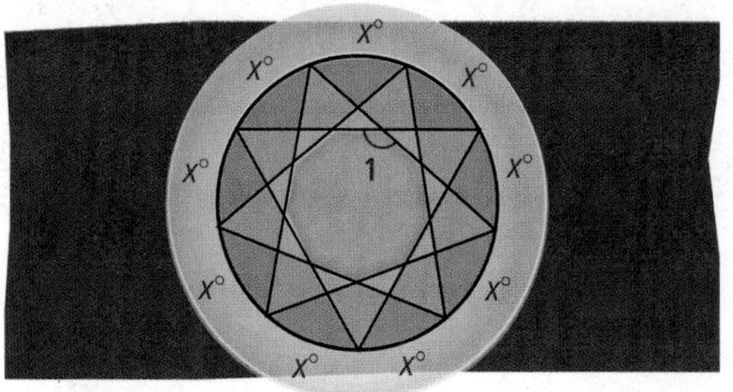


## ASSESSMENT PRACTICE

**28.** For what measure of $\overparen{UW}$ does $m\angle TVX = 34$?

$m\overparen{UW} =$ ________

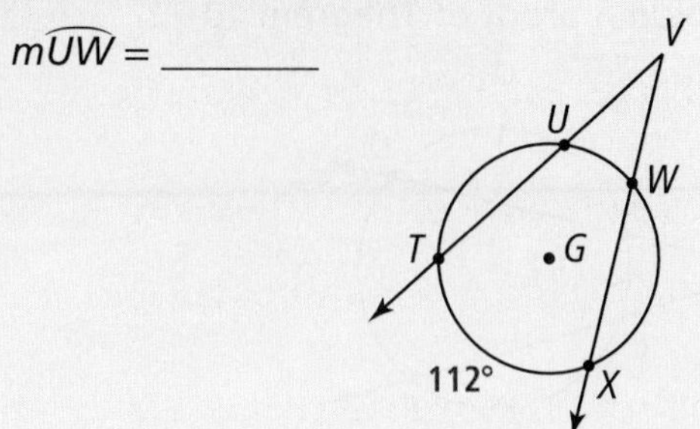


**29. SAT/ACT** Given ⊙$P$ and secants $\overline{FH}$ and $\overline{FK}$, what is $FG$?

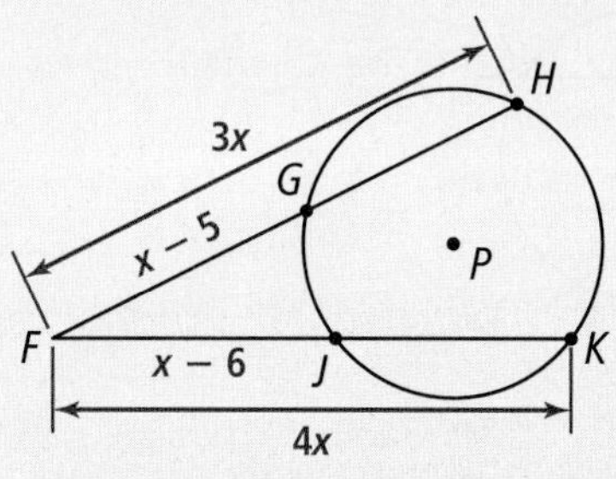


Ⓐ 3 Ⓑ 4 Ⓒ 9 Ⓓ 27 Ⓔ 36

**30. Performance Task** Alberto, Benson, Charles, and Deon sit at a round lunch table with diameter 54 inches. The salt shaker is 27 inches from Charles, 18 inches from Benson, 20 inches from Deon, and 30 inches from Alberto.

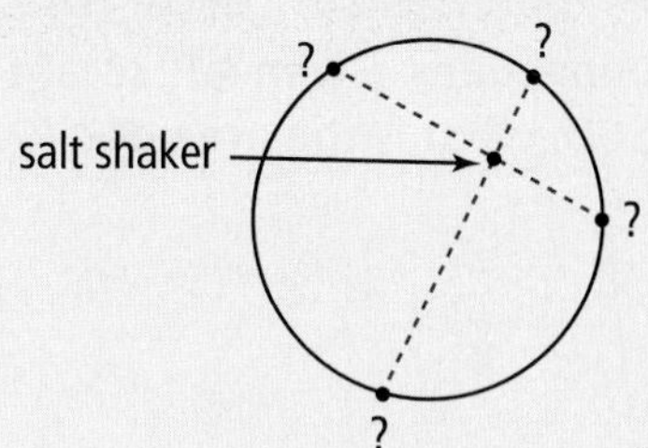


**Part A** In what order around the table are they seated? Explain.

**Part B** Alberto, Benson, Charles, and Deon change the positions of their seats and sit evenly spaced around the table. If the location of the salt shaker does not change, what is the closest that one of them could be from the salt shaker? What is the farthest?

TOPIC 10

# Topic Review

## TOPIC ESSENTIAL QUESTION

1. How are the figures formed related to the radius, circumference, and area of a circle when a line or line intersect a circle?

## Vocabulary Review

**Choose the correct term to complete each sentence.**

2. A(n) __________ is a region of a circle with two radii and an arc of the circle as borders.
3. A(n) __________ is an angle with its vertex on the circle.
4. A(n) __________ and the corresponding circle have exactly one point in common.
5. When both rays of an angle intersect a circle, the __________ is the portion of the circle between the rays.

- central angle
- chord
- inscribed angle
- intercepted arc
- secant
- sector of a circle
- segment of a circle
- tangent to a circle

## Concepts & Skills Review

### LESSON 10-1 Arcs and Sectors

#### Quick Review

**Arc length** and the area of a **sector of a circle** are proportional to the corresponding central angle.

The length of an arc is $\frac{n}{360}$ of the circumference, where $n$ is the measure of the central angle in degrees, and the area of a sector is $\frac{n}{360}$ of the area of the circle.

#### Example

**Circle $J$ has a radius of 6 cm. What is the area of a sector with a central angle of 80°?**

Write the formula for the area of a sector:

$$A = \frac{n}{360} \cdot \pi r^2$$

$$= \frac{80}{360} \cdot \pi(6)^2$$

$$\approx 25.1$$

The area of the sector is about 25.1 cm$^2$.

#### Practice & Problem Solving

**Find each arc length in terms of $\pi$.**

6. $\widehat{JK}$

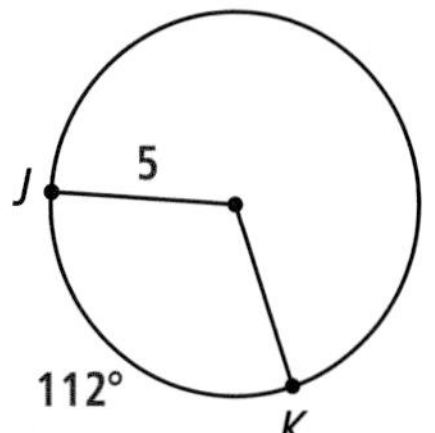


7. $\widehat{ABC}$

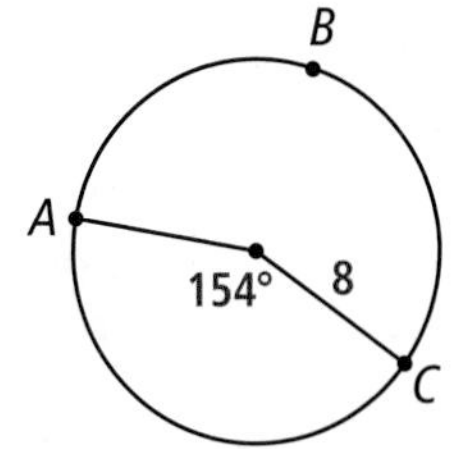


**Find the area of each sector in terms of $\pi$.**

8. sector $NRM$

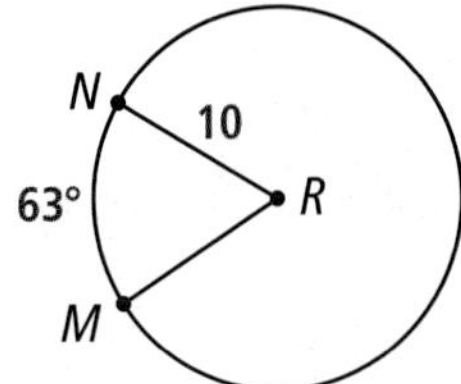


9. sector $DSE$

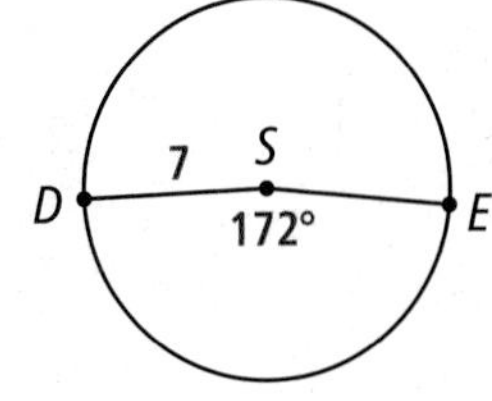


10. **Reason** If you know the circumference of a circle and the area of a sector of the circle, how could you determine the central angle of the sector? Explain.

TOPIC 10 REVIEW

## LESSON 10-2 Lines Tangent to a Circle

### Quick Review

A **tangent to a circle** is perpendicular to the radius of the circle at the **point of tangency**. You can use properties of right triangles to solve problems involving tangents.

### Example

**Lines $m$ and $n$ are tangent to $\odot T$. What is $m\angle ATB$?**

Since lines $m$ and $n$ are tangent lines, $m\angle SAT = m\angle SBT = 90$. Points $A$, $T$, $B$, and $S$ form a quadrilateral, so use the angle sum of a quadrilateral to solve the problem.

$$m\angle SAT + m\angle ASB + m\angle SBT + m\angle ATB = 360$$

$$90 + 61 + 90 + m\angle ATB = 360$$

$$m\angle ATB = 119$$

So, $m\angle ATB = 119$.

### Practice & Problem Solving

**For Exercises 11–12, $\overline{QR}$ and $\overline{AB}$ are tangent to the circle. Find each value.**

**11.** $QR$

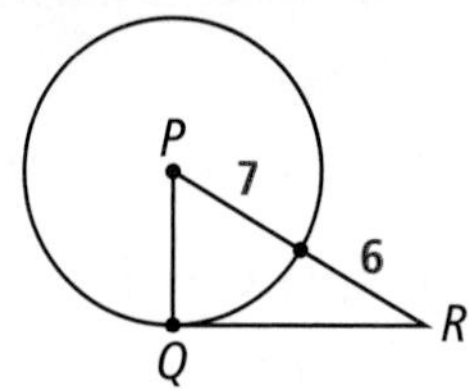


**12.** $m\angle CAB$

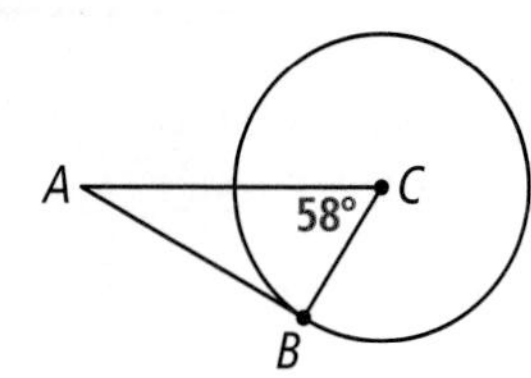


**13. Construct Arguments** If $\overline{GH}$ is a diameter of $\odot T$, is it possible to draw tangents to $G$ and $H$ from the same point external to $\odot T$? Explain.

**14.** Segment MN is tangent to $\odot L$. What is the radius of the circle? Explain.

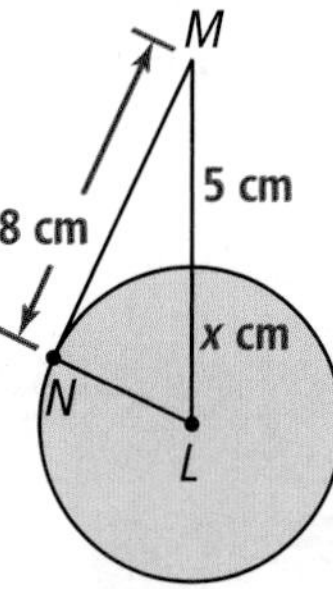


## LESSON 10-3 Chords

### Quick Review

**Chords** in a circle have the following properties:

- Two chords in the same circle with the same length have congruent central angles, have congruent arcs, and are equidistant from the center of the circle.
- Chords are bisected by the diameter of the circle that is perpendicular to the chord.

### Example

**What is the radius of $\odot T$?**

Since $\overline{CT} \perp \overline{AB}$, $\overline{CT}$ bisects $\overline{AB}$. So, $CB = 7$. Use the Pythagorean Theorem to find the radius.

$$(CT)^2 + (CB)^2 = (BT)^2$$

$$3^2 + 7^2 = (BT)^2$$

$$BT \approx 7.6$$

The radius of $\odot T$ is about 7.6.

### Practice & Problem Solving

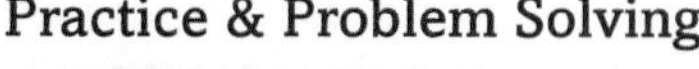

**For Exercises 15–17, the radius of $\odot T$ is 7. Find each value. Round to the nearest tenth.**

**15.** $FH$

**16.** $CD$

**17.** $m\angle BTA$

**18. Look for Relationships** Circles $T$ and $S$ intersect at points $A$ and $B$. What is the relationship between $\overline{AB}$ and $\overleftrightarrow{TS}$? Explain.

**19.** A contractor cuts off part of a circular countertop so that it fits against a wall. What should be the length $x$ of the cut? Round to the nearest tenth.

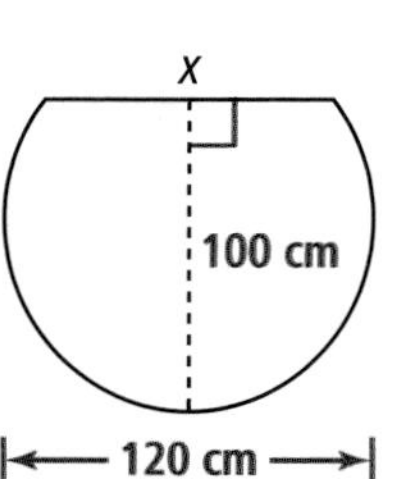

## LESSON 10-4 Inscribed Angles

### Quick Review

The measure of an **inscribed angle** is half the measure of its intercepted arc. As a result:

- Opposite angles of an inscribed quadrilateral are supplementary.
- The measure of an angle formed by a tangent and chord is half the measure of the intercepted arc.

### Example

**What are the angle measures of $\triangle ABC$?**

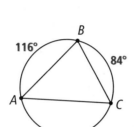

Use inscribed angles:

$m\angle BAC = \frac{1}{2}(84) = 42$

$m\angle BCA = \frac{1}{2}(116) = 58$

$m\angle ABC = 180 - 42 - 58 = 80$

### Practice & Problem Solving

**Find each value.**

20. $m\widehat{EF}$

21. $m\angle MNP$

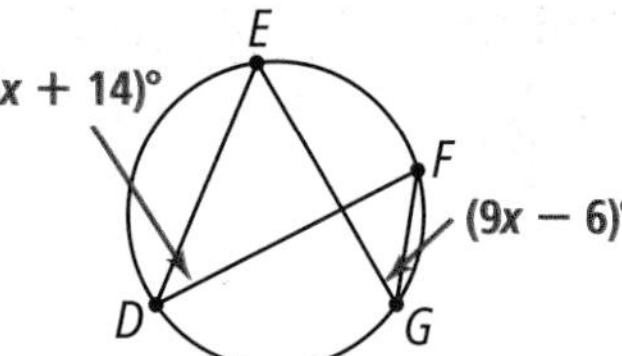


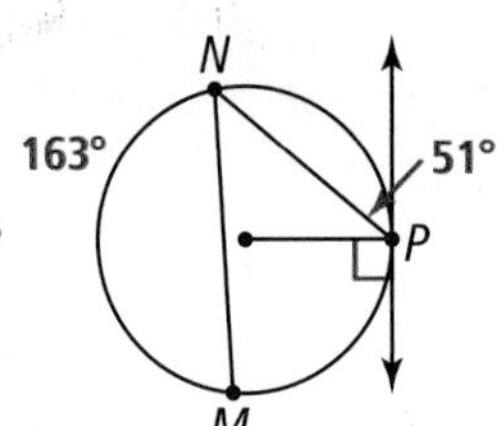


22. $m\angle WZY$

23. $m\angle QPR$

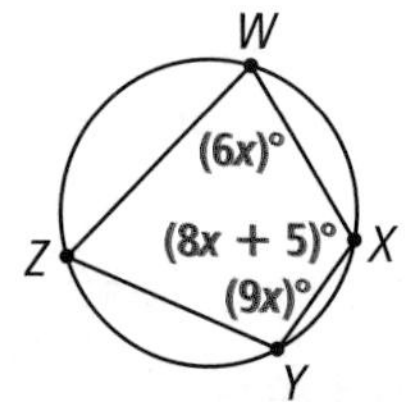


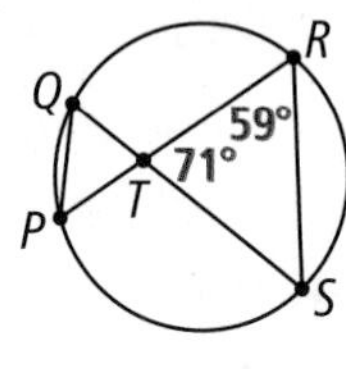


24. **Generalize** If a rectangle is inscribed in a circle, what must be true about the diagonals of the rectangle? Explain.

## LESSON 10-5 Secant Lines and Segments

### Quick Review

**Secant** lines form angles with special relationships:

- The measure of an angle formed by secants intersecting inside a circle is half the sum of the measures of the intercepted arcs.
- The measure of an angle formed by secants intersecting outside a circle is half the difference of the measures of the intercepted arcs.

### Example

**What is the value of $x$?**

Use secant segment relationships.

$$(AE)(AE + ED) = (AB)(AB + BC)$$
$$6(6 + 12) = 4(4 + x)$$
$$108 = 16 + 4x$$
$$92 = 4x$$
$$23 = x$$

The value of $x$ is 23.

### Practice & Problem Solving

**For Exercises 25 and 26, find each value in the figure shown.**

25. $QR$

26. $m\angle NRP$

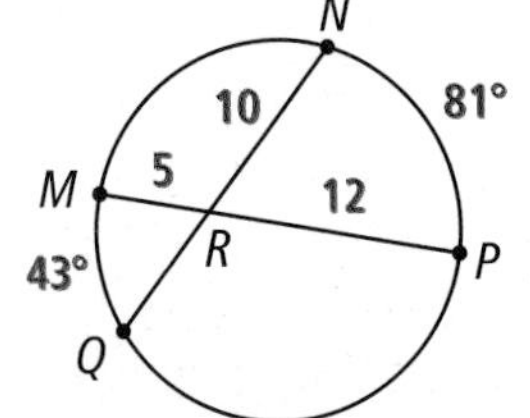


**For Exercises 27 and 28, find each value in the figure shown. The segment $\overline{WZ}$ is tangent to the circle.**

27. $WZ$

28. $m\widehat{XZ}$

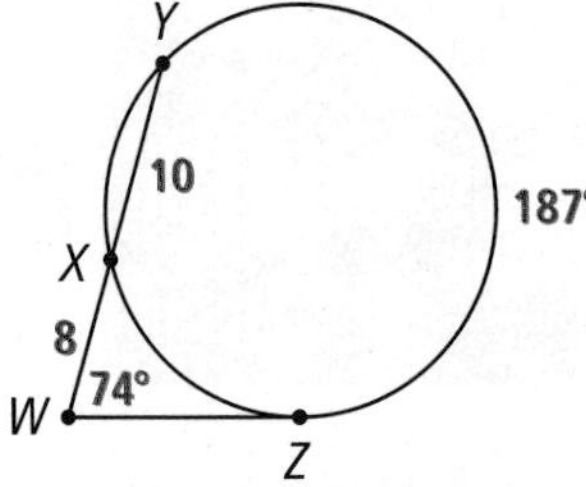


29. **Construct Arguments** A student said that if $\angle A$ is formed by two secants intersecting outside of a circle, then $m\angle A < 90$. Do you agree? Explain.

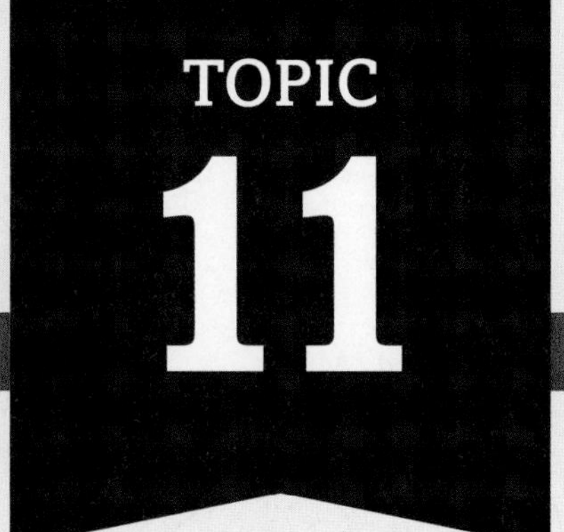


# Two- and Three-Dimensional Models

## TOPIC ESSENTIAL QUESTION

**How is Cavalieri's Principle helpful in understanding the volume formulas for solids?**

## Topic Overview

**enVision™ STEM Project:**
Design a Rigid Package

**11-1** Three-Dimensional Figures and Cross Sections

**11-2** Volumes of Prisms and Cylinders

**Mathematical Modeling in 3 Acts:**
Box 'Em Up

**11-3** Pyramids and Cones

**11-4** Spheres

## Topic Vocabulary

- Cavalieri's Principle
- hemisphere
- oblique cylinder
- oblique prism

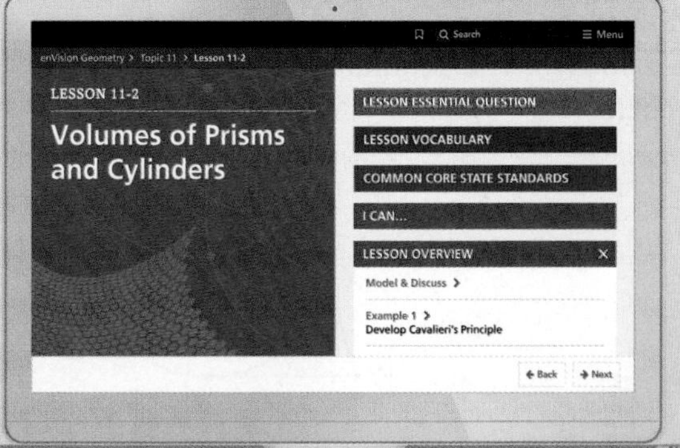

Go online | **PearsonRealize.com**

## Digital Experience

**INTERACTIVE STUDENT EDITION** Access online or offline.

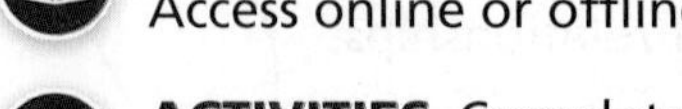
**ACTIVITIES** Complete ***Explore & Reason, Model & Discuss***, and ***Critique & Explain*** activities. Interact with Examples and Try Its.

**ANIMATION** View and interact with real-world applications.

**PRACTICE** Practice what you've learned.

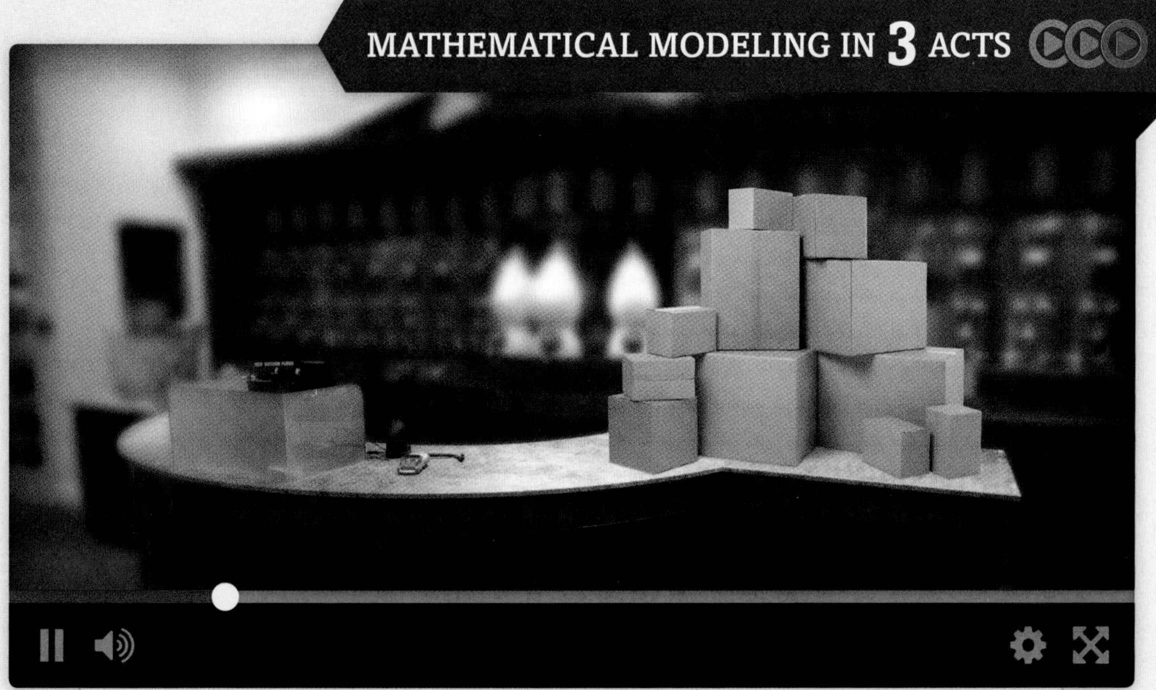


## Box 'Em Up

With so many people and businesses shopping online, retailers, and especially e-retailers, ship more and more packages every day. Some of the products people order have unusual sizes and shapes and need custom packaging. Imagine how you might package a surfboard, or a snow blower, or even live crawfish to ship to someone's house!

Think about this during the Mathematical Modeling in 3 Acts lesson.

TOPIC 11

**VIDEOS** Watch clips to support ***Mathematical Modeling in 3 Acts Lessons*** and **enVision™ *STEM Projects.***

**CONCEPT SUMMARY** Review key lesson content through multiple representations.

**ASSESSMENT** Show what you've learned.

**GLOSSARY** Read and listen to English and Spanish definitions.

**TUTORIALS** Get help from ***Virtual Nerd***, right when you need it.

**MATH TOOLS** Explore math with digital tools and manipulatives.

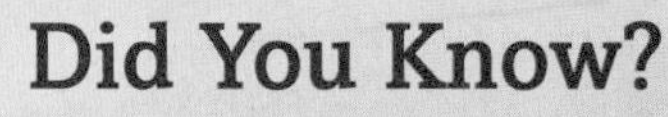



## Did You Know?

Cardboard boxes look simple, but the machines that make them are not. This **cartoning machine** is capable of making **15,000 boxes per day**.

Packages come in many shapes. The familiar milk carton shape is called a **gable-top carton** because of its resemblance to a house gable. **Cylindrical** packaging is often used for sugar, tea and grains that don't have rigid shapes.

Manufacturers consider many factors when designing a package.

- ☑ Marketing appeal
- ☑ Cost of materials
- ☑ Simplicity
- ☑ Safety
- ☑ Recyclability

## Your Task: Design a Rigid Package

You will design a rigid package for a product of your choice. Your design will address factors such as attractiveness, protection for the product, and cost. You will then draw two- and three-dimensional representations of your package and build a prototype.

Activity Assess

# 11-1 Three-Dimensional Figures and Cross Sections

I CAN… identify three-dimensional figures and their relationships with polygons to solve problems.

## EXPLORE & REASON

**Consider a cube of cheese. If you slice straight down through the midpoints of four parallel edges of the cube, the outline of the newly exposed surface is a square.**

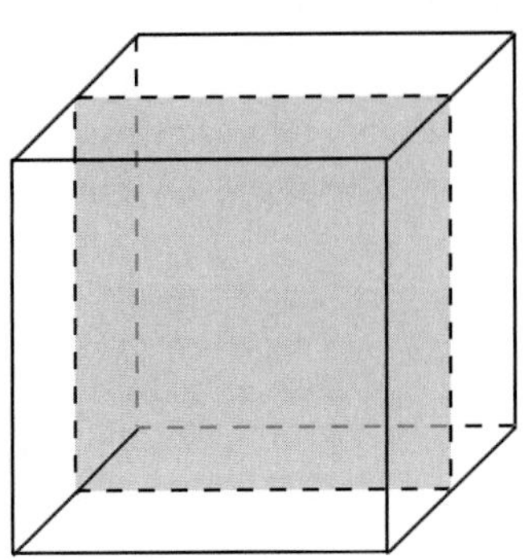

A. How would you slice the cube to expose a triangular surface?

B. **Communicate Precisely** How would you slice the cube to expose a triangular surface with the greatest possible area?

## ESSENTIAL QUESTION

**How are three-dimensional figures and polygons related?**

## EXAMPLE 1 Develop Euler's Formula

**How many faces, vertices, and edges does each prism contain? Do you notice any patterns in these quantities?**

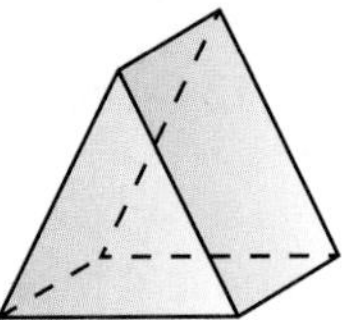
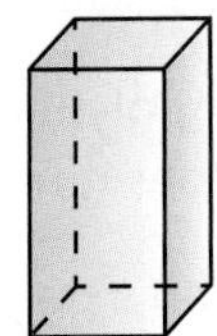
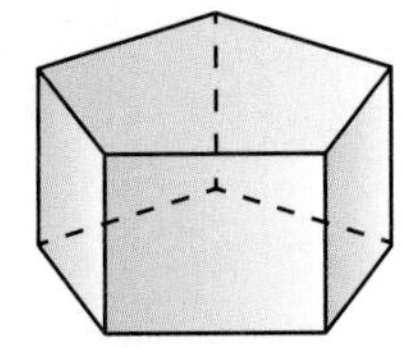
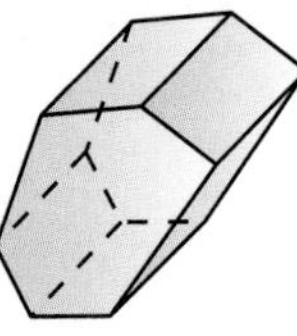

Make a table of the number of vertices, edges, and faces for each prism. Look for patterns and relationships.

| Type of Prism | Faces ($F$) | Vertices ($V$) | Edges ($E$) |
|---|---|---|---|
| triangular | 5 | 6 | 9 |
| rectangular | 6 | 8 | 12 |
| pentagonal | 7 | 10 | 15 |
| hexagonal | 8 | 12 | 18 |

For each additional face on the prism, the prism gains 2 vertices and 3 edges.

Look at the sums of the faces and vertices. Compare it to the number of edges.

$5 + 6 = 9 + 2$
$6 + 8 = 12 + 2$
$7 + 10 = 15 + 2$
$8 + 12 = 18 + 2$

The sum of the faces and vertices is always 2 more than the number of edges.

**MODEL WITH MATHEMATICS** Look at the relationships between the number of vertices, faces, and edges. How might you represent these relationships in an equation?

**Try It!** 1. How many faces, vertices, and edges do the pyramids have? Name at least three patterns you notice.

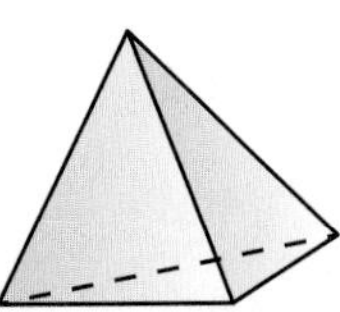
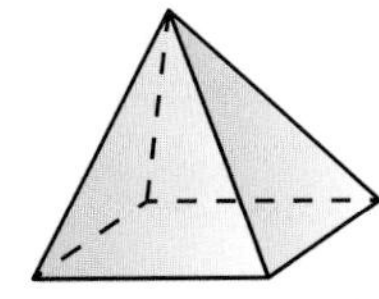
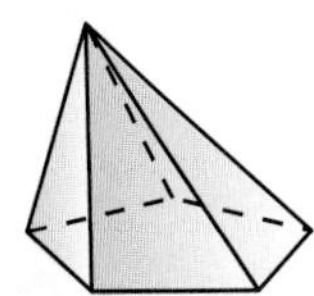
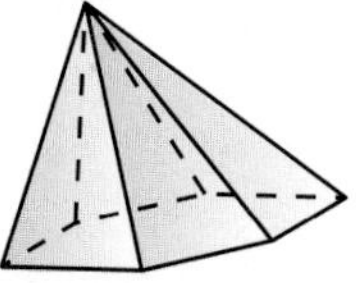

**CONCEPT** Euler's Formula

The sum of the number of faces ($F$) and vertices ($V$) of a polyhedron is 2 more than the number of its edges ($E$).

$F + V = E + 2$

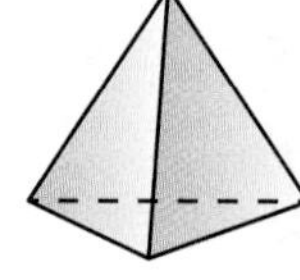

$F + V = E + 2$

$4 + 4 = E + 2$

$E = 6$

APPLICATION

## EXAMPLE 2 Apply Euler's Formula

**To make polyhedron-shaped game pieces using a 3D printer, Juanita enters the number of faces, edges, and vertices into a program. If she wants a game piece with 20 faces and 30 edges, how many vertices does the piece have?**

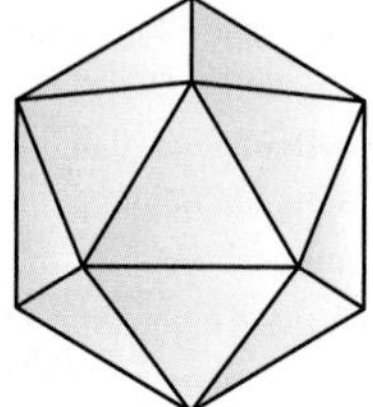

**COMMON ERROR**
Remember to add the number of faces and vertices on one side of the equation and to add the number of edges plus 2 on the other side of the equation.

$F + V = E + 2$

$20 + V = 30 + 2$ — Apply Euler's Formula.

$V = 12$

The game piece has 12 vertices.

**Try It!** 2. a. A polyhedron has 12 faces and 30 edges. How many vertices does it have?

b. Can a polyhedron have 4 faces, 5 vertices, and 8 edges? Explain.

## EXAMPLE 3 Describe a Cross Section

**Plane $M$ and plane $N$ intersect the regular octahedron as shown. What is the shape of each cross section?**

**STUDY TIP**
Recall that a *cross section* is the intersection of a solid and a plane.

Plane $M$ slices the octahedron in half through the top and bottom vertices. The cross section is a rhombus.

Plane $N$ slices horizontally between the bases of two square pyramids. The cross section is a square.

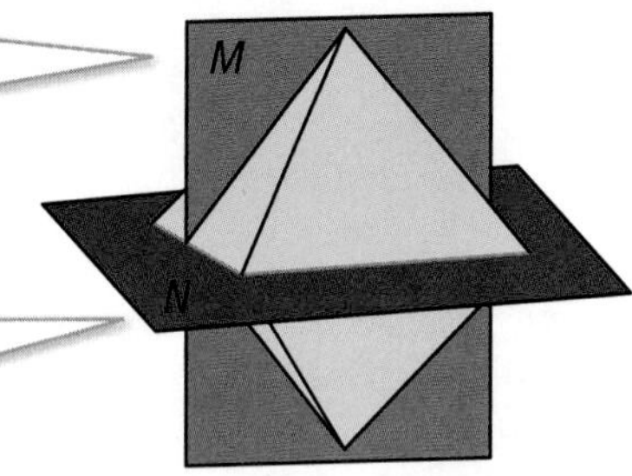

**Try It!** 3. a. What shape is the cross section shown?

b. What shape is the cross section if the plane is perpendicular to the base and passes through the vertex of the pyramid?

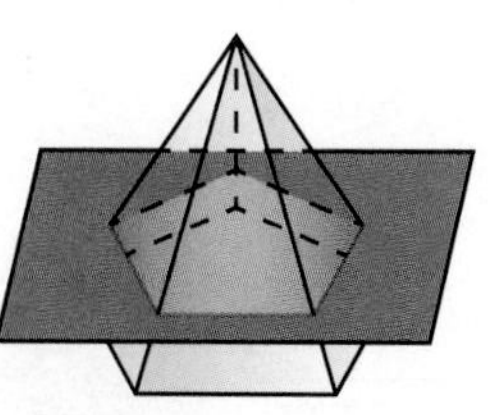

## EXAMPLE 4 Draw a Cross Section

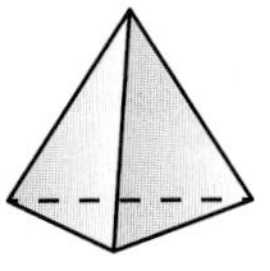

**A plane intersects a tetrahedron parallel to the base. How do you draw the cross section?**

**Step 1** Visualize the plane intersecting the tetrahedron.

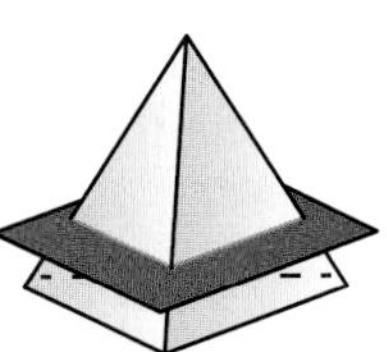

**Step 2** Draw lines where the plane cuts the surface of the polyhedron.

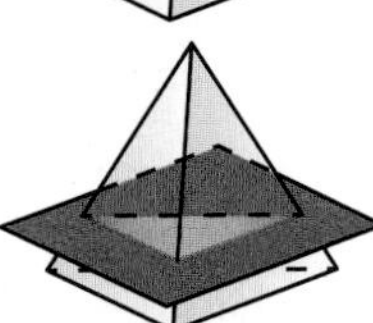

**STUDY TIP**
It is not possible for a polyhedron with *n* faces to have a cross section with more than *n* sides.

**Step 3** Shade the cross section.

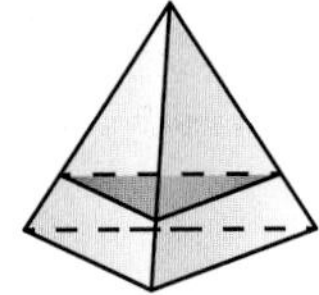

**Try It!** **4. a.** Draw the cross section of a plane intersecting the tetrahedron through the top vertex and perpendicular to the base.

**b.** Draw the cross section of a plane intersecting a hexagonal prism perpendicular to the base.

## EXAMPLE 5 Rotate a Polygon to Form a Three-Dimensional Figure

**If you rotate an isosceles triangle about the altitude, what three-dimensional figure does the triangle form?**

As the triangle rotates, each point on the sides traces out a circle about the axis of rotation.

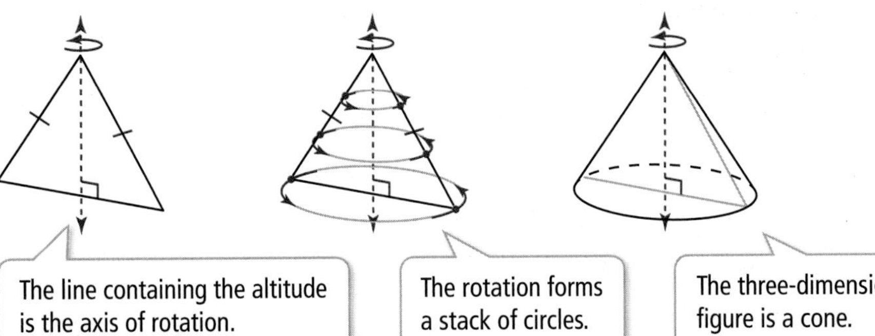

The line containing the altitude is the axis of rotation.
The rotation forms a stack of circles.
The three-dimensional figure is a cone.

**Try It!** **5. a.** What three-dimensional figure is formed by rotating equilateral triangle $\triangle ABC$ about $\overline{BD}$?

**b.** What three-dimensional figure is formed by rotating $\triangle ABC$ about $\overline{BC}$?

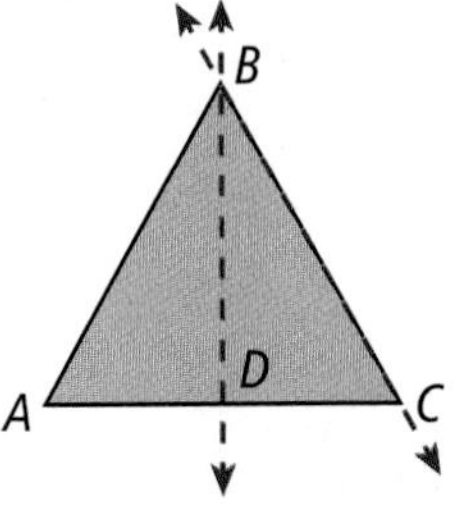

## CONCEPT SUMMARY Polyhedrons, Cross Sections, and Rotating a Polygon

| WORDS | DIAGRAMS |
|---|---|
| **Euler's Formula** The faces of a polyhedron are polygons. The sum of the number of faces $F$ and vertices $V$ of a polyhedron is 2 more than the number of its edges $E$. $F + V = E + 2$ | 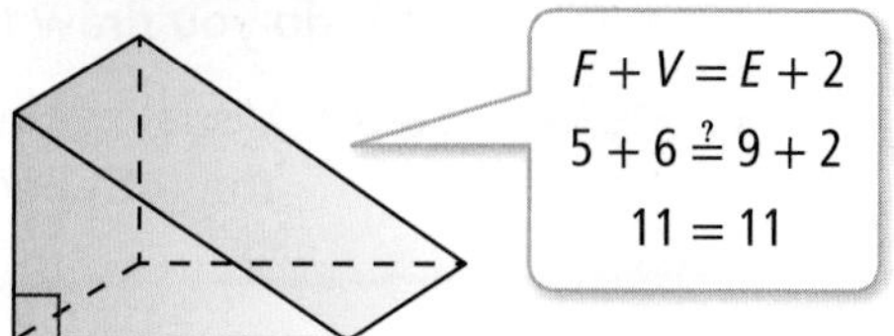 |
| **Cross Sections** A cross section is the intersection of a plane and a solid. The cross section of a plane and a convex polyhedron is a polygon. | 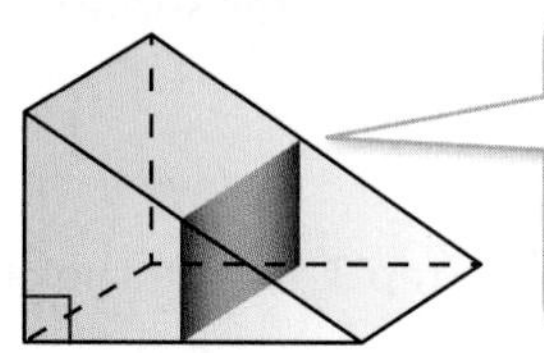 A cross section perpendicular to the base of the triangular prism is a rectangle. |
| **Rotation of Polygons** Rotating a polygon about an axis forms a three-dimensional figure with at least one circular cross section. | 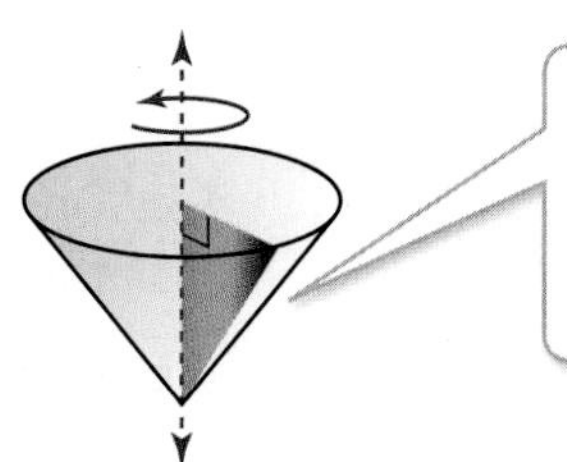 The right triangle is rotated about the line containing a leg to form a right cone. |



## Do You UNDERSTAND?

1. **ESSENTIAL QUESTION** How are three-dimensional figures and polygons related?

2. **Error Analysis** Nicholas drew a figure to find a cross section of an icosahedron, a polyhedron with 20 faces. What is Nicholas's error?

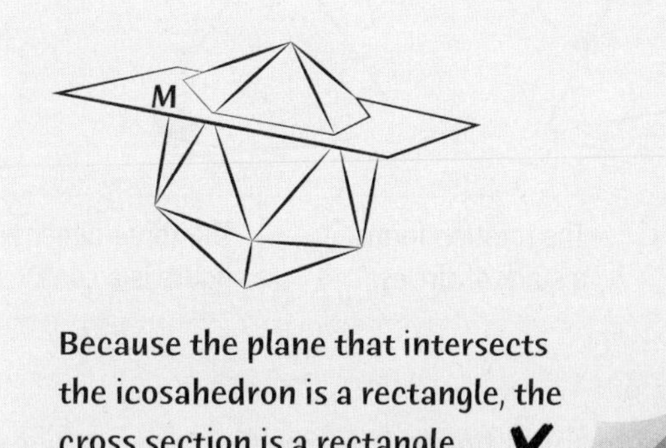

M
Because the plane that intersects the icosahedron is a rectangle, the cross section is a rectangle.
X


3. **Reason** Can a polyhedron have 3 faces, 4 vertices, and 5 edges? Explain.

## Do You KNOW HOW?

**For Exercises 4–7, copy and complete the table.**

| | Faces | Vertices | Edges |
|---|---|---|---|
| **4.** | 5 | 6 | |
| **5.** | 8 | | 18 |
| **6.** | | 12 | 20 |
| **7.** | 22 | 44 | |

8. What polygon is formed by the intersection of plane $N$ and the octagonal prism shown?

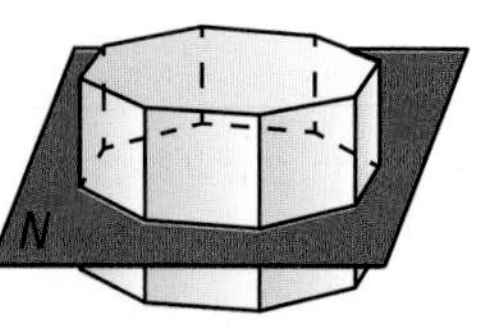


9. Describe the three-dimensional figure that is formed from rotating the isosceles right triangle about the hypotenuse.

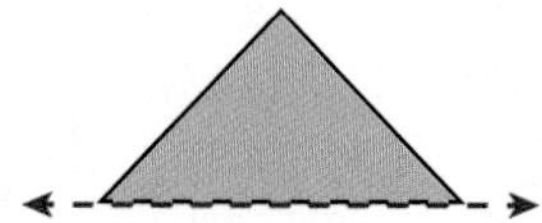

# PRACTICE & PROBLEM SOLVING

## UNDERSTAND

**10. Mathematical Connections** If you rotate rectangle *ABCD* about $\overleftrightarrow{CD}$, what is the volume of the resulting three-dimensional figure?

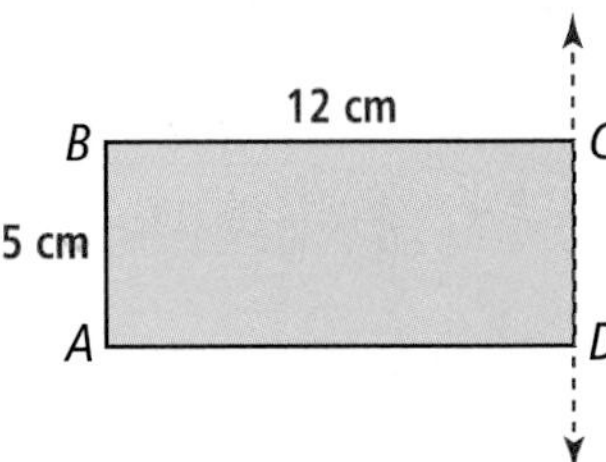


**11. Error Analysis** Philip was asked to find the number of vertices of a polyhedron with 32 faces and 60 edges. What is his error?

$$F + E = V + 2$$
$$32 + 60 = V + 2$$
$$90 = V$$

**12. Make Sense and Persevere** A tetrahedron is a polyhedron with four triangular faces. Can a plane intersect the tetrahedron shown to form a cross section with four sides? Explain.

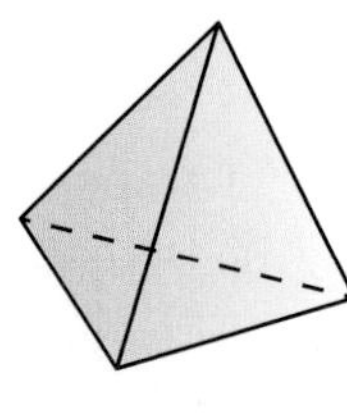

**13. Use Appropriate Tools** Can the intersection of a plane and a triangular prism produce a rectangular cross section? Draw a diagram to explain.

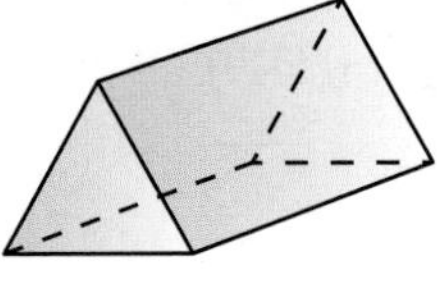

**14. Higher Order Thinking** Is it possible to rotate a polygon to form a cube? Explain.

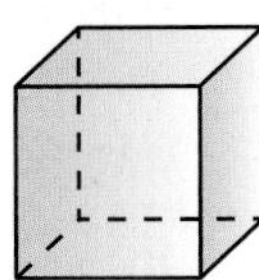

**15. Make Sense and Persevere** Use the polyhedron shown.

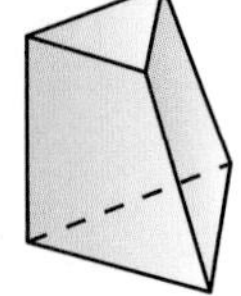

**a.** Does the figure have a cross section with five sides? Copy the figure and draw the cross section or explain why not.

**b.** What is the maximum number of sides that a cross section of this figure can have?

## PRACTICE

**For Exercises 16–20, find the missing number for each polyhedron.** SEE EXAMPLES 1 AND 2

**16.** A polyhedron has 24 edges and 12 vertices. How many faces does it have?

**17.** A polyhedron has 20 faces and 12 vertices. How many edges does it have?

**18.** A polyhedron has 8 faces and 15 edges. How many vertices does it have?

**19.** A polyhedron has 16 edges and 10 vertices. How many faces does it have?

**20.** Draw the cross section formed by the intersection of plane *A* and the polyhedron shown. What type of polygon is the cross section? SEE EXAMPLE 3

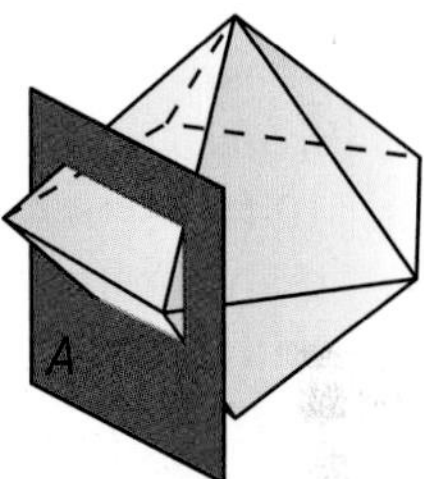


**For Exercises 20 and 21, use the square pyramid shown.** SEE EXAMPLE 4

**21.** Visualize a plane intersecting the square pyramid parallel to the base. Describe the cross section.

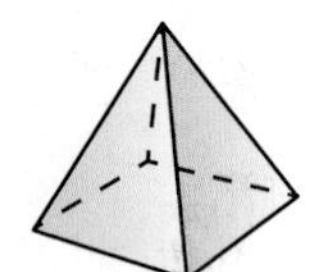

**22.** Visualize a plane intersecting the square pyramid through the vertex and perpendicular to opposite edges of the base. Describe the cross section.

**23.** Describe the three-dimensional figure that is formed from by rotating the rectangle about the side. SEE EXAMPLE 5

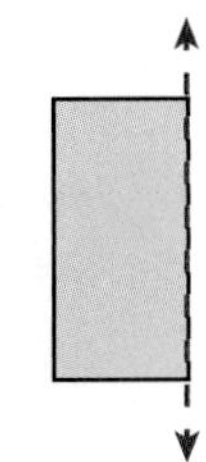

**24.** Describe the three-dimensional figure that is formed by rotating the pentagon about the line shown. SEE EXAMPLE 5

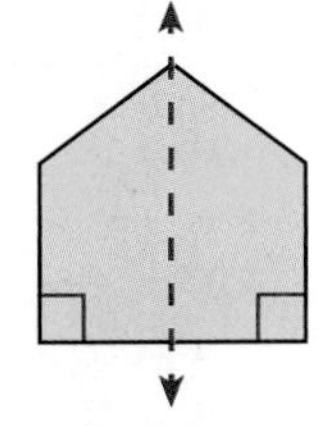

**25.** Describe the three-dimensional figure that is formed by rotating the circle about a diameter.

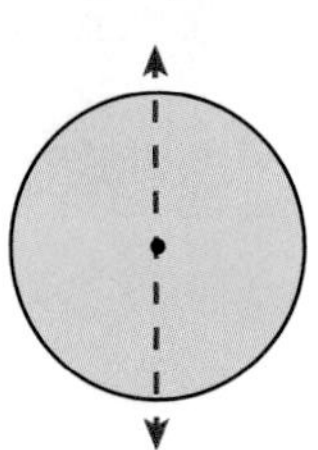

# PRACTICE & PROBLEM SOLVING

Practice Tutorial

Mixed Review Available Online

## APPLY

**26. Model With Mathematics** Parker cuts 12 pentagons and 20 hexagons out of fabric to make the pillow shown. The pillow has 60 vertices. If it takes 20 inches of thread per seam to connect the edges of the polygons, how many inches of thread does Parker need to make the pillow?

**27. Reason** A gem cutter cuts a polyhedral crystal from a garnet gemstone. The crystal has 10 fewer vertices than edges and twice as many edges as faces. How many faces, vertices, and edges does the crystal have?

**28. Communicate Precisely** Rebecca wants to install a safety mat under the path of a revolving door. What shape should she make the mat? Explain.

## ASSESSMENT PRACTICE

**29.** Complete the table for each polyhedron.

| Polyhedron | Faces ($F$) | Vertices ($V$) | Edges ($E$) |
|---|---|---|---|
| regular dodecahedron | 12 | | 30 |
| heptagonal pyramid | 8 | 9 | |
| octahedron | 8 | | 12 |
| rhombohedron | | 8 | 12 |

**30. SAT/ACT** Which best describes the cross section of plane $X$ and the polyhedron shown?

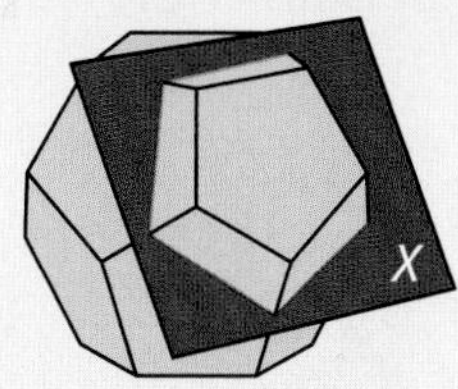


Ⓐ hexagon
Ⓑ pentagon
Ⓒ rectangle
Ⓓ trapezoid
Ⓔ triangle

**31. Performance Task** Draw a polyhedron with the fewest possible faces, vertices, and edges. Choose the faces from the polygons shown. You may use a polygon more than once.

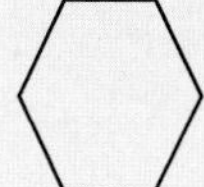 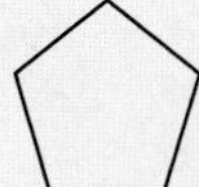  

**Part A** Explain why the polygon or polygons you chose minimize the number of vertices and edges.

**Part B** How do you know that there is no polyhedron with fewer faces, vertices, or edges than the one you drew?

# 11-2 Volumes of Prisms and Cylinders

**I CAN...** use the properties of prisms and cylinders to calculate their volumes.

**VOCABULARY**

- Cavalieri's Principle
- oblique cylinder
- oblique prism

## MODEL & DISCUSS

**The Environmental Club has a piece of wire mesh that they want to form into an open-bottom and open-top compost bin.**

A. Using one side as the height, describe how you can form a compost bin in the shape of a rectangular prism using all of the mesh with no overlap.

B. **Construct Arguments** Which height would result in the largest volume? Explain.

C. Suppose you formed a cylinder using the same height as a rectangular prism. How would the volumes compare?

## ESSENTIAL QUESTION

**How does the volume of a prism or cylinder relate to a cross section parallel to its base?**

CONCEPTUAL UNDERSTANDING

## EXAMPLE 1 Develop Cavalieri's Principle

**How are the volumes of the two different stacks of index cards related?**

The first stack forms a right prism. The second stack forms an *oblique prism*. An **oblique prism** is a prism such that some or all of the lateral faces are nonrectangular.

**VOCABULARY**
Remember that in a right prism, the sides are perpendicular to the bases. In an *oblique prism*, one or more sides are not perpendicular to the bases.

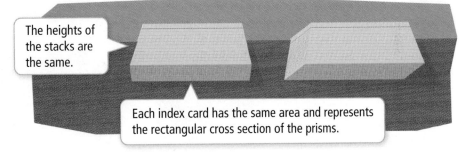

The heights of the stacks are the same.

Each index card has the same area and represents the rectangular cross section of the prisms.

The volumes of the two stacks are the same because the sums of the areas of the cards are the same.

**Try It!** 1. Do you think that right and oblique cylinders that have the same height and cross-sectional area also have equal volume? Explain.

## CONCEPT Cavalieri's Principle

**Cavalieri's Principle** states that if two three-dimensional figures have the same height and the same cross-sectional area at every level, then they have the same volume.

**If...**

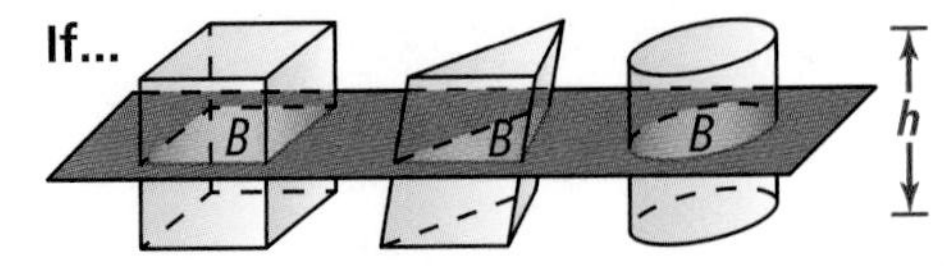


**Then...** the volumes are equal.

 Activity Assess

## CONCEPT Volumes of Prisms and Cylinders

The volume of a prism is the product of the area of the base and the height of the prism.

$V = Bh$

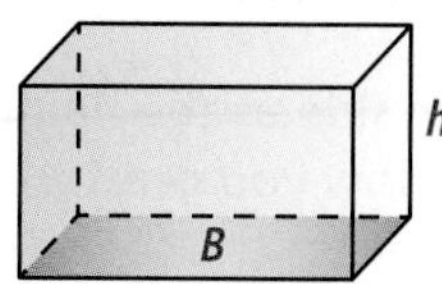


The volume of a cylinder is the product of the area of the base and the height of the cylinder.

$V = Bh$

$V = \pi r^2 h$

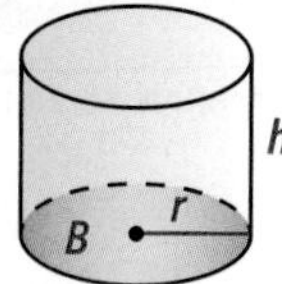


## EXAMPLE 2 Find the Volumes of Prisms and Cylinders

**A. Lonzell needs to store 20 ft$^3$ of firewood. Could he use the storage rack shown?**

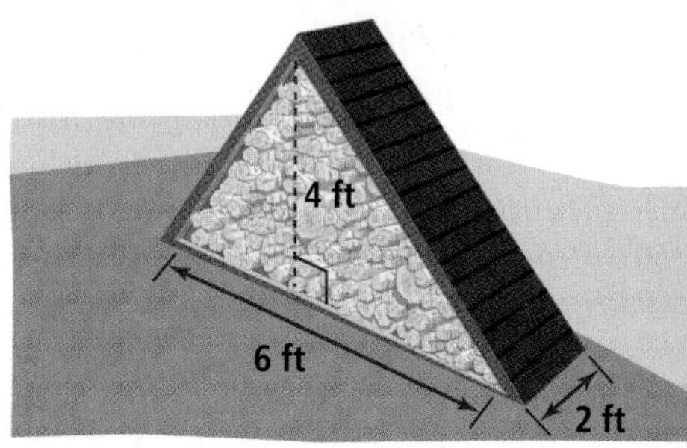


The rack is a triangular prism.

$$V = Bh$$

$$= \left[\frac{1}{2}(4)(6)\right](2) = 24$$

The volume of the storage rack is 24 ft$^3$, so Lonzell can store his firewood in the rack.

**B. Keisha is deciding between the two canisters shown. Which canister holds more? What is the volume of the larger canister?**

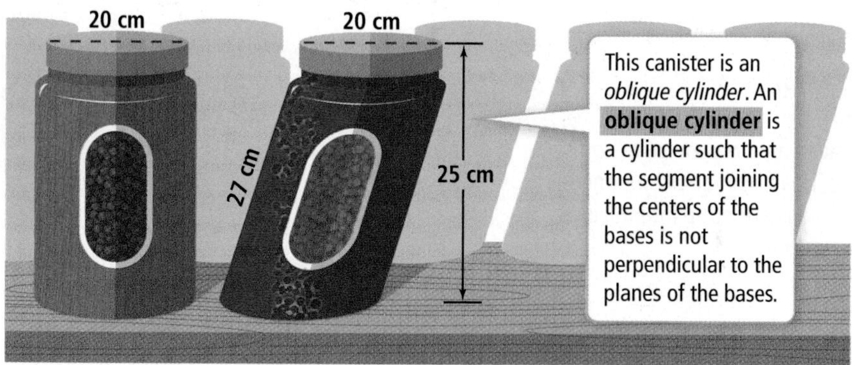

20 cm
20 cm
27 cm
25 cm
This canister is an *oblique cylinder*. An **oblique cylinder** is a cylinder such that the segment joining the centers of the bases is not perpendicular to the planes of the bases.


COMMON ERROR
The height of an oblique cylinder or prism is the length perpendicular to the bases, not the length of the sides of the figure.

The canisters have the same cross-sectional area at every height. So, by Cavalieri's Principle, the canisters have the same volume.

Use the volume formula to find the volume of the canister on the left.

$$V = \pi r^2 h$$

$$= \pi(10)^2(25) \approx 7{,}854$$

The diameter is 20 cm, so the radius is 10 cm.

The volume of both canisters is about 7,854 cm$^3$.

 **Try It!** 2. a. How would the volume of the storage shed change if the length of the triangular base is reduced by half?

b. How would the volume of the canisters change if the diameter is doubled?

APPLICATION

## EXAMPLE 3 Apply the Volumes of Prisms to Solve Problems

**Marta is repurposing a sandbox as a garden and is buying the soil from her school's fundraiser. Estimate the number of bags she should buy.**

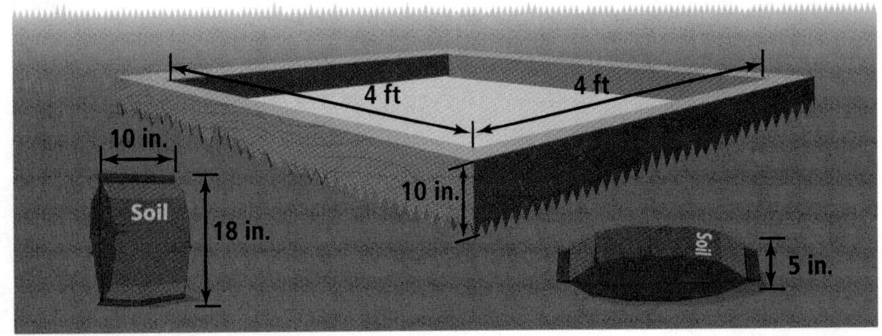


**Step 1** Determine the volume of soil needed.

Compute the volume of the sandbox in cubic inches.

$V = Bh$

$= (48 \cdot 48)(10)$ Use 4 ft = 48 in.

$= 23{,}040$

Marta needs 23,040 in.$^3$ of soil.

**Step 2** Estimate the volume of soil in each bag by modeling the bag of soil as a rectangular prism.

The height of the bag is tapered on the ends, but thicker in the middle, so we still use 5 inches to estimate the height.

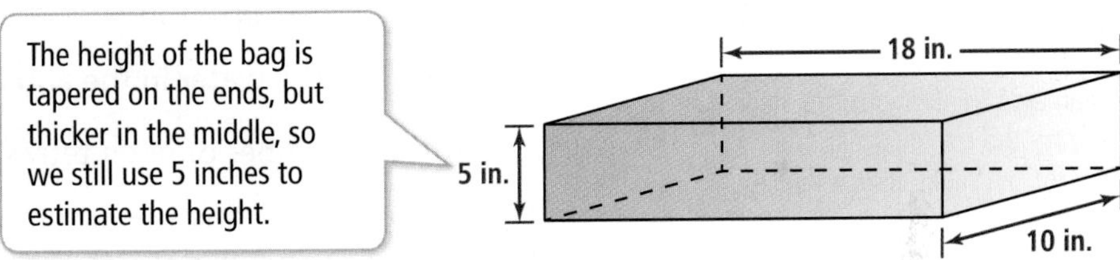


$V = Bh$

$= (10 \cdot 18)(5) = 900$

The volume of one bag of soil is about 900 in.$^3$.

**MODEL WITH MATHEMATICS**
Think about other ways to model the bag. Is a rectangular prism with the values used a reasonable model?

**Step 3** Estimate the number of bags needed.

$23{,}040 \div 900 \approx 26$

Marta should buy 26 bags of soil to fill the sandbox.

 **Try It!** 3. Kathryn is using cans of juice to fill a cylindrical pitcher that is 11 in. tall and has a radius of 4 in. Each can of juice is 6 in. tall with a radius of 2 in. How many cans of juice will Kathryn need?

## EXAMPLE 4 Apply Volume of Cylinders to Solve Problems

**Benito has 15 neon tetras in his aquarium. Each neon tetra requires at least 2 gallons of water. What is the maximum number of neon tetras that Benito should have in his aquarium? (*Hint:* 1 gal = 231 in.$^3$)**

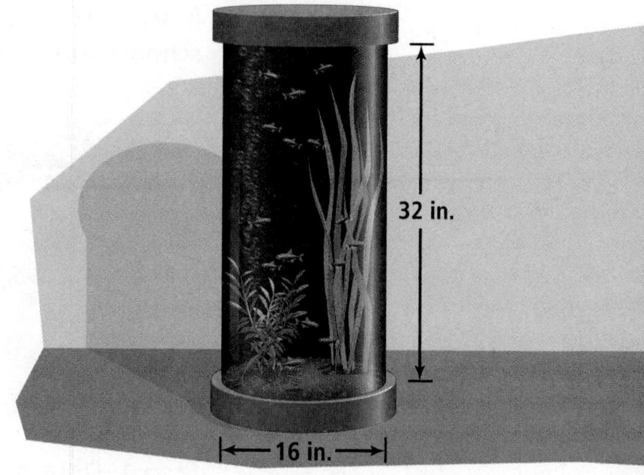


**Step 1** Compute the volume of water in cubic inches.

$$V = \pi r^2 h$$
$$= \pi(8)^2(32)$$
$$\approx 6{,}434$$

The radius is half the diameter.

The volume of the water in the aquarium is about 6,434 in.$^3$.

**Step 2** Find the volume of water in gallons.

$$6{,}434 \text{ in.}^3 \bullet \frac{1 \text{ gal}}{231 \text{ in.}^3} \approx 27.85 \text{ gal}$$

The volume of the water in the aquarium is about 27.85 gal.

STUDY TIP
You can also think about this step as finding the maximum number of fish for the tank using a density of 0.5 tetra per gallon.

**Step 3** Compute the number of neon tetras that Benito's tank should hold.

Use a proportion to find the maximum number $x$ of neon tetras that should be in 27.85 gal of water.

$$\frac{x \text{ fish}}{27.85 \text{ gal}} = \frac{1 \text{ fish}}{2 \text{ gal}}$$
$$\frac{x}{27.85} = \frac{1}{2}$$
$$2x = 27.85$$
$$x = 13.925$$

Benito should have no more than 13 neon tetras in his aquarium.

**Try It!** 4. Benito is considering the aquarium shown. What is the maximum number of neon tetras that this aquarium can hold?

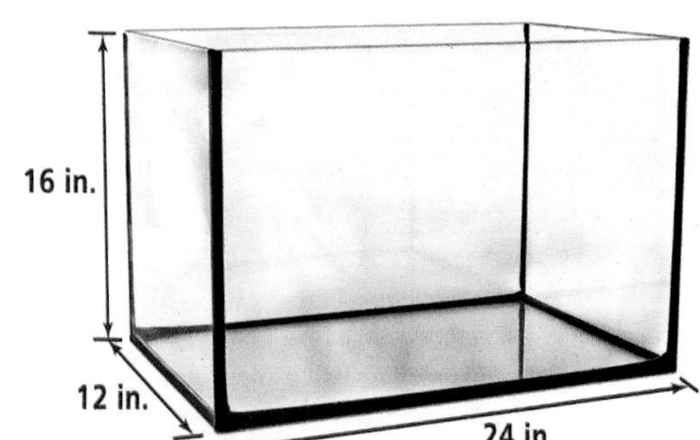

APPLICATION

## EXAMPLE 5 Determine Whether Volume or Surface Area Best Describes Size

**A forester surveys giant sequoias by gathering data about the heights and circumference of the trees.**

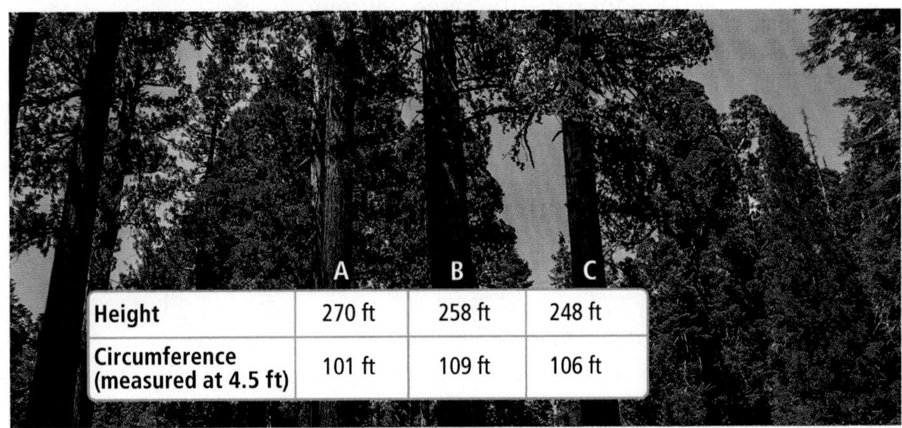

| | A | B | C |
|---|---|---|---|
| Height | 270 ft | 258 ft | 248 ft |
| Circumference (measured at 4.5 ft) | 101 ft | 109 ft | 106 ft |

**A. Should the forester use surface area or volume to describe the sizes of the sequoias? Explain.**

The amount of wood in a tree is represented by its volume, so she should use volume to determine the size of a giant sequoia.

**MODEL WITH MATHEMATICS**
Think about other shapes you could use to represent the tree. What is another mathematical model you could use for this problem?

**B. What are the sizes of the sequoias shown? Rank them in order by size from largest to smallest.**

Although the sequoias have branches and the trunk tapers gradually toward the top of the tree, each tree can be modeled as a cylinder. Find the volume of each cylinder to estimate the volume of each tree.

| | Radius (ft) | Volume of Trunk (ft$^3$) |
|---|---|---|
| Tree A<br>270 ft | $r = \frac{101}{2\pi} \approx 16.1$ | $V = \pi r^2 h$<br>$= \pi(16.1)^2(270)$<br>$\approx 219{,}870$ |
| Tree B<br>258 ft | $r = \frac{109}{2\pi} \approx 17.3$ | $V = \pi r^2 h$<br>$= \pi(17.3)^2(258)$<br>$\approx 242{,}584$ |
| Tree C<br>248 ft | $r = \frac{106}{2\pi} \approx 16.9$ | $V = \pi r^2 h$<br>$= \pi(16.9)^2(248)$<br>$\approx 222{,}523$ |

In order from largest to smallest, the three trees are: Tree B, Tree C, Tree A.

**Try It!** **5.** Describe a situation when surface area might be a better measure of size than volume.

## CONCEPT SUMMARY Volumes of Prisms and Cylinders

**WORDS**

**Cavalieri's Principle** Figures with the same height and same cross-sectional area at every level have the same volume.

As a result, right and oblique prisms and cylinders with the same base area and height have the same volume.

**DIAGRAMS**

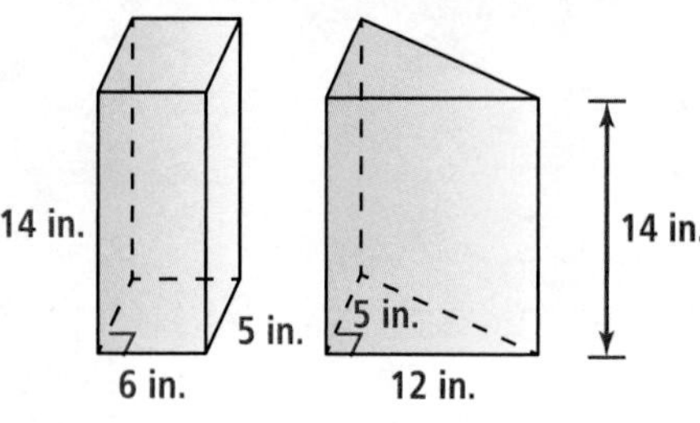


$V = Bh$

$V = 30 \cdot 14$

$V = 420$ cubic inches

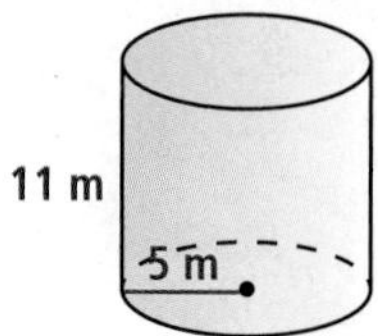


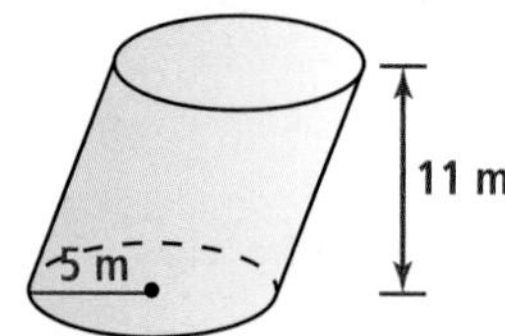


$V = Bh$

$V = \pi r^2 h$

$= \pi \cdot 5^2 \cdot 11$

$= 863.9$ cubic meters

## Do You UNDERSTAND?

1. **ESSENTIAL QUESTION** How does the volume of a prism or cylinder relate to a cross section parallel to its base?

2. **Error Analysis** Sawyer says that Cavalieri's Principle proves that the two prisms shown have the same volume. Explain Sawyer's error.

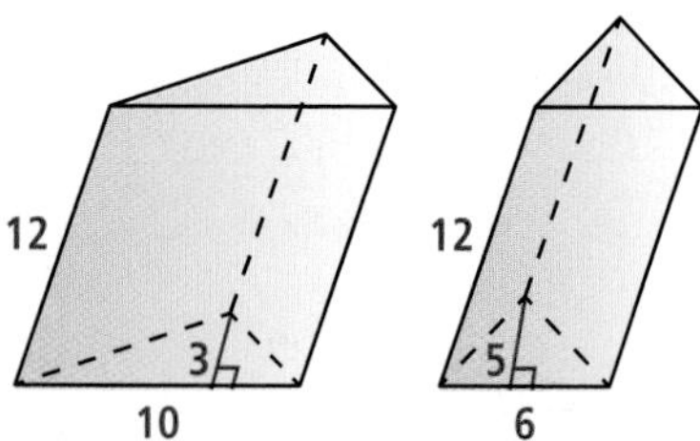


3. **Vocabulary** How are an oblique prism and an oblique cylinder alike and different?

4. **Reason** The circumference of the base of a cylinder is $x$, and the height of the cylinder is $x$. What expression gives the volume of the cylinder?

5. **Construct Arguments** Denzel kicks a large dent into a trash can and says that the volume does not change because of Cavalieri's Principle. Do you agree with Denzel? Explain.

## Do You KNOW HOW?

**For Exercises 6–11, find the volume of each figure. Round to the nearest tenth.**

6.

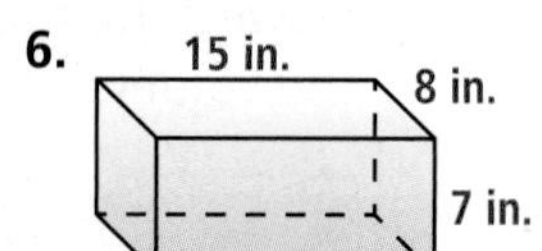


7.

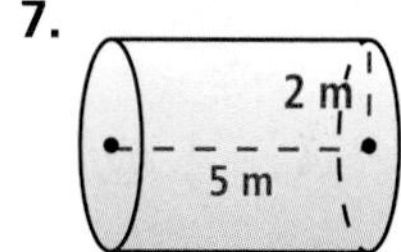


8.

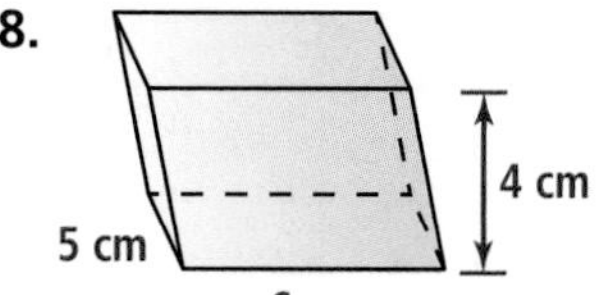


9.

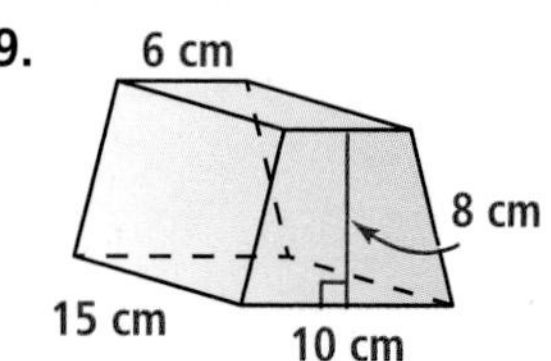


10.

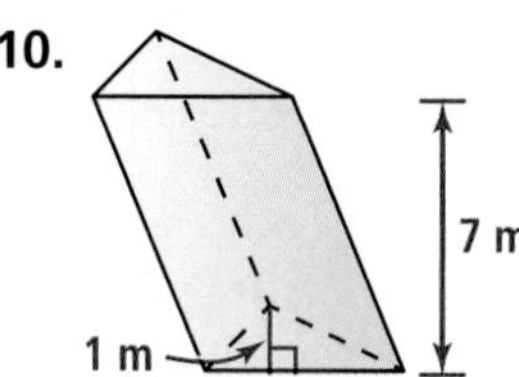


11.

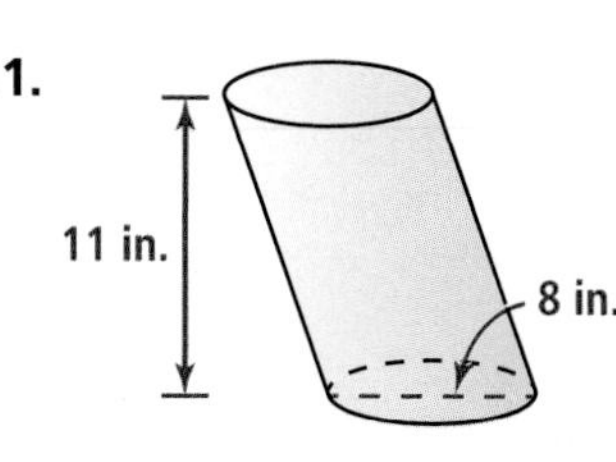


12. Which figures have the same volume? Explain.

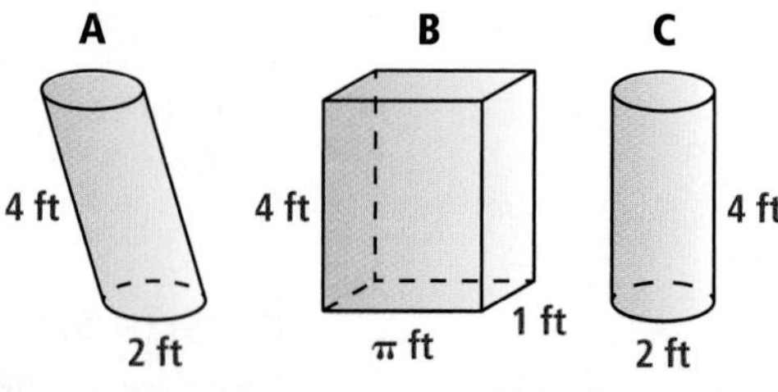

# PRACTICE & PROBLEM SOLVING

Scan for Multimedia

Additional Exercises Available Online

## UNDERSTAND

**13. Error Analysis** Dylan compares the volumes of two bottles. What is Dylan's error?

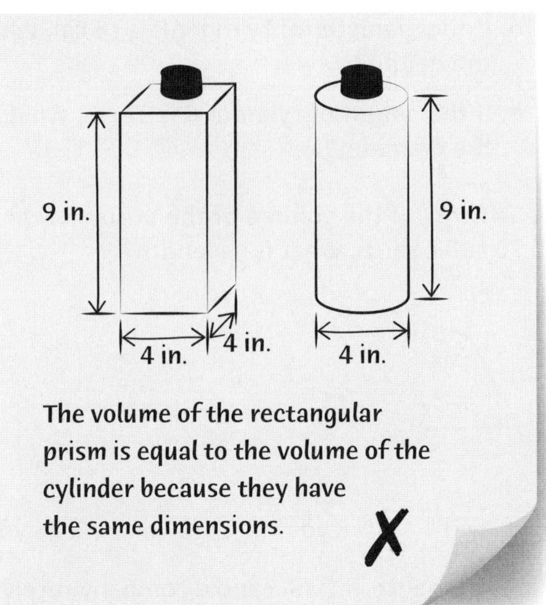

9 in.
9 in.
4 in.
4 in.
4 in.
The volume of the rectangular prism is equal to the volume of the cylinder because they have the same dimensions.
X


**14. Higher Order Thinking** Does Cavalieri's Principle apply to the volumes of the cones shown? Explain.

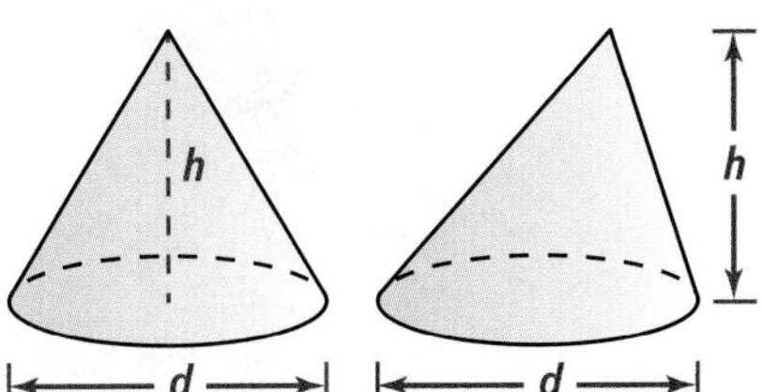


**15. Mathematical Connections** Does rotating the rectangle about line $m$ result in a cylinder with the same volume as rotating the rectangle about line $n$? Explain.

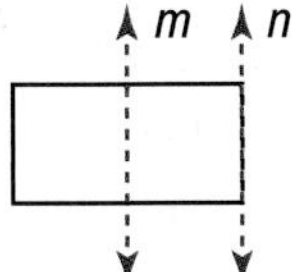


**16. Use Appropriate Tools** Do the prisms shown have equivalent volumes? Explain.

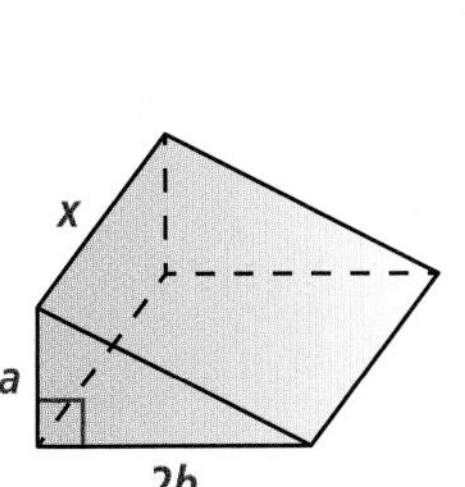


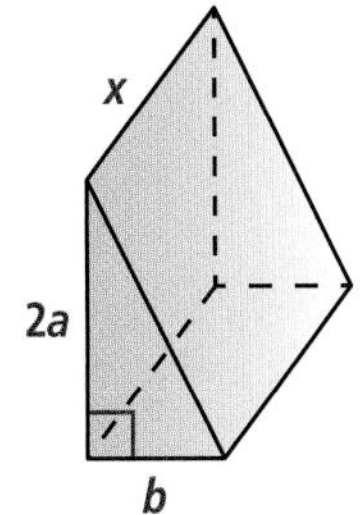


## PRACTICE

**17.** Katrina buys the two vases shown. How do the volumes of the vases compare? Explain. SEE EXAMPLE 1

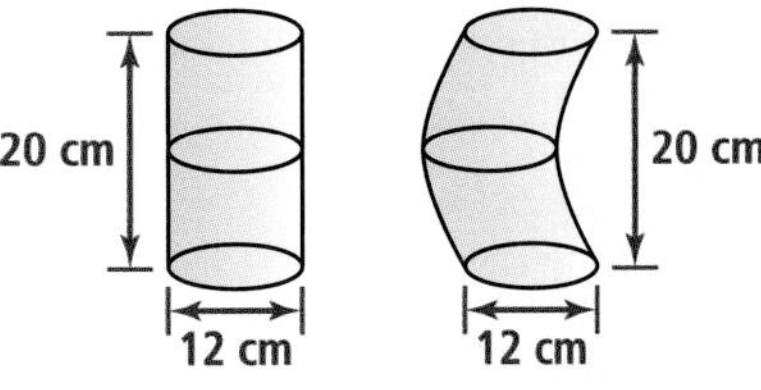


**18.** Talisa plans a 6-foot deep pond. While digging, she hits rock 5 feet down. How can Talisa modify the radius to maintain the original volume of the pond? SEE EXAMPLE 2

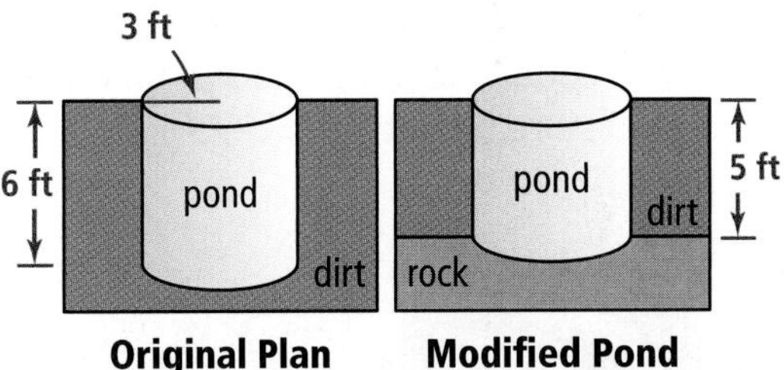


**19.** The instructions for plant food say to use 0.25 gram per cubic inch of soil. How many grams of plant food should Jordan use if the planter box shown is full of soil? SEE EXAMPLE 3

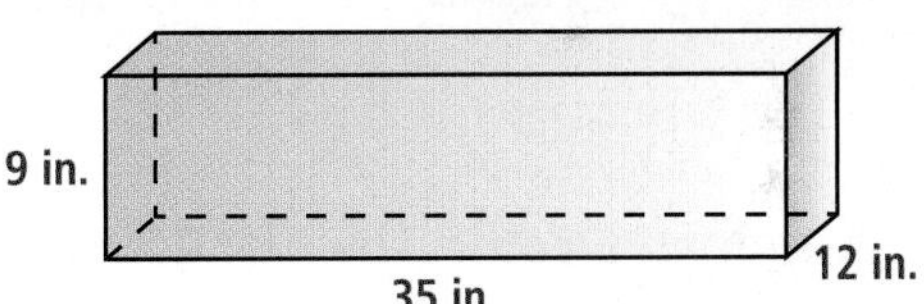


**20.** If a stack of 40 nickels fits snugly in the coin wrapper shown, how thick is 1 nickel? Round to the nearest hundredth. SEE EXAMPLE 4

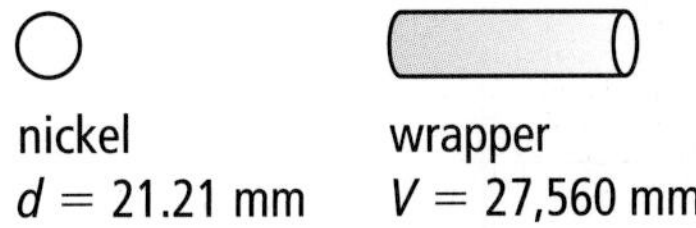

nickel
$d = 21.21$ mm

wrapper
$V = 27{,}560 \text{ mm}^3$

**21.** Sections of two flood-control ditches are shown. Which one holds the greater volume of water per foot? Explain. SEE EXAMPLE 5

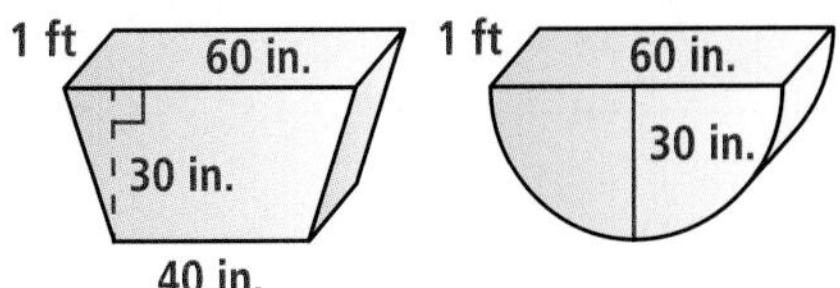

# PRACTICE & PROBLEM SOLVING

## APPLY

**22. Use Appropriate Tools** How many 3-inch-thick bags of mulch should Noemi buy to cover 100 square feet at a depth of 4 inches?

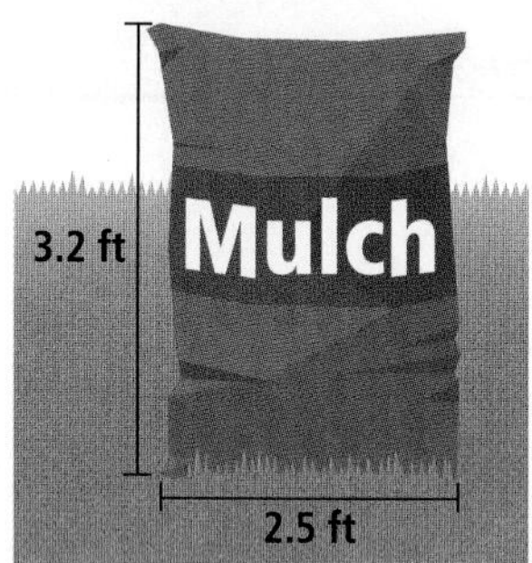


**23. Reason** Ines's younger brother will be home in a half hour. If her garden hose flows at a rate 24 gal/min, does she have enough time to fill the pool before he gets home? Explain. (*Hint:* 1 $ft^3$ = 7.48 gal)

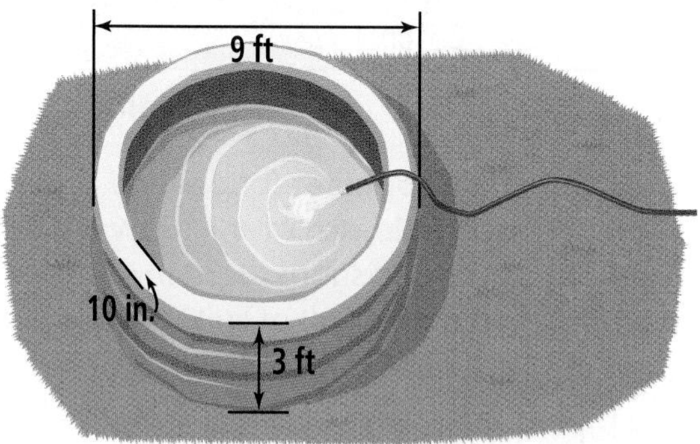


**24. Model With Mathematics** The ABC Cookie Company wants to promise an average of "12 chocolate chips per cookie." Assuming that the cookies fill about 80% of the box by volume, will 600 chocolate chips for each box of cookies be sufficient to make the claim? Explain.

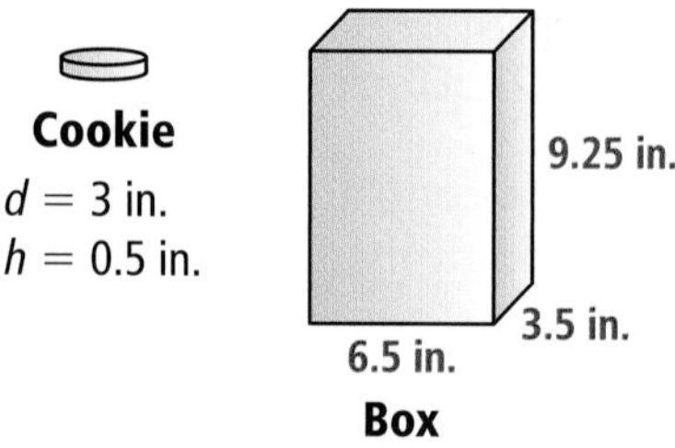


## ASSESSMENT PRACTICE

**25.** Cylinders A, B, and C have the same volume. Cylinder A has diameter 12 cm and height 8 cm.

**a.** If the diameter of cylinder B is 16 cm, what is the height?

**b.** If the height of cylinder C is 32 cm, what is the diameter?

**26. SAT/ACT** If the volume of the prism shown is 70 cubic yards, what is its length?

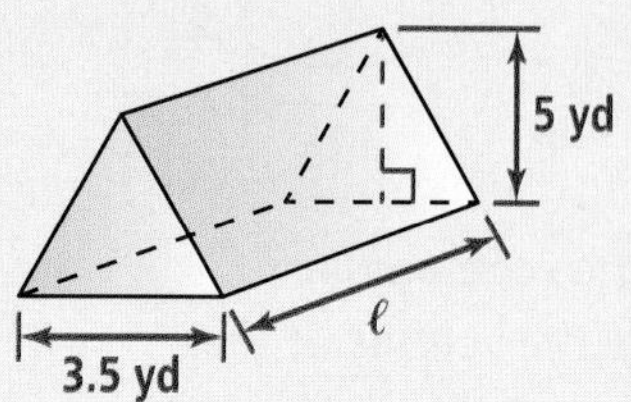


Ⓐ 4 yd Ⓑ 8 yd Ⓒ 16 yd Ⓓ 28 yd

**27. Performance Task** A candle company receives an order for an overnight delivery of 8 short candles and 6 tall candles. The overnight service has a weight limit of 23 kg.

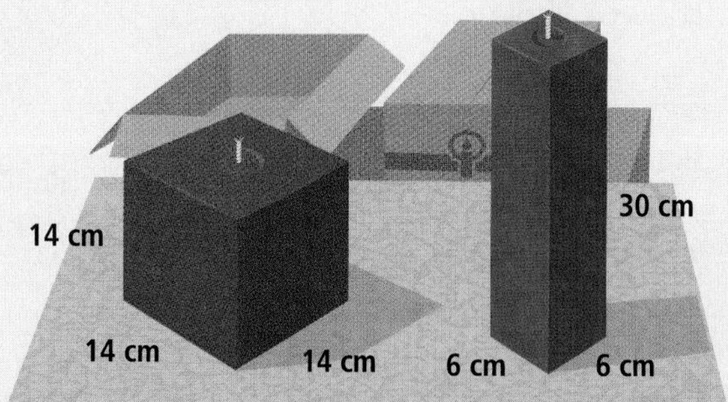


**Part A** The density of the wax used to make each candle is 0.0009 kg/$cm^3$. What is the weight of the order? Can the order be filled and shipped for delivery?

**Part B** If no tall candles are included in the order, what is the greatest number of short candles that can be delivered?

**Part C** What combination of tall and short candles can be delivered if the total number of candles delivered is 10?

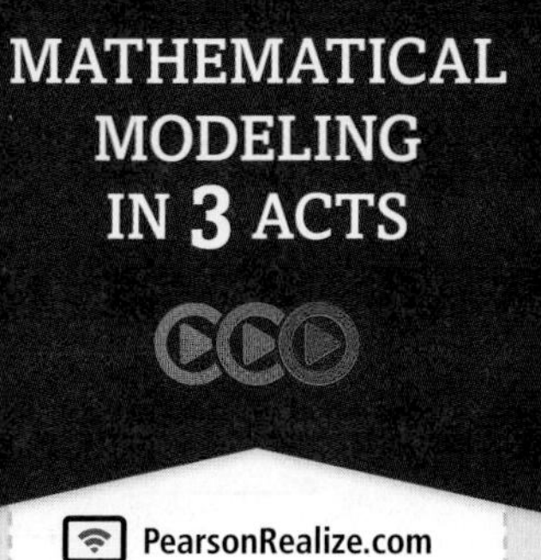


PearsonRealize.com

## Box 'Em Up

With so many people and businesses shopping online, retailers, and especially e-retailers, ship more and more packages every day. Some of the products people order have unusual sizes and shapes and need custom packaging. Imagine how you might package a surfboard, or a snow blower, or even live crawfish to ship to someone's house!

Think about this during the Mathematical Modeling in 3 Acts lesson.

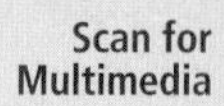

### ACT 1 Identify the Problem

1. What is the first question that comes to mind after watching the video?
2. Write down the main question you will answer about what you saw in the video.
3. Make an initial conjecture that answers this main question.
4. Explain how you arrived at your conjecture.
5. What information will be useful to know to answer the main question? How can you get it? How will you use that information?

### ACT 2 Develop a Model

6. Use the math that you have learned in this Topic to refine your conjecture.

### ACT 3 Interpret the Results

7. Did your refined conjecture match the actual answer exactly? If not, what might explain the difference?

# 11-3 Pyramids and Cones

PearsonRealize.com

**I CAN…** use the volumes of right and oblique pyramids and cones to solve problems.

## EXPLORE & REASON

**Consider the cube and pyramid.**

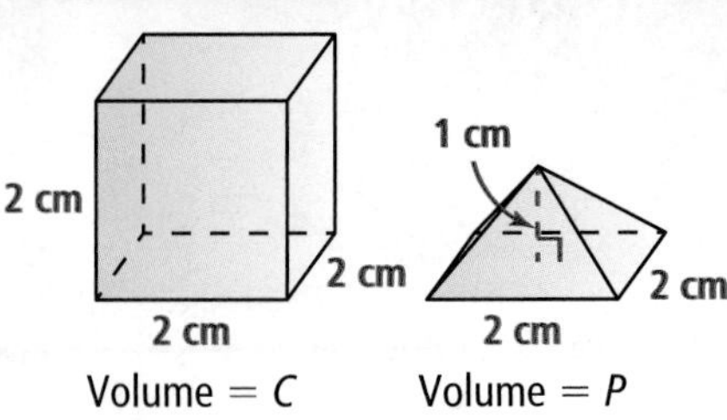


**A.** How many pyramids could you fit inside the cube? Explain.

**B.** Write an equation that shows the relationship between $C$ and $P$.

**C. Look for Relationships** Make a conjecture about the volume of any pyramid. Explain your reasoning.

**ESSENTIAL QUESTION** How are the formulas for volume of a pyramid and volume of a cone alike?

CONCEPTUAL UNDERSTANDING

## EXAMPLE 1 Apply Cavalieri's Principle to Pyramids and Cones

**How are the volumes of pyramids and cones with the same base area and height related?**

Imagine a set of cardboard discs, each with a slightly smaller radius than the previous disc. You can stack the discs in different ways.

**GENERALIZE**
Think about the shape formed by the stacks. What would happen if the number of discs increases while the difference in the radii and the thickness of each disc decreases?

The heights of the stacks are the same, and the area at each level is the same. The total volume of cardboard in each stack is the same.

The stacks approximate cones. You can apply Cavalieri's Principle to cones and pyramids.

If two figures have the same height and equal area at every cross section, they have equal volumes.

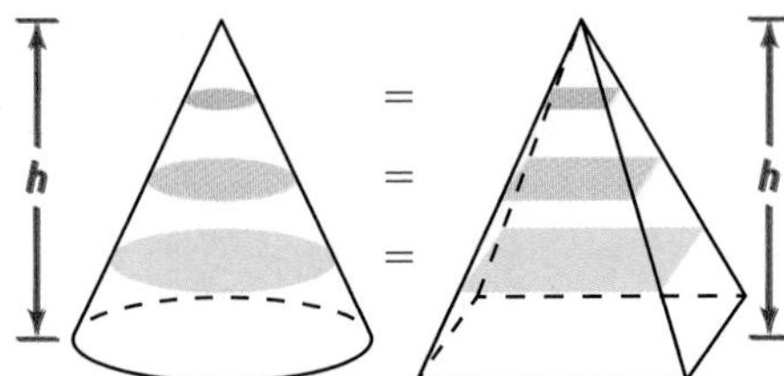

**Try It!** 1. Is it possible to use only Cavalieri's Principle to show that a cone and a cylinder have equal volumes? Explain.

## CONCEPT Volumes of Pyramids and Cones

The volume of a pyramid is one-third the product of the area of the base and the height of the pyramid.

$$V = \frac{1}{3}Bh$$

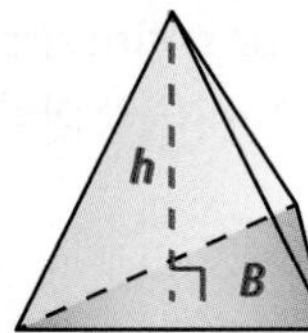


The volume of a cone is one-third the product of the area of the base and the height of the cone.

$$V = \frac{1}{3}Bh$$

$$V = \frac{1}{3}\pi r^2 h$$

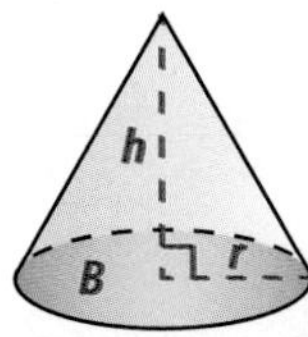

## EXAMPLE 2 Find the Volumes of Pyramids and Cones

**A. Kyle's truck can haul 1.75 tons of corn per load. One cubic meter of corn weighs 0.8 ton. How many loads will Kyle haul to move this pile of corn?**

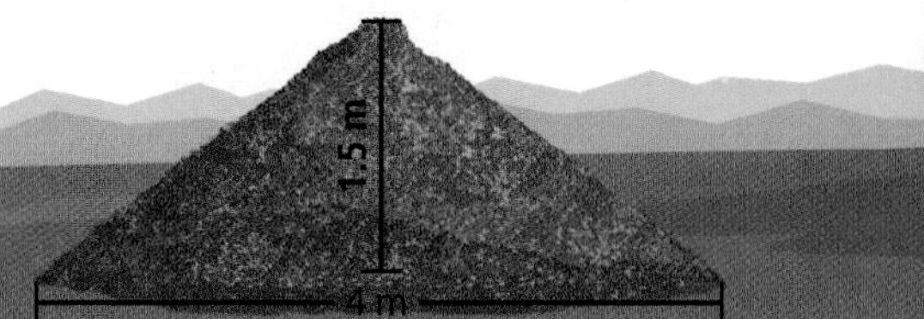


$V = \frac{1}{3}\pi r^2 h$

$= \frac{1}{3}\pi(2)^2(1.5) \approx 6.3 \text{ m}^3$

The pile is shaped like a cone, so use the volume formula for cones.

Since $6.3 \text{ m}^3 \cdot 0.8 \text{ ton/m}^3 = 5.04$ tons, Kyle will need to haul $5.04 \div 1.75 = 2.88$ or 3 loads.

**B. Jason is using the mold to make 12 candles. How many cubic inches of wax does he need?**

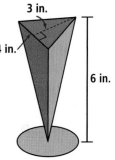

3 in.
4 in.
6 in.

$V = \frac{1}{3}Bh$

Use the volume formula for a pyramid.

$= \frac{1}{3}\left[\frac{1}{2}(4)(3)\right](6) = 12 \text{ in.}^3$

Use the area formula for a triangle to find the base.

For 12 candles, Jason needs $12 \text{ in.}^3 \cdot 12$, or $144 \text{ in.}^3$ of wax.

**STUDY TIP**
The base of a pyramid can be any polygon, so the formula you use to determine the area of the base *B* depends on the shape of the base.

**Try It!** 2. a. What is the volume of a cone with base diameter 14 and height 16?

b. What is the volume of a pyramid with base area 10 and height 7?

## EXAMPLE 3 Apply the Volumes of Pyramids to Solve Problems

**Dyani is 1.8 m tall and wants to be able to stand inside her new tent. Should she buy this tent?**

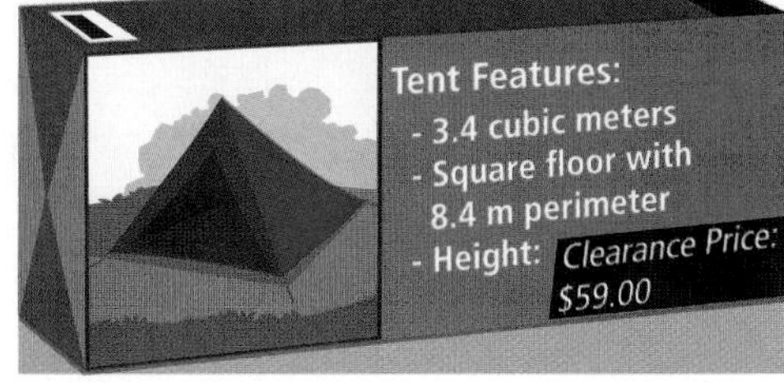


**Step 1** Draw and label a square pyramid to represent the tent.

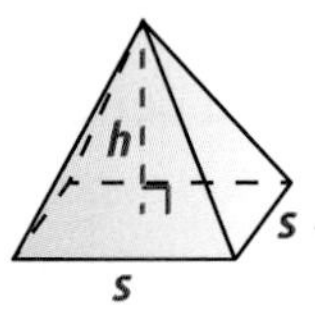


Since the perimeter of the square floor is 8.4 m, $s = 2.1$ m.

**Step 2** Find the height of the pyramid.

$V = \frac{1}{3}Bh$

$3.4 = \frac{1}{3}(2.1)^2 h$

$h \approx 2.3$

The height of the pyramid is approximately 2.3 m.

Dyani will be able to stand in the tent, so she should buy this tent.

CONTINUED ON THE NEXT PAGE

 **Try It!** **3.** A rectangular pyramid has a base that is three times as long as it is wide. The volume of the pyramid is 75 $ft^3$ and the height is 3 ft. What is the perimeter of the base?

APPLICATION

## EXAMPLE 4 Apply the Volumes of Cones to Solve Problems

**A restaurant sells smoothies in two sizes. Which size is a better deal?**

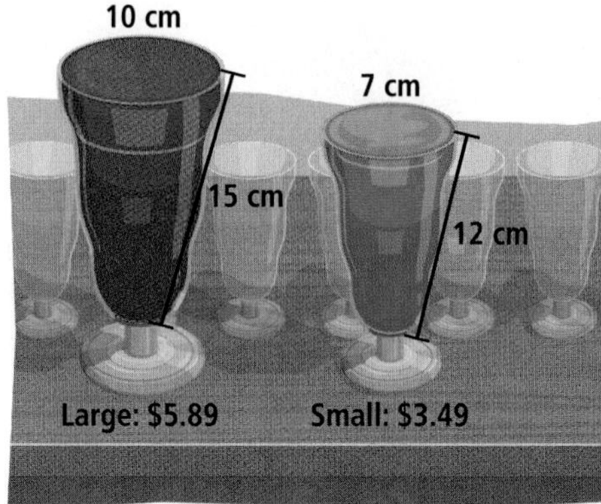


**Formulate** Compare the prices by determining the cost per cubic centimeter for each size.

The volume of fruit smoothie in each glass can be approximated as the volume of a cone.

**Compute** **Step 1** Calculate the height of each cone using the Pythagorean Theorem.

**Large**

$$5^2 + h^2 = 15^2$$
$$h^2 = 200$$
$$h \approx 14.1$$

The height of the large cone is approximately 14.1 cm.

**Small**

$$3.5^2 + h^2 = 12^2$$
$$h^2 = 131.75$$
$$h \approx 11.5$$

The height of the small cone is approximately 11.5 cm.

**Step 2** Calculate the volume of each cone.

**Large**

$$V = \frac{1}{3}\pi r^2 h$$
$$= \frac{1}{3}\pi(5)^2(14.1)$$
$$\approx 369.1$$

The volume of the large cone is approximately 369.1 $cm^3$.

**Small**

$$V = \frac{1}{3}\pi r^2 h$$
$$= \frac{1}{3}\pi(3.5)^2(11.5)$$
$$\approx 147.5$$

The volume of the small cone is approximately 147.5 $cm^3$.

**Step 3** Calculate the cost per cubic centimeter for each size.

**Large**

$$\frac{\$5.89}{369.1 \text{ cm}^3} \approx \$0.016 \text{ per cm}^3$$

**Small**

$$\frac{\$3.49}{147.5 \text{ cm}^3} \approx \$0.024 \text{ per cm}^3$$

**Interpret** The large size smoothie costs less per cubic centimeter, so the large size smoothie is a better deal.

CONTINUED ON THE NEXT PAGE

 **Try It!** **4.** A cone has a volume of $144\pi$ and a height of 12.

**a.** What is the radius of the base?

**b.** If the radius of the cone is tripled, what is the new volume? What is the relationship between the volumes of the two cones?

APPLICATION

## EXAMPLE 5 Measure a Composite Figure

**Kaitlyn is making a concrete animal sculpture. Each bag of concrete mix makes 0.6 ft$^3$ of concrete. How many bags of concrete mix does Kaitlyn need?**

Calculate the volume of each part.

**Step 1** Calculate the volume of one of the legs.

$$V = \pi r^2 h$$
$$= \pi(2)^2(16)$$
$$\approx 201 \text{ in.}^3$$

The legs are oblique cylinders.

**Step 2** Calculate the volume of the body.

$$V = Bh$$
$$= (22 \cdot 18)(15)$$
$$= 5{,}940 \text{ in.}^3$$

The body is a rectangular prism.

**Step 3** Calculate the volume of the head.

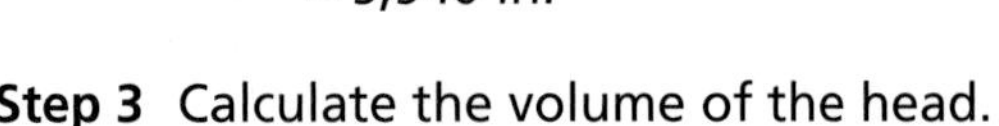

$$V = \frac{1}{3}Bh$$
$$= \frac{1}{3}(16 \cdot 16)(20)$$
$$\approx 1{,}707 \text{ in.}^3$$

The head is a square pyramid.

**COMMON ERROR**
When multiple parts of a composite figure have the same volume, make sure you account for each part in your total.

**Step 4** Calculate the total volume.

$$V = 4(201) + 5{,}940 + 1{,}707$$
$$= 8{,}451$$

Add the volumes of the parts of the sculpture.

The total volume is 8,451 in.$^3$. Convert to cubic feet to determine the amount of concrete needed.

$$8{,}451 \cdot \frac{1}{1{,}728} = 4.9$$

$1 \text{ ft}^3 = (12 \text{ in.})^3 = 1{,}728 \text{ in.}^3$

To make the sculpture, 4.9 ft$^3$ of concrete is needed. Kaitlyn needs $4.9 \div 0.6 \approx 8.2$ or 9 bags of concrete mix.

 **Try It!** **5.** A cone-shaped hole is drilled in a prism. The height of the triangular base is 12 cm. What is the volume of the remaining figure? Round to the nearest tenth.

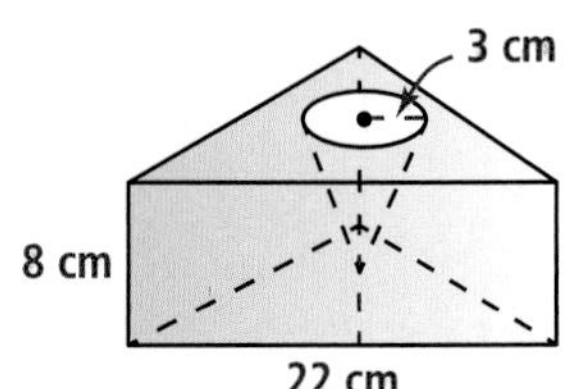

## CONCEPT SUMMARY Pyramids and Cones

**WORDS**

The volume of a pyramid is one-third the volume of a prism with the same base area and height.

The volume of a cone is one-third the volume of a cylinder with the same base area and height.

**DIAGRAMS**

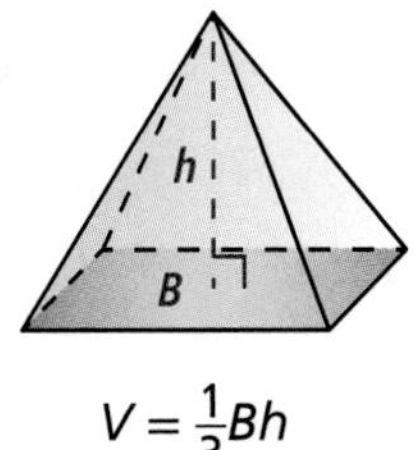


$V = \frac{1}{3}Bh$

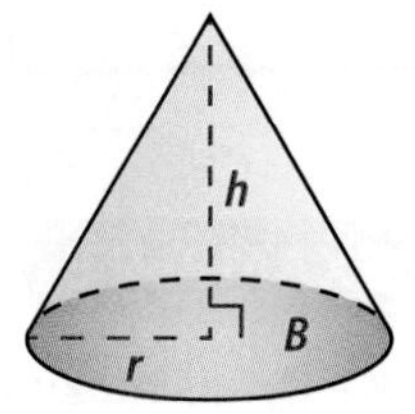


$V = \frac{1}{3}Bh$ or $V = \frac{1}{3}\pi r^2 h$

## Do You UNDERSTAND?

1. **ESSENTIAL QUESTION** How are the formulas for volume of a pyramid and volume of a cone alike?

2. **Error Analysis** Zhang is finding the height of a square pyramid with a base side length of 9 and a volume of 162. What is his error?

   $V = Bh$
   $162 = 9^2(h)$
   $h = 2$
   ✗

3. **Reason** A cone and cylinder have the same radius and volume. If the height of the cone is $h$, what is the height of the cylinder?

4. **Construct Arguments** Do you have enough information to compute the volume of the cone? Explain.

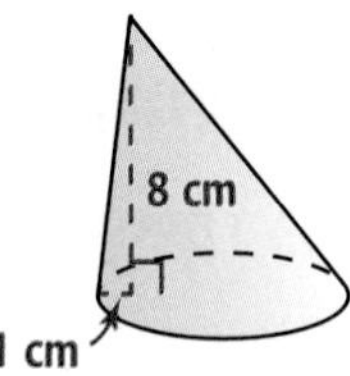


## Do You KNOW HOW?

**For Exercises 5–10, find the volume of each figure. Round to the nearest tenth. Assume that all angles in each polygonal base are congruent.**

5. 
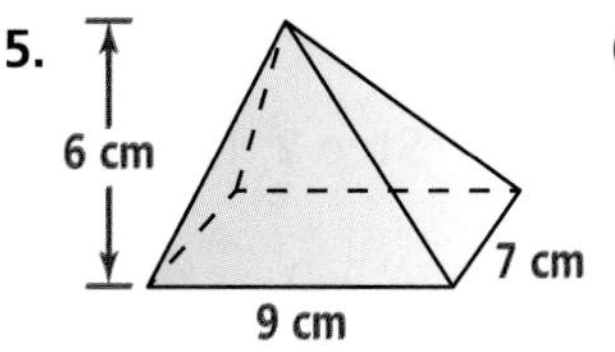


6. 
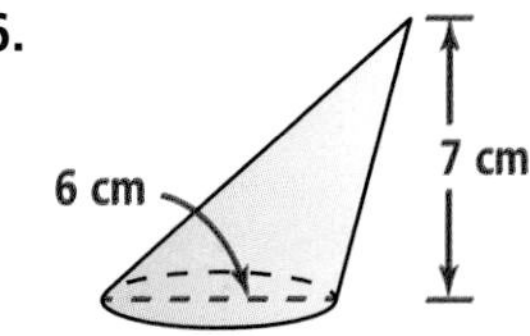


7. 8 in.; 3 in.

8. 
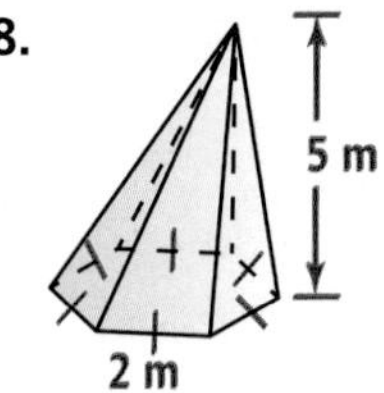


9. 24 ft; 11 ft; 18 ft; 12 ft

10. 
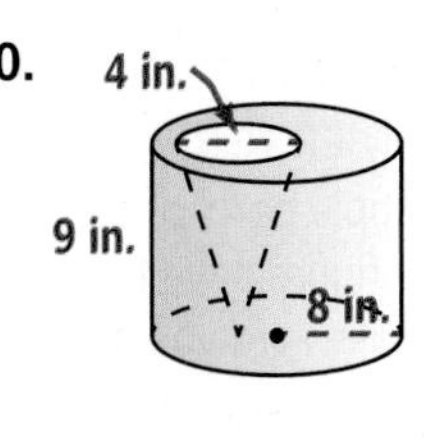


11. A solid metal square pyramid with a base side length of 6 in. and height of 9 in. is melted down and recast as a square pyramid with a height of 4 in. What is the base side length of the new pyramid?

# PRACTICE & PROBLEM SOLVING

Scan for Multimedia

Practice Tutorial

Additional Exercises Available Online

## UNDERSTAND

12. **Construct Arguments** A stack of 39 pennies is exactly as tall as a stack of 31 nickels. Do the two stacks have the same volume? Explain.

13. **Error Analysis** Jacob is finding the volume of the cylinder. What is his error?

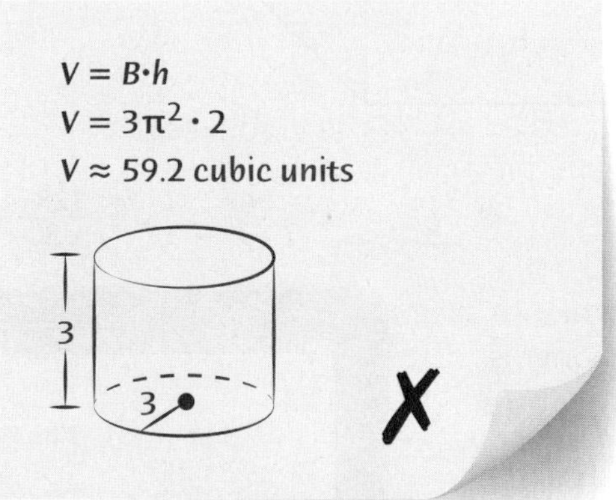


14. **Communicate Precisely** How would you find the volume of a right square pyramid with a base side length of 10 cm, and the altitude of a triangular side is 13 cm? Explain.

15. **Mathematical Connections** In terms of the radius $r$, what is the volume of a cone whose height is equal to its radius?

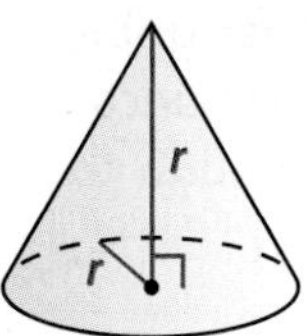


16. **Higher Order Thinking** A plane slices a cone parallel to the base at one-half of the height of the cone. What is the volume of the part of the cone lying below the plane?

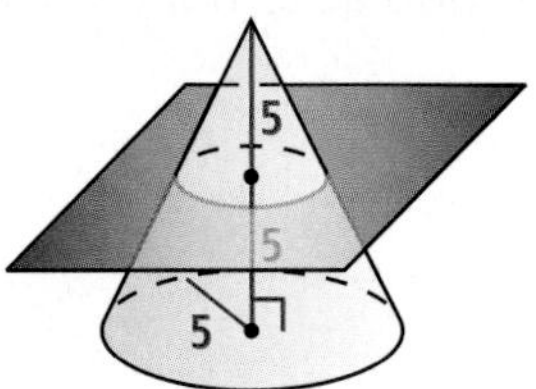


## PRACTICE

17. The plane intersects sections of equal area in the two solids. Are the volumes equal?
SEE EXAMPLE 1

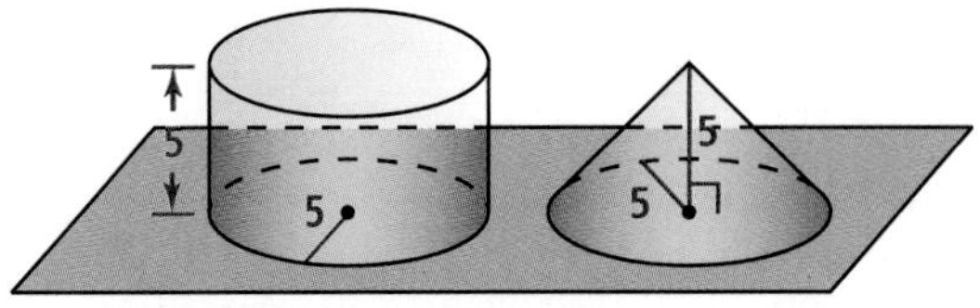


**For Exercises 18–21, find the volume of each solid. Assume that all angles in each polygonal base are congruent.** SEE EXAMPLE 2

18.

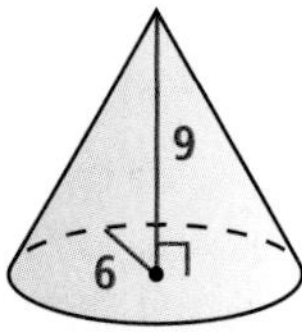


19.

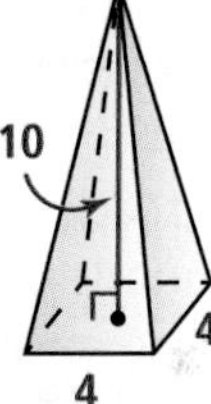

20.

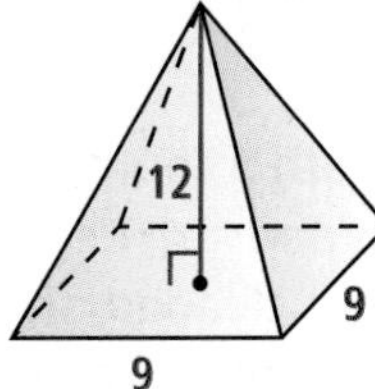


21.

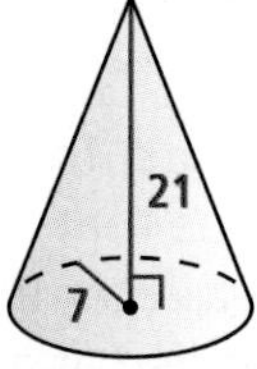


22. A cone is inscribed in a right square pyramid. What is the remaining volume if the cone is removed? SEE EXAMPLES 3 AND 4

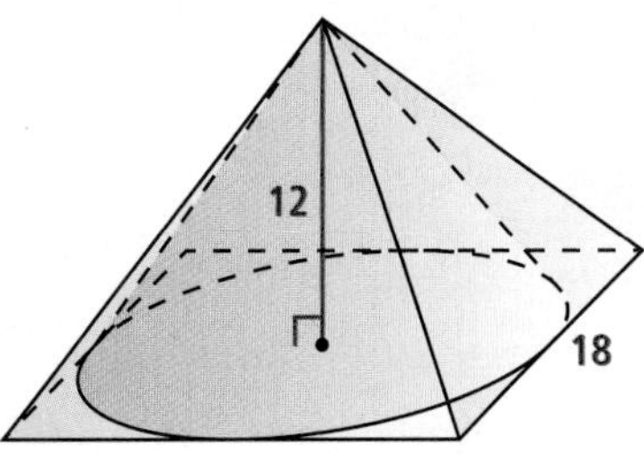


**For Exercises 23 and 24, find the volume of each composite figure.** SEE EXAMPLE 5

23.

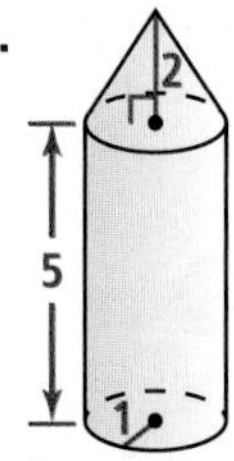


24.

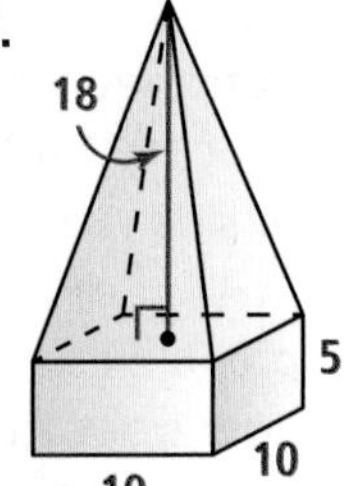

APPLY

25. **Make Sense and Persevere** Chiang makes gift boxes in the shape of a right square pyramid. She fills each box with chocolate cubes with $\frac{7}{8}$-in. sides. She can fill about 75% of a box. How many pieces can she fit in each box?

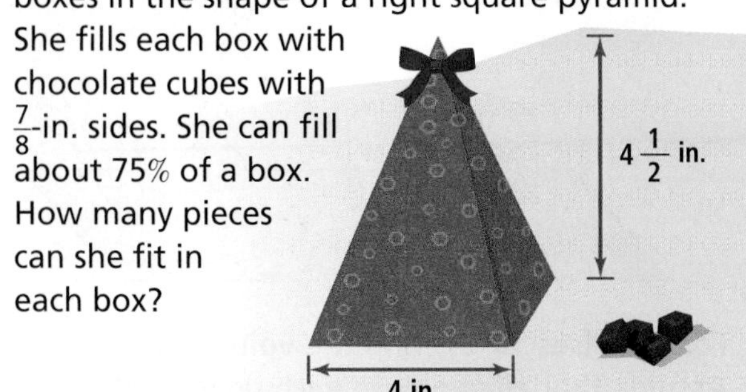


26. **Reason** A pile of snow is plowed into the shape of a right cone. How many trucks with a capacity of 10 $yd^3$ per truck will be needed to move the pile?

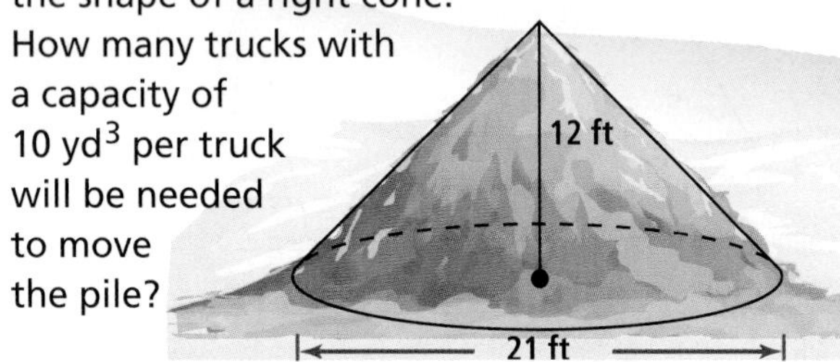


27. **Use Structure** The basin beneath a fountain is a right cone that is 7 m across and 1 m deep at the center. After the fountain is cleaned, the pool is refilled at a rate of 300 L/min. One cubic meter is 1,000 L. How long does it take to refill the pool?

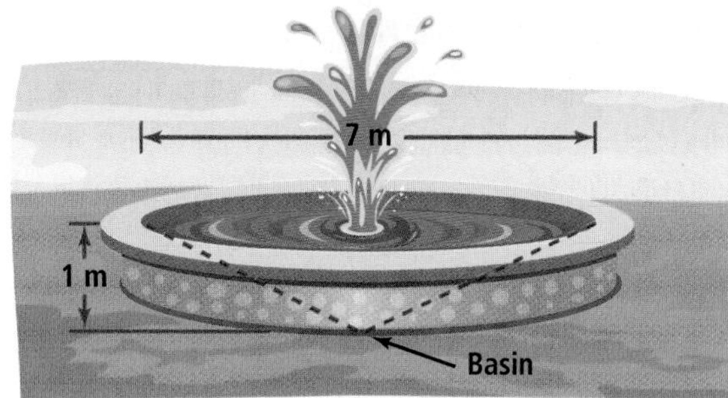


28. **Model With Mathematics** A physicist wants to know what percentage of gas is empty space. A molecule of methane can be modeled by a regular tetrahedron with side length 0.154 nm ($1 \text{ nm} = 1 \times 10^{-9}$ m). The altitude of each triangular side is 0.133 nm. If $6.022 \times 10^{23}$ molecules make up 0.0224 $m^3$ of gas, how does the volume of the molecules compare to the volume of the gas?

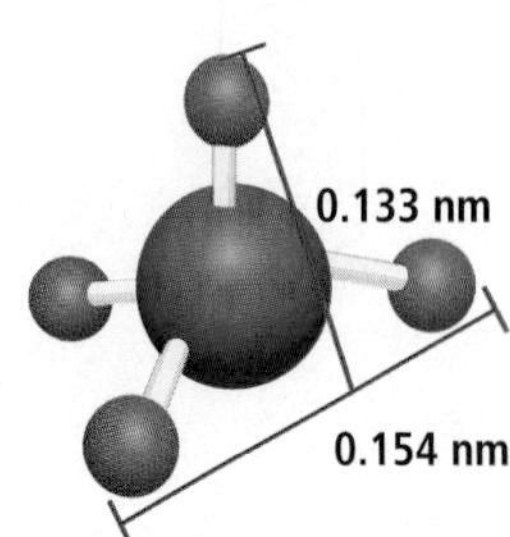


ASSESSMENT PRACTICE

29. Cavalieri's Principle states that if two solids have the same __?__ and the same __?__ at every cross section, then the two solids have the same __?__.

30. **SAT/ACT** Which is the volume of the largest cone that will fit entirely within the right square prism?

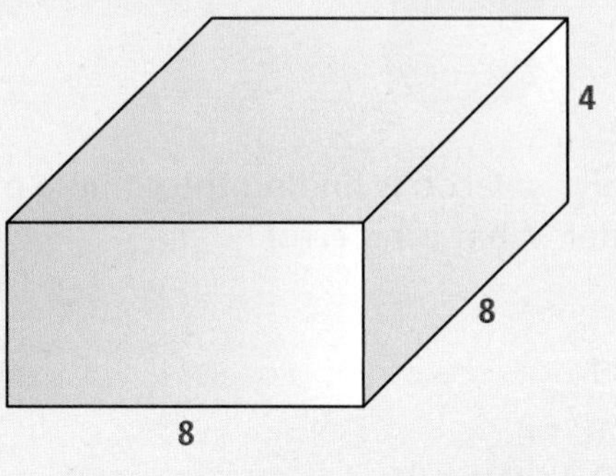


Ⓐ $\frac{16\pi}{3}$ Ⓑ $\frac{32\pi}{3}$ Ⓒ $\frac{64\pi}{3}$ Ⓓ $\frac{128\pi}{3}$

31. **Performance Task** A designer is working on a design for two goblets. Design A is based on a cylinder and design B is based on a cone. The client wants both goblets to be the same height and width.

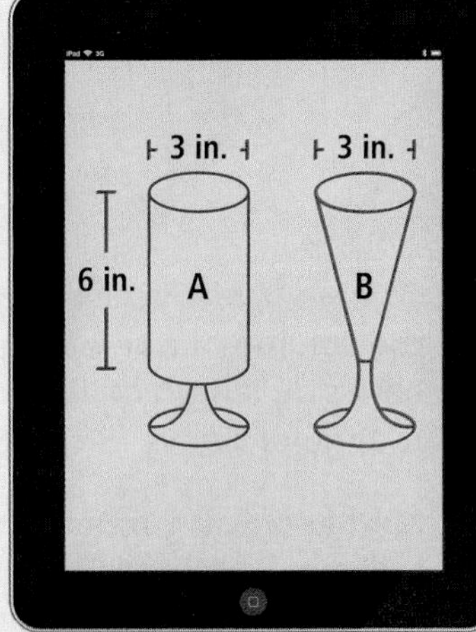


**Part A** The client wants the smaller goblet to hold at least 10 fl oz. One fluid ounce is 1.8 $in.^3$. Will design B be large enough to meet the client's requirements? Explain.

**Part B** The client wants the larger goblet to hold 20 fl oz. Does design A meet the client's requirement? Explain.

**Part C** How could design B be changed if the client wants the smaller goblet to hold at least 12 fl oz?

# 11-4 Spheres

PearsonRealize.com

**I CAN…** calculate the volume of a sphere and solve problems involving the volumes of spheres.

**VOCABULARY**

- hemisphere

## CRITIQUE & EXPLAIN

**Ricardo estimates the volume of a sphere with radius 2 by placing the sphere inside a cylinder and placing two cones inside the sphere. He says that the volume of the sphere is less than $16\pi$ and greater than $\frac{16}{3}\pi$.**

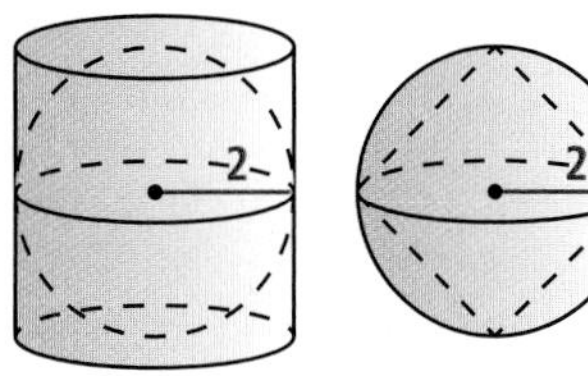


**A.** Do you agree with Ricardo? Explain.

**B. Reason** How might you estimate the volume of the sphere?

**ESSENTIAL QUESTION** **How does the volume of a sphere relate to the volumes of other solids?**

CONCEPTUAL UNDERSTANDING

## EXAMPLE 1 Explore the Volume of a Sphere

**What is the volume of a sphere? Why does the volume formula for a sphere make sense?**

A plane, parallel to the bases, intersects half of a sphere with radius $r$ and a cylinder with radius $r$ and height $r$. The cylinder has a cone with radius $r$ and height $r$ removed from its center.

**USE APPROPRIATE TOOLS**
Think about how you can draw the section of the cylinder with the cone removed. What does the cross section look like?

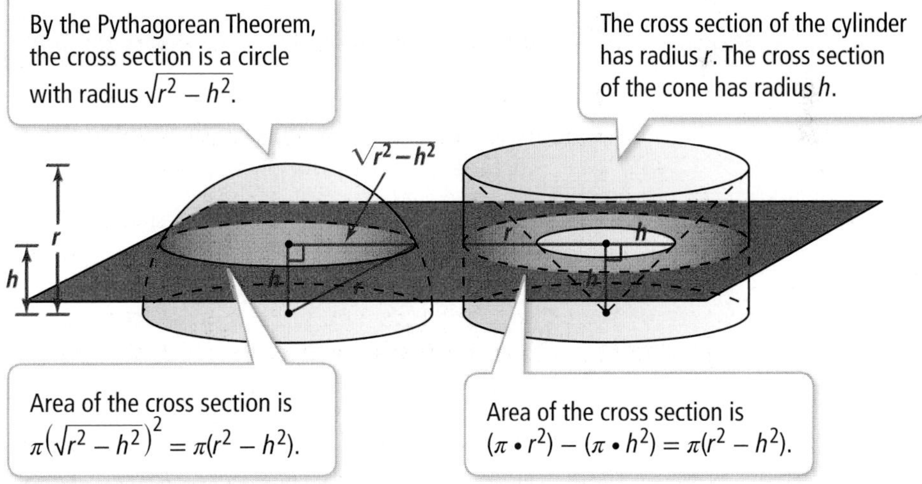

By the Pythagorean Theorem, the cross section is a circle with radius $\sqrt{r^2 - h^2}$.
The cross section of the cylinder has radius $r$. The cross section of the cone has radius $h$.
$\sqrt{r^2 - h^2}$
$r$
$h$
Area of the cross section is $\pi\left(\sqrt{r^2 - h^2}\right)^2 = \pi(r^2 - h^2)$.
Area of the cross section is $(\pi \cdot r^2) - (\pi \cdot h^2) = \pi(r^2 - h^2)$.


Once the cone is removed, the areas of the cross sections of the solids are equal at any height. Therefore, by Cavalieri's Principle, the two solids have the same volume.

$$\begin{aligned}\text{volume of half a sphere} &= \text{volume of cylinder} - \text{volume of cone}\\ &= \pi r^2 \cdot r - \frac{1}{3}\pi r^2 \cdot r\\ &= \frac{2}{3}\pi r^3\end{aligned}$$

The volume of a sphere is twice the volume of half of the sphere, so the volume of a sphere with radius $r$ is $\frac{4}{3}\pi r^3$.

CONTINUED ON THE NEXT PAGE

 **Try It!** **1.** Find the volumes of the three solids. What do you notice?

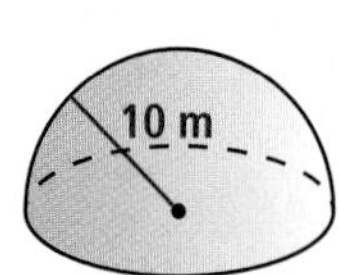


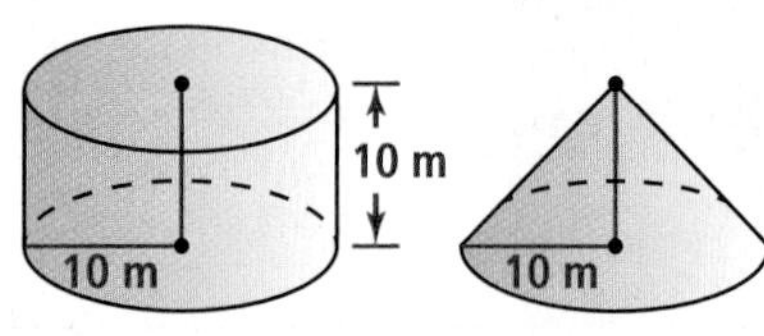


## CONCEPT Volume of a Sphere

The volume of a sphere is four-thirds of the product of $\pi$ and the cube of the radius of the sphere.

$V = \frac{4}{3}\pi r^3$

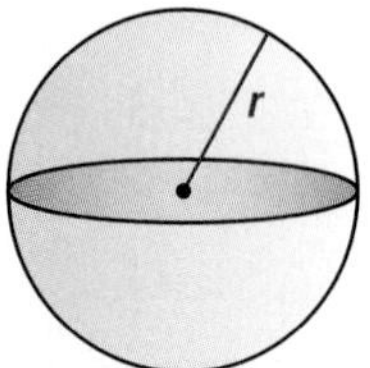


APPLICATION

## EXAMPLE 2 Use the Volumes of Spheres to Solve Problems

**The drama club makes a big ball from foam to hang above the stage for a play. They plan to cover the surface of the ball with metallic fabric. What is the minimum number of square meters of fabric that the club needs?**

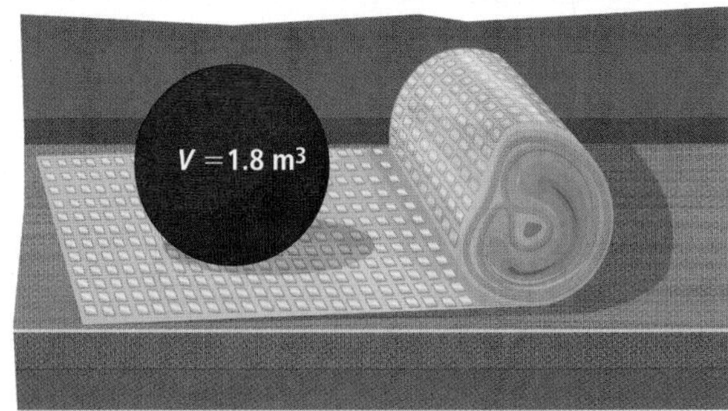


Use the volume formula to determine the radius of the ball. Then use the surface area formula of a sphere.

First find $r$ from the volume of the ball.

$V = \frac{4}{3}\pi r^3$ — Use the volume formula.

$1.8 = \frac{4}{3}\pi r^3$

$r^3 = \frac{1.35}{\pi}$ — Use a calculator to find the cube root.

$r \approx 0.75$

**STUDY TIP**
Remember that the surface area of a sphere is four times the area of a circle with the same radius.

The radius of the ball is about 0.75 m. Next, calculate the surface area.

The surface area of a sphere with radius $r$ is S.A. $= 4\pi r^2$.

S.A. $= 4\pi r^2$

S.A. $= 4\pi(0.75)^2$ — Substitute the radius into the surface area formula.

S.A. $\approx 7.1$

The club needs at least 7.1 $m^2$ of fabric.

 **Try It!** **2.** What is the largest volume a sphere can have if it is covered by 6 $m^2$ of fabric?

## EXAMPLE 3 Find the Volumes of Hemispheres

**What is the volume of the hemisphere?**

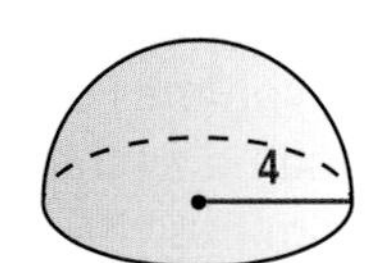


A *great circle* is the intersection of a sphere and a plane containing the center of the sphere.

**VOCABULARY**
The prefix *hemi* is from the Greek and means *half*. Thus, hemisphere means half-sphere.

A great circle divides a sphere into two **hemispheres**.

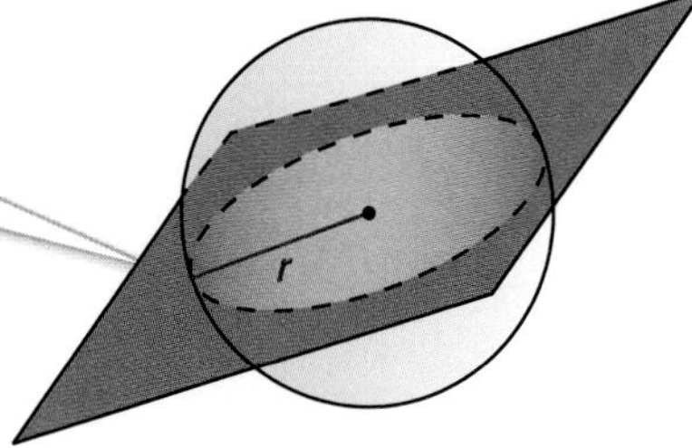


The volume of a hemisphere is one-half the volume of a sphere with the same radius.

$$V = \frac{2}{3}\pi r^3$$

$$V = \frac{2}{3}\pi \cdot 4^3 \approx 134.04$$

**Try It!** **3. a.** What is the volume of a hemisphere with radius 3 ft?

**b.** What is the volume of a hemisphere with diameter 13 cm?

## EXAMPLE 4 Find the Volumes of Composite Figures

**A solid is composed of a right cylinder and a hemisphere as shown. If the density of the solid is 100 kg/m$^3$, what is the mass of the solid?**

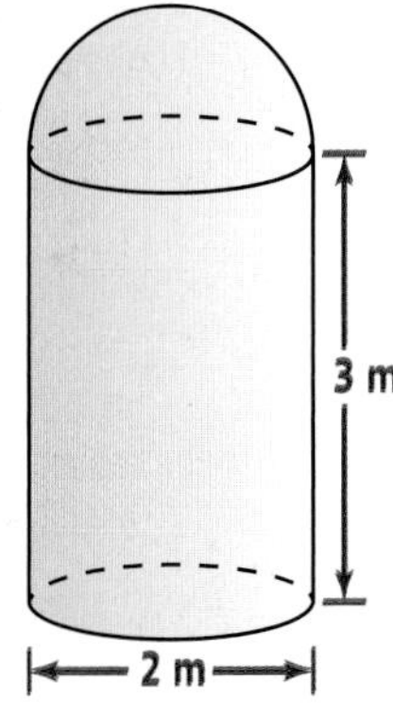


Find the volume of the solid.

**COMMON ERROR**
As you break a composite figure into figures or parts of figures you are familiar with, be careful not to mix up the measurements of each figure.

$$\begin{aligned} \text{volume of solid} &= \text{volume of cylinder} \\ &\quad + \text{volume of hemisphere} \\ &= \pi r^2 h + \frac{2}{3}\pi r^3 \\ &= \pi(1)^2(3) + \frac{2}{3}\pi(1)^3 \\ &\approx 11.5 \end{aligned}$$

The volume of the solid is about 11.5 m$^3$. Next, find the mass of the solid.

$$11.5 \cdot 100 = 1{,}150$$

The mass of the solid is about 1,150 kg.

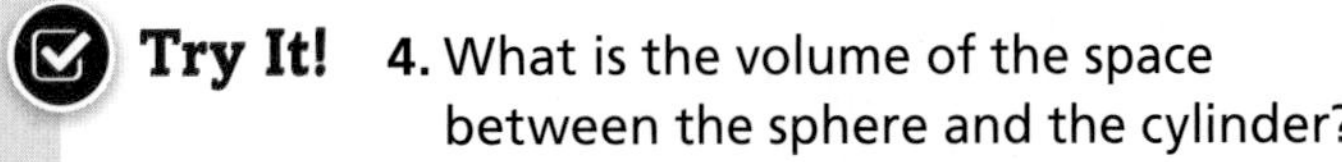

**Try It!** **4.** What is the volume of the space between the sphere and the cylinder?

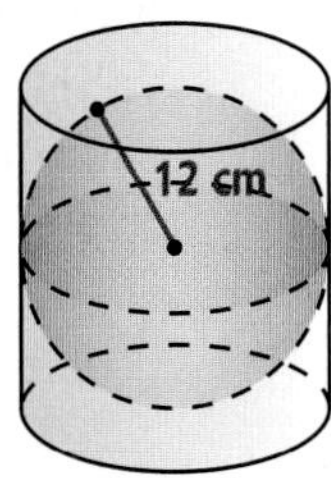

## CONCEPT SUMMARY Volume of Spheres

**WORDS** Cavalieri's Principle can be used to show how the volume of the sphere is related to the volumes of a cylinder and cone. The area of a cross section of a hemisphere is the same as the area of a cross section of a cylinder with height equal to the radius minus the cross section of a cone with height equal to the radius.

**DIAGRAMS**

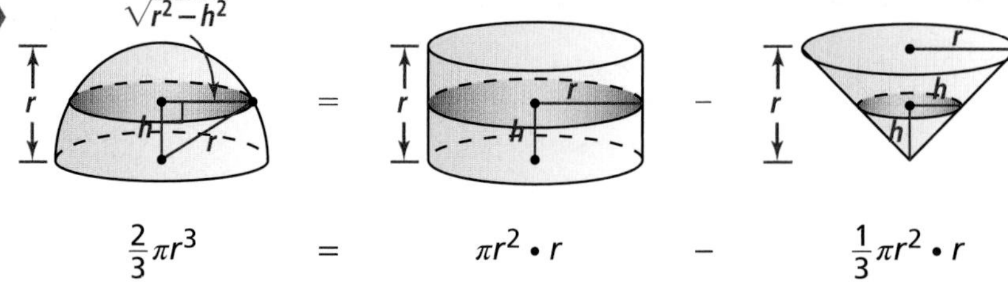


$$\frac{2}{3}\pi r^3 = \pi r^2 \cdot r - \frac{1}{3}\pi r^2 \cdot r$$

## Do You UNDERSTAND?

1. **ESSENTIAL QUESTION** How does the volume of a sphere relate to the volumes of other solids?

2. **Error Analysis** Reagan is finding the volume of the sphere. What is her error?

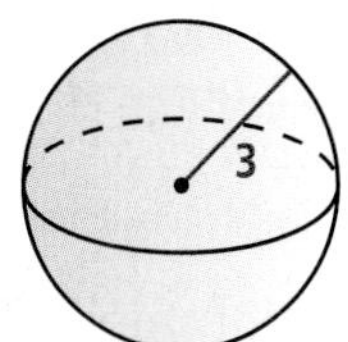


$$S.A. = \frac{4}{3}\pi r^3$$
$$S.A. = \frac{4}{3} \cdot \pi \cdot 3^3$$
$$S.A. \approx 113.1 \text{ square units}$$

3. **Vocabulary** How does a great circle define a hemisphere?

4. **Reason** The radius of a sphere, the base radius of a cylinder, and the base radius of a cone are $r$. What is the height of the cylinder if the volume of the cylinder is equal to the volume of the sphere? What is the height of the cone if the volume of the cone is equal to the volume of the sphere?

## Do You KNOW HOW?

**For Exercises 5 and 6, find the surface area of each solid.**

5.

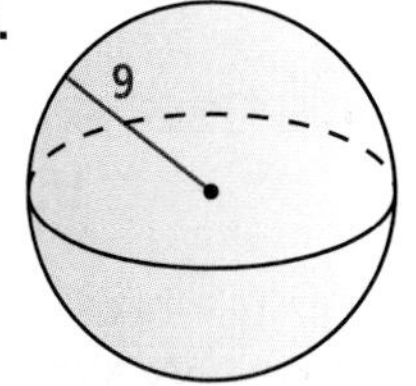


6.

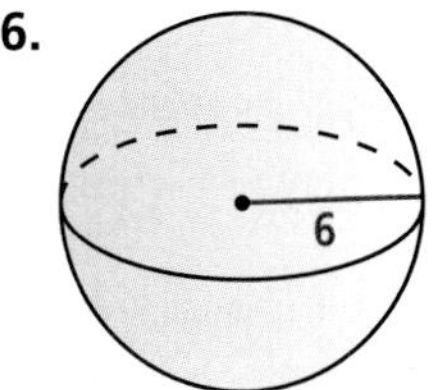


**For Exercises 7 and 8, find the volume of each solid.**

7.

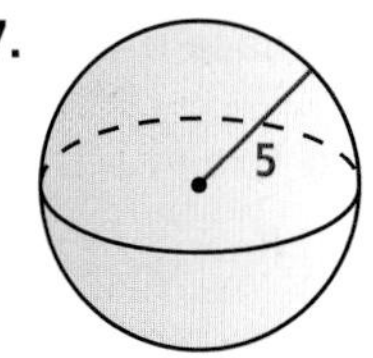


8.

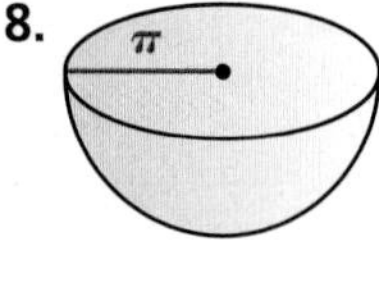


9. Find the volume of the largest sphere that can fit entirely in the rectangular prism.

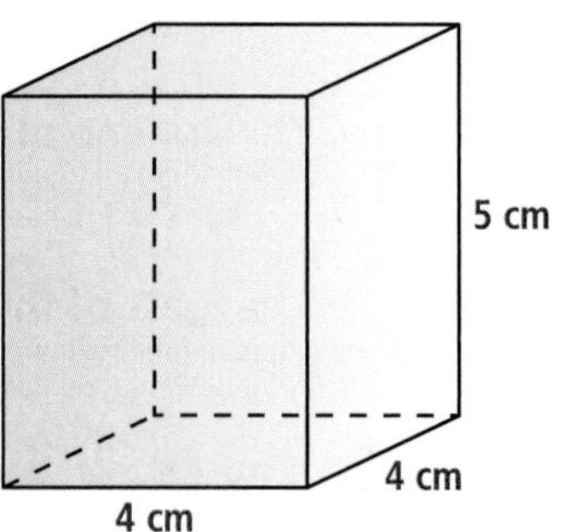


10. Find the volume and surface area of a sphere with radius 1.

## UNDERSTAND

**11. Construct Arguments** How does Cavalieri's Principle apply to finding the volume of a hemisphere? Explain.

**12. Error Analysis** Kayden is finding the surface area of the sphere. What is her error?

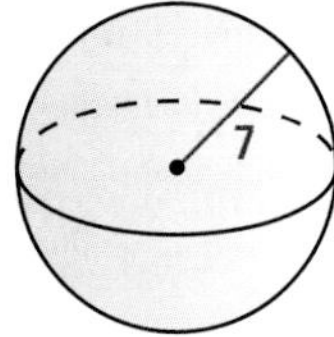


S.A. $= 4\pi r^2$
S.A. $= 4 \cdot \pi \cdot 14^2$
S.A. $\approx$ 2,463.0 square units

**13. Mathematical Connections** Given the surface area of a sphere, write a formula for the volume of a sphere in terms of the surface area.

**14. Construct Arguments** Fifteen cylinders and 15 rectangular prisms are stacked. Each cylinder has the same top surface area and height as each rectangular prism. What can you determine about the volumes of the two stacks of 15 solids? Explain.

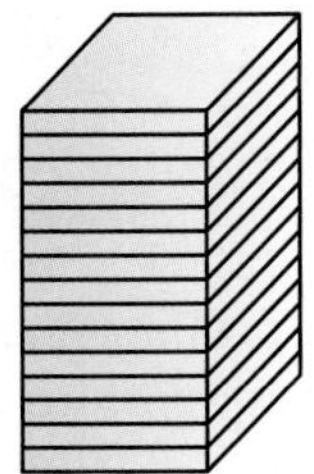

**15. Reason** A sphere is divided by two great circles that are perpendicular to each other. How would you find the surface area and volume of each part of the sphere between the two planes containing the great circles? Explain.

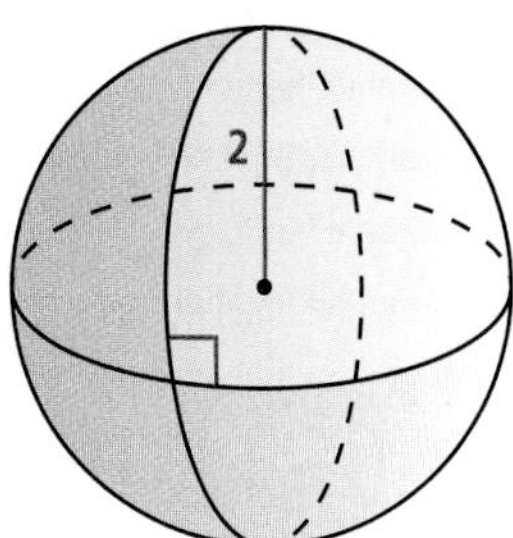


## PRACTICE

**For Exercises 16–18, find the area of each cross section.** SEE EXAMPLE 1

**16.**

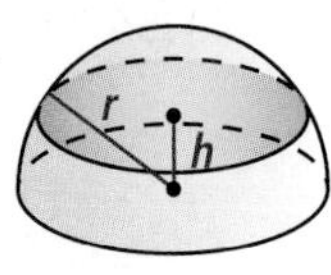


**17.**

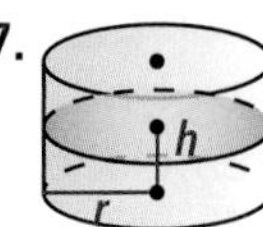


**18.**

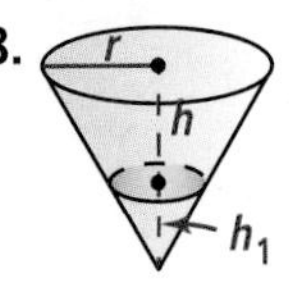


**For Exercises 19–22, find the surface area of each solid to the nearest tenth.** SEE EXAMPLE 2

**19.**

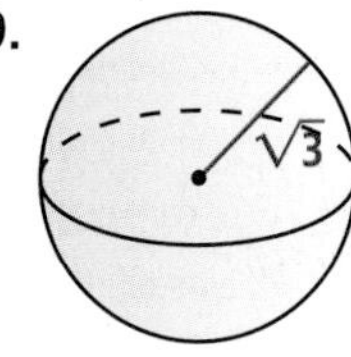


**20.**

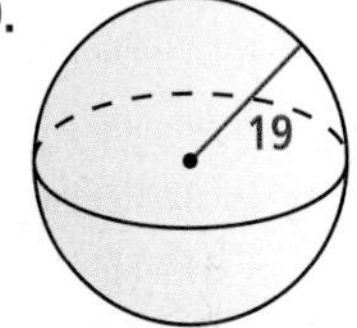


**21.** sphere with volume 35 $cm^3$

**22.** sphere with volume 100 $in.^3$

**For Exercises 23–26, find the volume of each solid to the nearest tenth.** SEE EXAMPLES 2 AND 3

**23.**

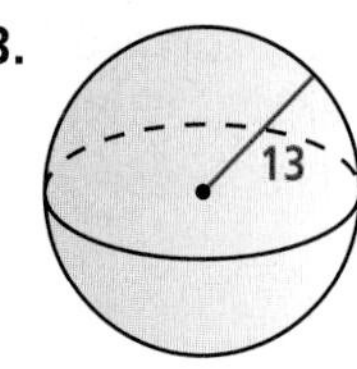


**24.**

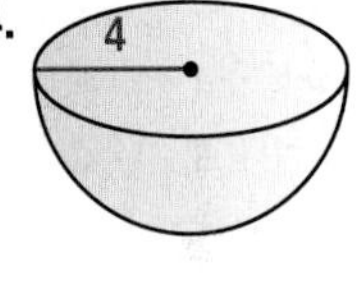


**25.** hemisphere with radius 12 ft

**26.** sphere with radius 25 m

**For Exercises 27 and 28, find the volume of each composite figure to the nearest tenth.**
SEE EXAMPLE 4

**27.**

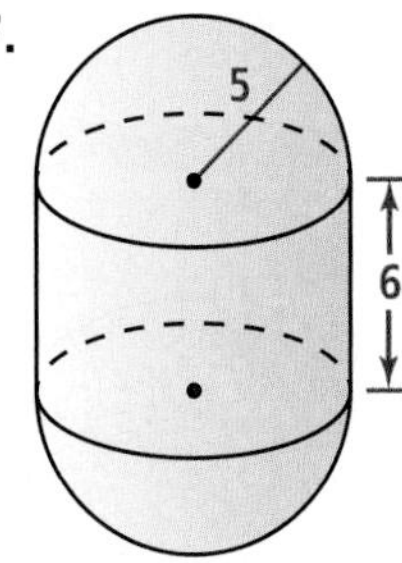


**28.**

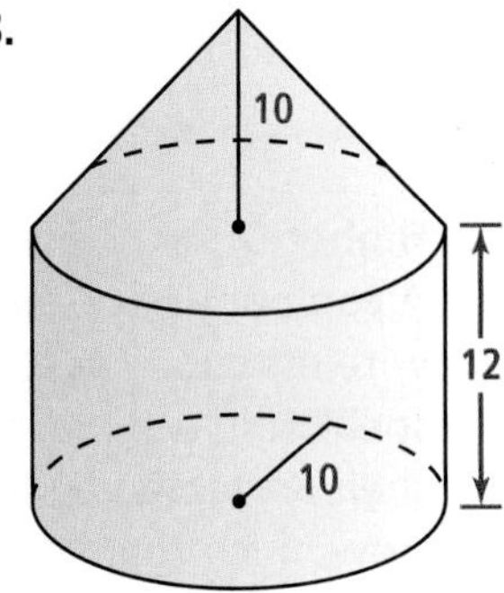

# PRACTICE & PROBLEM SOLVING

## APPLY

**29. Make Sense and Persevere** To reach the regulation pressure for a game ball, the amount of air pumped into a ball is 1.54 times the volume of the ball. A referee adds 15 in.$^3$ of air for each pump of air. How many pumps of air will it take the referee to fill an empty ball?

**30. Reason** Jeffery uses a block of clay to make round beads. How many beads can he make from the block?

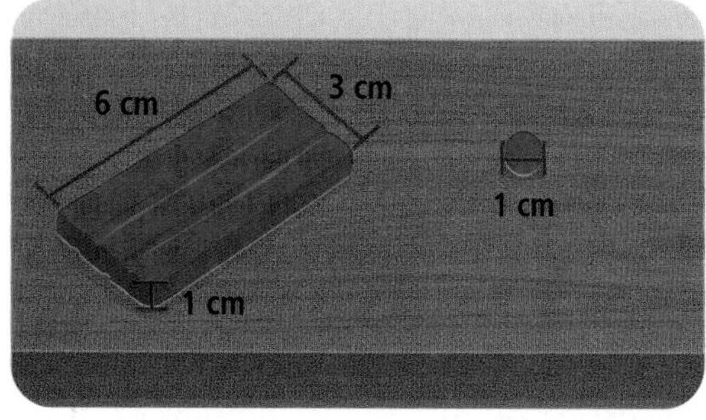


**31.** Felipe places a spherical round-bottom flask in a cylindrical beaker containing hot water. The flask must fit into the beaker with 2 cm of space around the flask. What is the minimum diameter $d$ of the beaker?

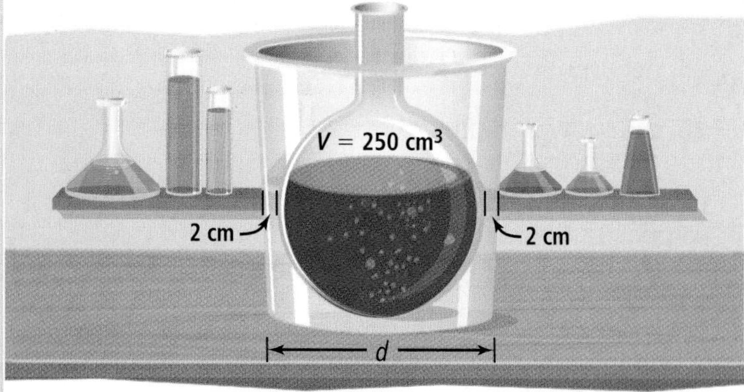


**32. Higher Order Thinking** A company packs each wireless cube-shaped speaker in a spherical shell protected by foam. How much foam does the company use for each speaker?

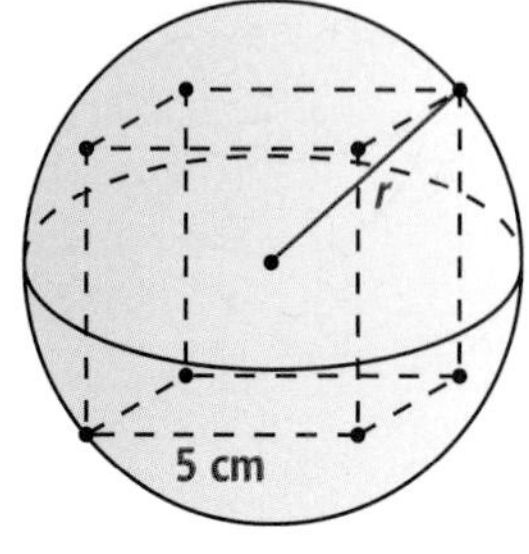


## ASSESSMENT PRACTICE

**33.** Match each description with its expression.

I. volume of a sphere with radius 1

II. surface area of a sphere with radius 2

III. circumference of a great circle for a sphere with radius 3

IV. volume of a hemisphere with radius 2

A. $\frac{4}{3}\pi$

B. $\frac{16}{3}\pi$

C. $6\pi$

D. $16\pi$

**34. SAT/ACT** The surface area of a sphere is $64\pi$ ft$^2$. What is the radius of the sphere?

Ⓐ 64 ft

Ⓑ 16 ft

Ⓒ 8 ft

Ⓓ 4 ft

**35. Performance Task** Jayesh is to fill the tank shown with liquid propane.

**Part A** The liquid propane expands and contracts as the temperature changes, so a propane tank is never filled to more than 80% capacity with liquid propane. How much liquid propane should Jayesh put in the tank?

**Part B** If Jayesh has 20 m$^3$ of liquid propane to fill another tank. What are the dimensions of the tank if the length of the cylindrical part is three times the diameter?

# TOPIC 11

# Topic Review

## TOPIC ESSENTIAL QUESTION

1. How is Cavalieri's Principle helpful in understanding the volume formulas for solids?

## Vocabulary Review

**Choose the correct term to complete each sentence.**

2. A prism is ________ if one or more faces are not perpendicular to the bases.
3. ________ describes the relationship between the volumes of three-dimensional figures that have the same height and the same cross sectional area at every level.
4. A great circle divides a sphere into two ________.

- Cavalieri's Principle
- cones
- cylinders
- hemispheres
- oblique
- right
- spheres

## Concepts & Skills Review

### LESSON 11-1 Three-Dimensional Figures and Cross Sections

#### Quick Review

The faces of a polyhedron are polygons. Euler's Formula states that the relationship between the number of faces $F$, number of vertices $V$, and number of edges $E$ is

$$F + V = E + 2$$

The cross section of a plane and a convex polyhedron is a polygon.

Rotating a polygon about an axis forms a three-dimensional figure.

#### Example

**A triangular prism has 5 faces and 9 edges. How many vertices does it have?**

$$F + V = E + 2$$

$$5 + V = 9 + 2$$

$$V = 6$$

The prism has 6 vertices.

#### Practice & Problem Solving

**For Exercises 5 and 6, use the pyramid shown.**

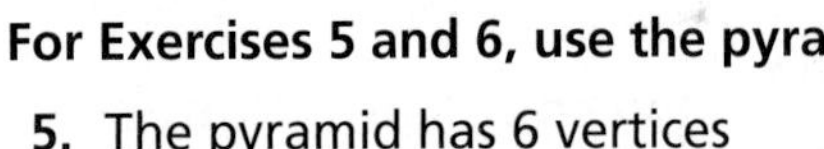

5. The pyramid has 6 vertices and 10 edges. How many faces does it have?

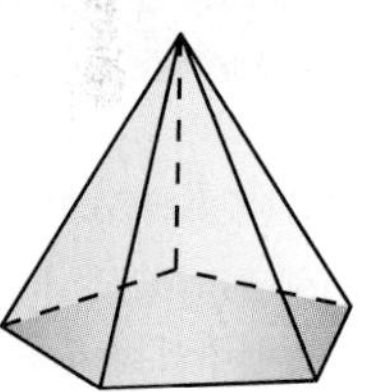

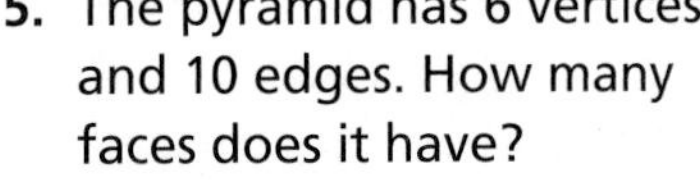

6. Visualize a plane intersecting the pyramid parallel to the base. Describe the cross section.

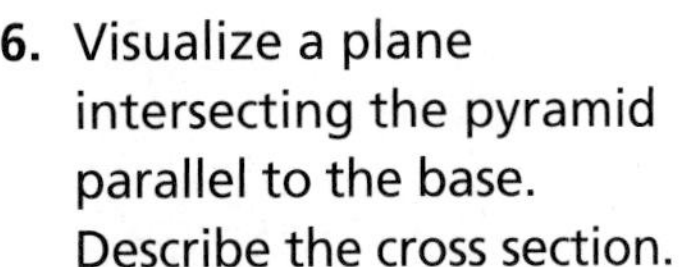

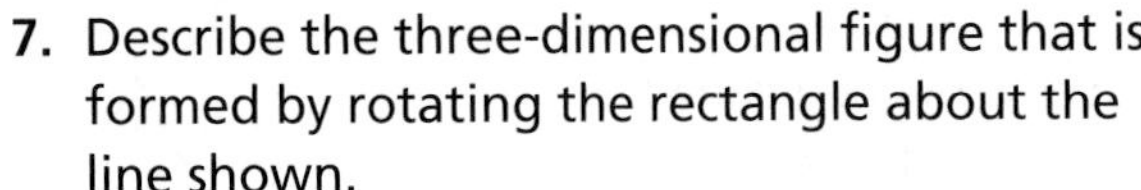

7. Describe the three-dimensional figure that is formed by rotating the rectangle about the line shown.

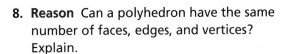

8. **Reason** Can a polyhedron have the same number of faces, edges, and vertices? Explain.

## LESSON 11-2 Volumes of Prisms and Cylinders

### Quick Review

**Cavalieri's Principle** states that figures with the same height and same area at every horizontal cross section have the same volume.

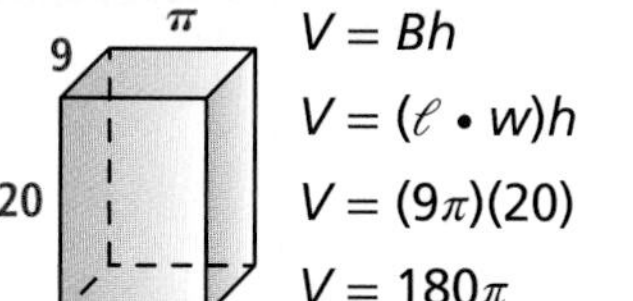


$V = Bh$
$V = (\ell \cdot w)h$
$V = (9\pi)(20)$
$V = 180\pi$

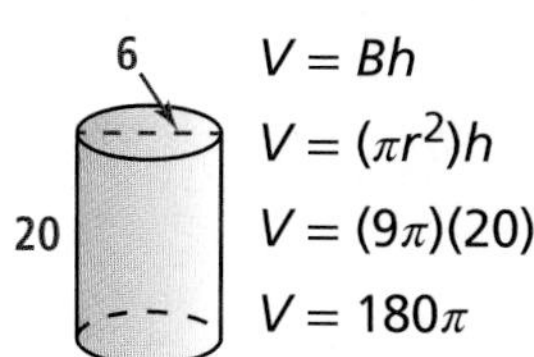


$V = Bh$
$V = (\pi r^2)h$
$V = (9\pi)(20)$
$V = 180\pi$

### Example

**Do the cylinders have the same volume? Explain.**

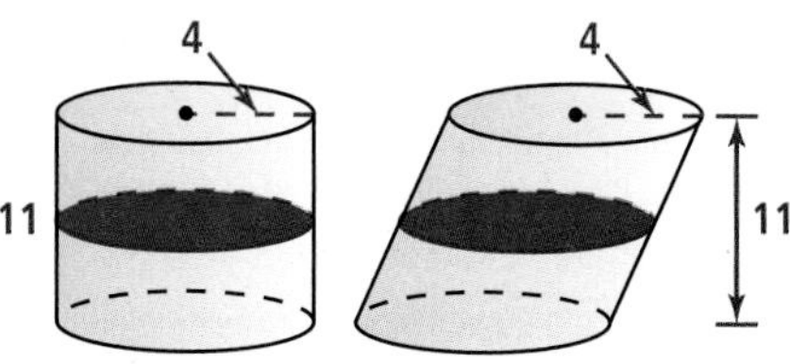


Yes, cylinders with the same base area and height have the same volume. The height of each cylinder is 11. The area of the base of each cylinder is $\pi(4)^2$, or $16\pi$.

### Practice & Problem Solving

**For Exercises 9 and 10, find the volume of each figure. Round to the nearest tenth.**

**9.**

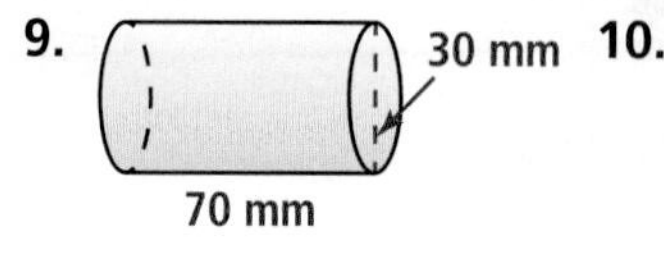


**10.**

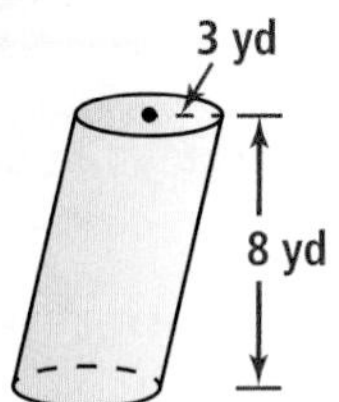


**11. Reason** What does the expression $\frac{3}{4}xyz$ represent for the prism shown?

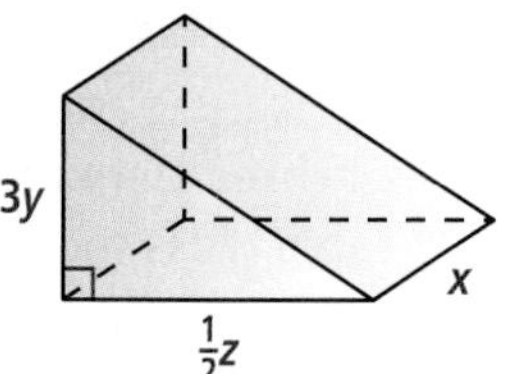


**12.** Malia pours wax in molds to make candles. Compare the amount of wax each mold holds.

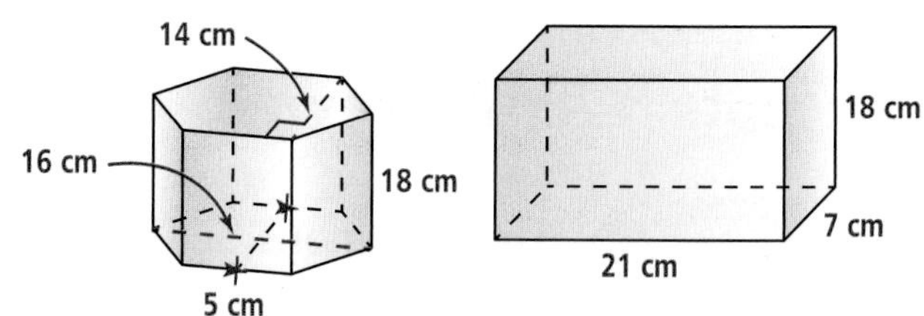


## LESSON 11-3 Pyramids and Cones

### Quick Review

The volume of a pyramid is one-third the volume of a prism with the same base area and height.

$V = \frac{1}{3}Bh$

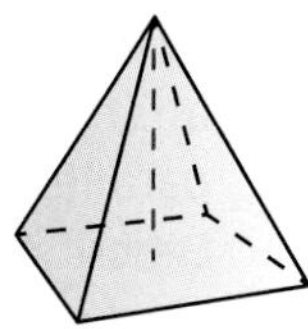

The volume of a cone is one-third the volume of a cylinder with the same base area and height.

$V = \frac{1}{3}Bh$

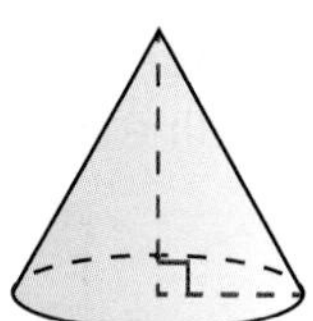

### Example

**What is the volume?**

$V = \frac{1}{3}Bh = \frac{1}{3} \cdot \frac{1}{2}(6 \cdot 3)(9)$

$= 27$

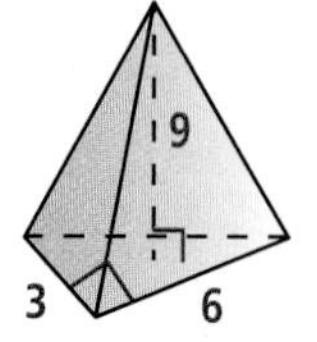


The volume of the pyramid is 27 cubic units.

### Practice & Problem Solving

**For Exercises 13 and 14, find the volume of each figure. Round to the nearest tenth.**

**13.**

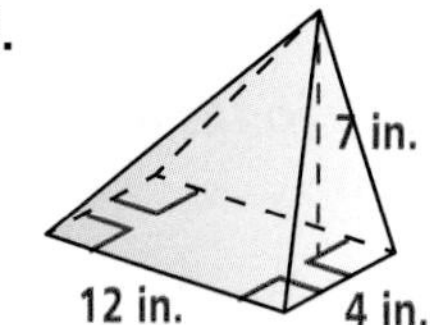


**14.**

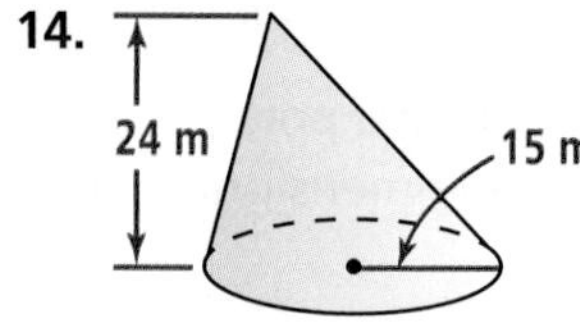


**15.** A sculptor cuts a pyramid from a marble cube with volume $t^3$ ft$^3$. The pyramid is $t$ ft tall. The area of the base is $t^2$ ft$^2$. Write an expression for the volume of marble removed.

**16.** A company cuts 2 in. from the tops of the solid plastic cones. How much less plastic is used in the new design?

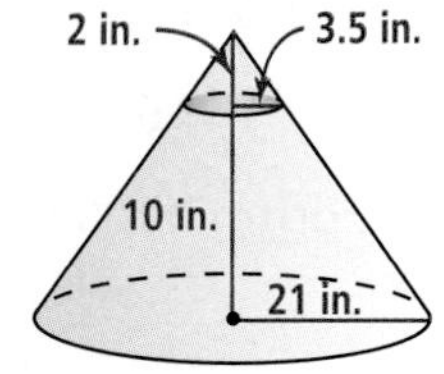

## LESSON 11-4 Spheres

### Quick Review

The volume of a sphere is $V = \frac{4}{3}\pi r^3$.

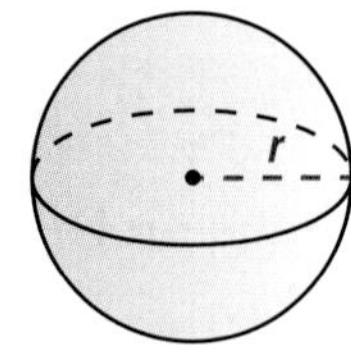


The volume of a hemisphere is one-half the volume of a sphere with the same radius, $V = \frac{2}{3}\pi r^3$.

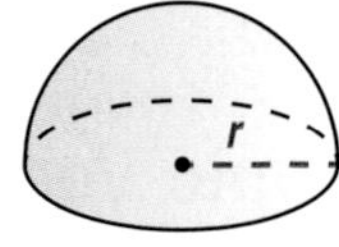


### Example

**What is the volume of the sphere shown?**

$$V = \frac{4}{3}\pi r^3$$
$$= \frac{4}{3}\pi(3)^3 = 36\pi$$

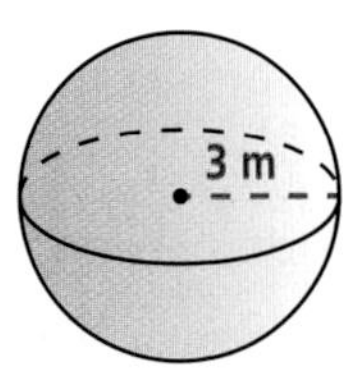


The volume of the sphere is $36\pi$ m$^3$.

### Practice & Problem Solving

**For Exercises 17 and 18, find the volume of each figure. Round to the nearest tenth.**

**17.**

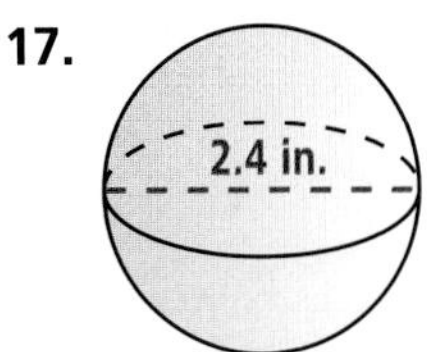


**18.**

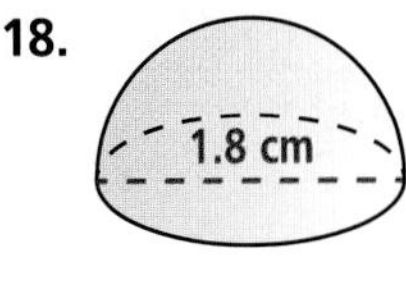


**19. Use Structure** A golf ball has a radius of $r$ centimeters. What is the least possible volume of a rectangular box that can hold 2 golf balls?

**20.** A capsule of liquid cold medicine is shown. If 1 dose is about 23 ml, how many capsules make up 1 dose? (*Hint:* 1 ml = 1 cm$^3$)

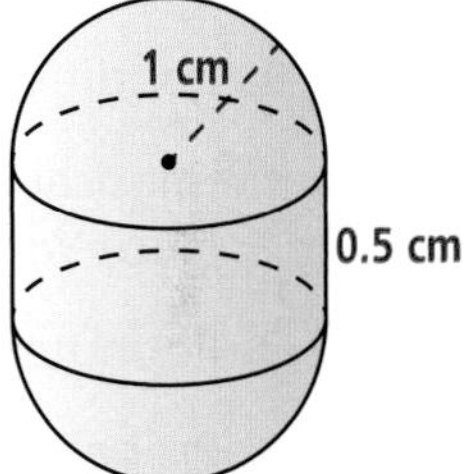


TOPIC 11 REVIEW

# Probability

## TOPIC ESSENTIAL QUESTION

**How can you find the probability of events and combinations of events?**

## Topic Overview



## Topic Vocabulary

- binomial distribution
- binomial experiment
- binomial probability
- combination
- complement
- conditional probability
- dependent events
- expected value
- factorial
- Fundamental Counting Principle
- independent events
- mutually exclusive
- permutation
- probability distribution
- uniform probability distribution

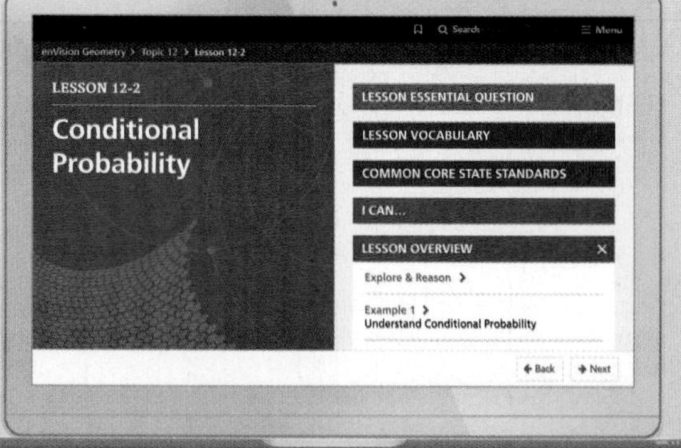

 Go online | **PearsonRealize.com**

## Digital Experience

 **INTERACTIVE STUDENT EDITION** Access online or offline.

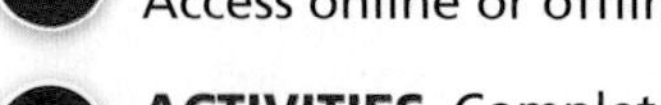 **ACTIVITIES** Complete ***Explore & Reason, Model & Discuss***, and ***Critique & Explain*** activities. Interact with Examples and Try Its.

 **ANIMATION** View and interact with real-world applications.

 **PRACTICE** Practice what you've learned.

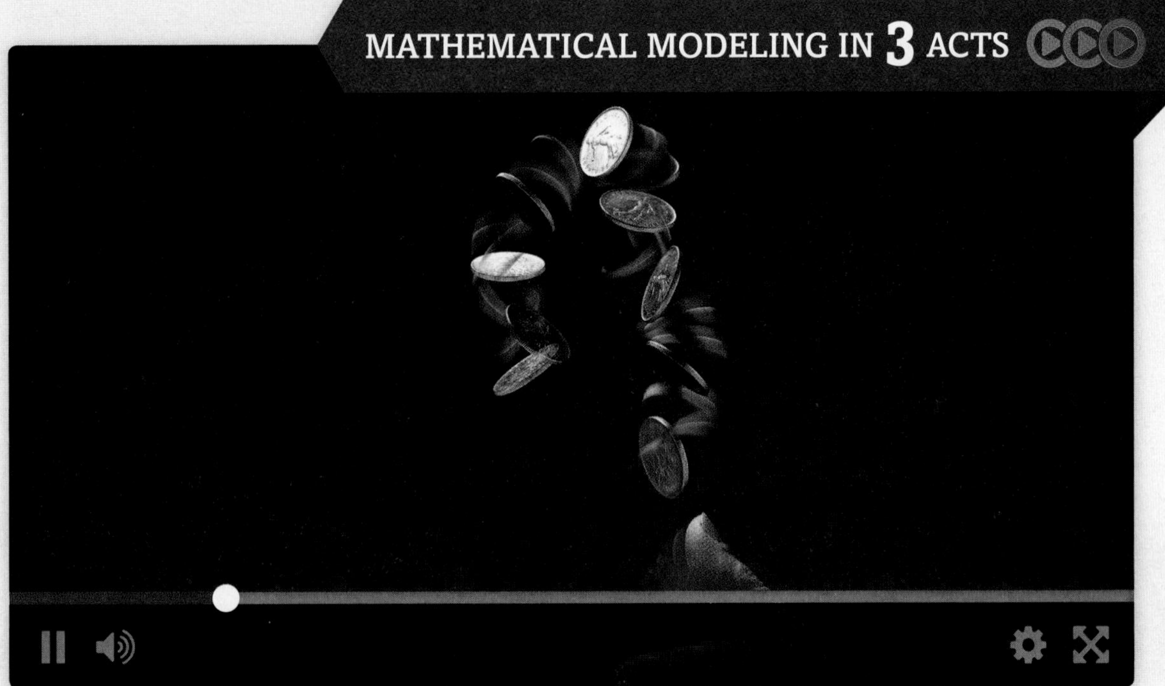


## Place Your Guess

A coin toss is a popular way to decide between two options or settle a dispute. The coin toss is popular because it is a simple and unbiased way of deciding. Assuming the coin being tossed is a fair coin, both parties have an equally likely chance of winning.

What other methods could you use to decide between two choices fairly? Think about this during the Mathematical Modeling in 3 Acts lesson.

TOPIC 12

**VIDEOS** Watch clips to support ***Mathematical Modeling in 3 Acts Lessons*** and **enVision™ *STEM Projects.***

**CONCEPT SUMMARY** Review key lesson content through multiple representations.

**ASSESSMENT** Show what you've learned.

**GLOSSARY** Read and listen to English and Spanish definitions.

**TUTORIALS** Get help from ***Virtual Nerd***, right when you need it.

**MATH TOOLS** Explore math with digital tools and manipulatives.

Video

## Did You Know?

**Meteorologists** use past climate data for a particular location and date as well as **weather models** to make weather predictions. Some regions in the U.S. are more predictable than others.

The **greatest temperature change** in a one-day period occurred in Loma, Montana, in 1972. The temperature rose an incredible **103 degrees**, from –54 to 49 °F, in 24 hours.

**Weather events** can surprise experts, and can vary greatly even within a few miles.

**Climate** is the long-term average of weather conditions. So the difference between weather and climate is a measure of time.

## Your Task: Simulate Weather Conditions

You and your classmates will research climate data for a specific location for one month. You'll use probability to simulate a plausible set of weather conditions for each day of February, including temperature and precipitation, and whether the precipitation will be rain or snow.

# 12-1 Probability Events

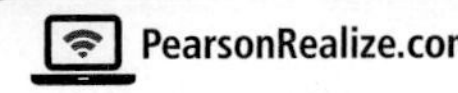

**I CAN…** use relationships among events to find probabilities.

**VOCABULARY**

- complement
- independent events
- mutually exclusive

## EXPLORE & REASON

**Allie spins the spinner and draws one card without looking. She gets a 3 on the spinner and the 3 card. Then she sets the card aside, spins again, and draws another card.**

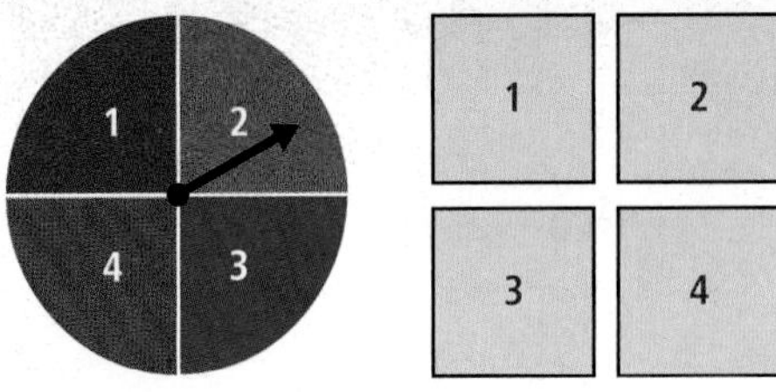


**A.** Is it possible for Allie to get a 3 on her second spin? On her second card? Explain.

**B. Construct Arguments** How does getting the 3 card on her first draw affect the probability of getting the 2 card on her second draw? Explain.

**ESSENTIAL QUESTION** How does describing events as mutually exclusive or independent affect how you find probabilities?

## EXAMPLE 1 Find Probabilities of Mutually Exclusive Events

**You roll a standard number cube once. Let *E* represent the event "roll an even number." Let *T* represent the event "roll a 3 or 5."**

**A. What is the probability that you roll an even number or roll a 3 or 5?**

Show the outcomes of events *E* and *T* as a subset of the sample space *S*.

Events *E* and *T* are **mutually exclusive** because there is no outcome in both sets.

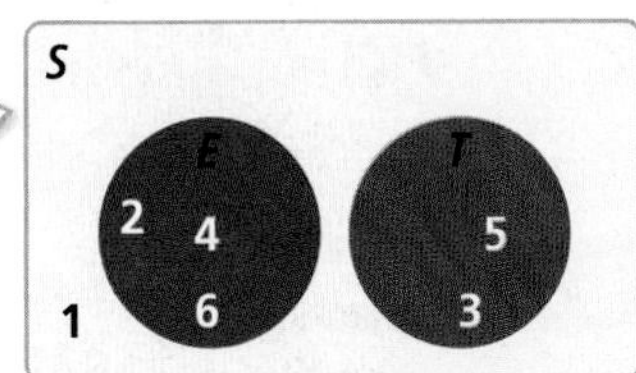


There are 5 outcomes that are even numbers or a 3 or 5. {2, 3, 4, 5, 6} There are a total of 6 possible outcomes in the sample space.

$$P(E \text{ or } T) = \frac{\text{number of favorable outcomes}}{\text{number of total possible outcomes}}$$

$$= \frac{3+2}{6}$$

There are 3 outcomes in event *E* and 2 outcomes in event *T*.

$$= \frac{3}{6} + \frac{2}{6}$$

This is equivalent to $P(E) + P(T)$.

$$= \frac{5}{6}$$

The probability of rolling an even number or rolling a 3 or a 5 is $\frac{5}{6}$.

**STUDY TIP**
Notice the roles of *or* and *and* when working with probability of mutually exclusive events.

**B. You roll a standard number cube once. What is the probability that you roll an even number and a 3 or 5?**

$$P(E \text{ and } T) = \frac{\text{number of favorable outcomes}}{\text{number of total possible outcomes}}$$

$$= \frac{0}{6}$$

$$= 0$$

Because events *E* and *T* are mutually exclusive, there are no outcomes that are in both sets.

The probability of rolling an even number and rolling a 3 or a 5 is 0.

CONTINUED ON THE NEXT PAGE

**GENERALIZE**
What is the probability of any pair of mutually exclusive events? Explain.

EXAMPLE 1 CONTINUED

**C. You roll a standard number cube once. What is the probability that you do *not* roll an even number?**

$P(\text{not } E) = \frac{3}{6}$ or $\frac{1}{2}$ — There are 3 outcomes that are not even numbers.

The probability of not rolling an even number is $\frac{1}{2}$.

**Try It!** 1. A box contains 100 balls. Thirty of the balls are purple and 10 are orange. If you select one of the balls at random, what is the probability of each of the following events?

**a.** The ball is purple or orange.

**b.** The ball is not purple and not orange.

## CONCEPT Probabilities of Mutually Exclusive Events

If $A$ and $B$ are mutually exclusive events, then

- $P(A \text{ or } B) = P(A) + P(B)$
- $P(A \text{ and } B) = 0$

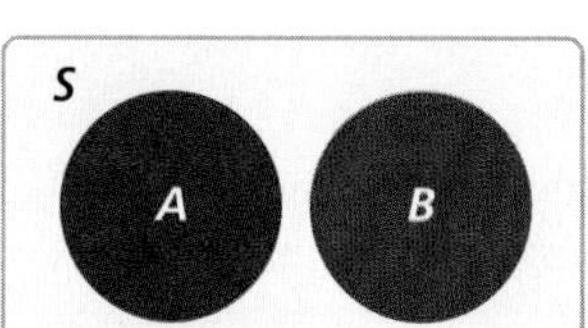


The **complement** of an event is the set of all outcomes in a sample space that are not included in the event.

If $C$ is the event that $A$ does not occur, then

$P(C) = 1 - P(A)$.

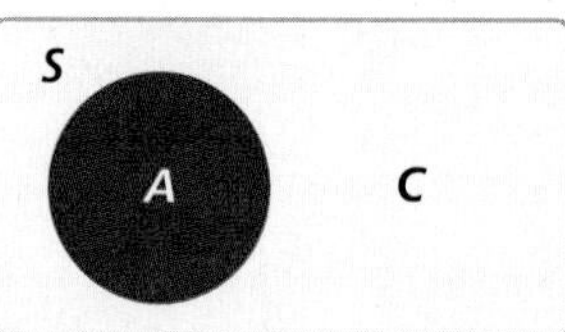

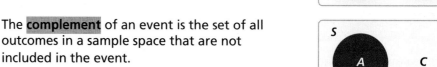

## EXAMPLE 2 Find the Probabilities of Non-Mutually Exclusive Events

**A student-made target includes two overlapping squares. Assume that a sticky ball thrown at the target is equally likely to land anywhere on the target. What is the probability that the ball lands inside one or both of the squares?**

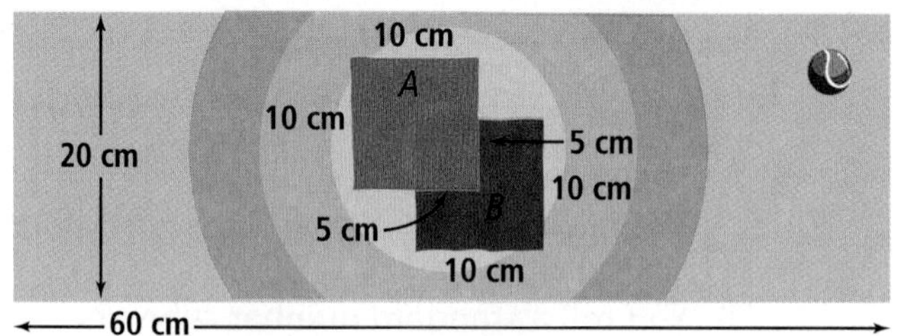


**Step 1** Find the area of the squares, and their overlapping area.

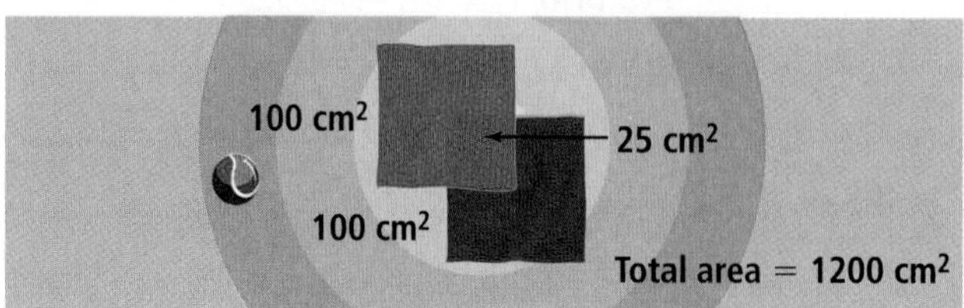


CONTINUED ON THE NEXT PAGE

EXAMPLE 2 CONTINUED

**Step 2** Find the probabilities.

**USE STRUCTURE**
What other method could you use to compute $P(A \text{ and } B)$?

$$P(A \text{ or } B) = \frac{100}{1,200} + \frac{100}{1,200} - \frac{25}{1,200}$$
$$= \frac{175}{1,200} = \frac{7}{48}$$

Subtract the probability of the overlapping area because it was included twice, once for each large square.

The probability that the ball will land inside one or both squares is $\frac{7}{48}$, or about 15%.

**Try It!** **2.** A video game is played on a 34 cm by 20 cm rectangular computer screen. A starship is represented by two overlapping circles of radius 6 cm whose area of overlap is 20 cm$^2$. A black hole is equally likely to appear at any point on the screen. To the nearest whole percent, what is the probability that the point will appear within the starship?

**CONCEPT** Probabilities of Non-Mutually Exclusive Events

If $A$ and $B$ are not mutually exclusive events, then $P(A \text{ or } B) = P(A) + P(B) - P(A \text{ and } B)$.

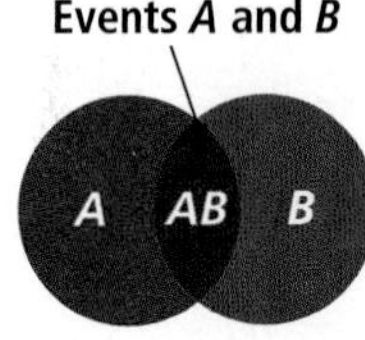

CONCEPTUAL UNDERSTANDING

## EXAMPLE 3 Identify Independent Events

**A jar contains 12 green marbles and 8 violet marbles.**

**A. A marble is chosen at random from the jar and replaced. Another marble is chosen at random from the jar. Does the color of the first marble chosen affect the possible outcomes for the second marble chosen?**

Determine the probabilities for each choice to decide whether the first marble chosen affects the possibilities for the second marble.

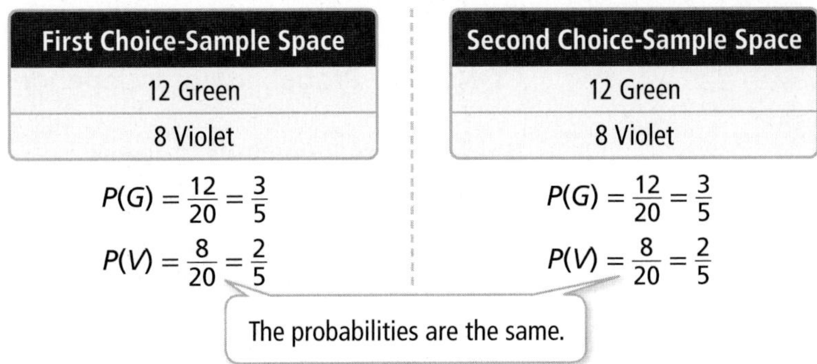

| First Choice-Sample Space |
|---|
| 12 Green |
| 8 Violet |

$P(G) = \frac{12}{20} = \frac{3}{5}$

$P(V) = \frac{8}{20} = \frac{2}{5}$

| Second Choice-Sample Space |
|---|
| 12 Green |
| 8 Violet |

$P(G) = \frac{12}{20} = \frac{3}{5}$

$P(V) = \frac{8}{20} = \frac{2}{5}$

The probabilities are the same.

The color of the first marble chosen does not affect the possible outcomes for the second marble chosen.

Two events are **independent events** if and only if the occurrence of one event does not affect the probability of a second event.

CONTINUED ON THE NEXT PAGE

EXAMPLE 3 CONTINUED

**B. A marble is chosen at random from the jar and not replaced. Another marble is chosen at random from the jar. Does the color of the first marble chosen affect the possible outcomes for the second marble chosen?**

Determine whether the events are independent.

| First Choice-Sample Space |
|---|
| 12 Green |
| 8 Violet |

**COMMON ERROR**
When two or more items are selected from the same set, you must determine whether the first item(s) is replaced before the next item is selected. Then find the probabilities.

$P(G) = \frac{12}{20} = \frac{3}{5}$

Assume a green marble was chosen first.

| Second Choice-Sample Space |
|---|
| 11 Green |
| 8 Violet |

$P(G) = \frac{11}{19}$ $\quad P(V) = \frac{8}{19}$

$P(V) = \frac{8}{20} = \frac{2}{5}$

Assume a violet marble is chosen first.

| Second Choice-Sample Space |
|---|
| 12 Green |
| 7 Violet |

$P(G) = \frac{12}{19}$ $\quad P(V) = \frac{7}{19}$

When the first marble is not replaced in the jar, the color of the first marble chosen does affect the possible outcomes for the second marble chosen. These events are not independent.

**Try It!** 3. There are 10 cards in a box, 5 black and 5 red. Two cards are selected from the box, one at a time.

a. A card is chosen at random and then replaced. Another card is chosen. Does the color of the first card chosen affect the possibilities of the second card chosen? Explain.

b. A card is chosen at random and *not* replaced. Another card is chosen. Does the color of the first card chosen affect the possibilities of the second card chosen? Explain.

**CONCEPT** Probability of Independent Events

If *A* and *B* are independent events, then $P(A \text{ and } B) = P(A) \cdot P(B)$.

If $P(A \text{ and } B) = P(A) \cdot P(B)$, then *A* and *B* are independent events.

Example: There are 12 possible results from the independent events rolling a number cube and tossing a coin.

$P(4) = \frac{1}{6}$ $\quad P(H) = \frac{1}{2}$

$P(4 \text{ and } H) = \frac{1}{6} \cdot \frac{1}{2} = \frac{1}{12}$

APPLICATION

## EXAMPLE 4 Find Probabilities of Independent Events

**Alex cannot decide which shirt to wear today, so she chooses one at random.**

**The probability of rain today is 40%, or $\frac{2}{5}$.**

**A. What is the probability that Alex chooses a yellow shirt and it does not rain today?**

Let $Y$ represent the event "yellow shirt." Let $N$ represent "no rain."

$Y$ and $N$ are independent because Alex's choice of shirt does not affect the weather, and the weather does not affect Alex's choice of shirt. Use the formula to find $P(Y \text{ and } N)$.

**STUDY TIP**
You can write probabilities as fractions, decimals, or percents. Choose the most convenient form for your purposes.

**Step 1** Find $P(N)$ and $P(Y)$.

$P(N) = 1 - \frac{2}{5} = \frac{3}{5}$.

Subtract the probability that it will rain, $\frac{2}{5}$, from 1 to find the probability that it will *not* rain.

$P(Y) = \frac{\text{number of favorable outcomes}}{\text{total number of outcomes}} = \frac{2}{4} \text{ or } \frac{1}{2}$

**Step 2** Apply the formula and multiply the probabilities of $Y$ and $N$.

$P(Y \text{ and } N) = P(Y) \bullet P(N) = \frac{1}{2} \bullet \frac{3}{5} = \frac{3}{10} = 30\%$

Use the rule for the probability of independent events.

The probability that Alex chooses a yellow shirt and it does not rain is 30%.

**B. What is the probability that Alex chooses a yellow shirt and it does not rain today or that Alex chooses a green shirt and it rains today?**

Let $G$ represent "green shirt." Let $R$ represent "rain."

The events "$Y$ and $N$" and "$G$ and $R$" are mutually exclusive because no outcomes are in both events.

**Step 1** Find $P(G \text{ and } R)$

$P(G \text{ and } R) = P(G) \bullet P(R) = \frac{1}{4} \bullet \frac{2}{5} = \frac{2}{20} = \frac{1}{10} = 10\%$

**Step 2** Find $P((Y \text{ and } N) \text{ or } (G \text{ and } R))$

$P((Y \text{ and } N) \text{ or } (G \text{ and } R)) = P(Y \text{ and } N) + P(G \text{ and } R)$

$= 30\% + 10\% = 40\%$

Add to find the probability that either event will occur.

The probability that Alex chooses a yellow shirt and it does not rain or that Alex chooses a green shirt and it rains is 40%.

**Try It!** 4. You spin the spinner two times. Assume that the probability of Blue each spin is $\frac{1}{3}$ and the probability of Orange each spin is $\frac{2}{3}$. What is the probability of getting the same color both times? Explain.

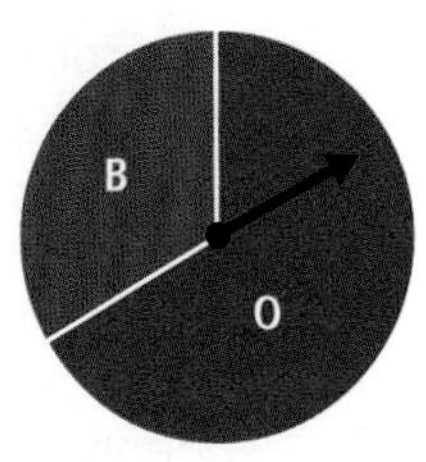

## CONCEPT SUMMARY Probability Events

| | Mutually Exclusive Events | Independent Events |
|---|---|---|
| **WORDS** | *A* and *B* are mutually exclusive because no outcome is in both *A* and *B*. | *D* and *M* are independent because the occurrence of one does not affect the probability of the other. |
| **ALGEBRA** | If *A* and *B* are mutually exclusive events, then $P(A \text{ or } B) = P(A) + P(B)$.<br><br>If *C* is the event that *A* does not occur, then $P(C) = 1 - P(A)$. | If *D* and *M* are independent events, then $P(D \text{ and } M) = P(D) \cdot P(M)$.<br><br>If $P(D \text{ and } M) = P(D) \cdot P(M)$, then *D* and *M* are independent events. |
| **EXAMPLES** | Experiment: spin the spinner.<br><br><br><br>Event *A*: number less than 3<br><br>Event *B*: number greater than 5<br><br>$P(A \text{ or } B) = P(A) + P(B) = \frac{2}{6} + \frac{1}{6} = \frac{1}{2}$ | Experiment: spin the spinner and roll a number cube<br><br><br><br>Event *D*: odd number on spinner<br><br>Event *M*: number greater than 4 on number cube<br><br>$P(D \text{ and } M) = P(D) \cdot P(M) = \frac{1}{2} \cdot \frac{1}{3} = \frac{1}{6}$ |

## Do You UNDERSTAND?

1. **ESSENTIAL QUESTION** How does describing events as independent or mutually exclusive affect how you find probabilities?

2. **Reason** Two marbles are chosen, one at a time, from a bag containing 6 marbles, 4 red marbles and 2 green marbles. Suppose the first marble chosen is green. Is the probability that the second marble will be red greater if the first marble is returned to the bag or if it is not returned to the bag? Explain.

3. **Error Analysis** The probability that Deshawn plays basketball (event *B*) after school is 20%. The probability that he talks to friends (event *T*) after school is 45%. He says that $P(B \text{ or } T)$ is 65%. Explain Deshawn's error.

4. **Vocabulary** What is the difference between mutually exclusive events and independent events?

## Do You KNOW HOW?

5. A bag contains 40 marbles. Eight are green and 2 are blue. You select one marble at random. What is the probability of each event?

   **a.** The marble is green or blue.

   **b.** The marble is not green and not blue.

6. A robot at a carnival booth randomly tosses a dart at a square target with 8 inch sides and a circle with a 3 inch radius in the middle. To the nearest whole percent, what is the probability that the dart will land in the circle?

**For Exercises 7 and 8, assume that you roll a standard number cube two times.**

7. What is the probability of rolling an even number on the first roll and a number less than 3 on the second roll?

8. What is the probability of rolling an odd number on the first roll and a number greater than 3 on the second roll?

# PRACTICE & PROBLEM SOLVING

Scan for Multimedia

Practice Tutorial

Additional Exercises Available Online

## UNDERSTAND

9. **Construct Arguments** Let $S$ be a sample space for an experiment in which every outcome is both equally likely and mutually exclusive. What can you conclude about the sum of the probabilities for all of the outcomes? Give an example.

10. **Error Analysis** At Lincoln High School, 6 students are members of both the Chess Club and the Math Club. There are 20 students in the Math Club, 12 students in the Chess Club, and 400 students in the entire school.

    Danielle calculated the probability that a student chosen at random belongs to the Chess Club or the Math Club. Explain her error.

    Event $C$: Student is in Chess Club
    Event $M$: Student is in Math Club

    $$P(C \text{ or } M) = P(C) + P(M)$$
    $$= \frac{12}{400} + \frac{20}{400}$$
    $$= \frac{32}{400} = 0.08$$

    ✗

11. **Higher Order Thinking** Murphy's math teacher sometimes wears scarves to class. Murphy has been documenting the relationship between his teacher wearing a scarf and when the class has a math quiz. The probabilities are as follows:

    - $P$(wearing a scarf) = 10%
    - $P$(math quiz) = 15%
    - $P$(wearing a scarf and math quiz) = 5%

    Are the events "the teacher is wearing a scarf" and "there will be a quiz" independent events? Explain.

**Reason A card is drawn from a box containing 5 cards, each showing a different number from 1 to 5. Consider the events "even number," "odd number," "less than 3," and "greater than 3." Determine whether each pair of events mutually exclusive.**

12. $< 3, > 3$

13. even, $> 3$

14. odd, $> 3$

15. odd, even

## PRACTICE

16. Hana is playing a virtual reality game in which she must toss a disc to land on the largest triangular section of the board. If the disc is equally likely to land anywhere on the board, what is the probability that she will succeed? Explain. SEE EXAMPLE 1

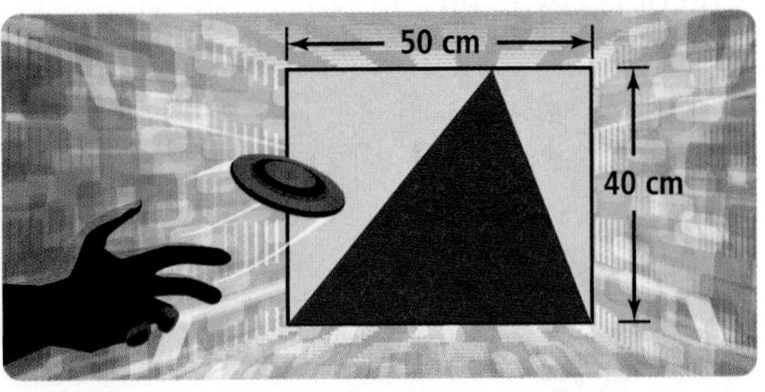


**In a class of 25 students, 8 students have heights less than 65 inches and 10 students have heights of 69 inches or more. For Exercises 17–19, find the probabilities described.** SEE EXAMPLE 1

17. $P$(less than 65 inches or greater than 69 inches)

18. $P$(greater than or equal to 65 inches)

19. $P$(greater than or equal to 65 inches and less than or equal to 69 inches)

20. A skydiver is equally likely to land at any point on a rectangular field. Two overlapping circular targets of radius 5 meters are marked on the field. To the nearest percent, what is the probability that the sky diver will land in one or both of the circles? SEE EXAMPLE 2

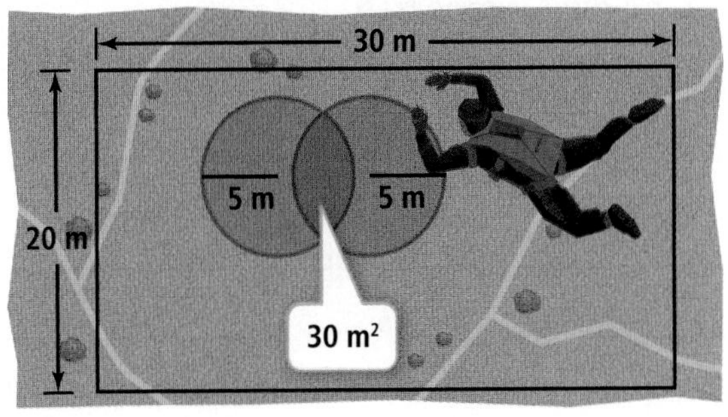


21. Two marbles are chosen at random, one at a time from a box that contains 7 marbles, 5 red and 2 green. SEE EXAMPLES 3 AND 4

    a. Find the probability of drawing 2 red marbles when the first marble is replaced before the second marble is chosen.

    b. Determine whether the situation described is independent.

## PRACTICE & PROBLEM SOLVING

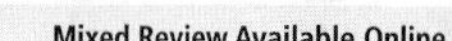


Mixed Review Available Online

### APPLY

22. **Mathematical Connections** For a science fair project, Paige wants to test whether ants prefer certain colors. She releases ants on the colored surface shown. If the ants are randomly distributed across the entire surface, what is the probability that any given ant will be within the blue circle, but not within the yellow circle? Round to the nearest whole percent.

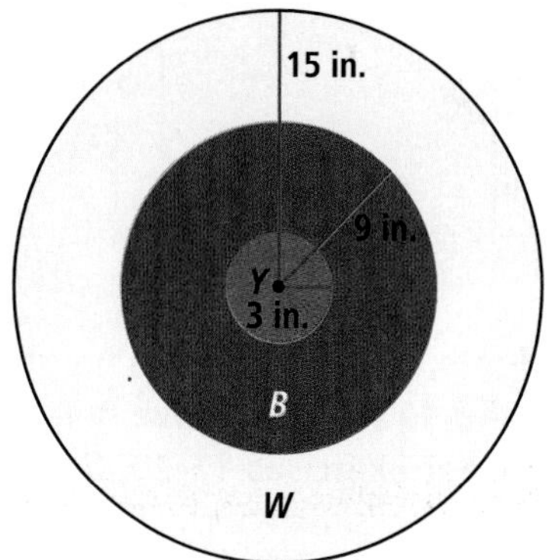


23. **Use Structure** A city issues 3-digit license plates for motorized scooters. The digits 0–9 are chosen at random by a computer program. What is the probability that a license plate issued meets each set of criteria?

   a. no digit is repeated

   b. all 3 digits are the same

   c. the 3-digit number formed is even

   d. the first two digits are the same and the third digit is different

24. **Model With Mathematics** During a football game, a kicker is called in twice to kick a field goal from the 30 yard line. Suppose that for each attempt, the probability that he will make the field goal is 0.8.

   a. What is the probability that he will make both field goals?

   b. What is the probability that he will make neither field goal?

### ASSESSMENT PRACTICE

25. The probability of events *A* and *B* both occurring is 15%. The probability of event *A* or *B* occurring is 60%. The probability of *B* occurring is 50%. What is the probability of *A* occurring?

26. **SAT/ACT** A robot spins the spinner shown twice. Assume that the outcomes 1, 2, 3, and 4 are equally likely for each spin. What is the probability that the sum of the two outcomes will be 6?

Ⓐ $\frac{1}{16}$

Ⓑ $\frac{1}{8}$

Ⓒ $\frac{3}{16}$

Ⓓ $\frac{1}{4}$

Ⓔ $\frac{3}{4}$

27. **Performance Task** Paula is packing to visit a friend in another city for a long weekend. She looks at the weather forecast shown below to find the chance of rain. Assume that whether it rains on each day is independent of whether it rains on any other day.

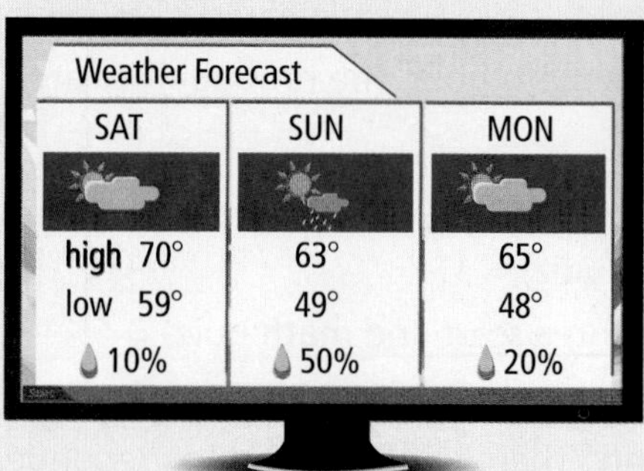


**Part A** What is the probability that it will not rain on any of the three days to the nearest percent?

**Part B** What is the probability that it will rain at least one of the three days to the nearest percent?

**Part C** Do you think Paula should pack an umbrella? Explain.

# 12-2 Conditional Probability

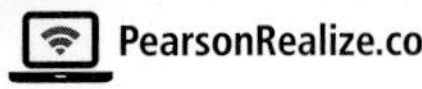
PearsonRealize.com

**I CAN…** find the probability of an event given that another event has occurred.

**VOCABULARY**
- conditional probability
- dependent events

## EXPLORE & REASON

**At Central High School, 85% of all senior girls attended and 65% of all senior boys attended the Spring Dance. Of all attendees, 20% won a prize.**

**A.** Assuming that the number of girls is about equal to the number of boys, estimate the probability that a randomly selected senior won a prize at the dance. Explain.

**B. Construct Arguments** If you knew whether the selected student was a boy or a girl, would your estimate change? Explain.

## ESSENTIAL QUESTION

**How are conditional probability and independence related in real-world experiments?**

## EXAMPLE 1 Understand Conditional Probability

**A student committee is being formed to decide how after-school activities will be funded. The committee members are selected at random from current club members. The frequency table shows the current club membership data.**

**Monday Club Memberships by Grade**

| | Drama | Science | Art | Total |
|---|---|---|---|---|
| Sophomore | 3 | 9 | 24 | 36 |
| Junior | 6 | 18 | 16 | 40 |
| Senior | 8 | 13 | 18 | 39 |
| Total | 17 | 40 | 58 | 115 |

**What is the probability that a member of the art club selected at random is a junior?**

**One Method** Use the frequency table to find the probability that the student chosen is a junior given that the student is a member of the art club.

The probability that an event $B$ will occur given that another event $A$ has already occurred is called a **conditional probability** and is written as $P(B \mid A)$.

$$P(\text{junior} \mid \text{member of the art club}) = \frac{\text{number of juniors in art club}}{\text{total number of art club members}}$$

$$= \frac{16}{58} = \frac{8}{29}$$

**COMMON ERROR**
Avoid confusing $P(A \mid B)$ with $P(B \mid A)$. In the first case the prior event is $B$, but in the second case the prior event is $A$.

**Another Method** Use the formula for conditional probability.

For any two events $A$ and $B$, with $P(A) \neq 0$, $P(B \mid A) = \dfrac{P(B \text{ and } A)}{P(A)}$.

$$P(\text{junior} \mid \text{art}) = \frac{P(\text{junior and art})}{P(\text{art})} = \frac{\frac{16}{115}}{\frac{58}{115}} = \frac{8}{29}$$

Of the 115 Monday club members and 58 art club members, 16 are juniors and in the art club.

The probability that the student chosen is a junior member from the art club is $\frac{8}{29}$.

CONTINUED ON THE NEXT PAGE

EXAMPLE 1 CONTINUED

 **Try It!** **1. a.** What is the probability that a member of the drama club is a sophomore, $P(\text{sophomore} \mid \text{drama})$?

**b.** What is the probability that a sophomore is a member of the drama club, $P(\text{drama} \mid \text{sophomore})$? Is $P(\text{sophomore} \mid \text{drama})$ the same as $P(\text{drama} \mid \text{sophomore})$? Explain.

## CONCEPT Conditional Probability and Independent Events

Let $A$ and $B$ be events with $P(A) \neq 0$ and $P(B) \neq 0$.

| | |
|---|---|
| If events $A$ and $B$ are independent, then the conditional probability of $B$ given $A$ equals the probability of $B$ and the conditional probability of $A$ given $B$ equals the probability of $A$. | If events $A$ and $B$ are independent, then $P(B \mid A) = P(B)$ and $P(A \mid B) = P(A)$. |
| If the conditional probability of $B$ given $A$ equals the probability of $B$ and the conditional probability of $A$ given $B$ equals the probability of $A$, then events $A$ and $B$ are independent. | If $P(B \mid A) = P(B)$ and $P(A \mid B) = P(A)$, then events $A$ and $B$ are independent. |

CONCEPTUAL UNDERSTANDING

##  EXAMPLE 2 Use the Test for Independence

**The table below shows the vehicles in a parking garage one afternoon. A vehicle in the garage will be selected at random. Let $B$ represent "the vehicle is black" and $V$ represent "the vehicle is a van." Are the events $B$ and $V$ independent or dependent?**

STUDY TIP
When looking at a table of probabilities, consider outcomes that are impossible or guaranteed to occur. For example, it is impossible to select a red van.

| | Car | Van | Pickup | Totals |
|---|---|---|---|---|
| Red | 5 | 0 | 2 | 7 |
| White | 0 | 0 | 2 | 2 |
| Black | 6 | 3 | 4 | 13 |
| Totals | 11 | 3 | 8 | 22 |

**One Method**

Since $P(B) = \frac{13}{22} \neq 0$ and $P(V \text{ and } B) = \frac{3}{22}$,

$$P(V \mid B) = \frac{P(V \text{ and } B)}{P(B)} = \frac{\frac{3}{22}}{\frac{13}{22}} = \frac{3}{13}$$

Since $P(V \mid B) \neq P(V)$, $B$ and $V$ are not independent events, they are **dependent events**.

CONTINUED ON THE NEXT PAGE

EXAMPLE 2 CONTINUED

**Another Method**

Since $P(V) = \frac{3}{22} \neq 0$ and $P(B \text{ and } V) = P(V \text{ and } B)$,

$$P(B \mid V) = \frac{P(B \text{ and } V)}{P(V)}$$

$$= \frac{\frac{3}{22}}{\frac{3}{22}} = 1$$

A probability of 1, or 100%, indicates an outcome that is certain. Given that a van is selected, it must be black.

Again, Since $P(B \mid V) \neq P(B)$, the events $B$ and $V$ are dependent events.

 **Try It!** 2. Let $R$ represent "selecting a red vehicle" and $C$ represent "selecting a car." Are the events $R$ and $C$ independent or dependent? Explain.

## EXAMPLE 3 Apply the Conditional Probability Formula

**A band's marketing agent conducted a survey to determine how many high school fans the band has. What is the probability that a surveyed student plans to attend the band's concert and is a fan of the group?**

**Concert Survey Results**

Students who plan to attend concert

- 70% of students plan to attend,
- 80% of students who plan to attend are fans of the band.

Students who do not plan to attend

- 30% of students do not plan to attend,
- 25% are fans of the band.

Use the conditional probability formula to find the combined probability.

Rewrite $P(B \mid A) = \frac{P(A \text{ and } B)}{P(A)}$ as $P(A \text{ and } B) = P(A) \cdot P(B \mid A)$.

$$P(A \text{ and } B) = P(A) \cdot P(B \mid A)$$

$$P(\text{attend and fan}) = P(\text{attend}) \cdot P(\text{fan} \mid \text{attend})$$

Event $A$ is "attend." Event $B$ is "fan."

$$= 0.7 \cdot 0.8$$

Substitute 0.7 for $P(\text{attend})$ and 0.8 for $P(\text{fan} \mid \text{attend})$.

$$= 0.56, \text{ or } 56\%$$

The probability that a surveyed student plans to attend the concert and is a fan of the group is 0.56, or 56%.

**LOOK FOR RELATIONSHIPS**
Why might $P(\text{fan} \mid \text{attend})$ not equal $P(\text{attend} \mid \text{fan})$ in this situation?

 **Try It!** 3. What is the probability that a surveyed student plans to attend but is not a fan of the group?

APPLICATION

## EXAMPLE 4 Use Conditional Probability to Make a Decision

**A marketer is looking at mobile phone statistics to help plan an online advertising campaign. She wants to find which product is most likely to be purchased after a related search.**

**Mobile Phone Search and Buying Behavior**

| Product | Search(S) | Search & Buy (S and B) |
|---|---|---|
| W | 46% | 16% |
| X | 32% | 14% |
| Y | 35% | 12% |
| Z | 40% | 15% |

Find the probability a mobile phone customer buys, given that they performed a related search. Use the formula $P(B \mid S) = \frac{P(S \text{ and } B)}{P(S)}$.

**MAKE SENSE AND PERSEVERE**
Product W has the highest $P(S \text{ and } B)$ of 16% but not the highest $P(B \mid S)$. Can you explain why?

| Product | $P(B \mid S)$ |
|---|---|
| W | $\frac{0.16}{0.46} \approx 0.348$ or about 34.8% |
| X | $\frac{0.14}{0.32} = 0.4375$ or 43.75% |
| Y | $\frac{0.12}{0.35} \approx 0.343$ or 34.3% |
| Z | $\frac{0.15}{0.40} = 0.375$ or 37.5% |

Product X has the highest probability of being purchased given that a related search was performed. So product X is probably a good choice for the online advertising campaign.

**Try It!** 4. The marketer also has data from desktop computers. Which product is most likely to be purchased after a related search?

**Computer Search and Buying Behavior (% of computer-based site visitors)**

| Product | Search | Search & Buy |
|---|---|---|
| J | 35% | 10% |
| K | 28% | 9% |
| L | 26% | 8% |
| M | 24% | 5% |



Go Online | PearsonRealize.com

  Concept Summary  Assess

## CONCEPT SUMMARY Conditional Probability

| | Conditional Probability Formula | Conditional Probability and Independent Events |
|---|---|---|
| WORDS | The probability that an event $B$ will occur given that another event $A$ has already occurred is called a **conditional probability**. | Events $A$ and $B$ are independent events if and only if the conditional probability of $A$ given $B$ is the same as the probability of $A$, and the conditional probability of $B$ given $A$ is the same as the probability of $B$. |
| ALGEBRA | For any two events $A$ and $B$, with $P(A) \neq 0$, $P(B \mid A) = \frac{P(A \text{ and } B)}{P(A)}$ | For any events $A$ and $B$ with $P(A) \neq 0$ and $P(B) \neq 0$, $A$ and $B$ are independent if and only if $P(B \mid A) = P(B)$ and $P(A \mid B) = P(A)$. |

## Do You UNDERSTAND?

1. ESSENTIAL QUESTION How are conditional probability and independence related in real-world experiments?

2. **Vocabulary** How is the sample space for $P(B \mid A)$ different from the sample space for $P(B)$?

3. **Vocabulary** Why does the definition of $P(B \mid A)$ have the condition that $P(A) \neq 0$?

4. **Use Structure** Why is $P(A) \cdot P(B \mid A) = P(B) \cdot P(A \mid B)$?

5. **Error Analysis** Taylor knows that $P(\text{red}) = 0.8$, $P(\text{blue}) = 0.2$, and $P(\text{red and blue}) = 0.05$. Explain Taylor's error.

$$P(\text{blue} \mid \text{red}) = \frac{0.05}{0.2} = 0.25$$ ✗

6. **Reason** At a sports camp, a coach wants to find the probability that a soccer player is a local camper. Because 40% of the students in the camp are local, the coach reasons that the probability is 0.4. Is his conclusion justified? Explain.

## Do You KNOW HOW?

7. Let $P(A) = \frac{3}{4}$, $P(B) = \frac{2}{3}$, and $P(A \text{ and } B) = \frac{1}{6}$. Find each probability.

   **a.** What is $P(B \mid A)$?

   **b.** What is $P(A \mid B)$?

8. Students randomly generate two digits from 0 to 9 to create a number between 0 and 99. Are the events "first digit 5" and "second digit 6" independent or dependent in each case? What is $P(56)$ in each experiment?

   **a.** The digits may not be repeated.

   **b.** The digits may be repeated.

9. Suppose that you select one card at random from the set of 6 cards below.

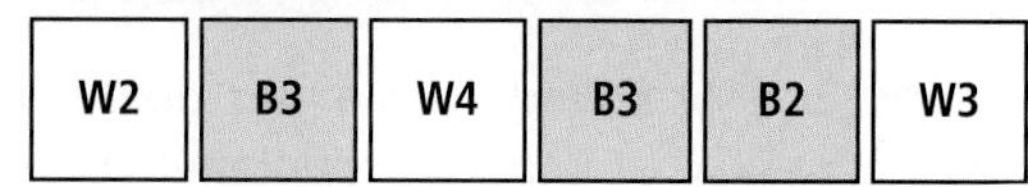


Let $B$ represent the event "select a blue card" and $T$ represent the event "select a card with a 3." Are $B$ and $T$ independent events? Explain your reasoning.

## PRACTICE & PROBLEM SOLVING

Scan for Multimedia

Additional Exercises Available Online

### UNDERSTAND

10. **Mathematical Connections** How can the formula $P(A \text{ and } B) = P(A) \cdot P(B \mid A)$ be simplified to find the probability of $A$ and $B$ when the events are independent? Explain.

11. **Error Analysis** From a bag containing 3 red marbles and 7 blue marbles, 2 marbles are selected without replacement. Esteban calculated the probability that two red marbles are selected. Explain Esteban's error.

$$P(\text{red}) = 0.3$$
$$P(\text{red and red}) = P(\text{red}) \cdot P(\text{red})$$
$$= 0.3 \cdot 0.3$$
$$= 0.09$$

✗

12. **Generalize** Kiyo is creating a table using mosaic tiles chosen and placed randomly. She is picking tiles without looking. How does P(yellow second | blue first) compare to P(yellow second | yellow first) if the tiles are selected without replacement? If the tiles are selected and returned to the pile because Kiyo wants a different color?

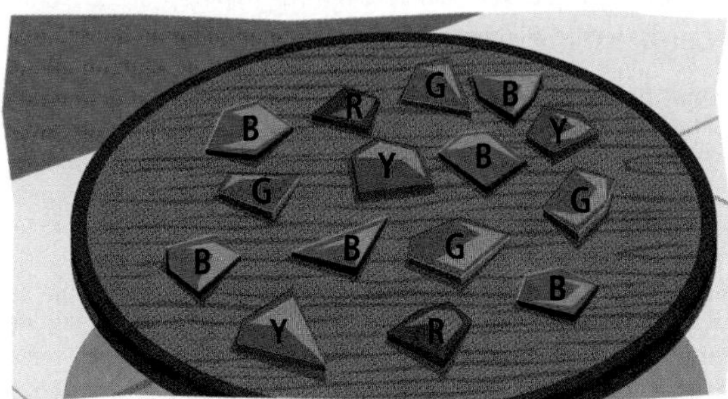


13. **Use Structure** At a fundraiser, a participant is asked to guess what is inside an unlabeled can for a possible prize. If there are two crates of cans to choose from, each having a mixture of vegetables and soup, what is the probability that the first participant will select a vegetable can from the left crate given each situation?

    a. The left crate has 2 cans of vegetables and 8 cans of soup, and the right crate has 7 cans of vegetables and 3 cans of soup.

    b. The left crate has 8 cans of vegetables and 2 cans of soup, and the right crate has 5 cans of vegetables and 5 cans of soup.

### PRACTICE

**For Exercises 14–18, use the data in the table to find the probability of each event.** SEE EXAMPLE 1

**Technology Class Enrollment by Year**

| | Sophomore | Junior |
|---|---|---|
| Robotics | 16 | 24 |
| Game Design | 18 | 22 |

14. P(Junior | Robotics)

15. P(Robotics | Junior)

16. P(Game Design | Sophomore)

17. P(Sophomore | Game Design)

18. Are year and technology class enrollment dependent or independent events? Explain. SEE EXAMPLE 2

19. At a high school, 40% of the students play an instrument. Of those students, 20% are freshmen. Of the students who do not play an instrument, 30% are freshmen. What is the probability that a student selected at random is a freshman who plays an instrument? SEE EXAMPLE 3

**In a study of an experimental medication, patients were randomly assigned to take either the medication or a placebo.**

**Effectiveness of New Medication As Compared to a Placebo**

| | Medication | Placebo |
|---|---|---|
| Health Improved | 53 | 47 |
| Health Did Not Improve | 65 | 35 |

20. What is the probability that a patient taking the medication showed improvement? Round to the nearest whole percent. SEE EXAMPLE 1

21. Are taking the medication and having improved health independent or dependent events? SEE EXAMPLE 2

22. Based on the data in the table, would you recommend that the medication be made available to doctors? Explain. SEE EXAMPLE 4

## PRACTICE & PROBLEM SOLVING

### APPLY

**23. Reason** In a recreation center with 1,500 members, 200 are high school students. Of the members, 300 regularly swim. The 45 students of the high school swim team are all members and practice at the pool every week. What is the probability that a high school member selected at random is on the swim team?

**24. Use Structure** At the school fair, 5% of students will win a prize. A winner has an equally likely chance to win each prize type shown. What is the probability that a student at the fair will win a comic book? Explain.

**25. Make Sense and Persevere** A box contains 50 batteries, of which 10 are dead and 5 are weak. Suppose you select batteries at random from the box and set them aside for recycling if they are dead or weak. If the first battery you select is dead and the second one is weak, what is the probability that the next battery you select will be weak?

**26. Higher Order Thinking** An inspector at a factory has determined that 1% of the flash drives produced by the plant are defective. If assembly line A produces 20% of all the flash drives, what is the probability that a defective flash drive chosen at random is from the corresponding conveyor belt A? Explain.

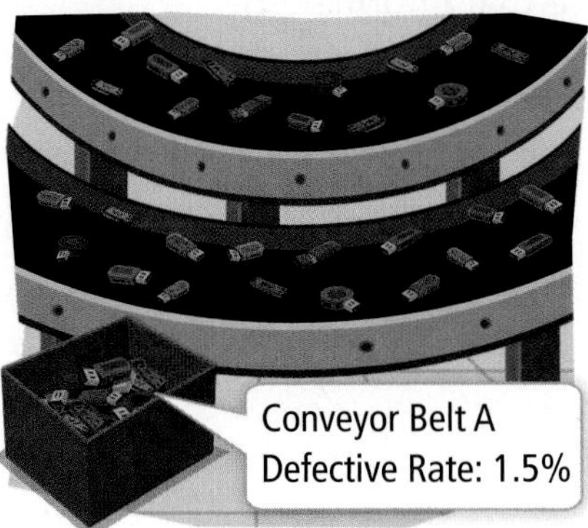


### ASSESSMENT PRACTICE

**27.** Which of the following pairs of events are independent? Select all that apply.

Ⓐ A student selected at random has a backpack. A student selected at random has brown hair.

Ⓑ Events $A$ and $B$, where $P(B \mid A) = \frac{1}{3}$, $P(A) = \frac{3}{5}$ and $P(B) = \frac{5}{9}$

Ⓒ A student selected at random is a junior. A student selected at random is a freshman.

Ⓓ Events $A$ and $B$, where $P(A) = 0.30$, $P(B) = 0.25$ and $P(A \text{ and } B) = 0.075$

Ⓔ Events $A$ and $B$, where $P(A) = 0.40$, $P(B) = 0.3$ and $P(A \text{ and } B) = 0.012$

**28. SAT/ACT** The table shows student participation in the newspaper and yearbook by year. A student on the newspaper staff is selected at random to attend a symposium. What is the probability that the selected student is a senior?

**Journalism Club Members**

| | Junior | Senior |
|---|---|---|
| Newspaper | 16 | 9 |
| Yearbook | 8 | 17 |

Ⓐ $\frac{9}{50}$

Ⓑ $\frac{9}{26}$

Ⓒ $\frac{9}{25}$

Ⓓ $\frac{9}{17}$

Ⓔ $\frac{9}{16}$

**29. Performance Task** In a survey of 50 male and 50 female high school students, 60 students said they exercise daily. Of those students, 32 were female.

**Part A** Use the data to make a two-way frequency table.

**Part B** What is the probability that a surveyed student who exercises daily is female? What is the probability that a surveyed student who exercises regularly is male?

**Part C** Based on the survey, what can you conclude about the relationship between exercise and gender? Explain.

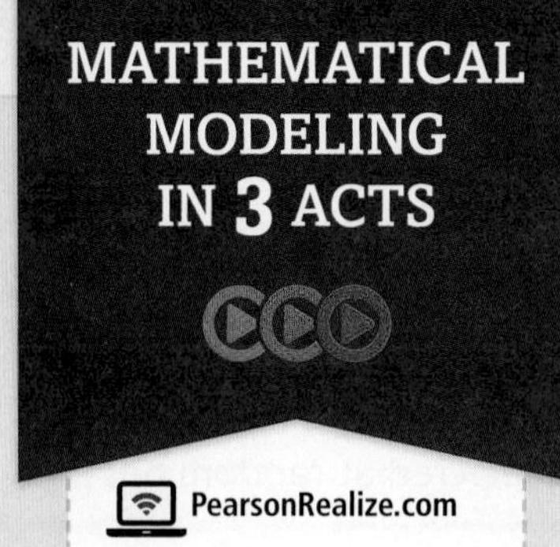


PearsonRealize.com

## Place Your Guess

A coin toss is a popular way to decide between two options or settle a dispute. The coin toss is popular because it is a simple and unbiased way of deciding. Assuming the coin being tossed is a fair coin, both parties have an equally likely chance of winning.

What other methods could you use to decide between two choices fairly? Think about this during the Mathematical Modeling in 3 Acts lesson.

### ACT 1 Identify the Problem

1. What is the first question that comes to mind after watching the video?
2. Write down the main question you will answer about what you saw in the video.
3. Make an initial conjecture that answers this main question.
4. Explain how you arrived at your conjecture.
5. What information will be useful to know to answer the main question? How can you get it? How will you use that information?

### ACT 2 Develop a Model

6. Use the math that you have learned in this Topic to refine your conjecture.

### ACT 3 Interpret the Results

7. Did your refined conjecture match the actual answer exactly? If not, what might explain the difference?

# 12-3 Permutations and Combinations

**I CAN…** use permutations and combinations to find the number of outcomes in a probability experiment.

**VOCABULARY**

- combination
- factorial
- Fundamental Counting Principle
- permutation

## EXPLORE & REASON

**Holly, Tia, Kenji, and Nate are eligible to be officers of the Honor Society. Two of the four students will be chosen at random as president and vice-president. The table summarizes the possible outcomes.**

**Honor Society Officers**

| President | Vice-President: Holly | Tia | Kenji | Nate |
|---|---|---|---|---|
| Holly | – | HT | HK | HN |
| Tia | TH | – | TK | TN |
| Kenji | KH | KT | – | KN |
| Nate | NH | NT | NK | – |

**A.** Holly wants to be an officer with her best friend Tia. How many outcomes make up this event?

**B.** How many outcomes show Holly as president and Tia as vice-president?

**C. Generalize** How many outcomes have only one of them as an officer? Explain.

**ESSENTIAL QUESTION** How are permutations and combinations useful when finding probabilities?

## EXAMPLE 1 Use the Fundamental Counting Principle

**Manuel wants to advertise the number of one-topping pizzas he offers to his customers. How many different one-topping pizzas are available at Manuel's Pizzeria?**

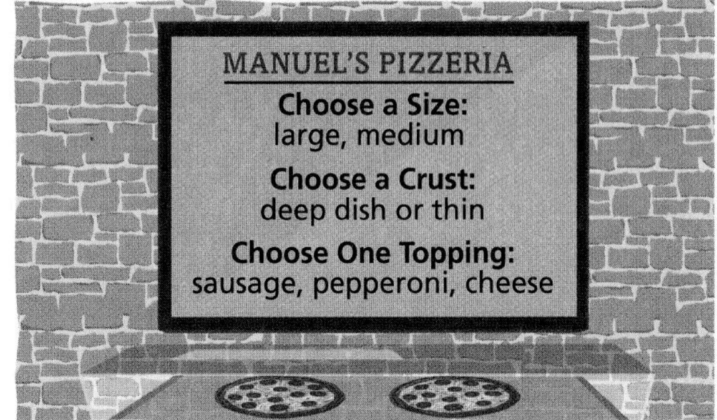

MANUEL'S PIZZERIA
Choose a Size:
large, medium
Choose a Crust:
deep dish or thin
Choose One Topping:
sausage, pepperoni, cheese


Make a tree diagram to find the number of pizzas.

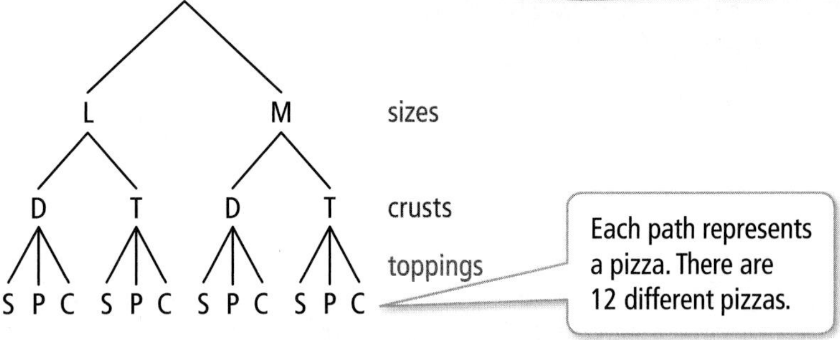


Each path represents a pizza. There are 12 different pizzas.

**COMMON ERROR**
When you compare a tree diagram to the Fundamental Counting Principle, remember to count the total number of paths from the beginning to the end of the tree diagram, not the number of branches in each section.

sizes × crusts × toppings = number of pizzas

$2 \times 2 \times 3 = 12$

This example illustrates the **Fundamental Counting Principle**. If there are $m$ ways to make the first selection and $n$ ways to make the second selection, then there are $m \times n$ ways to make the two selections. If a third selection, $p$, is added, then there are $m \times n \times p$ to make all three selections, and so on.

CONTINUED ON THE NEXT PAGE

EXAMPLE 1 CONTINUED

**Try It!** 1. The car that Ms. Garcia is buying comes with a choice of 3 trim lines (standard, sport, or luxury), 2 types of transmission (automatic or manual), and 8 colors. How many different option packages does Ms. Garcia have to choose from? Explain.

CONCEPTUAL UNDERSTANDING

## EXAMPLE 2 Find the Number of Permutations

**A. Gabriela is making a playlist with her 3 favorite songs. How many possible orders are there for the songs?**

**Method 1** Use an organized list.

Let A, B, and C represent the 3 songs.
There are 6 different possible orders for the songs.

| ABC | ACB |
|---|---|
| BAC | BCA |
| CAB | CBA |

**Method 2** Use the Fundamental Counting Principle.

$3 \cdot 2 \cdot 1$ — There are 3 choices for the first song, 2 choices for the second song, and 1 choice for the third song.

The **factorial** of a positive integer $n$ is the product of all positive integers less than or equal to $n$. It is written $n!$ and is read as *n factorial*. By definition, 0! equals 1.

$$n! = n \cdot (n-1) \cdot (n-2) \cdot \ldots \cdot 2 \cdot 1$$

The number of different possible orders for the songs is 3!

$$3! = 3 \cdot 2 \cdot 1 = 6$$

There are 6 different possible orders for the 3 songs.

**B. Gabriela wants to make another playlist using 5 of the 8 songs from her favorite artist's latest album. How many playlists are possible?**

**Method 1** Use the Fundamental Counting Principle.

There are 8 choices for the first song, 7 choices for the second song, and so on.

$$8 \cdot 7 \cdot 6 \cdot 5 \cdot 4 = 6{,}720$$

There are 6,720 possible playlists with 5 of the 8 songs.

**Method 2** Use factorials.

To count the number of ways to order 5 songs from A, B, C, D, E, F, G, and H, consider the list ABCDE. The diagram shows all the possible ways that sequence appears among the 8! ways to list all songs.

For any sequence of 5 songs, there are $(8-5)! = 3!$ ways that sequence appears as the first 5 songs when listing all 8! lists. So divide 8! by 3! to find the number of 5-song playlists.

| ABCDEFGH | ABCDEFHG |
|---|---|
| ABCDEGFH | ABCDEGHF |
| ABCDEHFG | ABCDEHGF |

$$\frac{8!}{3!} = \frac{8 \cdot 7 \cdot 6 \cdot 5 \cdot 4 \cdot 3 \cdot 2 \cdot 1}{3 \cdot 2 \cdot 1} = 6{,}720$$

There are 6,720 possible playlists with 5 of the 8 songs.

**LOOK FOR RELATIONSHIPS**
How is the Fundamental Counting Principle related to the number of permutations?

CONTINUED ON THE NEXT PAGE

 **Try It!** **2.** How many possible playlists are there for each situation?

**a.** Gabriela's 4 favorite songs **b.** 5 of the 10 most popular songs

## CONCEPT Permutations

A **permutation** is an arrangement of some or all objects of a set in a specific order.

The number of permutations of $n$ items arranged $r$ items at a time is

$$_{n}P_{r} = \frac{n!}{(n-r)!} \text{ for } 0 \le r \le n.$$

CONCEPTUAL UNDERSTANDING

## EXAMPLE 3 Find the Number of Combinations

**Marisol is planning to be a counselor at summer camp. She can choose 3 activities for her session. How many different combinations of 3 activities are possible?**

Use the formula to write an expression for the number of permutations of 10 choices taken 3 at a time.

$$_{10}P_{3} = \frac{10!}{(10-3)!} = 720$$

However, in this situation, the order of the 3 chosen activities does not matter, so you must adjust the formula.

A **combination** is a set of objects with no specific order.

3! Permutations 1 Combination

| | |
|---|---|
| ABC | ACB |
| BAC | BCA |
| CAB | CBA |

→ ABC

A group of 3 items can be arranged in 3! ways, so you must divide the the number of permutations, $_{10}P_{3}$, by the number of arrangements of the chosen items, 3!.

The notation $_{n}C_{r}$ indicates the number of combinations of $n$ items chosen $r$ items at a time.

$$_{10}C_{3} = \frac{_{10}P_{3}}{3!} = \frac{10!}{3!(10-3)!}$$

$$= \frac{720}{6}$$

$$= 120$$

$_{10}C_{3}$ denotes the number of combinations of 10 items taken 3 at a time.

**USE APPROPRIATE TOOLS**
Most scientific and graphing calculators can calculate permutations ($_{n}P_{r}$) and combinations ($_{n}C_{r}$).

There are 120 different combinations of activities that Marisol can choose.

 **Try It!** **3.** How many ways can a camper choose 5 activities from the 10 available activities at the summer camp?

Activity Assess

## CONCEPT Combinations

A **combination** is a set of objects with no specific order.

The number of combinations of $n$ items chosen $r$ at a time is

$${}_nC_r = \frac{n!}{r!(n-r)!} \text{ for } 0 \leq r \leq n.$$

APPLICATION

## EXAMPLE 4 Use Permutations and Combinations to Find Probabilities

**A teacher chooses 5 students at random from the names shown to work together on a group project. What is the probability that the 5 students' names begin with a consonant?**

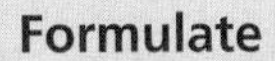

**Formulate** Determine if the problem is about permutations or combinations.

Since the order in which the students are chosen does not matter, use combinations to find the numbers of possible outcomes and desirable outcomes to calculate the probability.

**Compute** **Step 1** Find the total number of possible outcomes.

$${}_{18}C_5 = \frac{18!}{5!(18-5)!} = 8{,}568$$

There are 8,568 ways the teacher could choose 5 students.

**Step 2** Find the number of possible outcomes in which all the names begin with a consonant and none of the names begin with a vowel.

$${}_{13}C_5 = \frac{13!}{5!(13-5)!} = 1{,}287 \qquad {}_5C_0 = \frac{5!}{0!(5-0)!} = 1$$

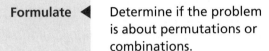

Choose 5 out of 13 names.

Choose 0 out of 5 names.

Use the Fundamental Counting Principle. Multiply the number of possible outcomes for the two subsets to find the total number of outcomes.

$${}_{13}C_5 \bullet {}_5C_0 = 1{,}287 \bullet 1 = 1{,}287$$

There are 1,287 outcomes with all the names beginning with consonants.

**Step 3** Find the probability.

$$P(\text{all consonants}) = \frac{\text{number of outcomes with all consonants}}{\text{total number of possible outcomes}} = \frac{1{,}287}{8{,}568} \approx 0.15$$

**Interpret** The probability that all 5 names begin with a consonant is about 0.15, or 15%.

**Try It!** 4. Using the data from Example 4, what is the probability that the 5 students' names end with a vowel?

## CONCEPT SUMMARY Permutations and Combinations

| | Permutation | Combination |
|---|---|---|
| WORDS | An arrangement of items in which the order of the items is important<br>${}_nP_r$ represents the number of permutations of $n$ items arranged $r$ at a time. | An arrangement of items in which the order of the items is not important<br>${}_nC_r$ represents the number of combinations of $n$ items chosen $r$ at a time. |
| ALGEBRA | ${}_nP_r = \frac{n!}{(n-r)!}$ for $0 \le r \le n$ | ${}_nC_r = \frac{n!}{r!(n-r)!}$ for $0 \le r \le n$ |
| NUMBERS | The number of permutations of 6 items taken 3 at a time is<br>${}_6P_3 = \frac{6!}{3!} = \frac{6 \cdot 5 \cdot 4 \cdot 3 \cdot 2 \cdot 1}{3 \cdot 2 \cdot 1} = 120$ | The number of combinations of 6 items taken 3 at a time is<br>${}_6C_3 = \frac{6!}{3!3!} = \frac{6 \cdot 5 \cdot 4 \cdot 3 \cdot 2 \cdot 1}{(3 \cdot 2 \cdot 1)(3 \cdot 2 \cdot 1)} = 20$ |

## Do You UNDERSTAND?

1. ESSENTIAL QUESTION How are permutations and combinations useful when finding probabilities?

2. **Use Structure** How is the formula for a combination related to the formula for a permutation?

3. **Vocabulary** Why is it important to distinguish between a *permutation* and a *combination* when counting items?

4. **Look for Relationships** How is ${}_9C_2$ related to ${}_9C_7$? Explain. How can you generalize this observation for any values of $n$ and $r$?

5. **Error Analysis** Explain Beth's error.

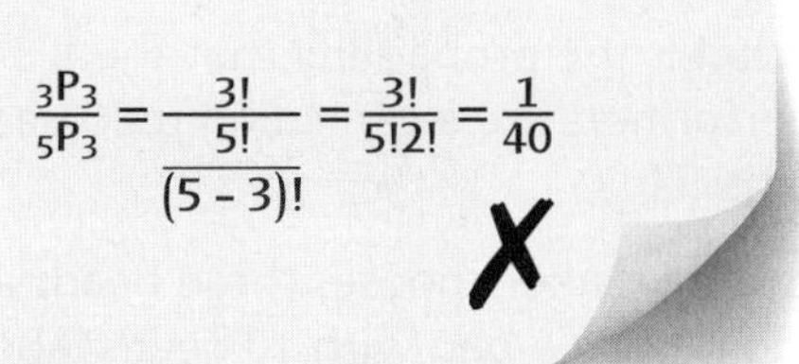

$\frac{{}_3P_3}{{}_5P_3} = \frac{3!}{\frac{5!}{(5-3)!}} = \frac{3!}{5!2!} = \frac{1}{40}$
X


6. **Construct Arguments** A company wants to form a committee of 4 people from its 12 employees. How can you use a combination to find the probability that the 4 people newest to the company will be selected?

## Do You KNOW HOW?

**Do the possible arrangements represent permutations or combinations?**

7. Jennifer will invite 3 of her 10 friends to a concert.

8. Jennifer must decide how she and her 3 friends will sit at the concert.

**Find the number of permutations.**

9. How many ways can 12 runners in a race finish first, second, and third?

**Find the number of combinations.**

10. In how many ways can 11 contestants for an award be narrowed down to 3 finalists?

11. How many different teams of 4 people can be chosen from a group of 8 people?

**Students will be chosen at random for school spirit awards. There are 6 athletes and 8 non-athletes who are eligible for 2 possible prizes. What is each probability?**

12. *P*(both prizes are awarded to athletes)

13. *P*(both prizes are awarded to non-athletes)

14. *P*(no prize is awarded to an athlete)

15. *P*(no prize is awarded to a non-athlete)

16. Explain how Exercises 12 and 13 are similar to Exercises 14 and 15.

## PRACTICE & PROBLEM SOLVING

Scan for Multimedia 

Additional Exercises Available Online

### UNDERSTAND

**17. Use Structure** Dwayne bought a new bike lock, and the lock came with instructions to choose 3 out of 30 numbers on a circular dial to keep his bike secure. The numbers cannot be repeated. How many possible arrangements can Dwayne choose for his lock? Do the arrangements represent permutations or combinations? Explain.

**18. Construct Arguments** Sage volunteers to read and play with sick children in a hospital. She selects some erasers at random from a bag to use as prizes. There are 8 alien erasers and 10 flying saucer erasers.

**a.** How many groups of 6 erasers can be formed from the 18 erasers? Explain.

**b.** In how many ways can 3 aliens be selected? Explain.

**c.** In how many ways can 3 aliens and 3 flying saucers be selected? Explain.

**d.** What is the probability that 3 aliens and 3 flying saucers will be selected? Explain.

**19. Error Analysis** There are 6 tiles numbered 1 to 6 in a box. Two tiles are selected at random without replacement to form a 2-digit number. Jeffrey found the probability that the number selected is 16. Explain his error.

The number of ways to select 1 and 6 is given by ${}_6C_2 = 15$

$$P(16) = \frac{1}{{}_6C_2} = \frac{1}{15}$$

**20. Mathematical Connections** How many lines are determined by the points, $P$, $Q$, $R$, and $S$? Explain.

**21. Higher Order Thinking** There are 11! different ways for a group of people to sit around a circular table. How many people are in the group? Explain.

### PRACTICE

**For Exercises 22–27, state if the possible arrangements represent permutations or combinations, then state the number of possible arrangements.** SEE EXAMPLES 1, 2, AND 3

**22.** A student chooses at random 4 books from a reading list of 11 books.

**23.** At the end of a season, 10 soccer teams are ranked by the state.

**24.** A committee of 5 people is being selected from a group of 9 to choose the food for a sport's banquet.

**25.** Hugo displays his 8 model planes in a single row.

**26.** A class president, secretary, and treasurer are chosen from 12 students running for office.

**27.** A food truck has a lunch special on tacos. Customers choose a shell, three toppings, and two sides for one price.

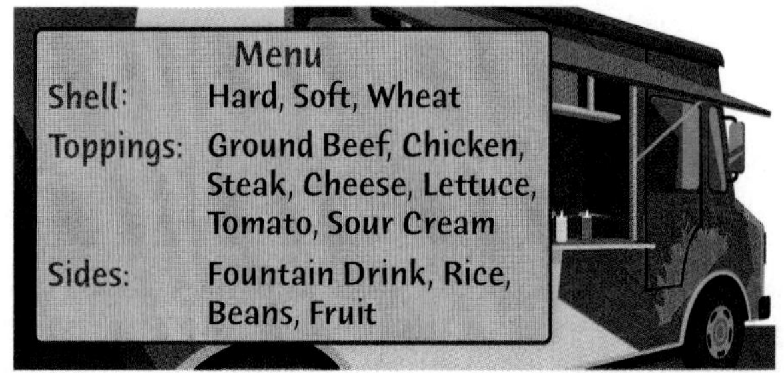

Menu
Shell: Hard, Soft, Wheat
Toppings: Ground Beef, Chicken, Steak, Cheese, Lettuce, Tomato, Sour Cream
Sides: Fountain Drink, Rice, Beans, Fruit


**28.** There are 4 comedians and 5 musicians performing in a variety show. The order in which the performers are chosen is random. SEE EXAMPLE 4

**a.** What is the probability that the first 3 performers are comedians?

**b.** What is the probability that the first two performers are a comedian followed by a musician?

**29.** A jewelry maker chooses three beads at random from a bag with 10 beads labeled A, B, C, D, E, F, G, H, I, and J. SEE EXAMPLES 2, 3, AND 4

**a.** How can you use permutations or combinations to find $P$(selected beads spell the initials DEB)? What is the probability?

**b.** How can you use permutations or combinations to find $P$(selected beads are all vowels)? What is the probability?

# PRACTICE & PROBLEM SOLVING

Practice Tutorial

Mixed Review Available Online

## APPLY

**30. Make Sense and Persevere** Amaya's wallet contains three \$1 bills, two \$5 bills, and three \$10 bills. If she pulls 2 bills without looking, what is the probability that she draws a \$1-bill and a \$10-bill? Explain.

**31. Model with Mathematics** Raul's favorite restaurant is running a prize game. Five of each of the winning tickets shown are available, and a customer must collect three winning tickets to receive the prize. What is the probability Raul will receive the prize for the baseball cap with his first 3 tickets?

**32. Look for Relationships** Smart Phones, Inc. chooses a 5-digit security code at random from the digits 0–9.

a. Suppose the digits cannot be repeated. What is the probability that the security code is 30429? Explain.

b. Suppose the digits can be repeated. What is the probability that the security code is 30429? Explain.

**33. Make Sense and Persevere** Edwin randomly plays 6 different songs from his playlist.

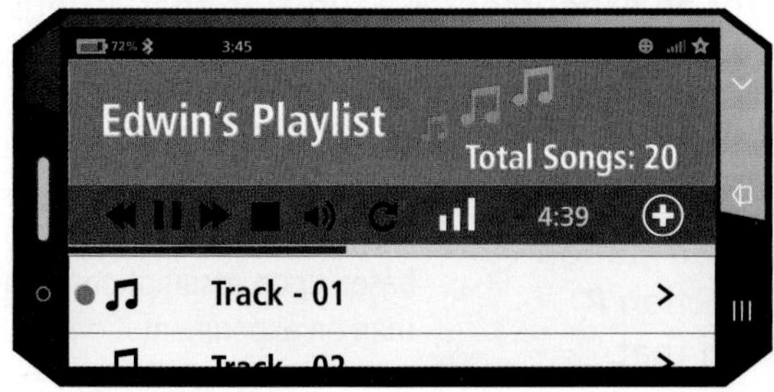


a. What is the probability that Edwin hears his 6 favorite songs?

b. What is the probability that he hears the songs in order from his most favorite to his sixth most favorite?

## ASSESSMENT PRACTICE

**34.** Consider an arrangement of 8 items taken 3 at a time in which order is not important. Does each expression give the correct number of arrangements? Select *Yes* or *No*.

| | Yes | No |
|---|---|---|
| ${}_8P_3$ | ❑ | ❑ |
| ${}_8C_3$ | ❑ | ❑ |
| $\frac{{}_8P_3}{3!}$ | ❑ | ❑ |
| $8! \cdot 3!$ | ❑ | ❑ |
| $\frac{8!}{3!}$ | ❑ | ❑ |
| $\frac{8!}{5!}$ | ❑ | ❑ |
| $\frac{8!}{3!5!}$ | ❑ | ❑ |
| $8 \cdot 7$ | ❑ | ❑ |

**35. SAT/ACT** Fifteen students enter a Safety Week poster contest in which prizes will be awarded for first through fourth place. In how many ways could the prizes be given out?

Ⓐ 4
Ⓑ 60
Ⓒ 1,365
Ⓓ 32,760
Ⓔ 50,625

**36. Performance Task** Use the word shown on the tiles below to find each probability.

**Part A** Two tiles are chosen at random without replacement. Use conditional probability to find the probability that both letters are vowels. Then find the probability using permutations or combinations. Explain.

**Part B** Four of the tiles are chosen at random and placed in the order in which they are drawn. Use conditional probability to find the probability the tiles spell the word SURF. Then find the probability using permutations or combinations. Explain.

Activity Assess

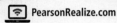

# 12-4 Probability Distributions

PearsonRealize.com

**I CAN…** define probability distributions to represent experiments and solve problems.

**VOCABULARY**

- binomial experiment
- binomial probability
- probability distribution
- uniform probability distribution

## MODEL & DISCUSS

**Mr. and Mrs. Mason have three children. Assume that the probability of having a baby girl is 0.5 and the probability of having a baby boy is also 0.5.**

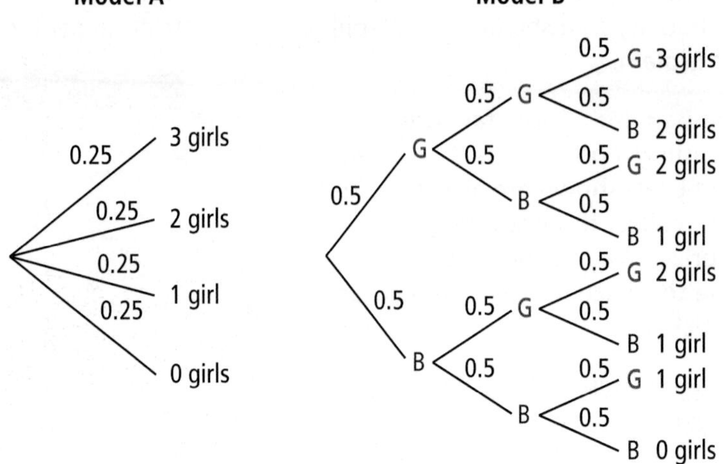


A. **Reason** Which model represents the situation correctly, Model A or Model B? Explain.

B. What is the probability that Mr. and Mrs. Mason have 3 girls?

C. Compare the probability that the Masons' first child was a boy and they then had two girls to the probability that their first two children were girls and they then had a boy. Does the order affect the probabilities? Explain.

## ESSENTIAL QUESTION

**What does a probability distribution tell you about an experiment?**

CONCEPTUAL UNDERSTANDING

## EXAMPLE 1 Develop a Theoretical Probability Distribution

**A. Teo and Henry are running for President of the Student Council. You will select a campaign button at random from the box containing 3 Teo buttons and 3 Henry buttons. You will record the number of Teo buttons that you get. What is the theoretical probability distribution for the sample space {0, 1}?**

**COMMUNICATE PRECISELY**
The sample space {0, 1} represents how many Teo buttons you can select in one trial.

A **probability distribution** for an experiment is a function that assigns a probability to each outcome of a sample space for the experiment.

Since you are selecting a button at random, you are equally likely to get 0 buttons or 1 button for Teo.

The theoretical probability distribution for this experiment is the function $P$, defined on the set {0, 1}, such that $P(0) = \frac{1}{2}$ and $P(1) = \frac{1}{2}$.

A theoretical probability is based upon assumptions rather than on experimentation.

CONTINUED ON THE NEXT PAGE

EXAMPLE 1 CONTINUED

**B. Now you plan to select a button at random, put it back in the box, and then select another button at random. You will record the total number of times that you get a Teo button in the experiment. Define the theoretical probability distribution for the sample space {0, 1, 2}. How does this probability distribution differ from the distribution in Part A?**

Make a tree diagram for the experiment.

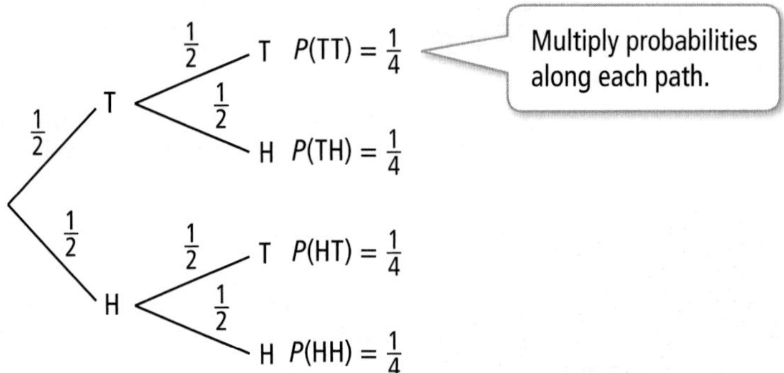


Add the probabilities of TH and HT to find the probability of getting one Teo button.

$$P(1) = \frac{1}{4} + \frac{1}{4} = \frac{1}{2}$$

**STUDY TIP**
One way to check your work is to check that the sum of the probabilities of all the outcomes is 1.

The theoretical probability distribution is the function $P$, defined on the set {0, 1, 2}, such that $P(0) = \frac{1}{4}$, $P(1) = \frac{1}{2}$, and $P(2) = \frac{1}{4}$.

Compare this probability distribution to the one in Part A.

A **uniform probability distribution** assigns the same probability to each outcome.

| Comparing Probability Distributions | | |
|---|---|---|
| **Select one button** | $P(0) = \frac{1}{2}, P(1) = \frac{1}{2}$. | uniform |
| **Select two buttons** | $P(0) = \frac{1}{4}, P(1) = \frac{1}{2}, P(2) = \frac{1}{4}$ | not uniform |

The probability distribution in Part A is a uniform probability distribution. The probability distribution in this part is not.

**Try It!** 1. You select two marbles at random from the bowl. For each situation, define the theoretical probability distribution for selecting a number of red marbles on the sample space {0, 1, 2}. Is it a uniform probability distribution?

**a.** You select one marble and put it back in the bowl. Then you select a second marble.

**b.** You select one marble and do not put it back in the bowl. Then you select a second marble.

APPLICATION

## EXAMPLE 2 Develop an Experimental Probability Distribution

**A cell phone company surveyed 500 households about the number of smartphones they have that are in use.**

| Number of Smartphones per Household | | | | | | | |
|---|---|---|---|---|---|---|---|
| Number | 0 | 1 | 2 | 3 | 4 | 5 | 6 or more |
| Frequency | 10 | 66 | 120 | 144 | 79 | 37 | 44 |

**Would you recommend that the company concentrate on selling data plans for individuals or plans for families with three or more smartphones? Explain.**

**Step 1** Define an experimental probability distribution on the sample space {0, 1, 2, 3, 4, 5, 6 or more}.

First divide each frequency by 500 to find each relative frequency. For convenience, round each relative frequency to the nearest whole percent.

| Number of Smartphones per Household | | | | | | | |
|---|---|---|---|---|---|---|---|
| Number | 0 | 1 | 2 | 3 | 4 | 5 | 6 or more |
| Frequency | 10 | 66 | 120 | 144 | 79 | 37 | 44 |
| Relative Frequency | 2% | 13% | 24% | 29% | 16% | 7% | 9% |

Each relative frequency represents the experimental probability that a household selected at random from the 500 households has a given number of smartphones.

An experimental probability is based upon collecting real-world data and finding relative frequencies.

An experimental probability distribution for the experiment is the function $P$ such that if $n$ is an outcome of the sample space, then $P(n)$ is the probability of that outcome. For example, $P(0) = 2\%$.

**Step 2** Graph the probability distribution.

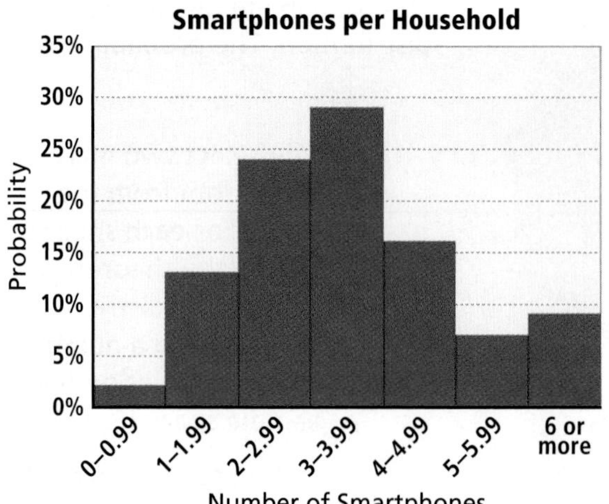


COMMON ERROR
When graphing a probability distribution, the heights of the bars represent the probabilities of each outcome, not their frequencies.

**Step 3** Interpret the results.

The probability that a household has 3 or more cell phones is 61%.

Therefore, the company should probably focus on family plans rather than individual plans.

CONTINUED ON THE NEXT PAGE

 **Try It!** 2. Suppose that you selected a student at random from the Drama Club and recorded the student's age.

| Ages of Students in Drama Club | | | | | |
|---|---|---|---|---|---|
| **Age** | 14 | 15 | 16 | 17 | 18 |
| **Number** | 4 | 7 | 10 | 7 | 9 |

a. Define an experimental probability distribution on the sample space {14, 15, 16, 17, 18}.

b. Graph the probability distribution you defined.

## CONCEPT Binomial Experiments

A **binomial experiment** is an experiment that consists of a fixed number of trials, with the following features.

- Each trial has two possible outcomes, one of which is denoted as "success."
- The results of the trials are independent events.
- The probability of "success" is the same for every trial.

## EXAMPLE 3 Binomial Experiments

**Is the experiment a binomial experiment?**

**A. This spinner is spun 3 times. Assume that the spinner is equally likely to stop in any of the sections. Success is landing on a section marked "Go Forward 2 Spaces."**

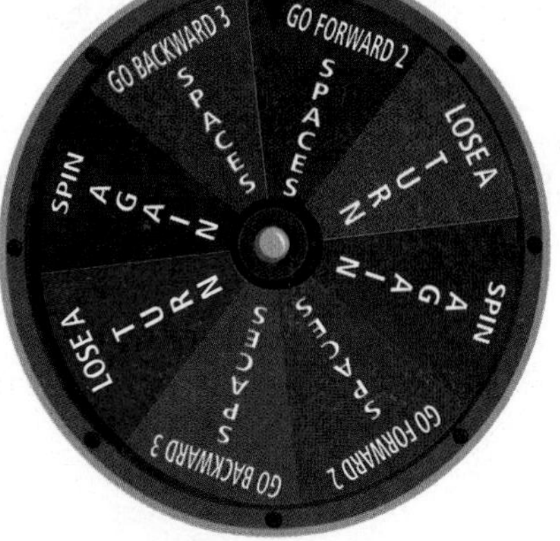


Compare the experiment to the requirements for a binomial experiment.

- There are two possible outcomes for each trial, landing on a section labeled "Go Forward 2 Spaces" (success) and not landing on one of those sections.
- The outcome of one spin does not affect the probability of success on any other spin.
- The probability of success is 0.25 for every trial.

The experiment is a binomial experiment.

**B. There are 7 students in a class of 23 students taking French. You are going to choose a student at random and then a second student at random. Success is choosing a student who is taking French.**

The probability that the first student is taking French is $\frac{7}{23}$.

If the first student is taking French, the probability that the second student is taking French is $\frac{6}{22}$. If the first student is not, the probability is $\frac{7}{22}$.

Because the probabilities for each trial are different, the experiment is not a binomial experiment.

**GENERALIZE**
Would the experiment be a binomial experiment if there were 25 students in the class? Some other number?

CONTINUED ON THE NEXT PAGE

 **Try It!** **3.** Is the experiment a binomial experiment? If so, find the probability of success. Explain.

**a.** You select one card at random from a set of 7 cards, 4 labeled A and 3 labeled B. Then you select another card at random from the cards that remain. Success is getting a card labeled A each time.

**b.** You roll a standard number cube 4 times. Assume that each time you roll the number cube, each number is equally likely to come up. For each trial, success is getting an even number.

## CONCEPT Binomial Probability Formula

For a binomial experiment consisting of $n$ trials with the probability of success $p$ for each trial, the probability of $r$ successes out of the $n$ trials is given by the following formula:

$$P(r) = {}_nC_r \cdot p^r(1-p)^{n-r}$$

The probability of having a given number of successes in a binomial experiment is called a **binomial probability**.

## EXAMPLE 4 Probabilities in a Binomial Experiment

**A grocery store gives away scratch-off cards with a purchase of more than \$100.**

**Terrell has 5 scratch-off cards. What is the probability that he has exactly 3 winning cards if each card has a 30% chance of being a winner?**

**Step 1** Determine whether the situation is a binomial experiment.

- Terrell's 5 cards represent 5 trials.
- Each card is either a winning card (success) or not.
- Whether one card is a winning card does not affect the probability that another card is a winning card.
- The probability of success, 0.3, is the same for every trial.

So this is a binomial experiment.

**REASON**
In the formula for binomial probability, what probability does the term $1-p$ represent?

**Step 2** Find the probability of 3 successes.

The formula $P(r) = {}_nC_r \cdot p^r(1-p)^{n-r}$ gives the probability of $r$ successes out of $n$ trials. Use $n = 5$, $r = 3$, and $p = 0.3$.

$$\begin{aligned} {}_5C_3 &= \frac{5!}{3!(5-3)!} \\ &= \frac{5 \cdot 4}{2 \cdot 1} \\ &= 10 \end{aligned}$$

$$\begin{aligned} P(3) &= {}_5C_3 \cdot (0.3)^3(1-0.3)^{5-3} \\ &= 10(0.3)^3(0.7)^2 \\ &= 10(0.027)(0.49) \\ &= 0.1323 \end{aligned}$$

The probability of having exactly 3 winning cards is about 13%.

 **Try It!** **4.** To the nearest tenth of a percent, what is the probability that Terrell has more than 3 winning cards? Explain.

## CONCEPT SUMMARY Probability Distributions

### TYPES OF DISTRIBUTIONS

A probability distribution for an experiment is a function that assigns a probability to each outcome of a sample space for the experiment.

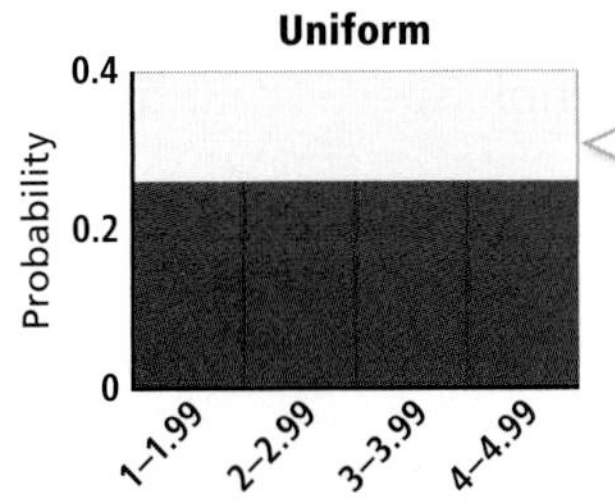


A uniform probability distribution assigns the same probability to each outcome.

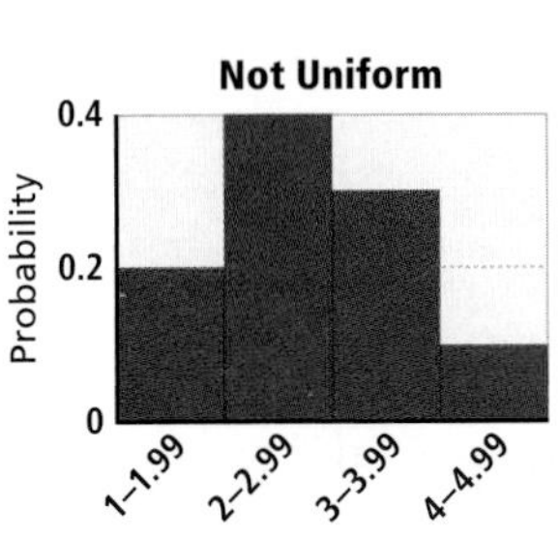


### BINOMIAL EXPERIMENT

A binomial experiment is an experiment that consists of a fixed number of trials, in which:

- each trial has two possible outcomes, one of which is denoted as "success";
- the results of the trials are independent events; and
- the probability of "success" is the same for every trial.

If the probability of success is $p$ for each trial, then the probability of $r$ successes out of $n$ trials is $P(r) = {}_nC_r \cdot p^r(1 - p)^{n-r}$.

## Do You UNDERSTAND?

1. **ESSENTIAL QUESTION** What does a probability distribution tell you about an experiment?

2. **Vocabulary** What is the difference between a binomial experiment and one that is not binomial?

3. **Error Analysis** A regular tetrahedron has four triangular sides, with one of the letters A, B, C, and D on each side. Assume that if you roll the tetrahedron, each of the letters is equally likely to end up on the bottom. {A, B, C, D} is a sample space for the experiment. Rochelle was asked to find the theoretical probability distribution for the experiment. Explain and correct the error.

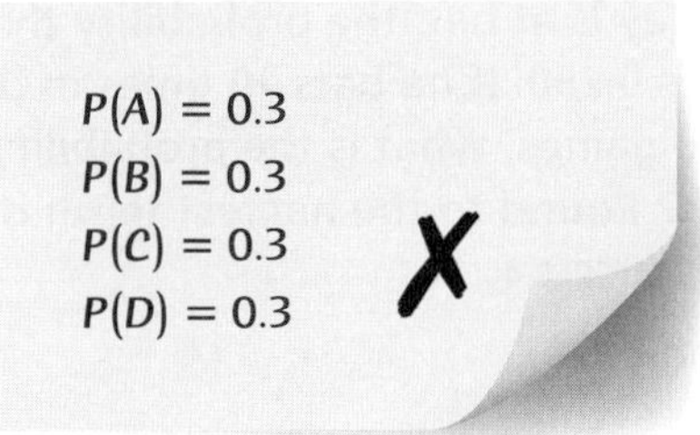


## Do You KNOW HOW?

**Graph the probability distribution $P$.**

4. Theoretical probability of selecting a student at random from a group of 3 students Jack, Alani, and Seth

5. Experimental probability of flipping a fair coin 3 times and counting the number of heads. The sample space is the set of numbers 0, 1, 2, 3. $P(0) = 0.125$, $P(1) = 0.375$, $P(2) = 0.375$, $P(3) = 0.125$

**A bag contains 5 balls: 3 green, 1 red, and 1 yellow. You select a ball at random 4 times, replacing the ball after each selection. Calculate the theoretical probability of each event to the nearest whole percent.**

6. getting a green ball exactly 3 times

7. getting a green ball exactly 4 times

8. getting a green ball at least 3 times

9. getting a yellow ball twice

10. getting only red and green balls

## PRACTICE & PROBLEM SOLVING

Scan for Multimedia

Practice Tutorial

Additional Exercises Available Online

### UNDERSTAND

**11. Communicate Precisely** Explain what it means for a coin to be a fair coin.

**12. Reason** You spin the spinner shown.

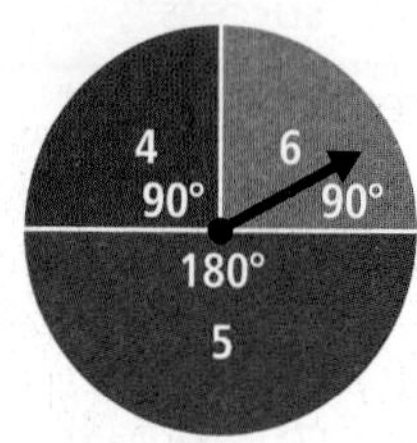


Describe a theoretical probability distribution for the experiment.

**13. Communicate Precisely** Five students in a class of 27 students ate hamburgers for lunch. Suppose the teacher selects a student in the class at random and then selects another student at random. Success for each selection is selecting a student who ate a hamburger. Is this a binomial experiment? Explain.

**14. Error Analysis** A standard number cube is rolled 7 times. Success for each roll is defined as getting a number less than 3. Abby tried to calculate the probability of 5 successes. Describe and correct her error.

$$P(5) = \left(\frac{1}{3}\right)^5\left(\frac{2}{3}\right)^2 \approx 0.002$$ ✗

**15. Mathematical Connections** A marble is selected from the bowl shown 4 times. The marble is returned to the bowl after each selection.

a. Show that there are exactly $_4C_2$ ways to get exactly 2 green marbles.

b. How are $_5C_3$ and $_5C_2$ related? Explain.

### PRACTICE

**A card is chosen at random from the box containing 10 cards: 3 yellow, 4 red, 2 green, and 1 blue.** SEE EXAMPLES 1 AND 2

**16.** Define a probability distribution for this experiment on the sample space {Y, R, G, B}.

**17.** Graph the probability distribution.

**In a certain game, the player can score 0, 1, 2, 3, or 4 points during their turn. The table shows the number of times Kennedy scored each number of points the last time she played the game.**
SEE EXAMPLE 2

| Score | 0 | 1 | 2 | 3 | 4 |
|---|---|---|---|---|---|
| Frequency | 3 | 7 | 9 | 6 | 5 |

**18.** Define an experimental probability distribution based on Kennedy's scores.

**19.** Graph the probability distribution you defined in Exercise 18.

**Is the experiment a binomial experiment? Explain.**
SEE EXAMPLE 3

**20.** A quality control specialist tests 50 LED light bulbs produced in a factory. Success is that a tested light bulb burns for at least 2,000 hours without dimming. For each light bulb, the probability of success is 0.9.

**21.** There are 10 black and 10 red cards face down on the table. One card is selected at random. Then another card is selected at random. Success is getting a red card.

**22.** A basketball player is shooting 2 free throws. The probability of her making the first free throw is 0.86. The probability of her making the second free throw is 0.92.

**Each time Bailey is at bat, the probability that he gets a hit is 0.250. If he bats 10 times in the course of two games, what is the probability of each result? Round to the nearest tenth of a percent.** SEE EXAMPLE 4

**23.** He gets no hits.

**24.** He gets exactly 1 hit.

**25.** He gets exactly 2 hits.

**26.** He gets fewer than 3 hits.

# PRACTICE & PROBLEM SOLVING

## APPLY

**27. Model with Mathematics** The circle graph shows the result of a survey of the most popular types of music in the U.S., based on sales, downloads, and streaming.

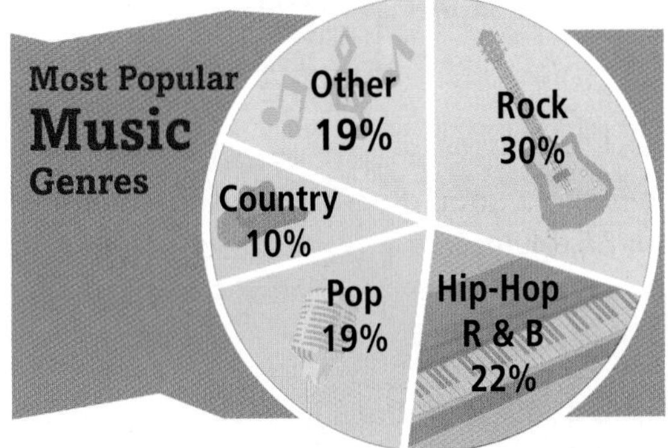


a. Define a probability distribution for the sample space.

b. Graph the probability distribution.

c. According to the survey, which is the most popular type of music in the United States?

**28. Higher Order Thinking** A pharmaceutical company is testing a new version of a medication. In a clinical trial of the old version of the medication, 18% of the subjects taking the old medication experienced headaches.

a. Suppose that 18% of the people taking the new medications will experience headaches. If 8 subjects are selected at random and given the new medication, what is the probability that less than two of them will experience headaches?

b. Suppose that two of the eight subjects experience headaches after taking the new medication. Is that cause for concern? Explain your reasoning.

**29. Communicate Precisely** In a quiz show, a contestant is asked 6 questions. Each question has 5 answer choices. Assume that the contestant picks an answer at random for each question and the probability of guessing the correct answer is 20%. What is the probability of guessing correctly on at least 4 of the questions? Round your answer to the nearest tenth of a percent.

## ASSESSMENT PRACTICE

**30.** You are going to roll a game piece two times. The game piece has 10 sides of equal area, each with one of the numbers 0 through 9. Assume that it is equally likely to land with any of the sides on top. Success is defined as getting a 3 on top.

Let $P$ be the function defined on {0, 1, 2} such that $P(n)$ is the probability of $n$ successes. Select all that apply.

Ⓐ This is a binomial experiment.

Ⓑ $P$ is a probability distribution for the sample space {0, 1, 2}.

Ⓒ $P(0) = 0.81$

Ⓓ $P(1) = 0.09$

Ⓔ $P(2) = 0.01$

**31. SAT/ACT** A standard number cube is rolled 6 times. Success is defined as getting a number greater than 4. Rounded to the nearest percent, what is the probability of exactly 2 successes?

Ⓐ 2% Ⓑ 8% Ⓒ 23% Ⓓ 33% Ⓔ 50%

**32. Performance Task** Get 5 index cards. Draw a picture on one side and no picture on the other side of each card.

**Part A** You are going to throw all 5 cards up in the air and count the number of cards that land face up. Assume that it is equally likely that each card will land face up and face down. Define a theoretical probability distribution for the sample space {0, 1, 2, 3, 4, 5}.

**Part B** Perform the experiment 20 times. Each time you perform the experiment, record the number of cards that land face up. Find the experimental probability for each outcome in the sample space {0, 1, 2, 3, 4, 5} and define an experimental probability distribution the sample space.

**Part C** Compare the results of Part A and B. If they are different, explain why you think they are different.

Activity Assess

# 12-5 Expected Value

PearsonRealize.com

**I CAN...** calculate, interpret, and apply expected value.

**VOCABULARY**

- binomial distribution
- expected value

## EXPLORE & REASON

**A company has 20 employees whose hourly wages are shown in the bar graph.**

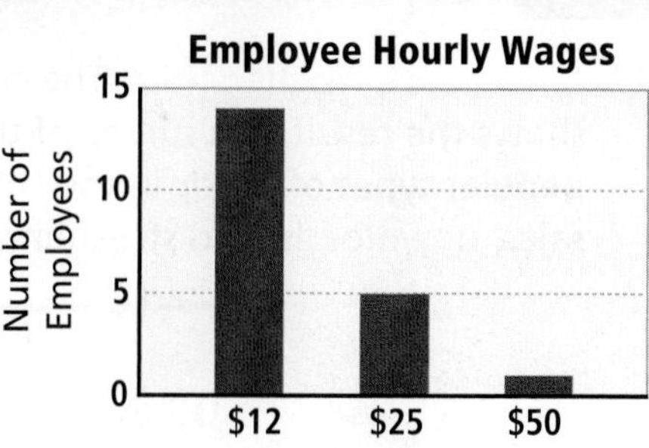


**A.** An employee is chosen at random. What is the probability that his or her hourly wage is \$12? \$25? \$50?

**B.** What is the mean hourly wage? Explain your method.

**C. Construct Arguments** Is the mean a good description of the typical hourly wage at this company? Explain.

**ESSENTIAL QUESTION** What does expected value tell you about situations involving probability?

CONCEPTUAL UNDERSTANDING

## EXAMPLE 1 Evaluate and Apply Expected Value

**The table shows data on sales in one month for each item on a restaurant menu. To estimate future profits, the owner evaluates the average profit from each meal.**

| Meal | Profit per Serving | Percent Sold |
|---|---|---|
| Stew | \$0.34 | 12% |
| Soup | \$0.41 | 7% |
| Lasagna | \$0.64 | 45% |
| Chili | \$0.73 | 36% |

**Expected value** is the sum of the value of each outcome multiplied by the probability of the outcome.

$$E(x) = x_1P(x_1) + x_2P(x_2) + x_3P(x_3) + \dots + x_nP(x_n)$$

**A. Based on the data, what is the average profit that the owner can expect to make from each meal?**

The outcomes are the profits for each meal. The probability for each meal is the percent sold. Multiply each outcome by its probability. Then add.

$$E(x) = 0.34(0.12) + 0.41(0.07) + 0.64(0.45) + 0.73(0.36) = 0.6203$$

Use the expected value formula when the probability of at least one event differs from any of the others.

If this weighted average continues, the owner can expect to earn about \$0.62 per meal.

**B. What is the expected profit for the next 200 meals ordered?**

$$\$0.6203 \times 200 = \$124.06$$

The owner can expect to net about \$124.06 for the next 200 meals.

**COMMON ERROR**
Note that average profit from each meal is not simply the average of the cost of 1 serving of each of the 4 meals because the number of each kind of meal varies.

CONTINUED ON THE NEXT PAGE

 **Try It!** **1. a.** What would happen to the expected value if fewer people ordered chili and more people ordered stew? Explain.

**b.** Suppose the owner of the restaurant increased the cost of an order of stew by \$.05 and decreased the cost of an order of chili by \$.05. How would these changes affect the average value per meal?

## EXAMPLE 2 Find Expected Payoffs

**A charity is considering a fundraising event in which donors will pay \$1 to spin the wheel 3 times. What is the expected payoff for the charity for each game?**

**EVEN THREES**

Spin 3 times
Get 3 even numbers
**Win an item worth \$4**

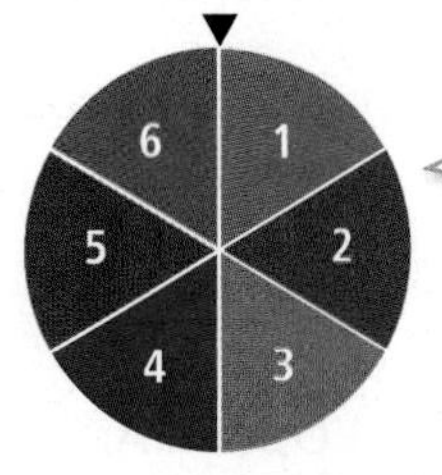


There are 6 possible outcomes. 3 of the possible outcomes are even numbers.

**MAKE SENSE AND PERSEVERE**
Think about methods used to find probabilities. What do you need to identify to find the probabilities for each situation?

**Step 1** Find the probabilities for the donor.

There are $6^3$, or 216 outcomes for spinning the wheel 3 times.

There are $3^3$, or 27, ways to spin 3 even numbers in a row, so the probability of a donor winning a \$4 prize is $\frac{27}{216}$, or $\frac{1}{8}$.

So, the probability of a donor not winning is $1 - \frac{1}{8}$, or $\frac{7}{8}$.

**Step 2** Find probabilities for the charity.

The probability that the charity gains \$1 is $P(1) = \frac{7}{8}$.

The probability that the charity loses \$3 is $P(-3) = \frac{1}{8}$.

**Step 3** Find the expected value of each game for the charity.

$$E(x) = 1\left(\frac{7}{8}\right) + (-3)\left(\frac{1}{8}\right)$$
$$= \frac{4}{8}$$
$$= \frac{1}{2}$$

The charity can expect to earn \$0.50 each game.

 **Try It!** **2.** What is the expected payoff for the person making the donation?

APPLICATION

## EXAMPLE 3 Use Expected Values to Evaluate Strategies

**A car owner is considering three options for an auto insurance policy. Statistics show that there is a 10% chance of needing a repair with an average cost of $500.**

**Car Insurance Policy Options**

| Option | Annual Premium ($) | Deductible ($) |
|---|---|---|
| A | 480 | 0 |
| B | 447 | 200 |
| C | 402 | 500 |

The deductible is the portion of repair costs that the car owner pays.

**A. Based on the owner's assumptions, which option has the least expected total annual cost to the owner?**

The total cost is the annual cost of insurance plus the cost of any deductible.

| | Annual premium | + | Annual deductible | • | Probability of repairs | = | Expected annual cost |
|---|---|---|---|---|---|---|---|
| Option A: | 480 | + | 0 | • | 0.10 | = | $480 |
| Option B: | 447 | + | 200 | • | 0.10 | = | $467 |
| Option C: | 402 | + | 500 | • | 0.10 | = | $452 |

Option C has the least expected total cost to the owner.

**MAKE SENSE AND PERSEVERE**
In most financial transactions, the parties have different goals. How would a consumer's goals be different from the insurance company's goals?

**B. Find the insurance company's expected income each year for each option. Which option provides the greatest income to the company?**

The income for the insurance company will be the premium minus what they expect to pay for repairs. The insurance company pays the difference between the cost of the repair and the deductible.

| | Annual premium | – | Payment for Repairs | • | Probability of repairs | = | Expected annual earnings |
|---|---|---|---|---|---|---|---|
| Option A: | 480 | – | 500 | • | 0.10 | = | $430 |
| Option B: | 447 | – | 300 | • | 0.10 | = | $417 |
| Option C: | 402 | – | 0 | • | 0.10 | = | $402 |

On average, the insurance company's annual income for Option A is greatest. The company's expected earnings are $430 per year.

**Try It!** **3.** Latoya is considering two options for a homeowner policy. She estimates there is a 5% chance she will need home repairs costing more than $500 in any given year. Which policy has the lesser expected total cost?

**Homeowner Policy Options**

| Option | Annual Cost ($) | Deductible ($) |
|---|---|---|
| A+ | 1400 | 0 |
| Economy | 1250 | 500 |

## EXAMPLE 4 Use Binomial Probability to Find Expected Value

**According to the weather app on Talisha's smartphone, there is a 40% chance of rain for each of the 5 days of her vacation. How many rainy days should Talisha expect during her vacation?**

STUDY TIP
Organize your work in a table that clearly shows each outcome and its probability.

| Days of Rain | Probability |
|---|---|
| 0 | ${}_5C_0(0.4)^0(0.6)^5 \approx 0.0777$ |
| 1 | ${}_5C_1(0.4)^1(0.6)^4 = 0.2592$ |
| 2 | ${}_5C_2(0.4)^2(0.6)^3 = 0.3456$ |
| 3 | ${}_5C_3(0.4)^3(0.6)^2 = 0.2304$ |
| 4 | ${}_5C_4(0.4)^4(0.6)^1 = 0.0768$ |
| 5 | ${}_5C_5(0.4)^5(0.6)^0 \approx 0.0102$ |

Find the binomial probability when $n = 5$, $p = 0.4$, and $1 - p = 0.6$ for the possibility of rain for each number of days of Talisha's vacation.

To find the expected number of rainy days, multiply each probability by the number of rainy days it corresponds to, and add those values together.

Expected number of rainy days

$= 0 \cdot P(0) + 1 \cdot P(1) + 2 \cdot P(2) + 3 \cdot P(3) + 4 \cdot P(4) + 5 \cdot P(5)$

$= 0(0.0777) + 1(0.2592) + 2(0.3456) + 3(0.2304) + 4(0.0768) + 5(0.0102) \approx 2$

Talisha should expect 2 rainy days during her vacation.

The table shows the probability of every outcome of a binomial experiment. This probability distribution is called a **binomial distribution**. A special relationship exists for the expected value for any binomial distribution.

$$E(x) = np$$

$$2 = 5(0.4)$$

$E(x)$ expected value; $n$ trials; $p$ probability

**Try It!** 4. A carnival game has 4 orange lights and 1 green light that flash rapidly one at a time in a random order. When a player pushes a button, the game stops, leaving one light on. If the light is green, the player wins a prize. Copy and complete the table, then determine the number of prizes that a player can expect to win if the game is played 4 times.

| Number of Green Lights | Probability |
|---|---|
| 0 | ${}_4C_0(0.2)^0(0.8)^4 = ■$ |
| 1 | ${}_4C_■(0.2)^■(0.8)^■ = ■$ |
| 2 | ${}_■C_■(0.2)^■(0.8)^■ = ■$ |
| 3 | ${}_■C_■(0.2)^■(0.8)^■ = ■$ |
| 4 | ${}_■C_■(0.2)^■(0.8)^■ = ■$ |

## CONCEPT SUMMARY Expected Value

**WORDS**

Expected value is the average outcome that will occur with many trials of an experiment. It is the sum of the value of each outcome times the probability of the outcome.

**ALGEBRA**

Let $x_1, x_2, x_3, \ldots x_n$ represent the values of the outcomes of a set of trials.

If $p_1, p_2, p_2, \ldots p_n$ is the probability of each outcome, then you can find the expected value, $E(x)$, with this formula.

$$E(x) = x_1p_1 + x_2p_2 + \ldots + x_np_n$$

## Do You UNDERSTAND?

1. **ESSENTIAL QUESTION** What does expected value tell you about situations involving probability?

2. **Error Analysis** What is Benjamin's error?

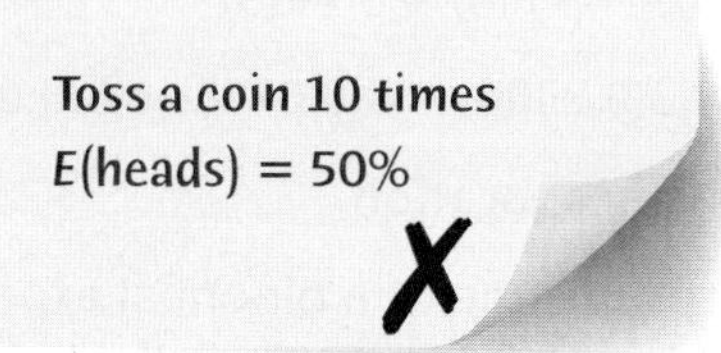

Toss a coin 10 times
$E(\text{heads}) = 50\%$

3. **Construct Arguments** A carnival game costs \$1 to play. The expected payout for each play of this game is \$1.12. Should the carnival operators modify the game in any way? Explain.

4. **Reason** The students in Ms. Kahn's class are raising money to help earthquake victims. They expect to raise \$0.52 for each raffle ticket they sell. If each raffle ticket is sold for \$2, what can you conclude?

5. **Vocabulary** When is the expected value of a set of items equal to the average of the items?

## Do You KNOW HOW?

6. What is the expected value when rolling a standard number cube?

7. What is the expected value of the sum when rolling two standard number cubes?

8. A travel website reports that in a particular European city, the probability of rain on any day in April is 40%. What is the expected number of rainy days in this city during the month of April?

9. You buy an airplane ticket for \$900. You discover that if you cancel or rebook your vacation flight to Europe, you will be charged an extra \$300. There is a 20% chance that you will not be able to travel on that flight.

   a. What is the expected value of the ticket?

   b. Does the expected value help you make a decision to buy the ticket? Explain.

10. A child-care service charges families an hourly rate based upon the age of the child. Their hourly rate per child is \$20 per hour for infants less than 1 year old, \$18 for toddlers 1 to 3 years old, \$15 per hour children 3 or more years old. The ratios of infants : toddlers : 3+ years is 2 : 3 : 5. What is the expected charge per child per hour?

# PRACTICE & PROBLEM SOLVING

Scan for Multimedia

Additional Exercises Available Online

## UNDERSTAND

11. **Error Analysis** For the dartboard shown, Deshawn calculated the expected number of points per dart. Explain Deshawn's error. What is the correct expected value?

$$\text{Expected value} = \frac{2}{7}(4) + \frac{5}{7}(1)$$
$$= \frac{8}{7} + \frac{5}{7}$$
$$= \frac{13}{7} \approx 1.86$$

X

12. **Reason** A nonrefundable plane ticket costs \$600, while a refundable ticket costs \$900. A traveler estimates there is a 20% chance he will have to cancel his upcoming trip. Should the traveler purchase a refundable or nonrefundable ticket? Explain.

13. **Construct Arguments** A consumer determines that her expected cost for Option B is \$528 per year.

| Option | Annual Premium | Deductible |
|---|---|---|
| A | \$600 | \$0 |
| B | \$500 | \$1,000 |

a. Why might this consumer select the policy with the \$1000 deductible?

b. Why might this consumer select the policy with no deductible?

14. **Mathematical Connections** How is expected value related to the mean?

## PRACTICE

**A farmer estimates her hens will produce 3,000 dozen more eggs this year than last year. She estimates the probability of her net profit or loss on each dozen eggs based on her costs.** SEE EXAMPLE 1

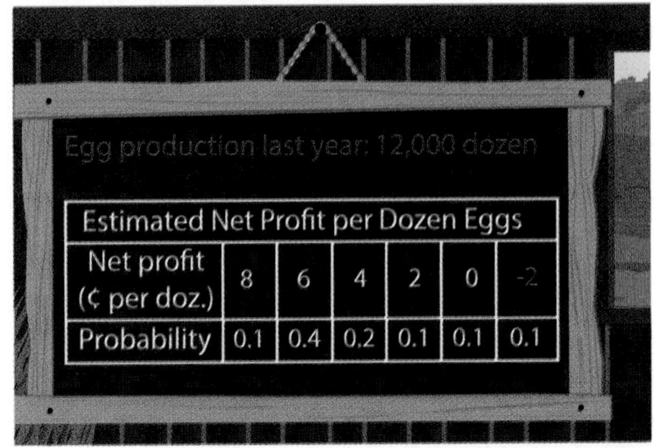


| Estimated Net Profit per Dozen Eggs | | | | | | |
|---|---|---|---|---|---|---|
| Net profit (¢ per doz.) | 8 | 6 | 4 | 2 | 0 | -2 |
| Probability | 0.1 | 0.4 | 0.2 | 0.1 | 0.1 | 0.1 |

15. What is her expected profit per dozen eggs?

16. What is her expected profit on the total egg production?

17. An electronics store offers students a discount of 10% on purchases of computers. They estimate that $\frac{1}{16}$ of computer sales are to students. The average sale per customer is \$498 and the store's profit is \$80 before the discount. What is the expected profit on the sale of a computer? SEE EXAMPLE 2

18. An insurance company offers three policy options. The probability a car will be damaged in a given year is 5%, and if a car is damaged, the cost of the repairs will be \$1000. Which option has the least expected annual cost for the car owner? Explain. SEE EXAMPLE 3

**Insurance Policy Options**

| Option | Annual Premium (\$) | Deductible (\$) |
|---|---|---|
| A | 900 | 0 |
| B | 800 | 400 |
| C | 700 | 1000 |

**On a tropical island, the probability of sunny weather is 90% each day.** SEE EXAMPLE 4

19. What is the expected number of sunny days in a non-leap year?

20. What is the expected number of sunny days during the month of June?

# PRACTICE & PROBLEM SOLVING

Mixed Review Available Online

## APPLY

21. **Model With Mathematics** A solar panel company has found that about 1% of its panels are defective. The company's cost to replace each defective panel is $600. A consultant recommends changes to the manufacturing process that will cost $200,000 and reduce the defective rate to 0.2%. The company estimates that it will sell 30,000 panels next year and that sales will increase by 5,000 panels per year for the next 10 years. Should the company follow the consultant's recommendation? Explain.

22. **Reason** A student tosses a coin 4 times and the results are heads, tails, heads, and heads. The student concludes that the expected number of heads for 100 tosses is 75. How did the student find this number? Do you agree with the student's reasoning? Explain.

23. **Higher Order Thinking** Your family is going to buy a new TV set for $599. You find out that the probability that the TV set will need to be serviced in the second year is 0.05 and the probability that the TV set will need to be serviced in the third year is 0.08. A 2-year warranty costs $55, and a 3-year warranty costs $80. The average cost of repairing the TV set is $278. What would you advise your family to do, get a 2-year extended warranty, a 3-year extended warranty or not to get any extended warranty? Explain your reasoning.

24. **Make Sense and Persevere** A company makes tablets that are guaranteed for one year. On average, one out of every 200 tablets needs to be repaired or replaced within the first year. If a tablet needs to be repaired, the company loses an average of $140. If the company sells 2,600,000 of the tablets in a year, what is their net profit on the sale of the tablets in that year?

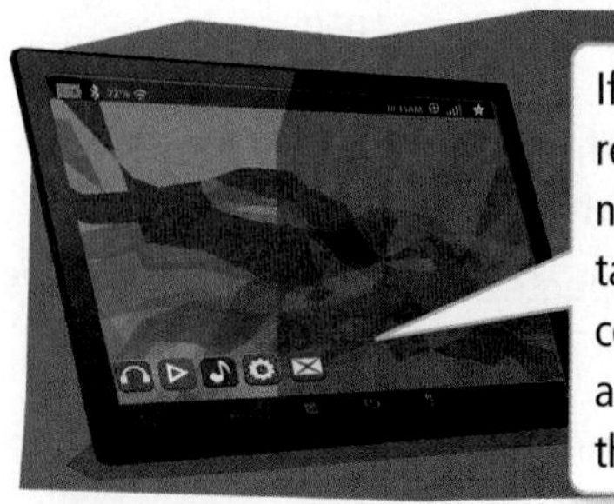

If no repairs or replacement is needed for a tablet, the company makes a $24 profit on that tablet.


## ASSESSMENT PRACTICE

25. A commuter recorded data on the arrival time of his morning train each weekday for 5 weeks. According to the data, he should expect the train to be 1.16 minutes late on any given day. What are the missing values in the commuter's table?

**Arrival Time for Train**

| Minutes late | 0 | 1 | 2 | 3 | 4 | 5 |
|---|---|---|---|---|---|---|
| Number of days | ■ | 5 | 1 | ■ | 1 | 3 |

26. **SAT/ACT** What is the expected total for 20 spins?

Ⓐ 100
Ⓑ 105
Ⓒ 110
Ⓓ 115
Ⓔ 120

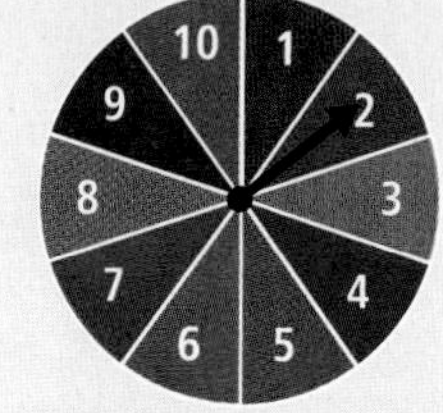


27. **Performance Task** A toy company is designing a children's game in which players toss chips onto a board. The square board will contain a smaller square at its center.

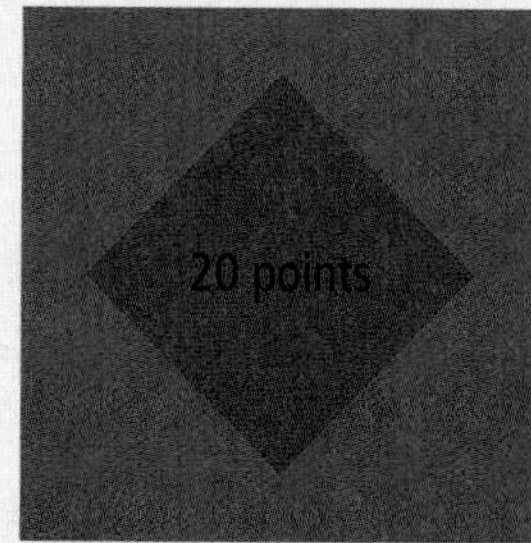


**Part A** Write design instructions for the board so that a chip tossed randomly onto the board is 8 times more likely to land in the outer region than in the inner square. Explain your reasoning.

**Part B** Assign a whole number of points to the outer region so that the expected score on a single toss is as close as possible to 5. Explain your reasoning.

**Part C** If the area of the inner square is doubled and the overall size of the board remains the same, how does the expected score change? Is it also doubled? Explain.

# 12-6 Probability and Decision Making

PearsonRealize.com

**I CAN…** use probability to make decisions.

## CRITIQUE & EXPLAIN

**Your friend offers to play the following game with you "If the product of the roll of two number cubes is 10 or less, I win. If not, you win!"**

**A.** If you were to play the game many times, what percent of the games would you expect to win?

**B.** Is the game fair? Should you take the offer? Explain.

**C. Make Sense and Persevere** Suggest a way to change the game from fair to unfair, or vice versa, while still using the product of the two number cubes. Explain.

## ESSENTIAL QUESTION

**How can you use probability to make decisions?**

APPLICATION

## EXAMPLE 1 Use Probability to Make Fair Decisions

**Sadie, Tamira, River, Victor, and Jae are candidates to represent their school at an event. How can you use random integers to select 2 students from the 5 candidates, so that each one is equally likely to be selected?**

**MAKE SENSE AND PERSEVERE**
Consider how you would assign integers from 1 to 10 among the 5 students. How do you adjust this for a random number generator that gives a number $r$ from the interval $0 \leq r < 1$?

There are 5 students. Assign a number to each student.

| 1 | 2 | 3 | 4 | 5 |
|---|---|---|---|---|
| Sadie | Tamira | River | Victor | Jae |

To select a student, use a calculator or other random number generator to generate a random integer from 1 to 5. Repeat to select the second student.

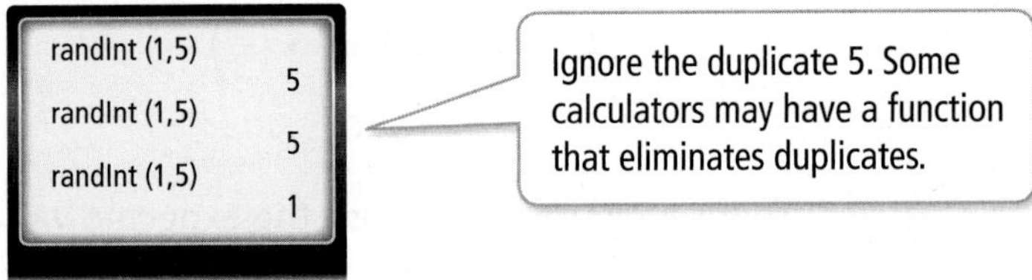
randInt (1,5)
5
randInt (1,5)
5
randInt (1,5)
1
Ignore the duplicate 5. Some calculators may have a function that eliminates duplicates.

Jae (5) and Sadie (1) are selected.

**Try It!** **1.** Your trainer creates training programs for you. How can you use index cards to randomly choose the following: Strength training 1 day per week; Cardio training 2 days per week, with no consecutive days; Swimming 1 day per week.

CONCEPTUAL UNDERSTANDING

## EXAMPLE 2 Determine Whether a Decision Is Fair or Unfair

**Thato places three cards in a hat and challenges Helena to a game.**

**A. Thato says, "If you draw a number greater than 2, you earn 2 points. Otherwise, I earn 2 points." Is the game fair or unfair? If it is unfair, which player has the advantage? Explain.**

In each round, Thato either wins 2 points or loses 2 points.

If Helena draws a "3" and gets 2 points, Thato considers this a loss of 2 points for himself.

Find the probability of each outcome. Then find the expected value.

$P(-2) = \frac{1}{3}$ and $P(+2) = \frac{2}{3}$.

$$E = -2 \cdot \left(\frac{1}{3}\right) + 2 \cdot \left(\frac{2}{3}\right)$$
$$= \frac{2}{3}$$

A game is considered "fair" if and only if the expected value is 0.

The game is unfair and is skewed to Thato's advantage. The probability of his scoring 2 points is twice the probability of Helena scoring 2 points.

**COMMON ERROR**
Recall that the expected value is the sum of the product of the value for each outcome and its probability. Be careful not to use the sum of the probabilities.

**B. Helena proposes a change to the scoring of the game. She says, "If I draw a number greater than 2, I get 2 points. Otherwise, you get 1 point." Is the game fair or unfair? If it is unfair, which player has the advantage? Explain.**

In each round, Thato either scores 1 point or he loses 2 points.

Find the probability of each outcome. Then find the expected value.

$P(-2) = \frac{1}{3}$ and $P(+1) = \frac{2}{3}$.

$$E = -2 \cdot \left(\frac{1}{3}\right) + 1 \cdot \left(\frac{2}{3}\right)$$
$$= -\frac{2}{3} + \frac{2}{3} = 0$$

This is a fair game because the expected value is 0. Neither player has an advantage over the other.

 **Try It!** 2. Justice and Tamika use the same 3 cards but change the game. In each round, a player draws a card and replaces it, and then the other player draws. The differences between the two cards are used to score each round. Order matters, so the difference can be negative. Is each game fair? Explain.

a. If the difference between the first and second cards is 2, Justice gets a point. Otherwise Tamika gets a point.

b. Each player subtracts the other person's number from her own to find the score. They take turns drawing first, and the first person who draws keeps the score for that turn.

APPLICATION

## EXAMPLE 3 Make a Decision Based on Expected Value

**The Silicon Valley Company manufactures tablets and computers. Their tablets are covered by a warranty for one year, so that if the tablet fails, the company replaces it. Since the failure rate of their model TAB5000 tablet is high, the head of production has a plan for replacing certain components inside the TAB5000 and calling the new model TAB5001.**

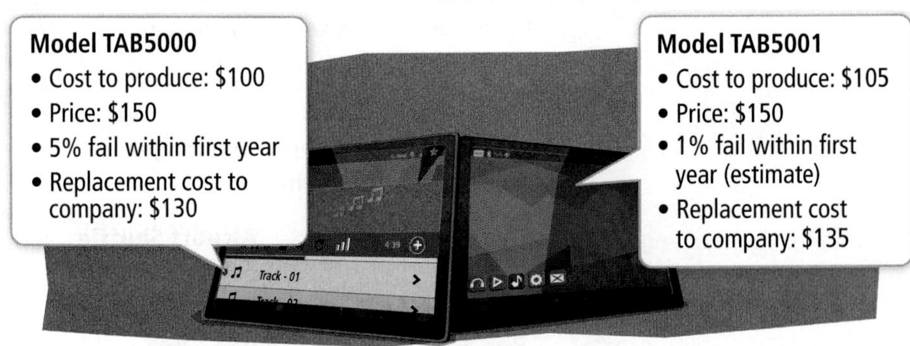

Model TAB5000
• Cost to produce: $100
• Price: $150
• 5% fail within first year
• Replacement cost to company: $130
Model TAB5001
• Cost to produce: $105
• Price: $150
• 1% fail within first year (estimate)
• Replacement cost to company: $135
Track - 01


**If you were the head of production, would you recommend replacing the TAB5000 with the TAB5001?**

**Formulate** ◀ Find the expected profit for each model.

Expected profit = price − cost − (cost to replace)(failure rate)

**Compute** ◀ Expected profit of TAB5000 $= \$150 - \$100 - (\$130)(0.05)$

$= \$50 - \$6.50$

$= \$43.50$

Expected profit of TAB5001 $= \$150 - \$105 - (\$135)(0.01)$

$= \$45 - \$1.35$

$= \$43.65$

**Interpret** ◀ The expected profit of the TAB5001 is more than the expected profit of the TAB5000. It makes sense to recommend replacing the TAB5000 with the TAB5001. Also, customers who bought a tablet would be more likely to be pleased with their purchase and buy from the same company in the future.

**Try It!** 3. Additional data is collected for the TAB5000 and TAB5001. The manufacturing cost and the replacement cost for the TAB5001 remain unchanged.

a. The manufacturing cost for the TAB5000 increased by $10. What would the expected profit be for the TAB5000?

b. The failure rate for the TAB5001 increased by 1%. What would the expected profit be for the TAB5001?

c. As a consultant for the company, what would you recommend they do to maximize their profit?

## EXAMPLE 4 Use a Binomial Distribution to Make Decisions

**An airport shuttle company takes 8 reservations for each trip because 25% of their reservations do not show up. Is this a reasonable policy?**

Find the probability that more passengers show up than the van can carry.

For 8 reservations, the graph shows the possible number of passenger combinations showing up.

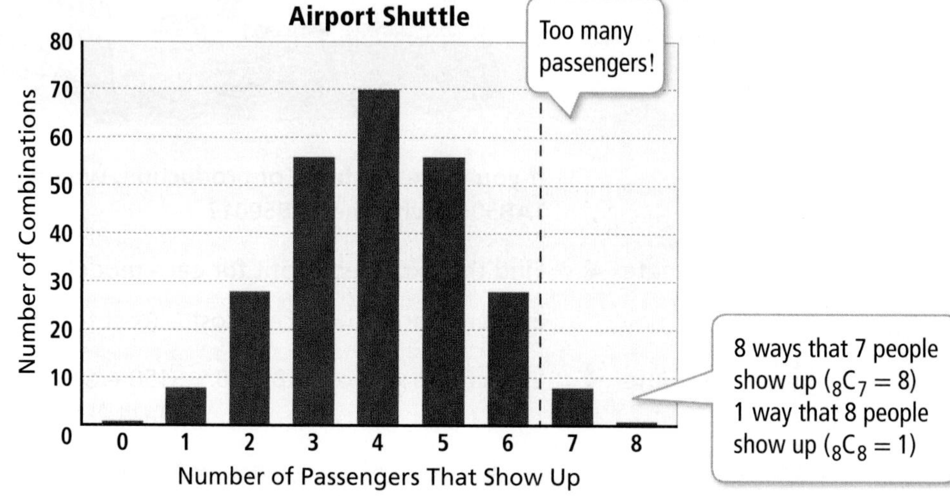


**USE APPROPRIATE TOOLS**
How does the graph of the binomial distribution help you think about the situation?

To find the probability that too many reservations show up, compute the probability that either 7 or 8 passengers show up. Each reservation has a 75% chance of showing up and a 25% chance of not showing up. Use $P(r) = {}_nC_r\, p^r(1 - p)^{n-r}$.

Find the probability that 7 reservations show up.

$$P(7) = {}_8C_7(0.75)^7(0.25)^1 \approx 8(0.1335)(0.25) \approx 0.267$$

Find the probability that 8 reservations show up.

$$P(8) = {}_8C_8(0.75)^8(0.25)^0 \approx 1(0.1001)(1) \approx 0.100$$

The probability that more reservations will show up than the van can carry is $P(7) + P(8)$, or about $0.267 + 0.100 = 0.367$.

Over one third of the trips will have passengers who can not get a seat in the van. This will result in dissatisfied customers, so this is not a reasonable policy.

**Try It!** 4. A play calls for a crowd of 12 extras with non-speaking parts. Because 10% of the extras have not shown up in the past, the director selects 15 students as extras. Find the probabilities that 12 extras show up to the performance, 15 extras show up to the performance, and more than 12 extras show up to the performance.

  Concept Summary  Assess

## CONCEPT SUMMARY Using Probability to Make Decisions

| METHOD | DESCRIPTION | APPLICATIONS |
|---|---|---|
| **Simple Probability** | Find the probability of random events. | • Select the most favorable among random events. |
| **Expected Value** | Multiply the probability of each outcome by its value. Add to find the expected value. | • Compare expected values to choose the best of several options.<br>• Compare expected values to decide if a game is fair. |
| **Probability Distribution** | Find the probability distribution of all possible outcomes. | • Compare expected values of several options.<br>• Create a graph of a probability distribution to present the distribution visually. |

## Do You UNDERSTAND?

1. ESSENTIAL QUESTION How can you use probability to make decisions?

2. **Reason** How can you use random numbers to simulate rolling a 6-sided number cube?

3. **Error Analysis** Explain the error in Diego's reasoning.

> If a game uses random numbers, it is always fair. ✗

4. **Use Structure** Describe what conditions are needed for a fair game.

5. **Use Appropriate Tools** Explain how you can visualize probability distributions to help you make decisions.

6. **Reason** Why must the expected value of a fair game equal zero?

## Do You KNOW HOW?

7. A teacher assigns 30 students a number from 1 to 30. The teacher uses the random numbers shown to select students for presentations. Which student was selected first? second?

```
randInt (1,30)
                 9
randInt (1,30)
                 9
randInt (1,30)
                 4
```

8. Three friends are at a restaurant and they all want the last slice of pizza. Identify three methods involving probability that they can use to determine who gets the last slice. Explain mathematically why each method will guarantee a fair decision.

9. Edgar rolls one number cube and Micah rolls two. If Edgar rolls a 6, he wins a prize. If Micah rolls a sum of 7, she gets a prize. Is this game fair? Explain.

10. The 10 parking spaces in the first row of the parking lot are reserved for the 12 members of the Student Council. Ten percent of Student Council members usually do not drive to school dances. What is the probability that more members of the Student Council will drive to a dance than there are reserved parking spaces?

Scan for Multimedia

Practice Tutorial

Additional Exercises Available Online

## UNDERSTAND

11. **Reason** Suppose Chris has pair of 4-sided dice, each numbered from 1 to 4, and Carolina has a pair of 10-sided dice, each numbered from 1 to 10. They decide to play a series of games against each other, using their own dice.

    a. Describe a game that would be fair. Explain.

    b. Describe an unfair game. Explain.

12. **Construct Arguments** Mr. and Ms. Mitchell have 3 children, Luke, Charlie, and Aubrey. All 3 children want to sit in the front seat. Charlie suggests that they flip a coin two times to decide who will sit in the front seat. The number of heads determines who sits in the front seat. Is this a fair method? Explain.

| Number of Heads | Front Seat Passenger |
|---|---|
| 0 | Luke |
| 1 | Charlie |
| 2 | Aubrey |

13. **Error Analysis** Mercedes is planning a party for 10 people. She knows from experience that about 20% of those invited will not show up. If she invites 12 people, how can she calculate the probability that more than 10 people will show up. What error did she make? What is the correct probability?

Use the binomial probability for 12, and more than 10 show up.
$(12)(0.80)^1(0.20)^{11} +$
$(1)(0.80)^0(0.20)^{12}$
✗

## PRACTICE

14. How can you use random integers to select 3 students from a group of 8 to serve as student body representatives, so that each student is equally likely to be selected? SEE EXAMPLE 1

**Explain whether each game is fair or unfair.** SEE EXAMPLE 2

15. When it is your turn, roll a standard number cube. If the number is even, you get a point. If it is odd, you lose a point.

16. When it is your turn, roll two standard number cubes. If the product of the numbers is even, you get a point. If the product is odd, you lose a point.

**Fatima is a contestant on a game show. So far, she has won \$34,000. She can keep the \$34,000 or spin the spinner shown below and add or subtract the amount shown from \$34,000.** SEE EXAMPLE 3

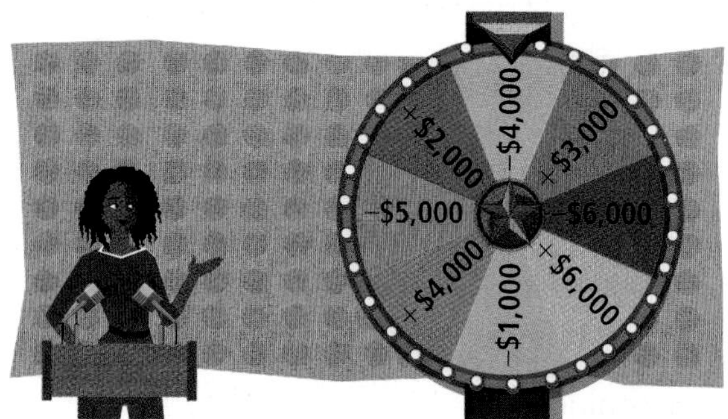


17. If Fatima spins the spinner, what are her expected total winnings?

18. Would you advise Fatima to keep the \$34,000 or to spin the spinner? Explain your reasoning.

19. Suppose 0.5% of people who file federal tax returns with an adjusted gross income (AGI) between \$50,000 and \$75,000 are audited. Of 5 people in that tax bracket for whom ABC Tax Guys prepared their taxes, 2 were audited. SEE EXAMPLE 4

    a. If 5 people with an AGI between \$50,000 and \$75,000 are selected at random from all the people who filed federal tax returns, what is the probability that at least 2 people are audited?

    b. Would you recommend that a friend with an AGI between \$50,000 and \$75,000 use ABC Tax Guys to prepare her tax returns? Explain.

# PRACTICE & PROBLEM SOLVING

## APPLY

**20. Model With Mathematics** For $5.49 per month, Ms. Corchado can buy insurance to cover the cost of repairing a leak in the natural gas lines within her house. She estimates that there is a 3% chance that she will need to have such repairs made next year.

**a.** What is the expected cost of a gas leak, if Ms. Corchado does not buy insurance? Use the cost shown in the middle of the graph.

**b.** With more recent information, Ms. Corchado learns that repair costs could be as much as $1,200 dollars with an 8% probability of a leak. What is the expected cost of a gas leak with these assumptions?

**c.** Would you advise Ms. Corchado to buy the insurance? Explain.

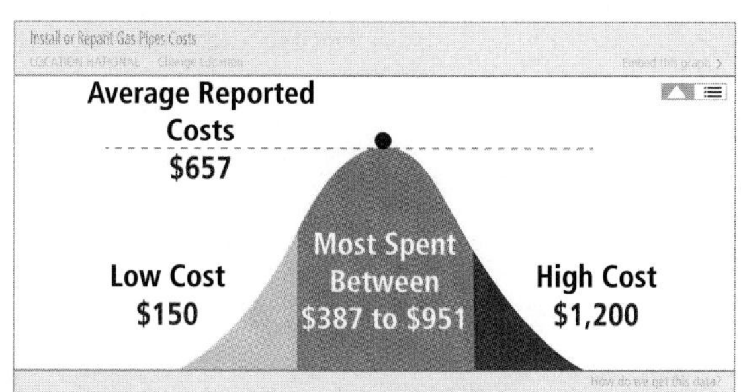


**21. Higher Order Thinking** You are a consultant to a company that manufactures components for cell phones. One of the components the company manufactures has a 4% failure rate. Design changes have improved the quality of the component. A test of 50 of the new components found that only one of the new components is defective.

**a.** Before the design improvements what was the probability that among 50 of the items, at most one of the items was defective?

**b.** Is it reasonable to conclude that the new components have a lower failure rate than 4%?

**c.** Would you recommend further testing to determine whether the new parts have a lower failure rate than 4%? Explain.

## ASSESSMENT PRACTICE

**22.** Paula, Sasha, and Yumiko live together. They want a system to determine who will wash the dinner dishes on any given night. Select all of the methods that are fair.

Ⓐ Roll a standard number cube. If the result is 1 or 2, Paula does the dishes; if 3 or 4, Sasha; if 5 or 6, Yumiko.

Ⓑ Roll a standard number cube. If the result is 1, Paula does the dishes; if 2, Sasha; if 4, Yumiko. If the result is 3, 5, or 6, roll again.

Ⓒ Roll two standard number cubes. If the sum of the numbers that come up is less than 6, Paula washes the dishes; if the sum is 8, 9, or 12, Sasha; if the sum is 6 or 7, Yumiko. If the sum is 10 or 11, roll again.

Ⓓ Write the name of each girl on a slip of paper, place the slips in a box, mix them up, and select one at random. The person whose name is selected does the dishes.

**23. SAT/ACT** A fair choice among a group of students may be made by flipping three coins in sequence, and noting the sequences of heads and tails. If each student is assigned one of these sequences, how many students can be selected fairly by this method?

Ⓐ 4 Ⓑ 5 Ⓒ 6 Ⓓ 7 Ⓔ 8

**24. Performance Task** Acme Tire Company makes two models of steel belted radial tires, Model 1001 and Model 1002.

| Model | 1001 |
|---|---|
| Blowouts per 200,000 tires | 2 |
| Profits before any lawsuits | $60 |

| Model | 1002 |
|---|---|
| Blowouts per 200,000 tires | 1 |
| Profits before any lawsuits | $56 |

If one of these tires fails and the company is sued, the average settlement is $1,200,000.

**Part A** Find the expected profit for both models of tires after any potential lawsuits. Explain.

**Part B** Would you recommend that the company continue selling both models? Explain.

TOPIC 12

# Topic Review

## TOPIC ESSENTIAL QUESTION

1. How can you find the probability of events and combinations of events?

## Vocabulary Review

**Choose the correct term to complete each sentence.**

2. An arrangement of items in a specific order is called a(n) ________.
3. Two events are ________ if there is no outcome that is in both events.
4. Two events are ________ if the occurrence of one event affects the probability of the other event.
5. An arrangement of items in which order is not important is called a(n) ________.
6. The predicted average outcome of many trials in an experiment is called the ________.

- combination
- complement
- conditional probability
- dependent events
- expected value
- independent events
- mutually exclusive
- permutation
- probability distribution

## Concepts & Skills Review

### LESSON 12-1 Probability Events

#### Quick Review

Two events are **mutually exclusive** if and only if there is no outcome that lies in the sample space of both events. Two events are **independent events** if and only if the outcome of one event does not affect the probability of a second event.

#### Example

**Let $A$ represent the event "even number," or $A = \{2, 4, 6, 8\}$.**

**Let $B$ represent the event "odd number," or $B = \{1, 3, 5, 7\}$.**

**Let $C$ represent the event "divisible by 3," or $C = \{3, 6\}$.**

1 2 3 4 5 6 7 8

Are $A$ and $B$ mutually exclusive? Explain.

Yes; all of their elements are different.

Are $A$ and $C$ mutually exclusive? Explain.

No; they both have a 3 in their sample space.

#### Practice & Problem Solving

**Ten craft sticks lettered A through J are in a coffee cup. Consider the events "consonant," "vowel," "letter before D in the alphabet," "letter after A in the alphabet," and "letter after E in the alphabet." State whether each pair of events is mutually exclusive.**

7. vowel, letter before D
8. letter before D, letter after E
9. letter after A, letter before D
10. **Communicate Precisely** Edward is rolling a number cube to decide on the new combination for his bicycle lock. If he only has one number to go, find the probability of each event. Use what you know about mutually exclusive events to explain your reasoning.
    a. Edward rolls a number that is both even and less than 2. Explain.
    b. Edward rolls a number that is even or less than 2. Explain.

## LESSON 12-2 Conditional Probability

### Quick Review

For any two events $A$ and $B$, with $P(A) \neq 0$, $P(A \text{ and } B) = P(A) \cdot P(B \mid A)$. Events $A$ and $B$ are independent if and only if $P(B \mid A) = P(B)$.

### Example

**The table shows the number of students on different teams by grade. One of these students is selected at random for an interview. Are selecting a sophomore and selecting a member of the track team independent events?**

**Team Enrollment by Year**

| | Sophomore | Junior |
|---|---|---|
| Cross Country | 9 | 6 |
| Track | 12 | 23 |

$P(\text{Sophomore and Track}) = 0.24$

$P(\text{Sophomore}) = 0.42 \quad P(\text{Track} \mid \text{Sophomore}) \approx 0.57$

$P(\text{Soph and Track}) \neq P(\text{Soph}) \cdot P(\text{Track} \mid \text{Soph})$ because $0.24 \neq 0.42 \cdot 0.57$

No, selecting a sophomore and selecting a member of the track team are dependent events.

### Practice & Problem Solving

**Use the table in the Example for Exercises 11–15. All students are selected at random.**

11. $P(\text{Junior})$

12. $P(\text{Cross Country})$

13. $P(\text{Junior} \mid \text{Cross Country})$

14. $P(\text{Cross Country} \mid \text{Junior})$

15. Are selecting a junior and selecting a cross country runner dependent or independent events?

16. **Error Analysis** One card is selected at random from five cards numbered 1–5. A student says that drawing an even number and drawing a prime number are dependent events because $P(\text{prime} \mid \text{even}) = 0.5$ and $P(\text{even}) = 0.4$. Describe and correct the error the student made.

17. **Use Structure** A person entered in a raffle has a 3% chance of winning a prize. A prize winner has a 25% chance of winning two theater tickets. What is the probability that a person entered in the raffle will win the theater tickets?

## LESSON 12-3 Permutations and Combinations

### Quick Review

The number of permutations of $n$ items taken $r$ at a time is ${}_nP_r = \frac{n!}{(n-r)!}$ for $0 \leq r \leq n$.

The number of combinations of $n$ items chosen $r$ at a time is ${}_nC_r = \frac{n!}{r!(n-r)!}$ for $0 \leq r \leq n$.

### Example

**A bag contains 4 blue tiles and 4 yellow tiles. Three tiles are drawn from the bag at random without replacement. What is the probability all three tiles are blue?**

Use combinations since order does not matter. Select 3 blue from 4 blue tiles ${}_4C_3$, or 4, ways.

Select 0 yellow from 4 yellow tiles ${}_4C_0$, or 1, way. Select 3 blue tiles from 8 total tiles ${}_8C_3$, or 56, ways.

$P(\text{3 blue}) = \frac{4 \cdot 1}{56} = \frac{1}{14} \approx 0.07 \approx 7\%$

### Practice & Problem Solving

**In Exercises 18 and 19, determine whether the situation involves finding permutations or combinations. Then find the number.**

18. How many ways can a team choose a captain and a substitute captain from 8 players?

19. How many ways can 3 numbers be selected from the digits 0–9 to set a lock code if the digits cannot be repeated?

20. **Error Analysis** A student computed ${}_5C_2$, and said that it is equal to 20. Describe and correct the error the student made.

21. **Look for Relationships** The formulas for permutations and combinations must always evaluate to a natural number. Explain why.

TOPIC 12 REVIEW

## LESSON 12-4 Probability Distributions

### Quick Review

For a binomial experiment consisting of $n$ trials, the probability of $r$ successes out of $n$ trials is called the **binomial probability** and given by:

$$P(r) = {}_nC_r \cdot p^r(1 - p)^{n-r}$$

### Example

**Curtis scores a touchdown 24% of the time he receives the ball. If Curtis receives the ball 7 times, what is the probability he scores a touchdown 4 of those times?**

$$P(4 \text{ touchdowns}) = {}_7C_4 \cdot 0.24^4(1 - 0.24)^{7-4}$$
$$= 35 \cdot 0.24^4(0.76)^3$$
$$\approx 0.051 \approx 5.1\%$$

### Practice & Problem Solving

**Rhoda finds that every seed she plants has a 56% chance to grow to full height. If she plants 10 seeds, what is the probability each number of plants grows to full height? Round to the nearest hundredth of a percent.**

**22.** 1 plant

**23.** 3 plants

**24.** 5 plants

**25.** 10 plants

**26. Error Analysis** Using the Example, Akasi tried to calculate Curtis' probable success rate of 3 touchdowns if he received the ball 5 times, but could not get an answer. Find and correct her mistake.

$$P(3) = {}_3C_5 \cdot 0.24^5\,(1\text{-}0.24)^{3\text{-}5}$$
$$= ?$$

X

## LESSON 12-5 Expected Value

### Quick Review

The **expected value** $E(x)$ of a trial of an experiment is the sum of the value of each possible outcome $x_n$ times its probability $p_n$ or $E(x) = x_1p_1 + x_2p_2 + \ldots + x_np_n$.

### Example

**The outer ring on a dartboard is worth 10 points, the middle ring is worth 25 points, and the bullseye is worth 100 points. When throwing darts, Ravi has a 45% chance of hitting the outer ring, a 40% chance of hitting the inner ring, a 5% chance of hitting the bullseye, and a 10% chance of missing the board. What is the expected value of a single dart throw?**

$$E(x) = 10(0.45) + 25(0.4) + 100(0.05) + 0(0.1)$$
$$= 4.5 + 10 + 5 + 0$$
$$= 19.5$$

### Practice & Problem Solving

**Use the information in the Example to find the expected value of 15 throws from each of the following people.**

**27.** Rosa: 20% outer ring; 65% inner ring, 10% bullseye, 5% miss

**28.** Vicki: 60% outer ring; 20% inner ring, 12% bullseye, 8% miss

**29. Higher Order Thinking** A basketball player takes 2 shots from the 3-point line and misses them both. She calculates the expected value of taking a shot from the 3-point line is 0 points. Do you agree with the player's calculation? Her reasoning? How could the player improve the accuracy of her estimate?

## LESSON 12-6 Probability and Decision Making

### Quick Review

Combined with probability, expected value can be used to help make decisions.

### Example

**Frederica is playing a game tossing 20 beanbags from a choice of three lines. Frederica has a 90% chance of success from the 5-point line, a 65% chance of success from the 10-point line, and a 20% chance from the 20-point line. Frederica wants to toss every beanbag from the same line, and thinks she should toss from the 5-point line since it has the highest probability of success. Is Frederica correct?**

Find the expected points per toss, or expected value.

**5-point line:**
5 points • 0.90 = 4.5 points per toss

**10-point line:**
10 points • 0.65 = 6.5 points per toss

**20-point line:**
20 points • 0.20 = 4 points per toss

Frederica should toss the beanbag from the 10-point line.

### Practice & Problem Solving

**Both situations have the same expected value. Find the missing information.**

**30.** Situation 1: Paul hits a dart target worth 15 points 45% of the time.

Situation 2: He hits a dart target worth 10 points $x$% of the time.

**31.** Situation 1: Lenora has a success rate of 25% when selling bracelets at $15 each.

Situation 2: She has a success rate of 20% when selling bracelets at $$x$ each.

**32.** **Make Sense of Problems** Use the information from the Example. Frederica practices her shots and increases her chances from the 20-point line to 30%. Should she now toss the beanbag from the 20-point line? Explain your reasoning.

TOPIC 12 REVIEW

# Visual Glossary

## English | Spanish

### A

**Acute angle** An acute angle is an angle whose measure is between 0 and 90.

**Ángulo agudo** Un ángulo agudo es un ángulo que mide entre 0 y 90.

**Example**

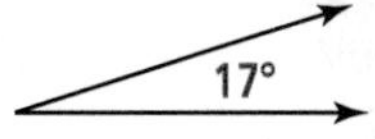


**Acute triangle** An acute triangle has three acute angles.

**Triángulo acutángulo** Un triángulo acutángulo tiene los tres ángulos agudos.

**Example**

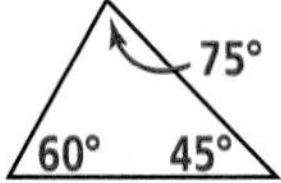


**Adjacent angles** Adjacent angles are two coplanar angles that have a common side and a common vertex but no common interior points.

**Ángulos adyacentes** Los ángulos adyacentes son dos ángulos coplanarios que tienen un lado común y el mismo vértice, pero no tienen puntos interiores comunes.

**Example**

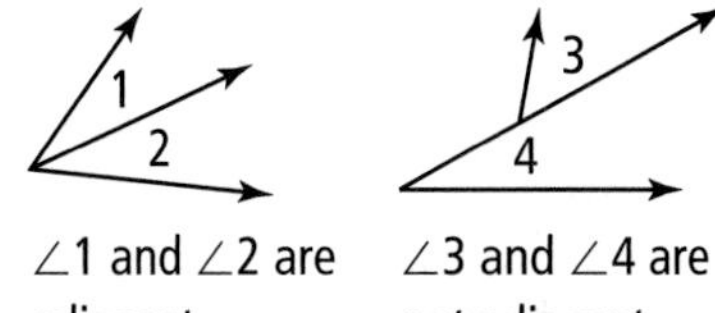


∠1 and ∠2 are adjacent. ∠3 and ∠4 are *not* adjacent.

**Alternate interior (exterior) angles** Alternate interior (exterior) angles are nonadjacent interior (exterior) angles that lie on opposite sides of the transversal.

**Ángulos alternos internos (externos)** Los ángulos alternos internos (externos) son ángulos internos (externos) no adyacentes situados en lados opuestos de la transversal.

**Example**

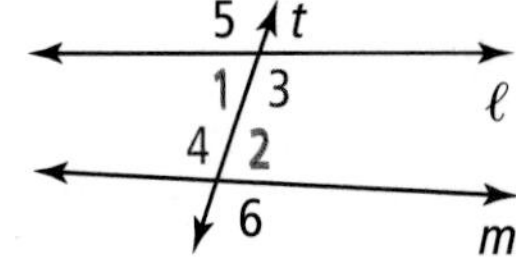


∠1 and ∠2 are alternate interior angles, as are ∠3 and ∠4. ∠5 and ∠6 are alternate exterior angles.

**Altitude** *See* **cone; cylinder; parallelogram; prism; pyramid; trapezoid; triangle.**

**Altura** *Ver* **cone; cylinder; parallelogram; prism; pyramid; trapezoid; triangle.**

**Altitude of a triangle** An altitude of a triangle is the perpendicular segment from a vertex to the line containing the side opposite that vertex.

**Altura de un triángulo** Una altura de un triángulo es el segmento perpendicular que va desde un vértice hasta la recta que contiene el lado opuesto a ese vértice.

**Example**

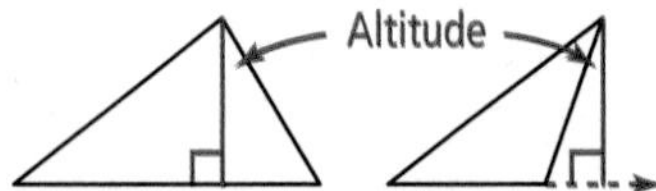

# English

# Spanish

**Angle** An angle is formed by two rays with the same endpoint. The rays are the *sides* of the angle and the common endpoint is the *vertex* of the angle.

**Ángulo** Un ángulo está formado por dos semirrectas que convergen en un mismo extremo. Las semirrectas son los *lados* del ángulo y los extremos en común son el *vértice*.

**Example**

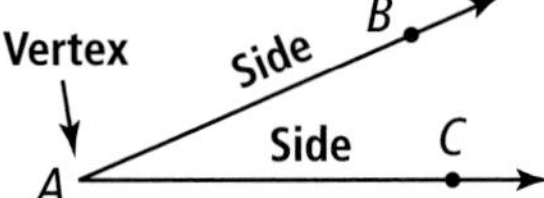


This angle could be named $\angle A$, $\angle BAC$, or $\angle CAB$.

**Angle bisector** An angle bisector is a ray that divides an angle into two congruent angles.

**Bisectriz de un ángulo** La bisectriz de un ángulo es una semirrecta que divide al ángulo en dos ángulos congruentes.

**Example**

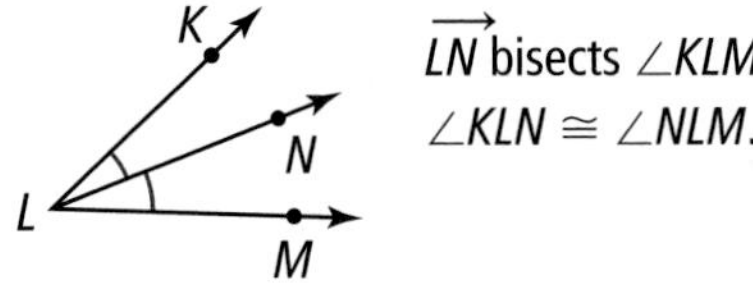


$\overrightarrow{LN}$ bisects $\angle KLM$.
$\angle KLN \cong \angle NLM$.

**Angle of elevation or depression** An angle of elevation (depression) is the angle formed by a horizontal line and the line of sight to an object above (below) the horizontal line.

**Ángulo de elevación o depresión** Un ángulo de elevación (depresión) es el ángulo formado por una línea horizontal y la recta que va de esa línea a un objeto situado arriba (debajo) de ella.

**Example**

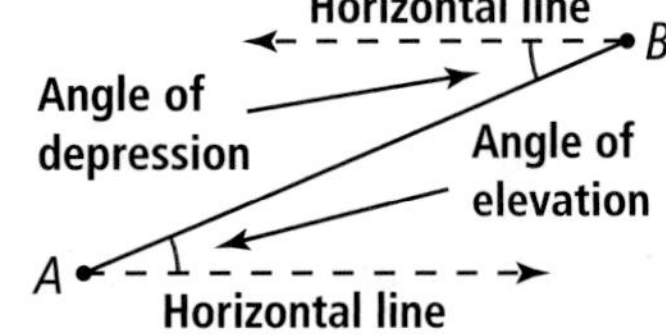


**Angle of rotation** *See* **rotation.**

**Ángulo de rotación** *Ver* **rotation.**

**Arc** *See* **major arc; minor arc.** *See also* **arc length; measure of an arc.**

**Arco** *Ver* **major arc; minor arc.** *Ver también* **arc length; measure of an arc.**

**Arc length** The length of an arc of a circle is the product of the circumference of the circle and the ratio of the corresponding central angle measure in degrees and 360. The length of the arc is also the product of the radius and central angle measure in radians.

**Longitud de un arco** La longitud del arco de un círculo es el producto de la circunferencia del círculo y la razón de la medida del ángulo central correspondiente en grados y 360. La longitud del arco es también el producto del radio y de la medida del ángulo central en radianes.

**Example**

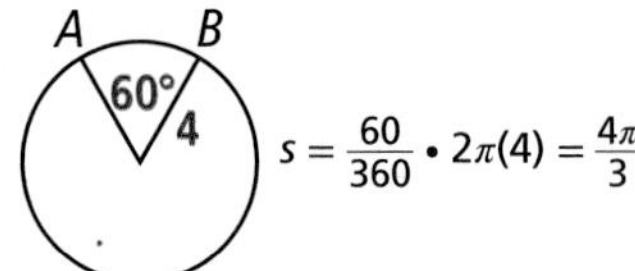


$s = \frac{60}{360} \cdot 2\pi(4) = \frac{4\pi}{3}$

$\frac{\pi}{4}$ radians

C

4

D

$s = \frac{\pi}{4}(4) = \pi$

VISUAL GLOSSARY

## English | Spanish

**Area** The area of a plane figure is the number of square units enclosed by the figure.

**Área** El área de una figura plana es la cantidad de unidades cuadradas que contiene la figura.

**Example** 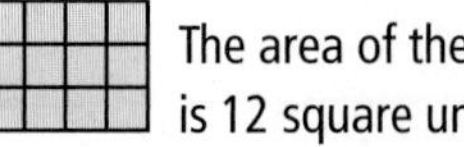 The area of the rectangle is 12 square units, or 12 units$^2$.

**Axes** *See* **coordinate plane.**

**Ejes** *Ver* **coordinate plane.**

**Base(s)** *See* **cone; cylinder; isosceles triangle; parallelogram; prism; pyramid; trapezoid; triangle.**

**Base(s)** *Ver* **cone; cylinder; isosceles triangle; parallelogram; prism; pyramid; trapezoid; triangle.**

**Base angles** *See* **trapezoid; isosceles triangle.**

**Ángulos de base** *Ver* **trapezoid; isosceles triangle.**

**Biconditional** A biconditional statement is the combination of a conditional statement, $p \rightarrow q$, and its converse, $q \rightarrow p$. A biconditional contains the words "if and only if."

**Bicondicional** Un enunciado bicondicional es la combinación de un enunciado condicional, $p \rightarrow q$, y su recíproco, $q \rightarrow p$. El enunciado bicondicional incluye las palabras "si y solo si".

**Example** This biconditional statement is true: Two angles are congruent *if and only if* they have the same measure.

**Binomial experiment** A binomial experiment is one in which the situation involves repeated trials. Each trial has two possible outcomes (success or failure), and the probability of success is constant throughout the trials.

**Experimento binomial** Un experimento binomial es un experimento que requiere varios ensayos. Cada ensayo tiene dos resultados posibles (éxito o fracaso), y la probabilidad de éxito es constante durante todos los ensayos.

**Binomial probability** For a binomial experiment consisting of *n* trials with probability of success *p* for each trial, the binomial probability is the probability of *r* successes out of *n* trials given by the function $P(r) = {}_nC_r \cdot p^r(1 - p)^{n-r}$.

**Probabilidad binomial** En un experimento que incluye *n* ensayos con una probabilidad *p* de cada ensayo, la probabilidad binomial es la probabilidad de *r* éxitos de *n* ensayos dados por la función $P(r) = {}_nC_r \cdot p^r(1 - p)^{n-r}$.

**Example** Suppose you roll a standard number cube and that you call rolling a 1 a success. Then $p = \frac{1}{6}$. The probability of rolling nine 1s in twenty rolls is ${}_{20}C_9 \left(\frac{1}{6}\right)^9 \left(1 - \frac{1}{6}\right)^{20-9} \approx 0.022$.

**Bisector** *See* **segment bisector; angle bisector.**

**Bisectriz** *Ver* **segment bisector; angle bisector.**

**Cavalieri's Principle** If two space figures have the same height and the same cross-sectional area at every level, then they have the same volume.

**Principio de Cavalieri** Si dos figuras sólidas tienen la misma altura y la misma área transversal en todos los niveles, entonces también tienen el mismo volumen.

**Example**

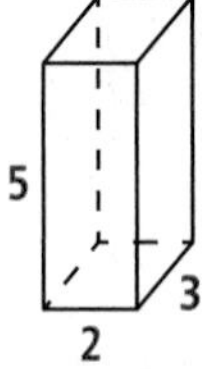



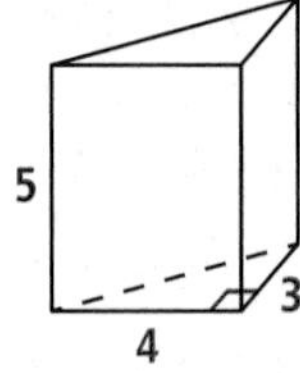



Both figures are prisms with height 5 units and horizontal cross-sectional area 6 square units.

$V = B \cdot h = (6)(5) = 30$ cubic units

**Center** *See* **circle; dilation; regular polygon; rotation; sphere.**

**Centro** *Ver* **circle; dilation; regular polygon; rotation; sphere.**

| English | Spanish |
| --- | --- |

**Central angle of a circle** A central angle of a circle is an angle formed by two radii with the vertex at the center of the circle.

**Ángulo central de un círculo** Un ángulo central de un círculo es un ángulo formado por dos radios que tienen el vértice en el centro del círculo.

**Example**

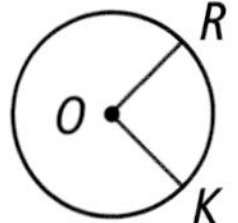


$\angle ROK$ is a central angle of $\odot O$.

**Centroid of a triangle** The centroid of a triangle is the point of concurrency of the medians of the triangle.

**Centroide de un triángulo** El centroide de un triángulo es el punto de intersección de sus medianas.

**Example** $P$ is the centroid of $\triangle ABC$.

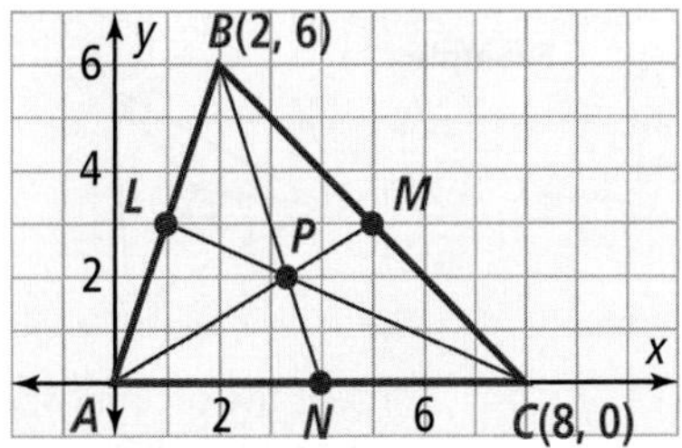


**Chord** A chord of a circle is a segment whose endpoints are on the circle.

**Cuerda** Una cuerda de un círculo es un segmento cuyos extremos son dos puntos del círculo.

**Example**

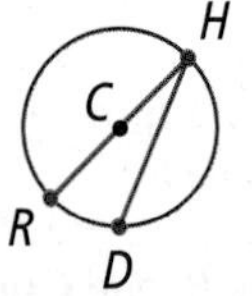


$\overline{HD}$ and $\overline{HR}$ are chords of $\odot C$.

**Circle** A circle is the set of all points in a plane that are a given distance, the radius, from a given point, the center. The standard form for an equation of a circle with center $(h, k)$ and radius $r$ is $(x - h)^2 + (y - k)^2 = r^2$.

**Círculo** Un círculo es el conjunto de todos los puntos de un plano situados a una distancia dada, el radio, de un punto dado, el centro. La fórmula normal de la ecuación de un círculo con centro $(h, k)$ y radio $r$ es $(x - h)^2 + (y - k)^2 = r^2$.

**Example**

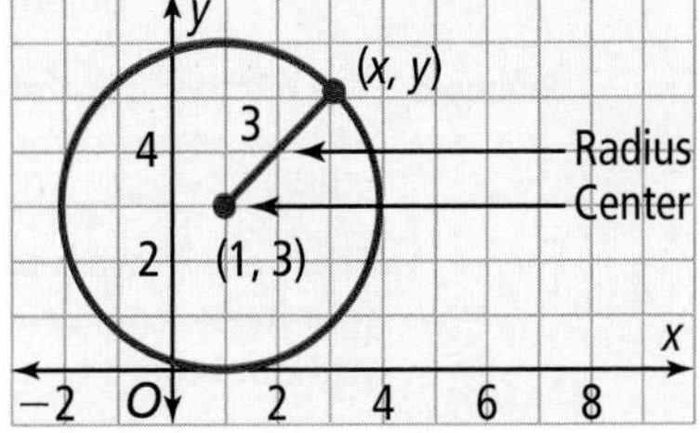


The equation of the circle whose center is (1, 3) and whose radius is 3 is $(x - 1)^2 + (y - 3)^2 = 9$.

**Circumcenter of a triangle** The circumcenter of a triangle is the point of concurrency of the perpendicular bisectors of the sides of the triangle.

**Circuncentro de un triángulo** El circuncentro de un triángulo es el punto de intersección de las bisectrices perpendiculares de los lados del triángulo.

**Example**

$QC = SC = RC$

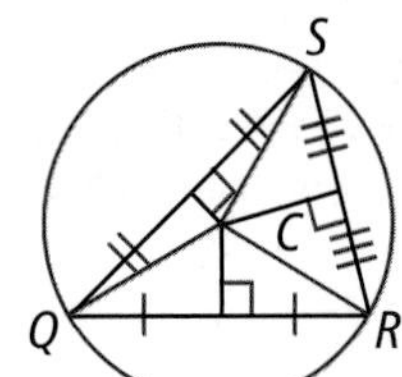


$C$ is the circumcenter.

# English

# Spanish

**Circumference** The circumference of a circle is the distance around the circle. Given the radius r of a circle, you can find its circumference $C$ by using the formula $C = 2\pi r$.

**Circunferencia** La circunferencia de un círculo es la distancia alrededor del círculo. Dado el radio r de un círculo, se puede hallar la circunferencia $C$ usando la fórmula $C = 2\pi r$.

**Example** 
$$\begin{aligned} C &= 2\pi r \\ &= 2\pi(4) \\ &= 8\pi \end{aligned}$$

4

Circumference is the distance around the circle.

---

**Circumference of a sphere** *See* **sphere**.

**Circunferencia de una esfera** Ver sphere.

---

**Circumscribed** A circumscribed circle of a triangle is the circle that contains the three vertices of the triangle.

**Circunscrito** El círculo circunscrito de un triángulo es el círculo que contiene los tres vértices del triángulo.

**Example**

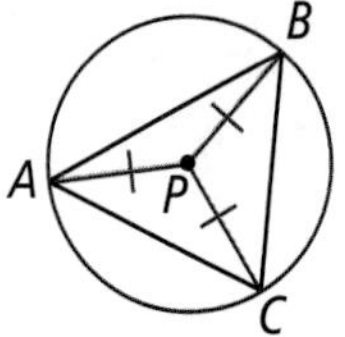


$\odot P$ is the circumscribed circle of $\triangle ABC$.

---

**Collinear points** Collinear points lie on the same line.

**Puntos colineales** Los puntos colineales son los que están sobre la misma recta.

**Example**

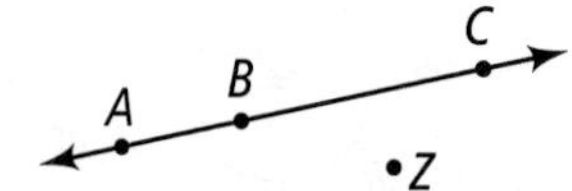


Points $A$, $B$, and $C$ are collinear, but points $A$, $B$, and $Z$ are noncollinear.

---

**Combination** Any unordered selection of $r$ objects from a set of $n$ objects is a combination. The number of combinations of $n$ objects taken $r$ at a time is ${}_nC_r = \frac{n!}{r!(n-r)!}$ for $0 \leq r \leq n$.

**Combinación** Cualquier selección no ordenada de $r$ objetos tomados de un conjunto de $n$ objetos es una combinación. El número de combinaciones de $n$ objetos, cuando se toman $r$ objetos cada vez, ${}_nC_r = \frac{n!}{r!(n-r)!}$ para $0 \leq r \leq n$.

**Example** The number of combinations of seven items taken four at a time is ${}_7C_4 = \frac{7!}{4!(7-4)!} = 35$. There are 35 ways to choose four items from seven items without regard to order.

---

**Compass** A compass is a tool for drawing arcs and circles of different sizes and can be used to copy lengths.

**Compás** El compás es un instrumento que se usa para dibujar arcos y círculos de diferentes tamaños, y que se puede usar para copiar longitudes.

---

**Complement of an event** All possible outcomes that are not in the event.
$P$(complement of event) = 1 − $P$(event)

**Complemento de un suceso** Todos los resultados posibles que no se dan en el suceso.
$P$(complemento de un suceso) = 1 − $P$(suceso)

**Example** The complement of rolling a 1 or a 2 on a standard number cube is rolling a 3, 4, 5, or 6.

## English

## Spanish

**Complementary angles** Two angles are complementary angles if the sum of their measures is 90.

**Ángulos complementarios** Dos ángulos son complementarios si la suma de sus medidas es igual a 90.

**Example**

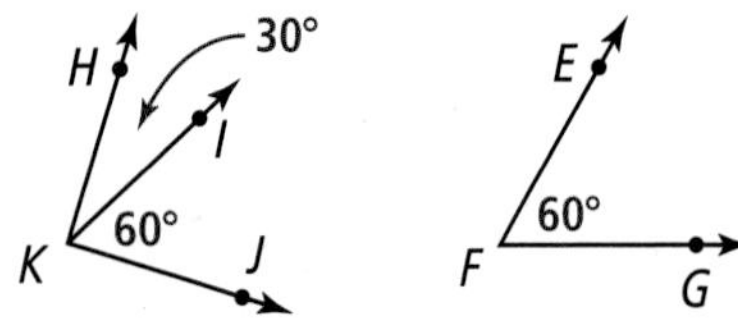


$\angle HKI$ and $\angle IKJ$ are complementary angles, as are $\angle HKI$ and $\angle EFG$.

**Composite space figures** A composite space figure is the combination of two or more figures into one object.

**Figuras geométricas compuestas** Una figura geométrica compuesta es la combinación de dos o más figuras en un mismo objeto.

**Example**

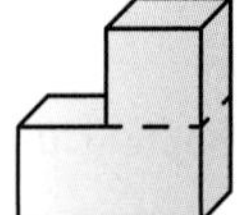

**Composition of rigid motions** A composition of rigid motions is a transformation with two or more rigid motions in which the second rigid motion is performed on the image of the first rigid motion.

**Composición de movimientos rígidos** Una composición de movimientos rígidos es una transformación de dos o más movimientos rígidos en la que el segundo movimiento rígido se realiza sobre la imagen del primer movimiento rígido.

**Example**

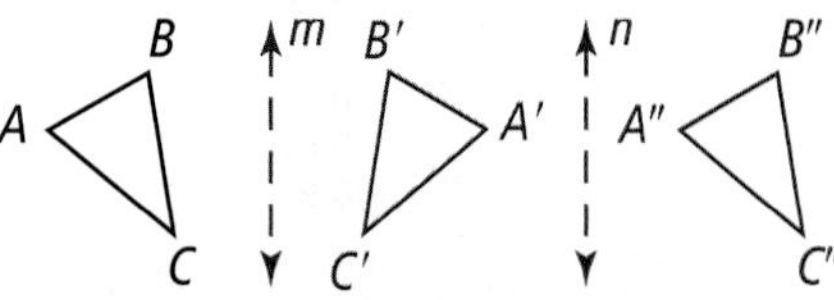


If you reflect $\triangle ABC$ across line $m$ to get $\triangle A'B'C'$ and then reflect $\triangle A'B'C'$ across line $n$ to get $\triangle A''B''C''$, you perform a composition of rigid motions.

**Compound event** A compound event is an event that consists of two or more events linked by the word *and* or the word *or*.

**Suceso compuesto** Un suceso compuesto es un suceso que consiste en dos o más sucesos unidos por medio de la palabra *y* o la palabra *o*.

**Example** Rolling a 5 on a standard number cube and then rolling a 4 is a compound event.

**Concave polygon** *See* **polygon.**

**Polígono cóncavo** *Ver* **polygon.**

**Concentric circles** Concentric circles lie in the same plane and have the same center.

**Círculos concéntricos** Los círculos concéntricos están en el mismo plano y tienen el mismo centro.

**Example**

The two circles both have center $D$ and are therefore concentric.

**Conclusion** The conclusion is the part of an *if-then* statement (conditional) that follows *then*.

**Conclusión** La conclusión es lo que sigue a la palabra entonces en un enunciado (condicional), *si . . ., entonces. . . .*

**Example** In the statement, "If it rains, then I will go outside," the conclusion is "I will go outside."

VISUAL GLOSSARY

## English | Spanish

**Concurrent** Three or more lines are concurrent if they intersect at one point. The point at which they intersect is the *point of concurrency.*

**Concurrente** Tres o más rectas son concurrentes si se intersecan en un punto. El punto en el que se intersecan es el *punto de concurrencia.*

**Example**

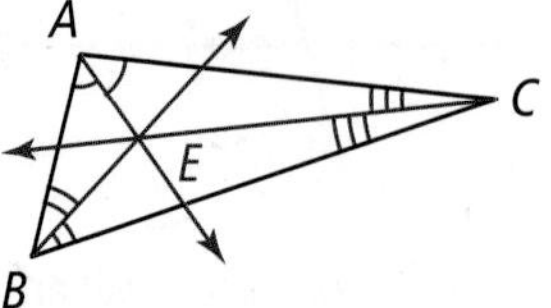


Point $E$ is the point of concurrency of the bisectors of the angles of $\triangle ABC$. The bisectors are concurrent.

**Conditional** A conditional is an *if-then* statement that relates a hypothesis, the part that follows if, to a conclusion, the part that follows then.

**Condicional** Un enunciado condicional es del tipo *si . . ., entonces. . . .*

**Example** *If* you act politely, *then* you will earn respect.

**Conditional probability** A conditional probability is the probability that an event $B$ will occur given that another event $A$ has already occurred. The notation $P(B|A)$ is read "the probability of event $B$, given event $A$." For any two events $A$ and $B$ in the sample space, $P(B|A) = \frac{P(A \text{ and } B)}{P(A)}$.

**Probabilidad condicional** Una probabilidad condicional es la probabilidad de que ocurra un suceso $B$ cuando ya haya ocurrido otro suceso $A$. La notación $P(B|A)$ se lee "la probabilidad del suceso $B$, dado el suceso $A$". Para dos sucesos cualesquiera $A$ y $B$ en el espacio muestral $P(B|A) = \frac{P(A \text{ and } B)}{P(A)}$.

**Example**
$$= \frac{P(\text{departs and arrives on time})}{P(\text{departs on time})}$$
$$= \frac{0.75}{0.83}$$
$$\approx 0.9$$

**Cone** A cone is a three-dimensional figure that has a circular *base*, a *vertex* not in the plane of the circle, and a curved lateral surface, as shown in the diagram. The *altitude* of a cone is the perpendicular segment from the vertex to the plane of the base. The *height* is the length of the altitude. In a *right* cone, the altitude contains the center of the base. The *slant height* of a right cone is the distance from the vertex to the edge of the base.

**Cono** Un cono es una figura tridimensional que tiene una *base* circular, un *vértice* que no está en el plano del círculo y una superficie lateral curvada (indicada en el diagrama). La *altura* de un cono es el segmento perpendicular desde el vértice hasta el plano de la base. La *altura*, por extensión, es la longitude de la altura. Un *cono recto* es un cono cuya altura contiene el centro de la base. La *longitude de la generatriz* de un cono recto es la distancia desde el vértice hasta el borde de la base.

**Example**

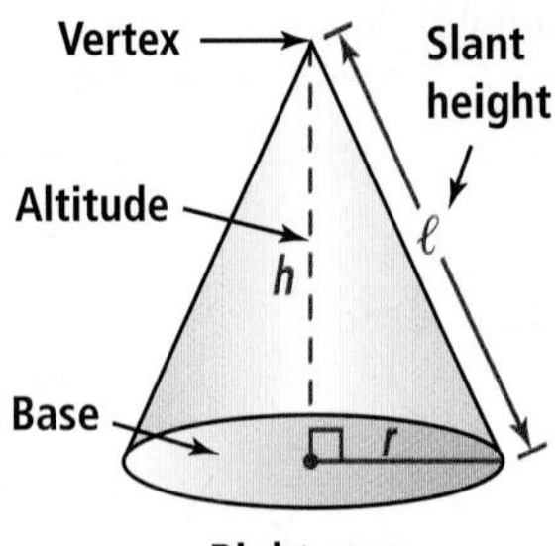


**Congruence transformation** A congruence transformation maps a figure to a congruent figure. A rigid motion is sometimes called a congruence transformation.

**Transformación de congruencia** En una transformación de congruencia, una figura es la imagen de otra figura congruente. Los movimientos rígidos son llamados a veces transformaciones de congruencia.

# English

# Spanish

**Congruent angles** Congruent angles are angles that have the same measure.

**Ángulos congruentes** Los ángulos congruentes son ángulos que tienen la misma medida.

**Example**

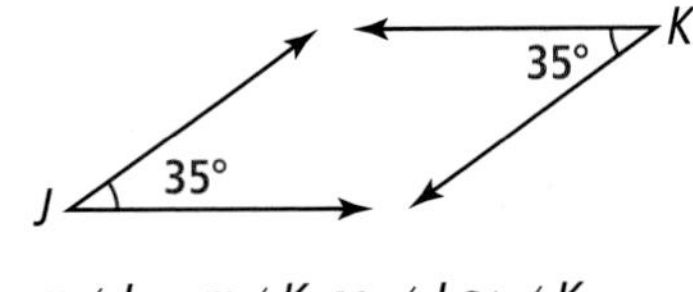


$m\angle J = m\angle K$, so $\angle J \cong \angle K$.

**Congruent arcs** Congruent arcs are arcs that have the same measure and are in the same circle or congruent circles.

**Arcos congruentes** Arcos congruentes son arcos que tienen la misma medida y están en el mismo círculo o en círculos congruentes.

**Example**

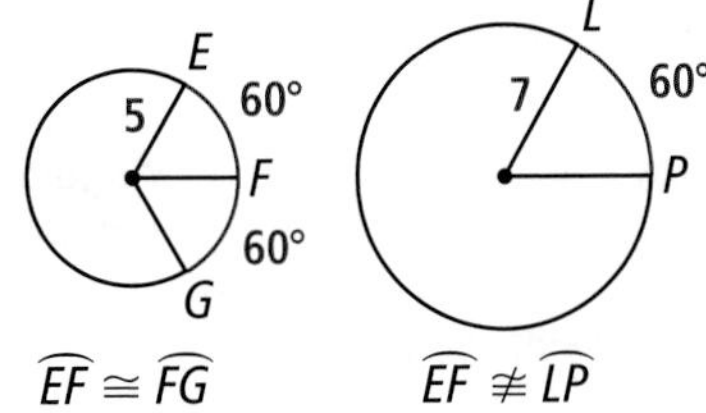


$\widehat{EF} \cong \widehat{FG}$ $\widehat{EF} \ncong \widehat{LP}$

**Congruent circles** Congruent circles are circles whose radii are congruent.

**Círculos congruentes** Los círculos congruentes son círculos cuyos radios son congruentes.

**Example**

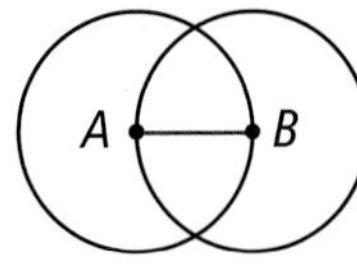


$\odot A$ and $\odot B$ have the same radius, so $\odot A \cong \odot B$.

**Congruent figures** Two figures are congruent if there is a rigid motion that maps one figure to the other.

**Figuras congruentes** Dos figuras son congruentes si hay un movimiento rígido en el que una figura es imagen de la otra.

**Example**

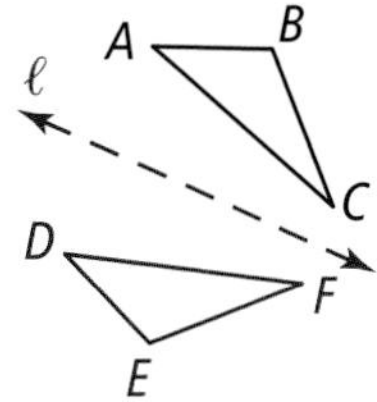


Since the reflection across line $\ell$ maps $\triangle ABC$ to $\triangle DEF$, $\triangle ABC$ and $\triangle DEF$ are congruent figures.

**Congruent polygons** Congruent polygons are polygons that have corresponding sides congruent and corresponding angles congruent.

**Polígonos congruentes** Los polígonos congruentes son polígonos cuyos lados correspondientes son congruentes y cuyos ángulos correspondientes son congruentes.

**Example**

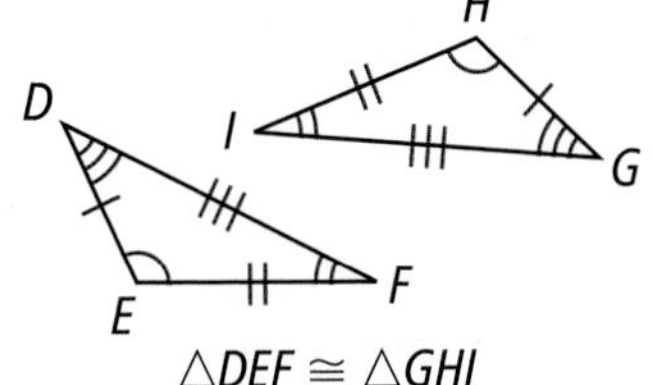


$\triangle DEF \cong \triangle GHI$

VISUAL GLOSSARY

## English | Spanish

**Congruent segments** Congruent segments are segments that have the same length.

**Segmentos congruentes** Los segmentos congruentes son segmentos que tienen la misma longitud.

**Example**

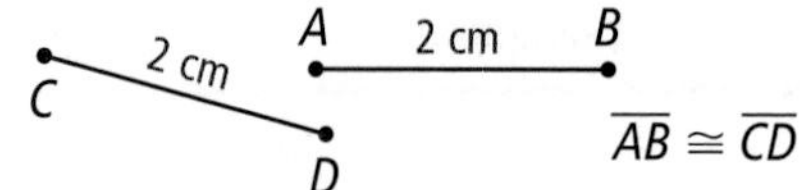


**Conjecture** A conjecture is an unproven statement or rule that is based on inductive reasoning.

**Conjetura** Una conjetura es una afirmación o regla no demostrada, que está fundamentada en un razonamiento inductivo.

**Example** As you walk down the street, you see many people holding unopened umbrellas. You make the conjecture that the forecast must call for rain.

**Consecutive angles** Consecutive angles of a polygon share a common side.

**Ángulos consecutivos** Los ángulos consecutivos de un polígono tienen un lado común.

**Example**

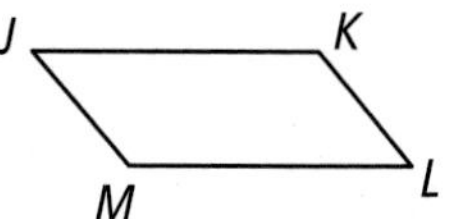


In ▱*JKLM*, $\angle J$ and $\angle M$ are consecutive angles, as are $\angle J$ and $\angle K$. $\angle J$ and $\angle L$ are *not* consecutive.

**Construction** A construction is a geometric figure made with only a straightedge and compass.

**Construcción** Una construcción es una figura geométrica trazada solamente con una regla sin graduación y un compás.

**Example**

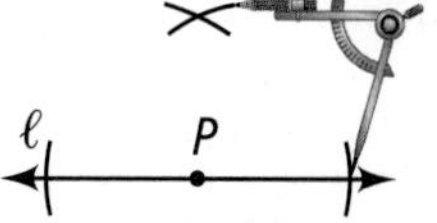


The diagram shows the construction (in progress) of a line perpendicular to a line $\ell$ through a point $P$ on $\ell$.

**Contrapositive** The contrapositive is obtained by negating and reversing the hypothesis and the conclusion of a conditional. The contrapositive of the conditional "if $p$, then $q$" is the conditional "if not $q$, then not $p$." A conditional and its contrapositive always have the same truth value.

**Contrapositivo** El contrapositivo se obtiene al negar e intercambiar la hipótesis y la conclusión de un condicional. El contrapositivo del condicional "si $p$, entonces $q$" es el condicional "si no $q$, entonces no $p$". Un condicional y su contrapositivo siempre tienen el mismo valor verdadero.

**Example** **Conditional:** If a figure is a triangle, then it is a polygon.
**Contrapositive:** If a figure is not a polygon, then it is not a triangle.

**Converse** The converse reverses the hypothesis and conclusion of a conditional.

**Expresión recíproca** La expresión recíproca intercambia la hipótesis y la conclusión de un condicional.

**Example** The converse of "If I was born in Houston, then I am a Texan" would be "If I am a Texan, then I am born in Houston."

**Convex polygon** *See* **polygon.**

**Polígono convexo** *Ver* **polygon.**

| English | Spanish |
|---|---|

**Coordinate(s) of a point** The coordinate of a point is its distance and direction from the origin of a number line. The coordinates of a point on a coordinate plane are in the form $(x, y)$, where $x$ is the $x$-coordinate and $y$ is the $y$-coordinate.

**Coordenada(s) de un punto** La coordenada de un punto es su distancia y dirección desde el origen en una recta numérica. Las coordenadas de un punto en un plano de coordenadas se expresan como $(x, y)$, donde $x$ es la coordenada $x$, e $y$ es la coordenada $y$.

**Example**

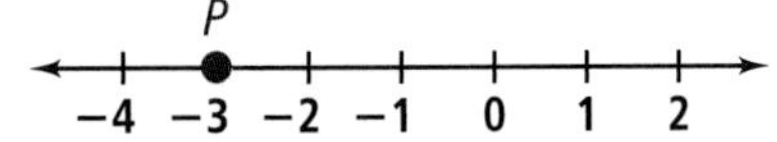


The coordinate of $P$ is $-3$.

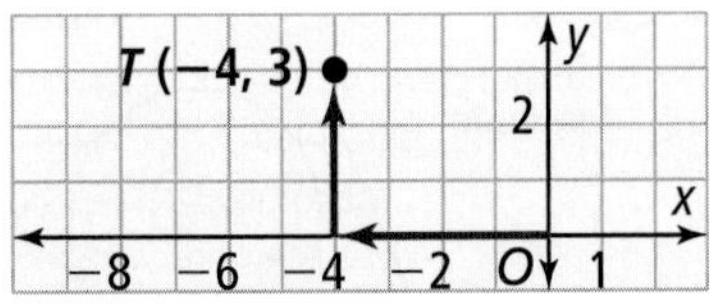


The coordinates of $T$ are $(-4, 3)$.

**Coordinate plane** The coordinate plane is formed by two number lines, called the axes, intersecting at right angles. The $x$-axis is the horizontal axis, and the $y$-axis is the vertical axis. The two axes meet at the origin, $O(0, 0)$. The axes divide the plane into four *quadrants*.

**Plano de coordenadas** El plano de coordenadas se forma con dos rectas numéricas, llamadas *ejes*, que se cortan en ángulos rectos. El eje $x$ es el eje horizontal y el eje $y$ es el eje vertical. Los dos ejes se unen en el *origen*, $O(0, 0)$. Los ejes dividen el plano de coordenadas en cuatro *cuadrantes*.

**Example**

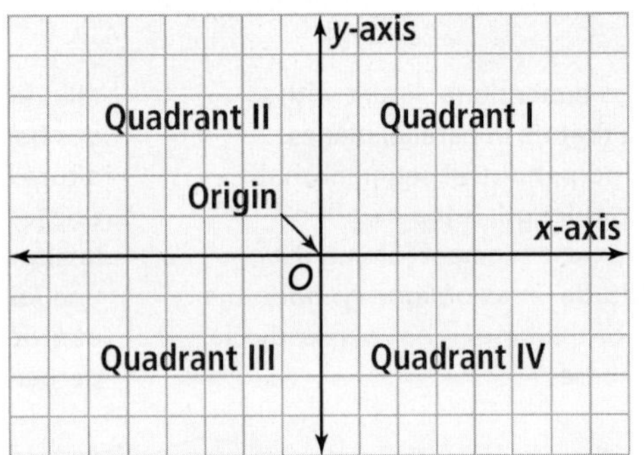


**Coordinate proof** *See* **proof.**

**Prueba de coordenadas** *Ver* **proof.**

**Corollary** A corollary is a theorem that can be proved easily using another theorem.

**Corolario** Un corolario es un teorema que se puede probar fácilmente usando otro teorema.

**Example** **Theorem:** If two sides of a triangle are congruent, then the angles opposite those sides are congruent.
**Corollary:** If a triangle is equilateral, then it is equiangular.

**Corresponding angles** Corresponding angles lie on the same side of the transversal $t$ and in corresponding positions relative to $\ell$ and $m$.

**Ángulos correspondientes** Los ángulos correspondientes están en el mismo lado de la transversal $t$ y en las correspondientes posiciones relativas a $\ell$ y $m$.

**Example**

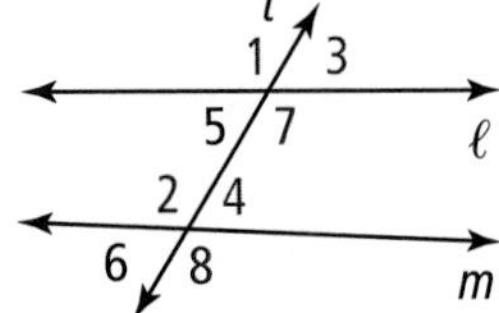


$\angle 1$ and $\angle 2$ are corresponding angles, as are $\angle 3$ and $\angle 4$, $\angle 5$ and $\angle 6$, and $\angle 7$ and $\angle 8$.

VISUAL GLOSSARY

## English

## Spanish

**Cosine ratio** See **trigonometric ratios.**

**Razón coseno** *Ver* **trigonometric ratios.**

**Counterexample** A counterexample is an example that shows a statement or conjecture is false.

**Contraejemplo** Un contraejemplo es un ejemplo que demuestra que una afirmación o conjetura es falsa.

**Example** **Statement:** All apples are red.
**Counterexample:** A Granny Smith Apple is green.

**Cross section** A cross section is the intersection of a solid and a plane.

**Sección de corte** Una sección de corte es la intersección de un plano y un cuerpo geométrico.

**Example**

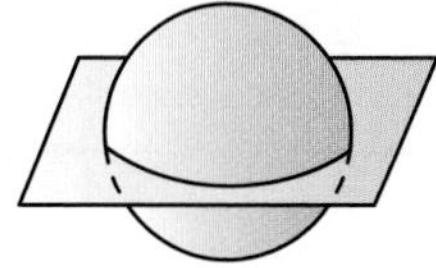

The cross section is a circle.

**Cube** A cube is a polyhedron with six faces, each of which is a square.

**Cubo** Un cubo es un poliedro de seis caras, cada una de las caras es un cuadrado.

**Example**

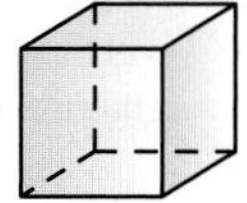

**Cylinder** A cylinder is a three-dimensional figure with two congruent circular bases that lie in parallel planes. An *altitude* of a cylinder is a perpendicular segment that joins the planes of the bases. Its length is the *height* of the cylinder. In a *right cylinder*, the segment joining the centers of the bases is an altitude. In an *oblique cylinder*, the segment joining the centers of the bases is not perpendicular to the planes containing the bases.

**Cilindro** Un cilindro es una figura tridimensional con dos bases congruentes circulares en planos paralelos. Una *altura* de un cilindro es un segmento perpendicular que une los planos de las bases. Su longitud es, por extensión, la *altura* del cilindro. En un *cilindro* recto, el segmento que une los centros de las bases es una altura. En un *cilindro oblicuo*, el segmento que une los centros de las bases no es perpendicular a los planos que contienen las bases.

**Example**

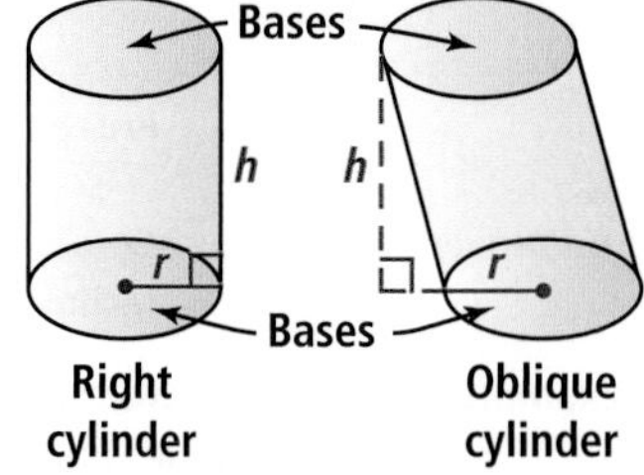


## D

**Decagon** A decagon is a polygon with ten sides.

**Decágono** Un decágono es un polígono de diez lados.

**Example**

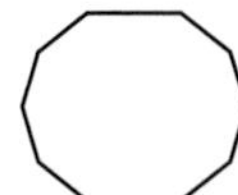

**Deductive reasoning** Deductive reasoning is a process of reasoning using given and previously known facts to reach a logical conclusion.

**Razonamiento deductivo** El razonamiento deductivo es un proceso de razonamiento en el que se usan hechos dados y previamente conocidos para llegar a una conclusión lógica.

**Example** Based on the fact that the sum of any two even numbers is even, you can deduce that the product of any whole number and any even number is even.

| English | Spanish |
|---|---|
| **Dependent events** When the outcome of one event affects the probability of a second event, the events are dependent events. | **Sucesos dependientes** Dos sucesos son dependientes si el resultado de un suceso afecta la probabilidad del otro. |

**Example** You have a bag with marbles of different colors. If you pick a marble from the bag and pick another without replacing the first, the events are dependent events.

**Diagonal** *See* **polygon.**

**Diagonal** *Ver* **polygon.**

**Diameter of a circle** A diameter of a circle is a segment that contains the center of the circle and whose endpoints are on the circle. The term *diameter* can also mean the length of this segment.

**Diámetro de un círculo** Un diámetro de un círculo es un segmento que contiene el centro del círculo y cuyos extremos están en el círculo. El término *diámetro* también puede referirse a la longitud de este segmento.

**Example**

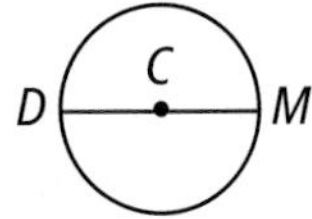


$\overline{DM}$ is a diameter of $\odot C$.

**Diameter of a sphere** The diameter of a sphere is a segment passing through the center, with endpoints on the sphere.

**Diámetro de una esfera** El diámetro de una esfera es un segmento que contiene el centro de la esfera y cuyos extremos están en la esfera.

**Example**

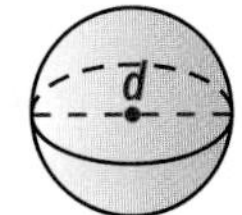


**Dilation** A dilation is a transformation that has *center C* and *scale factor n*, where $n > 0$, and maps a point $R$ to $R'$ in such a way that $R'$ is on $\overrightarrow{CR}$ and $CR' = n \cdot CR$. The center of a dilation is its own image. If $n > 1$, the dilation is an *enlargement*, and if $0 < n < 1$, the dilation is a *reduction*.

**Dilatación** Una dilatación, o *transformación de semejanza*, tiene *centro C* y *factor de escala n* para $n > 0$, y asocia un punto $R$ a $R'$ de tal modo que $R'$ está en $\overrightarrow{CR}$ y $CR' = n \cdot CR$. El centro de una dilatación es su propia imagen. Si $n > 1$, la dilatación es un aumento, y si $0 < n < 1$, la dilatación es una reducción.

**Example**

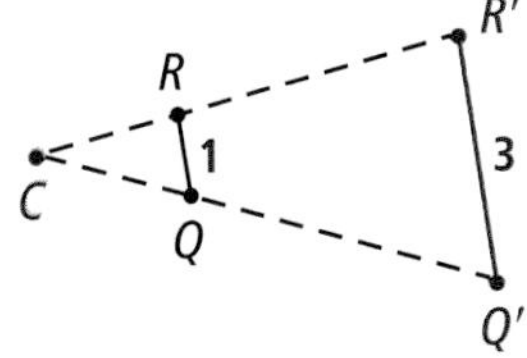


$\overline{R'Q'}$ is the image of $\overline{RQ}$ under a dilation with center $C$ and scale factor 3.

**Directrix** *See* **parabola.**

**Directriz** *Ver* **parabola.**

**Distance between two points on a line** The distance between two points on a line is the absolute value of the difference of the coordinates of the points.

**Distancia entre dos puntos de una línea** La distancia entre dos puntos de una línea es el valor absoluto de la diferencia de las coordenadas de los puntos.

**Example**

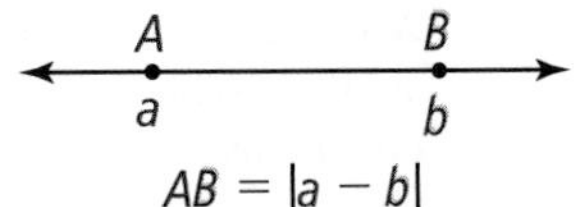

## English

## Spanish

**Distance from a point to a line** The distance from a point to a line is the length of the perpendicular segment from the point to the line.

**Distancia desde un punto hasta una recta** La distancia desde un punto hasta una recta es la longitud del segmento perpendicular que va desde el punto hasta la recta.

**Example** 

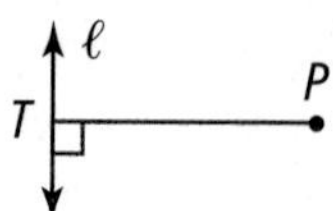


The distance from point $P$ to a line $\ell$ is $PT$.

## E

**Edge** *See* **polyhedron.**

**Arista** *Ver* **polyhedron.**

**Endpoint** *See* **ray; segment.**

**Extremo** *Ver* **ray; segment.**

**Enlargement** *See* **dilation.**

**Aumento** *Ver* **dilation.**

**Equiangular triangle** An equiangular triangle is a triangle whose angles are all congruent.

**Triángulo equiángulo** Un triángulo equiángulo es un triángulo cuyos ángulos son todos congruentes.

**Example**

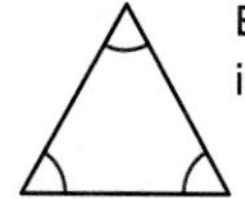

Each angle of the triangle is a 60° angle.

**Equidistant** A point is equidistant from two objects if it is the same distance from the objects.

**Equidistante** Un punto es equidistante de dos objetos si la distancia entre el punto y los objetos es igual.

**Example**

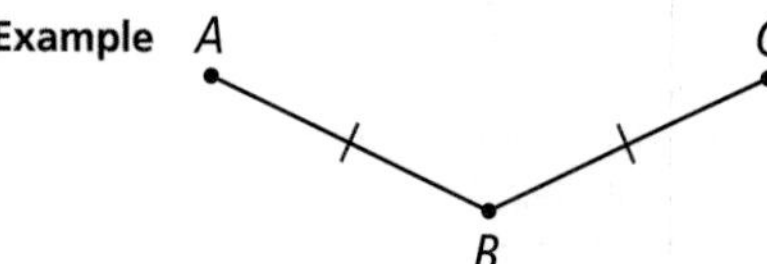


Point $B$ is equidistant from points $A$ and $C$.

**Equilateral triangle** An equilateral triangle is a triangle whose sides are all congruent.

**Triángulo equilátero** Un triángulo equilátero es un triángulo cuyos lados son todos congruentes.

**Example**

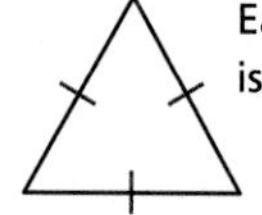

Each side of the triangle is 1.5 cm long.

**Equivalent statements** Equivalent statements are statements with the same truth value.

**Enunciados equivalentes** Los enunciados equivalentes son enunciados con el mismo valor verdadero.

**Example** The following statements are equivalent:
If a figure is a square, then it is a rectangle.
If a figure is not a rectangle, then it is not a square.

**Event** Any group of outcomes in a situation involving probability.

**Suceso** En la probabilidad, cualquier grupo de resultados.

**Example** When rolling a number cube, there are six possible outcomes. Rolling an even number is an event with three possible outcomes, 2, 4, and 6.

| English | Spanish |
|---|---|

**Expected value** The average value you can expect for a large number of trials of an experiment; the sum of each outcome's value multiplied by its probability.

**Valor esperado** El valor promedio que se puede esperar para una cantidad grande de pruebas en un experimento; la suma de los valores de los resultados multiplicados cada uno por su probabilidad.

**Example** In a game, a player has a 25% probability of earning 10 points by spinning an even number and a 75% probability of earning 5 points by spinning an odd number.

expected value = 0.25(10) + 0.75(5) = 6.25

**Experimental probability** The ratio of the number of times an event actually happens to the number of times the experiment is done.

$P(\text{event}) = \frac{\text{number of times an event happens}}{\text{number of times the experiment is done}}$

**Probabilidad experimental** La razón entre el número de veces que un suceso sucede en la realidad y el número de veces que se hace el experimento.

$P(\text{suceso}) = \frac{\text{número de veces que sucede un suceso}}{\text{número de veces que se hace el experimento}}$

**Example** A baseball player's batting average shows how likely it is that a player will get a hit, based on previous times at bat.

**Extended proportion** *See* **proportion.**

**Proporción extendida** *Ver* **proportion.**

**Extended ratio** *See* **ratio.**

**Razón extendida** *Ver* **ratio.**

**Exterior angle of a polygon** An exterior angle of a polygon is an angle formed by a side and an extension of an adjacent side.

**Ángulo exterior de un polígono** El ángulo exterior de un polígono es un ángulo formado por un lado y una extensión de un lado adyacente.

**Example**

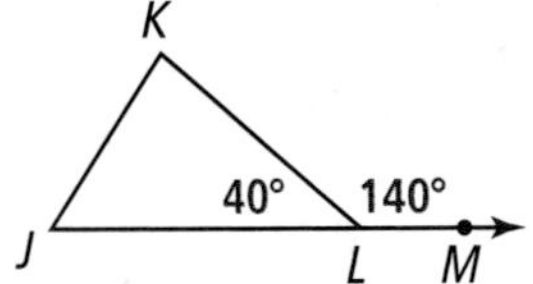


$\angle KLM$ is an exterior angle of $\triangle JKL$.

## F

**Factorial** The factorial of a positive integer *n* is the product of all positive integers less than or equal to *n* and written *n*!

**Factorial** El factorial de un número entero positivo *n* es el producto de todos los números positivos menores que o iguales a *n*, y se escribe *n*!

**Example** $4! = 4 \cdot 3 \cdot 2 \cdot 1 = 24$

**Flow proof** *See* **proof.**

**Prueba de flujo** *Ver* **proof.**

**Focus of a parabola** *See* **parabola.**

**Foco de una parábola** *Ver* **parabola.**

**Frequency table** A table that groups a set of data values into intervals and shows the frequency for each interval.

**Tabla de frecuencias** Tabla que agrupa un conjunto de datos en intervalos y muestra la frecuencia de cada intervalo.

**Example**

| Interval | Frequency |
|---|---|
| 0–9 | 5 |
| 10–19 | 8 |
| 20–29 | 4 |

VISUAL GLOSSARY

| English | Spanish |
|---|---|

**Fundamental Counting Principle** If there are $m$ ways to make the first selection and $n$ ways to make the second selection, then there are $m \cdot n$ ways to make the two selections.

**Principio fundamental de Conteo** Si hay $m$ maneras de hacer la primera selección y $n$ maneras de hacer la segunda selección, quiere decir que hay $m \cdot n$ maneras de hacer las dos selecciones.

**Example** For 5 shirts and 8 pairs of shorts, the number of possible outfits is $5 \cdot 8 = 40$.

**Geometric mean** The geometric mean is the number $x$ such that $\frac{a}{x} = \frac{x}{b}$, where $a$, $b$, and $x$ are positive numbers.

**Media geométrica** La media geométrica es el número $x$ tanto que $\frac{a}{x} = \frac{x}{b}$, donde $a$, $b$ y $x$ son números positivos.

**Example** The geometric mean of 6 and 24 is 12.

$$\frac{6}{x} = \frac{x}{24}$$
$$x^2 = 144$$
$$x = 12$$

**Geometric probability** Geometric probability is a probability that uses a geometric model in which points represent outcomes.

**Probabilidad geométrica** La probabilidad geométrica es una probabilidad que utiliza un modelo geométrico donde se usan puntos para representar resultados.

**Example**

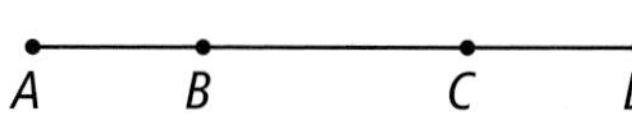


$P(H \text{ on } \overline{BC}) = \frac{BC}{AD}$

**Glide reflection** A glide reflection is the composition of a reflection followed by a translation in a direction parallel to the line of reflection.

**Reflexión deslizada** Una reflexión por deslizamiento es la composición de una reflexión seguida de una traslación en una dirección paralela a la recta de reflexión.

**Example**

The red G in the diagram is a glide reflection image of the black G.

**Great circle** A great circle is the intersection of a sphere and a plane containing the center of the sphere. A great circle divides a sphere into two *hemispheres*.

**Círculo máximo** Un círculo máximo es la intersección de una esfera y un plano que contiene el centro de la esfera. Un círculo máximo divide una esfera en dos *hemisferios*.

**Example**

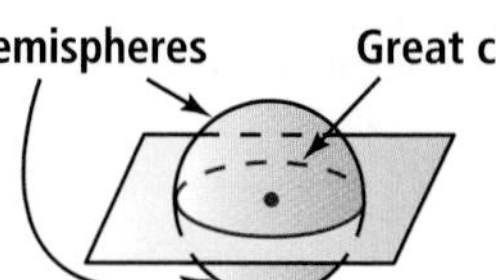


**H**

**Height** *See* **cone; cylinder; parallelogram; prism; pyramid; trapezoid; triangle.**

**Altura** *Ver* **cone; cylinder; parallelogram; prism; pyramid; trapezoid; triangle.**

**Hemisphere** *See* **great circle.**

**Hemisferio** *Ver* **great circle.**

**Hexagon** A hexagon is a polygon with six sides.

**Hexágono** Un hexágono es un polígono de seis lados.

**Example**

| English | Spanish |
|---|---|

**Hypotenuse** *See* **right triangle.**

**Hipotenusa** *Ver* **right triangle.**

**Hypothesis** In an *if-then* statement (conditional) the hypothesis is the part that follows *if*.

**Hipótesis** En un enunciado *si . . . entonces . . .* (condicional), la hipótesis es la parte del enunciado que sigue el *si*.

**Example** In the conditional "If an animal has four legs, then it is a horse," the hypothesis is "an animal has four legs."

**Image** *See* **transformation.**

**Imagen** *Ver* **transformation.**

**Incenter of a triangle** The incenter of a triangle is the point of concurrency of the angle bisectors of the triangle.

**Incentro de un triángulo** El incentro de un triángulo es el punto donde concurren las tres bisectrices de los ángulos del triángulo.

**Example**

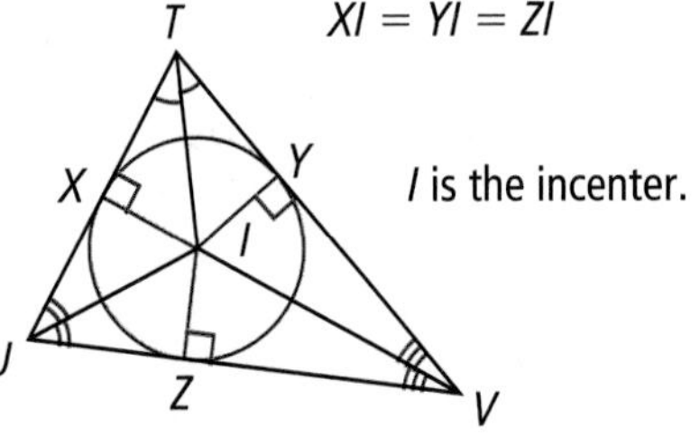


$XI = YI = ZI$

$I$ is the incenter.

**Independent events** When the outcome of one event does not affect the probability of a second event, the two events are independent.

**Sucesos independientes** Cuando el resultado de un suceso no altera la probabilidad de otro, los dos sucesos son independientes.

**Example** The results of two rolls of a number cube are independent. Getting a 5 on the first roll does not change the probability of getting a 5 on the second roll.

**Indirect proof** *See* **indirect reasoning; proof.**

**Prueba indirecta** *Ver* **indirect reasoning; proof.**

**Indirect reasoning** Indirect reasoning is a type of reasoning in which all possiblities are considered and then all but one are proved false. The remaining possibility must be true.

**Razonamiento indirecto** Razonamiento indirecto es un tipo de razonamiento en el que se consideran todas las posibilidades y se prueba que todas son falsas, a excepción de una. La posibilidad restante debe ser verdadera.

**Example** Eduardo spent more than \$60 on two books at a store. Prove that at least one book costs more than \$30.
**Proof:** Suppose neither costs more than \$30. Then he spent no more than \$60 at the store. Since this contradicts the given information, at least one book costs more than \$30.

**Inductive reasoning** Inductive reasoning is a type of reasoning that reaches conclusions based on a pattern of specific examples or past events.

**Razonamiento inductivo** El razonamiento inductivo es un tipo de razonamiento en el cual se llega a conclusiones con base en un patrón de ejemplos específicos o sucesos pasados.

**Example** You see four people walk into a building. Each person emerges with a small bag containing food. You use inductive reasoning to conclude that this building contains a restaurant.

| English | Spanish |
|---|---|

**Inscribed** The inscribed circle of a triangle is the circle that intersects each side of the triangle at exactly one point.

**Inscrito** El círculo inscrito de un triángulo es el círculo que interseca cada lado del triángulo en exactamente un punto.

**Example**

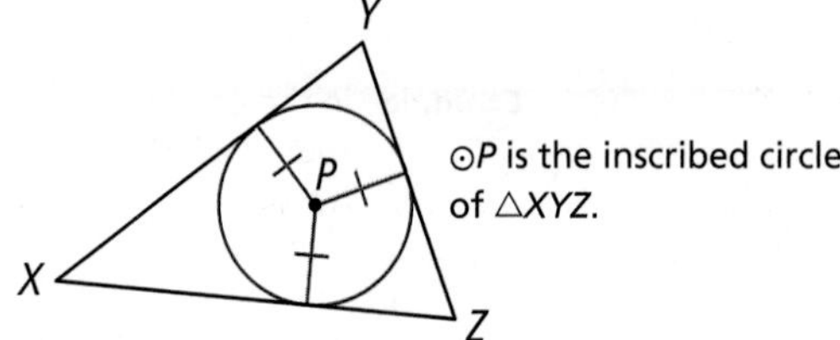


**Inscribed angle** An angle is inscribed in a circle if the vertex of the angle is on the circle and the sides of the angle are chords of the circle.

**Ángulo inscrito** Un ángulo está inscrito en un círculo si el vértice del ángulo está en el círculo y los lados del ángulo son cuerdas del círculo.

**Example**

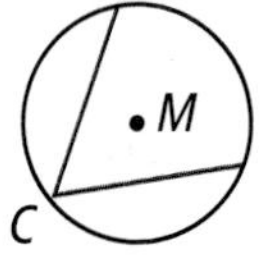


$\angle C$ is inscribed in $\odot M$.

**Intercepted arc** An intercepted arc is the part of a circle that lies between two segments that intersect the circle.

**Arco interceptor** Un arco interceptor es la parte de un círculo que yace entre dos segmentos de recta que intersecan al círculo.

**Example**

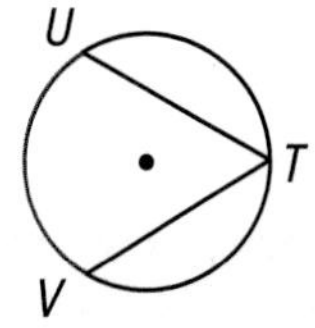


$\overset{\frown}{UV}$ is the intercepted arc of inscribed $\angle T$.

**Intersection** The intersection of two or more geometric figures is the set of points the figures have in common.

**Intersección** La intersección de dos o más figuras geométricas es el conjunto de puntos que las figuras tienen en común.

**Example**

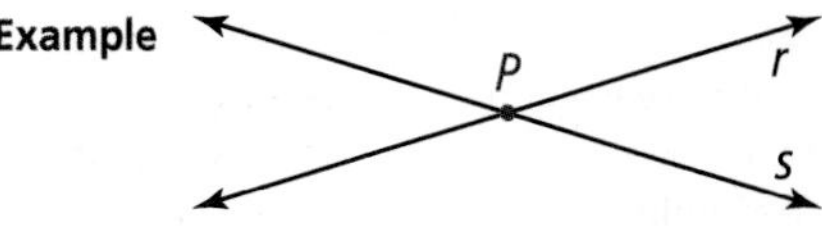


The intersection of lines $r$ and $s$ is point $P$.

**Inverse** The inverse is obtained by negating both the hypothesis and the conclusion of a conditional. The inverse of the conditional "if $p$, then $q$" is the conditional "if not $p$, then not $q$."

**Inverso** El inverso es la negación de la hipótesis y de la conclusión de un condicional. El inverso del condicional "si $p$, entonces $q$" es el condicional "si no $p$, entonces no $q$".

**Example** **Conditional:** If a figure is a square, then it is a parallelogram.
**Inverse:** If a figure is not a square, then it is not a parallelogram.

**Isosceles trapezoid** An isosceles trapezoid is a trapezoid whose nonparallel opposite sides are congruent.

**Trapecio isósceles** Un trapecio isosceles es un trapecio cuyos lados opuestos no paralelos son congruentes.

**Example**

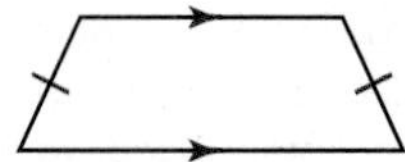

| English | Spanish |
|---|---|

**Isosceles triangle** An isosceles triangle is a triangle that has at least two congruent sides. If there are two congruent sides, they are called *legs*. The *vertex angle* is between them. The third side is called the *base* and the other two angles are called the *base angles*.

**Triángulo isósceles** Un triángulo isósceles es un triángulo que tiene por lo menos dos lados congruentes. Si tiene dos lados congruentes, éstos se llaman *catetos*. Entre ellos se encuentra el *ángulo del vértice*. El tercer lado se llama *base* y los otros dos ángulos se llaman *ángulos de base*.

**Example**

Vertex angle
Leg
Leg
Base angle
Base angle
Base

## K

**Kite** A kite is a quadrilateral with two pairs of consecutive sides congruent and no opposite sides congruent.

**Cometa** Una cometa es un cuadrilátero con dos pares de lados congruentes consecutivos y sin lados opuestos congruentes.

**Example**

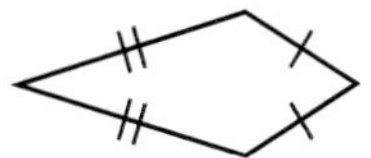

## L

**Lateral area** The lateral area of a prism or pyramid is the sum of the areas of the lateral faces. The lateral area of a cylinder or cone is the area of the curved surface.

**Área lateral** El área lateral de un prisma o pirámide es la suma de las áreas de sus caras laterals. El área lateral de un cilindro o de un cono es el área de la superficie curvada.

**Example**

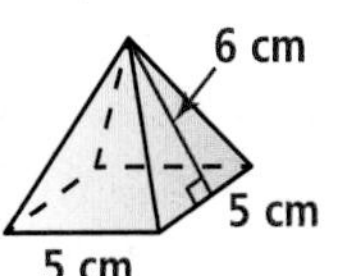


$$\text{L.A. of pyramid} = \frac{1}{2}p\ell$$
$$= \frac{1}{2}(20)(6)$$
$$= 60 \text{ cm}^2$$

**Lateral face** *See* **prism; pyramid.**

**Cara lateral** *Ver* **prism; pyramid.**

**Law of Cosines** In $\triangle ABC$, let $a$, $b$, and $c$ represent the lengths of the sides opposite $\angle A$, $\angle B$, and $\angle C$, respectively. Then
$a^2 = b^2 + c^2 - 2bc \cos A$,
$b^2 = a^2 + c^2 - 2ac \cos B$, and
$c^2 = a^2 + b^2 - 2ab \cos C$

**Ley de cosenos** En $\triangle ABC$, sean $a$, $b$ y $c$ las longitudes de los lados opuestos a $\angle A$, $\angle B$, y $\angle C$, respectivamente. Entonces
$a^2 = b^2 + c^2 - 2bc \cos A$,
$b^2 = a^2 + c^2 - 2ac \cos B$, y
$c^2 = a^2 + b^2 - 2ab \cos C$

**Example**

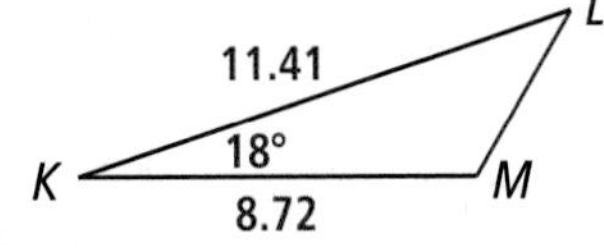


$$LM^2 = 11.41^2 + 8.72^2 - 2(11.42)(8.72)\cos 18^\circ$$
$$LM^2 = 16.9754$$
$$LM = 4.12$$

## English | Spanish

**Law of Detachment** The Law of Detachment is a law of logic that states if a conditional statement and its hypothesis are true, then its conclusion is also true. Symbolically, if $p \rightarrow q$ and $p$ are true, then $q$ is true.

**Regla de eliminación del condicional** La ley de eliminación del condicional es una regla lógica que establece que si un enunciado condicional y su hipótesis son ambos verdaderos, entonces la conclusión también será verdadera. Desde un punto de vista simbólico, si $p \rightarrow q$ y $p$ son verdaderos, entonces $q$ es verdadero.

**Example** Suppose the following statements are true.

- If Olivia has at least $10, she can buy the book she wants.
- Olivia has $12.

Then the following is true.

- Olivia can buy the book she wants.

**Law of Sines** In $\triangle ABC$, let $a$, $b$, and $c$ represent the lengths of the sides opposite $\angle A$, $\angle B$, and $\angle C$, respectively. Then $\frac{\sin A}{a} = \frac{\sin B}{b} = \frac{\sin C}{c}$.

**Ley de senos** En $\triangle ABC$, sean $a$, $b$ y $c$ las longitudes de los lados opuestos a $\angle A$, $\angle B$ y $\angle C$, respectivamente. Entonces $\frac{\sin A}{a} = \frac{\sin B}{b} = \frac{\sin C}{c}$.

**Example**

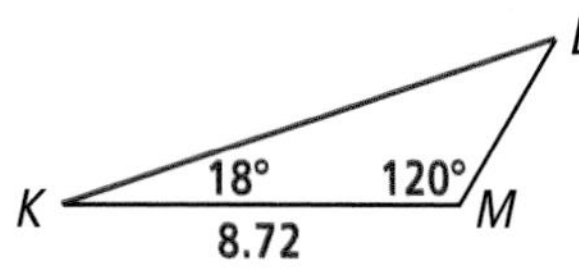


$$m\angle L = 180 - (120 + 18)$$
$$= \frac{KL}{\sin 120^\circ} = \frac{872}{\sin 42^\circ}$$
$$KL = \frac{872 \sin 120^\circ}{\sin 42^\circ}$$
$$KL = 11.26$$

**Law of Syllogism** The Law of Syllogism is a law of logic that states that given two true conditionals with the conclusion of the first being the hypothesis of the second, there exists a third true conditional having the hypothesis of the first and the conclusion of the second. Symbolically, if $p \rightarrow q$ and $q \rightarrow r$ are true, then $p \rightarrow r$ is true.

**Ley del silogismo hipotético** La ley del silogismo hipotético es una regla lógica que establece que si se tienen dos condicionales verdaderos en los que la conclusión del primero es la hipótesis del segundo, existe un tercer condicional verdadero compuesto por la hipótesis del primero y la conclusión del segundo. Desde un punto de vista simbólico, si $p \rightarrow q$ y $q \rightarrow r$ son verdaderos, entonces $p \rightarrow r$ es verdadero.

**Example** Suppose the following statements are true.

- If Renaldo works 20 hours this week, he earns $200.
- If Renaldo earns $200, he buys a new guitar.

Then the following is true.

- If Renaldo works 20 hours this week, he buys a new guitar.

**Leg** *See* **isosceles triangle; right triangle; trapezoid.**

**Cateto** *Ver* **isosceles triangle; right triangle; trapezoid.**

**Line** A line is undefined. You can think of a line as a straight path that extends in two opposite directions without end and has no thickness. A line contains infinitely many points. In spherical geometry, you can think of a line as a great circle of a sphere.

**Recta** Una recta es indefinida. Se puede pensar en una recta como un camino derecho que se extiende en direcciones opuestas sin fin ni grosor. Una recta tiene un número infinito de puntos. En la geometría esférica, se puede pensar en una recta como un gran círculo de una esfera.

**Example**

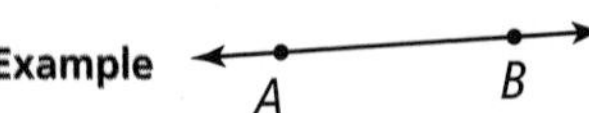


**Linear pair** A linear pair is a pair of adjacent angles whose noncommon sides are opposite rays.

**Par lineal** Un par lineal es un par de ángulos adjuntos cuyos lados no comunes son semirrectas opuestas.

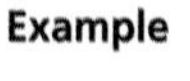

**Example**

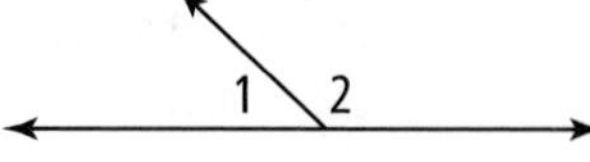

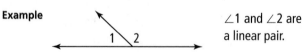

$\angle 1$ and $\angle 2$ are a linear pair.

| English | Spanish |
|---|---|

**Line of reflection** *See* **reflection.**

**Eje de reflexión** *Ver* **reflection.**

**Line of symmetry** *See* **reflectional symmetry.**

**Eje de simetría** *Ver* **reflectional symmetry.**

## M

**Major arc** A major arc of a circle is an arc that is larger than a semicircle.

**Arco mayor** Un arco mayor de un círculo es cualquier arco más grande que un semicírculo.

**Example**

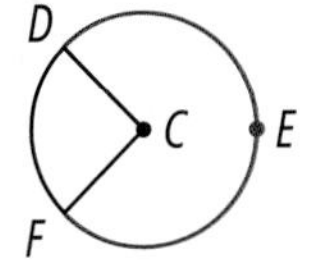


$\widehat{DEF}$ is a major arc of $\odot C$.

**Map** *See* **transformation.**

**Trazar** *Ver* **transformation.**

**Measure of an angle** Consider $\overrightarrow{OD}$ and a point $C$ on one side of $\overrightarrow{OD}$. Every ray of the form $\overrightarrow{OC}$ can be paired one to one with a real number from 0 to 180. The measure of $\angle COD$ is the absolute value of the difference of the real numbers paired with $\overrightarrow{OC}$ and $\overrightarrow{OD}$.

**Medida de un ángulo** Toma en cuenta $\overrightarrow{OD}$ y un punto $C$ a un lado de $\overrightarrow{OD}$. Cada semirrecta de la forma $\overrightarrow{OC}$ puede ser emparejada exactamente con un número real de 0 a 180. La medida de $\angle COD$ es el valor absoluto de la diferencia de los números reales emparejados con $\overrightarrow{OC}$ y $\overrightarrow{OD}$

**Example**

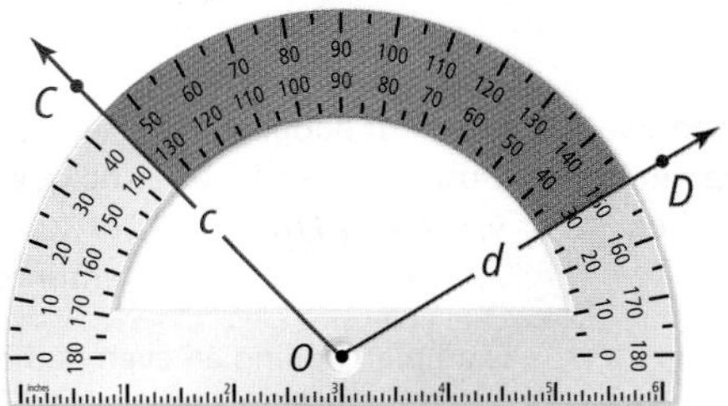


$m\angle COD = 105$

**Measure of an arc** The measure of a minor arc is the measure of its central angle. The measure of a major arc is 360° minus the measure of its related minor arc.

**Medida de un arco** La medida de un arco menor es la medida de su ángulo central. La medida de un arco mayor es 360° menos la medida en grados de su arco menor correspondiente.

**Example**

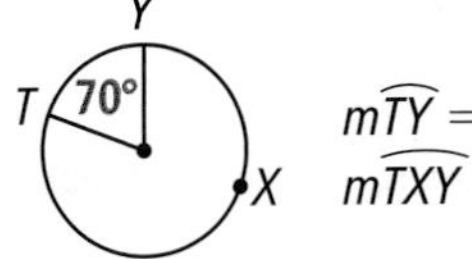


$m\widehat{TY} = 70$
$m\widehat{TXY} = 290$

**Median of a triangle** A median of a triangle is a segment that has as its endpoints at a vertex of the triangle and the midpoint of the opposite side.

**Mediana de un triángulo** Una mediana de un triángulo es un segmento que tiene en sus extremos el vértice del triángulo y el punto medio del lado opuesto.

**Example**

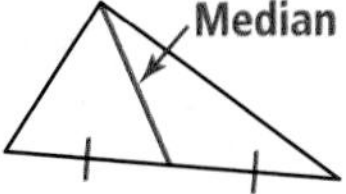


**Midpoint of a segment** A midpoint of a segment is the point that divides the segment into two congruent segments.

**Punto medio de un segmento** El punto medio de un segmento es el punto que divide el segmento en dos segmentos congruentes.

**Example**

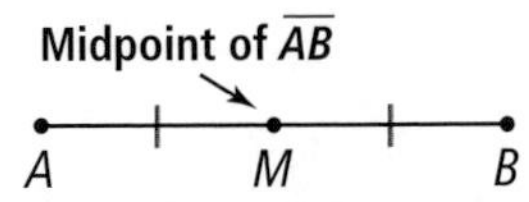

| English | Spanish |
|---|---|

**Midsegment of a trapezoid** The midsegment of a trapezoid is the segment that joins the midpoints of the nonparallel opposite sides of a trapezoid.

**Segmento medio de un trapecio** El segmento medio de trapecio es el segmento que une los puntos medios de los lados no paralelos de un trapecio.

**Example**

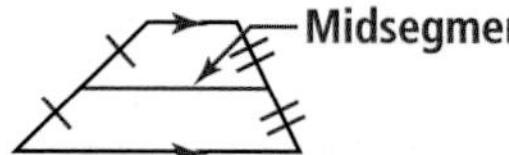


**Midsegment of a triangle** A midsegment of a triangle is a segment that joins the midpoints of two sides of the triangle.

**Segmento medio de un triángulo** Un segmento medio de un triángulo es un segmento que une los puntos medios de dos lados del triángulo.

**Example**

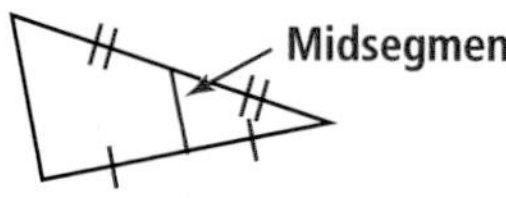


**Minor arc** A minor arc is an arc that is smaller than a semicircle.

**Arco menor** Un arco menor de un círculo es un arco más corto que un semicírculo.

**Example**

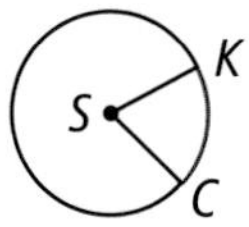


$\widehat{KC}$ is a minor arc of $\odot S$.

**Mutually exclusive events** When two events cannot happen at the same time, the events are mutually exclusive. If $A$ and $B$ are mutually exclusive events, then $P(A \text{ or } B) = P(A) + P(B)$.

**Sucesos mutuamente excluyentes** Cuando dos sucesos no pueden ocurrir al mismo tiempo, son mutuamente excluyentes. Si $A$ y $B$ son sucesos mutuamente excluyentes, entonces $P(A \text{ o } B) = P(A) + P(B)$.

**Example** Rolling an even number $E$ and rolling a multiple of five $M$ on a standard number cube are mutually exclusive events.

$$P(E \text{ or } M) = P(E) + P(M)$$
$$= \frac{3}{6} + \frac{1}{6}$$
$$= \frac{4}{6}$$
$$= \frac{2}{3}$$

## N

**Negation** The negation of a statement has the opposite meaning of the original statement.

**Negación** La negación de un enunciado tiene el sentido opuesto del enunciado original.

**Example** **Statement:** The angle is obtuse.
**Negation:** The angle is not obtuse.

***n*-gon** An $n$-gon is a polygon with $n$ sides.

***n*-ágono** Un $n$-ágono es un polígono de $n$ lados.

**Example** A polygon with 25 sides is a 25-gon.

**Nonagon** A nonagon is a polygon with nine sides.

**Nonágono** Un nonágono es un polígono de nueve lados.

**Example**

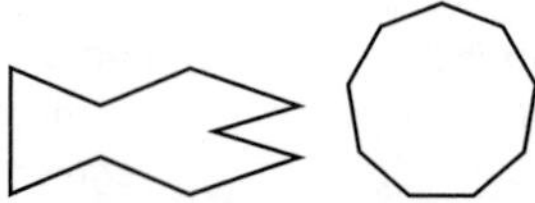

# English | Spanish

## O

**Oblique cylinder or prism** *See* **cylinder; prism.**

**Cilindro oblicuo o prisma** *Ver* **cylinder; prism.**

**Obtuse angle** An obtuse angle is an angle whose measure is between 90 and 180.

**Ángulo obtuso** Un ángulo obtuso es un ángulo que mide entre 90 y 180.

**Example**

**Obtuse triangle** An obtuse triangle has one obtuse angle.

**Triángulo obtusángulo** Un triángulo obtusángulo tiene un ángulo obtuso.

**Example**

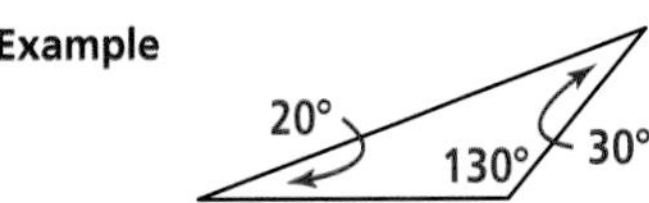


**Octagon** An octagon is a polygon with eight sides.

**Octágono** Un octágono es un polígono de ocho lados.

**Example**

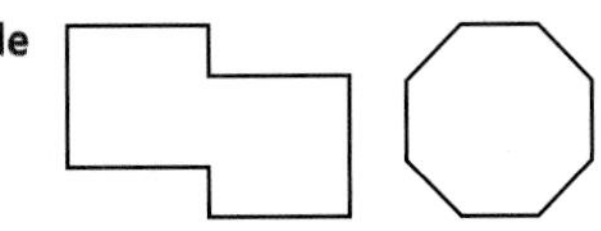

**Opposite angles** Opposite angles of a quadrilateral are two angles that do not share a side.

**Ángulos opuestos** Los ángulos opuestos de un cuadrilátero son dos ángulos que no comparten lados.

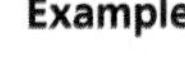

**Example**

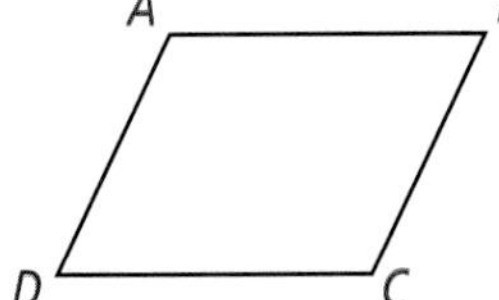


$\angle A$ and $\angle C$ are opposite angles, as are $\angle B$ and $\angle D$.

**Opposite rays** Opposite rays are collinear rays with the same endpoint. They form a line.

**Semirrectas opuestas** Las semirrectas opuestos son semirrectas colineales con el mismo extremo. Forman una recta.

**Example**

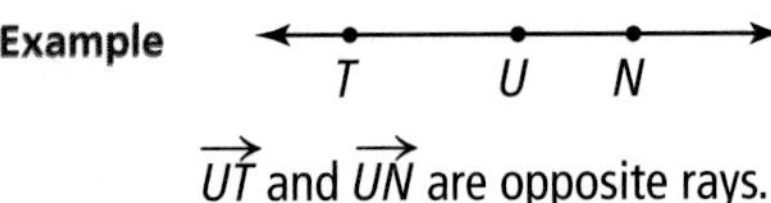


$\overrightarrow{UT}$ and $\overrightarrow{UN}$ are opposite rays.

**Opposite sides** Opposite sides of a quadrilateral are two sides that do not share a vertex.

**Lados opuestos** Los lados opuestos de un cuadrilátero son dos lados que no tienen un vértice en común.

**Example**

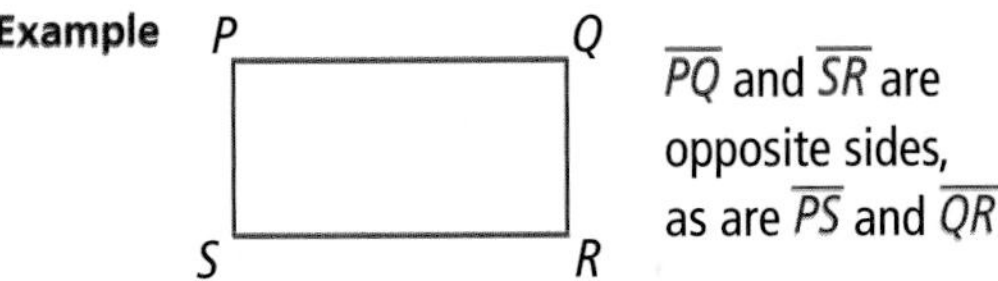


$\overline{PQ}$ and $\overline{SR}$ are opposite sides, as are $\overline{PS}$ and $\overline{QR}$.

**Orientation** Two figures have opposite orientation if a reflection is needed to map one onto the other. If a reflection is not needed to map one figure onto the other, the figures have the same orientation.

**Orientación** Dos figuras tienen orientación opuesta si una reflexión es necesaria para trazar una sobre la otra. Si una reflexión no es necesaria para trazar una figura sobre la otra, las figuras tienen la misma orientación.

**Example** R Я The two R's have opposite orientation.

## English — Spanish

**Origin** *See* **coordinate plane.**

**Origen** *Ver* **coordinate plane.**

**Orthocenter of a triangle** The orthocenter of a triangle is the point of concurrency of the lines containing the altitudes of the triangle.

**Ortocentro de un triángulo** El ortocentro de un triángulo es el punto donde se intersecan las alturas de un triángulo.

**Example**

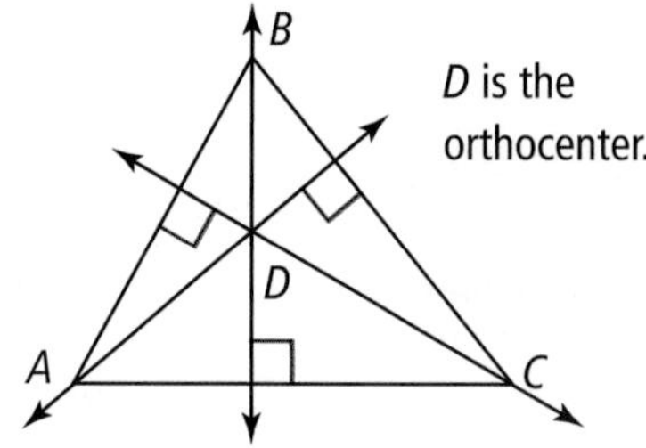


**Outcome** An outcome is the result of a single trial in a probability experiment.

**Resultado** Un resultado es que se obtiene al hacer una sola prueba en un experimento de probabilidad.

**Example** The outcomes of rolling a number cube are 1, 2, 3, 4, 5, and 6.

**Overlapping events** Overlapping events are events that have at least one common outcome. If $A$ and $B$ are overlapping events, then $P(A \text{ or } B) = P(A) + P(B) - P(A \text{ and } B)$.

**Sucesos traslapados** Sucesos traslapados son sucesos que tienen por lo menos un resultado en común. Si $A$ y $B$ son sucesos traslapados, entonces $P(A \text{ ó } B) = P(A) + P(B) - P(A \text{ y } B)$.

**Example** Rolling a multiple of 3 and rolling an odd number on a number cube are overlapping events.

$$P(\text{multiple of 3 or odd}) = P(\text{multiple of 3}) + P(\text{odd}) - P(\text{multiple of 3 and odd})$$
$$= \frac{1}{3} + \frac{1}{2} - \frac{1}{6}$$
$$= \frac{2}{3}$$

## P

**Parabola** A parabola is the set of all points $P$ in a plane that are the same distance from a fixed point $F$, the focus, as they are from a line $d$, the directrix.

**Parábola** La parábola es el conjunto de todos los puntos $P$ situados en un plano a la misma distancia de un punto fijo $F$, o foco, y de la recta $d$, o directriz.

**Example**

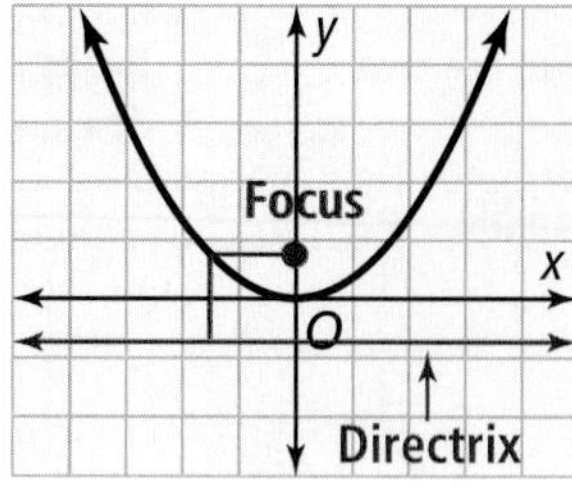


**Paragraph proof** *See* **proof.**

**Prueba de párrafo** *Ver* **proof.**

# English

# Spanish

**Parallel lines** Two lines are parallel if they lie in the same plane and do not intersect. The symbol || means "is parallel to."

**Rectas paralelas** Dos rectas son paralelas si están en el mismo plano y no se cortan. El símbolo || significa "es paralelo a".

**Example** $\ell \parallel m$

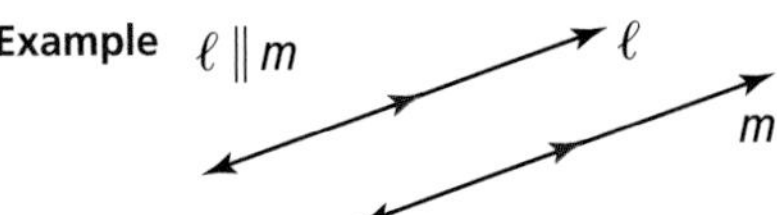


The red symbols indicate parallel lines.

**Parallelogram** A parallelogram is a quadrilateral with two pairs of parallel sides. You can choose any side to be the *base*. An *altitude* is any segment perpendicular to the line containing the base drawn from the side opposite the base. The *height* is the length of an altitude.

**Paralelogramo** Un paralelogramo es un cuadrilátero con dos pares de lados paralelos. Se puede escoger cualquier lado como la *base*. Una *altura* es un segmento perpendicular a la recta que contiene la base, trazada desde el lado opuesto a la base. La *altura*, por extensión, es la longitud de una altura.

**Example**

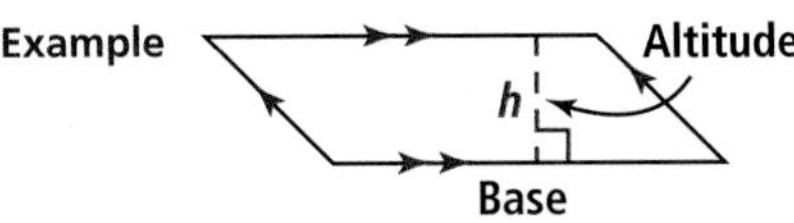


**Pentagon** A pentagon is a polygon with five sides.

**Pentágono** Un pentágono es un polígono de cinco lados.

**Example**

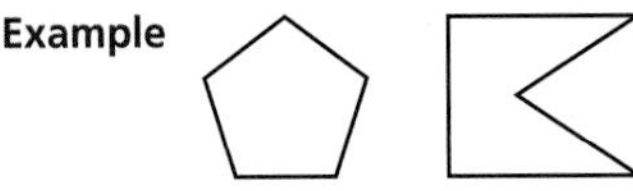

**Perimeter of a polygon** The perimeter of a polygon is the sum of the lengths of its sides.

**Perímetro de un polígono** El perímetro de un polígono es la suma de las longitudes de sus lados

**Example**

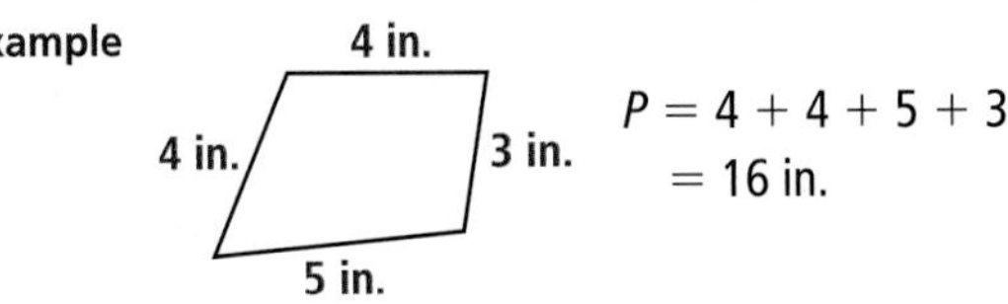


$$P = 4 + 4 + 5 + 3$$
$$= 16 \text{ in.}$$

**Permutation** A permutation is an arrangement of some or all of a set of objects in a specific order. You can use the notation ${}_nP_r$ to express the number of permutations, where $n$ equals the number of objects available and $r$ equals the number of selections to make.

**Permutación** Una permutación es una disposición de algunos o de todos los objetos de un conjunto en un orden determinado. El número de permutaciones se puede expresar con la notación ${}_nP_r$, donde $n$ es igual al número total de objetos y $r$ es igual al número de selecciones que han de hacerse.

**Example** How many ways can you arrange 5 objects 3 at a time?

$${}_5P_3 = \frac{5!}{(5-3)!} = \frac{5!}{2!} = \frac{5 \cdot 4 \cdot 3 \cdot 2 \cdot 1}{2 \cdot 1} = 60$$

There are 60 ways to arrange 5 objects 3 at a time.

**Perpendicular bisector** The perpendicular bisector of a segment is a line, segment, or ray that is perpendicular to the segment and divides the segment into two congruent segments.

**Mediatriz** La mediatriz de un segmento es una recta, segmento o semirrecta que es perpendicular al segmento y que divide al segmento en dos segmentos congruentes.

**Example**

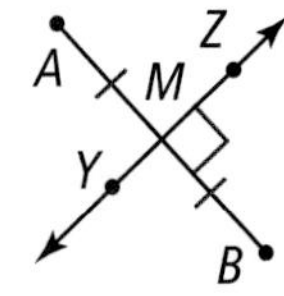


$\overleftrightarrow{YZ}$ is the perpendicular bisector of $\overline{AB}$. It is perpendicular to $\overline{AB}$ and intersects $\overline{AB}$ at midpoint $M$.

| English | Spanish |
|---|---|

**Perpendicular lines** Perpendicular lines are lines that intersect and form right angles. The symbol ⊥ means "is perpendicular to."

**Rectas perpendiculares** Las rectas perpendiculares son rectas que se cortan y forman ángulos rectos. El símbolo ⊥ significa "es perpendicular a".

**Example**

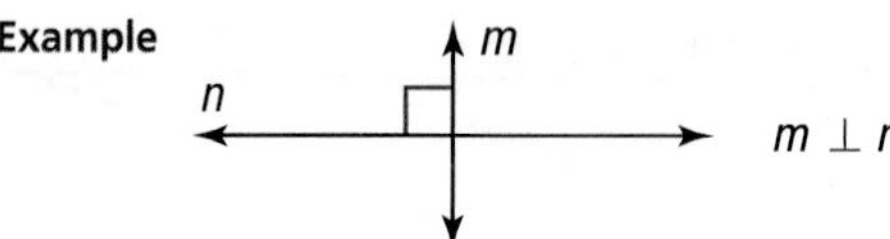


**Pi** Pi ($\pi$) is the ratio of the circumference of any circle to its diameter. The number $\pi$ is irrational and is approximately 3.14159.

**Pi** Pi ($\pi$) es la razón de la circunferencia de cualquier írculo a su diámetro. El número $\pi$ es irracional y se aproxima a $\pi \approx 3.14159$.

**Example**

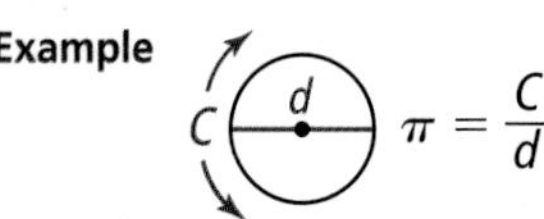


**Plane** A plane is undefined. You can think of a plane as a flat surface that extends without end and has no thickness. A plane contains infinitely many lines.

**Plano** Un plano es indefinido. Se puede pensar en un plano como una superficie plana sin fin, ni grosor. Un plano tiene un número infinito de rectas.

**Example**

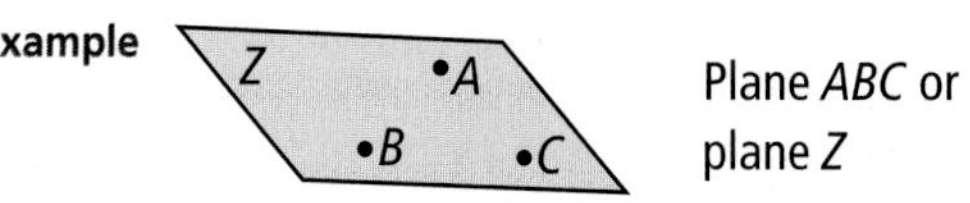


**Point** A point is undefined. You can think of a point as a location. A point has no size.

**Punto** Un punto es indefinido. Puedes imaginarte a un punto como un lugar. Un punto no tiene dimensión.

**Example** • $P$

**Point of concurrency** *See* **concurrent lines.**

**Punto de concurrencia** *Ver* **concurrent lines.**

**Point of tangency** *See* **tangent to a circle.**

**Punto de tangencia** *Ver* **tangent to a circle.**

**Point-slope form** The point-slope form for a nonvertical line with slope $m$ and through point $(x_1, y_1)$ is $y - y_1 = m(x - x_1)$.

**Forma punto-pendiente** La forma punto-pendiente para una recta no vertical con pendiente $m$ y que pasa por el punto $(x_1, y_1)$ es $y - y_1 = m(x - x_1)$.

**Example** $y + 1 = 3(x - 4)$
In this equation, the slope is 3 and $(x_1, y_1)$ is $(4, -1)$.

**Point symmetry** Point symmetry is the type of symmetry for which there is a rotation of 180° that maps a figure onto itself.

**Simetría central** La simetría central es un tipo de simetría en la que una figura se ha rotado 180° sobre sí misma.

**Example**

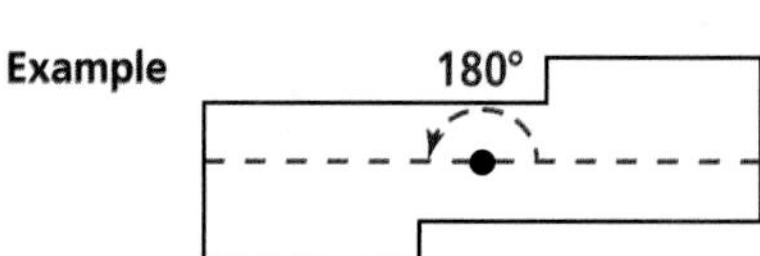

| English | Spanish |
|---|---|

**Polygon** A polygon is a closed plane figure formed by three or more segments. Each segment intersects exactly two other segments, but only at their endpoints, and no two segments with a common endpoint are collinear. The *vertices* of the polygon are the endpoints of the sides. A *diagonal* is a segment that connects two nonconsecutive vertices. A polygon is *convex* if no diagonal contains points outside the polygon. A polygon is *concave* if a diagonal contains points outside the polygon.

**Polígono** Un polígono es una figura plana compuesta por tres o más segmentos. Cada segmento interseca los otros dos segmentos exactamente, pero únicamente en sus puntos extremos y ningúno de los segmentos con extremos comunes son colineales. Los *vértices* del polígono son los extremos de los lados. Una *diagonal* es un segmento que conecta dos vértices no consecutivos. Un polígono es *convexo* si ninguna diagonal tiene puntos fuera del polígono. Un polígono es *cóncavo* si una diagonal tiene puntos fuera del polígono.

**Example**

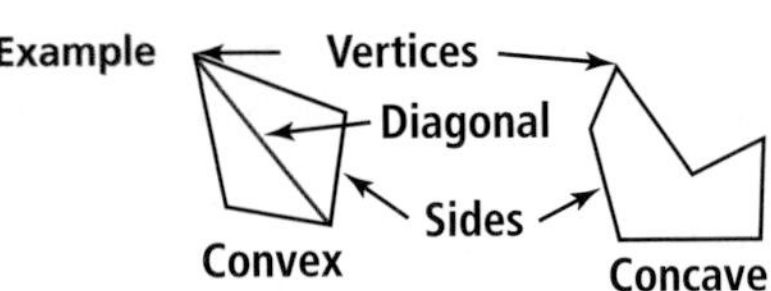


**Polyhedron** A polyhedron is a three-dimensional figure whose surfaces, or *faces*, are polygons. The vertices of the polygons are the *vertices* of the polyhedron. The intersections of the faces are the *edges* of the polyhedron.

**Poliedro** Un poliedro es una figura tridimensional cuyas superficies, o *caras*, son polígonos. Los vértices de los polígonos son los *vértices* del poliedro. Las intersecciones de las caras son las *aristas* del poliedro.

**Example**

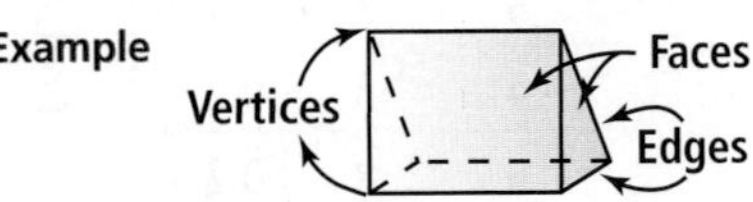


**Postulate** A postulate is an accepted statement of fact.

**Postulado** Un postulado es un enunciado que se acepta como un hecho.

**Example** **Postulate:** Through any two points there is exactly one line.

**Preimage** *See* **transformation**.

**Preimagen** *Ver* **transformation**.

**Prime notation** *See* **transformation**.

**Notación prima** *Ver* **transformation**.

**Prism** A prism is a polyhedron with two congruent and parallel faces, which are called the *bases*. The other faces, which are parallelograms, are called the *lateral faces*. An *altitude* of a prism is a perpendicular segment that joins the planes of the bases. Its length is the *height* of the prism. A *right prism* is one whose lateral faces are rectangular regions and a lateral edge is an altitude. In an *oblique prism*, some or all of the lateral faces are nonrectangular.

**Prisma** Un prisma es un poliedro con dos caras congruentes paralelas llamadas *bases*. Las otras caras son paralelogramos llamados *caras laterales*. La *altura* de un prisma es un segmento perpendicular que une los planos de las bases. Su longitud es también la *altura* del prisma. En un *prisma rectangular*, las caras laterales son rectangulares y una de las aristas laterales es la altura. En un *prisma oblicuo*, algunas o todas las caras laterales no son rectangulares.

**Example**

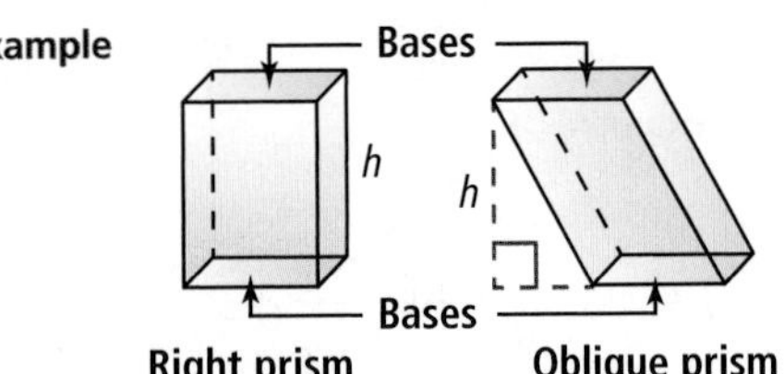

| English | Spanish |
|---|---|

**Probability** Probability is the likelihood that an event will occur (written formally as *P*(event)).

**Probabilidad** Probabilidad es la posibilidad de que un suceso ocurra, escrita formalmente *P*(suceso).

**Example** You have 4 red marbles and 3 white marbles. The probability that you select one red marble, and then, without replacing it, randomly select another red marble is $P(\text{red}) = \frac{4}{7} \cdot \frac{3}{6} = \frac{2}{7}$.

**Probability distribution** A probability distribution for an experiment is a function that assigns a probability to each outcome of a sample space for the experiment.

**Distribución de probabilidades** La distribución de probabilidades de un experimento es una función que asigna una probabilidad a cada resultado de un espacio muestral del experimento.

**Example**

| Roll | Fr. | Prob. |
|---|---|---|
| 1 | 5 | 0.125 |
| 2 | 9 | 0.225 |
| 3 | 7 | 0.175 |
| 4 | 8 | 0.2 |
| 5 | 8 | 0.2 |
| 6 | 3 | 0.075 |

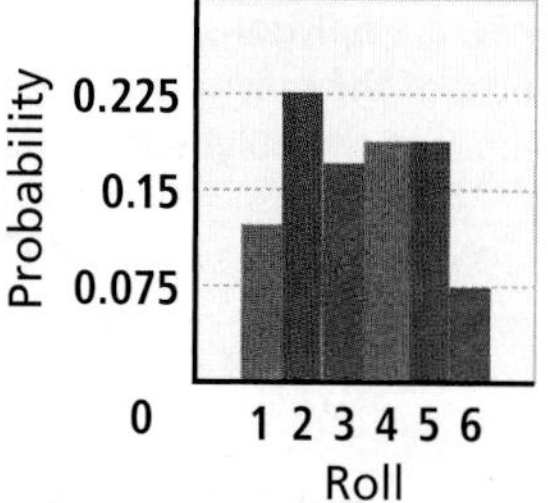


The table and graph both show the experimental probability distribution for the outcomes of 40 rolls of a standard number cube.

**Proof** A proof is a convincing argument that uses deductive reasoning. A proof can be written in many forms. In a two-column proof, the statements and reasons are aligned in columns. In a paragraph proof, the statements and reasons are connected in sentences. In a flow proof, arrows show the logical connections between the statements. In a coordinate proof, a figure is drawn on a coordinate plane and the formulas for slope, midpoint, and distance are used to prove properties of the figure. An indirect proof involves the use of indirect reasoning.

**Prueba** Una prueba es un argumento convincente en el cual se usa el razonamiento deductivo. Una prueba se puede escribir de varias maneras. En una *prueba de dos columnas*, los enunciados y las razones se alinean en columnas. En una *prueba de párrafo*, los enunciados y razones están unidos en oraciones. En una *prueba de flujo*, hay flechas que indican las conexiones lógicas entre enunciados. En una *prueba de coordenadas*, se dibuja una figura en un plano de coordenadas y se usan las fórmulas de la pendiente, punto medio y distancia para probar las propiedades de la figura. Una *prueba indirecta* incluye el uso de razonamiento indirecto.

**Example**

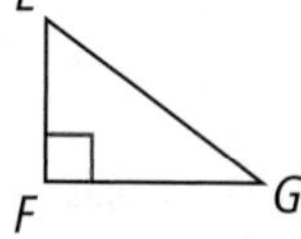


**Given:** $\triangle EFG$, with right angle $\angle F$
**Prove:** $\angle E$ and $\angle G$ are complementary.

**Paragraph Proof:** Because $\angle F$ is a right angle, $m\angle F = 90$. By the Triangle Angle-Sum Theorem, $m\angle E + m\angle F + m\angle G = 180$. By substitution, $m\angle E + 90 + m\angle G = 180$. Subtracting 90 from each side yields $m\angle E + m\angle G = 90$. $\angle E$ and $\angle G$ are complementary by definition.

| English | Spanish |
|---|---|

**Proportion** A proportion is a statement that two ratios are equal. An *extended proportion* is a statement that three or more ratios are equal.

**Proporción** Una proporción es un enunciado en el cual dos razones son iguales. Una *proporción extendida* es un enunciado que dice que tres razones o más son iguales.

**Example** $\frac{x}{5} = \frac{3}{4}$ is a proportion.

$\frac{9}{27} = \frac{3}{9} = \frac{1}{3}$ is an extended proportion.

**Pyramid** A pyramid is a polyhedron in which one face, the *base*, is a polygon and the other faces, the *lateral faces*, are triangles with a common vertex, called the *vertex* of the pyramid. An *altitude* of a pyramid is the perpendicular segment from the vertex to the plane of the base. Its length is the *height* of the pyramid. The *slant height* of a regular pyramid is the length of an altitude of a lateral face.

**Pirámide** Una pirámide es un poliedro en donde una cara, la *base*, es un polígono y las otras caras, las *caras laterales*, son triángulos con un vértice común, llamado el *vértice* de la pirámide. Una *altura* de una pirámide es el segmento perpendicular que va del vértice hasta el plano de la base. Su longitude es, por extensión, la *altura* de la pirámide. La *apotema* de una pirámide regular es la longitude de la altura de la cara lateral.

**Example**

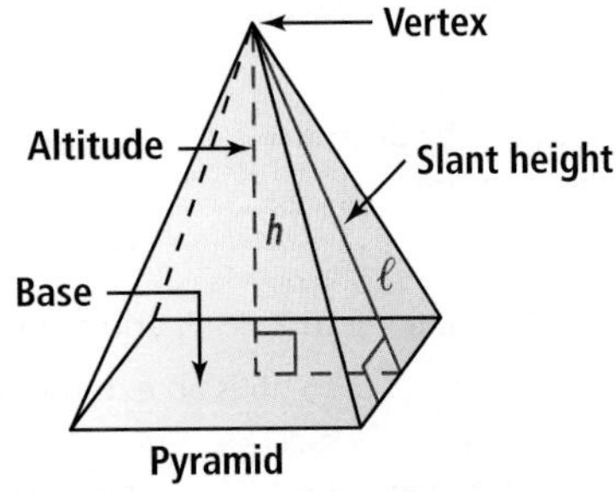


**Pythagorean triple** A Pythagorean triple is a set of three nonzero whole numbers *a*, *b*, and *c*, that satisfy the equation $a^2 + b^2 = c^2$.

**Tripleta de Pitágoras** Una tripleta de Pitágoras es un conjunto de tres números enteros positivos *a*, *b*, and *c* que satisfacen la ecuación $a^2 + b^2 = c^2$.

**Example** The numbers 5, 12, and 13 form a Pythagorean triple because $5^2 + 12^2 = 13^2 = 169$.

## Q

**Quadrant** *See* **coordinate plane.**

**Cuadrante** *Ver* **coordinate plane.**

**Quadrilateral** A quadrilateral is a polygon with four sides.

**Cuadrilátero** Un cuadrilátero es un polígono de cuatro lados.

**Example**

## R

**Radian** A radian is equal to the measure of a central angle that intercepts an arc with length equal to the radius of the circle.

**Radián** Un radián es igual a la medida de un ángulo central que interseca a un ángulo de la misma longitud que el radio del círculo.

**Example**

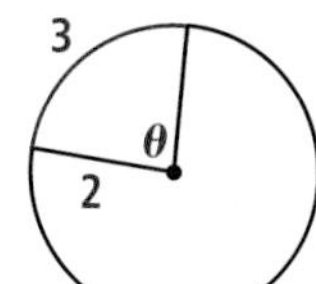


$s = \theta r$

$\theta = \frac{s}{r}$

$\theta = \frac{3}{2} = 1.5$ radians

## English | Spanish

**Radius of a circle** A radius of a circle is any segment with one endpoint on the circle and the other endpoint at the center of the circle. *Radius* can also mean the length of this segment.

**Radio de un círculo** Un radio de un círculo es cualquier segmento con extremo en el círculo y el otro extremo en el centro del círculo. *Radio* también se refiere a la longitude de este segmento.

**Example** 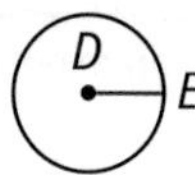

$\overline{DE}$ is a radius of $\odot D$.

**Radius of a sphere** The radius of a sphere is a segment that has one endpoint at the center and the other endpoint on the sphere.

**Radio de una esfera** El radio de una esfera es un segmento con un extremo en el centro y otro en la esfera.

**Example** 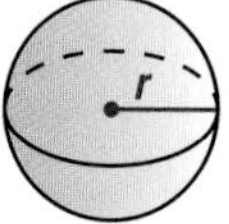


**Ratio** A ratio is a comparison of two quantities by division. An *extended ratio* is a comparison of three or more quantities by division.

**Razón** Una razón es una comparación de dos cantidades usando la división. Una *razón extendida* es una comparación de tres o más cantidades usando la división.

**Example** 5 to 7, 5 : 7, and $\frac{5}{7}$ are ratios.
3 : 5 : 6 is an extended ratio.

**Ray** A ray is the part of a line that consists of one *endpoint* and all the points of the line on one side of the endpoint.

**Semirrecta** Una semirrecta es la parte de una recta que tiene un *extremo* de donde parten todos los puntos de la recta.

**Example** 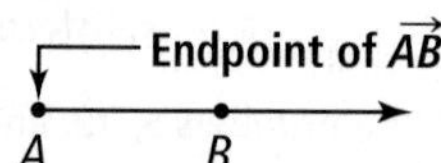


**Rectangle** A rectangle is a parallelogram with four right angles.

**Rectángulo** Un rectángulo es un paralelogramo con cuatro ángulos rectos.

**Example** 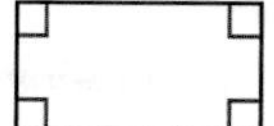

**Reduction** *See* **dilation.**

**Reducción** *Ver* **dilation.**

**Reflection** A reflection across line *r*, called the *line of reflection*, is a transformation such that if a point *A* is on line *r*, then the image of *A* is itself, and if a point *B* is not on line *r*, then its image *B′* is the point such that *r* is the perpendicular bisector of $\overline{BB'}$. A reflection is a rigid motion.

**Reflexión** Una reflexión a través de una línea *r*, llamada el *eje de reflexión*, es una transformación en la que si un punto *A* es parte de la línea *r*, la imagen de *A* es sí misma, y si un punto *B* no está en la línea *r*, su imagen *B′* es el punto en el cual la línea *r* es la bisectriz perpendicular de $\overline{BB'}$. Una reflexión es un movimiento rígido.

**Example** 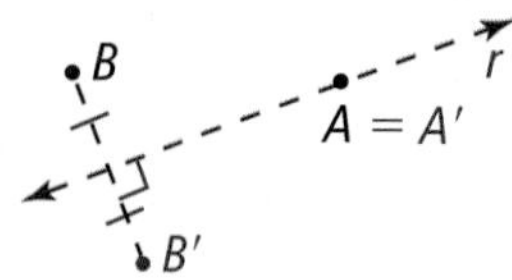

| English | Spanish |
|---|---|

**Reflectional symmetry** Reflectional symmetry is the type of symmetry for which there is a reflection that maps a figure onto itself. The reflection line is the *line of symmetry*. The line of symmetry divides a figure with reflectional symmetry into two congruent halves.

**Simetría reflexiva** Simetría reflexiva es el tipo de simetría donde hay una reflexión que ubica una figura en sí misma. El eje de reflexión es *el eje de simetría*. El eje de simetría divide una figura con simetría reflexiva en dos mitades congruentes.

**Example**

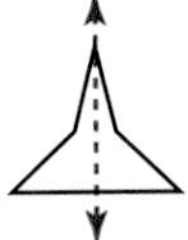

A reflection across the given line maps the figure onto itself.

**Regular polygon** A regular polygon is a polygon that is both equilateral and equiangular. Its *center* is the point that is equidistant from its vertices.

**Polígono regular** Un polígono regular es un polígono que es equilateral y equiangular. Su *centro* es el punto equidistante de sus vértices.

**Example**

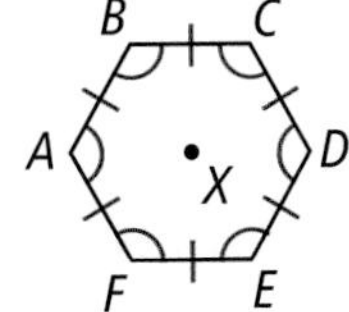


*ABCDEF* is a regular hexagon. Point *X* is its center.

**Relative frequency** The relative frequency of an event is the ratio of the number of times the event occurs to the total number of trials.

**Frecuencia relativa** La frecuencia relativa de un suceso es la razón del número de veces que ocurre un evento al número de eventos en el espacio muestral.

**Example**

| Archery Results | | | | | |
|---|---|---|---|---|---|
| **Scoring Region** | Yellow | Red | Blue | Black | White |
| **Arrow Strikes** | 52 | 25 | 10 | 8 | 5 |

$$\text{Relative frequency of striking red} = \frac{\text{frequency of striking red}}{\text{total frequencies}}$$

$$= \frac{25}{100} = \frac{1}{4}$$

**Remote interior angles** Remote interior angles are the two nonadjacent interior angles corresponding to each exterior angle of a triangle.

**Ángulos interiores remotos** Los ángulos interiores remotos son los dos ángulos interiores no adyacentes que corresponden a cada ángulo exterior de un triángulo.

**Example**

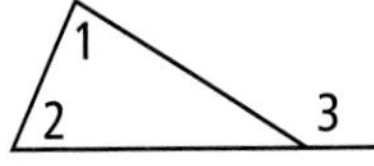


$\angle 1$ and $\angle 2$ are remote interior angles of $\angle 3$.

**Rhombus** A rhombus is a parallelogram with four congruent sides.

**Rombo** Un rombo es un paralelogramo de cuatro lados congruentes.

**Example**

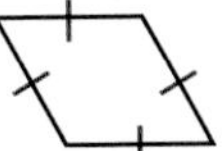

**Right angle** A right angle is an angle whose measure is 90.

**Ángulo recto** Un ángulo recto es un ángulo que mide 90.

**Example**

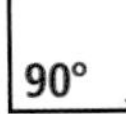


This symbol indicates a right angle.

VISUAL GLOSSARY

# English | Spanish

**Right cone** *See* **cone.**

**Cono recto** *Ver* **cone.**

**Right cylinder** *See* **cylinder.**

**Cilindro recto** *Ver* **cylinder.**

**Right prism** *See* **prism.**

**Prisma rectangular** *Ver* **prism.**

**Right triangle** A right triangle contains one right angle. The side opposite the right angle is the *hypotenuse* and the other two sides are the *legs*.

**Triángulo rectángulo** Un triángulo rectángulo contiene un ángulo recto. El lado opuesto del ángulo recto es la *hipotenusa* y los otros dos lados son los *catetos*.

**Example**

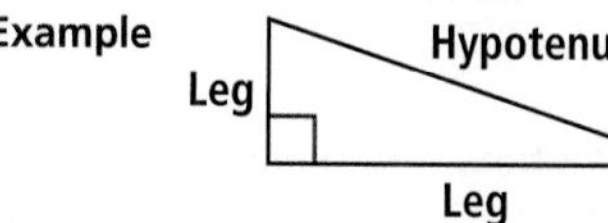


**Rigid motion** A rigid motion is a transformation that preserves distance and angle measure. A rigid motion is sometimes called a *congruence transformation*.

**Movimiento rígido** Un movimiento rígido es una transformación en el plano que no cambia la distancia ni la medida del ángulo. Los movimientos rígidos se conocen a veces como *transformaciones de congruencia*.

**Example** The four rigid motions are reflections, translations, rotations, and glide reflections.

**Rotation** A rotation of $x$ about a point $R$, called the *center of rotation*, is a transformation such that for any point $V$, its image is the point $V'$, where $RV = RV'$ and $m\angle VRV' = x$. The image of $R$ is itself. The positive number of degrees $x$ that a figure rotates is the *angle of rotation*. A rotation is a rigid motion.

**Rotación** Una rotación de $x$ sobre un punto $R$, llamado el *centro de rotación*, es una transformación en la que para cualquier punto $V$, su imagen es el punto $V'$, donde $RV = RV'$ y $m\angle VRV' = x$. La imagen de $R$ es sí misma. El número positivo de grados $x$ que una figura rota es el *ángulo de rotación*. Una rotación es un movimiento rígido.

**Example**

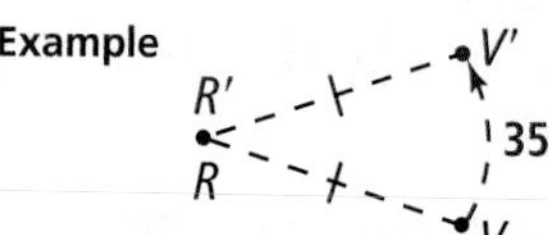


**Rotational symmetry** Rotational symmetry is the type of symmetry for which there is a rotation of 360° or less that maps a figure onto itself.

**Simetría rotacional** La simetría rotacional es un tipo de simetría en la que una rotación de 360° o menos vuelve a trazar una figura sobre sí misma.

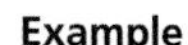
**Example**

The figure has 120° rotational symmetry.

**Same-side interior angles** Same-side interior angles lie on the same side of the transversal $t$ and between $\ell$ and $m$.

**Ángulos internos del mismo lado** Los ángulos internos del mismo lado están situados en el mismo lado de la transversal $t$ y dentro de $\ell$ y $m$.

**Example**

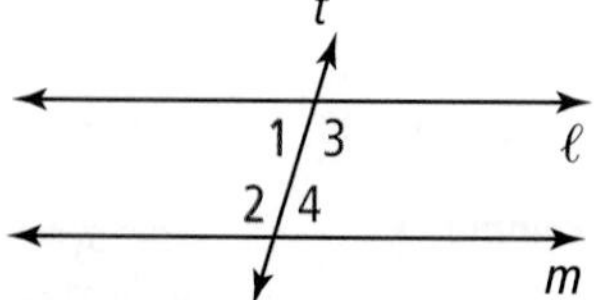


$\angle 1$ and $\angle 2$ are same-side interior angles, as are $\angle 3$ and $\angle 4$.

## English | Spanish

**Sample space** A sample space is the set of all possible outcomes of a situation or experiment.

**Espacio muestral** Un espacio muestral es el conjunto de todos los resultados posibles de un suceso.

**Example** When you roll a standard number cube, the sample space is {1, 2, 3, 4, 5, 6}.

**Scale** A scale is the ratio of any length in a scale drawing to the corresponding actual length. The lengths may be in different units.

**Escala** Una escala es la razón de cualquier longitud en un dibujo a escala en relación a la longitud verdadera correspondiente. Las longitudes pueden expresarse en distintas unidades.

**Example** 1 cm to 1 ft
1 cm = 1 ft
1 cm : 1 ft

**Scale drawing** A scale drawing is a drawing in which all lengths are proportional to corresponding actual lengths.

**Dibujo a escala** Un dibujo a escala es un dibujo en el que todas las longitudes son proporcionales a las longitudes verdaderas correspondientes.

**Example**

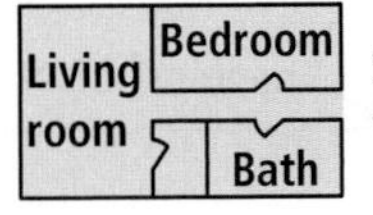


Scale:
1 in. = 30 ft

**Scale factor** A scale factor is the ratio of corresponding linear measurements of two similar figures.

**Factor de escala** El factor de escala es la razón de las medidas lineales correspondientes de dos figuras semejantes.

**Example**

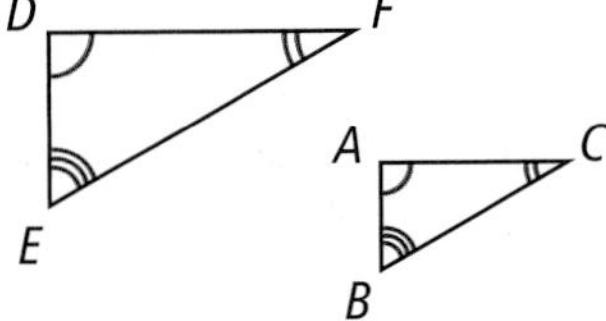


$\triangle ABC \sim \triangle DEF$

$\frac{AB}{DE} = \frac{BC}{EF} = \frac{CA}{FD}$

**Scale factor of a dilation** The scale factor of a dilation is the ratio of the distances from the center of dilation to an image point and to its preimage point.

**Factor de escala de dilatación** El factor de escala de dilatación es la razón de las distancias desde el centro de dilatación hasta un punto de la imagen y hasta un punto de la preimagen.

**Example**

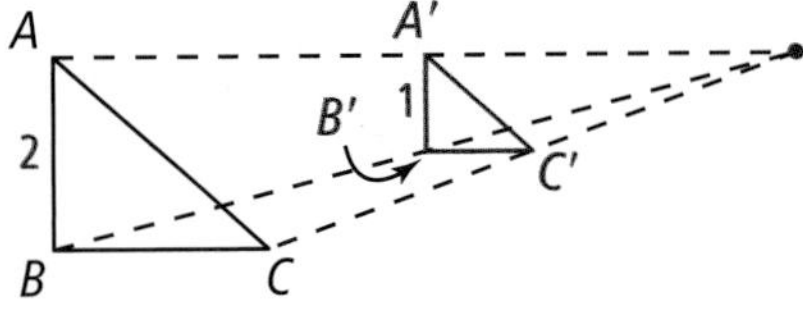


The scale factor of the dilation that maps $\triangle ABC$ to $\triangle A'B'C'$ is $\frac{1}{2}$.

**Scalene triangle** A scalene triangle has no congruent sides.

**Triángulo escaleno** Un triángulo escaleno no tiene lados congruentes.

**Example**

| English | Spanish |
|---|---|

**Secant** A secant is a line, ray, or segment that intersects a circle at two points.

**Secante** Una secante es una recta, semirrecta o segmento que corta un círculo en dos puntos.

**Example**

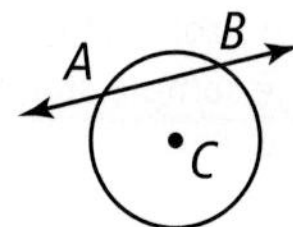


$\overleftrightarrow{AB}$ is a secant of $\odot C$.

**Sector of a circle** A sector of a circle is the region bounded by two radii and the intercepted arc.

**Sector de un círculo** Un sector de un círculo es la región limitada por dos radios y el arco abarcado por ellos.

**Example**

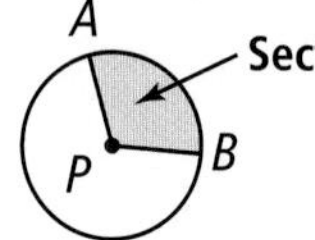


**Segment** A segment is the part of a line that consists of two points, called *endpoints*, and all points between them.

**Segmento** Un segmento es la parte de una recta que tiene dos puntos, llamados *extremos*, entre los cuales están todos los puntos de esa recta.

**Example**

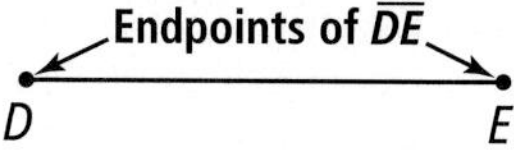


**Segment bisector** A segment bisector is a line, segment, ray, or plane that intersects a segment at the midpoint.

**Bisectriz de un segmento** La bisectriz de un segmento es una recta, segmento, semirrecta o plano que corta un segmento en el punto medio.

**Example**

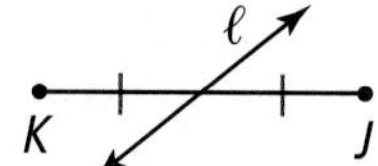


$\ell$ bisects $\overline{KJ}$.

**Segment of a circle** A segment of a circle is the part of a circle bounded by an arc and the segment joining its endpoints.

**Segmento de un círculo** Un segmento de un círculo es la parte de un círculo bordeada por un arco y el segmento que une sus extremos.

**Example**

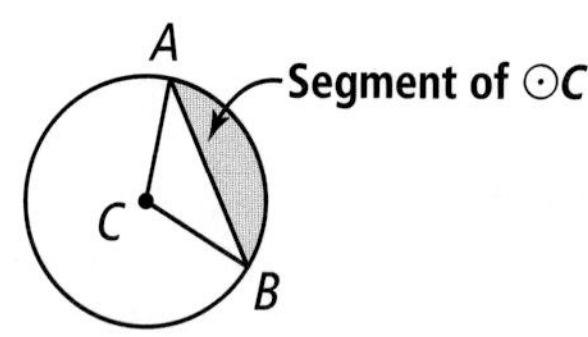


**Semicircle** A semicircle is half a circle.

**Semicírculo** Un semicírculo es la mitad de un círculo.

**Example**

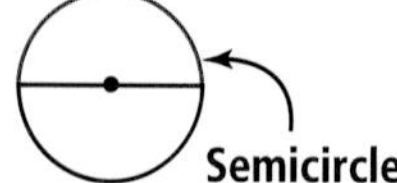


**Side** *See* **angle; polygon.**

**Lado** *Ver* **angle; polygon.**

# English / Spanish

**Similar figures** Similar figures are two figures that have the same shape, but not necessarily the same size. Two figures are similar if there is a similarity transformation that maps one figure to the other.

**Figuras semejantes** Los figuras semejantes son dos figuras que tienen la misma forma pero no necesariamente el mismo tamaño. Dos figuras son semejantes si hay una transformación de semajanza en la que una figura es la imagen de la otra.

**Example**

**Similarity transformation** A composition of one or more rigid motions and a dilation.

**Transformación de semejanza** Una composición de uno o más movimientos rígidos y una dilatación.

**Similar polygons** Similar polygons are polygons having corresponding angles congruent and the lengths of corresponding sides proportional. Similarity is denoted by $\sim$.

**Polígonos semejantes** Los polígonos semejantes son polígonos cuyos ángulos correspondientes son congruentes y las longitudes de los lados correspondientes son proporcionales. El símbolo $\sim$ significa "es semejante a".

**Example**

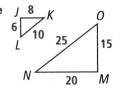

$\triangle JKL \sim \triangle MNO$

Scale factor $= \frac{2}{5}$

**Sine ratio** *See* **trigonometric ratios.**

**Razón seno** *Ver* **trigonometric ratios.**

**Slant height** *See* **cone; pyramid.**

**Generatriz (cono) o apotema (pirámide)** *Ver* **cone; pyramid.**

**Slope-intercept form** The slope-intercept form of a linear equation is $y = mx + b$, where $m$ is the slope of the line and $b$ is the $y$-intercept.

**Forma pendiente-intercepto** La forma pendiente-intercepto es la ecuación lineal $y = mx + b$, en la que $m$ es la pendiente de la recta y $b$ es el punto de intersección de esa recta con el eje $y$.

**Example** $y = \frac{1}{2}x - 3$

In this equation, the slope is $\frac{1}{2}$ and the $y$-intercept is $-3$.

**Slope of a line** The slope of a line is the ratio of its vertical change in the coordinate plane to the corresponding horizontal change. If $(x_1, y_1)$ and $(x_2, y_2)$ are points on a nonvertical line, then the slope is $\frac{y_2 - y_1}{x_2 - x_1}$. The slope of a horizontal line is 0, and the slope of a vertical line is undefined.

**Pendiente de una recta** La pendiente de una recta es la razón del cambio vertical en el plano de coordenadas en relación al cambio horizontal correspondiente. Si $(x_1, y_1)$ y $(x_2, y_2)$ son puntos en una recta no vertical, entonces la pendiente es $\frac{y_2 - y_1}{x_2 - x_1}$. La pendiente de una recta horizontal es 0, y la pendiente de una recta vertical es indefinida.

**Example**

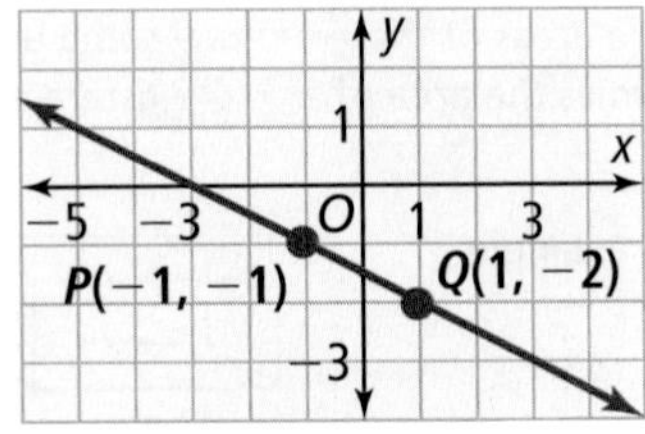


The line containing $P(-1, -1)$ and $Q(1, -2)$ has slope $\frac{-2-(-1)}{1-(-1)} = \frac{-1}{2} = -\frac{1}{2}$.

# English

# Spanish

**Sphere** A sphere is the set of all points in space that are a given distance $r$, the *radius*, from a given point $C$, the *center*. A *great circle* is the intersection of a sphere with a plane containing the center of the sphere. The *circumference* of a sphere is the circumference of any great circle of the sphere.

**Esfera** Una esfera es el conjunto de los puntos del espacio que están a una distancia dada $r$, el *radio*, de un punto dado $C$, el *centro*. Un *círculo máximo* es la intersección de una esfera y un plano que contiene el centro de la esfera. La *circunferencia* de una esfera es la circunferencia de cualquier círculo máximo de la esfera.

**Example**

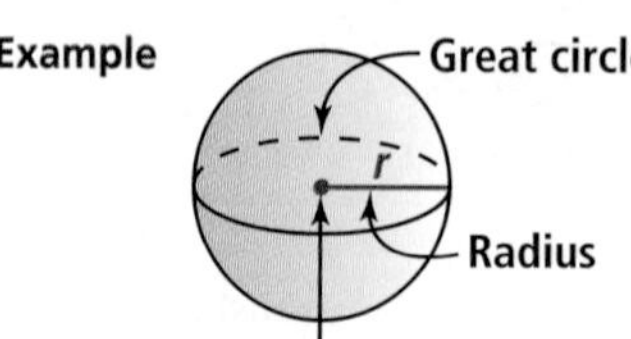


**Square** A square is a parallelogram with four congruent sides and four right angles.

**Cuadrado** Un cuadrado es un paralelogramo con cuatro lados congruentes y cuatro ángulos rectos.

**Example**

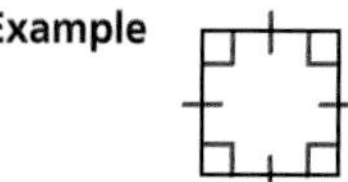

**Straight angle** A straight angle is an angle whose measure is 180.

**Ángulo llano** Un ángulo llano es un ángulo que mide 180.

**Example**

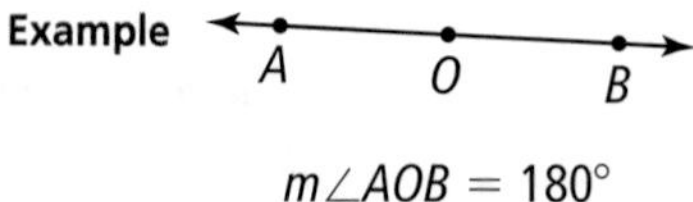


$m\angle AOB = 180°$

**Straightedge** A straightedge is a tool for drawing straight lines.

**Regla sin graduación** Una regla sin graduación es un instrumento para dibujar líneas rectas.

**Supplementary angles** Two angles are supplementary if the sum of their measures is 180.

**Ángulos suplementarios** Dos ángulos son suplementarios cuando sus medidas suman 180.

**Example**

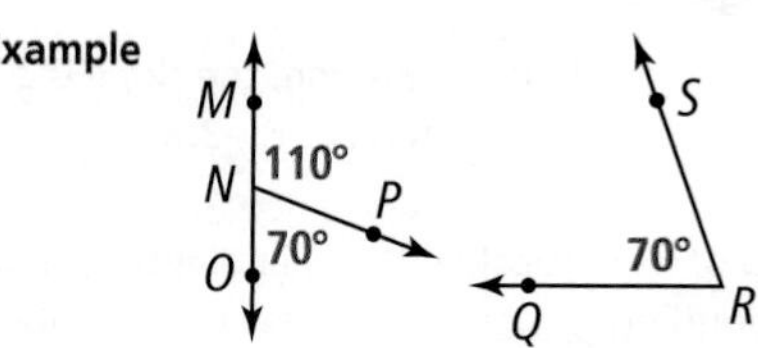


$\angle MNP$ and $\angle ONP$ are supplementary, as are $\angle MNP$ and $\angle QRS$.

**Surface area** The surface area of a prism, cylinder, pyramid, or cone is the sum of the lateral area and the areas of the bases. The surface area of a sphere is four times the area of a great circle.

**Área** El área de un prisma, pirámide, cilindro o cono es la suma del área lateral y las áreas de las bases. El área de una esfera es igual a cuatro veces el área de un círculo máximo.

**Example**

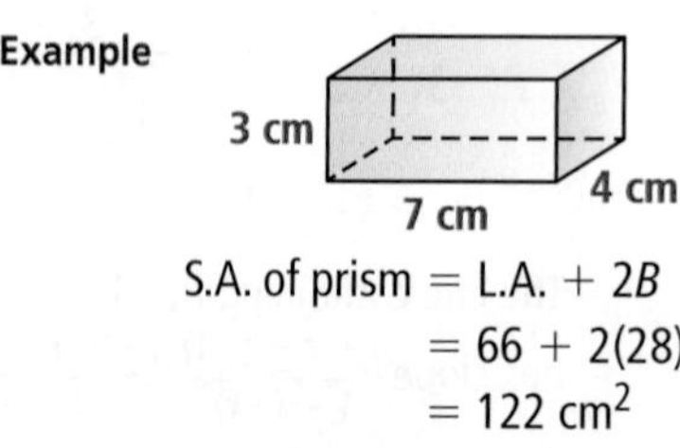


$$\begin{aligned} \text{S.A. of prism} &= \text{L.A.} + 2B \\ &= 66 + 2(28) \\ &= 122 \text{ cm}^2 \end{aligned}$$

# English

# Spanish

**Symmetry** A figure has symmetry if there is a rigid motion that maps the figure onto itself. *See also* **point symmetry; reflectional symmetry; rotational symmetry**.

**Simetría** Una figura tiene simetría si hay un movimiento rígido que traza la figura sobre sí misma. *Ver también* **point symmetry; reflectional symmetry; rotational symmetry**.

**Example**

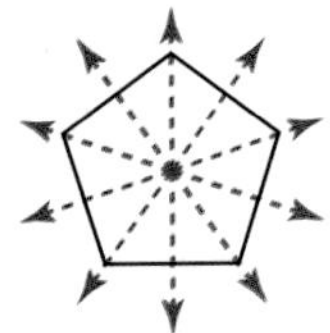

A regular pentagon has reflectional symmetry and 72° rotational symmetry.

## T

**Tangent ratio** *See* **trigonometric ratios.**

**Razón tangente** *Ver* **trigonometric ratios**.

**Tangent to a circle** A tangent to a circle is a line in the plane of the circle that intersects the circle in exactly one point. That point is the *point of tangency*.

**Tangente de un círculo** Una tangente de un círculo es una recta en el plano del círculo que corta el círculo en exactamente un punto. Ese punto es el *punto de tangencia*.

**Example**

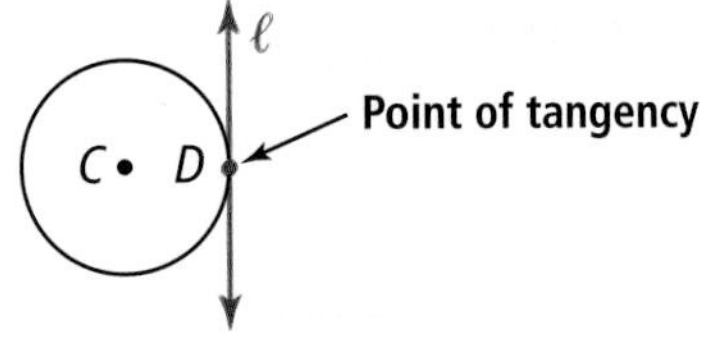


Line $\ell$ is tangent to $\odot C$. Point $D$ is the point of tangency.

**Theorem** A theorem is a conjecture that is proven.

**Teorema** Un teorema es una conjetura que se demuestra.

**Example** The theorem "Vertical angles are congruent" can be proven by using postulates, definitions, properties, and previously stated theorems.

**Theoretical probability** The theoretical probability is the ratio of the number of favorable outcomes to the number of possible outcomes if all outcomes have the same chance of happening.

$$P(\text{event}) = \frac{\text{number of favorable outcomes}}{\text{number of possible outcomes}}$$

**Probabilidad teórica** Si cada resultado tiene la misma probabilidad de darse, la probabilidad teórica de un suceso se calcula como la razón del número de resultados favorables al número de resultados posibles.

$$P(\text{suceso}) = \frac{\text{numero de resultados favorables}}{\text{numero de resultados posibles}}$$

**Example** In tossing a coin, the events of getting heads or tails are equally likely. The likelihood of getting heads is $P(\text{heads}) = \frac{1}{2}$.

VISUAL GLOSSARY

## English | Spanish

**Transformation** A transformation is a change in the position, size, or shape of a geometric figure. The given figure is called the *preimage* and the resulting figure is called the *image*. A transformation *maps* a figure onto its image. *Prime notation* is sometimes used to identify image points. In the diagram, $X'$ (read "$X$ prime") is the image of $X$.

**Transformación** Una transformación es un cambio en la posición, tamaño o forma de una figura. La figura dada se llama la *preimagen* y la figura resultante se llama la *imagen*. Una transformación *traza* la figura sobre su propia imagen. La *notación prima* a veces se utilize para identificar los puntos de la imagen. En el diagrama de la derecha, $X'$ (leído $X$ prima) es la imagen de $X$.

**Example**

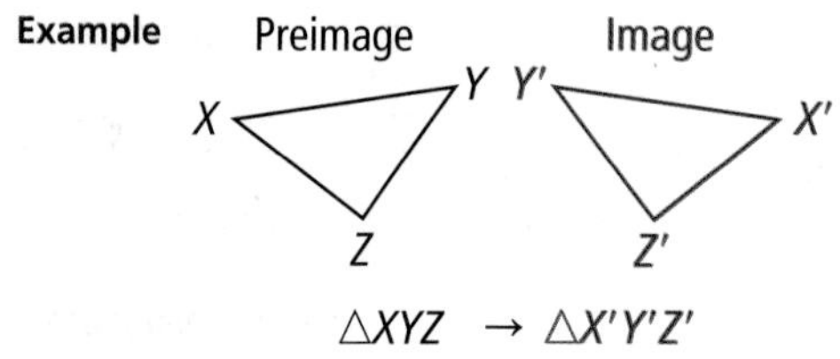


**Translation** A translation is a transformation that moves points the same distance and in the same direction. A translation is a rigid motion.

**Traslación** Una traslación es una transformación en la que se mueven puntos la misma distancia en la misma dirección. Una traslación es un movimiento rígido.

**Example**

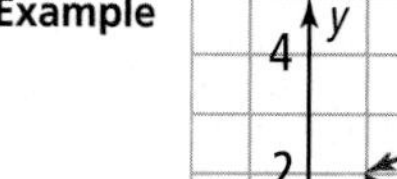
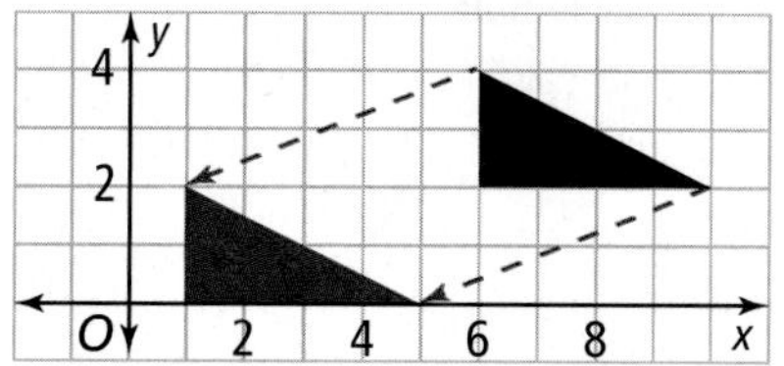


The blue triangle is the image of the black triangle under the translation $\langle -5, -2 \rangle$.

**Transversal** A transversal is a line that intersects two or more lines at distinct points.

**Transversal** Una transversal es una línea que interseca dos o más líneas en puntos precisos.

**Example**

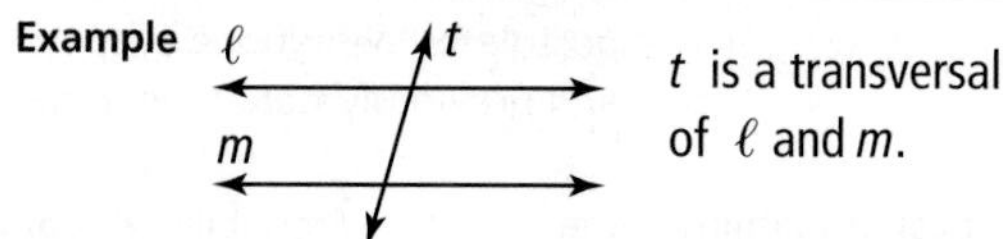


$t$ is a transversal of $\ell$ and $m$.

**Trapezoid** A trapezoid is a quadrilateral with exactly one pair of parallel sides, the *bases*. The nonparallel sides are called the *legs* of the trapezoid. Each pair of angles adjacent to a base are *base angles* of the trapezoid. An *altitude* of a trapezoid is a perpendicular segment from one base to the line containing the other base. Its length is called the *height* of the trapezoid.

**Trapecio** Un trapecio es un cuadrilátero con exactamente un par de lados paralelos, las *bases*. Los lados no paralelos se llaman los *catetos* del trapecio. Cada par de ángulos adyacentes a la base son los *ángulos de base* del trapecio. Una *altura* del trapecio es un segmento perpendicular que va de una base a la recta que contiene la otra base. Su longitud se llama, por extensión, la *altura* del trapecio.

**Example**

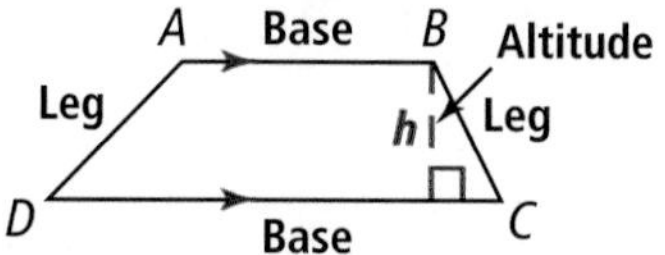


In trapezoid $ABCD$, $\angle ADC$ and $\angle BCD$ are one pair of base angles, and $\angle DAB$ and $\angle ABC$ are the other.

# English | Spanish

**Triangle** A triangle is a polygon with three sides. You can choose any side to be a *base*. The *height* is the length of the altitude drawn to the line containing that base.

**Triángulo** Un triángulo es un polígono con tres lados. Se puede escoger cualquier lado como *base*. La *altura*, entonces, es la longitud de la altura trazada hasta la recta que contiene la base.

**Example**

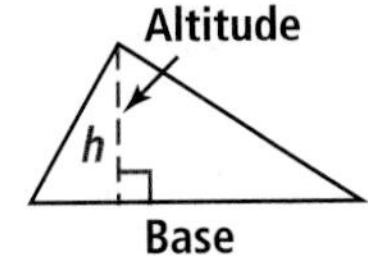


**Trigonometric ratios** The trigonometric ratios, or functions, relate the side lengths of a right triangle to its acute angles. In right $\triangle ABC$ with acute $\angle A$,

$$\text{sine } \angle A = \sin A = \frac{\text{length of leg opposite } \angle A}{\text{length of hypotenuse}}$$

$$\text{cosine } \angle A = \cos A = \frac{\text{length of leg adjacent to } \angle A}{\text{length of hypotenuse}}$$

$$\text{tangent } \angle A = \tan A = \frac{\text{length of leg opposite } \angle A}{\text{length of leg adjacent to } \angle A}$$

**Razones trigonométricas** Las razones trigonométricas, o funciones, relacionan las longitudes de lado de un triángulo rectángulo con sus ángulos agudos. En un triángulo rectángulo $\triangle ABC$ con ángulo agudo $\angle A$,

$$\text{seno } \angle A = \text{sen } A = \frac{\text{cateto opuesto a } \angle A}{\text{hipotenusa}}$$

$$\text{coseno } \angle A = \cos A = \frac{\text{cateto adyecente a } \angle A}{\text{hipotenusa}}$$

$$\text{tangente } \angle A = \tan A = \frac{\text{cateto opuesto a } \angle A}{\text{cateto adyecente a } \angle A}$$

**Example**

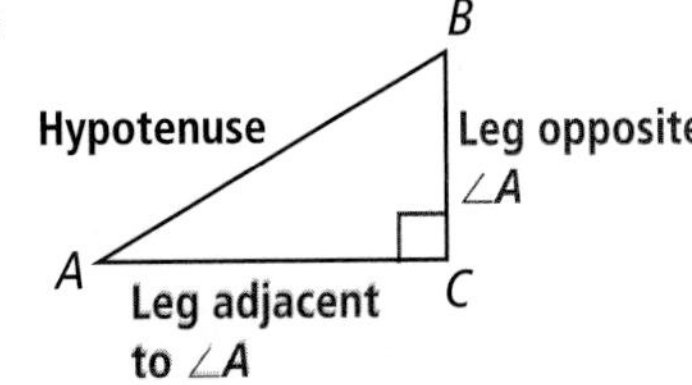


**Truth table** A truth table is a table that lists all the possible combinations of truth values for two or more statements.

**Tabla de verdad** Una tabla de verdad es una tabla que muestra todas las combinaciones posibles de valores de verdad de dos o más enunciados.

**Example**

| $p$ | $q$ | $p \to q$ |
|---|---|---|
| T | T | T |
| T | F | F |
| F | T | T |
| F | F | T |

**Truth value** The truth value of a statement is "true" (T) or "false" (F) according to whether the statement is true or false, respectively.

**Valor verdadero** El valor verdadero de un enunciado es "verdadero" (T) o "falso" (F) según el enunciado sea verdadero o falso, respectivamente.

**Two-column proof** *See* **proof**.

**Prueba de dos columnas** *Ver* **proof**.

## English

## Spanish

**Two-way frequency table** A two-way frequency table is a table that displays frequencies in two different categories.

**Tabla de frecuencias de doble entrada** Una tabla de frecuencias de doble entrada es una tabla de frecuencias que contiene dos categorías de datos.

**Example**

| | Male | Female | Totals |
|---|---|---|---|
| Juniors | 3 | 4 | 7 |
| Seniors | 3 | 2 | 5 |
| Totals | 6 | 6 | 12 |

The last column shows a total of 7 juniors and 5 seniors.
The last row shows a total of 6 males and 6 females.

**Uniform probability distribution** A uniform probability distribution assigns the same probability to each outcome.

**Distribución uniforme de probabilidad** Una distribución uniforme de probabilidad le asigna la misma probabilidad a cada resultado.

**Vertex** *See* **angle; cone; polygon; polyhedron; pyramid.** The plural form of *vertex* is *vertices*.

**Vértice** *Ver* **angle; cone; polygon; polyhedron; pyramid.**

**Vertex angle** *See* **isosceles triangle.**

**Ángulo del vértice** *Ver* **isosceles triangle.**

**Vertical angles** Vertical angles are two angles whose sides form two pairs of opposite rays.

**Ángulos opuestos por el vértice** Dos ángulos son ángulos opuestos por el vértice si sus lados son semirrectas opuestas.

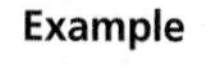
**Example**

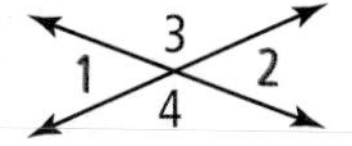


$\angle 1$ and $\angle 2$ are vertical angles, as are $\angle 3$ and $\angle 4$.

**Volume** Volume is a measure of the space a figure occupies.

**Volumen** El volumen es una medida del espacio que ocupa una figura.

# Index



INDEX

## D



## E



## F



## G



## H



## I



INDEX

## K



## L



## M



## N



## O



## P

# Q



# R



# S

## T

# Acknowledgments


## Photographs

### Cover:
**CVR** Vinciber/Fotolia;

### Topic 01:
**003** PaleMale/Getty Images; **020** Sabelskaya/Fotolia; **035** PaleMale/Getty Images; **058C** Arek_Malang/Shutterstock; **058L** Michaeljung/Shutterstock; **058R** Antonio Guillem/ Shutterstock;

### Topic 02:
**069** RAW/Fotolia; **099** RAW/Fotolia;

### Topic 03:
**103** Dennis van de Water/Shutterstock; **138** Ae in Wonder Land/Shutterstock; **139B** Shahril Khmd/Shutterstock; **139T** Steve Mann/Fotolia; **140** Steve Taylor ARPS/Alamy Stock Photo; **141** kichigin19/Fotolia; **142** Dennis van de Water/Shutterstock;

### Topic 04:
**147** Pearson Education, Inc.; **152BL** Amgadfoto/Fotolia; **152BR** Pearson Education, Inc.; **165B** Trekandphoto/Fotolia; **165T** kosmos111/Shutterstock; **181** Pearson Education, Inc.; **187** Chuck Eckert/Alamy Stock Photo;

### Topic 06:
**243** Africa Studio/Fotolia; **252** Africa Studio/Fotolia; **270** Rukawajung/Fotolia;

### Topic 07:
**299** Maxisport/Fotolia; **332** Maxisport/Fotolia; **339** Oleksii Nykonchuk/Fotolia;

### Topic 08:
**343** Science photo/Fotolia; **373** Science photo/Fotolia;

### Topic 09:
**383** Pearson Education.Inc; **391** Karen Doody/Stocktrek Images,Inc./Alamy Stock Photo; **392** Pearson Education.Inc; **405** Rgb Ventures/SuperStock/Ed Darack/Alamy Stock Photo; **409** Africa Rising/Shutterstock; **412** Stocker1970/Shutterstock;

### Topic 10:
**417** Paul Fleet/Shutterstock; **434** Songquan Deng/Shutterstock; **435** Paul Fleet/Shutterstock; **450** Vasilii Gubskii/Shutterstock; **458** Friedrich Saurer/Alamy Stock Photo;

### Topic 11:
**463** Andersphoto/Shutterstock; **470** Monkey Business/Fotolia; **470** Imfotograf/Fotolia; **470** Yellow Cat/Shutterstock; **470** Perutskyi Petro/Shutterstock; **474** Cynoclub/Fotolia; **475** Joerg Hackemann/123RF; **479** Andersphoto/Shutterstock; **492** Sorapong Chaipanya/123RF;

### Topic 12:
**497** Jacques Beauchamp/Glow Images; **497** Jacques Beauchamp/Glow Images; **542** Blackregis/123RF;

# Acknowledgments

## STEM

**FM** Andrew Orlemann/Shutterstock; **FM** Alexander Y/Shutterstock; **FM** Andrii Gorulko/Shutterstock; **FM** Aksonov/E+/Getty Images; **004B** Nd3000/Fotolia; **004C** Elena Ermakova/Fotolia; **004TL** Sergii Moscaliuk/Fotolia; **004TR** Evgeny Karandaev/Shutterstock; **070B** Praewpailin Phonsri/123RF; **070CL** Peter Rooney/Shutterstock; **070CM** Eric Fahrner/Shutterstock; **070CR** Marius Godoi/Shutterstock; **070TL** James Brey/E+/Getty Images; **070TR** Monkey Business Images/Shutterstock; **104B** Login/Fotolia; **104TR** World History Archive/Alamy Stock Photo; **148B** Lakeviewimages/Fotolia; **148C(a)** Michelle Lemon/Fotolia; **148C(b)** Eric Audras/ONOKY-Photononstop/Alamy Stock Photo; **148C(c)** Frankljunior/123RF; **148C(d)** Mr Twister/Shutterstock; **148T** Michelle Lemon/Fotolia; **200B** Aleksandr Simonov/Shutterstock; **200CL** Jacob Lund/Fotolia; **200CR** Maksym Protsenko/Fotolia; **200T** Neil Webb/Ikon Images/Alamy Stock Photo; **244B** Taina Sohlman/Fotolia; **244CL** Dushlik/Fotolia; **244CR** Julen Garces Carro/EyeEm/Alamy Stock Photo; **244T** Zastolskiy Victor/Shutterstock; **300** Pressmaster/Fotolia; **300** Chris Hill/National Geographic Creative/Alamy Stock Photo; **300** Juan Carlos Ulate/REUTERS/Alamy Stock Photo; **300** Petrovich12/Fotolia; **344** Kadmy/Fotolia; **344** Robert/Fotolia; **344** Okamigo/Fotolia; **344** Dariodv/Fotolia; **344** Makko3/Fotolia; **384** Makko3/Fotolia; **384** Hayate/Fotolia; **384** Aleksandr Lesik/Fotolia; **384** Andy Dean/Fotolia; **384** Mike Flippo/Shutterstock; **418** 3Dsculptor/Shutterstock; **418** Tryfonov/Fotolia; **418** Olekcii Mach/Alamy Stock Photo; **418** Algol/Shutterstock; **464** Heiner Heine/imageBROKER/Alamy Stock Photo; **464** AD Hunter/Shutterstock; **464** Katyr/Fotolia; **498** Vasin Lee/Shutterstock; **498** Harvepino/Shutterstock; **498** Tainar/Shutterstock; **498** Marina Zezelina/Shutterstock; **498** Zeljko Radojko/Fotolia;